Reading Rhetorical Theory

Reading Rhetorical Theory

Barry Brummett
University of Wisconsin–Milwaukee

Harcourt College Publishers
Fort Worth Philadelphia San Diego New York Orlando Austin San Antonio
Toronto Montreal London Sydney Tokyo

Publisher	Earl McPeek
Acquisitions Editor	Stephen Dalphin
Market Strategist	Laura Brennan
Developmental Editor	Peggy Howell
Art Director	Susan Journey
Production Manager	James McDonald

ISBN: 0-15-508304-X
Library of Congress Catalog Card Number: 99-64301

Address for Domestic Orders
Harcourt College Publishers, 6277 Sea Harbor Drive, Orlando, FL 32887-6777
800-782-4479

Address for International Orders
International Customer Service
Harcourt, Inc., 6277 Sea Harbor Drive, Orlando, FL 32887-6777
407-345-3800
(fax) 407-345-4060
(e-mail) hbintl@harcourtbrace.com

Address for Editorial Correspondence
Harcourt College Publishers, 301 Commerce Street, Suite 3700, Fort Worth, TX 76102

Web Site Address
hhtp://www.harcourtcollege.com

Printed in the United States of America

0 1 2 3 4 5 6 7 8 039 9 8 7 6 5 4 3 2

Harcourt College Publishers

For Robert L. Scott

Preface

In his book, *The Philosophy of Literary Form,* the great twentieth-century critic and rhetorical theorist Kenneth Burke invites us to "imagine that you enter a parlor. You come late. When you arrive, others have long preceded you, and they are engaged in a heated discussion, a discussion too heated for them to pause and tell you exactly what it is about. . . . You listen for a while, until you decide that you have caught the tenor of the argument; then you put in your oar" (p. 110). This famous passage describes the ongoing conversation about important issues that runs throughout history. That conversation takes place in many "parlors" of different disciplines and discourses, and all of us move from one parlor to another from time to time. The book you are holding is about what people have said in the parlor of rhetoric, one of the oldest discussions in recorded human history.

Rhetoric is the study of persuasion, of how humans influence one another, and in influencing each other, how we order our lives together. Since the ability to move others and to be moved by them through communication is fundamental to being human, we can learn much about ourselves by studying the centuries-long "conversation" that great thinkers and communicators have had about rhetoric. This "parlor" lies at the heart of the house of knowledge, if we may extend that metaphor.

Reading Rhetorical Theory invites you into that parlor to read a sample of what has been written for 2500 years and more about the experience of rhetoric. Yes, a "sample"! Weighty as this book may be, it is really only a representation of a very rich, complex, and diverse conversation about rhetoric. Furthermore, it is largely grounded in the European tradition; conversations about influence and persuasion have existed in one form or another in cultures around the world for centuries as well.

It might be easy to find the prospect of entering into this noisy parlor a little daunting. So many voices are waiting to be heard! Let us assure you that rhetoric is a subject that will repay careful study. While it may not become entirely clear from the start, slowly you, too, will form an opinion about what is being said and, who knows, may even put your own "oar" into the conversation!

The historical conversation about rhetoric into which you are about to enter is organized historically into some clear eras, defined in terms of social and cultural conditions and by the development of rhetorical theory in response to those conditions. The subject of rhetoric and some conceptual schemes for understanding it are introduced in the first editor's essay; then each historical period and each selection is in turn introduced by brief essays. In this book we have chosen to rely on original texts, or samples from original texts, as much as possible. Introductory essays are meant to help the reader put the texts into perspective and to develop thoughtful reactions to them. We hope you are enriched and rewarded by the conversation you are about to enter!

ACKNOWLEDGMENTS

The making of this book has been a monumental task for many others besides me. I am grateful to the editorial staff at Harcourt, especially Louise Slominsky, James McDonald, Peggy Howell, Jill Johnson, and Steve Dalphin, and at Elm Street Publishing Services, Inc. for their diligent work on many levels of this project. In many ways they have saved this book from errors I made. I would also like to acknowledge the reviewers of this book: Mark Lawrence McPhail, The University of Utah; George Dionisopoulos, San Diego State University; and John Louis Lucaites, Indiana University. I am grateful to two student assistants at the University of Wisconsin– Milwaukee who helped to gather original materials for inclusion in the book, Stephanie Garry and Alison Ebbers. The faculty at UW–Milwaukee, especially my rhetorical colleague Professor Kathryn Olson, has been supportive of this project, which has taken some time to complete. Thanks also to Dr. Detine Bowers for her support and assistance. Finally, I am grateful for the two courses I teach in the history of rhetorical theory and to the many students who have taught me as much about the subject as I have taught them.

Contents

INTRODUCTION

Human beings do many different things during the course of a day. One thing that we have the most in common is that we try to influence each other: We politely ask for coffee at breakfast, we urge a spouse to request a raise at work, we choose clothing that will create just the right impression for today's meeting, we discourage conversation by avoiding eye contact on the bus, or we complain about a bad product. Furthermore, we are constantly exposed to the efforts of other people to influence *us:* A lecturer tries to interest us in a subject, a political candidate pleads for our votes, an advertisement in the newspaper announces a one-day-only sale, and a brother asks to borrow our sweaters.

This business of influencing and being influenced has gone by many names ranging from *persuasion* to *marketing* to *relationship building.* But one term that has most consistently been used throughout history to mean "influence" is the word *rhetoric.* The study of rhetoric is ancient, dating at least to the sixth century B.C.E. in Greece and perhaps even earlier in Asia and Africa. Nearly every society has thought seriously about what it means to be rhetorical. The reason for this is that rhetoric is so much a part of our everyday lives. In fact, one can study what it means to be human by thinking about what it means to be rhetorical.

The purpose of this book is the study of rhetoric in the human experience. Beginning with the writings of some public speaking professors in ancient Greece, you will be reading what people throughout history have thought about rhetoric, the business of influencing one another, and how being rhetorical affects our personal, social, and political lives. Beginning with rhetoric, we will branch out to think about important issues such as what it means to have knowledge, to teach and to learn, and to live responsibly in a democratic society. To keep the focus of this study within bounds, we will be looking at some of the writers and thinkers in Europe, North Africa, and America who were the direct heirs of those early Greek rhetoricians.

Besides *rhetoric,* the other key term in this book is *theory.* What does it mean to theorize or to have a theory? A quick definition might be that a theory is the assertion of regular, systematic relationships among actions, objects, and events in the world. We make theories about those things that we can reliably generalize about.

The purpose of this introduction is to prepare you for this journey through a range of rhetorical theory. The introduction consists of two parts: *Thinking About Rhetoric* and *Thinking About Theory.* In the first part, you will learn some definitions and some key concepts that will help to organize the many different writers you will encounter along the way. In the second part, we will look at the varied ways of thinking and writing that can be called *rhetorical theory.* Not all the writings in this book are on the same level, nor do they all try to do the same thing.

Later, after the introduction, shorter essays will introduce the major historical periods and writers. For now, we begin thinking about rhetoric. Let's begin with a logical beginning, that of *definitions.*

THINKING ABOUT RHETORIC

Definitions of Rhetoric

Nearly every way of understanding *rhetoric* has centered around the idea of *influence:* the ways we use verbal and nonverbal signs to affect other people. But definitions have differed on two dimensions: *emphasis* and *weighting.* To understand what this means, let us consider just a few of the many definitions you will find stated or implied in this book.

Emphasis

For the ancient Sophists of Greece, such as Gorgias, the traveling teachers who first began talking and thinking about rhetoric, it simply meant the ability to plan and deliver effective public speaking. Plato, the philosophical adversary of the Sophists, saw rhetoric instead as flattery or pandering: saying to an audience whatever it wanted to hear so as to win its favor. For Aristotle, the first great systematizer of rhetorical theory, rhetoric meant the ability to discover the available means of persuasion in any situation. The Roman statesman Cicero thought of rhetoric as an important tool of statesmanship. One hundred years later, the Roman Quintilian used rhetoric mainly as a pedagogical device to teach young people. In the Renaissance, Peter Ramus thought of rhetoric as verbal embellishment and style. I. A. Richards, in the twentieth century, argued that rhetoric is the study of misunderstanding and its remedies. Kenneth Burke, the greatest rhetorical theorist of the twentieth century, defined rhetoric as inducing cooperation in people.

First, let's notice that each definition places a different *emphasis* on some aspect or dimension of influence. Cicero stressed influence in political struggles; Quintilian in educational contexts. Ramus emphasized the ability of rhetoric to make language beautiful; Richards stressed the importance of making language understandable. The Sophists saw rhetoric largely as public speaking, whereas Burke did not emphasize any type of communication so much as a function: specifically, that of creating cooperation. When we influence or are influenced, sometimes the language we use will be more important. Sometimes the logical reasoning we use is primary. Sometimes the context, whether political or interpersonal or religious, is the most important dimension of influence. A definition of rhetoric will emphasize what is most important to the theorist, for reasons having to do with the culture or politics of the era.

Weighting

Second, notice that each definition places a different *weighting* on being rhetorical—a weighting that predisposes people favorably or unfavorably toward the very thing being defined: influencing others. Clearly, Ramus's definition has a somewhat unfavorable weighting; he thought that persuasive influence was mere stylistic embellishment rather than substantive argument. Aristotle's definition is more neutral; rhetoric is depicted as a "faculty" or an ability to discover the means of persuasion. Whether that is good or bad, says Aristotle, depends on the discoverer's "moral purpose," not on rhetoric itself. Burke's and Richards's definitions seem to weight rhetoric favorably: Who can object to a remedy for misunderstanding or to an activity that increases cooperation? As with the dimension of emphasis, weighting occurs because of what is important to a theorist and because of the personal, social, or philosophical goals to which that writer is committed.

When any activity or object has historically been defined in many different ways, we know that it must be something both central to human life and central to the distribution of *power.* Were power not involved in how we think about (and in what we *do* about) influence, nobody would fuss much over how it is defined. A *pencil* is not defined in very many ways. Why? Because little is at stake in how it is defined. But when it comes to how we influence each other rhetorically, what is emphasized and how that activity is weighted will have a lot to do with how power is managed in any society. Think, for example, of the fact that an activity like rhetoric, which is central to our everyday lives, has been defined in so many ways precisely because of these possibilities of emphasis and weighting. So as you read this book, understand the variety of definitions of rhetoric as concealing a subtext of struggle over power. Instead, ask yourself who is being empowered or disempowered and whose interests are being served by defining rhetoric in this way or that.

We have briefly considered the idea that rhetoric is inseparable from our everyday lives and from power management. Why is this, and what is the connection between rhetoric and how we live and think? As we study the history of rhetorical theory, *four central issues* will run throughout every reading: *discourse, knowledge, media,* and *power.* Once you understand what is meant by these terms, you will be in a better position to compare theories and to track the development of some important issues through time. So let us turn to those four key terms to find out what they mean, what they have to do with influence, and how they interrelate with one another.

DISCOURSE

To understand our first central issue fully, we will need to "sneak up" on it gradually, since it is a rather complicated idea. Let us start with a parable of sorts: Imagine that it is many thousands of years ago and that you and some other people are living in caves on one side of a hill. You and the others hardly ever go out except to grab food and water and scurry back to shelter. You have very little contact with the others. Each one is isolated, each cave a city and a law unto itself. Now imagine that on the other side of the hill lives a tribe of people who mix freely with one another, who are organized, and who have designs on the food and water on *your* side of the hill. Who is in the better position here? Clearly, the people on the other side of the hill! In fact, you and your fellow hermits are in serious trouble, and you had better do something about it.

What will you do? Perhaps have a meeting? Talk it over down at the water hole? Form a committee? Maybe later. The *first* thing you must do is to lay the groundwork for all of the above. And the groundwork is that you must have *a way to communicate.* You must have some system of words and gestures and a way to understand what they mean. In short, you need a language and some understanding of how to use it. Without that, you will remain isolated in your caves, and woe betide you when that other tribe marches over the hill.

So you establish a language. But you soon discover that this is not sufficient. You find out that you cannot talk to each other when *organizing for war* in the same way that you talk to each other when *organizing for harvest.* The ways of communicating that seem to work well during *courtship* are likely to fail you when it comes time to join together in *religious* observances. So you need to diversify and devise different ways of communicating for different purposes, contexts, and occasions. In fact, it would not be too far-fetched to say that the way of communicating must *constitute the activity itself.* Specifically, you are not going to organize for war until you have an organizing-for-war vocabulary and set of rules and understandings for how to use it. How you talk therefore becomes foundational for how you interact.

Two Meanings of "Discourse"

The word *discourse* has two meanings. The first meaning is exactly what we've been talking about in the parable. Discourse means, in the first place, a set of rules, understandings, and practices for how language is used to constitute a human activity. For example, from time to time you may go to a classroom and hear a "college lecture." There is a set of rules, understandings, and practices for how language is used by both students and teachers to *create* the experience of the "college lecture." It is expected that the teacher will be the initiator of talk and will probably do most of the talking. It is understood that the talk will be scholarly and generally serious, and that it will relate to the subject matter being studied. It is the practice that students will follow the directions of the teacher and will communicate under terms generally set by her. Having those rules and expectations is what *makes* it a college lecture. If the professor came in to the classroom with three other people and proceeded to sing harmonious songs during the whole period, one could rightfully claim that the pattern of communication exhibited here did not constitute a college lecture, and that a college lecture had simply not been "done."

We move through the day going from one activity to another that is constituted by discourse in this first sense. You wake up and are *doing* the "family gathers around the breakfast table thing" *because* you are *communicating* in a certain way: You are employing the "family gathers around the breakfast table" discourse. You go to work, and you must use a different discourse so as to be able to do what you do at work. And so this goes on through the day.

A second, more limited sense of *discourse* is that it is a *particular* message or utterance. We form the specific things we want to say to people in the here and now by putting together messages that follow the parameters set by the first meaning of discourse (rules, understandings, and practices). If a professor is lecturing on the causes of the First World War, he is producing a discourse in this second sense of a specific utterance. But the utterance is being produced within the parameters of the first sense of discourse as a set of rules, understandings, and practices; otherwise, it may well be that a college lecture is simply not what is being done.

An analogy to games might help. The game of baseball exists in sort of an abstract sense as a set of rules, understandings, and practices: Each batter gets up to three strikes or four balls and then, if the batter has not placed a hit, must either walk or be out; each side gets three outs to an inning; if a batter is hit by a pitched ball, the batter gets a walk; and so forth. This is "baseball" that parallels the first sense of discourse; we can think of that meaning of discourse as if it were a game, in the abstract. Then, when the Brewers and the Twins take to the field on a particular Tuesday evening, they enact *a* baseball game within the parameters set by "baseball" in the abstract sense. And this second kind of baseball, a particular game, parallels the second sense of discourse as a specific message.

Discourse and Rhetoric

The relevance of this discussion of *discourse* to our study of rhetoric is this: *What kind of discourse is rhetoric?* The theorists you will study are going to argue about that question in several ways.

One issue will be: What sort of human activity is constituted by rhetoric? Here we will see arguments for different definitions, with their different emphases and weightings. When we use rhetoric, are we merely pandering to one another? Are we doing politics? Are we displaying linguistic skill and technique, i.e., entertaining each other?

A closely related issue is: Does rhetorical discourse constitute a distinct human activity? This question arises because when we influence someone, we are always influencing them *about* some other issue that has its own governing discourses. For instance, if legislators debate a tax increase, they are speaking about economic issues—yet economics has its own governing discourses. So should we say that the legislators are speaking and doing rhetoric or speaking and doing economics? The reason this question matters is that if rhetoric is not a distinct discourse constituting a distinct activity, then we might want to say that people should pay much more attention to other discourses than to rhetoric. In other words, would we be better off if legislators studied economics more than they studied rhetoric? This doubt can always be raised about rhetoric because we rarely or never simply "persuade" others, we always persuade them *about* some matter for which there are separate constituting discourses.

But the question might also be raised from the other direction: Can we engage in any other discourse without also engaging in rhetoric? The economist who is learning the discourse of her profession could also be said to be learning a way to persuade other economists, to influence the public to accept economic policy, and to be persuaded herself of the value of economic discourse. Can she "get away from" rhetoric? Can the physician employ the discourse of medicine to speak to his patients and colleagues without also employing the discourse of rhetoric to influence them to respect and agree with him?

As we will see throughout the book, there are other questions that will be asked about the discourse that is rhetoric. Some of those questions are best previewed in relation to our three other key issues. Let us turn now to the second of them, *knowledge.*

KNOWLEDGE

Knowledge is a good thing to have. There are few more damaging insults hurled, if true, than "You don't have a clue!" You can win a job or get fired because of how much knowledge you have or do not have. To anticipate our fourth central issue, we often hear it said that "knowledge is power." We have a sense that some people have more knowledge than others, and they usually find that to be to their advantage.

What Is Knowledge?

People who are thought to "have more knowledge" do not necessarily walk around with *more thoughts* in their heads than do others. If you are awake you are thinking, whether it be thoughts about trigonometry or thoughts about the taste of your bubble gum. Whether you are thinking up a cure for AIDS or wondering whether that "Full House" rerun is worth watching, your head is full of thoughts. So to say that we have knowledge is not to say that we have more thoughts than others. *The question of knowledge is a question of the status of thoughts.* Some thoughts are given higher status than others; these thoughts are sanctioned as being *knowledge.* If someone has the thought that nothing can exceed the speed of light, that thought has been "approved" as knowledge. Another person's thoughts may be equally occupied with the conviction that Elvis is alive and working in a donut shop in Kalamazoo, but few will say that such a person has knowledge.

To get the "seal of approval" as knowledge, specific ideas or bits of information in our heads must meet standards set by the cultures or societies in which we live. What counts as knowledge and how to get it will therefore vary from one culture to another. A religious vision of angels in the clouds may be certified as knowledge by one society and as hallucination by another. Your uncle's friends may agree that he *knows* that the lump in his side is cancer, whereas his physician may insist that he knows no such thing and that only a medical doctor can have such knowledge about his condition. Furthermore, some kinds of knowledge are counted as more valuable than others. Your neighbor has knowledge of how to fix your car, while your nephew has knowledge of how to solve the highest levels of a video game; which knowledge is considered more valuable?

In Western cultures, what have been some of the kinds of standards we set for what counts as knowledge and for what sorts of knowledge are more valuable than others? It will help us understand the standards that we hold for certifying knowledge if we focus on the issue of *teaching.* Throughout history, thinkers have usually argued that *the best knowledge is that which is teachable.* In general, theorists have thought that those ideas that can be passed on by a teacher to a student are most securely worthy of being called "knowledge."

What Is Teachable?

To understand this, let us think about what it means to say that something is teachable. We can identify four standards of teachability: *language, principles, commodification,* and a *priesthood.* That which is teachable tends to be that which can be *articulated in language.* Think of the difficulty we have in explaining to someone else a hunch, intuition, or gut reaction. We cannot put it into words—you have to experience those feelings yourself. For that very reason, we hesitate to call such hunches and intuition "knowledge." If someone says, "I don't know *how* I know, I just know," we will not value what they "know" as much as the knowledge that someone can pass on to us by fully articulating and explaining it.

To say that something is teachable means that a teacher *can* and *must* devise *systematic principles* that organize and sum up that which is taught. Compare "knowledge" of nuclear physics with "knowledge" of how to ride a bicycle. Nuclear physics *must* be taught through systematic principles. But it is difficult to learn how to ride a bike "in principle." You have to get on and do it! We would therefore say that knowledge of physics is of much higher status than is knowledge of how to ride a bike; we might even call the latter only a "knack" gained from experience rather than knowledge.

If something is teachable, then it becomes a sort of *exclusive commodity* that some may have but others may not until the latter are taught. That which is truly teachable is something that can be kept hidden and hoarded. It is therefore a controllable commodity, like gold. Medical science is teachable, and that knowledge is only handed out under strict and rigorous conditions such as medical school. A medical education is a commodity bought and sold at great price. Medical schools then become great and important institutions. In fact, every society has sanctioning *institutions* that are empowered to say what is knowledge and what is not. On the other hand, hardly anybody bothers to teach others how to climb a tree. Like the "knack" of riding a bike, knowledge of how to climb a tree seems to be open to any who try it; it doesn't need to be taught. It is not, therefore, valued nearly as much as is medicine.

And finally, that which is teachable must be taught by an *elite priesthood* of those who already possess and control the commodity of knowledge. That which is an exclusive commodity must be carefully protected by overseers. And when they claim to be able to teach, they lay a claim to their own advanced skills and status, as well. To learn accounting, one must go to business school and study with just the right sort of professors. Control over knowledge of accounting then enriches those who possess it with wealth and power. Nobody, however, goes to school to learn how to watch television, and therefore that sort of knowledge is hardly prized or even considered to be knowledge at all.

Knowledge and Rhetoric

The connection between *rhetoric* and *knowledge* may be the most highly debated, vigorously contested question addressed throughout the readings in this book. Three major issues about that relationship arise.

The first major issue follows from the discussion just above: *Is rhetoric teachable?* We will see that Plato gave a firm "No!" in response to that question, calling it a "knack" or something picked up from habit. The Sophists and Aristotle, however, did think it was teachable. We will find theorists disagreeing on how systematic those rhetorical principles need to be. They will disagree as to who ought to be the priesthood of rhetorical professors; Plato thought that if anyone even tried to teach rhetoric it should be philosophers, whereas Quintilian was himself a professor of rhetoric with a large, successful school.

Second, consider the question of *what one must know to be rhetorical.* Is knowledge of rhetorical technique itself enough? If one only learns how to argue, how to turn a phrase in a pleasing way, how to arrange a message, is that enough? Or must one learn the subject matters about which one may be called upon to be rhetorical? Few theorists argue that knowledge of technique alone is sufficient. But where one draws the line in terms of wider knowledge is hotly contested. The reason for this is that, as we noted above, rhetoricians may be called upon to address any issue whatsoever. Imagine that you open a public relations and advertising office. What sort of "subject" will walk in your door first? You can neither predict nor narrow your guess; it could be anyone from a nuclear power plant owner to a wig seller to a felonious politician, each one needing you to have some knowledge of nuclear engineering, wigs, or the law to be able to persuade others on their behalf. But it would seem to be true that nobody can learn *everything.* Does that mean that knowledge and rhetoric ultimately do not mix, or is there some approach to knowledge that is compatable with rhetoric? We will be on the lookout for how different theorists address this problem.

Third, is it *possible* to have *knowledge without rhetoric?* Some theorists will argue that knowledge is not objective and neutral, but is always something that the student has been influenced to believe. Even scientists, they argue, must persuade others of their findings before what they have discovered will be "certified" as knowledge. But others will object that this means that people could be talked into believing that 2 + 2 = 5. Surely, they argue, there must be some kinds of knowledge that are not created rhetorically. This issue is sometimes expressed as the difference between *opinion* and *belief.* Rhetoric always seems to create opinion, while teaching seems to create belief. Now, does it matter whether we get knowledge from opinion or belief? Suppose you believe that George Washington was the first president of the United States. Does it matter *how* you come to believe it? Does it matter whether you believe it because a teacher charmed you into believing it (rhetorically) or because you carefully examined the historical record and *learned* that it was true? And is it possible to learn objectively, or is all learning in some way influenced by rhetoric?

The question of how knowledge relates to rhetoric is a question of whether the *discourse* that is rhetoric can be knowledgeable, requires knowledge to use, or can even generate knowledge. So our first two key issues of discourse and knowledge are closely related. We will find further connections when we turn to *media,* our third major issue.

MEDIA

The term *media* is the plural form of the singular *medium.* What is a medium? Rhetorical theorists have used the word in at least three ways.

What Is a Medium?

First, a medium is a *channel of communication.* It is what conveys the content or information in a message. Right now, the medium you are using is a book; it is how some information about rhetorical theory is being conveyed from the author to you. The same information might have been conveyed in other ways: on an audiocassette or videocassette tape, by personal visits from your author, and so forth. The medium chosen here, a book, seemed to be the most efficient way to carry this message to you.

Medium is used in a second, broader sense of a *technology of communication plus the ways the technology is habitually used.* This sense of a medium asks us to think about not only the channel used to convey information but about how the channel is used in a society. In the United States today, the television is a technology of communication, but to say that does not fully express the nature of television as a medium. Televisions are used primarily in the home, primarily for entertainment purposes, and primarily as an advertising outlet for businesses. It does not have to be used that way; much television in Great Britain, for instance, carries little or no advertising. Because this definition of a medium takes into consideration its social uses, it urges us to think of media sociologically.

The broadest, third meaning of a medium is that it is any *extension of a person.* This definition comes from Marshall McLuhan, some of whose work you will read later in this book. Think about how the medium of the telephone works, for instance. You want to speak to your friend across town, but your voice and ears won't "reach" that far. So you use the telephone to extend yourself a few miles. This definition of a medium asks us to think about the relationship between media and human thought processes, and to think of the ways in which each influences the other. Media can then be thought of as extensions of the human psyche.

Media and Rhetoric

For most people, the medium used in communication makes a difference. Have you ever preferred to speak to someone about a complicated matter in person, rather than over the telephone? You know that the telephone restricts the kind of information that can be carried (no visual content, for instance), and that it shapes the sorts of messages that are effective when carried on that medium. Have you ever said something angry in an e-mail message that you would never have said face-to-face? You know that the computer medium insulates you from having direct personal contact with whom you are communicating. In short, we know that we often pick and choose among the media available to us because the media themselves have differing rhetorical effects above and beyond the messages conveyed through them.

For that reason, many of the rhetorical theorists you will read in this book have something to say about using the media that were available to rhetoricians in their times. In ancient Greek and Roman times, one of the classical "canons" or chief parts of rhetoric was *memory.* This was a direct result of the fact that many ancient speakers chose to speak without the use of notes (although writing instruments were certainly available) because they preferred that "oral/aural" (speaking and hearing) medium by itself. Plato is explicitly against communicating through writing because the written word cannot be questioned and cannot answer back. He preferred the give and take of the oral/aural medium. Campbell, Whately, and Blair, however, urged students of Enlightenment rhetoric to write in preparation for speaking. In the twentieth century, many rhetorical theorists have tried to explain how rhetoric works in the expanding range of electronic media: telephone, television, film, audio recordings, video, etc. Theorists studying the rhetorical practices of groups such as women who have historically been marginalized or ignored by those in power have tried to identify alternative media outlets for those rhetorical practices: face-to-face "gossip," child rearing, letter writing, and so forth.

Two sets of issues that we will want to track through the history of rhetorical theory are connected with the relationships of media to our first two key issues, discourse and knowledge. First, do some discourses have more rhetorical effectiveness when conveyed through some media rather than others? This question becomes particularly important given the claim that many theorists make that a given society at a given time will have a *dominant* medium, a medium that carries more of the messages and more of the important messages of a society. Some, like McLuhan, would argue that television is a dominant medium in our culture, although computers may well be replacing television quickly. During the Renaissance, writing was a dominant medium, especially after the "Gutenberg revolution" of the invention of the printing press. How did the dominance of writing affect the way that the discourse of rhetoric worked during the Renaissance? Did writing favor some discourses and discourage others? St. Augustine directed his rhetorical theory at preachers. How did that focus on an oral/aural medium affect his rhetorical theories, and how did Burke's penchant for writing book after book affect *his* theories of rhetoric? We will want to track the ways in which dominant or preferred media interact with rhetorical and other discourses in the theories we read throughout this book.

The interaction between media and knowledge is also interesting. In any given age and context, some media will be thought to be more productive of knowledge than other media. Suppose I tell you that I "know" that Montana has declared itself free and independent of the United States. You might skeptically ask me *how* I "know" this. If I tell you that I read it in the *National Enquirer,* or that my neighbor told me, your skepticism is likely to be reinforced; these are not media (tabloid newspapers, backyard gossip) that we typically associate with knowledge. Suppose I told you, "I saw it on the TV news last night." *Now* you may begin to think that I am serious. We tend to regard television as a highly reliable medium for conveying knowledge, for telling us the "truth."

The link between media and knowledge is firmly established. Medical doctors may be skeptical of scientific discoveries that are communicated through the medium of press conferences rather than through the medium of scholarly journals. A college class in which students gain knowledge by reading lots of dusty books may be more highly regarded than a college class in which students gain knowledge by watching movies; this is because the printed word, especially in the form of books, is thought of as a more natural medium for conveying knowledge than is the medium of film. Furthermore, different communities will have preferences for the media in which knowledge is *stored.* Increasingly, people seem to prefer accessing information that is stored digitally in computers; this preference is likely to challenge the academic preference for storing knowledge in printed form.

The link between media and knowledge is therefore a factor in rhetorical appeals. Part of the process of sanctioning certain ideas as knowledge is to identify the media by which we arrived at those ideas. We will be tracking the ways in which connections between media and knowledge take on rhetorical effectiveness in the theories we will read in this book. Finally, let us consider the fourth major issue that will concern us, that of *power.*

POWER

Power is a dimension of almost all writing on rhetorical theory that is nevertheless not always brought to the forefront of discussion. Power has been an issue present in our discussion of the other three key issues, although we have not often mentioned it. Power is an inescapable issue when we are thinking about the problem of how we influence other people to think or act.

The relationship of rhetoric to power is complex. Three key questions help us to understand that relationship: *What is power? Can rhetoric give power to the persuader? Is rhetorical power a good or bad thing?*

What Is Power?

The question of what power is would seem to be straightforward: the ability to work your will, to get your way, to do what you want. But we will see that the matter is much more complicated than that. Plato raises some questions first: What if you don't know what you *should* want? What if getting your way harms you? Is it really power, then, to get your way if your way is ignorant and uninformed? In other words, Plato wanted his audience to think about what power is *for,* and to consider that ends or goals are more important than means—yet power often seems to be merely a pursuit of means for their own sake. Imagine someone who has a powerful automobile but doesn't have a clue about where to drive it, or when. If that person uses the car's three hundred horsepower engine to run into a stone wall at top speed, would we say that the person *really* has power? Others in Plato's era and since have raised similar questions about power. Cicero and the Sophists were unabashed in viewing power as gaining personal and political advantage. For St. Augustine, power lay in the ability to spread the Word of God accurately and persuasively. For Hugh Blair in the eighteenth century, power was the ability to discern what is tasteful and what is not in art and discourse. One issue we will be on the lookout for, then, is what each rhetorical theorist thinks power is, because that will surely affect what each theorist thinks about how power can be attained.

Can Rhetoric Give Power?

Whether rhetoric can give power to the persuader depends in large part on the first question of what power is. If power is the ability to know the truth, then can rhetoric reveal and impart the truth? The question also arises about the domain of rhetorical influence, because if rhetoric has any power at all, it will be in the realm of whatever it can influence. If a theorist sees rhetoric as restricted to formal legal and political contexts, can rhetoric give power in interpersonal contexts? If rhetoric gives power to produce beautiful discourse, as Ramus and Blair suggest, does that deny it the power to alter political and social opinions? One more question concerning the power of rhetoric has to do with the ways that alternative rhetorics can empower marginalized groups. If women or people of color have often been excluded from the exercise of power in Western societies, what rhetorical resources do they have for finding and exercising power *in the margin?*

Are there *subversive* rhetorics that can give power to groups that are denied access to the traditional means of rhetorical influence?

Is Rhetorical Power Good or Bad?

Lord Acton is famous for his saying, "Power corrupts, and absolute power corrupts absolutely." If rhetoric is a way to get power, this might suggest that rhetoric is always to be avoided because of its tendency to corrupt. We may feel hard pressed to discover politicians, who have used rhetorical power to get elected, also using that power in exclusively ethical ways. Some theorists like Mikhail Bakhtin argue that because language use is always ideological, rhetorical struggles over power are unavoidable. Others will note that rhetoric grants the power to do *both* good and evil. Both Hitler and Dr. Martin Luther King, Jr. were masterful rhetoricians—without the power that their rhetoric gave them, neither would have been able to do what he did. The question of whether rhetoric must corrupt rhetoricians will be an ongoing issue in the rhetorical theories that we read.

Power, Discourse, Knowledge, Media

The relationship between power and the first three key issues of discourse, knowledge, and media is complicated. There seem to be some discourses that lead more easily to the acquisition and exercise of power, and of course that changes over the years. When St. Augustine was writing about the rhetoric of the discourse of religion, he was writing about a discourse that was empowered in the political and social realms of his time. Today, other discourses such as science and law seem to be more empowered politically than does religion. When Ramus and Blair write of rhetorical discourse in terms of style and taste, they seem to be regarding rhetoric as a discourse that is not very empowered beyond the aesthetic dimension. As we study the writings in this book, we will want to take note of which discourses are empowered and which are not, and whether the discourse of rhetoric is one of those so empowered.

An important use of power is the ability to certify certain ideas as being knowledge. For instance, Foucault will note how those who rise to power in the medical profession can certify which thoughts are sane and which are insane. They are gatekeepers for what counts as knowledge and what counts as delusion. On the other hand, possession of knowledge leads to power. Command over what a society regards as true information can be a major resource of rhetoric and can lead to power.

Some media will be regarded as more empowered for any given society at any given time. If the printed word is the dominant medium, then messages conveyed in print will have a more powerful impact and will be regarded more seriously. For instance, you may be advised that if you agree to any important commitment you should "get it in writing," which is a favoring of the printed word still in force even in an age of computers and television. One way in which marginalized groups may be excluded from power is therefore exclusion from dominant media, and that is why disempowered groups may be seen less on television or trained less in the use of computers today. Much of the rhetorical effect of media themselves will have to do with which media support power more readily.

We have thought about some basic definitions of rhetoric and have learned about four key issues that will surface again and again as writers address important questions of rhetoric. What exactly do these writers do, in writing about rhetoric? What is a rhetorical theory, and what can we expect to learn from studying them? We move now to the second part of this Introduction.

THINKING ABOUT THEORY

Early in this introduction we learned that a theory is the assertion of regular, systematic relationships among actions, objects, and events in the world. Although some people think that a theory is some abstraction separated from reality, in fact we need theories to help us get through the day. You may have a theory about how to deal with a co-worker who is sometimes difficult. You might have a theory about how to get the best deal on a new car. A theory about what is wrong with your VCR may lead you to correct it successfully. In each case, knowledge about regular, systematic relationships among actions, objects, and events is essential in understanding what is going on in life.

We also considered a wide range of definitions of rhetoric at the start of this introduction. It may come as no surprise that for a subject defined in as many ways as is *rhetoric,* there is also quite a variety of ways to *theorize* about rhetoric. Different kinds of systematic relationships may be asserted, and different kinds of actions, objects, and events may be the focus of those systematic relationships. When people say they are writing rhetorical theory, in fact they have written many different kinds of texts throughout history. So we are now going to review what one *can do* when one *does rhetorical theory.* Our survey of kinds of rhetorical theory will be based around seven pairs of dimensions: function and manifestation; practice and critique; philosophy and history; academic and popular; continuities and discontinuities; mainstream and marginal; and construction and deconstruction. As we will note when we are finished, these pairs are far from exclusive of one another; in fact they are all functions of one another. Therefore, the varieties of rhetorical theory can be amazingly complex. Before we understand that idea, we need to better understand our seven pairs of theoretical dimensions.

FUNCTION AND MANIFESTATION

Rhetoric can be theorized in terms of either the function it performs or the manifestation in which it appears within any given society. The *function* of rhetoric is what it does, and that will vary according to the role accorded influence and persuasion within a given society. In Giambattista Vico's vision of humane study, rhetoric was the key to knowledge of humankind. For John Locke, rhetoric is the efficient transfer of an idea from one mind to another. For Richard Whately in early-nineteenth century Britain, rhetoric performed the function of rational argument.

Rhetoric is also material—it is embodied. That means that it must take on some physical form, whether in a spoken speech or a written essay or some other *manifestation.* Many theorists such as William Hoffman focused on the manifestation which is public speaking. Others, such as Bernays, have thought about rhetoric as mass persuasion through mass media, a different sort of manifestation. For theorists of etiquette such as Eliza Leslie, rhetoric (especially for women) manifests itself in manners and comportment.

One way to distinguish among theories, then, is whether their main concern is with function or manifestation or some combination of the two. Is the theory about how rhetoric works in its social and cultural setting? Or is the theory about the particular way rhetoric manifests itself in a given time and place, offering advice on how to manipulate the material of that manifestation? Throughout history there has been a bias in most rhetorical theory to focus on manifestations that were *like public speeches* in being verbal, reasoned discourse. We will find that this bias sometimes blinds theorists to functions that rhetoric may be performing when it appears in manifestations other than traditional verbal discourse. Therefore we should be on the lookout for assumptions made by theorists about the functions rhetoric performs and about the manifestations in which it appears, and note where the emphasis in the theory lies.

PRACTICE AND CRITIQUE

This pair and the next set of theoretical dimensions are linked. First, someone might theorize about rhetorical *practice*. Regularities might be observed between specific rhetorical practices or techniques and outcomes. Some theorists such as George Campbell claimed that the best rhetorical theory does no more than this, taking note of what the most successful orators do to win the agreement of an audience. The purpose of this sort of theory is very often to advise prospective orators how to discover the most effective means of persuasion. Ultimately, this kind of theorizing is directed toward understanding how to improve practice.

Understanding any act of persuasion must be based upon observations. What rhetorical problems do people face when trying to influence others, and how are they overcome? How does unintentional influence work, sometimes at a very deep level of perceptual structure? To answer these questions, people might engage in a *critique* of rhetoric. A critique or criticism does not mean finding fault with rhetoric, it means examining and studying a rhetorical transaction so as to understand it better. This may eventually lead to an improved practice, but it need not do so, and understanding must always come before thinking about improved practice.

Critique itself is not yet theory, although it might be informed by or make use of theories of rhetoric. Critique is an engagement with a text so as to understand it better. Critique is not a rare or effete activity indulged in only by dusty professors! Every movie review or rock concert write-up is a critique. When you and your friends try to make sense of last night's NCAA basketball championship game, you are doing a critique.

But one might very well *theorize critique;* that is to say, think about different types and methods of critique. One might propose systematic ways of asking questions about a text, or suggest reliable techniques of noticing more effectively how a text works rhetorically. This theorizing about critique is called *methodology*—in this case specifically, methodology of *rhetorical criticism.* Blair was very much concerned with developing critical methodologies to help his readers discern taste in works of art. So one dimension of rhetorical theory might be directed either towards the practice of rhetoric or towards the methods by which we critique specific episodes of rhetoric.

HISTORY AND PHILOSOPHY

Methods for producing texts (practice) can be systematized, as can methods for understanding texts (critique). But there can be theories of theories, also—ways of systematically understanding what it is that we do when we systematically understand! In addition to theorizing about practice or about critique, one can also theorize about theory itself. In fact, this introduction is an example of theorizing about theory; it is presenting some conceptual schemes to help you understand how theory has been done throughout history.

There are two ways that scholars typically theorize about theory. One is to think *historically.* History may be understood in different ways because it is not composed of just one "obvious" story about a clear and simple string of events. The history of the United States would be very different from what one finds in most high school history textbooks if it were written by Asian-Americans or by African-Americans, for instance. History, therefore, needs to be theorized; systematic relationships among events, objects, and actions need to be asserted and argued for rather than simply "discovered." To theorize rhetorical theory historically is to propose a way to understand rhetorical theory as it chains out in history. The pattern of organization in this book arranges rhetorical theories according to an historical pattern in this way. The essay by Karlyn Kohrs Campbell is an example of theorizing history by proposing a particular way to see the history of women's public speaking.

One might also theorize about theories by asserting systematic relationships among them that are based on *philosophical* thinking. Theories might be grouped and thought about in terms of their underlying assumptions or goals. They might be systematized according to the fundamental definitions of reality that are contained within each theory. Theories might be grouped and then systematically studied according to theories that define rhetoric chiefly in terms of language, for instance; were this book to be organized in that way, one unit might consist of Longinus, perhaps Augustine, Ramus, Blair, Richards, and Burke. Or were we to theorize about theories according to their definitions of reality, Plato and Weaver might make up a unit on "idealist rhetoric." The essay by Spitzack and Carter organizes theories about women's rhetoric philosophically by noting the basic goals and assumptions that systematically link theories into some specific groups.

ACADEMIC AND POPULAR

One distinction between two different kinds of theorizing that has recently arisen is that of *academic* or *popular* theories of rhetoric. Before the late nineteenth or early twentieth century, this distinction was unimportant. Rhetorical theorists were writing for the benefit of a generally educated audience, which was the same audience that would make use of whatever advice the theories offered so as to engage in practice or critique. Although theorists have certainly held academic or teaching jobs throughout history (Aristotle, Quintilian, George Campbell and so forth), academics wrote for the general, educated population. Other than their source of employment, academic rhetoricians were indistinguishable from other rhetoricians who were offering rhetorical advice at the same time.

Only recently has there arisen a distinction between those who offer rhetorical theories for the general public and those who write rhetorical theories that are by and large read *within the academy* by students and other scholars. William Hoffman's book, *Public Speaking for Business Men,* and dozens like it, have never been considered academic, yet have served as rhetorical theory for millions of ordinary people who had to give speeches in business and social contexts. On the other hand, Kenneth Burke's *A Grammar of Motives* is a landmark book of rhetorical theory, but you will be hard pressed to find anyone reading it outside of colleges and universities.

One distinction you will want to notice as you read the theories in this book, then, is whether they are written for consumption within the academic community or in the general population. Take note of how that difference affects the ways the theories are written and the questions the theories address. Think about how this distinction generates a different way of thinking about what theory is good for.

Continuities and Discontinuities

One purpose that one might have in theorizing is to identify *continuities* in rhetorical theories, either within an era or culture or across wider spans of time and place. A theory of this sort might settle on one perspective or definition of rhetoric and track the ways in which rhetorical discourse throughout history and from one culture to another has matched that definition. To some extent, this introduction does this in asserting that discourse, knowledge, media, and power were four key issues relevant to all rhetorical theory. You will also find brief passages in some of the theories you read where the history of rhetorical theory is surveyed, as in chapter two of Whately's Introduction. It is easy to dismiss such passages as the theorist's quick and inconsequential survey of rhetoric, but such a dismissal would be a mistake. Instead, it is important to notice the continuities among histories being asserted by such theorists.

A theorist might also assert a discontinuity, however, exemplified by Weaver's complaint that recent rhetorical theory is bedeviled by scientism. One might survey rhetorical theories so as to find fault lines where the theory of one era or culture departs radically from that of another. This sort of theorizing typically links theories to history, culture, politics, and social circumstances, arguing that as those change, so do theories intended to account for rhetorical functioning.

An issue related to continuity and discontinuity is what one might call "family pride or scandals." We noted earlier that definitions of rhetoric differ in terms of weighting, or whether they "approve" of rhetoric or not. Constructions of rhetorical theories can sometimes work as extensions of such definitions, grouping together as rhetoric things that are "pride" or "scandal" depending on how one feels about rhetoric. These are assertions of continuities and discontinuities, as well. Plato, for instance, groups rhetoric within a whole class of things he calls "flattery," including cosmetics and cookery. He intends to scandalize rhetoric by putting it in some trivial company. Quintilian, on the other hand, defines the orator as "a good man skilled in speaking," thus *excluding* bad men from any consideration as rhetors, preserving family "pride" by setting such speakers as Hitler outside the pale of oratory. One way to study the continuities and discontinuities in theory construction, then, is to track what is included or excluded in the group that the theorist is calling "rhetoric."

MAINSTREAM OR MARGIN

You will notice that all the "business" of this introduction is done in the main part of the page. See all that empty white space around these printed words? That is the *margin*, where it is assumed that no important meanings are managed, no important information is contained. Every society likewise has its margins as well as its *mainstream*. The mainstream is where most attention is focused. It is where important decisions are made and where decisions about power and resources are managed. Rhetoric proceeds apace in both mainstream and margin, but most theories have looked only at the mainstream.

The Sophists, Plato, and Aristotle all talked about how rhetoric was conducted in Greek democracies, principally in that of Athens. They were theorizing about the mainstream of Greek society, however. Strangely enough, only about 15 percent of the population of Athens actually got to participate in that democracy. The rest of the population (women, children, the foreign-born) were surely engaging in some sort of rhetoric, but whatever their rhetorical practices were, they were *not* what the Sophists, Plato, and Aristotle looked at! Most of rhetorical theory throughout history has followed that pattern of theorizing the rhetorical experience of the mainstream.

Theorizing the rhetoric of the margin can be very interesting, and can add a needed complexity to our understanding of rhetoric. St. Augustine was theorizing a Christian rhetoric that was just entering an empowered, mainstream status after years of being in a marginalized state. Fell, K. K. Campbell, Spitzack, and Carter theorize about the experiences of women, whose rhetoric has usually and until very recently been marginalized by patriarchal societies. Molefi Asante theorizes about Afrocentric rhetoric and how it differs from mainstream Eurocentric rhetoric. So one way to distinguish among rhetorical theories is in terms of whether they theorize the mainstream or the margin.

CONSTRUCTION OR DECONSTRUCTION

One final distinction one might make is the use of theories to *construct* an understanding of systematic relationships in rhetorical transactions as opposed to the use of theories to *deconstruct* present understandings. The distinction is fairly straightforward. When we construct theories, it is for the purpose of guiding the understandings we have of how rhetoric works. When Chaim Perelman and L. Olbrechts-Tyteca propose the concept of the "universal audience," for instance, it is to introduce a concept that had not really been sufficiently noted before in rhetorical theory. Similarly, Stephen Toulmin's model of argumentation was a revolutionary new theoretical construction that was highly influential in helping people to understand how argument works in everyday contexts.

But one might also use theories to deconstruct understandings that are in place, often with the purpose of suggesting (constructing) new ones, but not necessarily so. Peter Ramus sets out explicitly to deconstruct Quintilian's popular rhetorical theories; Ramus's theory is much more of an attack on Quintilian than it is the construction of an alternative (although he is more constructive in other writings). Margaret Fell both deconstructs the patriarchal theories of rhetoric of her time, which tended to exclude women from public speaking, as well as proposes an alternative view of women's rhetoric as spiritually justified.

Complications and Interactions

We have reviewed seven pairs of dimensions describing what a rhetorical theory might do, might be about, or might feature. But it is important to realize that these are not exclusive categories. A given theory is unlikely *only* to function within just one of the pairs. Instead, what theories do and how they work can be incredibly complex, and that complexity can be realized by looking at the pairs as functions of one another. As an example, a given theory might theorize rhetorical *functions* with an emphasis on rhetorical *practice* rather than critique, philosophy, or history; or it might be a *popular* theory that announces itself as a *discontinuity* with previous practice because it is looking at rhetoric in the *margins*. Therefore, it performs a *constructive* theoretical function. On the other hand, a theory might theorize rhetorical *manifestations* . . . and then do everything else the first example did. Clearly, the possible combinations are enormous! For this reason, we should not be surprised at the variety that the wide range of theories you will read will display.

PREVIEW

It is now time to turn to the reason for this book—the actual survey of rhetorical theories. These theories are organized chronologically. The major categories of the book are:

Classical Greek Heritage

Classical Roman Heritage

Middle Ages and Renaissance

Enlightenment through the Nineteenth Century

Twentieth Century

Each unit begins with a brief essay introducing the major themes and concerns of that period. You will be given some ideas of what to look for as you read the material. Our four major issues of discourse, knowledge, media, and power will help us to organize our approach to each unit. Questions are posed to help you know what some of the most important points are in the readings. Each introductory essay suggests some books for further reading. Then the works of each particular theorist are introduced with a very brief essay telling you more about the professional and personal background of the writer.

Serious scholars spend lifetimes mining the ideas and issues within any one period—indeed, within any one author. Therefore, you should not expect to master the entirety of rhetorical theory in one pass-through. However, those of you who are new to rhetorical theory should still expect to learn a lot from this intellectual adventure, and you should expect an investment of your time and attention to pay off. These writings have endured not because they are obscure and difficult; some of them are, but most are not! They have endured because they are really about *us,* about how we talk to one another, and about our human condition. So as you read, be prepared to look for *yourself,* the society you live in, and the issues you confront in your everyday life.

FOR FURTHER READING

Black, Edwin. 1978. *Rhetorical Criticism: A Study in Method.* Madison: University of Wisconsin.

Black, Edwin. 1992. *Rhetorical Questions: Studies of Public Discourse.* Chicago: University of Chicago.

Blair, Carole. 1992. "Contested Histories of Rhetoric: The Politics of Preservation, Progress, and Change," *Quarterly Journal of Speech, 78:* 403–428.

Bryant, Donald C. 1953. "Rhetoric: Its Functions and Its Scope," *Quarterly Journal of Speech, 39:* 401–424.

Cherwitz, Richard A. 1990. *Rhetoric and Philosophy.* Hillsdale, NJ: Lawrence Erlbaum.

Covino, William A., and David A. Jolliffe. 1995. *Rhetoric: Concepts, Definitions, Boundaries.* Boston: Allyn and Bacon.

Ehninger, Douglas. 1975. "Colloquy II: A Synoptic View of Systems of Western Rhetoric," *Quarterly Journal of Speech, 56:* 448–453.

Enos, Theresa. 1996. *Encyclopedia of Rhetoric and Composition.* NY: Garland Publishing.

Foss, Karen A., and Sonja K. Foss. 1991. *Women Speak.* Prospect Heights, IL: Waveland.

Foss, Sonja K., Karen A. Foss, and Robert Trapp. 1991. *Contemporary Perspectives on Rhetoric,* 2nd ed. Prospect Heights, IL: Waveland.

Hart, Roderick P. 1990. *Modern Rhetorical Criticism.* Glenview, IL: Scott, Foresman.

Hauser, Gerard A. 1986. *Introduction to Rhetorical Theory.* Prospect Heights, IL: Waveland.

Kinneavy, James L. 1971. *A Theory of Discourse.* Englewood Cliffs, NJ: Prentice–Hall.

Scott, Robert L. 1975. "Colloquy I: A Synoptic View of Systems of Western Rhetoric," *Quarterly Journal of Speech, 56:* 439–447.

Vickers, Brian. 1988. *In Defence of Rhetoric.* Oxford: Clarendon Press.

Wallace, Karl R. 1963. "The Substance of Rhetoric: Good Reasons," *Quarterly Journal of Speech, 49:* 239–249.

Classical Greek Heritage

INTRODUCTION TO THE CLASSICAL GREEK HERITAGE

The most enduring influence on how rhetoric is understood and practiced in Western cultures has been ancient, democratic Greek civilization. Teachers and theorists of rhetoric, as well as famous orators who lived during that time, put down the foundation for rhetorical theory that followed. This essay introduces the main themes and concerns of rhetorical theory that were developed during the most fruitful part of the classical period, from about 500 to 300 B.C.E. Because those rhetorical ideas arose out of the social and cultural conditions of the Greek city-states, especially Athens, we first need to understand something about their history and society.

Historical Background

If you examine a map of Greece today, you will notice at least these two features: Much of the interior is mountainous, and much of the rest is exposed to the sea through bays, harbors, or islands. This means that civilization in ancient Greece arose in pockets here and there around the perimeter of the mainland and on islands. It was only later, initially with Alexander the Great, that really strong unified governments arose to create the political idea of Greece as one country. Instead, *city-states*—autonomous and relatively small political units—such as Athens, Sparta, and Corinth developed.

Because they settled by the sea, the Greeks had to be outward-going. They maintained active contact with other city-states and indeed, with the whole of the Mediterranean world. This meant that their civilizations, culturally as well as economically, grew rapidly from enrichment by other cultures and their ideas. Some scholars have argued, for instance, that much older African, specifically Egyptian, culture strongly influenced the development of Greek civilization as it was imported into Greece through trade.

Several of these city-states became true democracies, in which all the citizens participated directly in all governmental affairs (in the United States today, we live in a *republic* whereby we elect representatives who make decisions for us; very few public decisions are made democratically). Of these, Athens was the largest, with a population of about 150,000 at the time of Plato.

Being open to the sea, the city-states developed merchant fleets and trading empires that enriched them, attracting the attention of the military power to the east, Persia. Persia invaded, and most of the Greek city-states banded together to resist the threat. Against great odds, the Greeks defeated the Persians, and what is known as the Golden Age of Greece began in 479 B.C.E. A great statesman and orator, Pericles, was the main leader of Athens during this period. Under Pericles's wise leadership, democracy flourished and generated wise and effective government.

We can point to at least three important characteristics of most Greek thought at this time. One was a sense of unity in life and in the universe. The Greeks sought connectedness in their affairs. They assumed that a unity existed within the universe and between humanity and the universe that should be duplicated through harmonious human affairs. Second, the Greeks believed in achievement of well-rounded excellence in every dimension of humanity. The phrase "moderation in all things," which was born in and typical of this period, was a call for evenhanded development of excellence in all things, with no one trait being allowed to overshadow others to their detriment. Greeks expected people to be conversant with arts, athletics, and mathematics equally. Finally, the Greeks were a practical people. Although they were no strangers to philosophy and the consideration of abstract issues, it was usually in regards to the conduct of real human affairs and everyday life.

Athens maintained its dominance over the other city-states due to its size and power, a dominance that eventually became overbearing. Enmity arose between Athens and her fellow city-states around 447, followed by increasing hostilities and conflicts until the whole area erupted in what is known as the Peloponnesian War, around 432. It was the beginning of the end for Athenian dominance. In 430, Athens was ravaged by the plague. In 429, Pericles died, but he was soon replaced by a man named Alcibiades. The contrast between these two leaders exemplified the best and the worst of democracy and rhetoric's role in facilitating self rule. Alcibiades was a student and possibly a lover of Socrates, but he forsook his early training in philosophy to become a demagogue. Using his oratorical skill, Alcibiades persuaded the Athenians to engage in several unwise and disastrous wars. After he fell from power in 414, Athens spent several years alternating between basically two political forms, democracy or oligarchy (government by a few strong individuals), imposed on them by other victorious city-states. In general, when democracy was in place, Athenians were inspired by militant orators to undertake wars they ultimately lost. Under the direction of oligarchs, peace returned. In short, democracy was not a completely effective political form for Athens during this later period.

MAJOR FIGURES CONCERNED WITH RHETORIC

We are now ready to turn our attention to some of the major figures and groups of people who were thinking and teaching about rhetoric during this time period. The first important group is known as the *Sophists*. A sophist literally means a wise person or a lover of wisdom. As you can tell, the term is extremely broad, and indeed it was applied widely; Socrates himself was called a sophist. But eventually the term came to be associated with a particular group of traveling teachers of public speaking.

The triumph of the city-states over Persia prompted some serious reflection by the Greeks as to who they were and what their culture meant. They had a strong sense of being Greek, yet because of their political fragmentation their sense of being Greek was grounded in their language. They came to regard the Greek language as a particularly fine instrument of communication and thought. A related development was the growth of democracies. In a direct democracy, all decisions must be made through public discussion of serious problems. If you want a law passed, you must speak in favor of it yourself. If someone accuses you of a crime, you must defend yourself directly. Public speaking, therefore, became a vital skill for social and political life.

A demand therefore arose for instruction in how to use this marvelous Greek language in contexts of public debate, discussion, and oratory. A group of teachers of rhetoric came forward to meet the need: these were the Sophists. Although some, like Isocrates, were settled in one locale and opened formal schools, many of them, such as Gorgias, traveled from place to place, offering quick instruction usually for lucrative fees. Greeks eager to gain power and influence through the vital medium of public speaking flocked to these teachers. The Sophists generally were very practical, focused on the here and now, and concerned with everyday human affairs. They were more interested in practical action than in high principles.

The Sophists did not leave us very many writings. Some sophistic philosophers such as Heraclitus and Hermagoras left only fragments. The rhetorician Isocrates left a little more, such as his speech *Antidosis.* The *Antidosis* was a speech Isocrates gave defending himself against what he felt was an unjust tax. In it, he comments on several aspects of Athenian society. The excerpts printed here reflect his concerns for how his fellow Sophists were teaching rhetoric.

We also have here Isocrates's essay *Against the Sophists.* Now, why is the Sophist Isocrates writing against Sophists?! Because as time passed, the term came to be applied to those Sophists who were most likely to offer shallow and simplistic instruction. Although public speaking, and instruction in rhetoric, was as valued as ever, the public came to understand that as with any other subject, people could and did set themselves up as experts without truly possessing expertise. So it was with the Sophists, and thus Isocrates is really writing against Sophists who had fallen into ill repute by that time.

One of the greatest and most successful teachers of rhetoric was Gorgias, but even he was accused of teaching tricks and style rather than substance. Included here is a speech that he would give, the *Encomium of Helen,* as an example of the sort of rhetorical skills one could acquire by studying with him. We should read it for the techniques it demonstrates and for what its general style implies about how rhetoric should be conducted.

Other influential Greeks were not so charmed by the Sophists. Socrates was one of these skeptics. He lived in and around Athens, teaching and talking about philosophy. Socrates thought that cities should be governed by those who had the greatest knowledge, not by those who had the greatest persuasive power. Lucky democracies were swayed by wise leaders such as Pericles. But democracies work through rhetoric whether that persuasion turns out to be wise or not, and therefore Socrates argued that democracies could not guarantee that the people would be persuaded to make wise choices. He had the sad example of Alcibiades to make his point: a persuasive but foolish figure who did not know what Athens should do, and therefore persuaded the Athenians to make unwise decisions. Socrates's position was in the minority, and he so insulted the predominant democratic sensibilities of the time that he was put to death in 399 B.C.E.

The social and financial triumphs of the Sophists, coupled with the tragic death of Socrates, powerfully affected Socrates's most famous pupil, Plato. Unlike Socrates, who did not write anything that survives today, Plato wrote quite a lot of philosophy in the form of dialogues. Socrates appears as the major character and mouthpiece for Plato in these dialogues. Plato also vigorously opposed the idea of democracy and of persuasive public speaking that came with democracy, preferring instead that those with true knowledge, philosophers, should tell the people what to do. Plato's major works having to do with rhetoric are the dialogues *Gorgias* and *Phaedrus,* although many of his other famous works such as the *Republic* are also relevant to the study of rhetoric.

Plato was more settled than his teacher, and in 386 he founded a school called the Academy. One of the students there became a towering figure in Western culture and is the central thinker in the history of rhetorical theory: Aristotle. Aristotle wrote many books laying out his views on philosophy, science, and society in systematic, orderly structures of thought. One of his books is the *Rhetoric,* although many others such as the *Poetics* or the *Topics* are also directly concerned with rhetorical issues. The *Rhetoric* was the first exhaustive treatment of the purpose, contexts, and techniques of rhetoric. Aristotle founded his own school, called the Lyceum, in 334, and died in 322 B.C.E.

ISSUES IN CLASSICAL GREEK RHETORIC

With an understanding of the history, culture, and major figures of the Classical Greek Heritage in place, what are the major themes and issues to look out for in the readings that follow? We will organize our thinking around the four major themes of *discourse, knowledge, media,* and *power.*

At the beginning of Plato's dialogue, *Gorgias,* Socrates has come to the home of a powerful Athenian figure, Callicles, to hear the famous Sophist, Gorgias. Gorgias was engaged in an exercise common to many of the Sophists, which was that he offered to give a brief impromptu speech on *any* subject that anyone might propose to him or answer any question that might be put to him. The idea was that the public would be so impressed by this ability to speak on anything at a moment's notice that they would sign up with Gorgias for instruction in public speaking.

The Sophists had another sort of "advertisement" for their services, and that was to give a speech that had been carefully prepared and designed to show off the rhetorical skills that a student might learn. Because such speeches would be given across time and in many different contexts, they typically were not related to the "real world" of the here and now. Such is the speech that begins this collection of readings, Gorgias's *Encomium of Helen.* This speech is a defense of Helen of Troy, who even for these Greeks was a figure of ancient history and mythology.

So Plato puts Socrates into this dramatic situation of confronting a Sophist who is advertising his services. And what Socrates wants to know first is, what sort of *discourse* is this rhetoric that Gorgias claims to teach? The question is initially put in terms of what sort of job Gorgias has, as we might call one who makes shoes a shoemaker, or one who paints a painter. But since Gorgias's job is entirely wrapped up in teaching people how to make discourse, not shoes, the question is, as Socrates also says, one of "What is the function of his art, and what is it that he professes and teaches?" Socrates might have used as a focal example the same *Encomium* that you have in this book, to ask Gorgias the question, What kind of speaking and thinking is this?

Several issues need to be considered in answering the question of what sort of discourse rhetoric is. One, which is highlighted by Plato in the *Gorgias,* is the issue of whether rhetoric is a distinct kind of discourse. For as Socrates is made to point out in the dialogue, whenever one engages in rhetoric, one is always talking about something for which there is a proper body of knowledge and a separate discourse. He notes that when Gorgias's brother practices the profession of medicine, he is always speaking about medicine, which is grounded in its own distinct discourse. If one speaks about a proposed law to levy a tax on olive growers, one is speaking about economics and agriculture, both of which have their "own" discourses. One can never just speak about "nothing." Even Gorgias's *Encomium* is about something, albeit the mythic and distant Helen of Troy. So an issue to consider is, what is rhetoric *about?* What makes it distinct from other discourses? And if these thinkers identify distinctive characteristics of rhetoric, are those desirable characteristics, or is rhetoric the sort of discourse that must always lead to undesirable consequences?

A second issue concerning discourse is that of alternative discourses to rhetoric. A democracy must talk among itself to settle public questions. Plaintiffs and defendants must present reasons to support their cases. What discourses besides rhetoric are available for these purposes? For Plato, clearly the preferable alternative discourse is something called *dialectic.*

Dialectic is a discourse based on a free discussion among equal parties, based on questions and answers, designed to reach conclusions through achieving agreements based on categories, distinctions among categories, and divisions within categories. Let us suppose you wanted to know what *mental illness* is, for instance. You and another person might sit down and begin to discuss the issue. Is mental illness a good thing or a bad thing? A bad thing, surely. Is it a disease of the body or of the mind or both? Of the mind, or of both, you might decide. Then you might work to *distinguish* mental illness from other sorts of maladies as well as to *subdivide* mental illness into types or categories. As a result of this process, you might both come to an understanding of what mental illness is.

Plato is the great champion of dialectic; his dialogues are written in that form. Although we might well question whether he allows Socrates to slip into rhetorical discourse from time to time, his intention at least is to present Socrates as attempting to arrive at the truth about various matters dialectically. And clearly Socrates prefers dialectic to the discourse of rhetoric, with the latter involving single individuals holding forth for long periods of time to present their own views, backed up by reasoned argument and evidence. Notice how in the *Gorgias* he repeatedly cautions the other characters against such lengthy rhetorical display (although he is not shy about dominating the conversation himself). And although the *Phaedrus* is constructed around three speeches, note how *dialectical* the last, best speech is with its emphasis on definitions, comparisons, and contrasts. For Plato, dialectic was a way to arrive at *truth,* whereas rhetoric was a sort of discourse that could only generate *probability,* at best.

However, note that for Aristotle, *both* rhetoric and dialectic are counterparts of one another, *both* are discourses designed to answer questions for which we have no firm sciences and no well developed arts to guide us. If we want to know about the orbit of the moon, for instance, we have the art and science of astronomy to tell us about that orbit. Nor does that discourse generate merely probable conclusions; it can tell us for sure where the moon will be in the sky tonight. But if we want to know which candidate is better for an open political position, there are no definitive arts or sciences to help us with that question; therefore, we must argue it out, either through the give and take and categorizations of dialectic or through trading the more lengthy and developed arguments of rhetoric. So, when Aristotle wrote his *Rhetoric,* he was describing a kind of discourse that he saw, in contrast to Plato, as being similar to dialectic.

Two of these theorists introduce an idea that we will see echoed later in history: Rhetorical discourse is peculiar to being human; indeed, it defines us as such. Isocrates notes that only in rhetorical power do people exceed the abilities of animals. And Aristotle argues that people should be able to defend themselves verbally at least as well as they do physically, since the former rather than the latter defines humanity.

With our discussion above of truth and probability, we have segued into our second major issue of *knowledge.* You may recall that the issue of whether something can be taught is a major question in discussing knowledge. That issue arises often in the readings in this section. Attacking some of his fellow shallow Sophists, Isocrates raises the question of exactly what these teachers are teaching and what *can* be taught. For both Isocrates and Plato, the question of whether *virtue* can be taught is central to a discussion of rhetoric. Both writers note that to teach a person how to be persuasive without teaching the orator how to use that power responsibly—in other words, how to use it *virtuously*—can lead to abuses of power exemplified by Alcibiades. Yet the question arises for both theorists as to whether virtue *can* be taught, and specifically, whether the Sophists were teaching virtue and wisdom along with rhetorical skill. Is virtue something that can only be acquired through experience and wide, lengthy learning throughout life?

Related to that issue is the question of whether *rhetoric* can be taught. Note that in the *Gorgias,* Socrates defines rhetoric as merely a knack or habit picked up from experience. Compare the attitudes expressed there to those discussed in the *Phaedrus.* In that second dialogue, Plato seems to have Socrates express a more friendly attitude toward rhetoric. Socrates is in fact instructing young Phaedrus in the proper use of rhetoric, both in technique and in the ultimate *uses* of rhetoric (in other words, in virtue). Pay close attention to whether rhetoric is treated as a teachable discourse in that dialogue, and if so, on what terms (or, what dimensions or skills of rhetoric can be taught).

Isocrates is obliged to say that rhetoric is teachable, of course, since he himself founded a school to do that very thing. But as you read both *Against the Sophists* and the *Antidosis,* try to identify, in Isocrates's view, what is teachable about rhetoric and whether rhetorical principles can be extensively systematized. How much of rhetorical skill must be picked up from experience, according to Isocrates? To the extent that rhetoric can be taught, what suggestions does Isocrates offer for doing so?

Aristotle, the great systematizer, seems to present us with a view of rhetoric as extremely teachable. His exhaustive presentation of techniques, contexts, and purposes for rhetorical discourse could be designed to teach people how to engage in rhetorical practice. For centuries, his *Rhetoric* was treated in exactly that way by succeeding theorists who used it as the basis for instruction in public speaking.

One more knowledge-related issue that we will need to consider as we read these selections is whether rhetoric itself can be a route to knowledge. We might take a resounding "no!" to be the basis of both of the Platonic dialogues here. Follow the intricate lines of questioning throughout the *Gorgias* to note how Socrates separates knowledge and truth, which comes from dialectical discourse, from the mere opinion and belief, which comes from rhetorical discourse. Pay particular attention to Plato's arguments as to why that gap is inevitable and unavoidable and to why rhetoric *cannot* lead to knowledge, even with the best of intentions. When Plato defines rhetoric as flattery, note that he does so by comparing it to other "flattering" practices such as cooking or cosmetics that produce pleasure rather than true knowledge.

For Aristotle, rhetoric is not meant to lead to absolute, firm, scientific knowledge. Like dialectic (in his view, but not Plato's), it can only lead to probabilities: We can only "know" that the defendant is *probably* guilty; we can only "know" that passing this law is probably the best thing to do. We can never "know" that we should absolutely and definitely build this battleship for our navy now in the sense that we can "know" that the square root of sixteen is four.

The distinction Aristotle draws here is important and foundational for the succeeding centuries of rhetorical theory. He creates a great "divide" between issues that can be decided certainly, once and for all, and those that can only be settled with some measure of probability. Neither Plato nor the Sophists shared the idea of that division in quite the same way. Plato thought that *every* issue, from the mathematical to the moral, had some definite and sure answer (even if discovering that answer were difficult). The Sophists tended toward a kind of relativism, holding that truth and knowledge is changeable and shifting. By clearly defining two separate realms of knowledge, and by assigning rhetoric (and dialectic) to the management of one realm, Aristotle also created a great temptation to *shift* issues from the contingent, probable, uncertain realm over to the realm of sure and certain answers. This ultimately puts rhetoric on unstable ground, because people would *rather* manage difficult decisions with certainty than with mere probability. This means that people would prefer to settle issues absolutely, if they could, rather than talking things out. Think about what that implies for rhetoric and for social and political arrangements based on rhetoric.

Isocrates seems to share this practical and pragmatic view of the sort of knowledge that rhetoric can generate. Remember that he is training students for active participation in public life, not for philosophical contemplation. We can read his complaints against other Sophists as being against their shallow instruction and real-world relevance, but not as an indictment of them for being insufficiently philosophical. And Gorgias, of course, is little concerned with "the truth" at all. For him, training in technique is vital; whether that leads to the truth is not his business. Note how heavily technique-centered the *Encomium* is, how little concerned with giving students any knowledge or truth. Gorgias, like many of his fellow Sophists, was more interested in equipping his students to *act* than to *know.*

The issue of *media* is related to both knowledge and discourse. The classical Greeks definitely had command of writing, although much of their public business continued to be conducted in the oral/aural medium of public speaking. We might expect to find both influences in those theories. Note Plato's distrust of the written word, especially in the *Gorgias,* because it cannot answer questions and engage in his preferred discourse of dialectic. Plato wrote a great deal; however, note that it was in the form of a dialogue or spoken discourse. In both Plato and Isocrates, note the advice that is given for educating students in rhetoric, and whether the sorts of exercises prescribed are based on writing or on speaking.

It is interesting to note that although Gorgias's *Encomium of Helen* was meant to be spoken as an advertisement for the rhetorical skill one might learn at his school, it was also clearly a written text, meant to be recited over and over. As you read it, ask yourself whether it is for the ear or for the eye. Consider how it might appear in each separate medium.

Aristotle is clearly grounded in the written word. Think about the kind of advice he offers the student and the way in which it is offered; how does that compare to the professedly more oral/aural approach of Plato? Can we draw some conclusions here about the effect of writing or of speaking on the kind of knowledge conveyed and how it is conveyed? For instance, does the great complexity of his system of topics have any connection to a way of thinking that stores knowledge in written form? Does writing enable such complexity?

Finally, the issue of *power* is a very interesting one throughout the readings here. Gorgias is willing to excuse Helen's cooperation with her abductors if she was *persuaded* to do so. This was clearly meant to urge his listeners to think that persuasive oratory grants such power to the skillful user that nobody can resist it. Power was perhaps what Gorgias's students ultimately sought from his instructions.

Isocrates first raises the question of whether power in the absence of virtue is in fact to be desired. His colleague Gorgias may indeed have been among those Sophists who were teaching students how to gain power and advantage through oratory without teaching its responsible use.

But it is in Plato's dialogues that the question of power is most fully explored here. In the *Gorgias,* the question comes to the foreground in Socrates's exchange with Callicles. Callicles is presented as the archetypal "might makes right" man of public affairs, trained by Sophists to get advantage which he will turn to his own benefit, not that of the state or of others. Pay particular attention to the way in which Plato has Socrates undercut Polus and Callicles's entire argument by questioning what power itself is. How does Socrates define power in ways that make it something ultimately unattainable through rhetoric?

Also consider how Plato's way of thinking about the connection between rhetoric and power changes in the *Phaedrus.* What sort of power can rhetoric secure for its user in this dialogue? Pay particular attention to the fact that Socrates and Phaedrus both *model* three different kinds of speeches designed to secure power to one who is trying to seduce a loved one. Towards the end of the dialogue, Plato explains the uses for rhetoric that he finds justifiable.

The Classical Greek Heritage is foundational for rhetorical theory in the West. Themes and issues expressed in these readings will continue to arise throughout the rest of the history of rhetorical theory. Understanding how these writers addressed the questions of discourse, knowledge, media, and power will help us to understand writings of later periods as well.

FOR FURTHER READING

Backman, Mark. 1991. *Sophistication: Rhetoric and the Rise of Self-Consciousness.* Woodbridge, CT: Ox Bow Press.

Barrett, Harold. 1987. *The Sophists.* Novato, CA: Chandler & Sharp.

Benson, Thomas W., and Michael H. Prosser. 1988. *Readings in Classical Rhetoric.* Davis, CA: Hermagoras.

Clark, Donald Lemen. 1957. *Rhetoric in Greco-Roman Education.* NY: Columbia University.

Farrell, Thomas B. 1993. *Norms of Rhetorical Culture.* New Haven, CT: Yale University.

Jarratt, Susan C. 1991. *Rereading the Sophists: Classical Rhetoric Refigured.* Carbondale: Southern Illinois University.

Jarrett, James L. 1969. *Educational Theories of the Sophists.* NY: Teachers College, Columbia University.

Kennedy, George A. 1963. *The Art of Persuasion in Greece.* Princeton: Princeton University.

Kennedy, George A. 1972. *The Art of Rhetoric in the Roman World.* Princeton: Princeton University.

Kennedy, George A. 1980. *Classical Rhetoric and Its Christian and Secular Tradition from Ancient to Modern Times.* Chapel Hill: University of North Carolina.

Kitto, H.D.F. 1951. *The Greeks.* Baltimore: Penguin.

Murphy, James J. 1983. *A Synoptic History of Classical Rhetoric.* Davis, CA: Hermagoras.

Toynbee, Arnold J. 1952. *Greek Historical Thought.* NY: Mentor Books.

Untersteiner, Mario. 1954. *The Sophists.* Oxford: Basil Blackwell.

INTRODUCTION TO GORGIAS

Gorgias was born in the Sicilian town of Leontini around 483 B.C.E. He died around 376, making him roughly contemporaneous with Socrates. Gorgias originally came as an ambassador to Athens, and his oratorical style was so admired that he stayed there, traveling from city to city giving oratorical demonstrations and teaching others how to speak.

As an orator and teacher, Gorgias was quite successful and widely admired. He focused on ceremonial or display oratory in his own speaking, perhaps because its stylistic grandeur made it a good advertising tool for his public speaking instruction and perhaps because it allowed him to skirt the differing and difficult politics of the varying cities to which he traveled. In his teaching, he probably offered a more general course of instruction.

Throughout history, people have engaged in ceremonial oratory not only to mark important occasions in a culture but also for entertainment value. Picture the throngs of people who used to crowd public parks to hear stirring Fourth of July addresses! Think about the need still felt today to have entertaining and inspiring speakers at retirement dinners. Ceremonial speaking has therefore often featured a showy and carefully constructed verbal style more than hardheaded argument. The *Encomium of Helen* certainly illustrates that balance. Notice how much of it seems sing-songy to modern ears, and how much of it depends on the careful turning of a phrase rather than on serious, developed argument and evidence. When trying to understand the art, music, or oratory of other eras, we must not try to impose our own aesthetic standards on the work being examined. We should therefore take it as a given that the Greek people admired the verbal style of the *Encomium* and found its repetitive phrasing attractive.

The *Encomium of Helen* does develop one interesting substantive theme, however, and that is the power of persuasive language. Helen of Troy was a mythical Greek figure, a woman who was kidnapped by Paris, Prince of Troy, in Asia Minor. This event began the Trojan Wars, chronicled by the poet Homer in the *Iliad.* A sort of poetic controversy arose over the centuries as to whether Helen was to blame for having cooperated with her abduction. An "encomium" is a defense or praise of someone, and in this encomium of Helen, Gorgias argues that Helen was very likely *persuaded* by Paris to go with him and was therefore not to blame for her actions.

This alleged power of persuasion was consistent with the Sophists' perspective and with their approach to empowering people through teaching them public speaking. Gorgias's argument is also consistent with his more general philosophical stance of relativism, found in some of his other surviving fragments such as "On Nature." Our knowledge is always partial, always relative to the time and place in which we live, and always changing, according to Gorgias. And it changes because of changes wrought in the human mind and disposition by persuasion. For that reason, the "truths" that persuasion created in Helen's mind were valid for her, and cannot be second-guessed by people in other times and places. The *Encomium of Helen* therefore contains a more substantive argument in defense of rhetorical relativism that was key to the larger Sophistic philosophy.

GORGIAS

ENCOMIUM OF HELEN

The grace of a city is excellence of its men, of a body beauty, of a mind wisdom, of an action virtue, of a speech truth; the opposites of these are a disgrace. A man, a woman, a speech, a deed, a city, and an action, if deserving praise, one should honour with praise, but to the undeserving one should attach blame. For it is an equal error and ignorance to blame the praiseworthy and to praise the blameworthy. The man who says rightly what ought to be said should also refute those who blame Helen, a woman about whom both the belief of those who have listened to poets and the message of her name, which has become a reminder of the calamities, have been in unison and unanimity. I wish, by adding some reasoning to my speech, to free the slandered woman from the accusation and to demonstrate that those who blame her are lying, and both to show what is true and to put a stop to their ignorance.

That the woman who is the subject of this speech was pre-eminent among pre-eminent men and women, by birth and descent, is not obscure to even a few. It is clear that her mother was Leda, and her actual father was a god and her reputed father a mortal, Tyndareos and Zeus, of whom the one was believed to be because he was and the other was reputed to be because he said he was, and the one was the best of men and the other the master of all. Born of such parents, she had godlike beauty, which she acquired and had openly. In very many she created very strong amorous desires; with a single body she brought together many bodies of men who had great pride for great reasons; some of them had great amounts of wealth, others fame of ancient nobility, others vigour of personal strength, others power of acquired wisdom; and they all came because of a love which wished to conquer and a wish for honour which was unconquered. Who fulfilled his love by obtaining Helen, and why, and how, I shall not say; for to tell those who know what they know carries conviction but does not give pleasure. Passing over now in my speech that former time, I shall proceed to the beginning of my intended speech, and I shall propound the causes which made it reasonable for Helen's departure to Troy to occur.

Either it was because of the wishes of Chance and the purposes of the gods and the decrees of Necessity that she did what she did, or because she was seized by force, or persuaded by speeches, <or captivated by love>. Now, if it was because of the first, the accuser deserves to be accused; for it is impossible to hinder a god's predetermination by human preconsideration. It is not natural for the stronger to be hindered by the weaker, but for the weaker to be governed and guided by the stronger, and for the stronger to lead and the weaker to follow. A god is a stronger thing than a human being,

Edited and Translated by D. M. MacDowell

both in force and in wisdom and in other respects. So if the responsibility is to be attributed to Chance and God, Helen is to be released from the infamy.

But if she was seized by force and unlawfully violated and unjustly assaulted, clearly the man who seized or assaulted did wrong, and the woman who was seized or was assaulted suffered misfortune. So the barbarian who undertook a barbaric undertaking in speech and in law and in deed deserves to receive accusation in speech, debarment in law, and punishment in deed; but the woman who was violated and deprived of her country and bereaved of her family, would she not reasonably be pitied rather than reviled? He performed terrible acts, she suffered them; so it is just to sympathize with her but to hate him.

But if it was speech that persuaded and deceived her mind, it is also not difficult to make a defence for that and to dispel the accusation thus. Speech is a powerful ruler. Its substance is minute and invisible, but its achievements are superhuman; for it is able to stop fear and to remove sorrow and to create joy and to augment pity. I shall prove that this is so; I must also prove it by opinion to my hearers.

All poetry I consider and call speech with metre. Into those who hear it comes fearful fright and tearful pity and mournful longing, and at the successes and failures of others' affairs and persons the mind suffers, through speeches, a suffering of its own.

Now then, let me move from one speech to another. Inspired incantations through speeches are inducers of pleasure and reducers of sorrow; by intercourse with the mind's belief, the power of the incantation enchants and persuades and moves it by sorcery. Two arts of sorcery and magic have been invented; they are deviations of mind and deceptions of belief.

How many men have persuaded and do persuade how many, on how many subjects, by fabricating false speech! For if everyone, on every subject, possessed memory of the past and <understanding> of the present and foreknowledge of the future, speech would not be equally <powerful>; but as it is, neither remembering a past event nor investigating a present one nor prophesying a future one is easy, so that on most subjects most men make belief their mind's adviser. But belief, being slippery and unreliable, brings slippery and unreliable success to those who employ it. So what reason is there against Helen's also <having come under the influence of speech just as much against her will as if she had been seized by violence of violators? For persuasion expelled sense; and indeed persuasion, though not having an appearance of compulsion,> has the same power. For speech, the persuader, compelled mind, the persuaded, both to obey what was said and to approve what was done. So the persuader, because he compelled, is guilty; but the persuaded, because she was compelled by his speech, is wrongly reproached.

To show that persuasion, when added to speech, also moulds the mind in the way it wishes, one should note first the speeches of astronomers, who substituting belief for belief, demolishing one and establishing another, make the incredible and obscure become clear to the eyes of belief; and secondly compulsory contests conducted by means of speeches, in which a single speech pleases and persuades a large crowd, because written with skill, not spoken with truth; <and> thirdly conflicts of philosophical speeches, in which it is shown that quick-wittedness too makes the opinion which is based on belief changeable. The power of speech bears the same relation to the ordering of the mind as the ordering of drugs bears to the constitution of bodies. Just as different drugs expel different humours from the body, and some stop it from being ill but others stop it from living, so too some speeches cause sorrow, some cause pleasure, some cause fear, some give the hearers confidence, some drug and bewitch the mind with an evil persuasion.

That, if she was persuaded by speech, it was not a misdeed but a mischance, has been stated; and I shall examine the fourth cause in the fourth part of my speech. If it was love that brought all this about, she will without difficulty escape the accusation of the offence said to have been committed. Things that we see do not have the nature which we wish them to have but the nature which each of them actually has; and by seeing them the mind is moulded in its character too. For instance, when the sight surveys hostile persons and a hostile array of bronze and iron for hostile armament, offensive array of the one and shields of the other, it is alarmed, and it alarms the mind, so that often people flee in panic when some danger is imminent as if it were present. So strong is the disregard of law which is implanted in them because of the fear caused by the sight; when it befalls, it makes them disregard both the honour which is awarded for obeying the law and the benefit which accrues for doing right. And some people before now, on seeing frightful things, have also lost their presence of mind at the present moment; fear so extinguishes and expels thought. And many have fallen into groundless distress and terrible illness and incurable madness; so deeply does sight engrave on the mind images of actions that are seen. And as far as frightening things are concerned, many are omitted, but those omitted are similar to those mentioned.

But when painters complete out of many colours and objects a single object and form, they please the sight. The making of figures and the creation of statues provides a pleasant disease for the eyes. Thus some things naturally give distress and others pleasure to the sight. Many things create in many people love and desire of many actions and bodies. So if Helen's eye, pleased by Alexander's body, transmitted an eagerness and striving of love to her mind, what is surprising? If love is a god with a god's power, how would the weaker be able to repel and resist it? But if it is a human malady and incapacity of mind, it should not be blamed as an impropriety but considered as an adversity; for it comes, when it does come, through deceptions of mind, not intentions of thought, and through compulsions of love, not contrivances of skill.

So how should one consider the blame of Helen just? Whether she did what she did because she was enamoured <by sight> or persuaded by speech or seized by force or compelled by divine necessity, in every case she escapes the accusation.

I have removed by my speech a woman's infamy, I have kept to the purpose which I set myself at the start of my speech; I attempted to dispel injustice of blame and ignorance of belief, I wished to write the speech as an encomium of Helen and an amusement for myself.

INTRODUCTION TO ISOCRATES

Isocrates was a native of Athens and lived from 436 to 338 B.C.E. Isocrates was a student of such leading Sophists as Gorgias, Protagoras, and Prodicus, and he may have studied with Socrates as well. He was roughly contemporaneous with Plato. He founded a school around 393 B.C.E. in which he taught rhetoric.

Although Isocrates delivered speeches (he is one of the "Ten Attic Orators") and wrote speeches for others (as a "logographer"), he is best known as an educator. His school became a model for later academies, and was influential in shaping the practices and curricula of educators such as Aristotle. One can observe many favorable references to Isocrates in Aristotle's *Rhetoric.*

Isocrates required that boys entering his school have mastered grammar already. But he then taught rhetoric as a foundation for other studies and for life. For instance, he would teach political philosophy to his students through the study of famous political speeches and through the recitation of speeches. Composition of essays and speeches was a major pedagogical tool in his school, and students would learn about a wide variety of subject matters through writing and speaking. Because of this approach, Isocrates taught a way of thinking about rhetoric that was morally responsible. Students were made to consider the effect of their speeches on the social and political structure. In this way, he differed from some other Sophists who taught rhetoric only as a technique of immediate advantage over an audience or an opponent.

The rhetorical focus in Isocrates's school was epideictic, ceremonial oratory. A few examples of his own oratory survive. However, no purely theoretical work on rhetoric by Isocrates is known to exist. Therefore, we must deduce some of his views on rhetorical theory from his other writings. Two examples of such writings are included here.

Isocrates's *Against the Sophists* is his attempt to distinguish himself from unscrupulous Sophists or teachers of rhetoric who were concerned only with teaching tricks of the trade for obtaining persuasive effect. Those teachers would give their students general principles or maxims for how to speak. Isocrates opposes this practice in *Against the Sophists* because he believes that good speaking requires adaptation to particular circumstances. His students were broadly prepared on a wide variety of subjects, but they were then taught to think about choices and possibilities confronting the orator and the audience in each specific context of rhetoric. He therefore attacks his fellow Sophists for too much focus on general principles and not enough focus on "fitness for the occasion," or adaptation to the particular circumstances that call for rhetorical responses. But Isocrates likewise opposed philosophers such as Plato who were calling for attention to general *philosophical* ideals and principles, at the expense of particular circumstances. Isocrates mistrusted philosophical systems that would offer general rules for conduct without sensitivity to the changing circumstances of each situation. Therefore, in the *Antidosis,* note that he does not claim to be able to teach virtue, but rather how to assess and react to the rhetorical needs of the particular circumstance.

In ancient Athens, a person who was judged to be wealthy was required to fund some sort of public project, such as the building of a monument, statue, defensive fortification, or warship. Evidently Isocrates was assessed as wealthy, but he spoke against that charge in his speech *Antidosis.* The speech was given late in his life and was composed several years after *Against the Sophists.* In the *Antidosis,* Isocrates takes the stance that his wealth is exaggerated, perhaps because the public assumed he must be one of the wealthy, unscrupulous Sophists who charged high fees for shallow instruction in rhetoric. Isocrates uses the opportunity this speech affords to carefully define his life's work. Therefore, we may take from this speech some idea of his theories of rhetoric. As you read the *Antidosis,* note that although Isocrates still does not claim to teach virtue, he nevertheless emphasizes the virtuous results of an education in rhetoric. Pay particular attention to his claims for the effects of rhetorical training such as increased wisdom, civic participation, leadership, and so forth. Notice how Isocrates stands midway between other Sophists and philosophers such as Plato in arguing for the importance of both knowledge and the rhetorical application of knowledge in public affairs. In this way, he anticipates Cicero's theories of rhetoric in the Roman Republic.

ISOCRATES

AGAINST THE SOPHISTS[a]

If all who are engaged in the profession of education were willing to state the facts instead of making greater promises than they can possibly fulfil, they would not be in such bad repute with the lay-public. As it is, however, the teachers who do not scruple to vaunt their powers with utter disregard of the truth have created the impression that those who choose a life of careless indolence are better advised than those who devote themselves to serious study.

Indeed, who can fail to abhor, yes to contemn, those teachers, in the first place, who devote themselves to disputation,[b] since they pretend to search for truth, but straightway at the beginning of their professions attempt to deceive us with lies?[c] For I

[a] Isocrates regards himself as one of the sophists (see *Antid.* 220), but sets himself apart from the "common herd" of sophists (see *Panath.* 18).

English translation by George Norlin, Ph.D., LL.D. President of the University of Colorado Formerly Professor of Greek in the University of Colorado

[b] Captious argumentation in the field of ethics. He is not thinking of Socrates, who did not teach for pay, nor of Plato's dialectic, which was not yet famous, but of the minor Socratics, especially Antisthenes and Eucleides, who taught for money while affecting contempt for it. In general he is thinking of such quibblers as are later shown up in Plato's *Euthydemus.* See General Introd. pp. xxi ff.

[c] Theirs is a cloud morality, not truth to live by on earth. *Cf.* 20. See General Introd. p. xxii.

think it is manifest to all that foreknowledge of future events is not vouchsafed to our human nature, but that we are so far removed from this prescience[a] that Homer, who has been conceded the highest reputation for wisdom, has pictured even the gods as at times debating among themselves about the future[b]—not that he knew their minds but that he desired to show us that for mankind this power lies in the realms of the impossible.

But these professors have gone so far in their lack of scruple that they attempt to persuade our young men that if they will only study under them they will know what to do in life and through this knowledge will become happy and prosperous. More than that, although they set themselves up as masters and dispensers of goods so precious, they are not ashamed of asking for them a price of three or four minae![c] Why, if they were to sell any other commodity for so trifling a fraction of its worth they would not deny their folly; nevertheless, although they set so insignificant a price on the whole stock of virtue and happiness, they pretend to wisdom and assume the right to instruct the rest of the world. Furthermore, although they say that they do not want money and speak contemptuously of wealth as "filthy lucre," they hold their hands out for a trifling gain and promise to make their disciples all but immortal![d] But what is most ridiculous of all is that they distrust those from whom they are to get this money—they distrust, that is to say, the very men to whom they are about to deliver the science of just dealing—and they require that the fees advanced by their students be entrusted for safe keeping[a] to those who have never been under their instruction, being well advised as to their security, but doing the opposite of what they preach. For it is permissible to those who give any other instruction to be exacting in matters open to dispute, since nothing prevents those who have been made adept in other lines of training from being dishonourable in the matter of contracts. But men who inculcate virtue and sobriety—is it not absurd if they do not trust in their own students before all others?[b] For it is not to be supposed that men who are honourable and just-dealing with others will be dishonest with the very preceptors who have made them what they are.

When, therefore, the layman puts all these things together and observes that the teachers of wisdom and dispensers of happiness are themselves in great want[c] but exact only a small fee from their students, that they are on the watch for contradictions in words[d] but are blind to inconsistencies in deeds, and that, furthermore, they pretend to have knowledge of the future but are incapable either of saying anything pertinent or of giving any counsel regarding the present, and when he observes that those who follow their judgements are more consistent and more successful[e] than those who profess to have exact knowledge, then he has, I think, good reason to contemn such studies and regard them as stuff and nonsense, and not as a true discipline of the soul.

---

[a] There is, according to Isocrates, no "science" which can teach us to do under all circumstances the things which will insure our happiness and success. Life is too complicated for that, and no man can foresee exactly the consequences of his acts—"the future is a thing unseen." All that education can do is to develop a sound judgement (as opposed to knowledge) which will meet the contingencies of life with resourcefulness and, in most cases, with success. This is a fundamental doctrine of his "philosophy" which he emphasizes and echoes again and again in opposition to the professors of a "science of virtue and happiness." See General Introd. pp. xxvii ff.

[b] See *Iliad* xvi. 431 ff. and 652 ff.; xxii, 168 ff.

[c] Socrates (Plato, *Apology* 20 B) speaks with the same sarcasm of a sophist named Evenus, who professed to teach all the virtues necessary to a good man and a good citizen for five minae.

[d] That is, to make them all but gods.

---

[a] For their security, they required that the fees charged to their students be deposited with third parties until the end of the course.

[b] *Cf.* the same ridicule in Plato, *Gorg.* 519 C, 460 E.

[c] See the close of the *Paneg.*

[d] The aim of "eristic" (ἔρις means contention) is to show up the contradictions in the accepted morality.

[e] See 2, note *d; Panath.* 9; *Helen* 5.

But it is not these sophists alone who are open to criticism, but also those who profess to teach political discourse.[a] For the latter have no interest whatever in the truth,[b] but consider that they are masters of an art if they can attract great numbers of students by the smallness of their charges and the magnitude of their professions and get something out of them. For they are themselves so stupid and conceive others to be so dull that, although the speeches which they compose are worse than those which some laymen improvise, nevertheless they promise to make their students such clever orators that they will not overlook any of the possibilities which a subject affords. More than that, they do not attribute any of this power either to the practical experience or to the native ability of the student, but undertake to transmit the science of discourse as simply as they would teach the letters of the alphabet,[c] not having taken trouble to examine into the nature of each kind of knowledge, but thinking that because of the extravagance of their promises they themselves will command admiration and the teaching of discourse will be held in higher esteem—oblivious of the fact that the arts are made great, not by those who are without scruple in boasting about them, but by those who are able to discover all of the resources which each art affords.

For myself, I should have preferred above great riches that philosophy had as much power as these men claim; for, possibly, I should not have been the very last in the profession nor had the least share in its profits. But since it has no such power, I could wish that this prating might cease. For I note that the bad repute which results therefrom does not affect the offenders only, but that all the rest of us who are in the same profession share in the opprobium.[a]

But I marvel when I observe these men setting themselves up as instructors of youth who cannot see that they are applying the analogy of an art with hard and fast rules to a creative process. For, excepting these teachers, who does not know that the art of using letters remains fixed and unchanged, so that we continually and invariably use the same letters for the same purposes, while exactly the reverse is true of the art of discourse?[b] For what has been said by one speaker is not equally useful for the speaker who comes after him; on the contrary, he is accounted most skilled in this art who speaks in a manner worthy of his subject and yet is able to discover in it topics which are nowise the same as those used by others. But the greatest proof of the difference between these two arts is that oratory is good only if it has the qualities of fitness for the occasion,[c] propriety of style, and originality of treatment, while in the case of letters there is no such need whatsoever. So that those who make use of such analogies ought more justly to pay out than to accept fees, since they attempt to teach others when they are themselves in great need of instruction.

However, if it is my duty not only to rebuke others, but also to set forth my own views, I think all intelligent people will agree with me that while many of those who have pursued philosophy have remained in private life,[d] others, on the other hand, who have never taken lessons from any one of the sophists have become able orators and statesmen. For ability, whether in speech or in any other activity, is found in those who are well endowed by nature and have been schooled by practical

---

[a] The whole field of "deliberative" oratory, but the most "useful" branch of it in "litigious Athens" was the forensic.

[b] Their interest was not in the triumph of justice but in making "the worse reason appear the better." See General Introd. p. xxii.

[c] See General Introd. p. xxii.

[a] *Cf. Antid.* 168.

[b] That is, mechanical formulas are not sufficient. There must be inventiveness, resourcefulness, in a word, creative imagination.

[c] A fundamental requisite. See *Paneg.* 9; *Helen* 11, Vol. III., L.C.L.

[d] Isocrates himself.

experience.[a] Formal training makes such men more skillful and more resourceful in discovering the possibilities of a subject; for it teaches them to take from a readier source the topics which they otherwise hit upon in haphazard fashion. But it cannot fully fashion men who are without natural aptitude into good debaters or writers, although it is capable of leading them on to self-improvement and to a greater degree of intelligence on many subjects.

But I desire, now that I have gone this far, to speak more clearly on these matters. For I hold that to obtain a knowledge of the elements out of which we make and compose all discourses is not so very difficult if anyone entrusts himself, not to those who make rash promises, but to those who have some knowledge of these things. But to choose from these elements those which should be employed for each subject, to join them together, to arrange them properly, and also, not to miss what the occasion demands but appropriately to adorn the whole speech with striking thoughts and to clothe it in flowing and melodious phrase[b]—these things, I hold, require much study and are the task of a vigorous and imaginative mind:[c] for this, the student must not only have the requisite aptitude but he must learn the different kinds of discourse and practise himself in their use; and the teacher, for his part, must so expound the principles of the art with the utmost possible exactness as to leave out nothing that can be taught, and, for the rest, he must in himself set such an example of oratory that the students who have taken form under his instruction and are able to pattern after him will, from the outset, show in their speaking a degree of grace and charm which is not found in others. When all of these requisites are found together, then the devotees of philosophy will achieve complete success; but according as any one of the things which I have mentioned is lacking, to this extent must their disciples of necessity fall below the mark.

Now as for the sophists who have lately sprung up and have very recently embraced these pretensions,[a] even though they flourish at the moment, they will all, I am sure, come round to this position. But there remain to be considered those who lived before our time and did not scruple to write the so-called arts of oratory.[b] These must not be dismissed without rebuke, since they professed to teach how to conduct law-suits, picking out the most discredited of terms,[c] which the enemies, not the champions, of this discipline might have been expected to employ—and that too although this facility, in so far as it can be taught, is of no greater aid to forensic than to all other discourse. But they were much worse than those who dabble in disputation; for although the latter expounded such captious theories that were anyone to cleave to them in practice he would at once be in all manner of trouble, they did, at any rate, make professions of virtue and sobriety in their teaching, whereas the former, although exhorting others to study political discourse, neglected all the good things which this study affords, and became nothing more than professors of meddlesomeness and greed.[d]

And yet those who desire to follow the true precepts of this discipline may, if they will, be helped more speedily towards honesty of charac-

---

[a] Isocrates insists that the requisites of a good orator are first natural ability, second practical experience, and third formal training. See *Antid.* 186–188 and General Introd. p. xxvii, Vol. I., L.C.L.

[b] Prose should have the same finish and charm as poetry. See General Introd. p. xxiv.

[c] Unmistakably this phrase is parodied in Plato, *Gorgias* 463 A: *δοκεῖ τοίνυν μοι ὦ Γοργια, εἶναί τι ἐπιτήδευμα τεχνικὸν μὲν οὔ, ψυχῆς δὲ στοχαστικῆς καὶ ἀνδρείας καὶ φύσει δεινῆς προσομιλεῖν τοῖς ἀνθρώποις.*

---

[a] The sophists before mentioned. The teaching of the older sophists is discussed in the *Antidosis.*

[b] Especially the first to write such treatises, Corax and Tisias of Syracuse. *τέχνη*, like *ars* in Latin, was the accepted term for a treatise on rhetoric.

[c] Again and again Isocrates expresses his repugnance to this kind of oratory, and in general it was in bad odour. The precepts of Corax (Crow), for example, were called "the bad eggs of the bad Corax."

[d] The same complaint is made by Aristotle, *Rhet.* i. 1. 10.

ter[a] than towards facility in oratory. And let no one suppose that I claim that just living can be taught;[b] for, in a word, I hold that there does not exist an art of the kind which can implant sobriety and justice in depraved natures. Nevertheless, I do think that the study of political discourse can help more than any other thing to stimulate and form such qualities of character.

But in order that I may not appear to be breaking down the pretensions of others while myself making greater claims than are within my powers, I believe that the very arguments by which I myself was convinced will make it clear to others also that these things are true.

[a] For the kind of political discourse which Isocrates extols, and its ethical influence see *Antid.* 275 and General Introd. p. xxiv.

[b] See *Antid.* 274 ff.

• • •

ISOCRATES

ANTIDOSIS

• • •

In my treatment of the art of discourse, I desire, like the genealogists, to start at the beginning.[a] It is acknowledged that the nature of man is compounded of two parts, the physical and the mental, and no one would deny that of these two the mind comes first and is of greater worth; for it is the function of the mind to decide both on personal and on public questions, and of the body to be servant to the judgements of the mind. Since this is so, certain of our ancestors, long before our time, seeing that many arts had been devised for other things, while none had been prescribed for the body and for the mind, invented and bequeathed to us two disciplines: physical training for the body, of which gymnastics is a part, and, for the mind, philosophy, which I am going to explain. These are twin arts—parallel and complementary—by which their masters prepare the mind to become more intelligent and the body to become more serviceable, not separating sharply the two kinds of education, but using similar methods of instruction, exercise, and other forms of discipline.

For when they take their pupils in hand, the physical trainers instruct their followers in the postures which have been devised for bodily contests, while the teachers of philosophy impart all the forms of discourse in which the mind expresses itself. Then, when they have made them familiar and thoroughly conversant with these lessons, they set them at exercises, habituate them to work, and require them to combine in practice the particular things which they have learned, in order that they may grasp them more firmly and bring their theories into closer touch with the occasions for applying them—I say "theories," for no system of knowledge can possibly cover these occasions, since in all cases they elude our science.[a] Yet

[a] Literally, I desire first to discuss the art of discourse after the manner of the genealogists.

[a] The distinction usually drawn, in Plato for instance, between δόξα and ἐπιστήμη, the one "opinion," the other "knowledge," is not exactly that made by Isocrates. δόξα is here, not irresponsible opinion, but a working theory based on practical experience—judgement or insight in dealing with the uncertain contingencies of any human situation which presents itself. In this realm, he holds, there can be no exact science. *Cf.* 271; *Against the Sophists* 1–3. See General Introd. pp. xxii, xxvii.

those who most apply their minds to them and are able to discern the consequences which for the most part grow out of them, will most often meet these occasions in the right way.

Watching over them and training them in this manner, both the teachers of gymnastic and the teachers of discourse are able to advance their pupils to a point where they are better men and where they are stronger in their thinking or in the use of their bodies. However, neither class of teachers is in possession of a science by which they can make capable athletes or capable orators out of whomsoever they please. They can contribute in some degree to these results, but these powers are never found in their perfection save in those who excel by virtue both of talent and of training.[a]

I have given you now some impression of what philosophy is. But I think that you will get a still clearer idea of its powers if I tell you what professions I make to those who want to become my pupils. I say to them that if they are to excel in oratory or in managing affairs or in any line of work, they must, first of all, have a natural aptitude for that which they have elected to do; secondly, they must submit to training and master the knowledge of their particular subject, whatever it may be in each case; and, finally, they must become versed and practised in the use and application of their art; for only on these conditions can they become fully competent and pre-eminent in any line of endeavour. In this process, master and pupil each has his place; no one but the pupil can furnish the necessary capacity; no one but the master, the ability to impart knowledge; while both have a part in the exercises of practical application: for the master must painstakingly direct his pupil, and the latter must rigidly follow the master's instructions.

Now these observations apply to any and all the arts. If anyone, ignoring the other arts, were to ask me which of these factors has the greatest power in the education of an orator I should answer that natural ability is paramount and comes before all else. For given a man with a mind which is capable of finding out and learning the truth and of working hard and remembering what it learns, and also with a voice and a clarity of utterance which are able to captivate the audience, not only by what he says, but by the music of his words, and, finally, with an assurance[a] which is not an expression of bravado, but which, tempered by sobriety, so fortifies the spirit that he is no less at ease in addressing all his fellow-citizens than in reflecting to himself—who does not know that such a man might, without the advantage of an elaborate education and with only a superficial and common training, be an orator such as has never, perhaps, been seen among the Hellenes? Again, we know that men who are less generously endowed by nature but excel in experience and practice, not only improve upon themselves, but surpass others who, though highly gifted, have been too negligent of their talents. It follows, therefore, that either one of these factors may produce an able speaker or an able man of affairs, but both of them combined in the same person might produce a man incomparable among his fellows.

• • •

We ought, therefore, to think of the art of discourse just as we think of the other arts, and not to form opposite judgements about similar things, nor show ourselves intolerant toward that power which, of all the faculties which belong to the nature of man, is the source of most of our blessings. For in the other powers which we possess, as I have already said on a former occasion,[b] we are in no respect superior to other living creatures; nay, we are inferior to many in swiftness and in strength and in other resources; but, because there has been implanted in us the power to persuade each other and to make clear to each other whatever we de-

---

[a] For Isocrates' view as to the elements which produce the successful orator see General Introd. p. xxiv.

[a] Isocrates here mentions qualifications which he himself lacked, voice and assurance. See *Phil.* 81; *Panath.* 10.

[b] *Cf. Paneg.* 48.

sire, not only have we escaped the life of wild beasts, but we have come together and founded cities and made laws and invented arts; and, generally speaking, there is no institution devised by man which the power of speech has not helped us to establish. For this it is which has laid down laws concerning things just and unjust, and things honourable and base; and if it were not for these ordinances we should not be able to live with one another. It is by this also that we confute the bad and extol the good. Through this we educate the ignorant and appraise the wise; for the power to speak well is taken as the surest index of a sound understanding, and discourse which is true and lawful and just is the outward image of a good and faithful soul. With this faculty we both contend against others on matters which are open to dispute and seek light for ourselves on things which are unknown; for the same arguments which we use in persuading others when we speak in public, we employ also when we deliberate in our own thoughts; and, while we call eloquent those who are able to speak before a crowd, we regard as sage those who most skillfully debate their problems in their own minds. And, if there is need to speak in brief summary of this power, we shall find that none of the things which are done with intelligence take place without the help of speech, but that in all our actions as well as in all our thoughts speech is our guide, and is most employed by those who have the most wisdom.[a]

But without reflecting at all on these truths, Lysimachus has dared to attack those who aspire to an accomplishment which is the source of blessings so many and so great. But why should we be surprised at him when even among the professors of disputation[b] there are some who talk no less abusively of the art of speaking on general and useful themes than do the most benighted of men, not that they are ignorant of its power or of the advantage which it quickly gives to those who avail themselves of it, but because they think that by decrying this art they will enhance the standing of their own.

I could, perhaps, say much harsher things of them than they of me, but I refrain for a double reason. I want neither to descend to the level of men whom envy has made blind nor to censure men who, although they do no actual harm to their pupils are less able to benefit them than are other teachers. I shall, however, say a few words about them, first because they also have paid their compliments to me; second, in order that you, being better informed as to their powers, may estimate us justly in relation to each other; and, furthermore, that I may show you clearly that we who are occupied with political discourse and whom they call contentious are more considerate than they; for although they are always saying disparaging things of me, I shall not answer them in kind but shall confine myself to the simple truth.

For I believe that the teachers who are skilled in disputation and those who are occupied with astronomy and geometry and studies of that sort[a] do not injure but, on the contrary, benefit their pupils, not so much as they profess, but more than others give them credit for. Most men see in such studies nothing but empty talk and hair-splitting; for none of these disciplines has any useful application either to private or to public affairs; nay, they are not even remembered for any length of time after they are learned because they do not attend us through life nor do they lend aid in what we do, but are wholly divorced from our necessities. But I am neither of this opinion nor am I far removed from it; rather it seems to me both that those who hold that this training is of no use in practical life are right and that those who speak in praise of it have truth on their side. If there is a contradiction in this statement, it is because these disciplines are different in their nature from the

[a] 253–257 are quoted from *Nicocles* 5–9.

[b] The "eristics." *Cf. Epist.* v. 3 ff. See General Introd. p. xxi. In this passage, as well as in *Epist.* v. 3 ff., he may be resenting the criticisms of the Aristotelians. See Blass, *Die attische Beredsamkeit* ii. p. 65.

[a] Compare Socrates' views, Xen. *Memorabilia* iv. 7. 2 ff.

other studies which make up our education; for the other branches avail us only after we have gained a knowledge of them, whereas these studies can be of no benefit to us after we have mastered them unless we have elected to make our living from this source, and only help us while we are in the process of learning. For while we are occupied with the subtlety and exactness of astronomy and geometry and are forced to apply our minds to difficult problems, and are, in addition, being habituated to speak and apply ourselves to what is said and shown to us, and not to let our wits go wool-gathering, we gain the power, after being exercised and sharpened on these disciplines, of grasping and learning more easily and more quickly those subjects which are of more importance and of greater value.[a] I do not, however, think it proper to apply the term "philosophy" to a training which is no help to us in the present either in our speech or in our actions, but rather I would call it a gymnastic of the mind and a preparation for philosophy. It is, to be sure, a study more advanced than that which boys in school pursue, but it is for the most part the same sort of thing; for they also when they have laboured through their lessons in grammar, music,[b] and the other branches, are not a whit advanced in their ability to speak and deliberate on affairs, but they have increased their aptitude for mastering greater and more serious studies. I would, therefore, advise young men to spend some time on these disciplines,[c] but not to allow their minds to be dried up by these barren subtleties, nor to be stranded on the speculations of the ancient sophists, who maintain, some of them, that the sum of things is made up of infinite elements; Empedocles that it is made up of four, with strife and love operating among them; Ion, of not more than three; Alcmaeon, of only two; Parmenides and Melissus, of one; and Gorgias, of none at all.[a] For I think that such curiosities of thought are on a par with jugglers' tricks which, though they do not profit anyone, yet attract great crowds of the empty-minded, and I hold that men who want to do some good in the world must banish utterly from their interests all vain speculations and all activities which have no bearing on our lives.

[a] See *Panath.* 26; General Introd. p. xxiii.

[b] A broad term including the study of poetry.

[c] Compare Callicles' similar view about the study of philosophy in Plato, *Gorgias* 484 c.

Now I have spoken and advised you enough on these studies for the present. It remains to tell you about "wisdom" and "philosophy."[b] It is true that if one were pleading a case on any other issue it would be out of place to discuss these words (for they are foreign to all litigation), but it is appropriate for me, since I am being tried on such an issue, and since I hold that what some people call philosophy is not entitled to that name, to define and explain to you what philosophy, properly conceived, really is. My view of this question is, as it happens, very simple. For since it is not in the nature of man to attain a science by the possession of which we can know positively what we should do or what we should say, in the next resort I hold that man to be wise who is able by his powers of conjecture to arrive generally at the best course, and I hold that man to be a philosopher who occupies himself with the studies from which he will most quickly gain that kind of insight.[c]

What the studies are which have this power I can tell you, although I hesitate to do so; they are so contrary to popular belief and so very far removed from the opinions of the rest of the world,

[a] The fruitlessness of the speculations of the early philosophers (physicists) is shown, according to Isocrates, in the utter diversity of their views, for example, regarding the first principles or primary elements from which the world was created. At one extreme was Anaxagoras, who held that the primary elements were infinite in number; at the other was Gorgias, who in his nihilistic philosophy denied that there was any such thing as being or entity at all. *Cf. Hel.* 3; Xen. *Memorabilia* i. 1. 14 ff.; Plato, *Sophist* 242.

[b] See General Introd. pp. xxvi ff.

[c] See 184 and note.

that I am afraid lest when you first hear them you will fill the whole court-room with your murmurs and your cries. Nevertheless, in spite of my misgivings, I shall attempt to tell you about them; for I blush at the thought that anyone might suspect me of betraying the truth to save my old age and the little of life remaining to me.[a] But, I beg of you, do not, before you have heard me, judge that I could have been so mad as to choose deliberately, when my fate is in your hands, to express to you ideas which are repugnant to your opinions if I had not believed that these ideas follow logically on what I have previously said, and that I could support them with true and convincing proofs.

I consider that the kind of art which can implant honesty and justice in depraved natures has never existed and does not now exist, and that people who profess that power will grow weary and cease from their vain pretensions before such an education is ever found.[b] But I do hold that people can become better and worthier if they conceive an ambition to speak well,[c] if they become possessed of the desire to be able to persuade their hearers, and, finally, if they set their hearts on seizing their advantage—I do not mean "advantage" in the sense given to that word by the empty-minded, but advantage in the true meaning of that term;[d] and that this is so I think I shall presently make clear.

For, in the first place, when anyone elects to speak or write discourses which are worthy of praise and honour, it is not conceivable that he will support causes which are unjust or petty or devoted to private quarrels, and not rather those which are great and honourable, devoted to the welfare of man and our common good; for if he fails to find causes of this character, he will accomplish nothing to the purpose. In the second place, he will select from all the actions of men which bear upon his subject those examples which are the most illustrious and the most edifying; and, habituating himself to contemplate and appraise such examples, he will feel their influence not only in the preparation of a given discourse but in all the actions of his life.[a] It follows, then, that the power to speak well and think right will reward the man who approaches the art of discourse with love of wisdom and love of honour.

Furthermore, mark you, the man who wishes to persuade people will not be negligent as to the matter of character; no, on the contrary, he will apply himself above all to establish a most honourable name among his fellow-citizens; for who does not know that words carry greater conviction when spoken by men of good repute than when spoken by men who live under a cloud, and that the argument which is made by a man's life is of more weight than that which is furnished by words?[b] Therefore, the stronger a man's desire to persuade his hearers, the more zealously will he strive to be honourable and to have the esteem of his fellow-citizens.

And let no one of you suppose that while all other people realize how much the scales of persuasion incline in favour of one who has the approval of his judges, the devotees of philosophy alone are blind to the power of good will. In fact, they appreciate this even more thoroughly than others, and they know, furthermore, that probabilities and proofs and all forms of persuasion support only the points in a case to which they are severally applied, whereas an honourable reputation not only lends greater persuasiveness to the words of the man who possesses it, but adds greater lustre to his deeds, and is, therefore, more zealously to be sought after by men of intelligence than anything else in the world.

---

[a] *Cf.* Plato, *Apology* 38 c.

[b] *Cf. Against the Sophists* 21: Theognis 429 ff.; Xen. *Memorabilia* i. 2. 19 ff.; Plato, *Meno* 95 ff.

[c] *Cf. Against the Sophists* 15.

[d] Compare his discussion of true advantage in *Nicocles* 2; *Peace* 28–35.

[a] See General Introd. p. xxiv.

[b] *Cf.* Aristotle, *Rhet.* 1356 a: κυριωτάτη πίστις τὸ ἦθος.

I come now to the question of "advantage"[a]—the most difficult of the points I have raised. If any one is under the impression that people who rob others or falsify accounts or do any evil thing get the advantage, he is wrong in his thinking; for none are at a greater disadvantage throughout their lives than such men; none are found in more difficult straits, none live in greater ignominy; and, in a word, none are more miserable than they. No, you ought to believe rather that those are better off now and will receive the advantage in the future at the hands of the gods[b] who are the most righteous and the most faithful in their devotions, and that those receive the better portion at the hands of men who are the most conscientious in their dealings with their associates, whether in their homes or in public life, and are themselves esteemed as the noblest among their fellows.

This is verily the truth, and it is well for us to adopt this way of speaking on the subject, since, as things now are, Athens has in many respects been plunged into such a state of topsy-turvy and confusion that some of our people no longer use words in their proper meaning but wrest them from the most honourable associations and apply them to the basest pursuits.[c] On the one hand, they speak of men who play the buffoon and have a talent for mocking and mimicking as "gifted"[d]—an appellation which should be reserved for men endowed with the highest excellence; while, on the other hand, they think of men who indulge their depraved and criminal instincts and who for small gains acquire a base reputation as "getting the advantage," instead of applying this term to the most righteous and the most upright, that is, to men who take advantage of the good and not the evil things of life. They characterize men who ignore our practical needs and delight in the mental juggling of the ancient sophists as "students of philosophy," but refuse this name to whose who pursue and practise those studies which will enable us to govern wisely both our own households and the commonwealth—which should be the objects of our toil, of our study, and of our every act.

[a] *Cf.* 275.

[b] *Cf. Peace* 34.

[c] Reminiscent of Thuc. iii. 82 ff.

[d] *Cf. Areop.* 49.

It is from these pursuits that you have for a long time now been driving away our youth,[a] because you accept the words of those who denounce this kind of education. Yes, and you have brought it about that the most promising of our young men are wasting their youth in drinking-bouts, in parties, in soft living and childish folly, to the neglect of all efforts to improve themselves; while those of grosser nature are engaged from morning until night in extremes of dissipation which in former days an honest slave would have despised. You see some of them chilling their wine at the "Nine-fountains"[b]; others, drinking in taverns; others, tossing dice in gambling dens; and many, hanging about the training-schools of the flute-girls.

And as for those who encourage them in these things, no one of those who profess to be concerned for our youth has ever haled them before you for trial, but instead they persecute me, who, whatever else I may deserve, do at any rate deserve thanks for this, that I discourage such habits in my pupils.

But so inimical to all the world is this race of sycophants that when men pay a ransom[c] of a hundred and thirty minae[d] for women who bid fair to help them make away with the rest of their property besides, so far from reproaching them, they actually rejoice in their extravagance; but

[a] *Cf. Areop.* 50.

[b] A famous spring near the Acropolis, first called Callirrhoe (Fair-flowing). Later, when enclosed and adorned by Pisistratus, it was called the Fountain of Nine Spouts. See Thuc. ii. 15; Gardner, *Ancient Athens* p. 18.

[c] The ransom of slaves captured in war. Isocrates is probably thinking of some notorious case.

[d] The mina = 100 drachmas. A drachma was the standard wage of a day-labourer.

when men spend any amount, however small, upon their education, they complain that they are being corrupted. Could any charge be more unjust than this against our students? For, while in the prime of vigour, when most men of their age are most inclined to indulge their passions, they have disdained a life of pleasure; when they might have saved expense and lived softly, they have elected to pay out money and submit to toil; and, though hardly emerged from boyhood, they have come to appreciate what most of their elders do not know, namely, that if one is to govern his youth rightly and worthily and make the proper start in life, he must give more heed to himself than to his possessions, he must not hasten and seek to rule over others[a] before he has found a master to direct his own thoughts, and he must not take as great pleasure or pride in other advantages as in the good things which spring up in the soul under a liberal education. I ask you, then, when young men have governed themselves by these principles, ought they not to be praised rather than censured, ought they not to be recognized as the best and the most sober-minded among their fellows?

I marvel at men who felicitate those who are eloquent by nature on being blessed with a noble gift, and yet rail at those who wish to become eloquent, on the ground that they desire an immoral and debasing education. Pray, what that is noble by nature becomes shameful and base when one attains it by effort? We shall find that there is no such thing, but that, on the contrary, we praise, at least in other fields, those who by their own devoted toil are able to acquire some good thing more than we praise those who inherit it from their ancestors. And rightly so; for it is well that in all activities, and most of all in the art of speaking, credit is won, not by gifts of fortune, but by efforts of study. For men who have been gifted with eloquence by nature and by fortune, are governed in what they say by chance, and not by any standard of what is best, whereas those who have gained this power by the study of philosophy and by the exercise of reason never speak without weighing their words, and so are less often in error as to a course of action.

• • •

[a] *Cf. To Nicocles* 29; Plato, *Gorgias* 491.

INTRODUCTION TO PLATO

Plato lived from around 428 to 347 B.C.E. in Athens. He was born to an aristocratic, well-to-do family. Plato was the most famous student of Socrates, although Socrates founded no formal school or set course of study. Instead, Socrates taught through the methods illustrated in Plato's dialogues, the question and answer exchanges of *dialectic.* Socrates strongly influenced Plato, such that he is the main character in Plato's dialogues. Socrates was executed about 399 B.C.E., an event that powerfully formed many of Plato's views on rhetoric and politics. For a time after the execution, Plato traveled around the Mediterranean world, and some scholars think that during that period he was exposed to rhetorical practice and teachings in Italy, Sicily, and even Egypt. In 387 Plato opened his own settled school, the Academy, where he taught for the rest of his life. That school was in competition with the school of Isocrates and with the less formal instructions of the other Sophists.

Plato wrote prolifically in the form of dialogues. His theories of rhetoric may best be understood by grasping his philosophical foundation, which was that of *idealism.* As an idealist, Plato believed that the most fundamental reality is one of ideas, principles, and timeless truths, rather than the material things and events we encounter in everyday existence. Idealists note that people possess concepts that unify, underlie, and define different parts of our experience, no matter how diverse some of those experiences may be. We recognize as "chairs" many different and varied things. We call a wide variety of processes and outcomes "justice" or "kindness," and we think of a diverse group of movements as "running." In each example, the idealist would say that the *idea* or principle of a chair, justice, kindness, or running is a more fundamental and basic reality than is the particular material instance of each idea.

The "location" of ideas or principles may vary from one idealist to another. Plato thought that the human soul, moving between lives in human bodies, passes through a world of ideal forms in which we see the ideal chair, the ideal of justice or of kindness, or the ideal of running, and are therefore able to recognize the shadows or reflections of those ideals when we see them in this world again. This religious grounding for his idealism is explained in his *Republic* in the "cave metaphor." But modern readers who cannot share Plato's religious views may nevertheless find a fruitful understanding of his idealism by *psychologizing* his views; in other words, by locating ideal forms and principles in the human mind or in the conditions for human thought. One might then argue that people do not engage the particular things of this world so much as they deal with the ideas, the forms, and the patterns that organize the world for us. One might argue that you, the reader, did not sit down in the chair in which you are sitting! Instead, you sat down in your *idea* of a chair. Such a startling claim becomes more plausible when you reflect that you did not examine the particular chair to see how it "works," whether it would hold you, and so forth. You more than likely saw an *example* of "chair" and sat down according to your idea of how "chairs" work; in other words, you sat down in your *idea of a chair,* not that particular chair itself.

However one understands idealism, it is at the core of Plato's thinking. If the world of ideas is the most fundamental reality, then knowledge must always be knowledge of ideas rather than of the material things of this world. Because Plato also felt that ideas are unchanging (an assumption you may want to question), he felt that truths about ideas would likewise be unchanging. Because Plato felt that ideas undergirded every human experience, he felt that there were sure and certain unchanging truths to be discovered about every question that might arise in human experience. For Plato, questions of how to solve mathematics were no more or less certain than were questions of ethics or politics; all could be resolved by discovering the structure of ideas that undergirded experience.

Ideas underlie material reality as forms or patterns. It is the general form or pattern of justice that is real, not the particular example of justice one might witness in a courtroom today. It is the pattern of a chair that is most real, not this particular chair. For that reason the only method that could lead to true knowledge of those ideal forms was a method of inquiry designed to detect the ideal forms and patterns, divisions and classifications underlying material reality. That kind of formal method was *dialectic.* As we learned in the introduction to this book, dialectic is a kind of discourse designed, through questions and answers, to discover the categories and subdivisions by which reality is organized. Plato is strongly committed to dialectic as a formally attuned discourse that can discover the formal patterns of ideas underlying the reality of everyday experience.

Once we understand Plato's idealist grounding, the attitudes he displays in his two dialogues on rhetoric, *Gorgias* and *Phaedrus,* become clear. Most rhetoric seems to be concerned with advising an audience on how to behave in the here and now: how to choose a brand of coffee now in this grocery store; which candidate to elect this November; whether this specific law should be enacted; or whether this particular defendant should go free. Isocrates's stress on adapting to the situation is typical of rhetorical thinking—and anathema to Plato! Furthermore, rhetoric seems to be not at all concerned with timeless and unchanging truths; instead, it appears to be able to prove opposites and contradictions with carefree impunity. Rhetoric, as we have noted before, seeks to establish probability at best, rather than the certainty that Plato's idealism taught him was attainable. And rhetoric usually depends on individual persuaders presenting monologic appeals rather than on the give and take of dialectic. The objections raised against rhetoric in Plato's dialogues can therefore be understood by thinking about them as springing from his idealism.

Plato wrote the *Gorgias* around 386 B.C.E. As the dialogue begins, Gorgias has been giving one of his rhetorical demonstrations at the house of Callicles, a prominent Athenian. Socrates has come late to this demonstration in which Gorgias promised to answer any question that was posed to him. We must remember that Gorgias was a generation older than Socrates, and is pictured as somewhat weak and of declining powers. With Gorgias is his young, vigorous student Polus ("colt"). The dialogue is structured around exchanges between Socrates and, progressively, Gorgias, Polus, and Callicles.

The issues raised in the *Gorgias* are many and complicated. Socrates begins by wanting to know what it is that Gorgias does and what he teaches. He is given a preliminary answer that Gorgias, in teaching rhetoric, teaches about "speech." But this answer is problematic, since the characters agree that other disciplines also teach different kinds of speech. This stance is interesting, for it asserts a discursive basis to every kind of discipline. Medicine, for instance, is rather explicitly understood here as *speech* about diseases (rather than, say, knowledge of diseases, or knowledge of therapeutic techniques, or of treatments). Since all disciplines teach speech, Socrates demands to know what sort of speech rhetoric is about.

This query leads to a discussion with Gorgias and then with Polus about two kinds of speech: speech that induces belief and speech that induces knowledge. Plato's idealism can be seen clearly influencing this part of the dialogue, as Socrates stresses the importance of acquiring true knowledge and the harm that arises from acquiring a false opinion. The distinction between discourses that create knowledge and those that create mere opinion is further expressed as a distinction between true arts that depend on knowledge and their degraded counterparts that depend on merely flattering or pandering to an audience. Socrates contrasts four arts—medicine, gymnastic, legislation, and justice—with their flattering, pandering counterparts: respectively cookery, cosmetics, sophistry, and rhetoric. Rhetoric is therefore theorized as flattery, or saying whatever an audience wishes to hear, so as to create the semblance (and often a false semblance) of justice. Rhetoric, Socrates concludes, does not lead to power if it does not lead to knowledge; only knowledge can be the basis for power. And dialectic is the preferred type of discourse to lead to that knowledge.

At this point in the dialogue, Callicles intervenes. He is portrayed as the quintessential man of affairs, politician, and rhetorician. He praises the acquisition of power by any means, and names rhetoric as one of the chief means by which power may be obtained. Socrates and Callicles discuss the nature of power. Socrates wants Callicles to accept the idea that the only true power is the power to see the truth; Callicles takes the more traditional view that power is the ability to do what one likes, to satisfy one's desires, and to lead others. The dialogue is written so as to unmask the weaknesses in each of Callicles's successive explanations of what constitutes power and why it is desirable. The discussion is also therefore a critique of what good rhetoric *can* do, since if the power it gives is no power at all, then rhetoric is left with no purpose or end. The dialogue concludes with Callicles and Socrates both prophesying the latter's eventual demise at the hands of rhetoric before a court of uninformed Athenians.

The *Gorgias* is clearly an attack on rhetoric. Plato's later dialogue, the *Phaedrus,* is his attempt to put rhetoric in the best possible light he can given his philosophical dispositions. Socrates meets his young friend, Phaedrus, while walking outside the city. Phaedrus has just heard a speech which he very much admires by the Sophist Lysias. The speech is from a man who is attracted to a boy but instead of professing his love openly argues that not only does he *not* love the boy but that a nonlover such as himself is the sort of person with whom one should associate. We may think of the speech as a sort of clever seduction strategy.

Readers of the dialogue today may think in narrowly sexual terms about this subject matter of the speech. That would be a mistake. Although Greek males of that period did undeniably engage in same sex relations, the sexual dimensions of the relationships were often subordinated to the more important issue of education and socializing. It was the practice, especially among privileged classes, for older men to establish relationships with adolescent boys, or young men, for the purpose of educating and training them. Although sex sometimes became a part of that relationship, the responsibility of the older man to the younger to train him in how to be a responsible and successful adult was more important. So we may assume that Plato's audience for the *Phaedrus* would have disapproved of the purely, narrowly sexual purposes of the first speech by Lysias.

Lysias's speech is also not very well done, technically speaking. Socrates says so and later leads Lysias to that realization. The speech may seem poorly constructed even to our modern ears; there is little organization or flow to it, a plain and uninteresting style, and not much interesting argument. Socrates says that he thinks he can do better, and upon being challenged by Phaedrus, he gives the second speech of the dialogue in which he likewise takes the stance of a man disguising himself as a nonlover for the purposes of seduction. Socrates's speech is judged a technical success, but he stops midway through it in horror at the lies he is uttering. Love is a god, he explains, and not to be avoided or disguised. So Socrates gives a third speech that is technically skillful as well as truthful. Socrates and Phaedrus then reflect on what makes for good rhetoric, and here Plato expresses his best hopes for what a responsible rhetoric might do.

We should read the *Phaedrus* for its wit and style as well as content. Socrates often has good, sarcastic fun at Phaedrus's expense. The two characters sometimes flirt subtly with one another. This is a dialogue to enjoy as well as one from which we may learn.

The principles of good rhetoric explained at the end of the dialogue should be compared to the three speeches, for those speeches model what is good or bad about rhetorical practice, according to Plato. Rhetoric should always be in the service of truth, says Socrates, and should follow an exercise of thinking about principles, truths, definitions of key concepts, and so forth. Note that the first two speeches were not in the service of truth, and they are therefore examples of the sort of irresponsible sophistic rhetoric that Plato deplored.

Recall that the pursuit of ideal truth is facilitated, in Plato's philosophy, by a method attuned to categories, divisions, and basic principles—in other words, by dialectic. Many readers of the *Phaedrus* have noted that the principles of rhetorical technique agreed upon by Plato and Socrates in the last part of the dialogue strongly resemble dialectic in their stress on categorization and definition. Furthermore, the second and third speeches, the two technically good rhetorical efforts, incorporate many of those dialectical methods. Each begins with definitions, although the definition of love in the second speech is a lie. Note the heavy use of myth in the third speech—indeed, the heavy presence of mythical references throughout the dialogue—where myth is a way of achieving understanding by transcending material experience, which is very consistent with Plato's idealism. Each is concerned with categorizing different kinds of love or madness, different kinds of lovers, and so forth.

Plato is often regarded as the first great, and perhaps most influential, enemy of rhetoric. But we are indebted to him for the issues and questions he introduces about rhetoric. Without the challenge he posed to rhetors to be responsible and truthful, rhetoric might not have achieved the heights that it did in Western civilization in the centuries that followed.

PLATO

GORGIAS

or *On Rhetoric; Reputative*

CALLICLES: To join in a fight or a fray, as the saying is, Socrates, you have chosen your time well enough.

SOCRATES: Do you mean, according to the proverb, we have come too late for a feast?

CALLICLES: Yes, a most elegant feast; for Gorgias gave us a fine and varied display but a moment ago.

SOCRATES: But indeed, Callicles, it is Chaerephon here who must take the blame for this; he forced us to spend our time in the marketplace.

CHAEREPHON: No matter, Socrates: I will take the curing of it too; for Gorgias is a friend of mine, so that he will give us a display now, if you think fit, or if you prefer, on another occasion.

CALLICLES: What, Chaerephon? Has Socrates a desire to hear Gorgias?

CHAEREPHON: Yes, it is for that very purpose we are here.

CALLICLES: Then whenever you have a mind to pay me a call—Gorgias is staying with me, and he will give you a display.

SOCRATES: Thank you, Callicles: but would he consent to discuss with us? For I want to find out from the man what is the function of his art, and what it is that he professes and teaches. As for the rest of his performance, he must give it us, as you suggest, on another occasion.

CALLICLES: The best way is to ask our friend himself, Socrates: for indeed that was one of the features of his performance. Why, only this moment he was pressing for whatever questions anyone in the house might like to ask, and saying he would answer them all.

SOCRATES: What a good idea! Ask him, Chaerephon.

Translated by W. R. M. Lamb.

CHAEREPHON: What am I to ask?

SOCRATES: What he is.

CHAEREPHON: How do you mean?

SOCRATES: Just as, if he chanced to be in the shoemaking business, his answer would have been, I presume, "a shoemaker." Now, don't you see my meaning?

CHAEREPHON: I see, and will ask him. Tell me, Gorgias, is Callicles here correct in saying that you profess to answer any questions one may ask you?

GORGIAS: He is, Chaerephon; indeed, I was just now making this very profession, and I may add that nobody has asked me anything new for many years now.

CHAEREPHON: So I presume you will easily answer, Gorgias.

GORGIAS: You are free to make trial of that, Chaerephon.

POLUS: Yes, to be sure; and, if you like, Chaerephon, of me. For I think Gorgias must be quite tired out, after the long discourse he has just delivered.

CHAEREPHON: Why, Polus, do you suppose you could answer more excellently than Gorgias?

POLUS: And what does that matter, if I should satisfy you?

CHAEREPHON: Not at all; since it is your wish, answer.

POLUS: Ask.

CHAEREPHON: Then I ask you, if Gorgias chanced to be skilled in the same art as his brother Herodicus, what should we be justified in calling him? What we call his brother, should we not?

POLUS: Certainly.

CHAEREPHON: Then we should make a right statement if we described him as a doctor.

POLUS: Yes.

CHAEREPHON: And if he were expert in the same art as Aristophon, son of Aglaophon, or his brother,[1] what name should we rightly give him?

POLUS: Obviously that of painter.

CHAEREPHON: But as it is, we would like to know in what art he is skilled, and hence by what name we should rightly call him.

POLUS: Chaerephon, there are many arts among mankind that have been discovered experimentally, as the result of experiences: for experience conducts the course of our life according to art, but inexperience according to chance. Of these several arts various men partake in various ways, and the best men of the best. Gorgias here is one of these, and he is a partner in the finest art of all.

SOCRATES: Fine, at any rate, Gorgias, is the equipment for discourse that Polus seems to have got: but still he is not performing his promise to Chaerephon.

GORGIAS: How exactly, Socrates?

SOCRATES: He does not seem to me to be quite answering what he is asked.

GORGIAS: Well, will you please ask him?

SOCRATES: No, if you yourself will be so good as to answer, why, I would far rather ask you. For I see plainly, from what he has said, that Polus has had more practice in what is called rhetoric than in discussion.

POLUS: How so, Socrates?

SOCRATES: Because, Polus, when Chaerephon has asked in what art Gorgias is skilled, you merely eulogize his art as though it were under some censure, instead of replying what it is.

POLUS: Why, did I not reply that it was the finest?

SOCRATES: You certainly did: but nobody asked what was the quality of his art, only what it was, and by what name we ought to call Gorgias. Just as Chaerephon laid out the lines for you at first, and you answered him properly in brief words, in the same way you must now state what is that art, and what we ought to call Gorgias; or rather, Gorgias, do you tell us yourself in what art it is you are skilled, and hence, what we ought to call you.

GORGIAS: Rhetoric, Socrates.

SOCRATES: So we are to call you a rhetorician?

GORGIAS: Yes, and a good one, if you would call me what—to use Homer's phrase—"I vaunt myself to be."[2]

SOCRATES: Well, I shall be pleased to do so.

GORGIAS: Then call me such.

SOCRATES: And are we to say that you are able to make others like yourself?

GORGIAS: Yes, that is what I profess to do, not only here, but elsewhere also.

SOCRATES: Then would you be willing, Gorgias, to continue this present way of discussion, by alternate question and answer, and defer to some other time that lengthy style of speech in which Polus made a beginning? Come, be true to your promise, and consent to answer each question briefly.

GORGIAS: There are some answers, Socrates, that necessitate a lengthy expression: however, I will try to be as brief as possible; for indeed it is one of my claims that no one could express the same thing in briefer terms than myself.

SOCRATES: That is just what I want, Gorgias: give me a display of this very skill—in brevity of speech; your lengthy style will do another time.

GORGIAS: Well, I will do that, and you will admit that you never heard anyone speak more briefly.

SOCRATES: Come then; since you claim to be skilled in rhetorical art, and to be able to make anyone else a rhetorician, tell me with what particular thing rhetoric is concerned: as, for example, weaving is concerned with the manufacture of clothes, is it not?

GORGIAS: Yes.

SOCRATES: And music, likewise, with the making of tunes?

---

[1] Polygnotus, the famous painter who decorated public buildings in Athens from about 470 B.C. [Tr.]

[2] The regular phrase of a Homeric hero in boasting of his valor, parentage, etc.; *cf. Il.* vi. 2II, xiv. 113. [Tr.]

GORGIAS: Yes.

SOCRATES: Upon my word, Gorgias, I do admire your answers! You make them as brief as they well can be.

GORGIAS: Yes, Socrates, I consider myself a very fair hand at that.

SOCRATES: You are right there. Come now, answer me in the same way about rhetoric: with what particular thing is its skill concerned?

GORGIAS: With speech.

SOCRATES: What kind of speech, Gorgias? Do you mean that which shows sick people by what regimen they could get well?

GORGIAS: No.

SOCRATES: Then rhetoric is not concerned with all kinds of speech.

GORGIAS: No, I say.

SOCRATES: Yet it does make men able to speak.

GORGIAS: Yes.

SOCRATES: And to understand also the things about which they speak.

GORGIAS: Of course.

SOCRATES: Now, does the medical art, which we mentioned just now, make men able to understand and speak about the sick?

GORGIAS: It must.

SOCRATES: Hence the medical art also, it seems, is concerned with speech.

GORGIAS: Yes.

SOCRATES: That is, speech about diseases?

GORGIAS: Certainly.

SOCRATES: Now, is gymnastic also concerned with speech about the good and bad condition of our bodies?

GORGIAS: Quite so.

SOCRATES: And moreover it is the same, Gorgias, with all the other arts; each of them is concerned with that kind of speech which deals with the subject matter of that particular art.

GORGIAS: Apparently.

SOCRATES: Then why, pray, do you not give the name "rhetorical" to those other arts, when they are concerned with speech, if you call that "rhetoric" which has to do with speech?

GORGIAS: Because, Socrates, the skill in those other arts is almost wholly concerned with manual work and similar activities, whereas in rhetoric there is no such manual working, but its whole activity and efficacy is by means of speech. For this reason I claim for the rhetorical art that it is concerned with speech, and it is a correct description, I maintain.

SOCRATES: Now, do I understand what sort of art you choose to call it? Perhaps, however, I shall get to know this more clearly. But answer me this: we have arts, have we not?

GORGIAS: Yes.

SOCRATES: Then amongst the various arts some, I take it, consist mainly of work, and so require but brief speech; while others require none, for the art's object may be achieved actually in silence, as with painting, sculpture, and many other arts. It is to such as these that I understand you to refer when you say rhetoric has no concern with them; is not that so?

GORGIAS: Your supposition is quite correct, Socrates.

SOCRATES: But there is another class of arts which achieve their whole purpose through speech and—to put it roughly—require either no action to aid them, or very little; for example, numeration, calculation, geometry, draught-playing, and many other arts: some of these have the speech in about equal proportion to the action, but most have it as the larger part, or absolutely the whole of their operation and effect is by means of speech. It is one of this class of arts that I think you refer to as rhetoric.

GORGIAS: You are right.

SOCRATES: But, mind you, I do not think it is any one of these that you mean to call rhetoric; though, so far as your expression went, you did say that the art which has its effect through speech is rhetoric, and one might retort, if one cared to strain at mere words: So, Gorgias, you call numeration rhetoric! But I do not believe it is either numeration or geometry that you call rhetoric.

GORGIAS: Your belief is correct, Socrates, and your supposition just.

SOCRATES: Come now, and do your part in finishing off the answer to my question. Since rhetoric is in fact one of these arts which depend mainly on speech, and there are likewise other arts of the same nature, try if you can tell me with what this rhetoric, which has its effect in speech, is concerned. For instance, suppose some one asked me about one or other of the arts which I was mentioning just now: Socrates, what is the art of numeration? I should tell him, as you did me a moment ago, that it is one of those which have their effect through speech. And suppose he went on to ask: With what is its speech concerned? I should say: With the odd and even numbers, and the question of how many units there are in each. And if he asked again: What art is it that you call calculation? I should say that this also is one of those which achieve their whole effect by speech. And if he proceeded to ask: With what is it concerned? I should say—in the manner of those who draft amendments in the Assembly—that in most respects calculation is in the same case as numeration, for both are concerned with the same thing, the odd and the even; but that they differ to this extent, that calculation considers the numerical values of odd and even numbers not merely in themselves but in relation to each other. And suppose, on my saying that astronomy also achieves its whole effect by speech, he were to ask me: And the speech of astronomy, with what is it concerned? I should say: With the courses of the stars and sun and moon, and their relative speeds.

GORGIAS: And you would be right, Socrates.

SOCRATES: Come then and do your part, Gorgias: rhetoric is one of those arts, is it not, which carry out their work and achieve their effect by speech?

GORGIAS: That is so.

SOCRATES: Then tell me what they deal with: what subject is it, of all in the world, that is dealt with by this speech employed by rhetoric?

GORGIAS: The greatest of human affairs, Socrates, and the best.

SOCRATES: But that also, Gorgias, is ambiguous, and still by no means clear. I expect you have heard people singing over their cups the old catch, in which the singers enumerate the best things in life,—first health, then beauty, and thirdly, as the maker of the catch puts it, wealth got without guile.

GORGIAS: Yes, I have heard it; but what is the point of your quotation?

SOCRATES: I mean that, supposing the producers of those blessings which the maker of the catch commends—namely, the doctor, the trainer, and the money-getter—were to stand before you this moment, and the doctor first should say: "Gorgias is deceiving you, Socrates; for it is not his art, but mine, that deals with man's greatest good." Then supposing I were to ask him: "And who are you, to say so?" He would probably reply: "A doctor." "Well, what do you mean? That the work of your art is the greatest good?" "What else, Socrates," I expect he would reply, "is health? What greater good is there for men than health?" And supposing the trainer came next and said: "I also should be surprised indeed, Socrates, if Gorgias could show you a greater good in his art than I can in mine." Again I should say to him in his turn: "And who are you, sir? What is your work?" "A trainer," he would reply, "and my work is making men's bodies beautiful and strong." After the trainer would come the money-getter, saying—with, I fancy, a fine contempt for every one: "Pray consider, Socrates, if you can find a good that is greater than wealth, either in Gorgias' view or in that of anyone else at all." "Why then," we should say to him, "are you a producer of that?" "Yes," he would say. "And who are you?" "A money-getter." "Well then," we shall say to him, "do you judge wealth to be the greatest good for men?" "Of course," he will reply. "But look here," we should say; "our friend Gorgias contends that his own art is a cause of greater good than yours." Then doubtless his next question would be: "And what is that good? Let Gorgias answer." Now come, Gorgias; imagine yourself being questioned by those persons and by me, and tell us what is this thing that you say is the greatest good for men, and that you claim to produce.

GORGIAS: A thing, Socrates, which in truth is the greatest good, and a cause not merely of freedom to mankind at large, but also of dominion to single persons in their several cities.

SOCRATES: Well, and what do you call it?

GORGIAS: I call it the ability to persuade with speeches either judges in the law courts or statesmen in the council-chamber or the commons in the Assembly or an audience at any other meeting that may be held on public affairs. And I tell you that by virtue of this power you will have the doctor as your slave, and the trainer as your slave; your money-getter will turn out to be making money not for himself, but for another,—in fact for you, who are able to speak and persuade the multitude.

SOCRATES: I think now, Gorgias, you have come very near to showing us the art of rhetoric as you conceive it, and if I at all take your meaning, you say that rhetoric is a producer of persuasion, and has therein its whole business and main consummation. Or can you tell us of any other function it can have beyond that of effecting persuasion in the minds of an audience?

GORGIAS: None at all, Socrates; your definition seems to me satisfactory; that is the main substance of the art.

SOCRATES: Then listen, Gorgias: I, let me assure you, for so I persuade myself—if ever there was a man who debated with another from a desire of knowing the truth of the subject discussed, I am such a man; and so, I trust, are you.

GORGIAS: Well, what then, Socrates?

SOCRATES: I will now tell you. What the real nature of the persuasion is that you speak of as resulting from rhetoric, and what the matters are with which persuasion deals, I assure you I do not clearly understand; though I may have my suspicions as to what I suppose you to mean by it, and with what things you think it deals. But nevertheless I will ask you what you do mean by the persuasion that results from rhetoric, and with what matters you think it deals. Now why is it that, having a suspicion of my own, I am going to ask you this, instead of stating it myself? It is not on your account, but with a view to the argument, and to such a progress in it as may best reveal to us the point we are discussing. Just see if you do not think it fair of me to press you with my question: suppose I happened to ask you what Zeuxis was among painters, and you said "a figure painter," would it not be fair of me to ask you what sort of figures he painted, and where?

GORGIAS: Certainly.

SOCRATES: Would this be the reason—that there are also other painters who depict a variety of other figures?

GORGIAS: Yes.

SOCRATES: But if no one besides Zeuxis were a painter, your answer would have been right?

GORGIAS: Yes, of course.

SOCRATES: Come then, tell me now about rhetoric: do you think rhetoric alone effects persuasion, or can other arts do it as well? I mean, for example, when a man teaches anything, does he persuade in his teaching? Or do you think not?

GORGIAS: No, to be sure, Socrates, I think he most certainly does persuade.

SOCRATES: Then let us repeat our question with reference to the same arts that we spoke of just now: does not numeration, or the person skilled in numeration, teach us all that pertains to number?

GORGIAS: Certainly.

SOCRATES: And persuades also?

GORGIAS: Yes.

SOCRATES: So that numeration also is a producer of persuasion?

GORGIAS: Apparently.

SOCRATES: Then if we are asked what kind of persuasion, and dealing with what, we shall reply, I suppose: The instructive kind, which deals with the amount of an odd or an even number; and we shall be able to demonstrate that all the other arts which we mentioned just now are producers of persuasion, and what kind it is, and what it deals with, shall we not?

GORGIAS: Yes.

SOCRATES: Hence rhetoric is not the only producer of persuasion.

GORGIAS: You are right.

SOCRATES: Since then it is not the only one that achieves this effect, but others can also, we should be justified in putting this further question to the speaker, as we did concerning the painter: Then of what kind of persuasion, and of persuasion dealing with what, is rhetoric the art? Or do you not consider that such a further question would be justified?

GORGIAS: Yes, I do.

SOCRATES: Then answer me, Gorgias, since you agree with me on that.

GORGIAS: Well then, I mean that kind of persuasion, Socrates, which you find in the law courts and in any public gatherings, as in fact I said just now; and it deals with what is just and unjust.

SOCRATES: I, too, I may tell you, had a suspicion that it was this persuasion that you meant, and as dealing with those things, Gorgias; but you must not be surprised if I ask you by-and-by some such question as may seem to be obvious, though I persist in it; for, as I say, I ask my questions with a view to an orderly completion of our argument—I am not aiming at you, but only anxious that we do not fall into a habit of snatching at each other's words with a hasty guess, and that you may complete your own statement in your own way, as the premises may allow.

GORGIAS: And I think you are quite right in doing so, Socrates.

SOCRATES: Come then, let us consider another point. Is there something that you call "having learned"?

GORGIAS: There is.

SOCRATES: And again, "having believed"?

GORGIAS: Yes.

SOCRATES: Then do you think that having learned and having believed, or learning and belief, are the same thing, or different?

GORGIAS: In my opinion, Socrates, they are different.

SOCRATES: And your opinion is right, as you can prove in this way: if some one asked you—Is there, Gorgias, a false and a true belief?—you would say, Yes, I imagine.

GORGIAS: I should.

SOCRATES: But now, is there a false and a true knowledge?

GORGIAS: Surely not.

SOCRATES: So it is evident again that they[3] are not the same.

GORGIAS: You are right.

SOCRATES: But yet those who have learned have been persuaded, as well as those who have believed.

GORGIAS: That is so.

SOCRATES: Then would you have us assume two forms of persuasion—one providing belief without knowledge, and the other sure knowledge?

GORGIAS: Certainly.

SOCRATES: Now which kind of persuasion is it that rhetoric creates in law courts or any public meeting on matters of right and wrong? The kind from which we get belief without knowledge, or that from which we get knowledge?

GORGIAS: Obviously, I presume, Socrates, that from which we get belief.

SOCRATES: Thus rhetoric, it seems, is a producer of persuasion for belief, not for instruction in the matter of right and wrong.

GORGIAS: Yes.

SOCRATES: And so the rhetorician's business is not to instruct a law court or a public meeting in matters of right and wrong, but only to make them believe; since, I take it, he could not in a short while instruct such a mass of people in matters so important.

GORGIAS: No, to be sure.

SOCRATES: Come then, let us see what actually is our account of rhetoric: for I confess I am not yet able to distinguish what my own account of it is. When the city holds a meeting to appoint doctors or shipbuilders or any other set of craftsmen, there is no question then, is there, of the rhetorician giving advice? And clearly this is because in each appointment we have to elect the most skillful person. Again, in a case of building

---

[3] I.e., knowledge and belief. [Tr.]

walls or constructing harbors or arsenals, our only advisers are the master-builders; or in consulting on the appointment of generals, or on a maneuver against the enemy, or on a military occupation, it is the general staff who will then advise us, and not the rhetoricians. Or what do you say, Gorgias, to these instances? For as you claim to be an orator yourself and to make orators of others, it is proper to inquire of you concerning your own craft. And here you must regard me as furthering your own interest: for it is quite likely that some one within these walls has a wish to become your pupil—indeed I fancy I perceive more than one, yes, a number of them, who, perhaps, would be ashamed to press you with questions. So, when you are being pressed with mine, consider that you are being questioned by them as well: "What shall we get, Gorgias, by coming to hear you? On what matters shall we be enabled to give advice to the state? Will it be only on right and wrong, or on those things besides which Socrates was mentioning just now?" So try to give them an answer.

GORGIAS: Well, I will try, Socrates, to reveal to you clearly the whole power of rhetoric: and in fact you have correctly shown the way to it yourself. You know, I suppose, that these great arsenals and walls of Athens, and the construction of your harbors, are due to the advice of Themistocles, and in part to that of Pericles, not to your craftsmen.

SOCRATES: So we are told, Gorgias, of Themistocles; and as to Pericles, I heard him myself when he was advising us about the middle wall.[4]

GORGIAS: So whenever there is an election of such persons as you were referring to, Socrates, you see it is the orators who give the advice and get resolutions carried in these matters.

SOCRATES: That is just what surprises me, Gorgias, and has made me ask you all this time what in the world the power of rhetoric can be. For, viewed in this light, its greatness comes over me as something supernatural.

GORGIAS: Ah yes, if you knew all, Socrates,—how it comprises in itself practically all powers at once! And I will tell you a striking proof of this: many and many a time have I gone with my brother or other doctors to visit one of their patients, and found him unwilling either to take medicine or submit to the surgeon's knife or cautery; and when the doctor failed to persuade him I succeeded, by no other art than that of rhetoric. And I further declare that, if a rhetorician and a doctor were to enter any city you please, and there had to contend in speech before the Assembly or some other meeting as to which of the two should be appointed physician, you would find the physician was nowhere, while the master of speech would be appointed if he wished. And if he had to contend with a member of any other profession whatsoever, the rhetorician would persuade the meeting to appoint him before anyone else in the place: for there is no subject on which the rhetorician could not speak more persuasively than a member of any other profession whatsoever, before a multitude. So great, so strange, is the power of this art. At the same time, Socrates, our use of rhetoric should be like our use of any other sort of exercise. For other exercises are not to be used against all and sundry, just because one has learned boxing or wrestling or fighting in armor so well as to vanquish friend and foe alike: this gives one no right to strike one's friends, or stab them to death. Nor, in all conscience, if a man took lessons at a wrestling-school, and having got himself into good condition and learned boxing he proceeded to strike his father and mother, or some other of his relations or friends, should that be a reason for hating athletic trainers and teachers of fighting in armor, and ex-

---

[4] Built about 440 B.C. between the two walls built in 456 B.C., one connecting the Piraeus, and the other Phalerum, with Athens. The "middle wall" ran parallel to the former, and secured from hostile attack a narrow strip of land between Athens and the Piraeus. Socrates was born in 469 B.C. [Tr.]

pelling them from our cities. For they imparted their skill with a view to its rightful use against enemies and wrongdoers, in self-defense, not provocation; whereas the others have perverted their strength and art to an improper use. So it is not the teachers who are wicked, nor is the art either guilty or wicked on this account, but rather, to my thinking, those who do not use it properly. Now the same argument applies also to rhetoric: for the orator is able, indeed, to speak against every one and on every question in such a way as to win over the votes of the multitude, practically in any matter he may choose to take up: but he is no whit the more entitled to deprive the doctors of their credit, just because he could do so, or other professionals of theirs; he must use his rhetoric fairly, as in the case of athletic exercise. And, in my opinion, if a man becomes a rhetorician and then uses this power and this art unfairly, we ought not to hate his teacher and cast him out of our cities. For he imparted that skill to be used in all fairness, while this man puts it to an opposite use. Thus it is the man who does not use it aright who deserves to be hated and expelled and put to death, and not his teacher.

SOCRATES: I expect, Gorgias, that you as well as I have had no small practice in arguments, and have observed the following fact about them, that it is not easy for people to define to each other the matters which they take in hand to discuss, and to make such exchange of instruction as will fairly bring their debate to an end: no, if they find that some point is in dispute between them, and one of them says that the other is speaking incorrectly or obscurely, they are annoyed and think the remark comes from jealousy of themselves, and in a spirit of contention rather than of inquiry into the matter proposed for discussion. In some cases, indeed, they end by making a most disgraceful scene, with such abusive expressions on each side that the rest of the company are vexed on their own account that they allowed themselves to listen to such fellows. Well, what is my reason for saying this? It is because your present remarks do not seem to me quite in keeping or accord with what you said at first about rhetoric. Now I am afraid to refute you, lest you imagine I am contentiously neglecting the point and its elucidation, and merely attacking you. I therefore, if you are a person of the same sort as myself, should be glad to continue questioning you: if not, I can let it drop. Of what sort am I? One of those who would be glad to be refuted if I say anything untrue, and glad to refute anyone else who might speak untruly; but just as glad, mind you, to be refuted as to refute, since I regard the former as the greater benefit, in proportion as it is a greater benefit for oneself to be delivered from the greatest evil than to deliver some one else. For I consider that a man cannot suffer any evil so great as a false opinion on the subjects of our actual argument. Now if you say that you too are of that sort, let us go on with the conversation; but if you think we had better drop it, let us have done with it at once and make an end of the discussion.

GORGIAS: Nay, I too, Socrates, claim to be of the sort you indicate; though perhaps we should have taken thought also for the wishes of our company. For, let me tell you, some time before you and your friend arrived, I gave the company a performance of some length; and if we now have this conversation I expect we shall seriously protract our sitting. We ought, therefore, to consider their wishes as well, in case we are detaining any of them who may want to do something else.

CHAEREPHON: You hear for yourselves, Gorgias and Socrates, the applause by which these gentlemen show their desire to hear anything you may say; for my own part, however, Heaven forbid that I should ever be so busy as to give up a discussion so interesting and so conducted, because I found it more important to attend to something else.

CALLICLES: Yes, by all that's holy, Chaerephon; and let me say, moreover, for myself that among the many discussions which I have attended in my time I doubt if there was one that gave me such delight as this present one. So, for my part, I shall count it a favor even if you choose to continue it all day long.

SOCRATES: Why, Callicles, I assure you there is no hindrance on my side, if Gorgias is willing.

GORGIAS: After that, Socrates, it would be shameful indeed if I were unwilling, when it was I who challenged everybody to ask what questions they pleased. But if our friends here are so minded, go on with the conversation and ask me anything you like.

SOCRATES: Hark you then, Gorgias, to what surprises me in your statements: to be sure, you may possibly be right, and I may take your meaning wrongly. You say you are able to make a rhetorician of any man who chooses to learn from you?

GORGIAS: Yes.

SOCRATES: Now, do you mean, to make him carry conviction to the crowd on all subjects, not by teaching them, but by persuading?

GORGIAS: Certainly I do.

SOCRATES: You were saying just now, you know, that even in the matter of health the orator will be more convincing than the doctor.

GORGIAS: Yes, indeed, I was—meaning, to the crowd.

SOCRATES: And "to the crowd" means "to the ignorant"? For surely, to those who know, he will not be more convincing than the doctor.

GORGIAS: You are right.

SOCRATES: And if he is to be more convincing than the doctor, he thus becomes more convincing than he who knows?

GORGIAS: Certainly.

SOCRATES: Though not himself a doctor, you agree?

GORGIAS: Yes.

SOCRATES: But he who is not a doctor is surely without knowledge of that whereof the doctor has knowledge.

GORGIAS: Clearly.

SOCRATES: So he who does not know will be more convincing to those who do not know than he who knows, supposing the orator to be more convincing than the doctor. Is that, or something else, the consequence?

GORGIAS: In this case it does follow.

SOCRATES: Then the case is the same in all the other arts for the orator and his rhetoric: there is no need to know the truth of the actual matters, but one merely needs to have discovered some device of persuasion which will make one appear to those who do not know to know better than those who know.

GORGIAS: Well, and is it not a great convenience, Socrates, to make oneself a match for the professionals by learning just this single art and omitting all the others?

SOCRATES: Whether the orator is or is not a match for the rest of them by reason of that skill, is a question we shall look into presently, if our argument so requires: for the moment let us consider first whether the rhetorician is in the same relation to what is just and unjust, base and noble, good and bad, as to what is healthful, and to the various objects of all the other arts; he does not know what is really good or bad, noble or base, just or unjust, but he has devised a persuasion to deal with these matters so as to appear to those who, like himself, do not know to know better than he who knows. Or is it necessary to know, and must anyone who intends to learn rhetoric have a previous knowledge of these things when he comes to you? Or if not, are you, as the teacher of rhetoric, to teach the person who comes to you nothing about them—for it is not your business—but only to make him appear in the eyes of the multitude to know things of this sort when he does not know, and to appear to be good when he is not? Or will you be utterly unable to teach him rhetoric unless he previously knows the truth about these matters? Or what is the real state of the case, Gorgias? For Heaven's sake, as you proposed just now, draw aside the veil and tell us what really is the function of rhetoric.

GORGIAS: Why, I suppose, Socrates, if he happens not to know these things he will learn them too from me.

SOCRATES: Stop there: I am glad of that statement. If you make a man a rhetorician he must needs know what is just and unjust either previously or by learning afterwards from you.

GORGIAS: Quite so.

SOCRATES: Well now, a man who has learned building is a builder, is he not?

GORGIAS: Yes.

SOCRATES: And he who has learned music, a musician?

GORGIAS: Yes.

SOCRATES: Then he who has learned medicine is a medical man, and so on with the rest on the same principle; anyone who has learned a certain art has the qualification acquired by his particular knowledge?

GORGIAS: Certainly.

SOCRATES: And so, on this principle, he who has learned what is just is just?

GORGIAS: Absolutely, I presume.

SOCRATES: And the just man, I suppose, does what is just.

GORGIAS: Yes.

SOCRATES: Now the just man must *wish* to do what is just?

GORGIAS: Apparently.

SOCRATES: Hence the just man will never wish to act unjustly?

GORGIAS: That must needs be so.

SOCRATES: But it follows from our statements[5] that the rhetorician must be just.

GORGIAS: Yes.

SOCRATES: Hence the rhetorician will never wish to do wrong.

GORGIAS: Apparently not.

SOCRATES: Then do you remember saying a little while ago that we ought not to complain against the trainers or expel them from our cities, if a boxer makes not merely use, but an unfair use, of his boxing? So in just the same way, if an orator uses his rhetoric unfairly, we should not complain against his teacher or banish him from our city, but the man who does the wrong and misuses his rhetoric. Was that said or not?

GORGIAS: It was.

SOCRATES: But now we find that this very person, the rhetorician, could never be guilty of wrongdoing, do we not?

GORGIAS: We do.

SOCRATES: And in our first statements, Gorgias, we said that rhetoric dealt with speech, not on even and odd, but on the just and unjust, did we not?

GORGIAS: Yes.

SOCRATES: Well then, I supposed at the time when you were saying this that rhetoric could never be an unjust thing, since the speeches it made were always about justice; but when a little later you told us that the orator might make even an unjust use of his rhetoric, that indeed surprised me, and thinking the two statements were not in accord I made those proposals,—that if, like myself, you counted it a gain to be refuted, it was worth while to have the discussion, but if not, we had better have done with it. And now that we have come to examine the matter, you see for yourself that we agree once more that it is impossible for the rhetorician to use his rhetoric unjustly or consent to do wrong. Now, to distinguish properly which way the truth of the matter lies will require, by the Dog,[6] Gorgias, no short sitting.

POLUS: How is this, Socrates? Is that really your opinion of rhetoric, as you now express it? Or, think you, because Gorgias was ashamed not to admit your point that the rhetorician knows what is just and noble and good, and will himself teach these to anyone who comes to him without knowing them; and then from this admission I daresay there followed some inconsistency in the statements made—the result that

[5] I.e., that he must know what is just, and that he who knows this must be just. [Tr.]

[6] This favorite oath of Socrates was derived from Egypt, where the god Anubis was represented with a dog's head; *cf.* 482 B. [Tr.]

you are so fond of—when it was yourself who led him into that set of questions![7] For who do you think will deny that he has a knowledge of what is just and can also teach it to others? I call it very bad taste to lead the discussion in such a direction.

SOCRATES: Ah, sweet Polus, of course it is for this very purpose we possess ourselves of companions and sons, that when the advance of years begins to make us stumble, you younger ones may be at hand to set our lives upright again in words as well as deeds. So now if Gorgias and I are stumbling in our words, you are to stand by and set us up again—it is only your duty; and for my part I am willing to revoke at your pleasure anything that you think has been wrongly admitted, if you will kindly observe one condition.

POLUS: What do you mean by that?

SOCRATES: That you keep a check on that lengthy way of speaking, Polus, which you tried to employ at first.

POLUS: Why, shall I not be at liberty to say as much as I like?

SOCRATES: It would indeed be a hard fate for you, my excellent friend, if having come to Athens, where there is more freedom of speech than anywhere in Greece, you should be the one person there who could not enjoy it. But as a set-off to that, I ask you if it would not be just as hard on me, while you spoke at length and refused to answer my questions, not to be free to go away and avoid listening to you. No, if you have any concern for the argument that we have carried on, and care to set it on its feet again, revoke whatever you please, as I suggested just now; take your turn in questioning and being questioned, like me and Gorgias; and thus either refute or be refuted. For you claim, I understand, that you yourself know all that Gorgias knows, do you not?

POLUS: I do.

SOCRATES: Then are you with him also in bidding us ask at each point any questions we like of you, as one who knows how to answer?

POLUS: Certainly I am.

SOCRATES: So now, take whichever course you like: either put questions, or answer them.

POLUS: Well, I will do as you say. So answer me this, Socrates: since you think that Gorgias is at a loss about rhetoric, what is your own account of it?

SOCRATES: Are you asking what art I call it?

POLUS: Yes.

SOCRATES: None at all, I consider, Polus, if you would have the honest truth.

POLUS: But what do you consider rhetoric to be?

SOCRATES: A thing which you say—in the treatise which I read of late—"made art."

POLUS: What thing do you mean?

SOCRATES: I mean a certain habitude.

POLUS: Then do you take rhetoric to be a habitude?

SOCRATES: I do, if you have no other suggestion.

POLUS: Habitude of what?

SOCRATES: Of producing a kind of gratification and pleasure.

POLUS: Then you take rhetoric to be something fine—an ability to gratify people?

SOCRATES: How now, Polus? Have you as yet heard me tell you what I say it is, that you ask what should follow that—whether I do not take it to be fine?

POLUS: Why, did I not hear you call it a certain habitude?

SOCRATES: Then please—since you value "gratification"—be so good as gratify me in a small matter.

POLUS: I will.

SOCRATES: Ask me now what art I take cookery to be.

POLUS: Then I ask you, what art is cookery?

SOCRATES: None at all, Polus.

---

[7] The defective construction of this sentence is probably intended to mark the agitated manner of Polus in making his protest. [Tr.] The name "Polus" means young colt, and Polus's entry into the discussion here suggests in its style the awkward, impulsive gait of a colt. [Ed.]

POLUS: Well, what is it? Tell me.

SOCRATES: Then I reply, a certain habitude.

POLUS: Of what? Tell me.

SOCRATES: Then I reply, of production of gratification and pleasure, Polus.

POLUS: So cookery and rhetoric are the same thing?

SOCRATES: Not at all, only parts of the same practice.

POLUS: What practice do you mean?

SOCRATES: I fear it may be too rude to tell the truth; for I shrink from saying it on Gorgias' account, lest he suppose I am making satirical fun of his own profession. Yet indeed I do not know whether this is the rhetoric which Gorgias practices, for from our argument just now we got no very clear view as to how he conceives it; but what I call rhetoric is a part of a certain business which has nothing fine about it.

GORGIAS: What is that, Socrates? Tell us, without scruple on my account.

SOCRATES: It seems to me then, Gorgias, to be a pursuit that is not a matter of art, but showing a shrewd, gallant spirit which has a natural bent for clever dealing with mankind, and I sum up its substance in the name *flattery*. This practice, as I view it, has many branches, and one of them is cookery; which appears indeed to be an art but, by my account of it, is not an art but a habitude or knack. I call rhetoric another branch of it, as also personal adornment and sophistry—four branches of it for four kinds of affairs. So if Polus would inquire, let him inquire: he has not yet been informed to what sort of branch of flattery I assign rhetoric; but without noticing that I have not yet answered that, he proceeds to ask whether I do not consider it a fine thing. But I am not going to reply to the question whether I consider rhetoric a fine or a base thing, until I have first answered what it is; for it would not be fair, Polus: but if you want the information, ask me what sort of branch of flattery I assert rhetoric to be.

POLUS: I ask you then; so answer, what sort of branch it is.

SOCRATES: Now, will you understand when I answer? Rhetoric, by my account, is a semblance[8] of a branch of politics.

POLUS: Well then, do you call it a fine or a base thing?

SOCRATES: A base one, I call it—for all that is bad I call base—since I am to answer you as though you had already understood my meaning.

GORGIAS: Nor do I myself, upon my word, Socrates, grasp your meaning either.

SOCRATES: And no wonder, Gorgias, for as yet my statement is not at all clear; but Polus[9] here is so young and fresh!

GORGIAS: Ah, do not mind him; but tell me what you mean by rhetoric being a semblance of a branch of politics.

SOCRATES: Well, I will try to express what rhetoric appears to me to be: if it is not in fact what I say, Polus here will refute me. There are things, I suppose, that you call body and soul?

GORGIAS: Of course.

SOCRATES: And each of these again you believe to have a good condition?

GORGIAS: I do.

SOCRATES: And again, a good condition that may seem so, but is not? As an example, let me give the following: many people seem to be in good bodily condition when it would not be easy for anyone but a doctor, or one of the athletic trainers, to perceive that they are not so.

GORGIAS: You are right.

SOCRATES: Something of this sort I say there is in body and in soul, which makes the body or the soul seem to be in good condition, though it is none the more so in fact.

GORGIAS: Quite so.

SOCRATES: Now let me see if I can explain my meaning to you more clearly. There are two different affairs to which I assign two different arts: the one, which has to do with the soul, I

---

[8] I.e., an unreal image or counterfeit: Quintilian (ii. 15.25) renders *simulacrum*. [Tr.]

[9] Socrates alludes to the meaning of πῶλος (a colt). [Tr.]

call politics; the other, which concerns the body, though I cannot give you a single name for it offhand, is all one business, the tendance of the body, which I can designate in two branches as gymnastic and medicine. Under politics I set legislation in the place of gymnastic, and justice to match medicine. In each of these pairs, of course—medicine and gymnastic, justice and legislation—there is some intercommunication, as both deal with the same thing; at the same time they have certain differences. Now these four, which always bestow their care for the best advantage respectively of the body and the soul, are noticed by the art of flattery which, I do not say with knowledge, but by speculation, divides herself into four parts, and then, insinuating herself into each of those branches, pretends to be that into which she has crept, and cares nothing for what is the best, but dangles what is most pleasant for the moment as a bait for folly, and deceives it into thinking that she is of the highest value. Thus cookery assumes the form of medicine, and pretends to know what foods are best for the body; so that if a cook and a doctor had to contend before boys, or before men as foolish as boys, as to which of the two, the doctor or the cook, understands the question of sound and noxious foods, the doctor would starve to death. Flattery, however, is what I call it, and I say that this sort of thing is a disgrace, Polus—for here I address you—because it aims at the pleasant and ignores the best; and I say it is not an art, but a habitude, since it has no account to give of the real nature of the things it applies, and so cannot tell the cause of any of them. I refuse to give the name of art to anything that is irrational: if you dispute my views, I am ready to give my reasons. However, as I put it, cookery is flattery disguised as medicine; and in just the same manner self-adornment personates gymnastic: with its rascally, deceitful, ignoble, and illiberal nature it deceives men by forms and colors, polish and dress, so as to make them, in the effort of assuming an extraneous beauty, neglect the native sort that comes through gymnastic. Well, to avoid prolixity, I am willing to put it to you like a geometer[10]—for by this time I expect you can follow me: as self-adornment is to gymnastic, so is sophistry to legislation; and as cookery is to medicine, so is rhetoric to justice.[11] But although, as I say, there is this natural distinction between them,[12] they are so nearly related that sophists and orators are jumbled up as having the same field and dealing with the same subjects, and neither can they tell what to make of each other, nor the world at large what to make of them. For indeed, if the soul were not in command of the body, but the latter had charge of itself, and so cookery and medicine were not surveyed and distinguished by the soul, but the body itself were the judge, forming its own estimate of them by the gratifications they gave it, we should have a fine instance of what Anaxagoras described, my dear Polus—for you are versed in these matters: everything would be jumbled together, without distinction as between medicinal and healthful and tasty concoctions. Well now, you have heard what I state rhetoric to be—the counterpart of cookery in the soul, acting here as that does on the body. It may, indeed, be absurd of me, when I do not allow you to make long speeches, to have extended mine to so considerable a length. However, I can fairly claim indulgence: for when I spoke briefly you did not understand me; you were unable to make any use of the answer I gave you, but required a full exposition. Now if I on my part cannot tell what use to make of any answers you may give me, you shall extend your speech also; but if I can make some use of them, allow me to do it; that will only be fair. And

---

[10] I.e., in the concise mathematical manner, such as that which later appeared in the writings of Euclid. [Tr.]

[11] Administrative justice is here specially meant. [Tr.]

[12] I.e., sophistry and rhetoric. [Tr.]

now, if you can make any use of this answer of mine, do so.

POLUS: Then what is it you say? Do you take rhetoric to be flattery?

SOCRATES: Well, I said rather a branch of flattery. Why, at your age, Polus, have you no memory? What will you do later on?

POLUS: Then do you think that good orators are considered to be flatterers in their cities, and so worthless?

SOCRATES: Is that a question you are asking, or are you beginning a speech?

POLUS: I am asking a question.

SOCRATES: To my mind, they are not considered at all.

POLUS: How not considered? Have they not the chief power in their cities?

SOCRATES: No, if you mean power in the sense of something good for him who has it.

POLUS: Why, of course I mean that.

SOCRATES: Then, to my thinking, the orators have the smallest power of all who are in their city.

POLUS: What? Are they not like the despots, in putting to death anyone they please, and depriving anyone of his property and expelling him from their cities as they may think fit?

SOCRATES: By the Dog, I fear I am still in two minds, Polus, at everything you say, as to whether this is a statement on your own part, and a declaration of your own opinion, or a question you are putting to me.

POLUS: Why, I am asking you.

SOCRATES: Very well, my friend: then are you asking me two things at once?

POLUS: How two?

SOCRATES: Were you not this moment saying something like this: Is it not the case that the orators put to death anyone they wish, like the despots, and deprive people of property and expel them from their cities as they may think fit?

POLUS: I was.

SOCRATES: Then I tell you that there are two questions here, and I will give you answers to them both. For I say, Polus, that the orators and the despots alike have the least power in their cities, as I stated just now; since they do nothing that they wish to do, practically speaking, though they do whatever they think to be best.

POLUS: Well, and is not that a great power to have?

SOCRATES: No, judging at least by what Polus says.

POLUS: I say no! Pardon me, I say yes.

SOCRATES: No, by the ———, you do not; for you said that great power is a good to him who has it.

POLUS: Yes, and I maintain it.

SOCRATES: Then do you regard it as a good, when a man does what he thinks to be best, without having intelligence? Is that what you call having a great power?

POLUS: No, I do not.

SOCRATES: Then will you prove that the orators have intelligence, and that rhetoric is an art, not a flattery, and so refute me? Else, if you are going to leave me unrefuted, the orators who do what they think fit in their cities, and the despots, will find they have got no good in doing that, if indeed power is, as you say, a good, but doing what one thinks fit without intelligence is—as you yourself admit, do you not?—an evil.

POLUS: Yes, I do.

SOCRATES: How then can the orators or the despots have great power in their cities, unless Socrates is refuted by Polus, and admits that they do what they wish?

POLUS: Hark at the man———!

SOCRATES: I deny that they do what they wish: there, refute me.

POLUS: Did you not admit just now that they do what they think best?

SOCRATES: Yes, and I admit it now.

POLUS: Then do they not do what they wish?

SOCRATES: I say no.

POLUS: When they do what they think fit?

SOCRATES: Yes.

POLUS: What shocking, nay, monstrous answers, Socrates!

SOCRATES: Spare your invective, peerless Polus—if I may address you in your own style:[13] but if you have a question to ask me, expose my error; otherwise, make answer yourself.

POLUS: Well, I am ready to answer, in order that I may know what you mean.

SOCRATES: Then is it your view that people wish merely that which they do each time, or that which is the object of their doing what they do? For instance, do those who take medicine by doctor's orders wish, in your opinion, merely what they do—to take the medicine and suffer the pain of it—or rather to be healthy, which is the object of their taking it?

POLUS: To be healthy, without a doubt.

SOCRATES: And so with seafarers and such as pursue profit generally in trade; what they wish is not what they are doing at each moment—for who wishes to go on a voyage, and incur all its danger and trouble? It is rather, I conceive, the object of their voyage—to get wealth; since it is for wealth that they go on it.

POLUS: Certainly.

SOCRATES: And is it not just the same in every case? If a man does something for an object, he does not wish the thing that he does, but the thing for which he does it.

POLUS: Yes.

SOCRATES: Now is there any existent thing that is not either good or bad or between these—neither good nor bad?

POLUS: Most assuredly nothing, Socrates.

SOCRATES: Well, do you call wisdom and health and wealth and everything else of that kind good, and their opposites bad?

POLUS: I do.

SOCRATES: And by things neither good nor bad do you mean such things as sometimes partake of the good, sometimes of the bad, and sometimes of neither—for example, sitting, walking, running, and sailing, or again, stones and sticks and anything else of that sort? These are what you mean, are they not? Or are there other things that you describe as neither good nor bad?

POLUS: No, these are what I mean.

SOCRATES: Then do people do these intermediate things, when they do them, for the sake of the good things, or the good things for the intermediate?

POLUS: The intermediate, I presume, for the good.

SOCRATES: Thus it is in pursuit of the good that we walk, when we walk, conceiving it to be better; or on the contrary, stand, when we stand, for the sake of the same thing, the good: is it not so?

POLUS: Yes.

SOCRATES: And so we put a man to death, if we do put him to death, or expel him or deprive him of his property, because we think it better for us to do this than not?

POLUS: Certainly.

SOCRATES: So it is for the sake of the good that the doers of all these things do them?

POLUS: I agree.

SOCRATES: And we have admitted that when we do things for an object, we do not wish those things, but the object for which we do them?

POLUS: Quite so.

SOCRATES: Then we do not wish to slaughter people or expel them from our cities or deprive them of their property as an act in itself, but if these things are beneficial we wish to do them, while if they are harmful, we do not wish them. For we wish what is good, as you say; but what is neither good nor bad we do not wish, nor what is bad either, do we? Is what I say true in your opinion, Polus, or not? Why do you not answer?

POLUS: It is true.

SOCRATES: Then, as we agree on this, if a man puts anyone to death or expels him from a city

---

13 The assonance in *ὦ λῷστε Πῶλε* is a mocking allusion to the nicely balanced clauses and jingling phrases which Polus imitated from his master Gorgias. Something of this style appears in Polus's speech above, 448 c. [Tr.]

or deprives him of his property, whether he does it as a despot or an orator, because he thinks it better for himself though it is really worse, that man, I take it, does what he thinks fit, does he not?

POLUS: Yes.

SOCRATES: Now is it also what he wishes, supposing it to be really bad? Why do you not answer?

POLUS: No, I do not think he does what he wishes.

SOCRATES: Can such a man then be said to have great power in that city, if to have great power is something good, according to your admission?

POLUS: He cannot.

SOCRATES: Then I spoke the truth when I said that it is possible for a man to do what he thinks fit in a city and yet not to have great power nor to do what he wishes.

POLUS: As if you, Socrates, would not accept the liberty of doing what you think fit in your city rather than not, and would not envy a man whom you observed to have put some one to death as he thought fit, or deprived him of his property or sent him to prison!

SOCRATES: Justly, do you mean, or unjustly?

POLUS: Whichever way he does it, is it not enviable in either case?

SOCRATES: Hush, Polus!

POLUS: Why?

SOCRATES: Because we ought not to envy either the unenviable or the wretched, but pity them.

POLUS: What! Is that the state in which you consider those people, of whom I speak, to be?

SOCRATES: Yes, for so I must.

POLUS: Then do you consider that a man who puts another to death as he thinks fit, and justly puts him to death, is wretched and pitiable?

SOCRATES: Not I; but not enviable either.

POLUS: Did you not say just now that he was wretched?

SOCRATES: Only he who unjustly put some one to death, my friend, and I called him pitiable as well: if he acted justly, then he is unenviable.

POLUS: I suppose, at any rate, the man who is put to death unjustly is both pitiable and wretched.

SOCRATES: Less so than he who puts him to death, Polus, and less so than he who is put to death justly.

POLUS: In what way can that be, Socrates?

SOCRATES: In this, that to do wrong is the greatest of evils.

POLUS: What, is this the greatest? Is not to suffer wrong a greater?

SOCRATES: By no means.

POLUS: Then would you wish rather to suffer wrong than to do it?

SOCRATES: I should wish neither, for my own part; but if it were necessary either to do wrong or to suffer it, I should choose to suffer rather than do it.

POLUS: Then you would not accept a despot's power?

SOCRATES: No, if you mean by a despot's power the same as I do.

POLUS: Why, what I mean is, as I did just now, the liberty of doing anything one thinks fit in one's city—putting people to death and expelling them and doing everything at one's own discretion.

SOCRATES: My gifted friend, let me speak, and you shall take me to task in your turn. Suppose that in a crowded market I should hide a dagger under my arm and then say to you: "Polus, I have just acquired, by a wonderful chance, the power of a despot; for if I should think fit that one of those people whom you see there should die this very instant, a dead man he will be, just as I think fit; or if I think fit that one of them shall have his head broken, broken it will be immediately; or to have his cloak torn in pieces, torn it will be: so great is my power in this city." Then suppose that on your disbelieving this I showed you my dagger; I expect when you saw it you would say: "Socrates, at this rate every one would have great power, for any house you thought fit might be set ablaze on these methods, and the Athenian arsenals also, and the men-of-war and all the rest of the shipping, both public and private." But surely this is not what it is to have great power—merely doing what one thinks fit. Or do you think it is?

POLUS: Oh no, not in that way.

SOCRATES: Then can you tell me why you disapprove of this kind of power?

POLUS: I can.

SOCRATES: Why, then? Tell me.

POLUS: Because it is inevitable that he who acts thus will be punished.

SOCRATES: And is it not a bad thing to be punished?

POLUS: Certainly.

SOCRATES: So, my remarkable friend, you have come round again to the view that if doing what one thinks fit is attended by advantage in doing it, this is not merely a good thing but at the same time, it seems, the possession of great power; otherwise it is a bad thing and means little power. And let us consider another point besides; do we not admit that sometimes it is better to do those things that we were mentioning just now—to put people to death and banish them and deprive them of property—while sometimes it is not?

POLUS: To be sure.

SOCRATES: Then here is a point, it seems, that is admitted both on your side and on mine.

POLUS: Yes.

SOCRATES: Then when do you say it is better to do these things? Tell me where you draw the line.

POLUS: Nay, I would rather that you, Socrates, answered that.

SOCRATES: Well then I say, Polus, if you prefer to hear it from me, that it is better when these things are done justly, and worse when unjustly.

POLUS: So hard to refute you, Socrates! Nay, a mere child could do it, could he not, and prove your words are untrue?

SOCRATES: Then I shall be most grateful to the child, and equally to you, if you refute me and rid me of foolery. Come, do not grow weary in well-doing toward your friend, but refute me.

POLUS: Well, to be sure, Socrates, there is no need to refute you with ancient instances; for those happenings of but a day or two ago are enough to refute you, and prove that many a wrongdoer is happy.

SOCRATES: What sort of thing do you mean?

POLUS: I suppose you see that Archelaus, son of Perdiccas, is ruler of Macedonia?[14]

SOCRATES: Well, if I do not, at any rate I hear it.

POLUS: Do you consider him happy or wretched?

SOCRATES: I do not know, Polus; I have never met the man.

POLUS: What? Could you find out by meeting him, and cannot otherwise tell, straight off, that he is happy?

SOCRATES: No, indeed, upon my word.

POLUS: Then doubtless you will say, Socrates, that you do not know that even the Great King is happy.

SOCRATES: Yes, and I shall be speaking the truth; for I do not know how he stands in point of education and justice.

POLUS: Why, does happiness entirely consist in that?

SOCRATES: Yes, by my account, Polus; for a good and honorable man or woman, I say, is happy, and an unjust and wicked one is wretched.

POLUS: Then this Archelaus, on your statement, is wretched?

SOCRATES: Yes, my friend, supposing he is unjust.

POLUS: Well, but how can he be other than unjust? He had no claim to the throne which he now occupies, being the son of a woman who was a slave of Perdiccas' brother Alcetas, and in mere justice he was Alcetas' slave; and if he wished to do what is just, he would be serving Alcetas and would be happy, by your account;

---

[14] Archelaus usurped the throne of Macedonia in 413 B.C., and ruled till his death in 399 B.C. Euripides, Agathon, and other distinguished Athenians were guests at his court; Socrates was also invited, but declined to visit him (Aristot. *Rhet.* ii. 23. 8), and this is probably the point of Socrates' next remark. [Tr.]

but, as it is, he has become a prodigy of wretchedness, since he has done the most enormous wrong. First of all he invited this very master and uncle of his to his court, as if he were going to restore to him the kingdom of which Perdiccas had deprived him; and after entertaining him and his son Alexander—his own cousin, about the same age as himself—and making them drunk, he packed them into a carriage, drove them away by night, and murdered and made away with them both. And after all these iniquities he failed to observe that he had become a most wretched person, and had no repentance, but a while later he refused to make himself happy by bringing up, as he was justly bound, his brother, the legitimate son of Perdiccas, a boy about seven years old who had a just title to the throne, and restoring the kingdom to him; but he cast him into a well and drowned him, and then told his mother Cleopatra that he had fallen in and lost his life while chasing a goose. So now, you see, as the greatest wrongdoer in Macedonia, he is the most wretched of all the Macedonians, not the happiest; and I daresay some Athenians could be found who would join you in preferring to change places with any other Macedonian of them all, rather than with Archelaus!

SOCRATES: At the beginning of our discussion, Polus, I complimented you on having had, as I consider, a good training in rhetoric, while you seem to have neglected disputation; and now, accordingly, this is the argument, is it, with which any child could refute me? By this statement, you think, I now stand refuted at your hands, when I assert that the wrongdoer is not happy? How so, my good friend? Why, I tell you I do not admit a single point in what you say.

POLUS: No, because you do not want to; for you really agree with my statement.

SOCRATES: My gifted friend, that is because you attempt to refute me in rhetorical fashion, as they understand refuting in the law courts. For there, one party is supposed to refute the other when they bring forward a number of reputable witnesses to any statements they may make, whilst their opponent produces only one, or none. But this sort of refutation is quite worthless for getting at the truth; since occasionally a man may actually be crushed by the number and reputation of the false witnesses brought against him. And so now you will find almost everybody, Athenians and foreigners, in agreement with you on the points you state, if you like to bring forward witnesses against the truth of what I say: if you like, there is Nicias, son of Niceratus, with his brothers, whose tripods are standing in a row in the Dionysium;[15] or else Aristocrates, son of Scellias, whose goodly offering again is well known at Delphi; or if you choose, there is the whole house of Pericles or any other family you may like to select in this place. But I, alone here before you, do not admit it, for you fail to convince me: you only attempt, by producing a number of false witnesses against me, to oust me from my reality; the truth. But if on my part I fail to produce yourself as my one witness to confirm what I say, I consider I have achieved nothing of any account toward the matter of our discussion, whatever it may be; nor have you either, I conceive, unless I act alone as your one witness, and you have nothing to do with all these others. Well now, this is one mode of refutation, as you and many other people understand it; but there is also another which I on my side understand. Let us therefore compare them with each other and consider if there is a difference between them. For indeed the points which we have at issue are by no means of slight importance: rather, one might say, they are matters on which it is most honorable to have knowledge, and most disgraceful to lack

---

[15] These tripods were prizes won by dramatic performances supported as a public service by Nicias and his brothers, and they were placed in the precincts of the temple of Dionysus. The persons here mentioned are selected as instances of public men who won high reputation in their time through the pursuit of material wealth and influence. [Tr.]

it; for in sum they involve our knowing or not knowing who is happy and who is not. To start at once with the point we are now debating, you consider it possible for a man to be happy while doing wrong, and as a wrongdoer, since you regard Archelaus as a wrongdoer, and yet happy. We are to conclude, are we not, that this is your opinion?

POLUS: Certainly.

SOCRATES: And I say it is impossible. There we have one point at issue. Very good; but then, will a man be happy in wrongdoing if he comes in for requital and punishment?

POLUS: Not at all, since in that case he would be most wretched.

SOCRATES: But if the wrongdoer escapes requital, by your account he will be happy?

POLUS: Yes.

SOCRATES: Whereas in my opinion, Polus, the wrongdoer or the unjust is wretched anyhow; more wretched, however, if he does not pay the penalty and gets no punishment for his wrongdoing, but less wretched if he pays the penalty and meets with requital from gods and men.

POLUS: What a strange doctrine, Socrates, you are trying to maintain!

SOCRATES: Yes, and I will endeavor to make you too, my friend, maintain it with me: for I count you as a friend. Well now, these are the points on which we differ; just examine them yourself. I think I told you at an earlier stage that wrongdoing was worse than being wronged.

POLUS: Certainly you did.

SOCRATES: And you thought that being wronged was worse.

POLUS: Yes.

SOCRATES: And I said that wrongdoers were wretched, and I was refuted by you.

POLUS: Upon my word, yes.

SOCRATES: At least to your thinking, Polus.

POLUS: Yes, and true thinking too.

SOCRATES: Perhaps. But you said, on the other hand, that wrongdoers are happy, if they pay no penalty.

POLUS: Certainly.

SOCRATES: Whereas I say they are most wretched, and those who pay the penalty, less so. Do you wish to refute that as well?

POLUS: Why, that is still harder to refute, Socrates, than the other!

SOCRATES: Not merely so, Polus, but impossible; for the truth is never refuted.

POLUS: How do you mean? If a man be caught criminally plotting to make himself a despot, and he be straightway put on the rack and castrated and have his eyes burned out, and after suffering himself, and seeing inflicted on his wife and children, a number of grievous torments of every kind, he be finally crucified or burned in a coat of pitch, will he be happier than if he escape and make himself despot, and pass his life as the ruler in his city, doing whatever he likes, and envied and congratulated by the citizens and the foreigners besides? Impossible, do you tell me, to refute that?

SOCRATES: You are trying to make my flesh creep this time, my spirited Polus, instead of refuting me; a moment ago you were for calling witnesses. However, please refresh my memory a little: "criminally plotting to make himself a despot," you said?

POLUS: I did.

SOCRATES: Then neither of them will ever be happier than the other—neither he who has unjustly compassed the despotic power, nor he who pays the penalty; for of two wretched persons neither can be *happier;* but still more wretched is he who goes scot-free and establishes himself as despot. What is that I see, Polus? You are laughing? Here we have yet another form of refutation—when a statement is made, to laugh it down, instead of disproving it!

POLUS: Do you not think yourself utterly refuted, Socrates, when you make such statements as nobody in the world would assent to? You have only to ask anyone of the company here.

SOCRATES: Polus, I am not one of your statesmen: indeed, last year, when I was elected a member of the Council, and, as my tribe held the Presidency, I had to put a question to the vote, I got laughed at for not understanding the procedure.[16] So do not call upon me again to take the votes of the company now; but if, as I said this moment, you have no better disproof than those, hand the work over to me in my turn, and try the sort of refutation that I think the case requires. For I know how to produce one witness in support of my statements, and that is the man himself with whom I find myself arguing; the many I dismiss: there is also one whose vote I know how to take, whilst to the multitude I have not a word to say. See therefore if you will consent to be put to the proof in your turn by answering my questions. For I think, indeed, that you and I and the rest of the world believe that doing wrong is worse than suffering it, and escaping punishment worse than incurring it.

POLUS: And I, that neither I nor anyone else in the world believes it. You, it seems, would choose rather to suffer wrong than to do it.

SOCRATES: Yes, and so would you and everyone else.

POLUS: Far from it; neither I nor you nor anybody else.

SOCRATES: Then will you answer?

POLUS: To be sure I will, for indeed I am eager to know what on earth you will say.

SOCRATES: Well then, so that you may know, tell me, just as though I were asking you all over again, which of the two seems to you, Polus, to be the worse—doing wrong or suffering it?

POLUS: Suffering it, I say.

SOCRATES: Now again, which is fouler—doing wrong or suffering it? Answer.

POLUS: Doing it.

SOCRATES: And also more evil, if fouler.

POLUS: Not at all.

[16] Socrates refers humorously to his noble act in refusing to put to the vote an illegal proposal against the generals who fought at Arginusae, 406 B.C. By saying "last year" he fixes the supposed date of this conversation at 405 B.C. [Tr.]

SOCRATES: I see: you hold, apparently, that fair and good are not the same, nor evil and foul.

POLUS: Just so.

SOCRATES: But what of this? All fair things, like bodies and colors and figures and sounds and observances—is it according to no standard that you call these fair in each case? Thus in the first place, when you say that fair bodies are fair, it must be either in view of their use for some particular purpose that each may serve, or in respect of some pleasure arising when, in the act of beholding them, they cause delight to the beholder. Have you any description to give beyond this of bodily beauty?

POLUS: I have not.

SOCRATES: And so with all the rest in the same way, whether they be figures or colors, is it for some pleasure or benefit or both that you give them the name of "fair"?

POLUS: It is.

SOCRATES: And sounds also, and the effects of music, are not these all in the same case?

POLUS: Yes.

SOCRATES: And further, in all that belongs to laws and observances, surely the "fairness" of them cannot lie beyond those limits of being either beneficial or pleasant or both.

POLUS: I think not.

SOCRATES: And is it not just the same with the "fairness" of studies also?

POLUS: Doubtless; and this time, Socrates, your definition is quite fair, when you define what is fair by pleasure and good.

SOCRATES: And foul by their opposites, pain and evil?

POLUS: That needs must follow.

SOCRATES: Thus when of two fair things one is fairer, the cause is that it surpasses in either one or both of these effects, either in pleasure, or in benefit, or in both.

POLUS: Certainly.

SOCRATES: And again, when one of two foul things is fouler, this will be due to an excess either of pain or of evil: must not that be so?

POLUS: Yes.

SOCRATES: Come then, what was it we heard just now about doing and suffering wrong? Were you not saying that suffering wrong is more evil, but doing it fouler?

POLUS: I was.

SOCRATES: Well now, if doing wrong is fouler than suffering it, it is either more painful, and fouler by an excess of pain or evil or both; must not this also be the case?

POLUS: Yes, of course.

SOCRATES: Then let us first consider if doing wrong exceeds suffering it in point of pain—if those who do wrong are more pained than those who suffer it.

POLUS: Not so at all, Socrates.

SOCRATES: Then it does not surpass in pain.

POLUS: No, indeed.

SOCRATES: And so, if not in pain, it can no longer be said to exceed in both.

POLUS: Apparently.

SOCRATES: It remains, then, that it exceeds in the other.

POLUS: Yes.

SOCRATES: In evil.

POLUS: So it seems.

SOCRATES: Then it is by an excess of evil that doing wrong is fouler than suffering it.

POLUS: Yes, obviously.

SOCRATES: Now it is surely admitted by the mass of mankind, as it was too by you in our talk a while ago, that doing wrong is fouler than suffering it.

POLUS: Yes.

SOCRATES: And now it has been found to be more evil.

POLUS: So it seems.

SOCRATES: Then would you rather have the evil and foul when it is more than when it is less? Do not shrink from answering, Polus; you will get no hurt by it: but submit yourself bravely to the argument, as to a doctor, and reply yes or no to my question.

POLUS: Why, I should not so choose, Socrates.

SOCRATES: And would anybody else in the world?

POLUS: I think not, by this argument at least.

SOCRATES: Then I spoke the truth when I said that neither you nor anyone else in the world would choose to do wrong rather than suffer it, since it really is more evil.

POLUS: Apparently.

SOCRATES: So you see, Polus, that when one proof is contrasted with the other they have no resemblance, but whereas you have assent of every one else except myself, I am satisfied with your sole and single assent and evidence, and I take but your vote only and disregard the rest. Now let us leave this matter where it stands, and proceed next to examine the second part on which we found ourselves at issue—whether for a wrongdoer to pay the penalty is the greatest of evils, as you supposed, or to escape it is a greater, as I on my side held. Let us look at it this way: do you call paying the just penalty, and being justly punished, for wrongdoing the same thing?

POLUS: I do.

SOCRATES: And can you maintain that all just things are not fair, in so far as they are just? Consider well before you speak.

POLUS: No, I think they are, Socrates.

SOCRATES: Then take another point: if a man does anything, must there be something which is also acted upon by this doer of the thing?

POLUS: I think so.

SOCRATES: And does it suffer what the doer does, and is the effect such as the agent's action makes it? I mean, for example, when one strikes a blow something must needs be struck?

POLUS: It must.

SOCRATES: And if the striker strikes hard or quick, the thing struck is struck in the same way?

POLUS: Yes.

SOCRATES: Hence the effect in the thing struck is such as the striker makes it?

POLUS: Certainly.

SOCRATES: And so again, if one burns, something must be burned?

POLUS: Yes, of course.

SOCRATES: And if one burns severely or sorely, the thing burned is burned according as the burner burns it?

POLUS: Certainly.

SOCRATES: And again, if one cuts, the same may be said? For something is cut.

POLUS: Yes.

SOCRATES: And if the cut is large or deep or sore, the cut made in the thing cut is such as the cutter cuts it?

POLUS: Apparently.

SOCRATES: Then putting it all in a word, see if you agree that what I was just saying applies to all cases—that the patient receives an effect of the same kind as the agent's action.

POLUS: I do agree.

SOCRATES: Then this being admitted, is paying the penalty suffering something, or doing it?

POLUS: Suffering it must be, Socrates.

SOCRATES: And at the hands of an agent?

POLUS: Yes, of course; at the hands of the punisher.

SOCRATES: And he who punishes aright punishes justly?

POLUS: Yes.

SOCRATES: Doing what is just, or not?

POLUS: What is just.

SOCRATES: And he who pays the penalty by being punished suffers what is just?

POLUS: Apparently.

SOCRATES: And what is just, I think we have agreed, is fair?

POLUS: Certainly.

SOCRATES: Then of these two, the one does what is fair and the other, he who is punished, suffers it.

POLUS: Yes.

SOCRATES: And so, if fair, good? For that is either pleasant or beneficial.[17]

POLUS: It must be so.

SOCRATES: So he who pays the penalty suffers what is good?

POLUS: It seems so.

SOCRATES: Then he is benefited?

POLUS: Yes.

SOCRATES: Is it the benefit I imagine—that he becomes better in soul if he is justly punished?

POLUS: Quite likely.

SOCRATES: Then is he who pays the penalty relieved from badness of soul?

POLUS: Yes.

SOCRATES: And so relieved from the greatest evil? Look at it this way; in a man's pecuniary resources do you perceive any other badness than poverty?

POLUS: No, only poverty.

SOCRATES: And what in his bodily resources? You would say that badness there is weakness or disease or ugliness or the like?

POLUS: I would.

SOCRATES: And in soul too you believe there is a certain wickedness?

POLUS: Of course.

SOCRATES: And do you not call this injustice, ignorance, cowardice, and so forth?

POLUS: Certainly I do.

SOCRATES: So now in property, body, and soul, these three, you have mentioned three vices—poverty, disease, and injustice?

POLUS: Yes.

SOCRATES: Then which of these vices is the foulest? Is it not injustice—in short, the vice of the soul?

POLUS: Far the foulest.

SOCRATES: And if foulest, then also most evil?

POLUS: How do you mean, Socrates?

SOCRATES: Just this: the foulest is foulest in each case because it produces the greatest pain or harm or both; this follows from our previous admissions.

POLUS: Quite so.

SOCRATES: And foulest of all, we have just agreed, is injustice and, in general, vice of soul?

POLUS: Yes, we have.

SOCRATES: So then either it is most painful, that is, foulest of these vices by an excess of painfulness, or else of harmfulness, or in both ways?

POLUS: Necessarily.

SOCRATES: Then do you think that being unjust, licentious, cowardly, and ignorant is more painful than being poor and sick?

---

[17] As was agreed above, 474 D, E. [Tr.]

POLUS: No, I do not, Socrates, from what we have said.

SOCRATES: Portentous then must be the extent of harm, and astonishing the evil, by which the soul's vice exceeds all the others so as to be the foulest of all, since it is not by pain, on your view of the matter.

POLUS: Apparently.

SOCRATES: But further, I suppose, whatever has an excess of harm in the greatest measure, must be the greatest evil in the world.

POLUS: Yes.

SOCRATES: So injustice, licentiousness, and in general, vice of soul, are the greatest evils in the world?

POLUS: Apparently.

SOCRATES: Now what is the art that relieves from poverty? Is it not money-making?

POLUS: Yes.

SOCRATES: And what from disease? Is it not medicine?

POLUS: It must be.

SOCRATES: And what from wickedness and injustice? If you are not ready for that offhand, consider it thus: whither and to whom do we take those who are in bodily sickness?

POLUS: To the doctor, Socrates.

SOCRATES: And whither the wrongdoers and libertines?

POLUS: To the law court, do you mean?

SOCRATES: Yes, and to pay the penalty?

POLUS: I agree.

SOCRATES: Then is it not by employing a kind of justice that those punish who punish aright?

POLUS: Clearly so.

SOCRATES: Then money-making relieves us from poverty, medicine from disease, and justice from licentiousness and injustice.

POLUS: Apparently.

SOCRATES: Which then is the fairest of these things?

POLUS: Of what things, pray?

SOCRATES: Money-making, medicine, justice.

POLUS: Justice, Socrates, is far above the others.

SOCRATES: Now again, if it is fairest, it causes either most pleasure or benefit or both.

POLUS: Yes.

SOCRATES: Well then, is it pleasant to be medically treated, and do those who undergo such treatment enjoy it?

POLUS: I do not think so.

SOCRATES: But it is beneficial, is it not?

POLUS: Yes.

SOCRATES: Because one is relieved of a great evil, and hence it is worth while to endure the pain and be well.

POLUS: Of course.

SOCRATES: Is this then the happiest state of body for a man to be in—that of being medically treated—or that of never being ill at all?

POLUS: Clearly, never being ill.

SOCRATES: Yes, for what we regarded as happiness, it seems, was not this relief from evil, but its nonacquisition at any time.

POLUS: That is so.

SOCRATES: Well now, which is the more wretched of two persons who have something evil either in body or in soul, he who is medically treated and is relieved of the evil, or he who is not treated and keeps it?

POLUS: To my thinking, he who is not treated.

SOCRATES: And we found that paying the penalty is a relief from the greatest evil, wickedness?

POLUS: We did.

SOCRATES: Because, I suppose, the justice of the court reforms us and makes us juster, and acts as a medicine for wickedness.

POLUS: Yes.

SOCRATES: Happiest therefore is he who has no vice in his soul, since we found this to be the greatest of evils.

POLUS: Clearly so.

SOCRATES: Next after him, I take it, is he who is relieved of it.

POLUS: So it seems.

SOCRATES: And that was the man who is reproved, reprimanded, and made to pay the penalty.

POLUS: Yes.

SOCRATES: Hence the worst life is led by him who has the vice and is not relieved of it.

POLUS: Apparently.

SOCRATES: And this is the man who in committing the greatest wrongs and practicing the greatest injustice has contrived to escape reproof and chastisement and penalty alike, as you say Archelaus has succeeded in doing, and the rest of the despots and orators and overlords?

POLUS: So it seems.

SOCRATES: Because, I conceive, my excellent friend, what these persons have contrived for themselves is very much as though a man who was the victim of the worst diseases should contrive not to submit to the doctor's penalty for his bodily transgressions and take the prescribed treatment, from a childish fear of cautery or incision, as being so painful. Or do you not agree to this view of it?

POLUS: I do.

SOCRATES: Since he was ignorant, it would seem, of the virtue of bodily health and fitness. For it is very probable, from what we have just agreed, that something like this is done also by those who evade their due penalty, Polus; they perceive its painfulness, but are blind to its benefits, and are unaware how much more wretched than lack of health in the body it is to dwell with a soul that is not healthy, but corrupt, unjust, and unholy; and hence it is that they do all they can to avoid paying the penalty and being relieved of the greatest of evils, by providing themselves with money and friends and the ability to excel in persuasive speech. But if what we have agreed is true, Polus, do you observe the consequences of our argument? Or, if you like, shall we reckon them up together?

POLUS: Yes, if you do not mind.

SOCRATES: Then does it result that injustice and wrongdoing is the greatest evil?

POLUS: Yes, apparently.

SOCRATES: And further, it appeared that paying the penalty is a relief from this evil?

POLUS: It looks like it.

SOCRATES: Whereas not paying it is a retention of the evil in us?

POLUS: Yes.

SOCRATES: Thus wrongdoing is second of evils in greatness; but to do wrong and not pay the penalty is the greatest and takes the first place among all evils.

POLUS: It seems so.

SOCRATES: Well now, my friend, was this the point at issue between us, that you counted Archelaus, who did the greatest wrong, happy because he paid no penalty, whilst I on the contrary thought that anyone—whether Archelaus or any other person you please—who pays no penalty for the wrong he has done, is peculiarly and preeminently wretched among men, and that it is always the wrongdoer who is more wretched than the wronged, and the unpunished than the punished? Is not this what I stated?

POLUS: Yes.

SOCRATES: Then has it not been proved that this was a true statement?

POLUS: Apparently.

SOCRATES: Very well: so if this is true, Polus, what is the great use of rhetoric? For you see by what we have just agreed that a man must keep a close watch over himself so as to avoid wrongdoing, since it would bring a great deal of evil upon him; must he not?

POLUS: Certainly.

SOCRATES: But if he is guilty of wrongdoing, either himself or anyone else he may care for, he must go of his own freewill where he may soonest pay the penalty, to the judge as if to his doctor, with the earnest intent that the disease of his injustice shall not become chronic and cause a deep incurable ulcer in his soul. Or what are we to say, Polus, if our former conclusions stand? Must not our later ones accord with them in this way, and in this only?

POLUS: Yes, what else, indeed, are we to say, Socrates?

SOCRATES: Then for pleading in defense of injustice, whether it is oneself or one's parents or friends or children or country that has done the wrong, rhetoric is of no use to us at all, Polus; except one were to suppose, perchance, to the contrary, that a man ought to accuse himself first of all, and in the second place his relations or anyone else of his friends who may from time to time be guilty of wrong; and, instead of concealing the iniquity, to bring it to light in order that he may pay the penalty and be made healthy; and, moreover, to compel both himself and his neighbors not to cower away but to submit with closed eyes and good courage, as it were, to the cutting and burning of the surgeon, in pursuit of what is good and fair, and without reckoning in the smart: if his crimes have deserved a flogging, he must submit to the rod; if fetters, to their grip; if a fine, to its payment; if banishment, to be banished; or if death, to die; himself to be the first accuser either of himself or of his relations, and to employ his rhetoric for the purpose of so exposing their iniquities that they may be relieved of that greatest evil, injustice. Shall this be our statement or not, Polus?

POLUS: An extraordinary one, Socrates, it seems to me, though perhaps you do find it agrees with what went before.

SOCRATES: Well, either that must be upset, or this necessarily follows.

POLUS: Yes, that certainly is so.

SOCRATES: And so again conversely, supposing it is our duty to injure somebody, whether an enemy or anyone else—provided only that it is not against oneself that wrong has been done by such enemy, for this we must take care to avoid[18]—but supposing our enemy has wronged some one else, we must make every exertion of act and word to prevent him from being punished or coming to trial, or if he does, we must contrive that our enemy shall escape and not be punished; nay, if he has carried off a great lot of gold, that he shall not refund it but keep and spend it on himself and his, unjustly and godlessly, or if he has committed crimes that deserve death, that he shall not die; if possible, never die, but be deathless in his villainy, or failing that, live as long a time as may be in that condition. Such are the purposes, as it seems to me, Polus, for which rhetoric is useful, since to him who has no intention of doing wrong it is, I consider, of no great use, if indeed there is any use in it at all; for in our previous argument it was nowhere to be found.

CALLICLES: Tell me, Chaerephon, is Socrates in earnest over this, or only joking?

CHAEREPHON: To my thinking, Callicles, prodigiously in earnest: still, there is nothing like asking him.

CALLICLES: Upon my word, just what I want to do. Tell me, Socrates, are we to take you as serious just now, or joking? For if you are serious and what you say is really true, must not the life of us human beings have been turned upside down, and must we not be doing quite the opposite, it seems, of what we ought to do?

SOCRATES: Callicles, if men had not certain feelings, each common to one sort of people, but each of us had a feeling peculiar to himself and apart from the rest, it would not be easy for him to indicate his own impression to his neighbor. I say this because I notice that you and I are at this moment in much the same condition, since the two of us are enamored each of two things—I of Alcibiades, son of Cleinias, and philosophy, and you of two, the Athenian Demus, and the son of Pyrilampes.[19] Now I always observe that, for all your cleverness, you are unable to contradict your favorite, however much he may say or whatever may be his account of anything, but are ever changing over from side to side. In the Assembly, if the Athenian Demus disagrees with some statement you are making, you change over and say what it desires; and just the same thing happens to you in presence of that fair youth, the son of Pyrilampes; you are un-

---

[18] The parenthesis humorously anticipates an objection that might be made, in a particular case, to this theory of what a really thorough enmity would be: if our enemy has robbed *us* of gold, of course we cannot, as is presently urged, take care that "he shall not refund it." [Tr.]

[19] Pyrilampes' son was named Demus, and was famous for his beauty; *cf.* Aristoph. *Wasps,* 97. "Demus" was the ordinary word for the "people" of a city. [Tr.]

able to resist the counsels and statements of your darling, so that if anyone showed surprise at the strangeness of the things you are constantly saying under that influence, you would probably tell him, if you chose to speak the truth, that unless somebody makes your favorite stop speaking thus, you will never stop speaking thus either. Consider yourself therefore obliged to hear the same sort of remark from me now, and do not be surprised at my saying it, but make my darling, philosophy, stop talking thus. For she, my dear friend, speaks what you hear me saying now, and she is far less fickle to me than any other favorite: that son of Cleinias is ever changing his views, but philosophy always holds the same, and it is her speech that now surprises you, and she spoke it in your own presence. So you must either refute her, as I said just now, by proving that wrongdoing and impunity for wrong done is not the uttermost evil; or, if you leave that unproved, by the Dog, god of the Egyptians, there will be no agreement between you, Callicles, and Callicles, but you will be in discord with him all your life. And yet I, my very good sir, should rather choose to have my lyre, or some chorus that I might provide for the public, out of tune and discordant, or to have any number of people disagreeing with me and contradicting me, than that I should have internal discord and contradiction in my own single self.

CALLICLES: Socrates, you seem to be roistering recklessly in your talk, like the true demagogue that you are; and you are declaiming now in this way because Polus has got into the same plight as he was accusing Gorgias of letting himself be led into by you. For he said, I think, when you asked Gorgias whether, supposing a man came to him with no knowledge of justice but a desire to learn rhetoric, he would instruct the man, Gorgias showed some shame and said he would, because of the habit of mind in people which would make them indignant if refused—and so, because of this admission, he was forced to contradict himself, and that was just what suited you—and Polus was right, to my thinking, in mocking at you as he did then; but this time he has got into the very same plight himself. For my own part, where I am not satisfied with Polus is just that concession he made to you—that doing wrong is fouler than suffering it; for owing to this admission he too in his turn got entangled in your argument and had his mouth stopped, being ashamed to say what he thought. For you, Socrates, really turn the talk into such low, popular clap-trap, while you give out that you are pursuing the truth—into stuff that is "fair," not by nature, but by convention.[20] Yet for the most part these two—nature and convention—are opposed to each other, so that if a man is ashamed and dares not say what he thinks, he is forced to contradict himself. And this, look you, is the clever trick you have devised for our undoing in your discussions: when a man states anything according to convention you slip "according to nature" into your questions; and again, if he means nature, you imply convention. In the present case, for instance, of doing and suffering wrong, when Polus was speaking of what is conventionally fouler, you followed it up in the sense of what is naturally so. For by nature everything is fouler that is more evil, such as suffering wrong: doing it is fouler only by convention. Indeed this endurance of wrong done is not a man's part at all, but a poor slave's, for whom it is better to be dead than alive, as it is for anybody who, when wronged or insulted, is unable to protect himself or anyone else for whom he cares. But I suppose the makers of the laws are the weaker sort of men, and the more numerous. So it is with a view to themselves and their own interest that they make their laws and distribute their praises

---

[20] The distinction between "natural," or absolute, and "conventional," or legal, right, first made by the Ionian Archelaus who taught Socrates in his youth, is developed at length in the *Republic* (i. 388 foll.), and was a constant subject of discussion among the sophists of Plato's time. [Tr.]

and censures; and to terrorize the stronger sort of folk who are able to get an advantage, and to prevent them from getting one over *them,* they tell them that such aggrandizement is foul and unjust, and that wrongdoing is just this endeavor to get the advantage of one's neighbors: for I expect they are well content to see themselves on an equality, when they are so inferior. So this is why by convention it is termed unjust and foul to aim at an advantage over the majority, and why they call it wrongdoing: but nature, in my opinion, herself proclaims the fact that it is right for the better to have advantage of the worse, and the abler of the feebler. It is obvious in many cases that this is so, not only in the animal world, but in the states and races, collectively, of men—that right has been decided to consist in the sway and advantage of the stronger over the weaker. For by what manner of right did Xerxes march against Greece, or his father against Scythia? Or take the countless other cases of the sort that one might mention. Why, surely these men follow nature—the nature of right—in acting thus; yes, on my soul, and follow the law[21] of nature—though not that, I dare say, which is made by us; we mold the best and strongest amongst us, taking them from their infancy like young lions, and utterly enthral them by our spells and witchcraft, telling them the while that they must have but their equal share, and that this is what is fair and just. But, I fancy, when some man arises with a nature of sufficient force, he shakes off all that we have taught him, bursts his bonds, and breaks free; he tramples underfoot our codes and juggleries, our charms and "laws," which are all against nature; our slave rises in revolt and shows himself our master, and there dawns the full light of natural justice. And it seems to me that Pindar adds his evidence to what I say, in the ode where he says—

> Law the sovereign of all,
> Mortals and immortals,

which, so he continues,—

> Carries all with highest hand,
> Justifying the utmost force: in proof
> I take
> The deeds of Hercules, for
> unpurchased—

the words are something like that—I do not know the poem well—but it tells how he drove off the cows as neither a purchase nor a gift from Geryones; taking it as a natural right that cows or any other possessions of the inferior and weaker should all belong to the superior and stronger.

Well, that is the truth of the matter; and you will grasp it if you will now put philosophy aside and pass to greater things. For philosophy, you know, Socrates, is a charming thing, if a man has to do with it moderately in his younger days; but if he continues to spend his time on it too long, it is ruin to any man. However well endowed one may be, if one philosophizes far on into life, one must needs find oneself ignorant of everything that ought to be familiar to the man who would be a thorough gentleman and make a good figure in the world. For such people are shown to be ignorant of the laws of their city, and of the terms which have to be used in negotiating agreements with their fellows in private or in public affairs, and of human pleasures and desires; and, in short, to be utterly inexperienced in men's characters. So when they enter upon any private or public business they make themselves ridiculous, just as on the other hand, I suppose, when public men engage in your studies and discussions, they are quite ridiculous. The fact is, as Euripides has it—

---

[21] Callicles boldly applies the word νόμος, which so far has been used in the sense of man-made law or convention, in its widest sense of "general rule" or "principle." [Tr.]

> Each shines in that, to that end presses on,
> Allotting there the chiefest part o' the day,
> Wherein he haply can surpass himself—[22]

whereas that in which he is weak he shuns and vilifies; but the other he praises, in kindness to himself, thinking in this way to praise himself also. But the most proper course, I consider, is to take a share of both. It is a fine thing to partake of philosophy just for the sake of education, and it is no disgrace for a lad to follow it: but when a man already advancing in years continues in its pursuit, the affair, Socrates, becomes ridiculous; and for my part I have much the same feeling toward students of philosophy as toward those who lisp or play tricks. For when I see a little child, to whom it is still natural to talk in that way, lisping or playing some trick, I enjoy it, and it strikes me as pretty and ingenuous and suitable to the infant's age; whereas if I hear a small child talk distinctly, I find it a disagreeable thing, and it offends my ears and seems to me more befitting a slave. But when one hears a grown man lisp, or sees him play tricks, it strikes one as something ridiculous and unmanly, that deserves a whipping. Just the same, then, is my feeling toward the followers of philosophy. For when I see philosophy in a young lad I approve of it; I consider it suitable, and I regard him as a person of liberal mind: whereas one who does not follow it I account illiberal and never likely to expect of himself any fine or generous action. But when I see an elderly man still going on with philosophy and not getting rid of it, that is the gentleman, Socrates, whom I think in need of a whipping. For as I said just now, this person, however well endowed he may be, is bound to become unmanly through shunning the centers and marts of the city, in which, as the poet[23] said, "men get them note and glory"; he must cower down and spend the rest of his days whispering in a corner with three or four lads, and never utter anything free or high or spirited. Now I, Socrates, am quite fairly friendly to you, and so I feel very much at this moment as Zethus did, whom I have mentioned, towards Amphion in Euripides.[24] Indeed I am prompted to address you in the same sort of words as he did his brother: "You neglect, Socrates, what you ought to mind; you distort with a kind of boyish travesty a soul of such noble nature; and neither will you bring to the counsels of justice any rightly spoken word, nor will you accept any as probable or convincing, nor advise any gallant plan for your fellow." And yet, my dear Socrates—now do not be annoyed with me, for I am going to say this from goodwill to you—does it not seem to you disgraceful to be in the state I consider you are in, along with the rest of those who are ever pushing further into philosophy? For as it is, if somebody should seize hold of you or anyone else at all of your sort, and drag you off to prison, asserting that you were guilty of a wrong you had never done, you know you would be at a loss what to do with yourself, and would be all dizzy and agape without a word to say; and when you came up in court, though your accuser might be ever so paltry a rascal, you would have to die if he chose to claim death as your penalty. And yet what wisdom is there, Socrates, in "an art that found a man of goodly parts and made him worse," unable either to succor himself, or to deliver himself or anyone else from the greatest dangers, but like to be stripped by his enemies

[22] Eurip. fr. *Antiope* Zethus and Amphion, twins born to Zeus by Antiope, were left by her on Mt. Cithaeron, where Zethus grew up as a man of the field, and Amphion as a musician. Here probably Amphion is speaking in defense of the quieter life; further on, in the quotations given in 486 B.C., Zethus reproaches him with his effeminacy. [Tr.]

[23] Homer, *Il.* ix. 441. [Tr.]

[24] That is, Callicles reproaches Socrates for choosing private study over public, political action. [Ed.]

of all his substance, and to live in his city as an absolute outcast? Such a person, if one may use a rather low expression, can be given a box on the ear with impunity. No, take my advice, my good sir, "and cease refuting; some practical proficiency induce,"—something that will give you credit for sense: "to others leave these pretty toys,"—call them vaporings or fooleries as you will,—"which will bring you to inhabit empty halls"; and emulate, not men who probe these trifles, but who have means and repute and other good things in plenty.

SOCRATES: If my soul had happened to be made of gold, Callicles, do you not think I should have been delighted to find one of those stones with which they test gold, and the best one; which, if I applied it, and it confirmed to me that my soul had been properly tended, would give me full assurance that I am in a satisfactory state and have no need of other testing?

CALLICLES: What is the point of that question, Socrates?

SOCRATES: I will tell you. I am just thinking what a lucky stroke I have had in striking up with you.

CALLICLES: How so?

SOCRATES: I am certain that whenever you agree with me in any view that my soul takes, this must be the very truth. For I conceive that whoever would sufficiently test a soul as to rectitude of life or the reverse should go to work with three things which are all in your possession—knowledge, goodwill, and frankness. I meet with many people who are unable to test me, because they are not wise as you are; while others, though wise, are unwilling to tell me the truth, because they do not care for me as you do; and our two visitors here, Gorgias and Polus, though wise and friendly to me, are more lacking in frankness and inclined to bashfulness than they should be: nay, it must be so, when they have carried modesty to such a point that each of them can bring himself, out of sheer modesty, to contradict himself in face of a large company, and that on questions of the greatest importance. But you have all these qualities which the rest of them lack: you have had a sound education, as many here in Athens will agree; and you are well disposed to me. You ask what proof I have? I will tell you. I know, Callicles, that four of you have formed a partnership in wisdom—you, Tisander of Aphidnae, Andron, son of Androtion, and Nausicydes of Cholarges;[25] and I once overheard you debating how far the cultivation of wisdom should be carried, and I know you were deciding in favor of some such view as this—that one should not be carried away into the minuter points of philosophy, but you exhorted one another to beware of making yourselves overwise, lest you should unwittingly work your own ruin. So when I hear you giving me the same advice as you gave your own most intimate friends, I have proof enough that you really are well disposed to me. And further, as to your ability to speak out frankly and not be bashful, you not only claim this yourself, but you are borne out too by the speech that you made a short while ago. Well, this is clearly the position of our question at present: if you can bear me out in any point arising in our argument, that point can at once be taken as having been amply tested by both you and me, and there will be no more need of referring it to a further test; for no defect of wisdom or access of modesty could ever have been your motive in making this concession, nor again could you make it to deceive me: for you are my friend, as you say yourself. Hence any agreement between you and me must really have attained the perfection of truth. And on no themes could one make more honorable inquiry, Callicles, than on those which you have reproached me with—what character one should have, and what should be one's pursuits and up to what point, in later as

---

[25] Andron is one of the wise men who meet in the house of Callias, *Protag.* 315; Nausicydes may be the wealthy meal-merchant mentioned in Aristoph. *Eccles.* 426, and Xen. *Mem.* ii. 7. 6. Of Tisander nothing is known. [Tr.]

in earlier years. For I assure you that if there is any fault of conduct to be found in my own life it is not an intentional error, but due to my ignorance: so I ask you not to break off in the middle of your task of admonishing me, but to make fully clear to me what it is that I ought to pursue and by what means I may attain it; and if you find me in agreement with you now, and afterwards failing to do what I agreed to, regard me as a regular dunce and never trouble any more to admonish me again—a mere good-for-nothing. Now, go right back and repeat to me what you and Pindar hold natural justice to consist in: is it that the superior should forcibly despoil the inferior, the better rule the worse, and the nobler have more than the meaner? Have you some other account to give of justice, or do I remember aright?

CALLICLES: Why, that is what I said then, and I say it now also.

SOCRATES: Is it the same person that you call "better" and "superior"? For I must say I was no more able then to understand what your meaning might be. Is it the stronger folk that you call superior, and are the weaker ones bound to hearken to the stronger one—as for instance I think you were also pointing out then, that the great states attack the little ones in accordance with natural right, because they are superior and stronger, on the ground that the superior and the stronger and the better are all the same thing; or is it possible to be better and yet inferior and weaker, and to be superior and yet more wicked? Or is the definition of the better and the superior the same? This is just what I bid you declare in definite terms—whether the superior and the better and the stronger are the same or different.

CALLICLES: Well, I tell you plainly, they are all the same.

SOCRATES: Now, are the many superior by nature to the one? I mean those who make the laws to keep a check on the one, as you were saying yourself just now.

CALLICLES: Of course.

SOCRATES: Then the ordinances of the many are those of the superior.

CALLICLES: Certainly.

SOCRATES: And so of the better? For the superior are far better, by your account.

CALLICLES: Yes.

SOCRATES: And so their ordinances are by nature "fair," since they are superior who made them?

CALLICLES: I agree.

SOCRATES: Then is it the opinion of the many that—as you also said a moment ago—justice means having an equal share, and it is fouler to wrong than be wronged. Is that so, or not? And mind you are not caught this time in a bashful fit. Is it, or is it not, the opinion of the many that to have one's equal share, and not more than others, is just, and that it is fouler to wrong than be wronged? Do not grudge me an answer to this, Callicles, so that—if I find you agree with me—I may then have the assurance that comes from the agreement of a man so competent to decide.

CALLICLES: Well, most people do think so.

SOCRATES: Then it is not only by convention that doing wrong is fouler than suffering it, and having one's equal share is just, but by nature also: and therefore it looks as though your previous statement was untrue, and your count against me incorrect, when you said that convention and nature are opposites and that I, forsooth, recognizing that, am an unscrupulous debater, turning to convention when the assertion refers to nature, and to nature when it refers to convention.

CALLICLES: What an inveterate driveller the man is! Tell me, Socrates, are you not ashamed to be word-catching at your age, and if one makes a verbal slip, to take that as a great stroke of luck? Do you imagine that, when I said "being superior," I meant anything else than "better"? Have I not been telling you ever so long that I regard the better and the superior as the same thing? Or do you suppose I mean that if a pack of slaves and all sorts of fellows who are good for nothing, except perhaps in point of physical strength, gather together and say something, that is a legal ordinance?

SOCRATES: Very well, most sapient Callicles: you mean that, do you?

CALLICLES: Certainly I do.

SOCRATES: Why, my wonderful friend, I have myself been guessing ever so long that you meant something of this sort by "superior," and if I repeat my questions it is because I am so keen to know definitely what your meaning may be. For I presume you do not consider that two are better than one, or that your slaves are better than yourself, just because they are stronger than you are. Come now, tell me again from the beginning what it is you mean by the better, since you do not mean the stronger: only, admirable sir, do be more gentle with me over my first lessons, or I shall cease attending your school.

CALLICLES: You are sarcastic, Socrates.

SOCRATES: No, by Zethus, Callicles, whom you made use of just now[26] for aiming a good deal of sarcasm at me: but come, tell us whom you mean by the better.

CALLICLES: I mean the more excellent.

SOCRATES: So you see, you are uttering mere words yourself, and explaining nothing. Will you not tell us whether by the better and superior you mean the wiser, or some other sort?

CALLICLES: Why, to be sure, I mean those, and very much so.

SOCRATES: Then one wise man is often superior to ten thousand fools, by your account, and he ought to rule and they to be ruled, and the ruler should have more than they whom he rules. That is what you seem to me to intend by your statement—and I am not word-catching here—if the one is superior to the ten thousand.

CALLICLES: Why, that is my meaning. For this is what I regard as naturally just—that being better and wiser he should have both rule and advantage over the baser people.

SOCRATES: Stop there now. Once more, what is your meaning this time? Suppose that a number of us are assembled together, as now, in the same place, and we have in common a good supply of food and drink, and we are of all sorts—some strong, some weak; and one of us, a doctor, is wiser than the rest in this matter and, as may well be, is stronger than some and weaker than others; will not he, being wiser than we are, be better and superior in this affair?

CALLICLES: Certainly.

SOCRATES: Then is he to have a larger ration than the rest of us because he is better, or ought he as ruler to have the distribution of the whole stock, with no advantage in spending and consuming it upon his own person, if he is to avoid retribution, but merely having more than some and less than others? Or if he chance to be the weakest of all, ought he not to get the smallest share of all though he be the best, Callicles? Is it not so, good sir?

CALLICLES: You talk of food and drink and doctors and drivel: I refer to something different.

SOCRATES: Then tell me, do you call the wiser better? Yes or no?

CALLICLES: Yes, I do.

SOCRATES: But do you not think the better should have a larger share?

CALLICLES: Yes, but not of food and drink.

SOCRATES: I see; of clothes, perhaps; and the ablest weaver should have the largest coat, and go about arrayed in the greatest variety of the finest clothes?

CALLICLES: What have clothes to do with it?

SOCRATES: Well, shoes then; clearly he who is wisest in regard to these, and best, should have some advantage. Perhaps the shoemaker should walk about in the biggest shoes and wear the largest number.

CALLICLES: Shoes—what have they to do with it? You keep on drivelling.

SOCRATES: Well, if you do not mean things of that sort, perhaps you mean something like this: a farmer, for instance, who knows all about the land and is highly accomplished in the matter,

---

[26] Above, 486 A. [Tr.]

should perhaps have an advantage in sharing the seed, and have the largest possible amount of it for use on his own land.

CALLICLES: How you keep repeating the same thing, Socrates!

SOCRATES: Yes, and not only that, Callicles, but on the same subjects too.

CALLICLES: I believe, on my soul, you absolutely cannot ever stop talking of cobblers and fullers, cooks and doctors, as though our discussion had to do with them.

SOCRATES: Then will you tell me in what things the superior and wiser man has a right to the advantage of a larger share? Or will you neither put up with a suggestion from me nor make one yourself?

CALLICLES: Why, I have been making mine for some time past. First of all, by "the superior" I mean, not shoemakers or cooks, but those who are wise as regards public affairs and the proper way of conducting them, and not only wise but manly, with ability to carry out their purpose to the full; and who will not falter through softness of soul.

SOCRATES: Do you perceive, my excellent Callicles, that your count against me is not the same as mine against you? For you say I am ever repeating the same things, and reproach me with it, whereas I charge you, on the contrary, with never saying the same thing on the same subject; but at one moment you defined the better and superior as the stronger, and at another as the wiser, and now you turn up again with something else: "the manlier" is what you now tell us is meant by the superior and better. No, my good friend, you had best say, and get it over, whom you do mean by the better and superior, and in what sphere.

CALLICLES: But I have told you already: men of wisdom and manliness in public affairs. These are the persons who ought to rule our cities, and justice means this—that these should have more than other people, the rulers than the ruled.

SOCRATES: How so? Than themselves, my friend?

CALLICLES: What do you mean?

SOCRATES: I mean that every man is his own ruler; or is there no need of one's ruling oneself, but only of ruling others?

CALLICLES: What do you mean by one who rules himself?

SOCRATES: Nothing recondite; merely what most people mean—one who is temperate and self-mastering, ruler of the pleasures and desires that are in himself.

CALLICLES: You will have your pleasantry! You mean "the simpletons" by "the temperate."

SOCRATES: How so? Nobody can fail to see that I do not mean that.

CALLICLES: Oh, you most certainly do, Socrates. For how can a man be happy if he is a slave to anybody at all? No, natural fairness and justice, I tell you now quite frankly, is this—that he who would live rightly should let his desires be as strong as possible and not chasten them, and should be able to minister to them when they are at their height by reason of his manliness and intelligence, and satisfy each appetite in turn with what it desires. But this, I suppose, is not possible for the many; whence it comes that they decry such persons out of shame, to disguise their own impotence, and are so good as to tell us that licentiousness is disgraceful, thus enslaving—as I remarked before—the better type of mankind; and being unable themselves to procure achievement of their pleasures they praise temperance and justice by reason of their own unmanliness. For to those who started with the advantage of being either kings' sons or able by their own parts to procure some authority or monarchy or absolute power, what in truth could be fouler or worse than temperance and justice in such cases? Finding themselves free to enjoy good things, with no obstacle in the way, they would be merely imposing on themselves a master in the shape of the law, the talk and the rebuke of the multitude. Or how could they fail to be sunk in wretchedness by that "fairness" of justice and temperance, if they had no larger portion to give to their own friends than to their enemies, and that too when they were rulers in their own cities? No, in good truth, Socrates—which you claim to be seeking—the fact is this: luxury and licentiousness and liberty, if they have the support of force, are virtue and happiness, and the rest of these embellishments—the unnatural covenants of mankind—are all mere stuff and nonsense.

SOCRATES: Far from ignoble, at any rate, Callicles, is the frankness with which you develop your thesis: for you are now stating in clear terms what the rest of the world think indeed, but are loth to say. So I beg you not to give up on any account, that it may be made really evident how one ought to live. Now tell me: do you say the desires are not to be chastened if a man would be such as he ought to be, but he should let them be as great as possible and provide them with satisfaction from some source or other, and this is virtue?

CALLICLES: Yes, I say that.

SOCRATES: Then it is not correct to say, as people do, that those who want nothing are happy.

CALLICLES: No, for at that rate stones and corpses would be extremely happy.

SOCRATES: Well, well, as you say, life is strange. For I tell you I should not wonder if Euripides' words were true, when he says:

> Who knoweth if to live is to be dead,
> And to be dead, to live?

and we really, it may be, are dead; in fact I once heard one of our sages say that we are now dead, and the body is our tomb,[27] and the part of the soul in which we have desires is liable to be overpersuaded and to vacillate to and fro, and so some smart fellow, a Sicilian, I daresay, or Italian,[28] made a fable in which—by a play of words—he named this part, as being so impressionable and persuadable, a jar, and the thoughtless he called uninitiate: in these uninitiate that part of the soul where the desires are, the licentious and fissured part, he named a leaky jar in his allegory, because it is so insatiate. So you see this person, Callicles, takes the opposite view to yours, showing how of all who are in Hades—meaning of course the invisible—these uninitiate will be most wretched, and will carry water into their leaky jar with a sieve which is no less leaky. And then by the sieve, as my storyteller said, he means the soul: and the soul of the thoughtless he likened to a sieve, as being perforated, since it is unable to hold anything by reason of its unbelief and forgetfulness. All this, indeed, is bordering pretty well on the absurd; but still it sets forth what I wish to impress upon you, if I somehow can, in order to induce you to make a change, and instead of a life of insatiate licentiousness to choose an orderly one that is set up and contented with what it happens to have got. Now, am I at all prevailing upon you to change over to the view that the orderly people are happier than the licentious; or will no amount of similar fables that I might tell you have any effect in changing your mind?

CALLICLES: The latter is more like the truth, Socrates.

SOCRATES: Come now, let me tell you another parable from the same school[29] as that I have just told. Consider if each of the two lives, the temperate and the licentious, might be described by imagining that each of two men had a number of jars, and those of one man were sound and full, one of wine, another of honey, a third of milk, and various others of various things, and that the sources of each of these supplies were scanty and difficult and only available through much hard toil: well, one man, when he has taken his fill, neither draws off any more

[27] The sage was perhaps Philolaus, a Pythagorean philosopher contemporary with Socrates. The phrase σῶμα σῆμα, suggesting a mystical similarity between "body" and "tomb," was part of the Orphic doctrine. [Tr.]

[28] "Sicilian" may refer to Empedocles; "Italian" to one of the Pythagoreans. [Tr.]

[29] Probably of Pythagoras. [Tr.]

nor troubles himself a jot, but remains at ease on that score; while the other finds, like his fellow, that the sources are possible indeed, though difficult, but his vessels are leaky and decayed, and he is compelled to fill them constantly, all night and day, or else suffer extreme distress. If such is the nature of each of the two lives, do you say that the licentious man has a happier one than the orderly? Do I, with this story of mine, induce you at all to concede that the orderly life is better than the licentious, or do I fail?

CALLICLES: You fail, Socrates. For that man who has taken his fill can have no pleasure any more; in fact it is what I just now called living like a stone, when one has filled up and no longer feels any joy or pain. But a pleasant life consists rather in the largest possible amount of inflow.

SOCRATES: Well then, if the inflow be large, must not that which runs away be of large amount also, and must not the holes for such outflow be of great size?

CALLICLES: Certainly.

SOCRATES: Then it is a plover's life[30] you are describing this time, not that of a corpse or a stone. Now tell me, is the life you mean something like feeling hunger and eating when hungry?

CALLICLES: Yes, it is.

SOCRATES: And feeling thirst and drinking when thirsty?

CALLICLES: Yes, and having all the other desires, and being able to satisfy them, and so with these enjoyments leading a happy life.

SOCRATES: Bravo, my fine fellow! Do go on as you have begun, and mind you show no bashfulness about it. I too, it seems, must try not to be too bashful. First of all, tell me whether a man who has an itch and wants to scratch, and may scratch in all freedom, can pass his life happily in continual scratching.

CALLICLES: What an odd person you are, Socrates—a regular stump-orator!

SOCRATES: Why, of course, Callicles, that is how I upset Polus and Gorgias, and struck them with bashfulness; but you, I know, will never be upset or abashed; you are such a manly fellow. Come, just answer that.

CALLICLES: Then I say that the man also who scratches himself will thus spend a pleasant life.

SOCRATES: And if a pleasant one, a happy one also?

CALLICLES: Certainly.

SOCRATES: Is it so if he only wants to scratch his head? Or what more am I to ask you? See, Callicles, what your answer will be, if you are asked everything in succession that links on to that statement; and the culmination of the case, as stated—the life of catamites—is not that awful, shameful, and wretched? Or will you dare to assert that these are happy if they can freely indulge their wants?

CALLICLES: Are you not ashamed, Socrates, to lead the discussion into such topics?

SOCRATES: What, is it I who am leading it there, noble sir, or the person who says outright that those who enjoy themselves, with whatever kind of enjoyment, are happy, and draws no distinction between the good and bad sorts of pleasure? But come, try again now and tell me whether you say that pleasant and good are the same thing, or that there is some pleasure which is not good.

CALLICLES: Then, so that my statement may not be inconsistent through my saying they are different, I say they are the same.

SOCRATES: You are spoiling your first statements,[31] Callicles, and you can no longer be a fit partner with me in probing the truth, if you are going to speak against your own convictions.

CALLICLES: Why, you do the same, Socrates.

SOCRATES: Then I am just as much in the wrong if I do, as you are. But look here, my gifted

---

[30] Referring to this bird's habit of drinking water and then ejecting it. [Tr.]

[31] *Cf.* 482 D, where Callicles blamed Polus for not saying what he really thought. [Tr.]

friend, perhaps the good is not mere unconditional enjoyment: for if it is, we have to face not only that string of shameful consequences I have just shadowed forth, but many more besides.

CALLICLES: In your opinion, that is, Socrates.

SOCRATES: And do you, Callicles, really maintain that it is?

CALLICLES: I do.

SOCRATES: Then are we to set about discussing it as your serious view?

CALLICLES: Oh yes, to be sure.

SOCRATES: Come then, since that is your opinion, resolve me this: there is something, I suppose, that you call knowledge?

CALLICLES: Yes.

SOCRATES: And were you not saying just now that knowledge can have a certain courage coupled with it?

CALLICLES: Yes, I was.

SOCRATES: And you surely meant that they were two things, courage being distinct from knowledge?

CALLICLES: Quite so.

SOCRATES: Well now, are pleasure and knowledge the same thing, or different?

CALLICLES: Different, I presume, O sage of sages.

SOCRATES: And courage too, is that different from pleasure?

CALLICLES: Of course it is.

SOCRATES: Come now, let us be sure to remember this, that Callicles the Acharnian said pleasant and good were the same, but knowledge and courage were different both from each other and from the good.

CALLICLES: And Socrates of Alopece refuses to grant us this; or does he grant it?

SOCRATES: He does not; nor, I believe, will Callicles either, when he has rightly considered himself. For tell me, do you not regard people who are well off as being in the opposite condition to those who are badly off?

CALLICLES: I do.

SOCRATES: Then if these conditions are opposite to each other, must not the same hold of them as of health and disease? For, you know, a man is never well and ill at the same time, nor gets rid of health and disease together.

CALLICLES: How do you mean?

SOCRATES: Take, for instance, any part of the body you like by itself, and consider it. A man, I suppose, may have a disease of the eyes, called ophthalmia?

CALLICLES: Certainly.

SOCRATES: Then I presume he is not sound also at that time in those same eyes?

CALLICLES: By no conceivable means.

SOCRATES: And what say you, when he gets rid of his ophthalmia? Does he at that time get rid too of the health of his eyes, and so at last is rid of both things together?

CALLICLES: Far from it.

SOCRATES: Because, I imagine, this would be an astonishing and irrational result, would it not?

CALLICLES: Very much so.

SOCRATES: Whereas, I take it, he gets and loses either in turn?

CALLICLES: I agree.

SOCRATES: And so with strength and weakness in just the same way?

CALLICLES: Yes.

SOCRATES: And speed and slowness?

CALLICLES: Certainly.

SOCRATES: And so too with good things and happiness and their opposites—bad things and wretchedness—does one take on each of these in turn, and in turn put it off?

CALLICLES: Absolutely, I presume.

SOCRATES: Then if we find any things that a man puts off and retains at one and the same moment, clearly these cannot be the good and the bad. Do we admit this? Now consider very carefully before you answer.

CALLICLES: Oh, I admit it down to the ground.

SOCRATES: So now for our former admissions: did you say that being hungry was pleasant or painful? I mean, hunger itself.

CALLICLES: Painful, I said; though eating when one is hungry I call pleasant.

SOCRATES: I see; but at all events hunger itself is painful, is it not?

CALLICLES: I agree.

SOCRATES: And so too with thirst?

CALLICLES: Quite so.

SOCRATES: Then am I to ask you any further questions, or do you admit that all want and desire is painful?

CALLICLES: I admit it; no, do not question me further.

SOCRATES: Very good: but drinking when one is thirsty you surely say is pleasant?

CALLICLES: I do.

SOCRATES: Now, in this phrase of yours the words "when one is thirsty," I take it, stand for "when one is in pain"?

CALLICLES: Yes.

SOCRATES: But drinking is a satisfaction of the want, and a pleasure?

CALLICLES: Yes.

SOCRATES: So in the act of drinking, you say, one has enjoyment?

CALLICLES: Quite so.

SOCRATES: When one is thirsty?

CALLICLES: I agree.

SOCRATES: That is, in pain?

CALLICLES: Yes.

SOCRATES: Then do you perceive the conclusion,—that you say one enjoys oneself, though in pain at the same moment, when you say one drinks when one is thirsty? Or does this not occur at once, at the same place and time—in either soul or body, as you please? For I fancy it makes no difference. Is this so or not?

CALLICLES: It is.

SOCRATES: But further, you say it is impossible to be badly off, or to fare ill, at the same time as one is faring well.

CALLICLES: Yes, I do.

SOCRATES: But to enjoy oneself when feeling pain you have admitted to be possible.

CALLICLES: Apparently.

SOCRATES: Hence enjoyment is not faring well, nor is feeling pain faring ill, so that the pleasant is found to be different from the good.

CALLICLES: I cannot follow these subtleties of yours, Socrates.

SOCRATES: You can, but you play the innocent, Callicles. Just go on a little further, that you may realize how subtle is your way of reproving me. Does not each of us cease at the same moment from thirst and from the pleasure he gets by drinking?

CALLICLES: I cannot tell what you mean.

GORGIAS: No, no, Callicles, you must answer him, for our sakes also, that the arguments may be brought to a conclusion.

CALLICLES: But Socrates is always like this, Gorgias; he keeps on asking petty, unimportant questions until he refutes one.

GORGIAS: Why, what does that matter to you? In any case it is not your credit that is at stake, Callicles; just permit Socrates to refute you in such manner as he chooses.

CALLICLES: Well then, proceed with those little cramped questions of yours, since Gorgias is so minded.

SOCRATES: You are fortunate, Callicles, in having been initiated into the Great Mysteries before the Little:[32] I did not think that was the proper thing. So go on answering where you left off—as to whether each of us does not cease to feel thirst and pleasure at the same time.

CALLICLES: I grant it.

SOCRATES: And so with hunger and the rest, does he cease to feel the desires and pleasures at the same time?

CALLICLES: That is so.

SOCRATES: And also ceases to feel the pains and pleasures at the same time?

CALLICLES: Yes.

SOCRATES: But still he does not cease to have the good and bad at the same time, as you agreed; and now, you do not agree?

CALLICLES: I do; and what then?

SOCRATES: Only that we get the result, my friend, that the good things are not the same as the

[32] Socrates means that one cannot hope to know great things without first learning the truth about little things. [Tr.]

pleasant, nor the bad as the painful. For with the one pair the cessation is of both at once, but with the other two it is not, since they are distinct. How then can pleasant things be the same as good, or painful things as bad? Or if you like, consider it another way—for I fancy that even after that you do not admit it. Just observe: do you not call good people good owing to the presence of good things, as you call beautiful those in whom beauty is present?

CALLICLES: I do.

SOCRATES: Well now, do you give the name of good men to fools and cowards? It was not they just now but brave and wise men whom you so described. Or is it not these that you call good?

CALLICLES: To be sure it is.

SOCRATES: And now, have you ever seen a silly child enjoying itself?

CALLICLES: I have.

SOCRATES: And have you never seen a silly man enjoying himself?

CALLICLES: I should think I have; but what has that to do with it?

SOCRATES: Nothing; only answer.

CALLICLES: I have seen one.

SOCRATES: And again, a man of sense in a state of pain or enjoyment?

CALLICLES: Yes.

SOCRATES: And which sort are more apt to feel enjoyment or pain, the wise or the foolish?

CALLICLES: I should think there is not much difference.

SOCRATES: Well, that will suffice. In war have you ever seen a coward?

CALLICLES: Of course I have.

SOCRATES: Well now, when the enemy withdrew, which seemed to you to enjoy it more, the cowards or the brave?

CALLICLES: Both did, I thought; or if not that, about equally.

SOCRATES: No matter. Anyhow, the cowards do enjoy it?

CALLICLES: Very much.

SOCRATES: And the fools, it would seem.

CALLICLES: Yes.

SOCRATES: And when the foe advances, do the cowards alone feel pain, or the brave as well?

CALLICLES: Both.

SOCRATES: Alike?

CALLICLES: More, perhaps, the cowards.

SOCRATES: And when the foe withdraws, do they not enjoy it more?

CALLICLES: Perhaps.

SOCRATES: So the foolish and the wise, and the cowardly and the brave, feel pain and enjoyment about equally, according to you, but the cowardly more than the brave?

CALLICLES: I agree.

SOCRATES: But further, are the wise and brave good, and the cowards and fools bad?

CALLICLES: Yes.

SOCRATES: Then the good and the bad feel enjoyment and pain about equally?

CALLICLES: I agree.

SOCRATES: Then are the good and the bad about equally good and bad? Or are the bad in some yet greater measure good and bad?

CALLICLES: Why, upon my word, I cannot tell what you mean.

SOCRATES: You are aware, are you not, that you hold that the good are good by the presence of good things, and that the bad are so by the presence of bad things? And that the pleasures are the good things, and the pains bad things?

CALLICLES: Yes, I am.

SOCRATES: Hence in those who have enjoyment the good things—the pleasures—are present, so long as they enjoy?

CALLICLES: Of course.

SOCRATES: Then good things being present, those who enjoy are good?

CALLICLES: Yes.

SOCRATES: Well now, in those who feel pain are not bad things present, namely pains?

CALLICLES: They are.

SOCRATES: And it is by the presence of bad things, you say, that the bad are bad? Or do you no longer say so?

CALLICLES: I do say so.

SOCRATES: Then whoever enjoys is good, and whoever is pained, bad?

CALLICLES: Certainly.

SOCRATES: You mean, those more so who feel these things more, and those less who feel less, and those about equally who feel about equally?

CALLICLES: Yes.

SOCRATES: Now you say that the wise and the foolish, the cowardly and the brave, feel enjoyment and pain about equally, or the cowards even more?

CALLICLES: I do.

SOCRATES: Then just help me to reckon up the results we get from our admissions; for you know they say:

> That which seemeth well, 'tis well
> Twice and also thrice to tell,[33]

and to examine too. We say that the wise and brave man is good, do we not?

CALLICLES: Yes.

SOCRATES: And that the foolish and cowardly is bad?

CALLICLES: Certainly.

SOCRATES: And again, that he who enjoys is good?

CALLICLES: Yes.

SOCRATES: And that he who feels pain is bad?

CALLICLES: Necessarily.

SOCRATES: And that the good and the bad feel enjoyment and pain in a like manner, or perhaps the bad rather more?

CALLICLES: Yes.

SOCRATES: Then is the bad man made bad or good in a like manner to the good man, or even good in a greater measure? Does not this follow, along with those former statements, from the assumption that pleasant things and good things are the same? Must not this be so, Callicles?

CALLICLES: Let me tell you, Socrates, all the time that I have been listening to you and yielding you agreement, I have been remarking the puerile delight with which you cling to any concession one may make to you, even in jest. So you suppose that I or anybody else in the world does not regard some pleasures as better, and others worse!

SOCRATES: Oh ho, Callicles, what a rascal you are, treating me thus like a child—now asserting that the same things are one way, now another, to deceive me! And yet I started with the notion that I should not have to fear any intentional deception on your part, you being my friend; but now I find I was mistaken, and it seems I must, as the old saying goes, e'en make the best of what I have got, and accept just anything you offer. Well then, what you now state, it seems, is that there are certain pleasures, some good, and some bad; is not that so?

CALLICLES: Yes.

SOCRATES: Then are the beneficial ones good, and the harmful ones bad?

CALLICLES: Certainly.

SOCRATES: And are those beneficial which do some good, and those evil which do some evil?

CALLICLES: I agree.

SOCRATES: Now are these the sort you mean—for instance, in the body, the pleasures of eating and drinking that we mentioned a moment ago? Then the pleasures of this sort which produce health in the body, or strength, or any other bodily excellence,—are these good, and those which have the opposite effects, bad?

CALLICLES: Certainly.

SOCRATES: And similarly in the case of pains, are some worthy and some base?

CALLICLES: Of course.

SOCRATES: So it is the worthy pleasures and pains that we ought to choose in all our doings?

CALLICLES: Certainly.

SOCRATES: And the base ones not?

CALLICLES: Clearly so.

SOCRATES: Because, you know, Polus and I, if you recollect, decided[34] that everything we do should be for the sake of what is good. Do you agree with us in this view—that the good is the

---

[33] The saying—*καὶ δὶς γὰρ ὃ δεῖ καλόν ἐστιν ἐνισπεῖν*—was attributed by some to Empedocles. [Tr.]

[34] *Cf.* 468 C. [Tr.]

end of all our actions, and it is for its sake that all other things should be done, and not it for theirs? Do you add your vote to ours, and make a third?

CALLICLES: I do.

SOCRATES: Then it is for the sake of what is good that we should do everything, including what is pleasant, not the good for the sake of the pleasant.

CALLICLES: Certainly.

SOCRATES: Now is it in every man's power to pick out which sort of pleasant things are good and which bad, or is professional skill required in each case?

CALLICLES: Professional skill.

SOCRATES: Then let us recall those former points I was putting to Polus and Gorgias.[35] I said, if you remember, that there were certain industries, some of which extend only to pleasure, procuring that and no more, and ignorant of better and worse; while others know what is good and what bad. And I placed among those that are concerned with pleasure the habitude, not art, of cookery, and among those concerned with good the art of medicine. Now by the sanctity of friendship, Callicles, do not on your part indulge in jesting with me, or give me random answers against your conviction, or again, take what I say as though I were jesting. For you see that our debate is upon a question which has the highest conceivable claims to the serious interest even of a person who has but little intelligence—namely, what course of life is best; whether it should be that to which you invite me, with all those manly pursuits of speaking in Assembly and practicing rhetoric and going in for politics after the fashion of you modern politicians, or this life of philosophy; and what makes the difference between these two. Well, perhaps it is best to do what I attempted a while ago, and distinguish them; and then, when we have distinguished them and come to an agreement with each other as to these lives being really two, we must consider what is the difference between them and which of them is the one we ought to live. Now I daresay you do not yet grasp my meaning.

CALLICLES: No, I do not.

SOCRATES: Well, I will put it to you more plainly. Seeing that we have agreed, you and I, that there is such a thing as "good," and such a thing as "pleasant," and that the pleasant is other than the good, and that for the acquisition of either there is a certain practice or preparation—the quest of the pleasant in the one case, and that of the good in the other—but first you must either assent or object to this statement of mine: do you assent?

CALLICLES: I am with you entirely.

SOCRATES: Then try and come to a definite agreement with me on what I was saying to our friends here, and see if you now find that what I then said was true. I was saying, I think, that cookery seems to me not an art but a habitude, unlike medicine, which, I argued, has investigated the nature of the person whom she treats and the cause of her proceedings, and has some account to give of each of these things; so much for medicine: whereas the other, in respect of the pleasure to which her whole ministration is given, goes to work there in an utterly inartistic manner, without having investigated at all either the nature or the cause of pleasure, and altogether irrationally—with no thought, one may say, of differentiation, relying on routine and habitude for merely preserving a memory of what is wont to result; and that is how she is enabled to provide her pleasures. Now consider first whether you think that this account is satisfactory, and that there are certain other such occupations likewise, having to do with the soul; some artistic, with forethought for what is to the soul's best advantage, and others making light of this, but again, as in the former case, considering merely the soul's pleasure and how it may be contrived for her, neither inquiring which of the pleasures is a better or a worse one, nor caring for aught but mere gratification,

---

[35] *Cf.* 464–5. [Tr.]

whether for better or worse. For I, Callicles, hold that there are such, and for my part I call this sort of thing flattery, whether in relation to the body or to the soul or to anything else, whenever anyone ministers to its pleasure without regard for the better and the worse; and you now, do you support us with the same opinion on this matter, or do you gainsay us?

CALLICLES: Not I; I agree with you, in order that your argument may reach a conclusion, and that I may gratify Gorgias here.

SOCRATES: And is this the case with only one soul, and not with two or many?

CALLICLES: No, it is also the case with two or many.

SOCRATES: Then is it possible also to gratify them all at once, collectively, with no consideration of what is best?

CALLICLES: I should think it is.

SOCRATES: Then can you say what are the pursuits which effect this? Or rather, if you like, when I ask you, and one of them seems to you to be of this class, say yes, and when one does not, say no. And first let us consider flute-playing. Does it not seem to you one of this sort, Callicles, aiming only at our pleasure, and caring for naught else?

CALLICLES: It does seem so to me.

SOCRATES: And so too with all similar pursuits, such as harp-playing in the contests?

CALLICLES: Yes.

SOCRATES: And what of choral productions and dithyrambic compositions? Are they not manifestly, in your view, of the same kind? Or do you suppose Cinesias,[36] son of Meles, cares a jot about trying to say things of a sort that might be improving to his audience, or only what is likely to gratify the crowd of spectators?

CALLICLES: Clearly the latter is the case, Socrates, with Cinesias.

SOCRATES: And what of his father Meles? Did he ever strike you as looking to what was best in his minstrelsy? Or did he, perhaps, not even make the pleasantest his aim? For his singing used to be a pain to the audience. But consider now: do you not think that all minstrelsy and composing of dithyrambs have been invented for the sake of pleasure?

CALLICLES: I do.

SOCRATES: Then what of the purpose that has inspired our stately and wonderful tragic poetry? Are her endeavor and purpose, to your mind, merely for the gratification of the spectators, or does she strive hard, if there be anything pleasant and gratifying, but bad for them, to leave that unsaid, and if there be anything unpleasant, but beneficial, both to speak and sing that, whether they enjoy it or not? To which of these two aims, think you, is tragic poetry devoted?

CALLICLES: It is quite obvious, in her case, Socrates, that she is bent rather upon pleasure and the gratification of the spectators.

SOCRATES: Well now, that kind of thing, Callicles, did we say just now, is flattery?

CALLICLES: Certainly.

SOCRATES: Pray then, if we strip any kind of poetry of its melody, its rhythm and its meter, we get mere speeches as the residue, do we not?

CALLICLES: That must be so.

SOCRATES: And those speeches are spoken to a great crowd of people?

CALLICLES: Yes.

SOCRATES: Hence poetry is a kind of public speaking.

CALLICLES: Apparently.

SOCRATES: Then it must be a rhetorical public speaking; or do you not think that the poets use rhetoric in the theaters?

CALLICLES: Yes, I do.

SOCRATES: So now we have found a kind of rhetoric addressed to such a public as is compounded of children and women and men, and slaves as well as free; an art that we do not quite approve of, since we call it a flattering one.

CALLICLES: To be sure.

---

36 A dithyrambic poet whose extravagant style was ridiculed by Aristophanes (*Frogs*, 153; *Clouds*, 333; *Birds*, 1379). [Tr.]

SOCRATES: Very well; but now, the rhetoric addressed to the Athenian people, or to the other assemblies of freemen in the various cities—what can we make of that? Do the orators strike you as speaking always with a view to what is best, with the single aim of making the citizens as good as possible by their speeches, or are they, like the poets, set on gratifying the citizens, and do they, sacrificing the common weal to their own personal interest, behave to these assemblies as to children, trying merely to gratify them, nor care a jot whether they will be better or worse in consequence?

CALLICLES: This question of yours is not quite so simple; for there are some who have a regard for the citizens in the words that they utter, while there are also others of the sort that you mention.

SOCRATES: That is enough for me. For if this thing also is twofold, one part of it, I presume, will be flattery and a base mob-oratory, while the other is noble—the endeavor, that is, to make the citizens' souls as good as possible, and the persistent effort to say what is best, whether it prove more or less pleasant to one's hearers. But this is a rhetoric you never yet saw; or if you have any orator of this kind that you can mention, without more ado let me know who he is!

CALLICLES: No, upon my word, I cannot tell you of anyone, at least among the orators of today.

SOCRATES: Well then, can you mention one among those of older times whom the Athenians have to thank for any betterment that started at the time of his first harangues, as a change from the worse state in which he originally found them? For my part, I have no idea who the man is.

CALLICLES: Why, do you hear no mention of Themistocles and what a good man he was, and Cimon and Miltiades and the great Pericles, who has died recently,[37] and whom you have listened to yourself?

SOCRATES: Yes, Callicles, if that which you spoke of just now is true virtue—the satisfaction of one's own and other men's desires; but if that is not so, and the truth is—as we were compelled to admit in the subsequent discussion—that only those desires which make man better by their satisfaction should be fulfilled, but those which make him worse should not, and that this is a special art, then I for one cannot tell you of any man so skilled having appeared among them.

CALLICLES: Ah, but if you search properly you will find one.

SOCRATES: Then let us just consider the matter calmly, and see if any of them has appeared with that skill. Come now: the good man, who is intent on the best when he speaks, will surely not speak at random in whatever he says, but with a view to some object? He is just like any other craftsman, who having his own particular work in view selects the things he applies to that work of his, not at random, but with the purpose of giving a certain form to whatever he is working upon. You have only to look, for example, at the painters, the builders, the shipwrights, or any of the other craftsmen, whichever you like, to see how each of them arranges everything according to a certain order, and forces one part to suit and fit with another, until he has combined the whole into a regular and well-ordered production; and so of course with all the other craftsmen, and the people we mentioned just now, who have to do with the body—trainers and doctors; they too, I suppose, bring order and system into the body. Do we admit this to be the case, or not?

CALLICLES: Let it be as you say.

SOCRATES: Then if regularity and order are found in a house, it will be a good one, and if irregularity, a bad one?

CALLICLES: I agree.

SOCRATES: And it will be just the same with a ship?

CALLICLES: Yes.

SOCRATES: And further, with our bodies also, can we say?

---

37 429 B.C. We saw at 473 E that the supposed date of the discussion is 405 B.C., so that "recently" here is hardly accurate. [Tr.]

CALLICLES: Certainly.

SOCRATES: And what of the soul? If it shows irregularity, will it be good, or if it has a certain regularity and order?

CALLICLES: Our former statements oblige us to agree to this also.

SOCRATES: Then what name do we give to the effect of regularity and order in the body?

CALLICLES: Health and strength, I suppose you mean.

SOCRATES: I do. And what, again, to the effect produced in the soul by regularity and order? Try to find the name here, and tell it me as before.

CALLICLES: Why not name it yourself, Socrates?

SOCRATES: Well, if you prefer it, I will; and do you, if I seem to you to name it rightly, say so; if not, you must refute me and not let me have my way. For it seems to me that any regularity of the body is called healthiness, and this leads to health being produced in it, and general bodily excellence. Is that so or not?

CALLICLES: It is.

SOCRATES: And the regular and orderly states of the soul are called lawfulness and law, whereby men are similarly made law-abiding and orderly; and these states are justice and temperance. Do you agree or not?

CALLICLES: Be it so.

SOCRATES: Then it is this that our orator, the man of art and virtue, will have in view, when he applies to our souls the words that he speaks, and also in all his actions, and in giving any gift he will give it, and in taking anything away he will take it, with this thought always before his mind—how justice may be engendered in the souls of his fellow-citizens, and how injustice may be removed; how temperance may be bred in them and licentiousness cut off; and how virtue as a whole may be produced and vice expelled. Do you agree to this or not?

CALLICLES: I agree.

SOCRATES: For what advantage is there, Callicles, in giving to a sick and ill-conditioned body a quantity of even the most agreeable things to eat and drink, or anything else whatever, if it is not going to profit thereby any more, let us say, than by the opposite treatment, on any fair reckoning, and may profit less? Is this so?

CALLICLES: Be it so.

SOCRATES: Because, I imagine, it is no gain for a man to live in a depraved state of body, since in this case his life must be a depraved one also. Or is not that the case?

CALLICLES: Yes.

SOCRATES: And so the satisfaction of one's desires—if one is hungry, eating as much as one likes, or if thirsty, drinking—is generally allowed by doctors when one is in health; but they practically never allow one in sickness to take one's fill of things that one desires: do you agree with me in this?

CALLICLES: I do.

SOCRATES: And does not the same rule, my excellent friend, apply to the soul? So long as it is in a bad state—thoughtless, licentious, unjust, and unholy—we must restrain its desires and not permit it to do anything except what will help it to be better: do you grant this, or not?

CALLICLES: I do.

SOCRATES: For thus, I take it, the soul itself is better off?

CALLICLES: To be sure.

SOCRATES: And is restraining a person from what he desires correcting him?

CALLICLES: Yes.

SOCRATES: Then correction is better for the soul than uncorrected license, as you were thinking just now.

CALLICLES: I have no notion what you are referring to, Socrates; do ask some one else.

SOCRATES: Here is a fellow who cannot endure a kindness done him, or the experience in himself of what our talk is about—a correction!

CALLICLES: Well, and not a jot do I care, either, for anything *you* say; I only gave you those answers to oblige Gorgias.

SOCRATES: Very good. So now, what shall we do? Break off our argument midway?

CALLICLES: You must decide that for yourself.

SOCRATES: Why, they say one does wrong to leave off even stories in the middle; one should set a head on the thing, that it may not go about headless. So proceed with the rest of your answers, that our argument may pick up a head.

CALLICLES: How overbearing you are, Socrates! Take my advice, and let this argument drop, or find some one else to argue with.

SOCRATES: Then who else is willing? Surely we must not leave the argument there, unfinished?

CALLICLES: Could you not get through it yourself, either talking on by yourself or answering your own questions?

SOCRATES: So that, in Epicharmus's phrase,[38] "what two men spake erewhile" I may prove I can manage single-handed. And indeed it looks as though it must of sheer necessity be so. Still, if we are to do this, for my part I think we ought all to vie with each other in attempting a knowledge of what is true and what false in the matter of our argument; for it is a benefit to all alike that it be revealed. Now I am going to pursue the argument as my view of it may suggest; but if any of you think the admissions I am making to myself are not the truth, you must seize upon them and refute me. For I assure you I myself do not say what I say as knowing it, but as joining in the search with you; so that if anyone who disputes my statements is found to be on the right track, I shall be the first to agree with him. This, however, I say on the assumption that you think the argument should be carried through to a conclusion; but if you would rather it were not, let us have done with it now and go our ways.

GORGIAS: Well, my opinion is, Socrates, that we ought not to go away yet, but that you should go through with the argument; and I fancy the rest of them think the same. For I myself, in fact, desire to hear you going through the remainder by yourself.

SOCRATES: Why, to be sure, Gorgias, I myself should have liked to continue discussing with Callicles here until I had paid him an Amphion's speech in return for his of Zethus.[39] But since you, Callicles, are unwilling to join me in finishing off the argument, you must at any rate pull me up, as you listen, if it seems to you that my statements are wrong. And if you refute me, I shall not be vexed with you as you were with me; you will only be recorded in my mind as my greatest benefactor.

CALLICLES: Proceed, good sir, by yourself, and finish it off.

SOCRATES: Give ear, then; but first I will resume our argument from the beginning. Are the pleasant and the good the same thing? Not the same, as Callicles and I agreed. Is the pleasant thing to be done for the sake of the good, or the good for the sake of the pleasant? The pleasant for the sake of the good. And is that thing pleasant by whose advent we are pleased, and that thing good by whose presence we are good? Certainly. But further, both we and everything else that is good, are good by the advent of some virtue? In my view this must be so, Callicles. But surely the virtue of each thing, whether of an implement or of a body, or again of a soul or any live creature, does not arrive most properly by accident, but by an order or rightness or art that is apportioned to each. Is that so? I certainly agree. Then the virtue of each thing is a matter of regular and orderly arrangement? I at least should say so. Hence it is a certain order proper to each existent thing that by its advent in each makes it good? That is my view. So then a soul which has its own proper order is better than one which is unordered? Necessarily. But further, one that has order is orderly? Of course it will be. And the orderly one is temperate? Most necessarily. So the temperate soul is good. For my part, I can find nothing to say in objection to this, my dear Callicles; but if you can, do instruct me.

[38] Epicharmus of Cos produced philosophic comedies in Sicily during the first part of the fifth century. The saying is quoted in full by Athenaeus, vii. 308 *τὰ πϱὸ τοῦ δύ ἄνδϱες ἔλεγον εἷς ἐγων ἀποχϱέω*. [Tr.]

[39] *Cf.* 485 above. [Tr.]

CALLICLES: Proceed, good sir.

SOCRATES: I say, then, that if the temperate soul is good, one that is in the opposite state to this sensible[40] one is bad; and that was the senseless and dissolute one. Certainly. And further, the sensible man will do what is fitting as regards both gods and men; for he could not be sensible if he did what was unfitting. That must needs be so. And again, when he does what is fitting as regards men, his actions will be just, and as regards the gods, pious; and he who does what is just and pious must needs be a just and pious man. That is so. And surely he must be brave also: for you know a sound or temperate mind is shown, not by pursuing and shunning what one ought not, but by shunning and pursuing what one ought, whether they be things or people or pleasures or pains, and by steadfastly persevering in one's duty; so that it follows of strict necessity, Callicles, that the temperate man, as shown in our exposition, being just and brave and pious, is the perfection of a good man; and that the good man does well and fairly whatever he does; and that he who does well is blessed and happy,[41] while the wicked man or evil-doer is wretched. And this must be the man who is in an opposite case to the temperate,—the licentious man whom you were commending.

So there is my account of the matter, and I say that this is the truth; and that, if this is true, anyone, as it seems, who desires to be happy must ensure and practice temperance, and flee from licentiousness, each of us as fast as his feet will carry him, and must contrive, if possible, to need no correction; but if he have need of it, either himself or anyone belonging to him, either an individual or a city, then right must be applied and they must be corrected, if they are to be happy. This, in my opinion, is the mark on which a man should fix his eyes throughout life; he should concentrate all his own and his city's efforts on this one business of providing a man who would be blessed with the needful justice and temperance; not letting one's desires go unrestrained and in one's attempts to satisfy them—an interminable trouble—leading the life of a robber. For neither to any of his fellowmen can such a one be dear, nor to God; since he cannot commune with any, and where there is no communion, there can be no friendship. And wise men tell us, Callicles, that heaven and earth and gods and men are held together by communion and friendship, by orderliness, temperance, and justice; and that is the reason, my friend, why they call the whole of this world by the name of order,[42] not of disorder or dissoluteness. Now you, as it seems to me, do not give proper attention to this, for all your cleverness, but have failed to observe the great power of geometrical equality among both gods and men: you hold that self-advantage is what one ought to practice, because you neglect geometry. Very well: either we must refute this statement, that it is by the possession of justice and temperance that the happy are happy and by that of vice the wretched are wretched; or if this is true, we must investigate its consequences. Those former results, Callicles, must all follow, on which you asked me if I was speaking in earnest when I said that a man must accuse himself or his son or his comrade if he do any wrong, and that this is what rhetoric must be used for; and what you supposed Polus to be conceding from shame is after all true—that to do wrong is worse, in the same degree as it is baser, than to suffer it, and that whoever means to be the right sort of rhetorician must really be just and well-informed

---

40 The argument here makes use of a more literal meaning of *σώφρων*—"sound minded" (verging on "consciousness," as in what immediately follows). [Tr.]

41 As the various meanings of *σωφροσύνη* have been brought out to suggest that one side of that virtue involves the others, so here the apparent quibble of *εὖ πράττειν* ("act well" and "fare well") is intended to suggest a real dependence of happiness upon virtue. [Tr.]

42 *Κόσμος* ("order") was the name first given to the universe by the Pythagoreans. [Tr.]

of the ways of justice, which again Polus said that Gorgias was only shamed into admitting.

This being the case, let us consider what weight, if any, there is in the reproaches you cast upon me:[43] is it fairly alleged or not that I am unable to stand up for myself or any of my friends and relations, or to deliver them from the sorest perils, but am exposed like an outcast to the whim of anyone who chooses to give me—the dashing phrase is yours—a box on the ear; or strip me of my substance or expel me from the city; or, worst of all, put me to death; and that to be in such a case is the lowest depth of shame, as your account has it? But mine—though it has been frequently stated already, there can be no objection to my stating it once again—is this: I deny, Callicles, that to be wrongfully boxed on the ear is the deepest disgrace, or to have either my person cut or my purse; I hold that to strike or cut me or mine wrongfully is yet more of a disgrace and an evil, and likewise stealing and kidnapping and housebreaking, and in short any wrong whatsoever done to me or mine, are both worse and more shameful to the wrongdoer than to me the wronged. All this, which has been made evident in the form I have stated some way back in our foregoing discussion, is held firm and fastened—if I may put it rather bluntly—with reasons of steel and adamant (so it would seem, at least, on the face of it) which you or somebody more gallant than yourself must undo, or else accept this present statement of mine as the only possible one. For my story is ever the same, that I cannot tell how the matter stands, and yet of all whom I have encountered, before as now, no one has been able to state it otherwise without making himself ridiculous. Well now, once more I assume it to be so; but if it is so, and injustice is the greatest of evils to the wrongdoer, and still greater than this greatest, if such can be, when the wrongdoer pays no penalty, what rescue is it that a man must be able to effect for himself if he is not to be ridiculous in very truth? Is it not one which will avert from us the greatest harm? Nay, rescue must needs be at its shamefullest, if one is unable to rescue either oneself or one's own friends and relations, and second to it is inability in face of the second sort of evil, and third in face of the third, and so on with the rest; according to the gravity attaching to each evil is either the glory of being able to effect a rescue from each sort, or the shame of being unable. Is it so or otherwise, Callicles?

CALLICLES: Not otherwise.

SOCRATES: Then of these two, doing and suffering wrong, we declare doing wrong to be the greater evil, and suffering it the less. Now with what should a man provide himself in order to come to his own rescue, and so have both of the benefits that arise from doing no wrong on the one hand, and suffering none on the other? Is it power or will? What I mean is, will a man avoid being wronged by merely wishing not to be wronged, or will he avoid it by providing himself with power to avert it?

CALLICLES: The answer to that is obvious: by means of power.

SOCRATES: But what about doing wrong? Will the mere not wishing to do it suffice—since, in that case, he will not do it—or does it require that he also provide himself with some power or art, since unless he has got such learning or training he will do wrong? I really must have your answer on this particular point, Callicles—whether you think that Polus and I were correct or not in finding ourselves forced to admit, as we did in the preceding argument, that no one does wrong of his own wish, but that all who do wrong do it against their will.

CALLICLES: Let it be as you would have it, Socrates, in order that you may come to a conclusion of your argument.

SOCRATES: Then for this purpose also, of not doing wrong, it seems we must provide ourselves with a certain power or art.

CALLICLES: To be sure.

[43] Socrates proceeds to recall the reproaches of Callicles, above, 486. [Tr.]

SOCRATES: Now what can be the art of providing so that we suffer no wrong, or as little as possible? Consider if you take the same view of it as I do. For in my view it is this: one must either be a ruler, or even a despot, in one's city, or else an associate of the existing government.

CALLICLES: Do you note, Socrates, how ready I am to praise, when you say a good thing? This seems to me excellently spoken.

SOCRATES: Then see if this next statement of mine strikes you as a good one too. It seems to me that the closest possible friendship between man and man is that mentioned by the sages of old time as "like to like." Do you not agree?

CALLICLES: I do.

SOCRATES: So where you have a savage, uneducated ruler as despot, if there were some one in the city far better than he, I suppose the despot would be afraid of him and could never become a friend to him with all his heart?

CALLICLES: That is so.

SOCRATES: Nor a friend to anyone who was much inferior to him either; for the despot would despise him and never show him the attention due to a friend.

CALLICLES: That is true also.

SOCRATES: Then the only friend of any account that remains for such a person is a man of his own temper, who blames and praises the same things, and is thus willing to be governed by him and to be subject to his rule. He is a man who will have great power in that state; him none will wrong with impunity. Is it not so?

CALLICLES: Yes.

SOCRATES: Hence if one of the young men in the city should reflect: In what way can I have great power, and no one may do me wrong?—this, it would seem, is the path he must take, to accustom himself from his earliest youth to be delighted and annoyed by the same things as his master, and contrive to be as like the other as possible. Is it not so?

CALLICLES: Yes.

SOCRATES: And so this man will have attained to a condition of suffering no wrong and having great power—as your party maintain—in the city.

CALLICLES: Certainly.

SOCRATES: And of doing no wrong likewise? Or is it quite the contrary, if he is to be like his unjust ruler, and have great influence with him? Well, for my part, I think his efforts will be all the opposite way, that is, towards enabling himself to do as much wrong as possible and to pay no penalty for the wrong he does; will they not?

CALLICLES: Apparently.

SOCRATES: And thus he will find himself possessed of the greatest evil, that of having his soul depraved and maimed as a result of his imitation of his master and the power he has got.

CALLICLES: You have a strange way of twisting your arguments, at each point, this way or that, Socrates! Surely you know that this imitator will put to death anyone who does not imitate his master, if he pleases, and will strip him of his property.

SOCRATES: I know that, my good Callicles, if I am not deaf, as I have heard it so often of late from you and Polus, and from almost every one else in the town; but you in return must hear what I say—that he will put a man to death if he pleases, but it will be a villain slaying a good man and true.

CALLICLES: And is not this the very thing that makes one indignant?[44]

SOCRATES: Not if one is a man of sense, as our argument indicates. Or do you suppose that the object of a man's efforts should be to live as long a time as possible, and to cultivate those arts which preserve us from every danger; such as that which you bid me cultivate—rhetoric, the art that preserves us in the law courts?

CALLICLES: Yes, on my word I do, and sound advice it is that I give you.

---

[44] *Cf.* Callicles' warning (486 B) against the danger of being put to death on the false accusation of some paltry rascal. [Tr.]

SOCRATES: But now, my excellent friend, do you think there is anything grand in the accomplishment of swimming?

CALLICLES: No, in truth, not I.

SOCRATES: Yet, you know, that too saves men from death, when they have got into a plight of the kind in which that accomplishment is needed. But if this seems to you too small a thing, I will tell you of a more important one, the art of piloting, which saves not only our lives but also our bodies and our goods from extreme perils, as rhetoric does. And at the same time it is plain-fashioned and orderly, not giving itself grand airs in a pretense of performing some transcendent feat; but in return for performing the same as the forensic art—bringing one safely over, it may be, from Aegina—it charges a fee, I believe, of two obols[45] or if it be from Egypt or the Pontus, at the very most—for this great service of bringing safe home, as I said just now, oneself and children and goods and womenfolk—on landing us in harbor it charges a couple of drachmae;[46] and the actual possessor of the art, after performing all this, goes ashore and strolls on the quay by his vessel's side, with an unobtrusive demeanor. For he knows, I expect, how to estimate the uncertainty as to which of his passengers he has benefited by not letting them be lost at sea, and which he has injured, being aware that he has put them ashore not a whit better than when they came aboard, either in body or in soul. And so he reckons out how wrong it is that, whereas a victim of severe and incurable diseases of the body who has escaped drowning is miserable in not having died, and has got no benefit at his hands, yet, if a man has many incurable diseases in that part of him so much more precious than the body, his soul, that such a person is to live, and that he will be doing him the service of saving him either from the sea or from a law court or from any other peril whatsoever: no, he knows it cannot be better for a man who is vicious to live, since he must needs live ill.

This is why it is not the custom for the pilot to give himself grand airs, though he does save our lives; nor for the engineer either, my admirable friend, who sometimes has the power of saving lives in no less degree than a general—to say nothing of a pilot—or anyone else: for at times he saves whole cities. Can you regard him as comparable with the lawyer? And yet, if he chose to speak as you people do, Callicles, magnifying his business, he would bury you in a heap of words, pleading and urging the duty of becoming engineers, as the only thing; for he would find reasons in plenty. But you nonetheless despise him and his special art, and you would call him "engineer" in a taunting sense, and would refuse either to bestow your daughter on his son or let your own son marry his daughter. And yet after the praises you sing of your own pursuits what fair ground have you for despising the engineer and the others whom I was mentioning just now? I know you would claim to be a better man and of better birth. But if "better" has not the meaning I give it, but virtue means just saving oneself and one's belongings, whatever one's character may be, you are merely ridiculous in caviling at the engineer and the doctor and every other art that has been produced for our safety. No, my gifted friend, just see if the noble and the good are not something different from saving and being saved. For as to living any particular length of time, this is surely a thing that any true man should ignore, and not set his heart on mere life; but having resigned all this to Heaven and believing what the women say—that not one of us can escape his destiny—he should then proceed to consider in what way he will best live out his allotted span of life; whether in assimilating himself to the constitution of the state in which he may be dwelling—and so therefore now, whether it is your duty to make yourself as like as possible to

45 About fourpence. [Tr.]

46 About two shillings. [Tr.]

the Athenian people, if you intend to win its affection and have great influence in the city: see if this is to your advantage and mine, so that we may not suffer, my distinguished friend, the fate that they say befalls the creatures who would draw down the moon—the hags of Thessaly,[47] that our choice of this power in the city may not cost us all that we hold most dear. But if you suppose that anyone in the world can transmit to you such an art as will cause you to have great power in this state without conforming to its government either for better or for worse, in my opinion you are ill-advised, Callicles; for you must be no mere imitator, but essentially like them, if you mean to achieve any genuine sort of friendship with Demus the Athenian people, ay, and I dare swear, with Demus son of Pyrilampes[48] as well. So whoever can render you most like them is the person to make you a statesman in the way that you desire to be a statesman, and a rhetorician; for everybody is delighted with words that are designed for his special temper, but is annoyed by what is spoken to suit aliens—unless you have some other view, dear creature. Have we any objection to this, Callicles?

CALLICLES: It seems to me, I cannot tell how, that your statement is right, Socrates, but I share the common feeling; I do not quite believe you.

SOCRATES: Because the love of Demus, Callicles, is there in your soul to resist me: but if haply we come to examine these same questions more than once, and better, you will believe. Remember, however, that we said there were two treatments that might be used in the tendance of any particular thing, whether body or soul: one, making pleasure the aim in our dealings with it; the other, working for what is best, not indulging it but striving with it as hard as we can. Was not this the distinction we were making at that point?

CALLICLES: Certainly.

SOCRATES: Then the one, aiming at pleasure, is ignoble and really nothing but flattery, is it not?

CALLICLES: Be it so, if you like.

SOCRATES: And the aim of the other is to make that which we are tending, whether it be body or soul, as good as may be.

CALLICLES: To be sure.

SOCRATES: Then ought we not to make it our endeavor, in tending our city and its citizens, to make those citizens as good as possible? For without this, you see, as we found in our former argument, there is no use in offering any other service, unless the intentions of those who are going to acquire either great wealth or special authority or any other sort of power be fair and honorable. Are we to grant that?

CALLICLES: Certainly, if you so prefer.

SOCRATES: Then if you and I, Callicles, in setting about some piece of public business for the state, were to invite one another to see to the building part of it, say the most important erections either of walls or arsenals or temples, would it be our duty to consider and examine ourselves, first as to whether we understood the art of building or not, and from whom we had learned it? Would we have to do this, or not?

CALLICLES: Certainly.

SOCRATES: And so again, in the second place, whether we had ever erected any building privately for one of our friends or for ourselves, and whether such building was handsome or ugly? And if we found on consideration that we had been under good and reputable masters, and that there were many handsome buildings that had been erected by us with our masters' guidance, and many also by ourselves alone, after we had dispensed with our master, it might, in those circumstances, be open to men of sense to enter upon public works: but if we had neither a master of ourselves to point to, nor any buildings at all, or only a number of worthless ones, in that case surely it would be senseless to

[47] Socrates alludes to the popular theory that the practice of witchcraft is a serious danger or utter destruction to the practicer. [Tr.]

[48] *Cf.* above, 481 D. [Tr.]

attempt public works or invite one another to take them in hand. Shall we agree to the correctness of this statement or not?

CALLICLES: Yes, to be sure.

SOCRATES: And so too with all the rest: suppose, for instance, we had undertaken the duties of state-physicians, and were to invite one another to the work as qualified doctors, we should, I presume, have first inquired of each other, I of you and you of me: Let us see now, in Heaven's name; how does Socrates himself stand as regards his body's health? Or has anyone else, slave or free, ever had Socrates to thank for ridding him of a disease? And I also, I fancy, should make the same sort of inquiry about you; and then, if we found we had never been the cause of an improvement in the bodily condition of anyone, stranger or citizen, man or woman—by Heaven, Callicles, would it not in truth be ridiculous that men should descend to such folly that, before having plenty of private practice, sometimes with indifferent results, sometimes with success, and so getting adequate training in the art, they should, as the saying is, try to learn pottery by starting on a wine jar,[49] and start public practice themselves and invite others of their like to do so? Do you not think it would be mere folly to act thus?

CALLICLES: I do.

SOCRATES: And now, most excellent sir, since you are yourself just entering upon a public career, and are inviting me to do the same, and reproaching me for not doing it, shall we not inquire of one another: Let us see, has Callicles ever made any of the citizens better? Is there one who was previously wicked, unjust, licentious, and senseless, and has to thank Callicles for making him an upright, honorable man, whether stranger or citizen, bond or free? Tell me, if anyone examines you in these terms, Callicles, what will you say? What human being will you claim to have made better by your intercourse? Do you shrink from answering, if there really is some work of yours in private life that can serve as a step to your public practice?

CALLICLES: You are contentious, Socrates!

SOCRATES: No, it is not from contentiousness that I ask you this, but from a real wish to know in what manner you can imagine you ought to conduct yourself as one of our public men. Or can it be, then, that you will let us see you concerning yourself with anything else in your management of the city's affairs than making us, the citizens, as good as possible? Have we not more than once already admitted that this is what the statesman ought to do? Have we admitted it or not? Answer. We have: I will answer for you. Then if this is what the good man ought to accomplish for his country, recall now those men whom you mentioned a little while ago, and tell me if you still consider that they showed themselves good citizens—Pericles and Cimon and Miltiades and Themistocles.

CALLICLES: Yes, I do.

SOCRATES: Then if they were good, clearly each of them was changing the citizens from worse to better. Was this so, or not?

CALLICLES: Yes.

SOCRATES: So when Pericles began to speak before the people, the Athenians were worse than when he made his last speeches?

CALLICLES: Perhaps.

SOCRATES: Not "perhaps," as you say, excellent sir; it follows of necessity from what we have admitted, on the assumption that he was a good citizen.

CALLICLES: Well, what then?

SOCRATES: Nothing: but tell me one thing in addition,—whether the Athenians are said to have become better because of Pericles, or quite the contrary, to have been corrupted by him. What I, for my part, hear is that Pericles has made the Athenians idle, cowardly, talkative, and avaricious, by starting the system of public fees.[50]

---

[49] That is, instead of a small pot involving little waste in case of failure. [Tr.]

[50] This refers especially to the payment of dicasts or jurors, introduced by Pericles in 462-1 B.C. [Tr.]

CALLICLES: You hear that from the folk with battered ears,[51] Socrates.

SOCRATES: Ah, but what is no longer a matter of hearsay, but rather of certain knowledge, for you as well as for me, is that Pericles was popular at first, and the Athenians passed no degrading sentence upon him so long as they were "worse"; but as soon as they had been made upright and honorable by him, at the end of our Pericles' life they convicted him of embezzlement, and all but condemned him to death, clearly because they thought him a rogue.

CALLICLES: What then? Was Pericles a bad man on that account?

SOCRATES: Well, at any rate a herdsman in charge of asses or horses or oxen would be considered a bad one for being like that—if he took over animals that did not kick him or butt or bite, and in the result they were found to be doing all these things out of sheer wildness. Or do you not consider any keeper of any animal whatever a bad one, if he turns out the creature he received tame so much wilder than he found it? Do you, or do you not?

CALLICLES: Certainly I do, to oblige you.

SOCRATES: Then oblige me still further by answering this: is man also one of the animals, or not?

CALLICLES: Of course he is.

SOCRATES: And Pericles had charge of men?

CALLICLES: Yes.

SOCRATES: Well now, ought they not, as we admitted this moment, to have been made by him more just instead of more unjust, if he was a good statesman while he had charge of them?

CALLICLES: Certainly.

SOCRATES: And the just are gentle, as Homer said.[52] But what say you? Is it not so?

CALLICLES: Yes.

SOCRATES: But, however, he turned them out wilder than when he took them in hand, and that against himself, the last person he would have wished them to attack.

CALLICLES: You wish me to agree with you?

SOCRATES: Yes, if you consider I am speaking the truth.

CALLICLES: Then be it so.

SOCRATES: And if wilder, more unjust and worse?

CALLICLES: Be it so.

SOCRATES: Then Pericles was not a good statesman, by this argument.

CALLICLES: You at least say not.

SOCRATES: And you, too, I declare, by what you admitted. And now about Cimon once more, tell me, did not the people whom he tended ostracize him in order that they might not hear his voice for ten years? And Themistocles, did they not treat him in just the same way, and add the punishment of exile? And Miltiades, the hero of Marathon, they sentenced to be flung into the pit, and had it not been for the president, in he would have gone. And yet these men, had they been good in the way that you describe them, would never have met with such a fate. Good drivers, at any rate, do not keep their seat in the chariot at their first race to be thrown out later on, when they have trained their teams and acquired more skill in driving! This never occurs either in charioteering or in any other business; or do you think it does?

CALLICLES: No, I do not.

SOCRATES: So what we said before, it seems, was true, that we know of nobody who has shown himself a good statesman in this city of ours. You admitted there was nobody among those of the present day, but thought there were some among those of former times, and you gave these men the preference. But these we have found to be on a par with ours of the present day; and so, if they were orators, they employed neither the genuine art of rhetoric—else they would not have been thrown out—nor the flattering form of it.

CALLICLES: But still there can be no suggestion, Socrates, that any of the present-day men has

---

[51] I.e., people who show their Spartan sympathies by an addiction to boxing; *cf. Protag.* 342 B. [Tr.]

[52] Our text of Homer contains no such saying. The nearest is that in *Od.* vi. 120, and ix. 175—*ἤ ῥ' οἵ γ' ὑβρισταί τε καὶ ἄγριοι, οὐδὲ δίκαιοι*, "Wanton and wild are they, not just." [Tr.]

ever achieved anything like the deeds of anyone you may choose amongst those others.

SOCRATES: My admirable friend, neither do I blame the latter, at least as servants of the state; indeed, I consider they have shown themselves more serviceable than those of our time, and more able to procure for the city the things she desired. But in diverting her desires another way instead of complying with them—in persuading or compelling her people to what would help them to be better—they were scarcely, if at all, superior to their successors; and that is the only business of a good citizen. But in providing ships and walls and arsenals, and various other things of the sort, I do grant you that they were cleverer than our leaders. Thus you and I are doing an absurd thing in this discussion: for during all the time that we have been debating we have never ceased circling round to the same point and misunderstanding each other. I at all events believe you have more than once admitted and decided that this management of either body or soul is a twofold affair, and that on one side it is a menial service, whereby it is possible to provide meat for our bodies when they are hungry, drink when thirsty, and when they are cold, clothing, bedding, shoes, or anything else that bodies are apt to desire: I purposely give you the same illustrations, in order that you may the more easily comprehend. For as to being able to supply these things, either as a tradesman or a merchant or a manufacturer of any such actual things—baker or cook or weaver or shoemaker or tanner—it is no wonder that a man in such capacity should appear to himself and his neighbors to be a minister of the body; to every one, in fact, who is not aware that there is besides all these an art of gymnastics and medicine which really is, of course, ministration to the body, and which actually has a proper claim to rule over all those arts and to make use of their works, because it knows what is wholesome or harmful in meat and drink to bodily excellence, whereas all those others know it not; and hence it is that, while those other arts are slavish and menial and illiberal in dealing with the body, gymnastics and medicine can fairly claim to be their mistresses. Now, that the very same is the case as regards the soul you appear to me at one time to understand to be my meaning, and you admit it as though you knew what I meant; but a little later you come and tell me that men have shown themselves upright and honorable citizens in our city, and when I ask you who, you seem to me to be putting forward men of exactly the same sort in public affairs; as if, on my asking you who in gymnastics have ever been or now are good trainers of the body, you were to tell me, in all seriousness, "Thearion, the baker, Mithaecus, the author of the book on Sicilian cookery, Sarambus, the vintner—these have shown themselves wonderful ministers of the body; the first providing admirable loaves, the second tasty dishes, and the third wine." Now perhaps you would be indignant should I then say to you: "Sir, you know nothing about gymnastics; servants you tell me of, and caterers to appetites, fellows who have no proper and respectable knowledge of them, and who peradventure will first stuff and fatten men's bodies to the tune of their praises, and then cause them to lose even the flesh they had to start with; and these in their turn will be too ignorant to cast the blame of their maladies and of their loss of original weight upon their regalers, but any people who chance to be by at the time and offer them some advice—just when the previous stuffing has brought, after the lapse of some time, its train of disease, since it was done without regard to what is wholesome—these are the people they will accuse and chide and harm as far as they can, while they will sing the praises of that former crew who caused the mischief. And you now, Callicles, are doing something very similar to this: you belaud men who have regaled the citizens with all the good cheer they desired. People do say they have made the city great; but that it is with the swelling of an imposthume, due to those men of the former time, this they do not perceive. For with no regard for temperance and justice they have stuffed the city with harbors and arsenals and walls and tribute and suchlike trash; and so whenever that access of debility comes they will lay the blame on the advisers who are with them at the time, and belaud Themistocles and Cimon and Pericles, who caused all the trouble; and belike they will lay hold of you, if you are not on your guard, and my good friend Alcibiades, when they are losing what they had originally as well as what they have acquired, though you are not the authors, except perhaps part-authors, of the mischief. And yet there is a senseless thing which I see happening now, and hear of, in connection with the men of former times. For I observe that whenever the state proceeds against one of her statesmen as a wrongdoer, they are indignant and protest loudly against such monstrous treatment: after all their long and valuable services to the state they are unjustly ruined at her hands, so they protest. But the whole thing is a lie; since there is not a single case in which a ruler of a city could ever be unjustly ruined by the very city that he rules. For it is very much the same with pretenders to statesmanship as with professors of sophistry. The sophists, in fact, with all their other accomplishments, act absurdly in one point: claiming to be teachers of virtue, they often accuse their pupils of doing them an injury by cheating them of their fees and otherwise showing no recognition of the good they have done them. Now what can be more unreasonable than this plea? That men, after they have been made good and just, after all their injustice has been rooted out by their teacher and replaced by justice, should be unjust through something that they have not![53] Does not this seem to you absurd, my dear friend? In truth you have forced me to make quite a harangue, Callicles, by refusing to answer.

CALLICLES: And you are the man who could not speak unless somebody answered you?

SOCRATES: Apparently I can. Just now, at any rate, I am rather extending my speeches, since you will not answer me. But in the name of friendship, my good fellow, tell me if you do not think it unreasonable for a man, while professing to have made another good, to blame him for being wicked in spite of having been made good by him and still being so?

CALLICLES: Yes, I do.

SOCRATES: Well, and you hear such things said by those who profess to give men education in virtue?

CALLICLES: I do; but what is one to say of such worthless people?

SOCRATES: And what is one to say of those who, professing to govern the state and take every care that she be as good as possible, turn upon her and accuse her, any time it suits them, of being utterly wicked? Do you see any difference between these men and the others? Sophist and orator, my estimable friend, are the same thing, or very much of a piece, as I was telling Polus; but you in your ignorance think the one thing, rhetoric, a very fine affair, and despise the other. Yet in reality sophistic is a finer thing than rhetoric by so much as legislation is finer than judicature, and gymnastic than medicine; in fact, for my own part, I always regarded public speakers and sophists as the only people who have no call to complain of the thing that they themselves educate, for its wickedness towards them; as otherwise they must in the same words be also charging themselves with having been of no use to those whom they say they benefit. Is it not so?

CALLICLES: Certainly.

SOCRATES: And they alone, I presume, could most likely afford to give away their services without fee, if their words were true. For when a man has received any other service, for example, if he has acquired a fast pace from a trainer's lessons, he might possibly cheat him of his due if the trainer freely offered himself and did not

---

[53] Socrates rings changes here on a well-known story involving Corax and Tisias, the first rhetoricians. In this story Tisias is depicted as Corax's pupil, and he refuses to pay for his lessons. Corax takes him to court. Tisias argues that if the court decides against him, he should pay nothing, because obviously he has not been taught well enough to defend himself. Corax counters that if the court decides for Tisias, then obviously Tisias should pay for the lessons that enabled him to win. The case was dismissed. [Ed.]

stipulate for a fee to be paid down by the other as nearly as possible at the moment when he imparted to him the fast pace he required; for it is not through a slow pace, I conceive, that men act unjustly, but through injustice; is it not?

CALLICLES: Yes.

SOCRATES: And so whoever removed this particular thing, injustice, need never have a fear of being unjustly treated; this benefit alone may be freely bestowed without risk, granted that one really had the power of making people good. Is it not so?

CALLICLES: I agree.

SOCRATES: Then this, it seems, is the reason why there is no disgrace in taking money for giving every other kind of advice, as about building or the rest of the arts.

CALLICLES: It does seem so.

SOCRATES: But about this business of finding the way to be as good as possible, and of managing one's own household or city for the best, it is recognized to be a disgrace for one to decline to give advice except for a payment in cash, is it not?

CALLICLES: Yes.

SOCRATES: The reason evidently being that this is the only sort of service that makes the person so served desire to do one in return; and hence it is felt to be a good sign when this service that one has done is repaid to one in kind; but when this is not so, the contrary is felt. Is the case as I say?

CALLICLES: It is.

SOCRATES: Then please specify to which of these two ministrations to the state you are inviting me—that of struggling hard, like a doctor, with the Athenians to make them as good as possible, or that of seeking to serve their wants and humor them at every turn? Tell me the truth, Callicles; for it is only right that, as you began by speaking to me frankly, you should continue to tell me what you think. So now speak out like a good, generous man.

CALLICLES: I say then, the way of seeking to serve them.

SOCRATES: So it is to a flatterer's work, most noble sir, that you invite me?

CALLICLES: Work for a mean Mysian,[54] if you prefer the name, Socrates; for unless you do as I say—

SOCRATES: Do not tell me, what you have so often repeated, that anyone who pleases will put me to death, lest I on my side should have to tell you that it will be a villain killing a good man; nor that anyone may strip me of whatever I have, lest I should have to say in my turn: Well, but when he has stripped me, he will not know what use to make of his spoil, but as he stripped me unjustly so will he use his spoil unjustly, and if unjustly, foully, and if foully, ill.

CALLICLES: It quite strikes me, Socrates, that you believe not one of these troubles could befall you, as though you dwelt out of the way, and could never be dragged into a law court by some perhaps utterly paltry rascal.

SOCRATES: Then I am a fool, Callicles, in truth, if I do not suppose that in this city anyone, whoever he was, might find himself, as luck should have it, in any sort of plight. Of one thing, however, I am sure—that if ever I am brought before the court and stand in any such danger as you mention, it will be some villain who brings me there, for no honest man would prosecute a person who had done no wrong; and it would be no marvel if I were put to death. Would you like me to tell you my reason for expecting this?

CALLICLES: Do, by all means.

SOCRATES: I think I am one of few, not to say the only one, in Athens who attempts the true art of statesmanship, and the only man of the present time who manages affairs of state: hence, as the speeches that I make from time to time are not aimed at gratification, but at what is best instead of what is most pleasant, and as I

---

[54] The Mysians, like the Carians (*cf. Euthyd.* 285 C), were regarded as the lowest of the low. Callicles heatedly taunts Socrates with putting the matter in its worst light. [Tr.]

do not care to deal in "these pretty toys"[55] that you recommend, I shall have not a word to say at the bar. The same case that I made out to Polus will apply to me; for I shall be like a doctor tried by a bench of children on a charge brought by a cook.[56] Just consider what defense a person like that would make at such a pass, if the prosecutor should speak against him thus: "Children, this fellow has done you all a great deal of personal mischief, and he destroys even the youngest of you by cutting and burning, and starves and chokes you to distraction, giving you nasty bitter drafts and forcing you to fast and thirst; not like me, who used to gorge you with abundance of nice things of every sort." What do you suppose a doctor brought to this sad pass could say for himself? Or if he spoke the truth—"All this I did, my boys, for your health"—how great, think you, would be the outcry from such a bench as that? A loud one, would it not?

CALLICLES: I daresay: one must suppose so.

SOCRATES: Then you suppose he would be utterly at a loss what to say?

CALLICLES: Quite so.

SOCRATES: Such, however, I am sure would be my own fate if I were brought before the court. For not only shall I have no pleasures to plead as having been provided by me—which they regard as services and benefits, whereas I envy neither those who provide them nor those for whom they are provided—but if anyone alleges that I either corrupt the younger men by reducing them to perplexity, or revile the older with bitter expressions whether in private or in public, I shall be unable either to tell the truth and say—"It is on just grounds that I say all this, and it is your interest that I serve thereby, gentlemen of the jury"—or to say anything else; and so I daresay any sort of thing, as luck may have it, will befall me.

CALLICLES: Then do you think, Socrates, that a man in such a case and with no power of standing up for himself makes a fine figure in a city?

SOCRATES: Yes, if he had that one resource, Callicles, which you have repeatedly admitted; if he had stood up for himself by avoiding any unjust word or deed in regard either to men or to gods. For this has been repeatedly admitted by us to be the most valuable kind of self-protection. Now if I were convicted of inability to extend this sort of protection to either myself or another, I should be ashamed, whether my conviction took place before many or few, or as between man and man; and if that inability should bring about my death, I should be sorely vexed: but if I came to my end through a lack of flattering rhetoric, I am quite sure you would see me take my death easily. For no man fears the mere act of dying, except he be utterly irrational and unmanly; doing wrong is what one fears: for to arrive in the nether world having one's soul full fraught with a heap of misdeeds is the uttermost of all evils. And now, if you do not mind, I would like to tell you a tale to show you that the case is so.

CALLICLES: Well, as you have completed the rest of the business, go on and complete this also.

SOCRATES: Give ear then, as they say, to a right fine story, which you will regard as a fable, I fancy, but I as an actual account; for what I am about to tell you I mean to offer as the truth. By Homer's account, Zeus, Poseidon, and Pluto divided the sovereignty among them when they took it over from their father. Now in the time of Cronos there was a law concerning mankind, and it holds to this very day among the gods, that every man who has passed a just and holy life departs after his decease to the Isles of the Blessed, and dwells in all happiness apart from ill; but whoever has lived unjustly and impiously goes to the dungeon of requital and penance which, you know, they call Tartarus. Of these men there were judges in Cronos' time, and still

[55] Socrates retorts the phrase of Euripides, which Callicles applied (above, 486 C) to philosophic debate, upon the practical pursuits which Callicles recommended. [Tr.]

[56] *Cf.* 464 D. [Tr.]

of late in the reign of Zeus—living men to judge the living upon the day when each was to breathe his last; and thus the cases were being decided amiss. So Pluto and the overseers from the Isles of the Blessed came before Zeus with the report that they found men passing over to either abode undeserving. Then spake Zeus: "Nay," said he, "I will put a stop to these proceedings. The cases are now indeed judged ill; and it is because they who are on trial are tried in their clothing, for they are tried alive. Now many," said he, "who have wicked souls are clad in fair bodies and ancestry and wealth, and at their judgment appear many witnesses to testify that their lives have been just. Now, the judges are confounded not only by their evidence but at the same time by being clothed themselves while they sit in judgment, having their own soul muffled in the veil of eyes and ears and the whole body. Thus all these are a hindrance to them, their own habiliments no less than those of the judged. Well, first of all," he said, "we must put a stop to their foreknowledge of their death; for this they at present foreknow. However, Prometheus has already been given the word to stop this in them. Next they must be stripped bare of all those things before they are tried; for they must stand their trial dead. Their judge also must be naked, dead, beholding with very soul the very soul of each immediately upon his death, bereft of all his kin and having left behind on earth all that fine array, to the end that the judgment may be just. Now I, knowing all this before you, have appointed sons of my own to be judges; two from Asia, Minos and Rhadamanthus, and one from Europe, Aeacus. These, when their life is ended, shall give judgment in the meadow at the dividing of the road, whence are the two ways leading, one to the Isles of the Blessed, and the other to Tartarus. And those who come from Asia shall Rhadamanthus try, and those from Europe, Aeacus; and to Minos I will give the privilege of the final decision, if the other two be in any doubt; that the judgment upon this journey of mankind may be supremely just."

This, Callicles, is what I have heard and believe to be true; and from these stories, on my reckoning, we must draw some such moral as this: death, as it seems to me, is actually nothing but the disconnection of two things, the soul and the body, from each other. And so when they are disconnected from one another, each of them keeps its own condition very much as it was when the man was alive, the body having its own nature, with its treatments and experiences all manifest upon it. For instance, if anyone's body was large by nature or by feeding or by both when he was alive, his corpse will be large also when he is dead; and if he was fat, it will be fat too after his death, and so on for the rest; or again, if he used to follow the fashion of long hair, long-haired also will be his corpse. Again, if anyone had been a sturdy rogue, and bore traces of his stripes in scars on his body, either from the whip or from other wounds, while yet alive, then after death too his body has these marks visible upon it; or if anyone's limbs were broken or distorted in life, these same effects are manifest in death. In a word, whatever sort of bodily appearance a man had acquired in life, that is manifest also after his death either wholly or in the main for some time. And so it seems to me that the same is the case with the soul too, Callicles: when a man's soul is stripped bare of the body, all its natural gifts, and the experiences added to that soul as the result of his various pursuits, are manifest in it. So when they have arrived in presence of their judge, they of Asia before Rhadamanthus, these Rhadamanthus sets before him and surveys the soul of each, not knowing whose it is; nay, often when he has laid hold of the Great King or some other prince or potentate, he perceives the utter unhealthiness of his soul, striped all over with the scourge, and a mass of wounds, the work of perjuries and injustice; where every act has left its smirch upon his soul, where all is awry through falsehood and imposture, and nothing straight because of a nurture that knew not truth: or, as the result of an unbridled course of fastidiousness, insolence, and incontinence, he finds the soul full fraught with disproportion and ugliness. Beholding this he sends it away in dishonor straight to the place of custody, where on its arrival it is to endure the sufferings that are fitting. And it is fitting that every one under punishment rightly inflicted on him by another should either be made better and profit thereby, or serve as an example to the rest that others seeing the sufferings he endures may in fear amend themselves. Those who are benefited by the punishment they get from gods and men are they who have committed remediable offenses; but still it is through bitter throes of pain that they receive their benefit both here and in the nether world; for in no other way can there be riddance of iniquity. But of those who have done extreme wrong and, as a result of such crimes, have become incurable, of those are the examples made; no longer are they profited at all themselves, since they are incurable, but others are profited who behold them undergoing for their transgressions the greatest, sharpest, and most fearful sufferings evermore, actually hung up as examples there in the infernal dungeon, a spectacle and a lesson to such of the wrongdoers as arrive from time to time. Among them I say Archelaus also will be found, if what Polus tells us is true, and every other despot of his sort. And I think, moreover, that most of these examples have come from despots and kings and potentates and public administrators; for these, since they have a free hand, commit the greatest and most impious offenses. Homer also testifies to this; for he has represented kings and potentates as those who are punished everlastingly in the nether world—Tantalus and Sisyphus and Tityus; but Thersites, or any other private person who was wicked, has been portrayed by none as incurable and therefore subjected to heavy punishment; no doubt because he had not a free hand, and therefore was in fact happier than those who had. For in fact, Callicles, it is among the powerful that we find the specially wicked men. Still there is nothing to prevent good men being found even among these, and it deserves our special admiration when they are; for it is hard, Callicles, and deserving of no slight praise, when a man with a perfectly free hand for injustice lives always a just life. The men of this sort are but few; for indeed there have been, and I expect there yet will be, both here and elsewhere, men of honor and excellence in this virtue of administering justly what is committed to their charge. One in fact there has been whose fame stands high among us and throughout the rest of Greece, Aristeides, son of Lysimachus; but most of those in power, my excellent friend, prove to be bad. So, as I was saying, whenever the judge Rhadamanthus had to deal with such a one, he knows nothing else of him at all, neither who he is nor of what descent, but only that he is a wicked person; and on perceiving this he sends him away to Tartarus, first setting a mark on him to show whether he deems it a curable or an incurable case; and when the man arrives there he suffers what is fitting. Sometimes, when he discerns another soul that has lived a holy life in company with truth, a private man's or any other's—especially, as I claim, Callicles, a philosopher's who has minded his own business and not been a busybody in his lifetime—he is struck with admiration and sends it off to the Isles of the Blessed. And exactly the same is the procedure of Aeacus: each of these two holds a rod in his hand as he gives judgment; but Minos sits as supervisor, distinguished by the golden scepter that he holds, as Odysseus in Homer tells how he saw him—

> Holding a golden scepter, speaking dooms
> to the dead.

Now for my part, Callicles, I am convinced by these accounts, and I consider how I may be able to show my judge that my soul is in the best of health. So giving the go-by to the honors that most men seek I shall try, by inquiry into the truth, to be really good in as high a degree as I am able, both in my life and, when I come to die, in my death. And I invite all other men likewise, to the best of my power, and you particularly I invite in return[57] to this life and this contest, which I say is worth all other contests on this earth; and I make it a reproach to *you,* that you will not be able to deliver yourself when your trial comes and the judgment of which I told you just now; but when you go before your judge, the son of Aegina,[58] and he grips you and drags you up, you will gape and feel dizzy there no less than I do here, and some one perhaps will give you, yes, a degrading box on the ear, and will treat you with every kind of contumely.

Possibly, however, you regard this as an old wife's tale, and despise it; and there would be no wonder in our despising it if with all our searching we could somewhere find anything better and truer than this: but as it is, you observe that you three, who are the wisest of the Greeks in our day—you and Polus and Gorgias—are unable to prove that we ought to live any other life than this, which is evidently advantageous also in the other world. But among the many statements we have made, while all the rest are refuted this one alone is unshaken—that doing wrong is to be more carefully shunned than suffering it; that above all things a man should study not to seem but to be good both in private and in public; that if one becomes bad in any respect one must be corrected; that this is good in the second place,—next to being just, to become so and to be corrected by paying the penalty; and that every kind of flattery, with regard either to oneself or to others, to few or to many, must be avoided; and that rhetoric is to be used for this one purpose always, of pointing to what is just, and so in every other activity. Take my advice, therefore, and follow me where, if you once arrive, you will be happy both in life and after life's end, as this account declares. And allow anyone to condemn you as a fool and foully maltreat you if he chooses; yes, by Heaven, and suffer undaunted the shock of that ignominious cuff; for you will come to no harm if you be really a good and upright man, practicing virtue. And afterwards, having practiced it together, we shall in due course, if we deem it right, embark on politics, or proceed to consult on whatever we may think fit, being then better equipped for such counsel than we are now. For it is disgraceful that men in such a condition as we now appear to be in should put on a swaggering, important air when we never continue to be of the same mind upon the same questions, and those the greatest of all—we are so sadly uneducated. Let us therefore take as our guide the doctrine now disclosed, which indicates to us that this way of life is best—to live and die in the practice alike of justice and of all other virtue. This then let us follow, and to this invite every one else; not that to which you trust yourself and invite me, for it is nothing worth, Callicles.

---

[57] I.e., in return for Callicles' invitation to him to pursue the life of rhetoric and politics, 521 A. [Tr.]

[58] Aegina, daughter of the river god Asopus, was the mother of Aeacus by Zeus. [Tr.]

PLATO

PHAEDRUS

PERSONS OF THE DIALOGUE

SOCRATES
PHAEDRUS

Scene:—Under a plane-tree, by the banks of the Ilissus.

SOCRATES: My dear Phaedrus, whence come you, and whither are you going?

PHAEDRUS: I have come from Lysias the son of Cephalus, and I am going to take a walk outside the wall, for I have been sitting with him the whole morning; and our common friend Acumenus tells me that it is much more refreshing to walk in the open air than to be shut up in a cloister.

SOCRATES: There he is right. Lysias then, I suppose, was in the town?

PHAEDRUS: Yes, he was staying with Epicrates, here at the house of Morychus; that house which is near the temple of Olympian Zeus.

SOCRATES: And how did he entertain you? Can I be wrong in supposing that Lysias gave you a feast of discourse?

PHAEDRUS: You shall hear, if you can spare time to accompany me.

SOCRATES: And should I not deem the conversation of you and Lysias "a thing of higher import," as I may say in the words of Pindar, "than any business"?

PHAEDRUS: Will you go on?

SOCRATES: And will you go on with the narration?

PHAEDRUS: My tale, Socrates, is one of your sort, for love was the theme which occupied us—love after a fashion: Lysias has been writing about a fair youth who was being tempted, but not by a lover; and this was the point: he ingeniously proved that the non-lover should be accepted rather than the lover.

SOCRATES: O that is noble of him! I wish that he would say the poor man rather than the rich, and the old man rather than the young one;—then he would meet the case of me and of many a man; his words would be quite refreshing, and he would be a public benefactor. For my part, I do so long to hear his speech, that if you walk all the way to Megara, and when you have reached the wall come back, as Herodicus recommends, without going in, I will keep you company.

PHAEDRUS: What do you mean, my good Socrates? How can you imagine that my unpractised memory can do justice to an elaborate work, which the greatest rhetorician of the age spent a long time in composing? Indeed, I cannot; I would give a great deal if I could.

SOCRATES: I believe that I know Phaedrus about as well as I know myself, and I am very sure that the speech of Lysias was repeated to him, not once only, but again and again;—he insisted on hearing it many times over and Lysias was very willing to gratify him; at last, when nothing else would do, he got hold of the book, and looked at what he most wanted to see,—this occupied him during the whole morning;—and then when he was tired with sitting, he went out to take a walk, not until, by the dog, as I believe, he had simply learned by heart the entire discourse, unless it was unusually long, and he went to a place outside the wall that he might practise his lesson. There he saw a certain lover of discourse who had a similar weakness;—he saw and rejoiced; now thought he, "I shall have a partner in my revels." And he invited him to come and walk with him. But when the lover of discourse begged that he would repeat the tale, he gave himself airs and said, "No, I cannot," as if he were indisposed; although, if the hearer had refused, he would sooner or later have been compelled by him to listen whether he would or no. Therefore, Phaedrus, bid him do at once what he will soon do whether bidden or not.

PHAEDRUS: I see that you will not let me off until I speak in some fashion or other; verily therefore my best plan is to speak as I best can.

SOCRATES: A very true remark, that of yours.

PHAEDRUS: I will do as I say; but believe me, Socrates, I did not learn the very words—O no; nevertheless I have a general notion of what he said, and will give you a summary of the points in which the lover differed from the non-lover. Let me begin at the beginning.

SOCRATES: Yes, my sweet one; but you must first of all show what you have in your left hand under your cloak, for that roll, as I suspect, is the actual discourse. Now, much as I love you, I would not have you suppose that I am going to have your memory exercised at my expense, if you have Lysias himself here.

PHAEDRUS: Enough; I see that I have no hope of practising my art upon you. But if I am to read, where would you please to sit?

SOCRATES: Let us turn aside and go by the Ilissus; we will sit down at some quiet spot.

PHAEDRUS: I am fortunate in not having my sandals, and as you never have any, I think that we may go along the brook and cool our feet in the water; this will be the easiest way, and at midday and in the summer is far from being unpleasant.

SOCRATES: Lead on, and look out for a place in which we can sit down.

PHAEDRUS: Do you see that tallest plane-tree in the distance?

SOCRATES: Yes.

PHAEDRUS: There are shade and gentle breezes, and grass on which we may either sit or lie down.

SOCRATES: Move forward.

PHAEDRUS: I should like to know, Socrates, whether the place is not somewhere here at which Boreas is said to have carried off Orithyia from the banks of the Ilissus?

SOCRATES: Such is the tradition.

PHAEDRUS: And is this the exact spot? The little stream is delightfully clear and bright; I can fancy that there might be maidens playing near.

SOCRATES: I believe that the spot is not exactly here, but about a quarter of a mile lower down, where you cross to the temple of Artemis, and there is, I think, some sort of an altar of Boreas at the place.

PHAEDRUS: I have never noticed it; but I beseech you to tell me, Socrates, do you believe this tale?

SOCRATES: The wise are doubtful, and I should not be singular if, like them, I too doubted. I might have a rational explanation that Orithyia was playing with Pharmacia, when a northern gust carried her over the neighbouring rocks; and this being the manner of her death, she was said to have been carried away by Boreas. There is a discrepancy, however, about the locality; according to another version of the story she was taken from the Areopagus, and not from this place. Now I quite acknowledge that these allegories are very nice, but he is not to be envied who has to invent them; much labour and ingenuity will be required of him; and when he has once begun, he must go on and rehabilitate Hippocentaurs and chimeras dire. Gorgons and winged steeds flow in apace, and numberless other inconceivable and portentous natures. And if he is skeptical about them, and would fain reduce them one after another to the rules of probability, this sort of crude philosophy will take up a great deal of time. Now I have no leisure for such enquiries; shall I tell you why? I must first know myself, as the Delphian inscription says; to be curious about that which is not my concern, while I am still in ignorance of my own self, would be ridiculous. And therefore I bid farewell to all this; the common opinion is enough for me. For, as I was saying, I want to know not about this, but about myself: am I a monster more complicated and swollen with passion than the serpent Typho, or a creature of a gentler and simpler sort, to whom Nature has given a diviner and lowlier destiny? But let me ask you, friend: have we not reached the plane-tree to which you were conducting us?

PHAEDRUS: Yes, this is the tree.

SOCRATES: By Hera, a fair resting-place, full of summer sounds and scents. Here is this lofty and spreading plane-tree, and the agnus castus high and clustering, in the fullest blossom and the greatest fragrance; and the stream which flows beneath the plane-tree is deliciously cold to the feet. Judging from the ornaments and images, this must be a spot sacred to Achelous and the Nymphs. How delightful is the breeze:—so very sweet; and there is a sound in the air shrill and summerlike which makes answer to the chorus of the cicadae. But the greatest charm of all is the grass, like a pillow gently sloping to the head. My dear Phaedrus, you have been an admirable guide.

PHAEDRUS: What an incomprehensible being you are, Socrates: when you are in the country, as you say, you really are like some stranger who is led about by a guide. Do you ever cross the border? I rather think that you never venture even outside the gates.

SOCRATES: Very true, my good friend; and I hope that you will excuse me when you hear the reason, which is, that I am a lover of knowledge, and the men who dwell in the city are my teachers, and not the trees or the country. Though I do indeed believe that you have found a spell with which to draw me out of the city into the country, like a hungry cow before whom a bough or a bunch of fruit is waved. For only hold up before me in like manner a book, and you may lead me all round Attica, and over the wide world. And now having arrived, I intend to lie down, and do you choose any posture in which you can read best. Begin.

PHAEDRUS: Listen. You know how matters stand with me; and how, as I conceive, this affair may be arranged for the advantage of both of us. And I maintain that I ought not to fail in my suit, because I am not your lover: for lovers repent of the kindnesses which they have shown when their passion ceases, but to the non-lovers who are free and not under any compulsion, no time of repentance ever comes; for they confer their benefits according to the measure of their ability, in the way which is most conducive to their own interest. Then again, lovers consider how by reason of their love they have neglected their own concerns and rendered service to others: and when to these benefits conferred they add on the troubles which they have endured, they think that they have long ago made to the beloved a very ample return. But the non-lover has no such tormenting recollections; he has never neglected his affairs or quarrelled with his relations; he has no troubles to add up or excuses to invent; and being well rid of all these evils, why should he not freely do what will gratify the beloved? If you say that the lover is more to be esteemed, because his love is thought to be greater; for he is willing to say and do what is hateful to other men, in order to please his beloved;—that, if true, is only a proof that he will prefer any future love to his present, and will injure his old love at the pleasure of the new. And how, in a matter of such infinite importance, can a man be right in trusting himself to one who is afflicted with a malady which no experienced person would attempt to cure, for the patient himself admits that he is not in his right mind, and acknowledges that he is wrong in his mind, but says that he is unable to control himself? And if he came to his right mind, would he ever imagine that the desires were good which he conceived when in his wrong mind? Once more, there are many more non-lovers than lovers; and if you choose the best of the lovers, you will not have many to choose from; but if from the non-lovers, the choice will be larger, and you will be far more likely to find among them a person who is worthy of your friendship.

If public opinion be your dread, and you would avoid reproach, in all probability the lover, who is always thinking that other men are as emulous of him as he is of them, will boast to some one[1] of his successes, and make a show of them openly in the pride of his heart;—he wants others to know that his labour has not been lost; but the non-lover is more his own master, and is desirous of solid good, and not of the opinion of mankind. Again, the lover may be generally noted or seen following the beloved (this is his regular occupation), and whenever they are observed to exchange two words they are supposed to meet about some affair of love either past or in contemplation; but when non-lovers meet, no one asks the reason why, because people know that talking to another is natural, whether friendship or mere pleasure be the motive. Once more, if you fear the fickleness of friendship, consider that in any other case a quarrel might be a mutual calamity; but now, when you have given up what is most precious to you, you will be the greater loser, and therefore, you will have more reason in being afraid of the lover, for his vexations are many, and he is always fancying that every one is leagued against him. Wherefore also he debars his beloved from society; he will not have you intimate with the wealthy, lest they should exceed him in wealth, or with men of education, lest they should be his superiors in understanding; and he is equally afraid of anybody's influence who has any other advantage over himself. If he can persuade you to break with them, you are left without a friend in the world; or if, out of a regard to your own interest, you have more sense than to comply with his desire, you will have to quarrel with him. But those who are non-lovers, and whose success in love is the reward of their merit, will not be jealous of the companions of their beloved, and will rather hate those who refuse to be his associates, thinking that their favourite is slighted by the latter and benefited by the former; for more love than hatred may be expected to come to him out of his friendship with others. Many lovers too have loved the person of a youth before they knew his character or his belongings; so that when their passion has passed away, there is no knowing whether they will continue to be his friends; whereas, in the case of non-lovers who were always friends, the friendship is not lessened by the favours granted; but the recollection of these remains with them, and is an earnest of good things to come. Further, I say that you are likely to be improved by me, whereas the lover will spoil you. For they praise your words and actions in a wrong way; partly, because they are afraid of offending you, and also, their judgment is weakened by passion. Such are the feats which love exhibits; he makes things painful to the disappointed which give no pain to others; he compels the successful lover to praise what ought not to give him pleasure, and therefore the beloved is to be pitied rather than envied. But if you will listen to me, in the first place, I, in my intercourse with you, shall not merely regard present enjoyment, but also future advantage, being not mastered by love, but my own master; nor for small causes taking violent dislikes, but even when the cause is great, slowly laying up little wrath—unintentional offences I shall forgive, and intentional ones I shall try to prevent; and these are the marks of a friendship which will last. Do you think that a lover only can be a firm friend? Reflect:—if this were true, we should set small value on sons, or fathers, or mothers; nor should we ever have loyal friends, for our love of them arises not from passion, but from other associations. Further, if we ought to shower favours on those who are the most eager suitors,—on that principle, we ought always to do good, not to the most virtuous, but to the most needy; for they are the persons who will be most relieved,

[1] Reading *τῷ λέγειν*; cf. infra, *τῷ διαλέγεσθαι*.

and will therefore be the most grateful; and when you make a feast you should invite not your friend, but the beggar and the empty soul; for they will love you, and attend you, and come about your doors, and will be the best pleased, and the most grateful, and will invoke many a blessing on your head. Yet surely you ought not to be granting favours to those who besiege you with prayer, but to those who are best able to reward you; nor to the lover only, but to those who are worthy of love; nor to those who will enjoy the bloom of your youth, but to those who will share their possessions with you in age; nor to those who, having succeeded, will glory in their success to others, but to those who will be modest and tell no tales; nor to those who care about you for a moment only, but to those who will continue your friends through life; nor to those who, when their passion is over, will pick a quarrel with you, but rather to those who, when the charm of youth has left you, will show their own virtue. Remember what I have said; and consider yet this further point: friends admonish the lover under the idea that his way of life is bad, but no one of his kindred ever yet censured the non-lover, or thought that he was ill-advised about his own interests.

"Perhaps you will ask me whether I propose that you should indulge every non-lover. To which I reply that not even the lover would advise you to indulge all lovers, for the indiscriminate favour is less esteemed by the rational recipient, and less easily hidden by him who would escape the censure of the world. Now love ought to be for the advantage of both parties, and for the injury of neither.

"I believe that I have said enough; but if there is anything more which you desire or which in your opinion needs to be supplied, ask and I will answer."

Now, Socrates, what do you think? Is not the discourse excellent, more especially in the matter of the language?

SOCRATES: Yes, quite admirable; the effect on me was ravishing. And this I owe to you, Phaedrus, for I observed you while reading to be in an ecstasy, and thinking that you are more experienced in these matters than I am, I followed your example, and, like you, my divine darling, I became inspired with a phrenzy.

PHAEDRUS: Indeed, you are pleased to be merry.

SOCRATES: Do you mean that I am not in earnest?

PHAEDRUS: Now don't talk in that way, Socrates, but let me have your real opinion; I adjure you, by Zeus, the god of friendship, to tell me whether you think that any Hellene could have said more or spoken better on the same subject.

SOCRATES: Well, but are you and I expected to praise the sentiments of the author, or only the clearness, and roundness, and finish, and tournure of the language? As to the first I willingly submit to your better judgment, for I am not worthy to form an opinion, having only attended to the rhetorical manner; and I was doubting whether this could have been defended even by Lysias himself; I thought, though I speak under correction, that he repeated himself two or three times, either from want of words or from want of pains; and also, he appeared to me ostentatiously to exult in showing how well he could say the same thing[1] in two or three ways.

PHAEDRUS: Nonsense, Socrates; what you call repetition was the especial merit of the speech; for he omitted no topic of which the subject rightly allowed, and I do not think that any one could have spoken better or more exhaustively.

SOCRATES: There I cannot go along with you. Ancient sages, men and women, who have spoken and written of these things, would rise up in judgment against me, if out of complaisance I assented to you.

---

[1] Reading *ταὐτά*.

PHAEDRUS: Who are they, and where did you hear anything better than this?

SOCRATES: I am sure that I must have heard; but at this moment I do not remember from whom; perhaps from Sappho the fair, or Anacreon the wise; or, possibly, from a prose writer. Why do I say so? Why, because I perceive that my bosom is full, and that I could make another speech as good as that of Lysias, and different. Now I am certain that this is not an invention of my own, who am well aware that I know nothing, and therefore I can only infer that I have been filled through the ears, like a pitcher, from the waters of another, though I have actually forgotten in my stupidity who was my informant.

PHAEDRUS: That is grand:—but never mind where you heard the discourse or from whom; let that be a mystery not to be divulged even at my earnest desire. Only, as you say, promise[1] to make another and better oration, equal in length and entirely new, on the same subject; and I, like the nine Archons, will promise to set up a golden image at Delphi, not only of myself, but of you, and as large as life.

SOCRATES: You are a dear golden ass if you suppose me to mean that Lysias has altogether missed the mark, and that I can make a speech from which all his arguments are to be excluded. The worst of authors will say something which is to the point. Who, for example, could speak on this thesis of yours without praising the discretion of the non-lover and blaming the indiscretion of the lover? These are the commonplaces of the subject which must come in (for what else is there to be said?) and must be allowed and excused; the only merit is the arrangement of them, for there can be none in the invention; but when you leave the commonplaces, then there may be some originality.

PHAEDRUS: I admit that there is reason in what you say, and I too will be reasonable, and will allow you to start with the premise that the lover is more disordered in his wits than the non-lover; if in what remains you make a longer and better speech than Lysias, and use other arguments, then I say again, that a statue you shall have of beaten gold, and take your place by the colossal offerings of the Cypselids at Olympia.

SOCRATES: How profoundly in earnest is the lover, because to tease him I lay a finger upon his love! And so, Phaedrus, you really imagine that I am going to improve upon the ingenuity of Lysias?

PHAEDRUS: There I have you as you had me, and you must just speak, "as you best can." Do not let us exchange "tu quoque" as in a farce, or compel me to say to you as you said to me, "I know Socrates as well as I know myself, and he was wanting to speak, but he gave himself airs." Rather I would have you consider that from this place we stir not until you have unbosomed yourself of the speech; for here are we all alone, and I am stronger, remember, and younger than you:—Wherefore perpend, and do not compel me to use violence.

SOCRATES: But, my sweet Phaedrus, how ridiculous it would be of me to compete with Lysias in an extempore speech! He is a master in his art and I am an untaught man.

PHAEDRUS: You see how matters stand; and therefore let there be no more pretences; for, indeed, I know the word that is irresistible.

SOCRATES: Then don't say it.

PHAEDRUS: Yes, but I will; and my word shall be an oath. "I say, or rather swear"—but what good will be the witness of my oath?—"By this plane-tree I swear, that unless you repeat the discourse here in the face of this very plane-tree, I will never tell you another; never let you have word of another!"

SOCRATES: Villain! I am conquered; the poor lover of discourse has no more to say.

PHAEDRUS: Then why are you still at your tricks?

SOCRATES: I am not going to play tricks now that you have taken the oath, for I cannot allow myself to be starved.

---

[1] Reading ὑπόσχες εἰπεῖν.

PHAEDRUS: Proceed.

SOCRATES: Shall I tell you what I will do?

PHAEDRUS: What?

SOCRATES: I will veil my face and gallop through the discourse as fast as I can, for if I see you I shall feel ashamed and not know what to say.

PHAEDRUS: Only go on and you may do anything else which you please.

SOCRATES: Come, O ye Muses, melodious, as ye are called, whether you have received this name from the character of your strains, or because the Melians[1] are a musical race, help, O help me in the tale which my good friend here desires me to rehearse, in order that his friend whom he always deemed wise may seem to him to be wiser now than ever.

Once upon a time there was a fair boy, or, more properly speaking, a youth; he was very fair and had a great many lovers; and there was one special cunning one, who had persuaded the youth that he did not love him, but he really loved him all the same; and one day when he was paying his addresses to him, he used this very argument—that he ought to accept the non-lover rather than the lover; his words were as follows:—

"All good counsel begins in the same way; a man should know what he is advising about, or his counsel will all come to nought. But people imagine that they know about the nature of things, when they don't know about them, and, not having come to an understanding at first because they think that they know, they end, as might be expected, in contradicting one another and themselves. Now you and I must not be guilty of this fundamental error which we condemn in others; but as our question is whether the lover or non-lover is to be preferred, let us first of all agree in defining the nature and power of love, and then, keeping our eyes upon the definition and to this appealing, let us further enquire whether love brings advantage or disadvantage.

"Every one sees that love is a desire, and we know also that non-lovers desire the beautiful and good. Now in what way is the lover to be distinguished from the non-lover? Let us note that in every one of us there are two guiding and ruling principles which lead us whither they will; one is the natural desire of pleasure, the other is an acquired opinion which aspires after the best; and these two are sometimes in harmony and then again at war, and sometimes the one, sometimes the other conquers. When opinion by the help of reason leads us to the best, the conquering principle is called temperance; but when desire, which is devoid of reason, rules in us and drags us to pleasure, that power of misrule is called excess. Now excess has many names, and many members, and many forms, and any of these forms when very marked gives a name, neither honourable nor creditable, to the bearer of the name. The desire of eating, for example, which gets the better of the higher reason and the other desires, is called gluttony, and he who is possessed by it is called a glutton; the tyrannical desire of drink, which inclines the possessor of the desire to drink, has a name which is only too obvious, and there can be as little doubt by what name any other appetite of the same family would be called;—it will be the name of that which happens to be dominant. And now I think that you will perceive the drift of my discourse; but as every spoken word is in a manner plainer than the unspoken, I had better say further that the irrational desire which overcomes the tendency of opinion towards right, and is led away to the enjoyment of beauty, and especially of personal beauty, by the desires which are her own kindred—that supreme desire, I say, which by leading[1] conquers and by the force of passion

---

[1] In the original, *λίγειαι, Λίγυες*.

[1] Reading *ἀγωγῇ*.

is reinforced, from this very force, receiving a name, is called love (ἐρρωμένω; ἔρως)."

And now, dear Phaedrus, I shall pause for an instant to ask whether you do not think me, as I appear to myself, inspired?

PHAEDRUS: Yes, Socrates, you seem to have a very unusual flow of words.

SOCRATES: Listen to me, then, in silence; for surely the place is holy; so that you must not wonder, if, as I proceed, I appear to be in a divine fury, for already I am getting into dithyrambics.

PHAEDRUS: Nothing can be truer.

SOCRATES: The responsibility rests with you. But hear what follows, and perhaps the fit may be averted; all is in their hands above. I will go on talking to my youth. Listen:—

Thus, my friend, we have declared and defined the nature of the subject. Keeping the definition in view, let us now enquire what advantage or disadvantage is likely to ensue from the lover or the non-lover to him who accepts their advances.

He who is the victim of his passions and the slave of pleasure will of course desire to make his beloved as agreeable to himself as possible. Now to him who has a mind diseased anything is agreeable which is not opposed to him, but that which is equal or superior is hateful to him, and therefore the lover will not brook any superiority or equality on the part of his beloved; he is always employed in reducing him to inferiority. And the ignorant is the inferior of the wise, the coward of the brave, the slow of speech of the speaker, the dull of the clever. These, and not these only, are the mental defects of the beloved;—defects which, when implanted by nature, are necessarily a delight to the lover, and, when not implanted, he must contrive to implant them in him, if he would not be deprived of his fleeting joy. And therefore he cannot help being jealous, and will debar his beloved from the advantages of society which would make a man of him, and especially from that society which would have given him wisdom, and thereby he cannot fail to do him great harm. That is to say, in his excessive fear lest he should come to be despised in his eyes he will be compelled to banish from him divine philosophy; and there is no greater injury which he can inflict upon him than this. He will contrive that his beloved shall be wholly ignorant, and in everything shall look to him; he is to be the delight of the lover's heart, and a curse to himself. Verily, a lover is a profitable guardian and associate for him in all that relates to his mind.

Let us next see how his master, whose law of life is pleasure and not good, will keep and train the body of his servant. Will he not choose a beloved who is delicate rather than sturdy and strong? One brought up in shady bowers and not in the bright sun, a stranger to manly exercises and the sweat of toil, accustomed only to a soft and luxurious diet, instead of the hues of health having the colours of paint and ornament, and the rest of a piece?—such a life as any one can imagine and which I need not detail at length. But I may sum up all that I have to say in a word, and pass on. Such a person in war, or in any of the great crises of life, will be the anxiety of his friends and also of his lover, and certainly not the terror of his enemies; which nobody can deny.

And now let us tell what advantage or disadvantage the beloved will receive from the guardianship and society of his lover in the matter of his property; this is the next point to be considered. The lover will be the first to see what, indeed, will be sufficiently evident to all men, that he desires above all things to deprive his beloved of his dearest and best and holiest possessions, father, mother, kindred, friends, of all who he thinks may be hinderers or reprovers of their most sweet converse; he will even cast a jealous eye upon his gold and silver or other property, because these make him a less easy prey, and when caught less manageable; hence he is of necessity displeased at his possession of them and rejoices at their loss; and he would like him to be wifeless, childless, homeless, as well; and the longer the better, for the longer he is all this, the longer he will enjoy him.

There are some sort of animals, such as flatterers, who are dangerous and mischievous enough, and yet nature has mingled a temporary pleasure and grace in their composition. You may say that a courtesan is hurtful, and disapprove of such creatures and their practices, and yet for the time they are very pleasant. But the lover is not only hurtful to his love; he is also an extremely disagreeable companion. The old proverb says that "birds of a feather flock together"; I suppose that equality of years inclines them to the same pleasures, and similarity begets friendship; yet you may have more than enough even of this; and verily constraint is always said to be grievous. Now the lover is not only unlike his beloved, but he forces himself upon him. For he is old and his love is young, and neither day nor night will he leave him if he can help; necessity and the sting of desire drive him on, and allure him with the pleasure which he receives from seeing, hearing, touching, perceiving him in every way. And therefore he is delighted to fasten upon him and to minister to him. But what pleasure or consolation can the beloved be receiving all this time? Must he not feel the extremity of disgust when he looks at an old shrivelled face and the remainder to match, which even in a description is disagreeable, and quite detestable when he is forced into daily contact with his lover? Moreover he is jealously watched and guarded against everything and everybody, and has to hear misplaced and exaggerated praises of himself, and censures equally inappropriate, which are intolerable when the man is sober, and, besides being intolerable, are published all over the world in all their indelicacy and wearisomeness when he is drunk.

And not only while his love continues is he mischievous and unpleasant, but when his love ceases he becomes a perfidious enemy of him on whom he showered his oaths and prayers and promises, and yet could hardly prevail upon him to tolerate the tedium of his company even from motives of interest. The hour of payment arrives, and now he is the servant of another master; instead of love and infatuation, wisdom and temperance are his bosom's lords; but the beloved has not discovered the change which has taken place in him when he asks for a return and recalls to his recollection former sayings and doings; he believes himself to be speaking to the same person, and the other, not having the courage to confess the truth, and not knowing how to fulfil the oaths and promises which he made when under the dominion of folly, and having now grown wise and temperate, does not want to do as he did or to be as he was before. And so he runs away and is constrained to be a defaulter; the oyster-shell[1] has fallen with the other side uppermost—he changes pursuit into flight, while the other is compelled to follow him with passion and imprecation, not knowing that he ought never from the first to have accepted a demented lover instead of a sensible non-lover; and that in making such a choice he was giving himself up to a faithless, morose, envious, disagreeable being, hurtful to his estate, hurtful to his bodily health, and still more hurtful to the cultivation of his mind, than which there neither is nor ever will be anything more honoured in the eyes both of gods and men. Consider this, fair youth, and know that in the friendship of the lover there is no real kindness; he has an appetite and wants to feed upon you:

> "As wolves love lambs so lovers love their loves."

But I told you so, I am speaking in verse, and therefore I had better make an end; enough.

PHAEDRUS: I thought that you were only halfway and were going to make a similar speech

---

[1] In allusion to a game in which two parties fled or pursued according as an oyster-shell which was thrown into the air fell with the dark or light side uppermost.

about all the advantages of accepting the non-lover. Why do you not proceed?

SOCRATES: Does not your simplicity observe that I have got out of dithyrambics into heroics, when only uttering a censure on the lover? And if I am to add the praises of the non-lover what will become of me? Do you not perceive that I am already overtaken by the Nymphs to whom you have mischievously exposed me? And therefore I will only add that the non-lover has all the advantages in which the lover is accused of being deficient. And now I will say no more; there has been enough of both of them. Leaving the tale to its fate, I will cross the river and make the best of my way home, lest a worse thing be inflicted upon me by you.

PHAEDRUS: Not yet, Socrates; not until the heat of the day has passed; do you not see that the hour is almost noon? There is the midday sun standing still, as people say, in the meridian. Let us rather stay and talk over what has been said, and then return in the cool.

SOCRATES: Your love of discourse, Phaedrus, is superhuman, simply marvellous, and I do not believe that there is any one of your contemporaries who has either made or in one way or another has compelled others to make an equal number of speeches. I would except Simmias the Theban, but all the rest are far behind you. And now I do verily believe that you have been the cause of another.

PHAEDRUS: That is good news. But what do you mean?

SOCRATES: I mean to say that as I was about to cross the stream the usual sign was given to me,—that sign which always forbids, but never bids, me to do anything which I am going to do; and I thought that I heard a voice saying in my ear that I had been guilty of impiety, and that I must not go away until I had made an atonement. Now I am a diviner, though not a very good one, but I have enough religion for my own use, as you might say of a bad writer—his writing is good enough for him; and I am beginning to see that I was in error. O my friend, how prophetic is the human soul! At the time I had a sort of misgiving, and, like Ibycus, "I was troubled; I feared that I might be buying honour from men at the price of sinning against the gods." Now I recognize my error.

PHAEDRUS: What error?

SOCRATES: That was a dreadful speech which you brought with you, and you made me utter one as bad.

PHAEDRUS: How so?

SOCRATES: It was foolish, I say,—to a certain extent, impious; can anything be more dreadful?

PHAEDRUS: Nothing, if the speech was really such as you describe.

SOCRATES: Well, and is not Eros the son of Aphrodite, and a god?

PHAEDRUS: So men say.

SOCRATES: But that was not acknowledged by Lysias in his speech, nor by you in that other speech which you by a charm drew from my lips. For if love be, as he surely is, a divinity, he cannot be evil. Yet this was the error of both the speeches. There was also a simplicity about them which was refreshing; having no truth or honesty in them, nevertheless they pretended to be something, hoping to succeed in deceiving the manikins of earth and gain celebrity among them. Wherefore I must have a purgation. And I bethink me of an ancient purgation of mythological error which was devised, not by Homer, for he never had the wit to discover why he was blind, but by Stesichorus, who was a philosopher and knew the reason why; and therefore, when he lost his eyes, for that was the penalty which was inflicted upon him for reviling the lovely Helen, he at once purged himself. And the purgation was a recantation, which began thus,—

> "False is that word of mine—the truth is that thou didst not embark in ships, nor ever go to the walls of Troy";

and when he had completed his poem, which is called "the recantation," immediately his sight returned to him. Now I will be wiser than either Stesichorus or Homer, in that I am going to make my recantation for reviling love before I suffer; and this I will attempt, not as before, veiled and ashamed, but with forehead bold and bare.

PHAEDRUS: Nothing could be more agreeable to me than to hear you say so.

SOCRATES: Only think, my good Phaedrus, what an utter want of delicacy was shown in the two discourses; I mean, in my own and in that which you recited out of the book. Would not any one who was himself of a noble and gentle nature, and who loved or ever had loved a nature like his own, when we tell of the petty causes of lovers' jealousies, and of their exceeding animosities, and of the injuries which they do to their beloved, have imagined that our ideas of love were taken from some haunt of sailors to which good manners were unknown—he would certainly never have admitted the justice of our censure?

PHAEDRUS: I dare say not, Socrates.

SOCRATES: Therefore, because I blush at the thought of this person, and also because I am afraid of Love himself, I desire to wash the brine out of my ears with water from the spring; and I would counsel Lysias not to delay, but to write another discourse, which shall prove that "ceteris paribus" the lover ought to be accepted rather than the non-lover.

PHAEDRUS: Be assured that he shall. You shall speak the praises of the lover, and Lysias shall be compelled by me to write another discourse on the same theme.

SOCRATES: You will be true to your nature in that, and therefore I believe you.

PHAEDRUS: Speak, and fear not.

SOCRATES: But where is the fair youth whom I was addressing before, and who ought to listen now; lest, if he hear me not, he should accept a non-lover before he knows what he is doing?

PHAEDRUS: He is close at hand, and always at your service.

SOCRATES: Know then, fair youth, that the former discourse was the word of Phaedrus, the son of Vain Man, who dwells in the city of Myrrhina (Myrrhinusius). And this which I am about to utter is the recantation of Stesichorus the son of Godly Man (Euphemus), who comes from the town of Desire (Himera), and is to the following effect: "I told a lie when I said" that the beloved ought to accept the non-lover when he might have the lover, because the one is sane, and the other mad. It might be so if madness were simply an evil; but there is also a madness which is a divine gift, and the source of the chiefest blessings granted to men. For prophecy is a madness, and the prophetess at Delphi and the priestesses at Dodona when out of their senses have conferred great benefits on Hellas, both in public and private life, but when in their senses few or none. And I might also tell you how the Sibyl and other inspired persons have given to many a one many an intimation of the future which has saved them from falling. But it would be tedious to speak of what every one knows.

There will be more reason in appealing to the ancient inventors of names,[1] who would never have connected prophecy (*μαντική*), which foretells the future and is the noblest of arts, with madness (*μανική*), or called them both by the same name, if they had deemed madness to be a disgrace or dishonour;—they must have thought that there was an inspired madness which was a noble thing; for the two words, *μαντική* and *μανική*, are really the same, and the letter *τ* is only a modern and tasteless insertion. And this is confirmed by the name which was given by them to the rational investigation of futurity, whether made by the help of birds or of other signs—this, for as much as it is an art which supplies from the reasoning faculty mind (*νοῦς*) and information (*ἱστορία*) to human thought (*οἴησις*), they originally termed *οἰονοιστική*, but the word

[1] Cp. Cratylus 388 foll.

has been lately altered and made sonorous by the modern introduction of the letter Omega (οἰονοιστικὴ and οἰωνιστικὴ), and in proportion as prophecy (μαντικὴ) is more perfect and august than augury, both in name and fact, in the same proportion, as the ancients testify, is madness superior to a sane mind (σωφροσύνη), for the one is only of human, but the other of divine origin. Again, where plagues and mightiest woes have bred in certain families, owing to some ancient blood-guiltiness, there madness has entered with holy prayers and rites, and by inspired utterances found a way of deliverance for those who are in need; and he who has part in this gift, and is truly possessed and duly out of his mind, is by the use of purifications and mysteries made whole and exempt from evil, future as well as present, and has a release from the calamity which was afflicting him. The third kind is the madness of those who are possessed by the Muses; which taking hold of a delicate and virgin soul, and there inspiring frenzy, awakens lyrical and all other numbers; with these adorning the myriad actions of ancient heroes for the instruction of posterity. But he who, having no touch of the Muses' madness in his soul, comes to the door and thinks that he will get into the temple by the help of art—he, I say, and his poetry are not admitted; the sane man disappears and is nowhere when he enters into rivalry with the madman.

I might tell of many other noble deeds which have sprung from inspired madness. And therefore, let no one frighten or flutter us by saying that the temperate friend is to be chosen rather than the inspired, but let him further show that love is not sent by the gods for any good to lover or beloved; if he can do so we will allow him to carry off the palm. And we, on our part, will prove in answer to him that the madness of love is the greatest of heaven's blessings, and the proof shall be one which the wise will receive, and the witling disbelieve. But first of all, let us view the affections and actions of the soul divine and human, and try to ascertain the truth about them. The beginning of our proof is as follows:—

[1]The soul through all her being is immortal, for that which is ever in motion is immortal; but that which moves another and is moved by another, in ceasing to move ceases also to live. Only the self-moving, never leaving self, never ceases to move, and is the fountain and beginning of motion to all that moves besides. Now, the beginning is unbegotten, for that which is begotten has a beginning; but the beginning is begotten of nothing, for if it were begotten of something, then the begotten would not come from a beginning. But if unbegotten, it must also be indestructible; for if beginning were destroyed, there could be no beginning out of anything, nor anything out of a beginning; and all things must have a beginning. And therefore the self-moving is the beginning of motion; and this can neither be destroyed nor begotten, else the whole heavens and all creation would collapse and stand still, and never again have motion or birth. But if the self-moving is proved to be immortal, he who affirms that self-motion is the very idea and essence of the soul will not be put to confusion. For the body which is moved from without is soulless; but that which is moved from within has a soul, for such is the nature of the soul. But if this be true, must not the soul be the self-moving, and therefore of necessity unbegotten and immortal? Enough of the soul's immortality.

Of the nature of the soul, though her true form be ever a theme of large and more than mortal discourse, let me speak briefly, and in a figure. And let the figure be composite—a pair of winged horses and a charioteer. Now the winged horses and the charioteers of the gods are all of them noble and of noble descent, but those of other races are mixed; the human

---

[1] Translated by Cic. Tus. Quaest. s. 24.

charioteer drives his in a pair; and one of them is noble and of noble breed, and the other is ignoble and of ignoble breed; and the driving of them of necessity gives a great deal of trouble to him. I will endeavour to explain to you in what way the mortal differs from the immortal creature. The soul in her totality has the care of inanimate being everywhere, and traverses the whole heaven in divers forms appearing;—when perfect and fully winged she soars upward, and orders the whole world; whereas the imperfect soul, losing her wings and drooping in her flight, at last settles on the solid ground—there, finding a home, she receives an earthly frame which appears to be self-moved, but is really moved by her power; and this composition of soul and body is called a living and mortal creature. For immortal no such union can be reasonably believed to be; although fancy, not having seen nor surely known the nature of God, may imagine an immortal creature having both a body and also a soul which are united throughout all time. Let that, however, be as God wills, and be spoken of acceptably to him. And now let us ask the reason why the soul loses her wings!

The wing is the corporeal element which is most akin to the divine, and which by nature tends to soar aloft and carry that which gravitates downwards into the upper region, which is the habitation of the gods. The divine is beauty, wisdom, goodness, and the like; and by these the wing of the soul is nourished, and grows apace; but when fed upon evil and foulness and the opposite of good, wastes and falls away. Zeus, the mighty lord, holding the reins of a winged chariot, leads the way in heaven, ordering all and taking care of all; and there follows him the array of gods and demigods, marshalled in eleven bands; Hestia alone abides at home in the house of heaven; of the rest they who are reckoned among the princely twelve march in their appointed order. They see many blessed sights in the inner heaven, and there are many ways to and fro, along which the blessed gods are passing, every one doing his own work; he may follow who will and can, for jealousy has no place in the celestial choir. But when they go to banquet and festival, then they move up the steep to the top of the vault of heaven. The chariots of the gods in even poise, obeying the rein, glide rapidly; but the others labour, for the vicious steed goes heavily, weighing down the charioteer to the earth when his steed has not been thoroughly trained:—and this is the hour of agony and extremest conflict for the soul. For the immortals, when they are at the end of their course, go forth and stand upon the outside of heaven, and the revolution of the spheres carries them round, and they behold the things beyond. But of the heaven which is above the heavens, what earthly poet ever did or ever will sing worthily? It is such as I will describe; for I must dare to speak the truth, when truth is my theme. There abides the very being with which true knowledge is concerned; the colourless, formless, intangible essence, visible only to mind, the pilot of the soul. The divine intelligence, being nurtured upon mind and pure knowledge, and the intelligence of every soul which is capable of receiving the food proper to it, rejoices at beholding reality, and once more gazing upon truth, is replenished and made glad, until the revolution of the worlds brings her round again to the same place. In the revolution she beholds justice, and temperance, and knowledge absolute, not in the form of generation or of relation, which men call existence, but knowledge absolute in existence absolute; and beholding the other true existences in like manner, and feasting upon them, she passes down into the interior of the heavens and returns home; and there the charioteer putting up his horses at the stall, gives them ambrosia to eat and nectar to drink.

Such is the life of the gods; but of other souls, that which follows God best and is likest to him lifts the head of the charioteer into the outer world, and is carried round in the revolution, troubled indeed by the steeds, and with difficulty beholding true being; while another only rises and falls, and sees, and again fails to see by reason of the unruliness of the steeds. The rest of the souls are also longing after the upper world and they all follow, but not being strong enough they are carried round below the surface, plunging, treading on one another, each striving to be first; and there is confusion and perspiration and the extremity of effort; and many of them are lamed or have their wings broken through the ill-driving of the charioteers; and all of them after a fruitless toil, not having attained to the mysteries of true being, go away, and feed upon opinion. The reason why the souls exhibit this exceeding eagerness to behold the plain of truth is that pasturage is found there, which is suited to the highest part of the soul; and the wing on which the soul soars is nourished with this. And there is a law of Destiny, that the soul which attains any vision of truth in company with a god is preserved from harm until the next period, and if attaining always is always unharmed. But when she is unable to follow, and fails to behold the truth, and through some ill-hap sinks beneath the double load of forgetfulness and vice, and her wings fall from her and she drops to the ground, then the law ordains that this soul shall at her first birth pass, not into any other animal, but only into man; and the soul which has seen most of truth shall come to the birth as a philosopher, or artist, or some musical and loving nature; that which has seen truth in the second degree shall be some righteous king or warrior chief; the soul which is of the third class shall be a politician, or economist, or trader; the fourth shall be a lover of gymnastic toils, or a physician; the fifth shall lead the life of a prophet or hierophant; to the sixth the character of a poet or some other imitative artist will be assigned; to the seventh the life of an artisan or husbandman; to the eighth that of a sophist or demagogue; to the ninth that of a tyrant;—all these are states of probation, in which he who does righteously improves, and he who does unrighteously, deteriorates his lot.

Ten thousand years must elapse before the soul of each one can return to the place from whence she came, for she cannot grow her wings in less; only the soul of a philosopher, guileless and true, or the soul of a lover, who is not devoid of philosophy, may acquire wings in the third of the recurring periods of a thousand years; he is distinguished from the ordinary good man who gains wings in three thousand years:—and they who choose this life three times in succession have wings given them, and go away at the end of three thousand years. But the others[1] receive judgment when they have completed their first life, and after the judgment they go, some of them to the houses of correction which are under the earth, and are punished; others to some place in heaven whither they are lightly borne by justice, and there they live in a manner worthy of the life which they led here when in the form of men. And at the end of the first thousand years the good souls and also the evil souls both come to draw lots and choose their second life, and they may take any which they please. The soul of a man may pass into the life of a beast, or from the beast return again into the man. But the soul which has never seen the truth will not pass into the human form. For a man must have intelligence of universals, and be able to proceed from the many particulars of sense to one conception of reason;—this is the recollection of those things which our soul once saw while following God—when regardless of that which we now call being she raised her head up towards the true being. And therefore the mind of the philosopher alone has wings; and this is just, for he is always, according to the measure of his abilities, clinging in recollection to those things in which God abides, and in beholding which He is

[1] The philosopher alone is not subject to judgment (κρίσις), for he has never lost the vision of truth.

what He is. And he who employs aright these memories is ever being initiated into perfect mysteries and alone becomes truly perfect. But, as he forgets earthly interests and is rapt in the divine, the vulgar deem him mad, and rebuke him; they do not see that he is inspired.

Thus far I have been speaking of the fourth and last kind of madness, which is imputed to him who, when he sees the beauty of earth, is transported with the recollection of the true beauty; he would like to fly away, but he cannot; he is like a bird fluttering and looking upward and careless of the world below; and he is therefore thought to be mad. And I have shown this of all inspirations to be the noblest and highest and the offspring of the highest to him who has or shares in it, and that he who loves the beautiful is called a lover because he partakes of it. For, as has been already said, every soul of man has in the way of nature beheld true being; this was the condition of her passing into the form of man. But all souls do not easily recall the things of the other world; they may have seen them for a short time only, or they may have been unfortunate in their earthly lot, and, having had their hearts turned to unrighteousness through some corrupting influence, they may have lost the memory of the holy things which once they saw. Few only retain an adequate remembrance of them; and they, when they behold here any image of that other world, are rapt in amazement; but they are ignorant of what this rapture means, because they do not clearly perceive. For there is no light of justice or temperance or any of the higher ideas which are precious to souls in the earthly copies of them: they are seen through a glass dimly; and there are few who, going to the images, behold in them the realities, and these only with difficulty. There was a time when with the rest of the happy band they saw beauty shining in brightness,—we philosophers following in the train of Zeus, others in company with other gods; and then we beheld the beatific vision and were initiated into a mystery which may be truly called most blessed, celebrated by us in our state of innocence, before we had any experience of evils to come, when we were admitted to the sight of apparitions innocent and simple and calm and happy, which we beheld shining in pure light, pure ourselves and not yet enshrined in that living tomb which we carry about, now that we are imprisoned in the body, like an oyster in his shell. Let me linger over the memory of scenes which have passed away.

But of beauty, I repeat again that we saw her there shining in company with the celestial forms; and coming to earth we find her here too, shining in clearness through the clearest aperture of sense. For sight is the most piercing of our bodily senses; though not by that is wisdom seen; her loveliness would have been transporting if there had been a visible image of her, and the other ideas, if they had visible counterparts, would be equally lovely. But this is the privilege of beauty, that being the loveliest she is also the most palpable to sight. Now he who is not newly initiated or who has become corrupted, does not easily rise out of this world to the sight of true beauty in the other; he looks only at her earthly namesake, and instead of being awed at the sight of her, he is given over to pleasure, and like a brutish beast he rushes on to enjoy and beget; he consorts with wantonness, and is not afraid or ashamed of pursuing pleasure in violation of nature. But he whose initiation is recent, and who has been the spectator of many glories in the other world, is amazed when he sees any one having a godlike face or form, which is the expression of divine beauty; and at first a shudder runs through him, and again the old awe steals over him; then looking upon the face of his beloved as of a god he reverences him, and if he were not afraid of being thought a downright madman, he would sacrifice to his beloved as to the image of a god; then while he gazes on him there is a sort of reaction, and the shudder passes into an unusual heat and perspiration; for, as he receives the effluence of beauty through the eyes, the wing moistens and he warms. And as he warms, the parts out of which the wing grew, and which had been hitherto closed and rigid, and had prevented the wing from shooting forth, are melted, and as nourishment streams upon him, the lower end of the wing begins to swell and grow from the root upwards; and the growth extends under the whole soul—for once the whole was winged. During this process the whole soul is all in a state of ebullition and effervescence,—which may be compared to the irritation and uneasiness in the gums at the time of cutting teeth,—bubbles up, and has a feeling of uneasiness and tickling; but when in like manner the soul is beginning to grow wings, the beauty of the beloved meets her eye and she receives the sensible warm motion of particles which flow towards her, therefore called emotion (ἵμερος), and is refreshed and warmed by them, and then she ceases from her pain with joy. But when she is parted from her beloved and her moisture fails, then the orifices of the passage out of which the wing shoots dry up and close, and intercept the germ of the wing; which, being shut up with the emotion, throbbing as with the pulsations of an artery, pricks the aperture which is nearest, until at length the entire soul is pierced and maddened and pained, and at the recollection of beauty is again delighted. And from both of them together the soul is oppressed at the strangeness of her condition, and is in a great strait and excitement, and in her madness can neither sleep by night nor abide in her place by day. And wherever she thinks that she will behold the beautiful one, thither in her desire she runs. And when she has seen him, and bathed herself in the waters of beauty, her constraint is loosened, and she is refreshed, and has no more pangs and pains; and this is the sweetest of all pleasures at the time, and is the reason why the soul of the lover will never forsake his beautiful one, whom he esteems above all; he has forgotten mother and brethren and companions, and he thinks nothing of the neglect and loss of his property; the rules and proprieties of life, on which he formerly prided himself, he now despises, and is ready to sleep like a servant, wherever he is allowed, as near as he can to his desired one, who is the object of his worship, and the physician who can alone assuage the greatness of his pain. And this state, my dear imaginary youth to whom I am talking, is by men called love, and among the gods has a name at which you, in your simplicity, may be inclined to mock; there are two lines in the apocryphal writings of Homer in which the name occurs. One of them is rather outrageous, and not altogether metrical. They are as follows:—

> "Mortals call him fluttering love,
> But the immortals call him winged one,
> Because the growing of wings[1] is a necessity
> to him."

You may believe this, but not unless you like. At any rate the loves of lovers and their causes are such as I have described.

Now the lover who is taken to be the attendant of Zeus is better able to bear the winged god, and can endure a heavier burden; but the attendants and companions of Ares, when under the influence of love, if they fancy that they have been at all wronged, are ready to kill and put an end to themselves and their beloved. And he who follows in the train of any other god, while he is unspoiled and the impression lasts, honours and imitates him, as far as he is able; and after the manner of his god he behaves in his intercourse with his beloved and with the rest of the world during the first period of his earthly existence. Every one chooses his love from the ranks of beauty according to his character, and this he makes his god, and fashions and adorns as a sort of

[1] Or, reading *πτερόφοιτον*, "the movement of wings."

image which he is to fall down and worship. The followers of Zeus desire that their beloved should have a soul like him; and therefore they seek out some one of a philosophical and imperial nature, and when they have found him and loved him, they do all they can to confirm such a nature in him, and if they have no experience of such a disposition hitherto, they learn of any one who can teach them, and themselves follow in the same way. And they have the less difficulty in finding the nature of their own god in themselves, because they have been compelled to gaze intensely on him; their recollection clings to him, and they become possessed of him, and receive from him their character and disposition, so far as man can participate in God. The qualities of their god they attribute to the beloved, wherefore they love him all the more, and if, like the Bacchic Nymphs, they draw inspiration from Zeus, they pour out their own fountain upon him, wanting to make him as like as possible to their own god. But those who are the followers of Here seek a royal love, and when they have found him they do just the same with him; and in like manner the followers of Apollo, and of every other god walking in the ways of their god, seek a love who is to be made like him whom they serve, and when they have found him, they themselves imitate their god, and persuade their love to do the same, and educate him into the manner and nature of the god as far as they each can; for no feelings of envy or jealousy are entertained by them towards their beloved, but they do their utmost to create in him the greatest likeness of themselves and of the god whom they honour. Thus fair and blissful to the beloved is the desire of the inspired lover, and the initiation of which I speak into the mysteries of true love, if he be captured by the lover and their purpose is effected. Now the beloved is taken captive in the following manner:—

As I said at the beginning of this tale, I divided each soul into three—two horses and a charioteer; and one of the horses was good and the other bad: the division may remain, but I have not yet explained in what the goodness or badness of either consists, and to that I will now proceed. The right-hand horse is upright and cleanly made; he has a lofty neck and an aquiline nose; his colour is white, and his eyes dark; he is a lover of honour and modesty and temperance, and the follower of true glory; he needs no touch of the whip, but is guided by word and admonition only. The other is a crooked lumbering animal, put together anyhow; he has a short thick neck; he is flat-faced and of a dark colour, with grey eyes and blood-red complexion;[1] the mate of insolence and pride, shag-eared and deaf, hardly yielding to whip and spur. Now when the charioteer beholds the vision of love, and has his whole soul warmed through sense, and is full of the prickings and ticklings of desire, the obedient steed, then as always under the government of shame, refrains from leaping on the beloved; but the other, heedless of the pricks and of the blows of the whip, plunges and runs away, giving all manner of trouble to his companion and the charioteer, whom he forces to approach the beloved and to remember the joys of love. They at first indignantly oppose him and will not be urged on to do terrible and unlawful deeds; but at last, when he persists in plaguing them, they yield and agree to do as he bids them. And now they are at the spot and behold the flashing beauty of the beloved; which when the charioteer sees, his memory is carried to the true beauty, whom he beholds in company with Modesty like an image placed upon a holy pedestal. He sees her, but he is afraid and falls backwards in adoration, and by his fall is compelled to pull back the reins with such violence as to bring both the steeds on their haunches, the one willing and unresisting, the unruly one very

[1] Or with grey and blood-shot eyes.

unwilling; and when they have gone back a little, the one is overcome with shame and wonder, and his whole soul is bathed in perspiration; the other, when the pain is over which the bridle and the fall had given him, having with difficulty taken breath, is full of wrath and reproaches, which he heaps upon the charioteer and his fellow-steed, for want of courage and manhood, declaring that they have been false to their agreement and guilty of desertion. Again they refuse, and again he urges them on, and will scarce yield to their prayer that he would wait until another time. When the appointed hour comes, they make as if they had forgotten, and he reminds them, fighting and neighing and dragging them on, until at length he on the same thoughts intent, forces them to draw near again. And when they are near he stoops his head and puts up his tail, and takes the bit in his teeth and pulls shamelessly. Then the charioteer is worse off than ever; he falls back like a racer at the barrier, and with a still more violent wrench drags the bit out of the teeth of the wild steed and covers his abusive tongue and jaws with blood, and forces his legs and haunches to the ground and punishes him sorely. And when this has happened several times and the villain has ceased from his wanton way, he is tamed and humbled, and follows the will of the charioteer, and when he sees the beautiful one he is ready to die of fear. And from that time forward the soul of the lover follows the beloved in modesty and holy fear.

And so the beloved who, like a god, has received every true and loyal service from his lover, not in pretence but in reality, being also himself of a nature friendly to his admirer,[1] if in former days he has blushed to own his passion and turned away his lover, because his youthful companions or others slanderously told him that he would be disgraced, now as years advance, at the appointed age and time, is led to receive him into communion. For fate which has ordained that there shall be no friendship among the evil has also ordained that there shall ever be friendship among the good. And the beloved when he has received him into communion and intimacy, is quite amazed at the good-will of the lover; he recognises that the inspired friend is worth all other friends or kinsmen; they have nothing of friendship in them worthy to be compared with his. And when this feeling continues and he is nearer to him and embraces him, in gymnastic exercises and at other times of meeting, then the fountain of that stream, which Zeus when he was in love with Ganymede named Desire, overflows upon the lover, and some enters into his soul, and some when he is filled flows out again; and as a breeze or an echo rebounds from the smooth rocks and returns whence it came, so does the stream of beauty, passing through the eyes which are the windows of the soul, come back to the beautiful one; there arriving and quickening the passages of the wings, watering them and inclining them to grow, and filling the soul of the beloved also with love. And thus he loves, but he knows not what; he does not understand and cannot explain his own state; he appears to have caught the infection of blindness from another; the lover is his mirror in whom he is beholding himself, but he is not aware of this. When he is with the lover, both cease from their pain, but when he is away then he longs as he is longed for, and has love's image, love for love (Anteros) lodging in his breast, which he calls and believes to be not love but friendship only, and his desire is as the desire of the other, but weaker; he wants to see him, touch him, kiss, embrace him, and probably not long afterwards his desire is accomplished. When they meet, the wanton steed of the lover has a word to say to the charioteer; he would like to have a little pleasure in return for many pains, but the wanton steed of the beloved says not a word, for he is bursting with passion which he

---

[1] Omitting *εἰς ταὐτὸν ἄγει τὴν φιλίαν.*

understands not;—he throws his arms round the lover and embraces him as his dearest friend; and, when they are side by side, he is not in a state in which he can refuse the lover anything, if he ask him; although his fellow-steed and the charioteer oppose him with the arguments of shame and reason. After this their happiness depends upon their self-control; if the better elements of the mind which lead to order and philosophy prevail, then they pass their life here in happiness and harmony—masters of themselves and orderly—enslaving the vicious and emancipating the virtuous elements of the soul; and when the end comes, they are light and winged for flight, having conquered in one of the three heavenly or truly Olympian victories; nor can human discipline or divine inspiration confer any greater blessing on man than this. If, on the other hand, they leave philosophy and lead the lower life of ambition, then probably, after wine or in some other careless hour, the two wanton animals take the two souls when off their guard and bring them together, and they accomplish that desire of their hearts which to the many is bliss; and this having once enjoyed they continue to enjoy, yet rarely because they have not the approval of the whole soul. They too are dear, but not so dear to one another as the others, either at the time of their love or afterwards. They consider that they have given and taken from each other the most sacred pledges, and they may not break them and fall into enmity. At last they pass out of the body, unwinged, but eager to soar, and thus obtain no mean reward of love and madness. For those who have once begun the heavenward pilgrimage may not go down again to darkness and the journey beneath the earth, but they live in light always; happy companions in their pilgrimage, and when the time comes at which they receive their wings they have the same plumage because of their love.

Thus great are the heavenly blessings which the friendship of a lover will confer upon you, my youth. Whereas the attachment of the non-lover, which is alloyed with a worldly prudence and has worldly and niggardly ways of doling out benefits, will breed in your soul those vulgar qualities which the populace applaud, will send you bowling round the earth during a period of nine thousand years, and leave you a fool in the world below.

And thus, dear Eros, I have made and paid my recantation, as well and as fairly as I could; more especially in the matter of the poetical figures which I was compelled to use, because Phaedrus would have them.[1] And now forgive the past and accept the present, and be gracious and merciful to me, and do not in thine anger deprive me of sight, or take from me the art of love which thou hast given me, but grant that I may be yet more esteemed in the eyes of the fair. And if Phaedrus or I myself said anything rude in our first speeches, blame Lysias, who is the father of the brat, and let us have no more of his progeny; bid him study philosophy, like his brother Polemarchus; and then his lover Phaedrus will no longer halt between two opinions, but will dedicate himself wholly to love and to philosophical discourses.

PHAEDRUS: I join in the prayer, Socrates, and say with you, if this be for my good, may your words come to pass. But why did you make your second oration so much finer than the first? I wonder why. And I begin to be afraid that I shall lose conceit of Lysias, and that he will appear tame in comparison, even if he be willing to put another as fine and as long as yours into the field, which I doubt. For quite lately one of your politicians was abusing him on this very account; and called him a "speech-writer" again and again. So that a feeling of pride may probably induce him to give up writing speeches.

SOCRATES: What a very amusing notion! But I think, my young man, that you are much

[1] See 234 C.

mistaken in your friend if you imagine that he is frightened at a little noise; and, possibly, you think that his assailant was in earnest?

PHAEDRUS: I thought, Socrates, that he was. And you are aware that the greatest and most influential statesmen are ashamed of writing speeches and leaving them in a written form, lest they should be called Sophists by posterity.

SOCRATES: You seem to be unconscious, Phaedrus, that the "sweet elbow"[1] of the proverb is really the long arm of the Nile. And you appear to be equally unaware of the fact that this sweet elbow of theirs is also a long arm. For there is nothing of which our great politicians are so fond as of writing speeches and bequeathing them to posterity. And they add their admirers' names at the top of the writing, out of gratitude to them.

PHAEDRUS: What do you mean? I do not understand.

SOCRATES: Why, do you not know that when a politician writes he begins with the names of his approvers?

PHAEDRUS: How so?

SOCRATES: Why, he begins in this manner: "Be it enacted by the senate, the people, or both, on the motion of a certain person," who is our author; and so putting on a serious face, he proceeds to display his own wisdom to his admirers in what is often a long and tedious composition. Now what is that sort of thing but a regular piece of authorship?

PHAEDRUS: True.

SOCRATES: And if the law is finally approved, then the author leaves the theatre in high delight; but if the law is rejected and he is done out of his speech-making, and not thought good enough to write, then he and his party are in mourning.

PHAEDRUS: Very true.

SOCRATES: So far are they from despising, or rather so highly do they value the practice of writing.

PHAEDRUS: No doubt.

SOCRATES: And when the king or orator has the power, as Lycurgus or Solon or Darius had, of attaining an immortality of authorship in a State, is he not thought by posterity, when they see his compositions, and does he not think himself while he is yet alive, to be a god?

PHAEDRUS: Very true.

SOCRATES: Then do you think that any one of this class, however ill-disposed, would reproach Lysias with being an author?

PHAEDRUS: Not upon your view; for according to you he would be casting a slur upon his own favourite pursuit.

SOCRATES: Any one may see that there is no disgrace in the mere fact of writing.

PHAEDRUS: Certainly not.

SOCRATES: The disgrace begins when a man writes not well, but badly.

PHAEDRUS: Clearly.

SOCRATES: And what is well and what is badly—need we ask Lysias, or any other poet or orator, who ever wrote or will write either a political or any other work, in metre or out of metre, poet, or prose writer, to teach us this?

PHAEDRUS: Need we? For what should a man live if not for the pleasures of discourse? Surely not for the sake of bodily pleasures, which almost always have previous pain as a condition of them, and therefore are rightly called slavish.

SOCRATES: There is time enough. And I believe that the grasshoppers chirruping after their manner in the heat of the sun over our heads are talking to one another and looking down at us. What would they say if they saw that we, like the many, are not conversing, but slumbering at mid-day, lulled by their voices, too indolent to think? Would they not have a right to laugh at us? They might imagine that we were slaves, who, coming to rest at a place of resort of theirs, like sheep lie asleep at noon

---

[1] A proverb, like "the grapes are sour," applied to pleasures which cannot be had, meaning sweet things which, like the elbow, are out of the reach of the mouth. The promised pleasure turns out to be a long and tedious affair.

around the well. But if they see us discoursing, and like Odysseus sailing past them, deaf to their siren voices, they may perhaps, out of respect, give us of the gifts which they receive from the gods that they may impart them to men.

PHAEDRUS: What gifts do you mean? I never heard of any.

SOCRATES: A lover of music like yourself ought surely to have heard the story of the grass-hoppers, who are said to have been human beings in an age before the Muses. And when the Muses came and song appeared they were ravished with delight; and singing always, never thought of eating and drinking, until at last in their forgetfulness they died. And now they live again in the grasshoppers; and this is the return which the Muses make to them—they neither hunger, nor thirst, but from the hour of their birth are always singing, and never eating or drinking; and when they die they go and inform the Muses in heaven who honours them on earth. They win the love of Terpsichore for the dancers by their report of them; of Erato for the lovers, and of the other Muses for those who do them honour, according to the several ways of honouring them;—of Calliope the eldest Muse and of Urania who is next to her, for the philosophers, of whose music the grasshoppers make report to them; for these are the Muses who are chiefly concerned with heaven and thought, divine as well as human, and they have the sweetest utterance. For many reasons, then, we ought always to talk and not to sleep at mid-day.

PHAEDRUS: Let us talk.

SOCRATES: Shall we discuss the rules of writing and speech as we were proposing?

PHAEDRUS: Very good.

SOCRATES: In good speaking should not the mind of the speaker know the truth of the matter about which he is going to speak?

PHAEDRUS: And yet, Socrates, I have heard that he who would be an orator has nothing to do with true justice, but only with that which is likely to be approved by the many who sit in judgment; nor with the truly good or honourable, but only with opinion about them, and that from opinion comes persuasion, and not from the truth.

SOCRATES: The words of the wise are not to be set aside; for there is probably something in them; and therefore the meaning of this saying is not hastily to be dismissed.

PHAEDRUS: Very true.

SOCRATES: Let us put the matter thus:—Suppose that I persuaded you to buy a horse and go to the wars. Neither of us knew what a horse was like, but I knew that you believed a horse to be of tame animals the one which has the longest ears.

PHAEDRUS: That would be ridiculous.

SOCRATES: There is something more ridiculous coming:—Suppose, further, that in sober earnest I, having persuaded you of this, went and composed a speech in honour of an ass, whom I entitled a horse, beginning: "A noble animal and a most useful possession, especially in war, and you may get on his back and fight, and he will carry baggage or anything."

PHAEDRUS: How ridiculous!

SOCRATES: Ridiculous! Yes; but is not even a ridiculous friend better than a cunning enemy?

PHAEDRUS: Certainly.

SOCRATES: And when the orator instead of putting an ass in the place of a horse, puts good for evil, being himself as ignorant of their true nature as the city on which he imposes is ignorant; and having studied the notions of the multitude, falsely persuades them not about "the shadow of an ass," which he confounds with a horse, but about good which he confounds with evil,—what will be the harvest which rhetoric will be likely to gather after the sowing of that seed?

PHAEDRUS: The reverse of good.

SOCRATES: But perhaps rhetoric has been getting too roughly handled by us, and she might answer: What amazing nonsense you are talking! As if I forced any man to learn to speak in ignorance of the truth! Whatever my advice may be worth, I should have told him to arrive at the truth first, and then come to me. At the same time I boldly assert that mere knowledge of the truth will not give you the art of persuasion.

PHAEDRUS: There is reason in the lady's defence of herself.

SOCRATES: Quite true; if only the other arguments which remain to be brought up bear her witness that she is an art at all. But I seem to hear them arraying themselves on the opposite side, declaring that she speaks falsely, and that rhetoric is a mere routine and trick, not an art. Lo! a Spartan appears, and says that there never is nor ever will be a real art of speaking which is divorced from the truth.

PHAEDRUS: And what are these arguments, Socrates? Bring them out that we may examine them.

SOCRATES: Come out, fair children, and convince Phaedrus, who is the father of similar beauties, that he will never be able to speak about anything as he ought to speak unless he have a knowledge of philosophy. And let Phaedrus answer you.

PHAEDRUS: Put the question.

SOCRATES: Is not rhetoric, taken generally, a universal art of enchanting the mind by arguments; which is practised not only in courts and public assemblies, but in private houses also, having to do with all matters, great as well as small, good and bad alike, and is in all equally right, and equally to be esteemed—that is what you have heard?

PHAEDRUS: Nay, not exactly that; I should say rather that I have heard the art confined to speaking and writing in lawsuits, and to speaking in public assemblies—not extended farther.

SOCRATES: Then I suppose that you have only heard of the rhetoric of Nestor and Odysseus, which they composed in their leisure hours when at Troy, and never of the rhetoric of Palamedes?

PHAEDRUS: No more than of Nestor and Odysseus, unless Gorgias is your Nestor, and Thrasymachus or Theodorus your Odysseus.

SOCRATES: Perhaps that is my meaning. But let us leave them. And do you tell me, instead, what are plaintiff and defendant doing in a law-court—are they not contending?

PHAEDRUS: Exactly so.

SOCRATES: About the just and unjust—that is the matter in dispute?

PHAEDRUS: Yes.

SOCRATES: And a professor of the art will make the same thing appear to the same persons to be at one time just, at another time, if he is so inclined, to be unjust?

PHAEDRUS: Exactly.

SOCRATES: And when he speaks in the assembly, he will make the same things seem good to the city at one time, and at another time the reverse of good?

PHAEDRUS: That is true.

SOCRATES: Have we not heard of the Eleatic Palamedes (Zeno) who has an art of speaking by which he makes the same things appear to his hearers like and unlike, one and many, at rest and in motion?

PHAEDRUS: Very true.

SOCRATES: The art of disputation, then, is not confined to the courts and the assembly, but is one and the same in every use of language; this is the art, if there be such an art, which is able to find a likeness of everything to which a likeness can be found, and draws into the light of day the likenesses and disguises which are used by others?

PHAEDRUS: How do you mean?

SOCRATES: Let me put the matter thus: When will there be more chance of deception—when the difference is large or small?

PHAEDRUS: When the difference is small.

SOCRATES: And you will be less likely to be discovered in passing by degrees into the other extreme than when you go all at once?

PHAEDRUS: Of course.

SOCRATES: He, then, who would deceive others, and not be deceived, must exactly know the real likenesses and differences of things?

PHAEDRUS: He must.

SOCRATES: And if he is ignorant of the true nature of any subject, how can he detect the greater or less degree of likeness in other things to that of which by the hypothesis he is ignorant?

PHAEDRUS: He cannot.

SOCRATES: And when men are deceived and their notions are at variance with realities, it is clear that the error slips in through resemblances?

PHAEDRUS: Yes, that is the way.

SOCRATES: Then he who would be a master of the art must understand the real nature of everything; or he will never know either how to make the gradual departure from truth into the opposite of truth which is effected by the help of resemblances, or how to avoid it?

PHAEDRUS: He will not.

SOCRATES: He then, who being ignorant of the truth aims at appearances, will only attain an art of rhetoric which is ridiculous and is not an art at all?

PHAEDRUS: That may be expected.

SOCRATES: Shall I propose that we look for examples of art and want of art, according to our notion of them, in the speech of Lysias which you have in your hand, and in my own speech?

PHAEDRUS: Nothing could be better; and indeed I think that our previous argument has been too abstract and wanting in illustrations.

SOCRATES: Yes; and the two speeches happen to afford a very good example of the way in which the speaker who knows the truth may, without any serious purpose, steal away the hearts of his hearers. This piece of good-fortune I attribute to the local deities; and, perhaps, the prophets of the Muses who are singing over our heads may have imparted their inspiration to me. For I do not imagine that I have any rhetorical art of my own.

PHAEDRUS: Granted; if you will only please to get on.

SOCRATES: Suppose that you read me the first words of Lysias' speech.

PHAEDRUS: "You know how matters stand with me, and how, as I conceive, they might be arranged for our common interest; and I maintain that I ought not to fail in my suit, because I am not your lover. For lovers repent—"

SOCRATES: Enough:—Now, shall I point out the rhetorical error of those words?

PHAEDRUS: Yes.

SOCRATES: Every one is aware that about some things we are agreed, whereas about other things we differ.

PHAEDRUS: I think that I understand you; but will you explain yourself?

SOCRATES: When any one speaks of iron and silver, is not the same thing present in the minds of all?

PHAEDRUS: Certainly.

SOCRATES: But when any one speaks of justice and goodness we part company and are at odds with one another and with ourselves?

PHAEDRUS: Precisely.

SOCRATES: Then in some things we agree, but not in others?

PHAEDRUS: That is true.

SOCRATES: In which are we more likely to be deceived, and in which has rhetoric the greater power?

PHAEDRUS: Clearly, in the uncertain class.

SOCRATES: Then the rhetorician ought to make a regular division, and acquire a distinct notion of both classes, as well of that in which the many err, as of that in which they do not err?

PHAEDRUS: He who made such a distinction would have an excellent principle.

SOCRATES: Yes; and in the next place he must have a keen eye for the observation of particulars in speaking, and not make a mistake about the class to which they are to be referred.

PHAEDRUS: Certainly.

SOCRATES: Now to which class does love belong—to the debatable or to the undisputed class?

PHAEDRUS: To the debatable, clearly; for if not, do you think that love would have allowed you to say as you did, that he is an evil both to the lover and the beloved, and also the greatest possible good?

SOCRATES: Capital. But will you tell me whether I defined love at the beginning of my speech? for, having been in an ecstasy, I cannot well remember.

PHAEDRUS: Yes, indeed; that you did, and no mistake.

SOCRATES: Then I perceive that the Nymphs of Achelous and Pan the son of Hermes, who inspired me, were far better rhetoricians than Lysias the son of Cephalus. Alas! how inferior to them he is! But perhaps I am mistaken; and Lysias at the commencement of his lover's speech did insist on our supposing love to be something or other which he fancied him to be, and according to this model he fashioned and framed the remainder of his discourse. Suppose we read his beginning over again:

PHAEDRUS: If you please; but you will not find what you want.

SOCRATES: Read, that I may have his exact words.

PHAEDRUS: "You know how matters stand with me, and how, as I conceive, they might be arranged for our common interest; and I maintain I ought not to fail in my suit because I am not your lover, for lovers repent of the kindnesses which they have shown, when their love is over."

SOCRATES: Here he appears to have done just the reverse of what he ought; for he has begun at the end, and is swimming on his back through the flood to the place of starting. His address to the fair youth begins where the lover would have ended. Am I not right, sweet Phaedrus?

PHAEDRUS: Yes, indeed, Socrates; he does begin at the end.

SOCRATES: Then as to the other topics—are they not thrown down anyhow? Is there any principle in them? Why should the next topic follow next in order, or any other topic? I cannot help fancying in my ignorance that he wrote off boldly just what came into his head, but I dare say that you would recognize a rhetorical necessity in the succession of the several parts of the composition?

PHAEDRUS: You have too good an opinion of me if you think that I have any such insight into his principles of composition.

SOCRATES: At any rate, you will allow that every discourse ought to be a living creature, having a body of its own and a head and feet; there should be a middle, beginning, and end, adapted to one another and to the whole?

PHAEDRUS: Certainly.

SOCRATES: Can this be said of the discourse of Lysias? See whether you can find any more connexion in his words than in the epitaph which is said by some to have been inscribed on the grave of Midas the Phrygian.

PHAEDRUS: What is there remarkable in the epitaph?

SOCRATES: It is as follows:—

> "I am a maiden of bronze and lie on the tomb of Midas;
> So long as water flows and tall trees grow,
> So long here on this spot by his sad tomb abiding,
> I shall declare to passers-by that Midas sleeps below."

Now in this rhyme whether a line comes first or comes last, as you will perceive, makes no difference.

PHAEDRUS: You are making fun of that oration of ours.

SOCRATES: Well, I will say no more about your friend's speech lest I should give offence to you; although I think that it might furnish many other examples of what a man ought rather to avoid. But I will proceed to the other speech, which, as I think, is also suggestive to students of rhetoric.

PHAEDRUS: In what way?

SOCRATES: The two speeches, as you may remember, were unlike; the one argued that the lover and the other that the non-lover ought to be accepted.

PHAEDRUS: And right manfully.

SOCRATES: You would rather say "madly"; and madness was the argument of them, for, as I said, "love is a madness."

PHAEDRUS: Yes.

SOCRATES: And of madness there were two kinds; one produced by human infirmity, the other was a divine release of the soul from the yoke of custom and convention.

PHAEDRUS: True.

SOCRATES: The divine madness was subdivided into four kinds, prophetic, initiatory, poetic, erotic, having four gods presiding over them; the first was the inspiration of Apollo, the second that of Dionysus, the third that of the Muses, the fourth that of Aphrodite and Eros. In the description of the last kind of madness, which was also said to be the best, we spoke of the affection of love in a figure, into which we introduced a tolerably credible and possibly true though partly erring myth, which was also a hymn in honour of Love, who is your lord and also mine, Phaedrus, and the guardian of fair children, and to him we sung the hymn in measured and solemn strain.

PHAEDRUS: I know that I had great pleasure in listening to you.

SOCRATES: Let us take this instance and note how the transition was made from blame to praise.

PHAEDRUS: What do you mean?

SOCRATES: I mean to say that the composition was mostly playful. Yet in these chance fancies of the hour were involved two principles of which we should be too glad to have a clearer description if art could give us one.

PHAEDRUS: What are they?

SOCRATES: First, the comprehension of scattered particulars in one idea; as in our definition of love, which whether true or false certainly gave clearness and consistency to the discourse, the speaker should define his several notions and so make his meaning clear.

PHAEDRUS: What is the other principle, Socrates?

SOCRATES: The second principle is that of division into species according to the natural formation, where the joint is, not breaking any part as a bad carver might. Just as our two discourses, alike assumed, first of all, a single form of unreason; and then, as the body which from being one becomes double and may be divided into a left side and a right side, each having parts right and left of the same name—after this manner the speaker proceeded to divide the parts of the left side and did not desist until he found in them an evil or left-handed love which he justly reviled; and the other discourse leading us to the madness which lay on the right side, found another love, also having the same name, but divine, which the speaker held up before us and applauded and affirmed to be the author of the greatest benefits.

PHAEDRUS: Most true.

SOCRATES: I am myself a great lover of these processes of division and generalization; they help me to speak and to think. And if I find any man who is able to see "a One and Many" in nature, him I follow, and "walk in his footsteps as if he were a god." And those who have this art, I have hitherto been in the habit of calling dialecticians; but God knows whether the name is right or not. And I should like to know what name you would give to your or to Lysias' disciples, and whether this may not be that famous art of rhetoric which Thrasymachus and others teach and practise? Skilful speakers they are, and impart their skill to any who is willing to make kings of them and to bring gifts to them.

PHAEDRUS: Yes, they are royal men; but their art is not the same with the art of those whom you call, and rightly, in my opinion, dialecticians:—Still we are in the dark about rhetoric.

SOCRATES: What do you mean? The remains of it, if there be anything remaining which can be brought under rules of art, must be a fine thing; and, at any rate, is not to be despised by you and me. But how much is left?

PHAEDRUS: There is a great deal surely to be found in books of rhetoric?

SOCRATES: Yes; thank you for reminding me:—There is the exordium, showing how the speech should begin, if I remember rightly; that is what you mean—the niceties of the art?

PHAEDRUS: Yes.

SOCRATES: Then follows the statement of facts, and upon that witnesses; thirdly, proofs; fourthly, probabilities are to come; the great Byzantian word-maker also speaks, if I am not mistaken, of confirmation and further confirmation.

PHAEDRUS: You mean the excellent Theodorus.

SOCRATES: Yes; and he tells how refutation or further refutation is to be managed, whether in accusation or defence. I ought also to mention the illustrious Parian, Evenus, who first invented insinuations and indirect praises; and also indirect censures, which according to some he put into verse to help the memory. But shall I "to dumb forgetfulness consign" Tisias and Gorgias, who are not ignorant that probability is superior to truth, and who by force of argument make the little appear great and the great little, disguise the new in old fashions and the old in new fashions, and have discovered forms for everything, either short or going on to infinity? I remember Prodicus laughing when I told him of this; he said that he had himself discovered the true rule of art, which was to be neither long nor short, but of a convenient length.

PHAEDRUS: Well done, Prodicus!

SOCRATES: Then there is Hippias the Elean stranger, who probably agrees with him.

PHAEDRUS: Yes.

SOCRATES: And there is also Polus, who has treasuries of diplasiology, and gnomology, and eikonology, and who teaches in them the names of which Licymnius made him a present; they were to give a polish.

PHAEDRUS: Had not Protagoras something of the same sort?

SOCRATES: Yes, rules of correct diction and many other fine precepts; for the "sorrows of a poor old man," or any other pathetic case, no one is better than the Chalcedonian giant; he can put a whole company of people into a passion and out of one again by his mighty magic, and is first-rate at inventing or disposing of any sort of calumny on any grounds or none. All of them agree in asserting that a speech should end in a recapitulation, though they do not all agree to use the same word.

PHAEDRUS: You mean that there should be a summing up of the arguments in order to remind the hearers of them.

SOCRATES: I have now said all that I have to say of the art of rhetoric: have you anything to add?

PHAEDRUS: Not much; nothing very important.

SOCRATES: Leave the unimportant and let us bring the really important question into the light of day, which is: What power has this art of rhetoric, and when?

PHAEDRUS: A very great power in public meetings.

SOCRATES: It has. But I should like to know whether you have the same feeling as I have about the rhetoricians? To me there seem to be a great many holes in their web.

PHAEDRUS: Give an example.

SOCRATES: I will. Suppose a person to come to your friend Eryximachus, or to his father Acumenus, and to say to him: "I know how to apply drugs which shall have either a heating or a cooling effect, and I can give a vomit and also a purge, and all that sort of thing; and knowing all this, as I do, I claim to be a physician and to make physicians by imparting this knowledge to others,"—what do you suppose that they would say?

PHAEDRUS: They would be sure to ask him whether he knew "to whom" he would give his medicines, and "when," and "how much."

SOCRATES: And suppose that he were to reply: "No; I know nothing of all that; I expect the patient who consults me to be able to do these things for himself"?

PHAEDRUS: They would say in reply that he is a madman or a pedant who fancies that he is a physician because he has read something in a book, or has stumbled on a prescription or two, although he has no real understanding of the art of medicine.

SOCRATES: And suppose a person were to come to Sophocles or Euripides and say that he knows how to make a very long speech about a small matter, and a short speech about a great matter, and also a sorrowful speech, or a terrible, or threatening speech, of any other kind of speech, and in teaching this fancies that he is teaching the art of tragedy—?

PHAEDRUS: They too would surely laugh at him if he fancies that tragedy is anything but the arranging of these elements in a manner which will be suitable to one another and to the whole.

SOCRATES: But I do not suppose that they would be rude or abusive to him: Would they not treat him as a musician would a man who thinks that he is a harmonist because he knows how to pitch the highest and lowest note? Happening to meet such an one he would not say to him savagely, "Fool, you are mad!" But like a musician, in a gentle and harmonious tone of voice, he would answer: "My good friend, he who would be a harmonist must certainly know this, and yet he may understand nothing of harmony if he has not got beyond your stage of knowledge, for you only know the preliminaries of harmony and not harmony itself."

PHAEDRUS: Very true.

SOCRATES: And will not Sophocles say to the display of the would-be tragedian, that this is not tragedy but the preliminaries of tragedy? and will not Acumenus say the same of medicine to the would-be physician?

PHAEDRUS: Quite true.

SOCRATES: And if Adrastus the mellifluous or Pericles heard of these wonderful arts, brachylogies and eikonologies and all the hard names which we have been endeavouring to draw into the light of day, what would they say? Instead of losing temper and applying uncomplimentary epithets, as you and I have been doing, to the authors of such an imaginary art, their superior wisdom would rather censure us, as well as them. "Have a little patience, Phaedrus and Socrates," they would say; "you should not be in such a passion with those who from some want of dialectical skill are unable to define the nature of rhetoric, and consequently suppose that they have found the art in the preliminary conditions of it, and when these have been taught by them to others, fancy that the whole art of rhetoric has been taught by them; but as to using the several instruments of the art effectively, or making the composition a whole,—an application of it such as this is they regard as an easy thing which their disciples may make for themselves."

PHAEDRUS: I quite admit, Socrates, that the art of rhetoric which these men teach and of which they write is such as you describe—there I agree with you. But I still want to know where and how the true art of rhetoric and persuasion is to be acquired.

SOCRATES: The perfection which is required of the finished orator is, or rather must be, like the perfection of anything else, partly given by nature, but may also be assisted by art. If you have the natural power and add to it knowledge and practice, you will be a distinguished speaker; if you fall short in either of these, you will be to that extent defective. But the art, as far as there is an art, of rhetoric does not lie in the direction of Lysias or Thrasymachus.

PHAEDRUS: In what direction then?

SOCRATES: I conceive Pericles to have been the most accomplished of rhetoricians.

PHAEDRUS: What of that?

SOCRATES: All the great arts require discussion and high speculation about the truths of nature; hence come loftiness of thought and completeness of execution. And this, as I conceive, was the quality which, in addition to his natural gifts, Pericles acquired from his intercourse with Anaxagoras whom he happened to know. He was thus imbued with the higher philosophy, and attained the knowledge of Mind and the negative of Mind, which were favourite themes of Anaxagoras, and applied what suited his purpose to the art of speaking.

PHAEDRUS: Explain.

SOCRATES: Rhetoric is like medicine.

PHAEDRUS: How so?

SOCRATES: Why, because medicine has to define the nature of the body and rhetoric of the soul—if we would proceed, not empirically but scientifically, in the one case to impart health and strength by giving medicine and food, in the other to implant the conviction or virtue which you desire, by the right application of words and training.

PHAEDRUS: There, Socrates, I suspect that you are right.

SOCRATES: And do you think that you can know the nature of the soul intelligently without knowing the nature of the whole?

PHAEDRUS: Hippocrates the Asclepiad says that the nature even of the body can only be understood as a whole.[1]

SOCRATES: Yes, friend, and he was right:—still, we ought not to be content with the name of Hippocrates, but to examine and see whether his argument agrees with his conception of nature.

PHAEDRUS: I agree.

SOCRATES: Then consider what truth as well as Hippocrates says about this or about any other nature. Ought we not to consider first whether that which we wish to learn and to teach is a simple or multiform thing, and if simple, then to enquire what power it has of acting or being acted upon in relation to other things, and if multiform, then to number the forms; and see first in the case of one of them, and then in the case of all of them, what is that power of acting or being acted upon which makes each and all of them to be what they are?

PHAEDRUS: You may very likely be right, Socrates.

SOCRATES: The method which proceeds without analysis is like the groping of a blind man. Yet, surely, he who is an artist ought not to admit of a comparison with the blind, or deaf. The rhetorician, who teaches his pupil to speak scientifically, will particularly set forth the nature of that being to which he addresses his speeches; and this, I conceive, to be the soul.

PHAEDRUS: Certainly.

SOCRATES: His whole effort is directed to the soul; for in that he seeks to produce conviction.

PHAEDRUS: Yes.

SOCRATES: Then clearly, Thrasymachus or any one else who teaches rhetoric in earnest will give an exact description of the nature of the soul; which will enable us to see whether she be single and same, or, like the body, multiform. That is what we should call showing the nature of the soul.

PHAEDRUS: Exactly.

SOCRATES: He will explain, secondly, the mode in which she acts or is acted upon.

PHAEDRUS: True.

SOCRATES: Thirdly, having classified men and speeches, and their kinds and affections, and adapted them to one another, he will tell the reasons of his arrangement, and show why one soul is persuaded by a particular form of argument, and another not.

PHAEDRUS: You have hit upon a very good way.

SOCRATES: Yes, that is the true and only way in which any subject can be set forth or treated by rules of art, whether in speaking or writing. But the writers of the present day, at whose feet you have sat, craftily conceal the nature of the soul which they know quite well. Nor, until they adopt our method of reading and writing, can we admit that they write by rules of art?

PHAEDRUS: What is our method?

SOCRATES: I cannot give you the exact details; but I should like to tell you generally, as far as is in my power, how a man ought to proceed according to rules of art.

[1] Cp. Charmides, 156 C.

PHAEDRUS: Let me hear.

SOCRATES: Oratory is the art of enchanting the soul, and therefore he who would be an orator has to learn the differences of human souls—they are so many and of such a nature, and from them come the differences between man and man. Having proceeded thus far in his analysis, he will next divide speeches into their different classes:—"Such and such persons," he will say, "are affected by this or that kind of speech in this or that way," and he will tell you why. The pupil must have a good theoretical notion of them first, and then he must have experience of them in actual life, and be able to follow them with all his senses about him, or he will never get beyond the precepts of his masters. But when he understands what persons are persuaded by what arguments, and sees the person about whom he was speaking in the abstract actually before him, and knows that it is he, and can say to himself, "This is the man or this is the character who ought to have a certain argument applied to him in order to convince him of a certain opinion";—he who knows all this, and knows also when he should speak and when he should refrain, and when he should use pithy sayings, pathetic appeals, sensational effects, and all the other modes of speech which he has learned;—when, I say, he knows the times and seasons of all these things, then, and not till then, he is a perfect master of his art; but if he fail in any of these points, whether in speaking or teaching or writing them, and yet declares that he speaks by rules of art, he who says "I don't believe you" has the better of him. Well, the teacher will say, is this, Phaedrus and Socrates, your account of the so-called art of rhetoric, or am I to look for another?

PHAEDRUS: He must take this, Socrates, for there is no possibility of another, and yet the creation of such an art is not easy.

SOCRATES: Very true; and therefore let us consider this matter in every light, and see whether we cannot find a shorter and easier road; there is no use in taking a long rough roundabout way if there be a shorter and easier one. And I wish that you would try and remember whether you have heard from Lysias or any one else anything which might be of service to us.

PHAEDRUS: If trying would avail, then I might; but at the moment, I can think of nothing.

SOCRATES: Suppose I tell you something which somebody who knows told me.

PHAEDRUS: Certainly.

SOCRATES: May not "the wolf," as the proverb says, "claim a hearing"?

PHAEDRUS: Do you say what can be said for him.

SOCRATES: He will argue that there is no use in putting a solemn face on these matters, or in going round and round, until you arrive at first principles; for, as I said at first, when the question is of justice and good, or is a question in which men are concerned who are just and good, either by nature or habit, he who would be a skilful rhetorician has no need of truth—for that in courts of law men literally care nothing about truth, but only about conviction: and this is based on probability, to which he who would be a skilful orator should therefore give his whole attention. And they say also that there are cases in which the actual facts, if they are improbable, ought to be withheld, and only the probabilities should be told either in accusation or defence, and that always in speaking, the orator should keep probability in view, and say good-bye to the truth. And the observance of this principle throughout a speech furnishes the whole art.

PHAEDRUS: That is what the professors of rhetoric do actually say, Socrates. I have not forgotten that we have quite briefly touched upon this matter[1] already; with them the point is all-important.

---

[1] Cp. 259 E.

SOCRATES: I dare say that you are familiar with Tisias. Does he not define probability to be that which the many think?

PHAEDRUS: Certainly, he does.

SOCRATES: I believe that he has a clever and ingenious case of this sort:—He supposes a feeble and valiant man to have assaulted a strong and cowardly one, and to have robbed him of his coat or of something or other; he is brought into court, and then Tisias says that both parties should tell lies: the coward should say that he was assaulted by more men than one; the other should prove that they were alone, and should argue thus: "How could a weak man like me have assaulted a strong man like him?" The complainant will not like to confess his own cowardice, and will therefore invent some other lie which his adversary will thus gain an opportunity of refuting. And there are other devices of the same kind which have a place in the system. Am I not right, Phaedrus?

PHAEDRUS: Certainly.

SOCRATES: Bless me, what a wonderfully mysterious art is this which Tisias or some other gentleman, in whatever name or country he rejoices, has discovered. Shall we say a word to him or not?

PHAEDRUS: What shall we say to him?

SOCRATES: Let us tell him that, before he appeared, you and I were saying that the probability of which he speaks was engendered in the minds of the many by the likeness of the truth, and we had just been affirming that he who knew the truth would always know best how to discover the resemblances of the truth. If he has anything else to say about the art of speaking we should like to hear him; but if not, we are satisfied with our own view, that unless a man estimates the various characters of his hearers and is able to divide all things into classes and to comprehend them under single ideas, he will never be a skilful rhetorician even within the limits of human power. And this skill he will not attain without a great deal of trouble, which a good man ought to undergo, not for the sake of speaking and acting before men, but in order that he may be able to say what is acceptable to God and always to act acceptably to Him as far as in him lies; for there is a saying of wiser men than ourselves, that a man of sense should not try to please his fellow-servants (at least this should not be his first object) but his good and noble masters; and therefore if the way is long and circuitous, marvel not at this, for, where the end is great, there we may take the longer road, but not for lesser ends such as yours. Truly, the argument may say, Tisias, that if you do not mind going so far, rhetoric has a fair beginning here.

PHAEDRUS: I think, Socrates, that this is admirable, if only practicable.

SOCRATES: But even to fail in an honourable object is honourable.

PHAEDRUS: True.

SOCRATES: Enough appears to have been said by us of a true and false art of speaking.

PHAEDRUS: Certainly.

SOCRATES: But there is something yet to be said of propriety and impropriety of writing.

PHAEDRUS: Yes.

SOCRATES: Do you know how you can speak or act about rhetoric in a manner which will be acceptable to God?

PHAEDRUS: No, indeed. Do you?

SOCRATES: I have heard a tradition of the ancients, whether true or not they only know; although if we had found the truth ourselves, do you think that we should care much about the opinions of men?

PHAEDRUS: Your question needs no answer; but I wish that you would tell me what you say that you have heard.

SOCRATES: At the Egyptian city of Naucratis, there was a famous old god, whose name was Theuth; the bird which is called the Ibis is sacred to him, and he was the inventor of many arts, such as arithmetic and calculation and geometry and astronomy and draughts and dice, but his great discovery was the use of letters. Now in those days the god Thamus was the king of the whole country of Egypt; and he dwelt in that great city of Upper Egypt which the Hellenes call Egyptian Thebes, and the god himself is called by them Ammon. To him came Theuth and showed his inventions, desiring that the other Egyptians might be allowed to have the benefit of them; he enumerated them, and Thamus enquired about their several uses, and praised some of them and censured others, as he approved or disapproved of them. It would take a long time to repeat all that Thamus said to Theuth in praise or blame of the various arts. But when they came to letters, This, said Theuth, will make the Egyptians wiser and give them better memories; it is a specific both for the memory and for the wit. Thamus replied: O most ingenious Theuth, the parent or inventor of an art is not always the best judge of the utility or inutility of his own inventions to the users of them. And in this instance, you who are the father of letters, from a paternal love of your own children have been led to attribute to them a quality which they cannot have; for this discovery of yours will create forgetfulness in the learners' souls, because they will not use their memories; they will trust to the external written characters and not remember of themselves. The specific which you have discovered is an aid not to memory, but to reminiscence, and you give your disciples not truth, but only the semblance of truth; they will be hearers of many things and will have learned nothing; they will appear to be omniscient and will generally know nothing; they will be tiresome company, having the show of wisdom without the reality.

PHAEDRUS: Yes, Socrates, you can easily invent tales of Egypt, or of any other country.

SOCRATES: There was a tradition in the temple of Dodona that oaks first gave prophetic utterances. The men of old, unlike in their simplicity to young philosophy, deemed that if they heard the truth even from "oak or rock," it was enough for them; whereas you seem to consider not whether a thing is or is not true, but who the speaker is and from what country the tale comes.

PHAEDRUS: I acknowledge the justice of your rebuke; and I think that the Theban is right in his view about letters.

SOCRATES: He would be a very simple person, and quite a stranger to the oracles of Thamus or Ammon, who should leave in writing or receive in writing any art under the idea that the written word would be intelligible or certain; or who deemed that writing was at all better than knowledge and recollection of the same matters?

PHAEDRUS: That is most true.

SOCRATES: I cannot help feeling, Phaedrus, that writing is unfortunately like painting; for the creations of the painter have the attitude of life, and yet if you ask them a question they preserve a solemn silence. And the same may be said of speeches. You would imagine that they had intelligence, but if you want to know anything and put a question to one of them, the speaker always gives one unvarying answer. And when they have been once written down they are tumbled about anywhere among those who may or may not understand them, and know not to whom they should reply, to whom not; and, if they are maltreated or abused, they have no parent to protect them; and they cannot protect or defend themselves.

PHAEDRUS: That again is most true.

SOCRATES: Is there not another kind of word or speech far better than this, and having far greater power—a son of the same family, but lawfully begotten?

PHAEDRUS: Whom do you mean, and what is his origin?

SOCRATES: I mean an intelligent word graven in the soul of the learner, which can defend itself, and knows when to speak and when to be silent.

PHAEDRUS: You mean the living word of knowledge which has a soul, and of which the written word is properly no more than an image?

SOCRATES: Yes, of course that is what I mean. And now may I be allowed to ask you a question: Would a husbandman, who is a man of sense, take the seeds, which he values and which he wishes to bear fruit, and in sober seriousness plant them during the heat of summer, in some garden of Adonis, that he may rejoice when he sees them in eight days appearing in beauty? At least he would do so, if at all, only for the sake of amusement and pastime. But when he is in earnest he sows in fitting soil, and practises husbandry, and is satisfied if in eight months the seeds which he has sown arrive at perfection?

PHAEDRUS: Yes, Socrates, that will be his way when he is in earnest; he will do the other, as you say, only in play.

SOCRATES: And can we suppose that he who knows the just and good and honourable has less understanding, than the husbandman, about his own seeds?

PHAEDRUS: Certainly not.

SOCRATES: Then he will not seriously incline to "write" his thoughts "in water" with pen and ink, sowing words which can neither speak for themselves nor teach the truth adequately to others?

PHAEDRUS: No, that is not likely.

SOCRATES: No, that is not likely—in the garden of letters he will sow and plant, but only for the sake of recreation and amusement; he will write them down as memorials to be treasured against the forgetfulness of old age, by himself, or by any other old man who is treading the same path. He will rejoice in beholding the tender growth; and while others are refreshing their souls with banqueting and the like, this will be the pastime in which his days are spent.

PHAEDRUS: A pastime, Socrates, as noble as the other is ignoble, the pastime of a man who can be amused by serious talk, and can discourse merrily about justice and the like.

SOCRATES: True, Phaedrus. But nobler far is the serious pursuit of the dialectician, who, finding a congenial soul, by the help of science sows and plants therein words which are able to help themselves and him who planted them, and are not unfruitful, but have in them a seed which others brought up in different soils render immortal, making the possessors of it happy to the utmost extent of human happiness.

PHAEDRUS: Far nobler, certainly.

SOCRATES: And now, Phaedrus, having agreed upon the premises we may decide about the conclusion.

PHAEDRUS: About what conclusion?

SOCRATES: About Lysias, whom we censured, and his art of writing, and his discourses, and the rhetorical skill or want of skill which was shown in them—these are the questions which we sought to determine, and they brought us to this point. And I think that we are now pretty well informed about the nature of art and its opposite.

PHAEDRUS: Yes, I think with you; but I wish that you would repeat what was said.

SOCRATES: Until a man knows the truth of the several particulars of which he is writing or speaking, and is able to define them as they are, and having defined them again to divide them until they can be no longer divided, and until in like manner he is able to discern the nature of the soul, and discover the different modes of discourse which are adapted to different natures, and to arrange and dispose them in such a way that the simple form of speech may be addressed to the simpler nature, and the complex and composite to the more complex nature—until he has accomplished all this, he will be unable to handle arguments according to rules of art, as far as their nature allows them to be subjected to art, either for the purpose of teaching or persuading;—such is the view which is implied in the whole preceding argument.

PHAEDRUS: Yes, that was our view, certainly.

SOCRATES: Secondly, as to the censure which was passed on the speaking or writing of discourses, and how they might be rightly or wrongly censured—did not our previous argument show—?

PHAEDRUS: Show what?

SOCRATES: That whether Lysias or any other writer that ever was or will be, whether private man or statesman, proposes laws and so becomes the author of a political treatise, fancying that there is any greater certainty and clearness in his performance, the fact of his so writing is only a disgrace to him, whatever men may say. For not to know the nature of justice and injustice, and good and evil, and not to be able to distinguish the dream from the reality, cannot in truth be otherwise than disgraceful to him, even though he have the applause of the whole world.

PHAEDRUS: Certainly.

SOCRATES: But he who thinks that in the written word there is necessarily much which is not serious, and that neither poetry nor prose, spoken or written, is of any great value, if, like the compositions of the rhapsodes, they are only recited in order to be believed, and not with any view to criticism or instruction; and who thinks that even the best of writings are but a reminiscence of what we know, and that only in principles of justice and goodness and nobility taught and communicated orally for the sake of instruction and graven in the soul, which is the true way of writing, is there clearness and perfection and seriousness, and that such principles are a man's own and his legitimate offspring;—being, in the first place, the word which he finds in his own bosom; secondly, the brethren and descendants and relations of his idea which have been duly implanted by him in the souls of others;—and who cares for them and no others—this is the right sort or man; and you and I, Phaedrus, would pray that we may become like him.

PHAEDRUS: That is most assuredly my desire and prayer.

SOCRATES: And now the play is played out; and of rhetoric enough. Go and tell Lysias that to the fountain and school of the Nymphs we went down, and were bidden by them to convey a message to him and to other composers of speeches—to Homer and other writers of poems, whether set to music or not; and to Solon and others who have composed writings in the form of political discourses which they would term laws—to all of them we are to say that if their compositions are based on knowledge of the truth, and they can defend or prove them, when they are put to the test, by spoken arguments, which leave their writings poor in comparison of them, then they are to be called, not only poets, orators, legislators, but are worthy of a higher name, befitting the serious pursuit of their life.

PHAEDRUS: What name would you assign to them?

SOCRATES: Wise, I may not call them; for that is a great name which belongs to God alone,—lovers of wisdom or philosophers is their modest and befitting title.

PHAEDRUS: Very suitable.

SOCRATES: And he who cannot rise above his own compilations and compositions, which he has been long patching and piecing, adding some and taking away some, may be justly called poet or speech-maker or law-maker.

PHAEDRUS: Certainly.

SOCRATES: Now go and tell this to your companion.

PHAEDRUS: But there is also a friend of yours who ought not to be forgotten.

SOCRATES: Who is he?

PHAEDRUS: Isocrates the fair:—What message will you send to him, and how shall we describe him?

SOCRATES: Isocrates is still young, Phaedrus; but I am willing to hazard a prophecy concerning him.

PHAEDRUS: What would you prophesy?

SOCRATES: I think that he has a genius which soars above the orations of Lysias, and that his character is cast in a finer mould. My impression of him is that he will marvellously improve as he grows older, and that all former rhetoricians will be as children in comparison of him. And I believe that he will not be satisfied with rhetoric, but that there is in him a divine inspiration which will lead him to things higher still. For he has an element of philosophy in his nature. This is the message of the gods dwelling in this place, and which I will myself deliver to Isocrates, who is my delight; and do you give the other to Lysias, who is yours.

PHAEDRUS: I will; and now as the heat is abated let us depart.

SOCRATES: Should we not offer up a prayer first of all to the local deities?

PHAEDRUS: By all means.

SOCRATES: Beloved Pan, and all ye other gods who haunt this place, give me beauty in the inward soul; and may the outward and inward man be at one. May I reckon the wise to be the wealthy, and may I have such a quantity of gold as a temperate man and he only can bear and carry.—Anything more? The prayer, I think, is enough for me.

PHAEDRUS: Ask the same for me, for friends should have all things in common.

SOCRATES: Let us go.

INTRODUCTION TO ARISTOTLE

Aristotle lived from 384 to 322 B.C.E. He was born to Greek parents in the Macedonian city of Stagira and has sometimes been referred to as "The Stagirite." In 367 he traveled to Athens and began studying with Plato in his school, the Academy. Aristotle is thus heir to the line of illustrious Athenian theorists of rhetoric, from Socrates to Plato to Aristotle. Yet, since he was not a native Athenian, he could not take command of Plato's Academy upon Plato's death around 347. Aristotle returned to Macedon to serve as tutor for his most famous, if not illustrious, pupil, the military leader and dictator Alexander the Great. He later returned to Athens to teach in his own school, the Lyceum, but was forced to leave Athens again shortly before his death because of anti-Macedonian feelings brought on by the military conquests of Alexander and his father, Philip.

Aristotle wrote prolifically on a wide range of subjects. He taught and wrote about verbal arts such as logic and dialectic, natural sciences such as biology, philosophical matters such as ethics, and of course, rhetoric and politics. His work has been extremely influential in western thinking, particularly during the Middle Ages and the Renaissance.

The *Rhetoric,* from which several passages are reprinted here, is *the* seminal work on rhetorical theory. It would not be too extreme to say that every succeeding rhetorical theory must be read in the shadow of the *Rhetoric* as a continuation of or departure from the views it articulated.

As is the case for many of Aristotle's works, the *Rhetoric* was composed over several years and is comprised of several kinds of material. Some of it consists of Aristotle's lecture notes, while some of it is likely to be notes taken by his students on his lectures. Other passages are more conventionally written by Aristotle himself. This mix of materials is apparent while reading the work because some chapters are extremely dense and aphoristic while others are more fully developed and discursive.

The *Rhetoric* is in three books. Book I introduces the subject of rhetoric and places it in its social, political, and discursive context. Book II is concerned with invention, or the discovery of the substance of rhetorical appeals, in the form of *logos* or logical argument, *ethos* or the use of the speaker's character, and *pathos* or arousal of the audience's emotions. Book III explores matters that Aristotle considered less important although still part of rhetorical appeal: style, arrangement, and, to a lesser extent, delivery. Memory, which with invention, style, arrangement, and delivery are the "canons" of classical rhetoric, are explored in Aristotle's separate work *De Memoria.*

The first part of Book I is especially pithy and full of sentences with important implications for rhetorical theory. Aristotle does not formally define *rhetoric* until the start of the second chapter. Instead, he begins by placing rhetoric in its discursive context, as the counterpart of dialectic. As we discussed earlier, this move puts him at odds with Plato. Rhetoric and dialectic are both ways of dealing with decisions we must make for which there are no definite arts or sciences to guide us and to yield sure and certain answers. In those situations, we may talk out our decisions with friendly individuals (dialectic) or we may entertain competing arguments (rhetoric). With this categorization, Aristotle creates a great divide between the verbal and logical arts of rhetoric and dialectic on the one hand and the more formal sciences on the other hand. Only the latter can yield sure and certain knowledge. For Aristotle, this division left plenty of room for rhetoric and dialectic to guide human affairs, which rarely admit of sure and certain answers. As the centuries would pass and scientific knowledge grew, however, Aristotle's distinction created a temptation to shift many decisions and contexts of human action away from rhetorical management and towards objective, scientific management, to the detriment of rhetoric as a theory and a practice.

In the first chapter, Aristotle situates rhetoric in relationship to dialectic, and the study of rhetoric in relationship to the study of politics and other human affairs. He sees a wider role for rhetoric than that taught by some Sophists of his time, a role underlying political and social affairs generally. Aristotle explains four reasons why rhetoric is useful, and distinguishes honest rhetoric from sophism.

The second chapter begins by defining rhetoric in theoretical terms: It is a *faculty* of observing what will persuade in a given situation, in other words a speculative instrument, rather than the practical skill that many Sophists of his time restricted it to. Mastery of rhetoric must therefore be mastery of theory before it can be mastery of practice. In this busy chapter Aristotle also introduces the three kinds of proof (*logos, pathos, ethos*) and discusses the nature of the *enthymeme,* the argumentative form that is the basis for rhetoric.

Chapter three argues that there are three kinds of rhetoric: political or deliberative, forensic or legal, and ceremonial or display (epideictic). It is interesting that Aristotle defines each kind in terms of its audience. It is the audience's expectations, he claims, that dictate whether a given rhetorical situation calls for political, forensic, or ceremonial discourse.

At this point, the *Rhetoric* "thins out" to develop its subject matters more discursively. Due to space limitations, this anthology therefore does not include the whole of the *Rhetoric.* Aristotle takes up the three kinds of rhetoric and discusses the requirements of, successively, political, ceremonial, and forensic rhetoric. Book I thus ends by having defined rhetoric and by placing it in its social and political context.

Book II is organized around the three kinds of proof (*logos, ethos,* and *pathos*). Aristotle begins with an exhaustive review of the different kinds of emotions to which pathetic proof appeals. The chapters on specific emotions such as "calmness" or "fear" are omitted here, but they explain the nature of those emotions in depth. Next the different kinds of character are discussed, both with a view towards appealing to an audience as well as to using character in ethical proof. Chapters on the specific character of the elderly, or of the young, and so forth, are, like the other detailed chapters on specific emotions, omitted in this anthology.

The last third of Book II explains logical proof, largely by explaining Aristotle's notion of lines of argument, or *topoi,* and how those lines of argument can be used to generate the rhetorical arguments that are enthymemes. Aristotle identifies four general lines of argument and twenty-eight more specific lines, in addition to a discussion of maxims. These lines of argument, such as "the possible and the impossible," were meant to be applied to the subject matter on which one had to speak, and to suggest what might be said on that subject. They were *reminders* of the wide variety of ways to think about human affairs.

Book III begins with a brief discussion of delivery and a more extensive explanation of the virtues of attention to style in rhetoric. We have omitted here Aristotle's lengthy discussion of different kinds of figures of speech and stylistic devices. Later chapters in Book III that are included here explain his views on arrangement and how to order the parts of a speech for maximum effect.

You will recall that Plato ended his dialogue, *Phaedrus,* with a call for a rhetoric that would analyze and explain the different kinds of souls in an audience and how to move them. Aristotle saw a different, more complete use for rhetoric in human affairs than did Plato, but in a real sense his *Rhetoric* answers Plato's call. Many readers of the complete *Rhetoric* find his descriptions of character and human nature to be accurate even today, and therefore find it to be a good guide as to what will and will not persuade people. Aristotle in this work put down the foundation for rhetorical theory to come. The study of rhetorical theory after him is, whatever else it may be, a commentary upon the *Rhetoric.*

ARISTOTLE

THE RHETORIC OF ARISTOTLE

BOOK I

Rhetoric is an Art.

RHETORIC is the counterpart of Dialectic,—since both are concerned with things of which the cognizance is, in a manner, common to all men and belongs to no definite science. Hence all men in a manner use both; for all men to some extent make the effort of examining and of submitting to inquiry, of defending or accusing. People in general do these things either quite at random, or merely with a knack which comes from the acquired habit. Since both ways are possible, clearly it must be possible to reduce them to method; for it is possible to consider the cause why the practised or the spontaneous speaker hits his mark; and such an inquiry, all would allow, is the function of an art.

Hitherto, the essence of this Art has been neglected for the accidents.

Now hitherto the writers of treatises on Rhetoric have constructed only a small part of that art; for proofs form the only artistic element, all else being mere appendage. These writers, however, say nothing about enthymemes, which are the body of proof, but busy themselves chiefly with irrelevant matters. The exciting of prejudice, of pity, of anger, and such like emotions of the soul, has nothing to do with the fact, but has regard to the judge. So that if trials were universally managed, as they are at present managed in some at least of the cities, and for the most part in the best

Translated by Sir Richard Claverhouse Jebb, O.M., Litt.D., late Regius Professor of Greek in the University of Cambridge, edited by John Edwin Sandys, Litt.D., Fellow of St John's College, and Public Orator

governed, such people would have nothing to say. All the world over, men either admit that the laws ought so to forbid irrelevant speaking, or actually have laws which forbid it, as is the case in the procedure of the Areiopagos; a wise provision. For it is a mistake to warp the judge by moving him to anger or envy or pity; it is as if a man, who was going to use a rule, should make it crooked. Further, it is clear that the litigant's part is simply to prove that the fact is or is not, has occurred or has not occurred. Whether it is great or small, just or unjust, in any respects which the lawgiver has not defined, is a question, of course, on which the judge must decide for himself, instead of being instructed upon it by the litigant. Now it is most desirable that well-drawn laws should, as far as possible, define everything themselves, leaving as few points as possible to the discretion of the judges; first, because it is easier to get a small than a large number of men qualified by their intelligence to make laws and try causes; next, because legislative acts are done after mature deliberation, whereas judgments are given off-hand, so that it is hard for the judge to satisfy the demands of justice and expediency. Most important of all, the decision of the lawgiver concerns no special case, but is prospective and general; when we come to the ekklesiast and the dikast, they have to decide actual and definite cases; and they are often so entangled[1] with likings and hatreds and private interests, that they are not capable of adequately considering the truth, but have their judgment clouded by private pleasure or pain. On all other points, then, we say, the judge ought to be given as little discretionary power as possible; but the question whether a thing has or has not happened, will or will not be, is or is not, must perforce be left in his hands; these things the lawgiver cannot foresee. If, then, this is so, it is manifest that irrelevant matter is treated by all those technical writers who define the other points,—as what the proem, the narrative and each of the other parts should contain; for they busy themselves here solely with creating a certain mind in the judge,—but teach nothing about artificial proof, that is, about the way in which one is to become a master of enthymemes.

And the Deliberative branch has been neglected for the Forensic.

It is for this reason that, though the same method applies to public and to forensic speaking, and though the Deliberative branch is nobler and worthier of a citizen than that which deals with private contracts, they ignore the former, and invariably aim at systematizing the art of litigation. In public speaking it is less worth while to talk about things beside the subject. Deliberative oratory is less knavish than Forensic, and embraces larger interests. In a public debate, the judge judges in his own cause, so that nothing more is needful than to prove that the case stands as the adviser says. In forensic speaking this is not enough; it is important to win over the hearer. The judge's award concerns other men's affairs; and if he views these in reference to his own interest, and listens in a partial spirit, he indulges the litigant instead of deciding the cause. Hence it is that in many places, as we said before[1], the law forbids irrelevant pleading: in the public assembly, the judges themselves take care of that.

The master of Dialectic will be the true master of Rhetoric.

It is manifest that the artistic Rhetoric is concerned with proofs. The rhetorical proof is a sort of demonstration, for we entertain the strongest persuasion of a thing when we conceive that it has been demonstrated. A rhetorical demonstration is an enthymeme,—this being, generally speaking, the most authoritative of proofs. The enthymeme again is a sort of syllogism, and every kind of syl-

[1] συνήρτηται, printed in the text of the Venice ed. and preferred by Muretus. With the manuscript reading, συνήρηται, the sentence could only mean: 'and, in their case, likings etc., are often *taken into account*'.

[1] § 5 *supra.*

logism alike comes under the observation of Dialectic, either generally or in one of its departments. Hence it is clear that he who is best able to investigate the elements and the genesis of the syllogism will also be the most expert with the enthymeme, when he has further mastered its subject-matter and its differences from the logical syllogism. Truth and the likeness of truth come under the observation of the same faculty. (It may be added that men are adequately gifted for the quest of truth and generally succeed in finding it.) Hence the same sort of man who can guess about truth, must be able to guess about probabilities.

It is plain, then, that the mass of technical writers deal with irrelevant matter; it is plain, too, why[1] they have leaned by choice towards forensic speaking.

> Use of the Art of Rhetoric. It is
> (1) corrective:
> (2) instructive:
> (3) suggestive:
> (4) defensive.

Rhetoric is useful, first, because truth and justice are naturally stronger than their opposites; so that, when awards are not given duly, truth and justice must have been worsted by their own fault[2]. This is worth correcting. Again, supposing we had the most exact knowledge, there are some people whom it would not be easy to persuade with its help; for scientific exposition is in the nature of teaching, and teaching is out of the question; we must give our proofs and tell our story in popular terms,—as we said in the *Topics*[3] with reference to controversy with the many. Further,—one should be able to persuade, just as to reason strictly, on both sides of a question; not with a view to using the twofold power—one must not be the advocate of evil—but in order, first, that we may know the whole state of the case; secondly, that, if anyone else argues dishonestly, we on our part may be able to refute him. Dialectic and Rhetoric, alone among all arts, draw indifferently an affirmative or a negative conclusion: both these arts alike are impartial. The conditions of the subject-matter, however, are not the same; that which is true and better being naturally, as a rule, more easy to demonstrate and more convincing. Besides it would be absurd that, while incapacity for physical self-defence is a reproach, incapacity for mental defence should be none; mental effort being more distinctive of man than bodily effort. If it is objected that an abuser of the rhetorical faculty can do great mischief, this, at any rate, applies to all good things except virtue, and especially to the most useful things, as strength, health, wealth, generalship. By the right use of these things a man may do the greatest good, and by the unjust use, the greatest mischief.

> Summary:—The province of Rhetoric.
> Its fallacious branch—how related to the fallacious Dialectic.

It appears, then, that Rhetoric is not concerned with any single or definite class of subjects but is parallel to Dialectic: it appears, too, that it is useful; and that its function is not to persuade, but to discover the available means of persuasion in each case, according to the analogy of all other arts. The function of the medical art is not to cure, but to make such progress towards a cure as the case admits; since it is possible to treat judiciously even those who can never enjoy health. Further it is clear that it belongs to the same art to observe the persuasive and the apparent persuasive, as, in the case of Dialectic, to observe the real and the apparent syllogism. For the essence of Sophistry is not in the faculty but in the moral purpose: only, in the case of Rhetoric, a man is to be called a rhetorician with respect to his faculty, without distinction of his moral purpose; in the case of Dialectic, a man is 'sophist' in respect to his moral purpose; 'dialectician' in respect, not of his moral purpose, but of his faculty.

---

[1] διότι = ὅτι, 'that' (Cope).

[2] If those who have truth and right on their side are defeated, *their defeat must be due to themselves,* to their own neglect of Rhetoric (Cope).

[3] *Topica,* i 2.

Let us now attempt to speak of the method itself—the mode, and the means, by which we are to succeed in attaining our objects. By way of beginning we will once more define the art, and then proceed.

Definition of Rhetoric.

ii. Let Rhetoric be defined, then, as the faculty of discerning in every case the available means of persuasion. This is the function of no other art. Each of the other arts is instructive or persuasive about its proper subject-matter; as the medical art about things wholesome or unwholesome,—geometry, about the properties of magnitudes, arithmetic, about numbers,—and so with the rest of the arts and sciences. But Rhetoric appears to have the power of discerning the persuasive in regard (one may say) to any given subject; and therefore we describe it as having the quality of Art in reference to no special or definite class of subjects.

Proofs: I. Inartificial: II. Artificial.

Proofs are either artificial or inartificial. By 'inartificial' I mean such things as have not been supplied by our own agency, but were already in existence,—such as witnesses, depositions under torture, contracts, and the like: by 'artificial' I mean such things as may be furnished by our method and by our own agency; so that, of these, the 'inartificial' have only to be used; the 'artificial' have to be invented.

Artificial Proofs—
(1) ethical, (2) pathetic, 3) logical.

Of proofs provided by the speech there are three kinds; one kind depending on the character of the speaker; another, on disposing the hearer in a certain way; a third, a demonstration or apparent demonstration in the speech itself.

1. Ethical proof.

Ethical proof is wrought when the speech is so spoken as to make the speaker credible; for we trust good men more and sooner, as a rule, about everything; while, about things which do not admit of precision, but only of guess-work, we trust them absolutely. Now this trust, too, ought to be produced by means of the speech,—not by a previous conviction that the speaker is this or that sort of man. It is not true, as some of the technical writers assume in their systems, that the moral worth of the speaker contributes nothing to his persuasiveness; nay, it might be said that almost the most authoritative of proofs is that supplied by character.

2. Pathetic proof.

The hearers themselves become the instruments of proof when emotion is stirred in them by the speech; for we give our judgments in different ways under the influence of pain and of joy, of liking and of hatred; and this, I repeat, is the one point with which the technical writers of the day attempt to deal. This province shall be examined in detail when we come to speak of the emotions.

3. Logical proof.

Proof is wrought through the speech itself when we have demonstrated a truth or an apparent truth by the means of persuasion available in a given case.

> The faculty of Rhetoric has two elements, answering to (1) Dialectical skill; (2) Political Science.

These being the instruments of our proofs, it is clear that they may be mastered[1] by a man who can reason; who can analyse the several types of Character and the Virtues, and thirdly, the Emotions—the nature and quality of each emotion, the sources and modes of its production. It results that Rhetoric is, as it were, an offshoot of Dialectic and of that Ethical science which may fairly be called Politics. Hence it is that Rhetoric and its professors slip into the garb of Political Science—either

---

[1] ταύτας [τὰ τρία] ἐστὶν λαβεῖν.

through want of education, or from pretentiousness, or from other human causes. Rhetoric is a branch or an image[1] of Dialectic, as we said at the beginning. Neither of them is a science relating to the nature of any definite subject-matter. They are certain faculties of providing arguments.

3. Logical proof:
either (a) deductive, by Enthymeme; or
(b) inductive, by Example.

Enough has perhaps been said about the faculty of Dialectic and of Rhetoric and about their relation to each other. With regard to those proofs which are wrought by demonstration, real or apparent, just as in Dialectic there is Induction on the one hand, and Syllogism or apparent Syllogism on the other, so it is in Rhetoric. The Example is an Induction. The Enthymeme is a Syllogism; the Apparent Enthymeme is an Apparent Syllogism[2]. I call the Enthymeme a Rhetorical Syllogism[3] and the Example a Rhetorical Induction. All men effect their proofs by demonstration, either with examples or with enthymemes; there is no third way. Hence, since universally it is necessary to demonstrate anything whatever either by syllogism or by induction (and this we see from the *Analytics*[4]), it

---

[1] ὁμοίωμα, the reading of the inferior MSS: ὁμοία, that of the best MS (retained by Spengel and Roemer).

[2] Spengel's addition of these words is confirmed by Dionysius of Halicarnassus, *Ad Ammaeum,* c. vi.

[3] "By *enthymeme,* Aristotle meant a rhetorical syllogism: that is, a syllogism drawn, not from the premisses (ἀρχαί) proper to any particular science—such, for instance, as medicine—but from propositions relating to contingent things in the sphere of human action, which are the common property of all discussion; propositions which he classifies as general (ἐικότα) and particular (σημεῖα); and accordingly *defines* an enthymeme as 'a syllogism from probabilities and signs.' A misapprehension of Aristotle's meaning had, as early as the first century B.C., led to the conception of the enthymeme as not merely a syllogism of a particular subject-matter, but also as a syllogism *of which one premiss is suppressed*" (*Attic Orators,* ii 289 f, *q.v.*). Cope supported the former view in the text of *Introd.* 102f, and reverted to the latter view in the note.

[4] *An. Pr.* ii 23; *An. Post.* i 1.

follows that Induction and Syllogism must be identical respectively with Example and Enthymeme. The difference between Example and Enthymeme is manifest[1] from the *Topics*[2]. There, in reference to syllogism and induction, it has already been said that the proving of a proposition by a number of like instances, is, in Dialectic, Induction—answering to the Example in Rhetoric; and that, when certain things exist, and something else comes to pass through them, distinct from them but due to their existing, either as an universal or as an ordinary result, this is called in Dialectic, a Syllogism, as in Rhetoric it is called an Enthymeme. It is clear that the Rhetorical branch of Dialectic commands both these weapons. What has been said in the *Methodica* holds good here also; some rhetorical discourses rely on Example, some on Enthymeme; and so, likewise, some rhetoricians prefer the one and some the other. Arguments from Example are not the less persuasive; but arguments in the form of Enthymeme are the more applauded. The reason of this, and the way to use either, will be explained by and by[3]. Now let us define the things themselves more clearly.

Rhetoric must address itself to classes,
not individuals.
Its subjects are contingent things which
men can influence.

First, the notion of persuasion is relative; some things being at once persuasive and credible in themselves, other things because they are supposed to be demonstrated by persons who are so. Again, no art considers the particular; thus the medical art considers, not what is wholesome for Sokrates or

---

[1] 'Is manifest' (φανερόν)—*i.e.* may be inferred from the definitions of Induction and of the Syllogism in the *Topics.* Nothing is said in the *Topics* about Example or Enthymeme specially.

[2] *Top.* i 1, p. 100 A. 25 (syllogism): i 12, p. 105 A. 13 (induction).

[3] The cause and origin of them (so Victorius), and the mode of their employment, we will describe hereafter (ii 20–24). Cope, *Introd.* p. 155.

Kallias, but what is so for a certain sort of man or a certain class. This is characteristic of an Art, whereas particulars are infinite and cannot be known. Hence Rhetoric, too, will consider, not what is probable to the individual, as to Sokrates or Hippias, but what is probable to a given class, just as Dialectic does. Dialectic does not reason for *any* premisses—dotards have notions of their own—but from premisses which require discussion. So does Rhetoric reason only upon recognised subjects of debate. Its concern is with subjects on which we deliberate, not having reduced them to systems; and with hearers who cannot grasp the unity of an argument which has many stages, or follow a long chain of reasoning. We debate about things which seem capable of being either thus or thus. Matters which admit of no ambiguity, past, present, or future, are debated by no one, on that supposition: it is useless.

Its premisses must be probabilities.
One premiss of the enthymeme may be suppressed.

Now, one may construct a syllogism and draw a conclusion either from facts already reduced to syllogisms or from facts which have not been proved syllogistically, but which need such proof, because they are not probable. The former of these processes is necessarily difficult to follow owing to its length;—the umpire being assumed to be a plain man. Reasonings of the latter kind are not persuasive, because drawn from premisses which are not admitted or probable. Hence both the enthymeme and the example must deal with things which are (as a rule) contingent—the example, as a kind of induction, the enthymeme as a syllogism, and as a syllogism of few elements,—often, of fewer than the normal syllogism. Thus, if one of these elements is something notorious, it need not even be stated, as the hearer himself supplies it. For instance, to prove that Dorieus has been victor in a contest, for which the prize is a crown, it is enough to say that he has been victor in the Olympic games. It is needless to add that in the Olympic contests the prize is a crown; every one is aware of that.

Every premiss of the enthymeme is a Probability or a Sign.

The premisses of rhetorical syllogisms seldom belong to the class of necessary facts. The subject-matter of judgments and deliberations is usually contingent; for it is about their actions that men debate and take thought; but actions are all contingent, no one of them, one may say, being necessary. And results which are merely usual and contingent must be deduced from premisses of the same kind, as necessary results from necessary premisses:—this, too, has been shown in the *Analytics*[1]. It follows that the propositions from which enthymemes are taken will be sometimes necessarily true, but more often contingently true. Now the materials of the enthymeme are Probabilities and Signs. It follows that Probabilities and Signs must answer to the Contingent and the Necessary truths[2].

The Probable defined.

The Probable is that which usually happens; (with a limitation, however, which is sometimes forgotten—namely that the thing *may* happen otherwise:) the Probable being related to that in respect of which it is probable as Universal to Particular.

Signs.

One kind of Sign is as Particular to Universal; the other, as Universal to Particular. The Infallible Sign is called *tekmêrion;* the Fallible Sign has no distinctive name. By Infallible Signs I mean those which supply a strict Syllogism. Hence it is that this sort of Sign is called *tekmêrion,* for when people think that what they have said is irrefutable, then they think that they are bringing a *tekmêrion* (a *conclusive* proof)—as if the matter had been demonstrated and *concluded* (πεπερασμένον); for *tekmar* and *peras* mean the same thing ('*limit*') in the old language.

---

[1] *An. Pr.* i 8.

[2] See Cope's *Introduction*, p. 159.

The Sign which is as a Particular to a Universal would be illustrated by saying, 'Wise men are just; *for* Sokrates was wise and just.' This is a Sign, indeed, but it can be refuted, even though the statement be a fact; for it does not make a syllogism. On the other hand, if one said—'Here is a sign that he is ill—he is feverish'; or, 'she is a mother, for she has milk,' this is a strict proof. This is the only conclusive sign (or *tekmêrion*); for this alone, if the fact be true, is irrefutable. Another Sign, which is as Universal to Particular, would be exemplified by saying—'This is a sign that he has a fever, he breathes quick.' But this, too, even though it be true, is refutable. A man may breathe hard without having a fever.

The Example.

The nature of the Probable, of a Sign and of a conclusive Sign, and the nature of the difference between them have been explained sufficiently for our present purpose. In the *Analytics*[1] a fuller account of them has been given, and of the reason why some of them are inconclusive, while others are strictly logical. It has been said that an Example is an Induction, and the matters with which it is concerned have been stated. It is neither as part to whole nor as whole to part nor as whole to whole, but as part to part, as like to like. When both things come under the same class, but one is better known than the other, that better-known one is an Example. For instance, it is argued that Dionysios aims at a tyranny in asking for a body-guard; for Peisistratos formerly, when he had such a design, asked for a guard, and, having got it, became tyrant;—as did Theagenes at Megara; and so all the other cases known to the speaker become Examples in reference to Dionysios—as to whom they do not yet know that this was his motive for the request. All these cases come under the same general principle, that a man who aims at a tyranny asks for a bodyguard.

[1] *An. Pr.* ii 27.

Distinction between enthymemes proper and not proper to Rhetoric.
The Universal Commonplaces.
The Particular Commonplaces.

Such, then, are the sources from which the professedly demonstrative proofs are drawn. In regard to enthymemes, there is an important distinction which has been almost universally ignored; a distinction which applies equally to the syllogisms employed by Dialectic. Some enthymemes belong properly to Rhetoric, as some syllogisms belong properly to Dialectic; other enthymemes are peculiar to other arts and faculties, either existent or still to be formulated. Hence, though the speaker does not perceive it[1], the more he handles his subject with technical appropriateness, the more he is passing out of the province of Dialectic and Rhetoric[2]. My meaning will be plainer when expressed more fully. Dialectical and Rhetorical syllogisms deal properly with the so-called topics (or commonplaces), by which I mean here the *Universal* topics applicable to Justice, Physics, Politics, and a variety of other subjects of all sorts. Take the topic of More or Less. This topic will not help us to make a syllogism or an enthymeme about Justice rather than about Physics or anything else, different though these things are in kind. *Particular* Common-places are those arising from the propositions relative to the several species and classes of things. Thus there are propositions about Physics from which it is impossible to make a syllogism or an enthymeme about Ethics,—and others again, about Ethics from which one cannot reason upon Physics; and so in each case. The Universal Common-places will not make a man intelligent about any special class of things; since they have no special subject-matter. As to the Particular Common-places, the more carefully a speaker picks his propositions, the nearer he will be unconsciously coming to a science distinct from Dialectic and Rhetoric; for, if

[1] Omitting τοὺς ἀκροατὰς with Muretus and Spengel.

[2] Jebb's *Essays and Addresses*, 1907, p. 528.

he lights upon special first principles, this will be no longer Dialectic or Rhetoric, but that science of which he has the first principles. Most enthymemes are based upon these Particular or Special Common-places;—fewer upon the Universal. As in the *Topics*[1], then, so here we must distinguish, in regard to enthymemes, the Special Topics and the Universal Topics from which they are to be taken. By Special Topics I mean the propositions peculiar to any given subject; by Universal Topics, those which are common to all. We will begin with the Special Topics. But first of all we must determine how many branches of Rhetoric there are, in order that, having done this, we may ascertain separately the elements and the propositions of each.

The three species of Rhetoric.
Deliberative, forensic, and epideictic.

iii. The species of Rhetoric are three in number, for the hearers of speeches belong to that number of classes. The speech has three elements—the speaker, the subject, and the person addressed; and the end proposed has reference to this last, that is, to the hearer. Now the hearer must be either spectator or judge; and, if judge, then of the past or of the future. The judge of things future is (for instance) the ekklesiast; the judge of things past, the dikast; the other hearer is a spectator of the faculty. It follows that there must be three kinds of rhetorical speeches, the deliberative, the forensic, the epideictic.

Their elements.
Their times.

Now the elements of counsel are exhortation and dissuasion; since both private advisers and speakers in the public interest always either exhort or dissuade. The elements of litigation are accusation and defence; since the parties to a suit must be occupied with one or the other of these. The elements of an epideictic speech are praise and blame. The times which belong to these classes severally are:—to the deliberative speaker, the future; for he offers advice, exhorting or dissuading, about things to be;—to the litigant, the past; for the subjects of accusation on the one hand and defence on the other are always things past;—to the epideictic speaker, properly the present; for all men praise or blame in accordance with existing conditions, though they often avail themselves also of reminiscences from the past and conjectures about the future.

Their ends.

For these three classes there are three distinct ends, namely:—for the counsellor, utility or harm (since the exhorter advises a thing as being better, and the dissuader opposes it as being worse), and it is in reference to this topic that he uses the subsidiary topics of justice and injustice, honour and shame;—for litigants, justice and injustice,—and these, again, use subsidiary topics in reference to this one;—for those who praise or blame, the honourable and the shameful; and these, too, refer their other topics to this standard.

That the end of each class is such as has been stated is shown by this fact, that the other points are sometimes not contested by the speakers. For instance, the litigant will sometimes not dispute that a thing has happened or that he has done harm; but that he is guilty of an injustice, he will never admit; else there would be no need of a lawsuit. Similarly, speakers in debate often give up all other points, but will not allow that they are advising an inexpedient course, or dissuading from one which is advantageous; while, as to showing that it is no injustice to enslave a neighbouring and perhaps unoffending community, they often give themselves no anxiety. In the same way panegyrists and censurers do not consider whether such an one's acts were expedient or harmful; but often make it a ground of positive praise that, regardless of his own advantage, he did something or other noble. For instance they praise Achilles for coming to the rescue of his friend Patroklos, when he knew that he must die, though he might have lived. Now for Achilles such a death was nobler; but life was expedient.

[1] *Topica*, ix (*Soph. El.*), c. 9.

It appears from what has been said that we must first ascertain the propositions bearing upon these topics. Now signs, fallible or infallible, and probabilities are the propositions of Rhetoric; for as, universally, a syllogism is formed of propositions, so the enthymeme is a syllogism formed of the above-named propositions.

And as there can be no performance, past or future, of impossible things, but only of possible; and since things, which have not occurred, cannot have been done, and things, which are not to be, cannot be about to be done;—it is necessary alike for the Deliberative, for the Forensic, and for the Epideictic speaker to have propositions about the Possible and the Impossible, and on the question whether a thing has or has not happened, is or is not to be. Besides, since all men in praising or blaming, in exhorting or dissuading, in accusing or defending try to prove, not merely the above facts, but also that the good or evil, the honour or disgrace, the justice or injustice is great or small, whether they are taken absolutely or in comparison with each other, it is plain that it will be necessary to have propositions about greatness or smallness, and about greater or less, both universally and in particular cases; as on the question which is the greater or less good, the greater or less act of injustice—and so with the rest.

These, then, are the subjects in which it is necessary to ascertain the available propositions. Next, we must examine in detail each class of these subjects; namely, those of debate; those of epideictic speaking; and, thirdly, those of lawsuits.

The special Topics of deliberative Rhetoric.

iv. First, then, we must ascertain about what sort of goods or evils the speaker in debate offers counsel, since he does not do so about *all* things, but only about such as may or may not come to pass. As to things, which *necessarily* are or will be, or which cannot be or come to pass, no counsel can be given. Nor, of course, can it be given about all contingent things; for there are some goods of the contingent class, both natural and accidental, about which it is idle to offer advice. Evidently, advice can be given only on such subjects as admit of debate; and these are such as can be referred to ourselves, and which it rests with us to initiate. For our discussions are not carried beyond the point at which we find that things are impossible for us to do.

Now, accurately to enumerate and classify the several subjects on which men are wont to confer, and, further, to give of them, so far as possible, a really precise account, is an attempt which need not be made at present; first, because this is not the business of Rhetoric, but of a more intelligent and more exact method; next, because already Rhetoric has had assigned to it many more than its proper subjects of consideration. In fact it is true, as we have said before[1] that Rhetoric is made up of the science of logical analysis, and of that political science which is concerned with morals; and it has a resemblance, partly to Dialectic, partly to sophistical reasoning. But, in so far as any one attempts to construct either Dialectic or Rhetoric, not as faculties but as special sciences, he will unconsciously abolish their very essence, by shifting his ground and reconstructing them into sciences dealing with particular subjects and not with words alone[2]. Even here, however, we must notice these points which it is to our purpose to discriminate, though they still supply matter for inquiry to political science.

Now it may be said that the chief subjects, about which all men debate, and on which those who offer counsel speak, are five in number:—Ways and Means; War and Peace; Protection of the Country; Imports and Exports; Legislation.

---

[1] ii 7.

[2] *λήσεται τὴν φύσιν αὐτῶν ἀφανίσας τῷ μεταβαίνειν ἐπισκευάζων εἰς ἐπιστήμας ὑποκειμένων τινῶν πραγμάτων, ἀλλὰ μὴ μόνον λόγων*. Vater and Jebb, and Bonitz in the *Index Aristotelicus*, connect *εἰς ἐπιστήμας* with *ἐπισκευάζων*, and not with *μεταβαίνειν*. Cope prefers the latter construction: 'he will be unconsciously effacing their real nature by passing over (in his attempt to reconstruct them) into sciences of definite special subjects, instead of (confining himself to) those which deal with mere words,' *Comm.* i 61; *Introd.* 174.

Ways and Means.

He, then, who is to give counsel on Ways and Means, must know the sources of the public revenue, their nature and number, in order that, if any is neglected, it may be added, or, if any is too small, it may be increased; further, all the expense of the State, in order that, if any is superfluous, it may be taken away, or, if any is too large, it may be repressed; since, relatively to their actual property, men become richer, not only by acquiring, but by retrenching. A comprehensive view of these questions cannot be obtained simply by experience in private affairs; it is further necessary, with a view to giving counsel on these things, to be acquainted with the discoveries of others.[1]

War and Peace.

As to War and Peace, one must know how great the power of the State actually is, and is capable of becoming; also, the nature of the actual power, and of that which may be acquired; further, what wars the State has waged, and how. And these things must be known, not only in respect to one's own State, but in respect to its neighbours also, in order that it may keep peace with the stronger, and have the option of making war on the weaker. One must know, too, whether the power of the State is like or unlike that of its neighbours; for here, too, there is a possibility of advantage or loss. In regard to these points, again, one must have considered the issue, not only of one's own country's wars, but of the wars waged by other States too; for like causes produce like results.

Defence.

Further, in regard to the protection of the country, one must not be ignorant how it is guarded: one must know the strength and the species of the protecting force, and the sites of the forts; but this demands acquaintance with the country, in order that, if the garrison be too small, it may be increased, or, if superfluous, withdrawn; and that the important places may be especially watched.

Commerce.

Then, as to the food question, one must know how much outlay is enough for the State; what sort of food is produced in the country or can be imported; also what articles the citizens require to export or import, in order that treaties and pacts may be made with the right States; for there are two classes of States towards whom our citizens must be kept blameless:—the stronger, and those useful for commerce.

Legislation.

For safety, it is necessary to have the power of entertaining all these questions; but nothing is more necessary than to understand how to legislate, since on its laws depends the weal of the State. One must know, then, how many forms of government there are; what things are good for each form; and by what things, proper to it or adverse to it, each tends to be corrupted. When I talk of a polity being corrupted by things proper to it, I mean that all polities, except the best, are corrupted, both by relaxation and by tension. Democracy, for instance, is weakened, so that it must end in oligarchy, not only by relaxing but by over-straining: just as the aquiline and the snub-nosed type, which unbending brings to the right mean, may also be intensified to a point at which the very semblance of a nose is lost.

Now, with a view to legislative acts, it is useful to see what polity is expedient; not merely in the light of history, but by knowledge of actual foreign polities, and by seeing what form of government suits what sort of people. Evidently, then, books of travel are useful with a view to legislation, since from them one can ascertain the laws of the different nations; histories should be read with a view to giving political counsel. All this, however, is the business of Political Science, not of Rhetoric.

---

[1] ἱστορικὸν εἶναι κτλ., 'to be *inquisitive* as to the discoveries of others,' cp. Cope, *Comm.* i 64.

These, then, are all the chief subjects with which the intending debater should be conversant. Let us now state again the premisses, from which he must exhort or dissuade on these and on all other subjects[1].

Analysis of Happiness.

v. It may be said that all men, individually and in the aggregate, have some aim, with a view to which they choose or avoid; and this may be summarily described as Happiness, with its parts. So, for the sake of illustration, let us ascertain what, speaking broadly, we mean by Happiness, and what are the elements of its parts; for Happiness and the things which tend to it, and the things adverse to it, are the subjects of all attempts to exhort or dissuade; since we ought to do those things which tend to create it or any one of its parts, or to increase that part; but we ought not to do those things, which corrupt, or hinder it, or produce its opposite.

Let Happiness, then, be prosperity combined with virtue; or independence of life; or that existence which, being safe, is pleasantest; or a flourishing state of property and of body, with the faculty of guarding and producing this; for it may be said that all men allow Happiness to be one or more of these things.

If, then, Happiness is this sort of thing, these must be parts of it:—good birth, the possession of many friends, the possession of good friends, wealth, the possession of good children, the possession of many children, a happy old age; further, the excellences of the body, as health, beauty, strength, great stature, athletic power; also good repute, honour, good fortune, virtue. For a man would *then* be most independent, if he possessed both the personal and the external goods, since besides these there are no others. Personal goods are partly mental, partly bodily; external goods are birth, friends, money, honour. Further, we think that he ought to have influence and good fortune; for thus will his life be safest. So let us ascertain in like manner what each of these, too, is.

Good birth.

Good birth, then, means, for a nation or a city, that the people is indigenous or ancient; that its earliest representatives were conspicuous as leaders, and that many of their descendants have been conspicuous for those things which excite emulation. The individual's good birth may be either on the father's or the mother's side; it implies pure blood, and that (as in the case of the community) the founders of the line have been notable for virtue or for wealth or for something else which is honoured; and that the family has many conspicuous members, men and women, young and old.

Goodly and numerous offspring.

The possession of good children and the possession of many children are terms of plain meaning. The community has these things, if the youth be numerous and good, first as regards excellence of body, such as stature, beauty, strength, athletic power; the moral excellences of a young man are moderation and courage. The individual has these blessings, when his own children are numerous and good, both female and male; the bodily excellence of a woman being beauty and stature,—the moral, moderation and an industry which is not sordid. The existence of all such conditions is desirable both for the individual and for the state, and in regard to women as well as to men; for people among whom the state of women is low, as in Lacedæmon, have scarcely more than a half prosperity.

---

[1] The connexion of the next three chapters is as follows: "The deliberative speaker exhorts or dissuades with a view to the *happiness* of the persons addressed. Hence we must consider the popular notions of happiness which prevail among men. Here follows a series of *popular* definitions of happiness, and a list of the elements which are generally regarded as constituting it (c. 5). The deliberative speaker appeals to *the interest, τὸ συμφέρον*, of those whom he addresses. The συμφέρον is a kind of ἀγαθόν. Hence we must consider what are ἀγαθά. A popular analysis and list follow (c. 6). But the question will arise 'of two good things, which is the *better?*' Hence we must treat the κοινὸς τόπος of μᾶλλον καὶ ἧττον, or 'degree' (c. 7)" (R. C. J.).

Wealth.

The elements of wealth are—plenty of money—the possession of territory and of farms,—further, the possession of furniture, of cattle, and of slaves in great number, distinguished for their stature and beauty[1]; it being understood that all these things are[2] safe, worthy of a freeman, and useful. Those things are the more useful, which are the more productive; those things rather befit a freeman, which tend to enjoyment. By productive things I mean those from which revenues come; by things for enjoyment, such as yield nothing worth speaking of, except their use. The definition of secure possession is possession of things in such a place and manner, that the use of them depends on one's self:—the test of things being one's own, in one's having the power of alienating them; by alienation I mean giving and selling. Universally, wealth consists in using rather than in possessing; for wealth is the activity and the use of possessions.

Good repute.

Good repute consists in being respected by all men, or in being thought to have something which is desired by all men, or by most, or by the good, or by the prudent.

Honour.

Honour is a mark of good repute for beneficence. Those men are honoured justly and most, who have done benefits; not but that honour is paid also to a possible benefactor. A benefit has reference either to preservation or the other causes of being; or to wealth, or to some one of the other goods, of which the acquisition is not easy, either generally, or in a given circumstance, or at a given time; since many people get honour for things which look small; but the place and the moment account for it. The elements of honour are—sacrifices; records in verse or prose; privileges; grants of domain; chief seats; public funerals; statues; maintenance at the public cost; barbaric homage, such as salaams and giving place; and the gifts honourable among each people. The gift is the bestowal of a possession and a mark of honour: gifts, therefore, are desired both by the avaricious and by the ambitious, since for each it has what they want: it is a possession, which the *avaricious* desire; and it brings honour, which the *ambitious* desire.

Health.

The excellence of the body is health,—this health meaning that men are to be free from disease and to have the use of their bodies; for many people are healthy in the way in which Herodicus is said to have been, whom no one would count happy for their health, since they have to abstain from all, or nearly all, the things which men do. Beauty is different for each time of life: it is a youth's beauty that his body should be serviceable for the toils of the race and for feats of strength, while he is also pleasant to look upon;—so that the practices of the pentathlum are most beautiful, being formed at once for strength and for speed. The beauty of a man in his prime is that his body should be serviceable for the toils of war, while his aspect pleases and also strikes fear; the beauty of an old man is that his body should serve for the needful toils and be free from pain, through having none of those things which mar old age. Strength is the power of moving another as one likes, and one must do so by drawing or pushing or lifting or pressing or compressing; so that a strong man is strong either in all or in some of these things. Excellence of size is a superiority to the many in height and breadth, just so great as not thereby to make the movements slower. Athletic excellence of body results from size, strength and swiftness[1]; for the swift man is strong. He who can throw his legs in a certain way and move them quick and far,

---

[1] πλήθει καὶ μεγέθει καὶ κάλλει vulgo; πλήθει καὶ κάλλει Roemer, following the text written by the first hand in the margin of the Paris MS.

[2] <οἰκεῖα> is inserted here from the context by Roemer, 'are <one's very own, and are> safe.'

[1] καὶ τάχους, bracketed by Roemer. The next clause shows that it must have been omitted, as it adds the reason for its omission.

is fit for running; he who can compress and hold, for wrestling; he who can drive with a blow, for boxing; he who can do both the last, for the pancratium; he who can do all, for the pentathlum.

Happy old age.

Happy old age is old age which comes slowly, with painlessness; for a man has not a happy old age if he grows old, either quickly, or slowly indeed, yet with pain. It comes both from the excellences of the body, and from good fortune: for, if a man is not free from disease and is not strong, he will not escape suffering; nor, without good fortune[1], is he likely to have a long and painless life. There is, indeed, a distinct faculty of long life without strength or health; since many people live long without the excellences of the body; but precise discussion of these matters is of no use for our present purpose.

Friendship.

The possession of many friends—the possession of good friends—are plain terms, when 'friend' has been defined; your friend being a person who tends to do for your sake those things which he thinks good for you. A man, then, who has many such well-wishers, has many friends: he whose well-wishers are also worthy men, has good friends.

Good fortune.

Good fortune consists in those goods, of which fortune is the cause, coming to pass and belonging to us; either all of them, or most, or the chief. Fortune is the cause of some things of which the arts also are causes, and of many, too, which are *not* artificial,—as of those, for instance, which Nature gives (though the gifts of Fortune may be also contrary to Nature). Thus Art may be the cause of health, but Nature gives beauty and stature.—Generally, those goods are the gifts of Fortune which are the objects of envy. Fortune is also the cause of those goods which are beyond calculation. Suppose, for instance, that a man's brothers are ugly, but *he* is good-looking: or that *he* found a treasure, which everyone else had missed: or that the arrow hit the man next him, and not *him:* or that he alone did not go to a place which was his constant resort, while other people, going once in a way, were killed. All such things are counted pieces of good luck.

Virtue.

As to Virtue, since the topic of Praise has most to do with it, we must define it when we come to speak of praise.

• • •

The laudatory branch of Rhetoric.

ix. Let us next speak of Virtue and Vice and of the Noble and the Shameful (these being the objects of praise or blame); for, in speaking of these, we shall incidentally show the means of producing such or such an impression about our own characters (and this, we saw[1], is the second kind of proof); since the same means will enable us to make either another person or ourselves trustworthy in respect to virtue. And since it happens that people often praise, in jest or in earnest, not only a human being or a god, but this or that of the lower animals, as well as inanimate things, we must, in the same way as before, get our propositions about these. Let us, then, go on to speak of these matters, so far as is needful by way of illustration.

The popular conception of Virtue and Vice.

That, then, is Morally Beautiful or Noble, which, being desirable for its own sake, is also laudable; or which, being good, is pleasant because good. And if this is the Noble, it follows that

---

[1] *οὔτ' ἂν εὐτυχὴς*, the reading of the Paris MS, was corrected by Muretus into *οὔτ' ἄνευ τύχης*, where we should either omit *οὔτε*, with Hermolaus Barbarus, or alter it into *οὐκ*, with Roth. The former is the course adopted in this translation and in Roemer's text.

[1] ii 4.

Virtue is noble: for Virtue is at once a good and a laudable thing. Now Virtue seems to be a faculty of providing and preserving 'goods'; and a faculty of doing many and great benefits to all men in all cases. The parts of Virtue are Justice, Courage, Temperance, Magnificence, Magnanimity, Liberality, Gentleness, Prudence, Wisdom. And the great virtues must be those which are most useful to others, if virtue is a faculty of beneficence. For this reason men most honour the just and the brave; for Courage is useful to others in war, and justice in peace also. Next comes Liberality; for liberal men are open-handed and do not contend about money—the chief object of other people's desire. Now Justice is a virtue, through which everybody has his own according to the law; Injustice is a vice, through which a man has, against the law, what is *not* his own. Courage is a virtue, through which men tend to do noble deeds in perils and as the law commands, and to support the law; Cowardice is the opposite. Temperance is a virtue, through which men are disposed as the law enjoins towards the pleasures of the body; Intemperance is the opposite. Liberality is a virtue tending to confer pecuniary benefits; Illiberality is the opposite. Magnanimity is a virtue tending to confer great benefits; [Meanness of spirit is the opposite[1]]. Magnificence is a virtue productive of greatness in expenditure; Meanness of spirit and Shabbiness are the opposites. Prudence is a virtue of the intelligence, in respect to which men are able to consult for their own happiness about the goods and evils above-mentioned . . . [2]

Virtue and Vice, then, universally and in their parts, have been examined sufficiently for our immediate purpose; the Noble and the Shameful are not hard to discern. For manifestly those things which produce Virtue must be noble, since they tend to Virtue; and also those things which come from it; these being its signs and its works. And since these signs, and such deeds or sufferings as belong to the good man, are noble, it follows that all deeds or signs of courage, and all deeds courageously done, must be noble; likewise, just deeds and deeds done in a just way; (not, however, just sufferings; it is distinctive of this virtue that to suffer justly is not always noble,—as in the case of punishment it is more shameful to suffer it justly than unjustly;)—and so in regard to the other virtues. Also those deeds are noble, for which the prize is honour, or honour in a greater degree than money; and all desirable things which a man does, not in his own interest; also absolute goods,—such as the deeds which a man does for his country, regardless of his private interest; and natural goods; and goods which are not such for the individual, since things good for the individual are sought selfishly. Also those goods which may exist for one after death rather than in life; since goods to be enjoyed in life supply a stronger selfish motive. Also all things which are done on account of others, since here there is less selfishness. And all successes which benefit others and not oneself:—and good deeds done to one's benefactors, for this is just; and benefits generally—for they have no selfish bearing. Also the opposites of those things of which men are ashamed; for men are ashamed when they say, do, or mean to do shameful things; as Sappho has written, in answer to the words of Alcæus:

> 'Something I would say, but shame hinders me'[1]:—
>
> 'If thy desire were for good things or noble, and thy tongue were not labouring to utter something base, shame would not have covered thy eyes, but thou wouldest speak about thy rightful wish.'[2]

Those things are noble, too, about which men feel trepidation, without feeling fear; for it is by

[1] Bracketed by Spengel as redundant in view of § 12 ad fin.

[2] The definitions of the opposite of φρόνησις, and those of σοφία and its opposite, are here wanting. Roemer.

[1] Alcæus, fragm. 55, Bergk, ed. 4.

[2] Sappho, fragm. 28, *ib.*

those goods which tend to fame that they are thus affected. The naturally better persons or things have the nobler excellences and works,—as those of a man are nobler than those of a woman. Also those excellences are nobler which give enjoyment to others rather than to their possessors: whence justice and the just are noble. Again, it is noble to be avenged on one's enemies and not to make up the quarrel; for requital is just; and the just is noble; and it is the part of a courageous man not to be worsted. Victory, too, and honour are among noble things; for they are desirable though sterile; and they show a superior excellence. Memorable things are noble, and the more memorable, the nobler. So it is with those goods which do not wait on the living, and with those on which honour attends, and with signal things. Again, unique possessions are the nobler, since they are more memorable. So are possessions which yield no fruit; for they are more worthy of a free man. Those things, too, are noble which the special usage of a people makes so, and which are symbols of things which that people counts praiseworthy; thus in Lacedæmon it is noble to have long hair, for it is a sign of a free man; since it is not easy for a man with long hair to do any menial work. Again, it is noble not to ply any sordid trade; for it is the part of a free man not to live in dependence upon others. Then those qualities which border on a man's actual qualities must be assumed to be identical with them, for the purpose either of praise or of blame; thus, the cautious man may be called cold and designing; the foolish man may be called goodnatured, or the callous man, mild. And so each character may be interpreted by the character which ranges beside it—always in the better sense: for instance, the passionate and violent man may be called straightforward,—the arrogant man, majestic and dignified. Men who represent the extremes must be taken as representing the virtues; thus, the rash man must be called courageous; the prodigal, liberal; for it will seem so to most people, and at the same time a fallacy may be derived from the man's motive. Thus, if he runs risks where there is no need, much more (it will be thought) would he brave danger where honour required; or if he is lavish to the crowd, much more will he be generous to his friends: for it is an excess of virtue to do good to all. But one must consider too, to whom[1] the praise is addressed, for as Socrates said, it is not hard to praise Athenians to Athenians[2]. One must represent, as existing, that which is honoured by each set of people—as by Scythians, or Lacedæmonians, or philosophers. And, generally, one must draw the honourable into the sphere of the noble,—as, indeed, they seem to be neighbours. And all things may be treated as noble which befit the doers—deeds, for instance, worthy of their ancestors and their antecedents; for it is happy and noble to acquire fresh honour. Again a thing is noble, if done, beyond mere fitness, with a better and nobler tendency; for instance, if a man is moderate in prosperity, but magnanimous in adversity; or better and more conciliatory, the greater he becomes. An instance of this is the saying of Iphicrates about his origin as compared with his fortunes[3]; and the epigram on the Olympic victor:

> 'Of yore I had a rough yoke on my shoulders,' &c.[4]

also the verses of Simonides:

> 'She whose father, husband, and brothers were princes,' &c.[5]

> Episode on *ἔπαινος*, which expresses moral approbation; and *ἐγκώμιον*, which is given to *ἔργα*, as such.

Now, since praise is founded upon actions, and it is distinctive of the good man to act according

---

[1] *i.e.* 'the audience to whom.'

[2] *i.e.* 'before an audience of Athenians.' Plato, *Menexenus,* 235 D.

[3] 1 vii 32 *supra.*

[4] *ib.*

[5] *παίδων τ', οὐκ ἤρθη νοῦν ἐς ἀτασθαλίην*, Simonides, fragm. 111 Bergk ed. 4; Thuc. vi 59. Archedikê, daughter of Hippias, married Aeantides, son of Hippoklês, tyrant of Lampsakos. Her tomb was at Lampsakos.

to moral choice, we must try to show that our man acts by moral choice. It is a help towards this that he should be seen to have done the thing often. Therefore coincidences and accidents should be treated as results of moral choice; for, if many similar instances are brought forward, these will appear to show virtue and moral choice. Now praise is language which brings out the greatness of a virtue. We must make it evident, therefore, that the actions are of such or such a character. But encomium is concerned with achievements; the external circumstances, such as good birth and education, being used merely to increase the credibility; since it is likely that good men should come of good men, and that a man brought up in a given way should be of a given character. Hence we give encomium to men who *have done* something. The results achieved, however, are mere indications of the moral habit; for we should *praise* a man, even if he had not done the thing, if we were sure that he was of such or such a character. Felicitation and gratulation are synonymous terms, but not the same things as praise and encomium; rather, as happiness includes virtue, gratulation includes the rest.

Relation of Laudatory to Deliberative Rhetoric.

Laudatory and Deliberative Speaking have a topic in common; since those things which, in debate, one would suggest, become, when differently expressed, encomia. Given, then, the right actions and the right character, these, when we use them for admonition, must be expressed in an altered and inverted form. Thus 'A man should be proud, not of fortune's gifts, but of what he owes to himself.' So when you wish to praise, think what you would advise; and, when you wish to advise, think what you would praise. The modes of expression will necessarily be opposite, when the prohibitive and the non-prohibitive clauses are interchanged.

Of all the topics, that of amplification is most useful in Laudatory branch of Rhetoric, while examples are most useful to the Deliberative and Enthymemes to the Forensic branch.

One must use, too, many means of amplification. Suppose, for instance, that a man is the only one, or the first, or one of a few who has done something, or that he has done it in the highest degree; all these things are noble. The conditions of time and occasion may also be used; these serving to show that the deed was more than could have been expected. Note, too, if he has succeeded often in the same things, for this is great, and can seem no accident, but due to himself; or, if the incentives and prizes of achievement were first devised and established on his account. Such is the case of a man like Hippolochus[1] on whom the first encomium was written; or of Harmodius and Aristogeiton, on whose account the first statues were set up in the market-place[2]. And so with facts of the opposite kind. If you lack topics of absolute praise, you must praise by comparison, as Isokrates used to do from the habit of pleading law-suits[3]; and your comparison must be with eminent men; for this amplifies and is noble, if one is better than men of consideration. Amplification naturally falls in the province of Praise,—for it represents an excellence, and excellence belongs to noble things. Therefore, even if you do not compare your man

---

1 'Of Hippolochus nothing is known' (Cope, *Comm.*).

2 Demosthenes, *Lept.* p. 478 § 70, *χαλκῆν εἰκόνα* (of Konon), *ὥσπερ Ἁρμοδίου καὶ Ἀριστογείτονος, ἔστησαν πρώτου*. The first portrait-statues of the tyrannicides were the work of Antênor, and were carried off by Xerxes. Their place was taken by the work of Critios and Nêsiôtês, which was standing in the marketplace at the time when Aristotle wrote the *Rhetoric.* The earlier statues were recovered at a later date.

3 *διὰ τὴν συνήθειαν τοῦ δικολογεῖν*, the reading of the inferior MSS, was preferred by Jebb (1) for the reasons given by Vater, (2) because Cicero, *Brutus*, 48, describes Isokrates as having been in the habit of composing forensic orations for the use of others, and because six of these orations are still extant, (3) because Dionysius of Halicarnassus, *Isokr.* c. 18, refers to his forensic orations. Isokrates nowhere *denies* having written for the courts. On the other hand Spengel, Cope, and Roemer prefer accepting the reading of the Paris MS, *διὰ τὴν ἀσυνήθειαν*. 'Isocrates cultivated the habit of comparing his hero with others in consequence of his want of *actual* practice in the law-courts' (Cope, *Comm.* i 185).

with the eminent, at least you should compare him with the world in general, since excellence is held to reveal virtue. And, universally, of those topics which are common to all speeches, Amplification is most suitable to the Epideictic,—since the actions are taken for granted, so that it remains only to invest them with grandeur and beauty; Illustration is most suitable to Deliberative Speaking, for we judge the future by divination from the past;—Enthymemes are most suitable for Forensic Speaking; since the past, through its obscurity, gives the largest scope to explanation and demonstration.

These, then, are the premisses, from which, in almost every case, praise or blame is drawn; the objects, with a view to which we must praise or blame; and the sources of encomia and of reproaches. These ascertained, their opposites are manifest; blame being derived from the opposite things.

> Forensic Rhetoric. Accusation and Defence being the elements, and the end, justice or injustice, we must begin by analysing injustice, and inquiring what are the motives and aims of wrongdoing.

x. We must next state the number and the nature of the premisses from which syllogisms are to be derived in reference to Accusation and Defence. Three things, then, have to be ascertained; the nature and the number of the motives from which men do wrong; the states of mind in which they do wrong; the characters and situations of those whom they wrong. We will first define wrong-doing and then proceed.

> Actions are [1] Voluntary, from habit, reason, anger, or lust; [2] Involuntary, from chance, nature, or force.

Let wrong-doing, then, be defined as doing harm wilfully against the law. Law is either special or general. By special law I mean that written law, under which each community lives; by general laws, those unwritten ordinances, which seem to be acknowledged on all hands. Men do wilfully such things as they do knowingly, but not under compulsion. Not all wilful acts are done by moral choice, but all acts done by moral choice are wilful; since no man is ignorant of what he deliberately chooses. The causes, through which men elect to do harm and to do worthless acts contrary to the law, are Vice and Intemperance; for if people have a bad quality or bad qualities, in respect to this or these they are unjust, as well as bad; thus the illiberal man is unjust in respect to money, the intemperate man is unjust in respect to the pleasures of the body, the luxurious man in respect to the means of ease, the coward in respect to dangers; for cowards leave the comrades of their peril in the lurch through fear; as an ambitious man will betray for the sake of honour, a passionate man through anger, a lover of victory for the sake of victory, a bitter man for revenge, a foolish man because he is deceived about right or wrong, a shameless man through disregard for reputation. And so each of the rest will do wrong in respect to the subject-matter of his vice.

All this, however, is clear—partly from what has been said about the Virtues[1], partly from what will presently be said about the Affections[2]. It remains to say wherefore, and under what circumstances, men do wrong, and to whom. First, then, let us determine what things men want to get, or to shun, when they set about doing wrong; for it is plain that the accuser has to consider what and how many of those objects, with which all men rob their neighbours, exist for his adversary; the defendant has to consider what, and how many of them, do *not* exist. Now, all men do all things, either of themselves, or not of themselves. Of those things, which they do *not* of themselves, some are done by chance, some of necessity. And necessary acts are done either perforce or by nature; so that all things, which men do, *not* of themselves, are done either by chance or by nature or perforce. Actions which men do of themselves, and of which they are themselves the causes, are done either

---

[1] I ix *supra*.

[2] II i–xi *infra*.

from habit or from appetite, rational or irrational. Now *wish* is an appetite of good; for no one wishes, unless he thinks the thing good: the irrational appetites are anger and lust. So that every act of men must have one of seven causes—chance, nature, force, habit, reason, passion, lust. It is superfluous further to discriminate men's acts according to their ages, or their moral states; for, if it is incidental to youth to be passionate or lustful, yet youths do corresponding acts, not through their youth, but through anger or lust. Wealth, again, and poverty are not causes; rather it is incidental to the position of poor men that they desire money because they lack it, and to the position of rich men that they desire needless pleasures, because they command them: but these men, too, will act accordingly, not through wealth or poverty, but through desire. Likewise the just and the unjust and the rest, who are said to act in accordance with moral states, will act through the above-named causes; either from reason or from some affection; some, however, from good dispositions and affections, some from the opposite. It is incidental, however, to this or that kind of moral state to be attended by this or that kind of impulse; for, no sooner is a man temperate than, because he is so, he is presumably prone to good opinions and desires in regard to pleasant things; and the intemperate man, to their opposites. Such distinctions, then, may be left alone; we need only consider on what sort of conditions given results usually depend. For instance, no one of the results noticed above is regularly dependent on a man being fair or dark or tall or short; but, whether he is young or old, or just or unjust—*this* makes a difference. And generally all those accidents are important, which make a difference in men's characters; for instance, it will make a difference in a man whether he thinks himself rich or poor, prosperous or unfortunate. These points, then, shall be discussed by and by[1]: let us first finish the matter in hand.

[1] II xii–xvii *infra.*

Those things happen by chance, of which the cause is indefinite and which do not happen on account of anything, or always, or usually, or regularly: the definition of chance, however, will make all this clear. Things happen naturally, of which the cause is in themselves, and regular; for they have the same issue, either always or usually. As to things contrary to nature, there is no need to enquire minutely whether they happen according to *some* nature or other cause; chance, however, would seem to be the cause of these also. Acts are done perforce, which are done contrary to desire, or to calculation, by the agents themselves. Acts are done from habit, which men do because they have often done them. Acts are done by calculation when, being in the number of the above-mentioned goods, and seeming expedient as ends or means, they are done because they are expedient; since intemperate men, also, do some expedient things,—not, however, because they are expedient, but because they are pleasant. The acts done through passion and anger are acts of retribution. There is a difference between retribution and chastisement; chastisement being inflicted for the sake of the patient, retribution for the satisfaction of the agent. As to the nature of Anger, that will appear from what we say on the Affections[1]; the acts done through desire, are such as seem pleasant. A habit, whether unconsciously or painfully acquired, is among pleasant things; for there are many things which are not naturally pleasant, which people do with pleasure, when accustomed to them. Thus, to put it shortly, all things which men do of themselves are good or apparently good, pleasant or apparently pleasant: for I reckon among goods riddance from evils or apparent evils, and the exchange of a greater evil for a less, since these things are in their way desirable; and, similarly, I count among pleasures riddance from a pain or apparent pain, and the exchange of a greater pain for a less. We must ascertain, then, the number and nature

[1] II ii *infra.*

of things Expedient and Pleasant. The Expedient has already been discussed under the head of Deliberative Rhetoric[1]: let us now speak of the Pleasant. Our definition is to be considered adequate in each case if, without being exact, it is clear.

• • •

BOOK II[2]

> The speaker may produce a good impression of his character by means of his speech.

i. This, then, is an account of the premisses to be used in exhorting or dissuading, praising or blaming, accusing or defending, and of the popular notions and propositions available for producing belief in each case; since the enthymemes concern these and come from these, if we take each branch of Rhetoric by itself. And since Rhetoric has a view to judgment, for, both in debates and in lawsuits, there is judging, the speaker must not only see that the speech shall prove its point, or persuade, but must also develope a certain character in himself and in the judge, as it matters much for persuasiveness,—most of all in debate, but secondarily in lawsuits too—that the speaker should appear a certain sort of person, and that the judges should conceive him to be disposed towards them in a certain way;—further, that the judges themselves should be in a certain mood. The apparent character of the speaker tells more in debate, the mood of the hearer in lawsuits. Men have not the same views when they are friendly and when they hate, when they are angry or placid, but views either wholly different or different in a large measure. The friendly man regards the object of his judgment as either no wrong-doer or a doer of small wrong: the hater takes the opposite view. The man who desires and is hopeful (supposing the thing in prospect to be pleasant), thinks that it will be, and that it will be good; the man who is indifferent, or who feels a difficulty, thinks the opposite.

> He should make his audience feel that he possesses intelligence, virtue, and good-will.
> In this purpose we must analyse (*a*) the virtues and (*b*) the moral affections.
> In regard to each of the affections we have to see (1) its nature; (2) its antecedents; (3) its objects.

The speakers themselves are made trustworthy by three things; for there are three things, besides demonstrations, which make us believe. These are, intelligence, virtue and good-will. Men are false in their statements, and their counsels, from all or one of the following causes. Either through folly, they have not right opinions; or having right opinions, they say through knavery what they do not think; or they are sensible and honest, but not well-disposed; whence they may happen not to advise the best course, although they see it. Besides these cases there is no other. It follows that the man who is thought to have all the three qualities must win the belief of the hearers. Now the means of appearing intelligent and good are to be got from the analysis of the virtues[1]; for the same means will enable one to give such a character either to another person or to himself. Good-will and friendliness have now to be discussed under the head of the Affections.[2] The Affections are those things, being attended by pleasure or pain, by which men are altered in regard to their judgments;—as anger, pity, fear, and the like, with their opposites. In respect to each, three points are to

[1] 1 vi *supra*.

[2] The arrangement of Book II is singular. In Book I the λογικὴ πίστις,—the third of the ἔντεχνοι πίστεις, was partly analysed. Chapter 20 of Book II returns to this subject, and completes it. But the first eighteen chapters deal with the other two ἔντεχνοι πίστεις,—the ἠθικὴ and the παθητικὴ (R. C. J.).

[1] I ix *supra*.

[2] iv *infra*.

be determined; in respect to anger, for instance, in what state men are prone to anger,—with whom they are wont to be angry,—and at what things: for, supposing we knew one or two, but not all, of these things, it would be impossible to excite anger; and so in the other cases. As then, in the former part of the subject, we sketched the available propositions, so we propose to do here also, applying an analysis of the same kind.

Analysis of the affections. Anger and mildness.

ii. Anger, then, may be defined as an appetite, attended with pain, for revenge, on account of an apparent slighting of things which concern one, or of oneself, or of one's friends, when such slighting is unmeet. If, then, this is anger, it follows that the angry person is always angry with an individual (as with Kleon, not with the genus 'man'), and because that individual has done something, or intended something, against the angry person or his friends: it follows, too, that all anger is attended by a certain pleasure which comes from the hope of revenge; for it is pleasant to think that one will attain one's aim; and no one aims at things impossible for him—the angry man aims at things distinctly possible for him. So it has been well said of anger that

> 'It swells in men's breasts far sweeter than
> honey dripping from the rock.'[1]

A certain pleasure attends on it, not only for this reason, but also because men dwell in thought on the act of the revenge. So the image, which then arises, excites pleasure, like the imagery of dreams.

Now, slighting is an active form of opinion about something thought worthless. We think both bad things and good things worthy of earnestness—and the things which tend to them. But things which tend to them not at all, or very little, we deem worthless. There are three species of slighting—disdain, spite, and insolence. The man who disdains, slights; for people disdain all things which they fancy worthless; and what is worthless, they slight. Again, the man who spites appears to disdain; for spiting is a thwarting of wishes, not for the spiter's gain, but for the other's loss.

A man slights, then, not for his own gain. Clearly he supposes that the other can do him no harm (or he would fear instead of slighting); and also that he is not likely to do him any good worth mentioning (or he would give heed to be his friend). The man who insults, again, slights; for insolence is to do and say things which shame the sufferer; not in order that anything may accrue to the insulter, or because anything has been done to him, but in order that he may have joy. Requiters do not insult; they avenge. The source of pleasure to the insulters is this,—they fancy that, by ill-treating the other people, they are showing the greater superiority.

Hence young men and rich men are insolent; they fancy that, by insulting, they are superior. Dishonouring is a part of insolence; and the man who dishonours, slights. For what is worth nothing has no honour,—no *price* either as good or evil. So Achilles says in his wrath—

> 'He dishonoured me: for he hath taken
> the prize himself,'[1]

and

> 'Like some dishonoured vagabond,'[2]

—as if it was these things that made him angry. Men think that they ought to be made much of by their inferiors (1) in birth, (2) in power, (3) in goodness; and generally, a man expects honour for that in which he decidedly excels[3],—as, in respect to money, the rich man excels the poor,—in speak-

---

1 *Il.* xviii 109, quoted in I xi 9, *supra.*

1 *Il.* i 356.

2 *Il.* ix 648.

3 The translator here accepts *ἐν ᾧ ἄν τις ὑπερέχῃ πολύ*,—Spengel's conjecture for *ἐν ᾧ ἄν ταὐτῷ ὑπερέχῃ πολύ*. The Paris MS has *ταῦτα ὑπερέχει* and Roemer *ταῦτα ὑπερέχῃ*.

ing, the man of rhetorical faculty excels the man of none; as the ruler excels the ruled, and the man, who thinks himself worthy to rule, excels the man who deserves to be ruled. Whence the saying

> 'Great is the anger of Zeus-nurtured kings'[1]

and

> 'Yet afterwards he bears a grudge.'[2]

It is their superiority which makes them feel indignant. Again, (a man resents a slight) from those to whom good has been done, is meant or was meant, by himself, or by some one else at his instance, or by one of his friends.

It is now plain, therefore, from what has been said, in what moods men are angry, and with what persons, and at what things. Men are angry when they are pained; for the man who is pained is aiming at something. Whether, then, he is thwarted directly in anything—as, if a thirsty man were thwarted about drinking—or indirectly, the offence appears the same; whether one acts against him, or fails to act with him, or in any other way annoys him, while in this state of desire, he is alike angry. Hence people who are ill, who are in poverty, (who are at war,)[3] who are in love, who are thirsty,—generally, who have some ungratified desire—are irascible or easily incensed, chiefly against those who slight their present need. Thus, a sick man is enraged by want of sympathy with his illness,—a poor man, by indifference to his poverty, the wager of a war by indifference to his war, the lover by indifference to his love, and so in the other cases; . . .[4] each person being predisposed by his actual plight to his particular anger. Again, a man is made angry by a result contrary to that which he expects; for a great surprise is a greater pain, just as, when the desired thing happens, it is a greater joy. Hence it is plain what times and seasons, what circumstances, what periods of life, are favourable to the exciting of anger; and the more people are under these conditions, the more easily they can be excited.

These, then, are the moods in which men are prone to anger; the persons with whom they are angry are those who laugh at them and jeer them and mock them; for these insult;—and those who do them such harms as are signs of insolence. Such are necessarily those which are neither retributive nor of advantage to the doers; for it seems to remain that the motive is insolence. Men are angry, too, with those who disparage and despise them in regard to the things about which they are most in earnest; as those who pride themselves on their philosophy are made angry by disparagement of their philosophy, those who are proud of their appearance by disparagement of their appearance, and so forth; and they feel this much more strongly, if they suspect that the thing in question does not belong to them, or belongs to them insecurely, or is not recognised; for, as soon as they are quite sure that they possess the things about which they are mocked, they do not care. And the anger is felt against friends more than against those who are not such; for men think that from their friends they deserve good treatment rather than bad. A man is angry, too, with those who are wont to show him honour or regard, if they alter this behaviour; for he thinks that he is despised by these persons; else they would go on doing as before. He is angry, too, with those who do not requite his benefits, or who do not make an equal return; and with those who act the contrary way to himself, if they are inferiors; for all such persons seem to despise him,—the latter sort treating *him* as their inferior, the former sort treating (his benefits as coming) from an inferior.

And men especially resent a slight from men of no account; for the anger caused by a slight is

---

[1] *Il.* ii 196.

[2] *Il.* i 82.

[3] *πολεμοῦντες* added by Bekker, ed. 3.

[4] *<εἰ δὲ μὴ, κἂν ὁτιοῦν ἄλλο ὀλιγωρῇ τις>* is inserted in the text by Susemihl, followed by Roemer. The old Latin transl. has *si autem non, et quodcunque aliud parvipendat quis. εἰ δὲ μὴ* corresponds to *μάλιστα μὲν*, four lines earlier.

assumed to be directed against those whom it does not become to inflict it, and it does not become inferiors to do so. A man is angry with his friends for failing to speak well of him, and to do him good,—still more for speaking and doing evil; or for failing to perceive his need,—as Antiphon's[1] Plêxippos was angry with Meleager; for the non-perception is a sign of slighting; since things, about which we care, do not escape our notice. Again, we are angry with those who rejoice over our misfortunes, or who, in a general way, are made cheerful by them; since this is the token of an enemy or a contemner. And with those who do not care whether they give pain; hence men are angry with the bearers of bad news. And with those who hear of, or behold, their weaknesses; since these are like contemners or enemies, since friends share one's pain, and all men feel pain in contemplating their own weaknesses. Further, men are angry with those who slight them before five classes of people—(1) their rivals; (2) those whom they admire; (3) those by whom they wish to be admired; (4) those whom they revere; (5) those by whom they are revered; a slight in the presence of these makes men especially angry. Again, men are made angry by slights directed against objects which they are bound in honour to vindicate—as against their parents, children, wives, subjects. We are angry, too, with those who do not requite a favour; for the slighting is undue[2]. And with those who meet our earnestness with irony; for irony implies disdain. And with those who do good to all others, if they do not do good to us; for it is a mark of disdain to rate us below the whole world[3]. Forgetfulness, again, tends to produce anger,—forgetfulness of names, for instance, small as the matter is; since forgetfulness, too, seems to be a sign of slighting; for forgetfulness comes through carelessness, and carelessness is a kind of slighting.

The persons, then, with whom men are angry; the moods in which they are angry, and the causes of their anger, have been stated together. It is plain that it will be necessary to bring the judges by our speech into a mood which lends itself to anger, and to represent our adversaries as guilty of these things, at which men are angry, and as the sort of people, with whom they are angry.

• • •

Brief retrospect, with introduction to the analysis of the four 'universal' classes of argument, applicable to all special premisses derived from special branches of knowledge.

xviii. The use of all persuasive speech has a view to a decision[1]; for there is no further need of speaking about things which we know and have decided. This is no less the case when the speaker aims at encouraging or dissuading one man only,

---

[1] This Antiphon is the tragic poet mentioned in II vi 27. The text here refers to his *Meleager*, two lines of which are quoted in II xxiii 20. Plêxippos was the brother of Meleager's mother, Althea. Cp. Nauck, *Trag. Gr. Fragm.*, p. 792, ed. 2.

[2] *παρὰ τὸ προσῆκον γὰρ ἡ ὀλιγωρία*, 'for the slight is a violation of the *natural* claim, duty, or obligation' (Cope, *Comm.* ii 30 f).

[3] lit. 'to consider us unworthy to be treated in the same way as every one else' (Cope, ii 31).

---

[1] § I *ἐπεὶ δ' ἡ τῶν πιθανῶν λόγων χρῆσις—τοὺς λόγους ἠθικοὺς ποιητέον*. Here the protasis, *ἐπεὶ* etc., has no apodosis answering to it, either in grammar or in sense. (1) *Grammar.* This difficulty is not insuperable. Aristotle is often careless in the same way: *e.g. Poët.* 9, *ἐπεὶ δέ* . . . *ὥστε ἀνάγκη*, *Analyt. Post.* I 25 p. 866, *ἔτι εἰ ἀρχὴ* . . . *ὥστε βελτίων*. (3) *Sense.* '*Since* all rhetorical speech has a view to a judge—it follows that it has been shown how to make speeches characteristic.' This is a false connexion of protasis and apodosis. The following solutions have been suggested:—(*a*) Cope thinks that a sentence is lost after *βουλεύονται*, before the last sentence in § I. '*Since* all rhetoric is addressed to a judge, <I have therefore analysed the *ἤθη* and *πάθη*, in order to help the speaker to conciliate these judges;> the *πολιτειῶν ἤθη*, too, have been discussed, *and so* (*ὥστε*) this part of the subject is finished.' (*b*) Spengel thinks that *ἐπεὶ δ' ἡ τῶν πιθανῶν λόγων χρῆσις—βουλεύονται* is a mere amplification of II i 2 *ἐπεὶ δ' ἕνεκα κρίσεως—τὸν κριτὴν κατασκευάζειν*. In his *Rhetores Graeci* he brackets it as an interpolation. He thinks that the end of c. 17 and the first half of c. 18 hang together thus:—*περὶ μὲν οὖν τῶν καθ' ἡλικίαν—ἀδυνάτου· περὶ δὲ τῶν κατὰ τὰς πολιτείας ἠθῶν—ποιητέον. ἐπεὶ δὲ περὶ ἕκαστον μὲν*

as those who seek to admonish or to persuade may do. *That one* man is no less a judge; for he, whom we have to persuade, is, speaking generally, a judge. And it is so equally, whether we are speaking against a real adversary or against an imaginary case; since here we have to use our speech for the overthrow of arguments opposed to us, and to these arguments we address ourselves as to a living opponent. The same thing holds good of epideictic speaking: the speech is framed with reference to the spectator considered as a judge. As a rule, however, he alone is a judge in the simple sense, who decides a question in some issue of civil life; for there is a question of fact both in regard to the matter of a lawsuit and in regard to the subject of a debate. The characters of the several polities have already been treated under the head of Deliberative Rhetoric[1]. We may be considered, then, to have defined the way and the means of making our speech reflect a character.

And since each species of Rhetoric has, as we saw, a distinct end[2]; since, in regard to all of these, we have now got those popular principles and premisses from which men take their proofs in debate, in display, in forensic argument[3]; since, further, we have defined the available means of making speeches ethical[4];—it remains for us to discuss the *general* appliances[5]. All men are compelled in speaking to apply the topic of Possible and Impossible; and to try to show, either that a thing will be, or that it has been. Further, the topic of Size is common to all speeches; all men use depreciation and amplification in debate, in praising or blaming, in accusing or defending. When these topics have been defined, we must try to say what we have to say of Enthymemes generally, and of Examples, in order that, by the addition of what is still wanting, we may fulfil our original purpose. Of the general commonplaces, that of Amplification is, as has been said[1], most popular to Epideictic speaking; that of the Past to Forensic, for the decision concerns past facts; that of the Possible and Future to Deliberative.

γένος κτλ. Muretus and Vater think that the apodosis to *ἐπεὶ δ' ἡ τῶν πιθανῶν* is *λοιπὸν ἡμῖν διελθεῖν περὶ τῶν κοινῶν*. But the *second ἐπεὶ δὲ* (§ 2) is against this (R.C.J.). Spengel's view has been supported by Vahlen, *Zur Kritik Ar. Schriften* in the Transactions of the Vienna Academy, xxxviii (1861) 121–132; and opposed by Brandis, *Gesch. der gr. Philos.* III I, 195, and Thurot, *Études* (1861) 228–236. In Roemer's view, § I in the present chapter is the original form of the abridged sentence in II i 4, and this original was accidentally inserted in this place owing to the fortuitous fact that it began with *ἐπεὶ δὲ*, which is also the beginning of § 2 (*praef.* xcviii–ci).

[1] I viii.

[2] I iii.

[3] I iv–viii.

[4] I ix; x–xv.

[5] *κοινῶν*, *i.e.* both the *κοινοὶ τόποι* and the *κοιναὶ πίστεις*, Enthymeme and Example (R. C. J.).

The topic of the Possible and Impossible.

xix. First, then, let us speak of the Possible and Impossible. Now if, of two opposites, one can exist or come into existence, the other also would seem to be possible. For instance, if a man can be healed, he can also fall sick: for the potentiality of opposites, as such, is one. And, if of two like things one is possible, the other is. And, if the harder is possible, the easier is so. And, if the good and beautiful form of a thing can come into being, the thing generally can come into being; for it is harder for a fine house, than for a house, to exist. And, if there can be a beginning of anything, there can be an end; for no impossibility comes or begins to come into existence. Thus it neither happens, nor could begin to happen, that the diagonal of a square is commensurate with its side. And, if the end of a thing is possible, the beginning is so; for all things come from a beginning. And, if that which is later in existing, or in being born, can arise, that which is earlier can; for instance, if a man can come into existence, a boy can; for boyhood is the earlier stage—and, if a boy, then a man; for boyhood is the beginning. Those things, too, are possible, of which the love or desire is natural; for no one, as a rule, is enamoured or desirous of impossibilities. Those things, of which there are sciences and arts, can exist and come into

[1] I ix.

existence[1]. Things are possible, again, which have the beginning of birth in things which we can compel or persuade; such being those powers of which we are the superiors or the masters or the friends. When the parts of a thing are possible, the whole is so; and, when the whole is possible, the parts are so—as a rule. Thus, if the various parts of a shoe, the toe-piece, the strap, the side-leather, are possible, shoes are possible; and, if shoes are possible, the toe-piece, the strap, and the side-leather are possible, and, if the genus belongs to the number of possibilities, the species does; and *vice versa;* thus, if a sailing vessel can exist, a trireme can, and *vice versa.* If, of two things naturally interdependent, one is possible, the other is so; as, if double is possible, half is so; and *vice versa.* And, if a thing can come to pass without art or preparation, much more can it do so with them; whence Agathon's saying—

> 'Some things we have to effect by art;
> others come to us by necessity or chance.'[2]

If a thing is possible for the worse and weaker and more foolish, it is more so for their opposites; as Isokrates said that it was strange if Euthynos[3] had learned this, and *he* should not be able to discover it. The topics for Impossibility are of course to be found in the opposites of these.

Past and Future.

The question of Past Fact may be treated on these principles. First, if the less natural thing has happened, the more natural thing must have happened too. Again, if the usually later thing has happened, the earlier has happened; for instance, if he has forgotten a thing, he also learned it once. If he could and would, he has done the thing: for all men do what they would and can; there is nothing in the way. Again, if there was no external hindrance and he was angry; or, if he had the power and the *desire,* he has done the thing; for, as a rule, men do, if they can, the things for which they have an appetite,—bad men, through intemperance; good men, because they desire good things. Or, if he was going to do the thing[1], (you can say that he has done it); for it is *probable* that one, who intended an action, did it. A thing *has* happened, if those things have happened, of which it was the natural sequel or motive; thus, if it has lightened, it has thundered;—if he attempted the action, he did it. Or, if, again, those things have happened, to which it was the natural antecedent or means; thus, if it has thundered, it has lightened; or if he *did* the act, he made the attempt. In all such cases, the conclusion may be either necessarily or only generally true. The topics for the *negation* of Past Fact will obviously be found in the opposites of these.

The way to treat Fact Future appears from the same considerations. That *will* be, for which there is the power and the wish; or, which desire or anger[2], coupled with power, prompts. Hence, too,

---

[1] δυνατὸν ταῦτα καὶ εἶναι καὶ γενέσθαι, Bekker, with inferior MSS and the old Latin translation: δυνατὰ ταῦτα καὶ ἔστι καὶ γίγνεται, Spengel and Roemer, with the Paris MS. The former is the text here followed.

[2] Fragm. 8, Nauck, ed. 2,

> καὶ μὴν τὰ μέν γε χρὴ τέχνῃ πράσσειν, τὰ δὲ
> ἡμῖν ἀνάγκῃ καὶ τύχῃ προσγίγνεται

In 1. I all the MSS have τῃ τύχῃ; in 1. 2 all have τύχῃ, except Q, E, m, which have τέχνῃ (accepted by Muretus). Camozzi and others transferred τέχνῃ to 1. I, where τῃ τέχνῃ is accepted by Spengel and Roemer, while χρὴ τέχνῃ is proposed by Porson, on *Medea* 1090 (ed. 1826). For πράσσειν the Paris MS has πράσσει (adopted by Roemer).—Agathon follows the Sophists, who made all things happen either φύσει or τύχῃ or τέχνῃ, Plato, *Laws,* x, p. 185.

[3] Euthȳnos, not the Euthȳnous of Or. XXI (R. C. J.). Possibly a quotation from Or. XVIII (*Against Kallimachos*) 15, θαύμαζω δ' εἰ αὐτὸν μὲν ἱκανὸν γνῶναι νομίζει . . . ἐμὲ δ' οὐκ ἂν οἴεται τοῦτ' ἐξευρεῖν, in which case *Euthynos* (for which the scholiast has *Euthynous*) is a mistake for *Kallimachos;* cp. Usener, *Rhein. Mus.* xxv 603.

[1] εἰ ἔμελλε [γίγνεσθαι καὶ] ποιεῖν Spengel, Bekker (ed. 3), and Cope; the words bracketed (on the ground that the *things* come below) are defended by Vater, and by Vahlen on Ar. *Poët.* p. 153, and retained by Roemer.

[2] Most MSS add καὶ λογισμῷ, omitted by one MS, and bracketed by Spengel, but retained by Bekker and Roemer.

if[1] there is the impulse or the intention to do a thing, it *will* be; for, as a rule, things which are about to happen, come to pass rather than things which are *not* so. A thing *will* be, if its natural antecedents have already come to pass; thus, if it is cloudy, it is likely to rain. Or, if the means to an end have come into being, the end is likely to be; thus, if there is a foundation-stone, there will be a house.

More and Less.

As to the Greatness and Smallness of things, greater and less, and generally great things and small, all is clear from what has been already said by us. Under the Deliberative brand of Rhetoric we have discussed the relative greatness of goods[2], and the abstract greater and less[3]. Now, as in each kind of speaking the proposed end is a good,—namely, the Expedient, the Honourable, or the Just,—it follows that all speakers must derive their topics of amplification from these goods. It is waste of words to inquire further about *abstract* greatness and pre-eminence; for particulars are more momentous in practice than universals.

Enough, then, of the Possible and Impossible; Fact Past, Fact Future, the negation of these; and further of the Greatness or Smallness of things[4].

Proofs common to all Rhetoric.

xx. It remains to speak of the Proofs common to all Rhetoric, as we have spoken of their particular elements. The common proofs are generically two—Example and Enthymeme; for the maxim is part of an Enthymeme. First, then, we will speak of the Example; for the Example is like Induction, and Induction is the primary process.

[1] *διὰ ταῦτα καὶ εἰ*, so Bekker. *ταῦτα καὶ* (the reading of the Paris MS) is accepted by Roemer; Spengel suggests *καὶ τὰ* (omitting *διὰ ταῦτα* and *εἰ*).

[2] I vii.

[3] I vii, I.

[4] On c. xix see *Appendix* to Book II.

Examples.
Historical.
Artificial.

There are two kinds of Example. One kind consists in the use of historical parallel, another in the use of artificial parallel. Artificial parallel takes the form either of comparison or of fable, like Æsop's or the Libyan fables. It would be using historical parallel, if one were to say that we must arm against the Great King and not let him subdue Egypt; for, in a former instance, Darius did not come over till he had got Egypt, but, having got it, he came; and Xerxes, again, did not attack us till he had got it, but, having got it, he came[1]; and so this man[2] too, if he gets it, will come over—therefore he must not be allowed to get it. 'Comparison' means such illustrations as those of Sokrates—saying, for instance, that magistrates ought not to be appointed by lot, for it is like appointing athletes, not by athletic power, but by lot, or as if the appointment of a pilot from among the crew were to go, not by skill, but by lot[3]. Instances of fables are that of Stesichoros[4] about Phalaris, and that of Æsop on behalf of the demagogue.

When the people of Himera had made Phalaris their military dictator, and were going to give him a body-guard, Stesichoros told them, among other things, a story about a horse, who had a meadow all to himself, until a deer came and began to spoil his pasturage. When the horse, wishing

[1] Egypt became a Persian satrapy in 528 B.C., when it was conquered by Kambyses. In 490 Darius sent Datis and Artaphernes against Greece. In 486 Egypt revolted. In 485 Darius died. In 484 Xerxes reconquered Egypt, and in 480 invaded Greece (R. C. J.).

[2] Artaxerxes III (Ochus), 361–338. Ochus apparently made three expeditions against Egypt,—the first at an uncertain date, the second probably in the winter of 351–350 B.C., and the third (in which he reconquered Egypt) probably in 345. This last is the date accepted by A. Schaefer, in ed. 2 of his *Dem. u. s. Zeit* (i 482–4), instead of 340, the date adopted in ed. I (p. 437).

[3] Cp. Xen. *Mem.* I ii 9.

[4] Of Himera, *fl.* 610 B.C.; accession of Phalaris, 570.

to be avenged on the deer, asked a certain man whether this could be done with his help, 'Yes,' said the man, 'if you are bitted, and I mount you armed with javelins.' The horse agreed, and was mounted; but, instead of being avenged, he was himself enslaved to the man. 'So in your own case,' said Stesichoros—'take care that, in your desire to chastise your enemies, you do not fare like the horse. You have the bit in your mouths already; if you give him a guard, and allow him to mount, you will be finally enslaved to Phalaris.'

Æsop, defending at Samos a demagogue who was being tried for his life, said that a fox, trying to cross a river, was once swept into a crevice in the rocks, and, not being able to get out, suffered miseries for a long while, being covered with dog-fleas. A hedgehog in his wanderings, seeing the fox, took pity on her, and asked whether he should remove the fleas. The fox objected; and, on the hedgehog asking why, said—'These are sated, and draw little blood; but, if you take them away, others will come with an appetite, and drain what blood is left to me.' 'Now you, too, Samians, will take no more hurt from this man; for he is rich; but, if you kill him, others will come poor, and will fritter and waste your public wealth.'

Fables suit public speaking, and have this advantage, that, while it is hard to find historical parallels, it is comparatively easy to find fables in point; in fact, one must contrive them, as one contrives comparisons, if one can discover an analogy, which literary knowledge[1] will make easy. The fabulous parallels are more easy to provide, but the historical parallels are more useful for the purpose of debate; since, as a rule, the future is like the past.

When we have no Enthymemes, Examples must be used as demonstrations (for they are the means of proof); when we have, as testimonies;—using them as epilogue to the Enthymemes: for, when the Examples are put *first,* they seem like an induction, but induction is not appropriate to Rhetoric except in a few cases; whereas, if they are *subjoined,* they seem like testimonies; and, in all cases, a witness is persuasive. Hence, if you put the Examples first, you must use many; if at the end, even one is enough; for even one witness is useful, if good.

Maxims.

xxi. It has now been explained how many kinds of example there are, and how and when they should be used. As to the citation of Maxims; when a maxim has been defined, it will best appear, in regard to what subjects, and at what times, and by whom, maxims may fitly be used in speaking. A maxim is a statement, not about a particular fact, as about the character of Iphikrates, but general; not about all things, as about 'straight' being the opposite of 'curved,' but about those things which are the objects of action, and which it is desirable or undesirable to do. So, since the Enthymeme is that syllogism which concerns such things, maxims may be said to be the conclusions and the premisses of Enthymemes without the syllogism:—as

> 'No man of good sense should have his children brought up over-wise':

this is a maxim; when the cause, the *wherefore,* is added, it is the complete enthymeme, as:—

> 'for, besides the general charge of sloth, they reap jealous dislike from their fellow citizens.'[1]

Again:—

> 'There is no man who is wholly prosperous':—[2]

and

> 'There is no man who is free'—

---

[1] φιλοσοφίας, 'literature'; an Isokratic use of the word. Cp. *Rhet. ad Alex.*, c. I, ἡ τῶν λόγων φιλοσοφία, 'the study of literature' (cp. Cope, *Comm.* ii 256).

[1] Euripides, *Medea,* 296 ff.

[2] Euripides, Fragm. 661 Nauck, ed. 2.

are maxims; but, when placed beside the sequel, they are enthymemes:

> 'For he is the slave of money or of chance.'[1]

If, then, a maxim is what has been said, it follows that there are four kinds of maxims. The maxim either will, or will not, have a reason subjoined. Those maxims which need demonstration are such as state something unexpected or disputed; those which state nothing unexpected, have no reason added. Of the latter class, some will not need the added reason, because they are familiar beforehand; as—

> 'It is an excellent thing for a man to be healthy, to *our* thinking'—[2]

for most people think so. Others do not need the added reason, because they are plain at the first glance, as—

> 'A lover is ever kindly.'[3]

Of the maxims which have a reason added, some are imperfect enthymemes; as

> 'No man of good sense,' &c.;[4]

others are in the nature, but not in the form, of enthymemes; and these are the most popular. They are those in which the reason for the statement is *implied;* as

> 'Do not, being a mortal, cherish immortal anger.'[5]

To say that it is not right to cherish anger is a maxim: the added words, 'being a mortal,' are the wherefore. Similarly—

[1] Euripides, *Hecuba,* 858.

[2] Ascribed to Simonides or Epicharmus by the scholiast; the latter ascription is accepted by Meineke.

[3] Euripides, *Troades,* 1051.

[4] Euripides, *Medea,* 296 ff.

[5] Nauck, *Fragm. Adespota,* 79, ed. 2; cp. Bentley, *Phalaris,* pp. 229, 243, ed. Wagner.

> 'The mortal should have mortal, not immortal thoughts.'[1]

It is clear, then, from what has been said, how many kinds of maxim there are, and in what case each kind is suitable. When the statement is a disputed, or a startling one, the maxim should have its reason added. We may put this reason first, making a maxim of the conclusion:—as—'For my part, as it is not desirable to be envied or to be inactive, I hold that it is better not to be educated.' Or this maxim may be stated first, and the former clause added. When the statement is not startling, but merely not self-evident, the reason ought to be added in as terse a form as possible. Laconic or enigmatic sayings also suit cases of this kind: as the saying of Stesichoros to the Locrians, that it is better not to be insolent, lest the grasshoppers[2] should have to sing on the ground[3]. The use of maxims is suitable to elderly men, and in regard to subjects with which one is conversant; for sententiousness, like story-telling, is unbecoming in a younger man; while, in regard to subjects with which one is not conversant, it is stupid and shows want of culture. It is token enough of this that rustics are the greatest coiners of maxims, and the readiest to set forth their views.

Spurious generalization is most convenient in expressing bitter complaint or indignation[4]; and here, either at the outset, or when the fact has been proved. Even trite and common maxims should be used, if they can serve; since, just because they are common, they seem right, on the supposition that all the world is agreed about them. Thus, one who calls his men into danger before they have sacrificed, may quote—

[1] Ascribed by Bentley to Epicharmus.

[2] Or 'cicalas.'

[3] Implying that the trees would be cut down. The cicadas usually sit on trees when they chirp; *Il.* iii 151 (of *τέττιγες*), *δένδρῳ ἐφεζόμενοι*, and Ar. *Hist. An.* v 30, *οὐ γίγνονται δὲ τέττιγες ὅπου δένδρα μὴ ἐστι.*

[4] *σχετλιασμῷ καὶ δεινώσει*. In the former the sense of cruelty is uppermost; in the latter, the sense of injustice (R. C. J.).

> 'The one best omen is to fight for one's country';[1]

or, if he calls on them to face danger when they are the weaker—

> 'The war-god is for both sides.'[2]

Or, if he is urging them to destroy their enemies' children, though these are doing no wrong—

> 'He is a fool, who slays the father, and leaves the children.'[3]

Some proverbs, again, are also maxims;—as the proverb 'an Attic neighbour.'[4] Our maxims ought sometimes to controvert sayings which have become public property (as 'know thyself,'—'Do nothing excessively'[5]), if thus our character will appear better, or if our maxim expresses passion. It would express passion if, for instance, an angry speaker were to say—'The saying that it is well to "know thyself," is a lie. If this man had known himself, he would never have presumed to be general.' This would make our character more attractive—'We ought not, as some say, to love in the expectation of hating—rather we should hate in the expectation of loving.' One should make one's moral predilections plain by the very statement of the maxim; or, failing this, one should add one's reason[6],—as by saying—'We ought to love, not, as some say, but in the expectation of loving always; for the other sort of love is insidious.' Else thus:—'But I do not like the saying; for the genuine friend ought to love in the expectation of loving always.' 'Nor do I like the saying, Do nothing excessively. Bad men should be hated excessively.'

One great help, which maxims lend in speaking, arises from the vulgarity[1] of the hearers. They are delighted when a general statement of the speaker hits those opinions which they hold in a particular case. My meaning will be clearer when put as follows—and at the same time we shall be set on the track of the best maxims. A maxim is, as has been said, a general statement, and men are pleased when a sentiment, which they already entertain on special grounds, is stated in general terms. Thus, if a man is afflicted with bad neighbours or bad children, he will give ear to the statement, that nothing is so trying as neighbourhood[2], nothing so foolish as begetting children. Hence, we must guess what sort of prepossessions they have, and how they came by them; then we must express, in general terms, these views on these subjects. This, then, is one of the advantages of using maxims. It has another still greater:—it gives a moral character to our speech. Speeches have a moral character, when they show a moral purpose. All maxims do effect this, since the man who uses a maxim makes a general declaration of his moral predilections; so that, if the maxims are good, they give the appearance of a good character to him who uses them.

In regard to maxims, then—their nature, their kinds, the way to use them and the advantages they yield—this account may suffice.

xxii. Let us now speak of Enthymemes—first, generally, of the way to look for them—then, of their topics; for these two parts of the subject are distinct.

The Enthymeme. General precepts.

It has been said already[3] that the enthymeme is a syllogism, and in what sense it is a syllogism,

---

[1] *Il.* xii 243.

[2] *Il.* xviii 309.

[3] I xv 14 *supra.*

[4] Quoted by Zenobios II 28. The Corinthian envoy in Thucydides (I 70) describes it as the national character of the Athenians 'neither to remain in peace themselves, nor to suffer others to do so.'

[5] The maxims of Solon and Chilon, respectively.

[6] *i.e.* you must add the reason *why you disapprove of the received maxim;* xiii 4.

---

[1] *i.e.* their love of the commonplace.

[2] Demosthenes, Or. 55 § 1, *χαλεπώτερον οὐδὲν γείτονος πονηροῦ.*

[3] I ii §§ 8, 13.

and how it differs from the dialectical syllogism[1]. We must not draw conclusions from far back, and we must not take everything in. If we do the former, the length of the chain causes perplexity; if the latter, our statement of what is obvious is mere garrulity. This is the reason why the uneducated are more persuasive than the educated for popular audiences,—as the poets say of the uneducated, that 'they have a finer charm for the ear of the crowd.'[2] Educated men state general principles and draw general conclusions; uneducated men draw conclusions, which lie close at hand, from facts within their own experience. We must not argue, then, from all opinions, but from those of the sort defined,—as from those of the judges, or those of persons in whom they believe; it must be clear, too, that these opinions are universally or generally entertained. And we must reason, not exclusively from necessary premisses, but also from merely probable premisses.

Now, first of all, we must grasp the necessity of knowing all or some of the special facts belonging to the subject on which we are to speak and reason,—whether the subject of the reasoning be political or of any other kind; for, if you know none of these facts, you will have no premisses. How, for instance, could we advise the Athenians on the question of going to war, unless we knew the nature of their power,—whether it is a naval force or a land force, or both,—and its amount; then, what their revenues are, and who are their friends or enemies; further, what wars they have waged, and how; and so forth. How could we praise them, if we were not prepared with the seafight at Salamis, or the battle of Marathon, or the services rendered to the Herakleidæ, and such things;—since all men found their praise on the glories, real or seeming, of its object? Similarly, they rest their censure on the opposite things, considering what dishonour attaches or seems to attach to the censured—as that they brought the Greeks under the yoke, or enslaved those who had bravely fought with them against the barbarians—the men of Ægina[1] and Potidæa[2]—and so on; or, if there has been any like mistake on their part. In the same way, accusers and defenders have in their view the special conditions of the case. It makes no difference whether our subject is the Athenians or the Lacedæmonians, or a man or a god. Suppose we are advising Achilles, praising or blaming, accusing or defending him; we must take those things which are, or seem, peculiar to him, in order that our praise or blame may set out from his particular honours or dishonours, our accusation or defence from his injustice or justice, our advice from his interests or dangers. And so in regard to any subject whatever. Thus, the question whether Justice is or is not a good[3] must be argued from the attributes of Justice and of the Good.

So, since we always effect our proof by these means, whether our reasoning process is comparatively strict, or rather lax; since, that is, we do not take our premisses from things in general, but from things peculiar to our special subject—and it is plain that the properly logical proof can be wrought in no other way—it is plainly necessary, as we showed in the *Topics*[4], to have (first of all) a selection of premisses about the possible and the most convenient subjects; secondly, to deal with sudden contingencies on the same plan—that is, by referring, not to indefinite generalities, but to the special subject-matter of our speech,—bringing into the sphere of our argument as many facts as possible, which have the closest bearing on the subject; for, the larger our knowledge of its particular conditions, the easier will be the proof; and,

1 I ii § II.

2 Euripides, *Hippolytus,* 989.

1 Thuc. II 27; IV 57.

2 Thuc. II 70.

3 *ἢ μὴ ἀγαθόν*, omitted in the Paris MS and the Latin transl., and bracketed by Gaisford, is retained by Spengel, who regards it as a reference to the argument in Plato's *Republic.*

4 I 14.

the closer we keep to the subject, the more appropriate and the less general will be our topics. By 'general' topics I mean, for instance, praising Achilles for being a man and a hero and having gone against Troy—these things being true of many other persons, so that such a speaker praises Achilles no more than he praises Diomede. By 'special' topics I mean things which are attributes of Achilles and of no one else—as having slain Hektor, bravest of the Trojans, and Kyknos[1], the invulnerable, who hindered all the Greeks from landing—or because he was the youngest man of the expedition, and bound by no oath—and so forth.

> Enthymemes, (1) demonstrative, (2) refutative.

This, then, is one principle, and the first, on which our enthymemes are to be chosen—in reference to their special materials. Now let us speak of their elementary forms. By the 'elementary form' of an enthymeme I mean the *place* (or class) to which it belongs. There are two kinds of enthymemes. One kind is Demonstrative (affirmatively or negatively); the other kind is Refutative:—the distinction being the same as in Dialectic between Refutation and Syllogism. The Demonstrative Syllogism consists in drawing a conclusion from consistent propositions; the Refutative, in drawing a conclusion from conflicting propositions. Now it may be said that we are in possession of our topics in regard to the several special subjects, which are useful or necessary. We have chosen our propositions in regard to each; so that we have already ascertained the topics from which enthymemes are to be drawn about Good or Evil, Honourable or Shameful, Just or Unjust[2], likewise about characters, feelings, moral states[3]. But further, and from another point of view, let us get commonplaces for enthymemes in general. We will point out, side by side[1], the Refutative and the Demonstrative topics; and the topics of what appear to be enthymemes, but are not so, since they are not syllogisms. When these matters have been explained, we will determine the several modes of destroying[2] or attacking[3] enthymemes.

> An enumeration of heads of argument, from which Enthymemes can be constructed.

xxiii. *1.* One topic of Demonstrative Enthymemes is from opposites. We must see whether the opposite holds good of the opposite, for the purpose of refutation, if the argument is not on our side;—or, for the purpose of establishing the point, if it is so. Thus 'It is good to be temperate; for it is harmful to be intemperate.' Or, to take the instance in the *Messêniakos*[4]—'If war is the cause of the present evils, we must correct them by means of peace.'[5]

> 'If it is not just to wax wroth with unwitting wrong-doers, neither are thanks due to him who does a good deed because he must.'[6]
>
> 'But, if there is such a thing in the world as specious lying, thou mayest be sure of the opposite—that there is much truth, which does not win men's trust.'[7]

2. Another topic is supplied by the various inflexions of the stem. What can or cannot be said

---

[1] Pindar, *Ol.* II 82 (of Achilles) *ὅς Ἕκτορ' ἔσφαλε . . . Κύκνον τε θανάτῳ πόρεν.*

[2] I iv 7-xiv.

[3] The virtues and vices (II xii I); see, in general, II i–xviii.

[1] *παρασημαινόμενοι*, 'pointing out, side by side' (as if in parallel columns). This seems better than the sense given in the Berlin Index, *praeterea adnotare* and in Liddell and Scott, 'note in passing.'

[2] c. xxv *infra.*

[3] *ἐνστάσεων*, *instantiarum,* 'objections to one of the premisses.'

[4] Of Alkidamas, cp. I xiii 2, *supra.*

[5] Fragm. 2, Sauppe.

[6] Nauck, *Fragm. Adesp.* 80 ed. 2; ascribed to Agathon or Theodektes.

[7] Euripides, *Thyestes,* Fragm. 396 Nauck.

of one form, can or cannot be said of another. Thus—'The just is not always good; else *justly* would be always *well;* but the fact is that it is not desirable to be put to death justly.'[1]

3. Another topic is from Relative Terms. If it can be said of the one person that he *acted* well or justly, it can be said of the other that he has *suffered* well or justly; or, if the command was right, the execution of the command has been right. Thus Diomedon, the farmer of taxes[2], said of the taxes—'If it is no shame for you to sell, it is no shame for us to buy.' And, if 'well' or 'justly' can be predicated of the sufferer, it can be predicated of the doer. This argument, however, may be used fallaciously: for, granting that the man has deserved his fate, it does not follow that he deserved it from you. Hence we ought to consider separately the fitness of the suffering for the sufferer, and the fitness of the deed for the doer, and then turn the argument in whichever way is convenient;—for sometimes there is a discrepancy, and (the justice of the suffering) does not hinder (the deed from being wrong). Thus, in the *Alkmæon* of Theodektes[3]:

> 'But did no one in the world hate thy mother?'

Alkmæon answers—

> 'Nay, one should take the question in two parts.'

And when Alphesibœa asks 'how?', he rejoins—

> 'They doomed her to death, but spared my life.'

Take, again, the lawsuit about Demosthenes and the slayers of Nikânor[4]:—since they were judged to have slain him justly, he was held to have deserved his death. Or the case of the man who was killed at Thebes[1]—in which the accused asks that it may be decided whether that man deserved to die,—meaning that it cannot be wrong to have slain a man who deserved death.

4. Another topic is that of Degree; as—'If the very gods are not all-knowing, men are not likely to be so'; for this means that, if a condition is not present, where it would be *more* natural, of course it is not present, where it would be *less* so. The inference that a man strikes his neighbours, seeing that he strikes his father, comes from this argument—that, if the rarer thing exists, the more frequent thing exists also; for people strike their fathers more rarely than they strike their neighbours. The argument, then, may stand thus. Or it may be argued that, if a thing does not exist, where it is more frequent, it does not exist where it is rarer; or that, if it exists where it is rarer, it exists where it is more frequent—according as it may be needful to prove that it does or that it does not exist[2]. Again, this topic may be used in a case of parity:—hence the lines—

> 'Thy father is to be pitied for having lost his children; and is not Œneus to be pitied for having lost his famous son?'[3]

So it may be argued that, if Theseus did no wrong, neither did Paris; or that, if the Tyndaridæ

---

[1] I ix 15.

[2] Nothing more is known of him.

[3] 376–335 B.C., pupil of Isokrates; Fragm. 2, Nauck ed. 2. Alkmæon murdered his mother Eriphyle, for betraying Amphiaraos. Alphesibœa was the wife of Alkmæon.

[4] This lawsuit is unknown.

---

[1] Euphron, tyrant of Sikyon till about 364 B.C. When an oligarchy was reestablished, he fled. With the aid of Athens, he afterwards regained the city; but, finding it necessary to gain the support of Thebes, he went thither to obtain it. He was followed by some of his enemies, who murdered him in the *Kadmeia,* Xen. *Hellen.* vii 3 (R. C. J.).

[2] 'The inference'—'does not exist.' A translation of the longer form of this passage, preserved in the Paris MS, and adopted by Spengel and Roemer.

[3] *Fragm. Adesp.* 81 Nauck, from the *Meleager* of Euripides or of Antiphon. The scholiast suggests that Œneus may be speaking to Althæa—Althæa's brother having been killed by Meleager.

did none, neither did Paris; or that, if Hektor killed Patroklos, Paris killed Achilles[1]; or that, if other artists are not contemptible, neither are philosophers[2]; or that, if generals are not contemptible, because in many cases they are put to death[3], neither are sophists; or, 'if a private person ought to respect the opinion of Athens, Athens ought to respect that of Greece.'[4]

5. Another topic is from considerations of time. Thus Iphikrates said in his speech against Harmodios[5]—'If, before doing the deed, I had claimed the statue on condition of doing it, you would have given it: now that I have done the deed, will you not give it? You are ready to promise rewards, when you expect a benefit;—do not withdraw them, when you have reaped it.' Again, the argument about the Thebans allowing Philip to pass through into Attica:—'If he had asked this before he came to the help of Phocis, they would have promised it. It is absurd, then, if they are to refuse him a passage because he waived the point and trusted them.'[6]

6. Another topic is taken from things said (by the adversary), applied to our own case[7] as compared with his. The ways of doing this are

[1] Polykrates, Sauppe, *Fragm. Or. Att.* IX. 7. Theseus, with the aid of Peirithoüs, carried off Helen from Sparta, while she was a young girl, and placed her at Aphidnæ in Attica, under the care of Æthra, mother of Theseus. While Theseus was absent in Hades, the Dioskuri made an expedition into Attica,—took Athens, delivered Helen, and brought Æthra a slave to Sparta (R. C. J.).

[2] Isokrates, *Antid.* §§ 209–214.

[3] *θανατοῦνται* Paris MS, Spengel: vulgo *ἡττῶνται*.

[4] Lysias, Or. XVIII, Fragm. I Sauppe.

[5] Dionysios, *De Lysia,* c. 12, mentions the Speech *on the Statue of Iphikrates* as probably spurious on grounds of style and chronology (R. C. J.).

[6] Shortly before Chæronea, 338 B.C., Philip and his allies demanded that the Thebans should either join them in invading Attica, or give them a passage through Bœotia, Dem. *De Cor.* § 213. Spengel thinks this is quoted from the representations made by Philip's envoys (R. C. J.).

[7] *καθ' αὐτούς* vulgo; *καθ' αὑτοῦ*, 'against myself,' is conjectured by Bywater, and accepted by Roemer.

various[1]—as in the *Teucer*[2]. Iphikrates used this against Aristophon,—asking whether Aristophon would betray the ships for money?—and, when he said 'No,' rejoining—'So you, being Aristophon, would not betray them; would I, being Iphikrates?'[3] It is necessary that the adversary should be more liable to the suspicion of crime; else, the effect will be ludicrous—as if one were to say this in answer to the accusations of Aristeides. The argument is meant to create distrust of the accusers; for, as a rule, the accuser is by way of being better than the defendant: this assumption, then, should always be confuted. Generally speaking, a man is absurd when he upbraids others with what he himself does, or would do; or when he exhorts others to do what he himself does not, or is incapable of doing.

7. Another topic is from Definition. Thus—'What is the supernatural? Is it a god or the work of a god? He, however, who thinks that there is the work of a god, must needs think that there are gods.'[4] Or, take the saying of Iphikrates[5], that the best man is the noblest, for Harmodios and Aristogeiton had nothing noble about them, until they had done a noble deed;—and that he himself is more nearly akin to them:—'At all events my deeds are more nearly akin than yours to the deeds of Harmodios and Aristogeiton.'[6] Another example is the remark in the *Alexandros*[7]:—'all will

[1] *διαφέρει δ' ὁ τρόπος*, 'the character of the speaker is important,' 'it is the character that here makes the difference' (Spengel); 'this method excels all others' (Gaisford). *τρόπος* is interpreted as *τόπος* by Victorius and Muretus.

[2] Of Sophokles; cp. III xv 9. Teucer is here defending himself against Odysseus.

[3] Lysias, Or. LXV, Fragm. I. In 355, Aristophon, the Azenian, and Chares prosecuted Iphikrates for his failure in the last campaign of the Social War. Iphikrates was acquitted; cp. III x 7 (R. C. J.).

[4] Cp. Plato, *Apol. Socr.* 27 C–E.

[5] In the *ἀπολογία* against Harmodios, 371 B.C.; § 6 *supra* (cp. Cope, *Comm.* ii 256).

[6] Lysias, Or. XVIII, Fragm. 2.

[7] Polykrates, *Alexandros,* ix fragm. 2, p. 223 Sauppe.

allow that men of unruly life are not contented with the enjoyment of one love.' Or the reason which Sokrates gives for not going to Archelaos:—'It is an insolence not to be able to make an equal return for benefits, just as it is to requite them with evil'[1]. In all these cases the speaker defines and ascertains the meaning of a term with a view to reasoning on his subject.

8. Another commonplace is from the various senses of a word—of which 'rightly' was our example in the *Topics*[2].

9. Another is from Division: as 'All men do wrong from one of three motives—on account of *this,* or *this,* or *this;* here two of the motives are out of the question, and the accusers themselves do not impute the third.'

10. Another topic is from Induction: as, from the case of the woman of Peparêthos[3], it might be argued that women always discern the truth about their own children. Thus in an instance at Athens, when the orator Mantias was at law with his son, the mother settled the point for him[4]; in another instance at Thebes, the woman of Dodona declared Ismênias to be father of the son whom Stilbôn was disputing with him, and on this ground the Thebans held Thettaliskos to be the son of Ismênias[1]. Take, again, the example in the *Law* of Theodektês[2]: 'If men do not entrust their own horses to those who have taken bad care of other people's, neither will they entrust their own ships to those who have upset the ships of others. If it is so, then, in all cases, we ought not to use for our own protection those who have ill-guarded the safety of others.' Or, take the saying of Alkidamas[3], that 'all men honour the wise:—at least the Parians have paid honour to Archilochos, though he was a reviler; the Chians to Homer, though he was not their fellow-citizen; the Mytileneans to Sappho, though a woman,—the Lacedæmonians even raised Cheilon to their Senate, though they are anything but fond of letters; the Italiots honoured Pythagoras; the Lampsakenes gave burial, and still pay honours, to Anaxagoras, though an alien . . . <They who use the laws of philosophers always prosper> for the Athenians prospered by the use of Solon's laws, and the Lacedæmonians by using those of Lykurgos; and, at Thebes, no sooner did philosophers[4] become the leading men, than the State prospered.'

11. Another topic is taken from a decision on the same point, or on a like point, or on the opposite point—especially if it has been the decision of all men at all times; or else of a majority of mankind,—or of wise or good men, most or all,—or of our own judges, or of them to whom they listen; or of those whose decision, being that of the masters of the situation, it is impossible to reverse, or discreditable to reverse, as that of the gods, or

[1] Xenophon, *Apol. Socr.* 17; Diog. Laërt. *Vit. Socr.* II 5, 25.

[2] I 15. The word ὀρθῶς, however, is not used there as an example. Muretus omits the clause; Robortelli and Riccoboni propose περὶ τούτου ὀρθῶς εἴρηται.

[3] A small island off the coast of Thessaly, east of Halonnêsos. This passage is paraphrased by Eustath. on *Od.* i 215, 'A woman of Peparethos, by her deposition that a boy was her own son, solved the contention about him,' *i.e.* the mother, who had not seen her son for a long time, was able, by memory or insight, to bring some evidence which settled the point (R. C. J.).

[4] The general statement, that mothers always know their sons, is here confirmed by two instances:—Mantias had one legitimate, and two illegitimate sons. The legitimate son, Mantitheos, brings an action against the elder of the illegitimate sons, who claimed the name of Mantitheos, but who ought to bear the name of Bœôtos (Dem. Or. xxxix πρὸς Βοιωτὸν περὶ τοῦ ὀνόματος). The illegitimate Mantitheos had previously brought an action against Mantias; and his mother Plangôn had sworn to his being the son of Mantias and to his brother being so (Dem. *l. c.* § 4). Again in Or. xl (πρὸς Β. περὶ προικὸς) § 4, she is spoken of as ἐξαπατήσασα ὅρκῳ (R. C. J.).

[1] Ismênias and Stilbôn disputed the fathership of Thettaliskos. The story seems to be unknown (R. C. J.).

[2] § 17 *infra.* A declamation on the legal regulation of the position of mercenaries at Athens; Sauppe, *Or. Att.* III 247 *a.*

[3] *Fragm.* 5, from the Μουσεῖον, Sauppe, 155 *a.*

[4] Epameinôndas and Pelopidas.

our father or our teachers,—as Autoklês[1] said of Mixidêmidês, that it was strange, if trial before the Areiopagos was good enough for the 'Awful Goddesses, but not good enough for Mixidêmidês[2]. Or, take Sappho's saying that death is an evil—for the gods have so judged, or they would die. Or the remark of Aristippos, in answer to a saying of Plato's, which he thought rather compromising—'Well, at least our friend' (meaning Sokrates) 'said nothing of the kind.'[3] Again, Agêsipolis[4] asked the god at Delphi (after first consulting the oracle at Olympia), whether *he* took the same view as his father—implying that it would be indecent to contradict his father. And thus Isokrates represented Helen as good, since Theseus chose her[5]; Paris as good, seeing that the goddesses preferred him[6]; Evagoras, again, he says, is good, inasmuch as Konon after his misfortune[7] passed by all others and came to Evagoras[8].

12. Another topic consists in taking separately the parts of a subject[9]: as in the *Topics*[10]—what sort of motion is the soul? It must be *this* kind or *this* kind. The *Sokrates* of Theodektes affords an example—'Against what temple has he sinned? What gods, acknowledged by the city, has he failed to honour?'[11]

13. Since it happens, in most cases, that the same thing has the same result, good or bad, another topic consists in arguing from the Consequence,—whether in exhorting or dissuading, accusing or defending, praising or blaming. Thus:—'Culture has the bad consequence of exciting envy, and the good consequence of making one wise.'[1] Therefore 'we ought not to cultivate ourselves, for it is not well to be envied.' Or rather—'we *ought* to cultivate ourselves, for it is well to be wise.' The Art of Kallippos[2] is simply this topic, with the addition of the topic of Possibility and the rest, as described above (c. xix).

14. It is another topic, when we have either to exhort or dissuade in reference to two opposite things, and have to use the method just stated in regard to both. There is this difference that, in the former case, any two things are contrasted; here, the things contrasted are opposites. For instance, the priestess urged her son *not* to speak in public; 'for,' she said, 'if you speak justly, you will be hated by men; if unjustly, by the gods.' Or, '*No*—you *ought* to speak in public; for if you speak justly, the gods will love you; if unjustly, men.' This is the same thing as the saying about buying the salt along with the marsh[3]; and in this consists the 'retortion'[4] of the dilemma—when each of two opposite things has both a good and a bad consequence, opposite respectively to each other.

15. As men do not approve the same things in public and in their secret thoughts, but in public must approve just and honourable things, while, from their private point of view, they are apt to prefer their own advantage, another topic

---

[1] Autoklês, son of Strombichidês, one of the Athenian envoys at the congress of Sparta in 371 B.C.; Xen. *Hellen.* VI 3 § 2.

[2] Sauppe, p. 220.

[3] Cp. Grote's *Plato,* iii 471, and Cope's *Comm.* ii 265 f.

[4] Muretus and Bekker, ed. 3; cp. Xen. *Hellen.* IV 7 § 2, first quoted by Victorius. The MSS have '*Ηγήσιππος* retained by Roemer; Spengel points out that '*Ηγησίπολις* is the normal Ionic equivalent for' *Αγησίπολις*.

[5] Isokrates, *Helen,* 18–38.

[6] *Helen,* 41–48.

[7] In 405, after Ægospotami; Xen. *Hellen.* II I § 20.

[8] Isokrates, *Evagoras,* 51 f.

[9] No. 12 and no. 8 are hard to distinguish. Here, the idea of *dealing separately with the parts* is uppermost; there, the idea of showing what parts are comprised in the whole (R. C. J.).

[10] ii 4; iv 2, 6.

[11] Sauppe, 247 *a.*

---

[1] Cp. Euripides, *Medea,* 294; II 21 § 2 *supra.*

[2] § 21; one of the early writers on the Art of Rhetoric, possibly the person described as one of the first pupils of Isokrates in *Antid.* § 93. He is not to be confounded with the Kallippos mentioned in I xii 29 (Cope, *Comm.* ii 271 f).

[3] *i.e.* 'The unprofitable and unwholesome marsh with the profitable salt inseparably connected with it' (Cope); a proverb not found elsewhere.

[4] *βλαίσωσις* from *βλαισός, valgus,* 'with legs bent in,' here used of 'retorting' a dilemma.

consists in trying to infer either of these sentiments from the other. This is the most effective sort of paradox.

16. Another topic is taken from the symmetry of results. Thus Iphikrates[1], when they were trying to make his son take a public service, because though he was under age, he was a big boy, said that, 'if they count big boys as men, they must enact that little men are boys.' And Theodektes in his *Law*[2]: 'You make citizens of mercenaries, such as Strabax[3] and Charidêmos[4], for their merit; will you not make exiles of those, who have done fatal mischief with the mercenaries?'

17. Another topic consists in arguing identity of cause from identity of effect. Thus, Xenophanes[5] said that those who allege the gods to have come into existence are as impious as those who allege that they are dead; for, either way, it results that at one time the gods were not. And, universally, any given result may be treated as constant:—'You are about to decide the fate, not of Isokrates, but of the pursuit of Philosophy.'[6] Or, it may be argued, that 'to give earth and water'[7] means slavery—'to share in the Common Peace'[8] means obeying orders. (We must take whichever view may serve.)

18. Another topic is taken from the fact that men do not always make the same choice at a later as at an earlier time, but may reverse it. This enthymeme gives an example—'It is strange if, when we were in exile, we fought to return, and, having returned, are to go into exile to avoid fighting[1]. In the one case, they chose to keep their homes at the cost of fighting:—in the other, they chose *not* to fight at the cost of losing their homes.

19. Another topic consists in treating the conceivable as the actual reason for a thing existing or having come to pass. Suppose, for example, that one has given something to another for the purpose of paining him by withdrawing it:—whence the saying—

> 'The god bestows large blessings on many men, not in kindness, but that the troubles which they find may be more signal.'[2]

Or the passage from Antiphon's *Meleager:*—

> 'Not that they may slay the beast, but that they may witness the bravery of Meleager to Greece.'[3]

Or the remark in the *Ajax* of Theodektes, that Diomedes[4] chose Odysseus, not in order to honour him, but in order that his own follower might be a lesser man; for this motive is possible.[5]

20. Another topic is common to the law-courts and to debate—viz. to consider the inducements and drawbacks, the reasons for doing or avoiding an action; for these are the conditions which, according as they are present or absent, make an action desirable or undesirable: the former, if, for example, it is possible, easy, advantageous to the doer or his friends, hurtful and damaging to his enemies,—or if the penalty for the act is comparatively small. The grounds of suasion are these—the grounds of dissuasion are the opposite. The same motives form grounds of accusation or defence:—the deterring motives, of

---

[1] Sauppe, p. 219.

[2] Sauppe, p. 247.

[3] Mentioned by Dem. *Lept.* § 84, as having received *privileges* for the sake of Iphikrates.

[4] Of Ôreos in Eubœa; he first entered the Athenian service as a *mercenary* under Iphikrates about 367.

[5] The Eleatic, *c.* 620–520 B.C. 'The One is God.' Being is self-existent, and therefore eternal (R. C. J.). *Fragm. Incert.* 7 Mullach.

[6] Isokr. *Antid.* 173 f, quoted by Spengel in support of his substitution of Ἰσοκράτους (accepted by Roemer) for the manuscript reading Σωκράτους.

[7] Cp. Herodotus, IV 126.

[8] The 'Common Peace' made between the Greeks (except the Lacedæmonians) and Alexander, after Philip's death in 336 B.C. Pseudo-Demosthenes, Or. XVII 30, τῆς κοινῆς εἰρήνης μετέχειν.

[1] Lysias, Or. XXXIV II.

[2] *Fragm. Adesp.* 82 Nauck. Victorius quotes Cæsar, *De B. G.* I 14.

[3] p. 792 Nauck.

[4] *Il.* x 218–254.

[5] p. 801 Nauck.

defence; the inciting motives, of accusation. This topic represents the whole Art of Pamphilos[1] and of Kallippos.

21. Another topic concerns things which appear to have happened, but which are incredible. We may say, that men would not have fancied them, if they had not been true or nearly true. Or we may say, that this makes it *more* certain; for the things in which men believe are either facts or probabilities; if then it be incredible and not probable, it must be true; because its probability and plausibility are not the reason for this belief about it. Thus Androkles[2] the Pitthean said in arraigning the law, when they interrupted his speech—'The laws need a law to correct them, just as fish need salt—improbable and surprising as it is that creatures reared in brine should need salt—just as dried olives need olive-oil—though it is incredible that olive-oil should be needed by the sources of its own being.'[3]

22. Another topic, useful for Refutation, consists in taking account of any inconsistency in the series of dates or acts or statements, and this in three separate ways. First, in the case of the adversary—as:—'He says that he loves you, but he conspired with the Thirty.' Secondly, in our own case;—'And he says that I am litigious, but cannot prove that I have ever been engaged in a single lawsuit.' Thirdly, in our case, as compared with that of the adversary:—'*He* has never lent anything, but *I* have ransomed many of you.'

23. Another topic, useful for persons and causes discredited, or seemingly discredited, by a prejudice, is to give the reason of the paradox; for then there is something which accounts for the prejudice. Thus a woman, who had palmed off her son on another woman, was suspected from embracing him of being the youth's paramour; but, when the cause was stated, the prejudice was dispelled. Thus, again, in the *Ajax* of Theodektes[1], Odysseus tells Ajax *why* he is not thought braver than Ajax, though he is really so.

24. Another topic consists in arguing, from the presence or absence of the Cause, the existence or non-existence of the Effect; for Cause and Effect go together, and nothing is without a cause. Thus, when Thrasybulos[2] charged Leôdamas[3] with having been recorded as infamous[4] on the acropolis, and having erased the record in the time of the Thirty, Leôdamas said in his defence—'It is impossible; the Thirty would have trusted me the more for my enmity with the people being registered.'[5]

25. There is another topic, when it was or is possible to devise a better course than the speaker is recommending or taking, or has taken. Clearly, if the course is not this better course, he has not taken it; for no one willingly and wittingly chooses the worse. (This however is a fallacy; for the better plan often becomes clear after the event, though it was doubtful before it.)

26. When an intended action is contrary to some former action, another topic consists in viewing them together. Thus, when the people of Elea asked Xenophanes[6] whether they should sacrifice to Leukothea[7] and wail[8] for her, his advice was—

---

[1] Pamphilus, like Kallippos (§ 14), 'belonged to the early school of Rhetoricians of the age of Gorgias.' Cicero, *De Or.* III 82 (Cope, *Comm.* ii 285).

[2] Androkles denounced Alkibiades for the mutilation of the Hermæ, in 415 B.C.; he was put to death by the oligarchs at the beginning of the reign of terror which preceded the revolution of the Four Hundred, in 411. Thuc. VIII 65; Andok. *De Myst.* § 27 (R. C. J.).

[3] Sauppe, p. 153.

---

[1] p. 801 Nauck; his *Alkmæon* is quoted in § 3.

[2] Of Steiria, the restorer of the Democracy in 403 B.C.

[3] I vii 13 *supra* (cp. Cope, *Comm.* ii 291).

[4] *στηλίτης*, cp. Isokr. *De bigis,* § 9, *στηλίτην ἀναγράφειν* (of 'posting' Alkibiades as a public traitor), Dem. *Phil.* III 45; Andok. *de Myst.* 51. A similar argument is used by Lysias on behalf of the men denounced by Agoratos, Or. XIII 51 (R. C. J.).

[5] Sauppe, *Orat. Att., Fragm.*, p. 216.

[6] § 17 *supra.*

[7] The name of *Ino* after her death, just as Palæmon was the name of Melikertes.

[8] Probably the ritual represented her sufferings in life (R. C. J.).

'If you consider her a goddess, do not wail: if a woman, do not sacrifice.'

27. Another topic consists in founding accusation or defence upon mistakes. Thus, in the *Medea* of Karkinos[1], the accusers contend that she has slain her children—at any rate, they are not to be found;—for Medea had made the mistake of sending her children away. She says, in her defence, that she would have slain, *not* the children, but Jason; for, supposing her capable of the other murder, it would have been a blunder for her not to have done *this*. This special topic of enthymeme constitutes the whole of the Art in use before Theodôros[2].

28. Another topic is from a play on names. Thus Sophokles—

> 'Steel, truly, like the name thou bearest.'[3]

This is commonly used in praises of the gods. Thus, too, Konon punned on the name of Thrasybulos[4], Hêrodikos[5] on the names of Thrasymachos[6] and Pôlos[7], and said of Draco the lawgiver that his laws are 'not the laws of a man but of a dragon—they are so cruel.' And thus in Euripides, Hecuba says of 'Aphrodite (the Foam-born),'

> 'Well may her name be the beginning of folly.'[1]

And Chærêmôn—

> 'Pentheus, with name prophetic of his doom.'[2]

The Refutative Enthymemes seem more brilliant[3] than the Demonstrative, because the refutative enthymeme is the bringing together of opposites in a small compass; and, when two things are put side by side, they are plainer to the hearer. But, of all syllogisms, whether refutative or demonstrative, those are most applauded, of which we foresee the conclusion from the beginning—and this, not because they are superficial; for we are at the same time pleased with our own quickness[4].—or those, with which we can just keep up, as soon as they are stated.

• • •

BOOK III

i. There are three subjects of rhetorical inquiry,—first, as regards the sources of the proofs,—secondly, as regards the style,—thirdly, as to the order in which the parts of the speech are to be placed. We have spoken of the proofs, and of their several sources, showing that these are three in

---

1 Nauck's *Fragm. Tr. Gr.*, p. 798.

2 ἡ πρότερον Φεοδώρου τέχνη Spengel remarks that what is known of Korax and Tisias agrees with this. Inferior MSS have ἡ προτέρα, either (I) 'the former Art of Theodôros,' implying that he had written two Arts, or (2) 'the earlier Art of Theodôros,' as compared with Aristotle's own time. On Theodôros cp. III xiii 5, and Plato *Phaedr.* 266 E (R. C. J.).

3 Frag. 597, Nauck, ed. 2. The line refers to the cruelty of Sidêrô (the wife of Salmôneus) to her step-daughter Tyro. σιδήρῳ, the reading of the best MS, is preferred by Nauck and accepted by Roemer.

4 § 25 *supra.*

5 Hêrodikos of Selymbria, besides being a physician (cp. 1 v 10), was a sophist (πάσσοφος ἀνήρ, Plato, *Protag.* 316 A).

6 'αεὶ θρασύμαχος εἶ, Thrasymachos of Chalkêdon, the second of the technographers, Tisias being the first, Theodôrus the third (Ar. *De Soph. El.*). Cp. Plato, *Phœdr.* 361 C. 'Mitioris sophistae obiurgatio est in vehementiorem' (Spengel).

7 ἀεὶ σὺ πῶλος εἶ, 'Colt by name and colt by nature' (Thompson's Introd. to *Gorgias* p. v, n. 4). *Gorg.* 463 E.

1 *Troades,* 990. Aphrodite and ἀφροσύνη have the first half of the word in common (Cope).

2 Fragm. 4, Nauck. Chærêmôn, an Athenian tragedian, later than Aristophanes. Some think he was alive in Aristotle's time, *Poët.* I and 24, *Probl.* III 16. This line probably comes from his *Dionysos* (R. C. J.).

3 εὐδοκιμεῖ Cp. III ix 17.

4 We are pleased (not only with the speaker and his enthymeme, but) with ourselves also (ἅμα) for our sagacity in anticipating the conclusion; (and therefore we do not think it superficial). Cope, *Comm.* ii 300.

number[1],—showing, too, of what kind they are, and why their number is not larger,—viz. because all men are persuaded either by some affection of their own minds, when they are the judges, or by conceiving the speakers to be of a certain character, or by a demonstration.

Enthymemes, also, have been spoken of, and the sources from which they must be provided,—these being, on the one hand, the special commonplaces of enthymemes, on the other, the general commonplaces[2].

Diction, or Style.
Delivery.

We have next to speak of Diction; for it is not enough to know *what* we are to say;—we must say it in *the right way:*—this contributes much toward determining the character of the speech. The first subject of our inquiry was naturally that which comes first in nature—as to the means by which persuasiveness shall be given to our facts. The second question is how to dispose these in language; the third is one of the greatest importance, but one, with which it has not yet been attempted to deal—regarding the art of delivery. It was long before this art was applied even to tragic or epic recitation; for the earliest poets used to act their own tragedies. Now it is plain that delivery concerns rhetoric, just as it concerns poetry; and a few writers—Glaukon of Teôs among the rest—have treated it. The art of Delivery[3] is concerned with the voice: it is the art of knowing how to use it for the expression of each feeling; of knowing, for instance, when it should be loud, low, or moderate; of managing its pitch, shrill, deep, or middle;—and of adapting the rhythm to the subject. These are the three things, which speakers have in view—volume, harmony and rhythm. The honours of dramatic contests fall, as a rule, to the actors; and, just as, on the stage, the actors are at present of more importance than the poets, so it is, owing to the vices of society,[1] in the contests of civil life. The rules of delivery have not yet been reduced to an art—indeed, the art of Diction itself was of late development; and, properly viewed, the subject is thought vulgar. As, however, the whole discipline of rhetoric aims at appearance, we must give our attention to this subject, considered as necessary, not as desirable in itself; for, strictly speaking, our sole aim in our language should be to give neither pain nor pleasure; our facts ought to be our sole weapons, making everything superfluous which is outside the proof; owing to the infirmities of the hearer, however, style, as we have said, can do much. (At the same time, style has necessarily a certain small value in every kind of exposition; the mode of expression chosen makes some difference to the clearness,—not such a very great difference, however; it is all imagination and relative to the hearer; thus, no teacher commends geometry by graces of style.)

When the Art of Delivery comes to us, it will perform the function of the actor's art; hitherto, but slight progress has been made towards treating it, as by Thrasymachos in his work *on Pathos*[2]. The dramatic faculty is a gift of nature rather than of Art; but Diction is in the province of art. Hence those who are strong in diction gain honours in their turn, just as do speakers who excel in delivery; for speeches of the literary class are stronger in diction than in thought.

The first improvement in style was naturally made by the poets; for words are instruments of imitation, and the voice is the most imitative of all our organs. Thus the arts of recitation, the art of acting, and more besides, were formed. And, as the poets seemed to have won their present repu-

---

[1] I ii 3.

[2] Books I and II.

[3] αὐτὴ μὲν MSS: αὔτη schol.

[1] Or, 'owing to the defects (or depravity) of our political constitutions.'

[2] Sauppe, *Or. Att.* III p. 164, 4; Spengel, *Artium Scriptores,* p. 93 f.

tation[1], even when their thoughts were poor, by force of their style, the first prose style was led to become poetical[2], like that of Gorgias[3]. To this day, indeed, the mass of the uneducated think that such persons are the finest talkers. It is not so, however; the diction of prose and the diction of poetry are distinct. This appears from what is happening now: the writers of tragedies are themselves modifying their style; and, just as they passed from tetrameter to iambic, because the iambic measure is, of all, the most like conversation, so they have discarded all those words which violate the ordinary idiom, but which the earlier writers used for ornament[4], and which to this day the writers of hexameters so use[5]. It is absurd, then, to imitate those who have themselves dropped the fashion; and it becomes plain that we need not enter minutely into the whole question of style, but need discuss only that style of which we are speaking. The other style has been treated in the *Poetics*.

Clearness.
Appropriateness.

ii. These points, then, may be taken as discussed. One virtue of Diction may be defined to be clearness. This appears from the fact that, if our language does not express our meaning, it will not do its work. Again, diction ought to be neither low nor too dignified, but suitable to the subject. (The diction of poetry could hardly be called 'low,' yet it is not suitable to prose.) Diction is made clear by nouns and verbs used in their proper sense; it is raised and adorned by words of the other classes mentioned in the *Poetics*[1]. Deviation from the ordinary idiom makes diction more impressive; for, as men are differently impressed by foreigners and by their fellow-citizens, so are they affected by styles. Hence we ought to give a foreign air to our language; for men admire what is far from them, and what is admired is pleasant. In the case of *metrical* composition there are many things which produce this effect, and which are in place *there;* for the things and persons concerned are more out of the common. In prose the opportunities are much fewer, the subject-matter being humbler. Even in poetry, if fine language were used by a slave, or by a very young man, or about mere trifles, it would be somewhat unbecoming; even in poetry, there is a sliding scale of propriety. We must disguise our art, then, and seem to speak naturally, not artificially; the natural is persuasive, the artificial is the reverse; for men are prejudiced against it, as against an insidious design, just as they are suspicious of doctored wines. The difference is the same as between the voice of Theodôros[2] and that of other actors; *his* voice seems to belong to the speaker,—*theirs,* to other men. A successful illusion is wrought, when the composer picks his words from the language of daily life; this is what Euripides does, and first hinted the way to do[3].

Language is composed of nouns and verbs,—nouns being of the various classes which have been examined in the *Poetics*[4]. Strange words, compound words, words coined for the occasion, should be used sparingly and rarely:—*where,* we will say by and by[5]. The reason of this has been given

---

[1] *τὴν δὲ δόξαν* Paris MS, *τήνδε τὴν δόξαν* other MSS; *τήνδε* disapproved by Spengel and bracketed by Roemer.

[2] 'The language (of prose) first took a poetical colour' (Cope).

[3] Spengel, *Art. Scr.* p. 69.

[4] *οἷς δ' οἱ πρῶτοι ἐκόσμουν* : *οἷς οἱ πρότερον κτλ*, the Scholiast and Spengel: *οἷς [δ'] οἱ πρῶτοι κτλ*, Roemer. *ἀφείκασιν* is bracketed by Twining, Spengel, Bekker ed. 3, and Roemer; but retained by Vahlen, and by Bywater, *Journal of Philology,* xvii 73 f.

[5] c. 20–22.

---

[1] c. xxii.

[2] A celebrated tragic actor, mentioned in *Pol.* 1336 *b* 28, and in Dem. *De Fals. Leg.* § 274.

[3] He 'gave us the earliest glimpse of this kind of writing' (Cope); cp. Cope's *Introd.* 284 note 2.

[4] c. xxi.

[5] c. iii and vii.

already:—the effect is too odd to be fitting. Accepted terms, proper terms, and metaphors, are alone available for the diction of prose. This appears from the fact that all men confine themselves to these: all men in talking use metaphors, and the accepted or proper terms for things; so it is plain that, if the composer is skilful, the foreign air will be given, the art may be concealed, and he will be clear. And this, we saw, is the excellence of rhetorical language. Equivocal terms are the class of words most useful to the sophist, for it is with the help of these that he juggles; synonyms are most useful to the poet. By synonyms in ordinary use I mean, for instance, 'to go' and 'to walk':—these are at once accepted and synonymous terms[1].

Metaphor.

The nature of each of these kinds of words,—the number of sorts of metaphor,—and the supreme importance of metaphor both in poetry and in prose, have been explained, as we said, in the *Poetics*[2]. In prose the greater pains ought to be taken about metaphor, inasmuch as prose depends on fewer resources than verse. Clearness, pleasure, and distinction, are given in the highest degree by metaphor; and the art of metaphor cannot be taught.[3] Our metaphors, like our epithets, should be suitable. This will result from a certain proportion; if this is lost, the effect will be unbecoming, since the contrast between opposites is strongest when they are put side by side. As a crimson cloak suits a young man, what (we must inquire) suits an old man? The same dress will not suit him. If we wish to adorn, we must take our metaphor from something *better* in the same class of things; if to depreciate, from something *worse*. Thus (opposites being in the same class) it would be an example of this to say that the beggar 'prays' or that the man who prays 'begs'; as both are forms of asking. So Iphikrates said that Kallias was a 'begging priest,' not a 'torch-bearer'[1]; and Kallias replied that he must be uninitiated, or he would not call him a 'begging priest,' but a 'torch-bearer'[2]: both are concerned with a god, but one is a title of honour, the other of dishonour. Some people call actors 'creatures of Dionysos,' but they call themselves 'artists.'[3] Both terms are metaphors, the one calumnious, the other complimentary. Again, pirates nowadays call themselves 'purveyors.' So we may speak of the wrong-doer as 'making a mistake,' or the erring man as 'guilty of a wrong.' We may say that the thief has merely 'taken,' or that he has 'plundered.' The expression in the Têlephos of Euripides—

'*Ruling* the oar,
And, having landed on the Mysian coast,' . . .[4]

is unsuitable, because the word 'to rule' is above the dignity of the subject; so no illusion is produced. There is another fault, which may arise from the form of a word, when the sound which this symbolises is not pleasant. Thus Dionysios 'the brazen'[5] in his elegiacs calls poetry the 'scream of Kalliopê,'[6] both being sounds; the metaphor from inarticulate sounds, however, is unworthy.

---

1 § 7, 'Aristotelis quidem esse videntur, sed fortasse ex ampliore exemplar huic loco adnexa sunt' (Roemer, *Praef.* lxxx).

2 c. xxi, xxii.

3 Lit. 'it is impossible to acquire it from anyone else'; *Poet.* xxii 9, 'This alone cannot be imparted by another; it is a mark of genius,—for to make good metaphors implies an eye for resemblances' (Butcher).

---

1 *ἀλλ' οὐ δᾳδοῦχον*, bracketed by Diels and Roemer.

2 A hereditary office of high distinction, in connexion with the *Eleusinia*, here described as held by Kallias, the third of that name, the son of the third Hipponikos. Iphikrates is the self-made man of *Rhet.* I ix 31.

3 The term is so used by Dem. *De Fals. Leg.* 212. *Διονυσοκόλακες* became proverbial, as in Diogenes Laërtius, x 418; Athenæus, 538 F; and Alkiphron, iii 48.

4 The next line was *ἐτραυματίσθη πολεμίῳ βραχίονι*, 'was sorely wounded by a foeman's arm'; Fragm. 705 Nauck.

5 A poet and rhetorician of the early part of the fifth century, who was called 'the brazen' from his having been the first to suggest the use of bronze money at Athens.

6 Fragm. 7 Bergk, *P. L. G.* ed. 4.

Again, the metaphors, by which we give names to nameless things, must not be far-fetched, but drawn from things so kindred, and so similar, that the affinity appears at first sight: as in the well-known riddle—

> 'I saw a man who had glued bronze to a man with fire.'[1]

The operation has no name; but, both processes being applications, he has called the application of the cupping-instrument a 'glueing.' As a general rule, good riddles supply good metaphors; for metaphors are in the nature of riddles, and so of course the metaphors are happy. Also, metaphors should be taken from beautiful things:—the beauty or ugliness of a word consisting, as Likymnios[2] says, either in the sound or in the sense. There is yet a third consideration, which answers the sophistic argument. Bryson[3] said that there could be no such thing as foul language, if the *meaning* is the same, whether we use this or that term. This is false. One term may be more appropriate than another, more in the image of our thought, better suited to set it before the eyes. Again, this term and that term do not describe the thing in the same aspect—and so, on this ground also, one of them must be regarded as fairer or fouler than another. Both words denote the fair or foul things, but not *qua* fair or foul; or, if so, yet in different degrees. Our metaphors must be taken from this quarter,—from things beautiful in sound or in significance,—beautiful to the eye, or to some other sense. It makes a difference whether we say, for instance, 'rosy-fingered morn,'[1] or 'crimson-fingered,' or worse still, 'red-fingered.' In using epithets, too, we may characterise an object either from its mean or base side, as, 'Orestes, the matricide' or from its better side, as, 'avenger of his father.'[2] Thus Simônides, when the winner of the mule-race[3] offered him a small fee, declined to write, on the ground that he did not like to write about half-asses. But, when the pay was made enough, he wrote—

> 'Hail, daughters of wind-swift steeds!'[4]

(yet they were the daughters of the asses too). Then, without changing one's word, one may extenuate it.[5] This extenuation consists in making less either of the evil or of the good: as Aristophanes in the *Babylonians*[6] jokingly uses 'coinlet' for 'coin,' 'cloaklet' for 'cloak,' 'gibelet' for 'gibe,'—'plaguelet' &c.—Both in metaphors and in epithets, however, we must be cautious and observe the mean.

• • •

---

[1] The next line is preserved by Athenæus, 452 C, *οὕτω συγκόλλως ὥστε σύναιμα ποιεῖν*, 'I saw a man who welded brass with flame upon his fellow, so closely as to bring the blood together.' The riddle is ascribed by Plutarch to Cleobulina or Eumêtis; cp. Bergk, *P. L. G., Poëtae Eleg.* vii.

[2] A pupil of Gorgias, probably identical with Likymnios, the dithyrambic poet of Chios (c. 12 § 2). His *Art* of Rhetoric is mentioned below, in c. 13 § 5. Cp. Plato's *Phædrus*, 267 C; Blass, *Die Attische Beredsamkeit*, i 85 f, ed. 2.

[3] A sophist of Herakleia in Pontus; cp. Cope in *Journal of Cl. and Sacred Philol.* ii 143 and Natorp in Pauly-Wissowa.

---

[1] *Il.* i 477 etc.

[2] Eur. *Orestes*, 1587 f:—

Menelaus. ὁ μητροφόντες ἐπὶ φόνῳ πράσσει φόνον.

Orestes. ὁ πατρὸς ἀμύντωρ, ὃν σὺ προὔδωκας θανεῖν.

[3] Anaxilas of Rhêgium and Zanklê, who died in 476 B.C.; the name of the victor is preserved by Hêrakleides Ponticus, *Pol.* 25. Simônides died in 467, and the race with the Chariot drawn by mules, founded in 500 B.C., was abolished in 444. Cp. Bentley's *Diss. upon Phalaris*, 156 (198 Wagner).

[4] Fragm. 7 Bergk.

[5] Similarly Spengel (who doubts the genuineness of τὸ αὐτὸ), 'ut epithetis rem maiorem vel minorem reddere licet, sic verba ipsa extenuari possunt.' This implies that τὸ αὐτὸ is the accusative after ὑποκορίζεσθαι. In Liddell and Scott, however, the verb is regarded as intransitive:—'to use diminutives'; and Cope's paraphrase is as follows:—'Further the same thing may be effected (as by epithets in the way of elevation or depreciation) by diminutives,' *lit.* 'Diminutives are, or amount to, much the same thing as epithets.' Diminutives are only a special variety of epithets.

[6] Fragm. 90 Kock.

Arrangement.

xiii. Style has now been discussed, both generally[1] and in relation to each branch of Rhetoric[2]. It remains to speak of Arrangement. The speech has two parts:—it is necessary to *state* the matter which is our subject, and to *prove* it. We cannot, then, have a statement without a demonstration, or a demonstration without a previous statement; for the demonstrator must demonstrate something, and the expositor set a thing forth, in order to prove it. One of these processes is Statement, the other Proof:—just as one might divide Dialectic into Problem and Demonstration. The division now in use is absurd. 'Narrative' belongs, I presume, to Forensic speaking only. In Epideiktic or in Deliberative rhetoric, how can we have Narrative in their sense, or Refutation of the adversary, or Epilogue to the argument? Again, 'Proem,' 'Contrast,' 'Review,' have a place in Deliberative speaking, *only* where there is a personal controversy. Accusation and Defence, also, are often present in such a speech, but not *qua* Deliberative speech. The Epilogue, again, is not essential even to a Forensic speech—as, when the speech is short, or the matter easy to remember; for the advantage of Epilogue is abridgment[3]. The *necessary* parts of the speech, then, are Statement and Proof. These are proper to all. The greatest number that can be allowed is four—Proem, Statement, Proof, Epilogue. 'Refutation' comes under the head of Proof; 'Contrast' is a way of amplifying one's own argument, and is therefore a part of Proof, since he who does this, is demonstrating something. This is not true of the Proem, nor, again, of the Epilogue, which merely refreshes the memory. If, then, we are to follow Theodôros[1] in taking into our division such terms as the above, we shall have 'Narrative Proper' distinguished from 'Supplementary' or 'Preliminary Narrative'—'Refutation' from 'Supplementary Refutation.' Now a new term should be brought in, *only* where there is a distinct kind of thing to differentiate; otherwise, it is empty and nonsensical, like the terms used by Likymnios[2] in his Art—'Speeding on'—'Aberration'—'Ramifications.'

• • •

xvi. This may suffice in regard to the art of exciting prejudice.

Narrative.

In Epideiktic speeches the Narrative must be not continuous, but broken up. We have to relate the actions, on which the speech is founded. The speech is composed of two elements;—first, the inartificial, since the speaker is in no way the author of the actions; secondly, the artificial,—which consists in proving that the fact is so, if it be hard to believe,—or that it is of a certain character[3], or of a certain importance;—or in proving all these things. Hence it is sometimes undesirable to relate all our facts continuously, since this mode of exposition tasks the hearer's memory. Rather—'*These* facts show that our hero is brave'; '*these* facts show that he is wise or just.' This kind of statement is simple: the other is intricate and lacks plainness. Well-known facts should be merely recalled to the memory; hence[4] most people require no narrative—as when your purpose is to praise

---

[1] c. ii–xi.

[2] c. xii, note.

[3] συμβαίνει γὰρ τοῦ μήκους ἀφαιρεῖσθαι, 'contingit enim e longa magnaque re partem abscindere' (Victorius). 'For what happens (in an ordinary epilogue) is a subtraction from the length'—not the brevity of a speech; *i.e.* an epilogue is appropriate to a long speech, not a short one (Cope). 'E longa oratione licet delibare quibus peroremus' (Spengel). We may suggest συμβαίνει γὰρ τοῦ μήκους ἀφαιρεῖσθαι <ἕνεκα>, 'for the epilogue exists for the very purpose of subtracting from the length of the speech.'

---

[1] xi 6 *supra.* The superfluous subdivisions of Theodôros are noticed in Plato's *Phœdrus,* 266 D.

[2] A rhetorician, as well as a dithyrambic poet, xii 2 *supra.*

[3] Corresponding to (2) and (3) in c. xvii I.

[4] διὸ, 'since the facts *are* well-known' (R. C. J.).

Achilles; everyone knows his actions—you have only to *use* them. If Kritias, on the contrary, is your subject, narrative is needed—for not many people know[1].

An absurd rule is current to the effect that narrative should be rapid. When the baker asked whether he was to make the cake hard or soft, his customer asked—'Why cannot you make it *right?*' Just so here. Our narrative ought not to be lengthy, any more than our proem or the statement of our proofs; here, again, excellence lies neither in rapidity nor in brevity, but in the mean; that is, in saying just so much as will explain the matter; or, as will establish the fact, the injury, or the wrong,—or, so much as you wish to establish:—the adversary's aim being to negative this. And you should bring into your narrative anything that tends to show your own worth, or the adversary's worthlessness: 'Meanwhile, I was always urging him to the right course,—not to abandon his children to danger; but he answered that, wherever he might find himself, there he would find new children';—as Herodotus[2] says that the Egyptian rebels answered. Anything, too, may be brought in which will please the judges.

For the defendant, narrative is less important. His contention is either (1) that the fact has not occurred; or (2) that it was not harmful; or (3) that it was not unjust; or (4) that it was not of the importance alleged. He ought not to waste his time, then, on any admitted fact, unless this has some bearing on his own contention;—as on a contention that, admitting the act, it was not an unjust act. Again, he should give only a summary of past events, unless an account of them, as actually passing, tends to move pity or indignation. For instance, the story of Alkinoös[3], when told to Pênelopê, is comprised in sixty lines[4]. Such, too, is the treatment of the Epic Cycle by Phayllos[1], and the prologue in the *Œneus*[2].

Further, the narrative should have an ethical colour. The condition of effecting this is to know what gives *êthos*. One way, then, is to make the moral purpose of action clear, the quality of the *êthos* being determined by the quality of this purpose, and the quality of the purpose by the end. Hence mathematical discourses have no moral character, since they have no moral purpose, for they have no moral end. But the Sokratic discourses have such a character, since they deal with moral subjects. Different moral traits go with each character. Thus:—'As he was talking, he strode on'—this suggests the type of rowdy and boor. Then, one should speak, not (as it were) from the intellect, as is the fashion now, but from the moral purpose:—'However, I wished it to be';—'Yes, it was my deliberate intention'; 'Well, though I gained nothing by it, it is better thus.' One course would have shown a prudent man; the other shows a good man: the prudent man shows himself in the pursuit of advantage, the good man in that of honour. And, if any such trait seems incredible, then add the reason, as Sophokles does:—for instance in the *Antigone,* where she says that she cared more for her brother than she could have cared for husband or children. The latter, if lost, could have been replaced;

> 'But, now that sire and mother are with Death,
> No brother's life could bloom for me, again.'[3]

Or, if you have no reason to give, show at least that you are conscious of the statement being hard to believe;—'Such, however, is my nature':—for the world does find it hard to believe in any motive except self-interest.

---

[1] On the *lacuna* at this point, cp. Cope, *Introd.* 349, *Comm.* iii 188.

[2] ii. 30.

[3] *Od.* ix-xii.

[4] *Odyss.* xxiii 264–284, 310–343 (fifty-five lines).

[1] Of Phayllos nothing whatever is known (Cope).

[2] Eur. Frag. 558 f. Nauck.

[3] *Ant.* 911 f, where the MSS have *κεκευθότοιν* for Aristotle's *βεβηκότων*, 'a mere slip of memory'; cp. note on xiv 10, p. 184 n. 2 *supra.*

Use, too, in your narrative the traits of emotion,—the symptoms of it which are familiar to all, or which are peculiarly characteristic of yourself or of your adversary. 'He left me with a scowl'; or,—as Æschines[1] said of Kratylos—'hissing and shaking his fists.' These touches are persuasive, because the things which the hearers know become tokens to them of things which they do *not* know. Many similar touches may be borrowed from Homer:—

> 'So she spake, and the old woman covered her face with her hands':—[2]

(expressive), since people who are on the point of weeping put their hands to their eyes.

Present yourself in a definite character from the very outset, in order that the hearers may view you, as contrasted with your opponent, in this light; only, hide your art. How easy it is to do this, may be seen from the case of people bringing us news[3]:—though we have no idea what the tidings are, we get a foreboding.—The narrative should be distributed over the speech; and in some cases there should be none at the beginning.

In Deliberative Rhetoric there is least room for narrative, for no one can narrate the future. When, however, there *is* a narrative, its object will be merely to refresh the hearer's memory of the past, in order that he may judge better of the future. Or the object may be to excite a prejudice, or to praise. But, in narrating, the deliberative speaker is not doing his own work.

If a statement is incredible, the speaker must make himself responsible for the fact, and give the explanation at the outset, and marshal his reasons in a way acceptable to the hearers[4]. Thus, the Iokastê of Karkinos, in his *Œdipus,* goes on giving her word in answer to the inquiries of the man who is seeking her son; and so the Hæmon of Sophocles[1].

Proofs.

xvii. Our proofs must be demonstrative. There are four possible issues; our demonstration must have reference to the issue. Thus, (1) if one disputes a *fact,* this negative is the first thing which one has to prove in court; (2) if one says, 'I have done no harm,' that must be proved; (3) if one says 'I have not done so much harm,' or (4) 'I have done it justly,' then the truth of *this* becomes the issue.

It must not be forgotten that the issue of the *fact* is the only one, under which it may happen that one of the two parties is *necessarily* a knave. It may be impossible to plead ignorance,—as it is possible, when the justice of an act is the point at

---

[1] Supposed by Victorius to be Æschines Socraticus.

[2] *Od.* xix 361.

[3] How much the drama of modern life has lost in the extinction of the messenger! (R. C. J.)

[4] Reading διατάττειν ὡς βούλονται, for διατάττειν οἷς βούλονται, which is probably corrupt. The application of the examples in the text appears to be as follows:—(i) Iokastê tells the inquirer things about her son which he finds it hard to believe. She meets his unbelief by *pledging her word* for the facts. (ii) Kreon knows that Hæmon is in love with Antigone, and Hæmon thinks her sentence unjust. Kreon finds it 'incredible' that Hæmon should be at the same time dutiful to himself, but Hæmon explains the reason (*Ant.* 701–4). Cope (*Introd.* 354), who (like the scholiast) would omit τε after ὑπισχνεῖσθαι, appears to understand it thus:—'if the statement is incredible, the speaker must promise both to assign the cause, and to set forth his reasons in the terms his hearers desire.' He thinks that ὑπισχνεῖται, said of Iokastê, means 'promising to satisfy the questioner'; and he holds that Αἵμων is corrupt (similarly in *Comm.* iii 197). I object

> (i) to his ommission of τε, and to his way of taking ὑπισχνεῖσθαι, and (ii) to his version of οἷς βούλονται.

Victorius' explanation (as quoted by Cope) is: 'the speaker must promise to assign the reason, and to *refer the matter* (διατάττειν) to those whom the hearers approve.' But διατάττειν cannot mean *committere;* nor do I understand his explanation about Hæmon, unless he means (1) the thing 'incredible' to be Hæmon's defence of Antigone; (2) the 'promise,' his promise of obedience (R. C. J.).

διατάττειν οἷς βούλονται is translated *vadiare quibus volunt,* which suggests διαιτᾶσθαι or διαιτηταῖς (as observed by Roemer), or, possibly, διαιτηταῖς ἐπιτρέπειν οἷς, βούλονται.

[1] *Antigone,* 701–4.

issue. Hence, *in this case*[1], we should dwell (on this topic)[2]; but not so in the other cases[3].

In Epideiktic speaking, the greater part of the argument (as that certain things are honourable or advantageous) is amplification; the facts must be taken upon trust; it is but rarely that the speaker attempts demonstration of the facts themselves, only when they are incredible, or when he has some other special reason.

In Deliberative speaking, one may contend either (1) that certain things will not happen, or (2) that these things will result from our adversary's policy, but are unjust, (3) inexpedient, or (4) will result in a less degree than he says. We must see, too, whether he makes any false statement outside his immediate subject; for such statements seem to justify the inference that he is misrepresenting his subject itself. Examples are better suited to Deliberative speaking, Enthymemes to Forensic speaking:—Deliberative Rhetoric is concerned with the future, and so we must have examples from the past; Forensic Rhetoric is concerned with the existence or nonexistence of facts, and here rigorous demonstration is more possible; for the past has precision. Our enthymemes ought not to be given in a string, but worked in here and there; otherwise they hurt each other's effect. There is a limit of quantity:

> 'Friend, since thou hast said as much as
> a prudent man would say—'[4]

'as much as'—not '*such* things as.' Nor ought we to look for enthymemes on *all* subjects, else we shall do what some of the philosophers do, who apply demonstration to things which are better known, and more easily taken on trust, than their premisses. When you are trying to move feeling, use no enthymeme; it will either expel the feeling, or will have been used in vain; for simultaneous motions tend to expel each other; and either each destroys the other, or one overpowers the other. Nor should an enthymeme be sought, when you are seeking to make your speech ethical; for there is neither *êthos* nor moral purpose in a demonstration. Maxims, however, should be used both in narrative and in proof; for a maxim is ethical. Thus:—"I have given him this, and have given it, though I know the maxim, 'Trust no man.' " Or, if it is to be pathetic:—'Nor do I repent, though I have been injured:—the gain accrues to him, the sense of just conduct to me.'

Deliberative speaking is naturally more difficult than Forensic, since it concerns the future; the other concerns the past, which is already known, even to soothsayers, as Epimenides of Crete said. His divinations used not to concern the future, but only the dark things of the past. Again, in forensic speaking, we have the law for our theme; and, given a starting-point, it is easier to find our demonstration. Then, Deliberative speaking offers few topics, on which we can pause by the way, such as that of attack upon the adversary, discourse about oneself, or appeals to feeling; it admits these less than any branch of Rhetoric, unless the speaker leaves his proper ground. If, then, one is at a loss for topics, one must do like the Athenian orators and Isokrates; Isokrates brings accusation into his deliberative speeches; as accusation of the Lacedæmonians into his *Panegyricus*[1], and accusation of Chares into his *Speech about the Social War*[2]. An Epideiktic speech should be interwoven with laudatory episodes, in the manner of Isokrates, who is always bringing some one in[3]. This is what Gorgias meant by saying that matter of discourse never failed him.

---

1 *i.e.* where *fact* is in question (R. C. J.).

2 viz. that the adversary is *necessarily* a knave (R. C. J.).

3 Or, as Spengel, p. 444: Hence the speaker ought to dwell *on this point* (illa iudicatione: does Spengel mean the question of *fact*, or the argument that the adversary is necessarily a knave?), not on the others (R. C. J.).

4 *Od.* iv 204.

---

1 §§ 110–114.

2 *De Pace,* § 27.

3 Episodes on Theseus in the *Helena* §§ 22–38, and on Paris, *ib.* 41–48; on Pythagoras and the Egyptian priests in the *Busiris,* 21–29; on the poets, *ib.* 38–40; and on Agamemnon in the *Panathenaicus,* 72–84 (Spengel).

When, in speaking of Achilles, he praises Peleus, and then Æakos, and then the god, and valour, and this or that,—he is using the device in question.

When you have means of demonstration, you should use both the ethical and the demonstrative styles; if you have *no* enthymemes, the ethical style only; and, indeed, it better befits an estimable man that his character should appear in a good light than that his speech should be closely reasoned. Refutative enthymemes are more popular than Demonstrative, because in all refutative processes, the strictness of the conclusion is more evident, since opposites are more striking when set side by side.

Refutation of the adversary is not a distinct department of proof; his arguments are to be broken down, either by objection, or by counter-syllogism. Both in Deliberative and in Forensic speaking we should begin by bringing our own proofs, and then meet the arguments on the other side, refuting them and pulling them to pieces by anticipation. If, however, the adversary's case has a great number of points, we should begin with these, as Kallistratos did in the Messenian assembly, when he first disposed of the arguments about to be used against him, before he stated his own. The speaker who is replying should first address himself to his adversary's speech in the way of refutation and counter-syllogism—especially if the adverse arguments have gained applause; for the mind rejects a speech, against which it is prepossessed, just as it rejects a man, supposing the adversary to have made a good impression. It is necessary, then, to make room in the hearer's mind for the coming argument. This room will exist, if you remove the obstacles. Hence you should begin by combating the adverse arguments—all of them, or the chief, or the plausible, or those which are easy to refute—and then establish your own arguments.

> 'First I will come to the defence of the goddess. . . .
> Now I do not think that Hera . . .'[1]

[1] Eur. *Troades*, 969, 971.

Here he has laid hold first of the weakest point.

So much of argumentative proof. As to ethical proof[1], seeing that there are some things, which it is invidious to say of ourselves, or which expose us to the charge of tediousness or to contradiction, or which, if said of another, suggest that we are abusive or ill-bred, we must put these things into the mouth of some other person,—as Isokrates does in the *Philippos*[2], and in the *Antidosis*[3],—and as Archilochos does in his satire. Thus it is the father, whom he introduces speaking of the daughter in the verse:

> 'Nothing is beyond hope, against nothing should men make a vow',[4]

and thus he uses Charon the carpenter in the verse beginning

[1] It will be convenient to recall here the several connexions in which Aristotle has used *êthos* in relation to rhetorical persuasion. (1) 'Ethical proofs' proper are equivalent to 'proofs inherent in the *êthos* of the speaker' (I ii); this is further explained in II i. (2) In II xii 13 the *êthê* proper to youth, manhood, old age, noble birth, wealth, power, etc. are described. The advantage of knowing these is that we shall be able to give our speech the *general* colour or tone acceptable to the audience. They are really subservient, then, to the treatment of *pathê*,—to the exciting of certain feelings in the hearer's mind. (3) In III vii he says that 'style will have Propriety, if it is, first, *pathetic;* secondly *ethical;* thirdly, proportional to the subject.' By 'pathetic' he means, if the speaker appears to be himself affected in a way suitable to the facts which he is relating. 'Ethical style' he defines as 'the representation of facts by means of appropriate signs,' *i.e.* the presentation of the persons introduced, as speaking or acting in a characteristic way—with the marks or traits proper to their age, condition, etc. This has nothing to do with 'ethical proof' proper, *i.e.* the production in the hearer's mind of a good impression about the speaker's character. Nor has it anything to do with the *êthê* of II xii 13, which help us to come into a general sympathy with our hearers. It is merely a precept for effectiveness of style,—one of the characteristics essential to vivid, graphic description. (4) The *êthos* of III xvii is the '*êthos* of the speaker.' The special rule given is meant to guard us against spoiling our 'ethical proof' by seeming egotistic, abusive, or illbred (R. C. J.).

[2] §§ 4–7.

[3] §§ 132–9, 141–9.

[4] Fragm. 74, Bergk, ed. 4.

'Not Gyges' wealth......'[1]

Thus, too, in Sophokles, Hæmon pleads for Antigone with his father as it were in the words of others[2]. Enthymemes should sometimes, too, be thrown into the form of maxims;—for instance, 'Sensible men ought to make up their quarrels when they are prosperous—for so they will gain most.'[3] Put in the form of an enthymeme, this would be:—'If men ought to adjust their differences at the moment when it is most beneficial and gainful to do so, then they ought to do so when they are prosperous.'

• • •

Epilogue.

xix. The epilogue has four elements:—(1) the attempt to dispose the hearer favourably towards ourselves, and unfavourably towards the adversary;—(2) amplification and extenuation; (3) the attempt to excite certain feelings in the audience; (4) recapitulation.

(1) After we have proved our own truthfulness and the falseness of the adversary, the next thing is naturally to praise ourselves, vituperate him, and clinch our case. We must aim at proving either relative or absolute goodness on our part, and either relative or absolute badness on his part. The means of presenting people in either light—the topics, that is, by which they are to be made out good or bad—have been stated[4].

(2) The facts having been proved, the next thing in the natural order is to make much of them, or to make little of them. The facts must be admitted before one can discuss their magnitude; as the growth of the body implies something preexisting. The topics of amplification and extenuation have been set forth already[5].

(3) Next—the quality and the magnitude of the facts having been ascertained—we have to inspire the hearer with certain feelings;—namely, with pity or indignation or anger or hatred or envy or emulation or pugnacity. The topics for these, too, have been stated before[1].

(4) There remains, then, recapitulation. This should be managed *here* in the way commonly, but wrongly, recommended for the proem; we are advised to repeat our points over and over again, in order that they may be easily seized. Now, in the proem, we ought to state our subject, in order that the general issue may not be unknown; in the epilogue, we ought to state summarily the arguments by which our case has been proved. The starting-point should be the remark, that we have performed our undertaking; and then we may state *what* we have said, and *why*. One mode of doing this is by contrasting our own case with the adversary's; either by comparing what he and you have said on the same point, or without this direct comparison. 'This was *his* account of the matter, here is *mine;* and *my* reasons are these.' Or ironically:—'*He,* you know, spoke thus, and *I* thus.' Or 'What airs would he give himself, if he had proved all this, instead of merely proving *this?*' Or Interrogation may be used:—'What has not been proved?' Or 'What has *he* proved?'—The recapitulation, then, may either take this form of direct contrast, or follow the natural order of the statements,—taking first our own; then, if we like, the adversary's separately. An *asyndeton* is in place at the end of a speech, making the ordinary sentence into a true epilogue: 'I have spoken—you have heard; you have them;—judge.'[2]

---

[1] *οὔ μοι τὰ Γύγεω τοῦ πολυχρύσου μέλει*, Frag. 25, Bergk, ed. 4.

[2] *Antigone*, 688–700.

[3] Cp. Isokrates, *Archidamus*, 50.

[4] I ix.

[5] II xix.

---

[1] II i–xi.

[2] This illustration is doubtless a reminiscence of the epilogue of the speech of Lysias against Eratosthenes, Or. xii, *παύσομαι κατηγορῶν· ἀκηκόατε, ἑωράκατε, πεπόνθατε· ἔχετε, δικάζετε*. 'The speech for the prosecution must now close; I have appealed to your ears, to your eyes, to your hearts; the case is in your hands; I ask for your verdict.'

Classical Roman Heritage

INTRODUCTION TO THE CLASSICAL ROMAN HERITAGE

The age of great Greek rhetorical theorists came to an end with the death of Aristotle in 322 B.C.E. Two hundred sixteen years later, the Roman orator, statesman, and rhetorician Marcus Tullius Cicero was born, in 106 B.C.E. Thus began a short but illustrious period of vigorous development of rhetorical theory in ancient Rome.

Many people today have images of Rome given to us by the popular film industry: chariot races, debauched orgies, marching legions, Antony and Cleopatra, Julius Caesar and the Ides of March, and so forth. Some or all of these images may well have been true of certain periods of Roman history. However, to better understand Roman life and the place rhetoric had in it, we must be more careful in identifying different phases of Roman history and different types of government.

Rome began as a sort of city-state, much like those of Greece, and grew to be a commercial and military power in its sphere in the western end of the Mediterranean Sea. Its curve of development followed somewhat behind that of Athens, though. Rome emerged as a true regional power around the middle of the third century B.C.E., at which time it controlled all of what we now know as Italy. By the beginning of the second century B.C.E., Rome came to dominate the old Greek states in the eastern Mediterranean as well. Rome's position as master of the Mediterranean world laid the basis for its later expansion into Europe as far as the British Isles, north into Germany, east into lands around the Black Sea, and south into northern Africa.

The "movie" Rome of absolute dictators, dissolute luxury, and far flung conquest is not entirely true of this early period of Roman power and expansion. Rome during this period was a *republic,* and continued to be so until around the middle of the first century B.C.E., when the caesars or emperors took power and established the militarily-based dictatorships that would last until the end of the Roman era. We must therefore distinguish between Rome as a republic and Rome as an empire, because these different social and political conditions very much affected how rhetoric was practiced and theorized. Therefore we will start our overview of Roman rhetoric by examining the idea of *power.* Here and in consideration of our three other key concepts, a central theme will be the extent to which Roman civilization was in important ways both similar to and different from our way of life in late-twentieth century America.

POWER

A *republic* is a form of government in which representatives of the people pass most laws and conduct most government business. A republic is therefore much more commonly found today and throughout history than is a true democracy. A democracy requires the *direct* participation of citizens in public affairs, and therefore usually works best in small, compact political units—which are not typical of most modern states. Today in the United States we live in a republic rather than a democracy.

Until the middle of the first century B.C.E., Rome was for the most part a republic. It was a very interesting and peculiar kind of republic, though, especially for purposes of rhetorical theory. We can begin to understand the link between Rome's republican government and rhetoric if we consider the public offices and political bodies that governed Rome.

One political fact of life was that Roman society was more stratified by socioeconomic class than were most of the Greek cities. Roman society was organized around powerful noble families. A patronage system was in place for everything from jobs to the military structure—families would provide units for the army from among their dependents and hangers on, for instance. The image from the play *Romeo and Juliet* of an *Italian* city organized around rival Montague and Capulet families is a holdover from Roman social structure. So a real but "unofficial" source of power in the Roman world was the structure of powerful families or clans.

Representatives of the patrician, or noble, families were chosen to be part of the *Senate*. The Senate had direct power over finances, and any other power it had was technically of an advisory nature only. But, in fact, the social and intellectual leadership of the Senate went far beyond its legal boundaries. Great debates over public issues and great trials took place there. Very often, a decree made by the Senate was followed and respected, whether Romans "had to" do so or not.

The public *assembly* was composed of all adult male citizens, and it had the power to declare war. The *Tribunes* were ten representatives of the people, who usually turned out to be patricians. They had the power to convene the Senate and had veto power over it; however, each Tribune also had what amounted to veto power over one another. The *Consul* was the chief magistrate, very roughly equivalent to our president today, and had the power to convene the Senate. The Consul had no vote within the Senate, however.

Quaestors were financial administrators or paymasters, with power over how public money was spent. The *Censors* took the census and determined taxability, and also elected the members of the Senate. *Praetors* were like judges, presiding in law courts. *Aediles* were city supervisors, in charge of streets, markets, spectacles, and so forth—an important office in a nation centered in the city of Rome. From time to time a *Dictator* would be appointed with absolute although temporary power, usually in times of war or distress; this power was expected to be relinquished when the crisis passed. *Augurs* were religious officials who read signs and portents, and could forbid any public action as inauspicious. *Pontiffs* were chief priests and interpreted the will of the gods; they, too, could forbid any public action or undertaking as contrary to heavenly intentions.

The point of this quick review of offices in the Roman Republic is to note how loose and wide ranging were the sites of power. The Republic was in fact an odd assortment of democratic, republican, and oligarchic power bases. In the United States today, by contrast, we have more or less clear lines of how power is exercised: Congress has sole right to pass laws, but the president may veto them (and Congress may override, if it can). The Supreme Court has sole power to declare a law unconstitutional, yet it is appointed by the president with the consent of the Senate. The Congress and the states have sole power to alter the Constitution. In the Roman Republic, affairs were not this tidy. The Senate might pass a resolution to build a public monument that would be vetoed by a Tribune, who would in turn be blocked by another Tribune, until a Pontiff stepped in to say what the gods willed in the matter—and it might all depend in the end on whether the Quaestors were willing to fund the building. It *looks* as if the exercise of power in the Roman Republic was a sort of train wreck waiting to happen.

For the most part, however, the Republic "worked" very well for hundreds of years. It did so because of a widespread cultural commitment to *involvement in public, political life through rhetorical means*. Romans were committed to talking about their disagreements rhetorically, to settling troubling public questions through argument, and to persuading and allowing themselves to be persuaded. Power was very often exercised not through bottom line legalities but through the persuasiveness and force of argument of particular office holders or assemblies. The Roman Republic "worked" because it ran on tracks of rhetorical practice.

A commitment to persuade and to be persuaded in managing political affairs requires the corollary commitment to become involved in politics. Except for the lowest levels of society, Roman males were expected to be active in public affairs. They thought it was nothing but natural and healthy to be out and about in public, arguing over the latest issues, button-holing one another in the market to debate today's political problem, giving and listening to speeches, and participating in public discussions. As with the Greeks, this widespread involvement was within a sphere of inclusion of males and Roman citizens. We must bear in mind here, as for the Greeks, that women, slaves, and other "second class" people were marginalized. But for those admitted to the sphere of public life, participation was key.

How that value of participation contrasts to contemporary attitudes in the United States! Most of us participate in politics, if at all, as spectators of public events through the medium of television. Few of us see it as a duty, much less a pleasure, to be actively involved in political and public affairs. Relatively few citizens of the United States so much as send letters to public officials expressing their views. Some social observers today, therefore, point to the rhetorical theories of Cicero as a blueprint for rescuing Americans from their political apathy. The involvement in public affairs through rhetoric is seen as a way out of our perceived crisis of political lethargy.

Power in the Roman Republic, then, was exercised rhetorically. Arguing, talking, and personal involvement in public affairs was the order of the day. The cumbersome and motley assortment of public offices and governing bodies usually worked together because the citizenry as a whole was committed to the rhetorical management of public affairs.

Another interesting dimension of power in Roman rhetorical theory is evidenced by the characters in Cicero's dialogue treating power as if it were simply a good thing to have. Cicero sounds much like the Sophists of ancient Greece in this regard. The ability to exercise power over others through rhetoric is taken as an unabashedly good thing, much as Callicles might have argued in the *Gorgias*.

Quintilian, writing in the shadow of truly repressive, violent power in the Empire, is a little less enthusiastic about the virtues of power. He seems to echo Plato in hoping that the orator will be a *good* man skilled in speaking; ethics tempers the love of power for Quintilian. Longinus seems to retreat from an interest in worldly power entirely; for him, the power to move audiences through artistic use of language is quite enough. In this love for power, the ancient Romans of the Republic resemble today's pragmatic and results-oriented Americans.

Consider what a change occurred when the Roman Republic was overthrown in the first century B.C.E. as Julius Caesar became the first of the caesars, however briefly. Many of the offices and institutions of the Republic were kept during the Empire, but their *rhetorical* functions were greatly reduced or eliminated. Essentially, an emperor or a caesar has very little use for the sort of rhetoric that takes the form of open public discussion and management of important questions. Those questions will be settled by the emperor and his advisors! Often, important issues, and even the tenure of the emperor himself, was settled militarily rather than rhetorically. Therefore, Rome increasingly became a military dictatorship, ruled by whichever caesar had the support of its huge army. Rome became increasingly economically dependent on this military structure, and by the first century B.C.E. conquest, taxation, and tribute was the mainstay of its economy. Under such conditions, what use was there for free and open public debate?

When power becomes anchored by violence, the military, or a police state, the free exercise of rhetoric diminishes. Cicero lived at the end of the Roman Republic, and we will find him theorizing for a relatively free and open rhetorical practice. The contrast with the teacher and theorist Quintilian, living in the Empire in the first century C.E., is instructive. Quintilian is much less concerned with teaching his students rhetorical technique for political application because that function of rhetoric had withered under the Empire. We will note his greater preoccupation with rhetoric as a pedagogical device, with judicial and ceremonial applications of rhetoric. The pseudonymous theorist Longinus, probably also living in the first century C.E., writes about rhetoric as if it were purely stylistic embellishment or an aesthetic experience. Longinus is taking a "safe" route in theorizing about a rhetorical practice that does not risk confrontation with an absolute empire. The ways that power is distributed in a society thus affect how rhetoric is practiced and theorized. For the first time, with Quintilian and Longinus, we see what happens to rhetoric when power is concentrated in the hands of a few who are unfriendly to public argument and discussion.

KNOWLEDGE

The interesting political conditions of ancient Rome created the perspective that its rhetorical theorists took on the key question of knowledge. Whether under the Republic or the Empire, Roman thought is characterized by pragmatism, practicality, and common sense. Questions of what one can or should know and the relationship of knowledge to rhetorical practice are, for the Romans, subordinated to practical questions of what *works* in human affairs.

You will recall that the Greek theorist and philosopher Plato demanded that rhetors be well versed in the subject matters upon which they would speak. For him, the call for wide knowledge was based on ethical and philosophical considerations. The ability to convey knowledge of the truth to an audience was the most important rhetorical function. A speaker needed to know a lot because it was the *right* thing to do.

In contrast, the Romans took a stance much closer to that of the Sophists of Plato's day, which was that one acquires knowledge so as to be practically successful and effective in the world of human affairs. The characters in Cicero's dialogue are no longer calling for total mastery of all fields of knowledge. Although Cicero's mouthpiece character of Crassus comes close to such a sweeping requirement, he quickly modifies it as a result of discussion with his colleagues, and takes the much more realistic and practical stance that the orator must acquire wide learning in many subjects for *practical* reasons, so as to become a well-rounded leader and statesman.

The fact that knowledge had expanded between Plato's and Cicero's times is one factor contributing to Cicero's more limited call for being "well versed" in many subjects. It was simply less practical in Cicero's era to have mastered everything, as Plato would have the rhetor do. Of more importance for the Roman point of view, however, is the fact that practical success in oratory had become the standard for what one needed to know, replacing the need to possess absolute truth that had preoccupied Plato.

We will also want to track the development of rhetoric as a means to the acquisition of knowledge. For Cicero, and to a larger extent, for Quintilian, rhetoric is a pedagogical tool. Both theorists argue for the importance of putting students through exercises in rhetoric: reciting famous speeches, composing original speeches on set topics, reciting literature, arguing stock cases in law or ethics, and so forth. Exercising one's rhetorical ability was the way one became a widely educated, well-rounded person in Roman society.

MEDIA

The ancient Roman theorists we will read all reflect an interesting shift from the Greek context in terms of media. Although the Greeks were certainly literate, they were relatively closer to an oral/aural culture of the spoken word. By the time we come to Cicero, we are looking at a culture thoroughly immersed in the written word.

Longinus is writing straightforwardly about literature, and nearly all his examples come from written literature. The nature of his subject lends itself more to the written medium as well, for he is talking about some rather complicated stylistic devices or figures of speech that, although they are enjoyable to hear, may be more fully appreciated by seeing them in writing. A complicated metaphor may be thought about, mulled over, and repeated to one's self several times when we confront it in writing. Therefore, literature supports a more complicated view of linguistic style, which we see in Longinus.

Cicero and Quintilian both write in praise of the written word. Although there is certainly a place for orally recited exercises in their prescriptions for rhetorical training, they also emphasize the importance of writing. Both discuss the need to write out original speeches in several drafts, to copy famous speeches and literature, and to engage in training exercises employing the written word. Both shy away from requiring orators to have learned everything about every topic, as Plato did, and we may see in this relaxation of a demand for encyclopedic knowledge a reflection of the increase in reliance upon writing as a medium. Speakers need to know less, personally, because they can "look it up" or retrieve information from writing should they need to know certain facts for presentation in a speech. Our discussion above of different Roman attitudes towards the need for vast knowledge may in fact be a reflection of greater Roman reliance upon writing and its superior ability to store information for retrieval.

DISCOURSE

Roman theorists are, like their Greek predecessors, interested in the status of rhetoric as a distinct discourse. We will see Cicero's characters in *De Oratore* argue over whether "the orator" is a role one enters into from time to time or a calling or vocation that one assumes across many different contexts. The implications in terms of discourse seem to be related to whether rhetoric is a particular kind of discourse that one does occasionally and then quits, or is a way of thinking and acting through which one might engage in many discourses. Cicero seems to prefer the latter choice. For him, "the orator" is the epitome of the public man (*sic*), someone involved in a leadership role in many different contexts, and a well-educated man of affairs who approaches many different public problems from the rhetorical point of view.

Under the Republic, the kinds of discourse regarded as rhetorical were similar to those listed by the Greeks: judicial, political, and ceremonial. Under the Empire, the kinds of discourse that are regarded not only as rhetoric but as simply allowable became redefined and narrowed. A form of discourse that in previous theory, for better or worse, had found a role in the management of every kind of human affair now became a form of discourse for the management only of legal or ceremonial matters. We see under the Empire how the definition of a certain kind of discourse alters so as to follow social and political realities.

For Quintilian, rhetoric is a kind of discourse with legal, epideictic, or pedagogical uses but it is no longer the discourse that manages true power. Longinus's view of rhetoric is narrower still, being concerned only with aesthetics, style, and beauty. A retreat from politics was dictated for each theorist by the political demands of the Empire.

The Romans were unlike contemporary Americans in their greater involvement in the active politics of their day. In other ways, however, we are very much like them. Romans, whether in the Republic or the Empire, were above all pragmatists, as are we. They were interested in the practical uses and consequences of rhetoric, as are late twentieth century Americans immersed in advertising and spin doctoring. Less interested in a vision of absolute truth and more interested in what "works" for any given moment, the Romans as well as many of us today are direct descendants of the Sophists.

FOR FURTHER READING

Baldwin, Charles Sears. 1959. *Ancient Rhetoric and Poetic.* Gloucester, MA: Peter Smith.

Cicero. 1967. *Cicero: Nine Orations and the Dream of Scipio.* NY: Mentor Books.

Cowell, F. R. 1948. *Cicero and the Roman Republic.* Baltimore: Penguin Books.

Fortenbaugh, William W., and Mirhady, David C., eds. 1994. *Peripatetic Rhetoric After Aristotle.* New Brunswick, NJ: Transaction Publishers.

Hariman, Robert. 1995. *Political Style: The Artistry of Power.* Chicago: University of Chicago Press.

Kennedy, George. 1972. *The Art of Rhetoric in the Roman World.* Princeton, NJ: Princeton University Press.

McKeon, Richard. 1987. *Rhetoric: Essays in Invention and Discovery.* Woodbridge, CT: Ox Bow Press.

Scott, Izora. 1991. *Controversies of the Imitation of Cicero in the Renaissance.* Davis, CA: Hermagoras Press.

Vasaly, Ann. 1993. *Representations: Images of the Ancient World in Ciceronian Rhetoric.* Berkeley: University of California Press.

INTRODUCTION TO CICERO

Marcus Tullius Cicero was born in 106 B.C.E. and died in 43 B.C.E., assassinated by order of Antony as the Roman Republic was falling and the caesars establishing their power. Cicero epitomized the Roman ideal of the fully involved, active man of public affairs. By profession he was a lawyer, and his oratory in defense of clients is still celebrated as brilliant rhetoric. He was also a politician, and attained the office of Consul in 63. Late in his life he reemerged as a political leader, defending the Republic in opposition to the growing power of Julius Caesar, Antony, and other imperialists. That return to politics cost him his life. Antony had him killed as he attempted to flee Rome, and nailed his hands and head above the rostrum in the Senate where he had spoken so eloquently.

Cicero also wrote prolifically on philosophy and rhetoric, and published several of his speeches. Many consider him to be ancient Rome's greatest orator, and he was taken as an ideal model of oratory for aspiring speakers for centuries after his death. His masterpiece on rhetorical theory is considered to be *De Oratore,* which is excerpted here.

De Oratore is written in the form of a dialogue within a letter addressed to his brother. In the introduction to the letter, Cicero complains that there are few great orators left in Rome, and considers why that might be so. He then "recalls" a conversation he allegedly heard some years ago among several of Rome's political leaders, at a country house outside of Rome. This conversation is the substance of the rest of *De Oratore.* It is interesting from the point of view of media to note how Cicero's dialogue differs from Plato's: The characters speak at much greater length (in fact, keeping track of who is speaking is sometimes a challenge for the reader). This reflects a greater reliance on the printed word in Cicero's time; his characters are more "book-like" than were Plato's, although both appeared in writing.

Cicero does not appear in the dialogue, but the character Crassus is his "mouthpiece" character and generally expresses Cicero's views, as Socrates expresses the views of Plato. It is interesting to notice the general tone of Cicero's dialogue. Although there are some disagreements among the characters, their differences are cordially expressed and are moderate. In this way, they model the ideal of the Roman Republic, with its commitment to rhetorical argument and to the give and take of persuasion as the basis for social interaction. Furthermore, we will see that Crassus and his views are a model for Cicero's ideal man of public affairs and political involvement.

The conversation begins with a consideration of why one would want to be an orator and to practice rhetoric. Cicero defends to Scaevola the idea that the orator needs to have both wide knowledge and command of rhetorical style. The question is reasonably raised as to whether one *can* achieve wide knowledge when what there is to know is so vast. We are also invited to think about the type or level of knowledge that is required. Is it encyclopedic knowledge of detailed facts? Integrative knowledge of principles? Some other dimension of knowledge? Acknowledging the practical difficulties of "knowing everything," Crassus narrows his claims to argue that the orator must have knowledge of human life and conduct. In other words, the orator must be exposed to many different disciplines and areas of knowledge, but what the orator must know about them is their connection to how people live and act. Another way to put this is that Cicero, through Crassus, is claiming that the orator must have street smarts, or even *wisdom,* about how people think and act—and that this is a level of knowledge that is something other and perhaps higher than simply amassing information.

Antonius enters the argument by saying that the orator does not need special training in rhetorical technique as a separate art. Crassus agrees, and the two concur in mistrusting elaborate rules for rhetorical theory. Rules to guide rhetorical conduct must arise instead from what works in practical application, they agree. The characters then discuss what one must do, or be, to be a successful orator. The orator in training must perfect his linguistic style, practice constantly, and write so as to refine his ability to use language creatively. Note their stress upon such factors as appearance and style for the purpose of impressive delivery of speeches. These are dimensions of oratory that are very practical, not at all philosophically refined, and very similar to the preoccupations of today's rhetoricians who must appear attractive on television!

Book I concludes with an interesting distinction. Crassus and Antonius agree on the importance of training in style and delivery. But Crassus complains that Antonius sees the orator as a sort of "mechanic." By that he means that Antonius sees the orator as a role one steps into so as to give a speech from time to time—then steps out of the role to go on to other things.

In contrast, Crassus seems to have a very interesting concept of the orator. In his view, the orator is a sort of calling or vocation. It is someone trained to be a leader in all kinds of circumstances. Such a person must be widely educated, but not for the purposes of lofty philosophical analysis (note the occasional mistrust of philosophy that emerges in this dialogue). Instead, the orator is widely trained so as to be a leader in affairs of "human life and conduct."

It is interesting to compare this conception of "the orator" to other sorts of callings and vocations we have today. Certain professions are regarded in this way, as the sort of "job" one never puts down: priests and rabbis, medical doctors, and even professors. We can detect a sense of calling or vocation in those professions by the fact that they have titles that seem *always* to be applied to them. One is "the doctor" or "rabbi" constantly and is so addressed. One may be a "plumber" from nine to five and then never referred to as "the plumber" after hours in the way that "Father James" is *always* Father James. This sense of the orator as a calling or vocation is Cicero's model of the ideal kind of involvement in public life, an involvement to which the broadly trained rhetorician is ideally suited.

Book II is a very practical book, in keeping with the Romans' practical inclinations. It discusses the various techniques and purposes of rhetoric. Note that although it generally follows Aristotle's divisions of ethos and pathos, lines of argument, the need to know the facts of a case, and so forth, these Romans do not go into nearly the detail that Aristotle did. They are content to let theory arise from practice. They are not interested in a fully-developed theory for the purpose of being philosophically rigorous, as was Aristotle. Instead, they are offering practical advice for the aspiring Roman rhetorician.

Book III returns to Crassus's defense of the orator as a widely educated leader of the public. His views on philosophy are interesting here, for he claims that training in philosophy is admirable so long as it is coupled to training in rhetoric. In other words, it is acceptable for the orator to be trained to think, as long as the orator is also trained to put that thinking and knowledge into application as a leader of the state. Here Crassus bemoans a tendency to separate people of action (rhetoricians) from people of thought (philosophers) and lays the blame for that separation squarely at Plato's door! The discussion concludes with a reiteration of the view of orator as one broadly trained in both philosophical vision and the practical knowledge of how to apply that vision in worldy affairs.

Cicero's view of the orator was shortly to become irrelevant in the Roman world as the age of the caesars replaced the Roman Republic and made risky and unnecessary the political involvement of active citizens. Many observers have looked at our era of political apathy in the face of huge government and big business and have seen parallels to Roman times. Some of those observers have suggested that Cicero's vision of the orator is what we need to recover for our times: a sense of training in rhetoric, grounded in broad and liberal learning, that can equip our citizens for a return to active participation in public affairs.

CICERO

DE ORATORE

BOOK I

. . .

I. As I frequently contemplate and call to mind the times of old, those in general seem to me, brother Quintus, to have been supremely happy, who, while they were distinguished with honors and the glory of their actions in the best days of the republic, were enabled to pursue such a course of life that they could continue either in employment without danger, or in retirement with dignity. To myself, also, there was a time[1] when I thought that a season for relaxation, and for turning my thoughts again to the noble studies once pursued by both of us, would be fairly allowable, and be conceded by almost every one; if the infinite labor of forensic business and the occupations of ambition should be brought to a stand, either by the completion of my course of honors,[1] or by the decline of age. Such expectations, with regard to my studies and designs, not only the severe calamities resulting from public occurrences, but a variety of our own private

[1] After his consulship, A.U.C. 691, in the forty-fourth year of his age.

[1] There was a certain course of honors through which the Romans passed. After attaining the quæstorship, they aspired to the ædileship, and then to the prætorship and consulate. Cicero was augur, quæstor, ædile, prætor, consul, and proconsul of Asia. *Proust.*

troubles,[1] have disappointed. For in that period,[2] which seemed likely to offer most quiet and tranquillity, the greatest pressures of trouble and the most turbulent storms arose. Nor to our wishes and earnest desires has the enjoyment of leisure been granted, to cultivate and revive between ourselves those studies to which we have from early youth been addicted. For at our first entrance into life we fell amidst the perturbation[3] of all ancient order; in my consulship we were involved in struggles and the hazard of every thing;[4] and all the time since that consulship we have had to make opposition to those waves which, prevented by my efforts from causing a general destruction, have abundantly recoiled upon myself. Yet, amidst the difficulties of affairs, and the straitness of time, I shall endeavor to gratify my love of literature; and whatever leisure the malice of enemies, the causes of friends, or the public service will allow me, I shall chiefly devote to writing. As to you, brother, I shall not fail to obey your exhortations and entreaties; for no person can have more influence with me than you have both by authority and affection.

II. Here the recollection of an old tradition must be revived in my mind, a recollection not indeed sufficiently distinct, but adapted, I think, so far to reply to what you ask, that you may understand what opinions the most famous and eloquent men entertained respecting the whole art of oratory. For you wish, as you have often said to me (since what went abroad rough and incomplete[5] from our own note-books, when we were boys or young men, is scarcely worthy of my present standing in life, and that experience which I have gained from so many and such important causes as I have pleaded), that something more polished and complete should be offered by me on the same subjects; and you are at times inclined to dissent from me in our disputations on this matter; inasmuch as I consider eloquence to be the offspring of the accomplishments of the most learned men;[1] but you think it must be regarded as independent of elegant learning, and attributable to a peculiar kind of talent and practice.

Often, indeed, as I review in thought the greatest of mankind, and those endowed with the highest abilities, it has appeared to me worthy of inquiry what was the cause that a greater number of persons have been admirable in every other pursuit than in speaking. For which way soever you direct your view in thought and contemplation, you will see numbers excellent in every species, not only of the humble, but even of the highest arts. Who, indeed, is there, that, if he would measure the qualifications of illustrious men, either by the usefulness or magnitude of their actions, would not prefer a general to an orator? Yet who doubts that we can produce, from this city alone, almost innumerable excellent commanders, while we can number scarcely a few eminent in speaking? There have been many also in our own memory, and more in that of our fathers, and even of our forefathers, who had abilities to rule and govern affairs of state by their counsel and wisdom; while for a long period no tolerable orators were found, or scarcely one in every age. But lest any one should think that the art of speaking may more justly be compared with other pursuits, which depend upon abstruse studies, and a varied field of learning, than with the merits of a general, or the wisdom of a prudent senator, let him turn his thoughts to those particular sciences themselves, and contemplate who and how many have flourished in them, as he will thus be best enabled to judge how great a scarcity of orators there is and has ever been.

---

[1] He refers to his exile and the proposed union between Cæsar and Pompey to make themselves masters of the whole commonwealth; a matter to which he was unwilling to allude more plainly. *Ellendt.*

[2] *Qui locus.* Quæ vitæ pars. *Proust.*

[3] The civil wars of Marius and Sylla. *Ellendt.*

[4] Alluding to the conspiracy of Catiline.

[5] The two books *De Inventione Rhetoricâ.*

---

[1] *Prudentissimorum.* Equivalent to *doctissimorum.* Pearce. Some manuscripts have *eruditissimorum.*

III. It does not escape your observation that what the Greeks call PHILOSOPHY, is esteemed by the most learned men, the originator, as it were, and parent of all the arts which merit praise; philosophy, I say, in which it is difficult to enumerate how many distinguished men there have been, and of how great knowledge, variety, and comprehensiveness in their studies, men who have not confined their labors to one province separately, but have embraced whatever they could master either by scientific investigations, or by processes of reasoning. Who is ignorant in how great obscurity of matter, in how abstruse, manifold, and subtle an art they who are called mathematicians are engaged? Yet in that pursuit so many men have arrived at excellence, that not one seems to have applied himself to the science in earnest without attaining in it whatever he desired. Who has ever devoted himself wholly to music; who has ever given himself up to the learning which they profess who are called grammarians, without compassing, in knowledge and understanding, the whole substance and matter of those sciences, though almost boundless? Of all those who have engaged in the most liberal pursuits and departments of such sciences, I think I may truly say that a smaller number of eminent poets have arisen than of men distinguished in any other branch of literature; and in the whole multitude of the learned, among whom there rarely appears one of the highest excellence, there will be found, if you will but make a careful review of our own list and that of the Greeks, far fewer good orators than good poets. This ought to seem the more wonderful, as attainments in other sciences are drawn from recluse and hidden springs; but the whole art of speaking lies before us, and is concerned with common usage and the custom and language of all men; so that while in other things that is most excellent which is most remote from the knowledge and understanding of the illiterate, it is in speaking even the greatest of faults to vary from the ordinary kind of language, and the practice sanctioned by universal reason.

IV. Yet it can not be said with truth, either that more are devoted to the other arts, or that they are excited by greater pleasure, more abundant hope, or more ample rewards; for to say nothing of Greece, which was always desirous to hold the first place in eloquence, and Athens, that inventress of all literature, in which the utmost power of oratory was both discovered and brought to perfection, in this very city of ours, assuredly, no studies were ever pursued with more earnestness than those tending to the acquisition of eloquence. For when our empire over all nations was established, and after a period of peace had secured tranquillity, there was scarcely a youth ambitious of praise who did not think that he must strive, with all his endeavors, to attain the art of speaking. For a time, indeed, as being ignorant of all method, and as thinking there was no course of exercise for them, or any precepts of art, they attained what they could by the single force of genius and thought. But afterward, having heard the Greek orators, and gained an acquaintance with Greek literature, and procured instructors, our countrymen were inflamed with an incredible passion for eloquence. The magnitude, the variety, the multitude of all kind of causes, excited them to such a degree, that to that learning which each had acquired by his individual study, frequent practice, which was superior to the precepts of all masters, was at once added. There were then, as there are also now, the highest inducements offered for the cultivation of this study, in regard to public favor, wealth, and dignity. The abilities of our countrymen (as we may judge from many particulars) far excelled those of the men of every other nation. For which reasons, who would not justly wonder that in the records of all ages, times, and states, so small a number of orators should be found?

But the art of eloquence is something greater, and collected from more sciences and studies than people imagine.

V. For who can suppose that, amid the greatest multitude of students, the utmost abundance of masters, the most eminent geniuses among men, the infinite variety of causes, the most ample rewards offered to eloquence, there is any other reason to be found for the small number of orators than the incredible magnitude and difficulty of the art? A knowledge of a vast number of things is necessary, without which volubility of words is empty and ridiculous; speech itself is to be formed, not merely by choice, but by careful construction of words; and all the emotions of the mind, which nature has given to man, must be intimately known; for all the force and art of speaking must be employed in allaying or exciting the feelings of those who listen. To this must be added a certain portion of grace and wit, learning worthy of a well-bred man, and quickness and brevity in replying as well as attacking, accompanied with a refined decorum and urbanity. Besides, the whole of antiquity and a multitude of examples is to be kept in the memory; nor is the knowledge of laws in general, or of the civil law in particular, to be neglected. And why need I add any remarks on delivery itself, which is to be ordered by action of body, by gesture, by look, and by modulation and variation of the voice, the great power of which, alone and in itself, the comparatively trivial art of actors and the stage proves, on which though all bestow their utmost labor to form their look, voice, and gesture, who knows not how few there are, and have ever been, to whom we can attend with patience? What can I say of that repository for all things, the memory, which, unless it be made the keeper of the matter and words that are the fruits of thought and invention, all the talents of the orator, we see, though they be of the highest degree of excellence, will be of no avail? Let us, then, cease to wonder what is the cause of the scarcity of good speakers, since eloquence results from all those qualifications, in each of which singly it is a great merit to labor successfully; and let us rather exhort our children, and others whose glory and honor is dear to us, to contemplate in their minds the full magnitude of the object, and not to trust that they can reach the height at which they aim, by the aid of the precepts, masters, and exercises, that they are all now following, but to understand that they must adopt others of a different character.

VI. In my opinion, indeed, no man can be an orator possessed of every praiseworthy accomplishment, unless he has attained the knowledge of every thing important, and of all liberal arts, for his language must be ornate and copious from knowledge, since, unless there be beneath the surface matter understood and felt by the speaker, oratory becomes an empty and almost puerile flow of words. Yet I will not lay so great a burden upon orators, especially our own, amid so many occupations of public and private life, as to think it allowable for them to be ignorant of nothing; although the qualifications of an orator, and his very profession of speaking well, seem to undertake and promise that he can discourse gracefully and copiously on whatever subject is proposed to him. But because this, I doubt not, will appear to most people an immense and infinite undertaking, and because I see that the Greeks, men amply endowed not only with genius and learning, but also with leisure and application, have made a kind of partition of the arts, and have not singly labored in the whole circle of oratory, but have separated from the other parts of rhetoric that department of eloquence which is used in the forum on trials or in deliberations, and have left this species only to the orator; I shall not embrace in these books more than has been attributed to this kind of speaking[1] by the almost unanimous consent of the greatest men, after much examination and discussion of the subject; and I shall repeat, not a series of precepts drawn from the infancy of our old and boyish learning, but matters which I have heard were formerly argued in a discussion among some of our countrymen who were of the highest eloquence, and of the first rank in every kind of dignity. Not

---

[1] Deliberative and judicial oratory; omitting the epideictic or demonstrative kind.

that I contemn the instructions which the Greek rhetoricians and teachers have left us, but, as they are already public, and within the reach of all, and can neither be set forth more elegantly, nor explained more clearly by my interpretation, you will, I think, excuse me, my brother, if I prefer to the Greeks the authority of those to whom the utmost merit in eloquence has been allowed by our own countrymen.

VII. At the time, then, when the consul Philippus was vehemently inveighing against the cause of the nobility, and the tribuneship of Drusus, undertaken to support the authority of the senate, seemed to be shaken and weakened, I was told, I remember, that Lucius Crassus, as if for the purpose of collecting his thoughts, betook himself, during the days of the Roman games, to his Tusculan country seat, whither also Quintus Mucius, who had been his father-in-law, is said to have come at the same time, as well as Marcus Antonius, a sharer in all the political proceedings of Crassus, and united in the closest friendship with him. There went out with Crassus himself two young men besides, great friends of Drusus, youths of whom our ancestors then entertained sanguine hopes that they would maintain the dignity of their order; Caius Cotta, who was then a candidate for the tribuneship of the people, and Publius Sulpicius, who was thought likely to stand for that office in due course. These, on the first day, conferred much together until very late in the evening, concerning the condition of those times, and the whole commonwealth, for which purpose they had met. Cotta repeated to me many things then prophetically lamented and noticed by the three of consular dignity in that conversation; so that no misfortune afterward happened to the state which they had not perceived to be hanging over it so long before; and he said that, when this conversation was finished, there was such politeness shown by Crassus, that after they had bathed and sat down to table, all the seriousness of the former discourse was banished; and there appeared so much pleasantry in him, and so much agreeableness in his humor, that though the early part of the day might seem to have been passed by them in the senate house, the banquet showed all the delights of the Tusculan villa.

But on the next day, when the older part of the company had taken sufficient repose, and were come to their walk, he told me that Scævola, after taking two or three turns, said, "Why should not we, Crassus, imitate Socrates in the Phædrus of Plato?[1] for this plane-tree of yours has put me in mind of it, which diffuses its spreading boughs to overshade this place, not less widely than that did whose covert Socrates sought, and which seems to me to have grown not so much from the rivulet which is described, as from the language of Plato: and what Socrates, with the hardest of feet, used to do, that is, to throw himself on the grass, while he delivered those sentiments which philosophers say were uttered divinely, may surely, with more justice, be allowed to my feet." Then Crassus rejoined, "Nay, we will yet farther consult your convenience;" and called for cushions; when they all, said Cotta, sat down on the seats that were under the plane-tree.

VIII. There (as Cotta used to relate), in order that the minds of them all might have some relaxation from their former discourse, Crassus introduced a conversation on the study of oratory. After he had commenced in this manner, That indeed Sulpicius and Cotta did not seem to need his exhortations, but rather both to deserve his praise, as they had already attained such powers as not only to excel their equals in age, but to be admitted to a comparison with their seniors; "Nor does any thing seem to me," he added, "more noble than to be able to fix the attention of assemblies of men by speaking, to fascinate their minds, to direct their passions to whatever object the orator

---

[1] P. 229. Compare Ruhnken, ad Lex. Timæi, v. *ἀμφιλαφές*, and Manutius, ad Cic., Div., ii., 11, p. 254. Cicero aptly refers to that dialogue of Plato, because much is said about eloquence in it. The plane-tree was greatly admired by the Romans for its wide-spreading shade. See I. H. Vossius, ad Virg., Georg., ii., 70; Plin., H. N., xii., 1; xvii., 15; Hor., Od., ii., 15, 5; Gronov., Obss., i., 5. *Ellendt.*

pleases, and to dissuade them from whatsoever he desires. This particular art has constantly flourished above all others in every free state, and especially in those which have enjoyed peace and tranquillity, and has ever exercised great power. For what is so admirable as that, out of an infinite multitude of men, there should arise a single individual who can alone, or with only a few others, exert effectually that power which nature has granted to all? Or what is so pleasant to be heard and understood as an oration adorned and polished with wise thoughts and weighty expressions? Or what is so striking, so astonishing, as that the tumults of the people, the religious feelings of judges, the gravity of the senate, should be swayed by the speech of one man? Or what, moreover, is so kingly, so liberal, so munificent, as to give assistance to the suppliant, to raise the afflicted, to bestow security, to deliver from dangers, to maintain men in the rights of citizenship? What, also, is so necessary as to keep arms always ready, with which you may either be protected yourself, or defy the malicious, or avenge yourself when provoked? Or consider (that you may not always contemplate the forum, the benches, the rostra, and the senate) what can be more delightful in leisure, or more suited to social intercourse, than elegant conversation, betraying no want of intelligence on any subject? For it is by this one gift that we are most distinguished from brute animals, that we converse together, and can express our thoughts by speech. Who, therefore, would not justly make this an object of admiration, and think it worthy of his utmost exertions, to surpass mankind themselves in that single excellence by which they claim their superiority over brutes? But, that we may notice the most important point of all, what other power could either have assembled mankind, when dispersed, into one place, or have brought them from wild and savage life to the present humane and civilized state of society; or, when cities were established, have described for them laws, judicial institutions, and rights? And that I may not mention more examples, which are almost without number, I will conclude the subject in one short sentence; for I consider, that by the judgment and wisdom of the perfect orator, not only his own honor, but that of many other individuals, and the welfare of the whole state, are principally upheld. Go on, therefore, as you are doing, young men, and apply earnestly to the study in which you are engaged, that you may be an honor to yourselves, an advantage to your friends, and a benefit to the republic."

IX. Scævola then observed with courtesy, as was always his manner, "I agree with Crassus as to other points (that I may not detract from the art or glory of Lælius, my father-in-law, or of my son-in-law here),[1] but I am afraid, Crassus, that I can not grant you these two points; one, that states were, as you said, originally established, and have often been preserved by orators; the other, that, setting aside the forum, the assemblies of the people, the courts of judicature, and the senate-house, the orator is, as you pronounced, accomplished in every subject of conversation and learning. For who will concede to you, either that mankind, dispersed originally in mountains and woods, inclosed themselves in towns and walls, not so much from being convinced by the counsels of the wise, as from being charmed by the speeches of the eloquent? Or that other advantages, arising either from the establishment or preservation of states, were settled, not by wise and brave men, but by fluent and elegant speakers? Does Romulus seem to you to have assembled the shepherds, and those that flocked to him from all parts, or to have formed marriages with the Sabines, or to have repelled the power of the neighboring people, by eloquence, and not by counsel and eminent wisdom? Is there any trace of eloquence apparent in Numa Pompilius, in Servius Tullius, or in the rest of our kings, from whom we have many excellent regulations for maintaining our government? After the kings were expelled (though we see that their expulsion was effected by the mind of Lucius Brutus,

[1] Crassus.

and not by his tongue), do we not perceive that all the subsequent transactions are full of wise counsel, but destitute of all mixture of eloquence? But if I should be inclined to adduce examples from our own and other states, I could cite more instances of mischief than of benefit done to public affairs by men of eminent eloquence; but, to omit others, I think, Crassus, that the most eloquent men I ever heard, except you two,[1] were the Sempronii, Tiberius and Caius, whose father, a prudent and grave man, but by no means eloquent, on several other occasions, but especially when censor, was of the utmost service to the republic; and he, not by any faultless flow of speech, but by a word and a nod, transferred the freedmen into the city tribes;[2] and, if he had not done so, we should now have no republic, which we still maintain with difficulty; but his sons, who were eloquent, and qualified for speaking by all the helps of nature and of learning, having found the state in a most flourishing condition, both through the counsels of their father, and the arms of their ancestors, brought their country, by means of their oratory, that most excellent ruler of states as you call it, to the verge of ruin.

X. "Were our ancient laws, and the customs of our ancestors; were the auspices, over which you, Crassus, and I preside with great security to the republic; were the religious rites and ceremonies; were the civil laws, the knowledge of which has long prevailed in our family (and without any praise for eloquence), either invented, or understood, or in any way ordered by the tribe of orators? I can remember that Servius Galba, a man of godlike power in speaking, as well as Marcus Æmilius Porcina, and Cneius Carbo himself, whom you defeated when you were but a youth,[3] was ignorant of the laws, at a loss in the practices of our ancestors, and unlearned in civil jurisprudence; and, except you, Crassus, who, rather from your own inclination to study, than because it was any peculiar business of an orator, have learned the civil law from us, as I am sometimes ashamed to say, this generation of ours is ignorant of law.

"But what you assumed, as by a law of your own, in the last part of your speech, that an orator is able to speak fluently on any subject, I would not, if I were not here in your own domain, tolerate for a moment, but would head a party who should either oppose you by an interdict,[1] or summon you to contend with them at law, for having so unceremoniously invaded the possessions of others. In the first place, all the Pythagoreans, and the followers of Democritus, would institute a suit against you, with the rest of the natural philosophers, each in his own department, men who are elegant and powerful speakers, with whom you could not contend on equal terms.[2] Whole troops of other philosophers would assail you besides, even down from Socrates their origin and head, and would convince you that you had learned nothing about good and evil in life, nothing about the passions of the mind, nothing about the moral conduct of mankind, nothing about the proper course of life; they would show you that you have made no due inquiry after knowledge, and that you know nothing; and, when they had made an attack upon you

---

[1] Crassus and Antonius.

[2] Livy, xlv., 15, says that the freedmen were previously dispersed among all the four city tribes, and that Gracchus included them all in the Esquiline tribe. The object was to allow the freedmen as little influence as possible in voting.

[3] Caius Papirius Carbo, after having been a very seditious tribune, went over in his consulship to the side of the patricians, and highly extolled Lucius Opimius for killing Caius Gracchus. But, at the expiration of his consulship, being impeached by Crassus, on what grounds we do not know, he put himself to death. Cic., Orat., iii., 20, 74; Brut., 27, 103. *Ellendt.*

[1] An edict of the prætor forbidding something to be done, in contradistinction to a *decree,* which ordered something to be done. Ellendt refers to Gaius, iv., 139, 160.

[2] *Justo sacramento.* The *sacramentum* was a deposit of a certain sum of money laid down by two parties who were going to law; and when the decision was made, the victorious party received his money back, while that of the defeated party went into the public treasury. Varro, L. L., v., 180.

all together, then every sect would bring its separate action against you. The Academy would press you, and, whatever you asserted, force you to deny it. Our friends the Stoics would hold you entangled in the snares of their disputations and questions. The Peripatetics would prove that those very aids and ornaments to speaking, which you consider the peculiar property of the orators, must be sought from themselves; and they would show you that Aristotle and Theophrastus have written not only better, but also far more copiously, on these subjects, than all the masters of the art of speaking. I say nothing of the mathematicians, the grammarians, the musicians, with whose sciences this art of speaking of yours is not connected by the least affinity. I think, therefore, Crassus, that such great and numerous professions ought not to be made. What you can effect is sufficiently great, namely, that in judicial matters the cause which you plead shall seem the better and more probable; that in public assemblies, and in delivering opinions, your oratory shall have the most power to persuade; that, finally, you shall seem to the wise to speak with eloquence, and even to the simple to speak with truth. If you can do more than this, it will appear to me that it is not the orator, but Crassus himself that effects it by the force of talents peculiar to himself, and not common to other orators."

XI. Crassus then replied, "I am not ignorant, Scævola, that things of this sort are commonly asserted and maintained among the Greeks; for I was an auditor of their greatest men, when I came to Athens as quæstor from Macedonia,[1] and when the Academy was in a flourishing state, as it was represented in those days, for Charmadas, and Clitomachus, and Æschines were in possession of it. There was also Metrodorus, who, with the others, had been a diligent hearer of the famous Carneades himself, a man beyond all others, as they told me, a most spirited and copious speaker. Mnesarchus, too, was in great esteem, a hearer of your friend Panætius, and Diodorus, a scholar of Critolaus the Peripatetic; and there were many other famous men besides, highly distinguished in philosophy, by all of whom, with one voice as it were, I observed that the orator was repelled from the government of states, excluded from all learning and knowledge of great affairs, and degraded and thrust down into the courts of justice and petty assemblies, as into a workshop. But I neither assented to those men, nor to the originator of these disputations, and by far the most eloquent of them all, the eminently grave and oratorical Plato; whose Gorgias I then diligently read over at Athens with Charmadas; from which book I conceived the highest admiration of Plato, as he seemed to me to prove himself an eminent orator, even in ridiculing orators. A controversy indeed on the word ORATOR has long disturbed the minute Grecians, who are fonder of argument than of truth. For if any one pronounces him to be an orator who can speak fluently only on law in general, or on judicial questions, or before the people, or in the senate, he must yet necessarily grant and allow him a variety of talents; for he can not treat even of these matters with sufficient skill and accuracy without great attention to all public affairs, and without a knowledge of laws, customs, and equity, nor without understanding the nature and manners of mankind; and to him who knows these things, without which no one can maintain even the most minute points in judicial pleadings, how much is wanting of the knowledge even of the most important affairs? But if you allow nothing to belong to the orator but to speak aptly, ornately, and copiously, how can he even attain these qualities without that knowledge which you do not allow him? for there can be no true merit in speaking, unless what is said is thoroughly understood by him who says it. If, therefore, the natural philosopher Democritus spoke with elegance, as he is reported to have spoken, and as it appears to me that he did speak, the matter on

[1] Crassus was quæstor in Asia A.U.C. 645, and, on his return, at the expiration of his office, passed through Macedonia. *Ellendt.*

which he spoke belonged to the philosopher, but the graceful array of words is to be ascribed to the orator. And if Plato spoke divinely upon subjects most remote from civil controversies, as I grant that he did; if also Aristotle, and Theophrastus, and Carneades, were eloquent, and spoke with sweetness and grace on those matters which they discussed; let the subjects on which they spoke belong to other studies, but their speech itself, surely, is the peculiar offspring of that art of which we are now discoursing and inquiring. For we see that some have reasoned on the same subjects jejunely and dryly, as Chrysippus, whom they celebrate as the acutest of philosophers; nor is he on this account to be thought to have been deficient in philosophy, because he did not gain the talent of speaking from an art which is foreign to philosophy.

XII. "Where then lies the difference? Or by what term will you discriminate the fertility and copiousness of speech in those whom I have named, from the barrenness of those who use not this variety and elegance of phrase? One thing there will certainly be, which those who speak well will exhibit as their own; a graceful and elegant style, distinguished by a peculiar artifice and polish. But this kind of diction, if there be not matter beneath it clear and intelligible to the speaker, must either amount to nothing, or be received with ridicule by all who hear it. For what savors so much of madness, as the empty sound of words, even the choicest and most elegant, when there is no sense or knowledge contained in them? Whatever be the subject of a speech, therefore, in whatever art or branch of science, the orator, if he has made himself master of it, as of his client's cause, will speak on it better and more elegantly than even the very originator and author of it can.[1] If, indeed, any one shall say that there are certain trains of thought and reasoning properly belonging to orators, and a knowledge of certain things circumscribed within the limits of the forum, I will confess that our common speech is employed about these matters chiefly; but yet there are many things, in these very topics, which those masters of rhetoric, as they are called, neither teach nor understand. For who is ignorant that the highest power of an orator consists in exciting the minds of men to anger, or to hatred, or to grief, or in recalling them from these more violent emotions to gentleness and compassion? which power will never be able to effect its object by eloquence, unless in him who has obtained a thorough insight into the nature of mankind, and all the passions of humanity, and those causes by which our minds are either impelled or restrained. But all these are thought to belong to the philosophers, nor will the orator, at least with my consent, ever deny that such is the case; but when he has conceded to them the knowledge of things, since they are willing to exhaust their labors on that alone, he will assume to himself the treatment of oratory, which without that knowledge is nothing. For the proper concern of an orator, as I have already often said, is language of power and elegance accommodated to the feelings and understandings of mankind.

XIII. "On these matters I confess that Aristotle and Theophrastus have written.[1] But consider, Scævola, whether this is not wholly in my favor. For I do not borrow from them what the orator possesses in common with them; but they allow that what they say on these subjects belongs to oratory. Their other treatises, accordingly, they distinguish by the name of the science on which each is written; their treatises on oratory they entitle and designate as books of rhetoric. For when, in their discussions (as often happens), such topics present themselves as require them to speak of the immortal gods, of piety, of concord, of friendship, of the common rights of their fellow-citizens, or those of all mankind, of the law of nations, of equity, of temperance, of greatness of mind, of every kind of virtue, all the academies and schools of philosophy, I imagine, will cry out that all these

[1] See Quintilian, ii., 21.

[1] Though they are philosophers, and not orators or rhetoricians.

subjects are their property, and that no particle of them belongs to the orator. But when I have given them liberty to reason on all these subjects in corners to amuse their leisure, I shall give and assign to the orator his part, which is, to set forth with full power and attraction the very same topics which they discuss in such tame and bloodless phraseology. These points I then discussed with the philosophers in person at Athens, for Marcus Marcellus, our countryman, who is now curule ædile, obliged me to do so, and he would certainly have taken part in our present conversation, were he not now celebrating the public games; for he was then a youth marvelously given to these studies.

"Of the institution of laws, of war, of peace, of alliances, of tributes, of the civil law as relating to various ranks and ages respectively,[1] let the Greeks say, if they will, that Lycurgus or Solon (although I think that these should be enrolled in the number of the eloquent) had more knowledge than Hypereides or Demosthenes, men of the highest accomplishments and refinement in oratory; or let our countrymen prefer, in this sort of knowledge, the Decemviri who wrote the Twelve Tables, and who must have been wise men, to Servius Galba, and your father-in-law Lælius, who are allowed to have excelled in the glorious art of speaking. I, indeed, shall never deny that there are some sciences peculiarly well understood by those who have applied their whole study to the knowledge and consideration of them; but the accomplished and complete orator I shall call him who can speak on all subjects with variety and copiousness.

XIV. For often in those causes which all acknowledge properly to belong to orators, there is something to be drawn forth and adopted, not from the routine of the Forum, which is the only knowledge that you grant to the orator, but from some of the more obscure sciences. I ask whether a speech can be made for or against a general, without an acquaintance with military affairs, or often without a knowledge of certain inland and maritime countries? whether a speech can be made to the people about passing or rejecting laws, or in the senate on any kind of public transactions, without the greatest knowledge and judgment in political matters? whether a speech can be adapted to excite or calm the thoughts and passions (which alone is a great business of the orator) without a most diligent examination of all those doctrines which are set forth on the nature and manners of men by the philosophers? I do not know whether I may not be less successful in maintaining what I am going to say; but I shall not hesitate to speak that which I think. Physics, and mathematics, and those other things which you just now decided to belong to other sciences, belong to the peculiar knowledge of those who profess them; but if any one would illustrate those arts by eloquence, he must have recourse to the power of oratory. Nor, if, as is said, Philo,[1] the famous architect, who built an arsenal for the Athenians, gave that people an eloquent account of his work, is it to be imagined that his eloquence proceeded from the art of the architect, but from that of the orator. Or, if our friend Marcus Antonius had had to speak for Hermodorus[2] on the subject of dock-building, he would have spoken, when he had learned the case from Hermodorus, with elegance and copiousness, drawn from an art quite unconnected with dock-building. And Asclepiades,[3] whom we

[1] *Dejure civili generatim in ordines œtatesque descripto.* Instead of *civili,* the old reading was *civium,* in accordance with which Lambinus altered *descripto* into *descriptorum. Civili* was an innovation of Ernesti, which Ellendt condemns, and retains *civium;* observing that Cicero means *jura civium* plublica *singulis ordinibus et œtatibus assignata.* "By *ordines,*" says Ernesti, "are meant patricians and plebeians, senators, knights, and classes in the census; by *œtates,* younger and older persons."

[1] He is frequently mentioned by the ancients; the passages relating to him have been collected by Junius, de Picturâ in Catal. Artif. *Ernesti.* See Plin., H. N., vii., 38; Plut., Syll., c. 14; Val. Max., vii., 12.

[2] A Roman ship-builder. See Turneb., Advers., xi., 2.

[3] See Plin., H. N., vii., 37. Celsus often refers to his authority as the founder of a new party. *Ellendt.*

knew as a physician and a friend, did not, when he excelled others of his profession in eloquence, employ, in his graceful elocution, the art of physic, but that of oratory. What Socrates used to say, that *all men are sufficiently eloquent in that which they understand,* is very plausible, but not true. It would have been nearer truth to say that no man can be eloquent on a subject that he does not understand; and that, if he understands a subject ever so well, but is ignorant how to form and polish his speech, he can not express himself eloquently even about what he does understand.

XV. "If, therefore, any one desires to define and comprehend the whole and peculiar power of an orator, that man, in my opinion, will be an orator, worthy of so great a name, who, whatever subject comes before him, and requires rhetorical elucidation, can speak on it judiciously, in set form, elegantly, and from memory, and with a certain dignity of action. But if the phrase which I have used, "on whatever subject," is thought by any one too comprehensive, let him retrench and curtail as much of it as he pleases; but this I will maintain, that though the orator be ignorant of what belongs to other arts and pursuits, and understands only what concerns the discussions and practice of the Forum, yet if he has to speak on those arts, he will, when he has learned what pertains to any of them from persons who understand them, discourse upon them much better than the very persons of whom those arts form the peculiar province. Thus, if our friend Sulpicius have to speak on military affairs, he will inquire about them of my kinsman, Caius Marius,[1] and when he has received information, will speak upon them in such a manner, that he shall seem to Marius to understand them better than himself. Or if he has to speak on the civil law, he will consult with you, and will excel you, though eminently wise and learned in it, in speaking on those very points which he shall have learned from yourself. Or if any subject presents itself, requiring him to speak on the nature and vices of men, on desire, on moderation, on continence, on grief, on death, perhaps, if he thinks proper (though the orator ought to have a knowledge of these things), he will consult with Sextus Pompeius,[1] a man learned in philosophy. But this he will certainly accomplish, that, of whatever matter he gains a knowledge, or from whomsoever, he will speak upon it much more elegantly than the very person from whom he gained the knowledge. But, since philosophy is distinguished into three parts, inquiries into the obscurities of physics, the subtleties of logic, and the knowledge of life and manners, let us, if Sulpicius will listen to me, leave the two former, and consult our ease; but unless we have a knowledge of the third, which has always been the province of the orator, we shall leave him nothing in which he can distinguish himself. The part of philosophy, therefore, regarding life and manners, must be thoroughly mastered by the orator; other subjects, even if he has not learned them, he will be able, whenever there is occasion, to adorn by his eloquence, if they are brought before him and made known to him.

XVI. "For it is allowed among the learned that Aratus, a man ignorant of astronomy, has treated of heaven and the constellations in extremely polished and excellent verses; if Nicander,[2] of Colophon, a man totally unconnected with the country, has written well on rural affairs, with the

[1] The son of the great Caius Marius, seven times consul, had married Mucia, the daughter of the augur Scævola. In Cicero's Oration for Balbus, also, c. 21, 49, where the merits of that eminent commander are celebrated, Crassus is called his *affinis,* relation by marriage. *Henrichsen.*

[1] The uncle of Cneius Pompey the Great, who had devoted excellent talents to the attainment of a thorough knowledge of civil law, geometry, and the doctrines of the Stoics. See Cic., Brut., 47; Philipp., xii., 11; Beier, ad Off., i., 6, 19. *Ellendt.*

[2] Nicander, a physician, grammarian, and poet, flourished in the time of Attalus, the second king of Pergamus, about fifty years before Christ. His Theriaca and Alexipharmaca are extant; his Georgica, to which Cicero here alludes, has perished. *Henrichsen.*

aid of poetical talent, and not from understanding husbandry, what reason is there why an orator should not speak most eloquently on those matters of which he shall have gained a knowledge for a certain purpose and occasion? For the poet is nearly allied to the orator; being somewhat more restricted in numbers, but less restrained in the choice of words, yet in many kinds of embellishment his rival and almost equal; in one respect, assuredly, nearly the same, that he circumscribes or bounds his jurisdiction by no limits, but reserves to himself full right to range wherever he pleases with the same ease and liberty. For why did you say, Scævola,[1] that you would not endure, unless you were in my domain, my assertion, that the orator ought to be accomplished in every style of speaking, and in every part of polite learning? I should certainly not have said this if I had thought myself to be the orator whom I conceive in my imagination. But, as Caius Lucilius used frequently to say (a man not very friendly to you,[2] and on that account less familiar with me than he could wish, but a man of learning and good breeding), I am of this opinion, that no one is to be numbered among orators who is not thoroughly accomplished in all branches of knowledge requisite for a man of good breeding; and though we may not put forward such knowledge in conversation, yet it is apparent, and indeed evident, whether we are destitute of it, or have acquired it; as those who play at tennis do not exhibit, in playing, the gestures of the palæstra, but their movements indicate whether they have learned those exercises or are unacquainted with them; and as those who shape out any thing, though they do not then exercise the art of painting, yet make it clear whether they can paint or not; so in orations to courts of justice, before the people, and in the senate, although other sciences have no peculiar place in them, yet is it easily proved whether he who speaks has only been exercised in the parade of declamation, or has devoted himself to oratory after having been instructed in all liberal knowledge."

XVII. Then Scævola, smiling, said: "I will not struggle with you any longer, Crassus; for you have, by some artifice, made good what you asserted against me, so as to grant me whatever I refused to allow to the orator, and yet so as to wrest from me those very things again I know not how, and to transfer them to the orator as his property.[1] When I went as prætor to Rhodes, and communicated to Apollonius, that famous instructor in this profession, what I had learned from Panætius, Apollonius, as was his manner, ridiculed these matters,[2] threw contempt upon philosophy, and made many other observations with less wisdom than wit; but your remarks were of such a kind as not to express contempt for any arts or sciences, but to admit that they are all attendants and handmaids of the orator; and if ever any one should comprehend them all, and the same person should add to that knowledge the powers of supremely elegant oratory, I can not but say that he would be a man of high distinction and worthy of the greatest admiration. But if there should be such a one, or indeed has ever been, or can possibly be, you alone would be the person; who, not only in my

---

[1] See c. x.

[2] It is Lucilius the Satirist that is meant. What cause there had been for unfriendliness between him and Scævola is unknown; perhaps he might have spoken too freely, or made some satirical remark on the accusation of Scævola by Albucius for bribery, on which there are some verses in b. iii., c. 43. *Ellendt.*

---

[1] You granted me all that I desired when you said that all arts and sciences belong, as it were, respectively to those who have invented, or profess, or study them; . . . but when you said that those arts and sciences are necessary to the orator, and that he can speak upon them if he wishes, with more elegance and effect than those who have made them their peculiar study, you seemed to take them all from me again, and to transfer them to the orator as his own property. *Proust.*

[2] Orellius reads *Hœc—irrisit,* where the reader will observe that the pronoun is governed by the verb. Ellendt and some others read *Quœ* instead of *Hœc.* Several alterations have been proposed, but none of them bring the sentence into a satisfactory state.

judgment, but in that of all men, have hardly left to other orators (I speak it with deference to this company) any glory to be acquired. If, however, there is in yourself no deficiency of knowledge pertaining to judicial and political affairs, and yet you have not mastered all that additional learning which you assign to the complete orator, let us consider whether you do not attribute to him more than possibility and truth itself will allow." Here Crassus rejoined: "Remember that I have not been speaking of my own talents, but of those of the true orator. For what have I either learned or had a possibility of knowing, who entered upon pleading before I had any instruction; whom the pressure of business overtasked amid the occupations of the forum, of canvassing, of public affairs, and the management of the causes of friends, before I could form any true notion of the importance of such great employments? But if there seem to you to be so much in me, to whom, though capacity, as you think, may not greatly have been wanting, yet to whom learning, leisure, and that keen application to study which is so necessary, have certainly been wanting, what do you think would be the case if those acquirements, which I have not gained, should be united to some greater genius than mine? How able, how great an orator, do you think, would he prove?"

XVIII. Antonius then observed: "You prove to me, Crassus, what you advance; nor do I doubt that he will have a far greater fund of eloquence who shall have learned the reason and nature of every thing and of all sciences. But, in the first place, this is difficult to be achieved, especially in such a life as ours and such occupations; and next, it is to be feared that we may, by such studies, be drawn away from our exercise and practice of speaking before the people and in the forum. The eloquence of those men whom you mentioned a little before, seems to me to be of a quite different sort, though they speak with grace and dignity, as well on the nature of things as on human life. Theirs is a neat and florid kind of language, but more adapted for parade and exercise in the schools, than for these tumults of the city and forum. For when I, who late in life, and then but lightly, touched upon Greek learning, was going as proconsul into Cilicia, and had arrived at Athens, I waited there several days on account of the difficulty of sailing; and as I had every day with me the most learned men, nearly the same that you have just now named, and a report, I know not how, had spread among them that I, like you, was versed in causes of great importance, every one, according to his abilities, took occasion to discourse upon the office and art of an orator. Some of them, as Mnesarchus himself, said, that those whom we call orators were nothing but a set of mechanics with glib and well-practiced tongues, but that no one could be an orator but a man of true wisdom; and that eloquence itself, as it consisted in the art of speaking well, was a kind of virtue,[1] and that he who possessed one virtue possessed all, and that virtues were in themselves equal and alike; and thus he who was eloquent possessed all virtues, and was a man of true wisdom. But their phraseology was intricate and dry, and quite unsuited to my taste. Charmadas indeed spoke much more diffusely on those topics; not that he delivered his own opinion (for it is the hereditary custom of every one in the Academy to take the part of opponents to all in their disputations), but what he chiefly signified was, that those who were called rhetoricians, and laid down rules for the art of speaking, understood nothing; and that no man could attain any command of eloquence who had not mastered the doctrines of the philosophers.

XIX. "Certain men of eloquence at Athens, versed in public affairs and judicial pleadings, disputed on the other side; among whom was Menedemus, lately my guest at Rome; but when he had observed that there is a sort of wisdom which is employed in inquiring into the methods of settling and managing governments, he, though a ready speaker, was promptly attacked by the other,[2] a man of abundant learning, and of an al-

1 The Stoics called eloquence one of their virtues. See Quintilian, ii., 20.

2 Charmadas.

most incredible variety and copiousness of argument; who maintained that every portion of such wisdom must be derived from philosophy, and that whatever was established in a state concerning the immortal gods, the discipline of youth, justice, patience, temperance, moderation in every thing, and other matters, without which states would either not subsist at all, or be corrupt in morals, was nowhere to be found in the petty treatises of the rhetoricians. For if those teachers of rhetoric included in their art such a multitude of the most important subjects, why, he asked, were their books crammed with rules about proems and perorations, and such trifles (for so he called them), while about the modeling of states, the composition of laws, about equity, justice, integrity, about mastering the appetites, and forming the morals of mankind, not one single syllable was to be found in their pages? Their precepts he ridiculed in such a manner, as to show that the teachers were not only destitute of the knowledge which they arrogated to themselves, but that they did not even know the proper art and method of speaking; for he thought that the principal business of an orator was, that he might appear to those to whom he spoke to be such as he would wish to appear (that this was to be attained by a life of good reputation, on which those teachers of rhetoric had laid down nothing in their precepts); and that the minds of the audience should be affected in such a manner as the orator would have them to be affected, an object, also, which could by no means be attained, unless the speaker understood by what methods, by what arguments, and by what sort of language the minds of men are moved in any particular direction; but that these matters were involved and concealed in the profoundest doctrines of philosophy, which these rhetoricians had not touched even with the extremity of their lips. These assertions Menedemus endeavored to refute, but rather by *authorities* than by *arguments;* for, repeating from memory many noble passages from the orations of Demosthenes, he showed that the orator, while he swayed the minds of judges or of the people by his eloquence, was not ignorant by what means he attained his end, which Charmadas denied that any one could know without philosophy.

XX. "To this Charmadas replied, that he did not deny that Demosthenes was possessed of consummate ability and the utmost energy of eloquence; but whether he had these powers from natural genius, or because he was, as was acknowledged, a diligent hearer of Plato, it was not what Demosthenes could do, but what the rhetoricians taught, that was the subject of inquiry. Sometimes, too, he was carried so far by the drift of his discourse as to maintain that there was no art at all in speaking; and having shown by various arguments that we are so formed by nature as to be able to flatter, and to insinuate ourselves, as suppliants, into the favor of those from whom we wish to obtain any thing, as well as to terrify our enemies by menaces, to relate matters of fact, to confirm what we assert, to refute what is said against us, and, finally, to use entreaty or lamentation; particulars in which the whole faculties of the orator are employed; and that practice and exercise sharpened the understanding, and produced fluency of speech, he rested his cause, in conclusion, on a multitude of examples that he adduced; for first, as if stating an indisputable fact,[1] he affirmed that no writer on the art of rhetoric was ever even moderately eloquent, going back as far as I know not what Corax and Tisias,[2] who, he said, appeared to be the inventors and first authors of rhetorical science; and then named a vast number of the most eloquent men who had neither

---

[1] *Quasi deditâ operâ.* As if Charmadas himself had collected all the writers on the art of rhetoric, that he might be in a condition to prove what he now asserted; or, as if the writers on the art of rhetoric themselves had purposely abstained from attempting to be eloquent. But Charmadas was very much in the wrong; for Gorgias, Isocrates, Protagoras, Theophrastus, and other teachers of rhetoric were eminent for eloquence. *Proust.*

[2] Two Sicilians, said to have been the most ancient writers on rhetoric. See Quintilian, iii., 1.

learned, nor cared to understand the rules of art, and among whom (whether in jest, or because he thought, or had heard something to that effect) he instanced me as one who had received none of their instructions, and yet, as he said, had some abilities as a speaker; of which two observations I readily granted the truth of one, that I had never been instructed, but thought that in the other he was either joking with me, or was under some mistake. But he denied that there was any art, except such as lay in things that were known and thoroughly understood, things tending to the same object, and never misleading; but that every thing treated by the orators was doubtful and uncertain; as it was uttered by those who did not fully understand it, and was heard by them to whom knowledge was not meant to be communicated, but merely false, or at least obscure notions, intended to live in their minds only for a short time. In short, he seemed bent on convincing me that there was no art of speaking, and that no one could speak skillfully, or so as fully to illustrate a subject, but one who had attained that knowledge which is delivered by the most learned of the philosophers. On which occasions Charmadas used to say with a passionate admiration of your genius, Crassus, that I appeared to him very easy in listening, and you most pertinacious in disputation.

XXI. "Then it was that I, swayed by this opinion, remarked in a little treatise[1] which got abroad, and into people's hands, without my knowledge and against my will, that I had known many good speakers, but never yet any one that was truly eloquent; for I accounted him *a good speaker* who could express his thoughts with accuracy and perspicuity, according to the ordinary judgment of mankind, before an audience of moderate capacity; but I considered him alone *eloquent,* who could in a more admirable and noble manner amplify and adorn whatever subjects he chose, and who embraced in thought and memory all the principles of every thing relating to oratory. This, though it may be difficult to us, who, before we begin to speak in public, are overwhelmed by canvassings for office and by the business of the forum, is yet within the range of possibility and the powers of nature. For I, as far as I can divine by conjecture, and as far as I can estimate the abilities of our countrymen, do not despair that there may arise at some time or other a person, who, when, with a keener devotion to study than we feel, or have ever felt, with more leisure, with better and more mature talent for learning, and with superior labor and industry, he shall have given himself up to hearing, reading, and writing, may become such an orator as we desire to see—one who may justly be called not only a good speaker, but truly eloquent; and such a character, in my opinion, is our friend Crassus, or some one, if such ever was, of equal genius, who, having heard, read, and written more than Crassus, shall be able to make some little addition to it."

Here Sulpicius observed: "That has happened by accident, Crassus, which neither Cotta nor I expected, but which we both earnestly desired—I mean, that you should insensibly glide into a discourse of this kind. For, as we were coming hither, we thought it would be a pleasure, if, while you were talking on other matters, we might gather something worthy to be remembered from your conversation; but that you should go into a deep and full discussion on this very study, or art, or faculty, and penetrate into the heart of it, was what we could scarcely venture to hope. For I, who from my early youth have felt a strong affection for you both, and even a love for Crassus, having never left his company, could never yet elicit a word from him on the method and art of speaking, though I not only solicited him myself, but endeavored to move him by the agency of Drusus; on which subject you, Antonius (I speak but the truth), never failed to answer my requests and interrogatories, and have very often told me what you used to notice in speaking. And since each of you has opened a way to these subjects of our research, and since Crassus was the first to commence this discourse,

[1] See c. 47.—Cicero speaks of it as *exilis,* poor and dry, Brut., 44; Orat., 5.

do us the favor to acquaint us fully and exactly what you think about the various kinds of eloquence. If we obtain this indulgence from you, I shall feel the greatest obligation to this school of yours, Crassus, and to your Tusculan villa, and shall prefer your suburban place of study to the famous Academy and Lyceum."

XXII. "Nay rather, Sulpicius," rejoined Crassus, "let us ask Antonius, who is both capable of doing what you desire, and, as I hear you say, has been accustomed to do so. As to myself, I acknowledge that I have ever avoided all such kind of discourse, and have often declined to comply with your requests and solicitations, as you just now observed. This I did, not from pride or want of politeness, nor because I was unwilling to aid your just and commendable aspirations, especially as I knew you to be eminently and above others formed and qualified by nature to become a speaker, but, in truth, from being unaccustomed to such kind of discussions, and from being ignorant of those principles which are laid down as institutes of the art." "Then," said Cotta, "since we have got over what we thought the greatest difficulty, to induce you, Crassus, to speak at all upon these subjects, for the rest, it will be our own fault if we let you go before you have explained all that we have to ask." "I believe I must answer," says Crassus, "as is usually written in the formulæ for entering on inheritances,[1] concerning such points AS I KNOW AND SHALL BE ABLE." "And which of us," rejoined Cotta, "can be so presuming as to desire to know or to be able to do any thing that you do not know or can not do?" "Well, then," returned Crassus, "on condition that I may say that I can not do what I can not do, and that I may own that I do not know what I do not know, you may put questions to me at your pleasure." "We shall, then, first ask of you," said Sulpicius, "what you think of what Antonius has advanced; whether you think that there is any art in speaking?" "What!" exclaimed Crassus, "do you put a trifling question to me, as to some idle and talkative, though perhaps studious and learned Greek, on which I may speak according to my humor? When do you imagine that I have ever regarded or thought upon such matters, or have not always rather ridiculed the impudence of those men who, seated in the schools, would demand if any one, in a numerous assembly of persons, wished to ask any question, and desire him to speak? This Gorgias the Leontine is said to have first done, who was thought to undertake and promise something vast, in pronouncing himself prepared to speak on all subjects on which any one should be inclined to hear him. But afterward those men made it a common practice, and continue it to this day; so that there is no topic of such importance, or so unexpected, or so new, on which they do not profess that they will say all that can be said. But if I had thought that you, Cotta, or you, Sulpicius, were desirous to hear such matters, I would have brought hither some Greek to amuse you with their manner of disputation; for there is with M. Piso[1] (a youth already addicted to this intellectual exercise, and one of superior talents, and of great affection for me) the peripatetic Staseas, a man with whom I am well acquainted, and who, as I perceive is agreed among the learned, is of the first eminence in his profession."

XXIII. "Why do you speak to me," says Scævola, "of this Staseas, this peripatetic? You must comply with the wishes of these young gentlemen, Crassus, who do not want the common, profitless talk of any Greek, or any empty declamations of the schools, but desire to know the opinions of a man in whose footsteps they long to

---

[1] *Cretionibus.* An heir was allowed a certain time to determine, *cernere,* whether he would enter upon an estate bequeathed to him, or not. See Cic., ad Att., xi., 12; xiii., 46; Gaius, Instit., ii., 164; Ulpian, Fragm., xxii., 27; Heinecc., Syntagm., ii., 14, 17.

[1] Marcus Pupius Piso Calpurnianus, to whom Cicero was introduced by his father, that he might profit by his learning and experience. See Ascon., Ped. ad Pis., 26; Cic., Brut., 67; De Nat. De., i., 7, 16.

tread—one who is the wisest and most eloquent of all men, who is not distinguished by petty books of precepts, but is the first, both in judgment and oratory, in causes of the greatest consequence, and in this seat of empire and glory. For my part, as I always thought you a god in eloquence, so I have never attributed to you greater praises for oratory than for politeness; which you ought to show on this occasion especially, and not to decline a discussion on which two young men of such excellent ability invite you to enter." "I am certainly," replied Crassus, "desirous to oblige them, nor shall I think it any trouble to speak briefly, as is my manner, what I think upon any point of the subject. And to their first question (because I do not think it right for me to neglect your admonition, Scævola), I answer, that I think there is either no art of speaking at all, or but very little; but that all the disputation about it among the learned arises from a difference of opinion about the word. For if art is to be defined according to what Antonius just now asserted,[1] as lying in things thoroughly understood and fully known, such as are abstracted from the caprice of opinion and comprehended in the limits of science, there seems to me to be no art at all in oratory; since all the species of our forensic diction are various, and suited to the common understanding of the people. Yet if those things which have been observed in the practice and method of speaking have been noted and chronicled by ingenious and skillful men, have been set forth in words, illustrated in their several kinds, and distributed into parts (as I think may possibly be done), I do not understand why speaking may not be deemed an art, if not according to the exact definition of Antonius, at least according to common opinion. But whether it be an art, or merely the resemblance of an art, it is not, indeed, to be neglected; yet we must understand that there are other things of more consequence for the attainment of eloquence."

XXIV. Antonius then observed, that he was very strongly of opinion with Crassus; for he neither adopted such a definition of art as those preferred who attributed all the powers of eloquence to art, nor did he repudiate it entirely, as most of the philosophers had done. "But I imagine, Crassus," added he, "that you will gratify these two young men, if you will specify those particulars which you think may be more conducive to oratory than art itself." "I will indeed mention them," said he, "since I have engaged to do so, but must beg you not to publish my trifling remarks: though I will keep myself under such restraint as not to seem to speak like a master, or artist, but like one of the number of private citizens, moderately versed in the practice of the forum, and not altogether ignorant; not to have offered any thing from myself, but to have accidentally fallen in with the course of your conversation. Indeed, when I was a candidate for office, I used, at the time of canvassing, to send away Scævola from me, telling him I wanted to be foolish, that is, to solicit with flattery, a thing that can not be done to any purpose unless it be done foolishly; and that he was the only man in the world in whose presence I should least like to play the fool; and yet fortune has appointed him to be a witness and spectator of my folly.[1] For what is more foolish than to speak about speaking, when speaking itself is never otherwise than foolish, except it is absolutely necessary?" "Proceed, however, Crassus," said Scævola; "for I will take upon myself the blame which you fear."

XXV. "I am, then, of opinion," said Crassus, "that nature and genius in the first place contribute most aid to speaking; and that to those writers on the art, to whom Antonius just now alluded, it was not skill and method in speaking, but natural talent that was wanting; for there ought to

[1] Cap. xx.

[1] See Val. Max., iv., 5, 4.

be certain lively powers in the mind[1] and understanding, which may be acute to invent, fertile to explain and adorn, and strong and retentive to remember; and if any one imagines that these powers may be acquired by art (which is false, for it is very well if they can be animated and excited by art; but they certainly can not by art be ingrafted or instilled, since they are all the gifts of nature), what will he say of those qualities which are certainly born with the man himself, volubility of tongue, tone of voice, strength of lungs, and a peculiar conformation and aspect of the whole countenance and body? I do not say that art can not improve in these particulars (for I am not ignorant that what is good may be made better by education, and what is not very good may be in some degree polished and amended); but there are some persons so hesitating in their speech, so inharmonious in their tone of voice, or so unwieldy and rude in the air and movements of their bodies, that, whatever power they possess either from genius or art, they can never be reckoned in the number of accomplished speakers; while there are others so happily qualified in these respects, so eminently adorned with the gifts of nature, that they seem not to have been born like other men, but moulded by some divinity. It is, indeed, a great task and enterprise for a person to undertake and profess, that while every one else is silent, he alone must be heard on the most important subjects, and in a large assembly of men; for there is scarcely any one present who is not sharper and quicker to discover defects in the speaker than merits; and thus whatever offends the hearer effaces the recollection of what is worthy of praise. I do not make these observations for the purpose of altogether deterring young men from the study of oratory, even if they be deficient in some natural endowments. For who does not perceive that to C. Cælius, my contemporary, a new man, the mere mediocrity in speaking, which he was enabled to attain, was a great honor? Who does not know that Q. Varius, your equal in age, a clumsy, uncouth man, has obtained his great popularity by the cultivation of such faculties as he has?

XXVI. "But as our inquiry regards the COMPLETE ORATOR, we must imagine, in our discussion, an orator from whom every kind of fault is abstracted, and who is adorned with every kind of merit. For if the multitude of suits, if the variety of causes, if the rabble and barbarism of the forum afford room for even the most wretched speakers, we must not, for that reason, take our eyes from the object of our inquiry. In those arts, in which it is not indispensable usefulness that is sought, but liberal amusement for the mind, how nicely, how almost fastidiously, do we judge! For there are no suits or controversies which can force men, though they may tolerate indifferent orators in the forum, to endure also bad actors upon the stage. The orator therefore must take the most studious precaution not merely to satisfy those whom he necessarily must satisfy, but to seem worthy of admiration to those who are at liberty to judge disinterestedly. If you would know what I myself think, I will express to you, my intimate friends, what I have hitherto never mentioned, and thought that I never should mention. To me, those who speak best, and speak with the utmost ease and grace, appear, if they do not commence their speeches with some timidity, and show some confusion in the exordium, to have almost lost the sense of shame, though it is impossible that such should not be the case;[1] for the better qualified a man is to speak, the more he fears the difficulties of speaking, the uncertain success of a speech, and

[1] *Animi atque ingenii celeres quidam motus.* This sense of *motus,* as Ellendt observes, is borrowed from the Greek κίνησις, by which the philosophers intimated an *active power,* as, without motion, all things would remain unchanged, and nothing be generated. See Matth., ad Cic. pro Sext., 67, 143.

[1] *Tametsi id accidere non potest.* "Quamvis id fieri non possit, ut qui optimè dicit, in exordio non perturbetur." *Proust.*

the expectation of the audience. But he who can produce and deliver nothing worthy of his subject, nothing worthy of the name of an orator, nothing worthy the attention of his audience, seems to me, though he be ever so confused while he is speaking, to be downright shameless; for we ought to avoid a character for shamelessness, not by testifying shame, but by not doing that which does not become us. But the speaker who has no shame (as I see to be the case with many) I regard as deserving, not only of rebuke, but of personal castigation. Indeed, what I often observe in you I very frequently experience in myself, that I turn pale in the outset of my speech, and feel a tremor through my whole thoughts, as it were, and limbs. When I was a young man, I was on one occasion so timid in commencing an accusation, that I owed to Q. Maximus[1] the greatest of obligations for immediately dismissing the assembly, as soon as he saw me absolutely disheartened and incapacitated through fear." Here they all signified assent, looked significantly at one another, and began to talk together; for there was a wonderful modesty in Crassus, which, however, was not only no disadvantage to his oratory, but even an assistance to it, by giving it the recommendation of probity.

XXVII. Antonius soon after said, "I have often observed, as you mention, Crassus, that both you and other most accomplished orators, although in my opinion none was ever equal to you, have felt some agitation in entering upon their speeches. When I inquired into the reason of this, and considered why a speaker, the more ability he possessed, felt the greater fear in speaking, I found that there were two causes of such timidity: one, that those whom experience and nature had formed for speaking, well knew that the event of a speech did not always satisfy expectation even in the greatest orators; and thus, as often as they spoke, they feared, not without reason, that what sometimes happened might happen then; the other (of which I am often in the habit of complaining) is, that men, tried and approved in other arts, if they ever do any thing with less success than usual, are thought either to have wanted inclination for it, or to have failed in performing what they knew how to perform from ill health. 'Roscius,' they say, 'would not act to-day,' or, 'he was indisposed.' But if any deficiency is seen in the orator, it is thought to proceed from want of sense; and want of sense admits of no excuse, because nobody is supposed to have wanted sense because he 'was indisposed,' or because 'such was his inclination.' Thus we undergo a severer judgment in oratory, and judgment is pronounced upon us as often as we speak; if an actor is once mistaken in an attitude, he is not immediately considered to be ignorant of attitude in general; but if any fault is found in a speaker, there prevails forever, or at least for a very long time, a notion of his stupidity.

XXVIII. "But in what you observed as to there being many things in which, unless the orator has a full supply of them from nature, he can not be much assisted by a master, I agree with you entirely; and, in regard to that point, I have always expressed the highest approbation of that eminent teacher, Apollonius of Alabanda,[1] who, though he taught for pay, would not suffer such as he judged could never become orators, to lose their labor with him; and he sent them away with exhortations and encouragements to each of them to pursue that peculiar art for which he thought him naturally qualified. To the acquirement of other arts it is sufficient for a person to resemble a man, and to be able to comprehend in his mind, and retain in his memory, what is instilled, or, if he is very dull, inculcated into him; no volubility of tongue is requisite, no quickness of utterance; none of those things which we can not form for ourselves, aspect, countenance, look, voice. But in an orator, the acuteness of the

---

[1] He seems to be Quintus Fabius Maximus Eburnus, who was consul A.U.C. 638, and who, it is probable, presided as prætor on the occasion of which Crassus speaks. *Ellendt.*

[1] A town of Caria. The Apollonius mentioned above, c. 17, was Apollonius Molo, a native of Rhodes. *Proust.*

logicians, the wisdom of the philosophers, the language almost of poetry, the memory of lawyers, the voice of tragedians, the gesture almost of the best actors, is required. Nothing, therefore, is more rarely found among mankind than a consummate orator; for qualifications which professors of other arts are commended for acquiring in a moderate degree, each in his respective pursuit, will not be praised in the orator, unless they are all combined in him in the highest possible excellence."

"Yet observe," said Crassus, "how much more diligence is used in one of the light and trivial arts than in this, which is acknowledged to be of the greatest importance; for I often hear Roscius say that 'he could never yet find a scholar that he was thoroughly satisfied with; not that some of them were not worthy of approbation, but because, if they had any fault, he himself could not endure it.' Nothing, indeed, is so much noticed, or makes an impression of such lasting continuance on the memory, as that in which you give any sort of offense. To judge, therefore, of the accomplishments of the orator by comparison with this stage-player, do you not observe how every thing is done by him unexceptionably; every thing with the utmost grace; every thing in such a way as is becoming, and as moves and delights all? He has accordingly long attained such distinction, that in whatever pursuit a man excels, he is called a Roscius in his art. For my own part, while I desire this finish and perfection in an orator, of which I fall so far short myself, I act audaciously; for I wish indulgence to be granted to myself, while I grant none to others; for I think that he who has not abilities, who is faulty in action, who, in short, wants a graceful manner, should be sent off, as Apollonius advised, to that for which he has a capacity."

XXIX. "Would you then," said Sulpicius, "desire me, or our friend Cotta, to learn the civil law, or the military art?[1] for who can ever possibly arrive at that perfection of yours, that high excellence in every accomplishment?" "It was," replied Crassus, "because I knew that there was in both of you excellent and noble talents for oratory, that I have expressed myself fully on these matters; nor have I adapted my remarks more to deter those who had not abilities, than to encourage you who had; and though I perceive in you both consummate capacity and industry, yet I may say that the advantages of personal appearance, on which I have perhaps said more than the Greeks are wont to say, are in you, Sulpicius, even godlike. For any person better qualified for this profession by gracefulness of motion, by his very carriage and figure, or by the fullness and sweetness of his voice, I think that I have never heard speak; endowments which those, to whom they are granted by nature in an inferior degree, may yet succeed in managing, in such measure as they possess them, with judgment and skill, and in such a manner as not to be *unbecoming;* for that is what is chiefly to be avoided, and concerning which it is most difficult to give any rules for instruction, not only for me, who talk of these matters like a private citizen, but even for Roscius himself, whom I often hear say 'that the most essential part of art is to be *becoming,*' which yet is the only thing that can not be taught by art. But, if it is agreeable, let us change the subject of conversation, and talk like ourselves a little, not like rhetoricians."

"By no means," said Cotta, "for we must now entreat you (since you retain us in this study, and do not dismiss us to any other pursuit) to tell us something of your own abilities, whatever they are, in speaking; for we are not inordinately ambitious; we are satisfied with that mediocrity of eloquence of yours; and what we inquire of you is (that we may not attain more than that humble degree of oratory at which you have arrived)[1] what you think, since you say that the endowments to

[1] The young Roman nobles were accustomed to pursue one of three studies, jurisprudence, eloquence, or war. *Proust.*

[1] Cotta speaks ironically.

be derived from nature are not very deficient in us, we ought to endeavor to acquire in addition."

XXX. Crassus, smiling, replied, "What do you think is wanting to you, Cotta, but a passionate inclination, and a sort of ardor like that of love, without which no man will ever attain any thing great in life, and especially such distinction as you desire? Yet I do not see that you need any encouragement to this pursuit; indeed, as you press rather hard even upon me, I consider that you burn with an extraordinarily fervent affection for it. But I am aware that a desire to reach any point avails nothing, unless you know what will lead and bring you to the mark at which you aim. Since, therefore, you lay but a light burden upon me, and do not question me about the whole art of the orator, but about my own ability, little as it is, I will set before you a course, not very obscure, or very difficult, or grand, or imposing, the course of my own practice, which I was accustomed to pursue when I had opportunity, in my youth, to apply to such studies."

"O day much wished for by us, Cotta!" exclaimed Sulpicius; "for what I could never obtain, either by entreaty, or stratagem, or scrutiny (so that I was unable, not only to see what Crassus did, with a view to meditation or composition, but even to gain a notion of it from his secretary and reader, Diphilus), I hope we have now secured, and that we shall learn from himself all that we have long desired to know."

XXXI. "I conceive, however," proceeded Crassus, "that when you have heard me, you will not so much admire what I have said, as think that, when you desired to hear, there was no good reason for your desire; for I shall say nothing abstruse, nothing to answer your expectation, nothing either previously unheard by you, or new to any one. In the first place, I will not deny that, as becomes a man well born and liberally educated, I learned those trite and common precepts of teachers in general; first, that it is the business of an orator to speak in a manner adapted to persuade; next, that every speech is either upon a question concerning a matter in general, without specification of persons or times, or concerning a matter referring to certain persons and times. But that, in either case, whatever falls under controversy, the question with regard to it is usually, whether such a thing has been done, or, if it has been done, of what nature it is, or by what name it should be called; or, as some add, whether it seems to have been done rightly or not. That controversies arise also on the interpretation of writing, in which any thing has been expressed ambiguously, or contradictorily, or so that what is written is at variance with the writer's evident intention; and that there are certain lines of argument adapted to all these cases. But that of such subjects as are distinct from general questions, part come under the head of judicial proceedings, part under that of deliberations; and that there is a third kind which is employed in praising or censuring particular persons. That there are also certain commonplaces on which we may insist in judicial proceedings, in which equity is the object; others, which we may adopt in deliberations, all which are to be directed to the advantage of those to whom we give counsel; others in panegyric, in which all must be referred to the dignity of the persons commended. That, since all the business and art of an orator is divided into five parts,[1] he ought first to find out what he should say; next, to dispose and arrange his matter, not only in a certain order, but with a sort of power and judgment; then to clothe and deck his thoughts with language; then to secure them in his memory; and, lastly, to deliver them with dignity and grace. I had learned and understood also, that before we enter upon the main subject, the minds of the audience should be conciliated by an exordium; next, that the case should be clearly stated; then, that the point in controversy should be established; then, that what we maintain should be supported by proof, and that whatever was said on the other side should be refuted; and that, in the conclusion of our speech, whatever was in our favor should be amplified and enforced, and whatever made for our adversaries should be weakened and invalidated.

---

[1] Invention, disposition, embellishment, memory, and delivery. See ii., 19. *Ellendt.*

XXXII. "I had heard also what is taught about the costume of a speech; in regard to which it is first directed that we should speak correctly and in pure Latin; next, intelligibly and with perspicuity; then gracefully; then suitably to the dignity of the subject, and as it were becomingly; and I had made myself acquainted with the rules relating to every particular. Moreover, I had seen art applied to those things which are properly endowments of nature; for I had gone over some precepts concerning action, and some concerning artificial memory, which were short indeed, but requiring much exercise; matters on which almost all the learning of those artificial orators is employed; and if I should say that it is of no assistance, I should say what is not true; for it conveys some hints to admonish the orator, as it were, to what he should refer each part of his speech, and to what points he may direct his view, so as not to wander from the object which he has proposed to himself. But I consider that with regard to all precepts the case is this, not that orators by adhering to them have obtained distinction in eloquence, but that certain persons have noticed what men of eloquence practiced of their own accord, and formed rules accordingly;[1] so that eloquence has not sprung from art, but art from eloquence; not that, as I said before, I entirely reject art, for it is, though not essentially necessary to oratory, yet proper for a man of liberal education to learn. And by you, my young friends, some preliminary exercise must be undergone, though indeed you are already on the course; but those[2] who are to enter upon a race, and those who are preparing for what is to be done in the forum, as their field of battle, may alike previously learn, and try their powers by practicing in sport." "That sort of exercise," said Sulpicius, "is just what we wanted to understand; but we desire to hear more at large what you have briefly and cursorily delivered concerning art, though such matters are not strange even to us. Of that subject, however, we shall inquire hereafter; at present we wish to know your sentiments on exercise."

XXXIII. "I like that method," replied Crassus, "which you are accustomed to practice, namely, to lay down a case similar to those which are brought on in the forum, and to speak upon it, as nearly as possible, as if it were a real case.[1] But in such efforts the generality of students exercise only their voice (and not even that skillfully), and try their strength of lungs, and volubility of tongue, and please themselves with a torrent of their own words; in which exercise what they have heard deceives them, *that men by speaking succeed in becoming speakers.* For it is truly said also, *That men by speaking badly make sure of becoming bad speakers.* In those exercises, therefore, although it be useful even frequently to speak on the sudden, yet it is more advantageous, after taking time to consider, to speak with greater preparation and accuracy. But the chief point of all is that which (to say the truth) we hardly ever practice (for it requires great labor, which most of us avoid); I mean, to write as much as possible. *Writing* is said to be *the best and most excellent modeler and teacher of oratory;* and not without reason; for if what is meditated and considered easily surpasses sudden and extemporary speech, a constant and diligent habit of writing will surely be of more effect than meditation and consideration itself; since all the arguments relating to the subject on which we write, whether they are suggested by art, or by a certain power of genius and understanding, will present themselves, and occur to us, while we examine and contemplate it in the full light of our intellect; and all the thoughts and words, which are the most expressive of their kind, must of necessity come

---

[1] *Atque id egisse.* Most critics have supposed these words in some way faulty. Gesner conjectured *atque digessisse;* Lambinus, *atque in artem redegisse;* Ernesti, *ad artemque redegisse.* Ellendt supposes that *id egisse* may mean *ei rei operam dedisse.*

[2] *Sed iis, qui ingrediuntur.* Orellius and Ellendt retain this reading, though Ernesti had long before observed that there is no verb on which *iis* can be considered as dependent, and that we must read *ii* or *hi* as a nominative to the following *possunt.*

[1] *Quàm maximè ad veritatem accommodatè,* "with as much adaptation as possible to truth."

under and submit to the keenness of our judgment while writing; and a fair arrangement and collocation of the words is effected by writing, in a certain rhythm and measure, not poetical, but oratorical. Such are the qualities which bring applause and admiration to good orators; nor will any man ever attain them unless after long and great practice in writing, however resolutely he may have exercised himself in extemporary speeches; and he who comes to speak after practice in writing brings this advantage with him, that though he speak at the call of the moment, yet what he says will bear a resemblance to something written; and if ever, when he comes to speak, he brings any thing with him in writing, the rest of his speech, when he departs from what is written, will flow on in a similar strain. As, when a boat has once been impelled forward, though the rowers suspend their efforts, the vessel herself still keeps her motion and course during the intermission of the impulse and force of the oars; so, in a continued stream of oratory, when written matter fails, the rest of the speech maintains a similar flow, being impelled by the resemblance and force acquired from what is written.

XXXIV. "But in my daily exercises I used, when a youth, to adopt chiefly that method which I knew that Caius Carbo, my adversary,[1] generally practiced; which was, that, having selected some nervous piece of poetry, or read over such a portion of a speech as I could retain in my memory, I used to declaim upon what I had been reading in other words, chosen with all the judgment that I possessed. But at length I perceived that in that method there was this inconvenience, that Ennius, if I exercised myself on his verses, or Gracchus, if I laid one of his orations before me, had forestalled such words as were peculiarly appropriate to the subject, and such as were the most elegant and altogether the best; so that, if I used the same words, it profited nothing; if others, it was even prejudicial to me, as I habituated myself to use such as were less eligible. Afterward I thought proper, and continued the practice at a rather

[1] See c. x.

more advanced age,[1] to translate the orations of the best Greek orators;[2] by fixing upon which I gained this advantage, that while I rendered into Latin what I had read in Greek, I not only used the best words, and yet such as were of common occurrence, but also formed some words by imitation, which would be new to our countrymen, taking care, however, that they were unobjectionable.

"As to the exertion and exercise of the voice, of the breath, of the whole body, and of the tongue itself, they do not so much require art as labor; but in those matters we ought to be particularly careful whom we imitate and whom we would wish to resemble. Not only orators are to be observed by us, but even actors, lest by vicious habits we contract any awkwardness or ungracefulness. The memory is also to be exercised by learning accurately by heart as many of our own writings, and those of others, as we can. In exercising the memory, too, I shall not object if you accustom yourself to adopt that plan of referring to places and figures which is taught in treatises on the art.[3] Your language must then be brought forth from this domestic and retired exercise into the midst of the field, into the dust and clamor, into the camp and military array of the forum; you must acquire practice in every thing; you must try the strength of your understanding; and your retired lucubrations must be exposed to the light of reality. The poets must also be studied; an acquaintance must be formed with history; the writers and teachers in all the liberal arts and sciences must be read, and turned over, and must, for the sake of exercise, be praised, interpreted, corrected, censured, refuted; you must dispute on both sides of every question; and whatever may seem maintainable on any point must be brought forward and illustrated. The civil law must be thoroughly studied; laws in general must be understood; all antiquity must be known; the usages

[1] *Adolescens.* When he imitated the practice of Carbo, he was, he says, *adolescentulus.*

[2] A practice recommended by Quintilian, x., 5.

[3] This is sufficiently explained in book ii., c. 87. See also Quint., xi., 2.

of the senate, the nature of our government, the rights of our allies, our treaties and conventions, and whatever concerns the interests of the state, must be learned. A certain intellectual grace must also be extracted from every kind of refinement, with which, as with salt, every oration must be seasoned. I have poured forth to you all I had to say, and perhaps any citizen whom you had laid hold of in any company whatever would have replied to your inquiries on these subjects equally well."

XXXV. When Crassus had uttered these words a silence ensued. But, though enough seemed to have been said, in the opinion of the company present, in reference to what had been proposed, yet they thought that he had concluded his speech more abruptly than they could have wished. Scævola then said, "What is the matter, Cotta? why are you silent? Does nothing more occur to you which you would wish to ask Crassus?" "Nay," rejoined he, "that is the very thing of which I am thinking; for the rapidity of his words was such, and his oration was winged with such speed, that, though I perceived its force and energy, I could scarcely see its track and course; and, as if I had come into some rich and well-furnished house, where the furniture[1] was not unpacked, nor the plate set out, nor the pictures and statues placed in view, but a multitude of all these magnificent things laid up and heaped together; so just now, in the speech of Crassus, I saw his opulence and the riches of his genius through veils and curtains as it were, but when I desired to take a nearer view, there was scarcely opportunity for taking a glance at them; I can therefore neither say that I am wholly ignorant of what he possesses, nor that I have plainly ascertained and beheld it." "Then," said Scævola, "why do you not act in the same way as you would do if you had really come into a house or villa full of rich furniture? If every thing was put by as you describe, and you had a great curiosity to see it, you would not hesitate to ask the master to order it to be brought out, especially if he was your friend; in like manner you will now surely ask Crassus to bring forth into the light that profusion of splendid objects which are his property (and of which, piled together in one place, we have caught a glimpse, as it were through a lattice,[1] as we passed by), and set every thing in its proper situation." "I rather ask you, Scævola," says Cotta, "to do that for me (for modesty forbids Sulpicius and myself to ask of one of the most eminent of mankind, who has ever held in contempt this kind of disputation, such things as he perhaps regards only as rudiments for children); but do you oblige us in this, Scævola, and prevail on Crassus to unfold and enlarge upon those matters which he has crowded together, and crammed into so small a space in his speech." "Indeed," said Scævola, "I desired that before, more upon your account than my own; nor did I feel so much longing for this discussion from Crassus, as I experience pleasure from his orations in pleading. But now, Crassus, I ask you also on my own account, that since we have so much more leisure than has been allowed us for a long time, you would not think it troublesome to complete the edifice which you have commenced; for I see a finer and better plan of the whole work than I could have imagined, and one of which I strongly approve."

XXXVI. "I can not sufficiently wonder," says Crassus, "that even you, Scævola, should require of me that which I do not understand like those who teach it, and which is of such a nature that, if I understood it ever so well, it would be unworthy of your wisdom and attention." "Say you so?" replied Scævola. "If you think it scarcely worthy of my age to listen to those ordinary precepts, commonly known every where, can we possibly neglect those other matters which you said must be known by the orator, respecting the dispositions and manners of mankind, the means by which the minds of men are excited or calmed, history, antiquity, the administration of the republic, and, finally, of our own civil law itself? For I knew

[1] *Veste.* Under this word is included tapestry, coverings of couches, and other things of that sort.

[1] An illustration, says Proust, borrowed from the practice of traders, who allow goods on which they set a high value to be seen only through lattice-work.

that all this science, this abundance of knowledge, was within the compass of your understanding, but had never seen such rich furniture among the equipments of the orator."

"Can you then," says Crassus "(to omit other things innumerable and without limit, and come to your study, the civil law), can you account them orators for whom Scævola,[1] though in haste to go to the Campus Martius, waited several hours, sometimes laughing and sometimes angry, while Hypsæus, in the loudest voice, and with a multitude of words, was trying to obtain of Marcus Crassus, the prætor, that the party whom he defended might be allowed to lose his suit; and Cneius Octavius, a man of consular dignity, in a speech of equal length, refused to consent that his adversary should lose his cause, and that the party for whom he was speaking should be released from the ignominious charge of having been unfaithful in his guardianship, and from all trouble, through the folly of his antagonist?"[2]

[1] Not Quintus Scævola the augur, the father-in-law of Crassus, in whose presence Crassus is speaking, but another Quintus Scævola, who was an eminent lawyer, and held the office of pontifex; but at the time to which Crassus alludes he was tribune of the people, B.C. 105. *Proust.*

[2] The cause was as follows: As Scævola the pontiff was going into the field of Mars, to the election of consuls, he passed, in his way, through the forum, where he found two orators in much litigation, and blundering grievously through ignorance of the civil law. One of them was Hypsæus, the other Cneius Octavius, who had been consul B.C. 128. Hypsæus was accusing some guardian of maladministration of the fortunes of his ward. This sort of cause was called *judicium tutelœ.* Octavius defended the guardian. The judge of this controversy was Marcus Crassus, then city prætor, B.C. 105. He that was condemned on such a trial was decreed to pay damages to his ward to the amount of what his affairs had suffered through his means, and, in addition, by the law of the Twelve Tables, was to pay something by way of fine. But if the ward, or his advocate, sought to recover more from the defendant than was due, he lost his cause. Hypsæus proceeded in this manner, and therefore ought to have been nonsuited. Octavius, an unskillful defender of his client, should have rejoiced at this, for if he had made the objection and proved it, he would have obtained his cause; but he refused to permit Hypsæus to proceed for more than was due, though such proceeding would, by the law, have been fatal to his suit. *Proust.*

"I should have thought such men," replied Scævola "(for I remember Mucius[1] told me the story), not only unworthy of the name of orators, but unworthy even to appear to plead in the forum." "Yet," rejoined Crassus, "those advocates neither wanted eloquence, nor method, nor abundance of words, but a knowledge of the civil law; for in this case one, in bringing his suit, sought to recover more damages than the law of the Twelve Tables allowed, and, if he had gained those damages, would have lost his cause: the other thought it unjust that he himself should be proceeded against for more than was allowed in that sort of action, and did not understand that his adversary, if he proceeded in that manner, would lose his suit.

XXXVII. "Within these few days,[2] while we were sitting at the tribunal of our friend Quintus Pompeius, the city prætor, did not a man who is ranked among the eloquent pray that the benefit of the ancient and usual exception, *of which sum there is time for payment,* might be allowed to a

[1] Quintus Mucius Scævola, mentioned in the last note but one.

[2] The cause was this. One man owed another a sum of money, to be paid, for instance, in the beginning of January; the plaintiff would not wait till that time, but brought his action in December; the ignorant lawyer who was for the defendant, instead of contesting with the plaintiff this point, that he demanded his money before it was due (which if he had proved the plaintiff would have lost his cause), only prayed the benefit of the exception, which forbade an action to be brought for money before the day of payment, and so only put off the cause for that time. This he did not perceive to be a clause inserted for the advantage of the plaintiff, that he might know when to bring his suit. Thus the plaintiff, when the money became due, was at liberty to bring a new action, as if this matter had never come to trial, which action he could never have brought if the first had been determined on the other point, namely, its having been brought before the money was due; for then the defendant might have pleaded a former judgment, and precluded the plaintiff from the second action. See Justin., Instit., iv., 13, 5, *de re judicatâ.* "Of which sum there is a time for payment," were words of form in the exception from whence it was nominated; as, "That the matter had before come into judgment," were in the other exception *rei judicatœ.* Proust. *B.* See Gaius, Instit., iv., 131, and Heffter, Obs. on Gaius, iv., 23, p. 109, *seq. Ellendt.*

party from whom a sum of money was demanded; an exception which he did not understand to be made for the benefit of the creditor; so that if the defendant[1] had proved to the judge that the action was brought for the money before it became due, the plaintiff,[2] on bringing a fresh action, would be precluded by the exception *that the matter had before come into judgment*. What more disgraceful, therefore, can possibly be said or done, than that he who has assumed the character of an advocate, ostensibly to defend the causes and interests of his friends, to assist the distressed, to relieve such as are sick at heart, and to cheer the afflicted, should so err in the slightest and most trivial matters as to seem an object of pity to some, and of ridicule to others? I consider my relation, Publius Crassus, him who from his wealth had the surname of Dives,[3] to have been, in many other respects, a man of taste and elegance, but especially worthy of praise and commendation on this account, that (as he was the brother of Publius Scævola)[4] he was accustomed to observe to him *that neither could he*[5] *have satisfied the claims of the civil law if he had not added the power of speaking* (which his son here, who was my colleague in the consulate, has fully attained); *nor had he himself*[6] *begun to practice, and plead the causes of his friends, before he had gained a knowledge of the civil law.*

[1] *Infitiator.* The defendant or debtor.

[2] *Petitor.* The plaintiff or creditor.

[3] Publius Licinius Crassus Mucianus, son of Publius Mucius Scævola, who had been adopted into the Licinian family. He was consul with Lucius Valerins Flaccus, A.U.C. 623. . . . But the name of Dives had previously been in the family of the Crassi, for Publius Crassus, who was consul with Publius Africanus, A.U.C. 549, was so called. *Ellendt.*

[4] By birth. He had his name of Crassus from adoption, as stated in the preceding note.

[5] Publius Scævola, his brother. In the phrase, *neque illum in jure civili satis illi arti facere posse,* the words *illi arti* are regarded by Ernesti and Orellius as spurious, but Ellendt thinks them genuine, explaining *in jure civili* by *quod ad jus civile attinet.* I have followed Orellius and Ernesti in my translation.

[6] Publius Crassus.

What sort of character was the illustrious Marcus Cato? Was he not possessed of as great a share of eloquence as those times and that age[1] would admit in this city, and at the same time the most learned of all men in the civil law? I have been speaking for some time the more timidly on this point, because there is with us a man[2] eminent in speaking, whom I admire as an orator beyond all others, but who has ever held the civil law in contempt. But, as you desired to learn my sentiments and opinions, I will conceal nothing from you, but, as far as I am able, will communicate to you my thoughts upon every subject.

XXXVIII. "The almost incredible, unparalleled, and divine power of genius in Antonius appears to me, although wanting in legal knowledge, to be able easily to sustain and defend itself with the aid of other weapons of reason; let him therefore be an exception; but I shall not hesitate to condemn others, by my sentence, of want of industry in the first place, and of want of modesty in the next. For to flutter about the forum, to loiter in courts of justice and at the tribunals of the prætors, to undertake private suits in matters of the greatest concern, in which the question is often not about fact, but about equity and law, to swagger in causes heard before the centumviri,[3] in which the laws of prescriptive rights, of guardianship, of kindred,[4] of agnation,[5] of alluvions,

[1] *Illa tempora atque illa œtas.* By *tempora* is meant the state of the times as to political affairs; by *œtas,* the period of advancement in learning and civilization which Rome had reached.

[2] Antonius.

[3] A body of inferior *judices,* chosen three out of each tribe, so that the full number was a hundred and five. They took cognizance of such minor causes as the prætor intrusted to their decision.

[4] *Gentilitatum.* Kindred or family. Persons of the same family or descent had certain peculiar rights, *e.g.,* in entering upon an inheritance, in undertaking guardianship. In such rights slaves, freedmen, and *capite deminuti* had no participation. See Cic., Top., 6, 29. *Proust.*

[5] The *agnati,* as a brother by the same father, a brother's son or grandson, an uncle's son or grandson, had their peculiar rights. See Gaius, i., 156.

circumluvions,[1] of bonds, of transferring property, of party walls, lights, *stillicidia,*[2] of wills, transgressed or established, and innumerable other matters are debated, when a man is utterly ignorant what is properly his own and what his neighbor's, why any person is considered a citizen or a foreigner, a slave or a freeman, is a proof of extraordinary impudence. It is ridiculous arrogance for a man to confess himself unskillful in navigating smaller vessels, and yet say that he has learned to pilot galleys with five banks of oars, or even larger ships. You who are deceived by a quibble of your adversary in a private company, you who set your seal to a deed for your client, in which that is written by which he is overreached, can I think that any cause of greater consequence ought to be intrusted to you? Sooner assuredly shall he who oversets a two-oared boat in the harbor steer the vessel of the Argonauts in the Euxine Sea.

"But what if the causes are not trivial, but often of the utmost importance, in which disputes arise concerning points of civil law? What front must that advocate have who dares to appear in causes of such a nature without any knowledge of that law? What cause, for instance, could be of more consequence than that of the soldier, of whose death a false report having been brought home from the army, and his father, through giving credit to that report, having altered his will, and appointed another person, whom he thought proper, to be his heir, and having then died himself, the affair, when the soldier returned home, and instituted a suit for his paternal inheritance, came on to be heard before the centumviri? The point assuredly in that case was a question of civil law, whether a son could be disinherited of his father's possessions, whom the father neither appointed his heir by will, nor disinherited by name?[1]

XXXIX. "On the point, too, which the centumviri decided between the Marcelli and the Claudii, two patrician families, when the Marcelli said that an estate, which had belonged to the son of a freedman, reverted to them by right of *stirps,* and the Claudii alleged that the property of the man reverted to them by right of *gens,* was it not necessary for the pleaders in that cause to speak upon all the rights of *stirps* and *gens?*[2] As to that other matter also, which we have heard was contested at law before the centumviri, when an exile came to Rome (who had the privilege of living in exile at Rome if he attached himself to any citizen as a patron) and died intestate, was not, in a cause of that nature, the law of *attachment,*[3] obscure and indeed unknown, expounded and illustrated

---

[1] About these, various controversies might arise; as, when the force of a river has detached a portion from your land, and added it to that of your neighbor, to whom does that portion belong? Or if trees have been carried away from your land to that of your neighbor, and have taken root there, etc. *Proust.*

[2] When a person was obliged to let the water, which dropped from his house, run into the garden or area of his neighbor, or to receive the water that fell from his neighbor's house into his area. Adam's Roman Antiquities, p. 49.

---

[1] For he who had a son under his power should have taken care to institute him his heir, or to disinherit him by name; since if a father pretermitted or passed over his son in silence, the testament was of no effect. Just., Inst., ii., 13. And if the parents disinherited their children without cause, the civil law was, that they might complain that such testaments were invalid, under color that their parents were not of sound mind when they made them. Just., Inst., ii., 18. *B.*

[2] The son of a freedman of the Claudian family had died without making a will, and his property fell by law to the Claudii; but there were two families of them—the Claudii Pulchri, who were patricians, and the Claudii Marcelli, who were plebeians; and these two families went to law about the possession of the dead man's property. The patrician Claudii (whose family was the eldest of the name) claimed the inheritance by right of *gens,* on the ground that the freedman was of the *gens Claudia,* of which their family was the chief; . . . while the Claudii Marcelli, or plebeian Claudii, claimed it by right of *stirps,* on the ground that the freedman was more nearly related to them than to the Pulchri. *Pearce.* The term *gens* was used in reference to patricians; that of *stirps* to plebeians. *Proust.*

[3] *Jus applicationis.* This was a right which a Roman *quasi-patronus* had to the estate of a foreign client dying intestate. He was called *quasi-patronus,* because none but Roman citizens could have patrons. The difficulty in this cause proceeded from the obscurity of the law on which this kind of right was founded.

by the pleader? When I myself lately defended the cause of Sergius Aurata, on a private suit against our friend Antonius, did not my whole defense turn upon a point of law? For when Marius Gratidianus had sold a house to Aurata, and had not specified, in the deed of sale, that any part of the building owed service,[1] we argued that, for whatever encumbrance attended the thing sold, if the seller knew of it, and did not make it known, he ought to indemnify the purchaser.[2] In this kind of action our friend Marcus Bucculeius, a man not a fool in my opinion, and very wise in his own, and one who has no aversion to the study of law, made a mistake lately in an affair of a somewhat similar nature. For when he sold a house to Lucius Fufius, he engaged, in the act of conveyance, that the window-lights should remain as they then were. But Fufius, as soon as a building began to rise in some part of the city, which could but just be seen from that house, brought an action against Bucculeius, on the ground that whatever portion of the sky was intercepted, at however great a distance, the window-light underwent a change.[1] Amid what a concourse of people too, and with what universal interest, was the famous cause between Manius Curius and Marcus Coponius lately conducted before the centumviri! On which occasion Quintus Scævola, my equal in age, and my colleague,[2] a man of all others the most learned in the practice of the civil law, and of the most acute genius and discernment, a speaker most polished and refined in his language, and indeed, as I am accustomed to remark, the best orator among the lawyers, and the best lawyer among the orators, argued the law from the letter of the will, and maintained that he who was appointed second heir, after a posthumous son should be born and die, could not possibly inherit, unless such posthumous son had actually been born, and had died before he came out of tutelage: I, on the other side, argued that he who made the will had this intention, that if there was no son at all who could come of tutelage, Manius Curius should be his heir. Did either of us, in that cause, fail to exert ourselves in citing authorities, and precedents, and forms of wills, that is, to dispute on the profoundest points of civil law?[3]

XL. "I forbear to mention many examples of causes of the greatest consequence, which are indeed without number. It may often happen that even capital cases may turn upon a point of law; for, as an example, Publius Rutilius, the son of Marcus, when tribune of the people, ordered Caius Mancinus, a most noble and excellent man, and

---

[1] The services of city estates are those which appertain to buildings. It is required by city services that neighbors should bear the burdens of neighbors; and, by such services, one neighbor may be permitted to place a beam upon the wall of another; may be compelled to receive the droppings and currents from the gutter-pipes of another man's house upon his own house, area, or sewer; or may be exempted from receiving them; or may be restrained from raising his house in height, lest he should darken the habitation of his neighbor. Harris's Justinian, ii., 3. *B.*

[2] There is a more particular statement of this cause between Gratidianus and Aurata in Cicero's Offices, iii., 16. The Roman law, in that particular founded on the law of nature, ordained, to avoid deceit in bargain and sale, that the seller should give notice of all the bad qualities in the thing sold which he knew of, or pay damages to the purchaser for his silence; to which law Horace alludes, Sat., iii., 2:

> Mentem nisi litigiosus
> Exciperet dominus cum venderet.

But if he told the faults, or they were such as must be seen by a person using common care, the buyer suffered for his negligence, as Horace again indicates, Epist., ii., 2:

> Ille feret pretium pœnæ securus opinor:
> Prudens emisti vitiosum. Dicta tibi est Lex.

See also Grotius, ii., 12, and Puffendorf, v. 3, s. 4, 5. *B.*

[1] The mistake of Bucculeius seems to have consisted in this: he meant to restrain Fufius from raising the house in height, which might darken, or making any new windows which might overlook, some neighboring habitation which belonged to him; but by the use of words adapted by law for another purpose, he restrained himself from building within the prospect of those windows already made in the house which Fufius purchased. *B.*

[2] In the consulship.

[3] This celebrated cause is so clearly stated by Cicero as to require no explanation. It was gained by Crassus, the evident intention of the testator prevailing over the letter of the will. It is quoted as a precedent by Cicero, pro Cæcinâ, c. 18.

of consular dignity, to be put out of the senate; on the occasion when the chief herald had given him up to the Numantines, according to a decree of the senate, passed on account of the odium which he had incurred by his treaty with that people, and they would not receive him,[1] and he had then returned home, and had not hesitated to take his place in the senate; the tribune, I say, ordered him to be put out of the house, maintaining that he was not a citizen; because it was a received tradition, *That he whom his own father, or the people, had sold, or the chief herald had given up, had no* postliminium,[2] *or right of return.* What more important cause or argument can we find, among all the variety of civil transactions, than one concerning the rank, the citizenship, the liberty, the condition of a man of consular dignity, especially as the case depended, not on any charge which he might deny, but on the interpretation of the civil law? In a like case, but concerning a person of inferior degree, it was inquired among our ancestors whether, if a person belonging to a state in alliance with Rome had been in servitude among us, and gained his freedom, and afterward returned home, he returned by the right of *postliminium,* and lost the citizenship of this city. May not a dispute arise on a point of civil law respecting liberty, than which no cause can be of more importance, when the question is, for example, whether he who is enrolled as a citizen, by his master's consent, is free at once, or when the lustrum is completed? As to the case, also, that happened in the memory of our fathers, when the father of a family, who had come from Spain to Rome, and had left a wife pregnant in that province, and married another at Rome, without sending any notice of divorce to the former, and died intestate, after a son had been born of each wife, did a small matter come into controversy when the question was concerning the rights of two citizens, I mean concerning the boy who was born of the latter wife and his mother, who, if it were adjudged that a divorce was effected from a former wife by a certain set of words, and not by a second marriage, would be deemed a concubine? For a man, then, who is ignorant of these and other similar laws of his own country, to wander about the forum with a great crowd at his heels, erect and haughty, looking hither and thither with a gay and assured face and air, offering and tendering protection to his clients, assistance to his friends, and the light of his genius and counsel to almost all his fellow-citizens, is it not to be thought in the highest degree scandalous?

XLI. "Since I have spoken of the audacity, let me also censure the indolence and inertness of mankind. For if the study of the law were illimitable and arduous, yet the greatness of the advantage ought to impel men to undergo the labor of learning it; but, O ye immortal gods, I would not say this in the hearing of Scævola, unless he himself were accustomed to say it, namely, that *the attainment of no science seems to him more easy.* It is, indeed, for certain reasons, thought otherwise by most people, first, because those of old, who were at the head of this science, would not, for the sake of securing and extending their own influence, allow their art to be made public; in the next place, when it was published, the forms of actions at law being first set forth by Cneius Flavius, there were none who could compose a general system of those matters arranged under regular heads. For nothing can be reduced into a science unless he who understands the matters of which he would form a science has previously gained such knowledge as to enable him to constitute a science out of subjects in which there has never yet been any science. I perceive that, from desire to express this briefly, I have expressed it rather obscurely; but I will make an effort to explain myself, if possible, with more perspicuity.

XLII. "All things which are now comprised in sciences were formerly unconnected, and in a state, as it were, of dispersion; as in music, numbers, sounds, and measures; in geometry, lines, figures, spaces, magnitudes; in astronomy, the revolution of the heavens, the rising, setting,

[1] See Florus, ii., 18; Vell. Pat., ii., 1.

[2] See Cic., Topic., c. 8; Gaius, i., 129; Aul. Gell., vii., 18.

and other motions of the stars; in grammar, the study of the poets, the knowledge of history, the interpretation of words, the peculiar tone of pronunciation; and, finally, in this very art of oratory, invention, embellishment, arrangement, memory, delivery, seemed of old not to be fully understood by any, and to be wholly unconnected. A certain extrinsic art was therefore applied, adopted from another department of knowledge,[1] which the philosophers wholly claim to themselves, an art which might serve to cement things previously separate and uncombined, and unite them in a kind of system.

"Let, then, the end proposed in civil law be the preservation of legitimate and practical equity in the affairs and causes of the citizens. The general heads of it are then to be noted, and reduced to a certain number, as few as may be. A general head is that which comprehends two or more particulars, similar to one another by having something in common, but differing in species. Particulars are included under the general heads from which they spring. All names, which are given either to general heads, or particulars, must be limited by definitions, showing what exact meaning they have. A definition is a short and precise specification of whatever properly belongs to the thing which we would define. I should add examples on these points, were I not sensible to whom my discourse is addressed. I will now comprise what I proposed in a short space. For if I should have leisure to do what I have long meditated, or if any other person should undertake the task while I am occupied, or accomplish it after my death (I mean, to digest, first of all, the whole civil law under general heads, which are very few; next, to branch out those general heads, as it were, into members; then to explain the peculiar nature of each by a definition), you will have a complete system of civil law, large and full indeed, but neither difficult nor obscure. In the mean time, while what is unconnected is being combined, a person may,

[1] From philosophy.

even by gathering here and there, and collecting from all parts, be furnished with a competent knowledge of the civil law.

XLIII. "Do you not observe that Caius Aculeo,[1] a Roman knight, a man of the most acute genius in the world, but of little learning in other sciences, who now lives, and has always lived with me, understands the civil law so well, that none even of the most skillful, if you except my friend Scævola here, can be preferred to him? Every thing in it, indeed, is set plainly before our eyes, connected with our daily habits, with our intercourse among men, and with the forum, and is not contained in a vast quantity of writing, or many large volumes; for the elements that were at first published by several writers are the same; and the same things, with the change of a few words, have been repeatedly written by the same authors. Added to this, that the civil law may be more readily learned and understood, there is (what most people little imagine) a wonderful pleasure and delight in acquiring a knowledge of it. For, whether any person is attracted by the study of antiquity,[2] there is, in every part of the civil law, in the pontifical books, and in the Twelve Tables, abundance of instruction as to ancient matters, since not only the original sense of words is thence understood, but certain kinds of law proceedings illustrate the customs and lives of our ancestors; or if he has a view to the science of government (which Scævola

[1] This Aculeo married Cicero's aunt by the mother's side, as he tells us in the beginning of the second book of this treatise, c. 1, and his sons by that marriage, cousins to Cicero and his brother Quintus, were all bred up together with them, in a method approved by L. Crassus, the chief character in this dialogue, and by those very masters under whom Crassus himself had been. *B.*

[2] Orellius retains *hœc aliena studia* in his text, but acknowledges *aliena* to be corrupt. Wyttenbach conjectured *antiqua studia* for *antiquitatis studia.* Ellendt observes that Madvig proposed *Æliana,* from Lucius Ælius Stilo, the master of Varro, extolled by Cicero, Brut., 56; Acad., i., 2, 8; Legg., ii., 23. See Suetonius, de Ill. Gramm., c. 3; and Aul. Gell., x., 21. This conjecture, says Henrichsen, will suit very well with the word *hœc,* which Crassus may be supposed to have used, because Ælius Stilo was then alive, and engaged in those studies.

judges not to belong to the orator, but to science of another sort), he will find it all comprised in the Twelve Tables, every advantage of civil government, and every part of it being there described; or if authoritative and vaunting philosophy delight him (I will speak very boldly), he will find there the sources of all the philosophers' disputations, which lie in civil laws and enactments; for from these we perceive that virtue is above all things desirable, since honest, just, and conscientious industry is ennobled with honors, rewards, and distinctions; but the vices and frauds of mankind are punished by fines, ignominy, imprisonment, stripes, banishment, and death; and we are taught, not by disputations endless and full of discord, but by the authority and mandate of the laws, to hold our appetites in subjection, to restrain all our passions, to defend our own property, and to keep our thoughts, eyes, and hands, from that of others.

XLIV. "Though all the world exclaim against me, I will say what I think: that single little book of the Twelve Tables, if any one look to the fountains and sources of laws, seems to me, assuredly, to surpass the libraries of all the philosophers, both in weight of authority and in plenitude of utility. And if our country has our love, as it ought to have in the highest degree—our country, I say, of which the force and natural attraction is so strong, that one of the wisest of mankind preferred his Ithaca, fixed, like a little nest, among the roughest of rocks, to immortality itself—with what affection ought we to be warmed toward such a country as ours, which, pre-eminently above all other countries, is the seat of virtue, empire, and dignity? Its spirit, customs, and discipline ought to be our first objects of study, both because our country is the parent of us all, and because as much wisdom must be thought to have been employed in framing such laws, as in establishing so vast and powerful an empire. You will receive also this pleasure and delight from the study of the law, that you will then most readily comprehend how far our ancestors excelled other nations in wisdom, if you compare our laws with those of their Lycurgus, Draco, and Solon. It is indeed incredible how undigested and almost ridiculous is all civil law except our own; on which subject I am accustomed to say much in my daily conversation, when I am praising the wisdom of our countrymen above that of all other men, and especially of the Greeks. For these reasons have I declared, Scævola, that the knowledge of the civil law is indispensable to those who would become accomplished orators.

XLV. "And who does not know what an accession of honor, popularity, and dignity such knowledge, even of itself, brings with it to those who are eminent in it? As, therefore, among the Greeks, men of the lowest rank, induced by a trifling reward, offer themselves as assistants to the pleaders on trials (men who are by them called *pragmatici*),[1] so in our city, on the contrary, every personage of the most eminent rank and character, such as that Ælius Sextus,[2] who, for his

---

[1] It appears from Quintilian and Juvenal that this was a Roman custom as well as a Grecian, under the emperors; they are also mentioned by Ulpian. But in Cicero's time the *Patroni causarum,* or advocates, though they studied nothing but oratory, and were in general ignorant of the law, yet did not make use of any of these low people called *Pragmatici,* as the Greeks did at that time, but upon any doubts on the law, applied themselves to men of the greatest reputation in that science, such as the Scævolæ. But under the emperors there was not the same encouragement for these great men to study that science; the orators, therefore, fell of necessity into the Grecian custom. Quint., xii., 3: "Neque ego sum nostri moris ignarus, oblitusve eorum, qui velut ad Arculas sedent, et tela agentibus subministrant, neque idem Græcos nescio factitare, unde nomen his Pragmaticorum datum est." Juv., Sat., vii., 123:

Si quater egisti, si contigit aureus unus,
Inde cadunt partes ex fœdere Pragmaticorum. *B.*

[2] As the collection of forms published by Flavius, and from him called *Jus civile Flavianum,* soon grew defective, as new contracts arose every day, another was afterward compiled, or rather only made public, by Sextus Ælius, for the forms seem to have been composed as the different emergencies arose, by such of the patricians as understood the law, and to have been by them secreted to extend their own influence; however, this collection, wherein were many new forms adapted to the cases and circumstances which had happened since the time of Flavius, went under the title of *Jus Ælianum,* from the Ælius here praised by Ennius. *B.*

knowledge in the civil law, was called by our great poet,

> " '*A man of thought and prudence, nobly wise,*

and many besides, who, after arriving at distinction by means of their ability, attained such influence, that, in answering questions on points of law,[1] they found their authority of more weight than even their ability. For ennobling and dignifying old age, indeed, what can be a more honorable resource than the interpretation of the law? For myself, I have, even from my youth, been securing this resource, not merely with a view to benefit in pleadings in the forum, but also for an honor and ornament to the decline of life; so that, when my strength begins to fail me (for which the time is even now almost approaching), I may, by that means, preserve my house from solitude. For what is more noble than for an old man, who has held the highest honors and offices of the state, to be able justly to say for himself that which the Pythian Apollo says in Ennius, that he is the person from whom, if not nations and kings, yet all his fellow-citizens, solicit advice,

> " 'Uncertain how to act; whom, by my aid,
> I send away undoubting, full of counsel,
> No more with rashness things perplex'd to sway;'

for without doubt the house of an eminent lawyer is the oracle of the whole city. Of this fact the gate and vestibule of our friend Quintus Mucius is a proof, which, even in his very infirm state of health and advanced age, is daily frequented by a vast crowd of citizens, and by persons of the highest rank and splendor.

XLVI. "It requires no very long explanation to show why I think the public laws[1] also, which concern the state and government, as well as the records of history, and the precedents of antiquity, ought to be known to the orator; for, as in causes and trials relative to private affairs, his language is often to be borrowed from the civil law, and therefore, as we said before, the knowledge of the civil law is necessary to the orator; so in regard to causes affecting public matters, before our courts, in assemblies of the people, and in the senate, all the history of these and of past times, the authority of public law, the system and science of governing the state, ought to be at the command of orators occupied with affairs of government, as the very groundwork of their speeches.[2] For we are not contemplating, in this discourse, the character of an every-day pleader, bawler, or barrator, but that of a man who, in the first place, may be, as it were, the high-priest of this profession, for which, though nature herself has given rich endowments to man, yet it was thought to be a god that gave it, so that the very thing which is the distinguishing property of man might not seem to have been acquired by ourselves, but bestowed upon us by some divinity; who, in the next place, can move with safety even amid the weapons of his adversaries, distinguished not so much by a

---

[1] The custom *Respondendi de Jure,* and the interpretations and decisions of the learned, were so universally approved, that, although they were unwritten, they became a new species of law, and were called *Auctoritas,* or *Responsa Prudentum.* This custom continued to the time of Augustus without interruption, who selected particular lawyers, and gave them the sanction of a patent; but then grew into desuetude, till Hadrian renewed this office or grant, which made so considerable a branch of the Roman law. *B.*

[1] *Jura publica.* Dr. Taylor, in his History of the Roman Law, p. 62, has given us the heads of the Roman *Jus publicum,* which were, religion and divine worship—peace and war—legislation—exchequer and *res fisci,* escheats—the prerogative—law of treasons—taxes and imposts—coinage—jurisdiction—magistracies—regalia–embassies—honors and titles—colleges, schools, corporations—castles and fortifications—fairs, mercats, staple—forests—naturalization. *B.*

[2] *Tanquam aliqua materies.* Ernesti's text, says Orellius, has *alia* by mistake. *Aliqua* is not very satisfactory. Nobbe, the editor of Tauchnitz's text, retains Ernesti's *alia.*

herald's caduceus[1] as by his title of orator; who, likewise, is able, by means of his eloquence, to expose guilt and deceit to the hatred of his countrymen, and to restrain them by penalties; who can also, with the shield of his genius, protect innocence from punishment; who can rouse a spiritless and desponding people to glory, or reclaim them from infatuation, or inflame their rage against the guilty, or mitigate it, if incited against the virtuous; who, finally, whatever feeling in the minds of men his object and cause require, can either excite or calm it by his eloquence. If any one supposes that this power has either been sufficiently set forth by those who have written on the art of speaking, or can be set forth by me in so brief a space, he is greatly mistaken, and understands neither my inability nor the magnitude of the subject. For my own part, since it was your desire, I thought that the fountains ought to be shown you from which you might draw, and the roads which you might pursue, not so that I should become your guide (which would be an endless and unnecessary labor), but so that I might point out to you the way, and, as the practice is, might hold out my finger toward the spring."[2]

XLVII. "To me," remarked Scævola, "enough appears to have been said by you, and more than enough, to stimulate the efforts of these young men, if they are but studiously inclined; for as they say that the illustrious Socrates used to observe that his object was attained if any one was by his exhortations sufficiently incited to desire to know and understand virtue (since to those who were persuaded to desire nothing so much as to become good men, what remained to be learned was easy); so I consider that if you wish to penetrate into those subjects which Crassus has set before you in his remarks, you will, with the greatest ease, arrive at your object, after this course and gate has been opened to you." "To us," said Sulpicius, "these instructions are exceedingly pleasant and delightful; but there are a few things more which we still desire to hear, especially those which were touched upon so briefly by you, Crassus, in reference to oratory as an art, when you confessed that you did not despise them, but had learned them. If you will speak somewhat more at length on those points, you will satisfy all the eagerness of our long desire. For we have now heard to what objects we must direct our efforts, a point which is of great importance; but we long to be instructed in the ways and means of pursuing those objects."

"Then," said Crassus "(since I, to detain you at my house with less difficulty, have rather complied with your desires than my own habit or inclination), what if we ask Antonius to tell us something of what he still keeps in reserve, and has not yet made known to us (on which subjects he complained, a while ago, that a book has already dropped from his pen), and to reveal to us his mysteries in the art of speaking?" "As you please," said Sulpicius; "for, if Antonius speaks, we shall still learn what you think." "I request of you, then, Antonius," said Crassus, "since this task is put upon men of our time of life by the studious inclinations of these youths, to deliver your sentiments upon these subjects which, you see, are required from you."

XLVIII. "I see plainly, and understand indeed," replied Antonius, "that I am caught, not only because those things are required from me in which I am ignorant and unpracticed, but because these young men do not permit me to avoid, on the present occasion, what I always carefully avoid in my public pleadings, namely, not to speak after you, Crassus. But I will enter upon what you desire the more boldly, as I hope the same thing will happen to me in this discussion as usually happens to me at the bar, that no flowers of rhetoric will be expected from me. For I am not going to speak about *art,* which I never learned, but about my own practice; and those very particulars which I

---

[1] The herald's caduceus, or wand, renders his person inviolable. *Pearce.*

[2] *Ut fieri solet.* Ernesti conjectures *ut dici solet.* Ellendt thinks the common reading right, requiring only that we should understand *à commonstrantibus.*

have entered in my commonplace book are of this kind,[1] not expressed with any thing like learning, but just as they are treated in business and pleadings; and if they do not meet with approbation from men of your extensive knowledge, you must blame your own unreasonableness in requiring from me what I do not know; and you must praise my complaisance, since I make no difficulty in answering your questions, being induced, not by my own judgment, but your earnest desire." "Go on, Antonius," rejoined Crassus, "for there is no danger that you will say any thing otherwise than so discreetly that no one here will repent of having prompted you to speak."

"I will go on, then," said Antonius, "and will do what I think ought to be done in all discussions at the commencement; I mean, that the subject, whatever it may be, on which the discussion is held, should be defined; so that the discourse may not be forced to wander and stray from its course, from the disputants not having the same notion of the matter under debate. If, for instance, it were inquired, 'What is the art of a general?" I should think that we ought to settle, at the outset, what a general is; and when he was defined to be *a commander for conducting a war,* we might then proceed to speak of troops, of encampments, of marching in battle array, of engagements, of besieging towns, of provisions, of laying and avoiding ambuscades, and other matters relative to the management of a war; and those who had the capacity and knowledge to direct such affairs I should call generals; and should adduce the examples of the Africani and Maximi, and speak of Epaminondas, and Hannibal, and men of such character. But if we should inquire what sort of character he is, who should contribute his experience, and knowledge, and zeal to the management of the state, I should give this sort of definition, that *he who understands by what means the interests of the republic are secured and promoted, and employs those means, is worthy to be esteemed a director in affairs of government, and a leader in public councils;* and I should mention Publius Lentulus, the chief of the senate,[1] and Tiberius Gracchus the father, and Quintus Metellus, and Publius Africanus, and Caius Lælius, and others without number, as well of our own city as of foreign states. But if it should be asked 'Who truly deserved the name of a lawyer?' I should say that he deserves it *who is learned in the laws, and that general usage*[2] *which private persons observe in their intercourse in the community, who can give an answer on any point, can plead, and can take precautions for the interests of his client;* and I should name Sextus Ælius, Manius Manilius, Publius Mucius, as distinguished in those respects.

XLIX. In like manner, to notice sciences of a less important character, if a musician, if a grammarian, if a poet were the subject of consideration, I could state that which each of them possesses, and than which nothing more is to be expected from each. Even of the philosopher himself, who alone, from his abilities and wisdom, professes almost every thing, there is a sort of definition, signifying that *he who studies to learn the powers, nature, and causes of all things, divine and human, and to understand and explain the whole science of living virtuously,* may justly deserve this appellation.

"The orator, however, since it is about him that we are considering, I do not conceive to be exactly the same character that Crassus makes him, who seemed to me to include all knowledge of all matters and sciences under the single profession and name of an orator; but I regard him as *one who can use words agreeable to hear, and thoughts adapted to prove, not only in causes that are pleaded in the forum, but in causes in general.* Him I call an orator, and would have him, besides, accomplished in delivery and action, and with a certain degree of wit. But our friend Crassus

[1] Not recorded with any elegance, but in the plain style in which I am now going to express myself. *Ernesti.*

[1] *Principem illum.* Nempe *senatûs.* He was consul with Cneius Domitius, A.U.C. 592. *Ellendt.*

[2] The unwritten law.

seemed to me to define the faculty of an orator, not by the proper limits of his art, but by the almost immense limits of his own genius; for, by his definition, he delivered the helm of civil government into the hands of his orator; a point which it appeared very strange to me, Scævola, that you should grant him; when the senate has often given its assent on affairs of the utmost consequence to yourself, though you have spoken briefly and without ornament. And M. Scaurus, who I hear is in the country, at his villa not far off, a man eminently skilled in affairs of government, if he should hear that the authority which his gravity and counsels bear with them is claimed by you, Crassus, as you say that it is the property of the orator, he would, I believe, come hither without delay, and frighten us out of our talk by his very countenance and aspect; who, though he is no contemptible speaker, yet depends more upon his judgment in affairs of consequence than upon his ability in speaking; and, if any one has abilities in both these ways, he who is of authority in the public councils, and a good senator, is not on those accounts an orator; and if he that is an eloquent and powerful speaker be also eminent in civil administration, he did not acquire his political knowledge[1] through oratory. Those talents differ very much in their nature, and are quite separate and distinct from each other; nor did Marcus Cato, Publius Africanus, Quintus Metellus, Caius Lælius, who were all eloquent, give lustre to their own orations, and to the dignity of the republic, by the same art and method.

L. "It is not enjoined, let me observe, by the nature of things, or by any law or custom, that one man must not know more than one art; and therefore, though Pericles was the best orator in Athens, and was also for many years director of the public counsels in that city, the talent for both those characters must not be thought to belong to the same art because it existed in the same man; nor if Publius Crassus was both an orator and a lawyer, is the knowledge of the civil law for that reason included in the power of speaking. For if any man, who, while excelling in any art or science, has acquired another art or science in addition, shall represent that his additional knowledge is a part of that in which he previously excelled,[1] we may, by such a mode of argument, pretend that to play well at tennis or counters[2] is a part of the knowledge of civil law, because Publius Mucius was skilled in both; and, by parity of reasoning, those whom the Greeks call φυσικοί, 'natural philosophers,' may be regarded as poets, because Empedocles the natural philosopher wrote an excellent poem. But not even the philosophers themselves, who would have every thing, as their own right, to be theirs, and in their possession, have the confidence to say that geometry or music is a part of philosophy, because all acknowledge Plato to have been eminently excellent in those sciences. And if it be still your pleasure to attribute all sciences to the orator, it will be better for us, rather, to express ourselves to this effect, that since eloquence must not be bald and unadorned, but marked and distinguished by a certain pleasing variety of manifold qualities, it is necessary for a good orator to have heard and seen much, to have gone over many subjects in thought and reflection, and many also in reading; though not so as to have taken possession of them as his own property, but to have tasted of them as things belonging to others. For I confess that the orator should be a knowing man, not quite a tyro or novice in any

[1] *Aliquam scientiam.* For *aliquam* Manutius conjectured *illam,* which Lambinus, Ernesti, and Müller approve. Wyttenbach suggested *alienam,* which has been adopted by Schutz and Orellius. I have followed Manutius.

[1] *Sciet—excellet.* The commentators say nothing against these futures.

[2] *Duodecim scriptis.* This was a game played with counters on a board, moved according to throws of the dice, but different from our backgammon. The reader may find all that is known of it in Adam's Roman Antiquities, p. 423, and Smith's Dict. of Gr. and Rom. Ant., art. Latrunculi.

subject, not utterly ignorant or inexperienced in any business of life.

LI. "Nor am I discomposed, Crassus, by those tragic arguments of yours,[1] on which the philosophers dwell most of all; I mean, when you said, *That no man can, by speaking, excite the passions of his audience, or calm them when excited* (*in which efforts it is that the power and greatness of an orator are chiefly seen*), *unless one who has gained a thorough insight into the nature of all things, and the dispositions and motives of mankind; on which account philosophy must of necessity be studied by the orator;* a study in which we see that the whole lives of men of the greatest talent and leisure are spent; the copiousness and magnitude of whose learning and knowledge I not only do not despise, but greatly admire; but, for us who are engaged in so busy a state, and such occupations in the forum, it is sufficient to know and say just so much about the manners of mankind as is not inconsistent with human nature. For what great and powerful orator, whose object was to make a judge angry with his adversary, ever hesitated, because he was ignorant what anger was, whether 'a heat of temper,' or 'a desire of vengeance for pain received?'[2] Who, when he wished to stir up and inflame other passions in the minds of the judges or people by his eloquence, ever uttered such things as are said by the philosophers? part of whom deny that any passions whatever should be excited in the mind, and say that they who rouse them in the breasts of the judges are guilty of a heinous crime, and part, who are inclined to be more tolerant, and to accommodate themselves more to the realities of life, say that such emotions ought to be but very moderate and gentle. But the orator, by his eloquence, represents all those things which, in the common affairs of life, are considered evil and troublesome, and to be avoided, as heavier and more grievous than they really are; and at the same time amplifies and embellishes, by power of language, those things which to the generality of mankind seem inviting and desirable; nor does he wish to appear so very wise among fools as that his audience should think him impertinent or a pedantic Greek, or, though they very much approve his understanding, and admire his wisdom, yet should feel uneasy that they themselves are but idiots to him; but he so effectually penetrates the minds of men, so works upon their senses and feelings, that he has no occasion for the definitions of philosophers, or to consider in the course of his speech 'whether the chief good lies in the mind or in the body;' 'whether it is to be defined as consisting in virtue or in pleasure;' 'whether these two can be united and coupled together;' or 'whether,' as some think, 'nothing certain can be known, nothing clearly perceived and understood;' questions in which I acknowledge that a vast multiplicity of learning, and a great abundance of varied reasoning is involved; but we seek something of a far different character; we want a man of superior intelligence, sagacious by nature and from experience, who can acutely divine what his fellow-citizens, and all those whom he wishes to convince on any subject by his eloquence, think, feel, imagine, or hope.

LII. He must penetrate the inmost recesses of the mind of every class, age, and rank, and must ascertain the sentiments and notions of those before whom he is pleading,[1] or intends to plead; but his books of philosophy he must reserve to himself, for the leisure and tranquillity of such a Tusculan villa as this, and must not, when he is to speak on justice and honesty, borrow from Plato; who, when he thought that such subjects were to be illustrated in writing, imagined in his pages a new kind of commonwealth; so much was that which he thought necessary to be said of justice at

---

[1] *Istis tragœdiis tuis.* Persons are said *tragœdias in nugis agere* who make a small matter great by clamoring over it, as is done by actors in tragedies. *Proust.* See b. ii., c. 51; Quint., vi., 1, 36.

[2] See Aristotle, Rhetor., ii., 2; Cic., Tusc. Quæst., iv.

[1] Most copies have *aget;* Pearce, with the minority, prefers *agit.*

variance with ordinary life and the general customs of the world. But if such notions were received in existing communities and nations, who would have permitted you, Crassus, though a man of the highest character, and the chief leader in the city, to utter what you addressed to a vast assembly of your fellow-citizens?[1] DELIVER US FROM THESE MISERIES. DELIVER US FROM THE JAWS OF THOSE WHOSE CRUELTY CAN NOT BE SATIATED EVEN WITH BLOOD; SUFFER US NOT TO BE SLAVES TO ANY BUT YOURSELVES AS A PEOPLE, WHOM WE BOTH CAN AND OUGHT TO SERVE. I say nothing about the word MISERIES, in which, as the philosophers say,[2] a man of fortitude can not be; I say nothing of the JAWS from which you desire to be delivered, that your blood may not be drunk by an unjust sentence; a thing which they say can not happen to a wise man; but how durst you say that not only yourself, but the whole senate, whose cause you were then pleading, were SLAVES? Can virtue, Crassus, possibly be ENSLAVED, according to those whose precepts you make necessary to the science of an orator; virtue which is ever and alone free, and which, though our bodies be captured in war, or bound with fetters, yet ought to maintain its rights and liberty inviolate in all circumstances?[3] And as to what you added, that the senate not only CAN, but OUGHT to be SLAVES to the people, what philosopher is so effeminate, so languid, so enervated, so eager to refer every thing to bodily pleasure or pain, as to allow that the senate should be the SLAVES of the people, to whom the people themselves have delivered the power, like certain reins as it were, to guide and govern them?

[1] These words are taken from a speech which Crassus had a short time before delivered in an assembly of the people, and in which he had made severe complaints of the Roman knights, who exercised their judicial powers with severity and injustice, and gave great trouble to the senate. Crassus took the part of the senate, and addressed the exhortation in the text to the people. *Proust.* Crassus was supporting the Servilian law. *Manutius.*

[2] *Ut illi aiunt.* The philosophers, especially the Stoics, who affirmed that the wise man alone is happy. *Ellendt.*

[3] See the paradox of Cicero on the words *Omnes sapientes liberi, omnes stulti servi.*

LIII. "Accordingly, when I regarded these words of yours as the divinest eloquence, Publius Rutilius Rufus,[1] a man of learning, and devoted to philosophy, observed that what you had said was not only injudicious, but base and dishonorable. The same Rutilius used severely to censure Servius Galba, whom he said he very well remembered, because, when Lucius Scribonius brought an accusation against him, and Marcus Cato, a bitter and implacable enemy to Galba, had spoken with rancor and vehemence against him before the assembled people of Rome (in a speech which he published in his Origines[2]), Rutilius, I say, censured Galba for holding up, almost upon his shoulders, Quintus, the orphan son of Caius Sulpicius Gallus, his near relation, that he might, through the memory of his most illustrious father, draw tears from the people, and for recommending two little sons of his own to the guardianship of the public, and saying that he himself (as if he was making his will in the ranks before a battle,[3] without balance or writing-tables[4]) appointed the people of Rome protectors of their orphan condition. As Galba, therefore, labored under the ill opinion and dislike of the people, Rutilius said that he owed his deliverance to such tragic tricks as these; and I see it is also recorded in Cato's book, that *if he had not employed children and tears, he would have suffered.* Such proceedings Rutilius severely condemned, and said banishment, or even death, was more eligible than such

[1] Mentioned by Cic., Brut., c. 30. *Proust.* He was a perfect Stoic. *Ellendt.*

[2] A work on the origin of the people and cities of Italy, and other matters, now lost. Cic., Brut., c. 85; Corn. Nep., Life of Cato, c. 3.

[3] When a soldier, in the hearing of three or more of his comrades, named some one his heir in case he should fall in the engagement.

[4] When a person, in the presence of five witnesses and a *libripens,* assigned his property to somebody as his heir. Gaius, ii., 101; Aul. Gell., xv., 27.

meanness. Nor did he merely say this, but thought and acted accordingly; for being a man, as you know, of exemplary integrity, a man to whom no person in the city was superior in honesty and integrity, he not only refused to supplicate his judges, but would not allow his cause to be pleaded with more ornament or freedom of language than the simple plainness of truth carried with it.[1] Small was the part of it he assigned to Cotta here, his sister's son, and a youth of great eloquence; and Quintus Mucius also took some share in his defense, speaking in his usual manner, without ostentation, but simply and with perspicuity. But if you, Crassus, had then spoken—you, who just now said that the orator must seek assistance from those disputations in which the philosophers indulge, to supply himself with matter for his speeches—if you had been at liberty to speak for Publius Rutilius, not after the manner of philosophers, but in your own way, although his accusers had been, as they really were, abandoned and mischievous citizens, and worthy of the severest punishment, yet the force of your eloquence would have rooted all their unwarrantable cruelty from the bottom of their hearts. But, as it was, a man of such character was lost, because his cause was pleaded in such a manner as if the whole affair had been transacted in the imaginary commonwealth of Plato. Not a single individual uttered a groan; not one of the advocates gave vent to an exclamation; no one showed any appearance of grief; no one complained; no one supplicated, no one implored the mercy of the public. In short, no one even stamped a foot on the trial, for fear, I suppose, of renouncing the doctrine of the Stoics.

LIV. "Thus a Roman, of consular dignity, imitated the illustrious Socrates of old, who, as he was a man of the greatest wisdom, and had lived in the utmost integrity, spoke for himself, when on trial for his life, in such a manner as not to seem a suppliant or prisoner, but the lord and master of his judges. Even when Lysias, a most eloquent orator, brought him a written speech, which, if he pleased, he might learn by heart, and repeat at his trial, he willingly read it over, and said it was written in a manner very well suited to the occasion; but, said he, if you had brought me Sicyonian shoes,[1] I should not wear them, though they might be easy and suit my feet, because they would be effeminate; so that speech seems to me to be eloquent and becoming an orator, but not fearless and manly. In consequence, he also was condemned, not only by the first votes, by which the judges only decided whether they should acquit or condemn, but also by those which, in conformity with the laws, they were obliged to give afterward. For at Athens, if the accused person was found guilty, and if his crime was not capital, there was a sort of estimation of punishment; and when sentence was to be finally given by the judges, the criminal was asked what degree of punishment he acknowledged himself, at most, to deserve; and when this question was put to Socrates, he answered that he deserved to be distinguished with the noblest honors and rewards, and to be daily maintained at the public expense in the Prytaneum; an honor which, among the Greeks, is accounted the very highest. By which answer his judges were so exasperated that they condemned the most innocent of men to death. But had he been acquitted (which, indeed, though it is of no concern to us, yet I could wish to have been the case, because of the greatness of his genius), how could we have patience with those philosophers who now, though Socrates was condemned for no other crime but want of skill in speaking, maintain that the precepts of oratory should be learned from themselves, who are disciples of Socrates? With these men I have no dispute as to which of the two sciences is superior, or carries more truth in it; I only say that the one is distinct from the

[1] He was falsely accused of extortion in his province of Asia, and, being condemned, was sent into exile. Cic., Brut., c. 30. *Proust.*

[1] Shoes made at Sicyon, and worn only by the effeminate and luxurious. Lucret., iv., 1121.

other, and that oratory may exist in the highest perfection without philosophy.

LV. "In bestowing such warm approbation on the civil law, Crassus, I see what was your motive; when you were speaking, I did not see it.[1] In the first place, you were willing to oblige Scævola, whom we ought all to esteem most deservedly for his singularly excellent disposition; and seeing his science undowried and unadorned, you have enriched it with your eloquence as with a portion, and decorated it with a profusion of ornaments. In the next, as you had spent much pains and labor in the acquisition of it (since you had in your own house one[2] who encouraged and instructed you in that study), you were afraid that you might lose the fruit of your industry if you did not magnify the science by your eloquence. But I have no controversy with the science; let it be of as much consequence as you represent it; for without doubt it is of great and extensive concern, having relation to multitudes of people, and has always been held in the highest honor; and our most eminent citizens have ever been, and are still, at the head of the profession of it; but take care, Crassus, lest, while you strive to adorn the knowledge of the civil law with new and foreign ornaments, you spoil and denude her of what is granted and accorded to her as her own. For if you were to say that he who is a lawyer is also an orator, and that he who is an orator is also a lawyer, you would make two excellent branches of knowledge, each equal to the other, and sharers of the same dignity; but now you allow that a man may be a lawyer without the eloquence which we are considering, and that there have been many such; and you deny that a man can be an orator who has not acquired a knowledge of law. Thus the lawyer is, of himself, nothing with you

[1] *Tum, quum dicebas, non videbam.* Many copies omit the negative; an omission approved by Ernesti, Henrichsen, and Ellendt.

[2] Either Scævola, the father-in-law of Crassus, or Lucius Cœlius Antipater, whom Cicero mentions in his Brutus. *Proust.*

but a sort of wary and acute legalist, an instructor in actions,[1] a repeater of forms, a catcher at syllables; but because the orator has frequent occasion for the aid of the law in his pleadings, you have of necessity joined legal knowledge to eloquence as a handmaid and attendant.

LVI. "But as to your wonder at the effrontery of those advocates who, though they were ignorant of small things, profess great ones, or who ventured, in the management of causes, to treat of the most important points in the civil law, though they neither understood nor had ever learned them, the defense on both charges is easy and ready. For it is not at all surprising that he who is ignorant in what form of words a contract of marriage is made, should be able to defend the cause of a woman who has formed such a contract; nor, though the same skill in steering is requisite for a small as for a large vessel, is he therefore, who is ignorant of the form of words by which an estate is to be divided, incapable of pleading a cause relative to the division of an estate.[2] For though you appealed to causes of great consequence, pleaded before the centumviri, that

[1] *Prœco actionum.* One who informs those who are ignorant of law when the courts will be open; by what kind of suit any person must prosecute his claims on any other person; and acts in law proceedings as another sort of *prœco* acts at auctions. *Strebœus.*

[2] *Herctum cieri—herciscundœ familiœ.* Co-heirs, when an estate descended among them, were, by the Roman law, bound to each other by the action *familiœ herciscundœ;* that is, to divide the whole family inheritance, and settle all the accounts which related to it. Just., Inst., iii., 28, 4. The word *herctum,* says Festus, signifies whole or undivided, and *cio,* to divide; so, *familiam herctam ciere* was to divide the inheritance of the family, which two words, *herctum ciere,* were afterward contracted into *herciscere:* hence this law-term used here, *familiam herciscere.* Servius has, therefore, from Donatus, thus illustrated a passage in Virgil, at the end of the VIIIth Æneid,

Citæ Metium in diversa quadrigæ
Distulerant.

Citœ, says he, is a law-term, and signifies divided, as *hercto non cito,* the inheritance being undivided. *Citœ quadrigœ,* therefore, in that passage, does not mean *quick* or *swift,* as is generally imagined, but *drawing different ways.* B.

turned upon points of law, what cause was there among them all which could not have been ably pleaded by an eloquent man unacquainted with law? in all which causes, as in the cause of Manius Curius, which was lately pleaded by you,[1] and that of Caius Hostilius Mancinus,[2] and that of the boy who was born of a second wife, without any notice of divorce having been sent to the first,[3] there was the greatest disagreement among the most skillful lawyers on points of law. I ask, then, how in these causes a knowledge of the law could have aided the orator, when that lawyer must have had the superiority, who was supported, not by his own, but a foreign art, not by knowledge of the law, but by eloquence? I have often heard that, when Publius Crassus was a candidate for the ædileship, and Servius Galba, though older than he, and even of consular dignity, attended upon him to promote his interest (having betrothed Crassus's daughter to his son Caius), there came a countryman to Crassus to consult him on some matter of law; and when he had taken Crassus aside, and laid the affair before him, and received from him such an answer as was rather right than suited to his wishes, Galba, seeing him look dejected, called him by his name, and asked him on what matter he had consulted Crassus; when, having heard his case, and seeing the man in great trouble, 'I perceive,' said he, 'that Crassus gave you an answer while his mind was anxious, and preoccupied with other affairs.' He then took Crassus by the hand, and said, 'Hark you, how came it into your head to give this man such an answer?' Crassus, who was a man of great legal knowledge, confidently repeated that the matter was exactly as he had stated in his answer, and that there could be no doubt. But Galba, referring to a variety and multiplicity of matters, adduced abundance of similar cases, and used many arguments for equity against the strict letter of law; while Crassus, as he could not maintain his ground in the debate (for, though he was numbered among the eloquent, he was by no means equal to Galba), had recourse to authorities, and showed what he had asserted in the books of his brother Publius Mucius,[1] and in the commentaries of Sextus Ælius; though he allowed, at the same time, that Galba's arguments had appeared to him plausible, and almost true.

LVII. "But causes which are of such a kind that there can be no doubt of the law relative to them do not usually come to be tried at all. Does any one claim an inheritance under a will, which the father of a family made before he had a son born? Nobody; because it is clear that by the birth of a son the will is canceled.[2] Upon such points of law, therefore, there are no questions to be tried. The orator, accordingly, may be ignorant of all this part of the law relative to controversies,[3] which is, without doubt, the far greater part; but on those points which are disputed, even among the most skillful lawyers, it will not be difficult for the orator to find some writer of authority on that side, whichsoever it be, that he is to defend, from whom, when he has received his javelins ready for throwing, he will hurl them with the arm and strength of an orator. Unless we are to suppose, indeed (I would wish to make the observation without offending this excellent man Scævola), that you, Crassus, defended the cause of Manius Curius out of the writings and rules of your father-in-law. Did you not, on the contrary, undertake the defense of equity, the support of wills, and the

---

[1] See c. 39.

[2] C. 40.

[3] C. 40.

---

[1] The Crassus here mentioned was Publius Crassus Dives, brother of Publius Mucius, Pontifex Maximus. See c. 37. *Ellendt.*

[2] Cicero pro Cæcinâ, c. 25; Gaius, ii., 138.

[3] *Omnem hanc partem juris in controversiis.* For *in controversiis* Lambinus and Ernesti would read, from a correction in an old copy, *incontroversi;* but as there is no authority for this word, Ellendt, with Bakius, prefers *non controversi.* With this alteration, the sense will be, "all this uncontroverted part of the law."

intention of the dead? Indeed, in my opinion (for I was frequently present and heard you), you won the far greater number of votes by your wit, humor, and happy raillery, when you joked upon the extraordinary acuteness, and expressed admiration of the genius, of Scævola, who had discovered that *a man must be born before he can die;* and when you adduced many cases, both from the laws and decrees of the senate, as well as from common life and intercourse, not only acutely, but facetiously and sarcastically, in which, if we attended to the letter, and not the spirit, nothing would result. The trial, therefore, was attended with abundance of mirth and pleasantry; but of what service your knowledge of the civil law was to you upon it, I do not understand; your great power in speaking, united with the utmost humor and grace, certainly was of great service. Even Mucius himself, the defender of the father's right, who fought as it were for his own patrimony, what argument did he advance in the cause, when he spoke against you, that appeared to be drawn from the civil law? What particular law did he recite? What did he explain in his speech that was unintelligible to the unlearned? The whole of his oration was employed upon one point; that is, in maintaining that what was written ought to be valid. But every boy is exercised on such subjects by his master, when he is instructed to support, in such cases as these, sometimes the written letter, sometimes equity. In that cause of the soldier, I presume, if you had defended either him or the heir, you would have had recourse to the cases of Hostilius,[1] and not to your own power and talent as an orator. Nay, rather, if you had defended the will, you would have argued in such a manner that the entire validity of all wills whatsoever would have seemed to depend upon that single trial; or, if you had pleaded the cause of the soldier, you would have raised his father, with your usual eloquence, from the dead; you would have placed him before the eyes of the audience; he would have embraced his son, and with tears have recommended him to the Centumviri; you would have forced the very stones to weep and lament, so that all that clause, AS THE TONGUE HAD DECLARED, would seem not to have been written in the Twelve Tables, which you prefer to all libraries, but in some mere formula of a teacher.

LVIII. "As to the indolence of which you accuse our youth, for not learning that science, because, in the first place, it is very easy (how easy it is, let them consider who strut about before us, presuming on their knowledge of the science, as if it were extremely difficult; and do you yourself also consider that point, who say, that it is an easy science, which you admit as yet to be no science at all, but say that if somebody shall ever learn some other science, so as to be able to make this a science, it will then be a science); and because, in the next place, it is full of pleasure (but as to that matter, every one is willing to leave the pleasure to yourself, and is content to be without it, for there is not one of the young men who would not rather, if he must get any thing by heart, learn the Teucer of Pacuvius than the Manilian laws[1] on emption and vendition); and, in the third place, because you think that, from love to our country, we ought to acquire a knowledge of the practices of our ancestors; do you not perceive that the old laws are either grown out of date from their very antiquity, or are set aside by such as are new?[2] As to your opinion, that men are rendered good by learning the civil law, because, by laws, rewards are appointed for virtue, and punishment for vice; I, for my part, imagined that virtue was instilled into mankind (if it can be instilled by any means) by

---

[1] Certain legal formulæ, of which some lawyer named Hostilius was the author. *Ernesti.*

[1] *Manilianas—leges.* They were formulæ which those who wished not to be deceived might use in buying and selling; they are called *actiones* by Varro, R. R., ii., 5, 11. . . . The author was Manius Manilius, an eminent lawyer, who was consul A.U.C. 603. *Ernesti.*

[2] There is no proper grammatical construction in this sentence. Ernesti observes that it is, perhaps, in some way unsound.

instruction and persuasion, not by menaces, and force, and terror. As to the maxim that we should avoid evil, we can understand how good a thing it is to do so without a knowledge of the law. And as to myself, to whom alone you allow the power of managing causes satisfactorily, without any knowledge of law, I make you, Crassus, this answer: that I never learned the civil law, nor was ever at a loss for the want of knowledge in it, in those causes which I was able to defend in the courts.[1] It is one thing to be a master in any pursuit or art, and another to be neither stupid nor ignorant in common life, and the ordinary customs of mankind. May not every one of us go over our farms, or inspect our country affairs, for the sake of profit or delight at least?[2] No man lives without using his eyes and understanding, so far as to be entirely ignorant what sowing and reaping is; or what pruning vines and other trees means; or at what season of the year, and in what manner, those things are done. If, therefore, any one of us has to look at his grounds, or give any directions about agriculture to his steward, or any orders to his bailiff, must we study the books of Mago the Carthaginian,[3] or may we be content with our ordinary knowledge? Why, then, with regard to the civil law, may we not also, especially as we are worn out in causes and public business, and in the forum, be sufficiently instructed, to such a degree at least as not to appear foreigners and strangers in our own country? Or, if any cause, a little more obscure than ordinary, should be brought to us, it would, I presume, be difficult to communicate with our friend Scævola here; although indeed the parties, whose concern it is, bring nothing to us that has not been thoroughly considered and investigated. If there is a question about the nature of a thing itself under consideration; if about boundaries (as we do not go in person to view the property itself[1]); if about writings and bonds,[2] we of necessity have to study matters that are intricate and often difficult; and if we have to consider laws, or the opinions of men skilled in law, need we fear that we shall not be able to understand them, if we have not studied the civil law from our youth?

LIX. "Is the knowledge of the civil law, then, of no advantage to the orator? I can not deny that every kind of knowledge is of advantage, especially to him whose eloquence ought to be adorned with variety of matter; but the things which are absolutely necessary to an orator are numerous, important, and difficult, so that I would not distract his industry among too many studies. Who can deny that the gesture and grace of Roscius are necessary in the orator's action and deportment? Yet nobody would advise youths that are studying oratory to labor in forming their attitudes like players. What is so necessary to an orator as the voice? Yet, by my recommendation, no student in eloquence will be a slave to his voice like the Greeks and tragedians,[3] who pass whole years in sedentary declamation, and daily, before they venture upon delivery, raise their voice by degrees as they sit, and, when they have finished pleading, sit down again, and lower and recover

---

[1] *In jure.* "Apud tribunal prætoris." *Ernesti.*

[2] I translate the conclusion of the sentence in conformity with the text of Orellius, who puts *tamen* at the end of it, instead of letting it stand at the beginning of the next sentence, as is the case in other editions. His interpretation is, *invisere saltem.* "Though we be much occupied, yet we can visit our farms."

[3] He wrote eight-and-twenty books on country affairs in the Punic language, which were translated into Latin, by order of the senate, by Cassius Dionysius of Utica. See Varro, R. R., i., 1; and Columella, who calls him the father of farming. *Proust.*

[1] *Quum in rem præsentem non venimus.* We do not go *ad locum, unde præsentes rem et fines inspicere possimus.* Ellendt.

[2] *Perscriptionibus. Perscriptio* is considered by Ellendt to signify a draft or check to be presented to a banker.

[3] *Græcorum more et tragœdorum.* Lambinus would strike out *et,* on the authority of three manuscripts; and Pearce thinks that the conjunction ought to be absent. Ernesti thinks that some substantive belonging to *Græcorum* has dropped out of the text. A Leipsic edition, he observes, has *Græcorum more sophistarum et tragœdorum,* but on what authority he does not know.

it, as it were, through a scale, from the highest to the deepest tone. If we should do this, they whose causes we undertake would be condemned before we had repeated the *pœan* and the *munio*[1] as often as is prescribed. But if we must not employ ourselves upon gesture, which is of great service to the orator, or upon the culture of the voice, which alone is a great recommendation and support of eloquence; and if we can only improve in either in proportion to the leisure afforded us in this field of daily business, how much less must we apply to the occupation of learning the civil law? of which we may learn the chief points without regular study, and which is also unlike those other matters in this respect, that power of voice and gesture can not be got suddenly, or caught up from another person; but a knowledge of the law, as far as it is useful in any cause, may be gained on the shortest possible notice, either from learned men or from books. Those eminent Greek orators, therefore, as they are unskilled in the law themselves, have, in their causes, men acquainted with the law to assist them, who are, as you before observed, called *pragmatici.* In this respect our countrymen act far better, as they would have the laws and judicial decisions supported by the authority of men of the highest rank. But the Greeks would not have neglected, if they had thought it necessary, to instruct the orator in the civil law, instead of allowing him a *pragmaticus* for an assistant.

LX. "As to your remark that age is preserved from solitude by the science of the civil law, we may perhaps also say that it is preserved from solitude by a large fortune. But we are inquiring, not what is advantageous to ourselves, but what is necessary for the orator. Although (since we take so many points of comparison with the orator from one sort of artist) Roscius, whom we mentioned before, is accustomed to say that, as age advances upon him, he will make the measures of the flute-player slower, and the notes softer. But if he who is restricted to a certain modulation of numbers and feet, meditates, notwithstanding, something for his ease in the decline of life, how much more easily can we, I will not say lower our tones, but alter them entirely? For it is no secret to you, Crassus, how many and how various are the modes of speaking; a variety which I know not whether you yourself have not been the first to exhibit to us, since you have for some time spoken more softly and gently than you used to do; nor is this mildness in your eloquence, which carries so high authority with it, less approved than your former vast energy and exertion; and there have been many orators, as we hear of Scipio and Lælius, who always spoke in a tone only a little raised above that of ordinary conversation, but never exerted their lungs or throats like Servius Galba. But if you shall ever be unable or unwilling to speak in this manner, are you afraid that your house, the house of such a man and such a citizen, will, if it be not frequented by the litigious, be deserted by the rest of mankind? For my part, I am so far from having any similar feeling with regard to my own house, that I not only do not think that comfort for my old age is to be expected from a multitude of clients, but look for that solitude which you dread as for a safe harbor; for I esteem repose to be the most agreeable solace in the last stage of life.

"Those other branches of knowledge (though they certainly assist the orator)—I mean general history, and jurisprudence, and the course of things in old times, and variety of precedents—I will, if ever I have occasion for them, borrow from my friend Longinus,[1] an excellent man, and one of the greatest erudition in such matters. Nor will I dissuade these youths from reading every thing, hearing every thing, and acquainting themselves with every liberal study, and all polite learning, as

[1] *Pœanem aut munionem.* The word *munionem* is corrupt. Many editions have *nomium,* which is left equally unexplained. The best conjectural emendation, as Orellius observes, is *nomum,* proposed by a critic of Jena.

[1] Ernesti supposes him to be Caius Cassius Longinus, who is mentioned by Cicero, pro Planço, c. 24.

you just now recommended; but, upon my word, they do not seem likely to have too much time, if they are inclined to pursue and practice all that you, Crassus, have dictated; for you seemed to me to impose upon their youth obligations almost too severe (though almost necessary, I admit, for the attainment of their desires), since extemporary exercises upon stated cases, and accurate and studied meditations, and practice in writing, which you truly called the modeler and finisher of the art of speaking, are tasks of much difficulty; and that comparison of their own composition with the writings of others, and extemporal discussion on the work of another by way of praise or censure, confirmation or refutation, demand no ordinary exertion, either of memory or powers of imitation.

LXI. "But what you added was appalling, and indeed will have, I fear, a greater tendency to deter than to encourage. You would have every one of us a Roscius in our profession; and you said that what was excellent did not so much attract approbation, as what was faulty produced settled disgust; but I do not think that want of perfection is so disparagingly regarded in us as in the players; and I observe, accordingly, that we are often heard with the utmost attention, even when we are hoarse, for the interest of the subject itself and of the cause detains the audience; while Æsopus, if he has the least hoarseness, is hissed; for at those from whom nothing is expected but to please the ear, offense is taken whenever the least diminution of that pleasure occurs. But in eloquence there are many qualities that captivate; and, if they are not all of the highest excellence, and yet most of them are praiseworthy, those that are of the highest excellence must necessarily excite admiration.

"To return, therefore, to our first consideration, let the orator be, as Crassus described him, *one who can speak in a manner adapted to persuade;* and let him strictly devote himself to those things which are of common practice in civil communities, and in the forum, and, laying aside all other studies, however high and noble they may be, let him apply himself day and night, if I may say so, to this one pursuit, and imitate him to whom doubtless the highest excellence in oratory is conceded, Demosthenes the Athenian, in whom there is said to have been so much ardor and perseverance, that he overcame, first of all, the impediments of nature by pains and diligence; and, though his voice was so inarticulate that he was unable to pronounce the first letter of the very art which he was so eager to acquire, he accomplished so much by practice that no one is thought to have spoken more distinctly; and, though his breath was short, he effected such improvement by holding it in while he spoke, that in one sequence of words (as his writings show) two risings and two fallings of his voice were included;[1] and he also (as is related), after putting pebbles into his mouth, used to pronounce several verses at the highest pitch of his voice without taking breath, not standing in one place, but walking forward, and mounting a steep ascent. With such encouragements as these, I sincerely agree with you, Crassus, that youths should be incited to study and industry; other accomplishments which you have collected from various and distinct arts and sciences, though you have mastered them all yourself, I regard as unconnected with the proper business and duty of an orator."

LXII. When Antonius had concluded these observations, Sulpicius and Cotta appeared to be in doubt whose discourse of the two seemed to approach nearer to the truth. Crassus then said, "You make our orator a mere mechanic, Antonius, but I am not certain whether you are not really of another opinion, and whether you are not practicing upon us your wonderful skill in refutation, in which no one was ever your superior; a talent of which the exercise belongs properly to orators, but has now become common among philosophers, especially those who are accustomed

---

[1] In one period or sentence he twice raised and twice lowered his voice; he raised it in the former members of the period, and lowered it in the latter; and this he did in one breath. *Proust.* This seems not quite correct. Cicero appears to mean, that of the two members the voice was once raised and once lowered in each.

to speak fully and fluently on both sides of any question proposed. But I did not think, especially in the hearing of these young men, that merely such an orator was to be described by me as would pass his whole life in courts of justice, and would carry thither nothing more than the necessity of his causes required; but I contemplated something greater when I expressed my opinion that the orator, especially in such a republic as ours, ought to be deficient in nothing that could adorn his profession. But you, since you have circumscribed the whole business of an orator within such narrow limits, will explain to us with the less difficulty what you have settled as to oratorical[1] duties and rules; I think, however, that this may be done to-morrow, for we have talked enough for to-day. And Scævola, since he has appointed to go to his own Tusculan seat,[2] will now repose a little till the heat is abated; and let us also, as the day is so far advanced, consult our health."[3] The proposal pleased the whole company. Scævola then said, "Indeed, I could wish that I had not made an appointment with Lælius to go to that part of the Tusculan territory to-day. I would willingly hear Antonius;" and, as he rose from his seat, he smiled and added, "for he did not offend me so much when he pulled our civil law to pieces, as he amused me when he professed himself ignorant of it."

[1] Orellius's text has *prœceptis oratoris;* but we must undoubtedly read *oratoriis* with Pearce.

[2] Atticus was exceedingly pleased with this treatise, and commended it extremely, but objected to the dismission of Scævola from the disputation after he had been introduced into the first dialogue. Cicero defends himself by the example of their "god Plato," as he calls him, in his book *De Republicâ;* where the scene being laid in the house of an old gentleman, Cephalus, the old man, after bearing a part in the first conversation, excuses himself, saying that he must go to prayers, and returns no more, Plato not thinking it suitable to his age to be detained in the company through so long a discourse. With greater reason, therefore, he says that he had used the same caution in the case of Scævola, since it was not to be supposed that a person of his dignity, extreme age, and infirm health, would spend several successive days in another man's house; that the first day's dialogue related to his particular profession, but the other two chiefly to the rules and precepts of the art, at which it was not proper for one of Scævola's temper and character to be present only as a hearer. Ad Attic., iv., 16. *B.*

[3] Retire from the heat, like Scævola, and take rest.

BOOK II

THE ARGUMENT.

In this book Antonius gives instructions respecting invention in oratory, and the arrangements of the different parts of a speech; departments in which he was thought to have attained great excellence, though his language was not always highly studied or elegant. See Cic., de Clar. Orat., c. 37. As humor in speaking was considered as a part of invention, Caius Julius Cæsar, who was called the most facetious man of his time, speaks copiously on that subject, c. 54–71.

I. There was, if you remember, brother Quintus, a strong persuasion in us when we were boys, that Lucius Crassus had acquired no more learning than he had been enabled to gain from instruction in his youth, and that Marcus Antonius was entirely destitute and ignorant of all erudition whatsoever; and there were many who, though they did not believe that such was really the case, yet, that they might more easily deter us from the pursuit of learning, when we were inflamed with a desire of attaining it, took a pleasure in reporting what I have said of these orators; so that, if men of no learning had acquired the greatest wisdom, and an incredible degree of eloquence, all our industry might seem vain, and the earnest perseverance of our father, one of the best and most sensible of men, in educating us, might appear to be folly. These reasoners we, as boys, used at that time to refute with the aid of witnesses whom we had at home, our father, Caius Aculeo our relative, and Lucius Cicero our uncle; for our father, Aculeo (who married our mother's sister, and whom

Crassus esteemed the most of all his friends), and our own uncle (who went with Antonius into Cilicia, and quitted it at the same time with him), often told us many particulars about Crassus, relative to his studies and learning; and as we, with our cousins, Aculeo's sons, learned what Crassus approved, and were instructed by the masters whom he engaged, we had also frequent opportunities of observing (since, though boys,[1] we could understand this) that he spoke Greek so well that he might have been thought not to know any other language, and he put such questions to our masters, and discoursed upon such subjects in his conversation with them, that nothing appeared to be new or strange to him. But with regard to Antonius, although we had frequently heard from our uncle, a person of the greatest learning, how he had devoted himself, both at Athens and at Rhodes, to the conversation of the most learned men, yet I myself also, when quite a youth, often asked him many questions on the subject, as far as the bashfulness of my early years would permit. What I am writing will certainly not be new to you (for at that very time you heard it from me), namely, that from many and various conversations, he appeared to me neither ignorant nor unaccomplished in any thing in those branches of knowledge of which I could form any opinion. But there was such peculiarity in each, that Crassus desired not so much to be thought unlearned as to hold learning in contempt, and to prefer, on every subject, the understanding of our countrymen to that of the Greeks; while Antonius thought that his oratory would be better received by the Roman people if he were believed to have had no learning at all; and thus the one imagined that he should have more authority if he appeared to despise the Greeks, and the other if he seemed to know nothing of them.

But what their object was is certainly nothing to our present purpose. It is pertinent, however, to the treatise which I have commenced, and to this portion of it, to remark, that no man could ever excel and reach eminence in eloquence without learning, not only the art of oratory, but every branch of useful knowledge.

II. For almost all other arts can support themselves independently, and by their own resources; but to speak well, that is, to speak with learning, and skill, and elegance, has no definite province within the limits of which it is inclosed and restricted. Every thing that can possibly fall under discussion among mankind must be effectively treated by him who professes that he can practice this art, or he must relinquish all title to eloquence. For my own part, therefore, though I confess that both in our own country and in Greece itself, which always held this art in the highest estimation, there have arisen many men of extraordinary powers, and of the highest excellence in speaking,[1] without this absolute knowledge of every thing; yet I affirm that such a degree of eloquence as was in Crassus and Antonius could not exist without a knowledge of all subjects that contribute to form that wisdom and that force of oratory which were seen in them. On this account, I had the greater satisfaction in committing to writing that dialogue which they formerly held on these subjects; both that the notion which had always prevailed, that the one had no great learning, and that the other was wholly unlearned, might be eradicated, and that I might preserve, in the records of literature, the opinions which I thought divinely delivered by those consummate orators concerning eloquence, if I could by any means learn and fully register them; and also, indeed, that I might, as far as I should be able, rescue their fame, now upon the decline, from silence and oblivion. If they could have been known from

[1] The words *cùm essemus ejusmodi* in this parenthesis, which all commentators regard as corrupt, are left untranslated.

[1] *Multos et ingeniis et magnâ laude dicendi.* This passage, as Ellendt observes, is manifestly corrupt. He proposes *ingeniis magnos et laude dicendi;* but this seems hardly Ciceronian. Aldus Manutius noticed that an adjective was apparently wanting to *ingeniis,* but other editors have passed the passage in silence.

writings of their own, I should, perhaps, have thought it less necessary for me to be thus elaborate; but as one left but little in writing (at least, there is little extant), and that he wrote in his youth,[1] the other almost nothing, I thought it due from me to men of such genius, while we still retain a lively remembrance of them, to render their fame, if I could, imperishable. I enter upon this undertaking with the greater hopes of effecting my object,[2] because I am not writing of the eloquence of Servius Galba or Caius Carbo, concerning which I should be at liberty to invent whatever I pleased, as no one now living could confute me; but I publish an account to be read by those who have frequently heard the men themselves of whom I am speaking, that I may commend those two illustrious men to such as have never seen either of them, from the recollection, as a testimony, of those to whom both those orators were known, and who are now alive and present among us.

III. Nor do I now aim at instructing you, dearest and best of brothers, by means of rhetorical treatises, which you regard as unpolished (for what can be more refined or graceful than your own language?); but though, whether it be, as you used to say, from judgment, or, as Isocrates, the father of eloquence, has written of himself, from a sort of bashfulness and ingenuous timidity, that you have shrunk from speaking in public, or whether, as you sometimes jocosely remark, you thought one orator sufficient, not only for one family, but almost for a whole community, I yet think that these books will not appear to you of that kind which may deservedly be ridiculed on account of the deficiency in elegant learning in those who have discussed the art of speaking; for nothing seems to me to be wanting in the conversation of Crassus and Antonius that any one could imagine possible to be known or understood by men of the greatest genius, the keenest application, the most consummate learning, and the utmost experience; as you will very easily be able to judge, who have been pleased to acquire the knowledge and theory of oratory through your own exertions, and to observe the practice of it in mine. But that we may the sooner accomplish the task which we have undertaken, and which is no ordinary one, let us leave our exordium, and proceed to the conversation and arguments of the characters whom I have offered to your notice.

The next day, then, after the former conversation had taken place, about the second hour,[1] while Crassus was yet in bed, and Sulpicius sitting by him, and Antonius walking with Cotta in the portico, on a sudden Quintus Catulus[2] the elder, with his brother Caius Julius,[3] arrived there; and when Crassus heard of their coming, he arose in some haste, and they were all in a state of wonder, suspecting that the occasion of their arrival was of more than common importance. The parties having greeted each other with most friendly salutations, as their intimacy required, "What has brought you hither at last?" said Crassus; "is it any thing new?" "Nothing, indeed," said Catulus; "for you know it is the time of the public games. But (you may think us, if you please," added he, "either foolish or impertinent) when Cæsar came yesterday in the evening to my Tusculan villa from his own, he told me that he had met Scævola going from hence; from whom he said that he had heard a wonderful account, namely, that you, whom I

---

[1] See Brut., c. 43, 44.

[2] *Spe aggredior majore ad probandum.* That *ad probandum* is to be joined with *spe,* not with *aggredior,* is shown by Ellendt on b. i., c. 4.

---

[1] The second hour of the morning, answering to our eight o'clock.

[2] The same that was consul with Caius Marius, when they obtained, in conjunction, the famous victory over the Cimbri.

[3] He was the brother of Quintus Catulus by the mother's side, and about twenty years his junior. The mother's name was Popilia. *Ellendt.* See c. 11. He was remarkable for wit, but his oratory is said to have wanted nerve. Brut., c. 48. Cicero, with great propriety, makes Sulpicius sit with Crassus, and Cotta walk with Antonius; for Sulpicius wished to resemble Crassus in his style of oratory; Cotta preferred the manner of Antonius. Brutus, c. 55.

could never entice into such conversation, though I endeavored to prevail on you in every way, had held long dissertations with Antonius on eloquence, and had disputed, as in the schools, almost in the manner of the Greeks; and my brother, therefore, entreated me, not being of myself, indeed, averse to hear you, but, at the same time, afraid we might make a troublesome visit to you, to come hither with him; for he said that Scævola had told him that a great part of the discourse was postponed till to-day. If you think we have acted too forwardly, you will lay the blame upon Cæsar; if too familiarly, upon both of us; for we are rejoiced to have come, if we do not give you trouble by our visit."

IV. Crassus replied, "Whatever object had brought you hither, I should rejoice to see at my house men for whom I have so much affection and friendship; but yet (to say the truth) I had rather it had been any other object than that which you mention. For I (to speak as I think) was never less satisfied with myself than yesterday; though this happened more through my own good-nature than any other fault of mine; for, while I complied with the request of these youths, I forgot that I was an old man, and did that which I had never done even when young; I spoke on subjects that depended on a certain degree of learning. But it has happened very fortunately for me, that, as my part is finished, you have come to hear Antonius." "For my part, Crassus," returned Cæsar, "I am indeed desirous to hear you in that kind of fuller and continuous discussion, yet so that, if I can not have that happiness, I can be contented with your ordinary conversation. I will therefore endeavor that neither my friend Sulpicius, nor Cotta, may seem to have more influence with you than myself, and will certainly entreat you to show some of your good-nature even to Catulus and me. But if you are not so inclined I will not press you, nor cause you, while you are afraid of appearing impertinent yourself, to think me impertinent." "Indeed, Cæsar," replied Crassus, "I have always thought of all Latin words there was the greatest significance in that which you have just used; for he whom we call *impertinent* seems to me to bear an appellation derived from *not being pertinent;* and that appellation, according to our mode of speaking, is of very extensive meaning; for whoever either does not discern what occasion requires, or talks too much, or is ostentatious of himself, or is forgetful either of the dignity or convenience of those in whose presence he is, or is in any respect awkward or presuming, is called *impertinent.* With this fault that most learned nation of the Greeks abounds; and, consequently, because the Greeks do not feel the influence of this evil, they have not even found a name for the foible; for, though you make the most diligent inquiry, you will not find out how the Greeks designate an *impertinent* person. But of all their other impertinences, which are innumerable, I do not know whether there be any greater than their custom of raising the most subtile disputations on the most difficult or unnecessary points, in whatever place, and before whatever persons they think proper. This we were compelled to do by these youths yesterday, though against our will, and though we at first declined."

V. "The Greeks, however, Crassus," rejoined Catulus, "who were eminent and illustrious in their respective states, as you are, and as we all desire to be, in our own republic, bore no resemblance to those Greeks who force themselves on our ears; yet they did not in their leisure avoid this kind of discourse and disputation. And if they seem to you, as they ought to seem, impertinent, who have no regard to times, places, or persons, does this place, I pray, seem ill adapted to our purpose, in which the very portico where we are walking, and this field of exercise, and the seats in so many directions, revive in some degree the remembrance of the Greek gymnasia and disputations? Or is the time unseasonable, during so much leisure as is seldom afforded us, and is now afforded at a season when it is most desirable? Or are the company unsuited to this kind of discussion, when we are all of such a character as to think that life is nothing without these studies?" "I contemplate all these things," said Crassus, "in a quite different light; for I think that even the Greeks themselves originally contrived their palæstræ, and seats, and porticoes for exercise and amusement, not for disputation; since their gymnasia were invented many generations before the philosophers began to prate in them; and at this very day, when the philosophers occupy all the gymnasia, their audience would still rather hear the discus than a philosopher; and as soon as it begins to sound, they all desert the philosopher in the middle of his discourse, though discussing matters of the utmost weight and consequence, to anoint themselves for exercise; thus preferring the lightest amusement to what the philosophers represent to be of the utmost utility. As to the leisure which you say we have, I agree with you; but the enjoyment of leisure is not exertion of mind, but relaxation.

VI. I have often heard from my father-in-law, in conversation, that his father-in-law Lælius was almost always accustomed to go into the country with Scipio, and that they used to grow incredibly boyish again when they had escaped out of town, as if from a prison, into the open fields. I scarcely dare to say it of such eminent persons, yet Scævola is in the habit of relating that they used to gather shells and pebbles at Caieta and Laurentum, and to descend to every sort of pastime and amusement. For such is the case, that as we see birds form and build nests for the sake of procreation and their own convenience, and, when they have completed any part, fly abroad in freedom, disengaged from their toils, in order to alleviate their anxiety, so our minds, wearied with legal business and the labors of the city, exult and long to flutter about, as it were, relieved from care and solicitude. In what I said to Scævola, therefore, in pleading for Curius,[1] I said only what I thought. 'For if,' said I, 'Scævola, no will shall be properly made but what is of your writing, all of us citizens will come to you with our tablets, and you alone shall write all our wills; but then,' continued I, 'when will you attend to public business? when to that of your friends? when to your own? when, in a word, will you do nothing?' adding, 'for he does not seem to me to be a free man who does not sometimes *do nothing;*' of which opinion, Catulus, I still continue; and, when I come hither, the mere privilege of doing nothing, and of being fairly idle, delights me. As to the third remark which you added, that you are of such a disposition as to think life insipid without these studies, that observation not only does not encourage me to any discussion, but even deters me from it. For as Caius Lucilius, a man of great learning and wit, used to say, that what he wrote he would neither wish to have read by the most illiterate persons, nor by those of the greatest learning, since the one sort understood nothing, and the other perhaps more than himself; to which purpose he also wrote, *I do not care to read Persius*[1] (for he was, as we know, about the most learned of all our countrymen); *but I wish to read Lœlius Decimus* (with whom we were also acquainted, a man of worth and of some learning, but nothing to Persius); so I, if I am now to discuss these studies of ours, should not wish to do so before peasants, but much less before you; for I had rather that my talk should not be understood than be censured."

VII. "Indeed, Catulus," rejoined Cæsar, "I think I have already gained some profit[2] by coming hither; for these reasons for declining a discussion have been to me a very agreeable discussion. But why do we delay Antonius, whose part is, I hear, to give a dissertation upon eloquence in general, and for whom Cotta and Sulpicius have been some time waiting?" "But I," interposed Crassus, "will neither allow Antonius to speak a word, nor will I utter a syllable myself, unless I first obtain one favor from you." "What is it?" said Catulus.

---

[1] In the speech which he made on behalf of Curius, on the occasion mentioned in book i., c. 39. *Proust.*

[1] A learned orator, who wrote in the time of the Gracchi, and who is mentioned by Cicero, Brut., c. 26. *Proust.* Of Decimus Lælius nothing is known. *Ellendt.*

[2] *Navâsse operam;* that is, *bene collocâsse.* Ernesti.

"That you spend the day here." Then, while Catulus hesitated, because he had promised to go to his brother's house, "I," said Julius, "will answer for both. We will do so; and you would detain me even in case you were not to say a single word." Here Catulus smiled, and said, "My hesitation, then, is brought to an end; for I had left no orders at home, and he at whose house I was to have been has thus readily engaged us to you, without waiting for my assent."

They then all turned their eyes upon Antonius, who cried out, "Be attentive, I say, be attentive, for you shall hear a man from the schools, a man from the professor's chair, deeply versed in Greek learning;[1] and I shall, on this account, speak with the greater confidence, that Catulus is added to the audience, to whom not only we of the Latin tongue, but even the Greeks themselves, are wont to allow refinement and elegance in the Greek language. But since the whole process of speaking, whether it be an art or a business, can be of no avail without the addition of assurance, I will teach you, my scholars, that which I have not learned myself, what I think of *every kind of speaking*." When they all laughed, "It is a matter that seems to me," proceeded he, "to depend very greatly on talent, but only moderately on art; for art lies in things which are known; but all the pleading of an orator depends not on knowledge, but on opinion; for we both address ourselves to those who are ignorant, and speak of what we do not know ourselves; and, consequently, our hearers think and judge differently at different times concerning the same subjects, and we often take contrary sides, not only so that Crassus sometimes speaks against me, or I against Crassus, when one of us must of necessity advance what is false, but even that each of us, at different times, maintains different opinions on the same question, when more than one of those opinions can not possibly be right. I will speak, therefore, as on a subject which is of a character to defend falsehood, which rarely arrives at knowledge,[1] and which is ready to take advantage of the opinions and even errors of mankind, if you think that there is still reason why you should listen to me."

VIII. "We think, indeed, that there is very great reason," said Catulus, "and the more so, as you seem resolved to use no ostentation; for you have commenced, not boastfully, but rather, as you think, with truth, than with any fanciful notion of the dignity of your subject." "As I have acknowledged, then," continued Antonius, "that it is not one of the greatest of arts, so I allow, at the same time, that certain artful directions may be given for moving the feelings and gaining the favor of mankind. If any one thinks proper to say that the knowledge how to do this is a great art, I shall not contradict him; for as many speakers speak upon causes in the forum without due consideration or method, while others, from study, or a certain degree of practice, do their business with more address, there is no doubt that, if any one sets himself to observe what is the cause why some speak better than others, he may discover that cause; and, consequently, he who shall extend such observation over the whole field of eloquence, will find in it, if not an art absolutely, yet something resembling an art. And I could wish that, as I seem to see matters as they occur in the forum, and in pleadings, so I could now set them before you just as they are conducted!

"But I must consider my own powers. I now assert only that of which I am convinced, that although oratory is not an art, no excellence is superior to that of a consummate orator. For, to say nothing of the advantages of eloquence, which has the highest influence in every well-ordered and free state, there is such delight attendant on the very power of eloquent speaking, that nothing more

[1] Ironically spoken.

[1] *Quœ ad scientiam non sœpe perveniat.* Ellendt incloses these words in brackets as spurious, regarding them as a gloss on the preceding phrase that has crept into the text. Their absence is desirable.

pleasing can be received into the ears or understanding of man. What music can be found more sweet than the pronunciation of a well-ordered oration? What poem more agreeable than the skillful structure of prose? What actor has ever given greater pleasure in imitating, than an orator gives in supporting, truth? What penetrates the mind more keenly than an acute and quick succession of arguments? What is more admirable than thoughts illumined by brilliancy of expression? What nearer to perfection than a speech replete with every variety of matter? for there is no subject susceptible of being treated with elegance and effect that may not fall under the province of the orator.

IX. It is his, in giving counsel on important affairs, to deliver his opinion with clearness and dignity; it is his to rouse a people when they are languid, and to calm them when immoderately excited. By the same power of language, the wickedness of mankind is brought to destruction, and virtue to security. Who can exhort to virtue more ardently than the orator? Who reclaim from vice with greater energy? Who can reprove the bad with more asperity, or praise the good with better grace? Who can break the force of unlawful desire by more effective reprehension? Who can alleviate grief with more soothing consolation? By what other voice, too, than that of the orator, is history, the evidence of time, the light of truth, the life of memory, the directress of life, the herald of antiquity, committed to immortality? For if there be any other art which professes skill in inventing or selecting words; if any one, besides the orator, is said to form a discourse, and to vary and adorn it with certain distinctions, as it were, of words and thoughts; or if any method of argument, or expression of thought, or distribution and arrangement of matter, is taught, except by this one art, let us confess that either that, of which this art makes profession, is foreign to it, or possessed in common with some other art. But if such method and teaching be confined to this alone, it is not, though professors of other arts may have spoken well, the less on that account the property of this art; but as an orator can speak best of all men on subjects that belong to other arts, if he makes himself acquainted with them (as Crassus observed yesterday), so the professors of other arts speak more eloquently on their own subjects, if they have acquired any instruction from this art; for if any person versed in agriculture has spoken or written with eloquence on rural affairs, or a physician, as many have done, on diseases, or a painter upon painting, his eloquence is not, on that account, to be considered as belonging to any of those arts; although in eloquence, indeed, such is the force of human genius, many men of every class and profession[1] attain some proficiency even without instruction; but, though you may judge what is peculiar to each art when you have observed what they severally teach, yet nothing can be more certain than that all other arts can discharge their duties without eloquence, but that an orator can not even acquire his name without it; so that other men, if they are eloquent, borrow something from him; while he, if he is not supplied from his own stores, can not obtain the power of speaking from any other art."

X. Catulus then said, "Although, Antonius, the course of your remarks ought by no means to be retarded by interruption, yet you will bear with me and grant me pardon; *for I can not help crying out,* as he in the Trinummus[2] says, so ably do you seem to me to have described the powers of the orator, and so copiously to have extolled them, as the eloquent man, indeed, must necessarily do; he must extol eloquence best of all men; for to praise it he has to employ the very eloquence which he praises. But proceed, for I agree with you, that to speak eloquently is all your own; and that, if any one does so on any other art, he employs an accomplishment borrowed from something else, not peculiar to him

---

[1] The reader will observe that the construction in the text is *multi omnium generum atque artium,* as Ellendt observes, referring to Matthiæ.

[2] iii., 2, 7.

or his own." "The night," added Crassus, "has made you polite to us, Antonius, and humanized you; for in yesterday's address to us,[1] you described the orator as a man that can do only one thing, like *a waterman or a porter,* as Cæcilius[2] says; a fellow void of all learning and politeness." "Why yesterday," rejoined Antonius, "I had made it my object, if I refuted you, to take your scholars from you;[3] but now, as Catulus and Cæsar make part of the audience, I think I ought not so much to argue against you as to declare what I myself think. It follows, then, that, as the orator of whom we speak is to be placed in the forum, and in the view of the public, we must consider what employment we are to give him, and to what duties we should wish him to be appointed. For Crassus[4] yesterday, when you, Catulus and Cæsar, were not present, made, in a few words, the same statement in regard to the division of the art that most of the Greeks have made; not expressing what he himself thought, but what was said by them; that there are two principal sorts of questions about which eloquence is employed—one indefinite, the other definite. He seemed to me to call that indefinite in which the subject of inquiry is general, as, *Whether eloquence is desirable; whether honors should be sought;* and that definite in which there is an inquiry with respect to particular persons, or any settled and defined point; of which sort are the questions agitated in the forum, and in the causes and disputes of private citizens. These appear to me to consist either in judicial pleadings, or in giving counsel; for that third kind, which was noticed by Crassus, and which, I hear, Aristotle[5] himself, who has fully illustrated these subjects, added, is, though it be useful, less necessary." "What kind do you mean?" said Catulus; "is it panegyric? for I observe that that is introduced as a third kind."

XI. "It is so," says Antonius; "and as to this kind of oratory, I know that I myself, and all who were present, were extremely delighted when your mother Popilia[1] was honored with a panegyric by you; the first woman, I think, to whom such honor was ever paid in this city. But it does not seem to me that all subjects on which we speak are to be included in art, and made subject to rules; for from those fountains, whence all the ornaments of speech are drawn, we may also take the ornaments of panegyric, without requiring elementary instructions; for who is ignorant, though no one teach him, what qualities are to be commended in any person? For if we but look to those things which Crassus has mentioned in the beginning of the speech which he delivered when censor in opposition to his colleague,[2] *That in those things which are bestowed on mankind by nature or fortune, he could contentedly allow himself to be excelled; but that in whatever men could procure for themselves, he could not suffer himself to be excelled,* he who would pronounce the panegyric of any person will understand that he must expatiate on the blessings of fortune; and these are advantages of birth, wealth, relationship, friends, resources, health, beauty, strength, talent, and such other qualities as are either personal, or dependent on circumstances; and, if he possessed these, he must show that he made a proper use of them; if not, that he managed wisely without them; if he lost them, that he bore the loss with resignation; he must then state what he whom he praises did or suffered with wisdom, or with liberality, or with fortitude, or with justice, or with honor, or with piety, or with gratitude, or with humanity, or, in a

---

[1] See b. i., c. 62.

[2] The writer of Comedies, *Vincere Cœcilius gravitate, Terentius arte.* Hor.

[3] I wished to refute you yesterday, that I might draw Scævola and Cotta from you. This is spoken in jest. *Proust.*

[4] B. i., c. 31.

[5] Rhet., i., 3, 1.

---

[1] See note on c. 3.

[2] Domitius Ahenobarbus. Plin., II. N., xvii., I.

word, under the influence of any virtue. These particulars, and whatever others are of similar kind, he will easily observe who is inclined to praise any person; and he who is inclined to blame him the contrary." "Why, then, do you hesitate," said Catulus, "to make this a third kind, since it is so in the nature of things? for if it is more easy than others, it is not, on that account, to be excluded from the number." "Because I am unwilling," replied Antonius, "to treat of all that falls under the province of an orator, as if nothing, however small it may be, could be uttered without regard to stated rules. Evidence, for instance, is often to be given, and sometimes with great exactness, as I was obliged to give mine against Sextus Titius,[1] a seditious and turbulent member of the commonwealth; when, in delivering my evidence, I explained all the proceedings of my consulate, in which I, on behalf of the commonwealth, opposed him as tribune of the people, and exposed all that I thought he had done contrary to the interest of the state; I was detained long, I listened to much, I answered many objections; but would you therefore wish, when you give precepts on eloquence, to add any instructions on giving evidence as a portion of the art of oratory?"

XII. "There is, indeed," said Catulus, "no necessity." "Or if (as often happens to the greatest men) communications are to be delivered, either in the senate from a commander in chief, or to such a commander, or from the senate to any king or people, does it appear to you that because, on such subjects, we must use a more accurate sort of language than ordinary, this kind of speaking should be counted as a department of eloquence, and be furnished with peculiar precepts?" "By no means," replied Catulus; "for an eloquent man, in speaking on subjects of that sort, will not be at a loss for that talent which he has acquired by practice on other matters and topics." "Those other kinds of subjects, therefore," continued Antonius, "which often require to be treated with eloquence, and which, as I said just now (when I was praising eloquence), belong to the orator, have neither any place in the division of the parts of oratory, nor fall under any peculiar kind of rules, and yet must be handled as eloquently as arguments in pleadings; such are reproof, exhortation, consolation, all which demand the finest graces of language; yet these matters need no rules from art." "I am decidedly of that opinion," said Catulus. "Well, then, to proceed," said Antonius, "what sort of orator, or how great a master of language, do you think it requires to write history?" "If to write it as the Greeks have written, a man of the highest powers," said Catulus; "if as our own countrymen, there is no need of an orator; it is sufficient for the writer to tell the truth." "But," rejoined Antonius, "that you may not despise those of our own country, the Greeks themselves too wrote at first just like our Cato, and Pictor, and Piso. For history was nothing else but a compilation of annals; and accordingly, for the sake of preserving the memory of public events, the pontifex maximus used to commit to writing the occurrences of every year, from the earliest period of Roman affairs to the time of the pontifex Publius Mucius, and had them engrossed on white tablets, which he set forth as a register in his own house, so that all the people had liberty to inspect it; and these records are yet called the Great Annals. This mode of writing many have adopted, and, without any ornaments of style, have left behind them simple chronicles of times, persons, places, and events. Such, therefore, as were Pherecydes, Hellanicus, Acusilas,[1] and many others among the Greeks, are Cato, and Pictor, and Piso with us, who neither understand how composition is to be adorned (for ornaments of style have

[1] A tribune of the people, A.U.C. 655, whom Antonius opposed about the Agrarian law. He is mentioned also in c. 66, and appears to be the same that is said to have played vigorously at ball, ii., 62; iii., 23. *Ellendt.* See also Cic., Brut., c. 62.

[1] Of these, Acusilas or Acusilaus, a native of Argos, was the most ancient, according to Suidas. *Ellendt.* The others are better known.

been but recently introduced among us), and, provided what they related can be understood, think brevity of expression the only merit. Antipater,[1] an excellent man, the friend of Crassus, raised himself a little, and gave history a higher tone; the others were not embellishers of facts, but mere narrators."

XIII. "It is," rejoined Catulus, "as you say; but Antipater himself neither diversified his narrative by variety of thoughts, nor polished his style by an apt arrangement of words, or a smooth and equal flow of language, but rough-hewed it as he could, being a man of no learning, and not extremely well qualified for an orator; yet he excelled, as you say, his predecessors." "It is far from being wonderful," said Antonius, "if history has not yet made a figure in our language; for none of our countrymen study eloquence, unless that it may be displayed in causes and in the forum; whereas among the Greeks, the most eloquent men, wholly unconnected with public pleading, applied themselves as well to other honorable studies as to writing history; for of Herodotus himself, who first embellished this kind of writing, we hear that he was never engaged in pleading; yet his eloquence is so great as to delight me extremely, as far as I can understand Greek writing. After him, in my opinion, Thucydides has certainly surpassed all historians in the art of composition; for he is so abundant in matter, that he almost equals the number of his words by the number of his thoughts; and he is so happy and judicious in his expressions,[2] that you are at a loss to decide whether his facts are set off by his style, or his style by his thoughts; and of him, too, we do not hear, though he was engaged in public affairs, that he was of the number of those who pleaded causes, and he is said to have written his books at a time when he was removed from all civil employments, and, as usually happened to every eminent man at Athens, was driven into banishment. He was followed by Philistus[1] of Syracuse, who, living in great familiarity with the tyrant Dionysius, spent his leisure in writing history, and, as I think, principally imitated Thucydides. But afterward, two men of great genius, Theopompus and Ephorus, coming from what we may call the noblest school of rhetoric, applied themselves to history by the persuasion of their master Isocrates, and never attended to pleading at all.

XIV. At last historians arose also among the philosophers; first Xenophon, the follower of Socrates, and afterward Callisthenes, the pupil of Aristotle and companion of Alexander. The latter wrote in an almost rhetorical manner; the former used a milder strain of language, which has not the animation of oratory, but, though perhaps less energetic, is, as it seems to me, much more pleasing. Timæus, the last of all these, but, as far as I can judge, by far the most learned, and abounding most with richness of matter and variety of thought, and not unpolished in style, brought a large store of eloquence to this kind of writing, but no experience in pleading causes."

When Antonius had spoken thus, "What is this, Catulus?" said Cæsar. "Where are they who say that Antonius is ignorant of Greek? how many historians has he named! and how learnedly and judiciously has he spoken of each!" "On my word," said Catulus, "while I wonder at this, I cease to wonder at what I regarded with much greater wonder before, namely, that he, being unacquainted with these matters, should have such power as a speaker." "But, Catulus," said Antonius, "my custom is to read these books, and some others, when I have leisure, not to hunt for any thing that may improve me in speaking, but for my own amusement. What profit is there from it, then? I own that

---

1 Lucius Cælius Antipater published a history of the Punic Wars, as Cicero says in his Orator, and was the master of Crassus, the speaker in these dialogues, as appears from Cic., Brut., c. 26. *Proust.*

2 *Aptus et pressus.* A *scriptor,* or *orator aptus,* will be one "structâ et rotundâ compositione verborum utens;" and *pressus* will be "in verborum circuitione nec superfluens nee claudicans." *Ellendt.*

1 He is called *Pusillus Thucydides* by Cicero, Ep. ad Q. Fratr., xii.

there is not much; yet there is some; for as, when I walk in the sun, though I may walk for another purpose, yet it naturally happens that I gain a deeper color; so, when I have read those books attentively at Misenum[1] (for at Rome I have scarcely opportunity to do so), I can perceive that my language acquires a complexion,[2] as it were, from my intercourse with them. But, that you may not take what I say in too wide a sense, I only understand such of the Greek writings as their authors wished to be understood by the generality of people. If I ever fall in with the philosophers, deluded by the titles to their books, as they generally profess to be written on well-known and plain subjects, as virtue, justice, probity, pleasure, I do not understand a single word of them, so restricted are they to close and exact disputations. The poets, as speaking in a different language, I never attempt to touch at all; but amuse myself, as I said, with those who have written history, or their own speeches,[3] or who have adopted such a style that they seem to wish to be familiar to us who are not of the deepest erudition."

• • •

XIX. "You are wrong, Catulus," said Antonius, "for I myself have met with many Phormios. Who, indeed, is there among those Greeks that seems to think any of us understand any thing? To me, however, they are not so very troublesome; I easily bear with and endure them all; for they either produce something which diverts me, or make me repent less of not having learned from them. I dismiss them less contumeliously than Hannibal dismissed the philosopher, and on that account, perhaps, have more trouble with them; but certainly all their teaching, as far as I can judge, is extremely ridiculous. For they divide the whole matter of oratory into two parts, the controversy about the cause and about the question. The cause they call the matter relating to the dispute or litigation affecting the persons concerned;[1] the question, a matter of infinite doubt. Respecting the cause they give some precepts; on the other part of pleading they are wonderfully silent. They then make five parts, as it were, of oratory; to invent what you are to say, to arrange what you have invented, to clothe it in proper language, then to commit it to memory, and at last to deliver it with due action and elocution; a task, surely, requiring no very abstruse study. For who would not understand without assistance that nobody can make a speech unless he has settled what to say, and in what words, and in what order, and remembers it? Not that I find any fault with these rules, but I say that they are obvious to all, as are likewise those four, five, six, or even seven partitions (since they are differently divided by different teachers) into which every oration is by them distributed; for they bid us adopt such an exordium as to make the hearer favorable to us, and willing to be informed and attentive; then to state our case in such a manner that the detail may be probable, clear, and concise; next, to divide or propound the question; to confirm what makes for us by arguments and reasoning, and refute what makes for the adversary; after this some place the conclusion of the speech, and peroration as it were; others direct you, before you come to the peroration, to make a digression by way of embellishment or amplification, then to sum up and conclude. Nor do I altogether condemn these divisions; for they are made with some

---

[1] A promontory of Campania, where Antonius had a country house.

[2] Ruhnken, in a note on Timæus's Lex., p. 78, expresses a suspicion that Cicero, when he wrote this, was thinking of a passage in Plato's Letters, Ep. vii., p. 718, F. *Greenwood.* Orellius very judiciously inserts *tactu,* the conjecture of Ernesti, in his text, instead of the old reading *cantu,* which, though Ellendt retains and attempts to defend it, can not be made to give any satisfactory sense.

[3] Cicero means orators. The speeches which historians have written are not given as their own, but put into the mouths of others. *Ellendt.*

[1] *Reorum.* This reading is very properly adopted by Orellius and Ellendt in place of the old *rerum.* Ellendt refers to c. 43 and 79 for the sense of *reus.*

nicety, though without sufficient judgment, as must of necessity be the case with men who had no experience in real pleading. For the precepts which they confine to the exordium and statement of facts are to be observed through the whole speech; since I can more easily make a judge favorable to me in the progress of my speech, than when no part of the cause has been heard; and desirous of information, not when I promise that I will prove something, but when I actually prove and explain; and I can best make him attentive, not by the first statement, but by working on his mind through the whole course of the pleading. As to their direction that the statement of facts should be probable, and clear, and concise, they direct rightly; but in supposing that these qualities belong more peculiarly to the statement of facts than to the whole of the speech, they seem to me to be greatly in error; and their whole mistake lies assuredly in this, that they think oratory an art or science, not unlike other sciences, such as Crassus said yesterday might be formed from the civil law itself; so that the general heads of the subject must first be enumerated, when it is a fault if any head be omitted; next, the particulars under each general head, when it is a fault if any particular be either deficient or redundant; then the definitions of all the terms, in which there ought to be nothing either wanting or superfluous.

XX. "But if the more learned can attain this exactness in the civil law, as well as in other studies of a small or moderate extent, the same can not, I think, be done in an affair of this compass and magnitude. If, however, any are of opinion that it can be done, they must be introduced to those who profess to teach these things as a science; they will find every thing ready set forth and complete; for there are books without number on these subjects, neither concealed nor obscure. But let them consider what they mean to do; whether they will take up arms for sport or for real warfare; for with us a regular engagement and field of battle require one thing, the parade and school of exercise another. Yet preparatory exercise in arms is of some use both to the gladiator and the soldier; but it is a bold and ready mind, acute and quick at expedients, that renders men invincible, and certainly not less effectively if art be united with it.

"I will now, therefore, form an orator for you, if I can, commencing so as to ascertain, first of all, what he is able to do. Let him have a tincture of learning; let him have heard and read something; let him have received those very instructions in rhetoric to which I have alluded. I will try what becomes him; what he can accomplish with his voice, his lungs, his breath, and his tongue. If I conceive that he may reach the level of eminent speakers, I will not only exhort him to persevere in labor, but, if he seem to me to be a good man,[1] will entreat him; so much honor to the whole community do I think that there is in an excellent orator, who is at the same time a good man. But if he shall appear likely, after he has done his utmost in every way, to be numbered only among tolerable speakers, I will allow him to act as he pleases, and not be very troublesome to him. But if he shall be altogether unfit for the profession, and wanting in sense, I will advise him to make no attempts, or to turn himself to some other pursuit. For neither is he, who can do excellently, to be left destitute of encouragement from us, nor is he, who can do some little, to be deterred; because one seems to be the part of a sort of divinity; the other, either to refrain from what you can not do extremely well, or to do what you can perform not contemptibly, is the part of a reasonable human being; but the conduct of the third character, to declaim in spite of decency and natural deficiency, is that of a man who, as you said, Catulus, of

---

[1] Cato defined an orator *vir bonus dicendi peritus.* Cicero in this passage, under the character of Antonius, and in his own person, De Inv., i., 3, 4, signifies that, though he thinks a good character of great importance in an orator, he does not deny that much eloquence may at times be found in a man of bad character. Cato and Cicero spoke each according to the character of his own age. Quintilian, xii., 1, goes back to the opinion of Cato. Aristotle had previously required good morals in an orator, Rhet., i., 2, 4; ii., 1, 5. *Ellendt.*

a certain haranguer, collects as many witnesses as possible of his folly by a proclamation from himself. Of him, then, who shall prove such as to merit our exhortation and encouragement, let me speak so as to communicate to him only what experience has taught myself, that, under my guidance, he may arrive at that point which I have reached without any guide; for I can give him no better instructions."

• • •

XXII. "Let this, then, be the first of my precepts, to point out to the student whom he should imitate, and in such a manner that he may most carefully copy the chief excellencies of him whom he takes for his model. Let practice then follow, by which he may represent in his imitation the exact resemblance of him whom he chose as his pattern; not as I have known many imitators do, who endeavor to acquire by imitation what is easy, or what is remarkable, or almost faulty; for nothing is easier than to imitate any person's dress, or attitude, or carriage; or if there is any thing offensive in a character, it is no very difficult matter to adopt it, and be offensive in the same way; in like manner as that Fusius, who even now, though he has lost his voice, rants on public topics, could never attain that nervous style of speaking which Caius Fimbria had, though he succeeds in imitating his distortion of features and broad prounciation; but he neither knew how to choose a pattern whom he would chiefly resemble, and in him that he did choose he preferred copying the blemishes. But he who shall act as he ought must first of all be very careful in making this choice, and must use the utmost diligence to attain the chief excellencies of him whom he has approved.

"What, let me ask, do you conceive to be the reason why almost every age has produced a peculiar style of speaking? a matter on which we can not so easily form a judgment in regard to the orators of our own country (because they have, to say the truth, left but few writings from which such judgment might be formed), as those of the Greeks, from whose writings it may be understood what was the character and tendency of eloquence in each particular age. The most ancient, of whom there are any works extant, are Pericles[1] and Alcibiades,[2] and, in the same age, Thucydides, writers perspicacious, pointed, concise, abounding more in thoughts than in words. It could not possibly have happened that they should all have the same character, unless they had proposed to themselves some one example for imitation. These were followed in order of time by Critias, Theramenes, and Lysias. There are extant many writings of Lysias, some of Critias;[3] of Theramenes[4] we only hear. They all still retained the vigorous style of Pericles, but had somewhat more exuberance. Then behold Isocrates arose, from whose school,[5] as from the Trojan horse, none but real heroes proceeded; but some of them were desirous to be distinguished on parade, some in the field of battle."

---

[1] Cicero, Brut., c. 7, says that some compositions were in circulation under the name of Pericles; and Quintilian, iii., 1, 12, looking to that observation of Cicero, tacitly assents to those who denied the genuineness of those compositions. See also Quint., x., 2, 22; 10, 49. *Ellendt.*

[2] That Alcibiades left nothing in writing, though he had great reputation as a speaker, seems to be rightly inferred by Ruhnken from Demosth., De Cor., c. 40. Thucydides is here mentioned among orators on account of the orations which he inserted in his history. *Ellendt.*

[3] He wrote not only orations, which are mentioned by Dionys. Halicarn., de Lysiâ jud., c. 2; cf. de Isæo, c. 2; by Phrynichus, ap. Phot., Cod. 158, and by others, but also tragedies, elegies, and other works. That he was eloquent and learned we are told by Cicero, De Or., iii., 34; Brut., c. 7. *Henrichsen.* The remains of his writings were collected by Bach, 1827. *Ellendt.*

[4] The eloquence of Theramenes is mentioned by Cicero, iii., 16; Brut., c. 7. The writings which Suidas enumerates as being his were doubtless spurious. See Ruhnken, Hist. Crit. Or. Gr., p. xl. *Ellendt.*

[5] The words *magister istorum omnium* which, though retained by Orellius, are pronounced spurious by Lambinus, Ernesti, Ruhnken, Schutz, and Ellendt, are left untranslated. "They can not be Cicero's words," says Ellendt, "even though they are found quoted by Nonius, p. 344."

• • •

XXIV. "But to conduct, at length, him whom we are forming to the management of causes, and those in which there is considerable trouble, judicial trials, and contested suits (somebody will perhaps laugh at the precept which I am going to give, for it is not so much sagacious as necessary, and seems rather to proceed from a monitor who is not quite a fool than from a master of profound learning), our first precept for him shall be, That, whatever causes he undertakes to plead, he must acquire a minute and thorough knowledge of them. This is not a precept laid down in the schools; for easy causes are given to boys. 'The law forbids a stranger to ascend the wall; he ascends it; he beats back the enemy; he is accused.' It is no trouble to understand such a cause as this. They are right, therefore, in giving no precepts about learning the cause; for such is generally the form of causes in the schools. But in the forum, wills, evidence, contracts, covenants, stipulations, relationship by blood, by affinity, decrees, opinions of lawyers, and even the lives and characters of those concerned in the cause, are all to be investigated; and by negligence in these particulars we see many causes lost, especially those relative to private concerns, as they are often of greater intricacy. Thus some, while they would have their business thought very extensive, that they may seem to fly about the whole forum, and to go from one cause to another, speak upon causes which they have not mastered, whence they incur much censure; censure for negligence if they voluntarily undertake the business, or for perfidiousness if they undertake it under any engagement;[1] but such censure is assuredly of worse consequence than they imagine, since nobody can possibly speak on a subject which he does not understand otherwise than to his own disgrace; and thus, while they despise the imputation of ignorance, which is in reality the greater fault, they incur that of stupidity also, which they more anxiously avoid.

"It is my custom to use my endeavor that every one of my clients may give me instructions in his own affairs himself, and that nobody else be present, so that he may speak with the greater freedom.[1] I am accustomed also to plead to him the cause of his adversary, in order to engage him to plead his own, and state boldly what he thinks of his own case. When he is gone, I conceive myself in three characters—my own, that of the adversary, and that of the judge. Whatever circumstance is such as to promise more support or assistance than obstruction, I resolve to speak upon it; wherever I find more harm than good, I set aside and totally reject that part entirely; and thus I gain this advantage, that I consider at one time what I shall say, and say it at another; two things which most speakers, relying upon their genius, do at one and the same time; but certainly those very persons would speak considerably better if they would but resolve to take one time for premeditation, and another for speaking.

"When I have acquired a thorough understanding of the business and the cause, it immediately becomes my consideration what ground there may be for doubt. For of all points that are disputed among mankind, whether the case is of a criminal nature, as concerning an act of violence; or controversial, as concerning an inheritance; or deliberative, as on going to war; or personal, as in panegyric; or argumentative, as on modes of life, there is nothing in which the inquiry is not either what has been done, or is being done, or will be done, or of what nature a thing is, or how it should be designated.

---

[1] *Magna offensio vel negligentiœ, susceptis rebus, vel perfidiœ, receptis. Recipere* is used with a reference to others, by whom we allow some duty to be laid upon us; *suscipere* regards only ourselves. *Ellendt.*

[1] *Inertia.* This passage puzzled Lambinus and others, who did not see how the reproach of *inertia* in an orator could be greater than that of *tarditas,* or stupidity. But *inertia* here signifies *artis ignorantia,* ignorance of his art, which is doubtless the greatest fault in an orator. *Verburg.*

• • •

XXVII. "But to return to my own method. When, after hearing and understanding the nature of a cause, I proceed to examine the subject-matter of it, I settle nothing until I have ascertained to what point my whole speech, bearing immediately on the question and case, must be directed. I then very diligently consider two other points; the one, how to recommend myself, or those for whom I plead; the other, how to sway the minds of those before whom I speak to that which I desire. Thus the whole business of speaking rests upon three things for success in persuasion: that we prove what we maintain to be true; that we conciliate those who hear; that we produce in their minds whatever feeling our cause may require. For the purpose of proof, two kinds of matter present themselves to the orator; one, consisting of such things as are not invented by him, but, as appertaining to the cause, are judiciously treated by him, as deeds, testimonies, covenants, contracts, examinations, laws, acts of the senate, precedents, decrees, opinions of lawyers, and whatever else is not found out by the orator, but brought under his notice by the cause and by his clients; the other, consisting entirely in the orator's own reasoning and arguments: so that, as to the former head, he has only to handle the arguments with which he is furnished; as to the latter, to invent arguments likewise. Those who profess to teach eloquence, after dividing causes into several kinds, suggest a number of arguments for each kind, which method, though it may be better adapted to the instruction of youth, in order that when a case is proposed to them they may have something to which they may refer, and from whence they may draw forth arguments ready prepared; yet it shows a slowness of mind to pursue the rivulets, instead of seeking for the fountain-head; and it becomes our age and experience to derive what we want to know from the source, and to ascertain the spring from which every thing proceeds.

"But that first kind of matters which are brought before the orator ought to be the constant subject of our contemplation for general practice in affairs of that nature. For in support of deeds and against them, for and against evidence, for and against examinations by torture, and in other subjects of that sort, we usually speak either of each kind in general and abstractedly, or as confined to particular occasions, persons, and causes; and such commonplaces (I speak to you, Cotta and Sulpicius) you ought to keep ready and prepared with much study and meditation. It would occupy too much time at present to show by what means we should confirm or invalidate testimony, deeds, and examinations. These matters are all to be attained with a moderate share of capacity, though with very great practice; and they require art and instruction only so far as they should be illustrated with certain embellishments of language. So also those which are of the other kind, and which proceed wholly from the orator, are not difficult of invention, but require perspicuous and correct exposition. As these two things, therefore, are the objects of our inquiry in causes, first, what we shall say, and, next, how we shall say it, the former, which seems to be wholly concerned with art, though it does indeed require some art, is yet an affair of but ordinary understanding, namely, to see what ought to be said; the latter is the department in which the divine power and excellence of the orator is seen; I mean in delivering what is to be said with elegance, copiousness, and variety of language."

• • •

XXIX. "For my part," said Catulus, "what I am accustomed most to admire in you both is, that while you are totally unlike each other in your manner of speaking, yet each of you speaks so well, that nothing seems either to have been denied you by nature, or not to have been bestowed on you by learning. You, therefore, Crassus, from your obliging disposition, will neither withhold from us the illustration of whatever may have been inadvertently or purposely omitted by Antonius; nor if you, Antonius, do not speak on every point, we shall think, not that you could not speak on it, but that you preferred that it should be treated by Crassus." Here Crassus said, "Do you rather, Antonius, omit those particulars which you have proposed to treat, and which no one here needs, namely, from what topics the statements made in pleadings are to be derived, which, though they would be treated by you in a new and excellent way, are in their nature very easy, and commonly set forth in books of rules; but show us those resources whence you draw that eloquence which you frequently exert, and always divinely." "I will indeed show you them," said Antonius; "and that I may the more easily obtain from you what I require, I will refuse you nothing that you ask. The supports of my whole eloquence, and that power of speaking which Crassus just now extolled to the skies, are, as I observed before, three processes; the first, that of conciliating my hearers; the second, that of instructing them; and the third, that of moving them. The first of these divisions requires mildness of address; the second penetration; the third energy; for it is impossible but that he, who is to determine a cause in our favor, must either lean to our side from propensity of feeling, or be swayed by the arguments of our defense, or be forced by action upon his mind. But since that part, in which the opening of the case itself and the defense lie, seems to comprehend all that is laid down as doctrine on this head, I shall speak on that first, and say but few words; for I seem to have but few observations gained from experience, and imprinted as it were on my memory.

XXX. "We shall willingly consent to your judicious proposal, Crassus, to omit those defenses for every sort of causes which the masters of rhetoric are accustomed to teach boys, and to open those sources whence all arguments for every cause and speech are derived. For neither, as often as we have occasion to write any word, need the letters of that word be so often collected in our thoughts; nor, as often as we are to plead a cause, need we turn to the separate arguments for that cause; but we should have certain commonplaces which, like letters for forming a word, immediately occur to us to aid in stating a cause. But these commonplaces can be of advantage only to that orator who is conversant in business, and has that experience which age at length brings with it; or one who has so much attention and power of thought as to anticipate age by study and diligence. For if you bring to me a man of ever so deep erudition, of ever so acute and subtile an intellect, or ever so ready an elocution, if he be a stranger to the customs of civil communities, to the examples, to the institutions, to the manners and inclinations of his fellow-citizens, the commonplaces from which arguments are drawn will be of little benefit to him. I must have a well-cultivated genius, like a field not once plowed only, but again and again, with renewed and repeated tillage, that it may produce better and larger crops; and the cultivation here required is experience, attentive hearing of other orators, reading, and writing.

"First, then, let him examine the nature of his cause, which is never obscure so far as the inquiry 'whether a thing has been done or not;' or 'of what nature it is;' or 'what name it should receive;' and when this is ascertained, it immediately occurs, with the aid of natural good sense, and not of those artifices which teachers of rhetoric inculcate, 'what constitutes the cause,' that is, the point without which there would be no controversy; then, 'what is the matter for trial,' which they direct you to ascertain in this manner: Opimius slew Gracchus: what constitutes the cause? 'That he slew him for the good of the republic, when he had called the people to arms, in consequence of a decree of the senate.' Set this point aside, and there will be no question for trial. But Decius denies that such a deed could be authorized contrary to the laws. The point therefore to be tried will be 'whether Opimius had authority to do so from the decree of the senate, for the good of the commonwealth.' These matters are indeed clear, and may be settled by common sense; but it remains to be considered what arguments, relative to the point for trial, ought to be advanced, as well by the accuser as by him who has undertaken the defense.

XXXI. "Here we must notice a capital error in those masters to whom we send our children; not that it has much to do with speaking, but that you may see how stupid and unpolished a set of men they are who imagine themselves learned. For, in distinguishing the different kinds of speaking, they make two species of causes. One they call 'that in which the question is about a general proposition, without reference to persons and times;' the other, 'that which is confined to certain persons and times;' being ignorant that all controversies must have relation to the force and nature of the general position; for in that very cause which I mentioned, the person of Opimius or Decius has nothing to do with the common arguments of the orator; since the inquiry has unrestricted reference to the question in general, 'whether he seems deserving of punishment who has slain a citizen under a decree of the senate for the preservation of his country, when such a deed was not permitted by the laws.' There is, indeed, no cause in which the point that falls under dispute is considered with reference to the parties to the suit, and not from arguments relating to such questions in general. But even in those very cases where the dispute is about a fact, as 'whether Publius Decius[1] has taken money contrary to law,' the arguments both for the accusation and for the defense must have reference to the general question, and the general nature of the case; as, to show that the defendant is expensive, the arguments must refer to luxury; that he is covetous of another's property, to avarice; that he is seditious, to turbulent and ill-designing citizens in general; that he is convicted by many proofs, to the general nature of evidence: and, on the other side, whatever is said for the defendant must of necessity be abstracted from the occasion and individual, and referred to the general notions of things and questions of the kind. These, perhaps, to a man who can not readily comprehend in his mind all that is in the nature of things, may seem extremely numerous to come under consideration when the question is about a single fact; but it is the number of charges, and not of modes of defense, or topics for them, that is infinite.[1]

[1] He was accused of having been bribed to bring Opimius to trial for having caused the death of Caius Gracchus. See Smith's Dict. of Biog. and Mythol., art. Decius, n. 4.

• • •

XXXIV. "This is indeed the end," continued Antonius, "of that part on which I just now entered; for it is now understood that all matters which admit of doubt are to be decided, not with reference to individuals, who are innumerable, or to occasions, which are infinitely various, but to general considerations and the nature of things; that general considerations are not only limited in number, but very few; that those who are studious of speaking should embrace in their minds the subjects peculiar to the several departments of eloquence, arranged under general heads, as well as arrayed and adorned, I mean with thoughts and illustrations. These will, by their own force, beget words, which always seem to me to be elegant enough, if they are such that the subject seems to have suggested them. And if you ask the truth (as far, that is, as it is apparent to me, for I can affirm nothing more than my own notions and opinions), we ought to carry this preparatory stock of general questions and commonplaces into the forum with us, and not, when any cause is brought before us, begin then to seek for topics from which we may draw our arguments; topics which, indeed, by all who have made them the subjects of but moderate consideration, may be thoroughly prepared by means of study and practice; but the thoughts must still revert to those general heads and commonplaces to which I have so often alluded, and from

[1] Innumerable accusations may be brought against a person, as against Verres by Cicero; but the *loci*, common topics or grounds, on which the attack or defense will rest (respecting, for instance, avarice, luxury, violence, treason), will be but few. *Ellendt.*

which all arguments are drawn for every species of oratory. All that is required, whether it result from art, or observation, or practice, is but to know those parts of the field in which you may hunt for, and trace out, what you wish to find; for when you have embraced in your thoughts the whole of any topic, if you are but well practiced in the treatment of subjects, nothing will escape you, and every circumstance material to the question will occur and suggest itself to you.

XXXV. "Since, then, in speaking, three things are requisite for finding argument—genius, method (which, if we please, we may call art), and diligence, I can not but assign the chief place to genius; yet diligence can raise even genius itself out of dullness; diligence, I say, which, as it avails in all things, is also of the utmost moment in pleading causes. Diligence is to be particularly cultivated by us; it is to be constantly exerted; it is capable of effecting almost every thing. That a cause is thoroughly understood, as I said at first, is owing to diligence; that we listen to our adversary attentively, and possess ourselves, not only of his thoughts, but even of his every word; that we observe all the motions of his countenance, which generally indicate the workings of the mind, is owing to diligence [but to do this covertly, that he may not seem to derive any advantage to himself, is the part of prudence];[1] that the mind ruminates on those topics which I shall soon mention, that it insinuates itself thoroughly into the cause, that it fixes itself on it with care and attention, is owing to diligence; that it applies the memory like a light, to all these matters, as well as the tone of voice and power of delivery, is owing to diligence. Betwixt genius and diligence there is very little room left for art; art only shows you where to look, and where that lies which you want to find; all the rest depends on care, attention, consideration, vigilance, assiduity, industry; all which I include in that one word which I have so often repeated, diligence; a single virtue, in which all other virtues are comprehended. For we see how the philosophers abound in copiousness of language, who, as I think (but you, Catulus, know these matters better), lay down no precepts of eloquence, and yet do not, on that account, the less undertake to speak with fullness and fluency on whatever subject is proposed to them."

XXXVI. Catulus then observed, "It is as you say, Antonius, that most philosophers deliver no precepts of eloquence, and yet are prepared with something to say on any subject. But Aristotle, he whom I admire more than any of them, has set forth certain topics from which every line of argument may be deduced, not only for the disputations of philosophy, but even for the reasoning which we use in pleading causes; from whose notions your discourse, Antonius, has for some time past not varied; whether you, from a resemblance to that divine genius, hit upon his track, or whether you have read and made yourself master of his writings—a supposition, indeed, which seems to be more probable than the other, for I see that you have paid more attention to the Greek writers than we had imagined." "You shall hear from myself," said he, "Catulus, what is really the case: I always thought that an orator would be more agreeable to the Roman people, and better approved, who should give, above all, as little indication as possible of artifice, and none at all of having studied Grecian literature. At the same time, when the Greeks undertook, professed, and executed such great things, when they offered to teach mankind how to penetrate the most obscure subjects, to live virtuously and to speak eloquently, I thought it the part of an irrational animal rather than a man not to pay them some degree of attention, and, if we can not venture to hear them openly, for fear of diminishing our authority with our own fellow-citizens, to catch their words at least by listening privately, and hearkening at a distance to what they stated; and thus I have acted, Catulus, and have gained a general notion of the arguments and subjects of all their writers."

• • •

[1] The words in brackets are regarded by all the best critics as the production of some interpolator.

XXXVIII. "But that our conversation may return to the point from which it digressed, do you observe that of those three illustrious philosophers, who, as you said, came to Rome, one was Diogenes, who professed to teach the art of reasoning well, and distinguishing truth from falsehood, which he called by the Greek name *διαλεκτική*, or logic? In this art, if it be an art, there are no directions how truth may be discovered, but only how it may be judged. For every thing of which we speak we either affirm to be or not to be;[1] and if it be expressed absolutely, the logicians take it in hand to judge whether it be true or false; or, if it be expressed conditionally, and qualifications are added, they determine whether such qualifications are rightly added, and whether the conclusion of each syllogism is true; and at last they torment themselves with their own subtilties, and, after much disquisition, find out not only what they themselves can not resolve, but even arguments, by which what they had before begun to resolve, or rather had almost made clear, is again involved in obscurity. Here, then, that Stoic[2] can be of no assistance to me, because he does not teach me how to find out what to say; he is rather even an impediment to me; for he finds many difficulties which he says can by no means be cleared, and unites with them a kind of language that is not clear, easy, and fluent, but poor, dry, succinct, and concise; and if any one shall approve of such a style, he will approve it with the acknowledgment that it is not suited to the orator. For our mode of speaking is to be adapted to the ear of the multitude, to fascinate and excite their minds, and to prove matters that are not weighed in the scales of the goldsmith, but in the balance, as it were, of popular opinion; we may therefore entirely dismiss an art which is too silent about the invention of arguments, and too full of words in pronouncing judgment on them. That Critolaus, whom you mention as having come hither with Diogenes, might, I fancy, have been of more assistance to our studies, for he was out of the school of that Aristotle from whose method I seem to you not greatly to differ. Between this Aristotle (of whom I have read, as well that book in which he explains the rhetorical systems of all who went before him, as those in which he gives us some notions of his own on the art), between him, I say, and the professed teachers of the art, there appeared to me to be this difference: that he, with the same acuteness of intellect with which he had penetrated the qualities and nature of things throughout the universe, saw into every thing that pertained to the art of rhetoric, which he thought beneath him; but they, who thought this art alone worthy of cultivation, passed their whole lives in contemplating this one subject, not with as much ability as he, but with constant practice in their single pursuit, and greater devotion to it. As to Carneades, that extraordinary force and variety of eloquence which he possessed would be extremely desirable for us; a man who never took up any argument in his disputations which he did not prove; never attacked any argument that he did not overthrow. But this is too arduous an accomplishment to be expected from those who profess and teach rhetoric.

XXXIX. "If it were my desire that a person totally illiterate should be instructed in the art of speaking, I would willingly send him to these perpetual workers at the same employment, who hammer day and night on the same anvil, and who would put his literary food into his mouth, in the smallest pieces, minced as fine as possible, as nurses put theirs into the mouths of children. But if he were one who had had a liberal education, and some degree of practice, and seemed to have some acuteness of genius, I would instantly conduct him, not where a little brook of water was confined by itself, but to the source whence a whole flood gushed forth; to an instructor who would show him the seats and abodes, as it were, of every sort of arguments, and would illustrate

[1] In this passage I adopt the correction, or rather restoration, of Ellendt, *Nam et omne, quod eloquimur, fit, ut id aut esse dicamus aut non esse.* All other modern editions for *fit* have *sic*.

[2] Diogenes, and other Stoics like him. *Proust.*

them briefly, and define them in proper terms. For what point is there in which he can hesitate, who shall see that whatever is assumed in speaking, either to prove or to refute, is either derived from the peculiar force and nature of the subject itself, or borrowed from something foreign to it? From its own peculiar force: as when it is inquired, 'what the nature of a whole thing is,' or 'a part of it,' or 'what name it has,' or whatever belongs to the whole matter. From what is foreign to it: as when circumstances which are extrinsic, and not inherent in the nature of the thing, are enumerated in combination. If the inquiry regard the whole, its whole force is to be explained by a definition, thus: 'If the majesty of a state be its greatness and dignity, he is a traitor to its majesty who delivers up an army to the enemies of the Roman people, not he who delivers up him who has violated it into the power of the Roman people.' But if the question respect only a part, the matter must be managed by partition in this manner: 'Either the senate should have been obeyed concerning the safety of the republic, or some other authority should have been constituted, or he should have acted on his own judgment: to constitute another authority had been haughty; to act on his own judgment had been arrogant; he had therefore to obey the direction of the senate.' If we argue from a name, we may express ourselves like Carbo: 'If he be a consul who consults the good of his country, what else has Opimius done?' But if we argue from what is intimately connected with the subject, there are many sources of arguments and commonplaces; for we shall look to adjuncts, to general views, to particulars falling under general views, to things similar and dissimilar, contrary, consequential; to such as agree with the case, and are, as it were, forerunners of it, and such as are at variance with it; we shall investigate the causes of circumstances, and whatever has arisen from those causes; and shall notice cases that are stronger, or similar, or weaker.

• • •

XLI. "I have been as brief in the exemplification of these matters as their nature would permit. For as, if I wished to make known to any one a quantity of gold, that was buried in separate heaps, it ought to be sufficient if I told him the signs and marks of the places, with the knowledge of which he might dig for himself, and find what he wished with very little trouble, and without any mistake; so I wished to specify such marks, as it were, of arguments, as would let him who seeks them know where they are;[1] what remains is to be brought out by industry and thought. What kind of arguments is most suitable to any particular kind of cause it requires no exquisite skill to prescribe, but merely moderate capacity to determine. For it is not now my design to set forth any system of rhetoric, but to communicate to men of eminent learning some hints drawn from my own experience. These commonplaces, therefore, being fixed in the mind and memory, and called forth on every subject proposed to be discussed, there will be nothing that can escape the orator, not merely in matters litigated in the forum, but in any department of eloquence whatever. But if he shall attain such success as to seem to be what he would wish to seem, and to affect the minds of those before whom he pleads in such a manner as to lead or rather force them in whatever direction he pleases, he will assuredly require nothing else to render him accomplished in oratory.

"We now see that it is by no means sufficient to find out what to say, unless we can handle it skillfully when we have found it. This treatment ought to be diversified, that he who listens may neither discover any artifice, nor be tired and satiated with uniformity. Whatever you advance should be laid down as a proposition, and you

---

[1] I follow Ellendt's text: *Sic has ego argumentorum volui notas quœrenti demonstrare ubi sint.* Orellius and most other editors have *Sic has ego argumentorum novi notas, quœ illa mihi quœrenti demonstrant,* "sententiâ perineptâ," as Ellendt observes; for it was not what Antonius himself knew that was to be specified, but how he wished learners to be assisted.

should show why it is so; and, from the same premises, you should sometimes form a conclusion, and sometimes leave it to be formed by the hearer, and make a transition to something else. Frequently, however, you need make no proposition, but show, by the reasoning which you shall use, what proposition might have been made. If you produce a comparison to any thing, you should first confirm what you offer as a comparison, and then apply to it the point in question. In general, you should shade the distinctive points of your arguments so that none of your hearers may count them; and that, while they appear clear as to matter, they may seem blended in your mode of speaking on them.

XLII. "I run over these matters cursorily, as addressing men of learning, and, being myself but half-learned, that we may at length arrive at matters of greater consequence. For there is nothing, Catulus, of more importance in speaking than that the hearer should be favorable to the speaker, and be himself so strongly moved that he may be influenced more by impulse and excitement of mind than by judgment or reflection. For mankind make far more determinations through hatred, or love, or desire, or anger, or grief, or joy, or hope, or fear, or error, or some other affection of mind, than from regard to truth, or any settled maxim, or principle of right, or judicial form, or adherence to the laws. Unless any thing else, therefore, be agreeable to you, let us proceed to consider these points."

"There seems," observed Catulus, "to be still some little wanting to those matters which you have discussed, Antonius, something that requires to be explained before you proceed to what you propose." "What is it?" asked Antonius. "What order," replied Catulus, "and arrangement of arguments, has your approbation; for in that department you always seem a god to me." "You may see how much of a god I am in that respect, Catulus," rejoined Antonius, "for I assure you the matter would never have come into my thoughts if I had not been reminded of it; so that you may suppose I am generally led by mere practice in speaking, or rather perhaps by chance, to fix on that arrangement of matter by which I seem at times to produce some effect. However, that very point which I, because I had no thought of it, passed by as I should by a person unknown to me, is of such efficacy in oratory that nothing is more conducive to victory; but yet you seem to me to have required from me prematurely an account of the order and disposition of the orator's material; for if I had placed all his power in argumentation, and in proving his case from its own inherent merits, it might be time to say something on the order and arrangement of his arguments; but as three heads were specified by me, and I have spoken on only one, it will be proper, after I have attended to the other two, to consider, last of all, about the general arrangement of a speech.

XLIII. "It contributes much to success in speaking that the morals, principles, conduct, and lives of those who plead causes, and of those for whom they plead, should be such as to merit esteem, and that those of their adversaries should be such as to deserve censure; and also that the minds of those before whom the cause is pleaded should be moved as much as possible to a favorable feeling, as well toward the speaker as toward him for whom he speaks. The feelings of the hearers are conciliated by a person's dignity, by his actions, by the character of his life; particulars which can more easily be adorned by eloquence if they really exist, than be invented if they have no existence. But the qualities that attract favor to the orator are a soft tone of voice, a countenance expressive of modesty, a mild manner of speaking; so that if he attacks any one with severity, he may seem to do so unwillingly and from compulsion. It is of peculiar advantage that indications of good-nature, of liberality, of gentleness, of piety, of grateful feelings, free from selfishness and avarice, should appear in him; and every thing that characterizes men of probity and humility, not acrimonious, nor pertinacious, nor litigious, nor harsh, very much conciliates benevolence, and alienates the affections from those in whom such qualities are not apparent. The contrary qualities to these, therefore, are to be imputed to your opponents. This mode of address is extremely excellent in those causes in which the mind of the judge can not well be inflamed by ardent and vehement incitation; for energetic oratory is not always desirable, but often smooth, submissive, gentle language, which gains much favor for *rei,* or defendants, a term by which I designate not only such as are accused, but all persons about whose affairs there is any litigation; for in that sense people formerly used the word. To describe the character of your clients in your speeches, therefore, as just, full of integrity, religious, unpresuming, and patient of injuries, has an extraordinary effect; and such a description, either in the commencement, or in your statement of facts, or in the peroration, has so much influence, if it is agreeably and judiciously managed, that it often prevails more than the merits of the cause. Such influence, indeed, is produced by a certain feeling and art in speaking, that the speech seems to represent, as it were, the character of the speaker; for, by adopting a peculiar mode of thought and expression, united with action that is gentle and indicative of amiableness, such an effect is produced that the speaker seems to be a man of probity, integrity, and virtue.

XLIV. "To this mode of speaking we may subjoin the opposite method, which moves the minds of the judges by very different means, and impels them to hate, or love, or envy, or benevolence, or fear, or hope, or desire, or abhorrence, or joy, or grief, or pity, or severity; or leads them to whatever feelings resemble and are allied to these and similar emotions of mind. It is desirable, too, for the orator, that the judges may voluntarily bring to the hearing of the cause some feelings in their breasts favorable to the object of the speaker. For it is easier, as they say, to increase the speed of him that is already running, than to excite to motion him that is torpid. But if such shall not be the case, or be somewhat doubtful, then, as a careful physician, before he proceeds to administer any medicine to a patient, must not only understand the disease of him whom he would cure, but also his habit and constitution of body when in health, so I, for my part, when I undertake a cause of such doubt and importance as is likely to excite the feelings of the judges, employ all my sagacity on the care and consideration of ascertaining, as skillfully as I can, what their sentiments and opinions are, what they expect, to which side they incline, and to what conclusion they are likely to be led, with the least difficulty, by the force of oratory. If they yield themselves up, and, as I said before, voluntarily incline and preponderate to the side to which I would impel them, I embrace what is offered, and turn my sails to that quarter from whence any breath of wind is perceived to blow. But if the judge is unbiased, and free from all passion, it is a work of greater difficulty; for every feeling must then be moved by the power of oratory, without any assistance from nature. But so great are the powers of that which was rightly termed by a good poet,[1]

> *"Incliner of the soul, and queen of all things,"*

Eloquence, that it can not only make him upright who is biased, or bias him who is steadfast, but can, like an able and resolute commander, lead even him captive who resists and opposes.

XLV. "These are the points about which Crassus just now jocosely questioned me when he said that I treated them divinely, and praised what I did as being meritoriously done in the causes of Manius Aquilius,[2] Caius Norbanus,[3] and some others; but really, Crassus, when such arts are adopted by you in pleading, I used to feel terrified; such power of mind, such impetuosity, such passion, is expressed in your eyes, your countenance, your gesture, and even in your very finger;[4] such a

---

[1] Pacuvius in his Hermione, as appears from Nonius v. *flexanima.* The thought is borrowed from Euripides, Hec., 816. *Ellendt.*

[2] See note on c. 28.

[3] See note on c. 47.

[4] The forefinger, which Crassus is said to have pointed with wonderful effect. See Quintilian, xi., 3, 94.

torrent is there of the most emphatic and best chosen words, such noble thoughts, so just, so new, so free from all disguise or puerile embellishment, that you seem not only to me to fire the judge, but to be yourself on fire. Nor is it possible that the judge should feel concern, or hate, or envy, or fear in any degree, or that he should be moved to compassion and tears, unless all these sensations which the orator would awaken in the judge shall appear to be deeply felt and experienced by the orator himself. For if a counterfeit passion were to be assumed, and if there were nothing in a speech of that kind but what was false and simulated, still greater art would perhaps be necessary. What is the case with you, however, Crassus, or with others, I do not know; as to myself, there is no reason why I should say what is false to men of your great good sense and friendship for me—I never yet, upon my honor, tried to excite sorrow, or compassion, or envy, or hatred, when speaking before a court of judicature, but I myself, in rousing the judges, was affected with the very same sensations that I wished to produce in them. For it is not easy to cause the judge to be angry with him with whom you desire him to be angry, if you yourself appear to take the matter coolly; or to make him hate him whom you wish him to hate, unless he first see you burning with hatred; nor will he be moved to pity unless you give him plain indications of your own acute feelings by your expressions, sentiments, tone of voice, look, and, finally, by sympathetic tears; for as no fuel is so combustible as to kindle without the application of fire, so no disposition of mind is so susceptible of the impressions of the orator as to be animated to strong feeling unless he himself approach it full of inflammation and ardor.

XLVI. "And that it may not appear to you extraordinary and astonishing that a man should so often be angry, so often grieve, and be so often excited by every passion of the mind, especially in other men's concerns, there is such force, let me assure you, in those thoughts and sentiments which you apply, handle, and discuss in speaking, that there is no occasion for simulation or deceit; for the very nature of the language which is adopted to move the passions of others moves the orator himself in a greater degree than any one of those who listen to him. That we may not be surprised, too, that this happens in causes, in criminal trials, in the danger of our friends, and before a multitude in the city and in the forum, where not only our reputation for ability is at stake (for that might be a slight consideration; although, when you have professed to accomplish what few can do, it is not wholly to be neglected), but where other things of greater importance are concerned, fidelity, duty to our clients, and earnestness in discharging that duty; we are so much moved by such considerations, that even while we defend the merest strangers we can not regard them as strangers, if we wish to be thought honest men ourselves. But, as I said, that this may not appear surprising in us, what can be more fictitious than poetry, than theatrical representations, than the argument of a play? Yet on the stage I myself have often observed the eyes of the actor, through his mask, appear inflamed with fury while he was repeating these verses,[1]

> "Have you, then, dared to separate him from you,
> Or enter Salamis without your brother?
> And dreaded not your father's countenance?"

He never uttered the word 'countenance' but Telamon seemed to me to be distracted with rage and grief for his son. And how, lowering his voice to a tone of sorrow, did he appear to weep and bewail, as he exclaimed,

> "Whom childless now in the decline of life
> You have afflicted, and bereaved, and killed;
> Regardless of your brother's death, regardless

---

[1] *Spondalia.* For this word I have given "verses." "That it is corrupt," says Ellendt, "all the commentators agree." Hermann, Opusc., i., p. 304, conjectures *è spondâ illâ,* "from that couch," on which he supposes Telamon may have been reclining.

> Of his young son intrusted to your
> keeping!"

And if even the player who pronounced these verses every day could not yet pronounce them efficiently without a feeling of real grief, can you suppose that Pacuvius, when he wrote them, was in a cool and tranquil state of mind? Such could not be the case; for I have often heard that no man can be a good poet (as they say is left recorded in the writings of both Democritus and Plato) without ardor of imagination, and the excitement of something similar to phrensy."

• • •

L. "In good truth, Antonius," interposed Sulpicius, "you recall these circumstances to my memory with justice, since I never saw any thing slip out of any person's hands as that cause then slipped out of mine. For whereas, as you observed, I had given you not a cause to plead, but a flame to extinguish; what a commencement was it (immortal gods!) that you made! What timidity was there! What distrust! What a degree of hesitation and slowness of speech! But, as soon as you had gained that by your exordium, which was the only thing that the assembly allowed you as an excuse, namely, that you were pleading for a man intimately connected with you, and your own quæstor, how quickly did you secure your way to a fair audience! But lo! when I thought that you had reaped no other benefit than that the hearers would think they ought to excuse you for defending a pernicious citizen, on account of the ties of union betwixt you, you began to proceed gradually and tacitly, while others had as yet no suspicion of your designs, though I myself felt some apprehension, to maintain in your defense that what had happened was not sedition in Norbanus, but resentment on the part of the Roman people, resentment not excited unjustly, but deservedly, and in conformity with their duty. In the next place, what argument did you omit against Cæpio? How did you confound all the circumstances of the case by allusions to hatred, ill-will, and compassion? Nor was this the case only in your defense, but even in regard to Scaurus and my other witnesses, whose evidence you did not confute by disproving it, but by having recourse to the same impetuosity of the people. When those circumstances were mentioned by you just now, I felt no desire for any rules of instruction; for the very demonstration of your methods of defense, as stated by yourself, I regard as no ordinary instruction." "But if you are so disposed," said Antonius, "I will tell you what maxims I adopt in speaking, and what I keep principally in view; for a long life and experience in important affairs have taught me to discern by what means the minds of men are to be moved.

LI. "The first thing I generally consider is whether the cause requires that the minds of the audience should be excited; for such fiery oratory is not to be exerted on trivial subjects, nor when the minds of men are so affected that we can do nothing by eloquence to influence their opinions, lest we be thought to deserve ridicule or dislike, if we either act tragedies about trifles or endeavor to pluck up what can not be moved. For as the feelings on which we have to work in the minds of the judges, or whoever they may be before whom we may plead, are *love, hatred, anger, envy, pity, hope, joy, fear, anxiety,* we are sensible that *love* may be gained if you seem to advocate what is advantageous to the persons before whom you are speaking; or if you appear to exert yourself in behalf of good men, or at least for such as are good and serviceable to them; for the latter case more engages favor, the former, the defense of virtue, esteem; and if a hope of future advantage is proposed, it has a greater effect than the mention of past benefits. You must endeavor to show that in the cause which you defend, either your dignity or advantage is concerned; and you should signify that he for whom you solicit their love has referred nothing to his own private benefit, and done nothing at all for his own sake; for dislike is felt for the selfish gains of individuals, while favor is shown to their desires to serve others. But we must take care, while we are on this topic, not to appear to extol the merit and glory of those whom we would wish to be esteemed for their good deeds, too highly, as these qualities are usually the greatest objects of envy. From these considerations, too, we shall learn how to draw *hatred* on our adversaries, and to avert it from ourselves and our friends. The same means are to be used, also, either to excite or allay *anger;* for if you exaggerate every fact that is hurtful or disadvantageous to the audience, their hatred is excited; but if any thing of the kind is thrown out against men of worth, or against characters on whom no one ought to cast any reflection, or against the public, there is then produced, if not so violent a degree of hatred, at least an unfavorable feeling, or displeasure near akin to hatred. *Fear* is also inculcated either from people's own dangers or those of the public. Personal fear affects men more deeply; but that which is common to all is to be treated by the orator as having similar influence.[1]

LII. "Similar, or rather the same, is the case with regard to *hope, joy,* and *anxiety;* but I know not whether the feeling of *envy* is not by far the most violent of all emotions; nor does it require less power to suppress than to excite it. Men envy chiefly their equals or inferiors when they perceive themselves left behind, and are mortified that the others have outstripped them; but there is often a strong unfavorable feeling toward superiors, which is the stronger if they are intolerably arrogant, and transgress the fair bounds of common justice through super-eminence in dignity or fortune. If such advantages are to be made instruments to kindle dislike,[2] the chief thing to be said is, 'that they are not the acquisitions of virtue, that they have been gained perhaps by vice and crime; and that, however honorable or imposing they may appear, no merit was ever carried so high as the insolence of mankind and their contumelious disdain.' To allay envy, it may be observed, 'that such advantages have been gained by extreme toil and imminent perils; that they have not been applied to the individual's own private benefit, but that of others; that he himself, if he appear to have gained any glory, although it might not be an undue reward for danger, was not elated with it, but wholly set it aside and undervalued it;' and such an effect must by all means be produced (since most men are envious, and it is a most common and prevalent vice, and envy is felt toward all super-eminent and flourishing fortune), that the opinion entertained of such characters be lowered, and that their fortunes, so excellent in people's imaginations, may appear mingled with labor and trouble.

"*Pity* is excited if he who hears can be induced to apply to his own circumstances those unhappy particulars which are lamented in the case of others, particulars which they have either suffered or fear to suffer; and while he looks at another, to glance frequently at himself. Thus, as all the circumstances incident to human suffering are heard with concern, if they are pathetically represented, so virtue in affliction and humiliation is the most powerful of all objects of contemplation; and as that other department of eloquence which, by its recommendation of goodness, ought to give the picture of a virtuous man, should be in a gentle and (as I have often observed) a submissive strain, so this, which is adopted by the orator to effect a change in the minds of the audience, and to work upon them in every way, should be vehement and energetic.

• • •

LXXVI. "I now return therefore to that point, Catulus, on which you a little while ago accorded me praise; the order and arrangement of facts and topics of argument. On this head, two methods may be observed; one, which the nature of causes dictates; the other, which is suggested by the orator's judgment and prudence. For, to premise something before we come to the main point; then to explain the matter in question; then

---

[1] Since public or common fear must affect individuals.

[2] *Quæ si inflammanda sunt.* An elegant mode of expression, for "si ad animos invidiâ inflammandos adhibenda sunt tanquam faces." *Ernesti.*

to support it by strengthening our own arguments, and refuting those on the other side; next, to sum up, and come to the peroration, is a mode of speaking that nature herself prescribes. But to determine how we should arrange the particulars that are to be advanced in order to prove, to inform, to persuade, more peculiarly belongs to the orator's discretion. For many arguments occur to him; many, that seem likely to be of service to his pleading; but some of them are so trifling as to be utterly contemptible; some, if they are of any assistance at all, are sometimes of such a nature, that there is some defect inherent in them; while that which appears to be advantageous, is not of such import that it need be advanced in conjunction with any thing prejudicial. And as to those arguments which are to the purpose, and deserving of trust, if they are (as it often happens) very numerous, I think that such of them as are of least weight, or as are of the same tendency with others of greater force, ought to be set aside, and excluded altogether from our pleading. I myself, indeed, in collecting proofs, make it a practice rather to weigh than to count them.

LXXVII. "Since, too, as I have often observed, we bring over people in general to our opinions by three methods, by instructing their understandings, conciliating their benevolence, or exciting their passions, one only of these three methods is to be professed by us, so that we may appear to desire nothing else but to instruct; the other two, like blood throughout the body, ought to be diffused through the whole of our pleading; for both the beginning, and the other parts of a speech, on which we will by-and-by say a few words, ought to have this power in a great degree, so that they may penetrate the minds of those before whom we plead, in order to excite them. But in those parts of the speech which, though they do not convince by argument, yet by solicitation and excitement produce great effect, though their proper place is chiefly in the exordium and the peroration, still, to make a digression from what you have proposed and are discussing, for the sake of exciting the passions, is often advantageous. Since, after the statement of the case has been made, an opportunity often presents itself of making a digression to rouse the feelings of the audience; or this may be properly done after the confirmation of our own arguments, or the refutation of those on the other side, or in either place, or in all, if the cause has sufficient copiousness and importance; and those causes are the most considerable, and most pregnant with matter for amplification and embellishment, which afford the most frequent opportunities for that kind of digression in which you may descant on those points by which the passions of the audience are either excited or calmed. In touching on this matter, I can not but blame those who place the arguments to which they trust least in the front; and, in like manner, I think that they commit an error who, if ever they employ several advocates (a practice which never had my approbation), will have him to speak first in whom they confide least, and rank the others also according to their abilities.[1] For a cause requires that the expectations of the audience should be met with all possible expedition; and if nothing to satisfy them be offered in the commencement, much more labor is necessary in the sequel; for that case is in a bad condition which does not at the commencement of the pleading at once appear to be the better. For this reason, as, in regard to pleaders,[2] he who is the most able should speak first, so in regard to a speech, let the arguments of most weight be put foremost; yet so that this rule be observed with respect to both, that some of superior efficiency be reserved for the peroration; if any are but of moderate strength (for to the weak no place should be given at all), they may be thrown into the main body and into the midst of the group. All these things

---

[1] *Ut in quoque eorum minimum putant esse, ita eum primum volunt dicere.* "As in each of them they think that there is least, so they wish him to speak first."

[2] *Ut in oratore.* Schutz conjectures *in oratoribus,* but he had better, as Ellendt observes, have conjectured *ex oratoribus.* But the text may be correct.

being duly considered, it is then my custom to think last of that which is to be spoken first, namely, what exordium I shall adopt. For whenever I have felt inclined to think of that first, nothing occurs to me but what is jejune, or nugatory, or vulgar and ordinary.

LXXVIII. "The beginnings of speeches ought always to be accurate and judicious, well furnished with thoughts, and happy in expression, as well as peculiarly suited to their respective causes; for our earliest acquaintance with a speech, as it were, and the first recommendation of it to our notice, is at the commencement, which ought at once to propitiate and attract the audience. In regard to this point, I can not but feel astonished, not indeed at such as have paid no attention to the art, but at a man of singular eloquence and erudition, I mean Philippus, who generally rises to speak with so little preparation, that he knows not what word he shall utter first; and he says, that when he has warmed his arm, then it is his custom to begin to fight; but he does not consider that those from whom he takes this simile hurl their first lances gently, so as to preserve the utmost grace in their action, and at the same time to husband their strength. Nor is there any doubt, but that the beginning of a speech ought very seldom to be vehement and pugnacious; but if even in the combat of gladiators for life, which is decided by the sword, many passes are made previous to the actual encounter, which appear to be intended, not for mischief, but for display, how much more naturally is such prelude to be expected in a speech, in which an exhibition of force is not more required than gratification? Besides, there is nothing in the whole nature of things that is all produced at once, and that springs entire into being in an instant; and nature herself has introduced every thing that is done and accomplished most energetically with a moderate beginning. Nor is the exordium of a speech to be sought from without, or from any thing unconnected with the subject, but to be derived from the very essence of the cause. It is, therefore, after the whole cause has been considered and examined, and after every argument has been excogitated and prepared, that you must determine what sort of exordium to adopt; for thus it will easily be settled,[1] as it will be drawn from those points which are most fertile in arguments, or in those matters on which I said[2] you ought often to make digressions. Thus our exordia will give additional weight, when they are drawn from the most intimate parts of our defense; and it will be shown that they are not only not common, and can not be transferred to other causes, but that they have wholly grown out of the cause under consideration.

LXXIX. "But every exordium ought either to convey an intimation of the whole matter in hand, or some introduction and support to the cause, or something of ornament and dignity. But, like vestibules and approaches to houses and temples, so the introductions that we prefix to causes should be suited to the importance of the subjects. In small and unimportant[3] causes, therefore, it is often more advisable to commence with the subject-matter itself without any preface. But, when we are to use an exordium (as will generally be the case), our matter for it may be derived either from the suitor, from the adversary, from the subject, or from those before whom we plead. From the suitor (I call all those suitors whom a suit concerns) we may deduce such particulars as characterize a worthy, generous, or unfortunate man, or one deserving of compassion; or such particulars as avail against a false accusation. From the adversary we may deduce almost the contrary particulars from the same points. From the subject, if the matter under consideration be cruel, or heinous, or beyond expectation, or undeserved, or pitiable, or savoring of ingratitude or indignity, or unprecedented, or not admitting restitution or satisfaction.

---

[1] *Reperientur . . . sumentur.* These words are plural in Orellius's text, but Ellendt and others seem rightly to determine that they should be singular.

[2] C. 77.

[3] *Infrequentibus causis. Infrequens causa* is a cause at the pleading of which few auditors are likely to attend. *Ernesti.*

From those before whom we plead we may draw such considerations as to procure their benevolence and good opinion; an object better attained in the course of pleading than by direct entreaty. This object indeed is to be kept in view throughout the whole oration, and especially in the conclusion; but many exordia, however, are wholly based upon it; for the Greeks recommend us to make the judge, at the very commencement, attentive and desirous of information; and such hints are useful, but not more proper for the exordium than for other parts; but they are indeed easier[1] to be observed in the beginning, because the audience are then most attentive, when they are in expectation of the whole affair, and they may also, in the commencement, be more easily informed, as the particulars stated in the outset are generally of greater perspicuity than those which are spoken by way of argument, or refutation, in the body of the pleading. But we shall derive the greatest abundance and variety of matter for exordia, either to conciliate or to arouse the judge, from those points in the cause which are adapted to create emotion in the mind; yet the whole of these ought not to be brought forward in the exordium; the judge should only receive a slight impulse at the outset, so that the rest of our speech may come with full force upon him when he is already impressed in our favor.

LXXX. "Let the exordium, also, be so connected with the sequel of the speech, that it may not appear, like a musician's prelude, to be something attached merely from imagination, but a coherent member of the whole body; for some speakers, when they have delivered their premeditated exordium, make such a transition to what is to follow, that they seem positively unwilling to have an audience. But a prolusion of that kind ought not to be like that of gladiators,[2] who brandish spears before the fight, of which they make no use in the encounter; but should be such, that speakers may even use as weapons the thoughts which they advanced in the prelude.

"But as to the directions which they give to consult brevity in the narration, if that is to be called brevity where there is no word redundant, the language of Lucius Crassus is distinguished by brevity; but if that kind of brevity is intended when only just so many words are used as are absolutely necessary, such conciseness is indeed sometimes proper; but it is often prejudicial, especially in narration; not only as it produces obscurity, but also because it destroys that which is the chief excellence of narration, that it be pleasing and adapted to persuade. For instance, the narrative,

> "For he, as soon as he became of age,"
> etc.,[1]

how long is it! The manners of the youth himself, the inquiries of the servant, the death of Chrysis, the look, figure, and affliction of the sister, and the other circumstances, are told with the utmost variety and agreeableness. But if he had been studious of such brevity as this,

> "She's carried forth; we go; we reach the place
> Of sepulture; she's laid upon the pile,"

he might have comprised the whole in ten lines: although 'She's carried forth, we go,' is only so far concise, as to consult, not absolute brevity, but elegance; for if there had been nothing expressed but 'she's laid upon the pile,' the whole matter would have been easily comprehended. But a narration referring to various characters, and intersected by dialogue, affords much gratification; and that becomes more probable which you report to have been done, when you describe the manner in which it was done; and it is much more clearly understood

---

[1] *Faciliora etiam in principiis.* Ellendt justly observes that *etiam* must be corrupt, and that *autem* should probably be substituted for it.

[2] *Samnitium.* A kind of gladiators so called, that fought with Samnite arms. They had their origin among the Campanians. Liv., ix., 40.

[1] Terence, Andr., Act I., Sc. 1.

if you sometimes pause for that purpose, and do not hurry over it with affected brevity. For the narrative parts of a speech, as well as the other parts, ought to be perspicuous, and we ought to take the more pains with that part, because it is more difficult not to be obscure in stating a case, than either in an exordium, in argumentation, in refuting of an accusation, or in a peroration: and obscurity in this part of a speech is attended with greater danger than in other parts; both because, if any thing be obscurely expressed in any other part, only that is lost which is so expressed; but obscurity in the narrative part spreads darkness over the whole speech; and because, as to other parts, if you have expressed any thing obscurely in one place, you may explain it more clearly in another; while for the narrative part of a speech there is but one place. But your narrative will be clear if it be given in ordinary language, with adherence to the order of time and without interruption.

LXXXI. "But when we ought to introduce a statement of facts, and when we ought not, requires judicious consideration. For we ought to make no such statement, either if the matter is notorious, or if the circumstances are free from doubt, or if the adversary has related them, unless, indeed, we wish to confute his statement; and whenever we do make a statement of facts, let us not insist too eagerly upon points which may create suspicion and ill-feeling, and make against us, but let us extenuate such points as much as possible; lest that should happen which, whenever it occurs, Crassus thinks is done through treachery, not through folly, namely, that we damage our own cause; for it concerns the fortune of the whole cause, whether the case is stated with caution or otherwise, because the statement of the case is the foundation of all the rest of the speech.

"What follows is, that the matter in question be laid down, when we must settle what is the point that comes under dispute; then the chief grounds of the cause are to be laid down conjunctively, so as to weaken your adversary's supports, and to strengthen your own; for there is in causes but one method for that part of your speech, which is of efficacy to prove your arguments; and that needs both confirmation and refutation; but because what is alleged on the other side can not be refuted unless you confirm your own statements, and your own statements can not be confirmed unless you refute the allegations on the opposite side, these matters are in consequence united both by their nature, by their object, and by their mode of treatment. The whole speech is then generally brought to a conclusion by some amplification on the different points, or by exciting or mollifying the judge; and every particular, not only in the former parts of the speech, but more especially toward the conclusion, is to be adapted to excite as much as possible the feelings of the judges, and to incline them in our favor.

"Nor does there now appear to be any reason, indeed, why we should make a distinct head of those precepts which are given concerning suasory or panegyrical speeches; for most of them are common to all kinds of oratory; yet, to speak in favor of any important matter, or against it, seems to me to belong only to the most dignified character; for it is the part of a wise man to deliver his opinion on momentous affairs, and that of a man of integrity and eloquence, to be able to provide for others by his prudence, to confirm by his authority, and to persuade by his language.

LXXXII. "Speeches are to be made in the senate with less display; for it is an assembly of wise men;[1] and opportunity is to be left for many others to speak. All suspicion, too, of ostentation of ability is to be avoided. A speech to the people, on the other hand, requires all the force, weight, and various coloring of eloquence. For persuading, then, nothing is more desirable than worth; for he who thinks that expediency is more desirable, does not consider what the counselor chiefly wishes, but what he prefers upon occasion to follow; and there is no man, especially in so noble a state as this, who does not think that worth ought

---

[1] *Sapiens enim est consilium.* These words I regard as a scholium that has crept into the text. *Ernesti.*

chiefly to be regarded; but expediency commonly prevails, there being a concealed fear, that even worth can not be supported if expediency be disregarded. But the difference between the opinions of men lies either in this question, 'which of two things is of the greater utility?' or, if that point is agreed, it is disputed 'whether honor or expediency ought rather to be consulted.' As these seem often to oppose each other, he who is an advocate for expediency, will enumerate the benefits of peace, of plenty, of power, of riches, of settled revenues, of troops in garrison, and of other things, the enjoyment of which we estimate by their utility; and he will specify the disadvantages of a contrary state of things. He who exhorts his audience to regard honor, will collect examples from our ancestors, which may be imitated with glory, though attended with danger; he will expatiate on immortal fame among posterity; he will maintain that advantage arises from the observance of honor, and that it is always united with worth. But what is possible or impossible, and what is necessary or unnecessary, are questions of the greatest moment in regard to both; for all debate is at an end, if it is understood that a thing is impossible, or if any necessity for it appears; and he who shows what the case is, when others have overlooked it, sees farthest of all. But for giving counsel in civil affairs the chief qualification is a knowledge of the constitution; and, to speak on such matters so as to be approved, an acquaintance with the manners of the people is required; and, as these frequently vary, the fashion of speaking must often be varied; and, although the power of eloquence is mostly the same, yet, as the highest dignity is in the people, as the concerns of the republic are of the utmost importance, and as the commotions of the multitude are of extraordinary violence, a more grand and imposing manner of addressing them seems necessary to be adopted; and the greatest part of a speech is to be devoted to the excitement of the feelings, either by exhortation, or the commemoration of some illustrious action, or by moving the people to hope, or to fear, or to ambition, or desire of glory; and often also to dissuade them from temerity, from rage, from ardent expectation, from injustice, from envy, from cruelty.

LXXXIII. "But it happens that, because a popular assembly appears to the orator to be his most enlarged scene of action,[1] he is naturally excited in it to a more magnificent species of eloquence; for a multitude has such influence, that, as the flute-player can not play without his flutes, so the orator can not be eloquent without a numerous audience. And, as the inclinations of popular assemblies take many and various turns, an unfavorable expression of feeling from the whole people must not be incurred; an expression which may be excited by some fault in the speech, if any thing appears to have been spoken with harshness, with arrogance, in a base or mean manner, or with any improper feeling whatever; or it may proceed from some offense taken, or ill-will conceived, at some particular individuals, which is either just, or arising from some calumny or bad report; or it may happen if the subject be displeasing; or if the multitude be swayed by any impulse from their own hopes or fears. To these four causes as many remedies may be applied: the severity of rebuke, if you have sufficient authority for it; admonition, which is a milder kind of rebuke; an assurance, that if they will give you a hearing, they will approve what you say; and entreaty, which is the most condescending method, but sometimes very advantageous. But on no occasion is facetiousness and ready wit[2] of more effect, and any smart saying that is consistent with dignity and true jocularity; for nothing is so easily diverted from gloom, and often from rancor, as a multitude, even by a single expression uttered opportunely, quickly, smartly, and with good humor."

---

[1] *Quia maxima quasi oratori scena videtur concionis.* "Because the greatest stage, as it were, for an orator, appears [to be that] of a public assembly."

[2] *Celeritas.* The same word is used in c. 54: *hoc quod in celeritate atque dicto est.* Schutz conjectured *hilaritas.*

• • •

BOOK III

V. As soon, therefore, as they had withdrawn before noon, and reposed themselves a little, Cotta said that he particularly observed that Crassus employed all the time about the middle of the day in the most earnest and profound meditation; and that he himself, who was well acquainted with the countenance which he assumed whenever he was going to speak in public, and the nature of his looks when he was fixed in contemplation, and had often remarked them in causes of the greatest importance, came on purpose, while the rest were asleep, into the room in which Crassus had lain down on a couch prepared for him, and that, as soon as he perceived him to be settled in a thoughtful posture, he immediately retired; and that almost two hours passed in that perfect stillness. Afterward, when they all, as the day was now verging to the afternoon, waited upon Crassus, Cæsar said, "Well, Crassus, shall we go and take our seats? though we only come to put you in mind of your promise, and not to demand the performance of it." Crassus then replied, "Do you imagine that I have the assurance to think that I can continue longer indebted to such friends as you, especially in an obligation of this nature?" "What place then will suit you?" said Cæsar; "a seat in the middle of the wood, for that is the most shady and cool?" "Very well," replied Crassus, "for there is in that spot a seat not at all unsuited for this discourse of ours." This arrangement being agreeable to the rest of the company, they went into the wood, and sat down there with the most earnest desire to listen.

Crassus then said, "Not only the influence of your authority and friendship, but also the ready compliance of Antonius, have taken from me all liberty of refusal, though I had an excellent pretext for refusing. In the partition, however, of this dissertation between us, Antonius, when he assumed to himself the part of speaking upon those matters which form the subject of the orator's speech, and left to me to explain how they should be embellished, divided things which are in their nature incapable of separation; for as every speech consists of the matter and the language, the language can have no place if you take away the matter, nor the matter receive any illustration if you take away the language. Indeed, the great men of antiquity, embracing something of superior magnificence in their ideas, appear to me to have seen farther into the nature of things than the visual faculties of our minds can penetrate; as they said that all these things, above and below, formed one system, and were linked together in strict union by one and the same power, and one principle of universal harmony in nature; for there is no order of things which can either of itself, if forcibly separated from the rest, preserve a permanent existence, or without which the rest can maintain their power and eternal duration.

VI. "But, if this reasoning appear to be too comprehensive to be embraced by human sense and understanding, yet that saying of Plato is true, and certainly not unknown to you, Catulus, 'that all the learning of these liberal and polite departments of knowledge is linked together in one bond of union; for when the power of that reason, by which the causes and events of things are known, is once thoroughly discerned, a certain wonderful agreement and harmony, as it were, in all the sciences is discovered.' But, if this also appear to be too sublime a thought for us to contemplate who are prostrate on the earth, it, however, certainly is our duty to know and remember that which we have embraced, which we profess, which we have taken upon ourselves. Since eloquence, as I observed yesterday, and Antonius signified in some passages of his discourse this morning, is one and the same, into whatever tracts or regions of debate it may be carried: for whether it discourses concerning the nature of the heavens or of the earth—whether of divine or human power—whether it speaks from a lower, or an equal, or a superior place—whether to impel an audience, or to instruct, or to deter, or to incite, or to dissuade, or to inflame, or to soothe—whether to a small or to a large assembly—whether to strangers, to friends, or alone—its language is derived through different channels, not from different sources; and, wherever it directs its course, it is attended with the same equipment and decoration. But since we are overwhelmed by opinions, not only those of the vulgar, but those also of men imperfectly instructed, who treat of those things more easily when divided and torn asunder which they have not capacity to comprehend in a general view, and who sever the language from the thoughts like the body from the soul, neither of which separations can be made without destruction, I will not undertake in this discourse more than that which is imposed upon me; I will only signify briefly, that neither can embellishments of language be found without arrangement and expression of thoughts, nor can thoughts be made to shine without the light of language. But before I proceed to touch upon those particulars by which I think language is beautified and illumined, I will state briefly what I think concerning eloquence in general.

VII. "There is no one of the natural senses, in my opinion, which does not include under its general comprehension many things dissimilar one to another, but which are still thought deserving of similar approbation; for we both perceive many things by the ear, which, although they all charm us with their sounds, are yet often so various in themselves, that that which we hear last appears to be the most delightful; and almost innumerable pleasures are received by the eye, which all captivate us in such a manner as to delight the same sense in different ways; and pleasures that bear no sort of resemblance to each other charm the rest of the senses in such a manner that it is difficult to determine which affords the most exquisite enjoyment. But the same observation which is to be made in regard to nature may be applied also to the different kinds of art. Sculpture is a single art, in which Myro, Polycletus, and Lysippus excelled; all of whom differed one from another, but so that you would not wish any one of them to be unlike himself. The art and science of painting is one, yet Zeuxis, Aglaophon, and Apelles are quite unlike one another in themselves, though to none of them does any thing seem wanting in his peculiar style. And if this be wonderful, and yet true, in these, as it were, mute arts, how much more wonderful is it in language and speech? which, though employed about the same thoughts and words, yet admits of the greatest variations; and not so that some speakers are to be censured and others commended, but that those who are allowed to merit praise, merit it for different excellences. This is fully exemplified in poets, who have the nearest affinity to orators: how distinct from each other are Ennius, Pacuvius, and Accius; how distinct, among the Greeks, Æschylus, Sophocles, and Euripides; though almost equal praise may be attributed to them all in different kinds of writing. Then, behold and contemplate those whose art is the subject of our present inquiry; what a wide distinction there is between the accomplishments and natural abilities of orators! Isocrates possessed sweetness, Lysias delicacy, Hyperides pointedness, Æschines sound, and Demosthenes energy; and which of them was not excellent? yet which of them resembled any one but himself? Africanus had weight, Lælius smoothness, Galba asperity, Carbo something of fluency and harmony; but which of these was not an orator of the first rank in those times? and yet every one attained that rank by a style of oratory peculiar to himself.

VIII. "But why should I search into antiquity for examples, when I can point to present and living characters? What was ever more pleasing to the ear than the language of our friend Catulus? language of such purity, that he appears to be almost the only orator that speaks pure Latin; and of such power, that with its peculiar dignity there is yet blended the utmost politeness and wit. In a word, when I hear him, I always think that whatever you should add, or alter, or take away, his language would be impaired and deteriorated. Has not our friend Cæsar here, too, introduced a new kind of oratory, and brought before us an almost peculiar style of eloquence? Who has ever, besides him, treated tragical subjects in an almost comic manner, serious subjects with pleasantry, grave subjects with gayety, and subjects suited to the forum with a grace peculiar to the stage? in such a way that neither is the jocular style excluded by the importance of the subject, nor is the weight of the matter lessened by the humor with which it is treated. Here are present with us two young men, almost of equal age, Sulpicius and Cotta; what things were ever so dissimilar as they are one to another? yet what is so excellent as they are in their respective styles? One is polished and refined, explaining things with the greatest propriety and aptitude of expression; he always adheres to his cause, and, when he has discovered, with his keen discernment, what he ought to prove to the judge, he directs his whole attention and force of oratory to that point, without regarding other arguments; while Sulpicius has a certain irresistible energy of mind, a most full and powerful voice, a most vigorous action, and consummate dignity of motion, united with such weight and copiousness of language, that he appears of all men the best qualified by nature for eloquence.

• • •

X. "I thought it necessary to premise these particulars, that if every remark of mine did not exactly adapt itself to the inclinations of you all, and to that peculiar style of speaking which each of you most admired, you might be sensible that I described that character of eloquence of which I myself most approved.

"Those matters, therefore, of which Antonius has treated so explicitly, are to be endowed with action and elocution by the orator in some certain manner. What manner of elocution can be better (for I will consider action by-and-by) than that of speaking in pure Latin, with perspicuity, with gracefulness, and with aptitude and congruity to the subject in question? Of the two which I mentioned first, purity and clearness of language, I do not suppose that any account is expected from me; for we do not attempt to teach him to be an orator who can not speak; nor can we hope that he who can not speak grammatical Latin will speak elegantly; nor that he who can not speak what we can understand, will ever speak any thing for us to admire. Let us, therefore, omit these matters, which are easy of attainment, though necessary in practice; for the one is taught in school-learning and the rudiments of children; the other[1] is cultivated for this reason, that what every person says may be understood—a qualification which we perceive indeed to be necessary, yet that none can be held in less estimation.[2] But all elegance of language, though it receive a polish from the science of grammar, is yet augmented by the reading of orators and poets; for those ancients, who could not then adorn what they expressed, had almost all a kind of nobleness of diction; and those who are accustomed to their style can not express themselves otherwise than in pure Latin, even though they desire to do so. Yet we must not make use of such of their words as our modern mode of speaking does not admit, unless sometimes for the sake of ornament, and but sparingly, as I shall explain; but he who is studious and much conversant with ancient writers, will make such use of common expressions as always to adopt the most eligible."

• • •

XIV. "You see," said Antonius, "how inattentive we are, and how unwillingly we listen to you,[3] when we might be induced (I judge from myself) to neglect all other concerns to follow you and give you our attention; so elegant are your remarks upon unpleasing, so copious upon barren, so new upon common subjects."

"Those two parts, indeed, Antonius," continued Crassus, "which I have just run over, or rather have almost passed by, that of speaking in pure Latin, and with perspicuity, were easy to treat;

---

[1] Perspicuity.

[2] This seems to be speaking rather too lightly of the merit of perspicuity, which Quintilian pronounces the chief virtue of language.

[3] Ironically.

those which remain are important, intricate, diversified, weighty, on which depends all the admiration bestowed upon ability and all the praise given to eloquence; for nobody ever admired an orator for merely speaking good Latin; if he speaks otherwise, they ridicule him; and not only do not think him an orator, but not even a man. Nor has any one ever extolled a speaker for merely speaking in such a manner that those who were present understood what he said; though every one has despised him who was not able to do so. Whom, then, do men regard with awe? What speaker do they behold with astonishment? At whom do they utter exclamations? Whom do they consider as a deity, if I may use the expression, among mortals? Him who speaks distinctly, explicitly, copiously, and luminously, both as to matter and words; who produces in his language a sort of rhythm and harmony; who speaks, as I call it, *gracefully.* Those also who treat their subject as the importance of things and persons requires, are to be commended for that peculiar kind of merit, which I term *aptitude* and *congruity.* Antonius said that he had never seen any who spoke in such a manner, and observed that to such only was to be attributed the distinguishing title of *eloquence.* On my authority, therefore, deride and despise all those who imagine that from the precepts of such as are now called rhetoricians they have gained all the powers of oratory, and have not yet been able to understand what character they hold, or what they profess; for indeed, by an orator, every thing that relates to human life, since that is the field on which his abilities are displayed, and is the subject for his eloquence, should be examined, heard, read, discussed, handled, and considered; since eloquence is one of the most eminent virtues; and though all the virtues are in their nature equal and alike, yet one species is more beautiful and noble than another; as is this power, which, comprehending a knowledge of things, expresses the thoughts and purposes of the mind in such a manner, that it can impel the audience whithersoever it inclines its force; and, the greater is its influence, the more necessary it is that it should be united with probity and eminent judgment; for if we bestow the faculty of eloquence upon persons destitute of these virtues, we shall not make them orators, but give arms to madmen.

XV. "This faculty, I say, of thinking and speaking, this power of eloquence, the ancient Greeks denominated wisdom. Hence the Lycurgi, the Pittaci, the Solons; and, compared with them, our Coruncanii, Fabricii, Catos, and Scipios, were perhaps not so learned, but were certainly of a like force and inclination of mind. Others, of equal ability, but of dissimilar affection toward the pursuits of life, preferred ease and retirement, as Pythagoras, Democritus, Anaxagoras, and transferred their attention entirely from civil polity to the contemplation of nature; a mode of life which, on account of its tranquillity, and the pleasure derived from science, than which nothing is more delightful to mankind, attracted a greater number than was of advantage to public concerns. Accordingly, as men of the most excellent natural talents gave themselves up to that study, in the enjoyment of the greatest abundance of free and unoccupied time, so men of the greatest learning, blessed with excess of leisure and fertility of thought, imagined it their duty to make more things than were really necessary the objects of their attention, investigation, and inquiry. That ancient learning, indeed, appears to have been at the same time the preceptress of living rightly and of speaking well; nor were there separate masters for those subjects, but the same teachers formed the morals and the language; as Phœnix in Homer, who says that he was appointed a companion in war to the young Achilles by his father Peleus, to make him an orator in words and a hero in deeds. But as men accustomed to constant and daily employment, when they are hindered from their occupation by the weather, betake themselves to play at ball, or dice, or draughts, or even invent some new game of their own to amuse their leisure; so they, being either excluded from public employments, as from business, by the state of the times, or being idle from inclination, gave themselves up wholly, some to the poets, some to the geometers, some to music; others even, as the logicians, found out a new study and exercise for themselves, and consumed their whole time and lives in those arts which have been discovered to form the minds of youth to learning and to virtue.

XVI. "But, because there were some, and those not a few, who either were eminent in public affairs, through their twofold excellence in acting and speaking, excellences which are indeed inseparable, as Themistocles, Pericles, Theramenes; or who, though they were not employed themselves in public affairs, were teachers of others in that science, as Gorgias, Thrasymachus, Isocrates; there appeared others who, being themselves men of abundant learning and ingenuity, but averse to political business and employments, derided and despised the exercise of oratory; at the head of which party was Socrates. He, who, by the testimony of all the learned, and the judgment of all Greece, was the first of all men as well in wisdom and penetration, grace and refinement, as in eloquence, variety, and copiousness of language on whatever subject he took in hand, deprived of their common name those who handled, treated, and gave instruction in those matters which are the objects of our present inquiry, when they were previously comprised under one appellation; as all knowledge in the best arts and sciences, and all exercise in them, was denominated *philosophy;* and he separated in his discussions the ability of thinking wisely and speaking gracefully, though they are naturally united; Socrates, I say, whose great genius and varied conversation Plato has in his Dialogues consigned to immortality, he himself having left us nothing in writing. Hence arose that divorce, as it were, of the tongue from the heart, a division certainly absurd, useless, and reprehensible, that one class of persons should teach us to think, and another to speak, rightly; for, as many reasoners had their origin almost from Socrates, and as they caught up some one thing, some another, from his disputations, which were various, diversified, and diffusive upon all subjects, many sects as it were became propagated, dissenting one from another, and much divided and very dissimilar in opinions, though all the philosophers wished to be called, and thought that they were, Socratics.

• • •

XIX. "But the streams of learning have flowed from the common summit of science,[1] like rivers from the Apennines, in different directions, so that the philosophers have passed, as it were, into the Upper or Ionian Sea, a Greek sea abounding with harbors, but the orators have fallen into the Lower or Tuscan, a barbarian sea infested with rocks and dangers, in which even Ulysses himself had mistaken his course. If, therefore, we are content with such a degree of eloquence, and such an orator as has the common discretion to know that you ought either to deny the charge which is brought against you, or, if you can not do that, to show that what he who is accused has committed, was either done justifiably, or through the fault or wrong of some other person, or that it is agreeable to law, or at least not contrary to any law, or that it was done without design, or from necessity; or that it does not merit the term given it in the accusation; or that the pleading is not conducted as it ought to have been or might have been; and if you think it sufficient to have learned the rules which the writers on rhetoric have delivered, which, however, Antonius has set forth with much more grace and fullness than they are treated by them; if, I say, you are content with these qualifications, and those which you wished to be specified by me, you reduce the orator from a spacious and immense field of action into a very narrow compass; but if you are desirous to emulate Pericles, or Demosthenes, who is more familiar to us from his numerous writings; and if you are captivated with this noble and illustrious idea and excellence of a perfect orator, you must include in your minds all the powers of Carneades, or those of Aristotle. For, as I observed before, the ancients, till the time of Socrates, united all knowledge and science in all things, whether they appertained to morality, to the duties of life,

[1] *Ex communi sapientium jugo.* I read *sapientiœ* with Ellendt. It is a comparison, as he observes, of Socrates to a hill.

to virtue, or to civil government, with the faculty of speaking; but afterward, the eloquent being separated by Socrates from the learned (as I have already explained), and this distinction being continued by all the followers of Socrates, the philosophers disregarded eloquence, and the orators philosophy; nor did they at all encroach upon each other's provinces, except that the orators borrowed from the philosophers, and the philosophers from the orators, such things as they would have taken from the common stock if they had been inclined to remain in their pristine union. But as the old pontiffs, on account of the multitude of religious ceremonies, appointed three officers called Epulones,[1] though they themselves were instituted by Numa to perform the *epulare sacrificium* at the games; so the followers of Socrates excluded the pleaders of causes from their own body, and from the common title of philosophers, though the ancients were of opinion that there was a miraculous harmony between speaking and understanding.

XX. "Such being the case, I shall crave some little indulgence for myself, and beg you to consider that whatever I say, I say not of myself, but of the complete orator. For I am a person, who, having been educated in my boyhood, with great care on the part of my father, and having brought into the forum such a portion of talent as I am conscious of possessing, and not so much as I may perhaps appear to you to have, can not aver that I learned what I now comprehend, exactly as I shall say that it ought to be learned; since I engaged in public business most early of all men, and at one-and-twenty years of age brought to trial a man of the highest rank, and the greatest eloquence;[2] and the forum has been my school, and practice, with the laws and institutions of the Roman people, and the customs of our ancestors, my instructors. I got a small taste of those sciences of which I am speaking, feeling some thirst for them, while I was quæstor in Asia, having procured a rhetorician about my own age from the Academy, that Metrodorus, of whose memory Antonius has made honorable mention; and, on my departure from Asia, at Athens, where I should have staid longer, had I not been displeased with the Athenians, who would not repeat their mysteries, for which I came two days too late. The fact, therefore, that I comprise within my scheme so much science, and attribute so much influence to learning, makes not only not in my favor, but rather against me (for I am not considering what I, but what a perfect orator can do), and against all those who put forth treatises on the art of rhetoric, and who are indeed obnoxious to extreme ridicule; for they write merely about the several kinds of suits, about exordia, and statements of facts; but the real power of eloquence is such, that it embraces the origin, the influence, the changes of all things in the world, all virtues, duties, and all nature, so far as it affects the manners, minds, and lives of mankind. It can give an account of customs, laws, and rights, can govern a state, and speak on every thing relating to any subject whatsoever with elegance and force. In this pursuit I employ my talents as well as I can, as far as I am enabled by natural capacity, moderate learning, and constant practice; nor do I conceive myself much inferior in disputation to those who have as it were pitched their tent for life in philosophy alone.

XXI. "For what can my friend Caius Velleius[1] allege to show why pleasure is the chief good, which I can not either maintain more fully, if I were so inclined, or refute, with the aid of those commonplaces which Antonius has set forth, and that habit of speaking in which Velleius himself is unexercised, but every one of us experienced? What is there that either Sextus Pompeius, or the two Balbi,[2] or my acquaintance Marcus Vigellius,

---

[1] See Liv., xxxiii., 42.

[2] Carbo. See note on i., 10.

[1] The same that speaks, in the dialogue *De Naturâ Deorum,* on the tenets of the Epicureans.

[2] One Balbus is a speaker in the *De Nat. Deorum,* on the doctrines of the Stoics. The other, says Ellendt, is supposed to be the lawyer who is mentioned by Cicero, Brut., c. 42, and who was the master of Servius Sulpicius. Of Vigellius nothing is known.

who lived with Panætius, all men of the Stoic sect, can maintain concerning virtue, in such a manner that either I, or any one of you, should give place to them in debate? For philosophy is not like other arts or sciences; since what can he do in geometry, or in music, who has never learned? He must be silent, or be thought a madman; but the principles of philosophy are discovered by such minds as have acuteness and penetration enough to extract what is most probable concerning any subject, and are elegantly expressed with the aid of exercise in speaking. On such topics, a speaker of ordinary abilities, if he has no great learning, but has had practice in declaiming, will, by virtue of such practice, common to others as well as to him, beat our friends the philosophers, and not suffer himself to be despised and held in contempt; but if ever a person shall arise who shall have abilities to deliver opinions on both sides of a question on all subjects, after the manner of Aristotle, and, from a knowledge of the precepts of that philosopher, to deliver two contradictory orations on every conceivable topic, or shall be able, after the manner of Arcesilas or Carneades, to dispute against every proposition that can be laid down, and shall unite with those powers rhetorical skill, and practice and exercise in speaking, he will be the true, the perfect, the only orator. For neither without the nervous eloquence of the forum, can an orator have sufficient weight, dignity, and force; nor, without variety of learning, sufficient elegance and judgment. Let us suffer that old Corax of yours,[1] therefore, to hatch his young birds in the nest, that they may fly out disagreeable and troublesome bawlers; and let us allow Pamphilus, whoever he was,[2] to depict a science of such consequence upon flags, as if for an amusement for children; while we ourselves describe the whole business of an orator, in so short a disputation as that of yesterday and to-day; admitting, however, that it is of such extent as to be spread through all the books of the philosophers, into which none of those rhetoricians[1] has ever dipped."

XXII. Catulus then said, "It is, indeed, by no means astonishing, Crassus, that there should appear in you either such energy, or such agreeableness, or such copiousness of language; though I previously supposed that it was merely from the force of natural genius that you spoke in such a way as to seem to me not only the greatest of orators, but the wisest of men; but I now understand that you have always given precedence to matters relating to philosophy, and your copious stream of eloquence has flowed from that source; and yet, when I recollect the different stages of your life, and when I consider your manner of living and pursuits, I can neither conceive at what time you acquired that learning, nor can I imagine you to be strongly addicted to those studies, or men, or writings; nor can I determine at which of these two things I ought most to feel surprised, that you could obtain a thorough knowledge of those matters which you persuade me are of the utmost assistance to oratory, amid such important occupations as yours, or that, if you could not do so, you can speak with such effect." Here Crassus rejoined, "I would have you first of all, Catulus, persuade yourself of this, that, when I speak of an orator, I speak not much otherwise than I should do if I had to speak of an actor; for I should say that he could not possibly give satisfaction in his gesture unless he had learned the exercises of the

[1] See i., 20. He jokes on the name of Corax, which signifies *a crow*.

[2] *Pamphilum nescio quem*. Some suppose him to be the painter that is mentioned as the instructor of Apelles by Pliny, H. N., xxxv., 36, 8. He seems, whoever he was, to have given some fanciful map-like view of the rules of rhetoric. But it is not intimated by Pliny that the Pamphilus of whom he speaks was, though a learned painter, any thing more than a painter. A Pamphilus is mentioned by Quintilian, iii., 6, 34; xii., 10, 6; and by Aristotle Rhet., ii., 23. By *infulæ* in the text, which I have rendered "flags," Ellendt supposes that something similar to our printed cotton handkerchiefs, or flags hung out at booths at fairs, is meant. Talæus thinks that the tables of rules might have been called *infulæ* in ridicule, from their shape.

[1] Such "disagreeable and troublesome bawlers," as those from the nest of Corax just mentioned. *Ernesti.*

palæstra, and dancing; nor would it be necessary that, when I said this, I should be myself a player, though it perhaps would be necessary that I should be a not unskillful critic in another man's profession. In like manner I am now, at your request, speaking of the orator, that is, the perfect orator; for, about whatever art or faculty inquiry is made, it always relates to it in its state of absolute perfection; and if, therefore, you now allow me to be a speaker, if even a pretty good one, or a positively good one, I will not contradict you (for why should I, at my time of life, be so foolish? I know that I am esteemed such); but, if it be so, I am certainly not perfect. For there is not among mankind any pursuit of greater difficulty or effort, or that requires more aids from learning; but, since I have to speak of the orator, I must of necessity speak of the perfect orator; for unless the powers and nature of a thing be set before the eyes in their utmost perfection, its character and magnitude can not be understood. Yet I confess, Catulus, that I do not at present live in any great familiarity with the writings or the professors of philosophy, and that, as you have rightly observed, I never had much leisure to set apart for the acquisition of such learning, and that I have only given to study such portions of time as my leisure when I was a youth, and vacations from the business of the forum, have allowed me.

XXIII. "But if, Catulus, you inquire my sentiments on that learning, I am of opinion that so much time need not be spent on it by a man of ability, and one who studies with a view to the forum, to the senate, to causes, to civil administration, as those have chosen to give to it whom life has failed while they were learning. For all arts are handled in one manner by those who apply them to practice; in another by those who, taking delight in treating of the arts themselves, never intend to do any thing else during the whole course of their lives. The master of the gladiators[1] is now in the extremity of age, yet daily meditates upon

[1] See note on ii., 80.

the improvement of his science, for he has no other care; but Quintus Velocius[1] had learned that exercise in his youth, and, as he was naturally formed for it, and had thoroughly acquired it, he was, as it is said in Lucilius,

> " 'Though as a gladiator in the school
> Well skill'd, and bold enough to match
> with any,'

yet resolved to devote more attention to the duties of the forum, and of friendship, and to his domestic concerns. Valerius[2] sung every day; for he was on the stage; what else was he to do? But our friend Numerius Furius sings only when it is agreeable to him; for he is the head of a family, and of equestrian dignity; he learned when a boy as much as it was necessary for him to learn. The case is similar with regard to sciences of the greatest importance; we have seen Quintus Tubero,[3] a man of eminent virtue and prudence, engaged in the study of philosophy night and day, but his uncle Africanus[4] you could scarcely ever perceive paying any attention to it, though he paid a great deal. Such knowledge is easily gained, if you only get as much of it as is necessary, and have a faithful and able instructor, and know how to learn yourself. But if you are inclined to do nothing else all your life, your very studies and inquiries daily give rise to something for you to investigate as an amusement at your leisure; thus it happens, that the investigation of particular points is endless, though general knowledge is easy, if practice establish learning once acquired, moderate exercise be devoted to it, and memory and inclination continue. But it is pleasant to be constantly learning, if we wish to be thoroughly masters of any thing; as if I, for instance, had a desire to play excellently at backgammon, or had a strong attachment to tennis, though perhaps I should not attain perfection in those games; but others, because they excel

[1] This name was introduced on the conjecture of Victorius. Previously the passage was unintelligible.

[2] Of Valerius and Furius nothing is known. *Ellendt.*

[3] Cic., Tusc. Quæst., iv., 2; Fin., iv., 9.

[4] See ii., 37.

in any performance, take a more vehement delight in it than the object requires, as Titius[1] in tennis, Brulla in backgammon. There is no reason, therefore, why any one should dread the extent of the sciences because he perceives old men still learning them; for either they were old men when they first applied to them, or have been detained in the study of them till they became old; or are of more than ordinary stupidity. And the truth in my opinion is, that a man can never learn thoroughly that which he has not been able to learn quickly."

XXIV. "Now, now," exclaimed Catulus, "I understand, Crassus, what you say, and readily assent to it; I see that there has been time enough for you, a man of vigor and ability to learn, to acquire a knowledge of what you mention." "Do you still persist," rejoined Crassus, "to think that I say what I say of myself, and not of my subject? But, if it be agreeable to you, let us now return to our stated business." "To me," said Catulus, "it is very agreeable."

"To what end, then," continued Crassus, "does this discourse, drawn out to so great a length, and brought from such deep sources, tend? The two parts which remain for me, that of adorning language, and contemplating eloquence in general in its highest perfection—one of which requires that we should speak gracefully, the other aptly—have this influence, that eloquence is rendered by their means productive of the utmost delight, made to penetrate effectually into the inmost hearts of the audience, and furnished with all possible variety of matter. But the speech which we use in the forum, adapted for contest, full of acrimony, formed to suit the taste of the vulgar, is poor indeed and beggarly; and, on the other hand, even that which they teach who profess themselves masters of the art of speaking, is not of much more dignity than the common style of the forum. We have need of greater pomp,[2] of choice matter collected, imported, and brought together from all parts; such a provision as must be made by you, Cæsar, for the next year,[1] with such pains as I took in my ædileship, because I did not suppose that I could satisfy such a people as ours with ordinary matters, or those of their own country.

"As for choosing and arranging words, and forming them into proper periods, the art is easy, or, I may say, the mere practice without any art at all. Of matter, the quantity and variety are infinite; and as the Greeks[2] were not properly furnished with it, and our youth in consequence almost grew ignorant while they were learning, even Latin teachers of rhetoric, please the gods, have arisen within the last two years; a class of persons whom I had suppressed by my edict,[3] when I was censor, not because I was unwilling (as some I know not who, asserted), that the abilities of our youth should be improved, but because I did not wish that their understandings should be weakened and their impudence strengthened. For among the Greeks, whatever was their character, I perceived that there was, besides exercise of the tongue, some degree of learning, as well as politeness suited to liberal knowledge; but I knew that these new masters could teach youth nothing but effrontery, which, even when joined with good qualities, is to be avoided, and in itself especially so; and as this, therefore, was the only thing that was taught by the Latins, their school being indeed a school of impudence, I thought it became the censor to take care that the evil should not spread farther. I do not, however, determine and decree on the point, as if I despaired that the subjects which we are discussing can be delivered, and treated with

---

[1] Titius is mentioned ii., 62. Of Brulla nothing is known. *Ellendt.*

[2] *Apparatu.* In allusion, says Petavius, to the shows given by the ædiles.

---

[1] *Ad annum.* That of his ædileship. *Ernesti.*

[2] The Greek rhetoricians. *Pearce.*

[3] Quintilian refers to this passage, ii., 4, 42. . . . . The edict of the censors Crassus and Ahenobarbus, which was marked by all the ancient severity, is preserved in Aul. Gell., xv., 11; and Suetonius, De Clar. Rhet., procem. Crassus intimates that that class of men sprung up again after his edict; for the censors had not such power that their mere prohibitions could continue in force after their term of office was expired. *Ellendt.*

elegance, in Latin; for both our language and the nature of things allows the ancient and excellent science of Greece to be adapted to our customs and manners; but for such a work are required men of learning, such as none of our countrymen have been in this department; but if ever such arise, they will be preferable to the Greeks themselves.

• • •

XXVI. "Though such expressions of applause, therefore, as 'very well,' 'excellent,' may be often repeated to me, I would not have 'beautifully,' 'pleasantly,' come too often; yet I would have the exclamation, 'Nothing can be better,' very frequent. But this high excellence and merit in speaking should be attended with some portions of shade and obscurity, that the part on which a stronger light is thrown may seem to stand out, and become more prominent. Roscius never delivers this passage with all the spirit that he can,

> " 'The wise man seeks for honor, not for spoil,
> As the reward of virtue;'

but rather in an abject manner, that into the next speech,

> " 'What do I see? the steel-girt soldier holds
> The sacred seats,'

he may throw his whole powers, may gaze, may express wonder and astonishment. How does the other great actor[1] utter

> " 'What aid shall I solicit?'

How gently, how sedately, how calmly! For he proceeds with

> " 'O father! O my country! House of Priam!'

in which so much action could not be exerted if it had been consumed and exhausted by any preceding emotion. Nor did the actors discover this before the poets themselves, or, indeed, before even those who composed the music, by both of whom their tone is sometimes lowered, sometimes heightened, sometimes made slender, sometimes full, with variation and distinction. Let our orator, then, be thus graceful and delightful (nor can he indeed be so otherwise); let him have a severe and solid grace, not a luscious and delicious sweetness; for the precepts relative to the ornament of eloquence, which are commonly given, are of such a nature that even the worst speaker can observe them. It is first of all necessary, therefore, as I said before, that a stock of matter and thoughts be got together; a point on which Antonius has already spoken; these are to be interwoven into the very thread and essence of the oration, embellished by words, and diversified by illustrations.

"But the greatest glory of eloquence is to exaggerate a subject by embellishment; which has effect not only in amplifying and extolling any thing in a speech to an extraordinary degree, but also in extenuating it, and making it appear contemptible.

XXVII. This is required on all those points which Antonius said must be observed in order to gain credit to our statements, when we explain any thing, or when we conciliate the feelings, or when we excite the passions of our audience; but in the particular which I mentioned last, amplification is of the greatest effect; and excellence in it the peculiar and appropriate praise of the orator. Even that exercise is of more than ordinary importance which Antonius illustrated[1] in the latter part of his dissertation (in the beginning[2] he set it aside), I mean that of panegyric and satire; for nothing is a better preparative for exaggeration and amplification in a speech than the talent of performing both these parts in a most effective manner. Consequently, even those topics are of use which, though

---

[1] Æsopus, as I suppose. *Ellendt;* who observes that the verses are from the Andromache of Ennius. See c. 47, 58; Tusc. Disp., iii., 19.

[1] B. ii., c. 84.

[2] B. ii., c. 10.

they ought to be *proper* to causes, and to be inherent in their very vitals, yet, as they are commonly applied to general subjects, have been by the ancients denominated *common places;* of which *some* consist in bitter accusations and complaints against vices and crimes, with a certain amplification (in opposition to which nothing is usually said, or can be said), as against an embezzler of the public money, or a traitor, or a parricide; remarks which we ought to introduce when the charges have been proved, for otherwise they are jejune and trifling; *others* consist in entreaty or commiseration; *others* relate to contested points of argument, whence you may be enabled to speak fully on either side of any general question, an exercise which is now imagined to be peculiar to those two sects of philosophy[1] of which I spoke before; among those of remote antiquity it belonged to those from whom all the art and power of speaking in forensic pleadings was derived;[2] for concerning virtue, duty, justice and equity, dignity, utility, honor, ignominy, rewards and punishments, and similar subjects, we ought to possess the spirit, and talent, and address, to speak on either side of the question. But since, being driven from our own possessions, we are left in a poor little farm, and even that the subject of litigation, and since, though the patrons of others, we have not been able to preserve and protect our own property, let us borrow what is requisite for us (which is a notable disgrace) from those[3] who have made this irruption into our patrimony.

• • •

XXX. "But those which relate to action, either concern controverted points of moral duty, under which head it may be inquired, 'What is right and to be practiced;' of which head the whole train of virtues and of vices is the subject-matter; or refer to the excitement, or alleviation, or removal of some emotion of the mind. Under this head are included exhortation, reproof, consolation, compassion, and all that either gives impulse to any emotion of the mind, or, if it so happen, mitigates it. These kinds, then, and modes of all questions being explained, it is of no consequence if the partition of Antonius in any particular disagrees with my division; for there are the same parts in both our dissertations, though divided and distributed by me a little otherwise than by him. Now I will proceed to the sequel, and recall myself to my appointed task and business. For the arguments for every kind of question are to be drawn from those commonplaces which Antonius enumerated; but some commonplaces will be more adapted to some kinds than to others; concerning which there is no necessity for me to speak, not because it is a matter of any great length, but of sufficient perspicuity.

"Those speeches, then, are the most ornate which spread over the widest field, and, from some private and single question, apply and direct themselves to show the nature of such questions in general, so that the audience, from understanding its nature, and kind, and whole bearing, may determine as to particular individuals, and as to all suits criminal and civil. Antonius has encouraged you, young men, to perseverance in this exercise, and intimated that you were to be conducted by degrees from small and confined questions to all the power and varieties of argument. Such qualifications are not to be gained from a few small treatises, as they have imagined who have written on the art of speaking; nor are they work merely for a Tusculan villa, or for a morning walk and afternoon sitting, such as these of ours; for we have not only to point and fashion the tongue, but have to store the mind with the sweetness, abundance, and variety of most important and numerous subjects.

XXXI. "For ours is the possession (if we are indeed orators, if we are to be consulted as persons of authority and leaders in the civil contests and perils of the citizens and in public councils), ours, I say, is the entire possession of all that

[1] The Academic and Peripatetic; see iii., 17, 18. *Proust.*

[2] Those who taught forensic eloquence. *Proust.*

[3] The philosophers.

wisdom and learning, upon which, as if it were vacant and had fallen in to them, men abounding in leisure have seized, taking advantage of us, and either speak of the orator with ridicule and sarcasm, as Socrates in the Gorgias, or write something on the art of oratory in a few little treatises, and call them books on rhetoric; as if all those things did not equally concern the orator, which are taught by the same philosophers on justice, on the duties of life, on the establishment and administration of civil government, and on the whole systems of moral and even natural philosophy. These matters, since we can not get them elsewhere, we must now borrow from those very persons by whom we have been pillaged; so that we apply them to the knowledge of civil affairs, to which they belong, and have a regard; nor let us (as I observed before) consume all our lives in this kind of learning, but, when we have discovered the fountains (which he who does not find out immediately will never find at all), let us draw from them as much as occasion may require, as often as we need. For neither is there so sharp a discernment in the nature and understanding of man, that any one can descry things of such importance, unless they are pointed out; nor yet is there so much obscurity in the things, that a man of penetrating genius can not obtain an insight into them, if he only direct his view toward them. As the orator therefore has liberty to expatiate in so large and immense a field, and, wherever he stops, can stand upon his own territory, all the furniture and embellishments of eloquence readily offer themselves to him. For copiousness of matter produces copiousness of language; and, if there be an inherent dignity in the subjects on which he speaks, there must be, from the nature of the thing, a certain splendor in his expression. If the speaker or writer has but been liberally instructed in the learning proper for youth, and has an ardent attachment to study, and is assisted by natural endowments, and exercised in those indefinite questions on general subjects, and has chosen, at the same time, the most elegant writers and speakers to study and imitate, he will never, be assured, need instruction from such preceptors how to compose or embellish his language; so readily, in an abundance of matter, will nature herself, if she be but stimulated, fall without any guide into all the art of adorning eloquence."

XXXII. Catulus here observed, "Ye immortal gods, what an infinite variety, force, and extent of matter have you, Crassus, embraced, and from how narrow a circle have you ventured to lead forth the orator, and to place him in the domains of his ancestors! For we have understood that those ancient masters and authors of the art of speaking considered no kind of disputation to be foreign to their profession, but were always exercising themselves in every branch of oratory. Of which number was Hippias of Elis, who, when he came to Olympia, at the time of the vast concourse at the games celebrated every fifth year, boasted, in the hearing of almost all Greece, that there was no subject in any art or science of which he was ignorant; as he understood not only those arts in which all liberal and polite learning is comprised, geometry, music, grammar, and poetry, and whatever is said on the natures of things, the moral duties of men, and the science of government, but that he had himself made, with his own hand, the ring which he wore, and the cloak and shoes which he had on.[1] He indeed went a little too far; but, even from his example, we may easily conjecture how much knowledge those very orators desired to gain in the most noble arts, when they did not shrink from learning even the more humble. Why need I allude to Prodicus of Chios, Thrasymachus of Chalcedon, or Protagoras of Abdera? every one of whom in those days disputed and wrote much even on the nature of things. Even Gorgias the Leontine himself, under whose advocacy (as Plato represented) the orator yielded to the philosopher;[2] who was either never defeated in

---

[1] See Plato, Hipp. Min., p. 231, G.

[2] Gorgias, in the Dialogue of Plato, undertakes the defense of oratory against Socrates, whom Plato represents as maintaining the dignity of philosophy. Gorgias is vanquished by Socrates. *Proust.*

argument by Socrates (and then the Dialogue of Plato is wholly fictitious), or, if he was so defeated, it was because Socrates was the more eloquent and convincing, or, as you term it, the more powerful and better orator; but this Gorgias, in that very book of Plato, offers to speak most copiously on any subject whatever, that could be brought under discussion or inquiry; and he was the first of all men that ventured to demand, in a large assembly, on what subject any one desired to hear him speak; and to whom such honors were paid in Greece, that to him alone, of all great men, a statue was erected at Delphi, not gilded, but of solid gold. Those whom I have named, and many other most consummate masters in the art of speaking, flourished at the same time; from whose examples it may be understood that the truth is really such as you, Crassus, have stated, and that the name of the orator was distinguished among the ancients in Greece in a more extensive sense, and with greater honor than among ourselves. I am therefore the more in doubt whether I should attribute a greater degree of praise to you, or of blame to the Greeks; since you, born under a different language and manners, in the busiest of cities, occupied either with almost all the private causes of the people, or with the government of the world and the direction of the mightiest of empires, have mastered such numbers of subjects, and acquired so extensive a knowledge, and have united all this with the science and practice of one who is of authority in the republic by his counsels and eloquence; while they, born in an atmosphere of learning, ardently attached to such studies, but dissolved in idleness, have not only made no acquisitions, but have not even preserved as their own that which was left and consigned to them."

XXXIII. Crassus then said, "Not only in this particular, Catulus, but in many others, the grandeur of the sciences has been diminished by the distribution and separation of their parts. Do you imagine, that when the famous Hippocrates of Cos flourished, there were then some of the medical faculty who cured diseases, others wounds, and a third class the eyes? Do you suppose that geometry under Euclid and Archimedes, that music under Damon and Aristoxenus, that grammar itself when Aristophanes and Callimachus treated of it, were so divided into parts, that no one comprehended the universal system of any of those sciences, but different persons selected different parts on which they meant to bestow their labor? I have, indeed, often heard from my father and father-in-law, that even our own countrymen, who were ambitious to excel in renown for wisdom, were wont to comprehend all the objects of knowledge which this city had then learned. They mentioned, as an instance of this, Sextus Ælius; and we ourselves have seen Manius Manilius walking across the forum; a signal that he who did so gave all the citizens liberty to consult him upon any subject; and to such persons, when thus walking or sitting at home upon their seats of ceremony, all people had free access, not only to consult them upon points of civil law, but even upon the settlement of a daughter in marriage, the purchase of an estate, or the cultivation of a farm, and indeed upon any employment or business whatsoever. Such was the wisdom of the well-known elder Publius Crassus, such that of Titus Coruncanius, such that of the great-grandfather Scipio, my son-in-law, a person of great judgment; all of whom were supreme pontiffs, so that they were consulted upon all affairs, divine and human; and the same men gave their counsel and discharged their duty in the senate, before the people, and in the private causes of their friends, in civil and military service, both at home and abroad. What was deficient in Marcus Cato, except the modern polish of foreign and adventitious learning? Did he, because he was versed in the civil law, forbear from pleading causes? or, because he could speak, neglect the study of jurisprudence? He labored in both these kinds of learning, and succeeded in both. Was he, by the popularity which he acquired by attending to the business of private persons, rendered more tardy in the public service of the state? No man spoke with more courage before the people, none was ever a better senator; he was at the same time a most excellent commander-in-chief; and indeed nothing in those days could possibly be known or learned in this city which he did not investigate and thoroughly understand, and on which he did not also write. Now, on the contrary, men generally come to assume offices and the duties of public administration unarmed and defenseless; prepared with no science, nor any knowledge of business. But if any one happen to excel the multitude, he is elevated with pride by the possession of any single talent, as military courage, or a little experience in war (which indeed has now fallen into decay[1]), or a knowledge of the law (not of the whole law, for nobody studies the pontifical law, which is annexed to civil jurisprudence[2]), or eloquence (which they imagine to consist in declamation and a torrent of words), while none have any notion of the alliance and affinity that connects all the liberal arts and sciences, and even the virtues themselves.

• • •

XXXV. "I do not imagine that they were different; for I see that one and the same course of study comprised all those branches of knowledge which were esteemed necessary for a man of learning, and one who wished to become eminent in civil administration; and that they who had received this knowledge, if they had sufficient powers for speaking in public, and devoted themselves, without any impediment from nature, to oratory, became distinguished for eloquence. Aristotle himself, accordingly, when he saw Isocrates grow remarkable for the number and quality of his scholars [because he himself had diverted his lectures from forensic and civil causes to mere elegance of language[1]], changed on a sudden almost his whole system of teaching, and quoted a verse from the tragedy of Philoctetes[2] with a little alteration; for the hero said that *It was disgraceful for him to be silent while he allowed barbarians to speak;* but Aristotle said that *it was disgraceful for him to be silent while he allowed Isocrates to speak.* He therefore adorned and illustrated all philosophical learning, and associated the knowledge of things with practice in speaking. Nor did this escape the knowledge of that very sagacious monarch Philip, who sent for him as a tutor for his son Alexander, that he might acquire from the same teacher instructions at once in conduct and in language. Now, if any one desires either to call that philosopher, who instructs us fully in things and words, an *orator,* he may do so without opposition from me; or if he prefer to call that orator, of whom I speak as having wisdom united with eloquence, a *philosopher,* I shall make no objection, provided it be allowed that neither *his* inability to speak, who understands his subject, but can not set it forth in words, nor *his* ignorance, to whom matter is wanting though words abound, can merit commendation; and if I had to choose one of the two, I should prefer uneloquent good sense to loquacious folly. But if it be inquired which is the more eminent excellence, the palm is to be given to the learned orator; and if they allow the same person to be a philosopher, there is an end of controversy; but if they distinguish them, they will acknowledge their inferiority in this respect, that all their knowledge is inherent in the *complete orator;* but in the knowledge of the *philosophers* eloquence is not necessarily inherent; which, though it may be

---

[1] For, except Metellus Numidicus and Marius, no one in those days had gained any great reputation by his conduct in the field.

[2] *Quod est conjunctum.* That is, "conjunctum cum jure civili." *Proust.* What Cicero says here is somewhat at variance with what he says, De Legg., ii., 19, where he shows, at some length, that only a small part of the civil law is necessary to be combined with the knowledge of the pontifical law. *Ellendt.*

[1] The words in brackets, says Ellendt, are certainly spurious, for they could not possibly have been written by Cicero. In the original, *quod ipse,* etc., *ipse* necessarily refers to Aristotle, of whom what is here said could never have been true.

[2] The Philoctetes of Euripides, as is generally supposed.

undervalued by them, must of necessity be thought to give a finishing grace to their sciences." When Crassus had spoken thus, he made a pause for a while, and the rest kept silence.

XXXVI. Cotta then observed, "I can not indeed complain, Crassus, that you seem to me to have given a dissertation upon a different subject from that on which you had undertaken to speak; for you have contributed to our conversation more than was either laid upon you by us, or given notice of by yourself. But certainly it was the part that belonged to you, to speak upon the embellishments of language, and you had already entered upon it, and distributed the whole excellence of eloquence into four parts; and, when you had spoken upon the first two, as we indeed thought sufficiently, but, as you said yourself, cursorily and slightly, you had two others left: how we should speak, first, *elegantly,* and next, *aptly.* But when you were proceeding to these particulars, the tide, as it were, of your genius suddenly hurried you to a distance from land, and carried you out into the deep, almost beyond the view of us all; for, embracing all knowledge of every thing, you did not indeed teach it us (for that was impossible in so short a space of time), but—I know not what improvement you may have made in the rest of the company—as for myself, you have carried me altogether into the heart of the academy, in regard to which I could wish that that were true which you have often asserted that it is not necessary to consume our lives in it, but that he may see every thing in it who only turns his eyes toward it: but even if the view be somewhat obscure, or I should be extraordinarily dull, I shall assuredly never rest, or yield to fatigue, until I understand their doubtful ways and arts of disputing for and against every question." Cæsar then said, "One thing in your remarks, Crassus, struck me very much, that you said that he who did not learn any thing soon, could never thoroughly learn it at all; so that I can have no difficulty in making the trial, and either immediately understanding what you extolled to the skies in your observations, or, if I can not do so, losing no time, as I may remain content with what I have already acquired." Here Sulpicius observed, "I, indeed, Crassus, neither desire any acquaintance with your Aristotle, nor Carneades, nor any of the philosophers; you may either imagine that I despair of being able to acquire their knowledge, or that, as is really the case, I despise it. The ordinary knowledge of common affairs, and such as are litigated in the forum, is great enough for me, for attaining that degree of eloquence which is my object; and even in that narrow circle of science I am ignorant of a multitude of things, which I begin to study, whenever any cause in which I am to speak requires them. If, therefore, you are not now fatigued, and if we are not troublesome to you, revert to those particulars which contribute to the merit and splendor of language; particulars which I desired to hear from you, not to make me despair that I can ever possibly attain eloquence, but to make some addition to my stock of learning."

XXXVII. "You require of me," said Crassus, "to speak on matters which are very well known, and with which you, Sulpicius, are not unacquainted; for what rhetorician has not treated of this subject, has not given instructions on it, has not even left something about it in writing? But I will comply with your request, and briefly explain to you at least such points as are known to me; but I shall still think that you ought to refer to those who are the authors and inventors of these minute precepts. All speech, then, is formed of words, which we must first consider singly, then in composition; for there is one merit of language which lies in single words, another which is produced by words joined and compounded. We shall therefore either use such words as are the proper and fixed names as it were of things, and apparently almost born at the same time with the things themselves; or such as are metaphorical, and placed as it were in a situation foreign to them; or such as we invent and make ourselves. In regard, then, to words taken in their own proper sense, it is a merit in the orator to avoid mean and obsolete ones, and to use such as are choice and ornamental; such as have in them some fullness and force of sound. But in this kind of *proper* words, selection is necessary, which must be decided in some measure by the judgment of the ear; in which point the mere habit of speaking well is of great effect. Even what is vulgarly said of orators by the illiterate multitude, *He uses proper words,* or *Such a one uses improper words,* is not the result of any acquired skill, but is a judgment arising from a natural sense of what is right; in which respect it is no great merit to avoid a fault (though it is of great importance to do so); yet this is the groundwork, as it were, and foundation of the whole, namely, the use and command of proper words. But the superstructure which the orator himself is to raise upon this, and in which he is to display his art, appears to be a matter for us to examine and illustrate.

XXXVIII. "There are three qualities, then, in a simple word, which the orator may employ to illustrate and adorn his language; he may choose either an *unusual* word; or one that is *new* or *metaphorical. Unusual* words are generally of ancient date and fashion, and such as have been long out of use in daily conversation; these are allowed more freely to poetical license than to ours; yet a poetical word gives occasionally dignity also to oratory; nor would I shrink from saying, with Cœlius, *Quâ tempestate Pœnus in Italiam venit,* 'At the season when the Carthaginian came into Italy:' nor *proles,* 'progeny;' nor *suboles,* 'offspring;' nor *effari,* 'to utter;' nor *nuncupari,* 'to declare;' nor, as you are in the habit of saying, Catulus, *non rebar,* 'I did not deem;' nor *non opinabar,* 'I did not opine;' nor many others, from which, if properly introduced, a speech assumes an air of greater grandeur. *New* words are such as are produced and formed by the speaker; either by joining words together, as these,

> " '*Tum pavor sapientiam omnem mî exanimato expectorat,*
> Then fear expels all wisdom from the breast
> Of me astonished;'

or,

> " '*Num non vis hujus me versutiloquas malitias?*
> Would you not have me dread his cunning malice?'

for you see that *versutiloquas* and *expectorat* are words not newly produced, but merely formed by composition. But words are often invented, without composition, as the expression of Ennius,[1] *Dii genitales,* 'the genial gods;' or *baccarum ubertate incurviscere,* 'to bend down with the fertile crop of berries.'

"The third mode, that of using words in a *metaphorical* sense, is widely prevalent, a mode of which necessity was the parent, compelled by the sterility and narrowness of language; but afterward delight and pleasure made it frequent; for as a dress was first adopted for the sake of keeping off the cold, but in process of time began to be made an ornament of the body and an emblem of dignity, so the metaphorical use of words was originally invented on account of their paucity, but became common from the delight which it afforded. For even the countrymen say, *gemmare vites,* that 'the vines are budding;' *luxuriem esse in herbis,* that 'there is a luxuriancy in the grass;' and *lœtas segetes,* that 'there is a bountiful crop;' for when that which can scarcely be signified by its proper word is expressed by one used in a metaphorical sense, the similitude taken from that which we indicate by a foreign term gives clearness to that which we wish to be understood. These metaphors, therefore, are a species of borrowing, as you take from something else that which you have not of your own. Those have a greater degree of boldness which do not show poverty, but bring some accession of splendor to our language. But why should I specify to you either the modes of their production or their various kinds?

XXXIX. "A metaphor is a brief similitude contracted into a single word; which word being put in the place of another, as if it were in its own place, conveys, if the resemblance be acknowledged, delight; if there is no resemblance, it is

---

[1] All the editions retain *ille senius,* though universally acknowledged to be corrupt. The conjecture of Turnebus, *ille Ennius,* has found most favor; that of Orellius, *illud Ennii,* is approved by Ellendt. That the words *dî genitales* were used by Ennius appears from Servius on Virg., Æn., vi., 764.

condemned. But such words should be metaphorically used as may make the subject clearer; as all these:[1]

> " '*Inhorrescit mare,*
> *Tenebrœ conduplicantur, noctisque et nimbúm occœcat nigror,*
> *Flamma inter nubes coruscat, cœlum tonitru contremit,*
> *Grando mixta imbri largifluo subita prœcipitans cadit;*
> *Undique omnes venti erumpunt, sœvi existunt turbines;*
> *Fervit œstu pelagus.*
>
> *The sea begins to shudder,*
> *Darkness is doubled; and the black of night*
> *And of the tempest thickens; fire gleams vivid*
> *Amid the clouds; the heavens with thunder shake;*
> *Hail mixed with copious rain sudden descends*
> *Precipitate; from all sides every blast*
> *Breaks forth; fierce whirlwinds gather, and the flood*
> *Boils with fresh tumult.*'

Here almost every thing is expressed in words metaphorically adapted from something similar, that the description may be heightened. Or metaphors are employed that the whole nature of any action or design may be more significantly expressed, as in the case of him who indicates, by two metaphorical words, that another person was designedly obscure, in order that what he intended might not be understood,

> " '*Quandoquidem is se circumvestit dictis, sœpit sedulò,*
> Since thus he clothes himself around with words,
> And hedges constantly.'

"Sometimes, also, brevity is the object attained by metaphor; as, *Si telum manu fugit,* 'If from his hand the javelin fled.' The throwing of a missile weapon unawares could not be described with more brevity in the proper words than it is signified by one used metaphorically. On this head, it often appears to me wonderful why all men are more delighted with words used in a metaphorical or foreign sense than in their own proper and natural signification.

XL. "For if a thing has not a name of its own, and a term peculiar to it—as the *pes,* or 'hawser,' in a ship; *nexum,* a 'bond,' which is a ceremony performed with scales;[1] *divortium,* a 'divorce,' with reference to a wife[2]—necessity compels you to borrow from another what you have not yourself; but, even in the greatest abundance of proper words, men are much more charmed with such as are uncommon, if they are used metaphorically with judgment. This happens, I imagine, either because it is some manifestation of wit to jump over such expressions as lie before you, and catch at others from a greater distance; or because he who listens is led another way in thought, and yet does not wander from the subject, which is a very great pleasure; or because a subject, and entire comparison, is dispatched in a single word; or because every metaphor that is adopted with judgment, is directed immediately to our senses, and principally to the sense of sight, which is the keenest of them all. For such expressions as the *odor* of urbanity, the *softness* of humanity, the *murmur* of the sea, and *sweetness* of language, are derived from the other senses; but those which relate to the sight are much more striking, for they place almost in the eye of the mind such objects as we can not see and discern by the natural eyes. There is, indeed, nothing in universal nature, the proper name and term of which we may not use with regard to other matters; for whencesoever a simile may be drawn (and it may be drawn from any thing), from thence a

---

[1] From Pacuvius. See Cic., Divin., i., 14.

---

[1] See Smith's Dict. of Gr. and Rom. Ant., art. *Nexum.*

[2] *Divortium,* in its proper sense, denoted the separation of roads or waters.

single word, which contains the resemblance, metaphorically applied, may give illustration to our language. In such metaphorical expressions, dissimilitude is principally to be avoided; as,

> " '*Cœli ingentes fornices,*
> The arch immense of heaven;'

for though Ennius[1] is said to have brought a globe upon the stage, yet the semblance of an arch can never be inherent in the form of a globe.

> " '*Vive, Ulixes, dum licet:*
> *Oculis postremum lumen radiatum rape:*[2]
>
> *Live, live, Ulysses, while you may, and snatch,*
> *Snatch with thine eyes the last light shining on them.*'

He did not say *cape,* 'take,' nor *pete,* 'seek,' for such expressions might have implied delay, as of one hoping to live longer; but *rape,* 'snatch,' a word which was peculiarly suitable to what he had said before, *dum licet,* 'while you may.'

XLI. "Care is next to be taken that the simile be not too far-fetched; as, for 'the Syrtis of his patrimony,' I should rather have said, 'the rock;' for 'the Charybdis of his possessions,' rather 'the gulf:' for the eyes of the mind are more easily directed to those objects which we have seen, than to those of which we have only heard. And since it is the greatest merit in a metaphorical word that what is metaphorical should strike the senses, all offensiveness is to be avoided in those objects to which the comparison must naturally draw the minds of the audience. I would not have it said that the republic was 'castrated' by the death of Africanus; I would not have Glaucia called 'the excrement of the senate;' for though there may be a resemblance, yet it is a depraved imagination in both cases that gives rise to such a comparison. I would not have the metaphor grander than the subject requires, as 'a tempest of reveling;' nor meaner, as 'the reveling of the tempest.' I would not have the metaphorical be of a more confined sense than the proper and peculiar term would have been; as,

> " '*Quidnam est, obsecro, quid te adiri abnutas?*[1]
>
> Why is it, prithee, that thou nodd'st us back
> From coming to thee?'

Vetas, prohibes, absterres, 'forbid,' 'hinder,' 'terrify,' had been better, because he had before said,

> " '*Fly quickly hence,*[2]
> *Lest my contagion or my shadow fall*
> *On men of worth.*'

Also, if you apprehend that the metaphor may appear too harsh, it may frequently be softened by prefixing a word or words to it; as if, in old times, on the death of Marcus Cato, any one had said that the senate was left 'an orphan,' the expression had been rather bold; but, 'so to speak, an orphan,' is somewhat milder; for a metaphor ought not to be too daring, but of such a nature that it may appear to have been introduced into the place of another expression, not to have sprung into it; to have come in by entreaty, and not by violence. And there is no mode of embellishment more effective as regards single words, nor any that throws a greater lustre upon language; for the ornament that flows from this figure does not consist merely in a single metaphorical word, but may be connected by a continuation of many, so that

---

[1] In his tragedy of Hecuba, as is supposed by Hermann, ad Eurip., Hec., p. 167. See Varro, L. L., v., p. 8.

[2] Supposed by Bothe, Trag. Lat. Fragm., p. 278, to be from the Niptra of Pacuvius. See Cic., Quæst. Acad., ii., 28.

[1] From the Thyestes of Ennius. Cic., Tusc., iii., 12.

[2] Orellius's text has *istim,* which is considered to be the same as *istinc.* See Victorius, ad Cic. Ep. ad Div., vi., 6.

one thing may be expressed and another understood; as,

> " 'Nor will I allow
> Myself again to strike the Grecian fleet
> On the same rock and instrument of ruin.'[1]

And this,

> " 'You err, you err, for the strong reins of law
> Shall hold you back, exulting and confiding
> Too much in your own self, and make you bow
> Beneath the yoke of empire.'

Something being assumed as similar, the words which are proper to it are metaphorically transferred (as I termed it before) to another subject.

XLII. "This is a great ornament to language, but obscurity is to be avoided in it; for from this figure arise what are called ænigmas. Nor is this rule to be observed in single words only, but in phrases, that is, in a continuation of words. Nor have metonymy and hypallage[2] their form from a single word, but from a phrase or sentence; as,

> " 'Grim Afric trembles with an awful tumult;'[3]

where for the *Africans* is used *Afric;* not a word newly compounded, as in *Mare saxifragis undis,* 'The sea with its rock-breaking waves;' nor a metaphorical one, as, *Mollitur mare,* 'The sea is softened;' but one proper name exchanged for another, for the sake of embellishment. Thus, 'Cease, Rome, thy foes to cherish,' and, 'The spacious plains are witnesses.' This figure contributes exceedingly to the ornament of style, and is frequently to be used; of which kind of expression these are examples: that the *Mars,* or fortune, *of war is common;* and to say *Ceres,* for corn; *Bacchus,* for wine; *Neptune,* for the sea; the *curia,* or *house,* for the senate; the *campus,* for the comitia or elections; the *gown,* for peace; *arms* or *weapons,* for war. Under this figure, the virtues and vices are used for the persons in whom they are inherent: '*Luxury* has broken into that house;' or, 'whither *avarice* has penetrated;' or, '*honesty* has prevailed;' or, '*justice* has triumphed.' You perceive the whole force of this kind of figure, when, by the variation or change of a word, a thing is expressed more elegantly; and to this figure is closely allied another,[1] which, though less ornamental, ought not to be unknown; as when we would have the whole of a thing understood from a part; as we say *walls* or *roof* for a whole building; or a part from the whole, as when we call one troop *the cavalry of the Roman people;* or when we signify the plural by the singular, as,

> " 'But still the Roman, though the affair has been
> Conducted well, is anxious in his heart;'[2]

or when the singular is understood from the plural,

> " 'We that were *Rudians* once are *Romans* now;'

or in whatever way, by this figure, the sense is to be understood, not as it is expressed, but as it is meant.

• • •

LII. "I have now shown, as far as I could, what I deemed most conducive to the embellish-

---

[1] Whence this and the following quotation are taken is uncertain.

[2] *Traductio atque immutatio.* See Cic., Orat., 27; Quint., viii., 6; ix., 3; infra, c. 43, 54.

[3] From the Annals of Ennius. See Cic., Ep. ad Div., ix., 7; Orat., 27; Festus v. *metonymia.*

[1] Synecdoche.

[2] This quotation and the following are from the Annals of Ennius.

ment of language; for I have spoken of the merits of single words; I have spoken of them in composition; I have spoken of the harmony of numbers and structure. But if you wish me to speak also of the form and, as it were, complexion of eloquence, there is one sort which has a fullness, but is free from tumor; one which is plain, but not without nerve and vigor; and one which, participating of both these kinds, is commended for a certain middle quality. In each of these three forms there ought to be a peculiar complexion of beauty, not produced by the daubing of paint, but diffused throughout the system by the blood. Then, finally,[1] this orator of ours is so to be finished as to his style and thoughts in general, that, as those who study fencing and polite exercises, not only think it necessary to acquire a skill in parrying and striking, but also grace and elegance of motion, so he may use such words as are suited to elegant and graceful composition, and such thoughts as contribute to the impressiveness of language. Words and thoughts are formed in almost innumerable ways, as is, I am sure, well known to you; but betwixt the formation of words and that of thoughts there is this difference, that that of the words is destroyed if you change them, that of the thoughts remains, whatever words you think proper to use. But I think that you ought to be reminded (although, indeed, you act agreeably to what I say) that you should not imagine there is any thing else to be done by the orator, at least any thing else to produce a striking and admirable effect, than to observe these three rules with regard to single words; to use frequently *metaphorical* ones, sometimes *new* ones, and rarely *very old* ones.

"But with regard to continuous composition, when we have acquired that smoothness of junction and harmony of numbers which I have explained, our whole style of oratory is to be distinguished and frequently interspersed with brilliant lights, as it were, of thoughts and of words."

• • •

---

[1] *Tum denique.* Ellendt incloses *tum* in brackets, and thinks that much of the language of the rest of the chapter is confused and incorrect. The words *ut ii, qui in armorum tractatione versantur,* which occur a little below, and which are generally condemned, are not translated.

INTRODUCTION TO QUINTILIAN

Marcus Fabius Quintilianus, commonly referred to as Quintilian, lived around 35 to 95 C.E. Quintilian is widely regarded as the second most important Roman rhetorical theorist (with Cicero being first). He was born in Spain and received his early education there, moving later to Rome to begin a career as a teacher and occasional advocate in court. Quintilian occupied the first endowed chair of rhetoric in the Roman Empire and was primarily known throughout his life as a teacher of rhetoric. Late in life he published his book, *Institutio Oratoria,* or *The Education of an Orator.* This volume appeared around 93 C.E.

The *Institutio Oratoria* is quite a lengthy work, and it has survived intact. It is comprised of twelve books. Books I and II are concerned with the nature and purpose of both education and of rhetoric itself. The rest of the books develop what has become known as the five canons of classical rhetoric. Books three through seven discuss *invention* and *arrangement.* Books eight through ten are concerned with *style.* Book eleven is about *memory* and *delivery.* Book twelve returns to the idea of oratory in general, and discusses what the ideal or perfect orator would be.

This book is a plan for a lifetime of education, with special emphasis on the training of the young in a rhetorically-grounded curriculum. The verbal arts, including recitation of famous literature and speeches; composing original orations, essays, and poems; writing and composition; logic; and dialectic are the basis for a well-rounded education. This work is therefore more than a manual or set of instructions for public speaking. Rather, it takes rhetoric as the core discipline for a lifetime of broadly-based liberal learning.

Several themes may be noted throughout Quintilian. First, he endorses and extends Cicero's idea of the orator as a calling, especially in his view of the orator as a broadly-prepared leader. This view is ironic given the fact that he lived during the Roman Empire, and the scope for rhetorically-based leadership was greatly reduced.

Quintilian's endorsement of Cicero's view of oratory as a life's commitment may help us to understand his puzzling definitions, which occur more than once throughout his work, of oratory as the art of speaking well and of the orator as a good man skilled in speaking. Critics have commented for centuries that these definitions sound like wishful thinking: People often do something that any reasonable person would call oratory yet it is not done well, and history is full of bad men and women who were skilled in speaking yet who seem nevertheless to have been orators. These puzzling definitions are best understood in the light of Cicero's view of the orator. In this view, if one took oratory as a calling or vocation, or as a commitment to lead the state in public affairs, then one would rise above petty ambition or slovenly work and strive for both goodness and skill. A commitment to a life of public leadership through rhetoric, in other words, raises one to a higher purpose. Those of us living in a cynical age might still question whether Quintilian's high ambitions for oratory and the orator justify his writing morals and excellence as *definitional* attributes of either one.

We should also note the frequent references in this excerpt to the psychology of the student. Quintilian often refers to how students think and are motivated in a sort of educational rhetoric designed to aid the teacher in appealing to the class. Quintilian, of course, devotes much attention to describing specific rhetorical exercises that he would give to students, such as confirming and refuting propositions, praising or censuring famous characters from myth or history, or arguing stock questions.

We should note Quintilian's stress on the importance of adapting to an audience rather than following rigid rhetorical rules. Although he is laying out a rhetorical theory, it has a minimum of firm dictates as to what the speaker should and should not do. Instead, he stresses that the speaker should do what is *expedient* and what is *becoming;* one might see in these very practical suggestions the need to adapt, in the Empire, to changing political circumstances.

Quintilian continued to be influential in rhetorical theory for centuries after his death. His *Institutio Oratoria* is certainly the longest and arguably the most complete work of any influence to survive from the classical age. Although he cannot be said to have broken much new ground theoretically, he is valuable for his summation of the canons of rhetoric and for laying a basis of pedagogy and theory that would ground the curriculum in many schools through the Middle Ages and beyond.

QUINTILIANUS, MARCUS FABIUS

THE INSTITUTIO ORATORIA OF QUINTILIAN

BOOK I

PREFACE

Having at length, after twenty years devoted to the training of the young, obtained leisure for study, I was asked by certain of my friends to write something on the art of speaking. For a long time I resisted their entreaties, since I was well aware that some of the most distinguished Greek and Roman writers had bequeathed to posterity a number of works dealing with this subject, to the composition of which they had devoted the utmost care. This seemed to me to be an admirable excuse for my refusal, but served merely to increase their enthusiasm. They urged that previous writers on the subject had expressed different and at times contradictory opinions, between which it was very difficult to choose. They thought therefore that they were justified in imposing on me the task, if not of discovering original views, at least of passing definite judgment on those expressed by my predecessors. I was moved to comply not so much because I felt confidence that I was equal to the task, as because I had a certain compunction about refusing. The subject proved more extensive than I had first imagined; but finally I volunteered to shoulder a

English Translation by H. E. Butler, M.A., Professor of Latin in London University

task which was on a far larger scale than that which I was originally asked to undertake. I wished on the one hand to oblige my very good friends beyond their requests, and on the other to avoid the beaten track and the necessity of treading where others had gone before. For almost all others who have written on the art of oratory have started with the assumption that their readers were perfect in all other branches of education and that their own task was merely to put the finishing touches to their rhetorical training; this is due to the fact that they either despised the preliminary stages of education or thought that they were not their concern, since the duties of the different branches of education are distinct one from another, or else, and this is nearer the truth, because they had no hope of making a remunerative display of their talent in dealing with subjects, which, although necessary, are far from being showy: just as in architecture it is the superstructure and not the foundations which attracts the eye. I on the other hand hold that the art of oratory includes all that is essential for the training of an orator, and that it is impossible to reach the summit in any subject unless we have first passed through all the elementary stages. I shall not therefore refuse to stoop to the consideration of those minor details, neglect of which may result in there being no opportunity for more important things, and propose to mould the studies of my orator from infancy, on the assumption that his whole education has been entrusted to my charge. This work I dedicate to you, Marcellus Victorius. You have been the truest of friends to me and you have shown a passionate enthusiasm for literature. But good as these reasons are, they are not the only reasons that lead me to regard you as especially worthy of such a pledge of our mutual affection. There is also the consideration that this book should prove of service in the education of your son Geta, who, young though he is, already shows clear promise of real talent. It has been my design to lead my reader from the very cradle of speech through all the stages of education which can be of any service to our budding orator till we have reached the very summit of the art. I have been all the more desirous of so doing because two books on the art of rhetoric are at present circulating under my name, although never published by me or composed for such a purpose. One is a two days' lecture which was taken down by the boys who were my audience. The other consists of such notes as my good pupils succeeded in taking down from a course of lectures on a somewhat more extensive scale: I appreciate their kindness, but they showed an excess of enthusiasm and a certain lack of discretion in doing my utterances the honour of publication. Consequently in the present work although some passages remain the same, you will find many alterations and still more additions, while the whole theme will be treated with greater system and with as great perfection as lies within my power.

My aim, then, is the education of the perfect orator. The first essential for such an one is that he should be a good man, and consequently we demand of him not merely the possession of exceptional gifts of speech, but of all the excellences of character as well. For I will not admit that the principles of upright and honourable living should, as some have held, be regarded as the peculiar concern of philosophy. The man who can really play his part as a citizen and is capable of meeting the demands both of public and private business, the man who can guide a state by his counsels, give it a firm basis by his legislation and purge its vices by his decisions as a judge, is assuredly no other than the orator of our quest. Wherefore, although I admit I shall make use of certain of the principles laid down in philosophical textbooks, I would insist that such principles have a just claim to form part of the subject-matter of this work and do actually belong to the art of oratory. I shall frequently be compelled to speak of such virtues as courage, justice, self-control; in fact scarcely a case comes up in which some one of these virtues is not involved; every one of them requires illustration and consequently makes a demand on the imagination and eloquence of the pleader. I ask you then, can there be any doubt that, wherever imaginative power and amplitude of diction are required, the orator has a specially important part to play? These two branches of knowledge were, as Cicero has clearly shown,[1] so closely united, not merely in theory but in practice, that the same men were regarded as uniting the qualifications of orator and philosopher. Subsequently this single branch of study split up into its component parts, and thanks to the indolence of its professors was regarded as consisting of several distinct subjects. As soon as speaking became a means of livelihood and the practice of making an evil use of the blessings of eloquence came into vogue, those who had a reputation for eloquence ceased to study moral philosophy, and ethics, thus abandoned by the orators, became the prey of weaker intellects. As a consequence certain persons, disdaining the toil of learning to speak well, returned to the task of forming character and establishing rules of life and kept to themselves what is, if we *must* make a division, the better part of philosophy, but presumptuously laid claim to the sole possession of the title of philosopher, a distinction which neither the greatest generals nor the most famous statesmen and administrators have ever dared to claim for themselves. For they preferred the performance to the promise of great deeds. I am ready to admit that many of the old philosophers inculcated the most excellent principles and practised what they preached. But in our own day the name of philosopher has too often been the mask for the worst vices. For their attempt has not been to win the name of philosopher by virtue and the earnest search for wisdom; instead they have sought to disguise the depravity of their characters by the assumption of a stern and austere mien accompanied by the wearing of a garb differing from that of their fellow men. Now as a matter of fact we all of us frequently handle those themes which philosophy claims for its own. Who, short of being an utter villain, does not speak of justice, equity and virtue? Who (and even common country-folk are no exception) does not make some inquiry into the causes of natural phenomena? As for the special uses and distinctions of words, they should be a subject of study common to all who give any thought to the meaning of language. But it is surely the orator who will have the greatest mastery of all such departments of knowledge and the greatest power to express it in words. And if ever he had reached perfection, there would be no need to go to the schools of philosophy for the precepts of virtue. As things stand, it is occasionally necessary to have recourse to those authors who have, as I said above, usurped the better part of the art of oratory after its desertion by the orators and to demand back what is ours by right, not with a view to appropriating their discoveries, but to show them that they have appropriated what in truth belonged to others. Let our ideal orator then be such as to have a genuine title to the name of philosopher: it is not sufficient that he should be blameless in point of character (for I cannot agree with those who hold this opinion): he must also be a thorough master of the science and the art of speaking, to an extent that perhaps no orator has yet attained. Still we must none the less follow the ideal, as was done by not a few of the ancients, who, though they refused to admit that the perfect sage had yet been found, none the less handed down precepts of wisdom for the use of posterity. Perfect eloquence is assuredly a reality, which is not beyond the reach of human intellect. Even if we fail to reach it, those whose aspirations are highest, will attain to greater heights than those who abandon themselves to premature despair of ever reaching the goal and halt at the very foot of the ascent.

I have therefore all the juster claim to indulgence, if I refuse to pass by those minor details which are none the less essential to my task. My first book will be concerned with the education preliminary to the duties of the teacher of rhetoric. My second will deal with the rudiments of the schools of rhetoric and with problems connected with the essence of rhetoric itself. The next five will be concerned with Invention, in which I include Arrangement. The four following will be assigned to Eloquence, under which head I include Memory and Delivery. Finally there will be one book in which our complete orator will be delineated; as far as my feeble powers permit, I shall discuss his character, the rules which should guide him in undertaking, studying and pleading cases, the style of his eloquence, the time at which he should cease to plead cases and the studies to which he should devote himself after such cessation. In the course of these discussions I shall deal in its proper place with the method of teaching by which students will acquire not merely a knowledge of those things to which the name of art is restricted by certain theorists, and will not only come to understand the laws of rhetoric, but will acquire that which will increase their powers of speech and nourish their eloquence. For as a rule the result of the dry textbooks on the art of rhetoric is that by straining after excessive subtlety they impair and cripple all the nobler elements of style, exhaust the life-blood of the imagination and leave but the bare bones, which, while it is right and necessary that they should exist and be bound each to each by their respective ligaments, require a covering of flesh as well. I shall therefore avoid the precedent set by the majority and shall not restrict myself to this narrow conception of my theme, but shall include in my twelve books a brief demonstration of everything which may seem likely to contribute to the education of an orator. For if I were to attempt to say all that might be said on each subject, the book would never be finished.

There is however one point which I must emphasise before I begin, which is this. Without natural gifts technical rules are useless. Consequently the student who is devoid of talent will derive no more profit from this work than barren soil from a treatise on agriculture. There are, it is true, other natural aids, such as the possession of a good voice and robust lungs, sound health, powers of endurance and grace, and if these are possessed only to a moderate extent, they may be improved by methodical training. In some cases, however, these gifts are lacking to such an extent that their absence is fatal to all such advantages as talent and study can confer, while, similarly, they are of no profit in themselves unless cultivated by skilful teaching, persistent study and continuous and extensive practice in writing, reading and speaking.

• • •

BOOK II

I. The custom has prevailed and is daily growing commoner of sending boys to the schools of rhetoric much later than is reasonable: this is always the case as regards Latin rhetoric and occasionally applies to Greek as well. The reason for this is twofold: the rhetoricians, more especially our own, have abandoned certain of their duties and the teachers of literature have undertaken tasks which rightly belong to others. For the rhetorician considers that his duty is merely to declaim and give instruction in the theory and practice of declamation and confines his activities to deliberative and judicial themes, regarding all others as beneath the dignity of his profession; while the teacher of literature is not satisfied to take what is left him (and we owe him a debt of gratitude for this), but even presumes to handle declamations in character and deliberative themes,[1] tasks which impose the very heaviest burden on the speaker. Consequently subjects which once formed the first stages of rhetoric have come to form the final stages of a literary education, and boys who are ripe for more advanced study are kept back in the inferior school and practise rhetoric under the direction of teachers of literature. Thus we get the absurd result that a boy is not regarded as fit to go on to the schools of declamation till he knows how to declaim.

The two professions must each be assigned their proper sphere. *Grammatice,* which we translate as the science of letters, must learn to know its own limits, especially as it has encroached so far beyond the boundaries to which its unpretentious name should restrict it and to which its earlier professors actually confined themselves. Springing from a tiny fountain-head, it has gathered strength from the historians and critics and has swollen to the dimensions of a brimming river, since, not content with the theory of correct speech, no inconsiderable subject, it has usurped the study of practically all the highest departments of knowledge. On the other hand rhetoric, which derives its name from the power of eloquence, must not shirk its peculiar duties nor rejoice to see its own burdens shouldered by others. For the neglect of these is little less than a surrender of its birthright. I will of course admit that there may be a few professors of literature who have acquired sufficient knowledge to be able to teach rhetoric as well; but when they do so, they are performing the duties of the rhetorician, not their own.

A further point into which we must enquire concerns the age at which a boy may be considered sufficiently advanced to profit by the instructions of the rhetorician. In this connexion we must consider not the boy's actual age, but the progress he has made in his studies. To put it briefly, I hold that the best answer to the question "When should a boy be sent to the school of rhetoric?" is this, "When he is fit." But this question is really dependent on that previously raised. For if the duties of the teacher of literature are prolonged to include instruction in deliberative declamation, this will postpone the need for the rhetorician. On the other hand if the rhetorician does not refuse to undertake the first duties of his task, his instruction will be required from the moment the boy begins to compose narratives and his first attempts at passages of praise or denunciation. We know that the orators of earlier days improved their eloquence by declaiming themes and common-places[1] and other forms of rhetorical exercises not involving particular circumstances or persons such as provide the material for real or imaginary causes.[2] From this we can clearly see what a scandalous dereliction of duty it is for the schools of rhetoric to abandon this department of their work, which was not merely its first, but for a long time its sole task. What is there in those exercises of which I have just spoken that does not involve matters which are the special concern of rhetoric and further are typical of actual legal cases? Have we not to narrate facts in the law-courts? Indeed I am not sure that this is not the most important department of rhetoric in actual practice. Are not eulogy and denunciation frequently introduced in the course of the contests of the courts? Are not common-places frequently inserted in the very heart of lawsuits, whether, like those which we find in the works of Cicero, they are directed against vice, or, like those published by Quintus Hortensius, deal with questions of general interest such as "whether small points of argument should carry weight," or are employed to defend or impugn the credibility of witnesses? These are weapons which we should always have stored in our armoury ready for immediate use as occasion may demand. The critic who denies that such matters concern an orator is one who will refuse to believe that a statue is being begun when its limbs are actually being cast. Some will think that I am in too great a hurry, but let no one accuse me of thinking that the pupil who has been entrusted to the rhetorician should forthwith be withdrawn from the teacher of literature. The latter will still have certain hours allotted him, and there is no reason to fear that a boy will be overloaded by receiving instruction from two different masters. It will not mean any increase of work, but merely the division among two masters of the studies which were previously indiscriminately combined under one: and the efficiency of either teacher will be increased. This method is still in vogue among the Greeks, but has been abandoned by us, not perhaps without some excuse, as there were others ready to step into the rhetorician's shoes.

• • •

IV. I shall now proceed to indicate what I think should be the first subjects in which the rhetorician should give instruction, and shall postpone for a time our consideration of the art of rhetoric in the narrow sense in which that term is popularly used. For in my opinion it is most desirable that we should commence with something resembling the subjects already acquired under the teacher of literature.

Now there are three forms of narrative, without counting the type used in actual legal cases. First there is the fictitious narrative as we get it in tragedies and poems, which is not merely not true but has little resemblance to truth.[1] Secondly, there is the realistic narrative as presented by comedies, which, though not true, has yet a certain verisimilitude. Thirdly there is the historical narrative, which is an exposition of actual fact. Poetic narratives are the property of the teacher of literature. The rhetorician therefore should begin with the historical narrative, whose force is in proportion to its truth. I will, however, postpone my demonstration of what I regard as the best method of narration till I come to deal with narration as required in the courts.[2] In the meantime, it will be sufficient to urge that it should be neither dry nor jejune (for why spend so much labour over our studies if a bald and naked statement of fact is regarded as sufficiently expressive?); nor on the other hand must it be tortuous or revel in elaborate descriptions, such as those in which so many are led to indulge by a misguided imitation of poetic licence. Both these extremes are faults; but that which springs from poverty of wit is worse than that which is due to imaginative excess. For we cannot demand or expect a perfect style from boys. But there is greater promise in a certain luxuriance of mind, in ambitious effort and an ardour that leads at times to ideas bordering on the extravagant. I have no objection to a little exuberance in the young learner. Nay, I would urge teachers too like nurses to be careful to provide softer food for still undeveloped minds and to suffer them to take their fill of the milk of the more attractive studies. For the time being the body may be somewhat plump, but maturer years will reduce it to a sparer habit. Such plumpness gives hope of strength; a child fully formed in every limb is likely to grow up a puny weakling. The young should be more daring and inventive and should rejoice in their inventions, even though correctness and severity are still to be acquired. Exuberance is easily remedied, but barrenness is incurable, be your efforts what they may. To my mind the boy who gives least promise is one in whom the critical faculty develops in advance of the imagination. I like to see the firstfruits of the mind copious to excess and almost extravagant in their profusion. The years as they pass will skim off much of the froth, reason will file away many excrescences, and something too will be removed by what I may perhaps call the wear and tear of life, so long as there is sufficient material to admit of cutting and chiselling away. And there will be sufficient, if only we do not draw the plate too thin to begin with, so that it runs the risk of being broken if the graver cut too deep. Those of my readers who know their Cicero will not be surprised that I take this view: for does he not say "I would have the youthful mind run riot in the luxuriance of its growth"?[3]

We must, therefore, take especial care, above all where boys are concerned, to avoid a dry teacher, even as we avoid a dry and arid soil for plants that are still young and tender. For with such a teacher their growth is stunted and their eyes are turned earthwards, and they are afraid to rise above the level of daily speech. Their leanness is regarded as a sign of health and their weakness as a sign of sound judgment, and while they are content that their work should be devoid of faults they fall into the fault of being devoid of merit. So let not the ripeness of vintage come too soon nor the must turn harsh while yet in the vat; thus it will last for years and mellow with age.

It is worth while too to warn the teacher that undue severity in correcting faults is liable at times to discourage a boy's mind from effort. He loses hope and gives way to vexation, then last of all comes to hate his work and fearing everything attempts nothing. This phenomenon is familiar to farmers, who hold that the pruning-hook should not be applied while the leaves are yet young, for they seem to "shrink from the steel"[4] and to be unable as yet to endure a scar. The instructor therefore should be as kindly as possible at this stage; remedies, which are harsh by nature, must be applied with a gentle hand: some portions of the work must be praised, others tolerated and others altered: the reason for the alterations should however be given, and in some cases the master will illumine an obscure passage by inserting something of his own. Occasionally again the teacher will find it useful to dictate whole themes himself that the boy may imitate them and for the time being love them as if they were his own. But if a boy's composition is so careless as not to admit of correction, I have found it useful to give a fresh exposition of the theme and to tell him to write it again, pointing out that he was capable of doing better: for there is nothing like hope for making study a pleasure. Different ages however demand different methods: the task set and the standard of correction must be proportioned to the pupil's strength. When boys ventured on something that was too daring or exuberant, I used to say to them that I approved of it for the moment, but that the time would come when I should no longer tolerate such a style. The result was that the consciousness of ability filled them with pleasure, without blinding their judgment.

However, to return to the point from which I had digressed. Written narratives should be composed with the utmost care. It is useful at first, when a child has just begun to speak, to make him repeat what he has heard with a view to improving his powers of speech; and for the same purpose, and with good reason, I would make him tell his story from the end back to the beginning or start in the middle and go backwards or forwards, but only so long as he is at his teacher's knee and while he is incapable of greater effort and is beginning to connect words and things, thereby strengthening the memory. Even so when he is beginning to understand the nature of correct and accurate speech, extempore effusions, improvised without waiting for thought to supply the matter or a moment's hesitation before rising to the feet, must not be permitted: they proceed from a passion for display that would do credit to a common mountebank. Such proceedings fill ignorant parents with senseless pride, while the boys themselves lose all respect for their work, adopt a conceited bearing, and acquire the habit of speaking in the worst style and actually practising their faults, while they develop an arrogant conviction of their own talents which often proves fatal even to the most genuine proficiency. There will be a special time for acquiring fluency of speech and I shall not pass the subject by unnoticed. For the meantime it will suffice if a boy, by dint of taking pains and working as hard as his age will permit, manages to produce something worthy of approval. Let him get used to this until it becomes a second nature. It is only he who learns to speak correctly before he can speak with rapidity who will reach the heights that are our goal or the levels immediately below them.

To narratives is annexed the task of refuting and confirming them, styled *anaskeue* and *kataskeue,* from which no little advantage may be derived. This may be done not merely in connexion with fiction and stories transmitted by the poets, but with the actual records of history as well. For instance we may discuss the credibility of the story that a raven settled on the head of Valerius in the midst of a combat and with its wings and beak struck the eyes of the Gaul who was his adversary, and a quantity of arguments may be produced on either side: or we may discuss the tradition that Scipio[1] was begotten by a serpent, or that Romulus was suckled by the she-wolf, or the story of Numa and Egeria. As regards Greek history, it allows itself something very like poetic licence. Again the time and place of some particular occurrence and sometimes even the persons concerned often provide matter for discussion: Livy for instance is frequently in doubt as to what actually occurred and historians often disagree.

From this our pupil will begin to proceed to more important themes, such as the praise of famous men and the denunciation of the wicked. Such tasks are profitable in more than one respect. The mind is exercised by the variety and multiplicity of the subject matter, while the character is moulded by the contemplation of virtue and vice. Further wide knowledge of facts is thus acquired, from which examples may be drawn if circumstances so demand, such illustrations being of the utmost value in every kind of case. It is but a step from this to practice in the comparison of the respective merits of two characters. This is of course a very similar theme to the preceding, but involves a duplication of the subject matter and deals not merely with the nature of virtues and vices, but with their degree as well. But the method to be followed in panegyric and invective will be dealt with in its proper place, as it forms the third department of rhetoric.[1]

As to *commonplaces* (I refer to those in which we denounce vices themselves such as adultery, gambling or profligacy without attacking particular persons), they come straight from the courts and, if we add the name of the defendant, amount to actual accusations. As a rule, however, the general character of a commonplace is usually given a special turn: for instance we make our adulterer blind, our gambler poor and our profligate far advanced in years. Sometimes too they entail defence: for we may speak on behalf of luxury or love, while a pimp or a parasite may be defended in such a way that we appear as counsel not for the character itself, but to rebut some specific charge that is brought against him.

Theses on the other hand are concerned with the comparison of things and involve questions such as "Which is preferable, town or country life?" or "Which deserves the greatest praise, the lawyer or the soldier?" These provide the most attractive and copious practice in the art of speaking, and are most useful whether we have an eye to the duties of deliberative oratory or the arguments of the courts. For instance Cicero in his *pro Murena*[2] deals very fully with the second of the two problems mentioned above. Other *theses* too belong entirely to the deliberative class of oratory, as for instance the questions as to "Whether marriage is desirable" or "Whether a public career is a proper object of ambition." Put such discussions into the mouths of specific persons and they become deliberative declamations at once.

My own teachers used to prepare us for conjectural cases by a form of exercise which was at once useful and attractive: they made us discuss and develop questions such as "Why in Sparta is Venus represented as wearing armour?"[3] or "Why is Cupid believed to be a winged boy armed with arrows and a torch?" and the like. In these exercises our aim was to discover the intention implied, a question which frequently occurs in controversial declamations. Such themes may perhaps be regarded as a kind of *chria* or moral essay.

That certain topics such as the question as to whether we should always believe a witness or whether we should rely on circumstantial evidence, are part and parcel of actual forensic pleading is so obvious that certain speakers, men too who have held civil office with no small distinction, have written out passages dealing with such themes, committed them to memory and kept them ready for immediate use, with a view to employing them when occasion arose as a species of ornament to be inserted into their extempore speeches. This practice—for I am not going to postpone expressing my judgment on it—I used to regard a confession of extreme weakness. For how can such men find appropriate arguments in the course of actual cases which continually present new and different features? How can they answer the points that their opponents may bring up? how deal a rapid counterstroke in debate or cross-examine a witness? if, even in those matters which are of common occurrence and crop up in the majority of cases, they cannot give expression to the most familiar thoughts except in words prepared so far in advance. And when they produce the same passage in a number of different cases, they must come to loathe it like food that has grown cold or stale, and they can hardly avoid a feeling of shame at displaying this miserable piece of furniture to an audience whose memory must have detected it so many times already: like the furniture of the ostentatious poor, it is sure to show signs of wear through being used for such a variety of different purposes. Also it must be remembered that there is hardly a single commonplace of such universal application that it will fit any actual case, unless some special link is provided to connect it with the subject: otherwise it will seem to have been tacked on to the speech, not interwoven in its texture, either because it is out of keeping with the circumstances or like most of its kind is inappropriately employed not because it is wanted, but because it is ready for use. Some speakers, for example, introduce the most long-winded commonplaces just for the sake of the sentiments they contain, whereas rightly the sentiments should spring from the context. Such disquisitions are at once ornamental and useful, only if they arise from the nature of the case. But the most finished eloquence, unless it tend to the winning of the case, is to say the least superfluous and may even defeat its own purpose. However I must bring this digression to a close.

The praise or denunciation of laws requires greater powers; indeed they should almost be equal to the most serious tasks of rhetoric. The answer to the question as to whether this exercise is more nearly related to deliberative or controversial oratory depends on custom and law and consequently varies in different states. Among the Greeks the proposer of a law was called upon to set forth his case before a judge,[1] while in Rome it was the custom to urge the acceptance or rejection of a law before the public assembly. But in any case the arguments advanced in such cases are few in number and of a definite type. For there are only three kinds of law, *sacred, public* and *private.* This division is of rhetorical value chiefly when a law is to be praised. For example the orator may advance from praise to praise by a series of gradations, praising an enactment first because it is *law,* secondly because it is *public,* and, finally, designed for the support of *religion.* As regards the questions which generally arise, they are common to all cases. Doubts may be raised as to whether the mover is legally in a position to propose a law, as happened in the case of Publius Clodius, whose appointment as tribune of the plebs was alleged to be unconstitutional.[2] Or the legality of the proposal itself may be impugned in various ways; it may for instance be urged that the law was not promulgated within seventeen[3] days, or was proposed, or is being proposed on an improper day, or in defiance of the tribunicial veto or the auspices or any other legal obstacle, or again that it is contrary to some existing law. But such points are not suitable to elementary rhetorical exercises, which are not concerned with persons, times or particular cases. Other subjects, whether the dispute be real or fictitious, are generally treated on the following lines. The fault must lie either in the words or the matter. As regards the words, the question will be whether they are sufficiently clear or contain some ambiguity, and as regards the matter whether the law is consistent with itself or should be retrospective or apply to special individuals. The point however which is most commonly raised is the question whether the law is right or expedient. I am well aware that many rhetoricians introduce a number of sub-divisions in connexion with this latter enquiry. I however include under the term *right* all such qualities as justice, piety and religion. Justice is however usually discussed under various aspects. A question may be raised about the acts with which the law is concerned, as to whether they deserve punishment or reward or as to the degree of punishment or reward that should be assigned, since excess in either direction is open to criticism. Again expediency is sometimes determined by the nature of things, sometimes by the circumstances of the time. Another common subject of controversy is whether a law can be enforced, while one must not shut one's eyes to the fact that exception is sometimes taken to laws in their entirety, but sometimes only in part, examples of both forms of criticism being found in famous speeches. I am well aware, too, that there are laws which are not proposed with a view to perpetuity, but are concerned with temporary honours or commands, such as the *lex Manilia*[4] which is the subject of one of Cicero's speeches. This however is not the place for instructions on this topic, since they depend on the special circumstances of the matters under discussion, not on their general characteristics.

Such were the subjects on which the ancients as a rule exercised their powers of speaking, though they called in the assistance of the logicians as well to teach them the theory of argument. For it is generally agreed that the declamation of fictitious themes in imitation of the questions that arise in the lawcourts or deliberative assemblies came into vogue among the Greeks about the time of Demetrius of Phalerum. Whether this type of exercise was actually invented by him I have failed to discover, as I have acknowledged in another work.[1] But not even those who most strongly assert his claim to be the inventor, can produce any adequate authority in support of their opinion. As regards Latin teachers of rhetoric, of whom Plotius was the most famous, Cicero[2] informs us that they came into existence towards the end of the age of Crassus.

V. I will speak of the theory of declamation a little later. In the mean time, as we are discussing the elementary stages of a rhetorical education, I think I should not fail to point out how greatly the rhetorician will contribute to his pupils' progress, if he imitates the teacher of literature whose duty it is to expound the poets, and gives the pupils whom he has undertaken to train, instruction in the reading of history and still more of the orators. I myself have adopted this practice for the benefit of a few pupils of suitable age whose parents thought it would be useful. But though my intentions were excellent, I found that there were two serious obstacles to success: long custom had established a different method of teaching, and my pupils were for the most part full-grown youths who did not require this form of teaching, but were taking my work as their model. However, the fact that I have been somewhat late in making the discovery is not a reason why I should be ashamed to recommend it to those who come after me. I now know that this form of teaching is practised by the Greeks, but is generally entrusted to assistants, as the professors themselves consider that they have no time to give individual instruction to each pupil as he reads. And I admit that the form of lecture which this requires, designed as it is to make boys follow the written word with ease and accuracy, and even that which aims at teaching the meaning of any rare words that may occur, are to be regarded as quite below the dignity of the teacher of rhetoric. On the other hand it is emphatically part of his profession and the undertaking which he makes in offering himself as a teacher of eloquence, to point out the merits of authors or, for that matter, any faults that may occur: and this is all the more the case, as I am not asking teachers to undertake the task of recalling their pupils to stand at their knee once more and of assisting them in the reading of whatever book they may select. It seems to me at once an easier and more profitable method to call for silence and choose some one pupil—and it will be best to select them by turns—to read aloud, in order that they may at the same time learn the correct method of elocution. The case with which the speech selected for reading is concerned should then be explained, for if this be done they will have a clearer understanding of what is to be read. When the reading is commenced, no important point should be allowed to pass unnoticed either as regards the resourcefulness or the style shown in the treatment of the subject: the teacher must point out how the orator seeks to win the favour of the judge in his *exordium,* what clearness, brevity and sincerity, and at times what shrewd design and well-concealed artifice is shown in the statement of facts. For the only true art in pleading is that which can only be understood by one who is a master of the art himself. The teacher will proceed further to demonstrate what skill is shown in the division into heads, how subtle and frequent are the thrusts of argument, what vigour marks the stirring and what charm the soothing passage, how fierce is the invective and how full of wit the jests, and in conclusion how the orator establishes his sway over the emotions of his audience, forces his way into their very hearts and brings the feelings of the jury into perfect sympathy with all his words. Finally as regards the style, he will emphasise the appropriateness, elegance or sublimity of particular words, will indicate where the amplification of the theme is deserving of praise and where there is virtue in a diminuendo; and will call attention to brilliant metaphors, figures of speech and passages combining smoothness and polish with a general impression of manly vigour.

It will even at times be of value to read speeches which are corrupt and faulty in style, but still meet with general admiration thanks to the perversity of modern tastes, and to point out how many expressions in them are inappropriate, obscure, high-flown, grovelling, mean, extravagant or effeminate, although they are not merely praised by the majority of critics, but, worse still, praised just because they are bad. For we have come to regard direct and natural speech as incompatible with genius, while all that is in any way abnormal is admired as exquisite. Similarly we see that some people place a higher value on figures which are in any way monstrous or distorted than they do on those who have not lost any of the advantages of the normal form of man. There are even some who are captivated by the shams of artifice and think that there is more beauty in those who pluck out superfluous hair or use depilatories, who dress their locks by scorching them with the curling iron and glow with a complexion that is not their own, than can ever be conferred by nature pure and simple, so that it really seems as if physical beauty depended entirely on moral hideousness.

It will, however, be the duty of the rhetorician not merely to teach these things, but to ask frequent questions as well, and test the critical powers of his class. This will prevent his audience from becoming inattentive and will secure that his words do not fall on deaf ears. At the same time the class will be led to find out things for themselves and to use their intelligence, which is after all the chief aim of this method of training. For what else is our object in teaching, save that our pupils should not always require to be taught? I will venture to say that this particular form of exercise, if diligently pursued, will teach learners more than all the text-books of all the rhetoricians: these are no doubt of very considerable use, but being somewhat general in their scope, it is quite impossible for them to deal with all the special cases that are of almost daily occurrence. The art of war will provide a parallel: it is no doubt based on certain general principles, but it will none the less be far more useful to know the methods employed, whether wisely or the reverse, by individual generals under varying circumstances and conditions of time and place. For there are no subjects in which, as a rule, practice is not more valuable than precept. Is a teacher to declaim to provide a model for his audience, and will not more profit be derived from the reading of Cicero or Demosthenes? Is a pupil to be publicly corrected if he makes a mistake in declaiming, and will it not be more useful, and more agreeable too, to correct some actual speech? For everyone has a preference for hearing the faults of others censured rather than his own. I might say more on the subject. But every one can see the advantages of this method. Would that the reluctance to put it into practice were not as great as the pleasure that would undoubtedly be derived from so doing!

This method once adopted, we are faced by the comparatively easy question as to what authors should be selected for our reading. Some have recommended authors of inferior merit on the ground that they were easier to understand. Others on the contrary would select the more florid school of writers on the ground that they are likely to provide the nourishment best suited to the minds of the young. For my part I would have them read the best authors from the very beginning and never leave them, choosing those, however, who are simplest and most intelligible. For instance, when prescribing for boys, I should give Livy the preference over Sallust; for, although the latter is the greater historian, one requires to be well-advanced in one's studies to appreciate him properly. Cicero, in my opinion, provides pleasant reading for beginners and is sufficiently easy to understand: it is possible not only to learn much from him, but to come to love him. After Cicero I should, following the advice of Livy, place such authors as most nearly resemble him.

There are two faults of taste against which boys should be guarded with the utmost care.

Firstly no teacher suffering from an excessive admiration of antiquity, should be allowed to cramp their minds by the study of Cato and the Gracchi and other similar authors. For such reading will give them a harsh and bloodless style, since they will as yet be unable to understand the force and vigour of these authors, and contenting themselves with a style which doubtless was admirable in its day, but is quite unsuitable to ours, will come to think (and nothing could be more fatal) that they really resemble great men. Secondly the opposite extreme must be equally avoided: they must not be permitted to fall victims to the pernicious allurements of the precious blooms produced by our modern euphuists, thus acquiring a passion for the luscious sweetness of such authors, whose charm is all the more attractive to boyish intellects because it is so easy of achievement. Once, however, the judgment is formed and out of danger of perversion, I should strongly recommend the reading of ancient authors, since if, after clearing away all the uncouthness of those rude ages, we succeed in absorbing the robust vigour and virility of their native genius, our more finished style will shine with an added grace: I also approve the study of the moderns at this stage, since even they have many merits. For nature has not doomed us to be dullards, but we have altered our style of oratory and indulged our caprices over much. It is in their ideals rather than their talents that the ancients show themselves our superiors. It will therefore be possible to select much that is valuable from modern writers, but we must take care that the precious metal is not debased by the dross with which it is so closely intermingled. Further I would not merely gladly admit, but would even contend that we have recently had and still have certain authors who deserve imitation in their entirety. But it is not for everyone to decide who these writers are. Error in the choice of earlier authors is attended with less danger, and I have therefore postponed the study of the moderns, for fear that we should imitate them before we are qualified to judge of their merits.

• • •

VIII. It is generally and not unreasonably regarded as the sign of a good teacher that he should be able to differentiate between the abilities of his respective pupils and to know their natural bent. The gifts of nature are infinite in their variety, and mind differs from mind almost as much as body from body. This is clear from a consideration of the orators themselves, who differ in style to such an extent that no one is like another, in spite of the fact that numbers have modelled their style on that of their favorite authors. Many again think it useful to direct their instruction to the fostering of natural advantages and to guide the talents of their pupils along the lines which they instinctively tend to follow. Just as an expert gymnast, when he enters a gymnasium full of boys, after testing body and mind in every way, is able to decide for what class of athletic contest they should be trained, even so, they say, a teacher of oratory after careful observation of a boy's stylistic preferences, be they for terseness and polish, energy, dignity, charm, roughness, brilliance or wit, will so adapt his instructions to individual needs that each pupil will be pushed forward in the sphere for which his talents seem specially to design him; for nature, when cultivated, goes from strength to strength, while he who runs counter to her bent is ineffective in those branches of the art for which he is less suited and weakens the talents which he seemed born to employ. Now, since the critic who is guided by his reason is free to dissent even from received opinions, I must insist that to my thinking this view is only partially true. It is undoubtedly necessary to note the individual gifts of each boy, and no one would ever convince me that it is not desirable to differentiate courses of study with this in view. One boy will be better adapted for the study of history, another for poetry, another for law, while some perhaps had better be packed off to the country. The teacher of rhetoric will distinguish such special aptitudes, just as our gymnast will turn one pupil into a runner, another into a boxer or wrestler or an expert at some other of the athletic accomplishments for which prizes are awarded at the sacred games. But on the other hand, he who is destined for the bar must study not one department merely, but must perfect himself in all the accomplishments which his profession demands, even though some of them may seem too hard for him when he approaches them as a learner. For if natural talent alone were sufficient, education might be dispensed with. Suppose we are given a pupil who, like so many, is of depraved tastes and swollen with his own conceit; shall we suffer him to go his own sweet way? If a boy's disposition is naturally dry and jejune, ought we not to feed it up or at any rate clothe it in fairer apparel? For, if in some cases it is necessary to remove certain qualities, surely there are others where we may be permitted to add what is lacking. Not that I would set myself against the will of nature. No innate good quality should be neglected, but defects must be made good and weaknesses made strong. When Isocrates, the prince of instructors, whose works proclaim his eloquence no less than his pupils testify to his excellence as a teacher, gave his opinion of Ephorus and Theopompus to the effect that the former needed the spur and the latter the curb, what was his meaning? Surely not that the sluggish temperament of the one and the headlong ardour of the other alike required modification by instruction, but rather that each would gain from an admixture of the qualities of the other.

In the case of weaker understandings however some concession must be made and they should be directed merely to follow the call of their nature, since thus they will be more effective in doing the only thing that lies in their power. But if we are fortunate enough to meet with richer material, such as justifies us in the hope of producing a real orator, we must leave no oratorical virtue uncared for. For though he will necessarily have a natural bent for some special department of oratory, he will not feel repelled by the others, and by sheer application will develop his other qualities until they equal those in which he naturally excels. The skilled gymnast will once again provide us with a parallel: if he undertakes to train a pancratiast,[1] he will not merely teach him how to use his fists or his heels, nor will he restrict his instructions to the holds in wrestling, giving special attention to certain tricks of this kind, but will train him in every department of the science. Some will no doubt be incapable of attaining proficiency in certain exercises; these must specialise on those which lie within their powers. For there are two things which he must be most careful to avoid: first, he must not attempt the impossible, secondly he must not switch off his pupil from what he can do well to exercises for which he is less well suited. But if his pupil is like the famous Nicostratus, whom we saw when he was old and we were boys, he will train him equally in every department of the science and will make him a champion both in boxing and wrestling, like Nicostratus himself who won the prize for both contests within a few days of each other. And how much more important is the employment of such methods where our future orator is concerned! It is not enough to be able to speak with terseness, subtlety or vehemence, any more than it would be for a singing master to excel in the upper, middle or lower register only, or in particular sections of these registers alone. Eloquence is like a harp and will never reach perfection, unless all its strings be taut and in tune.

• • •

XI. I have now arrived at the point when I must begin to deal with that portion of the art at which those who have omitted the preceding stages generally commence. I can see, however, that certain critics will attempt to obstruct my path at the very outset: for they will urge that eloquence can dispense with rules of this kind and, in smug satisfaction with themselves and the ordinary methods and exercises of the schools, will laugh at me for my pains; in which they will be only following the example of certain professors of no small reputation. One of these gentlemen, I believe, when asked to define a *figure* and a *thought,* replied that he did not know what they were, but that, if they had anything to do with the subject, they would be found in his declamation. Another when asked whether he was a follower of Theodorus or Apollodorus, replied, "Oh! as for me, I am all for the Thracians."[1] To do him justice, he could hardly have found a neater way to avoid confessing his ignorance. These persons, just because, thanks to their natural gifts, they are regarded as brilliant performers and have, as a matter of fact, uttered much that deserves to be remembered, think that, while most men share their careless habits, few come near them for talent. Consequently they make it their boast that they speak on impulse and owe their success to their native powers; they further assert that there is no need of proof or careful marshalling of facts when we are speaking on fictitious themes, but only of some of those sounding epigrams, the expectation of which has filled the lecture-room; and these they say are best improvised on the spur of the moment. Further, owing to their contempt for method, when they are meditating on some future effusion, they spend whole days looking at the ceiling in the hope that some magnificent inspiration may occur to them, or rock their bodies to and fro, booming inarticulately as if they had a trumpet inside them and adapting their agitated movements, not to the delivery of the words, but to their pursuit. Some again settle on certain definite openings long before they have thought what they are going to say, with a view to using them as pegs for subsequent snatches of eloquence, and then after practising their delivery first in silent thought and then aloud for hours together, in utter desperation of providing any connecting links, abandon them and take refuge in one formula after another, each no less hackneyed and familiar than the last. The least unreasonable of them devote their attention not to the actual cases, but to their purple patches, in the composition of which they pay no attention to the subject-matter, but fire off a series of isolated thoughts just as they happen to come to hand. The result is a speech which, being composed of disconnected passages having nothing in common with each other, must necessarily lack cohesion and can only be compared to a schoolboy's notebook, in which he jots down any passages from the declamations of others that have come in for a word of praise. None the less they do occasionally strike out some good things and some fine epigrams, such as they make their boast. Why not? slaves and barbarians sometimes achieve the same effects, and if we are to be satisfied with this sort of thing, then good-bye to any theory of oratory.

• • •

XIII. Let no one however demand from me a rigid code of rules such as most authors of text-books have laid down, or ask me to impose on students of rhetoric a system of laws immutable as fate, a system in which injunctions as to the *exordium* and its nature lead the way; then come the *statement of facts* and the laws to be observed in this connexion: next the *proposition* or, as some prefer, the *digression*, followed by prescriptions as to the order in which the various questions should be discussed, with all the other rules, which some speakers follow as though they had no choice but to regard them as orders and as if it were a crime to take any other line. If the whole of rhetoric could be thus embodied in one compact code, it would be an easy task of little compass: but most rules are liable to be altered by the nature of the case, circumstances of time and place, and by hard necessity itself. Consequently the all-important gift for an orator is a wise adaptability since he is called upon to meet the most varied emergencies. What if you should instruct a general, as often as he marshals his troops for battle, to draw up his front in line, advance his wings to left and right, and station his cavalry to protect his flank? This will perhaps be the best plan, if circumstances allow. But it may have to be modified owing to the nature of the ground, if, for instance, he is confronted by a mountain, if a river bars his advance, or his movements are hampered by hills, woods or broken country. Or again it may be modified by the character of the enemy or the nature of the crisis by which he is faced. On one occasion he will fight in line, on another in column, on one he will use his auxiliary troops, on another his legionaries; while occasionally a feint of flight may win the day. So, too, with the rules of oratory. Is the *exordium* necessary or superfluous? should it be long or short? addressed entirely to the judge or sometimes directed to some other quarter by the employment of some figure of speech?[1] Should the statement of facts be concise or developed at some length? continuous or divided into sections? and should it follow the actual or an artificial order of events? The orator will find the answers to all these questions in the circumstances of the case. So, too, with the order in which questions should be discussed, since in any given debate it may often suit one party best that such and such a question come up first, while their opponents would be best suited by another. For these rules have not the formal authority of laws or decrees of the plebs, but are, with all they contain, the children of expediency. I will not deny that it is generally expedient to conform to such rules, otherwise I should not be writing now; but if our friend expediency suggests some other course to us, why, we shall disregard the authority of the professors and follow her.

For my part above all things

"This I enjoin and urge and urge anew"[2]

that in all his pleadings the orator should keep two things constantly in view, what is becoming and what is expedient. But it is often expedient and occasionally becoming to make some modification in the time-honoured order. We see the same thing in pictures and statues. Dress, expression and attitude are frequently varied. The body when held bolt upright has but little grace, for the face looks straight forward, the arms hang by the side, the feet are joined and the whole figure is stiff from top to toe. But that curve, I might almost call it motion, with which we are so familiar, gives an impression of action and animation. So, too, the hands will not always be represented in the same position, and the variety given to the expression will be infinite. Some figures are represented as running or rushing forward, others sit or recline, some are nude, others clothed, while some again are half-dressed, half-naked. Where can we find a more violent and elaborate attitude than that of the Discobolus of Myron? Yet the critic who disapproved of the figure because it was not upright, would merely show his utter failure to understand the sculptor's art, in which the very novelty and difficulty of execution is what most deserves our praise. A similar impression of grace and charm is produced by rhetorical figures, whether they be *figures of thought* or *figures of speech*. For they involve a certain departure from the straight line and have the merit of variation from the ordinary usage. In a picture the full face is most attractive. But Apelles painted Antigonus in profile, to conceal the blemish caused by the loss of one eye. So, too, in speaking, there are certain things which have to be concealed, either because they ought not to be disclosed or because they cannot be expressed as they deserve. Timanthes, who was, I think, a native of Cythnus, provides an example of this in the picture with which he won the victory over Colotes of Teos. It represented the sacrifice of Iphigenia, and the artist had depicted an expression of grief on the face of Calchas and of still greater grief on that of Ulysses, while he had given Menelaus an agony of sorrow beyond which his art could not go. Having exhausted his powers of emotional expression he was at a loss to portray the father's face as it deserved, and solved the problem by veiling his head and leaving his sorrow to the imagination of the spectator. Sallust[3] did something similar when he wrote "I think it better to say nothing of Carthage rather than say too little." It has always, therefore, been my custom not to tie myself down to *universal* or *general* rules (this being the nearest equivalent I can find for the Greek *catholic rules*). For rules are rarely of such a kind that their validity cannot be shaken and overthrown in some particular or other. But I must reserve each of these points for fuller treatment in its proper place. For the present I will only say that I do not want young men to think their education complete when they have mastered one of the small text-books of which so many are in circulation, or to ascribe a talismanic value to the arbitrary decrees of theorists. The art of speaking can only be attained by hard work and assiduity of study, by a variety of exercises and repeated trial, the highest prudence and unfailing quickness of judgement. But rules are helpful all the same so long as they indicate the direct road and do not restrict us absolutely to the ruts made by others. For he who thinks it an unpardonable sin to leave the old, old track, must be content to move at much the same speed as a tight-rope walker. Thus, for example, we often leave a paved military road to take a short cut or, finding that the direct route is impossible owing to floods having broken down the bridges, are forced to make a circuit, while if our house is on fire and flames bar the way to the front door, we make our escape by breaking through a party wall. The orator's task covers a large ground, is extremely varied and develops some new aspect almost every day, so that the last word on the subject will never have been said. I shall however try to set forth the traditional rules and to point out their best features, mentioning the changes, additions and subtractions which seem desirable.

XIV. Rhetoric is a Greek term which has been translated into Latin by *oratoria* or *oratrix*. I would not for the world deprive the translators of the praise which is their due for attempting to increase the vocabulary of our native tongue; but translations from Greek into Latin are not always satisfactory, just as the attempt to represent Latin words in a Greek dress is sometimes equally unsuccessful. And the translations in question are fully as harsh as the *essentia* and *queentia*[1] of Plautus,[2] and have not even the merit of being exact. For *oratoria* is formed like *elocutoria* and *oratrix* like *elocutrix,* whereas the rhetoric with which we are concerned is rather to be identified with *eloquentia,* and the word is undoubtedly used in two senses by the Greeks. In the one case it is an adjective i.e. *ars rhetorica,* the rhetorical art, like piratic in the phrase *nauis piratica,* in the other it is a noun like philosophy or friendship. It is as a substantive that we require it here; now the correct translation of the Greek *grammatice* is *litteratura* not *litteratrix* or *litteratoria,* which would be the forms analogous to *oratrix* and *oratoria.* But in the case of "rhetoric" there is no similar Latin equivalent. It is best therefore not to quarrel about it, more especially as we have to use Greek terms in many other cases. For I may at least use the words *philosophus, musicus* and *geometres* without outraging them by changing them into clumsy Latin equivalents. Finally, since Cicero gave a Greek title[3] to the earlier works which he wrote on this subject, I may without fear of rashness accept the great orator as sufficient authority for the name of the art which he professed.

To resume, then, rhetoric (for I shall now use the name without fear of captious criticism) is in my opinion best treated under the three following heads, the art, the artist and the work. The art is that which we should acquire by study, and is the art of speaking well. The artist is he who has acquired the art, that is to say, he is the orator whose task it is to speak well. The work is the achievement of the artist, namely good speaking. Each of these three *general* divisions is in its turn divided into *species.* Of the two latter divisions I shall speak in their proper place. For the present I shall proceed to a discussion of the first.

XV. The first question which confronts us is "What is rhetoric?" Many definitions have been given; but the problem is really twofold. For the dispute turns either on the quality of the thing itself or on the meaning of the words in which it is defined. The first and chief disagreement on the subject is found in the fact that some think that even bad men may be called orators, while others, of whom I am one, restrict the name of orator and the art itself to those who are good. Of those who divorce eloquence from that yet fairer and more desirable title to renown, a virtuous life, some call rhetoric merely a power, some a science, but not a virtue, some a practice, some an art, though they will not allow the art to have anything in common with science or virtue, while some again call it a perversion of art or κακοτεχνία. These persons have as a rule held that the task of oratory lies in persuasion or speaking in a persuasive manner: for this is within the power of a bad man no less than a good. Hence we get the common definition of rhetoric as the power of persuading. What I call a power, many call a capacity, and some a faculty. In order therefore that there may be no misunderstanding I will say that by power I mean δύναμις. This view is derived from Isocrates, if indeed the treatise on rhetoric[1] which circulates under his name is really from his hand. He, although far from agreeing with those whose aim is to disparage the duties of an orator, somewhat rashly defined rhetoric as πειθοῦς δημιουργός, the "worker of persuasion": for I cannot bring myself to use the peculiar derivative which Ennius[2] applies to Marcus Cethegus in the phrase *suadae medulla,* the "marrow of persuasion." Again Gorgias,[3] in the dialogue of Plato that takes its title from his name, says practically the same thing, but Plato intends it to be taken as the opinion of Gorgias, not as his own. Cicero[4] in more than one passage defined the duty of an orator as "speaking in a persuasive manner." In his *Rhetorica*[5] too, a work which it is clear gave him no satisfaction, he makes the end to be persuasion. But many other things have the power of persuasion, such as money, influence, the authority and rank of the speaker, or even some sight unsupported by language, when for instance the place of words is supplied by the memory of some individual's great deeds, by his lamentable appearance or the beauty of his person. Thus when Antonius in the course of his defence of Manius Aquilius tore open his client's robe and revealed the honourable scars which he had acquired while facing his country's foes, he relied no longer on the power of his eloquence, but appealed directly to the eyes of the Roman people. And it is believed that they were so profoundly moved by the sight as to acquit the accused. Again there is a speech of Cato, to mention no other records, which informs us that Servius Galba escaped condemnation solely by the pity which he aroused not only by producing his own young children before the assembly, but by carrying round in his arms the son of Sulpicius Gallus. So also according to general opinion Phryne was saved not by the eloquence of Hyperides, admirable as it was, but by the sight of her exquisite body, which she further revealed by drawing aside her tunic. And if all these have power to persuade, the end of oratory, which we are discussing, cannot adequately be defined as persuasion. Consequently those who, although holding the same general view of rhetoric, have regarded it as the *power of persuasion by speaking,* pride themselves on their greater exactness of language. This definition is given by Gorgias, in the dialogue[6] mentioned above, under compulsion from the inexorable logic of Socrates. Theodectes agrees with him, whether the treatise on rhetoric which has come down to us under his name is really by him or, as is generally believed, by Aristotle. In that work the end of rhetoric is defined as the *leading of men by the power of speech to the conclusion desired by the orator.* But even this definition is not sufficiently comprehensive, since others besides orators persuade by speaking or lead others to the conclusion desired, as for example harlots, flatterers and seducers. On the other hand the orator is not always engaged on persuasion, so that sometimes persuasion is not his special object, while sometimes it is shared by others who are far removed from being orators. And yet Apollodorus is not very far off this definition when he asserts that the first and all-important task of forensic oratory is *to persuade the judge and lead his mind to the conclusions desired by the speaker.* For even Apollodorus makes the orator the sport of fortune by refusing him leave to retain his title if he fails to persuade. Some on the other hand pay no attention to results, as for example Aristotle,[7] who says "*rhetoric is the power of discovering all means of persuading by speech.*" This definition has not merely the fault already mentioned, but the additional defect of including merely the power of invention, which without style cannot possibly constitute oratory. Hermagoras, who asserts that its end is to *speak persuasively,* and others who express the same opinion, though in different words, and inform us that the end is to *say everything which ought to be said with a view to persuasion,* have been sufficiently answered above, when I proved that persuasion was not the privilege of the orator alone. Various additions have been made to these definitions. For some hold that rhetoric is concerned with everything, while some restrict its activity to politics. The question as to which of these views is the nearer to the truth shall be discussed later in its appropriate place. Aristotle seems to have implied that the sphere of the orator was all-inclusive when he defined rhetoric as the *power to detect every element in any given subject which might conduce to persuasion;* so too does Patrocles who omits the words *in any given subject,* but since he excludes nothing, shows that his view is identical. For he defines rhetoric as the *power to discover whatever is persuasive in speech.* These definitions like that quoted above include no more than the power of *invention* alone. Theodorus avoids this fault and holds that it is the *power to discover and to utter forth in elegant language whatever is credible in every subject of oratory.* But, while others besides orators may discover what is credible as well as persuasive, by adding the words *in every subject* he, to a greater extent than the others, concedes the fairest name in all the world to those who use their gifts as an incitement to crime. Plato makes Gorgias[1] say that he is a master of persuasion in the law-courts and other assemblies, and that his themes are justice and injustice, while in reply Socrates allows him the power of persuading, but not of teaching. Those who refused to make the sphere of oratory all-inclusive, have been obliged to make somewhat forced and long-winded distinctions: among these I may mention Ariston, the pupil of the Peripatetic Critolaus, who produced the following definition, "*Rhetoric is the science of seeing and uttering what ought to be said on political questions in language that is likely to prove persuasive to the people.*" Being a Peripatetic he regards it as a science, not, like the Stoics, as a virtue, while in adding the words "*likely to prove persuasive to the people*" he inflicts a positive insult on oratory, in implying that it is not likely to persuade the learned. The same criticism will apply to all those who restrict oratory to political questions, for they exclude thereby a large number of the duties of an orator, as for example panegyric, the third department of oratory, which is entirely ignored. Turning to those who regard rhetoric as an art, but not as a virtue, we find that Theodorus of Gadara is more cautious. For he says (I quote the words of his translators), "*rhetoric is the art which discovers and judges and expresses, with an elegance duly proportioned to the importance of all such elements of persuasion as may exist in any subject in the field of politics.*" Similarly Cornelius Celsus defines the end of rhetoric as *to speak persuasively on any doubtful subject within the field of politics.* Similar definitions are given by others, such for instance as the following:—"*rhetoric is the power of judging and holding forth on such political subjects as come before it with a certain persuasiveness, a certain action of the body and delivery of the words.*" There are countless other definitions, either identical with this or composed of the same elements, which I shall deal with when I come to the questions concerned with the subject matter of rhetoric. Some regard it as neither a power, a science or an art; Critolaus calls it the *practice of speaking* (for this is the meaning of τριβή), Athenaeus styles it the *art of deceiving,* while the majority, content with reading a few passages from the Gorgias of Plato, unskilfully excerpted by earlier writers, refrain from studying that dialogue and the remainder of Plato's writings, and thereby fall into serious error. For they believe that in Plato's view rhetoric was not an art, but a certain *adroitness in the production of delight and gratification,*[2] or with reference to another passage the *shadow of a small part of politics*[3] and the *fourth department of flattery.* For Plato assigns[4] two departments of politics to the body, namely medicine and gymnastic, and two to the soul, namely law and justice, while he styles the art of cookery[5] a form of flattery of medicine, the art of the slave-dealer a flattery of gymnastic, for they produce a false complexion by the use of paint and a false robustness by puffing them out with fat: sophistry he calls a dishonest counterfeit of legal science, and rhetoric of justice. All these statements occur in the *Gorgias* and are uttered by Socrates who appears to be the mouthpiece of the views held by Plato. But some of his dialogues were composed merely to refute his opponents and are styled *refutative,* while others are for the purpose of teaching and are called *doctrinal.* Now it is only rhetoric as practised in their own day that is condemned by Plato or Socrates, for he speaks of it as "the manner in which you engage in public affairs"[1]: rhetoric in itself he regards as a genuine and honourable thing, and consequently the controversy with Gorgias ends with the words, "The rhetorician therefore must be just and the just man desirous to do what is just."[2] To this Gorgias makes no reply, but the argument is taken up by Polus, a hot-headed and headstrong young fellow, and it is to him that Socrates makes his remarks about "shadows" and "forms of flattery." Then Callicles,[3] who is even more hot-headed, intervenes, but is reduced to the conclusion that "he who would truly be a rhetorician ought to be just and possess a knowledge of justice." It is clear therefore that Plato does not regard rhetoric as an evil, but holds that true rhetoric is impossible for any save a just and good man. In the *Phaedrus*[4] he makes it even clearer that the complete attainment of this art is impossible without the knowledge of justice, an opinion in which I heartily concur. Had this not been his view, would he have ever written the Apology of Socrates or the Funeral Oration[5] in praise of those who had died in battle for their country, both of them works falling within the sphere of oratory. It was against the class of men who employed their glibness of speech for evil purposes that he directed his denunciations. Similarly Socrates thought it incompatible with his honour to make use of the speech which Lysias composed for his defence, although it was the usual practice in those days to write speeches for the parties concerned to speak in the courts on their own behalf, a device designed to circumvent the law which forbade the employment of advocates. Further the teachers of rhetoric were regarded by Plato as quite unsuited to their professed task. For they divorced rhetoric from justice and preferred plausibility to truth, as he states in the *Phaedrus.*[6] Cornelius Celsus seems to have agreed with these early rhetoricians, for he writes "The orator only aims at the semblance of truth," and again a little later "The reward of the party to a suit is not a good conscience, but victory." If this were true, only the worst of men would place such dangerous weapons at the disposal of criminals or employ the precepts of their art for the assistance of wickedness. However I will leave those who maintain these views to consider what ground they have for so doing.

For my part, I have undertaken the task of moulding the ideal orator, and as my first desire is that he should be a good man, I will return to those who have sounder opinions on the subject. Some however identify rhetoric with politics, Cicero[7] calls it a *department of the science of politics* (and science of politics and philosophy are identical terms), while others again call it a *branch of philosophy,* among them Isocrates. The definition which best suits its real character is that which makes rhetoric the *science of speaking well.* For this definition includes all the virtues of oratory and the character of the orator as well, since no man can speak well who is not good himself. The definition given by Chrysippus, who derived it from Cleanthes, to the effect that it is the *science of speaking rightly,* amounts to the same thing. The same philosopher also gives other definitions, but they concern problems of a different character from that on which we are now engaged. Another definition defines oratory as the power of *persuading men to do what ought to be done,* and yields practically the same sense save that it limits the art to the result which it produces. Areus again defines it well as *speaking according to the excellence of speech.* Those who regard it as the science of political obligations, also exclude men of bad character from the title of orator, if by science they mean virtue, but restrict it overmuch by confining it to political problems. Albutius, a distinguished author and professor of rhetoric, agrees that rhetoric is the science of speaking well, but makes a mistake in imposing restrictions by the addition of the words *on political questions* and *with credibility;* with both of these restrictions I have already dealt. Finally those critics who hold that the aim of rhetoric is *to think and speak rightly,* were on the correct track.

These are practically all the most celebrated and most discussed definitions of rhetoric. It would be both irrelevant and beyond my power to deal with all. For I strongly disapprove of the custom which has come to prevail among writers of text-books of refusing to define anything in the same terms as have been employed by some previous writer. I will have nothing to do with such ostentation. What I say will not necessarily be my own invention, but it will be what I believe to be the right view, as for instance that oratory is the science of speaking well. For when the most satisfactory definition has been found, he who seeks another, is merely looking for a worse one.

Thus much being admitted we are now in a position to see clearly what is the end, the highest aim, the ultimate goal of rhetoric, that *τέλος* in fact which every art must possess. For if rhetoric is the science of speaking well, its end and highest aim is to speak well.

XVI. There follows the question as to whether rhetoric is useful. Some are in the habit of denouncing it most violently and of shamelessly employing the powers of oratory to accuse oratory itself. "It is eloquence" they say "that snatches criminals from the penalties of the law, eloquence that from time to time secures the condemnation of the innocent and leads deliberation astray, eloquence that stirs up not merely sedition and popular tumult, but wars beyond all expiation, and that is most effective when it makes falsehood prevail over the truth." The comic poets even accuse Socrates of teaching how to make the worse cause seem the better, while Plato says that Gorgias and Tisias made similar professions. And to these they add further examples drawn from the history of Rome and Greece, enumerating all those who used their pernicious eloquence not merely against individuals but against whole states and threw an ordered commonwealth into a state of turmoil or even brought it to utter ruin; and they point out that for this very reason rhetoric was banished from Sparta, while its powers were cut down at Athens itself by the fact that an orator was forbidden to stir the passions of his audience. On the showing of these critics not only orators but generals, magistrates, medicine and philosophy itself will all be useless. For Flaminius was a general, while men such as the Gracchi, Saturninus and Glaucia were magistrates. Doctors have been caught using poisons, and those who falsely assume the name of philosopher have occasionally been detected in the gravest crimes. Let us give up eating, it often makes us ill; let us never go inside houses, for sometimes they collapse on their occupants; let never a sword be forged for a soldier, since it might be used by a robber. And who does not realise that fire and water, both necessities of life, and, to leave mere earthly things, even the sun and moon, the greatest of the heavenly bodies, are occasionally capable of doing harm.

On the other hand will it be denied that it was by his gift of speech that Appius the Blind broke off the dishonourable peace which was on the point of being concluded with Pyrrhus? Did not the divine eloquence of Cicero win popular applause even when he denounced the Agrarian laws,[1] did it not crush the audacious plots of Catiline and win, while he still wore the garb of civil life, the highest honour that can be conferred on a victorious general, a public thanksgiving to heaven? Has not oratory often revived the courage of a panic-stricken army and persuaded the soldier faced by all the perils of war that glory is a fairer thing than life itself? Nor shall the history of Sparta and Athens move me more than that of the Roman people, who have always held the orator in highest honour. Never in my opinion would the founders of cities have induced their unsettled multitudes to form communities had they not moved them by the magic of their eloquence: never without the highest gifts of oratory would the great legislators have constrained mankind to submit themselves to the yoke of law. Nay, even the principles which should guide our life, however fair they may be by nature, yet have greater power to mould the mind to virtue, when the beauty of things is illumined by the splendour of eloquence. Wherefore, although the weapons of oratory may be used either for good or ill, it is unfair to regard that as an evil which can be employed for good.

These problems, however, may be left to those who hold that rhetoric is the power to persuade. If our definition of rhetoric as the science of speaking well implies that an orator must be a good man, there can be no doubt about its usefulness. And in truth that god, who was in the beginning, the father of all things and the architect of the universe, distinguished man from all other living creatures that are subject to death, by nothing more than this, that he gave him the gift of speech. For as regards physical bulk, strength, robustness, endurance or speed, man is surpassed in certain cases by dumb beasts, who also are far more independent of external assistance. They know by instinct without need of any teacher how to move rapidly, to feed themselves and swim. Many too have their bodies clothed against cold, possess natural weapons and have not to search for their food, whereas in all these respects man's life is full of toil. Reason then was the greatest gift of the Almighty, who willed that we should share its possession with the immortal gods. But reason by itself would help us but little and would be far less evident in us, had we not the power to express our thoughts in speech; for it is the lack of this power rather than thought and understanding, which they do to a certain extent possess, that is the great defect in other living things. The construction of a soft lair, the weaving of nests, the hatching and rearing of their young, and even the storing up of food for the coming winter, together with certain other achievements which we cannot imitate, such as the making of honey and wax, all these perhaps indicate the possession of a certain degree of reason; but since the creatures that do these things lack the gift of speech they are called dumb and unreasoning beasts. Finally, how little the heavenly boon of reason avails those who are born dumb. If therefore we have received no fairer gift from heaven than speech, what shall we regard as so worthy of laborious cultivation, or in what should we sooner desire to excel our fellow-men, than that in which mankind excels all other living things? And we should be all the more eager to do so, since there is no art which yields a more grateful recompense for the labour bestowed upon it. This will be abundantly clear if we consider the origins of oratory and the progress it has made; and it is capable of advancing still further. I will not stop to point out how useful and how becoming a task it is for a good man to defend his friends, to guide the senate by his counsels, and to lead peoples or armies to follow his bidding; I merely ask, is it not a noble thing, by employing the understanding which is common to mankind and the words that are used by all, to win such honour and glory that you seem not to speak or plead, but rather, as was said of Pericles, to thunder and lighten?[1]

XVII. However, if I were to indulge my own inclinations in expatiating on this subject, I should go on for ever. Let us therefore pass to the next question and consider whether rhetoric is an art. No one of those who have laid down rules for oratory has ever doubted that it is an art. It is clear even from the titles of their books that their theme is the art of rhetoric, while Cicero[2] defines rhetoric as *artistic eloquence.* And it is not merely the orators who have claimed this distinction for their studies with a view to giving them an additional title to respect, but the Stoic and Peripatetic philosophers for the most part agree with them. Indeed I will confess that I had doubts as to whether I should discuss this portion of my inquiry, for there is no one, I will not say so unlearned, but so devoid of ordinary sense, as to hold that building, weaving or moulding vessels from clay are arts, and at the same time to consider that rhetoric, which, as I have already said, is the noblest and most sublime of tasks, has reached such a lofty eminence without the assistance of art. For my own part I think that those who have argued against this view did not realise what they were saying, but merely desired to exercise their wits by the selection of a difficult theme, like Polycrates, when he praised Busiris and Clytemnestra; I may add that he is credited with a not dissimilar performance, namely the composition of a speech which was delivered against Socrates.

Some would have it that rhetoric is a natural gift though they admit that it can be developed by practice. So Antonius in the *de Oratore*[1] of Cicero styles it a *knack derived from experience,* but denies that it is an art: this statement is however not intended to be accepted by us as the actual truth, but is inserted to make Antonius speak in character, since he was in the habit of concealing his art. Still Lysias is said to have maintained this same view, which is defended on the ground that uneducated persons, barbarians and slaves, when speaking on their own behalf, say something that resembles an *exordium,* state the facts of the case, prove, refute and plead for mercy just as an orator does in his peroration. To this is added the quibble that nothing that is based on art can have existed before the art in question, whereas men have always from time immemorial spoken in their own defence or in denunciation of others: the teaching of rhetoric as an art was, they say, a later invention dating from about the time of Tisias and Corax: oratory therefore existed before art and consequently cannot be an art. For my part I am not concerned with the date when oratory began to be taught. Even in Homer we find Phoenix[2] as an instructor not only of conduct but of speaking, while a number of orators are mentioned, the various styles are represented by the speeches of three of the chiefs[3] and the young men are set to contend among themselves in contests of eloquence:[4] moreover lawsuits and pleaders are represented in the engravings on the shield of Achilles.[5] It is sufficient to call attention to the fact that everything which art has brought to perfection originated in nature. Otherwise we might deny the title of art to medicine, which was discovered from the observation of sickness and health, and according to some is entirely based upon experiment: wounds were bound up long before medicine developed into an art, and fevers were reduced by rest and abstention from food, long before the reason for such treatment was known, simply because the state of the patient's health left no choice. So too building should not be styled an art; for primitive man built himself a hut without the assistance of art. Music by the same reasoning is not an art; for every race indulges in some kind of singing and dancing. If therefore any kind of speech is to be called eloquence, I will admit that it existed before it was an art. If on the other hand not every man that speaks is an orator and primitive man did not speak like an orator, my opponents must needs acknowledge that oratory is the product of art and did not exist before it. This conclusion also rules out their argument that men speak who have never learnt how to speak, and that which a man does untaught can have no connexion with art. In support of this contention they adduce the fact that Demades was a waterman and Aeschines an actor, but both were orators. Their reasoning is false. For no man can be an orator untaught and it would be truer to say that these orators learned oratory late in life than that they never learned at all; although as a matter of fact Aeschines had an acquaintance with literature from childhood since his father was a teacher of literature, while as regards Demades, it is quite uncertain that he never studied rhetoric and in any case continuous practice in speaking was sufficient to bring him to such proficiency as he attained: for experience is the best of all schools. On the other hand it may fairly be asserted that he would have achieved greater distinction, if he had received instruction: for although he delivered his speeches with great effect, he never ventured to write them for others. Aristotle, it is true, in his *Gryllus*[6] produces some tentative arguments to the contrary, which are marked by characteristic ingenuity. On the other hand he also wrote three books on the art of rhetoric, in the first of which he not merely admits that rhetoric is an art, but treats it as a department of politics and also of logic. Critolaus and Athenodorus of Rhodes have produced many arguments against this view, while Agnon renders himself suspect by the very title of his book in which he proclaims that he is going to indict rhetoric. As to the statements of Epicurus on this subject, they cause me no surprise, for he is the foe of all systematic training.

These gentlemen talk a great deal, but the arguments on which they base their statements are few. I will therefore select the most important of them and will deal with them briefly, to prevent the discussion lasting to all eternity. Their first contention is based on the subject-matter; for they assert that all arts have their own subject-matter (which is true) and go on to say that rhetoric has none, which I shall show in what follows to be false. Another slander is to the effect that no art will acquiesce in false opinions: since an art must be based on direct perception, which is always true: now, say they, rhetoric does give its assent to false conclusions and is therefore not an art. I will admit that rhetoric sometimes substitutes falsehood for truth, but I will not allow that it does so because its opinions are false, since there is all the difference between holding a certain opinion oneself and persuading someone else to adopt an opinion. For instance a general frequently makes use of falsehood: Hannibal when hemmed in by Fabius persuaded his enemy that he was in retreat by tying brushwood to the horns of oxen, setting fire to them by night and driving the herds across the mountains opposite.[1] But though he deceived Fabius, he himself was fully aware of the truth. Again when the Spartan Theopompus changed clothes with his wife and escaped from custody disguised as a woman, he deceived his guards, but was not for a moment deceived as to his own identity.[2] Similarly an orator, when he substitutes falsehood for the truth, is aware of the falsehood and of the fact that he is substituting it for the truth. He therefore deceives others, but not himself. When Cicero boasted that he had thrown dust in the eyes of the jury in the case of Cluentius, he was far from being blinded himself. And when a painter by his artistic skill makes us believe that certain objects project from the picture, while others are withdrawn into the background, he knows perfectly well that they are really all in the same plane. My opponents further assert that every art has some definite goal towards which it directs its efforts, but that rhetoric as a rule has no such goal, while at other times it professes to have an aim, but fails to perform its promise. They lie: I have already shown that rhetoric has a definite purpose and have explained what it is. And, what is more, the orator will always make good his professions in this respect, for he will always speak well. On the other hand this criticism may perhaps hold good as against those who think persuasion the end of oratory. But our orator and his art, as we define it, are independent of results. The speaker aims at victory, it is true, but if he speaks well, he has lived up to the ideals of his art, even if he is defeated. Similarly a pilot will desire to bring his ship safe to harbour; but if he is swept out of his course by a storm, he will not for that reason cease to be a pilot, but will say in the well-known words of the old poet[3] "Still let me steer straight on!" So too the doctor seeks to heal the sick; but if the violence of the disease or the refusal of the patient to obey his regimen or any other circumstance prevent his achieving his purpose, he will not have fallen short of the ideals of his art, provided he has done everything according to reason. So too the orator's purpose is fulfilled if he has spoken well. For the art of rhetoric, as I shall show later, is realised in action, not in the result obtained. From this it follows that there is no truth in yet another argument which contends that arts know when they have attained their end, whereas rhetoric does not. For every speaker is aware when he is speaking well. These critics also charge rhetoric with doing what no art does, namely making use of vices to serve its ends, since it speaks the thing that is not and excites the passions. But there is no disgrace in doing either of these things, as long as the motive be good: consequently there is nothing vicious in such action. Even a philosopher is at times permitted to tell a lie, while the orator must needs excite the passions, if that be the only way by which he can lead the judge to do justice. For judges are not always enlightened and often have to be tricked to prevent them falling into error. Give me philosophers as judges, pack senates and assemblies with philosophers, and you will destroy the power of hatred, influence, prejudice and false witness; consequently there will be very little scope for eloquence whose value will lie almost entirely in its power to charm. But if, as is the case, our hearers are fickle of mind, and truth is exposed to a host of perils, we must call in art to aid us in the fight and employ such means as will help our case. He who has been driven from the right road cannot be brought back to it save by a fresh détour.

The point, however, that gives rise to the greatest number of these captious accusations against rhetoric, is found in the allegation that orators speak indifferently on either side of a case. From which they draw the following arguments: no art is self-contradictory, but rhetoric does contradict itself; no art tries to demolish what itself has built, but this does happen in the operations of rhetoric; or again:—rhetoric teaches either what ought to be said or what ought not to be said; consequently it is not an art because it teaches what ought not to be said, or because, while it teaches what ought to be said, it also teaches precisely the opposite. Now it is obvious that all such charges are brought against that type of rhetoric with which neither good men nor virtue herself will have anything to do; since if a case be based on injustice, rhetoric has no place therein and consequently it can scarcely happen even under the most exceptional circumstances that an orator, that is to say, a good man, will speak indifferently on either side. Still it is in the nature of things conceivable that just causes may lead two wise men to take different sides, since it is held that wise men may fight among themselves, provided that they do so at the bidding of reason. I will therefore reply to their criticisms in such a way that it will be clear that these arguments have no force even against those who concede the name of orator to persons of bad character. For rhetoric is not self-contradictory. The conflict is between case and case, not between rhetoric and itself. And even if persons who have learned the same thing fight one another, that does not prove that what they have learned is not an art. Were that so, there could be no art of arms, since gladiators trained under the same master are often matched against each other; nor would the pilot's art exist, because in sea-fights pilots may be found on different sides; nor yet could there be an art of generalship, since general is pitted against general. In the same way rhetoric does not undo its own work. For the orator does not refute his own arguments, nor does rhetoric even do so, because those who regard persuasion as its end, or the two good men whom chance has matched against one another seek merely for probabilities: and the fact that one thing is more credible than another, does not involve contradiction between the two. There is no absolute antagonism between the probable and the more probable, just as there is none between that which is white and that which is whiter, or between that which is sweet and that which is sweeter. Nor does rhetoric ever teach that which ought not to be said, or that which is contrary to what ought to be said, but solely what ought to be said in each individual case. But though the orator will as a rule maintain what is true, this will not always be the case: there are occasions when the public interest demands that he should defend what is untrue.

The following objections are also put forward in the second book of Cicero's *de Oratore*[1]:—"Art deals with things that are known. But the pleading of an orator is based entirely on opinion, not on knowledge, because he speaks to an audience who do not know, and sometimes himself states things of which he has no actual knowledge." Now one of these points, namely whether the judges have knowledge of what is being said to them, has nothing to do with the art of oratory. The other statement, that art is concerned with things that are known, does however require an answer. Rhetoric is the art of speaking well and the orator knows how to speak well. "But," it is urged, "he does not know whether what he says is true." Neither do they, who assert that all things derive their origin from fire or water or the four elements or indivisible atoms; nor they who calculate the distances of the stars or the size of the earth and sun. And yet all these call the subject which they teach an art. But if reason makes them seem not merely to hold opinions but, thanks to the cogency of the proofs adduced, to have actual knowledge, reason will do the same service to the orator. "But," they say, "he does not know whether the cause which he has undertaken is true." But not even a doctor can tell whether a patient who claims to be suffering from a headache, really is so suffering: but he will treat him on the assumption that his statement is true, and medicine will still be an art. Again what of the fact that rhetoric does not always aim at telling the truth, but always at stating what is probable? The answer is that the orator knows that what he states is no more than probable. My opponents further object that advocates often defend in one case what they have attacked in another. This is not the fault of the art, but of the man. Such are the main points that are urged against rhetoric; there are others as well, but they are of minor importance and drawn from the same sources.

That rhetoric is an art may, however, be proved in a very few words. For if Cleanthes'[1] definition be accepted that "Art is a power reaching its ends by a definite path, that is, by ordered methods," no one can doubt that there is such method and order in good speaking: while if, on the other hand, we accept the definition which meets with almost universal approval that art consists in perceptions agreeing and cooperating to the achievement of some useful end, we shall be able to show that rhetoric lacks none of these characteristics. Again it is scarcely necessary for me to point out that like other arts it is based on examination and practice. And if logic is an art, as is generally agreed, rhetoric must also be an art, since it differs from logic in *species* rather than in *genus*. Nor must I omit to point out that where it is possible in any given subject for one man to act without art and another with art, there must necessarily be an art in connexion with that subject, as there must also be in any subject in which the man who has received instruction is the superior of him who has not. But as regards the practice of rhetoric, it is not merely the case that the trained speaker will get the better of the untrained. For even the trained man will prove inferior to one who has received a better training. If this were not so, there would not be so many rhetorical rules, nor would so many great men have come forward to teach them. The truth of this must be acknowledged by everyone, but more especially by us, since we concede the possession of oratory to none save the good man.[2]

XVIII. Some arts, however, are based on examination, that is to say on the knowledge and proper appreciation of things, as for instance astronomy, which demands no action, but is content to understand the subject of its study: such arts are called *theoretical.* Others again are concerned with action: this is their end, which is realised in action, so that, the action once performed, nothing more remains to do: these arts we style *practical,* and dancing will provide us with an example. Thirdly there are others which consist in producing a certain result and achieve their purpose in the completion of a visible task: such we style *productive,* and *painting* may be quoted as an illustration. In view of these facts we must come to the conclusion that, in the main, rhetoric is concerned with action; for in action it accomplishes that which it is its duty to do. This view is universally accepted, although in my opinion rhetoric draws largely on the two other kinds of art. For it may on occasion be content with the mere examination of a thing. Rhetoric is still in the orator's possession even though he be silent, while if he gives up pleading either designedly or owing to circumstances over which he has no control, he does not therefore cease to be an orator, any more than a doctor ceases to be a doctor when he withdraws from practice. Perhaps the highest of all pleasures is that which we derive from private study, and the only circumstances under which the delights of literature are unalloyed are when it withdraws from action, that is to say from toil, and can enjoy the pleasure of self-contemplation. But in the results that the orator obtains by writing speeches or historical narratives, which we may reasonably count as part of the task of oratory, we shall recognise features resembling those of a productive art. Still, if rhetoric is to be regarded as one of these three classes of art, since it is with action that its practice is chiefly and most frequently concerned, let us call it an active or administrative art, the two terms being identical.

XIX. I quite realise that there is a further question as to whether eloquence derives most from nature or from education. This question really lies outside the scope of our inquiry, since the ideal orator must necessarily be the result of a blend of both. But I do regard it as of great importance that we should decide how far there is any real question on this point. For if we make an absolute divorce between the two, nature will still be able to accomplish much without the aid of education, while the latter is valueless without the aid of nature. If, on the other hand, they are blended in equal proportions, I think we shall find that the average orator owes most to nature, while the perfect orator owes more to education. We may take a parallel from agriculture. A thoroughly barren soil will not be improved even by the best cultivation, while good land will yield some useful produce without any cultivation; but in the case of really rich land cultivation will do more for it than its own natural fertility. Had Praxiteles attempted to carve a statue out of a millstone, I should have preferred a rough block of Parian marble to any such statue. On the other hand, if the same artist had produced a finished statue from such a block of Parian marble, its artistic value would owe more to his skill than to the material. To conclude, nature is the raw material for education: the one forms, the other is formed. Without material art can do nothing, material without art does possess a certain value, while the perfection of art is better than the best material.

XX. More important is the question whether rhetoric is to be regarded as one of the indifferent arts, which in themselves deserve neither praise nor blame, but are useful or the reverse according to the character of the artist; or whether it should, as not a few even among philosophers hold, be considered as a virtue. For my own part I regard the practice of rhetoric which so many have adopted in the past and still follow to-day, as either no art at all, or, as the Greeks call it, ἀτεχνία (for I see numbers of speakers without the least pretension to method or literary training rushing headlong in the direction in which hunger or their natural shamelessness calls them); or else it is a bad art such as is styled κακοτεχνία. For there have, I think, been many persons and there are still some who have devoted their powers of speaking to the destruction of their fellow-men. There is also an unprofitable imitation of art, a kind of ματαιοτεχνία, which is neither good nor bad, but merely involves a useless expenditure of labour, reminding one of the man who shot a continuous stream of vetch-seeds from a distance through the eye of a needle, without ever missing his aim, and was rewarded by Alexander, who was a witness of the display, with the present of a bushel of vetch-seeds, a most appropriate reward. It is to such men that I would compare those who spend their whole time at the expense of much study and energy in composing declamations, which they aim at making as unreal as possible. The rhetoric on the other hand, which I am endeavouring to establish and the ideal of which I have in my mind's eye, that rhetoric which befits a good man and is in a word the only true rhetoric, will be a virtue. Philosophers arrive at this conclusion by a long chain of ingenious arguments; but it appears to me to be perfectly clear from the simpler proof of my own invention which I will now proceed to set forth.

The philosophers state the case as follows. If self-consistency as to what should and should not be done is an element of virtue (and it is to this quality that we give the name of prudence), the same quality will be revealed as regards what should be said and what should not be said, and if there are virtues, of which nature has given us some rudimentary sparks, even before we were taught anything about them, as for instance justice, of which there are some traces even among peasants and barbarians, it is clear that man has been so formed from the beginning as to be able to plead on his own behalf, not, it is true, with perfection, but yet sufficiently to show that there are certain sparks of eloquence implanted in us by nature. The same nature, however, is not to be found in those arts which have no connexion with virtue. Consequently, since there are two kinds of speech, the continuous which is called rhetoric, and the concise which is called dialectic (the relation between which was regarded by Zeno as being so intimate that he compared the latter to the closed fist, the former to the open hand), even the art of disputation will be a virtue. Consequently there can be no doubt about oratory whose nature is so much fairer and franker.

I should like, however, to consider the point more fully and explicitly by appealing to the actual work of oratory. For how will the orator succeed in panegyric unless he can distinguish between what is honourable and the reverse? How can he urge a policy, unless he has a clear perception of what is expedient? How can he plead in the law-courts, if he is ignorant of the nature of justice? Again, does not oratory call for courage, since it is often directed against the threats of popular turbulence and frequently runs into peril through incurring the hatred of the great, while sometimes, as for instance in the trial of Milo, the orator may have to speak in the midst of a crowd of armed soldiers? Consequently, if oratory be not a virtue, perfection is beyond its grasp. If, on the other hand, each living thing has its own peculiar virtue, in which it excels the rest or, at any rate, the majority (I may instance the courage of the lion and the swiftness of the horse), it may be regarded as certain that the qualities in which man excels the rest are, above all, reason and powers of speech. Why, therefore, should we not consider that the special virtue of man lies just as much in eloquence as in reason? It will be with justice then that Cicero[1] makes Crassus say that "eloquence is one of the highest virtues," and that Cicero himself calls it a virtue in his letters to Brutus[2] and in other passages. "But," it may be urged, "a bad man will at times produce an *exordium* or a *statement of facts,* and will argue a case in a manner that leaves nothing to be desired." No doubt; even a robber may fight bravely without courage ceasing to be a virtue; even a wicked slave may bear torture without a groan, and we may still continue to regard endurance of pain as worthy of praise. We can point to many acts which are identical with those of virtue, but spring from other sources. However, what I have said here must suffice, as I have already dealt with the question of the usefulness of oratory.

XXI. As to the material of oratory, some have asserted that it is speech, as for instance Gorgias[3] in the dialogue of Plato. If this view be accepted in the sense that the word "speech" is used of a discourse composed on any subject, then it is not the material, but the work, just as a statue is the work of the sculptor. For speeches like statues require art for their production. If on the other hand we interpret "speech" as indicating the words themselves, they can do nothing unless they are related to facts. Some again hold that the material consists of persuasive arguments. But they form part of the work, are produced by art and require material themselves. Some say that political questions provide the material. The mistake made by these lies not in the quality of their opinion but in its limitation. For political questions are material for eloquence but not the only material. Some, on the ground that rhetoric is a virtue, make the material with which it deals to be the whole of life. Others, on the ground that life regarded as a whole does not provide material for every virtue, since most of them are concerned only with departments of life (justice, courage and self-control each having their own duties and their own end), would consequently restrict oratory to one particular department of life and place it in the practical or pragmatic department of ethics, that is to say the department of morals which deals with the business of life.

For my own part, and I have authority to support me, I hold that the material of rhetoric is composed of everything that may be placed before it as a subject for speech. Plato, if I read him aright, makes Socrates[1] say to Gorgias that its material is to be found in things not words; while in the *Phaedrus*[2] he clearly proves that rhetoric is concerned not merely with law-courts and public assemblies, but with private and domestic affairs as well: from which it is obvious that this was the view of Plato himself. Cicero also in a passage[3] of one of his works, states that the material of rhetoric is composed of the things which are brought before it, but makes certain restrictions as to the nature of these things. In another passage,[4] however, he expresses his opinion that the orator has to speak about all kinds of things; I will quote his actual words: "although the very meaning of the name of orator and the fact that he professes to speak well seem to imply a promise and undertaking that the orator will speak with elegance and fullness on any subject that may be put before him." And in another passage[5] he says, "It is the duty of the true orator to seek out, hear, read, discuss, handle and ponder everything that befalls in the life of man, since it is with this that the orator is concerned and this that forms the material with which he has to deal."

But this material, as we call it, that is to say the things brought before it, has been criticised by some, at times on the ground that it is limitless, and sometimes on the ground that it is not peculiar to oratory, which they have therefore dubbed a *discursive* art, because all is grist that comes to its mill. I have no serious quarrel with these critics, for they acknowledge that rhetoric is concerned with every kind of material, though they deny that it has any peculiar material just because of that material's multiplicity. But in spite of this multiplicity, rhetoric is not unlimited in scope, and there are other minor arts whose material is characterised by the same multiplicity: such for instance is architecture, which deals with everything that is useful for the purpose of building: such too is the engraver's art which works on gold, silver, bronze, iron. As for sculpture, its activity extends to wood, ivory, marble, glass and precious stones in addition to the materials already mentioned. And things which form the material for other artists, do not for that reason cease forthwith to be material for rhetoric. For if I ask what is the material of the sculptor, I shall be told bronze; and if I ask what is the material of the maker of vessels (I refer to the craft styled *χαλκευτική* by the Greeks), the answer will again be bronze: and yet there is all the difference in the world between vessels and statues. Similarly medicine will not cease to be an art, because, like the art of the gymnast, it prescribes rubbing with oil and exercise, or because it deals with diet like the art of cookery. Again, the objection that to discourse of what is good, expedient or just is the duty of philosophy presents no difficulty. For when such critics speak of a philosopher, they mean a good man. Why then should I feel surprised to find that the orator whom I identify with the good man deals with the same material? There is all the less reason, since I have already shown in the first book[6] that philosophers only usurped this department of knowledge after it had been abandoned by the orators: it was always the peculiar property of rhetoric and the philosophers are really trespassers. Finally, since the discussion of whatever is brought before it is the task of dialectic, which is really a concise form of oratory, why should not this task be regarded as also being the appropriate material for continuous oratory?

There is a further objection made by certain critics, who say "Well then, if an orator has to speak on every subject, he must be the master of all the arts." I might answer this criticism in the words of Cicero,[7] in whom I find the following passage:—"In my opinion no one can be an absolutely perfect orator unless he has acquired a knowledge of all important subjects and arts." I however regard it as sufficient that an orator should not be actually ignorant of the subject on which he has to speak. For he cannot have a knowledge of all causes, and yet he should be able to speak on all. On what then will he speak? On those which he has studied. Similarly as regards the arts, he will study those concerning which he has to speak, as occasion may demand, and will speak on those which he has studied.

What then?—I am asked—will not a builder speak better on the subject of building and a musician on music? Certainly, if the orator does not know what is the question at issue. Even an illiterate peasant who is a party to a suit will speak better on behalf of his case than an orator who does not know what the subject in dispute may be. But on the other hand if the orator receive instruction from the builder or the musician, he will put forward what he has thus learned better than either, just as he will plead a case better than his client, once he has been instructed in it. The builder and the musician will, however, speak on the subject of their respective arts, if there should be any technical point which requires to be established. Neither will be an orator, but he will perform his task like an orator, just as when an untrained person binds up a wound, he will not be a physician, but he will be acting as one. Is it suggested that such topics never crop up in panegyric, deliberative or forensic oratory? When the question of the construction of a port at Ostia came up for discussion, had not the orator to state his views? And yet it was a subject requiring the technical knowledge of the architect. Does not the orator discuss the question whether livid spots and swellings on the body are symptomatic of ill-health or poison? And yet that is a question for the qualified physician. Will he not deal with measurements and figures? And yet we must admit that they form part of mathematics. For my part I hold that practically all subjects are under certain circumstances liable to come up for treatment by the orator. If the circumstances do not occur, the subjects will not concern him.

We were therefore right in asserting that the material of rhetoric is composed of everything that comes before the orator for treatment, an assertion which is confirmed by the practice of everyday speech. For when we have been given a subject on which to speak, we often preface our remarks by calling attention to the fact that the matter has been laid before us. Gorgias indeed felt so strongly that it was the orator's duty to speak on every subject, that he used to allow those who attended his lectures to ask him questions on any subject they pleased. Hermagoras also asserted that the material of oratory lay in the cause and the questions it involved, thereby including every subject that can be brought before it. If he denies that general questions[1] are the concern of oratory, he disagrees with me: but if they do concern rhetoric, that supports my contention. For there is nothing which may not crop up in a cause or appear as a question for discussion. Aristotle[2] himself also by his tripartite division of oratory, into forensic, deliberative and demonstrative, practically brought everything into the orator's domain, since there is nothing that may not come up for treatment by one of these three kinds of rhetoric.

A very few critics have raised the question as to what may be the *instrument* of oratory. My definition of an instrument is *that without which the material cannot be brought into the shape necessary for the effecting of our object.* But it is not the art which requires an instrument, but the artist. Knowledge needs no instruments, for it may be complete although it produces nothing, but the artist must have them. The engraver cannot work without his chisel nor the painter without his brush. I shall therefore defer this question until I come to treat of the orator as distinct from his art.

BOOK III

• • •

III. The art of oratory, as taught by most authorities, and those the best, consists of five parts:—*invention, arrangement, expression, memory,* and *delivery* or *action* (the two latter terms being used synonymously). But all speech expressive of purpose involves also a *subject* and *words.* If such expression is brief and contained within the limits of one sentence, it may demand nothing more, but longer speeches require much more. For not only what we say and how we say it is of importance, but also the circumstances under which we say it. It is here that the need of arrangement comes in. But it will be impossible to say everything demanded by the subject, putting each thing in its proper place, without the aid of memory. It is for this reason that memory forms the fourth department. But a delivery, which is rendered unbecoming either by voice or gesture, spoils everything and almost entirely destroys the effect of what is said. Delivery therefore must be assigned the fifth place.

Those (and Albutius is among them), who maintain that there are only three departments on the ground that memory and delivery (for which I shall give instructions in their proper place[1]) are given us by nature not by art, may be disregarded, although Thrasymachus held the same views as regards delivery. Some have added a sixth department, subjoining *judgment* to *invention,* on the ground that it is necessary first to *invent* and then to *exercise our judgment.* For my own part I do not believe that *invention* can exist apart from *judgment,* since we do not say that a speaker has *invented* inconsistent, two-edged or foolish arguments, but merely that he has failed to avoid them. It is true that Cicero in his Rhetorica[2] includes *judgment* under *invention;* but in my opinion *judgment* is so inextricably mingled with the first three departments of rhetoric (for without *judgment* neither *expression* nor *arrangement* are possible), that I think that even delivery owes much to it. I say this with all the greater confidence because Cicero in his *Partitiones oratoriae*[3] arrives at the same five-fold division of which I have just spoken. For after an initial division of oratory into *invention* and *expression,* he assigns *matter* and *arrangement* to *invention, words* and *delivery* to *expression,* and makes *memory* a fifth department common to them all and acting as their guardian. Again in the *Orator*[4] he states that eloquence consists of five things, and in view of the fact that this is a later work we may accept this as his more settled opinion. Others, who seem to me to have been no less desirous than those mentioned above to introduce some novelty, have added *order,* although they had already mentioned arrangement, as though *arrangement* was anything else than the marshalling of arguments in the best possible order. Dion taught that oratory consisted only of *invention* and *arrangement,* but added that each of these departments was twofold in nature, being concerned with words and things, so that *expression* comes under *invention,* and *delivery* under *arrangement,* while *memory* must be added as a fifth department. The followers of Theodorus divide *invention* into two parts, the one concerned with *matter* and the other with *expression,* and then add the three remaining departments. Hermagoras places *judgment, division, order* and everything relating to *expression* under the heading of *economy,* a Greek word meaning the management of domestic affairs which is applied metaphorically to oratory and has no Latin equivalent.

A further question arises at this point, since some make *memory* follow *invention* in the list of departments, while others make it follow *arrangement.* Personally I prefer to place it fourth. For we ought not merely to retain in our minds the fruits of our *invention,* in order that we may be able to arrange them, or to remember our *arrangement* in order that we may express it, but we must also commit to memory the words which we propose to use, since *memory* embraces everything that goes to the composition of a speech.

There are also not a few who have held that these are not *parts* of rhetoric, but rather *duties* to be observed by the orator. For it is his business to invent, arrange, express, etcetera. If, however, we accept this view, we leave nothing to art. For although the orator's task is to speak well, rhetoric is the science of speaking well. Or if we adopt another view, the task of the artist is to persuade, while the power of persuasion resides in the art. Consequently, while it is the duty of the orator to invent and arrange, *invention* and *arrangement* may be regarded as belonging to rhetoric. At this point there has been much disagreement, as to whether these are *parts* or *duties* of rhetoric, or, as Athenaeus believes, *elements* of rhetoric, which the Greeks call *στοιχεῖα.* But they cannot correctly be called *elements.* For in that case we should have to regard them merely as first-principles, like the moisture, fire, matter or atoms of which the universe is said to be composed. Nor is it correct to call them duties, since they are not performed by others, but perform something themselves. We must therefore conclude that they are *parts.* For since rhetoric is composed of them, it follows that, since a whole consists of parts, these must be parts of the whole which they compose. Those who have called them *duties* seem to me to have been further influenced by the fact that they wished to reserve the name of *parts* for another division of rhetoric: for they asserted that the *parts* of rhetoric were, *panegyric, deliberative* and *forensic* oratory. But if these are parts, they are parts rather of the material than of the art. For each of them contains the whole of rhetoric, since each of them requires *invention, arrangement, expression, memory* and *delivery.* Consequently some writers have thought it better to say that there are three *kinds* of oratory; those whom Cicero[1] has followed seem to me to have taken the wisest course in terming them *kinds of causes.*

IV. There is, however, a dispute as to whether there are three kinds or more. But it is quite certain that all the most eminent authorities among ancient writers, following Aristotle who merely substituted the term *public* for *deliberative,* have been content with the threefold division. Still a feeble attempt has been made by certain Greeks and by Cicero in his *de Oratore,*[2] to prove that there are not merely more than three, but that the number of kinds is almost past calculation: and this view has almost been thrust down our throats by the greatest authority[3] of our own times. Indeed if we place the task of praise and denunciation in the third division, on what kind of oratory are we to consider ourselves to be employed, when we complain, console, pacify, excite, terrify, encourage, instruct, explain obscurities, narrate, plead for mercy, thank, congratulate, reproach, abuse, describe, command, retract, express our desires and opinions, to mention no other of the many possibilities? As an adherent of the older view I must ask for indulgence and must enquire what was the reason that led earlier writers to restrict a subject of such variety to such narrow bounds. Those who think such authorities in error hold that they were influenced by the fact that these three subjects practically exhausted the range of ancient oratory. For it was customary to write panegyrics and denunciations and to deliver funeral orations, while the greater part of their activities was devoted to the law-courts and deliberative assemblies; as a result, they say, the old writers of text-books only included those kinds of oratory which were most in vogue. The defenders of antiquity point out that there are three kinds of audience: one which comes simply for the sake of getting pleasure, a second which meets to receive advice, a third to give judgement on causes. In the course of a thorough enquiry into the question it has occurred to me that the tasks of oratory must either be concerned with the law-courts or with themes lying outside the law-courts. The nature of the questions into which enquiry is made in the courts is obvious. As regards those matters which do not come before a judge, they must necessarily be concerned either with the past or the future. We praise or denounce past actions, we deliberate about the future. Again everything on which we have to speak must be either certain or doubtful. We praise or blame what is certain, as our inclination leads us: on the other hand where doubt exists, in some cases we are free to form our own views, and it is here that deliberation comes in, while in others, we leave the problem to the decision of others, and it is on these that litigation takes place.

Anaximenes regarded forensic and public oratory as *genera* but held that there were seven *species:*—exhortation, dissuasion, praise, denunciation, accusation, defence, inquiry, or as he called it ἐξεταστικόν. The first two, however, clearly belong to deliberative, the next to demonstrative, the three last to forensic oratory. I say nothing of Protagoras, who held that oratory was to be divided only into the following heads: question and answer, command and entreaty, or as he calls it εὐχωλή. Plato in his *Sophist*[4] in addition to public and forensic oratory introduces a third kind which he styles προσομιλητική, which I will permit myself to translate by "conversational." This is distinct from forensic oratory and is adapted for private discussions, and we may regard it as identical with dialectic. Isocrates[1] held that praise and blame find a place in every kind of oratory.

The safest and most rational course seems to be to follow the authority of the majority. There is, then, as I have said, one kind concerned with praise and blame, which, however, derives its name from the better of its two functions and is called *laudatory;* others however call it *demonstrative.* Both names are believed to be derived from the Greek in which the corresponding terms are *encomiastic,* and *epideictic.* The term *epideictic* seems to me however to imply display rather than demonstration, and to have a very different meaning from *encomiastic.* For although it includes laudatory oratory, it does not confine itself thereto. Will any one deny the title of *epideictic* to *panegyric?* But yet *panegyrics* are advisory in form and frequently discuss the interests of Greece. We may therefore conclude that, while there are three kinds of oratory, all three devote themselves in part to the matter in hand, and in part to display. But it may be that Romans are not borrowing from Greek when they apply the title *demonstrative,* but are merely led to do so because praise and blame demonstrate the nature of the object with which they are concerned. The second kind is *deliberative,* the third *forensic* oratory. All other *species* fall under these three *genera:* you will not find one in which we have not to praise or blame, to advise or dissuade, to drive home or refute a charge, while conciliation, narration, proof, exaggeration, extenuation, and the moulding of the minds of the audience by exciting or allaying their passions, are common to all three kinds of oratory. I cannot even agree with those who hold that *laudatory* subjects are concerned with the question of what is honourable, *deliberative* with the question of what is expedient, and *forensic* with the question of what is just: the division thus made is easy and neat rather than true: for all three kinds rely on the mutual assistance of the other. For we deal with justice and expediency in *panegyric* and with honour in *deliberations,* while you will rarely find a *forensic* case, in part of which at any rate something of those questions just mentioned is not to be found.

V. Every speech however consists at once of that which is expressed and that which expresses, that is to say of matter and words. Skill in speaking is perfected by nature, art and practice, to which some add a fourth department, namely imitation, which I however prefer to include under art. There are also three aims which the orator must always have in view; he must instruct, move and charm his hearers. This is a clearer division than that made by those who divide the task of oratory into that which relates to things and that which concerns the emotions, since both of these will not always be present in the subjects which we shall have to treat. For some themes are far from calling for any appeal to the emotions, which, although room cannot always be found for them, produce a most powerful effect wherever they do succeed in forcing their way. The best authorities hold that there are some things in oratory which require proof and others which do not, a view with which I agree. Some on the other hand, as for instance Celsus, think that the orator will not speak on any subject unless there is some question involved in it; but the majority of writers on rhetoric are against him, as is also the threefold division of oratory, unless indeed to praise what is allowed to be honourable and to denounce what is admittedly disgraceful are no part of an orator's duty.

• • •

That which I call the *basis* some style the *constitution,* others the *question,* and others again *that which may be inferred from the question,* while Theodorus calls it the most *general head,* κεφάλαιου γενικώτατον, to which everything must be referred. These different names, however, all mean the same thing, nor is it of the least importance to students by what special name things are called, as long as the thing itself is perfectly clear.

• • •

We must therefore accept the view of the authorities followed by Cicero,[1] to the effect that there are three things on which enquiry is made in every case: we ask *whether a thing is, what it is,* and *of what kind it is.* Nature herself imposes this upon us. For first of all there must be some subject for the question, since we cannot possibly determine *what a thing is,* or *of what kind it is,* until we have first ascertained *whether it is,* and therefore the first question raised is *whether it is.* But even when it is clear that a thing *is,* it is not immediately obvious *what it is.* And when we have decided what it is, there remains the question of its *quality.* These three points once ascertained, there is no further question to ask. These heads cover both *definite* and *indefinite questions.* One or more of them is discussed in every demonstrative, deliberative or forensic theme. These heads again cover all cases in the courts, whether we regard them from the point of view of *rational* or *legal questions.* For no legal problem can be settled save by the aid of *definition, quality* and *conjecture.* Those, however, who are engaged in instructing the ignorant will find it useful at first to adopt a slightly less rigid method: the road will not be absolutely straight to begin with, but it will be more open and will provide easier going. I would have them therefore learn above all things that there are four different methods which may be employed in every case, and he who is going to plead should study them as first essentials. For, to begin with the defendant, far the strongest method of self-defence is, if possible, to deny the charge. The second best is when it is possible to reply that the particular act with which you are charged was never committed. The third and most honourable is to maintain that the act was justifiable. If none of these lines of defence are feasible, there remains the last and only hope of safety: if it is impossible either to deny the charge or justify the act, we must evade the charge with the aid of some point of law, making it appear that the action has been brought against us illegally. Hence arise those questions of *legal action* or *competence.* For there are some things, which, although not laudable in themselves, are yet permitted by law; witness the passage in the Twelve Tables authorising creditors to divide up a debtor's body amongst themselves, a law which is repudiated by public custom. There are also certain things which although equitable are prohibited by law; witness the restrictions placed on testamentary disposition.[2] The accuser likewise has four things which he must keep in mind: he must prove that something was done, that a particular act was done, that it was wrongly done, and that he brings his charge according to law. Thus every cause will turn on the same sorts of questions, though the parts of plaintiff and defendant will sometimes be interchanged: for instance in the case of a claim for a reward, it will be the plaintiff's task to show that what was done was right.

• • •

VII. I will begin with the class of *causes* which are concerned with praise and blame. This class appears to have been entirely divorced by Aristotle,[3] and following him by Theophrastus, from the practical side of oratory (which they call *πραγματική*) and to have been reserved solely for the delectation of audiences, which indeed is shown to be its peculiar function by its name, which implies display.[4] Roman usage on the other hand has given it a place in the practical tasks of life. For funeral orations are often imposed as a duty on persons holding public office, or entrusted to magistrates by decree of the senate. Again the award of praise or blame to a witness may carry weight in the courts, while it is also a recognised practice to produce persons to praise the character of the accused. Further the published speeches of Cicero directed against his rivals in the election to the consulship,[5] and against Lucius Piso, Clodius and Curio,[6] are full of denunciation, and were notwithstanding delivered in the senate as formal expressions of opinion in the course of debate. I do not deny that some compositions of this kind are composed solely with a view to display, as, for instance, panegyrics of gods and heroes of the past, a consideration which provides the solution of a question which I discussed a little while back,[1] and proves that those are wrong who hold that an orator will never speak on a subject unless it involves some problem. But what problem is involved by the praise of Jupiter Capitolinus, a stock theme of the sacred Capitoline contest,[2] which is undoubtedly treated in regular rhetorical form?

However, just as panegyric applied to practical matters requires proof, so too a certain semblance of proof is at times required by speeches composed entirely for display. For instance, a speaker who tells how Romulus was the son of Mars and reared by the she-wolf, will offer as proofs of his divine origin the facts that when thrown into a running stream he escaped drowning, that all his achievements were such as to make it credible that he was the offspring of the god of battles, and that his contemporaries unquestionably believed that he was translated to heaven. Some arguments will even wear a certain semblance of defence: for example, if the orator is speaking in praise of Hercules, he will find excuses for his hero having changed raiment with the Queen of Lydia and submitted to the tasks which legend tells us she imposed upon him. The proper function however of panegyric is to amplify and embellish its themes.

This form of oratory is directed in the main to the praise of gods and men, but may occasionally be applied to the praise of animals or even of inanimate objects. In praising the gods our first step will be to express our veneration of the majesty of their nature in general terms. Next we shall proceed to praise the special power of the individual god and the discoveries whereby he has benefited the human race. For example, in the case of Jupiter, we shall extol his power as manifested in the governance of all things, with Mars we shall praise his power in war, with Neptune his power over the sea; as regards inventions we shall celebrate Minerva's discovery of the arts, Mercury's discovery of letters, Apollo's of medicine, Ceres' of the fruits of the earth, Bacchus' of wine. Next we must record their exploits as handed down from antiquity. Even gods may derive honour from their descent, as for instance is the case with the sons of Jupiter, or from their antiquity, as in the case of the children of Chaos, or from their offspring, as in the case of Latona, the mother of Apollo and Diana. Some again may be praised because they were born immortal, others because they won immortality by their valour, a theme which the piety of our sovereign has made the glory even of these present times.[3]

There is greater variety required in the praise of men. In the first place there is a distinction to be made as regards time between the period in which the objects of our praise lived and the time preceding their birth; and further, in the case of the dead, we must also distinguish the period following their death. With regard to things preceding a man's birth, there are his country, his parents and his ancestors, a theme which may be handled in two ways. For either it will be creditable to the objects of our praise not to have fallen short of the fair fame of their country and of their sires or to have ennobled a humble origin by the glory of their achievements. Other topics to be drawn from the period preceding their birth will have reference to omens or prophecies foretelling their future greatness, such as the oracle which is said to have foretold that the son of Thetis would be greater than his father. The praise of the individual himself will be based on his character, his physical endowments and external circumstances. Physical and accidental advantages provide a comparatively unimportant theme, which requires variety of treatment. At times for instance we extol beauty and strength in honorific terms, as Homer does in the case of Agamemnon[4] and Achilles[5]; at times again weakness may contribute largely to our admiration, as when Homer says[6] that Tydeus was small of stature but a good fighter. Fortune too may confer dignity as in the case of kings and princes (for they have a fairer field for the display of their excellences) but on the other hand the glory of good deeds may be enhanced by the smallness of their resources. Moreover the praise awarded to external and accidental advantages is given, not to their possession, but to their honourable employment. For wealth and power and influence, since they are the sources of strength, are the surest test of character for good or evil; they make us better or they make us worse. Praise awarded to character is always just, but may be given in various ways. It has sometimes proved the more effective course to trace a man's life and deeds in due chronological order, praising his natural gifts as a child, then his progress at school, and finally the whole course of his life, including words as well as deeds. At times on the other hand it is well to divide our praises, dealing separately with the various virtues, fortitude, justice, self-control and the rest of them and to assign to each virtue the deeds performed under its influence. We shall have to decide which of these two methods will be the more serviceable, according to the nature of the subject; but we must bear in mind the fact that what most pleases an audience is the celebration of deeds which our hero was the first or only man or at any rate one of the very few to perform: and to these we must add any other achievements which surpassed hope or expectation, emphasising what was done for the sake of others rather than what he performed on his own behalf. It is not always possible to deal with the time subsequent to our hero's death: this is due not merely to the fact that we sometimes praise him, while still alive, but also that there are but few occasions when we have a chance to celebrate the award of divine honours, posthumous votes of thanks, or statues erected at the public expense. Among such themes of panegyric I would mention monuments of genius that have stood the test of time. For some great men like Menander have received ampler justice from the verdict of posterity than from that of their own age. Children reflect glory on their parents, cities on their founders, laws on those who made them, arts on their inventors and institutions on those that first introduced them; for instance Numa first laid down rules for the worship of the gods, and Publicola first ordered that the lictors' rods should be lowered in salutation to the people.

The same method will be applied to denunciations as well, but with a view to opposite effects. For humble origin has been a reproach to many, while in some cases distinction has merely served to increase the notoriety and unpopularity of vices. In regard to some persons, as in the story of Paris, it has been predicted that they would be the cause of destruction to many, some like Thersites and Irus have been despised for their poverty and mean appearance, others have been loathed because their natural advantages were nullified by their vices: the poets for instance tell us that Nireus[1] was a coward and Pleisthenes[2] a debauchee. The mind too has as many vices as virtues, and vice may be denounced, as virtue may be praised, in two different ways. Some have been branded with infamy after death like Maelius, whose house was levelled with the ground, or Marcus Manlius, whose first name was banished from his family for all generations to come. The vices of the children bring hatred on their parents; founders of cities are detested for concentrating a race which is a curse to others, as for example the founder of the Jewish superstition;[3] the laws of Gracchus are hated, and we abhor any loathsome example of vice that has been handed down to posterity, such as the criminal form of lust which a Persian is said to have been the first to practise on a woman of Samos. And even in the case of the living the judgment of mankind serves as a proof of their character, and the fairness or foulness of their fame proves the orator's praise or blame to be true.

• • •

VIII. I am surprised that *deliberative* oratory also has been restricted by some authorities to questions of expediency. If it should be necessary to assign one single aim to deliberative I should prefer Cicero's[4] view that this kind of oratory is primarily concerned with what is honourable. I do not doubt that those who maintain the opinion first mentioned adopt the lofty view that nothing can be expedient which is not good. That opinion is perfectly sound so long as we are fortunate enough to have wise and good men for counsellors. But as we most often express our views before an ignorant audience, and more especially before popular assemblies, of which the majority is usually uneducated, we must distinguish between what is honourable and what is expedient and conform our utterances to suit ordinary understandings.

• • •

The majority of Greek writers have held that this kind of oratory is entirely concerned with addressing public assemblies and have restricted it to politics. Even Cicero[1] himself deals chiefly with this department. Consequently those who propose to offer advice upon peace, war, troops, public works or revenue must thoroughly acquaint themselves with two things, the resources of the state and the character of its people, so that the method employed in tendering their advice may be based at once on political realities and the nature of their hearers. This type of oratory seems to me to offer a more varied field for eloquence, since both those who ask for advice and the answers given to them may easily present the greatest diversity.

Consequently there are three points which must be specially borne in mind in advice or dissuasion: first the nature of the subject under discussion, secondly the nature of those who are engaged in the discussion, and thirdly the nature of the speaker who offers them advice. As to the subject under discussion its practicability is either certain or uncertain. In the latter case this will be the chief, if not the only point for consideration; for it will often happen that we shall assert first that something ought not to be done, even if it can be done, and secondly, that it cannot be done. Now when the question turns on such points as to whether the Isthmus can be cut through, the Pontine Marshes drained, or a harbour constructed at Ostia, or whether Alexander is likely to find land beyond the Ocean,[2] we make use of *conjecture.* But even in connection with things that are undoubtedly feasible, there may at times be room for *conjecture,* as for instance in questions such as whether Rome is ever likely to conquer Carthage, whether Hannibal will return to Africa if Scipio transports his army thither, or whether the Samnites are likely to keep faith if the Romans lay down their arms.[3] There are some things too which we may believe to be both feasible and likely to be carried into effect, but at another time or place or in another way.

When there is no scope for conjecture, our attention will be fixed on other points. In the first place advice will be asked either on account of the actual thing on which the orator is required to express his views, or on account of other causes which affect it from without. It is on the actual thing that the senate for instance debates, when it discusses such questions as whether it is to vote pay for the troops. In this case the material is simple. To this however may be added reasons for taking action or the reverse, as for example if the senate should discuss whether it should deliver the Fabii to the Gauls when the latter threaten war,[4] or Gaius Caesar should deliberate whether he should persist in the invasion of Germany, when his soldiers on all sides are making their wills.[5] These deliberative themes are of a twofold nature. In the first case the reason for deliberation is the Gallic threat of war, but there may still be a further question as to whether even without such threat of war they should surrender those who, contrary to the law of nations, took part in a battle when they had been sent out as ambassadors and killed the king with whom they had received instructions to treat. In the second case Caesar would doubtless never deliberate on the question at all, but for the perturbation shown by his soldiers; but there is still room for enquiry whether quite apart from this occurrence it would be wise to penetrate into Germany. But it must be remembered that we shall always speak first on that subject which is capable of discussion quite apart from the consequences.

Some have held that the three main considerations in an advisory speech are honour, expediency and necessity. I can find no place for the last.

For however great the violence which may threaten us, it may be necessary for us to suffer something, but we are not compelled to do anything; whereas the subject of deliberation is primarily whether we shall do anything. Or if by necessity they mean that into which we are driven by fear of worse things, the question will be one of expediency. For example, if a garrison is besieged by overwhelmingly superior forces and, owing to the failure of food and water supplies, discusses surrender to the enemy, and it is urged that it is a matter of necessity, the words "otherwise we shall perish" must needs be added: consequently there is no necessity arising out of the circumstances themselves, for death is a possible alternative. And as a matter of fact the Saguntines[1] did not surrender, nor did those who were surrounded on the raft from Opitergium.[2] It follows that in such cases also the question will be either one of expediency alone or of a choice between expediency and honour. "But," it will be urged, "if a man would beget children, he is under the necessity of taking a wife." Certainly. But he who wishes to become a father must needs be quite clear that he must take a wife. It appears to me, therefore, that where necessity exists, there is no room for deliberation, any more than where it is clear that a thing is not feasible. For deliberation is always concerned with questions where some doubt exists. Those therefore are wiser who make the third consideration for deliberative oratory to be τὸ δυνατόν or "possibility" as we translate it; the translation may seem clumsy, but it is the only word available. That all these considerations need not necessarily obtrude themselves in every case is too obvious to need explanation. Most writers, however, say that there are more than three. But the further considerations which they would add are really but *species* of the three *general* considerations just mentioned. For right, justice, piety, equity and mercy (for thus they translate τὸ ἥμερον), with any other virtues that anyone may be pleased to add, all come under the heading of that which is honourable. On the other hand, if the question be whether a thing is easy, great, pleasant or free from danger, it comes under questions of expediency. Such topics arise from some contradiction; for example a thing is expedient, but difficult, or trivial, or unpleasant, or dangerous. Some however hold that at times deliberation is concerned solely with the question whether a thing is pleasant, as for instance when discussion arises as to whether a theatre should be built or games instituted. But in my opinion you will never find any man such a slave to luxury as not to consider anything but pleasure when he delivers an advisory speech. For there must needs be something on every occasion that takes precedence of pleasure: in proposing the institution of public games there is the honour due to the gods; in proposing the erection of a theatre the orator will consider the advantages to be derived from relaxation from toil, and the unbecoming and undesirable struggle for places which will arise if there is no proper accommodation; religion, too, has its place in the discussion, for we shall describe the theatre as a kind of temple for the solemnization of a sacred feast. Often again we shall urge that honour must come before expediency; as for instance when we advise the men of Opitergium not to surrender to the enemy, even though refusal to do so means certain death. At times on the other hand we prefer expediency to honour, as when we advise the arming of slaves in the Punic War.[3] But even in this case we must not openly admit that such a course is dishonourable: we can point out that all men are free by nature and composed of the same elements, while the slaves in question may perhaps be sprung from some ancient and noble stock; and in the former case when the danger is so evident, we may add other arguments, such as that they would perish even more cruelly if they surrendered, should the enemy fail to keep faith, or Caesar (a more probable supposition) prove victorious. But in such a conflict of principles it is usual to modify the names which we give them. For expediency is often ruled out by those who assert not merely that honour comes before expediency, but that nothing can be expedient that is not honourable, while others say that what we call honour is vanity, ambition and folly, as contemptible in substance as it is fair in sound. Nor is expediency compared merely with inexpediency. At times we have to choose between two advantageous courses after comparison of their respective advantages. The problem may be still more complicated, as for instance when Pompey deliberated whether to go to Parthia, Africa or Egypt.[1] In such a case the enquiry is not which of two courses is better or worse, but which of three or more. On the other hand in *deliberative* oratory there will never be any doubt about circumstances wholly in our favour. For there can clearly be no doubt about points against which there is nothing to be said. Consequently as a rule all *deliberative* speeches are based simply on comparison, and we must consider what we shall gain and by what means, that it may be possible to form an estimate whether there is more advantage in the aims we pursue or greater disadvantage in the means we employ to that end. A question of expediency may also be concerned with time (for example, "it is expedient, but not now") or with place ("it is expedient, but not here") or with particular persons ("it is expedient, but not for us" or "not as against these") or with our method of action ("it is expedient, but not thus") or with degree ("it is expedient, but not to this extent").

But we have still more often to consider personality with reference to what is becoming, and we must consider our own as well as that of those before whom the question is laid. Consequently, though examples are of the greatest value in deliberative speeches, because reference to historical parallels is the quickest method of securing assent, it matters a great deal whose authority is adduced and to whom it is commended. For the minds of those who deliberate on any subject differ from one another and our audience may be of two kinds. For those who ask us for advice are either single individuals or a number, and in both cases the factors may be different. For when advice is asked by a number of persons it makes a considerable difference whether they are the senate or the people, the citizens of Rome or Fidenae, Greeks or barbarians, and in the case of single individuals, whether we are urging Cato or Gaius Marius to stand for office, whether it is the elder Scipio or Fabius who is deliberating on his plan of campaign. Further sex, rank, and age, must be taken into account, though it is character that will make the chief difference. It is an easy task to recommend an honourable course to honourable men, but if we are attempting to keep men of bad character to the paths of virtue, we must take care not to seem to upbraid a way of life unlike our own. The minds of such an audience are not to be moved by discoursing on the nature of virtue, which they ignore, but by praise, by appeals to popular opinion, and if such vanities are of no avail, by demonstration of the advantage that will accrue from such a policy, or more effectively perhaps by pointing out the appalling consequences that will follow the opposite policy. For quite apart from the fact that the minds of unprincipled men are easily swayed by terror, I am not sure that most men's minds are not more easily influenced by fear of evil than by hope of good, for they find it easier to understand what is evil than what is good. Sometimes again we urge good men to adopt a somewhat unseemly course, while we advise men of poor character to take a course in which the object is the advantage of those who seek our advice. I realise the thought that will immediately occur to my reader: "Do you then teach that this should be done or think it right?" Cicero[2] might clear me from blame in the matter; for he writes to Brutus in the following terms, after setting forth a number of things that might honourably be urged on Caesar: "Should I be a good man to advise this? No. For the end of him who gives advice is the advantage of the man to whom he gives it. But, you say, your advice is right. Certainly, but there is not always room for what is right in giving advice." However, this is a somewhat abstruse question, and does not concern deliberative oratory alone. I shall therefore reserve it for my twelfth and concluding book.[3] For my part I would not have anything done dishonourably. But for the meantime let us regard these questions as at least belonging to the rhetorical exercises of the schools: for knowledge of evil is necessary to enable us the better to defend what is right. For the present I will only say that if anyone is going to urge a dishonourable course on an honourable man, he should remember not to urge it as being dishonourable, and should avoid the practice of certain declaimers who urge Sextus Pompeius to piracy just because it is dishonourable and cruel. Even when we address bad men, we should gloss over what is unsightly. For there is no man so evil as to wish to seem so.

• • •

IX. I now come to the forensic kind of oratory, which presents the utmost variety, but whose duties are no more than two, the bringing and rebutting of charges. Most authorities divide the forensic speech into five parts: the *exordium,* the *statement of facts,* the *proof,* the *refutation,* and the *peroration.* To these some have added the *partition into heads, proposition* and *digression,* the two first of which form part of the *proof.* For it is obviously necessary to *propound* what you are going to *prove* as well as to conclude. Why then, if *proposition* is a part of a speech, should not *conclusion* be also? *Partition* on the other hand is merely one aspect of *arrangement,* and *arrangement* is a part of rhetoric itself, and is equally distributed through every theme of oratory and their whole body, just as are *invention* and *style.* Consequently we must regard *partition* not as one part of a whole speech, but as a part of each individual question that may be involved. For what question is there in which an orator cannot set forth the order in which he is going to make his points? And this of course is the function of *partition.* But how ridiculous it is to make each question an aspect of *proof,* but *partition* which is an aspect of a question a part of the whole speech. As for *digression* (*egressio,* now more usually styled *excessus*), if it lie outside the case, it cannot be part of it, while, if it lie within it, it is merely an accessory or ornament of that portion of the case from which *digression* is made. For if anything that lies within the case is to be called part of it, why not call *argument, comparison, commonplace, pathos, illustration* parts of the case? On the other hand I disagree with those who, like Aristotle,[1] would remove *refutation* from the list on the ground that it forms part of the *proof:* for the *proof* is constructive, and the *refutation* destructive. Aristotle[2] also introduces another slight novelty in making *proposition,* not *statement of facts,* follow the *exordium.* This however he does because he regards *proposition* as the *genus* and *statement of facts* as the *species,* with the result that he holds that, whereas the former is always and everywhere necessary, the latter may sometimes be dispensed with.

It is however necessary to point out as regards these five parts which I have established, that that which has to be spoken first is not necessarily that which requires our first consideration. But above all we must consider the nature of the case, the question at issue and the arguments for and against. Next we must consider what points are to be made, and what refuted, and then how the facts are to be stated. For the *statement of facts* is designed to prepare the way for the *proofs* and must needs be unprofitable, unless we have first determined what *proofs* are to be promised in the *statement.* Finally we must consider how best to win the judge to take our view. For we cannot be sure until we have subjected all the parts of the case to careful scrutiny, what sort of impression we wish to make upon the judge: are we to mollify him or increase his severity, to excite or relax his interest in the case, to render him susceptible to influence or the reverse?

I cannot however approve the view of those who think that the *exordium* should actually be written last. For though we must collect all our material and determine the proper place for each portion of it, before we begin to speak or write, we must commence with what naturally comes first. No one begins a portrait by painting or modelling the feet, and no art finds its completion at the point where it should begin. Otherwise what will happen if we have not time to write our speech? Will not the result of such a reversal of the proper order of things be that we shall be caught napping? We must therefore review the subject-matter in the order laid down, but write our speech in the order in which we shall deliver it.

X. Every cause in which one side attacks and the other defends consists either of one or more controversial questions. In the first case it is called *simple,* in the second *complex.* An example of the first is when the subject of enquiry is a theft or an adultery taken by itself. In *complex* cases the several questions may all be of the same kind, as in cases of extortion, or of different kinds, as when a man is accused at one and the same time of homicide and sacrilege. Such cases no longer arise in the public courts, since the praetor allots the different charges to different courts in accordance with a definite rule; but they still are of frequent occurrence in the Imperial or Senatorial courts, and were frequent in the days when they came up for trial before the people.[1] Private suits again are often tried by one judge, who may have to determine many different points of law. There are no other *species* of *forensic* causes, not even when one person brings the same suit on the same grounds against two different persons, or two persons bring the same suit against one, or several against several, as occasionally occurs in lawsuits about inheritances. Because although a number of parties may be involved, there is still only one suit, unless indeed the different circumstances of the various parties alter the questions at issue.

There is however said to be a third and different class, the *comparative.* Questions of comparison frequently require to be handled in portions of a cause, as for instance in the centumviral court,[2] when after other questions have been raised the question is discussed as to which of two claimants is the more deserving of an inheritance. It is rare however for a case to be brought into court on such grounds alone, as in *divinations*[3] which take place to determine who the accuser shall be, and occasionally when two informers dispute as to which has earned the reward. Some again have added a fourth class, namely *mutual accusation,* which they call ἀντικατηγορία. Others, however, regard it as belonging to the *comparative* group, to which indeed the common case of reciprocal suits on different grounds bears a strong resemblance. If this latter case should also be called ἀντικατηγορία (for it has no special name of its own), we must divide *mutual accusation* into two classes, in one of which the parties bring the same charge against each other, while in the other they bring different charges. The same division will also apply to claims.

As soon as we are clear as to the kind of cause on which we are engaged, we must then consider whether the act that forms the basis of the charge is denied or defended, or given another name or excepted from that class of action. Thus we determine the *basis* of each case.

• • •

BOOK V

• • •

I. To begin with it may be noted that the division laid down by Aristotle[4] has met with almost universal approval. It is to the effect that there are some proofs adopted by the orator which lie outside the art of speaking, and others which he himself deduces or, if I may use the term, begets out of his case. The former therefore have been styled ἄτεχνοι or *inartificial* proofs, the latter ἔντεχνοι or *artificial.* To the first class belong decisions of previous courts, rumours, evidence extracted by torture, documents, oaths, and witnesses, for it is with these that the majority of forensic arguments are concerned. But though in themselves they involve no art, all the powers of eloquence are as a rule required to disparage or refute them. Consequently in my opinion those who would eliminate the whole of this class of proof from their rules of oratory, deserve the strongest condemnation. It is not, however, my intention to embrace all that can be said for or against these views. I do not for instance propose to lay down rules for commonplaces, a task requiring infinite detail, but merely to sketch out the general lines and method to be followed by the orator.

• • •

VIII. The second class of proofs are wholly the work of art and consist of matters specially adapted to produce belief. They are, however, as a rule almost entirely neglected or only very lightly touched on by those who, avoiding arguments as rugged and repulsive things, confine themselves to pleasanter regions and, like those who, as poets tell, were bewitched by tasting a magic herb in the land of the Lotus-eaters or by the song of the Sirens into preferring pleasure to safety, follow the empty semblance of renown and are robbed of that victory which is the aim of eloquence. And yet those other forms of eloquence, which have a more continuous sweep and flow, are employed with a view to assisting and embellishing the arguments and produce the appearance of superinducing a body upon the sinews, on which the whole case rests; thus if it is asserted that some act has been committed under the influence of anger, fear or desire, we may expatiate at some length on the nature of each of these passions. It is by these same methods that we praise, accuse, exaggerate, attenuate, describe, deter, complain, console or exhort. But such rhetorical devices may be employed in connexion with matters about which there is no doubt or at least which we speak of as admitted facts. Nor would I deny that there is some advantage to be gained by pleasing our audience and a great deal by stirring their emotions. Still, all these devices are more effective, when the judge thinks he has gained a full knowledge of the facts of the case, which we can only give him by argument and by the employment of every other known means of proof.

Before, however, I proceed to classify the various species of artificial proof, I must point out that there are certain features common to all kinds of proof. For there is no question which is not concerned either with things or persons, nor can there be any ground for argument save in connexion with matters concerning things or persons, which may be considered either by themselves or with reference to something else; while there can be no proof except such as is derived from things consequent or things opposite, which must be sought for either in the time preceding, contemporaneous with or subsequent to the alleged fact, nor can any single thing be proved save by reference to something else which must be greater, less than or equal to it. As regards arguments, they may be found either in the questions raised by the case, which may be considered by themselves quite apart from any connexion with individual things or persons, or in the case itself, when anything is discovered in it which cannot be arrived at by the light of common reason, but is peculiar to the subject on which judgment has to be given. Further, all proofs fall into three classes, necessary, credible, and not impossible. Again there are four forms of proof. First, we may argue that, because one thing is, another thing is not; as *It is day and therefore not night.* Secondly, we may argue that, because one thing is, another thing is; as *The sun is risen, therefore it is day.* Thirdly, it may be argued that because one thing is not, another thing is; as *It is not night, therefore it is day.* Finally, it may be argued that, because one thing is not, another thing is not; as *He is not a reasoning being, therefore he is not a man.* These general remarks will suffice by way of introduction and I will now proceed to details.

IX. Every artificial proof consists either of indications, arguments or examples. I am well aware that many consider indications to form part of the arguments. My reasons for distinguishing them are two-fold. In the first place indications as a rule come under the head of inartificial proofs: for a bloodstained garment, a shriek, a dark blotch and the like are all evidence analogous to documentary or oral evidence and rumours; they are not discovered by the orator, but are given him with the case itself. My second reason was that indications, if indubitable, are not arguments, since they leave no room for question, while arguments are only possible in controversial matters. If on the other hand they are doubtful, they are not arguments, but require arguments to support them.

The two first species into which artificial proofs may be divided are, as I have already said, those which involve a conclusion and those which do not. The former are those which cannot be otherwise and are called τεκμήρια by the Greeks, because they are indications from which there is no getting away. These however seem to me scarcely to come under the rules of art. For where an indication is irrefutable, there can be no dispute as to facts. This happens whenever there can be no doubt that something is being or has been done, or when it is impossible for it to be or have been done. In such cases there can be no dispute as to the fact. This kind of proof may be considered in connexion with past, present or future time. For example, a woman who is delivered of a child must have had intercourse with a man, and the reference is to the past. When there is a high wind at sea, there must be waves, and the reference is to the present. When a man has received a wound in the heart, he is bound to die, and the reference is to the future. Nor again can there be a harvest where no seed has been sown, nor can a man be at Rome when he is at Athens, nor have been wounded by a sword when he has no scar. Some have the same force when reversed: a man who breathes is alive, and a man who is alive breathes. Some again cannot be reversed: because he who walks moves it does not follow that he who moves walks. So too a woman, who has not been delivered of a child, may have had intercourse with a man, there may be waves without a high wind, and a man may die without having received a wound in the heart. Similarly seed may be sown without a harvest resulting, a man, who was never at Athens, may never have been at Rome, and a man who has a scar may not have received a sword-wound.

There are other indications or εἰκότα, that is probabilities, as the Greeks call them, which do not involve a necessary conclusion. These may not be sufficient in themselves to remove doubt, but may yet be of the greatest value when taken in conjunction with other indications. The Latin equivalent of the Greek σημεῖον is *signum,* a sign, though some have called it *indicium,* an indication, or *vestigium,* a trace. Such signs or indications enable us to infer that something else has happened; blood for instance may lead us to infer that a murder has taken place. But bloodstains on a garment may be the result of the slaying of a victim at a sacrifice or of bleeding at the nose. Everyone who has a bloodstain on his clothes is not necessarily a murderer. But although such an indication may not amount to proof in itself, yet it may be produced as evidence in conjunction with other indications, such for instance as the fact that the man with the bloodstain was the enemy of the murdered man, had threatened him previously or was in the same place with him. Add the indication in question to these, and what was previously only a suspicion may become a certainty. On the other hand there are indications which may be made to serve either party, such as livid spots, swellings which may be regarded as symptoms either of poisoning or of bad health, or a wound in the breast which may be treated as a proof of murder or of suicide. The force of such indications depends on the amount of extraneous support which they receive.

Hermagoras would include among such indications as do not involve a necessary conclusion, an argument such as the following, "Atalanta cannot be a virgin, as she has been roaming the woods in the company of young men." If we accept this view, I fear that we shall come to treat all inferences from a fact as indications. None the less such arguments are in practice treated exactly as if they were indications. Nor do the Areopagites, when they condemned a boy for plucking out the eyes of quails, seem to have had anything else in their mind than the consideration that such conduct was an indication of a perverted character which might prove hurtful to many, if he had been allowed to grow up. So, too, the popularity of Spurius Maelius and Marcus Manlius was regarded as an indication that they were aiming at supreme power. However, I fear that this line of reasoning will carry us too far. For if it is an indication of adultery that a woman bathes with men, the fact that she revels with young men or even an intimate friendship will also be indications of the same offence. Again depilation, a voluptuous gait, or womanish attire may be regarded as indications of effeminacy and unmanliness by anyone who thinks that such symptoms are the result of an immoral character, just as blood is the result of a wound: for anything, that springs from the matter under investigation and comes to our notice, may properly be called an indication. Similarly it is also usual to give the names of signs to frequently observed phenomena, such as prognostics of the weather which we may illustrate by the Vergilian

> *"For wind turns Phoebe's face to ruddy gold"*[1]

and

> *"The crow with full voice, good-for-naught, invites the rain."*[2]

If these phenomena are caused by the state of the atmosphere, such an appellation is correct enough. For if the moon turns red owing to the wind, her hue is certainly a sign of wind. And if, as the same poet infers,[3] the condensation and rarification of the atmosphere causes that "concert of bird-voices" of which he speaks, we may agree in regarding it as a sign. We may further note that great things are sometimes indicated by trivial signs, witness the Vergilian crow; that trivial events should be indicated by signs of greater importance is of course no matter for wonder.

X. I now turn to arguments, the name under which we comprise the ἐνθυμήματα, ἐπιχειρήματα, and ἀποδείξεις of the Greeks, terms which, in spite of their difference, have much the same meaning. For the *enthymeme* (which we translate by *commentum* or *commentatio,* there being no alternative, though we should be wiser to use the Greek name) has three meanings: firstly it means anything conceived in the mind (this is not however the sense of which I am now speaking); secondly it signifies a proposition with a reason, and thirdly a conclusion of an argument drawn either from denial of consequents or from incompatibles[4]; although there is some controversy on this point. For there are some who style a conclusion from consequents an *epicheireme,* while it will be found that the majority hold the view that an *enthymeme* is a conclusion from incompatibles[5]: wherefore Cornificius styles it a *contrarium* or argument from contraries. Some again call it a rhetorical syllogism, others an incomplete syllogism, because its parts are not so clearly defined or of the same number as those of the regular syllogism, since such precision is not specially required by the orator. Valgius[6] translates ἐπιχείρημα by *aggressio,* that is an attempt. It would however, in my opinion, be truer to say that it is not our handling of the subject, but the thing itself which we attempt which should be called an ἐπιχείρημα, that is to say the argument by which we try to prove something and which, even if it has not yet been stated in so many words, has been clearly conceived by the mind. Others regard it not as an attempted or imperfect proof, but a complete proof, falling under the most special[7] species of proof; consequently, according to its proper and most generally received appellation it must be understood in the sense of a definite conception of some thought consisting of at least three parts.[8] Some call an ἐπιχείρημα a *reason,* but Cicero[9] is more correct in calling it a *reasoning,* although he too seems to derive this name from the syllogism rather than anything else; for he calls the *syllogistic basis*[10] a *ratiocinative basis* and quotes philosophers to support him. And since there is a certain kinship between a syllogism and an *epicheireme,* it may be thought that he was justified in his use of the latter term. An ἀπόδειξις is a clear proof; hence the use of the term γραμμικαὶ ἀποδείξεις, "linear demonstrations"[11] by the geometricians. Caecilius holds that it differs from the *epicheireme* solely in the kind of conclusion arrived at and that an *apodeixis* is simply an incomplete *epicheireme* for the same reason that we said an enthymeme differed from a syllogism. For an *epicheireme* is also part of a syllogism. Some think that an *apodeixis* is portion of an *epicheireme,* namely the part containing the proof. But all authorities, however much they may differ on other points, define both in the same way, in so far as they call both a method of proving what is not certain by means of what is certain. Indeed this is the nature of all arguments, for what is certain cannot be proved by what is uncertain. To all these forms of argument the Greeks give the name of πίστεις, a term which, though the literal translation is *fides* "a warrant of credibility," is best translated by *probatio* "proof." But *argument* has several other meanings. For the plots of plays composed for acting in the theatre are called arguments, while Pedianus, when explaining the themes of the speeches of Cicero, says *The argument is as follows.* Cicero[1] himself in writing to Brutus says, *Fearing that I might transfer something from that source to my Cato, although the argument is quite different.* It is thus clear that all subjects for writing are so called. Nor is this to be wondered at, since the term is also in common use among artists; hence the Vergilian phrase *A mighty argument.*[2] Again a work which deals with a number of different themes is called "rich in argument." But the sense with which we are now concerned is that which provides proof. Celsus indeed treats the terms, proof, indication, credibility, attempt, simply as different names for the same things, in which, to my thinking, he betrays a certain confusion of thought. For proof and credibility are not merely the result of logical processes, but may equally be secured by inartificial arguments. Now I have already[3] distinguished signs or, as he prefers to call them, indications from arguments. Consequently, since an argument is a process of reasoning which provides proof and enables one thing to be inferred from another and confirms facts which are uncertain by reference to facts which are certain, there must needs be something in every case which requires no proof. Otherwise there will be nothing by which we can prove anything; there must be something which either is or is believed to be true, by means of which doubtful things may be rendered credible. We may regard as certainties, first, those things which we perceive by the senses, things for instance that we hear or see, such as signs or indicatons; secondly, those things about which there is general agreement, such as the existence of the gods or the duty of loving one's parents; thirdly, those things which are established by law or have passed into current usage, if not throughout the whole world, at any rate in the nation or state where the case is being pleaded—there are for instance many rights which rest not on law, but on custom; finally, there are the things which are admitted by either party, and whatever has already been proved or is not disputed by our adversary. Thus for instance it may be argued that since the world is governed by providence, the state should similarly be governed by some controlling power: it follows that the state must be so governed, once it is clear that the world is governed by providence. Further, the man who is to handle arguments correctly must know the nature and meaning of everything and their usual effects. For it is thus that we arrive at probable arguments or εἰκότα as the Greeks call them. With regard to credibility there are three degrees. First, the highest, based on what usually happens, as for instance the assumption that children are loved by their parents. Secondly, there is the highly probable, as for instance the assumption that a man in the enjoyment of good health will probably live till tomorrow. The third degree is found where there is nothing absolutely against an assumption, such as that a theft committed in a house was the work of one of the household. Consequently Aristotle in the second book of his *Rhetoric*[4] has made a careful examination of all that commonly happens to things and persons, and what things and persons are naturally adverse or friendly to other things or persons, as for instance, what is the natural result of wealth or ambition or superstition, what meets with the approval of good men, what is the object of a soldier's or a farmer's desires, and by what means everything is sought or shunned. For my part I do not propose to pursue this subject. It is not merely a long, but an impossible or rather an infinite task; moreover it is within the compass of the common understanding of mankind. If, however, anyone wishes to pursue the subject, I have indicated where he may apply. But all credibility, and it is with credibility that the great majority of arguments are concerned, turns on questions such as the following: whether it is credible that a father has been killed by his son, or that a father has committed incest with his daughter, or to take questions of an opposite character, whether it is credible that a stepmother has poisoned her stepchild, or that a man of luxurious life has committed adultery; or again whether a crime has been openly committed, or false evidence given for a small bribe, since each of these crimes is the result of a special cast of character as a rule, though not always; if it were always so, there would be no room for doubt, and no argument.

Let us now turn to consider the "places" of arguments, although some hold that they are identical with the topics which I have already discussed above.[1] But I do not use this term in its usual acceptance, namely, commonplaces[2] directed against luxury, adultery, and the like, but in the sense of the secret places where arguments reside, and from which they must be drawn forth. For just as all kinds of produce are not provided by every country, and as you will not succeed in finding a particular bird or beast, if you are ignorant of the localities where it has its usual haunts or birthplace, as even the various kinds of fish flourish in different surroundings, some preferring a smooth and others a rocky bottom, and are found on different shores and in divers regions (you will for instance never catch a sturgeon or wrasse in Italian waters), so not every kind of argument can be derived from every circumstance, and consequently our search requires discrimination. Otherwise we shall fall into serious error, and after wasting our labour through lack of method we shall fail to discover the argument which we desire, unless assisted by some happy chance. But if we know the circumstances which give rise to each kind of argument, we shall easily see, when we come to a particular "place," what arguments it contains.

Firstly, then, arguments may be drawn from persons; for, as I have already said,[3] all arguments fall into two classes, those concerned with things and those concerned with persons, since causes, time, place, occasion, instruments, means and the like are all accidents of things. I have no intention of tracing all the accidents of persons, as many have done, but shall confine myself to those from which arguments may be drawn. Such are birth, for persons are generally regarded as having some resemblance to their parents and ancestors, a resemblance which sometimes leads to their living disgracefully or honourably, as the case may be; then there is nationality, for races have their own character, and the same action is not probable in the case of a barbarian, a Roman and a Greek; country is another, for there is a like diversity in the laws, institutions and opinions of different states; sex, since for example a man is more likely to commit a robbery, a woman to poison; age, since different actions suit different ages; education and training, since it makes a great difference who were the instructors and what the method of instruction in each individual case; bodily constitution, for beauty is often introduced as an argument for lust, strength as an argument for insolence, and their opposites for opposite conduct; fortune, since the same acts are not to be expected from rich and poor, or from one who is surrounded by troops of relations, friends or clients and one who lacks all these advantages; condition, too, is important, for it makes a great difference whether a man be famous or obscure, a magistrate or a private individual, a father or a son, a citizen or a foreigner, a free man or a slave, married or unmarried, a father or childless. Nor must we pass by natural disposition, for avarice, anger, pity, cruelty, severity and the like may often be adduced to prove the credibility or the reverse of a given act; it is for instance often asked whether a man's way of living be luxurious, frugal or parsimonious. Then there is occupation, since a rustic, a lawyer, a man of business, a soldier, a sailor, a doctor all perform very different actions. We must also consider the personal ambitions of individuals, for instance whether they wish to be thought rich or eloquent, just or powerful. Past life and previous utterances are also a subject for investigation, since we are in the habit of inferring the present from the past. To these some add passion, by which they mean some temporary emotion such as anger or fear; they also add design, which may refer to the past, present or future. These latter, however, although accidents of persons, should be referred to that class of arguments which we draw from causes, as also should certain dispositions of mind, for example when we inquire whether one man is the friend or enemy of another. Names also are treated as accidents of persons; this is perfectly true, but names are rarely food for argument, unless indeed they have been given for some special reasons, such as the titles of Wise, Great, Pious, or unless the name has suggested some special thought to the bearer. Lentulus[1] for instance had the idea of conspiracy suggested to him by the fact that according to the Sibylline books and the Responses of the soothsayers the tyranny was promised to three members of the Cornelian family, and he considered himself to be the third in succession to Sulla and Cinna, since he too bore the name Cornelius. On the other hand the conceit employed by Euripides[2] where he makes Eteocles taunt his brother Polynices on the ground that his name is evidence of character, is feeble in the extreme. Still a name will often provide the subject for a jest,[3] witness the frequent jests of Cicero on the name of Verres. Such, then, and the like are the accidents of persons. It is impossible to deal with them all either here or in other portions of this work, and I must content myself with pointing out the lines on which further enquiry should proceed.

• • •

Well, then, to give a brief summary of the whole question, arguments are drawn from persons, causes, place and time (which latter we have divided into preceding, contemporary and subsequent), from resources (under which we include instruments), from manner (that is, how a thing has been done), from definition, genus, species, difference, property, elimination, division, beginnings, increase, consummation, likes, unlikes, contradictions, consequents, efficients, effects, results, and comparison, which is subdivided into several species.

• • •

BOOK VIII

• • •

I. What the Greeks call φράσις, we in Latin call *elocutio* or style. Style is revealed both in individual words and in groups of words. As regards the former, we must see that they are Latin, clear, elegant and well-adapted to produce the desired effect. As regards the latter, they must be correct, aptly placed and adorned with suitable figures. I have already, in the portions of the first book dealing with the subject of grammar, said all that is necessary on the way to acquire idiomatic and correct speech. But there my remarks were restricted to the prevention of positive faults, and it is well that I should now point out that our words should have nothing provincial or foreign about them. For you will find that there are a number of writers by no means deficient in style whose language is precious rather than idiomatic. As an illustration of my meaning I would remind you of the story of the old woman at Athens, who, when Theophrastus, a man of no mean eloquence, used one solitary word in an affected way, immediately said that he was a foreigner, and on being asked how she detected it, replied that his language was too Attic for Athens. Again Asinius Pollio held that Livy, for all his astounding eloquence, showed traces of the idiom of Padua. Therefore, if possible, our voice and all our words should be such as to reveal the native of this city, so that our speech may seem to be of genuine Roman origin, and not merely to have been presented with Roman citizenship.

II. Clearness results above all from *propriety* in the use of words. But *propriety* is capable of more than one interpretation. In its primary sense it means calling things by their right names, and is consequently sometimes to be avoided, for our language must not be obscene, unseemly or mean. Language may be described as mean when it is beneath the dignity of the subject or the rank of the speaker. Some orators fall into serious error in their eagerness to avoid this fault, and are afraid of all words that are in ordinary use, even although they may be absolutely necessary for their purpose. There was, for example, the man who in the course of a speech spoke of "Iberian grass," a meaningless phrase intelligible only to himself. Cassius Severus, however, by way of deriding his affectation, explained that he meant Spanish broom. Nor do I see why a certain distinguished orator thought "fishes conserved in brine" a more elegant phrase than the word which he avoided.[1] But while there is no special merit in the form of *propriety* which consists in calling things by their real names, it is a fault to fly to the opposite extreme. This fault we call *impropriety,* while the Greeks call it *ἄκυρον*. As examples I may cite the Virgilian,[2] "Never could I have hoped for such great woe," or the phrase, which I noted had been corrected by Cicero in a speech of Dolabella's, "To bring death," or again, phrases of a kind that win praise from some of our contemporaries, such as, "His words fell from the cross."[3] On the other hand, everything that lacks appropriateness will not necessarily suffer from the fault of positive *impropriety,* because there are, in the first place, many things which have no proper term either in Greek or Latin. For example, the verb *iaculari* is specially used in the sense of "to throw a javelin," whereas there is no special verb appropriated to the throwing of a ball or a stake. So, too, while *lapidare* has the obvious meaning of "to stone," there is no special word to describe the throwing of clods or potsherds. Hence abuse or *catachresis* of words becomes necessary, while metaphor, also, which is the supreme ornament of oratory, applies words to things with which they have strictly no connexion. Consequently *propriety* turns not on the actual term, but on the meaning of the term, and must be tested by the touchstone of the understanding, not of the ear. The second sense in which the word *propriety* is used occurs when there are a number of things all called by the same name: in this case the original term from which the others are derived is styled the *proper* term. For example, the word *vertex* means a whirl of water, or of anything else that is whirled in a like manner: then, owing to the fashion of coiling the hair, it comes to mean the top of the head, while finally, from this sense it derives the meaning of the highest point of a mountain. All these things may correctly be called *vertices,* but the *proper* use of the term is the first. So, too, *solea* and *turdus* are employed as names of fish, to mention no other cases.[4] The third kind of *propriety* is found in the case where a thing which serves a number of purposes has a special name in some one particular context; for example, the proper term for a funeral *song* is *naenia,* and for the general's *tent augurale.* Again, a term which is common to a number of things may be applied in a *proper* or special sense to some one of them. Thus we use *urbs* in the special sense of Rome, *venales* in the special sense of newly-purchased slaves, and *Corinthia* in the special sense of bronzes, although there are other cities besides Rome, and many other things which may be styled *venales* besides slaves, and gold and silver are found at Corinth as well as bronze. But the use of such terms implies no special excellence in an orator. There is, however, a form of *propriety* of speech which deserves the highest praise, that is to say, the employment of words with the maximum of significance, as, for instance, when Cato[5] said that "Caesar was thoroughly sober when he undertook the task of overthrowing the constitution," or as Virgil[6] spoke of a "thin-drawn strain," and Horace[7] of the "shrill pipe," and "dread Hannibal." Some also include under this head that form of *propriety* which is derived from characteristic epithets, such as in the Virgilian[8] phrases, "sweet unfermented wine," or "with white teeth." But of this sort of propriety I shall have to speak elsewhere.[9] *Propriety* is also made to include the appropriate use of words in metaphor, while at times the salient characteristic of an individual comes to be attached to him as a *proper* name: thus Fabius was called "Cunctator," the Delayer, on account of the most remarkable of his many military virtues. Some, perhaps, may think that words which mean more than they actually say deserve mention in connexion with clearness, since they assist the understanding.

I, however, prefer to place *emphasis*[1] among the ornaments of oratory, since it does not make a thing intelligible, but merely more intelligible.

Obscurity, on the other hand, results from the employment of obsolete words, as, for instance, if an author should search the records of the priests, the earliest treaties and the works of long-forgotten writers with the deliberate design of collecting words that no man living understands. For there are persons who seek to gain a reputation for erudition by such means as this, in order that they may be regarded as the sole depositories of certain forms of knowledge. Obscurity may also be produced by the use of words which are more familiar in certain districts than in others, or which are of a technical character, such as the wind called "Atabalus,"[2] or a "sack-ship," or *in malo cosanum.* Such expressions should be avoided if we are pleading before a judge who is ignorant of their meaning, or, if used, should be explained, as may have to be done in the case of what are called homonyms. For example, the word *taurus* may be unintelligible unless we make it clear whether we are speaking of a bull, or a mountain, or a constellation, or the name of a man, or the root of a tree.[3]

A greater source of obscurity is, however, to be found in the construction and combination of words, and the ways in which this may occur are still more numerous. Therefore, a sentence should never be so long that it is impossible to follow its drift, nor should its conclusion be unduly postponed by transposition or an excessive use of *hyperbaton.*[4] Still worse is the result when the order of the words is confused as in the line[5]

> *"In the midmost sea*
> *Rocks are there by Italians altars*
> *called."*

Again, parenthesis, so often employed by orators and historians, and consisting in the insertion of one sentence in the midst of another, may seriously hinder the understanding of a passage, unless the insertion is short. For example, in the passage where Vergil[6] describes a colt, the words

> *"Nor fears he empty noises,"*

are followed by a number of remarks of a totally different form, and it is only four lines later that the poet returns to the point and says,

> *"Then, if the sound of arms be heard afar,*
> *How to stand still he knows not."*

Above all, ambiguity must be avoided, and by ambiguity I mean not merely the kind of which I have already spoken, where the sense is uncertain, as in the clause *Chremetem audivi percussisse Demean,*[7] but also that form of ambiguity which, although it does not actually result in obscuring the sense, falls into the same verbal error as if a man should say *visum a se hominem librum scribentem* (that he had seen a man writing a book). For although it is clear that the book was being written by the man,[8] the sentence is badly put together, and its author has made it as ambiguous as he could.

Again, some writers introduce a whole host of useless words; for, in their eagerness to avoid ordinary methods of expression, and allured by false ideals of beauty they wrap up everything in a multitude of words simply and solely because they are unwilling to make a direct and simple statement of the facts: and then they link up and involve one of those long-winded clauses with others like it, and extend their periods to a length beyond the compass of mortal breath. Some even expend an infinity of toil to acquire this vice, which, by the way, is nothing new: for I learn from the pages of Livy[9] that there was one, a teacher, who instructed his pupils to make all they said obscure, using the Greek word σκότισον ("darken it.") It was this same habit that gave rise to the famous words of praise, "So much the better: even I could not understand you." Others are consumed with a passion for brevity and omit words which are actually necessary to the sense, regarding it as a matter of complete indifference whether their meaning is intelligible to others, so long as they know what they mean themselves. For my own part, I regard as useless words which make such a demand upon the ingenuity of the hearer. Others, again, succeed in committing the same fault by a perverse misuse of figures. Worst of all are the phrases which the Greeks call ἀδιανόητα, that is to say, expressions which, though their meaning is obvious enough on the surface, have a secret meaning, as for example in the phrase *cum ductus est caecus secundum viam stare,* or where the man, who is supposed in the scholastic theme to have torn his own limbs with his teeth, is said to have *lain upon himself.*[1] Such expressions are regarded as ingenious, daring and eloquent, simply because of their ambiguity, and quite a number of persons have become infected by the belief that a passage which requires a commentator must for that very reason be a masterpiece of elegance. Nay, there is even a class of hearer who find a special pleasure in such passages; for the fact that they can provide an answer to the riddle fills them with an ecstasy of self-congratulation, as if they had not merely heard the phrase, but invented it.

For my own part, I regard clearness as the first essential of a good style: there must be propriety in our words, their order must be straightforward, the conclusion of the period must not be long postponed, there must be nothing lacking and nothing superfluous. Thus our language will be approved by the learned and clear to the uneducated. I am speaking solely of clearness in style, as I have already dealt with clearness in the presentation of facts in the rules I laid down for the *statement of the case.* But the general method is the same in both. For if what we say is not less nor more than is required, and is clear and systematically arranged, the whole matter will be plain and obvious even to a not too attentive audience. For we must never forget that the attention of the judge is not always so keen that he will dispel obscurities without assistance, and bring the light of his intelligence to bear on the dark places of our speech. On the contrary, he will have many other thoughts to distract him unless what we say is so clear that our words will thrust themselves into his mind even when he is not giving us his attention, just as the sunlight forces itself upon the eyes. Therefore our aim must be not to put him in a position to understand our argument, but to force him to understand it. Consequently we shall frequently repeat anything which we think the judge has failed to take in as he should. We shall say, for example, "I fear that this portion of our case has been somewhat obscurely stated: the fault is mine, and I will therefore re-state it in plainer and simpler language"; for the pretended admission of a fault on our part creates an excellent impression.

III. I now come to the subject of ornament, in which, more than in any other department, the orator undoubtedly allows himself the greatest indulgence. For a speaker wins but trifling praise if he does no more than speak with correctness and lucidity; in fact his speech seems rather to be free from blemish than to have any positive merit. Even the untrained often possess the gift of invention, and no great learning need be assumed for the satisfactory arrangement of our matter, while if any more recondite art is required, it is generally concealed, since unconcealed it would cease to be an art, while all these qualities are employed solely to serve the interests of the actual case. On the other hand, by the employment of skilful ornament the orator commends himself at the same time, and whereas his other accomplishments appeal to the considered judgment of the learned, this gift appeals to the enthusiastic approval of the world at large, and the speaker who possesses it fights not merely with effective, but with flashing weapons. If in his defence of Cornelius Cicero had confined himself merely to instructing the judge and speaking in clear and idiomatic Latin without a thought beyond the interests of his case, would he ever have compelled the Roman people to proclaim their admiration not merely by acclamation, but by thunders of applause? No, it was the sublimity and splendour, the brilliance and the weight of his eloquence that evoked such clamorous enthusiasm. Nor, again, would his words have been greeted with such extraordinary approbation if his speech had been like the ordinary speeches of every day. In my opinion the audience did not know what they were doing, their applause sprang neither from their judgment nor their will; they were seized with a kind of frenzy and, unconscious of the place in which they stood, burst forth spontaneously into a perfect ecstasy of delight.

But rhetorical ornament contributes not a little to the furtherance of our case as well. For when our audience find it a pleasure to listen, their attention and their readiness to believe what they hear are both alike increased, while they are generally filled with delight, and sometimes even transported by admiration. The flash of the sword in itself strikes something of terror to the eye, and we should be less alarmed by the thunderbolt if we feared its violence alone, and not its flash as well. Cicero was right when, in one of his letters[1] to Brutus, he wrote, "Eloquence which evokes no admiration is, in my opinion, unworthy of the name." Aristotle[2] likewise thinks that the excitement of admiration should be one of our first aims.

But such ornament must, as I have already said,[3] be bold, manly and chaste, free from all effeminate smoothness and the false hues derived from artificial dyes, and must glow with health and vigour. So true is this, that although, where ornament is concerned, vice and virtue are never far apart, those who employ a vicious style of embellishment disguise their vices with the name of virtue. Therefore let none of our decadents accuse me of being an enemy to those who speak with grace and finish. I do not deny the existence of such a virtue, I merely deny that they possess it. Shall I regard a farm as a model of good cultivation because its owner shows me lilies and violets and anemones and fountains of living water in place of rich crops and vines bowed beneath their clusters? Shall I prefer the barren plane and myrtles trimly clipped, to the fruitful olive and the elm that weds the vine? No, let such luxuries delight the rich: but where would their wealth be if they had nought save these?

• • •

Its most important exhibitions are to be found in the following: δείνωσις, or a certain sublimity in the exaggerated denunciation of unworthy conduct, to mention no other topics; φαντασία, or imagination, which assists us to form mental pictures of things; ἐξεργασία, or finish, which produces completeness of effect; ἐπεξεργασία, an intensified form of the preceding, which reasserts our proofs and clinches the argument by repetition; and ἐνέργεια, or vigour, a near relative of all these qualities, which derives its name from action and finds its peculiar function in securing that nothing that we say is tame. Bitterness, which is generally employed in abuse, may be of service as in the following passage from Cassius: "What will you do when I invade your special province, that is, when I show that, as far as abuse is concerned, you are a mere ignoramus?"[4] Pungency also may be employed, as in the following remark of Crassus: "Shall I regard you as a consul, when you refuse to regard me as a senator?" But the real power of oratory lies in enhancing or attenuating the force of words. Each of these departments has the same number of methods; I shall touch on the more important; those omitted will be of a like character, while all are concerned either with words or things. I have, however, already dealt with the methods of invention and arrangement, and shall therefore now concern myself with the way in which style may elevate or depress the subject in hand.

IV. The first method of *amplification* or *attenuation* is to be found in the actual word employed to describe a thing. For example, we may say that a man who was *beaten* was *murdered,* or that a *dishonest* fellow is a *robber,* or, on the other hand, we may say that one who *struck* another merely *touched* him, and that one who *wounded* another merely *hurt* him. The following passage from the *pro Caelio,*[5] provides examples of both: "If a widow lives freely, if being by nature bold she throws restraint to the winds, makes wealth an excuse for luxury, and strong passions for playing the harlot, would this be a reason for my regarding a man who was somewhat free in his method of saluting her to be an adulterer?" For here he calls an immodest woman a harlot, and says that one who had long been her lover saluted her with a certain freedom. This sort of *amplification* may be strengthened and made more striking by pointing the comparison between words of stronger meaning and those for which we propose to substitute them, as Cicero does in denouncing Verres:[1] "I have brought before you, judges, not a thief, but a plunderer; not an adulterer, but a ravisher; not a mere committer of sacrilege, but the enemy of all religious observance and all holy things; not an assassin, but a bloodthirsty butcher who has slain our fellow-citizens and our allies." In this passage the first epithets are bad enough, but are rendered still worse by those which follow. I consider, however, that there are four principal methods of *amplification: augmentation, comparison, reasoning* and *accumulation.*

Of these, *augmentation* is most impressive when it lends grandeur even to comparative insignificance. This may be effected either by one step or by several, and may be carried not merely to the highest degree, but sometimes even beyond it. A single example from Cicero[2] will suffice to illustrate all these points. "It is a sin to bind a Roman citizen, a crime to scourge him, little short of the most unnatural murder to put him to death; what then shall I call his crucifixion?" If he had merely been scourged, we should have had but one step, indicated by the description even of the lesser offence as a *sin,* while if he had merely been killed, we should have had several more steps; but after saying that it was "little short of the most unnatural murder to put him to death," and mentioning the worst of crimes, he adds, "What then shall I call his crucifixion?" Consequently, since he had already exhausted his vocabulary of crime, words must necessarily fail him to describe something still worse.

• • •

VI. By a *trope* is meant the artistic alteration of a word or phrase from its proper meaning to another. This is a subject which has given rise to interminable disputes among the teachers of literature, who have quarrelled no less violently with the philosophers than among themselves over the problem of the *genera* and *species* into which *tropes* may be divided, their number and their correct classification. I propose to disregard such quibbles as in no wise concern the training of an orator, and to proceed to discuss those *tropes* which are most necessary and meet with most general acceptance, contenting myself merely with noting the fact that some *tropes* are employed to help out our meaning and others to adorn our style, that some arise from words used *properly* and others from words used *metaphorically,* and that the changes involved concern not merely individual words, but also our thoughts and the structure of our sentences. In view of these facts I regard those writers as mistaken who have held that *tropes* necessarily involved the substitution of word for word. And I do not ignore the fact that as a rule the *tropes* employed to express our meaning involve ornament as well, though the converse is not the case, since there are some which are intended solely for the purpose of embellishment.

Let us begin, then, with the commonest and by far the most beautiful of *tropes,* namely, *metaphor,* the Greek term for our *translatio.* It is not merely so natural a turn of speech that it is often employed unconsciously or by uneducated persons, but it is in itself so attractive and elegant that however distinguished the language in which it is embedded it shines forth with a light that is all its own. For if it be correctly and appropriately applied, it is quite impossible for its effect to be commonplace, mean or unpleasing. It adds to the copiousness of language by the interchange of words and by borrowing, and finally succeeds in accomplishing the supremely difficult task of providing a name for everything. A noun or a verb is transferred from the place to which it properly belongs to another where there is either no *literal* term or the *transferred* is better than the *literal.* We do this either because it is necessary or to make our meaning clearer or, as I have already said, to produce a decorative effect. When it secures none of these results, our metaphor will be out of place. As an example of a necessary metaphor I may quote the following usages in vogue with peasants when they call a vinebud *gemma,* a gem (what other term is there which they could use?), or speak of the *crops being thirsty* or the *fruit suffering.* For the same reason we speak of a *hard* or *rough* man, there being no *literal* term for these temperaments. On the other hand, when we say that a man is *kindled to anger* or *on fire with greed* or that he has *fallen into error,* we do so to enhance our meaning. For none of these things can be more literally described in its own words than in those which we import from elsewhere. But it is a purely ornamental metaphor when we speak of *brilliance of style, splendour of birth, tempestuous public assemblies, thunderbolts of eloquence,* to which I may add the phrase employed by Cicero[1] in his defence of Milo where he speaks of Clodius as the *fountain,* and in another place as *the fertile field and material* of his client's *glory.* It is even possible to express facts of a somewhat unseemly character by a judicious use of metaphor, as in the following passage:[2]

> *"This do they lest too much indulgence make*
> *The field of generation slothful grow*
> *And choke its idle furrows."*

On the whole *metaphor* is a shorter form of *simile,* while there is this further difference, that in the latter we compare some object to the thing which we wish to describe, whereas in the former this object is actually substituted for the thing. It is a comparison when I say that a man did something *like a lion,* it is a metaphor when I say of him, *He is a lion.* Metaphors fall into four classes. In the first we substitute one living thing for another, as in the passage where the poet, speaking of a charioteer,[3] says,

> *"The steersman then*
> *With mighty effort wrenched his charger round."*

or when Livy[4] says that Scipio was continually *barked at* by Cato. Secondly, inanimate things may be substituted for inanimate, as in the Virgilian.

> *"And gave his fleet the rein,"*[5]

or inanimate may be substituted for animate, as in

> *"Did the Argive bulwark fall by sword or fate?"*[6]

or animate for inanimate, as in the following lines:

> *"The shepherd sits unknowing on the height*
> *Listening the roar from some far mountain brow."*[7]

But, above all, effects of extraordinary sublimity are produced when the theme is exalted by a bold and almost hazardous metaphor and inanimate objects are given life and action, as in the phrase

> *"Araxes' flood that scorns a bridge,"*[8]

or in the passage of Cicero,[9] already quoted, where he cries, "What was that sword of yours doing, Tubero, the sword you drew on the field of Pharsalus? Against whose body did you aim its point? What meant those arms you bore?" Sometimes the effect is doubled, as in Virgil's.

> *"And with venom arm the steel."*[10]

For both "to arm the steel" and "to arm with venom" are metaphors. These four kinds of metaphor are further subdivided into a number of *species,* such as transference from rational beings to rational and from irrational to irrational and the reverse, in which the method is the same, and finally from the whole to its parts and from the parts to the whole. But I am not now teaching boys: my readers are old enough to discover the *species* for themselves when once they have been given the *genus.*

While a temperate and timely use of metaphor is a real adornment to style, on the other hand, its frequent use serves merely to obscure our language and weary our audience, while if we introduce them in one continuous series, our language will become allegorical and enigmatic. There are also certain metaphors which fail from meanness, such as that of which I spoke above[11]:

"There is a rocky wart upon the mountain's brow."

or they may even be coarse. For it does not follow that because Cicero was perfectly justified in talking of "the sink of the state,"[1] when he desired to indicate the foulness of certain men, we can approve the following passage from an ancient orator: "You have lanced the boils of the state." Indeed Cicero[2] himself has demonstrated in the most admirable manner how important it is to avoid grossness in metaphor, such as is revealed by the following examples, which he quotes:— "The state was gelded by the death of Africanus," or "Glaucia, the excrement of the senate-house." He also points out that a metaphor must not be too great for its subject or, as is more frequently the case, too little, and that it must not be inappropriate. Anyone who realises that these are faults, will be able to detect instances of them only too frequently. But excess in the use of metaphor is also a fault, more especially if they are of the same species. Metaphors may also be harsh, that is, far-fetched, as in phrases like "the snows of the head" or

"Jove with white snow the wintry Alps bespewed."[3]

The worst errors of all, however, originate in the fact that some authors regard it as permissible to use even in prose any metaphors that are allowed to poets, in spite of the fact that the latter aim solely at pleasing their readers and are compelled in many cases to employ metaphor by sheer metrical necessity. For my own part I should not regard a phrase like "the shepherd of the people" as admissible in pleading, although it has the authority of Homer, nor would I venture to say that winged creatures "swim through the air," despite the fact that this metaphor has been most effectively employed by Virgil to describe the flight of bees and of Daedalus.[4] For metaphor should always either occupy a place already vacant, or if it fills the room of something else, should be more impressive than that which it displaces.

What I have said above applies perhaps with even greater force to *synecdochè.* For while *metaphor* is designed to move the feelings, give special distinction to things and place them vividly before the eye, *synecdochè* has the power to give variety to our language by making us realise many things from one, the whole from a part, the *genus* from a *species,* things which follow from things which have preceded; or, on the other hand, the whole procedure may be reversed. It may, however, be more freely employed by poets than by orators. For while in prose it is perfectly correct to use *mucro,* the point, for the whole sword, and *tectum,* roof, for a whole house, we may not employ *puppis,* stern, to describe a ship, nor *abies,* fir, to describe planks; and again, though *ferrum,* the steel, may be used to indicate a sword, *quadrupes* cannot be used in the sense of horse. It is where numbers are concerned that *synecdochè* can be most freely employed in prose. For example, Livy frequently says, "The Roman won the day," when he means that the *Romans* were victorious; on the other hand, Cicero in a letter to Brutus[5] says, "We have imposed on the people and are regarded as orators," when he is speaking of himself alone. This form of *trope* is not only a rhetorical ornament, but is frequently employed in everyday speech. Some also apply the term *synecdochè* when something is assumed which has not actually been expressed, since one word is then discovered from other words, as in the sentence,

"The Arcadians to the gates began to rush;"[6]

when such omission creates a blemish, it is called an *ellipse.* For my own part, I prefer to regard this as a figure, and shall therefore discuss it under that head. Again, one thing may be suggested by another, as in the line,

"Behold, the steers
Bring back the plough suspended from the yoke,"[7]

from which we infer the approach of night. I am not sure whether this is permissible to an orator except in arguments, when it serves as an indication of some fact. However, this has nothing to do with the question of style.

It is but a short step from *synecdochè* to *metonymy,* which consists in the substitution of one name for another, and, as Cicero[1] tells us, is called *hypallage* by the rhetoricians. These devices are employed to indicate an invention by substituting the name of the inventor, or a possession by substituting the name of the possessor. Virgil, for example, writes:[2]

"Ceres by water spoiled,"

and Horace:

"Neptune admitted to the land
Protects the fleets from blasts of Aquilo."[3]

If, however, the process is reversed, the effect is harsh. But it is important to enquire to what extent *tropes* of this kind should be employed by the orator. For though we often hear "Vulcan" used for fire and to say *vario Marte pugnatum est* for "they fought with varying success" is elegant and idiomatic, while *Venus* is a more decent expression than *coitus,* it would be too bold for the severe style demanded in the courts to speak of *Liber* and *Ceres* when we mean bread and wine. Again, while usage permits us to substitute that which contains for that which is contained, as in phrases such as "civilised cities," or "a cup was drunk to the lees," or "a happy age," the converse procedure would rarely be ventured on by any save a poet: take, for example, the phrase:

"Ucalegon burns next."[4]

It is, however, perhaps more permissible to describe what is possessed by reference to its possessor, as, for example, to say of a man whose estate is being squandered, "the man is being eaten up." Of this form there are innumerable species. For example, we say "sixty thousand men were slain by Hannibal at Cannae," and speak of "Virgil" when we mean "Virgil's poems"; again, we say that supplies have "come," when they have been "brought," that a "sacrilege," and not a "sacrilegious man" has been detected, and that a man possesses a knowledge of "arms," not of "the art of arms." The type which indicates cause by effect is common both in poets and orators. As examples from poetry I may quote:

"Pale death with equal foot knocks at the
poor man's door"[5]

and

"There pale diseases dwell and sad old age;"[6]

while the orator will speak of "headlong anger," "cheerful youth" or "slothful ease."

The following type of *trope* has also some kinship with *synecdochè.* For when I speak of a man's "looks" instead of his "look," I use the plural for the singular, but my aim is not to enable one thing to be inferred from many (for the sense is clear enough), but I merely vary the form of the word. Again, when I call a "gilded roof" a "golden roof," I diverge a little from the truth, because gilding forms only a part of the roof. But to follow out these points is a task involving too much minute detail even for a work whose aim is not the training of an orator.

Antonomasia, which substitutes something else for a proper name, is very common in poets: it may be done in two ways: by the substitution of an epithet as equivalent to the name which it replaces, such as "Tydides," "Pelides,"[7] or by indicating the most striking characteristics of an individual, as in the phrase

"Father of gods and king of men,"[8]

or from acts clearly indicating the individual, as in the phrase,

"The arms which he, the traitor, left
Fixed on the chamber wall."[9]

This form of *trope* is rare in oratory, but is occasionally employed, For although an orator would not say "Tydides" or "Pelides," he will speak of certain definite persons as "the impious parricides," while I should have no hesitation in speaking of Scipio as "the destroyer of Carthage and Numantia," or of Cicero as "the prince of Roman orators." Cicero himself, at any rate, availed himself of this licence, as, for example, in the following case: "Your faults are not many, said the old praeceptor to the hero,"[1] where neither name is given, though both are clearly understood.

On the other hand, *onomatopoea,* that is to say, the creation of a word, although regarded with the highest approbation by the Greeks, is scarcely permissible to a Roman. It is true that many words were created in this way by the original founders of the language, who adapted them to suit the sensation which they expressed. For instance, *mugitus,* lowing, *sibilus,* a hiss, and *murmur* owe their origin to this practice. But to-day we consider that all has been done that can be done in this line, and do not venture on fresh creations, in spite of the fact that many of the words thus formed in antiquity are daily becoming obsolete. Indeed, we scarcely permit ourselves to use new derivatives, so they are called, which are formed in various ways from words in common use, such as *Sullaturit,*[2] "he wishes to be a second Sulla," or *proscripturit,* "he wishes to have a proscription," while *laureati postes,* "laurelled doorposts," for *lauru coronati,* "crowned with laurel," are similar formations.[3]

These facts make *catachresis* (of which *abuse* is a correct translation) all the more necessary. By this term is meant the practice of adapting the nearest available term to describe something for which no actual term exists, as in the line

"A horse they build by Pallas' art divine,"[4]

or as in the expression found in tragedy,

"To Aigialeus
His sire bears funeral offerings,"[5]

The following examples are of a similar character. Flasks are called *acetabula,*[6] whatever they contain, and caskets *pyxides,*[7] of whatever material they are made, while *parricide* includes the murder of a mother or a brother. We must be careful to distinguish between *abuse* and *metaphor,* since the former is employed where there is no proper term available, and the latter when there is another term available. As for poets, they indulge in the abuse of words even in cases where proper terms do exist, and substitute words of somewhat similar meaning. But this is rare in prose. Some, indeed, would give the name of *catachresis* even to cases such as where we call temerity valour or prodigality liberality. I, however, cannot agree with them; for in these instances word is not substituted for word, but thing for thing, since no one regards prodigality and liberality as meaning the same, but one man calls certain actions liberal and another prodigal, although neither for a moment doubts the difference between the two qualities.

There is but one of the *tropes* involving change of meaning which remains to be discussed, namely, *metalepsis* or *transumption,* which provides a transition from one *trope* to another. It is (if we except comedy) but rarely used in Latin, and is by no means to be commended, though it is not infrequently employed by the Greeks, who, for example, call Χείρων the centaur Ησσων[8] and substitute the epithet θοαί (swift) for ὀξειαι[9] in referring to sharp-pointed islands. But who would endure a Roman if he called Verres *sus*[10] or changed the name of Aelius Catus to Aelius *doctus?* It is the nature of *metalepsis* to form a kind of intermediate step between the term transferred and the thing to which it is transferred, having no meaning in itself, but merely providing a transition. It is a *trope* with which to claim acquaintance, rather than one which we are ever likely to require to use. The commonest example is the following: *cano* is a synonym for *canto* and *canto*[11] for *dico,* therefore *cano* is a synonym for *dico,* the intermediate step being provided by *canto.* We need not waste any more time over it. I can see no use in it except, as I have already said, in comedy.

The remaining *tropes* are employed solely to adorn and enhance our style without any reference to the meaning. For the *epithet,* of which the correct translation is *appositum,* though some call it *sequens,* is clearly an ornament. Poets employ it with special frequency and freedom, since for them it is sufficient that the epithet should suit the word to which it is applied: consequently we shall not blame them when they speak of "white teeth" or "liquid wine."[1] But in oratory an epithet is redundant unless it has some point. Now it will only have point when it adds something to the meaning, as for instance in the following: "O abominable crime, O hideous lust!" But its decorative effect is greatest when it is metaphorical, as in the phrases "unbridled greed"[2] or "those mad piles of masonry."[3] The epithet is generally made into a *trope* by the addition of something to it, as when Virgil speaks of "disgraceful poverty" or "sad old age."[4] But the nature of this form of embellishment is such that, while style is bare and inelegant without any epithets at all, it is overloaded when a large number are employed. For then it becomes long-winded and cumbrous, in fact you might compare it to an army with as many camp-followers as soldiers, an army, that is to say, which has doubled its numbers without doubling its strength. None the less, not merely single epithets are employed, but we may find a number of them together, as in the following passage from Virgil:[5]

> *"Anchises, worthy deigned*
> *Of Venus' glorious bed, [beloved of heaven,*
> *Twice rescued from the wreck of Pergamum.]"*

Be this as it may, two epithets directly attached to one noun are unbecoming even in verse. There are some writers who refuse to regard an *epithet* as a *trope,* on the ground that it involves no change. It is not always a *trope,* but if separated from the word to which it belongs, it has a significance of its own and forms an *antonomasia.* For if you say, "The man who destroyed Numantia and Carthage," it will be an *antonomasia,* whereas, if you add the word "Scipio," the phrase will be an *epithet.* An epithet therefore cannot stand by itself.

Allegory, which is translated in Latin by *inversio,* either presents one thing in words and another in meaning, or else something absolutely opposed to the meaning of the words. The first type is generally produced by a series of metaphors. Take as an example:

> *"O ship, new waves will bear thee back to sea.*[6]
> *What dost thou? Make the haven, come what may,"*

and the rest of the ode, in which Horace represents the state under the semblance of a ship, the civil wars as tempests, and peace and good-will as the haven. Such, again, is the claim of Lucretius:[7]

> "Pierian fields I range untrod by man,"

and such again the passage where Virgil says,

> *"But now*
> *A mighty length of plain we have travelled o'er;*
> *'Tis time to loose our horses' steaming necks."*[8]

On the other hand, in the Bucolics[9] he introduces an allegory without any metaphor:

> *"Truth, I had heard*
> *Your loved Menalcas by his songs had saved*
> *All those fair acres, where the hills begin*
> *To sink and droop their ridge with easy slope*
> *Down to the waterside and that old beech*
> *With splintered crest."*

For in this passage, with the exception of the proper name, the words bear no more than their literal meaning. But the name does not simply denote the shepherd Menalcas, but is a pseudonym for Virgil himself. Oratory makes frequent use of such allegory, but generally with this modification, that there is an admixture of plain speaking. We get allegory pure and unadulterated in the following passage of Cicero:[10] "What I marvel at and complain of is this, that there should exist any man so set on destroying his enemy as to scuttle the ship on which he himself is sailing." The following is an example of the commonest type, namely, the mixed allegory:[1] "I always thought that Milo would have other storms and tempests to weather, at least in the troubled waters of political meetings." Had he not added the words "at least in the troubled waters of political meetings," we should have had pure allegory: their addition, however, converted it into a mixed allegory. In this type of allegory the ornamental element is provided by the metaphorical words and the meaning is indicated by those which are used literally. But far the most ornamental effect is produced by the artistic admixture of simile, metaphor and allegory, as in the following example:[2] "What strait, what tide-race, think you, is full of so many conflicting motions or vexed by such a variety of eddies, waves and fluctuations, as confuse our popular elections with their wild ebb and flow? The passing of one day, or the interval of a single night, will often throw everything into confusion, and one little breath of rumour will sometimes turn the whole trend of opinion." For it is all-important to follow the principle illustrated by this passage and never to mix your metaphors. But there are many who, after beginning with a tempest, will end with a fire or a falling house, with the result that they produce a hideously incongruous effect. For the rest, allegory is often used by men of little ability and in the conversation of everyday life. For those hackneyed phrases of forensic pleading, "to fight hand to hand," "to attack the throat," or "to let blood" are all of them allegorical, although they do not strike the attention: for it is novelty and change that please in oratory, and what is unexpected always gives special delight. Consequently we have thrown all restraint to the wind in such matters, and have destroyed the charm of language by the extravagant efforts which we have made to attain it. Illustrative examples also involve allegory if not preceded by an explanation; for there are numbers of sayings available for use like the "Dionysius is at Corinth,"[3] which is such a favourite with the Greeks. When, however, an allegory is too obscure, we call it a riddle: such riddles are, in my opinion, to be regarded as blemishes, in view of the fact that lucidity is a virtue; nevertheless they are used by poets, as, for example, by Virgil[4] in the following lines:

> *"Say in what land, and if thou tell me true,*
> *I'll hold thee as Apollo's oracle,*
> *Three ells will measure all the arch of heaven."*

Even orators sometimes use them, as when Caelius[5] speaks of the "Clytemnestra who sold her favours for a farthing, who was a Coan in the dining-room and a Nolan in her bedroom." For although we know the answers, and although they were better known at the time when the words were uttered, they are riddles for all that; and other riddles are, after all, intelligible if you can get someone to explain them.

On the other hand, that class of allegory in which the meaning is contrary to that suggested by the words, involve an element of irony, or, as our rhetoricians call it, *illusio*. This is made evident to the understanding either by the delivery, the character of the speaker or the nature of the subject. For if any one of these three is out of keeping with the words, it at once becomes clear that the intention of the speaker is other than what he actually says. In the majority of *tropes* it is, however, important to bear in mind not merely what is said, but about whom it is said, since what is said may in another context be literally true. It is permissible to censure with counterfeited praise and praise under a pretence of blame. The following will serve as an example of the first.[6] "Since Gaius Verres, the urban praetor, being a man of energy and blameless character, had no record in his register of this substitution of this man for another on the panel." As an example of the reverse process we may take the following:[7] "We are regarded as orators and have imposed on the people." Sometimes, again, we may speak in mockery when we say the opposite of what we desire to be understood, as in Cicero's denunciation of Clodius[8]: "Believe me, your well-known integrity has cleared you of all blame, your modesty has saved you, your past life has been your salvation." Further, we may employ *allegory,* and disguise bitter taunts in gentle words by way of wit, or we may indicate our meaning by saying exactly the contrary or . . . [1] If the Greek names for these methods are unfamiliar to any of my readers, I would remind him that they are σαρκασμός, ἀστεϊσμός, 'αντίφρασις and παροιμία (sarcasm, urbane wit, contradiction and proverbs). There are, however, some writers who deny that these are species of *allegory,* and assert that they are actually *tropes* in themselves: for they argue shrewdly that allegory involves an element of obscurity, whereas in all these cases our meaning is perfectly obvious. To this may be added the fact that when a *genus* is divided into *species,* it ceases to have any peculiar properties of its own: for example, we may divide tree into its species, pine, olive, cypress, etc., leaving it no properties of its own, whereas allegory always has some property peculiar to itself. The only explanation of this fact is that it is itself a species. But this, of course, is a matter of indifference to those that use it. To these the Greeks add μυκτηρισμός, or mockery under the thinnest of disguises.

When we use a number of words to describe something for which one, or at any rate only a few words of description would suffice, it is called *periphrasis,* that is, a circuitous mode of speech. It is sometimes necessary, being of special service when it conceals something which would be indecent, if expressed in so many words: compare the phrase "To meet the demands of nature" from Sallust.[2] But at times it is employed solely for decorative effect, a practice most frequent among the poets:

> "*Now was the time*
> *When the first sleep to weary mortals comes*
> *Stealing its way, the sweetest boon of heaven.*"[3]

Still it is far from uncommon even in oratory, though in such cases it is always used with greater restraint. For whatever might have been expressed with greater brevity, but is expanded for purposes of ornament, is a *periphrasis,* to which we give the name *circumlocution,* though it is a term scarcely suitable to describe one of the virtues of oratory. But it is only called *periphrasis* so long as it produces a decorative effect: when it passes into excess, it is known as *perissology:* for whatever is not a help, is a positive hindrance.

Again, *hyperbaton,* that is, the transposition of a word, is often demanded by the structure of the sentence and the claims of elegance, and is consequently counted among the ornaments of style. For our language would often be harsh, rough, limp or disjointed, if the words were always arranged in their natural order and attached each to each just as they occur, despite the fact that there is no real bond of union. Consequently some words require to be postponed, others to be anticipated, each being set in its appropriate place. For we are like those who build a wall of unhewn stone: we cannot hew or polish our words in order to make them fit more compactly, and so we must take them as they are and choose suitable positions for them. Further, it is impossible to make our prose rhythmical except by artistic alterations in the order of words, and the reason why those four words in which Plato[4] in the noblest of his works states that he had gone down to the Piraeus were found written in a number of different orders upon his wax tablets, was simply that he desired to make the rhythm as perfect as possible. When, however, the transposition is confined to two words only, it is called *anastrophe,* that is, a reversal of order. This occurs in everyday speech in *mecum* and *secum,* while in orators and historians we meet with it in the phrase *quibus de rebus.* It is the transposition of a word to some distance from its original place, in order to secure an ornamental effect, that is strictly called *hyperbaton:* the following passage will provide an example: *animadverti, iudices, omnem accusatoris orationem in duas divisam esse partes.*[5] ("I noted, gentlemen, that the speech of the accuser was divided into two parts.") In this case the strictly correct order would be *in duas partes divisam esse,* but this would have been harsh and ugly. The poets even go so far as to secure this effect by the division of words, as in the line:

> *Hyperboreo septem subiecta trioni*[1]
> *("Under the Hyperborean Wain"),*

a licence wholly inadmissible in oratory. Still there is good reason for calling such a transposition a *trope,* since the meaning is not complete until the two words have been put together. On the other hand, when the transposition makes no alteration in the sense, and merely produces a variation in the structure, it is rather to be called a *verbal figure,* as indeed many authorities have held. Of the faults resulting from long or confused *hyperbata* I have spoken in the appropriate place.[2]

I have kept *hyperbole* to the last, on the ground of its boldness. It means an elegant straining of the truth, and may be employed indifferently for exaggeration or attenuation. It can be used in various ways. We may say more than the actual facts, as when Cicero says,[3] "He vomited and filled his lap and the whole tribunal with fragments of food, or when Virgil speaks of

> *"Twin rocks that threaten heaven."*[4]

Again, we may exalt our theme by the use of simile, as in the phrase:

> *"Thou wouldst have deemed*
> *That Cyclad isles uprooted swam*
> *the deep."*[5]

Or we may produce the same result by introducing a comparison, as in the phrase:

> "Swifter than the levin's wings;"[6]

or by the use of indications, as in the lines:

> *"She would fly*
> *Even o'er the tops of the unsickled*
> *corn,*
> *Nor as she ran would bruise the*
> *tender ears."*[7]

Or we may employ a metaphor, as the verb *to fly* is employed in the passage just quoted. Sometimes, again, one *hyperbole* may be heightened by the addition of another, as when Cicero in denouncing Antony says:[8] "What Charybdis was ever so voracious? Charybdis, do I say? Nay, if Charybdis ever existed, she was but a single monster. By heaven, even Ocean's self, methinks, could scarce have engulfed so many things, so widely scattered in such distant places, in such a twinkling of the eye." I think, too, that I am right in saying that I noted a brilliant example of the same kind in the Hymns[9] of Pindar, the prince of lyric poets. For when he describes the onslaught made by Hercules upon the Meropes, the legendary inhabitants of the island of Cos, he speaks of the hero as like not to fire, winds or sea, but to the thunderbolt, making the latter the only true equivalent of his speed and power, the former being treated as quite inadequate. Cicero has imitated his method in the following passage from the Verrines:[10] "After long lapse of years the Sicilians saw dwelling in their midst, not a second Dionysius or Phalaris (for that island has produced many a cruel tyrant in years gone by), but a new monster with all the old ferocity once familiar to those regions. For, to my thinking, neither Scylla nor Charybdis were ever such foes as he to the ships that sailed those same narrow seas." The methods of hyperbole by attenuation are the same in number. Compare the Virgilian[11]

> *"Scarce cling they to their bones,"*

or the lines from a humorous work[12] of Cicero's,

> *"Fundum Vetto vocat quem possit mit-*
> *tere funda;*
> *Ni tamen exciderit, qua cava funda*
> *patet."*

> "Vetto gives the name of farm to an estate
> which might easily be hurled from a sling,
> though it might well fall through the hole
> in the hollow sling, so small is it."

But even here a certain proportion must be observed. For although every *hyperbole* involves the incredible, it must not go too far in this direction, which provides the easiest road to extravagant affectation. I shrink from recording the faults to which the lack of this sense of proportion has given rise, more especially as they are so well known and obvious. It is enough to say that *hyperbole* lies, though without any intention to deceive. We must therefore be all the more careful to consider how far we may go in exaggerating facts which our audience may refuse to believe. Again, *hyperbole* will often cause a laugh. If that was what the orator desired, we may give him credit for wit; otherwise we can only call him a fool. *Hyperbole* is employed even by peasants and uneducated persons, for the good reason that everybody has an innate passion for exaggeration or attenuation of actual facts, and no one is ever contented with the simple truth. But such disregard of truth is pardonable, for it does not involve the definite assertion of the thing that is not. *Hyperbole* is, moreover, a virtue, when the subject on which we have to speak is abnormal. For we are allowed to amplify, when the magnitude of the facts passes all words, and in such circumstances our language will be more effective if it goes beyond the truth than if it falls short of it. However, I have said enough on this topic, since I have already dealt with it in my work on the causes of the decline of oratory.

NOTES

BOOK I

p. 297: 1. *de Or.* iii. 15.

BOOK II

p. 298: 1. *suasoriae* are declamations on deliberative themes (*e.g.* Hannibal deliberates whether he should cross the Alps).

p. 299: 1. *communes loci* = passages dealing with some general principle of theme. For *theses* see II. iv. 24.

2. *controversiae* are declamations on controversial or judicial themes. A general rule of law is stated: then a special case, which has to be solved in accordance with the law. An abbreviated *controversia* is to be found in I. x. 33, and they occur frequently hereafter (cp. esp. III. vi. 96).

p. 300: 1. With special reference to the element of the miraculous. Ovid's *Metamorphoses* would give a good example. 2. Book IV. chap. ii. 3. *de Or.* II. xxi. 88. 4. *cp.* Verg. G. ii. 369, *ante reformidant ferrum.*

p. 301: 1. Sec Aul. Gall. vii. i.

p. 302: 1. Book III. Chap. vii. 2. *Pro Mur.* ix. 21. *sqq.* 3. The reason according to Lactantius (*Inst. Div.* i. 20) was the bravery of the Spartan women in one of the Messenian wars.

p. 303: 1. *i.e.* a court of *nomothetae* appointed by the Athenian assembly, who examined the provisions of the proposed law. 2. Clodius was a patrician and got himself made a plebeian by adoption to enable him to hold the tribunate. The question of the legality of this procedure is discussed by Cicero in the *de Domo,* 13–17. 3. Lit. within the space of three market-days. *nundinum* = 9 days, the second market-day being the ninth, and forming the last day of the first *nundinum* and the first of the second. Similarly the third market-day is the last day of the second *nundinum* and the first of the third. 4. The *lex Manilia* proposed to give Pompey the command against Mithridates.

p. 304: 1. Probably the lost treatise on "The causes of the decline of oratory" (*De causis corruptae eloquentiae*). 2. See Cic. *de Or.* iii. 24, 93.

p. 307: 1. The *pancration* was a mixture of wrestling and boxing.

p. 308: 1. i.e. I care naught for your rival schools of rhetoric. I give all my favor to the men armed with the bucklet (the gladiators know as *Thraces*). Such contests of the amphitheatre interest me far more than the contests between rival schools of rhetoric.

p. 309: 1. *i.e.* by the figure known as *apostrophe,* in which the orator diverts his speech from the judge to some other person: See IX. ii. 38. 2. Verg. *Aen.* iii. 436. 3. *Jug.* xix.

p. 310: 1. *sc.* essence and possibility. 2. A *stoic. cp.* X. i. 124. 3. See § 6 of next chapter.

p. 311: 1. This treatise is lost. It may have been the work of the younger Isocrates. 2. *Ann.* ix. 309 (Vahlen). The derivative to which he objects is the rare word *suada.* 3. *Gorg.* 453 A. 4. *de Inv.* I. v. 6, *de Or.* I. xxxi. 138. 5. *cp.* III. i. 20 and Cic. *de Or.* I. ii. 5. The work in question is better known as the *de Inventione.* 6. *Gorg.* p. 452. E. 7. *Rhet.* i. 2.

p. 312: 1. *Gorg.* 454 B. 2. *Gorg.* 462 C. 3. *ib.* 463 D. 4. *ib.* 464 B. 5. *ib.* 464 B-465 E.

p. 313: 1. 500 C. 2. 460 C. 3. 508 C. 4. 261A–273E. 5. *Menexenus.* 6. 267A, with special reference to Tisias and Gorgias. 7. *de Inv.* I. v. 6.

p. 314: 1. *i.e.* though denouncing laws which would naturally be popular.

p. 315: 1. *cp.* Aristoph. *Ach.* 530; "Then in his wrath Pericles the Olympian lightened and thundered and threw all Greece into confusion." 2. *de Inv.* I. v. 6. The titles in question are such as *Ars rhetorica, Ars Hermagorae,* etc.

p. 316: 1. II. lvii. 232. 2. *Il.* ix. 432. 3. *i.e.* the copious style by Nester, the plain by Menelaus, the intermediate by Ulysses. 4. *Il.* xv. 284. 5. *Il.* xviii. 497 *sqq.* 6. A lost treatise, named after Gryllus, the son of Xenophon.

p. 317: 1. See Livy, XXII. xvi. 2. Probably a king of Sparta, 770–720 B. C. 3. Ennius, *Ann.* 483 (Vahlen).

p. 318: 1. II. vii. 30.

p. 319: 1. Fr. 790. 2. *i.e.* since our ideals are so high.

p. 321: 1. *de Or.* III. xiv. 55. 2. Lost. 3. *Gorg.* 449E.

p. 322: 1. *Gorg.* 449E. 2. *Phaedr.* 261 A. 3. *de Inv.* i. 5. 4. *de Or.* I. vi. 21. "I will not demand omniscience from an orator, although" etc. 5. *ib.* III. xiv. 54. 6. Pref. § 10 *sqq.* 7. *de Or.* I. vi. 20.

p. 323: 1. See III. v. 12–16. 2. *Rhet.* I. iii. 3.

p. 324: 1. Book II. chaps. ii. and iii. 2. No such statement is found in the *de Inventione.* 3. i. 3. 4. 14–17.

p. 325: 1. *de Or.* I. xxxi. 141; *Top.* xxiv. 91. 2. *de Or.* ii. 10 *sq.* 3. Unknown. Perhaps the elder Pliny. 4. 222 C.

p. 326: 1. Fr. 3 s.

p. 327: 1. See § 44. 2. *e.g.* that the legal heir must receive at least a quarter of the property. 3. *Rhet.* 1358 b. 2. 4. *sc.* ἐπιδεικτική. 5. The speech was known as *in Toga Candida.* Only fragments survive. 6. The *in Pisonem* survives, the *in Clodium et Curionem,* to which he refers again (V. x. 92), is lost.

p. 328: 1. III. v. 3. 2. The quinquennial contest in honour of Jupiter Capitolinus, founded by Domitian in 86. 3. *sc.* by Domitian's deification of his father Vespasian and his brother Titus. 4. *Iliad,* ii. 477. 5. *Iliad,* ii. 180. 6. *Iliad,* v. 801.

p. 329: 1. The handsomest warrior among the Greeks of Troy. 2. Son of Atreus: the allusion is not known. 3. Moses. 4. *de Or.* II. lxxxii. 334.

p. 330: 1. *de Orat.* ii. 82. 2. The theme of a *suasoria* of the elder Seneca (*Suas.* i.). "Alexander deliberates whether to sail forth into the ocean." 3. *sc.* at the Claudine Forks: See above, § 3. 4. See Livy, v. 36. 5. See Caesar, *Gallic War,* i. 39, where this detail is recorded, also 40 where the speech made to his troops is given.

p. 331: 1. In 218 B.C., when besieged by Hannibal. See Livy, xxi. 14. 2. C. Antonius was blockaded in an island off the Dalmatian coast which he held for Caesar 49 B.C. Most were captured; but in one case, of a raft carrying 1,000 men from Opitergium in Venetia, surrender was scorned and the men slew each other rather than yield. See Lucan, iv. 462; Florus, ii. 33. 3. After the battle of Cannae: Livy, xxii, 57.

p. 332: 1. After his defeat at Pharsalus. 2. The letter is lost. The argument of the quotation is as follows. The policy which I advise is honourable, but it would be wrong for me to urge Caesar to follow it, since it is contrary to his interests. 3. Chap. xii.

p. 333: 1. *Rhet.* ii. 26. 2. *Rhet.* iii. 13.

p. 334: 1. In the permanent courts (*questiones perpetuae*). There were separate courts for different offences. In cases brought before the Senate or the Emperor a number of different charges might be dealt with at once. 2. A civil court specially concerned with questions of inheritance. 3. *Divinatio* is a trial to decide between the claims of two persons to appear as accuser, there being no public prosecutor at Rome. *cp.* Cicero's *Divinatio in Caecilium.*

BOOK V

4. *Rhet.* I. ii. 2.

p. 337: 1. Verg. *G.* i. 431. 2. *ib.* i. 388. 3. Verg. *G.* i. 422. 4. V. viii. 5; xiv. 2. *n.* 5. See V. xiv. 2, VIII. v. 9. 6. See III. i. 18. A rhetorician of the reign of Augustus. 7. The last or lowest species. *cp* § 56 and VII. i. 23. 8. *i.e.* the major and minor premisses and the conclusion. See V. xiv. 6 *sqq.* 9. *de Inv.* I. xxxi. 34. 10. See III. vi. 43, 46, 51. 11. See I. x. 38.

p. 338: 1. In some letter now lost. 2. *Aen.* vii. 791, with reference to the design on the shield of Turnus. 3. V. ix. 2. 4. 1–17.

p. 339: 1. In previous chapter. 2. See II. iv. 22, V. xii. 6 and xiii. 57. 3. V. viii. 4.

p. 340: 1. Publius, Cornelius, Lentulus Sura, Catilinarian conspirator. *cp.* Sall *Cat.* c. 46. 2. *Phoeniss.* 636. "With truth did our father call thee Polynices with divine foreknowledge naming thee after 'strife.' " 3. See VI. iii. 53.

BOOK VIII

p. 341: 1. Probably *salsamenta.* 2. *Aen.* IV. 419. 3. Presumably in the sense, "He spoke like one in bodily pain." 4. Lit. i.e. in the *proper* sense *the sole of the foot* and a *thrush.* 5. *Suet. Caes.* 53. 6. *Ecl.* vi. 5. 7. *Odes* I. xii. 1, and III. vi. 36. 8. *Georg.* i. 295 and *Aen* xi. 681. 9. *sc.* ch. vi.

p. 342: 1. See IX ii. 64. 2. An Apulian term for the Scirocco. What is the peculiarity of a *sack-ship* is unknown. It is possible that with Haupt we should read *stlataria,* "a broad-beamed merchant-vessel." 3. Reference unknown. 4. See VIII. vi. 62. 5. *Aen* i. 109. The awkwardness of the order cannot be brought out in English. 6. *Georg.* iii. 79–83. 7. See VII. ix. 10. 8. *i.e.* and not the man by the book! 9. Perhaps in his letter to his son, for which see II. v. 20.

p. 343: 1. Like a wild beast devouring his prey.

p. 344: 1. Now lost. 2. *Rhet.* III. ii. 5. 3. In the introduction to this book, 19. 4. Cassius Severus was famous for his powers of abuse. His opponent was abusive. Cassius says that he will take a leaf out of his book and show him what real abuse is. 5. xvi. 38.

p. 345: 1. *Verr.* I. iii. 9. 2. *Verr.* V. lxvi. 170.

p. 346: 1. *Pro Mil.* xiii. 34, 35. 2. Virg. *Georg.* iii. 1. 3. Probably from Ennius. 4. Liv. XXXVIII. liv. 5. *Aen.* vi. 1. 6. From an unknown tragedian. 7. *Aen.* ii. 307. 8. *Aen.* viii. 728. 9. *Pro Lig.* iii. 9. See VIII. iv. 27. 10. *Aen.* ix. 773. 11. See VIII. iii. 48.

p. 347: 1. In *Cat.* I. v. 12. 2. *De Or.* III. xli. 164. 3. From Furius, an old epic poet of the second century (not Furius Bibaculus), *cp* Hor. *S.* II. v. 11. 4. *Georg.* iv. 59. *Aen.* vi. 16 and 19. 5. This letter is lost. 6. *Aen.* xi. 142. A false explanation of the historic infinitive as involving the ommission of some such word as *coepcrunt.* 7. *Ed.* ii. 66.

p. 348: 1. *Orat.* xxvii. 93. 2. *Aen.* i. 177. 3. *A. P.* 63. 4. *Aen.* ii. 311. 5. Hor. *Od.* I. iv. 13. 6. *Aen.* vi. 275. 7. The son of Tydeus=Diomede, the son of Peleus=Achilles. 8. *Aen.* i. 65. 9. *Aen.* iv. 495. This third example does not correspond with the twofold division given by *utroque* and may be spurious.

p. 349 1. *Pro Muren.* xxix. 60. The passage continues (a quotation from some old play) "But you have faults and I can correct them." Phoenix is addressing his pupil Achilles. 2. Cic. *ad Att.* IX. x. 6. 3. This passage is too corrupt to admit of emendation or translation. There seem to be references to *vio* for *eo* and to *arquitollens,* for which cp. *arquitenens. Septemtriones* can hardly be selected for censure, as it is not uncommon. 4. *Aen.* II. xv. It is an abuse to say *aedificant,* which means literally, "they make a house." 5. Perhaps from the Medus of Pacuvius. It is an abuse to use *parentat* of funeral offerings made by father to son. 6. Lit. vinegar flasks. 7. *i.e.* made of boxwood. 8. *χείρων* and *ἥσσων* both mean inferior. 9. *cp. Od.* xv. 298. *Θοός* is used elsewhere to express sharpness. 10. Verres=boar; Catus=wise. 11. In the sense of to *repeat.*

p. 350: 1. *Georg.* III. 364. 2. Cic. in *Cat.* I. x. 25. 3. *Pro Mil.* xx. 53. 4. *Aen.* vi. 276 and 275. Here the addition is *metonymy, turpis* and *tristis* both substituting *effect* in place of *cause: cp.* § 27. 5. *Aen.* iii. 475. I have translated 476 (*cura deum, bis Pergameis erepte ruinis*) as well to bring out Quintilian's meaning. Quintilian assumes the rest of quotation to be known. 6. Hor. *Od.* i. xiv. 1. 7. *Lucr.* IV. 1. 8. *Georg.* II. 541. 9. *Buc.* IX. 7. 10. From an unknown speech.

p. 351: 1. *Pro Mil.* ii, 5. 2. *Pro Mur.* xvii. 35. 3. The allusion must be to the fact that Dionysius II, tyrant of Syracuse, on his expulsion from the throne, migrated to Corinth and set up as a schoolmaster. Its application is uncertain, but it would obviously be a way of saying, "How the mighty are fallen!" 4. *Ecl.* iii. 104; the solution is lost. 5. The references are to the licentious character of Clodia. *Coa* was probably intended to suggest *coitus,* while *nola* is best derived from *nolle,* and is to be regarded as the opposite of *Coa.* 6. Cic. *Pro Cluent.* xxxiii. 91. 7. *cp.* § 20. 8. From the lost speech *in Clodium et Curionem.*

p. 352: 1. The passage is hopelessly corrupt. The concluding portion of the sentence must have referred to the use of proverbs, of which it may have contained an example. This is clear from the next sentence. Sarcasm, urbane wit and contradiction are covered by the first three clauses, but there has been no allusion to proverbs such as demands. 2. Presumably from the Histories. 3. *Aen.* ii. 268. 4. At the beginning of the *Republic.* 5. Cic. *pro Cluent.* i. 1.

p. 353: 1. *Georg.* iii. 381. 2. VIII. ii. 14. 3. *Phil.* II. xxv. 63. 4. *Aen.* i. 162. 5. *Aen.* viii. 691. 6. *Aen.* v. 319. 7. *Aen.* vii. 808. 8. *Phil.* II. xxvii. 67. 9. A lost work. 10. V. lvi. 145. 11. *Ecl* iii. 103. Describing a flock of starved sheep. 12. Unknown.

INTRODUCTION TO LONGINUS

We do not really know who "Longinus" was. He is the author of the short treatise *On the Sublime.* This book has not survived intact, and much of the text is lost to us. It is believed to have been written around the first century C.E. There is an internal reference, in chapter twelve, to his being Greek, but it emerged and was used in the context of the Roman rhetorical tradition.

On the Sublime introduces a type of discourse that we have not seen to this point in history, at least not so explicitly and at such length. That discourse is *criticism.* By criticism we mean, of course, not finding fault or carping over some text or performance, but rather, writing that appreciates and attempts to interpret some other text. People have always criticized the latest play or song, of course. Today we are surrounded by criticism of popular music, sports, literature, and so forth. But here we see Longinus first set out some systematic principles designed to help his reader understand a kind of text or discourse.

The type of discourse or text that Longinus wants to explain is *the sublime.* He is not very specific in defining and explaining just what the sublime is. It appears to be the highest aesthetic, emotional experience that one can have, especially to be found in drama and in literature, which is Longinus's focus here. Without laying out specific characteristics of the sublime, Longinus nevertheless attempts to show what its general parameters are and how it might arise, especially through manipulation of language *style.*

An emergence of a concern for criticism is theoretically interesting. Criticism is something that an audience, rather than a rhetor, writer, or orator, does. It is something that can be done in private, and in order to explain one's personal and private reactions to a text. Therefore it is interesting that Longinus's treatise on criticism emerged during the Roman Empire under the dictatorial caesars. The ability to speak was curtailed from what it had been in Cicero's time; people were therefore much more often audiences than they were speakers. And the ability to speak in public was risky; people were safer forming judgments in private about literature that they could read to themselves. Thus, Longinus's treatise of criticism fits the political and social environment in which he lived.

The reader will want to note the development of theory of style in *On the Sublime.* Longinus reflects a theoretical development that will continue until its culmination in the Renaissance, which is the proliferation of types and categories of figures of speech or stylistic devices. His theory of language is, in that sense, already more complex than was Aristotle's or Cicero's, although in another sense it is narrower by being focused largely on stylistic devices. The broader, more common uses of language as an instrument of communication do not concern Longinus here.

In Longinus's insistence that the sublime must be grounded in sublimity of thought we find echoes of Cicero's orator and Quintilian's good man skilled in speaking: the idea that moral virtue is somehow connected with rhetorical skill. His treatise ends with a return to that theme, in bemoaning the decay of eloquence. Perhaps Longinus wished to say, in a covert way because of the repressive political circumstances, that democratic or republican values themselves entail rhetorical excellence. If so, then his message to our time is that a decline in the quality of public discourse reflects, rather than causes, a decline in the moral and civic virtue of our citizens.

LONGINUS

ON THE SUBLIME

CHAPTER I

FIRST THOUGHTS ON SUBLIMITY

Since you have urged me in my turn to write down my thoughts on the sublime for your gratification, we should consider whether my views contain anything of value to men in public life. And as your nature and your sense of fitness prompt you, my dear friend, you will help me to form the truest possible judgements on the various details; for it was a sound answer that was given by the man who, when asked what we have in common with the gods, replied, 'Benevolence and truth'.

As I am writing for you, Terentianus, who are a man of some erudition, I almost feel that I can dispense with a long preamble showing that sublimity consists in a certain excellence and distinction in expression, and that it is from this source alone that the greatest poets and historians have acquired their preeminence and won for themselves an eternity of fame. For the effect of elevated language is, not to persuade the hearers, but to entrance them; and at all times, and in every way, what transports us with wonder is more telling than what merely persuades or gratifies us. The extent to which we can be persuaded is usually under our own control, but these sublime passages exert an irresistible force and mastery and get the upper hand with every hearer. Inventive skill and the proper order and disposition of material are not manifested in a good touch here and there, but reveal themselves by slow degrees as they run through the whole texture of the composition; on the other hand, a well-timed stroke of sublimity scatters everything before it like a thunderbolt, and in a flash reveals the full power of the speaker. But I should think, my dear Terentianus, that you could develop these points and others of the same kind from your own experience.

Translated by T. S. Dorsch

CHAPTER 2

IS THERE AN ART OF THE SUBLIME?

BEFORE going any farther, I must take up the question whether there is such a thing as an art of sublimity or profundity, for some people think that those who relate matters of this kind to a set of artistic precepts are on a completely wrong track. Genius, they say, is innate; it is not something that can be learnt, and nature is the only art that begets it. Works of natural genius are spoilt, they believe, are indeed utterly debased, when they are reduced to the bare bones of rules and systems. However, I suggest that there is a case for the opposite point of view when it is considered that, although nature is in the main subject only to her own laws where sublime feelings are concerned, she is not given to acting at random and wholly without system. Nature is the first cause and the fundamental creative principle in all activities, but the function of a system is to prescribe the degree and the right moment for each, and to lay down the clearest rules for use and practice. Furthermore, sublime impulses are exposed to greater dangers when they are left to themselves without the ballast and stability of knowledge; they need the curb as often as the spur.

Speaking of the life of mankind as a whole, Demosthenes declares that the greatest of all blessings is good fortune, and that next to it comes good counsel, which, however, is no less important, since its absence leads to the complete destruction of what good fortune brings. Applying this to diction, we might say that nature fills the place of good fortune, and art that of good counsel. Most important, we must remember that the very fact that certain linguistic effects derive from nature alone cannot be learnt from any other source than art. If then the critic who censures those who want to learn this art would take these points into consideration, he would no longer, I imagine, regard the study of the topic I am treating as superfluous and unprofitable.

(Here two pages of the manuscript are missing)

CHAPTER 3

DEFECTS THAT MILITATE AGAINST SUBLIMITY

. . . Quell they the oven's far-flung splendour-glow!
Ha, let me but one hearth-abider mark—
One flame-wreath torrent-like I'll whirl on high;
I'll burn the roof, to cinders shrivel it!—
Nay, now my chant is not of noble strain.[1]

SUCH things as this are not tragic, but pseudo-tragic—the 'flame-wreaths', the 'vomiting forth to heaven', the representation of Boreas as a flute-player, and all the rest. They are turbid in expression, and the imagery is confused rather than suggestive of terror; each phrase, when examined in the light of day, sinks gradually from the terrible to the contemptible.

Now even in tragedy, which by its very nature is majestic and admits of some bombast, misplaced tumidity is unpardonable; still less, I think, would it be appropriate to factual narration. This is why people laugh at Gorgias of Leontini[2] when he writes of 'Xerxes the Zeus of the Persians', or of 'vultures, animated sepulchres'. Similarly certain expressions of Callisthenes[3] are ridiculed as being high-flown and not sublime; still more are some of Cleitarchus's[4]—a frivolous fellow who, in the words of Sophocles,[5] blows 'on wretched pipes without control of breath'. Such effects will be found also in Amphicrates and Hegesias and Matris,[6] for often when they believe themselves to

---

1 I have adopted the translation provided by A. S. Way for Roberts's edition, since it brings out so well the bombastic, pseudo-tragic quality to which Longinus takes exception. The lines probably come from a lost *Orithyia* by Aeschylus.

2 A Sicilian rhetorician of the fifth century B.C.

3 A historian who wrote at the end of the fourth and beginning of the third centuries B.C.

4 Another historian, contemporary with Callisthenes; celebrated the deeds of Alexander the Great.

5 The words, probably from a lost *Orithyia* by Sophocles, are quoted in a fuller form by Cicero (*Ad Atticum*).

6 Amphicrates of Athens (*fl.* 90 B.C.), Hegesias of Magnesia (*fl.* 270 B.C.), and Matris of Thebes (*fl.* ? 200 B.C.) were rhetoricians.

be inspired they are not really carried away, but are merely being puerile.

Tumidity seems, on the whole, to be one of the most difficult faults to guard against. For somehow or other, all those who aim at grandeur in the hope of escaping the charge of feebleness and aridity fall naturally into this very fault, putting their trust in the maxim that 'to fall short of a great aim is at any rate a noble failure'. As in the human body, so also in diction swellings are bad things, mere flabby insincerities that will probably produce an effect opposite to that intended; for as they say, there is nothing drier than a man with dropsy.

Tumidity, then, arises from the desire to outdo the sublime. Puerility, on the other hand, is the complete antithesis of grandeur, for it is entirely low and mean-spirited, and is indeed the most ignoble of faults. What then is puerility? Is it not, surely, a thought which is pedantically elaborated until it tails off into frigidity? Writers slip into this kind of fault when they strive for unusual and well-wrought effects, and above all for attractiveness, and instead flounder into tawdriness and affectation.

Related to this there is a third type of fault in impassioned writing which Theodorus[1] called *parenthyrsus,* or false sentiment. This is misplaced, hollow emotionalism where emotion is not called for, or immoderate passion where restraint is what is needed. For writers are often carried away, as though by drunkenness, into outbursts of emotion which are not relevant to the matter in hand, but are wholly personal, and hence tedious. To hearers unaffected by this emotionalism their work therefore seems atrocious, and naturally enough, for while they are themselves in an ecstasy, their hearers are not. However, I am leaving this matter of the emotions for treatment in another place.

[1] Theodorus of Gadara, a rhetorician (*fl.* 30 B.C.).

CHAPTER 4

FRIGIDITY

OF the second fault I mentioned, that is, frigidity, there are plenty of examples in Timaeus,[1] in other respects a writer of some ability, and not incapable of occasional grandeur—a man, indeed, of much learning and inventiveness. However, while he was very fond of criticizing the failings of others, he remained blind to his own, and his passion for continually embarking upon odd conceits often led him into the most trifling puerilities. I shall give you only one or two examples from this author, since Cecilius has anticipated me with most of them. In his eulogy of Alexander the Great he says of him that 'he gained possession of the whole of Asia in fewer years than Isocrates[2] took to write his *Panegyric* advocating war against the Persians.' How remarkable is this comparison of the great Macedonian with the rhetorician! For it is obvious, Timaeus, that, seen in this light, the Spartans were far inferior in prowess to Isocrates, since they took thirty years over the conquest of Messene, whereas he took no more than ten over the composition of his *Panegyric.* Then look at the way in which he speaks of the Athenians captured in Sicily: 'They had behaved sacrilegiously towards Hermes and mutilated statues of him, and it was for this reason that they were punished, very largely through the efforts of a single man, Hermocrates the son of Hermon, who on his father's side was descended from the outraged god.' I am surprised, my dear Terentianus, that he does not write of the tyrant Dionysius that, 'having been guilty of impious conduct towards

[1] Timaeus of Tauromenium (*fl.* 310 B.C.), a Sicilian historian who was so fond of finding faults in the work of other writers that he was nicknamed Epitimaeus, i.e., 'fault-finder'.

[2] Isocrates (436–338 B.C.), the great Athenian orator and rhetorician. In his *Panegyric* (380 B.C.) he urged the Athenians and the Spartans to lay aside their rivalry and unite against Persia.

Zeus and Heracles, he was therefore deprived of his sovereignty by Dion and Heracleides.'[1]

But why speak of Timaeus when even such demigods as Xenophon and Plato, trained as they were in the school of Socrates, forget themselves at times for the sake of such trivial effects? In his *Constitution of Sparta* Xenophon writes: 'In fact you would hear their voices less than those of marble statues, and would turn aside their gaze less easily than those of bronze figures; and you would think them more modest even than the maidens in their eyes.'[2] It would have been more characteristic of Amphicrates[3] than Xenophon to speak of the pupils of our eyes as modest maidens. And good heavens, to ask us to believe that every single one of them had modest eyes, when it is said that the shamelessness of people is revealed in nothing so much as in their eyes! 'You drunken sot with the eyes of a dog,' as the saying goes.[4] However, Timaeus could not let Xenophon keep even this frigid conceit to himself, but laid his thieving hands on it. At all events, speaking of Agathocles, and how he abducted his cousin from the unveiling ceremony when she had been given in marriage to another man, he asks, 'Who would have done this if he had not had strumpets in his eyes instead of maidens?'

As for the otherwise divine Plato, he says, when he means, merely wooden tablets, 'They will inscribe memorials of cypress-wood and place them in the temples;'[5] and again, 'With regard to walls, Megillus, I would agree with Sparta that the walls be allowed to remain lying asleep in the ground, and not rise again.'[1] And Herodotus's phrase for beautiful women, when he calls them 'tortures for the eyes',[2] is not much better. However, Herodotus can in some measure be defended, for it is barbarians who use this phrase in his book, and they in their cups. All the same, it is not proper to put low terms into the mouths even of such people as these, and thereby lay oneself open to the censure of later ages.

CHAPTER 5

THE ORIGINS OF LITERARY IMPROPRIETY

ALL these ignoble qualities in literature arise from one cause—from that passion for novel ideas which is the dominant craze among the writers of today; for our faults spring, for the most part, from very much the same sources as our virtues. Thus while a fine style, sublime conceptions, yes, and happy turns of phrase, too, all contribute towards effective composition, yet these very factors are the foundation and origin, not only of success, but also of its opposite. Something of the kind applies also to variations in manner, to hyperbole, and to the idiomatic plural, and I shall show later the dangers which these devices seem to involve. At the moment I must cast about and make some suggestions how we may avoid the defects that are so closely bound up with the achievement of the sublime.

CHAPTER 6

CRITICISM AND THE SUBLIME

THE way to do this, my friend, is first of all to get a clear understanding and appreciation of what constitutes the true sublime. This, however, is no easy

---

[1] The genitive of Zeus is Dios, and Longinus ironically bases on this a conceit in the manner of Timaeus's far-fetched pun on Hermes and Hermocrates the son of Hermon.

[2] Because it reflects a tiny image of the person gazing into it, the pupil of the eye was called *korē*, or maiden.

[3] An Athenian rhetorician at the beginning of the first century B.C.

[4] *Iliad* I, 225.

[5] *Laws* V, 741 C.

[1] ibid. VI, 778 D.

[2] Herodotus, V, 18.

undertaking, for the ability to judge literature is the crowning achievement of long experience. Nevertheless, if I am to speak by way of precept, we can perhaps learn discrimination in these matters from some such considerations as those which follow.

CHAPTER 7
THE TRUE SUBLIME

IT must be understood, my dear friend, that, as in everyday life nothing is great which it is considered great to despise, so is it with the sublime. Thus riches, honours, reputation, sovereignty, and all the other things which possess in marked degree the external trappings of a showy splendour, would not seem to a sensible man to be great blessings, since contempt for them is itself regarded as a considerable virtue; and indeed people admire those who possess them less than those who could have them but are high-minded enough to despise them. In the same way we must consider, with regard to the grand style in poetry and literature generally, whether certain passages do not simply give an impression of grandeur by means of much adornment indiscriminately applied, being shown up as mere bombast when these are stripped away—passages which it would be more noble to despise than to admire. For by some innate power the true sublime uplifts our souls; we are filled with a proud exaltation and a sense of vaunting joy, just as though we had ourselves produced what we had heard.

If an intelligent and well-read man can hear a passage several times, and it does not either touch his spirit with a sense of grandeur or leave more food for reflection in his mind than the mere words convey, but with long and careful examination loses more and more of its effectiveness, then it cannot be an example of true sublimity—certainly not unless it can outlive a single hearing. For a piece is truly great only if it can stand up to repeated examination, and if it is difficult, or, rather, impossible to resist its appeal, and it remains firmly and ineffaceably in the memory. As a generalization, you may take it that sublimity in all its truth and beauty exists in such works as please all men at all times. For when men who differ in their pursuits, their ways of life, their ambitions, their ages, and their languages all think in one and the same way about the same works, then the unanimous judgement, as it were, of men who have so little in common induces a strong and unshakeable faith in the object of admiration.

CHAPTER 8
FIVE SOURCES OF SUBLIMITY

IT may be said that there are five particularly fruitful sources of the grand style, and beneath these five there lies as a common foundation the command of language, without which nothing worth while can be done. The first and most important is the ability to form grand conceptions, as I have explained in my commentary on Xenophon. Second comes the stimulus of powerful and inspired emotion. These two elements of the sublime are very largely innate, while the remainder are the product of art—that is, the proper formation of the two types of figure, figures of thought and figures of speech, together with the creation of a noble diction, which in its turn may be resolved into the choice of words, the use of imagery, and the elaboration of the style. The fifth source of grandeur, which embraces all those I have already mentioned, is the total effect resulting from dignity and elevation.

We must consider, then, what is involved under each of these heads, with a preliminary reminder that Cecilius has left out of account some of the five divisions, one of them obviously being that which relates to emotion. Now if he thought that these two things, sublimity and emotion, were the same thing, and that they were essentially bound up with each other, he is mistaken. For some emotions can be found that are mean and not in the least sublime, such as pity, grief, and fear; and on the other hand many sublime passages convey no emotion, such as, among countless examples, the poet's daring lines about the Aloadae:

> *Keenly they strove to set Ossa upon*
> *Olympus, and upon Ossa the forest-clad*
> *Pelion, that they might mount up to*
> *heaven;*

and the still greater conception that follows:

> *And this would they have accomplished.*[1]

With the orators, again, their eulogies, ceremonial addresses, and occasional speeches contain touches of majesty and grandeur at every point, but as a rule lack emotion; thus emotional speakers are the least effective eulogists, while, on the other hand, those who excel as panegyrists avoid emotionalism. But if Cecilius believed that emotion contributes nothing at all to the sublime, and for this reason considered it not worth mentioning, once again he was making a very serious mistake; for I would confidently maintain that nothing contributes so decisively to the grand style as a noble emotion in the right setting, when it forces its way to the surface in a gust of frenzy, and breathes a kind of divine inspiration into the speaker's words.

CHAPTER 9

NOBILITY OF SOUL

NOW since the first of these factors, that is to say, nobility of soul,[2] plays the most important part of them all, here too, even though it is a gift rather than an acquired characteristic, we should do all we can to train our minds towards the production of grand ideas, perpetually impregnating them, so to speak, with a noble inspiration. By what means, you will ask, is this to be done? Well, I have written elsewhere to this effect: 'Sublimity is the echo of a noble mind.' Thus, even without being spoken, a simple idea will sometimes of its own accord excite admiration by reason of the greatness of mind that it expresses; for example, the silence of Ajax in 'The Calling Up of the Spirits'[1] is grand, more sublime than any words.

First, then, it is absolutely necessary to indicate the source of this power, and to show that the truly eloquent man must have a mind that is not mean or ignoble. For it is not possible that those who throughout their lives have feeble and servile thoughts and aims should strike out anything that is remarkable, anything that is worthy of an immortality of fame; no, greatness of speech is the province of those whose thoughts are deep, and stately expressions come naturally to the most high-minded of men.

• • •

CHAPTER 10

THE SELECTION AND ORGANIZATION OF MATERIAL

NEXT we must consider whether there is anything else that makes for sublimity of style. Now as we naturally associate with all things certain elements that are inherent in their substance, so it necessarily follows that we shall find one source of the sublime in the unerring choice of the most felicitous of these elements, and in the ability to relate them to one another in such a way as to make of them a single organism, so to speak. For one writer attracts the hearer by his choice of matter, another by the cumulative effect of the ideas he chooses.

---

[1] *Odyssey* XI, 315–16; 317.

[2] The first of the five sources of sublimity, listed in the previous chapter as 'the ability to form grand conceptions'.

[1] *Odyssey* XI, 543 ff.

For example, Sappho in her poetry always chooses the emotions attendant on the lover's frenzy from among those which accompany this passion in real life. And wherein does she demonstrate her excellence? In the skill with which she selects and fuses the most extreme and intense manifestations of these emotions.

• • •

CHAPTER 11

AMPLIFICATION

A MERIT associated with those already presented is that which is called amplification, that is, when the matters under discussion or the points of an argument allow of many pauses and many fresh starts from section to section, and the grand phrases come rolling out one after another with increasing effect.

This may be managed either by the rhetorical development of a commonplace, or by exaggeration, whether facts or arguments are to be stressed, or by the orderly disposition of factual points or of appeals to the feelings. There are, indeed, countless forms of amplification. Yet the speaker must be aware that, without the help of sublimity, none of these methods can of itself form a complete whole, unless indeed in the expression of pity or disparagement. In other forms of amplification, when you take away the element of the sublime, it will be like taking the soul out of the body; for their vigour will be completely drained away without the sustaining power of the sublime.

However, in the interests of clarity I must briefly indicate how my present precepts differ from those about which I have just spoken, that is, the marking-out of the most striking points and their organization into a single whole, and in what general respects sublimity is to be distinguished from the effects of amplification.

CHAPTER 12

AMPLIFICATION DEFINED

NOW the definition of the writers on rhetoric is not, in my view, acceptable. Amplification, they say, is language which invests the subject with grandeur. But obviously this definition could apply equally well to sublimity and to the emotional and the figurative styles, since these too invest language with some degree of grandeur. As I see it, they are to be distinguished from one another by the fact that sublimity consists in elevation, amplification in quantity; thus sublimity is often contained in a single idea, whereas amplification is always associated with quantity and a certain amount of redundancy. To sum it up in general terms, amplification is the accumulation of all the small points and incidental topics bearing on the subject-matter; it adds substance and strength to the argument by dwelling on it, differing from proof in that, while the latter demonstrates the point at issue . . .

(Here two pages of the manuscript are lost)

. . . extremely rich; like some ocean, he[1] often swells into a mighty expanse of grandeur. From this I should say that, where language is concerned, the orator,[2] being more concerned with the emotions, shows much fire and vehemence of spirit, whilst Plato, standing firmly based upon his supreme dignity and majesty, though indeed he is not cold, has not the same vehemence.

It seems to me that it is on these same grounds, my dear Terentianus—if we Greeks may be allowed an opinion in this matter—that Cicero is to be differentiated from Demosthenes in his use of the grand style. Demosthenes is characterized by a sublimity which is for the most part rugged, Cicero by profusion. Demosthenes, by reason of his force, yes, and his speed and power and intensity,

---

[1] Chapter 13 makes it clear that this refers to Plato.

[2] Demosthenes.

may be likened to a thunderbolt or flash of lightning, as it were burning up or seizing as his own all that he falls upon. But Cicero is, in my opinion, like a wide-spreading conflagration that rolls on to consume everything far and wide; he has within him an abundance of steady and enduring flame which can be let loose at whatever point he desires, and which is fed from one source after another.

However, you Romans should be able to form a better judgement in this matter. But the right place for the Demosthenean sublimity and intensity is in passages where hyperbole and powerful emotions are involved, and where the audience are to be swept off their feet. On the other hand, profusion is in order when it is necessary to flood them with words. It is for the most part appropriate to the treatment of rhetorical commonplaces, and of perorations and digressions; well suited, too, to all descriptive and epideictic[1] writings, to works of history and natural philosophy, and to a number of other types of literature.

CHAPTER 13

PLATO AND THE SUBLIME: IMITATION

NOW although Plato—for I must return to him—flows with such a noiseless stream, he none the less achieves grandeur. You are familiar with his *Republic* and know his manner. 'Those, therefore,' he says,[2] 'who have no experience of wisdom and goodness, and are always engaged in feasting and similar pleasures, are brought down, it would seem, to a lower level, and there wander about all their lives. They have never looked up towards the truth, nor risen higher, nor tasted of any pure and lasting pleasure. In the manner of cattle, they bend down with their gaze fixed always on the ground and on their feeding-places, grazing and fattening and copulating, and in their insatiable greed for these pleasures they kick and butt one another with horns and hoofs of iron, and kill one another if their desires are not satisfied.'

Provided that we are ready to give him due attention, this author shows us that, in addition to those already mentioned, there is another way that leads to the sublime. And what kind of a way is this? It is the imitation and emulation of the great historians and poets of the past. Let us steadfastly keep this aim in mind, my dear fellow. For many authors catch fire from the inspiration of others—just as we are told that the Pythian priestess, when she approaches the tripod standing by a cleft in the ground from which, they say, there is breathed out a divine vapour, is impregnated thence with the heavenly power, and by virtue of this afflatus is at once inspired to speak oracles. So too, as though also issuing from sacred orifices, certain emanations are conveyed from the genius of the men of old into the souls of those who emulate them, and, breathing in these influences, even those who show very few signs of inspiration derive some degree of divine enthusiasm from the grandeur of their predecessors.

Was Herodotus alone an extremely Homeric writer? No, for even earlier there was Stesichorus,[1] and Archilochus, and above all others Plato, who for his own use drew upon countless tributary streams from the great Homeric river. I should perhaps have had to prove this had not Ammonius[2] and his followers selected and recorded the facts.

---

[1] Epideictic orations were one of the types of set speech defined in the rhetorical systems of the ancients—in Latin *genus demonstrativum;* they include such things as funeral orations, panegyrics, and speeches of dispraise.

[2] *Republic* IX, 586.

[1] Stesichorus (*c.* 640–*c.* 555 B.C.), one of the great lyrical poets.

[2] Ammonius (*fl.* 140 B.C.) carried on at Alexandria the work of his master Aristarchus, who has been described as 'the founder of scientific scholarship'.

Now this procedure is not plagiarism; rather it is like taking impressions from beautiful pictures or statues or other works of art. I do not think there would have been so fine a bloom on Plato's philosophical doctrines, or that he would so often have embarked on poetic subject-matter and phraseology, had he not been striving heart and soul with Homer for first place, like a young contestant entering the ring with a long-admired champion, perhaps showing too keen a spirit of emulation in his desire to break a lance with him, so to speak, yet getting some profit from the endeavour. For as Hesiod says,[1] 'This strife is good for mortals.' And indeed the fight for fame and the crown of victory are noble and very well worth the winning where even to be worsted by one's predecessors carries no discredit.

• • •

CHAPTER 15

IMAGERY AND THE POWER OF THE IMAGINATION

FURTHERMORE, my dear boy, dignity, grandeur, and powers of persuasion are to a very large degree derived from images—for that is what some people call the representation of mental pictures. In a general way the term 'image' is used of any mental conception, from whatever source it presents itself, which gives rise to speech; but in current usage the word is applied to passages in which, carried away by your feelings, you imagine you are actually seeing the subject of your description, and enable your audience as well to see it. You will have noticed that imagery means one thing with orators and another with poets—that in poetry its aim is to work on the feelings, in oratory to produce vividness of description, though indeed in both cases an attempt is made to stir the feelings.

> Mother, I beseech you, do not set upon me those blood-boltered and snake-like hags. See there, see there, they approach, they leap upon me![1]

and again,

> Ah! She will slay me! Whither shall I fly?[2]

In these passages the poet himself had 'seen' the Furies, and he almost compelled his audience, too, to see what he had imagined.

Now Euripides expends his highest powers in giving tragic expression to these two passions, madness and love, and he is more brilliantly successful with these, I think, than with any others, although he is not afraid to make incursions into other realms of the imagination. While he is very far from possessing a natural grandeur, yet on many occasions he forces his genius to tragic heights, and where sublimity is concerned, each time, in the words of Homer,

> with his tail he lashes his ribs and flanks on both sides, and goads himself on to fight.[3]

For example, when the Sun hands the reins to Phaethon, he says:

> 'And do not as you drive venture into the Libyan sky, for being tempered with no moisture it will burn up your wheel.'[4]

And he goes on,

---

[1] *Works and Days* 24.

[1] Euripides, *Orestes* 255–7.

[2] Euripides, *Iphigenia in Tauris* 291.

[3] *Iliad* XX, 170–1.

[4] This and the following passage are taken from the lost *Phaethon* of Euripides.

> 'But speed your course towards the seven Pleiades.' And hearing this, the boy took hold of the reins, and lashed the flanks of his winged team, and they winged their path up to the cloudy ridges of the sky. And hard behind rode his father, astride the Dog-Star's back, schooling his son: 'Drive that way! Now this way guide the chariot, this way!'

Now would you not say that the soul of the poet goes into the chariot with the boy, sharing his danger and joining the horses in their flight? For he could never have formed such an image had he not been swept along neck by neck with these celestial activities. You will find the same in the words he gives to Cassandra:

> Yet, you Trojans, lovers of steeds . . .[1]

Aeschylus, too, ventures on images of a most heroic cast, as when he says in his *Seven against Thebes:*

> Seven resistless warrior-captains have slit a bullock's throat over an iron-rimmed shield, and have brushed their hands over the bullock's blood and sworn an oath by War and Havoc and Terror, the lover of blood . . .[2]

Here they pledge themselves by a joint oath to a pitiless death. Sometimes, however, Aeschylus introduces ideas that are unfinished and crude and harsh; yet Euripides in a desire to emulate him comes dangerously near to committing the same faults. For example, in Aeschylus the palace of Lycurgus at the appearance of Dionysus is described in unusual terms as being divinely possessed:

> Then the house is in an ecstasy, and the roof is inspired with a Bacchic frenzy.[3]

[1] From another lost play of Euripides.

[2] *Seven against Thebes,* 42–6.

[3] From a lost play of Aeschylus.

Euripides has expressed the same idea differently, softening it down:

> And the whole mountain joined with them in their Bacchic frenzy.[1]

Sophocles, too, has used excellent imagery in describing the death of Oedipus as he entombs himself amid portents from the sky,[2] and in his account of how, at the departure of the Greeks, Achilles shows himself above his tomb to those who are sailing away,[3] a scene which I think no one has depicted more vividly than Simonides.

But it would be out of the question to quote all the examples. However, as I have said, those from the poets display a good deal of romantic exaggeration, and everywhere exceed the bounds of credibility, whereas the finest feature of the orator's imagery is always its adherence to reality and truth. Whenever the texture of the speech becomes poetical and fabulous, and falls into all sorts of impossibilities, such deviations seem strange and unnatural. Our brilliant modern orators, for example, see Furies, heaven help us, just as though they were tragedians, and, noble fellows that they are, they cannot even understand that when Orestes says,

> Be off, for you are one of my avenging Furies clasping my waist to hurl me down to hell,[4]

he is imagining this because he is mad.

What, then, is the effect of imagery when it is used in oratory? Among other things, it can infuse much passion and energy into speeches, but when it is combined with the argumentative passages it not only persuades the hearer, but actually masters him.

[1] Euripides, *Bacchae* 726.

[2] Sophocles, *Oedipus at Colonus* I, 586–666.

[3] In his lost *Polyxena.* The poem in which Simonides describes the same episode is also lost.

[4] Euripides, *Orestes* 264–5.

'Suppose,' says Demosthenes,[1] to give an example, 'suppose that at this very moment an uproar were to be heard in front of the courts, and someone were to tell us that the prison had been broken open and the prisoners were escaping, there is no one, old or young, so irresponsible that he would not give all the help in his power; moreover, if someone were to come and tell us that so-and-so was the person who let them out, he would at once be put to death without a hearing.' Then of course there is Hyperides,[2] who was put on trial when he had proposed the enfranchisement of the slaves after the great defeat; his answer was that it was not himself, the advocate, who had framed the measure, but the battle of Chaeronea. Here the orator has at one and the same time developed an argument and used his imagination, and his conception has therefore transcended the bounds of mere persuasion. In all such cases our ears always, by some natural law, seize upon the stronger element, so that we are attracted away from the demonstration of fact to the startling image, and the argument lies below the surface of the accompanying brilliance. And it is not unreasonable that we should be affected in this way, for when two forces are combined to produce a single effect, the greater always attracts to itself the virtues of the lesser.

I have gone far enough in my discussion of sublimity of thought, as it is produced by greatness of mind, imitation, or imagery.

[1] Demosthenes, *Timocrates* 208.

[2] Hyperides (389–22 B.C.), a distinguished Attic orator. See Chapter 34. Plutarch relates (*Moralia* 849 A) that after the Athenian defeat at Chaeronea Hyperides proposed an extension of the franchise, and, when he was impeached for the illegality of his proposal, declared, 'The arms of the Macedonians obscured my vision; it was not I who proposed the measure, but the battle of Chaeronea.'

CHAPTER 16
RHETORICAL FIGURES: ADJURATION

WE now come to the place which I have duly set aside for rhetorical figures, for they too, when properly handled, will contribute in no small measure, as I have said, to the effect of grandeur. However, since it would be a toilsome and indeed endless business to consider them all closely at this stage, I shall merely, in order to confirm my proposition, run over a few of those which make for grandeur of utterance.

In the following passage Demosthenes is putting forward an argument in support of his policy. What was the natural procedure for doing this? 'You were not wrong, you who undertook the struggle for the freedom of the Greeks, and you have a precedent for this here at home. For those who fought at Marathon were not wrong, nor those at Salamis, nor those at Plataea.'[1] But when, as though carried away by a divine enthusiasm and by the inspiration of Phoebus himself, he uttered his oath by the champions of Greece, 'By those who stood the shock at Marathon, it cannot be that you were wrong,' it would seem that, by his use of this single figure of adjuration, which I here give the name of apostrophe, he has deified his ancestors by suggesting that we ought to swear by men who have died such deaths as we swear by gods; he has instilled into his judges the spirit of the men who stood there in the fore-front of the danger, and has transformed the natural flow of his argument into a passage of transcending sublimity, endowing it with the passion and the power of conviction that arise from unheard-of and extraordinary oaths. At the same time he has infused into the minds of his audience words which act in some sort as an antidote and a remedy, so that,

[1] *De Corona* 208. Demosthenes is defending, by reference to the past, his aggressive policy which resulted in the Athenian defeat at Chaeronea.

uplifted by these eulogies, they come to feel just as proud of the war against Philip as of the triumphs at Marathon and Salamis. By all these means he has been able to carry his hearers away with the figure he has employed.

It is said, indeed, that Demosthenes found the germ of this oath in Eupolis:[1]

> For by the fight I fought at Marathon, no
> one of them shall vex my heart and not
> pay for it.

But there is nothing grand about the mere swearing of an oath; we must take into account the place, the manner, the circumstances, and the motive. In the Eupolis there is nothing but an oath, and that addressed to the Athenians while they were still enjoying prosperity and in no need of consolation. Moreover, the poet has not in his oath deified the warriors in order to engender in his audience a high opinion of their valour, but has wandered away from those who stood the shock to something inanimate, that is, the fight. In Demosthenes the oath is designed for men who have suffered defeat, so that the Athenians may no longer regard Chaeronea as a disaster; and at the same time it is, as I said, a proof that no wrong has been done, an example, a demonstration of the efficacy of oaths, a eulogy, and an exhortation. And since the orator was likely to be faced with the objection, 'You are speaking of a defeat that resulted from your policy, yet your oath relates to victories,' in what follows he keeps on the safe side and measures every word, showing that even in orgies of the imagination it is necessary to remain sober. 'Those who stood in the forefront of the battle at Marathon,' he says, 'and those who fought aboard ship at Salamis and Artemisium, and those who stood shoulder to shoulder at Plataea.' Nowhere does he speak of the 'victors'; everywhere he cunningly avoids mention of the result, since it was a happy one and the reverse of what happened at Chaeronea. Thus he anticipates objections and carries his audience with him. 'To all of whom, Aeschines,' he adds, 'the state gave a public funeral, not only to those who were successful.'

[1] Eupolis (*c.* 446–*c.* 411 B.C.) was a poet of the Old Comedy. The lines come from his lost comedy *Demi*.

CHAPTER 17

RHETORICAL FIGURES AND SUBLIMITY

IN this matter, my dear friend, I must not omit an observation of my own, which, however, shall be quite concisely stated. This is that, by some quality innate in them, the rhetorical figures reinforce the sublime, and in their turn derive a marvellous degree of support from it. I will tell you where and how this happens. The unconscionable use of figures is peculiarly subject to suspicion, and engenders impressions of hidden traps and plots and fallacies. This is true when the speech is addressed to a judge with absolute authority, and still more to despots, kings, or rulers in high places, for such a one is at once annoyed if, like a simple child, he is caught on the wrong foot by the rhetorical devices of a highly-skilled orator. Accepting the fallacy as a personal insult, he sometimes turns quite savage, and even if he masters his rage, he becomes utterly impervious to the persuasive quality of the speech. Thus a rhetorical figure would appear to be most effective when the fact that it is a figure is not apparent.

Sublimity and the expression of strong feeling are, therefore, a wonderfully helpful antidote against the suspicion that attends the use of figures. The cunning artifice remains out of sight, associated from now on with beauty and sublimity, and all suspicion is put to flight. Sufficient evidence of this is the passage already mentioned, 'I swear by the men of Marathon!' But by what means has the orator here concealed his figure? Obviously by its very brilliance. For in much the same way as dim lights vanish in the radiance of the sun, so does the all-pervading effluence of grandeur utterly obscure the artifices of rhetoric.

Something of the same kind occurs also in painting. For although light and shade as represented by colours may lie side by side on the same surface, it is the light that first catches the eye and seems not only to stand out, but also to be much nearer. So also is it with literature: by some natural affinity and by their brilliance, things that appeal to our feelings and sublime conceptions lie nearer to our hearts, and always catch our attention before the figures, overshadowing their artistry, and keeping it out of sight, so to speak.

CHAPTER 18
RHETORICAL QUESTIONS

BUT what are we to say on the matter of questions and answers? Does not Demosthenes aim at enhancing the grandeur and effectiveness of his speeches very considerably by the very way in which he exploits these figures and their appeal to the imagination? 'Now tell me, do you want to go about asking one another, "Is there any news?"? For what stranger news could there be than that of a Macedonian conquering Greece? "Is Philip dead?" "No, but he is ill." What difference does it make to you? For even if anything should happen to him, you will soon invent another Philip.'[1] And again, 'Let us sail against Macedonia,' he says. '"But where shall we land?" someone asks. The mere fact of our fighting will find out the weak spots in Philip's strategy.'[2] If this had been given as a bald statement, it would have been completely ineffective; but as it is, the inspired rapidity in the play of question and answer, together with the device of meeting his own objections as though they were someone else's, has not only added to the sublimity of his words, but also given them greater conviction, and all this by the use of this particular figure. For a display of feeling is more effective when it seems not to be premeditated on the part of the speaker, but to have arisen from the occasion; and this method of asking questions and providing your own answers gives the appearance of being a natural outburst of feeling. Those who are being questioned by others are stimulated into answering the questions spontaneously, and with energy and complete candour; in the same way the rhetorical figure of question and answer beguiles the audience into thinking that each deliberately considered point has been struck out and put into words on the spur of the moment. Furthermore—for the following passage has been accepted as one of the most sublime in Herodotus—if thus . . .

> *(Here two pages of the manuscript are missing)*

CHAPTER 19
ASYNDETON, OR THE OMISSION OF CONJUNCTIONS

. . . the words come gushing out, as it were, set down without connecting links, and almost outstripping the speaker himself. 'And, locking their shields,' says Xenophon,[1] 'they pressed forward, fought, slew, were slain.' Then there are the words of Eurylochus:

> We came through the oak-coppice, as
> you bade, renowned Odysseus. We saw
> amid the forest-glens a beautiful palace.[2]

The phrases, disconnected, but none the less rapid, give the impression of an agitation which at the same time checks the utterance and urges it on. And the poet has produced such an effect by his use of asyndeton.

---

[1] Demosthenes, *Philippic* I, 10.

[2] ibid. 44.

[1] Xenophon, *Historia Graeca* IV, 3, 19.

[2] *Odyssey* X, 251–2.

CHAPTER 20

THE ACCUMULATION OF FIGURES

A COMBINATION of figures for a common purpose usually has a very moving effect—when two or three unite in a kind of partnership to add force, persuasiveness, and beauty. Thus in Demosthenes' speech against Meidias you will find examples of asyndeton interwoven with the figures of anaphora and diatyposis:[1] 'For the aggressor might do many things, some of which the victim would be unable to describe to anyone else, by his manner, his looks, his voice.' Then, in order that the speech may not, as it proceeds, remain at a standstill as far as these particular effects are concerned (for standing still connotes calm, whereas emotion, being an upheaval or agitation of the soul, connotes disorder), he at once hurries on to fresh examples of asyndeton and anaphora: 'By his manner, his looks, his voice, when he acts with insolence, when he acts with hostility, when he strikes you with his fists, when he strikes you like a slave.' In this way the orator does just the same as the aggressor; he belabours the judges' minds with blow after blow. He goes on from here to make yet another hurricane onslaught: 'When he strikes you with his fists,' he says, 'when he beats you about the face—this rouses you, this drives men out of their wits when they are not used to being trampled underfoot. No one describing this could bring out the strength of its effect.' Thus all the way through, although with continual variations, he preserves the essential character of the repetitions and the asyndeta, and thus too his order is disordered, and similarly his disorder embraces a certain element of order.

[1] Anaphora is the repetition of words; diatyposis is vivid description.

CHAPTER 21

CONJUNCTIONS: SOME DISADVANTAGES

NOW, if you will, try putting in the conjunctions, in the manner of Isocrates[1] and his disciples: 'Furthermore, this too must not be overlooked, that the aggressor might do many things, first by his manner, then by his looks, and then again by his mere voice.' If you amplify it like this, phrase by phrase, you will see that the drive and ruggedness of the emotion that is being exploited, toned down into smoothness by the use of the conjunctions, lapse into pointlessness and at once lose all their fire. If you tie runners together you will deprive them of their speed; in exactly the same way emotion resents being hampered by conjunctions and other appendages of the kind, for it then loses its freedom of motion and the impression it gives of being shot from a catapult.

CHAPTER 22

THE FIGURE OF HYPERBATON, OR INVERSION

HYPERBATA, or inversions, must be put into the same class. These consist in the arrangement of words or ideas out of their normal sequence, and they carry, so to speak, the genuine stamp of powerful emotion. There are people who, when they are angry or frightened or irritated or carried away by jealousy or any other feeling—for there are innumerable forms of emotion, and indeed no one would be able to say just how many—will sometimes let themselves be deflected; and often, after

[1] Isocrates (436–338 B.C.), a great Athenian orator. His disciples included Hyperides (see Chapters 15 and 34) and Theopompus (see Chapters 31 and 43).

they have brought forward one point, they will drop in others without rhyme or reason, and then, under the stress of their agitation, they will come right round to their original position just as though they were being chased by a whirlwind. Dragged in every direction by their rapid changes of mood, they will keep altering the arrangement of their words and ideas, losing their natural sequence and introducing all sorts of variations. In the same way the best authors will use inversion in such a way that their representations will assume the aspect of natural processes at work. For art is perfect only when it looks like nature, and again, nature hits the mark only when she conceals the art that is within her.

This may be exemplified by the words of Dionysius the Phocaean in Herodotus:[1] 'For our affairs stand on a razor's edge, men of Ionia, whether we are to be free men or slaves, and runaway slaves at that. Now, therefore, if you are prepared to accept hardships, straightway there is toil for you, but you will be able to overcome your enemies.' Here the normal order would have been, 'O men of Ionia, now is the time for you to take toil upon you; for our affairs stand on a razor's edge.' However, the speaker has transposed 'men of Ionia', starting at once with the thought of the fear, as though in this pressing danger he would not even address his hearers first. Furthermore, he has inverted the order of his ideas; for instead of saying that they must endure toil, which is the point of his exhortation, he first gives them the reason why they must toil when he says, 'Our affairs stand on a razor's edge.' Thus what he says does not seem premeditated, but forced out of him.

Thucydides is even more skilful in his use of inversions to dissociate things which are by their nature one and indivisible. Demosthenes, though indeed he is not as wilful as Thucydides, is the most immoderate of all in his use of this kind of figure, and through inversions he gives the impression of speaking extremely masterfully, and, what is more, of speaking impromptu; moreover, he carries his audience with him to share in the dangers of his long inversions. For he will often hold up the sense of what he has begun to express, and meanwhile he will in a strange and unlikely order pile one idea on top of another, drawn from any kind of source and just dropped into the middle of what he is saying, inducing in his hearer the fear that the whole structure of the sentence will fall to pieces, and compelling him in his agitation to share in the risk the speaker is taking; and then unexpectedly, after a long interval, he will bring out the long-awaited phrase just where it is most effective, at the very end, and thus, by the very audacity and recklessness of his inversions, he administers a much more powerful shock. I forbear to give examples, since there are so many of them.

[1] Herodotus, VI, II.

CHAPTER 23

POLYPTOTON: INTERCHANGE OF SINGULAR AND PLURAL

THE figures called polyptota[1] (accumulations, variations, and climaxes) are, as you know, very powerful auxiliaries in the production of elegance and of every kind of sublime and emotional effect. Observe, too, how greatly an exposition is diversified and enlivened by changes in case, tense, person, number, and gender. In the matter of number, I can say that the decorative quality of a passage

[1] Strictly speaking, polyptoton is the use of more than one case of the same word, but Longinus seems to apply it also to rhetorical effects gained by changes in number, person, tense, or gender.

is not enhanced only by words which are singular in form, but which on close examination are found to have a plural meaning, as in

> Straightway a countless host ranged along
> the beaches send out a cry, 'Tunny!'[1]

But it is more noteworthy that at times the use of the plural in place of the singular has a more resounding effect, and impresses us by the very idea of multitude implied in the plural number. This is exemplified by Sophocles in some lines spoken by Oedipus:

> O marriages, marriages, it is you that begot me and gave me birth, and then brought to light again the same seed, and showed fathers, brothers, and sons as being all kindred blood, and brides, wives, and mothers, too, and all the foulest deeds that are done among men.[2]

All these relate to a single name, that of Oedipus, with that of Jocasta on the other side; however, the expansion of the number serves to pluralize the misfortunes as well.

There is the same kind of multiplication in the line, 'Forth came Hectors, and Sarpedons too;'[3] and again in Plato's passage on the Athenians which I have also quoted in another work: 'For no Pelopes nor Cadmi nor Aegypti and Danai, nor any other hordes of barbarians by birth share our home with us, but we who are pure Greeks and not semi-barbarians live here', and the rest of it.[4] For naturally the facts sound more impressive from this accumulation of names in groups. However, this should not be done except on occasions when the subject admits of amplification or redundancy or exaggeration or emotionalism—any one or more of these; for to be hung all over with bells is altogether too pretentious.[1]

[1] Author unknown. Presumably the passage refers to a crowd of fisherfolk hailing the appearance of a shoal of tunny.

[2] *Oedipus Tyrannus* 1403–8.

[3] Author unknown.

[4] Plato, *Menexenus* 245 D.

CHAPTER 24

POLYPTOTON: CONVERSION OF PLURAL TO SINGULAR

FURTHERMORE, the opposite process, the contraction of plural ideas into a singular form, sometimes achieves an outstanding effect of sublimity. 'Afterwards,' says Demosthenes,[2] 'the whole Peloponnese was at variance.' Again, 'And when Phrynicus produced his play *The Capture of Miletus* the theatre burst into tears.'[3] To compress the number from multiplicity into unity gives a stronger impression of a single entity. In both examples the reason for the striking effect is, I think, the same. Where the words are singular, to turn them into the plural suggests an unexpected burst of feeling; where they are plural, and are fused into a fine-sounding singular, the change in the opposite direction produces an effect of surprise.

CHAPTER 25

POLYPTOTON: INTERCHANGE OF TENSES

AGAIN, if you introduce circumstances that are past in time as happening at the present moment,

[1] The metaphor here refers to the bells hung on the trappings of a war-horse. Roberts translates, 'a richly caparisoned style'.

[2] *De Corona* 18.

[3] Herodotus, VI, 21. Phrynicus was a tragic playwright contemporary with Aeschylus. Herodotus continues the anecdote quoted here by recounting that the Athenians fined Phrynicus 1000 drachmas for reminding them in *The Capture of Miletus* of a disaster which had befallen a friendly state, and ordered that the play should never again be performed.

you will turn the passage from mere narrative into vivid actuality. 'Someone,' says Xenophon, 'has fallen under Cyrus's horse, and being trampled on, strikes the horse in the belly with his sword. It rears and throws Cyrus, and he falls to the ground.'[1] Thucydides is particularly fond of this device.

CHAPTER 26

POLYPTOTON: VARIATIONS OF PERSON, OR PERSONAL ADDRESS

IN the same way the change of person is striking, and often makes the hearer feel that he is moving in the thick of the danger:

> You would say that they met in the shock of war, all unwearied and undaunted, so impetuously did they rush into the fray.[2]

Then there is Aratus's

> Do not in that month entrust yourself to the surges of the ocean.[3]

Herodotus does much the same kind of thing: 'From the city of Elephantine you will sail upwards, until you come to a level plain; and after you have crossed this tract, you will board again another ship and sail for two days, and then you will come to a great city whose name is Meroe.'[4] You see, my friend, how, as he takes you in imagination through the places in question, he transforms hearing into sight. All such passages, by their direct personal form of address, bring the hearer right into the middle of the action being described. When you seem to be addressing, not the whole audience, but a single member of it

> But you would not have known of Tydeus's son for which of the armies he fought—[1]

you will affect him more profoundly, and make him more attentive and full of active interest, if you rouse him by these appeals to him personally.

CHAPTER 27

POLYPTOTON: CONVERSION TO THE FIRST PERSON

AGAIN, there are times when a writer, while speaking of a character, suddenly breaks off and converts himself into that character. A figure of this kind is in a way an outburst of emotion:

> And with a far-echoing shout Hector cried out to the Trojans to rush against the ships and leave the blood-spattered spoils. And if I spy anyone who of his own will holds back from the ships, I will surely bring about his death.[2]

Here the poet has taken upon himself the presentation of the narrative, as is appropriate, and then suddenly, without any warning, has attributed the abrupt threat to the angry chieftain. Had he inserted, 'Hector said so and so', it would have given a frigid effect; as it is, the change in form of the passage has anticipated the sudden change of speakers. Accordingly this figure should be used for preference when a sudden crisis will not give the author time to linger, but compels him to change at once from one character to another.

There is another example in Hecataeus:[3] 'Ceyx took this badly and at once ordered the descendants of Heracles to depart. For it is not in my

---

[1] Xenophon, *Cyropaedia* VII, i, 37.

[2] *Iliad* XV, 697–8.

[3] Aratus (*fl.* 270 B.C.), one of the didactic poets of Alexandria. This is line 299 of his *Phaenomena.*

[4] Herodotus, II, 29.

[1] *Iliad* V, 85.

[2] *Iliad* XV, 346–9.

[3] Hecataeus of Miletus (*fl.* 520 B.C.), historian and geographer.

power to help you. Therefore, in order that you may not perish yourselves and injure me, take yourselves off to some other country.'

In his *Aristogeiton* Demosthenes has by a rather different method used change of person to indicate a rapid play of emotion. 'And will none of you,' he says, 'be found to feel disgust and indignation at the violence of this vile and shameless creature, who—O, you most abandoned of men—whose unbridled speech is not shut in by gates and doors which might well be opened. . . .'[1] With his sense incomplete, he has made a sudden change, and in his indignation has all but split a single phrase between two persons—'who—O, you most abandoned . . . '. Thus, while he has turned his speech round to address Aristogeiton, and seems to have left him out of account,[2] yet with this display of passion he has turned it on him much more forcefully. The same thing occurs in Penelope's speech:

> Herald, why have those highborn suitors sent you here? Is it to tell the handmaids of the godlike Odysseus to cease from their labours and prepare a banquet for them? Would that they had never wooed me, nor elsewhere gathered together, that this now were the latest and last of their feasting, you that assemble together and waste so much of our substance, the store of the prudent Telemachus. Nor did you ever in the bygone days of your childhood hear from your fathers what manner of man Odysseus was.[3]

[1] Demosthenes, *Aristogeiton* I, 27.

[2] There is an inconsistency here. W. Hamilton Fyfe has in his translation accepted a conjectural emendation which enables him to read, 'while swinging his speech round on to Aristogeiton and appearing to abandon the jury. . . .'

[3] *Odyssey* IV, 681–9.

CHAPTER 28

PERIPHRASIS

NO one, I think, would dispute that periphrasis contributes to the sublime. For as in music the sweetness of the dominant melody is enhanced by what are known as the decorative additions, so periphrasis often harmonizes with the direct expression of a thought and greatly embellishes it, especially if it is not bombastic or inelegant, but pleasantly tempered.

This is pretty well illustrated by Plato at the beginning of his Funeral Oration:[1] 'We have done what gives them the tribute that is their due, and having gained this, they proceed along their appointed path, escorted publicly by their country, and each man privately by his kinsfolk.' Death, you see, he calls 'their appointed path', and their having been granted the accustomed rites he describes as a kind of 'public escort on the part of their native land'. Surely he has considerably increased the dignity of his conception here. Has he not made music of the unadorned diction that was his starting-point, and shed over it with something of a tuneful harmony the melodiousness that arises from his periphrasis?

Then there is Xenophon: 'You regard toil as the guide to a life of pleasure; you have garnered in your hearts the best of all possessions and the fittest for warriors. For nothing rejoices you so much as praise.'[2] By rejecting 'you are willing to work hard' in favour of 'you make toil the guide to a life of pleasure', and by expanding the rest of the sentence in the same way, he has added to his eulogy a certain grandeur of thought. And this is true also of that inimitable sentence in Herodotus: 'Upon those Scythians who despoiled her temple the goddess cast a malady that made women of them.'[3]

[1] Plato, *Menexenus* 236 D.

[2] Xenophon, *Cyropaedia* I, v, 12.

[3] Herodotus, I, 105.

CHAPTER 29

THE DANGERS OF PERIPHRASIS

HOWEVER, periphrasis is a hazardous business, more so than any other figure, unless it is used with a certain sense of proportion. For it quickly lapses into insipidity, akin to empty chatter and dullness of wit. This is why even Plato, who always uses figures with skill, but sometimes with a certain lack of timeliness, is mocked when he says in his *Laws* that 'neither golden nor silver treasure should be allowed to establish itself and dwell in a city';[1] so that if he had been forbidding people to possess herds, says the critic, he would obviously have said 'ovine and bovine treasure'.

However, my digression on the use of figures and their bearing on the sublime has gone on long enough, my dear Terentianus. They are all means of increasing the animation and the emotional impact of style, and emotional effects play as large a part in the production of the sublime as the study of character does in the production of pleasure.

[1] *Laws* 801 B.

CHAPTER 30

THE PROPER CHOICE OF DICTION

SINCE in discourse thought and diction are for the most part mutually interdependent, we must further consider whether any other elements that come under the heading of diction remain to be studied. It is probably superfluous to explain to those who already know it how wonderfully the choice of appropriate and high-sounding words moves and enchants an audience, and to remind them that such a choice is the highest aim of all orators and authors; for of itself it imparts to style, as though to the finest statues, at once grandeur, beauty, mellowness, weight, force, power, and any other worthy quality you can think of, and endows the facts as it were with a living voice. For words finely used are in truth the very light of thought. Yet it would not do to use such grand diction all the time, for to apply great and stately terms to trifling matters would be like putting a big tragic mask on a tiny child. However, in poetry and . . .

(Here four pages of the manuscript are missing)

CHAPTER 31

FAMILIAR LANGUAGE

. . . very thought-provoking and powerful; so too is Anacreon's 'No longer do I care for the Thracian filly.'[1] In this way also that unusual term employed by Theopompus deserves praise, for by reason of the analogy implied it seems to me to be highly expressive, although Cecilius for some reason finds fault with it: 'Philip,' says Theopompus, 'had a genius for stomaching things.' Now the homely term is sometimes much more expressive than elegant diction, for, being taken from everyday life, it is at once recognized, and carries the more conviction from its familiarity. Thus, in connexion with a man whose greedy nature makes him put up patiently and cheerfully with things that are shameful and sordid, the words 'stomaching things' are extremely vivid.[2] Much the same may be said of Herodotus's expressions: 'Cleomenes in his madness cut his own flesh into strips with a dagger until, having made a thorough mince of himself, he perished;' and 'Pythes continued fighting on the ship until he was all cut into shreds.'[3] These expressions are on the very

[1] From a fragment of Anacreon, the sixth-century lyric poet. The word 'filly' used here is derived from a conjectural emendation which is suggested by the context, and which seems appropriate to the point that Longinus is making.

[2] Theopompus was a historian of the mid fourth century B.C., a disciple of Isocrates.

[3] Herodotus, VI, 75; VII, 181.

edge of vulgarity, but their expressiveness saves them from actually being vulgar.

CHAPTER 32

METAPHOR

WITH regard to the appropriate number of metaphors, Cecilius appears to side with those who lay down that two, or at most three, should be brought together in the same passage. Demosthenes is again the standard in this context. The appropriate occasion for their use is when the emotions come pouring out like a torrent, and irresistibly carry along with them a host of metaphors. 'Men,' he says, 'who are steeped in blood, who are flatterers, who have each of them mutilated the limbs of their own fatherlands, who have pledged their liberty by drinking first to Philip, and now to Alexander, measuring their happiness by their bellies and their basest appetites, and who have uprooted that liberty and that freedom from despotism which were to the Greeks of earlier days the rules and standards of integrity.'[1] Here the orator's indignation against the traitors casts a veil over the number of figurative expressions he has used.

Now Aristotle and Theophrastus declare that the following phrases have a softening effect on bold metaphors: 'as if', and 'as it were', and 'if one may put it like this', and 'if one may venture the expression'; for the qualifications, they say, mitigate the boldness. I accept this, but at the same time, as I said when I was talking about rhetorical figures, the timely expression of violent emotions, together with true sublimity, is the appropriate antidote for the number and boldness of metaphors. For the onward rush of passion has the property of sweeping everything before it, or rather of requiring bold imagery as something altogether indispensable; it does not allow the hearer leisure to consider the number of metaphors, since he is carried away by the enthusiasm of the speaker.

[1] *De Corona* 296.

Furthermore, in the handling of commonplaces and of description nothing so much confers distinction as a continuous series of metaphors. It is by this means that the anatomy of the human body is superbly depicted in Xenophon,[1] and still more divinely in Plato.[2] The head, says Plato, is a citadel, and the neck is constructed as an isthmus between the head and the breast; and the vertebrae, he says, are set below like pivots. Pleasure tempts men to evil, and the tongue is the touchstone of taste. The heart is the fuel-store of the veins, the fountain from which the blood begins its vigorous course, and it keeps its station in the guard-house of the body. The various passages he calls the lanes. 'And for the thumping of the heart which takes place when danger is imminent or when anger is rising, when it becomes fiery-hot, the gods,' he says, 'have devised some relief by implanting the lungs, which, being soft and bloodless, and pierced inwardly with pores, serve as a kind of buffer, so that when anger boils up in the heart, it may throb against a yielding substance and not be damaged.' The seat of the desires he compares with the women's apartments, and that of anger with the men's. Then the spleen is the napkin of the entrails, from which it is filled with waste matter, and swells and festers. 'And after this,' he says, 'they covered everything over with flesh, which they put there, like felt matting, as a protection against attacks from outside.' And he called the blood the fodder of the flesh, adding that, 'in order to provide nourishment, they irrigated the body, cutting channels as is done in gardens, so that, the body being perforated with conduits, the rivulets of the veins might flow on as though from some never-failing

[1] *Memorabilia* I, iv, 5.

[2] The descriptions are drawn from the *Timaeus* 65 C–85 E.

source.' And when the end comes, he says, the cables of the soul, like those of a ship, are loosed, and she is set free. These and innumerable similar metaphors form a continuous succession. But those I have mentioned are enough to show that figurative language is a natural source of grandeur, and that metaphors contribute to sublimity; and also that it is emotional and descriptive passages that most gladly find room for them.

However, it is obvious, even without my stating it, that the use of metaphors, like all the other beauties of style, is liable to lead to excess. In this respect even Plato is severely criticized, on the ground that he is often carried away by a kind of linguistic frenzy into harsh and intemperate metaphors and bombastic allegory. 'For it is not easy to see,' he says, 'that a city needs to be mixed like a bowl of wine, in which the strong, raging wine seethes as it is poured in, but when it is chastened by another god who is sober, its association with such good company turns it into an excellent and temperate drink.'[1] To call water 'a sober god', say the critics, and to describe mixing as 'chastening', is to use the language of some poet who is not in fact sober.

Cecilius, too, has picked on such defects as these, and in the works he has written in praise of Lysias he has actually dared to represent Lysias as being in all respects superior to Plato. But here he has given way to two uncritical impulses; for although he is even fonder of Lysias than of himself, his hatred for Plato altogether surpasses his love for Lysias. However, he is merely being contentious, and his premisses are not, as he thought, admitted. For he prefers the orator, whom he regards as faultless and without blemish, to Plato, who often made mistakes. But this is not the truth of the matter, nor anything like the truth.

[1] Plato, *Laws* 773 C.

CHAPTER 33

SUPERIORITY OF FLAWED SUBLIMITY TO FLAWLESS MEDIOCRITY

SUPPOSE we take some writer who really may be considered flawless and beyond reproach. In this context we must surely ask ourselves in general terms, with reference to both verse and prose, which is superior, grandeur accompanied by a few flaws, or mediocre correctness, entirely sound and free from error though it may be. Yes, and further, whether in literature the first place should rightly be given to the greater number of virtues, or to virtues which are greater in themselves. For these questions are proper to a study of sublimity, and for every reason they should be resolved.

Now I am well aware that the highest genius is very far from being flawless, for entire accuracy runs the risk of descending to triviality, whereas in the grand manner, as in the possession of great wealth, something is bound to be neglected. Again, it may be inevitable that men of humble or mediocre endowments, who never run any risks and never aim at the heights, should in the normal course of events enjoy a greater freedom from error, while great abilities remain subject to danger by reason of their very greatness. And in the second place, I know that it is always the less admirable aspects of all human endeavours that are most widely noticed; the remembrance of mistakes remains ineradicable, while that of virtues quickly melts away.

I have myself observed a good many faults in Homer and other authors of the highest distinction, and I cannot say that I enjoy finding these slips; however, I would not call them wilful errors, but rather careless oversights let in casually and at random by the heedlessness of genius. I am none the less certain that the greater virtues, even if they are not consistently shown throughout the composition, should always be voted into the first place—for the greatness of mind that they represent, if for no other reason. Now Apollonius reveals himself in his *Argonautica*[1] as an impeccable poet, and Theocritus is extremely successful in his pastorals, apart from a few surface blemishes. Yet would you not rather choose to be Homer than Apollonius?

And again, is Eratosthenes in his *Erigone*,[2] which is an entirely flawless little poem, a greater poet than Archilochus, whose verse is often ill-arranged, but who has surges of a divine inspiration which it would be difficult to bring under the control of rules? Furthermore, would you choose as a lyrical poet to be Bacchylides rather than Pindar? And in tragedy Ion of Chios rather than Sophocles? Bacchylides and Ion are, it is true, faultless and elegant writers in the polished manner. But Pindar and Sophocles seem at times in their impetuous career to burn up everything in their path, although their fire is often unaccountably quenched, and they lapse into a most miserable flatness. Yet would anyone in his senses put the whole series of Ion's works on the same footing as the single play of *Oedipus*?

CHAPTER 34

HYPERIDES AND DEMOSTHENES

IF success in composition were not judged according to true standards, then Hyperides would be ranked altogether higher than Demosthenes. For he has more variety of tone than Demosthenes, and more numerous merits. In every branch of his art he is very nearly in the first flight, like the pentathlete; in each contest he is inferior to the champions among his rivals, but comes first among the amateurs.

Now Hyperides not only imitates all the virtues of Demosthenes except his talent in composition; he has also with uncommon success taken to his province the merits and graces of Lysias. For he talks plainly, when this is required, and does not like Demosthenes make all his points in a monotonous series. He has, too, a gift for characterization, seasoned with charm and simplicity. Moreover, he has considerable wit, a most urbane raillery, true nobility of manner, a ready skill in exchanges of irony, a fund of jokes which, in the Attic manner, are neither tasteless nor ill-bred, but always to the point, a clever touch in satire, and plenty of comic force and pointed ridicule combined with a well-directed sense of fun—and all this invested with an inimitable elegance. He is very well endowed by nature with the power to awaken pity. He is a fluent story-teller, and with his easy flow of inspiration has an excellent faculty for winding his way through a digression, as of course he shows in his somewhat poetic handling of the story of Leto. And he has treated his Funeral Oration as, I think, no one else could have done it.

Demosthenes, on the other hand, is not good at describing character. He is not concise, nor has he any fluency nor any talent for delivering set orations. In general he partakes of none of the merits that have just been listed. When he is forced into attempting a joke or a witticism, he does not so much raise laughter at what he says as make himself the object of laughter, and when he wants to exert a little charm, he comes nowhere near doing so. If he had tried to write the little speeches on Phryne or Athenogenes, he would have made us think even more highly of Hyperides.[1] All the same, in my opinion the virtues of Hyperides, many as they may be, are wanting in the requisite grandeur; the productions of a sober-hearted fellow, they are staid and do not disturb the peace of mind of the audience—certainly no one who reads Hyperides is frightened by him. But when Demosthenes takes up

---

[1] Apollonius Rhodius (*fl.* 240 B.C.) was the foremost Alexandrian epic poet; his *Argonautica,* an epic in four books on the story of Jason and the Argonauts, is extant.

[2] Eratosthenes, a versatile Alexandrian author and scholar of the third century B.C. The *Erigone* is an elegy based on the story of Icarius, his daughter Erigone, and his dog Maera.

---

[1] Hyperides's speech against Athenogenes was recovered last century; his defence of Phryne is lost.

the tale, he displays the virtues of great genius in their highest form: a sublime intensity, lifelike passions, copiousness, readiness, speed, where it is appropriate, and his own unapproachable power and vehemence. Having, I say, made himself master of all the riches of these mighty, heaven-sent gifts—for it would not be right to call them human—he invariably, by reason of the virtues he possesses, puts down all his rivals, and this even where the qualities he does not possess are concerned; it might be said, indeed, that he overpowers with his thunder and lightning the orators of every age. One could more easily outface a descending thunderbolt than meet unflinchingly his continual outbursts of passion.

CHAPTER 35

PLATO AND LYSIAS

IN the case of Plato and Lysias there is, as I have said, a further point of difference. Lysias is much inferior to Plato in both the greatness and the number of his merits, and at the same time he surpasses him in his faults even more than he falls short of him in his virtues.

What then was in the mind of those godlike authors who, aiming at the highest flights of composition, showed no respect for detailed accuracy? Among many other things this—that nature has adjudged us men to be creatures of no mean or ignoble quality. Rather, as though inviting us to some great festival, she has brought us into life, into the whole vast universe, there to be spectators of all that she has created and the keenest aspirants for renown; and thus from the first she has implanted in our souls an unconquerable passion for all that is great and for all that is more divine than ourselves. For this reason the entire universe does not satisfy the contemplation and thought that lie within the scope of human endeavour; our ideas often go beyond the boundaries by which we are circumscribed, and if we look at life from all sides, observing how in everything that concerns us the extraordinary, the great, and the beautiful play the leading part, we shall soon realize the purpose of our creation.

This is why, by some sort of natural instinct, we admire, not, surely, the small streams, beautifully clear though they may be, and useful too, but the Nile, the Danube, the Rhine, and even more than these the Ocean. The little fire that we have kindled ourselves, clear and steady as its flame may be, does not strike us with as much awe as the heavenly fires, in spite of their often being shrouded in darkness; nor do we think it a greater marvel than the craters of Etna, whose eruptions throw up from their depths rocks and even whole mountains, and at times pour out rivers of that pure Titanian fire. In all such circumstances, I would say only this, that men hold cheap what is useful and necessary, and always reserve their admiration for what is out of the ordinary.

CHAPTER 36

SUBLIMITY AND LITERARY FAME

NOW with regard to authors of genius, whose grandeur always has some bearing on questions of utility and profit,[1] it must be observed at the outset that, while writers of this quality are far from being faultless, yet they all rise above the human level. All other attributes prove their possessors to be men, but sublimity carries one up to where one is close to the majestic mind of God. Freedom from error escapes censure, but the grand style excites admiration as well. It need scarcely be added that each of these outstanding authors time and again redeems all his failures by a single happy stroke of sublimity; and, most decisive of all, that if we were to pick out all the blunders of Homer,

[1] Which is not the case with all the grandeurs of nature named in the previous chapter.

Demosthenes, Plato, and the greatest of all our other authors, and were to put them all together, it would be found that they amounted to a very small part, say rather an infinitesimal fraction, of the triumphs achieved by these demigods on every page. That is why the judgement of all ages, which envy itself cannot convict of perversity, has awarded them the palm of victory, guarding it as their inalienable right, and likely so to preserve it 'as long as rivers run and tall trees flourish'.[1]

As for the writer who maintains that the faulty Colossus is not superior to Polycleitus's spearman, one obvious retort, among many others, is to point out that meticulous accuracy is admired in art, grandeur in the works of nature, and that it is by nature that man is endowed with the power of speech. Moreover, in statues we look for the likeness of a man, whereas in literature, as I have said, we look for something transcending the human. However, to revert to the doctrine with which I began my commentary,[2] since freedom from faults is usually the result of art, and distinction of style, however unevenly sustained, is due to genius, it is right that art should everywhere be employed as a supplement to nature, for in cooperation the two may bring about perfection.

So much it has been necessary to say in order to resolve the problems before us. But everyone is welcome to his own taste.

CHAPTER 37

COMPARISONS AND SIMILES

CLOSELY related to metaphors—for we must go back to them—are comparisons and similes, which differ only in this. . . .

[1] Author unknown. Also quoted in a slightly different form as part of a longer quotation in Plato, *Phaedrus* 264 C.

[2] See Chapter 2.

(Here two pages of the manuscript are missing)

CHAPTER 38

HYPERBOLES

. . . and such hyperboles as, 'Unless you carry your brains trodden down in your heels'.[1] One must therefore know in each case where to draw the line, for sometimes if one overshoots the mark one spoils the effect of the hyperbole, and if such expressions are strained too far they fall flat, and sometimes produce the opposite effect to that which was intended. Isocrates, for example, unaccountably lapsed into childishness through the ambition which led to his fondness for exaggeration. The theme of his *Panegyric* is that Athens is superior to Sparta in the benefits that she has conferred on the Greeks, but at the very beginning he declares: 'Moreover, words have such power that they can make what is grand humble, and endow petty things with greatness; they can express old ideas in a new way, and discuss what has just happened in the style of long ago.'[2] 'Do you then by these means, Isocrates,' says someone, 'intend to interchange the roles of the Athenians and the Spartans?' For in his eulogy of the power of language he has all but made a prefatory announcement to his auditors that he himself is not to be trusted. Perhaps then, as I said earlier about rhetorical figures,[3] the best hyperboles are those which conceal the fact that they are hyperboles. And this happens when, under the influence of powerful emotion, they are used in connexion with some great circumstance, as is the case with Thucydides when he speaks of those who perished in Sicily. 'For the Syracusans,' he says, 'went down and began their slaughter, especially of those who

[1] From a work at one time ascribed to Demosthenes, *De Halonneso* 45.

[2] Isocrates, *Panegyric* 8.

[3] Chapter 17.

were in the river. And the water was immediately polluted; but none the less it was drunk, thick though it was with mud and blood, and most of them still thought it was worth fighting for.'[1] That a drink of mud and blood should still be worth fighting for is made credible by the height of the emotions excited by the circumstances.

The same is true of Herodotus's account of those who fought at Thermopylae. 'In this place,' he says, 'as they were defending themselves with their daggers, such of them as still had daggers, and with their very hands and mouths, the barbarians buried them.'[2] Here you may ask what is meant by fighting against armed men 'with their very mouths', and being 'buried' with arrows. At the same time the expressions carry conviction, for the incident does not seem to be introduced for the sake of the hyperbole, but the hyperbole seems to take its rise quite plausibly from the incident. For as I keep on saying, actions and feelings which come close to sweeping us off our feet serve as an excuse and a lenitive for any kind of daring phraseology. This is why, even when they reach the point of being actually incredible, the shafts of comedy also seem plausible from their very laughability, as in

> The field he had was smaller than a letter.[3]

For laughter, too, is an emotion, related as it is to pleasure.

Hyperboles may apply just as much to petty things as to great, an overstraining of the facts being the common element. In a sense satire is the exaggeration of pettiness.

[1] Thucydides, VII, 84.

[2] Herodotus, VII, 255.

[3] Author unknown.

CHAPTER 39

COMPOSITION, OR DISPOSITION OF MATERIAL

THE fifth of the factors contributing to the sublime which I specified at the beginning remains to be dealt with, my friend, and that is the arrangement of the words in due order. On this matter I have already in two treatises given an adequate account of such conclusions as I could reach; for my present purpose I need only add the essential fact that men find in a harmonious arrangement of sounds, not only a natural medium of persuasion and pleasure, but also a marvellous instrument of grandeur and passion. For does not the flute instil certain emotions into those that hear it, seeming to carry them away and fill them with a divine frenzy? Does it not give rhythmic movement, and compel the hearer to conform to the melody and adapt his own movements to this rhythm, even if he is not in the least musical? Then the tones of the harp, in themselves meaningless, often cast a wonderful spell, as you know, by their variations in sound and the throbbing interplay and harmonious blending of the notes struck.

Yet these are mere semblances, spurious counterfeits of the art of persuasion, and not, as I have mentioned, a genuine expression of human nature. Now composition is a kind of harmony of the words which are implanted in man at his birth, and which affect not his hearing alone but his very soul, and it is my belief that it brings out manifold patterns of words, thoughts, deeds, beauty, and melody, all of them originally born and bred in us; moreover, by the blending of its myriad tones it brings into the hearts of the bystanders the actual emotion of the speaker, and always induces them to share it; and finally it builds up an accumulation of phrases into a grand and harmonious structure. Are we not to believe that by these means it casts a spell on us, and draws our thoughts towards what is majestic and dignified and sublime, and towards any other potentialities which it embraces, gaining a complete mastery over our minds? But it is madness to dispute on matters which are the subject of such general agreement, since experience is sufficient proof.

An idea which appears sublime, and which is certainly to be admired, is that which Demosthenes associates with his decree: 'This decree caused the peril which at that time encompassed the city to pass away just like a cloud.'[1] But its ring owes no less to the harmony than to the thought, for its delivery rests entirely on the dactylic rhythms, which are the noblest of rhythms and make for grandeur—which is why the heroic measure, the most beautiful of known measures, is composed of dactyls. And indeed, if you moved it wherever you liked away from its proper place,[2] and said, 'this decree, just like a cloud, caused the peril at that time to pass away', or if you cut out a single syllable and said, 'caused to pass away like a cloud', you would realize how far the harmony of sound chimes in with the sublimity. For 'just like a cloud' starts off with a long rhythm, consisting of four metrical beats, and if you remove a single syllable and write 'like a cloud', by this abbreviation you at once mutilate the effect of grandeur. And again, if you stretch the phrase out with 'caused to pass away just as if a cloud', the meaning is the same, but it no longer falls on the ear with the same effect because, by the drawing out of the final beats, the sheer sublimity of the passage is robbed of its solidity and of its tension.

[1] *De Corona* 188.

[2] The awkwardness here is due to corruption in the text, the loss perhaps of a phrase, perhaps of a preceding sentence, which would have indicated that 'it' refers to the last phrase of the decree, 'just like a cloud'. It is difficult to find English equivalents for most of the technicalities of this paragraph.

CHAPTER 40

THE STRUCTURE OF THE SENTENCE

AMONG the chief agents in the formation of the grand style is the proper combination of the constituent members—as is true of the human body and its members. Of itself no single member, when dissociated from any other, has anything worthy of note about it, but when they are all mutually interconnected they make up a perfect whole. Similarly, when the elements of grandeur are separated from one another, they carry the sublimity along with them, dispersing it in every direction; but when they are combined into a single organism, and, moreover, enclosed within the bonds of harmony, they form a rounded whole, and their voice is loud and clear, and in the periods thus formed the grandeur receives contributions, as it were, from a variety of factors. I have, however, sufficiently demonstrated that many writers both of prose and verse who have no natural gift of sublimity, or even of grandeur, and who for the most part employ common and popular words which carry no extraordinary associations, have nevertheless, by merely combining and fitting these words together in the right order, achieved dignity and distinction and an appearance of grandeur—among many others Philistus,[1] for example, Aristophanes at times, and Euripides as a rule.

After the slaughter of his children Heracles says,

> I am stowed to the hatches with woes,
> and there is no room for more.[2]

The expression is extremely vulgar, but it becomes sublime by reason of its aptness to its setting. If you fit the passage together in any other way, you will realize that Euripides is a poet rather by virtue

[1] A Sicilian historian of the fourth century.

[2] Euripides, *Hercules Furens* 1245.

of his power of composition than of his ideas. Writing of Dirce being dragged away by the bull, he says:

> And wheresoever he chanced to wheel around, he seized and dragged along at once woman or rock or oak, now this, now that.[1]

This idea is excellent in itself, but gains further strength from the fact that the rhythm is not hurried or as it were carried along on rollers, but the words offer resistance to one another and derive support from the pauses, and take their stand in a firmly-based grandeur.

CHAPTER 41

SOME IMPEDIMENTS TO SUBLIMITY

WHERE the sublime is concerned nothing has so debasing an effect as broken or agitated rhythms, such as pyrrhics (⏑⏑), trochees (-⏑), and dichorees (-⏑-⏑), which drop right down to the level of dance-music. For all over-rhythmical styles are at once felt to be cheap and affected; the monotonous jingle seems superficial, and does not penetrate our feelings—and the worst of it is that, just as choral lyrics distract the audience's attention from the action of the play and forcibly turn it to themselves, so also an over-rhythmical style does not communicate the feeling of the words, but only of the rhythm. And so there are times when the hearers foresee the likely endings and themselves break in on the speaker, and, as might happen in dancing, they anticipate the steps and finish too soon.

Equally wanting in grandeur are passages which are too close-packed, or cut up into tiny phrases and words with short syllables, giving the impression of being roughly and unevenly held together with pins.

CHAPTER 42

CONCISENESS

FURTHERMORE, excessive conciseness in expression reduces sublimity, for grandeur is marred when it is too closely compressed. You must take this to mean, not compression that is properly used, but what is entirely broken up into fragments and thus frittered away. For excessive conciseness curtails the sense where brevity goes straight to the point. On the other hand, it is clear that prolixity is lifeless, since it entails an unseasonable length.

CHAPTER 43

TRIVIALITY OF EXPRESSION, AND AMPLIFICATION

THE use of trivial words terribly disfigures passages in the grand style. For example, as far as content is concerned, the storm in Herodotus is marvellously described, but the description contains certain details which are, heaven knows, too far below the dignity of the subject. One might perhaps instance 'when the sea boiled', where the word 'boiled' is so cacophonous as to detract greatly from the sublimity. Then 'the wind,' he says, 'grew fagged'; and 'an unpleasant end' awaited those who were clinging to the wreck.[1] The phrase 'grew fagged' is uncouth, and lacks dignity, and 'unpleasant' is inappropriate to so great a disaster.

Similarly, when Theopompus had given a marvellous account of the Persian King's descent into

---

[1] From the lost *Antiope* of Euripides.

[1] Herodotus, VII, 188; VII, 191; VIII, 13.

Egypt, he spoiled the whole description by the use of some trivial words. 'For which city and which tribe of all those in Asia,' he says, 'did not send envoys to the King? And which of the products of the earth or of the beautiful or precious achievements of art was not brought to him as an offering? Were there not many costly coverlets and mantles, purple and white and multi-coloured, many pavilions of gold furnished with all things needful, many robes of state and costly couches? Further, there was silver and gold plate richly wrought, goblets and mixing-bowls, some of which you might have seen studded with jewels, others embellished in a cunning and costly fashion. In addition to these there were countless myriads of weapons, both Greek and barbarian, and beasts of burden beyond number, and sacrificial victims fattened for the slaughter; and many bushels of spices, and bags and sacks and sheets of papyrus and all other useful things; and such a store of preserved flesh from every kind of victim as to form piles so large that anyone approaching them from a distance took them for mounds and hills confronting them.'

Here Theopompus runs from the sublime to the trivial where he ought, on the contrary, to have been heightening his effects. By mixing bags and spices and sacks with the wonderful report of the equipment as a whole, he has almost given the impression of a cook-shop. Suppose that among all those decorative objects, among the golden and jewelled mixing bowls, the silver plate, the pavilions of pure gold, and the goblets—suppose that someone had actually brought paltry bags and sacks and placed them in the midst of all these, his action would have produced an effect that offended the eye. Well, in the same way the untimely introduction of such words as these as it were disfigures and debases the description. He could have given a general account, as he speaks of the 'hills' of flesh being built up, and with regard to the rest of the provisions have spoken of wagons and camels and a host of baggage-animals laden with everything that ministers to the luxury and the pleasures of the table; or he could have called them piles of all kinds of grain and of all that conduces to fine cooking and good living; or if he had to put it so explicitly, he could have spoken of all the delicacies of caterers and good cooks.

In sublime passages we ought not to resort to sordid and contemptible terms unless constrained by some extreme necessity. We should use words that suit the dignity of the subject, and imitate nature, the artist who has fashioned man, for she has not placed in full view our private parts or the means by which our whole frame is purged, but as far as possible has concealed them, and, as Xenophon says,[1] has put their passages into the farthest background so as not to sully the beauty of the whole figure.

However, there is no urgent need to enumerate and classify the things that lead to triviality. For as I have previously indicated the qualities that furnish style with nobility and sublimity, it is obvious that their opposities will for the most part make it mean and ugly.

CHAPTER 44

THE DECAY OF ELOQUENCE

HOWEVER, as in view of your love of learning I will not hesitate to add, my dear Terentianus, there remains to be cleared up a problem to which a certain philosopher has recently applied his wits. 'I wonder,' he said, 'as no doubt do many other people, why it is that in our age there are men well fitted for public life who are extremely persuasive, who are keen and shrewd, and especially well endowed with literary charm, and yet really sublime and transcendent natures are, with few exceptions, no longer produced. Such a great and world-wide dearth of literature attends our age! Are we,' he

[1] *Memorabilia* I, iv, 6.

went on, 'are we to accept the well-worn view that democracy is the kindly nurse of great men, and that great men of letters may be said to have flourished only under democracy and perished with it? For freedom, they say, has the power to foster the imaginations of high-souled men and to inspire them with hope, and with it there spreads the keenness of mutual rivalry and an eager competition for the first place. Furthermore, by reason of the prizes which are open to all in republics, the intellectual gifts of orators are continually sharpened by practice and as it were kept bright by rubbing, and, as might be expected, these gifts, fostered in freedom, help to shed light on the affairs of state. Nowadays,' he continued, 'we seem to absorb from our childhood onwards the lessons of the slavery to which we are accustomed, all but swaddled in the infancy of our minds as we are in slavish customs and observances, and never tasting of the finest and most productive source of eloquence, by which I mean freedom; and thus we emerge as nothing but sublime flatterers.'

This, he maintained, was the reason why, although all other faculties may fall to the lot even of menials, no slave ever becomes an orator; for the fact that he has no freedom of speech, that he lives as it were a dungeoned life, and that he is always liable to be beaten, comes bubbling up to the surface. As Homer puts it, 'The day of our enslavement takes away half our manhood.'[1] 'And so,' went on the philosopher, 'just as the cages in which they keep the Pygmies, or dwarfs, as they call them, not only stunt the growth of these who are imprisoned in them, if what I hear is true, but also shrink them by reason of the fetters fixed round their bodies, so all slavery, however just it may be, could well be described as a cage of the soul, a common prison-house.'

However, I took him up and said: 'It is easy, my good sir, and a characteristic of human nature, always to be finding fault with the present state of affairs. But consider whether it may be that it is not the peace of this world of ours that corrupts great natures, but much rather this endless war which holds our desires in its grasp, yes, and further still the passions that garrison our lives nowadays and utterly devastate them. For the love of money, that insatiable craving from which we all now suffer, and the love of pleasure make us their slaves, or rather, one might say, sink our lives (body and soul) into the depths, the love of money being a disease that makes us petty-minded, and the love of pleasure an utterly ignoble attribute.

'On further reflection, indeed, I do not see how, if we value the possession of unlimited wealth, or, to give the truth of the matter, make a god of it, we can avoid allowing the evils that naturally attend its entry into our souls. For vast and unlimited wealth is closely followed—step by step, as they say—by extravagance, and no sooner has the one opened the gates of cities and houses than the other comes in and joins it in setting up house there. With the passing of time, according to the philosophers, they build nests in our lives, and soon set about begetting offspring, giving birth to pretentiousness, vanity, and luxury—no bastards these, but very much their true-born issue. And if these children of wealth are allowed to reach maturity they soon breed in our hearts implacable masters, insolence and lawlessness and shamelessness. This will inevitably happen, and then men will no longer lift up their eyes nor take any further thought for their good name; the ruin of their lives will gradually be completed as their grandeur of soul withers and fades until it sinks into contempt, when they become lost in admiration of their mortal capabilities and neglect to develop the immortal.

'A man who has accepted a bribe for a verdict would never be a sound and unbiased judge of what is just and honourable, for a corrupt judge must necessarily regard his own private interests as honourable and just. And where bribery now governs all our lives, and we hunt others to death,

[1] *Odyssey* XVII, 332.

and lay traps for legacies, and bargain our souls for gain from any and every source, having become slaves to [luxury], can we expect, in this pestilential ruin of our lives, that there should still remain an unbiased and incorruptible judge of works which possess grandeur or enduring life, and that he would not be overcome by his passion for gain? For such men as we are, indeed, it is perhaps better that we should be ruled than live in freedom. If we were given complete liberty, like released prisoners, our consuming greed for our neighbours' possessions might set the world on fire with our deeds of evil.'

In short, I maintained that what wears down the spirit of the present generation is the apathy in which, with few exceptions, we all pass our lives; for we do no work nor show any enterprise from any other motives than those of being praised or being able to enjoy our pleasures—never from an eager and honourable desire to serve our fellows.

'It is best to leave such things at a guess',[1] and to pass on to the next problem, that is, the emotions, about which I previously undertook to write in a separate treatise, for they seem to me to share a place in literature generally, and especially in the sublime . . .

(The rest is lost)

---

[1] Euripides, *Electra* 379.

❖

Middle Ages and Renaissance

INTRODUCTION TO THE MIDDLE AGES AND RENAISSANCE

Development of Roman rhetorical theory stymied after the first century C.E. The repressions of the military dictatorships took their toll on the exercise and theory of rhetoric. The Roman Empire itself eventually began to decline, a victim of its own size, corruption, and the growing military power of Germanic and Slavic tribes to the north and east.

The Roman Empire at its peak spread from the British Isles into what is now Russia and Turkey beyond the Black Sea. In an age of limited communication technology and relatively slow transportation, it became unwieldy to manage these holdings entirely from Rome. Eventually a second capital of the Empire was established at the city of Byzantium, or Constantinople, now known as Istanbul, Turkey.

Roman government and society grew progressively more decadent, more dependent on conquest and military power for its economic base, and more unstable as incompetent caesars replaced one another through violent overthrows. Tribes to the north and east such as the Goths, Visigoths, Huns, and Vandals grew more powerful militarily and began moving into Roman territory. Many theories have been advanced for why Rome decayed and fell; some have suggested that the high presence of lead in Roman drinking and eating vessels weakened the population through poisoning!

Whatever the reason, the military pressures from outside the Empire grew and defeats mounted until eventually the Empire in the west, grounded in Rome, fell in the sacking of Rome in the year 410. The Empire completed its process of collapse and its distant outposts were taken over by indigenous populations. However, the Empire in the east continued to hold together for several centuries thereafter. What became the Byzantine Empire perpetuated stable government and society under an imperial form of government.

These political and military developments must also be considered in light of another development of absolutely vital importance: the growth of the Christian Church. Founded in the first century C.E. and persecuted in the first years of its existence, by the time of the fall of Rome the Church had become an established power. Some of the caesars had been

Christians at least in name. A system of churches, abbies, monasteries, and convents spread throughout the Roman Empire, a religious empire occupying the same space as the political empire. When the political empire fell, the religious empire remained standing as the only unified organizational structure linking together the Western world. The Church was suddenly empowered as the largest and most effective institution in Europe.

The Church functioned as a kind of government. It owned vast amounts of land, had huge financial resources, and up through the Renaissance maintained its own standing armies based around its center in Rome. But the most interesting dimension of the Church from the perspective of rhetorical theory was that it represented a distinct way of *knowing,* a perspective on how life ought to be lived, and a philosophy of how people should influence one another. Understanding the Church is key to understanding what rhetoric became in the Middle Ages, that period from the fall of Rome to roughly 1300. In fact, the chief rhetorical theorist of the period was a man of the Church, St. Augustine. We will begin by considering the key term of *knowledge* in the development of rhetorical theory in the Middle Ages.

Knowledge

Two major points about the relationships among knowledge, the Church, and rhetoric in the Middle Ages need to be considered. First, Christianity is a way of knowing. It makes certain claims, as does any religion, about what is true and about how one can come to know those truths. Like most religions, those claims rest upon a bedrock of beliefs that are dogmatic: beliefs that are statements of faith and doctrine, to be taken at face value as absolute truths. This way of knowing is often in conflict with ways of knowing common to other institutions or ways of life in secular society. Faith is often taken to be at odds with, or at least different from, science, common sense, or commerce.

The Church's stance towards knowledge affected its stance toward rhetoric in two ways. First, old ways of knowing keyed to secular (or "pagan") thoughts and practices were suspect—and rhetoric was one of those old ways of knowing. The Church was suspicious of many of the ways of the old Empire, especially since it had persecuted the Church for many years. Even under the restrictions of the caesars, rhetoric was part of that imperial society. So the Church was suspicious of the practice of argument and persuasion in general because of its cultural connections. Second, rhetoric has always been antagonistic towards absolutist ways of knowing. Rhetoric proves opposites; today it shows that one should vote for Smith yet tomorrow it proves that one should vote for Jones. Rhetoric, taken as a way of knowing, has therefore always been a highly relativistic way of knowing. That does not comport well with the absolutist and dogmatic beliefs of the Church. The Church was committed to ways of knowing that were *not arguable,* which would seem to run counter to what rhetoric does.

St. Augustine was key in formulating a truce between the Church and rhetoric, given these reservations about truth and knowledge. Rather than finding a role for rhetoric in the discovery of truths, he situated rhetoric *after* its discovery, much as did Plato. The teachings of the Church, of holy writings, or the promptings of the spirit were sufficient to tell a speaker (more specifically, a preacher) what to say. Yet *how* to say it so as to influence wide audiences was a problem. We will see that Augustine finds a role for rhetoric in disseminating religious truths.

A second important point in the relationships among knowledge, rhetoric, and the Church is that the Church made extraordinary efforts to monopolize knowledge in the Middle Ages. All learning became the province of the Church. Even nobles were likely to be illiterate, and to require the services of a cleric (or clerk) who could read and write as a member of their courts. Books were more likely to be found in abbeys and cathedrals than in the houses of even the rich and powerful. Augustine is writing for an audience of preachers who will pass on knowledge to a largely illiterate audience. His rhetorical theory is thus predicated upon the possession of a knowledge that the audience could not share or have any access to except through the efforts of the Church. This monopoly over knowledge gave the Church an extraordinary rhetorical advantage.

Media

The importance of media in the Middle Ages is interesting and complicated. It is complicated because, as noted above, much of western culture returned to an oral/aural condition. Illiteracy was widespread. On the other hand, the Church and its leaders were immersed in a highly literate culture, having a monopoly over knowledge and control over most of the books in which knowledge was stored.

The connection between media and rhetorical theory is interesting. If a society regards the written word as a storehouse of knowledge, then the characteristics of writing may come to influence what people think about the characteristics of knowledge. Think about what happens to knowledge when it is written down and put in a book. The words in a book do not change. The ink on the page remains the same. Therefore, a society based on written media is one prone to thinking of knowledge as unchanging and stable.

We should note that the Church was becoming an increasingly text-based institution even in the early Middle Ages. The idea of the Bible as a unified text, and, more important, as a foundation for faith, was in the process of formation at this time. The idea of dogmatic, absolute, and unchanging truths was very consistent with a commitment to the written word (which is absolute and unchanging). So it should not surprise us that a commitment to the written medium goes hand-in-hand with the Church's beliefs. Let us consider further that Augustine is theorizing rhetoric not for the writer of Church teachings or of holy texts but for the *speaker* who will explain and interpret truths to an audience. Augustine's rhetoric, then, is located in the second tier medium of speaking. We must remember that marker of rhetoric's "second class" standing (behind religious truth) in Augustine's thinking.

Discourse

At least two new forms of rhetorical discourse began to be theorized during the Middle Ages. The importance of Augustine in the Middle Ages indicates the development of the discourse of preaching. Sometimes taken to be an extension of the Aristotelian idea of ceremonial or epideictic speaking, preaching nevertheless had some distinct characteristics, as we discussed above. St. Augustine's selection in this book addresses the rhetorical problems of preaching. Other rhetorical theorists of the time such as Robert of Basevorn and Boethius also contributed to theories of preaching.

Of course, Christianity was not the only religion in the West. It may be instructive to compare the experience of the Church with that of the Jews during this period. The rhetorical needs of the Jewish faith were different from those of the Church. In the first century C.E. the Roman occupiers of the Jewish homeland in what is now Israel reacted to constant rebellions by Jewish nationalists by destroying much of Jerusalem (and its Temple) and expelling many of the Jews. Thus began a great diaspora, a situation in which a people is dispersed geographically. Jews who were forced to flee into many countries across Europe nevertheless wanted to maintain a sense of their own community, as distinct and special, in contrast to the communities in which they were forced to live. This rhetorical challenge of maintaining community differed from the Christian desire to expand community through converts.

The discursive needs of Christians and Jews differed. Judaism is a highly text-centered faith, and its leaders and teachers have always been concerned with proper interpretation of holy writings. Therefore, *hermeneutics,* or the art of interpretation, has always been of more importance for Judaism than is rhetoric, and has created different discursive preoccupations than those of the Church.

Another kind of discourse that appeared in the Middle Ages was letter writing. Letters became important legal documents during this time. They often took the form of contracts and deeds. They were important in exercising influence in distant places. Letters became a means by which the Church communicated among itself.

Because it was difficult and expensive to send a letter across the distances between one castle and another, or from one monastery to another, the writing of a letter became an important task. One would scarcely want to write carelessly what might take many weeks and much effort to convey from one place to another. So the writing of letters became a common form of rhetorical discourse, and theories likewise arose to advise letter writers on the best strategies to pursue.

Power

We have touched upon the relationships among knowledge, media, and power already. Control over knowledge and over the written media that contained it was a major source of power for the Church. Forms of rhetoric designed to exploit the location of power in written media began to be developed during this period.

One last issue of power that needs to be considered is that in general, the scope for rhetoric was not much expanded during the Middle Ages from what it had been in the Roman Empire. This was especially true for the dialogic, give and take rhetoric of democracies and republics. These restrictions on rhetoric were due to the forms of power in place during the Middle Ages. Neither the Church nor the earls and barons of Europe wanted rhetorical discussion of policies and laws any more than did the Roman caesars. Augustine demonstrates a one-way rhetoric of preaching, but it is designed to flow from Church to public as a form of enforcement of the faith. The reflowering of rhetoric would have to wait until new forms of power could be developed.

THE RENAISSANCE

The term *renaissance* means "rebirth." In many ways the Middle Ages were a period of conserving and retaining culture, fostered by the essentially conservative institutions of the Church and the feudal aristocracy. There came a time in the Western world, however, when old knowledge from the classical period was rediscovered and new learning increased at a remarkable rate. This period is what we call the Renaissance. It is useful to think in terms of an early and a late Renaissance, and of the direction of its movement. The Renaissance began in the south of Europe, principally in Italy, and moved north. Whatever generalizations one may make about the Renaissance are usually true earlier for southern nations such as Italy and France and later for northern nations such as Great Britain and the Scandinavian countries. The early Renaissance was roughly from 1300 to 1500 C.E., while the later Renaissance was approximately from 1500 to 1700 C.E. The rebirth that created the Renaissance was a rebirth of different forms and discoveries of knowledge, so it is with that key term that we begin our review of this period and its rhetorical theory.

Knowledge

One development of supreme importance in the early Renaissance was the breakup of the monopoly of the Church over knowledge, learning, and educational institutions. This diffusion of knowledge happened for several reasons. One reason was growing discontent with the doctrines and dogma of the Church from within. Various schisms and controversies arose, culminating in the beginning of the Reformation in the early sixteenth century. Martin Luther founded Protestant reforms and rejection of Church authority in Germany, while King Henry VIII broke the authority of the Church in England, founding the Church of England in its place and declaring himself its head.

One important development in the diffusion of knowledge was the rise of cities. There have always been cities in human history, of course, but in the late Middle Ages more and more people began to flock to towns and villages, forsaking the predominantly rural, agricultural lifestyle of the feudal system. Higher concentrations of population in the cities enabled the rise of larger businesses that could ground factories and other commercial enterprises in the increasing pools of cheap labor. These cities were relatively independent of Church and aristocratic nobles. Guilds, or organizations of business people, were formed and grew in power.

Business needs educated people who can read, write, and do mathematics. It became the interest of the growing commercial and civic interests of the cities to break the monopoly of the Church over knowledge. One way in which that was done was through the sponsorship of universities that, although most of them retained some connection to the Church, were relatively independent of it. Libraries developed outside of monasteries and abbeys. Scholars began to produce new knowledge from new research. Some of that knowledge was rhetorical.

The growing need for educated people in cities and businesses included a need for those skilled in persuasion, which has always been an essential tool of commerce. Furthermore, the old traditions of rhetoric as the foundation for a broadly-based education had never died, and continued into the Renaissance to create a need to study rhetoric. Chairs of rhetoric, logic, dialectic, and other verbal arts were established in universities across the West.

The new interest in rhetorical studies went hand-in-hand with a renewed interest in classical learning. The older "pagan" learning of ancient Greece and Rome in general was rediscovered once the Church lost its power to suppress competition with its own doctrine and ideas. Many of the ancient rhetorical theories that had been suppressed or neglected by a Church distrustful of persuasion were rediscovered. The recovery of ancient mathematical and scientific knowledge began to fuel a renewal of discovery.

You will recall that one of the principles of classical Greek thought was an interest in *unity:* a belief that the universe is ordered and unified, with a connection among all things and all branches of knowledge. This belief was reborn in the Renaissance in several ways. The expression "Renaissance man" refers to a person who is widely educated in a vast array of subjects. An interest in this Platonic or Ciceronian concept of broad learning returned during the Renaissance, fueled by a belief that such broad learning could be unified into a single system of thought. Often, rhetoric was taken to be the foundation of that learning, since it is an art that addresses itself to many different subject matters. Erasmus, whose work we will read in this section, is an example of one who defended the rhetorical practice of *copia* as one of the cornerstones of a liberal education.

This search for a way of coordinating all subject matters of learning was a search for what became known as a *universal method.* Many scholars and universities expended much effort in attempting to discover a perspective from which all branches of knowledge might seem connected. As we shall see, Ramus proposed a new system of ten "topics" that he thought would serve as the basis for a universal method.

Another result of the rediscovery of classical learning was a renewed interest in relativism and humanism. Relativism is the belief that truths and values arise from and are relevant for the particular social groups and contexts that generate them; in other words, it rejects the idea of absolute or timeless truths. Humanism is the belief that the human is the center of the universe, of most interest and value, and most worthy to be studied. Both relativism and humanism are inherently rhetorical concepts, since rhetoric is always concerned with establishment of truths and values here and now, not on a timeless plane, and rhetoric is always keyed to the human and what will persuade humans to respond to the discourses of others. Humanism gave rise to new theories of psychology that would assist rhetorical theory. Francis Bacon was an early proponent of a new *faculty psychology,* as we will see later in this section, that would find wide acceptance among rhetorical theorists.

Humanism and relativism were cornerstones of sophistic thinking, and perhaps the chief reasons that Plato rejected sophistry and was deeply suspicious of the rhetoric that supported it. Humanism and relativism were also strongly opposed by the dogmatic Church, which insisted on the primacy of God and its own absolute truths. A rediscovery of humanism and relativism were therefore part of both a rediscovery of rhetoric and a rejection of the monopoly of the Church over knowledge in the early Renaissance.

Finally, we must note that in the late Renaissance, science, engineering, mathematics, and other technical disciplines began to grow at a dramatic rate. Discoveries in navigation enabled the start of European conquest and imperialism around the world. Chemistry and astronomy made great strides. The calculus was developed in mathematics. Towards the end of the Renaissance, these "hard" sciences began to acquire a prestige and status above that of the older verbal, humanist arts—including rhetoric. It began to appear that with objective, scientific methods much knowledge could be acquired. Increasingly, people began turning to science to find the universal method that had been a Renaissance ideal. The prestige and success of science during this period would culminate in the Enlightenment's enshrinement of science and reason, sometimes at the expense of other forms of knowing.

Discourse

As the Middle Ages turned over into the Renaissance, the noble classes concentrated administration of their earldoms, dukedoms, and kingdoms in "courts": locations where trials were heard, decisions made, advisors and aides consulted, and policies planned. Those who have visited or seen pictures of the palace of Versailles or its predecessor the Louvre, in France, can visualize a vast building full of people laying plots and schemes to acquire political power or the personal favor of the monarch.

Nation states arose in the West as central governments united what had been semi-independent principalities. These nations became larger and more complex as populations grew and cities prospered. As the population grew and power became more concentrated, so did the importance of the decisions that would be made in the seats of power, the courts. So it became very much worth the while of those who wanted to influence the decisions made by powerful nobles to move about the court using persuasion to gain the cooperation of advisors and confidants. A new form of discourse arose to enable this persuasion: *courtly rhetoric.* Courtly rhetoric was a kind of interpersonal rhetoric designed to be used by individuals to persuade and impress other individuals in places of power and influence.

In these relatively more domestic and personal settings, women began to have rhetorical influence closer to the centers of power than they had ever been. In this section we include our first female theorist, Christine de Pizan. She is offering rhetorical advice to other women in courtly positions as to how they might obtain and wield this kind of courtly influence. We will note how her rhetoric differs from the traditional forms of public speaking with which the idea of rhetoric had long been associated.

Power

In our discussion above, two contradictory developments may be noted in terms of power during the Renaissance. One development was a diffusion of power that had previously been concentrated in the Church. As noted, this occurred on many fronts: religious, educational, and organizational. The Church simply no longer had a monopoly over either knowledge or religious belief, and so its power declined.

Diffusion of power occurred through the establishment of other sources of knowledge, in institutions such as other faiths and denominations, the secular universities and corporations, and in other disciplines such as the rise of science. As more people began to be educated outside of the restrictions of the institutional Church, previously marginalized individuals such as women moved closer to the centers of power through discourses such as courtly rhetoric. Our second female theorist, Margaret Fell, is more identifiably feminist than Christine de Pisan. Fell argues for the inclusion of women in the public sphere of argument.

A contradictory development was the concentration of power in increasingly centralized governments of the increasingly large nation states of the West. In some nations such as Britain, this centralization also included the development of a strong parliamentary tradition. This form of republican government began a long tradition of vigorous rhetorical debate in the British House of Commons. Rhetoric was alive and well in the traditions of England. But in other nations without a parliamentary government, such as France and the Germanic principalities, rhetoric took the form of courtly rhetoric in intrigues and plots. The Ciceronian model of the politically active rhetorical leader was not found universally in the West.

Media

In the Renaissance, print continued its move towards ascendancy. Courtly rhetoric was carried out through writing as much as through oral communication. The rise of big businesses was made possible by, and also engendered, huge enterprises of writing so as to keep records, communicate with clients and customers, and manage far-flung outposts of commercial empire. The breakup of the Church's monopoly over learning also meant the collapse of its monopoly over literacy. Increasingly, the privileged classes of most nations began to learn to read and write.

We noted in our discussion of the Middle Ages how a commitment to print creates a commitment to stable and unchanging truths. During the Middle Ages, this bias of the printed medium was employed by the Church to further its dogmatic principles. During the Renaissance, the secular enterprises of science and commerce captured the "rhetoric" of the printed medium for their own purposes. Belief in the value of big business and of science was reinforced by seeing each as objective, producing sure and certain truths (science) or values (business). Enshrining the truths and principles of science and commerce in the written medium thus helped to empower those enterprises.

FOR FURTHER READING

Jeanneret, Michel. 1991. *A Feast of Words: Banquets and Table Talk in the Renaissance.* Chicago: University of Chicago Press.

Kahn, Victoria. 1994. *Machiavellian Rhetoric: From the Counter-Reformation to Milton.* Princeton, NY: Princeton University Press.

King, Margaret L. 1991. *Women of the Renaissance.* Chicago: University of Chicago Press.

Litfin, Duane. 1994. *St. Paul's Theology of Proclamation, 1 Corinthians 1–4 and Greco-Roman Rhetoric.* Cambridge: Cambridge University Press.

Llull, Ramon. 1994. *Ramon Llull's New Rhetoric: Text and Translation of Llull's Rhethorica Nova.* Mark D. Johnston, ed. and transl. Davis, CA: Hermagoras Press.

Mack, Peter. 1993. *Renaissance Argument: Calla and Agricola in the Traditions of Rhetoric and Dialectic.* Leiden: E.J. Brill.

Mack, Peter, ed. 1994. *Renaissance Rhetoric.* NY: St. Martin's Press.

Murphy, James J. 1974. *Rhetoric in the Middle Ages: A History of Rhetorical Theory from St. Augustine to the Renaissance.* Berkeley: University of California Press.

Ong, Walter J. 1967. *The Presence of the Word: Some Prolegomena for Cultural and Religious History.* NY: Clarion.

Ong, Walter J. 1979. *Ramus, Method, and the Decay of Dialogue: From the Art of Discourse to the Art of Reason.* NY: Octagon Books.

Wallace, Karl R. 1943. *Francis Bacon on Communication and Rhetoric.* Chapel Hill: University of North Carolina Press.

INTRODUCTION TO ST. AUGUSTINE

Aurelius Augustine lived from 354 to 430 C.E. He was born in Tagaste, northern Africa. Augustine taught grammar at Tagaste, and later was a professor of rhetoric in the city of Carthage. Seeking better students and higher fees, he moved to Rome to teach. Later, he was appointed to a chair of rhetoric at Milan, where he came under the influence of Bishop Ambrose's preaching. At first entranced by the Bishop's words, he eventually realized that Ambrose's preaching style was so effective that it had implanted in him the ideas of Christian faith. During a process of conversion, Augustine became increasingly disenchanted with the standard course of rhetoric that he was teaching. Grounded in the Greek and Roman tradition, it taught students techniques for outwitting opponents in argument. But Augustine was becoming increasingly concerned not with victory but with truth, specifically with the truths of the Christian faith as he understood them. He was finally converted to the faith in 386 and resigned his professorship of rhetoric. Eventually Augustine returned to lead the Church in northern Africa, eventually becoming bishop of the city of Hippo there. He is canonized as a saint of the Roman Catholic Church.

As Augustine advanced in leadership in the Church, he was forced to return to consideration of the problems of rhetoric that he thought he had left behind. Christianity is one of the world's most rhetorical religions in that it seeks converts. It actively takes the stance that it is important to bring others to accept its principles. The methods of including people in the Church are often rhetorical. Yet Augustine knew firsthand how dishonest rhetoric could be, how shifting in its principles, how unconcerned with truth. So in his work he confronted the question of how absolute truth might use a method that recognizes no absolute truths, how a doctrine of love and kindness could use a technique that seems attuned only to winning, and how a religion concerned with human ends could use a discourse that regarded itself only as a means.

Augustine's solution to those problems is expressed in his book *De Doctrina Christiana*, or *On Christian Doctrine*. This work is divided into four books, directed towards the issue of how Christian doctrine might be spread. The first three books are concerned with how those who are passing the faith on to others might "discover the thought" to be explained. It is interesting that this process of discovering what to say, which for centuries had been regarded as *invention* in the classical canons of rhetoric, is *not* seen as part of rhetoric for Augustine. Instead, discovering what to say is seen as a matter of learning, interpreting, and understanding sacred writings and Church teachings. The preacher, it is clear, is not to think up the *substance* of what to say, as did the classical orator. That substance is already given by the faith.

In book four of *De Doctrina Christiana,* excerpted here, Augustine claims that he is not writing a rhetorical theory. By that he means that he is not presenting the traditional rhetorical teachings that he had taught as a younger man, telling his reader that one may find them elsewhere. He is, however, in fact presenting what amounts to a rhetorical theory for the preacher. It is a theory of how to most effectively pass on the truths that the preacher would have secured through the interpretive methods outlined in the first three books. The preacher, in Augustine's view, is therefore a kind of *teacher,* and words denoting teaching or educating occur throughout the fourth book. In this way Augustine resembles Plato: both want the speaker to convey secured truths to an audience for its improvement and enlightenment.

The beginning of our reading asserts that rhetorical theory is best acquired from other authors, and quickly, as a general guide to speaking rather than as a system of hard and fast rules. Augustine stresses the importance of wisdom for the task of preaching, a wisdom acquired through reading Scripture and from Church doctrine. This is the kind of inspiration that is entirely sufficient for preaching, he claims.

Early in the selection given here we find the key move in Augustine's rhetorical theory. He argues that the preacher has three duties: to instruct, to please, and to persuade. Augustine then turns to a scheme of language *style* that had been around since the anonymous Roman book, *Ad Herennium* some four hundred years earlier, which holds that there are three levels of speaking style: plain, middle, and grand. Augustine links the three levels with the three duties of the speaker: Teaching is suited to the plain style, pleasing is suited to the middle style, and persuasion is suited to the grand style. This theory of rhetorical style and its three uses grounds the rest of the reading.

It is interesting to note that what amounts to rhetoric for Augustine has become concentrated largely in matters of language style. Invention has been rendered useless by reliance on sacred writings and church dogma. The power of holy script is taken to be so impressive that little more is needed in the way of delivery, arrangement, or memory. Style alone is used as a means to convey the truths of the Church.

Augustine explains the intricacies and relationships among the three purposes and their corresponding three levels of style. Note his disapproval of using the middle style for pleasing alone; his loftier purposes seem to require instruction or persuasion as well. Consider his admission that a given sermon may require all three levels of style. Finally, note his advice to those priests who may nevertheless have little rhetorical ability to preach: one's *life* has persuasive force, he argues, so that action "as a flowing speech" can win people to the faith.

In the centuries to follow, rhetoric would turn more and more to a preoccupation with verbal style. Augustine's theory laid a solid foundation for the serious purposes to which the manipulation of language might be put. Later theorists would begin to focus on language for its own sake, as a sort of game or embellishment. But Augustine offers a way to think of language as an important rhetorical instrument serving the purposes of an established and serious truth.

ST. AUGUSTINE

ON CHRISTIAN DOCTRINE

The Enchiridion.

BOOK FOURTH

ARGUMENT.

Passing to the second part of his work, that which treats of expression, the author premises that it is no part of his intention to write a treatise on the laws of rhetoric. These can be learned elsewhere, and ought not to be neglected, being indeed specially necessary for the Christian teacher, whom it behoves to excel in eloquence and power of speech. After detailing with much care and minuteness the various qualities of an orator, he recommends the authors of the holy scriptures as the best models of eloquence, far excelling all others in the combination of eloquence with wisdom. He points out that perspicuity is the most essential quality of style, and ought to be cultivated with especial care by the teacher, as it is the main requisite for instruction, although other qualities are required for delighting and persuading the hearer. All these gifts are to be sought in earnest prayer from God, though we are not to forget to be zealous and diligent in study. He shows that there are three species of style, the subdued, the elegant, and the majestic; the first serving for instruction, the second for praise, and the third for exhortation: and of each of these he gives examples, selected both from scripture and from early teachers of the church, Cyprian and Ambrose. He shows that these various styles may be mingled, and when and for what purposes they are mingled; and that they all have the same end in view, to bring home the truth to the hearer, so that he may understand it, hear it with gladness, and practise it in his life. Finally, he exhorts the Christian teacher himself, pointing out the dignity and responsibility of the office he holds, to lead a life in harmony with his own teaching, and to show a good example to all.

Translated by Professor J. F. Shaw, Londonderry.

CHAP. I.—*This Work Not Intended as a Treatise on Rhetoric*

1. THIS work of mine, which is entitled *On Christian Doctrine,* was at the commencement divided into two parts. For, after a preface, in which I answered by anticipation those who were likely to take exception to the work, I said, "There are two things on which all interpretation of Scripture depends: the mode of ascertaining the proper meaning, and the mode of making known the meaning when it is ascertained. I shall treat first of the mode of ascertaining, next of the mode of making known, the meaning."[1] As, then, I have already said a great deal about the mode of ascertaining the meaning, and have given three books to this one part of the subject, I shall only say a few things about the mode of making known the meaning, in order if possible to bring them all within the compass of one book, and so finish the whole work in four books.

2. In the first place, then, I wish by this preamble to put a stop to the expectations of readers who may think that I am about to lay down rules of rhetoric such as I have learnt, and taught too, in the secular schools, and to warn them that they need not look for any such from me. Not that I think such rules of no use, but that whatever use they have is to be learnt elsewhere; and if any good man should happen to have leisure for learning them, he is not to ask me to teach them either in this work or any other.

[1] Book i. chap. 1.

Chap. II.—It Is Lawful for a Christian Teacher to Use the Art of Rhetoric

3. Now, the art of rhetoric being available for the enforcing either of truth or falsehood, who will dare to say that truth in the person of its defenders is to take its stand unarmed against falsehood? For example, that those who are trying to persuade men of what is false are to know how to introduce their subject, so as to put the hearer into a friendly, or attentive, or teachable frame of mind, while the defenders of the truth shall be ignorant of that art? That the former are to tell their falsehoods briefly, clearly, and plausibly, while the latter shall tell the truth in such a way that it is tedious to listen to, hard to understand, and in fine, not easy to believe it? That the former are to oppose the truth and defend falsehood with sophistical arguments, while the latter shall be unable either to defend what is true, or to refute what is false? That the former, while imbuing the minds of their hearers with erroneous opinions, are by their power of speech to awe, to melt, to enliven, and to rouse them, while the latter shall in defence of the truth be sluggish, and frigid, and somnolent? Who is such a fool as to think this wisdom? Since, then, the faculty of eloquence is available for both sides, and is of very great service in the enforcing either of wrong or right, why do not good men study to engage it on the side of truth, when bad men use it to obtain the triumph of wicked and worthless causes, and to further injustice and error?

Chap. III.—The Proper Age and the Proper Means for Acquiring Rhetorical Skill

4. But the theories and rules on this subject (to which, when you add a tongue thoroughly skilled by exercise and habit in the use of many words and many ornaments of speech, you have what is called *eloquence* or *oratory*) may be learnt apart from these writings of mine, if a suitable space of time be set aside for the purpose at a fit and proper age. But only by those who can learn them quickly; for the masters of Roman eloquence themselves did not shrink from saying that any one who cannot learn this art quickly can never thoroughly learn it at all.[1] Whether this be true or not, why need we inquire? For even if this art can occasionally be in the end mastered by men of slower intellect, I do not think it of so much importance as to wish men who have arrived at mature age to spend time in learning it. It is enough that boys should give attention to it; and even of these, not all who are to be fitted for usefulness in the Church, but only those who are not yet engaged in any occupation of more urgent necessity, or which ought evidently to take precedence of it. For men of quick intellect and glowing temperament find it easier to become eloquent by reading and listening to eloquent speakers than by following rules for eloquence. And even outside the canon, which to our great advantage is fixed in a place of secure authority, there is no want of ecclesiastical writings, in reading which a man of ability will acquire a tinge of the eloquence with which they are written, even though he does not aim at this, but is solely intent on the matters treated of; especially, of course, if in addition he practise himself in writing, or dictating, and at last also in speaking, the opinions he has formed on grounds of piety and faith. If, however, such ability be wanting, the rules of rhetoric are either not understood, or if, after great labour has been spent in enforcing them, they come to be in some small measure understood, they prove of no service. For even those who have learnt them, and who speak with fluency and elegance, cannot always think of them when they are speaking so as to speak in accordance with them, unless they are discussing the rules themselves. Indeed, I think there are scarcely any who can do both things—that is, speak well, and, in order to do this, think of the rules of speaking while they are speaking. For we must be careful that what we have got to say does not

---

[1] Cicero, *de Oratore,* iii. 31; Quinctil. *Inst. Orat.* i. 1, 2.

escape us whilst we are thinking about saying it according to the rules of art. Nevertheless, in the speeches of eloquent men, we find rules of eloquence carried out which the speakers did not think of as aids to eloquence at the time when they were speaking, whether they had ever learnt them, or whether they had never even met with them. For it is because they are eloquent that they exemplify these rules; it is not that they use them in order to be eloquent.

5. And, therefore, as infants cannot learn to speak except by learning words and phrases from those who do speak, why should not men become eloquent without being taught any art of speech, simply by reading and learning the speeches of eloquent men, and by imitating them as far as they can? And what do we find from the examples themselves to be the case in this respect? We know numbers who, without acquaintance with rhetorical rules, are more eloquent than many who have learnt these; but we know no one who is eloquent without having read and listened to the speeches and debates of eloquent men. For even the art of grammar, which teaches correctness of speech, need not be learnt by boys, if they have the advantage of growing up and living among men who speak correctly. For without knowing the names of any of the faults, they will, from being accustomed to correct speech, lay hold upon whatever is faulty in the speech of any one they listen to, and avoid it; just as city-bred men, even when illiterate, seize upon the faults of rustics.

CHAP. IV.—*The Duty of the Christian Teacher*

6. It is the duty, then, of the interpreter and teacher of Holy Scripture, the defender of the true faith and the opponent of error, both to teach what is right and to refute what is wrong, and in the performance of this task to conciliate the hostile, to rouse the careless, and to tell the ignorant both what is occurring at present and what is probable in the future. But once that his hearers are friendly, attentive, and ready to learn, whether he has found them so, or has himself made them so, the remaining objects are to be carried out in whatever way the case requires. If the hearers need teaching, the matter treated of must be made fully known by means of narrative. On the other hand, to clear up points that are doubtful requires reasoning and the exhibition of proofs. If, however, the hearers require to be roused rather than instructed, in order that they may be diligent to do what they already know, and to bring their feelings into harmony with the truths they admit, greater vigour of speech is needed. Here entreaties and reproaches, exhortations and upbraidings, and all the other means of rousing the emotions, are necessary.

7. And all the methods I have mentioned are constantly used by nearly every one in cases where speech is the agency employed.

CHAP. V.—*Wisdom of More Importance than Eloquence to the Christian Teacher*

But as some men employ these coarsely, inelegantly, and frigidly, while others use them with acuteness, elegance, and spirit, the work that I am speaking of ought to be undertaken by one who can argue and speak with wisdom, if not with eloquence, and with profit to his hearers, even though he profit them less than he would if he could speak with eloquence too. But we must beware of the man who abounds in eloquent nonsense, and so much the more if the hearer is pleased with what is not worth listening to, and thinks that because the speaker is eloquent what he says must be true. And this opinion is held even by those who think that the art of rhetoric should be taught: for they confess that "though wisdom without eloquence is of little service to states, yet eloquence without wisdom is frequently a positive injury, and is of service never."[1] If, then, the men who teach the principles of eloquence have been forced by truth to confess this in the very books which treat of eloquence, though they were ignorant of the true, that is, the heavenly wisdom which comes down

---

[1] Cicero, *de Inventione Rhetorica*, i. 1.

from the Father of Lights, how much more ought we to feel it who are the sons and the ministers of this higher wisdom! Now a man speaks with more or less wisdom just as he has made more or less progress in the knowledge of Scripture; I do not mean by reading them much and committing them to memory, but by understanding them aright and carefully searching into their meaning. For there are who read and yet neglect them; they read to remember the words, but are careless about knowing the meaning. It is plain we must set far above these the men who are not so retentive of the words, but see with the eyes of the heart into the heart of Scripture. Better than either of these, however, is the man who, when he wishes, can repeat the words, and at the same time correctly apprehends their meaning.

8. Now it is especially necessary for the man who is bound to speak wisely, even though he cannot speak eloquently, to retain in memory the words of Scripture. For the more he discerns the poverty of his own speech, the more he ought to draw on the riches of Scripture, so that what he says in his own words he may prove by the words of Scripture; and he himself, though small and weak in his own words, may gain strength and power from the confirming testimony of great men. For his proof gives pleasure when he cannot please by his mode of speech. But if a man desire to speak not only with wisdom, but with eloquence also (and assuredly he will prove of greater service if he can do both), I would rather send him to read, and listen to, and exercise himself in imitating, eloquent men, than advise him to spend time with the teachers of rhetoric; especially if the men he reads and listens to are justly praised as having spoken, or as being accustomed to speak, not only with eloquence, but with wisdom also. For eloquent speakers are heard with pleasure; wise speakers with profit. And, therefore, Scripture does not say that the multitude of the eloquent, but "the multitude of the wise is the welfare of the world."[1] And as we must often swallow wholesome bitters, so we must always avoid unwholesome sweets. But what is better than wholesome sweetness or sweet wholesomeness? For the sweeter we try to make such things, the easier it is to make their wholesomeness serviceable. And so there are writers of the Church who have expounded the Holy Scriptures, not only with wisdom, but with eloquence as well; and there is not more time for the reading of these than is sufficient for those who are studious and at leisure to exhaust them.

Chap. vi.—The Sacred Writers Unite Eloquence with Wisdom

9. Here, perhaps, some one inquires whether the authors whose divinely-inspired writings constitute the canon, which carries with it a most wholesome authority, are to be considered wise only, or eloquent as well. A question which to me, and to those who think with me, is very easily settled. For where I understand these writers, it seems to me not only that nothing can be wiser, but also that nothing can be more eloquent. And I venture to affirm that all who truly understand what these writers say, perceive at the same time that it could not have been properly said in any other way. For as there is a kind of eloquence that is more becoming in youth, and a kind that is more becoming in old age, and nothing can be called eloquence if it be not suitable to the person of the speaker, so there is a kind of eloquence that is becoming in men who justly claim the highest authority, and who are evidently inspired of God. With this eloquence they spoke; no other would have been suitable for them; and this itself would be unsuitable in any other, for it is in keeping with their character, while it mounts as far above that of others (not from empty inflation, but from solid merit) as it seems to fall below them. Where, however, I do not understand these writers, though their eloquence is then less apparent, I have no doubt but that it is of the same kind as that I do understand. The very obscurity, too, of these divine and wholesome words was a necessary element in eloquence of a kind that was designed to profit our understandings, not

[1] Wisd. vi. 24.

only by the discovery of truth, but also by the exercise of their powers.

10. I could, however, if I had time, show those men who cry up their own form of language as superior to that of our authors (not because of its majesty, but because of its inflation), that all those powers and beauties of eloquence which they make their boast, are to be found in the sacred writings which God in His goodness has provided to mould our characters, and to guide us from this world of wickedness to the blessed world above. But it is not the qualities which these writers have in common with the heathen orators and poets that give me such unspeakable delight in their eloquence; I am more struck with admiration at the way in which, by an eloquence peculiarly their own, they so use this eloquence of ours that it is not conspicuous either by its presence or its absence: for it did not become them either to condemn it or to make an ostentatious display of it; and if they had shunned it, they would have done the former; if they had made it prominent, they might have appeared to be doing the latter. And in those passages where the learned do note its presence, the matters spoken of are such, that the words in which they are put seem not so much to be sought out by the speaker as spontaneously to suggest themselves; as if wisdom were walking out of its house,—that is, the breast of the wise man, and eloquence, like an inseparable attendant, followed it without being called for.[1]

CHAP. VII.—*Examples of True Eloquence Drawn from the Epistles of Paul and the Prophecies of Amos*

11. For who would not see what the apostle meant to say, and how wisely he has said it, in the following passage: "We glory in tribulations also: knowing that tribulation worketh patience; and patience, experience; and experience, hope: and hope maketh not ashamed; because the love of God is shed abroad in our hearts by the Holy Ghost which is given unto us"?[1] Now were any man unlearnedly learned (if I may use the expression) to contend that the apostle had here followed the rules of rhetoric, would not every Christian, learned or unlearned, laugh at him? And yet here we find the figure which is called in Greek κλίμαξ (climax), and by some in Latin *gradatio,* for they do not care to call it *scala* (a ladder), when the words and ideas have a connection of dependency the one upon the other, as we see here that patience arises out of tribulation, experience out of patience, and hope out of experience. Another ornament, too, is found here; for after certain statements finished in a single tone of voice, which we call clauses and sections (*membra et cæsa*), but the Greeks κῶλα and κόμματα,[2] there follows a rounded sentence (*ambitus sive circuitus*) which the Greeks call περίοδος,[3] the clauses of which are suspended on the voice of the speaker till the whole is completed by the last clause. For of the statements which precede the period, this is the first clause, "knowing that tribulation worketh patience;" the second, "and patience, experience;" the third, "and experience, hope." Then the period which is subjoined is completed in three clauses, of which the first is, "and hope maketh not ashamed;" the second, "because the love of God is shed abroad in our hearts;" the third, "by the Holy Ghost which is given unto us." But these and other matters of the same kind are taught in the art of elocution. As then I do not affirm that the apostle was guided by the rules of eloquence, so I do not deny that his wisdom naturally produced, and was accompanied by, eloquence.

---

[1] Cf. Cicero, *Orator.* 21: "Sed est eloquentiæ, sicut reliquarum rerum, fundamentum sapientia."

[1] Rom. v. 3–5.

[2] Cf. Cicero, *Orator.* 62: "Quæ nescio cur, cum Græci κόμματα et κωλα nominent, nos non recte incisa et membra dicamus."

[3] Cf. Cicero, *de Claris Oratoribus,* 44: "Comprehensio et ambitus ille verborum (si sic periodum appellari placet)."

12. In the Second Epistle to the Corinthians, again, he refutes certain false apostles who had gone out from the Jews, and had been trying to injure his character; and being compelled to speak of himself, though he ascribes this as folly to himself, how wisely and how eloquently he speaks! But wisdom is his guide, eloquence his attendant; he follows the first, the second follows him, and yet he does not spurn it when it comes after him. "I say again," he says, "Let no man think me a fool: if otherwise, yet as a fool receive me, that I may boast myself a little. That which I speak, I speak it not after the Lord, but as it were foolishly, in this confidence of boasting. Seeing that many glory after the flesh, I will glory also. For ye suffer fools gladly, seeing ye yourselves are wise. For ye suffer, if a man bring you into bondage, if a man devour you, if a man take of you, if a man exalt himself, if a man smite you on the face. I speak as concerning reproach, as though we had been weak. Howbeit, whereinsoever any is bold (I speak foolishly), I am bold also. Are they Hebrews? so am I. Are they Israelites? so am I. Are they the seed of Abraham? so am I. Are they ministers of Christ? (I speak as a fool), I am more: in labours more abundant, in stripes above measure, in prisons more frequent, in deaths oft. Of the Jews five times received I forty stripes save one, thrice was I beaten with rods, once was I stoned, thrice I suffered shipwreck, a night and a day I have been in the deep; in journeyings often, in perils of waters, in perils of robbers, in perils by mine own countrymen, in perils by the heathen, in perils in the city, in perils in the wilderness, in perils in the sea, in perils among false brethren; in weariness and painfulness, in watchings often, in hunger and thirst, in fastings often, in cold and nakedness. Besides those things which are without, that which cometh upon me daily, the care of all the churches. Who is weak, and I am not weak? who is offended, and I burn not? If I must needs glory, I will glory of the things which concern my infirmities."[1] The thoughtful and attentive perceive how much wisdom there is in these words. And even a man sound asleep must notice what a stream of eloquence flows through them.

[1] 2 Cor. xi. 16–30.

13. Further still, the educated man observes that those sections which the Greeks call *κόμματα*, and the clauses and periods of which I spoke a short time ago, being intermingled in the most beautiful variety, make up the whole form and features (so to speak) of that diction by which even the unlearned are delighted and affected. For, from the place where I commenced to quote, the passage consists of periods: the first the smallest possible, consisting of two members; for a period cannot have less than two members, though it may have more: "I say again, let no man think me a fool." The next has three members: "if otherwise, yet as a fool receive me, that I may boast myself a little." The third has four members: "That which I speak, I speak it not after the Lord, but as it were foolishly, in this confidence of boasting." The fourth has two: "Seeing that many glory after the flesh, I will glory also." And the fifth has two: "For ye suffer fools gladly, seeing ye yourselves are wise." The sixth again has two members: "for ye suffer, if a man bring you into bondage." Then follow three sections (*cæsa*): "if a man devour you, if a man take of you, if a man exalt himself." Next three clauses (*membra*): "if a man smite you on the face. I speak as concerning reproach, as though we had been weak." Then is subjoined a period of three members: "Howbeit, whereinsoever any is bold (I speak foolishly), I am bold also." After this, certain separate sections being put in the interrogatory form, separate sections are also given as answers, three to three: "Are they Hebrews? so am I. Are they Israelites? so am I. Are they the seed of Abraham? so am I." But a fourth section being put likewise in the interrogatory form, the answer is given not in another section (*cæsum*) but in a clause (*membrum*):[1] "Are they the ministers of

[1] The only apparent difference between *membrum* and *cæsum* is, that the former is the longer of the two. It is impossible to express the difference in English.

Christ? (I speak as a fool.) I am more." Then the next four sections are given continuously, the interrogatory form being most elegantly suppressed: "in labours more abundant, in stripes above measure, in prisons more frequent, in deaths oft." Next is interposed a short period; for, by a suspension of the voice, "of the Jews five times" is to be marked off as constituting one member, to which is joined the second, "received I forty stripes save one." Then he returns to sections, and three are set down: "Thrice was I beaten with rods, once was I stoned, thrice I suffered shipwreck." Next comes a clause: "a night and a day I have been in the deep." Next fourteen sections burst forth with a vehemence which is most appropriate: "In journeyings often, in perils of waters, in perils of robbers, in perils by mine own countrymen, in perils by the heathen, in perils in the city, in perils in the wilderness, in perils in the sea, in perils among false brethren, in weariness and painfulness, in watchings often, in hunger and thirst, in fastings often, in cold and nakedness." After this comes in a period of three members: "Besides those things which are without, that which cometh upon me daily, the care of all the churches." And to this he adds two clauses in a tone of inquiry: "Who is weak, and I am not weak? who is offended, and I burn not?" In fine, this whole passage, as if panting for breath, winds up with a period of two members: "If I must needs glory, I will glory of the things which concern mine infirmities." And I cannot sufficiently express how beautiful and delightful it is when after this outburst he rests himself, and gives the hearer rest, by interposing a slight narrative. For he goes on to say: "The God and Father of our Lord Jesus Christ, which is blessed for evermore, knoweth that I lie not." And then he tells very briefly the danger he had been in, and the way he escaped it.

14. It would be tedious to pursue the matter further, or to point out the same facts in regard to other passages of Holy Scripture. Suppose I had taken the further trouble, at least in regard to the passages I have quoted from the apostle's writings, to point out figures of speech which are taught in the art of rhetoric? Is it not more likely that serious men would think I had gone too far, than that any of the studious would think I had done enough? All these things when taught by masters are reckoned of great value; great prices are paid for them, and the vendors puff them magniloquently. And I fear lest I too should smack of that puffery while thus descanting on matters of this kind. It was necessary, however, to reply to the ill-taught men who think our authors contemptible; not because they do not possess, but because they do not display, the eloquence which these men value so highly.

15. But perhaps some one is thinking that I have selected the Apostle Paul because he is our great orator. For when he says, "Though I be rude in speech, yet not in knowledge,"[1] he seems to speak as if granting so much to his detractors, not as confessing that he recognised its truth. If he had said, "I am indeed rude in speech, but not in knowledge," we could not in any way have put another meaning upon it. He did not hesitate plainly to assert his knowledge, because without it he could not have been the teacher of the Gentiles. And certainly if we bring forward anything of his as a model of eloquence, we take it from those epistles which even his very detractors, who thought his bodily presence weak and his speech contemptible, confessed to be weighty and powerful.[2]

I see, then, that I must say something about the eloquence of the prophets also, where many things are concealed under a metaphorical style, which the more completely they seem buried under figures of speech, give the greater pleasure when brought to light. In this place, however, it is my duty to select a passage of such a kind that I shall not be compelled to explain the matter, but only to

---

[1] 2 Cor. xi. 6.

[2] 2 Cor. x. 10.

commend the style. And I shall do so, quoting principally from the book of that prophet who says that he was a shepherd or herdsman, and was called by God from that occupation, and sent to prophesy to the people of God.[1] I shall not, however, follow the Septuagint translators, who, being themselves under the guidance of the Holy Spirit in their translation, seem to have altered some passages with the view of directing the reader's attention more particularly to the investigation of the spiritual sense; (and hence some passages are more obscure, because more figurative, in their translation;) but I shall follow the translation made from the Hebrew into Latin by the presbyter Jerome, a man thoroughly acquainted with both tongues.

16. When, then, this rustic, or *quondam* rustic prophet, was denouncing the godless, the proud, the luxurious, and therefore the most neglectful of brotherly love, he called aloud, saying: "Woe to you who are at ease in Zion, and trust in the mountain of Samaria, who are heads and chiefs of the people, entering with pomp into the house of Israel! Pass ye unto Calneh, and see; and from thence go ye to Hamath the great; then go down to Gath of the Philistines, and to all the best kingdoms of these: is their border greater than your border? Ye that are set apart for the day of evil, and that come near to the seat of oppression; that lie upon beds of ivory, and stretch yourselves upon couches; that eat the lamb of the flock, and the calves out of the midst of the herd; that chant to the sound of the viol. They thought that they had instruments of music like David; drinking wine in bowls, and anointing themselves with the costliest ointment: and they were not grieved for the affliction of Joseph."[2] Suppose those men who, assuming to be themselves learned and eloquent, despise our prophets as untaught and unskilful of speech, had been obliged to deliver a message like this, and to men such as these, would they have chosen to express themselves in any respect differently—those of them, at least, who would have shrunk from raving like madmen?

17. For what is there that sober ears could wish changed in this speech? In the first place, the invective itself; with what vehemence it throws itself upon the drowsy senses to startle them into wakefulness: "Woe to you who are at ease in Zion, and trust in the mountains of Samaria, who are heads and chiefs of the people, entering with pomp into the house of Israel!" Next, that he may use the favours of God, who has bestowed upon them ample territory, to show their ingratitude in trusting to the mountain of Samaria, where idols were worshipped: "Pass ye unto Calneh," he says, "and see; and from thence go ye to Hamath the great; then go down to Gath of the Philistines, and to all the best kingdoms of these: is their border greater than your border?" At the same time also that these things are spoken of, the style is adorned with names of places as with lamps, such as "Zion," Samaria," "Calneh," "Hamath the great," and "Gath of the Philistines." Then the words joined to these places are most appropriately varied: "ye are at ease," "ye trust," "pass on," "go," "descend."

18. And then the future captivity under an oppressive king is announced as approaching, when it is added: "Ye that are set apart for the day of evil, and come near to the seat of oppression." Then are subjoined the evils of luxury: "ye that lie upon beds of ivory, and stretch yourselves upon couches; that eat the lamb from the flock, and the calves out of the midst of the herd." These six clauses form three periods of two members each. For he does not say: Ye who are set apart for the day of evil, who come near to the seat of oppression, who sleep upon beds of ivory, who stretch yourselves upon couches, who eat the lamb from the flock, and calves out of the herd." If he had so expressed it, this would have had its beauty: six separate clauses running on, the same pronoun being repeated each time, and each clause finished

---

[1] Amos i. 1, vii. 14.

[2] Amos vi. 1-6. The version given above, which is a literal translation of Jerome's Latin, as quoted by Augustine, differs slightly from the English authorized version.

by a single effort of the speaker's voice. But it is more beautiful as it is, the clauses being joined in pairs under the same pronoun, and forming three sentences, one referring to the prophecy of the captivity: "Ye that are set apart for the day of evil, and come near the seat of oppression;" the second to lasciviousness: "ye that lie upon beds of ivory, and stretch yourselves upon couches;" the third to gluttony: "who eat the lamb from the flock, and the calves out of the midst of the herd." So that it is at the discretion of the speaker whether he finish each clause separately and make six altogether, or whether he suspend his voice at the first, the third, and the fifth, and by joining the second to the first, the fourth to the third, and the sixth to the fifth, make three most elegant periods of two members each: one describing the imminent catastrophe; another, the lascivious couch; and the third, the luxurious table.

19. Next he reproaches them with their luxury in seeking pleasure for the sense of hearing. And here, when he had said, "Ye who chant to the sound of the viol," seeing that wise men may practise music wisely, he, with wonderful skill of speech, checks the flow of his invective, and not now speaking to, but of, these men, and to show us that we must distinguish the music of the wise from the music of the voluptuary, he does not say, "Ye who chant to the sound of the viol, and think that ye have instruments of music like David;" but he first addresses to themselves what it is right the voluptuaries should hear, "Ye who chant to the sound of the viol;" and then, turning to others, he intimates that these men have not even skill in their art: "they thought that they had instruments of music like David; drinking wine in bowls, and anointing themselves with the costliest ointment." These three clauses are best pronounced when the voice is suspended on the first two members of the period, and comes to a pause on the third.

20. But now as to the sentence which follows all these: "and they were not grieved for the affliction of Joseph." Whether this be pronounced continuously as one clause, or whether with more elegance we hold the words, "and they were not grieved," suspended on the voice, and then add, "for the affliction of Joseph," so as to make a period of two members; in any case, it is a touch of marvellous beauty not to say, "and they were not grieved for the affliction of their brother;" but to put Joseph for brother, so as to indicate brothers in general by the proper name of him who stands out illustrious from among his brethren, both in regard to the injuries he suffered and the good return he made. And, indeed, I do not know whether this figure of speech, by which Joseph is put for brothers in general, is one of those laid down in that art which I learnt and used to teach. But how beautiful it is, and how it comes home to the intelligent reader, it is useless to tell any one who does not himself feel it.

21. And a number of other points bearing on the laws of eloquence could be found in this passage which I have chosen as an example. But an intelligent reader will not be so much instructed by carefully analysing it as kindled by reciting it with spirit. Nor was it composed by man's art and care, but it flowed forth in wisdom and eloquence from the Divine mind; wisdom not aiming at eloquence, yet eloquence not shrinking from wisdom. For if, as certain very eloquent and acute men have perceived and said, the rules which are laid down in the art of oratory could not have been observed, and noted, and reduced to system, if they had not first had their birth in the genius of orators, is it wonderful that they should be found in the messengers of Him who is the author of all genius? Therefore let us acknowledge that the canonical writers are not only wise but eloquent also, with an eloquence suited to a character and position like theirs.

CHAP. VIII.—The Obscurity of the Sacred Writers, though Compatible with Eloquence, Not to Be Imitated by Christian Teachers

22. But although I take some examples of eloquence from those writings of theirs which there is no difficulty in understanding, we are not by any means to suppose that it is our duty to imitate them in those passages where, with a view to exercise and train the minds of their readers, and to break in upon the satiety and stimulate the zeal of those who are willing to learn, and with a view also to throw a veil over the minds of the godless either that they may be converted to piety or shut out from a knowledge of the mysteries, from one or other of these reasons they have expressed themselves with a useful and wholesome obscurity. They have indeed expressed themselves in such a way that those who in after ages understood and explained them aright have in the Church of God obtained an esteem, not indeed equal to that with which they are themselves regarded, but coming next to it. The expositors of these writers, then, ought not to express themselves in the same way, as if putting forward their expositions as of the same authority; but they ought in all their deliverances to make it their first and chief aim to be understood, using as far as possible such clearness of speech that either he will be very dull who does not understand them, or that if what they say should not be very easily or quickly understood, the reason will lie not in their manner of expression, but in the difficulty and subtilty of the matter they are trying to explain.

CHAP. IX.—How, and with Whom, Difficult Passages Are to Be Discussed

23. For there are some passages which are not understood in their proper force, or are understood with great difficulty, at whatever length, however clearly, or with whatever eloquence the speaker may expound them; and these should never be brought before the people at all, or only on rare occasions when there is some urgent reason. In books, however, which are written in such a style that, if understood, they, so to speak, draw their own readers, and if not understood, give no trouble to those who do not care to read them, and in private conversations, we must not shrink from the duty of bringing the truth which we ourselves have reached within the comprehension of others, however difficult it may be to understand it, and whatever labour in the way of argument it may cost us. Only two conditions are to be insisted upon, that our hearer or companion should have an earnest desire to learn the truth, and should have capacity of mind to receive it in whatever form it may be communicated, the teacher not being so anxious about the eloquence as about the clearness of his teaching.

CHAP. X.—The Necessity for Perspicuity of Style

24. Now a strong desire for clearness sometimes leads to neglect of the more polished forms of speech, and indifference about what sounds well, compared with what clearly expresses and conveys the meaning intended. Whence a certain author, when dealing with speech of this kind, says that there is in it "a kind of careful negligence."[1] Yet while taking away ornament, it does not bring in vulgarity of speech; though good teachers have, or ought to have, so great an anxiety about teaching that they will employ a word (which cannot be made pure Latin without becoming obscure or ambiguous, but which when used according to the vulgar idiom is neither ambiguous nor obscure) not in the way the learned, but rather in the way the unlearned employ it. For if our translators did not shrink from saying, "Non congregabo conventicula eorum de sanguinibus,"[2] because they felt that it was important for the sense to put a word here in the plural which in Latin is only used in the singular; why should a teacher of godliness who is addressing an unlearned audience shrink from using *ossum* instead of *os,* if he fear that the latter might be taken not as the singular of *ossa,* but as

---

[1] Cicero, *Orator.* 23: "Quædam etiam negligentia est diligens."

[2] "I shall not assemble their assemblies of blood," Ps. xvi. 4. (Vulgate.) "Their drink-offerings of blood will I not offer." (A. V.)

the singular of *ora,* seeing that African ears have no quick perception of the shortness or length of vowels? And what advantage is there in purity of speech which does not lead to understanding in the hearer, seeing that there is no use at all in speaking, if they do not understand us for whose sake we speak? He, therefore, who teaches will avoid all words that do not teach; and if instead of them he can find words which are at once pure and intelligible, he will take these by preference; if, however, he cannot, either because there are no such words, or because they do not at the time occur to him, he will use words that are not quite pure, if only the substance of his thought be conveyed and apprehended in its integrity.

25. And this must be insisted on as necessary to our being understood, not only in conversations, whether with one person or with several, but much more in the case of a speech delivered in public: for in conversation any one has the power of asking a question; but when all are silent that one may be heard, and all faces are turned attentively upon him, it is neither customary nor decorous for a person to ask a question about what he does not understand; and on this account the speaker ought to be especially careful to give assistance to those who cannot ask it. Now a crowd anxious for instruction generally shows by its movements if it understands what is said; and until some indication of this sort be given, the subject discussed ought to be turned over and over, and put in every shape and form and variety of expression, a thing which cannot be done by men who are repeating words prepared beforehand and committed to memory. As soon, however, as the speaker has ascertained that what he says is understood, he ought either to bring his address to a close, or pass on to another point. For if a man gives pleasure when he throws light upon points on which people wish for instruction, he becomes wearisome when he dwells at length upon things that are already well known, especially when men's expectation was fixed on having the difficulties of the passage removed. For even things that are very well known are told for the sake of the pleasure they give, if the attention be directed not to the things themselves, but to the way in which they are told. Nay, even when the style itself is already well known, if it be pleasing to the hearers, it is almost a matter of indifference whether he who speaks be a speaker or a reader. For things that are gracefully written are often not only read with delight by those who are making their first acquaintance with them, but re-read with delight by those who have already made acquaintance with them, and have not yet forgotten them; nay, both these classes will derive pleasure even from hearing another man repeat them. And if a man has forgotten anything, when he is reminded of it he is taught. But I am not now treating of the mode of giving pleasure. I am speaking of the mode in which men who desire to learn ought to be taught. And the best mode is that which secures that he who hears shall hear the truth, and that what he hears he shall understand. And when this point has been reached, no further labour need be spent on the truth itself, as if it required further explanation; but perhaps some trouble may be taken to enforce it so as to bring it home to the heart. If it appear right to do this, it ought to be done so moderately as not to lead to weariness and impatience.

CHAP. XI.—The Christian Teacher Must Speak Clearly, but Not Inelegantly

26. For teaching, of course, true eloquence consists, not in making people like what they disliked, nor in making them do what they shrank from, but in making clear what was obscure; yet if this be done without grace of style, the benefit does not extend beyond the few eager students who are anxious to know whatever is to be learnt, however rude and unpolished the form in which it is put; and who, when they have succeeded in their object, find the plain truth pleasant food enough. And it is one of the distinctive features of good intellects not to love words, but the truth in words. For of what service is a golden key, if it cannot open what we want it to open? Or what objection is there to a wooden one if it can, seeing that to open what is shut is all we want? But as there is a certain analogy between learning and eating, the very food without which it is impossible to live must be flavoured to meet the tastes of the majority.

Chap. xii.—The Aim of the Orator, according to Cicero, Is to Teach, to Delight, and to Move. Of These, Teaching Is the Most Essential

27. Accordingly a great orator has truly said that "an eloquent man must speak so as to teach, to delight, and to persuade."[1] Then he adds: "To teach is a necessity, to delight is a beauty, to persuade is a triumph."[2] Now of these three, the one first mentioned, the teaching, which is a matter of necessity, depends on what we say; the other two on the way we say it. He, then, who speaks with the purpose of teaching should not suppose that he has said what he has to say as long as he is not understood; for although what he has said be intelligible to himself, it is not said at all to the man who does not understand it. If, however, he is understood, he has said his say, whatever may have been his manner of saying it. But if he wishes to delight or persuade his hearer as well, he will not accomplish that end by putting his thought in any shape no matter what, but for that purpose the style of speaking is a matter of importance. And as the hearer must be pleased in order to secure his attention, so he must be persuaded in order to move him to action. And as he is pleased if you speak with sweetness and elegance, so he is persuaded if he be drawn by your promises, and awed by your threats; if he reject what you condemn, and embrace what you commend; if he grieve when you heap up objects for grief, and rejoice when you point out an object for joy; if he pity those whom you present to him as objects of pity, and shrink from those whom you set before him as men to be feared and shunned. I need not go over all the other things that can be done by powerful eloquence to move the minds of the hearers, not telling them what they ought to do, but urging them to do what they already know ought to be done.

28. If, however, they do not yet know this, they must of course be instructed before they can be moved. And perhaps the mere knowledge of their duty will have such an effect that there will be no need to move them with greater strength of eloquence. Yet when this is needful, it ought to be done. And it is needful when people, knowing what they ought to do, do it not. Therefore, to teach is a necessity. For what men know, it is in their own hands either to do or not to do. But who would say that it is their duty to do what they do not know? On the same principle, to persuade is not a necessity: for it is not always called for; as, for example, when the hearer yields his assent to one who simply teaches or gives pleasure. For this reason also to persuade is a triumph, because it is possible that a man may be taught and delighted, and yet not give his consent. And what will be the use of gaining the first two ends if we fail in the third? Neither is it a necessity to give pleasure; for when, in the course of an address, the truth is clearly pointed out (and this is the true function of teaching), it is not the fact, nor is it the intention, that the style of speech should make the truth pleasing, or that the style should of itself give pleasure; but the truth itself, when exhibited in its naked simplicity, gives pleasure, because it is the truth. And hence even falsities are frequently a source of pleasure when they are brought to light and exposed. It is not, of course, their falsity that gives pleasure; but as it is true that they are false, the speech which shows this to be true gives pleasure.

Chap. xiii.—The Hearer Must Be Moved as well as Instructed

29. But for the sake of those who are so fastidious that they do not care for truth unless it is put in the form of a pleasing discourse, no small place has been assigned in eloquence to the art of pleasing. And yet even this is not enough for those stubborn-minded men who both understand and are pleased with the teacher's discourse, without deriving any

---

[1] Cicero, *Orator.* 21: "Est igitur eloquens qui ita dicet, ut probet, ut delectet, ut flectat." Not quoted accurately by Augustine.

[2] "Probare, necessitatis est; delectare, suavitatis; flectere, victoriæ."

profit from it. For what does it profit a man that he both confesses the truth and praises the eloquence, if he does not yield his consent, when it is only for the sake of securing his consent that the speaker in urging the truth gives careful attention to what he says? If the truths taught are such that to believe or to know them is enough, to give one's assent implies nothing more than to confess that they are true. When, however, the truth taught is one that must be carried into practice, and that is taught for the very purpose of being practised, it is useless to be persuaded of the truth of what is said, it is useless to be pleased with the manner in which it is said, if it be not so learnt as to be practised. The eloquent divine, then, when he is urging a practical truth, must not only teach so as to give instruction, and please so as to keep up the attention, but he must also sway the mind so as to subdue the will. For if a man be not moved by the force of truth, though it is demonstrated to his own confession, and clothed in beauty of style, nothing remains but to subdue him by the power of eloquence.

CHAP. XIV.—Beauty of Diction to Be in Keeping with the Matter

30. And so much labour has been spent by men on the beauty of expression here spoken of, that not only is it not our duty to do, but it is our duty to shun and abhor, many and heinous deeds of wickedness and baseness which wicked and base men have with great eloquence recommended, not with a view to gaining assent, but merely for the sake of being read with pleasure. But may God avert from His Church what the prophet Jeremiah says of the synagogue of the Jews: "A wonderful and horrible thing is committed in the land: the prophets prophesy falsely, and the priests applaud them with their hands;[1] and my people love to have it so: and what will ye do in the end thereof?"[2]

[1] "And the priests bear rule by their means." (A. V.)

[2] Jer. v. 30, 31 (LXX.)[1] Jer. xxiii. 29.

O eloquence, which is the more terrible from its purity, and the more crushing from its solidity! Assuredly it is "a hammer that breaketh the rock in pieces." For to this God Himself has by the same prophet compared His own word spoken through His holy prophets.[1] God forbid, then, God forbid that with us the priest should applaud the false prophet, and that God's people should love to have it so. God forbid, I say, that with us there should be such terrible madness! For what shall we do in the end thereof? And assuredly it is preferable, even though what is said should be less intelligible, less pleasing, and less persuasive, that truth be spoken, and that what is just, not what is iniquitous, be listened to with pleasure. But this, of course, cannot be, unless what is true and just be expressed with elegance.

31. In a serious assembly, moreover, such as is spoken of when it is said, "I will praise Thee among much people,"[2] no pleasure is derived from that species of eloquence which indeed says nothing that is false, but which buries small and unimportant truths under a frothy mass of ornamental words, such as would not be graceful or dignified even if used to adorn great and fundamental truths. And something of this sort occurs in a letter of the blessed Cyprian, which, I think, came there by accident, or else was inserted designedly with this view, that posterity might see how the wholesome discipline of Christian teaching had cured him of that redundancy of language, and confined him to a more dignified and modest form of eloquence, such as we find in his subsequent letters, a style which is admired without effort, is sought after with eagerness, but is not attained without great difficulty. He says, then, in one place, "Let us seek this abode: the neighbouring solitudes afford a retreat where, whilst the spreading shoots of the vine trees, pendulous and intertwined, creep amongst the supporting reeds, the

[1] Jer. xxiii. 29.

[2] Ps. xxxv. 18.

leafy covering has made a portico of vine."[1] There is wonderful fluency and exuberance of language here; but it is too florid to be pleasing to serious minds. But people who are fond of this style are apt to think that men who do not use it, but employ a more chastened style, do so because they cannot attain the former, not because their judgment teaches them to avoid it. Wherefore this holy man shows both that he can speak in that style, for he has done so once, and that he does not choose, for he never uses it again.

CHAP. XV.—The Christian Teacher Should Pray before Preaching

32. And so our Christian orator, while he says what is just, and holy, and good (and he ought never to say anything else), does all he can to be heard with intelligence, with pleasure, and with obedience; and he need not doubt that if he succeed in this object, and so far as he succeeds, he will succeed more by piety in prayer than by gifts of oratory; and so he ought to pray for himself, and for those he is about to address, before he attempts to speak. And when the hour is come that he must speak, he ought, before he opens his mouth, to lift up his thirsty soul to God, to drink in what he is about to pour forth, and to be himself filled with what he is about to distribute. For, as in regard to every matter of faith and love there are many things that may be said, and many ways of saying them, who knows what it is expedient at a given moment for us to say, or to be heard saying, except God who knows the hearts of all? And who can make us say what we ought, and in the way we ought, except Him in whose hand both we and our speeches are? Accordingly, he who is anxious both to know and to teach should learn all that is to be taught, and acquire such a faculty of speech as is suitable for a divine. But when the hour for speech arrives, let him reflect upon that saying of our Lord's, as better suited to the wants

[1] Cyprian, *ad Donat.* Ep. i.

of a pious mind: "Take no thought how or what ye shall speak; for it shall be given you in that same hour what ye shall speak. For it is not ye that speak, but the Spirit of your Father which speaketh in you."[1] The Holy Spirit, then, speaks thus in those who for Christ's sake are delivered to the persecutors; why not also in those who deliver Christ's message to those who are willing to learn?

CHAP. XVI.—Human Directions Not to Be Despised, though God Makes the True Teacher

33. Now if any one says that we need not direct men how or what they should teach, since the Holy Spirit makes them teachers, he may as well say that we need not pray, since our Lord says, "Your Father knoweth what things ye have need of before ye ask Him;"[2] or that the Apostle Paul should not have given directions to Timothy and Titus as to how or what they should teach others. And these three apostolic epistles ought to be constantly before the eyes of every one who has obtained the position of a teacher in the Church. In the First Epistle to Timothy do we not read: "These things command and teach"?[3] What these things are, has been told previously. Do we not read there: "Rebuke not an elder, but entreat him as a father"?[4] Is it not said in the Second Epistle: "Hold fast the form of sound words, which thou hast heard of me"?[5] And is he not there told: "Study to show thyself approved unto God, a workman that needeth not to be ashamed, rightly dividing the word of truth"?[6] And in the same place: "Preach the word; be instant in season, out of season; reprove, rebuke, exhort, with all long-

[1] Matt. x. 19, 20.

[2] Matt. vi. 8.

[3] 1 Tim. iv. 11.

[4] 1 Tim. v. 1.

[5] 2 Tim. i. 13.

[6] 2 Tim. ii. 15.

suffering and doctrine."[1] And so in the Epistle to Titus, does he not say that a bishop ought to "hold fast the faithful word as he hath been taught, that he may be able by sound doctrine both to exhort and to convince the gainsayers"?[2] There, too, he says: "But speak thou the things which become sound doctrine: that the aged men be sober," and so on.[3] And there, too: "These things speak, and exhort, and rebuke with all authority. Let no man despise thee. Put them in mind to be subject to principalities and powers,"[4] and so on. What then are we to think? Does the apostle in any way contradict himself, when, though he says that men are made teachers by the operation of the Holy Spirit, he yet himself gives them directions how and what they should teach? Or are we to understand, that though the duty of men to teach even the teachers does not cease when the Holy Spirit is given, yet that neither is he who planteth anything, nor he who watereth, but God who giveth the increase?[5] Wherefore though holy men be our helpers, or even holy angels assist us, no one learns aright the things that pertain to life with God, until God makes him ready to learn from Himself, that God who is thus addressed in the psalm: "Teach me to do Thy will; for Thou art my God."[6] And so the same apostle says to Timothy himself, speaking, of course, as teacher to disciple: "But continue thou in the things which thou hast learned, and hast been assured of, knowing of whom thou hast learned them."[7] For as the medicines which men apply to the bodies of their fellow-men are of no avail except God gives them virtue (who can heal without their aid, though they cannot without His), and yet they are applied; and if it be done from a sense of duty, it is esteemed a work of mercy or benevolence; so the aids of teaching, applied through the instrumentality of man, are of advantage to the soul only when God works to make them of advantage, who could give the gospel to man even without the help or agency of men.

CHAP. XVII.—*Threefold Division of the Various Styles of Speech*

34. He then who, in speaking, aims at enforcing what is good, should not despise any of those three objects, either to teach, or to give pleasure, or to move, and should pray and strive, as we have said above, to be heard with intelligence, with pleasure, and with ready compliance. And when he does this with elegance and propriety, he may justly be called eloquent, even though he do not carry with him the assent of his hearer. For it is these three ends, viz. teaching, giving pleasure, and moving, that the great master of Roman eloquence himself seems to have intended that the following three directions should subserve: "He, then, shall be eloquent, who can say little things in a subdued style, moderate things in a temperate style, and great things in a majestic style:"[1] as if he had taken in also the three ends mentioned above, and had embraced the whole in one sentence thus: "He, then, shall be eloquent, who can say little things in a subdued style, in order to give instruction, moderate things in a temperate style, in order to give pleasure, and great things in a majestic style, in order to sway the mind."

CHAP. XVIII.—*The Christian Orator Is Constantly Dealing with Great Matters*

35. Now the author I have quoted could have exemplified these three directions, as laid down by himself, in regard to legal questions: he could not,

---

1 2 Tim. iv. 2.
2 Tit. i. 9.
3 Tit. ii. 1, 2.
4 Tit. ii. 15, iii. 1.
5 1 Cor. iii. 7.
6 Ps. cxliii. 10.
7 2 Tim. iii. 14.

---

1 Cicero, *Orator.* 29: "Is igitur erit eloquens, qui poterit parva summisse, modica temperate, magna granditer dicere."

however, have done so in regard to ecclesiastical questions,—the only ones that an address such as I wish to give shape to is concerned with. For of legal questions those are called small which have reference to pecuniary transactions; those great where a matter relating to man's life or liberty comes up. Cases, again, which have to do with neither of these, and where the intention is not to get the hearer to do, or to pronounce judgment upon anything, but only to give him pleasure, occupy as it were a middle place between the former two, and are on that account called middling, or moderate. For moderate things get their name from *modus* (a measure); and it is an abuse, not a proper use of the word *moderate,* to put it for *little.* In questions like ours, however, where all things, and especially those addressed to the people from the place of authority, ought to have reference to men's salvation, and that not their temporal but their eternal salvation, and where also the thing to be guarded against is eternal ruin, everything that we say is important; so much so, that even what the preacher says about pecuniary matters, whether it have reference to loss or gain, whether the amount be great or small, should not seem unimportant. For justice is never unimportant, and justice ought assuredly to be observed, even in small affairs of money, as our Lord says: "He that is faithful in that which is least, is faithful also in much."[1] That which is least, then, is very little; but to be faithful in that which is least is great. For as the nature of the circle, viz. that all lines drawn from the centre to the circumference are equal, is the same in a great disk that it is in the smallest coin; so the greatness of justice is in no degree lessened, though the matters to which justice is applied be small.

36. And when the apostle spoke about trials in regard to secular affairs (and what were these but matters of money?), he says: "Dare any of you, having a matter against another, go to law before the unjust, and not before the saints? Do ye not know that the saints shall judge the world? and if the world shall be judged by you, are ye unworthy to judge the smallest matters? Know ye not that we shall judge angels? how much more things that pertain to this life? If, then, ye have judgments of things pertaining to this life, set them to judge who are least esteemed in the Church. I speak to your shame. Is it so, that there is not a wise man among you? no, not one that shall be able to judge between his brethren? But brother goeth to law with brother, and that before the unbelievers. Now therefore there is utterly a fault among you, because ye go to law one with another: why do ye not rather take wrong? why do ye not rather suffer yourselves to be defrauded? Nay, ye do wrong, and defraud, and that your brethren. Know ye not that the unrighteous shall not inherit the kingdom of God?"[1] Why is it that the apostle is so indignant, and that he thus accuses, and upbraids, and chides, and threatens? Why is it that the changes in his tone, so frequent and so abrupt, testify to the depth of his emotion? Why is it, in fine, that he speaks in a tone so exalted about matters so very trifling? Did secular matters deserve so much at his hands? God forbid. No; but all this is done for the sake of justice, charity, and piety, which in the judgment of every sober mind are great, even when applied to matters the very least.

37. Of course, if we were giving men advice as to how they ought to conduct secular cases, either for themselves or for their connections, before the church courts, we would rightly advise them to conduct them quietly as matters of little moment. But we are treating of the manner of speech of the man who is to be a teacher of the truths which deliver us from eternal misery and bring us to eternal happiness; and wherever these truths are spoken of, whether in public or private, whether to one or many, whether to friends or enemies, whether in a continuous discourse or in conversation, whether in tracts, or in books, or in

[1] Luke xvi. 10.

[1] 1 Cor. vi. 1–9.

letters long or short, they are of great importance. Unless indeed we are prepared to say that, because a cup of cold water is a very trifling and common thing, the saying of our Lord that he who gives a cup of cold water to one of His disciples shall in no wise lose his reward,[1] is very trivial and unimportant. Or that when a preacher takes this saying as his text, he should think his subject very unimportant, and therefore speak without either eloquence or power, but in a subdued and humble style. Is it not the case that when we happen to speak on this subject to the people, and the presence of God is with us, so that what we say is not altogether unworthy of the subject, a tongue of fire springs up out of that cold water which inflames even the cold hearts of men with a zeal for doing works of mercy in hope of an eternal reward?

CHAP. XIX.—The Christian Teacher Must Use Different Styles on Different Occasions

38. And yet, while our teacher ought to speak of great matters, he ought not always to be speaking of them in a majestic tone, but in a subdued tone when he is teaching, temperately when he is giving praise or blame. When, however, something is to be done, and we are speaking to those who ought, but are not willing, to do it, then great matters must be spoken of with power, and in a manner calculated to sway the mind. And sometimes the same important matter is treated in all these ways at different times, quietly when it is being taught, temperately when its importance is being urged, and powerfully when we are forcing a mind that is averse to the truth to turn and embrace it. For is there anything greater than God Himself? Is nothing, then, to be learnt about Him? Or ought he who is teaching the Trinity in unity to speak of it otherwise than in the method of calm discussion, so that in regard to a subject which it is not easy to comprehend, we may understand as much as it is given us to understand? Are we in this case to seek out ornaments instead of proofs? Or is the hearer to be moved to do something instead of being instructed so that he may learn something? But when we come to praise God, either in Himself, or in His works, what a field for beauty and splendour of language opens up before man, who can task his powers to the utmost in praising Him whom no one can adequately praise, though there is no one who does not praise Him in some measure! But if He be not worshipped, or if idols, whether they be demons or any created being whatever, be worshipped with Him or in preference to Him, then we ought to speak out with power and impressiveness, show how great a wickedness this is, and urge men to flee from it.

[1] Matt. x. 42.

CHAP. XX.—Examples of the Various Styles Drawn from Scripture

39. But now to come to something more definite. We have an example of the calm, subdued style in the Apostle Paul, where he says: "Tell me, ye that desire to be under the law, do ye not hear the law? For it is written, that Abraham had two sons; the one by a bond maid, the other by a free woman. But he who was of the bond woman was born after the flesh; but he of the free woman was by promise. Which things are an allegory: for these are the two covenants; the one from the Mount Sinai, which gendereth to bondage, which is Hagar. For this Hagar is Mount Sinai in Arabia, and answereth to Jerusalem which now is, and is in bondage with her children. But Jerusalem which is above is free, which is the mother of us all;"[1] and so on. And in the same way where he reasons thus: "Brethren, I speak after the manner of men: Though it be but a man's covenant, yet if it be confirmed, no man disannulleth, or addeth thereto. Now to Abraham and his seed were the promises made. He saith not, And to seeds, as of many; but

[1] Gal. iv. 21–26.

as of one, And to thy seed, which is Christ. And this I say, that the covenant, that was confirmed before of God in Christ, the law, which was four hundred and thirty years after, cannot disannul, that it should make the promise of none effect. For if the inheritance be of the law, it is no more of promise: but God gave it to Abraham by promise."[1] And because it might possibly occur to the hearer to ask, If there is no inheritance by the law, why then was the law given? he himself anticipates this objection and asks, "Wherefore then serveth the law?" And the answer is given: "It was added because of transgressions, till the seed should come to whom the promise was made; and it was ordained by angels in the hand of a mediator. Now a mediator is not a mediator of one; but God is one." And here an objection occurs which he himself has stated: "Is the law then against the promises of God?" He answers: "God forbid." And he also states the reason in these words: "For if there had been a law given which could have given life, verily righteousness should have been by the law. But the Scripture hath concluded all under sin, that the promise by faith of Jesus Christ might be given to them that believe."[2] It is part, then, of the duty of the teacher not only to interpret what is obscure, and to unravel the difficulties of questions, but also, while doing this, to meet other questions which may chance to suggest themselves, lest these should cast doubt or discredit on what we say. If, however, the solution of these questions suggest itself as soon as the questions themselves arise, it is useless to disturb what we cannot remove. And besides, when out of one question other questions arise, and out of these again still others; if these be all discussed and solved, the reasoning is extended to such a length, that unless the memory be exceedingly powerful and active, the reasoner finds it impossible to return to the original question from which he set out. It is, however, exceedingly desirable that whatever occurs to the mind as an objection that might be urged should be stated and refuted, lest it turn up at a time when no one will be present to answer it, or lest, if it should occur to a man who is present but says nothing about it, it might never be thoroughly removed.

[1] Gal. iii. 15–18.

[2] Gal. iii. 19–22.

40. In the following words of the apostle we have the temperate style: "Rebuke not an elder, but entreat him as a father; and the younger men as brethren; the elder women as mothers, the younger as sisters."[1] And also in these: "I beseech you, therefore, brethren, by the mercies of God, that ye present your bodies a living sacrifice, holy, acceptable unto God, which is your reasonable service."[2] And almost the whole of this hortatory passage is in the temperate style of eloquence; and those parts of it are the most beautiful in which, as if paying what was due, things that belong to each other are gracefully brought together. For example: "Having then gifts, differing according to the grace that is given to us, whether prophecy, let us prophesy according to the proportion of faith; or ministry, let us wait on our ministering; or he that teacheth, on teaching; or he that exhorteth, on exhortation: he that giveth, let him do it with simplicity; he that ruleth, with diligence; he that showeth mercy, with cheerfulness. Let love be without dissimulation. Abhor that which is evil, cleave to that which is good. Be kindly affectioned one to another with brotherly love; in honour preferring one another; not slothful in business; fervent in spirit; serving the Lord; rejoicing in hope; patient in tribulation; continuing instant in prayer; distributing to the necessity of saints; given to hospitality. Bless them which persecute you: bless, and curse not. Rejoice with them that do rejoice, and weep with them that weep. Be of the same mind one toward another."[3] And how gracefully all this is brought to a close in a period of two members:

[1] 1 Tim. v. 1, 2.

[2] Rom. xii. 1.

[3] Rom. xii. 6–16.

"Mind not high things, but condescend to men of low estate!" And a little afterwards: "Render therefore to all their dues: tribute to whom tribute is due; custom to whom custom; fear to whom fear; honour to whom honour."[1] And these also, though expressed in single clauses, are terminated by a period of two members: "Owe no man anything, but to love one another." And a little farther on: "The night is far spent, the day is at hand: let us therefore cast off the works of darkness, and let us put on the armour of light. Let us walk honestly, as in the day; not in rioting and drunkenness, not in chambering and wantonness, not in strife and envying: but put ye on the Lord Jesus Christ, and make not provision for the flesh, to fulfil the lusts thereof."[2] Now if the passage were translated thus, "et carnis providentiam ne in concupiscentiis feceritis,"[3] the ear would no doubt be gratified with a more harmonious ending; but our translator, with more strictness, preferred to retain even the order of the words. And how this sounds in the Greek language, in which the apostle spoke, those who are better skilled in that tongue may determine. My opinion, however, is, that what has been translated to us in the same order of words does not run very harmoniously even in the original tongue.

41. And, indeed, I must confess that our authors are very defective in that grace of speech which consists in harmonious endings. Whether this be the fault of the translators, or whether, as I am more inclined to believe, the authors designedly avoided such ornaments, I dare not affirm; for I confess I do not know. This I know, however, that if any one who is skilled in this species of harmony would take the closing sentences of these writers and arrange them according to the law of harmony (which he could very easily do by changing some words for words of equivalent meaning, or by retaining the words he finds and altering their arrangement), he will learn that these divinely-inspired men are not defective in any of those points which he has been taught in the schools of the grammarians and rhetoricians to consider of importance; and he will find in them many kinds of speech of great beauty,—beautiful even in our language, but especially beautiful in the original,—none of which can be found in those writings of which they boast so much. But care must be taken that, while adding harmony, we take away none of the weight from these divine and authoritative utterances. Now our prophets were so far from being deficient in the musical training from which this harmony we speak of is most fully learnt, that Jerome, a very learned man, describes even the metres employed by some of them,[1] in the Hebrew language at least; though, in order to give an accurate rendering of the words, he has not preserved these in his translation. I, however (to speak of my own feeling, which is better known to me than it is to others, and than that of others is to me), while I do not in my own speech, however modestly I think it done, neglect these harmonious endings, am just as well pleased to find them in the sacred authors very rarely.

42. The majestic style of speech differs from the temperate style just spoken of, chiefly in that it is not so much decked out with verbal ornaments as exalted into vehemence by mental emotion. It uses, indeed, nearly all the ornaments that the other does; but if they do not happen to be at hand, it does not seek for them. For it is borne on by its own vehemence; and the force of the thought, not the desire for ornament, makes it seize upon any beauty of expression that comes in its way. It is enough for its object that warmth of feeling should suggest the fitting words; they need not be selected by careful elaboration of speech. If

[1] Rom. xiii. 7.

[2] Rom. xiii. 12–14.

[3] Instead of "*ne feceritis in concupiscentiis,*" which is the translation as quoted by Augustine.

[1] In his preface to Job.

a brave man be armed with weapons adorned with gold and jewels, he works feats of valour with those arms in the heat of battle, not because they are costly, but because they are arms; and yet the same man does great execution, even when anger furnishes him with a weapon that he digs out of the ground.[1] The apostle in the following passage is urging that, for the sake of the ministry of the gospel, and sustained by the consolations of God's grace, we should bear with patience all the evils of this life. It is a great subject, and is treated with power, and the ornaments of speech are not wanting: "Behold," he says, "now is the accepted time; behold, now is the day of salvation. Giving no offence in anything, that the ministry be not blamed: but in all things approving ourselves as the ministers of God, in much patience, in afflictions, in necessities, in distresses, in strifes, in imprisonments, in tumults, in labours, in watchings, in fastings; by pureness, by knowledge, by long-suffering, by kindness, by the Holy Ghost, by love unfeigned, by the word of truth, by the power of God, by the armour of righteousness on the right hand and on the left, by honour and dishonour, by evil report and good report: as deceivers, and yet true; as unknown, and yet well known; as dying, and, behold, we live; as chastened, and not killed; as sorrowful, yet alway rejoicing; as poor, yet making many rich; as having nothing, and yet possessing all things."[2] See him still burning: "O ye Corinthians, our mouth is opened unto you, our heart is enlarged," and so on; it would be tedious to go through it all.

43. And in the same way, writing to the Romans, he urges that the persecutions of this world should be overcome by charity, in assured reliance on the help of God. And he treats this subject with both power and beauty: "We know," he says, "that all things work together for good to them that love God, to them who are the called according to His purpose. For whom He did foreknow, He also did predestinate to be conformed to the image of His Son, that He might be the first-born among many brethren. Moreover, whom He did predestinate, them He also called; and whom He called, them He also justified; and whom He justified, them He also glorified. What shall we then say to these things? If God be for us, who can be against us? He that spared not His own Son, but delivered Him up for us all, how shall He not with Him also freely give us all things? Who shall lay anything to the charge of God's elect? It is God that justifieth; who is he that condemneth? It is Christ that died, yea rather, that is risen again, who is even at the right hand of God, who also maketh intercession for us. Who shall separate us from the love of Christ? shall tribulation, or distress, or persecution, or famine, or nakedness, or peril, or sword? (As it is written, For Thy sake we are killed all the day long; we are accounted as sheep for the slaughter.) Nay, in all these things we are more than conquerors, through Him that loved us. For I am persuaded, that neither death, nor life, nor angels, nor principalities, nor powers, nor things present, nor things to come, nor height, nor depth, nor any other creature, shall be able to separate us from the love of God, which is in Christ Jesus our Lord."[1]

44. Again, in writing to the Galatians, although the whole epistle is written in the subdued style, except at the end, where it rises into a temperate eloquence, yet he interposes one passage of so much feeling that, notwithstanding the absence of any ornaments such as appear in the passages just quoted, it cannot be called anything but powerful: "Ye observe days, and months, and times, and years. I am afraid of you, lest I have bestowed upon you labour in vain. Brethren, I beseech you, be as I am; for I am as ye are: ye have not injured me at all. Ye know how, through infirmity of the flesh, I preached the gospel unto you at the first.

[1] An allusion to Virgil's *Æneid,* vii. 508: "Quod cuique repertum Rimanti, telum ira fecit."

[2] 2 Cor. vi. 2–10.

[1] Rom. viii. 28–39.

And my temptation which was in my flesh ye despised not, nor rejected; but received me as an angel of God, even as Christ Jesus. Where is then the blessedness ye spake of? for I bear you record, that, if it had been possible, ye would have plucked out your own eyes, and have given them to me. Am I therefore become your enemy, because I tell you the truth? They zealously affect you, but not well; yea, they would exclude you, that ye might affect them. But it is good to be zealously affected always in a good thing, and not only when I am present with you. My little children, of whom I travail in birth again until Christ be formed in you, I desire to be present with you now, and to change my voice; for I stand in doubt of you."[1] Is there anything here of contrasted words arranged antithetically, or of words rising gradually to a climax, or of sonorous clauses, and sections, and periods? Yet, notwithstanding, there is a glow of strong emotion that makes us feel the fervour of eloquence.

CHAP. XXI.—Examples of the Various Styles, Drawn from the Teachers of the Church, Especially Ambrose and Cyprian

45. But these writings of the apostles, though clear, are yet profound, and are so written that one who is not content with a superficial acquaintance, but desires to know them thoroughly, must not only read and hear them, but must have an expositor. Let us, then, study these various modes of speech as they are exemplified in the writings of men who, by reading the Scriptures, have attained to the knowledge of divine and saving truth, and have ministered it to the Church. Cyprian of blessed memory writes in the subdued style in his treatise on the sacrament of the cup. In this book he resolves the question, whether the cup of the Lord ought to contain water only, or water mingled with wine. But we must quote a passage by way of illustration. After the customary introduction, he proceeds to the discussion of the point in question. "Observe," he says, "that we are instructed, in presenting the cup, to maintain the custom handed down to us from the Lord, and to do nothing that our Lord has not first done for us: so that the cup which is offered in remembrance of Him should be mixed with wine. For, as Christ says, 'I am the true vine,'[1] it follows that the blood of Christ is wine, not water; and the cup cannot appear to contain His blood by which we are redeemed and quickened, if the wine be absent; for by the wine is the blood of Christ typified, that blood which is foreshadowed and proclaimed in all the types and declarations of Scripture. For we find that in the book of Genesis this very circumstance in regard to the sacrament is foreshadowed, and our Lord's sufferings typically set forth, in the case of Noah, when he drank wine, and was drunken, and was uncovered within his tent, and his nakedness was exposed by his second son, and was carefully hidden by his elder and his younger sons.[2] It is not necessary to mention the other circumstances in detail, as it is only necessary to observe this point, that Noah, foreshadowing the future reality, drank, not water, but wine, and thus showed forth our Lord's passion. In the same way we see the sacrament of the Lord's supper prefigured in the case of Melchizedek the priest, according to the testimony of the Holy Scriptures, where it says: 'And Melchizedek king of Salem brought forth bread and wine: and he was the priest of the most high God. And he blessed Abraham.'[3] Now, that Melchizedek was a type of Christ, the Holy Spirit declares in the Psalms, where the Father addressing the Son says, 'Thou art a priest for ever after the order of Melchizedek.'[4]"[5] In this passage, and in all of the letter that follows,

---

[1] Gal. iv. 10–20.

[1] John xv. 1.

[2] Gen. ix. 20–24.

[3] Gen. xiv. 18, 19.

[4] Ps. cx. 4.

[5] *Ad Cœcilium,* Ep. 63. 1, 2.

the subdued style is maintained, as the reader may easily satisfy himself.

46. St. Ambrose also, though dealing with a question of very great importance, the equality of the Holy Spirit with the Father and the Son, employs the subdued style, because the object he has in view demands, not beauty of diction, nor the swaying of the mind by the stir of emotion, but facts and proofs. Accordingly, in the introduction to his work, we find the following passage among others: "When Gideon was startled by the message he had heard from God, that, though thousands of the people failed, yet through one man God would deliver His people from their enemies, he brought forth a kid of the goats, and by direction of the angel laid it with unleavened cakes upon a rock, and poured the broth over it; and as soon as the angel of God touched it with the end of the staff that was in his hand, there rose up fire out of the rock and consumed the offering.[1] Now this sign seems to indicate that the rock was a type of the body of Christ, for it is written, 'They drank of that spiritual rock that followed them, and that rock was Christ;'[2] this, of course, referring not to Christ's divine nature, but to His flesh, whose ever-flowing fountain of blood has ever satisfied the hearts of His thirsting people. And so it was at that time declared in a mystery that the Lord Jesus, when crucified, should abolish in His flesh the sins of the whole world, and not their guilty acts merely, but the evil lusts of their hearts. For the kid's flesh refers to the guilt of the outward act, the broth to the allurement of lust within, as it is written, 'And the mixed multitude that was among them fell a lusting; and the children of Israel also wept again and said, Who shall give us flesh to eat?'[3] When the angel, then, stretched out his staff and touched the rock, and fire rose out of it, this was a sign that our Lord's flesh, filled with the Spirit of God, should burn up all the sins of the human race. Whence also the Lord says, 'I am come to send fire on the earth.' "[1] And in the same style he pursues the subject, devoting himself chiefly to proving and enforcing his point.[2]

47. An example of the *temperate* style is the celebrated encomium on virginity from Cyprian: "Now our discourse addresses itself to the virgins, who, as they are the objects of higher honour, are also the objects of greater care. These are the flower on the tree of the Church, the glory and ornament of spiritual grace, the joy of honour and praise, a work unbroken and unblemished, the image of God answering to the holiness of the Lord, the brighter portion of the flock of Christ. The glorious fruitfulness of their mother the Church rejoices in them, and in them flourishes more abundantly; and in proportion as bright virginity adds to her numbers, in the same proportion does the mother's joy increase.'[3] And at another place in the end of the epistle, 'As we have borne,' he says, 'the image of the earthly, we shall also bear the image of the heavenly.'[4] Virginity bears this image, integrity bears it, holiness and truth bear it; they bear it who are mindful of the chastening of the Lord, who observe justice and piety, who are strong in faith, humble in fear, steadfast in the endurance of suffering, meek in the endurance of injury, ready to pity, of one mind and of one heart in brotherly peace. And every one of these things ought ye, holy virgins, to observe, to cherish, and fulfil, who having hearts at leisure for God and for Christ, and having chosen the greater and better part, lead and point the way to the Lord, to whom you have pledged your vows. Ye who are advanced in age, exercise control over the younger. Ye who are younger, wait upon the elders, and encourage your equals; stir up one another by mutual exhortations; provoke one another to glory by emulous examples of virtue; endure bravely, advance in spirituality, finish your course

---

[1] Judg. vi. 14–21.

[2] 1 Cor. x. 4.

[3] Num. xi. 4.

[1] Luke xii. 49.

[2] *De Spiritu Sancto,* lib. i. Prol.

[3] *De habitu Virginum,* chap. vii.

[4] 1 Cor. xv. 49.

with joy; only be mindful of us when your virginity shall begin to reap its reward of honour."[1]

48. Ambrose also uses the temperate and ornamented style when he is holding up before virgins who have made their profession a model for their imitation, and says: "She was a virgin not in body only, but also in mind; not mingling the purity of her affection with any dross of hypocrisy; serious in speech; prudent in disposition; sparing of words; delighting in study; not placing her confidence in uncertain riches, but in the prayer of the poor; diligent in labour; reverent in word; accustomed to look to God, not man, as the guide of her conscience; injuring no one, wishing well to all; dutiful to her elders, not envious of her equals; avoiding boastfulness, following reason, loving virtue. When did she wound her parents even by a look? When did she quarrel with her neighbours? When did she spurn the humble, laugh at the weak, or shun the indigent? She is accustomed to visit only those haunts of men that pity would not blush for, nor modesty pass by. There is nothing haughty in her eyes, nothing bold in her words, nothing wanton in her gestures: her bearing is not voluptuous, nor her gait too free, nor her voice petulant; so that her outward appearance is an image of her mind, and a picture of purity. For a good house ought to be known for such at the very threshold, and show at the very entrance that there is no dark recess within, as the light of a lamp set inside sheds its radiance on the outside. Why need I detail her sparingness in food, her superabundance in duty,—the one falling beneath the demands of nature, the other rising above its powers? The latter has no intervals of intermission, the former doubles the days by fasting; and when the desire for refreshment does arise, it is satisfied with food such as will support life, but not minister to appetite."[2] Now I have cited these latter passages as examples of the temperate style, because their purpose is not to induce those who have not yet devoted themselves to take the vows of virginity, but to show of what character those who have taken vows ought to be. To prevail on any one to take a step of such a nature and of so great importance, requires that the mind should be excited and set on fire by the majestic style. Cyprian the martyr, however, did not write about the duty of taking up the profession of virginity, but about the dress and deportment of virgins. Yet that great bishop urges them to their duty even in these respects by the power of a majestic eloquence.

49. But I shall select examples of the majestic style from their treatment of a subject which both of them have touched. Both have denounced the women who colour, or rather discolour, their faces with paint. And the first, in dealing with this topic, says: "Suppose a painter should depict in colours that rival nature's the features and form and complexion of some man, and that, when the portrait had been finished with consummate art, another painter should put his hand over it, as if to improve by his superior skill the painting already completed; surely the first artist would feel deeply insulted, and his indignation would be justly roused. Dost thou, then, think that thou wilt carry off with impunity so audacious an act of wickedness, such an insult to God the great artificer? For, granting that thou art not immodest in thy behaviour towards men, and that thou art not polluted in mind by these meretricious deceits, yet, in corrupting and violating what is God's, thou provest thyself worse than an adulteress. The fact that thou considerest thyself adorned and beautified by such arts is an impeachment of God's handiwork, and a violation of truth. Listen to the warning voice of the apostle: 'Purge out the old leaven, that ye may be a new lump, as ye are unleavened. For even Christ our passover is sacrificed for us: therefore let us keep the feast, not with old leaven, neither with the leaven of malice and wickedness; but with the unleavened bread of sincerity and truth.'[1] Now

[1] *De habitu Virginum,* chap. xviii.

[2] *De Virginibus,* lib. ii. chap. i.

[1] 1 Cor. v. 7, 8.

can sincerity and truth continue to exist when what is sincere is polluted, and what is true is changed by meretricious colouring and the deceptions of quackery into a lie? Thy Lord says, 'Thou canst not make one hair white or black;'[1] and dost thou wish to have greater power so as to bring to nought the words of thy Lord? With rash and sacrilegious hand thou wouldst fain change the colour of thy hair: I would that, with a prophetic look to the future, thou shouldst dye it the colour of flame."[2] It would be too long to quote all that follows.

50. Ambrose again, inveighing against such practices, says: "Hence arise these incentives to vice, that women, in their fear that they may not prove attractive to men, paint their faces with carefully-chosen colours, and then from stains on their features go on to stains on their chastity. What folly it is to change the features of nature into those of a painting, and from fear of incurring their husband's disapproval, to proclaim openly that they have incurred their own! For the woman who desires to alter her natural appearance pronounces condemnation on herself; and her eager endeavours to please another prove that she has first been displeasing to herself. And what testimony to thine ugliness can we find, O woman, that is more unquestionable than thine own, when thou art afraid to show thyself? If thou art comely, why dost thou hide thy comeliness? If thou art plain, why dost thou lyingly pretend to be beautiful, when thou canst not enjoy the pleasure of the lie either in thine own consciousness or in that of another? For he loves another woman, thou desirest to please another man; and thou art angry if he love another, though he is taught adultery in thee. Thou art the evil promptress of thine own injury. For even the woman who has been the victim of a pander shrinks from acting the pander's part, and though she be vile, it is herself she sins against and not another. The crime of adultery is almost more tolerable than thine; for adultery tampers with modesty, but thou with nature."[1] It is sufficiently clear, I think, that this eloquence calls passionately upon women to avoid tampering with their appearance by deceitful arts, and to cultivate modesty and fear. Accordingly, we notice that the style is neither subdued nor temperate, but majestic throughout. Now in these two authors whom I have selected as specimens of the rest, and in other ecclesiastical writers who both speak the truth and speak it well,—speak it, that is, judiciously, pointedly, and with beauty and power of expression,—many examples may be found of the three styles of speech, scattered through their various writings and discourses; and the diligent student may by assiduous reading, intermingled with practice on his own part, become thoroughly imbued with them all.

CHAP. XXII.—*The Necessity of Variety in Style*

51. But we are not to suppose that it is against rule to mingle these various styles: on the contrary, every variety of style should be introduced so far as is consistent with good taste. For when we keep monotonously to one style, we fail to retain the hearer's attention; but when we pass from one style to another, the discourse goes off more gracefully, even though it extend to greater length. Each separate style, again, has varieties of its own which prevent the hearer's attention from cooling or becoming languid. We can bear the subdued style, however, longer without variety than the majestic style. For the mental emotion which it is necessary to stir up in order to carry the hearer's feelings with us, when once it has been sufficiently excited, the higher the pitch to which it is raised, can be maintained the shorter time. And therefore we must be on our guard, lest, in striving to carry to a higher point the emotion we have excited, we rather lose what we have already gained. But after

[1] Matt. v. 36.

[2] Cyprian, *de habitu Virginum,* chap. xii.

[1] Ambrose, *de Virginibus,* lib. ii.

the interposition of matter that we have to treat in a quieter style, we can return with good effect to that which must be treated forcibly, thus making the tide of eloquence to ebb and flow like the sea. It follows from this, that the majestic style, if it is to be long continued, ought not to be unvaried, but should alternate at intervals with the other styles; the speech or writing as a whole, however, being referred to that style which is the prevailing one.

CHAP. XXIII.—*How the Various Styles Should Be Mingled*

52. Now it is a matter of importance to determine what style should be alternated with what other, and the places where it is necessary that any particular style should be used. In the majestic style, for instance, it is always, or almost always, desirable that the introduction should be temperate. And the speaker has it in his discretion to use the subdued style even where the majestic would be allowable, in order that the majestic when it is used may be the more majestic by comparison, and may as it were shine out with greater brilliance from the dark background. Again, whatever may be the style of the speech or writing, when knotty questions turn up for solution, accuracy of distinction is required, and this naturally demands the subdued style. And accordingly this style must be used in alternation with the other two styles whenever questions of that sort turn up; just as we must use the temperate style, no matter what may be the general tone of the discourse, whenever praise or blame is to be given without any ulterior reference to the condemnation or acquittal of any one, or to obtaining the concurrence of any one in a course of action. In the majestic style, then, and in the quiet likewise, both the other two styles occasionally find place. The temperate style, on the other hand, not indeed always, but occasionally, needs the quiet style; for example, when, as I have said, a knotty question comes up to be settled, or when some points that are susceptible of ornament are left unadorned and expressed in the quiet style, in order to give greater effect to certain exuberances (as they may be called) of ornament. But the temperate style never needs the aid of the majestic; for its object is to gratify, never to excite, the mind.

CHAP. XXIV.—*The Effects Produced by the Majestic Style*

53. If frequent and vehement applause follows a speaker, we are not to suppose on that account that he is speaking in the majestic style; for this effect is often produced both by the accurate distinctions of the quiet style, and by the beauties of the temperate. The majestic style, on the other hand, frequently silences the audience by its impressiveness, but calls forth their tears. For example, when at Cæsarea in Mauritania I was dissuading the people from that civil, or worse than civil, war which they called *Caterva* (for it was not fellow-citizens merely, but neighbours, brothers, fathers and sons even, who, divided into two factions and armed with stones, fought annually at a certain season of the year for several days continuously, every one killing whomsoever he could), I strove with all the vehemence of speech that I could command to root out and drive from their hearts and lives an evil so cruel and inveterate; it was not, however, when I heard their applause, but when I saw their tears, that I thought I had produced an effect. For the applause showed that they were instructed and delighted, but the tears that they were subdued. And when I saw their tears I was confident, even before the event proved it, that this horrible and barbarous custom (which had been handed down to them from their fathers and their ancestors of generations long gone by, and which like an enemy was besieging their hearts, or rather had complete possession of them) was overthrown; and immediately that my sermon was finished I called upon them with heart and voice to give praise and thanks to God. And, lo, with the blessing of Christ, it is now eight years or more since anything of the sort was attempted there. In many other cases besides I have observed that men show the effect made on them by the powerful elo-

quence of a wise man, not by clamorous applause so much as by groans, sometimes even by tears, finally by change of life.

54. The quiet style, too, has made a change in many; but it was to teach them what they were ignorant of, or to persuade them of what they thought incredible, not to make them do what they knew they ought to do but were unwilling to do. To break down hardness of this sort, speech needs to be vehement. Praise and censure, too, when they are eloquently expressed, even in the temperate style, produce such an effect on some, that they are not only pleased with the eloquence of the encomiums and censures, but are led to live so as themselves to deserve praise, and to avoid living so as to incur blame. But no one would say that all who are thus delighted change their habits in consequence, whereas all who are moved by the majestic style act accordingly, and all who are taught by the quiet style know or believe a truth which they were previously ignorant of.

CHAP. XXV.—*How the Temperate Style Is to Be Used*

55. From all this we may conclude, that the end arrived at by the two styles last mentioned is the one which it is most essential for those who aspire to speak with wisdom and eloquence to secure. On the other hand, what the temperate style properly aims at, viz. to please by beauty of expression, is not in itself an adequate end; but when what we have to say is good and useful, and when the hearers are both acquainted with it and favourably disposed towards it, so that it is not necessary either to instruct or persuade them, beauty of style may have its influence in securing their prompter compliance, or in making them adhere to it more tenaciously. For as the function of all eloquence, whichever of these three forms it may assume, is to speak persuasively, and its object is to persuade, an eloquent man will speak persuasively, whatever style he may adopt; but unless he succeeds in persuading, his eloquence has not secured its object. Now in the subdued style, he persuades his hearers that what he says is true; in the majestic style, he persuades them to do what they are aware they ought to do, but do not; in the temperate style, he persuades them that his speech is elegant and ornate. But what use is there in attaining such an object as this last? They may desire it who are vain of their eloquence and make a boast of panegyrics, and such-like performances, where the object is not to instruct the hearer, or to persuade him to any course of action, but merely to give him pleasure. We, however, ought to make that end subordinate to another, viz. the effecting by this style of eloquence what we aim at effecting when we use the majestic style. For we may by the use of this style persuade men to cultivate good habits and give up evil ones, if they are not so hardened as to need the vehement style; or if they have already begun a good course, we may induce them to pursue it more zealously, and to persevere in it with constancy. Accordingly, even in the temperate style we must use beauty of expression not for ostentation, but for wise ends; not contenting ourselves merely with pleasing the hearer, but rather seeking to aid him in the pursuit of the good end which we hold out before him.

CHAP. XXVI.—*In Every Style the Orator Should Aim at Perspicuity, Beauty, and Persuasiveness*

56. Now in regard to the three conditions I laid down a little while ago[1] as necessary to be fulfilled by any one who wishes to speak with wisdom and eloquence, viz. perspicuity, beauty of style, and persuasive power, we are not to understand that these three qualities attach themselves respectively to the three several styles of speech, one to each, so that perspicuity is a merit peculiar to the subdued style, beauty to the temperate, and persuasive power to the majestic. On the contrary, all speech, whatever its style, ought constantly to aim

[1] Chaps. xv. and xvii.

at, and as far as possible to display, all these three merits. For we do not like even what we say in the subdued style to pall upon the hearer; and therefore we would be listened to, not with intelligence merely, but with pleasure as well. Again, why do we enforce what we teach by divine testimony, except that we wish to carry the hearer with us, that is, to compel his assent by calling in the assistance of Him of whom it is said, "Thy testimonies are very sure"?[1] And when any one narrates a story, even in the subdued style, what does he wish but to be believed? But who will listen to him if he do not arrest attention by some beauty of style? And if he be not intelligible, is it not plain that he can neither give pleasure nor enforce conviction? The subdued style, again, in its own naked simplicity, when it unravels questions of very great difficulty, and throws an unexpected light upon them; when it worms out and brings to light some very acute observations from a quarter whence nothing was expected; when it seizes upon and exposes the falsity of an opposing opinion, which seemed at its first statement to be unassailable; especially when all this is accompanied by a natural, unsought grace of expression, and by a rhythm and balance of style which is not ostentatiously obtruded, but seems rather to be called forth by the nature of the subject: this style, so used, frequently calls forth applause so great that one can hardly believe it to be the subdued style. For the fact that it comes forth without either ornament or defence, and offers battle in its own naked simplicity, does not hinder it from crushing its adversary by weight of nerve and muscle, and overwhelming and destroying the falsehood that opposes it by the mere strength of its own right arm. How explain the frequent and vehement applause that waits upon men who speak thus, except by the pleasure that truth so irresistibly established, and so victoriously defended, naturally affords? Wherefore the Christian teacher and speaker ought, when he uses the subdued style, to endeavour not only to be clear and intelligible, but to give pleasure and to bring home conviction to the hearer.

[1] Ps. xciii. 5.

57. Eloquence of the temperate style, also, must, in the case of the Christian orator, be neither altogether without ornament, nor unsuitably adorned nor is it to make the giving of pleasure its sole aim, which is all it professes to accomplish in the hands of others; but in its encomiums and censures it should aim at inducing the hearer to strive after or hold more firmly by what it praises, and to avoid or renounce what it condemns. On the other hand, without perspicuity this style cannot give pleasure. And so the three qualities, perspicuity, beauty, and persuasiveness, are to be sought in this style also; beauty, of course, being its primary object.

58. Again, when it becomes necessary to stir and sway the hearer's mind by the majestic style (and this is always necessary when he admits that what you say is both true and agreeable, and yet is unwilling to act accordingly), you must, of course, speak in the majestic style. But who can be moved if he does not understand what is said? and who will stay to listen if he receives no pleasure? Wherefore, in this style, too, when an obdurate heart is to be persuaded to obedience, you must speak so as to be both intelligible and pleasing, if you would be heard with a submissive mind.

Chap. XXVII.—The Man Whose Life Is in Harmony with His Teaching Will Teach with Greater Effect

59. But whatever may be the majesty of the style, the life of the speaker will count for more in securing the hearer's compliance. The man who speaks wisely and eloquently, but lives wickedly, may, it is true, instruct many who are anxious to learn; though, as it is written, he "is unprofitable to himself."[1] Wherefore, also, the apostle says:

[1] Ecclus. xxxvii. 19.

"Whether in pretence or in truth Christ is preached."[1] Now Christ is the truth; yet we see that the truth can be preached, though not in truth,—that is, what is right and true in itself may be preached by a man of perverse and deceitful mind. And thus it is that Jesus Christ is preached by those that seek their own, and not the things that are Jesus Christ's. But since true believers obey the voice, not of any man, but of the Lord Himself, who says, "All therefore whatsoever they bid you observe, that observe and do: but do not ye after their works; for they say and do not;"[2] therefore it is that men who themselves lead unprofitable lives are heard with profit by others. For though they seek their own objects, they do not dare to teach their own doctrines, sitting as they do in the high places of ecclesiastical authority, which is established on sound doctrine. Wherefore our Lord Himself, before saying what I have just quoted about men of this stamp, made this observation: "The scribes and the Pharisees sit in Moses' seat."[3] The seat they occupied, then, which was not theirs but Moses', compelled them to say what was good, though they did what was evil. And so they followed their own course in their lives, but were prevented by the seat they occupied which belonged to another, from preaching their own doctrines.

60. Now these men do good to many by preaching what they themselves do not perform; but they would do good to very many more if they lived as they preach. For there are numbers who seek an excuse for their own evil lives in comparing the teaching with the conduct of their instructors, and who say in their hearts, or even go a little further, and say with their lips: Why do you not do yourself what you bid me do? And thus they cease to listen with submission to a man who does not listen to himself, and in despising the preacher they learn to despise the word that is preached. Wherefore the apostle, writing to Timothy, after telling him, "Let no man despise thy youth," adds immediately the course by which he would avoid contempt: "but be thou an example of the believers, in word, in conversation, in charity, in spirit, in faith, in purity."[1]

[1] Phil. i. 18.

[2] Matt. xxiii. 3.

[3] Matt. xxiii. 2.

Chap. xxviii.—Truth Is More Important than Expression. What Is Meant by Strife about Words

61. Such a teacher as is here described may, to secure compliance, speak not only quietly and temperately, but even vehemently, without any breach of modesty, because his life protects him against contempt. For while he pursues an upright life, he takes care to maintain a good reputation as well, providing things honest in the sight of God and men,[2] fearing God, and caring for men. In his very speech even he prefers to please by matter rather than by words; thinks that a thing is well said in proportion as it is true in fact, and that a teacher should govern his words, not let the words govern him. This is what the apostle says: "Not with wisdom of words, lest the cross of Christ should be made of none effect."[3] To the same effect also is what he says to Timothy: "Charging them before the Lord that they strive not about words to no profit, but to the subverting of the hearers."[4] Now this does not mean that, when adversaries oppose the truth, we are to say nothing in defence of the truth. For where, then, would be what he says when he is describing the sort of man a bishop ought to be: "that he may be able by sound doctrine both to exhort and convince the gainsayers"?[5] To strive about words is not to be

[1] 1 Tim. iv. 12.

[2] 2 Cor. viii. 21.

[3] 1 Cor. ii. 17.

[4] 2 Tim ii. 14.

[5] Tit. i. 9.

careful about the way to overcome error by truth, but to be anxious that your mode of expression should be preferred to that of another. The man who does not strive about words, whether he speak quietly, temperately, or vehemently, uses words with no other purpose than to make the truth plain, pleasing, and effective; for not even love itself, which is the end of the commandment and the fulfilling of the law,[1] can be rightly exercised unless the objects of love are true and not false. For as a man with a comely body but an ill-conditioned mind is a more painful object than if his body too were deformed, so men who teach lies are the more pitiable if they happen to be eloquent in speech. To speak eloquently, then, and wisely as well, is just to express truths which it is expedient to teach in fit and proper words,—words which in the subdued style are adequate, in the temperate, elegant, and in the majestic, forcible. But the man who cannot speak both eloquently and wisely should speak wisely without eloquence, rather than eloquently without wisdom.

CHAP. XXIX.—It Is Permissible for a Preacher to Deliver to the People What Has Been Written by a More Eloquent Man than Himself

If, however, he cannot do even this, let his life be such as shall not only secure a reward for himself, but afford an example to others; and let his manner of living be an eloquent sermon in itself.

62. There are, indeed, some men who have a good delivery, but cannot compose anything to deliver. Now, if such men take what has been written with wisdom and eloquence by others, and commit it to memory, and deliver it to the people, they cannot be blamed, supposing them to do it without deception. For in this way many become preachers of the truth (which is certainly desirable), and yet not many teachers; for all deliver the discourse which one real teacher has composed, and there are no divisions among them. Nor are such men to be alarmed by the words of Jeremiah the prophet, through whom God denounces those who steal His words every one from his neighbour.[1] For those who steal take what does not belong to them, but the word of God belongs to all who obey it; and it is the man who speaks well, but lives badly, who really takes the words that belong to another. For the good things he says seem to be the result of his own thought, and yet they have nothing in common with his manner of life. And so God has said that they steal His words who would appear good by speaking God's words, but are in fact bad, as they follow their own ways. And if you look closely into the matter, it is not really themselves who say the good things they say. For how can they say in words what they deny in deeds? It is not for nothing that the apostle says of such men: "They profess that they know God, but in works they deny Him."[2] In one sense, then, they do say the things, and in another sense they do not say them; for both these statements must be true, both being made by Him who is the Truth. Speaking of such men, in one place He says, "Whatsoever they bid you observe, that observe and do; but do not ye after their works;"—that is to say, what ye hear from their lips, that do; what ye see in their lives, that do ye not;—"for they say and do not."[3] And so, though they do not, yet they say. But in another place, upbraiding such men, He says, "O generation of vipers, how can ye, being evil, speak good things?"[4] And from this it would appear that even what they say, when they say what is good, it is not themselves who say, for in will and in deed they deny what they say. Hence it happens that a

[1] 1 Tim. i. 5 and Rom. xiii. 10.

[1] Jer. xxiii. 30.

[2] Tit. i. 16.

[3] Matt. xxiii. 3.

[4] Matt. xii. 34.

wicked man who is eloquent may compose a discourse in which the truth is set forth to be delivered by a good man who is not eloquent; and when this takes place, the former draws from himself what does not belong to him, and the latter receives from another what really belongs to himself. But when true believers render this service to true believers, both parties speak what is their own, for God is theirs, to whom belongs all that they say; and even those who could not compose what they say make it their own by composing their lives in harmony with it.

CHAP. XXX.—*The Preacher Should Commence His Discourse with Prayer to God*

63. But whether a man is going to address the people or to dictate what others will deliver or read to the people, he ought to pray God to put into his mouth a suitable discourse. For if Queen Esther prayed, when she was about to speak to the king touching the temporal welfare of her race, that God would put fit words into her mouth,[1] how much more ought he to pray for the same blessing who labours in word and doctrine for the eternal welfare of men? Those, again, who are to deliver what others compose for them ought, before they receive their discourse, to pray for those who are preparing it; and when they have received it, they ought to pray both that they themselves may deliver it well, and that those to whom they address it may give ear; and when the discourse has a happy issue, they ought to render thanks to Him from whom they know such blessings come, so that all the praise may be His "in whose hand are both we and our words."[1]

[1] Esth. iv. 16 (LXX.).

CHAP. XXXI.—*Apology for the Length of the Work*

64. This book has extended to a greater length than I expected or desired. But the reader or hearer who finds pleasure in it will not think it long. He who thinks it long, but is anxious to know its contents, may read it in parts. He who does not care to be acquainted with it need not complain of its length. I, however, give thanks to God that with what little ability I possess I have in these four books striven to depict, not the sort of man I am myself (for my defects are very many), but the sort of man he ought to be who desires to labour in sound, that is, in Christian doctrine, not for his own instruction only, but for that of others also.

[1] Wisd. vii. 16.

INTRODUCTION TO CHRISTINE DE PIZAN

One of the changes ushered in by the Renaissance in the general cultural scene in the West was an increased opportunity for education for girls and women. Sometimes in private schools, sometimes with private tutors, young women of the upper classes began to receive a broadly based liberal education. In keeping with the times, that education was often rhetorically based and involved extensive exercises and learning in the verbal arts.

Opportunities for the practice of rhetoric, or for other public roles or professions, expanded somewhat for women although not at the same pace as did improved educational venues. Some powerful female political leaders such as Catherine de'Medici, Isabella of Aragon, and Elizabeth of England emerged in the Renaissance. But opportunities for careers in universities, the Church, or commerce remained severely limited for women.

Perhaps because of the presence of powerful queens and female nobles, one of the best chances for privileged women to pursue active careers on the Ciceronian model so popular during the Renaissance was in the political courts. The role of the *courtier* emerged, as one who practiced the courtly rhetoric to which we referred in the introduction to this period. A courtier was a member of a royal or noble court, skilled in the arts of interpersonal persuasion, and adept at forming alliances and practicing diplomacy. The courtier could have been male or female, but in either case it was an inherently rhetorical career.

Christine de Pizan was born in Italy but lived in France during the early Renaissance, in the fourteenth and early fifteenth centuries. The French King Charles V was a patron of de Pizan and her family. De Pizan was a courtier and became adept at the practice of courtly rhetoric. She was also a writer of poetry, history, and biography.

We have here an excerpt from her book, *The Treasure of the City of Ladies,* written in 1405. Of particular interest is the advice she gives to women of how to act behind the scenes to achieve political and personal ends, to maintain a standing in court, and to secure a good reputation. Note how the advice she gives is for women to act in accord with their traditional roles as much as possible, while manipulating men in the latter's more active roles. The oppression of gender politics prevented her from defending a more independent role for women. But this reading is an excellent example of a growing rhetorical role for women. It is also a good example of what amounts to a rhetorical theory that may never be called by that name. We have noted that women, excluded from traditional rhetorical roles, nevertheless continued to practice rhetoric in other forms. De Pizan's advocacy of a courtly rhetoric is a rhetorical theory from the margin, showing how women of the early Renaissance found persuasive influence in effective ways even if excluded from the center of political activity.

CHRISTINE DE PIZAN

A MEDIEVAL WOMAN'S MIRROR OF HONOR

The Treasury of the City of Ladies

• • •

PART I

• • •

8. WHICH SHOWS HOW THE GOOD PRINCESS WISHES TO ATTRACT VIRTUE TO HER.

Guided by divine inspiration, the good princess will think of all these things. Here is how she will act. She will choose well-informed, ethical, and wise advisers to help her elect what is good and avoid what is evil. Although every mortal creature, by nature, is inclined to sin, she will strive to avoid specific mortal sins. As in medicine, she will be the good doctor who cures ills by their opposites. She will follow Chrysostom's *Commentary on the Gospel of Saint Matthew* which says: "Whoever wishes importance in Heaven must observe humility on earth." The most significant in the eyes of God is not the most honored on earth, but whoever is most just on earth will be exalted in Heaven. Since the good princess knows that honors generally inflate pride yet befit her husband's status and her own authority, she will direct her heart toward humility, protecting it from damage by arrogance and puffery by pride. She will thank God and attribute all honor to Him, never ceasing to recognize that she is poor, mortal, frail, and sinful, and that her worldly status is only an office for which she will be accountable to God shortly. In the eyes of eternity, her life's span is very short.

Though the dignity of her position requires this noble princess to receive homage from others, she will not take undue pleasure when it is rendered to her. She will avoid it whenever possible. Her manner, her bearing, and her speech will be gentle and kindly, her face friendly, her eyes lowered. Returning greetings to all who greet her, she will be so humane and courteous that her words will be pleasing to God and to all the world. This virtue of humility will make the noble lady patient. Although the world brings ample adversity to great lords and ladies as well as to the lowly, she never will be resentful no matter what happens. She will accept all adversity for the love of Our Lord, thanking Him humbly. If people wrong or injure her, as they might by accident or intention, she will not punish or pursue them. If they are rightfully and justly punished, she will pity them, remembering that God commands one to love one's enemies. Saint Paul says that charity is not self-seeking. Therefore she will pray to God to give them patience in suffering and to be merciful to them.

This noble lady's great constancy, courage, and force of character will not heed the darts of the envious. If she learns of frivolous slander against her, as happens every day to the best of people no matter how great they are, she will not be troubled nor take offence but will pardon readily. Nor because of her greatness will she suspect ill will if anyone slights her, recalling what Our Lord suffered for us and nevertheless prayed for His tormenters. Instead, this humble lady will question whether she could have offended in any manner, remembering virtuous Seneca's teaching to princes, princesses, and people in power: "It is great merit in the sight of God, praiseworthy in the world, and a sign of nobility to let pass lightly the slight which might easily be avenged." That is also a good example to lesser people.

Saint Gregory speaks similarly in the twenty-second book of the *Moralia:* "Nobody is perfect

Translated by Charity Cannon Willard
Edited by Madeleine Pelner Cosman

who does not have patience with the damage his neighbors may inflict upon him." He who cannot bear the trespasses of others shows by impatience that he is far from virtuous himself. The same saint's praise of patience says that just as the rose smells sweet and looks beautiful among sharp thorns, a patient creature shines victoriously among those who attempt to wrong her. The princess trying to amass virtue upon virtue should remember that Saint Paul says: "Whoever has all the other virtues, prays unceasingly, goes on pilgrimages, fasts at length, and does all good, but has no charity, profits in nothing."

Therefore, the princess contemplating all this will be so merciful toward everyone that she will suffer for them as for herself. Not content merely to note people in trouble, she will put her hand to the task of helping. As a sage said: "Charity is extended not only through aiding others with money from one's purse but also through comforting words, fitting advice, and all other good one can do." Through charity, this great lady will be the advocate of peace between the prince, her husband (or her son, if she is a widow), and her people, those to whom she has a duty to offer her assistance. If the prince, because of poor advice or for any other reason, should be tempted to harm his subjects, they will know their lady to be full of kindness, pity, and charity. They will come to her, humbly petitioning her to intercede for them before the prince. Poor and unable to request it themselves, they merit the lady's clemency.

9. Wherein It Is Explained How the Good and Wise Princess Will Attempt to Make Peace between the Prince and His Barons if There Is Any Difficulty between Them.

If any neighboring or foreign prince wars for any grievance against her lord, or if her lord wages war against another, the good lady will weigh the odds carefully. She will balance the great ills, infinite cruelties, losses, deaths, and destruction to property and people against the war's outcome, which is usually unpredictable. She will seriously consider whether she can preserve the honor of her lord and yet prevent the war. Working wisely and calling on God's aid, she will strive to maintain peace. So also, if any prince of the realm or the country, or any baron, knight, or powerful subject should hold a grudge against her lord, or if he is involved in any such quarrel and she foresees that for her lord to take a prisoner or make a battle would lead to trouble in the land, she will strive toward peace. In France the discontent of an insignificant baron (named Bouchart) against the King of France, the great prince, has recently resulted in great trouble and damage to the kingdom. The *Chronicles of France* recount the tale of many such misadventures. Again, not long ago, in the case of Lord Robert of Artois, a disagreement with the king harmed the French realm and gave comfort to the English.

Mindful of such terrible possibilities, the good lady will strive to avoid destruction of her people, making peace and urging her lord (the prince) and his council to consider the potential harm inherent in any martial adventure. Furthermore, she must remind him that every good prince should avoid shedding blood, especially that of his subjects. Since making a new war is a grave matter, only long thought and mature deliberation will devise the better way toward the desired result. Thus, always saving both her own honor and her lord's, the good lady will not rest until she has spoken, or has had someone else speak to those who have committed the misdeed in question, alternately soothing and reproving them. While their error is great and the prince's displeasure reasonable, and though he ought to punish them, she would always prefer peace. Therefore, if they would be willing to correct their ways or make suitable amends, she gladly would try to restore them to her lord's good graces.

With such words as these, the good princess will be peacemaker. In such manner, Good Queen Blanche, mother of Saint Louis, always strove to reconcile the king with his barons, and, among others, the Count of Champagne. The proper role of a good, wise queen or princess is to maintain peace and concord and to avoid wars and their resulting disasters. Women particularly should concern themselves with peace because men by nature are more foolhardy and headstrong, and their overwhelming desire to avenge themselves prevents them from foreseeing the resulting dangers and terrors of war. But woman by nature is more gentle and circumspect. Therefore, if she has sufficient will and wisdom she can provide the best possible means to pacify man. Solomon speaks of peace in the twenty-fifth chapter of the *Book of Proverbs.* Gentleness and humility assuage the prince. The gentle tongue (which means the soft word) bends and breaks harshness. So water extinguishes fire's heat by its moisture and chill.

Queens and princesses have greatly benefitted this world by bringing about peace between enemies, between princes and their barons, or between rebellious subjects and their lords. The Scriptures are full of examples. The world has no greater benevolence than a good and wise princess. Fortunate is that land which has one. I have listed as examples many of these wondrous women in *The Book of the City of Ladies.*

What results from the presence of such a princess? All her subjects who recognize her wisdom and kindness come to her for refuge, not only as their mistress but almost as the goddess on earth in whom they have infinite hope and confidence. Keeping the land in peace and tranquility, she and her works radiate charity.

• • •

11. Which Begins to Expound the Moral Teachings which Worldly Prudence Will Give the Princess.

Worldly Prudence's teachings and advice do not depart greatly from God's, but rather arise from them and depend on them. Therefore, we shall speak of the wise governance of life according to Prudence, who will teach the princess or noble lady to cherish honor and good reputation above all things in this earthly world. Prudence also will say that God is not in the least displeased with a creature living morally in the world, and she who lives the moral life will love the good renown called honor. Saint Augustine's *Book of Corrections* tells us that two things necessary for living well are conscience and good repute. Similarly, the wise author of the *Book of Ecclesiasticus* exhorts: "Cherish good repute for it will endure longer than any other treasure."

Agreeing that, above all earthly things, nothing so suits the noble as honor, the good princess will ask what qualities belong to true honor. Certainly not worldly riches, at least not according to the world's normal habits. Riches are of meager value in perfecting honor. What things, then, are suitable? Good morals. What in the world is the use of good morals? They perfect the noble creature, achieving the good repute wherein lies perfect honor. No matter what wealth a prince or princess possesses, if she does not lead a life of reputation and praise through doing good, she lacks honor regardless of the blandishments of her entourage to suggest that she has it. True honor must be above reproach. How greatly should the noble lady love honor? Certainly more than her life, for she would pay more dearly for the loss of it. The reason for this is clear. Whoever dies well is saved, but the one who is dishonored suffers reproach, living or dead, so long as she is remembered.

Good reputation is the greatest treasure a princess or noble lady can acquire. No other is so great or should be sought more eagerly. Ordinary treasure is useful only in the locale in which she finds herself, but the treasure which is the reputation of her honor serves her in lands near and far. Like the odor of sanctity, good repute is a sweet fragrance from the body wafting across the world so that everyone is aware of it. The fragrance of good repute thus goes forth from a worthy person so that everyone else may sense her good example.

After this admonishment by Prudence, the princess might well ask what she must do to put these ideas into practice. Her life will pivot around two particular points. One is the morals she will observe and abide by, and the other is the style of life which will direct her. Two moral considerations are especially necessary for women who desire honor, for without them it is unattainable: namely, Sobriety and Chastity.

Sobriety, the first, does not concern merely eating and drinking, but indeed all else serving to restrain and moderate excess. Sobriety will prevent a lady from being difficult to serve, for she will not be unreasonable in her demands. Despite her high estate she will be well satisfied with whatever is served of wines and foods. Not dwelling on such matters, she will partake of only the necessities life requires. Sobriety also will keep her from excessive sleep, because Prudence tells her that too much repose encourages sin and vice. Furthermore, Sobriety will deflect her from avarice. A small amount of wealth will be a great sufficiency for her. Above all, Prudence will restrain her from coveting extravagant clothes, jewels, headdresses, and an unreasonable mode of life. Unfailingly, Prudence will tell her that although all princesses and wealthy ladies customarily ought to be richly adorned with robes, headgear, and ornaments corresponding to their station in life, discretion must rule decoration. If you, good princess, are not content with your station nor the traditional styles and would prefer to acquire something finer or desire to introduce new styles, you are mistaken. For all frivolous things redound to your dishonor and insult the virtue of Sobriety. Therefore, do not do it. It benefits no one unless somehow it is in accord with the desires of one's lord. Even so, the good princess should not imitate anything extravagant without good advice, counsel, and just cause.

Sobriety also should be evident in all the lady's senses, as well as in her actions and costume. Her glance will be slow, deliberate, and without vagueness. Sobriety will protect her from too great curiosity about sweet scents, to which many ladies give great attention, spending large quantities of money on perfume. Likewise, it will tell her that she should not seek out or indulge the body in such delights, when she would do better to give the money to the poor. The same Sobriety will duly correct her tongue, for her speech must be free from extravagances so unbecoming to great ladies, and, indeed, to all worthy women. Heartily despising the vice of falsehood, she will prefer truth, which will be so habitual in her mouth that always what she says will be believed and respected. She will be known as a person who never lies. The virtue of truth is more necessary in the mouths of princes and princesses than in others because everyone must trust them. Sobriety also will prevent her from speaking words she has not carefully considered in advance, especially in those places where they will be weighed or reported.

Prudence and Sobriety teach a lady well-ordered speech and wise eloquence. She never will be coy, but will speak well-considered words, soft and rather low-pitched, uttered with a pleasant face and without excessive motion of the hands or body, nor facial grimaces. She will avoid excessive or uncalled-for laughter. Refraining from speaking ill of others, she will not blame, but rather will encourage goodness. Gladly she will keep in check vague, dishonest words, nor will she permit others to speak them to her. Her humor also will be discreet.

In the midst of her own entourage, the princess will speak a virtuous language of good example, so that those who listen to her directly, as well as those who hear later reports, will perceive that her words come from her goodness, wisdom, and honesty. Never speaking ungraciously to her companions or servants, nor quarreling or speaking viciously, instead she will instruct her household retainers and friends gently, correcting their shortcomings softly, politely, threatening to expel them if they do not reform, punishing them in a quiet voice without being needlessly unkind. Crude brutality from the mouth of a lady or, indeed, any woman turns more against herself than against the one to whom it is addressed. Moreover, her commands must be reasonable for the time and place, as well as suitable for the person receiving them, each according to his own proper duty.

The lady willingly will read books inculcating good habits, as well as studying on occasion devotional books. She will disdain volumes describing dishonest habits or vice. Never allowing them in her household, she will not permit them in the presence of any daughter, relative, or lady-in-waiting. Examples of good or of evil doubtlessly attract the attention of those who see or hear them. Hence the noble lady who takes pleasure in remembering or in speaking good words likewise will be pleased to listen to them; above all, she will delight in the words of God. Whoever belongs to God willingly hears His word. As it is set forth in Scripture: "Those who love me hear my word with a full heart and observe it." Consequently, she will invite good, notable clerics to deliver sermons on feast days, sharing these with her daughters, ladies, and her whole family, desiring the refinement of her own knowledge of our faith's articles, commandments, and ideas on Salvation.

Regarding worldly affairs, she will listen gladly to worthy people, brave knights, and gentlemen who speak of their deeds and accomplishments, as well as to great churchmen cherished for their knowledge, and to all noble men and women worthy of hearing for their fine sensibilities and exemplary lives. Appreciating them with honor, she also will lavish upon them suitable gifts. Similarly, the wise noblewoman will gather about her those who lead admirable, elevated lives of devotion. Seeking them out and receiving them humbly, she will talk to them in private, listening to them devotedly, and requesting remembrance in their prayers.

Thus the virtue of Sobriety will govern the noble princess. From this will follow naturally the regime of the second of the two virtues: the practice of Chastity. It will direct her to such purity that her word, deed, appearance, dress, countenance, bearing, status, and high regard will be unreproachable.

• • •

PART II

• • •

8. Which Tells How Unsuitable It Is for Women at Court to Talk about Each Other and to Say Unkind Things.

Women of the court must not slander or malign one another. Not only is it sinful and wrong because of the pertinent reasons already mentioned, but also, she who speaks ill of another deserves the same fate. The woman who knows others are maligning her will tend to combat gossip with gossip. No one, however, is sufficiently righteous to be able to say: "I do not fear a soul. What could anyone say about me? I am pure. And so, I boldly can speak of others." This is foolishness. Everyone has something that can be criticized. As the Scriptures say: "No man is without crime which means without sin." If you don't have a particular vice, you may actually discover you have a worse one, or two or three. If you examine your conscience well, you will find faults aplenty. Sins hidden from the world are known to God, who alone knows who is a good pilgrim.

Women of the court bicker; it is said around the town that the women of the court speak ill of one another. The court of a princess should resemble a well-run abbey, where the monks are under oath not to speak to lay-people or to others about what goes on in their midst in secret. Similarly, women of a court should love and support one another like sisters. They should not quarrel with each other in the ladies' quarters, nor talk behind each others' backs like fishwives. Unsuitable for the court of a princess, such behavior should not be permitted.

Envy, the third cause inspiring slander, is the least excusable, most wicked, and farthest removed from right reason. If the hate-filled person slanders the one who has wronged her, it is natural retribution for injury. If God did not forbid it, such slander would be understandable. Likewise, she who slanders because of opinion at least can base her accusations upon some vague appearances and misunderstandings. On the other hand, speaking ill from envy has no cause but sheer wickedness dwelling and flourishing in the human heart. This wickedness poisons the slanderous speaker and imperils the one slandered. Not the bite of a serpent, nor the blow of a sword, nor any other sharp thrust was ever as dangerous as the tongue of an envious person. This pointed barb strikes and kills aggressor and victim alike in both body and soul. If we were to count, good Lord, how many kingdoms, countries, and good people have been destroyed by false reports founded on envy, our sum would be staggering. But for brevity, we will omit these examples.

Envious slander also comes from pure malice, without another motive. How does the person who is good, or who has been blessed with certain gifts of grace or fortune, deserve to have anyone speak evil of him or to cause him difficulties? Good things surely may have come to him rightfully. He may be particularly happy or fortunate. Thus, slander coming from no reasonable cause must derive from sheer perniciousness, and for this reason it is most damnable. Since we already have spoken of this envy in the fourth and fifth chapters of this second part, we will say no more. Let this suffice as a warning to ladies, noblewomen, and others at court.

• • •

INTRODUCTION TO MARGARET FELL

Margaret Fell was an English woman living in the late Renaissance from 1614 to 1702. Fell was a member of the Society of Friends, or the Quaker Church, during its early years. The Friends developed doctrines of equality between the sexes, largely due to the efforts of Fell and her second husband, George Fox. Fell was an active public speaker during a period in which women were rarely found on the platform. Her speaking was rhetorically sophisticated for it used Biblical teachings to support the idea of women's equality, which Christian churches had not acknowledged much prior to this time.

Because of her political activity in speaking on behalf of equal rights, Fell often experienced trouble and persecution. The Friends were not the established Church of England, and like other such denominations were suppressed from time to time. During a period of imprisonment, Fell wrote her *Women's Speaking Justified, Proved, and Allowed by the Scriptures,* which is included here. This tract is a powerful example of rhetoric in its own right. It is also an example of rhetorical theory in that it attempts to make a place for the rhetorical practices of women in the social and political mainstream.

MARGARET FELL

WOMEN'S SPEAKING JUSTIFIED, PROVED, AND ALLOWED BY THE SCRIPTURES

Whereas it hath been an objection in the minds of many, and several times hath been objected by the clergy, or ministers, and others, against womens speaking in the Church; and so consequently may be taken, that they are condemned for meddling in the things of God; the ground of which objection, is taken from the Apostles[1] words, which he writ in his first Epistle to the *Corinthians,* chap. 14. vers. 34, 35. And also what he writ to *Timothy* in the first Epistle, chap. 2, vers. 11, 12. But how far they wrong the Apostles intentions in these Scriptures, we shall shew clearly when we come to them in their course and order. But first let me lay down how God himself hath manifested his Will and Mind concerning women, and unto women.

And first, when *God created Man in his own image; in the image of God created he them, male and female: and God blessed them, and God said unto them, Be fruitful, and multiply: And God said, Behold, I have given you of every herb,* etc.,

[1] The Apostle is Paul. [Ed.]

Gen. 1. Here God joins them together in his own image, and makes no such distinctions and differences as men do; for though they be weak, he is strong; and as he said to the Apostle, *His grace is sufficient,* and his *strength is made manifest in weakness,* 2 Cor. 12.9. And such hath the Lord chosen, even *the weak things of the world, to confound the things which are mighty; and things which are despised, hath God chosen, to bring to nought things that are,* 1 Cor. 1. And God hath put no such difference between the male and female as men would make.

It is true, *The serpent that was more subtle than any* other *beast of the field,* came unto the woman, with his temptations, and with a lie; his subtilty discerning her to be more inclinable to hearken to him; when he said, *If ye eat, your eyes shall be opened:* and the woman saw that *the fruit was good to make one wise,* there the temptation got into her, and *she did eat, and gave to her husband, and he did eat* also, and so they were both tempted into the transgression and disobedience; and therefore God said unto *Adam,* when that he hid himself when he heard his voice, *Hast thou eaten of the tree which I commanded thee that thou shouldest not eat?* And Adam said, *The woman which thou gavest me, she gave me of the tree, and I did eat.* And the Lord said unto the woman, *What is this that thou hast done?* and the woman said, *The serpent beguiled me, and I did eat.* Here the woman spoke the truth unto the Lord. See what the Lord saith, vers. 15, after he had pronounced sentence on the serpent: *I will put enmity between thee and the woman, and between thy seed and her seed; it shall bruise thy head, and thou shalt bruise his heel,* Gen. 3.

Let this word of the Lord, which was from the beginning, stop the mouths of all that oppose womens speaking in the power of the Lord; for he hath put enmity between the woman and the serpent; and if the seed of the woman speak not, the seed of the serpent speaks; for God hath put enmity between the two seeds, and it is manifest, that those that speak against the woman and her seeds speaking, speak out of the enmity of the old serpents seed; and God hath fulfilled his word and his promise, *When the fulness of time was come, he hath sent forth his Son, made of a woman, made under the Law, that we might receive the adoption of sons,* Gal. 4.4, 5. . . .

Thus we see that Jesus owned the love and grace that appeared in women, and did not despise it, and by what is recorded in the Scriptures, he received as much love, kindness, compassion, and tender dealing towards him from women, as he did from any others, both in his life time, and also after they had exercised their cruelty upon him, for *Mary Magdalene,* and *Mary* the *Mother of Joseph,* beheld where he was laid: *And when the Sabbath was past,* Mary Magdalene, *and* Mary *the* Mother of James, *and* Salome, *had brought sweet spices that they might anoint him. And very early in the morning, the first day of the week, they came unto the sepulchre at the rising of the sun, And they said among themselves, Who shall roll us away the stone from the door of the sepulchre? And when they looked, the stone was rolled away for it was very great,* Mark 16.1, 2, 3, 4. Luke 24.1, 2. *and they went down into the sepulchre,* and as *Matthew* saith, *The angel rolled away the stone, and he said unto the women, Fear not, I know whom ye seek,* Jesus *which was crucified: he is not here, he is risen,* Mat. 28. Now *Luke* saith thus, That there stood two men by them in shining apparel, and as they were perplexed and afraid, the men said unto them, he is not here; remember how he said unto you when he was in Galilee, that the *Son of Man* must be delivered into the hands of sinful men, and be crucified, and the third day rise again, and they remembered his words, and returned from the sepulchre, and told all these things to the eleven,[2] and to all the rest.

It was *Mary Magdalene,* and *Joanna,* and *Mary* the *Mother of James,* and the other women that were with them, which told these things to the Apostles, *And their words seemed unto them as idle tales, and they believed them not.* Mark this, ye de-

[2] The eleven are the men Jesus chose to be his disciples, without Judas who left them after he betrayed Jesus to the Romans. [Ed.]

spisers of the weakness of women, and look upon your selves to be so wise: but Christ Jesus doth not so, for he makes use of the weak: for when he met the women after he was risen, he said unto them, *All hail,* and they came and held him by the feet, and worshipped him, then said Jesus unto them, *Be not afraid, go tell my brethren that they go into Galilee, and there they shall see me,* Mat. 28.10; Mark 16.9. And *John* saith, when *Mary* was weeping at the sepulchre, that Jesus said unto her, *Woman, why weepest thou? what seekest thou? And when she supposed him to be the Gardener, Jesus saith unto her,* Mary; *she turned herself, and saith unto him,* Rabboni, *which is to say master; Jesus saith unto her, Touch me not, for I am not yet ascended to my Father, but go to my brethren, and say unto them I ascend unto my Father, and to my God, and your God,* John 20.16, 17.

Mark this, you that despise and oppose the message of the Lord God that he sends by women, what had become of the redemption of the whole body of mankind, if they had not believed the message that the Lord Jesus sent by these women, of and concerning his resurrection? And if these women had not thus, out of their tenderness and bowels of love, who had received mercy, and grace, and forgiveness of sins, and virtue, and healing from him, which many men also had received the like, if their hearts had not been so united, and knit unto him in love, that they could not depart as the men did, but sat watching, and waiting, and weeping about the sepulchre until the time of his resurrection, and so were ready to carry his message, as is manifested, else how should his Disciples have known, who were not there?

Oh! blessed and glorified be the glorious Lord, for this may all the whole body of mankind say, though the wisdom of man, that never knew God, is always ready to except against the weak; but the weakness of God is stronger than men, and the foolishness of God is wiser than men.

And in *Act.* 18 you may read how *Aquila* and *Priscilla* took unto them *Apollos,* and expounded unto him the way of God more perfectly; who was an eloquent man, and mighty in the Scriptures: yet we do not read that he despised what *Priscilla* said, because she was a woman, as many now do.

And now to the Apostles words, which is the ground of the great objection against womens speaking. And first, 1 *Cor.* 14. let the reader seriously read that chapter, and see the end and drift of the Apostle in speaking these words: for the Apostle is there exhorting the Corinthians unto charity, and to desire spiritual gifts, and not to speak in an unknown tongue, and not to be children in understanding, but to be children in malice, but in understanding to be men; and that the spirits of the prophets should be subject to the prophets, for God is not the author of confusion, but of peace: And then he saith, *Let your women keep silence in the Church,* etc.

Where it doth plainly appear that the women, as well as others, that were among them, were in confusion, for he saith, *How is it brethren? when ye come together, every one of you hath a psalm, hath a doctrine, hath a tongue, hath a revelation, hath an interpretation? let all things be done to edifying.* Here was no edifying, but all was in confusion speaking together. Therefore he saith, *If any man speak in an unknown tongue, let it be by two, or at most by three, and that by course, and let one interpret, but if there be no interpreter, let him keep silence in the Church.* Here the man is commanded to keep silence as well as the woman, when they are in confusion and out of order.

But the Apostle saith further, *They are commanded to be in obedience,* as also saith the Law; and *if they will learn any thing, let them ask their husbands at home, for it is a shame for a woman to speak in the Church.*

Here the Apostle clearly manifests his intent; for he speaks of women that were under the Law,[3] and in that transgression as *Eve* was, and such as were to learn, and not to speak publicly, but they

---

[3] Women under the Law were those who, because they had not yet accepted Jesus and the new dispensation he offered, were still subject to Jewish law, or what Christians would call the law of the Old Testament. Fell regards such women as morally inferior to converts and deserving of sterner controls. [Ed.]

must first ask their husbands at home, and it was a shame for such to speak in the Church. And it appears clearly, that such women were speaking among the *Corinthians,* by the Apostles exhorting them from malice and strife, and confusion, and he preacheth the Law unto them, and he saith, in the Law it is written, *With men of other tongues, and other lips, will I speak unto this people,* vers. 2. 21.

And what is all this to women speaking? that have the everlasting Gospel to preach, and upon whom the promise of the Lord is fulfilled, and his Spirit poured upon them according to his word, *Acts* 2. 16, 17, 18. And if the Apostle would have stopped such as had the Spirit of the Lord poured upon them, why did he say just before, *If any thing be revealed to another that sitteth by, let the first hold his peace?* and *you may all prophesy one by one.* Here he did not say that such women should not prophesy as had the revelation and Spirit of God poured upon them, but their women that were under the Law, and in the transgression, and were in strife, confusion and malice in their speaking, for if he had stopped womens praying or prophesying, why doth he say: *Every man praying or prophesying having his head covered, dishonoureth his head; but every woman that prayeth or prophesieth with her head uncovered, dishonoureth her head? Judge in yourselves, Is it comely that a woman pray or prophesy uncovered? For the woman is not without the man, neither is the man without the woman, in the Lord,* 1 Cor. 11.3, 4, 13.

Also that other Scripture, in 1 *Tim.* 2., where he is exhorting that prayer and supplication be made everywhere, lifting up holy hands without wrath and doubting; he saith in the like manner also, that *Women must adorn themselves in modest apparel, with shamefastness and sobriety, not with broidered hair, or gold, or pearl, or costly array.* He saith, *Let women learn in silence with all subjection, but I suffer not a woman to teach, nor to usurp authority over the man, but to be in silence; for* Adam *was first formed, then* Eve; *and* Adam *was not deceived, but the woman being deceived was in the transgression.*

Here the Apostle speaks particularly to a woman in relation to her husband, to be in subjection to him, and not to teach, nor usurp authority over him, and therefore he mentions *Adam* and *Eve.* But let it be strained to the utmost, as the opposers of women's speaking would have it, that is, that they should not preach nor speak in the Church, of which there is nothing here. Yet the Apostle is speaking to such as he is teaching to wear their apparel, what to wear, and what not to wear; such as were not come to wear modest apparel, and such as were not come to shamefastness and sobriety, but he was exhorting them from broidered hair, gold, and pearls, and costly array; and such are not to usurp authority over the man, but to learn in silence with all subjection, as it becometh women professing godliness with good works.

And what is all this to such as have the power and spirit of the Lord Jesus poured upon them, and have the message of the Lord Jesus given unto them? must not they speak the Word of the Lord because of these undecent and unreverent women that the Apostle speaks of, and to, in these two Scriptures? And how are the men of this generation blinded, that bring these Scriptures, and pervert the Apostles words, and corrupt his intent in speaking of them? and by these Scriptures, endeavour to stop the message and Word of the Lord God in women, by condemning and despising of them. If the Apostle would have had womens speaking stopped, and did not allow of them, why did he entreat his true yoke-fellow to help those women who laboured with him in the Gospel? *Phil.* 4.3. And why did the Apostles join together in prayer and supplication with the women, and *Mary* the *Mother of Jesus,* and with his brethren, *Acts* 1.14, if they had not allowed, and had union and fellowship with the Spirit of God, wherever it was revealed in women as well as others? But all this opposing and gainsaying of womens speaking, hath risen out of the bottomless pit, and spirit of darkness that hath spoken for these many hundred years together in this night of apostacy, since the revelations have ceased and been hid, and so that spirit hath limited and bound all up within its bond and compass, and so would suffer none to speak, but such as that spirit of darkness, approved of, man or woman. . . .

And so here hath been the misery of these last Ages past, in the time of the Reign of the Beast, that John saw when he stood upon the Sand of the Sea, rising out of the Sea, and out of the Earth, having seven Heads and ten Horns, *Rev.* 13. In this great city of *Babylon,* which is the woman that hath sitteth so long upon the Scarlet-coloured Beast, full of names of Blasphemy, having seven Heads and ten Horns; and this Woman hath been arrayed and decked with gold, and pearls, and precious stones; and she hath had a golden Cup in her hand, full of Abominations, and hath made all Nations drunk with the Cup of her Fornication; and all the world hath wondered after the Beast, and hath worshipped the Dragon that gave power to the Beast; and this woman hath been drunk with the blood of the Saints, and with the blood of the Martyrs of Jesus; and this hath been the woman that hath been speaking and usurping authority for many hundred years together: And let the times and ages past testify how many have been murdered and slain, in Ages and Generations past; every Religion and Profession (as it hath been called) killing and murdering one another, that would not join one with another: And thus the Spirit of Truth, and the Power of the Lord Jesus Christ hath been quite lost among them that have done this; and this mother of Harlots hath sitten as a Queen, and said, *She should see no sorrow,* but though her days have been long, even many hundred of years, for there was power, given unto the Beast, to continue forty and two months, and to make war with the Saints, and to overcome them; and all that have dwelt upon the earth have worshipped him, whose names are not written in the Book of the Life of the Lamb, slain from the foundation of the world.

But blessed be the Lord, his time is over, which was above twelve hundred Years, and the darkness is past, and the night of Apostacy draws to an end, and the true light now shines, the morning-Light the bright morning Star, the Root and Off-spring of *David,* he is risen, he is risen, glory to the highest for evermore; and the joy of the morning is come, and the Bride, the Lambs *Wife,* is making her self ready, as a Bride that is adorning for her Husband, and to her is granted that she shall be arrayed in fine linnen, clean and white, and the fine linnen is the Righteousness of the Saints: The *Holy Jerusalem* is descending out of Heaven from God, having the Glory of God, and her light is like a Jasper stone, clear as Christal.

And this is that free Woman that all the Children of the Promise are born of; not the Children of the bond-woman, which is *Hagar,* which genders to strife and to bondage, and which answers to *Jerusalem* which is in bondage with her Children; but this is *the Jerusalem which is free, which is the Mother of us all;* And to this bond-woman and her children, that are born after the flesh, have persecuted them that are born after the Spirit, even until now; but now the bond-woman and her Seed is to be cast out, that hath kept so long in bondage and in slavery, and under limits; this bond-woman and her brood is to be cast out, and our Holy City, the *New Jerusalem,* is coming down from heaven, and her Light will shine throughout the whole earth, even as a *Jasper stone, clear as Christal,* which brings freedom and liberty, and perfect Redemption to her whole Seed; and this is that woman and Image of the Eternal God, that God hath owned, and doth own, and will own for evermore.

More might be added to this purpose, both out of the Old Testament and New, where it is evident that God made no difference, but gave his good spirit, as it pleased him both to Man and Woman, as *Deborah, Huldah,* and *Sarah.* The Lord calls by his prophet *Isaiah: Hearken, unto me, ye that follow after Righteousness, ye that seek the Lord, look unto the Rock from whence ye were hewn, and to the hole of the Pit from whence ye were digged, look unto Abraham your Father, and to Sarah that bare you, for the Lord will comfort Sion,* etc. Isa. 5. *And* Anna *the Prophetess, who was a widow of fourscore and four years of age, which departed not from the Temple, but served God with fastings and prayers night and day, she coming in at that instant* (when old *Simeon* took the Child Jesus in his arms, and) *she gave thanks unto the Lord, and spake of him to all them who looked for Redemption* in

Jerusalem, *Luke* 2.36, 37, 38. And *Philip* the Evangelist, into whose house the Apostle *Paul* entered, who was one of the Seven, *Acts* 6.3. He had four Daughters which were Virgins, that did prophesy, *Acts* 21.

And so let this serve to stop that opposing Spirit that would limit the Power and Spirit of the Lord Jesus, whose Spirit is poured upon all flesh, both Sons and Daughters, now in his Resurrection; and since that the Lord God in the Creation, when he made man in his own Image, he made them *male* and *female;* and since that Christ Jesus, as the Apostle saith, was made of a Woman, and the power of the Highest overshadowed her, and the holy Ghost came upon her, and the holy thing that was born of her, was called *the Son of God,* and when he was upon the Earth, he manifested his *love,* and his *will,* and his *mind,* both to the Woman of *Samaria,* and *Martha,* and *Mary* her Sister, and several others, as hath been shewed; and after his Resurrection also manifested himself unto them first of all, even before he ascended unto his Father. *Now when Jesus was risen, the first day of the week, he appeared first unto Mary Magdalene,* Mark 16.9. And thus the Lord Jesus hath manifested himself and his Power, without respect of Persons; and so let all mouths be stopt that would limit him, whose Power and Spirit is infinite, that is pouring it upon all flesh.

And thus much in answer to these *two* Scriptures, which have been such a stumbling block, that the ministers of Darkness have made such a mountain of; But the Lord is removing all this, and taking it out of the way.

A further Addition in Answer to the Objection concerning Women keeping silent in the Church; For it is not permitted for them to speak, but to be under obedience; as also saith the Law, If they will learn any thing, let them ask their Husbands at home, for it is a shame for a Woman to speak in the Church: *Now this as* Paul *writeth* in 1 Cor. 14.34. *is one with that of* 1 Tim. 2. 11. *Let Women learn in silence, with all subjection.*

To which I say, If you tie this to all outward Women, then there were many Women that were Widows which had no Husbands to learn of, and many were Virgins which had no Husbands; and *Philip* had four Daughters that were Prophets; such would be despised, which the Apostle did not forbid: And if it were to all Women, that no Woman might speak, then *Paul* would have contradicted himself; but they were such Women that the Apostle mentions in *Timothy,* That *grew wanton, and were busie-bodies, and tatlers, and kicked against Christ:* For Christ in the Male and in the Female is one, and he is the Husband, and his Wife is the Church, and God hath said, that his *Daughters* should Prophesie as well as his *Sons:* And where he hath poured forth his Spirit upon them, they must prophesie, though blind Priests say to the contrary, and will not permit holy Women to speak.

And whereas it is said, *I permit not a Woman to speak, as saith the Law:* but where Women are led by the Spirit of God, they are not under the Law, for Christ in the Male and in the Female is one; and where he is made manifest in Male and Female, he may speak, for *he is the end of the Law for Righteousness to all them that believe.* So here you ought to make a distinction what sort of Women are forbidden to speak, such as were under the Law, who were not come to Christ, nor to the Spirit of Prophesie: For *Hulda, Miriam,* and *Hanna,* were Prophets, who were not forbidden in the time of the Law, for they all prophesied in the time of the Law: as you may read, in 2 *Kings* 22. what *Hulda* said unto the Priest, and to the Ambassadors that were sent to her from the King, *Go, saith she, and tell the Man that sent you to me, Thus saith the Lord God of Israel, Behold, I will bring evil upon this place, and on the Inhabitants thereof, even all the words of the Book which the King of* Judah *hath read, because they have forsaken me, and have burnt Incense to other Gods, to anger me with all the works of their hands: Therefore my wrath shall be kindled against this place, and shall not be quenched. But to the King of* Judah *that sent you to me to ask counsel of the Lord, so shall you say to him, Thus saith the Lord God of Israel, because thy heart did melt, and thou humblest thyself before the Lord, when thou heardest what I spake against this place, and against the Inhabitants of the same, how they should be destroyed; Behold I will receive thee to thy Father, and thou shalt be put into thy Grave in peace, and thine eyes shall not see all the evil which I will bring upon this place.* Now let us see if any of you blind Priests can speak after this manner, and see if it be not a better Sermon than any of you can make, who are against Womens speaking? And *Isaiah,* that went to the Prophetess, did not forbid her Speaking or Prophesying, *Isa.* 8. And was it not prophesied in *Joel* 2. that *Hand-maids should Prophesie?* And are not Hand-maids Women? Consider this, ye that are against Womens Speaking, how in the *Acts* the Spirit of the Lord was poured forth upon Daughters as well as Sons. In the time of the Gospel, when *Mary* came to salute *Elizabeth in the Hill Country in* Judea, *and when* Elizabeth *heard the salutation of* Mary, *the Babe leaped in her Womb, and she was filled with the Holy Spirit; and* Elizabeth *spake with a loud voice, Blessed art thou amongst Women, blessed is the fruit of thy Womb; whence is this to me, that the Mother of my Lord should come to me for lo, as soon as thy Salutation came to my ear, the Babe leaped in my Womb for joy, for blessed is she that believes, for there shall be a performance of those things which were told her from the Lord.* And this was *Elizabeths* Sermon concerning Christ, which at this day stands upon Record: And then *Mary* said, *My soul doth magnifie the Lord, and my Spirit rejoiceth in God my saviour, for he hath regarded the low estate of his Hand-maid: for behold, from henceforth all Generations shall call me blessed; for he that is mighty, hath done to me great things, and holy is his Name; and his Mercy is on them that fear him, from Generation to Generation; he hath shewed strength with his Arms; he hath scattered the proud in the imaginations of their own hearts; he hath put down the mighty from their Seats, and exalted them of low degree; he hath filled the hungry with good things, and the rich he hath sent empty away: He hath holpen his servant* Israel, *in remembrance of his mercy, as he spake to his Father, to* Abraham, *and to his Seed forever.* Are you not here beholding to the Woman for her Sermon, to use her words to put into your Common Prayer?[4] and yet you forbid Womens Speaking. Now here you may see how these two women prophesied of Christ, and Preached better than all the blind Priests did in that Age, and better than this Age also, who are beholding to women to make use of their words. And see in the Book of *Ruth,* how the women blessed her in the Gate of the City, of whose stock came Christ. *The Lord make the woman that is come unto thy House like* Rachel *and* Leah, *which built the house of* Israel; *and that thou mayest do worthily in* Ephrata, *and be famous in* Bethlehem; *let thy house be like the house of* Pharez, *whom* Tamar *bare unto* Judah, *of the Seed which the Lord shall give thee of this young woman. And blessed be the Lord, which hath not left thee this day without a Kinsman, and his Name shall be continued in* Israel. And also see in the first Chapter of *Samuel,* how *Hannah* prayed and spake in the *Temple* of the *Lord, Oh Lord of Hosts, if thou wilt look on the trouble of thy Hand-maid, and remember me, and not forget thy Hand-maid.* And read in the second Chapter of *Samuel,* How she rejoyced in God, and said, *My heart rejoyceth in the Lord; My Horn is exalted in the Lord and my mouth is enlarged over my enemies, because I rejoyce in thy Salvation; there is none holy as the Lord, yea, there is none besides thee; and there is no God like our God: Speak no more presumptuously, let not arrogancy come out of your mouth, for the Lord is a God of knowledge, and by him enterprises are established; the Bow, and the mighty Men are broken, and the weak hath girded to themselves strength; they that were full, are hired forth for bread, and the hungry are no more hired; so that the barren hath born seven and she that had many Children, is feeble; the Lord killeth, and maketh alive; bringeth*

---

[4] Common Prayer: that is, the Anglican Book of Common Prayer, read aloud by the priest during the worship service, in which these words of Mary's are quoted. [Ed.]

down to the Grave, and raiseth up: the Lord maketh poor, and maketh rich, bringeth low and exalteth, he raiseth up the poor out of the dust, and lifteth up the Beggars from the dunghil to set them among Princes, to make them inherit the seat of Glory; for the Pillars of the earth are the Lords, and he hath set the world upon them; he will keep the feet of his Saints, and the wicked shall keep silence in darkness, for in his own might shall no man be strong; the Lords Adversaries shall be destroyed, and out of Heaven shall be thunder upon them; the Lord shall judge the ends of the World, and shall give power to his King; and exalt the Horn of his Anointed. Thus you may see what a woman hath said, when old *Ely* the Priest thought she had been drunk, and see if any of you blind Priests that speak against Womens Speaking, can Preach after this manner? who cannot make such a Sermon as this woman did, and yet will make a trade of this Woman and other womens words. And did not the Queen of *Sheba* speak, that came to *Solomon,* and received the *Law of God,* and *preached* it in her own Kingdom, and *blessed the Lord God that loved* Solomon, *and set him on the throne of* Israel, *because the Lord loved* Israel *for ever; and made the King to do Equity and Righteousness?* And this was the language of the Queen of *Sheba.* And see what glorious expressions Queen *Hester* used to comfort the People of God, which was the Church of God; as you may read in the book of *Hester* which caused *joy* and gladness of heart among the Jews, who prayed and worshipped the Lord in all places, who jeoparded her life contrary to the Kings command, went and spoke to the King, in the wisdom and fear of the Lord, by which means she saved the lives of the People of God; and righteous *Mordecai* did not forbid her speaking, but said, *If she held her peace, her and her Fathers house should be destroyed;* and herein you blind Priests are contrary to Righteous *Mordecai.*

Likewise you may read how *Judith* spoke, and what noble acts she did, and how she spoke to the Elders of *Israel,* and said, *Dear Brethren, seeing ye are the honorable and elders of the People of God, call to remembrance how our Fathers in time past were tempted, that they might be proved if they would worship God aright; they ought also to remember how our Father* Abraham, *being tryed through manifold tribulations, was found a friend of God, so was* Isaac, Jacob, *and* Moses, *and all they pleased God, and were stedfast in Faith through manifold troubles.* And read also her prayer in the Book of *Judith,* and how the Elders commended her, and said, *All that thou speakest is true, and no man can reprove thy words, pray therefore for us, for thou art an holy Woman, and fearest God.* So these elders of *Israel* did not forbid her speaking, as you blind Priests do; yet you will make a Trade of Womens words to get money by, and take Texts, and Preach Sermons upon Womens words; and still cry out, Women must not speak, Women must be silent; so you are far from the minds of the Elders of *Israel,* who praised God for a Womans speaking. But the *Jezebel,* and the Woman, the false Church, the great Whore, and tatling women, and busie-bodies, which are forbidden to Preach, which have a long time spoke and tatled, which are forbidden to speak by the True Church, which Christ is the Head of; such Women as were in transgression under the Law, which are called a Woman in the *Revelations.* And see further how the wife Woman cryed to *Joab* over the Wall, and saved the city of *Abel,* as you may read, 2 *Sam.* 20. how in her wisdom she spoke to *Joab,* saying, *I am one of them that are peaceable and faithful in* Israel, *and thou goest about to destroy a City and Mother in* Israel; *Why wilt thou destroy the Inheritance of the Lord? Then went the woman to the people in her wisdom, and smote off the head of* Sheba, *that rose up against* David, *the Lords Anointed: Then* Joab *blew the Trumpet, and all the People departed in peace.* And this deliverance was by the means of a Womans Speaking; but tatlers, and busie-bodies, are forbidden to preach by the True Woman, whom Christ is the Husband to the Woman as well as the Man, all being comprehended to be the Church; and so in this True Church, Sons and Daughters do Prophesie, Women labour in the Gospel; but the Apostle permits not tatlers, busie-bodies, and such as usurp authority over the Man would not have Christ Reign, nor speak neither in the Male nor Female; Such the Law permits not to speak, such must learn of their Husbands: But what Husbands have Widows to learn of, but Christ? And was not Christ the Husband of *Philips* four Daughters? And may not they that learn of their Husbands speak then? But *Jezebel,* and Tatlers, and the Whore that denies Revelation and Prophesie, are not permitted, which will not learn of Christ; and they that be out of the Spirit and Power of Christ, that the Prophets were in, who are in the Transgression, are ignorant of the Scriptures; and such are against Womens Speaking, and Mens too, who Preach that which they have received of the Lord God; but that which they have preached, and do preach, will come over all your heads, yea, over the head of the false Church, the Pope; for the Pope is the Head of the False Church, and the False Church is the Popes Wife: and so he and they that be of him, and come from him, are against Womens Speaking in the True Church, when both he and the false Church are called *Woman,* in *Rev.* 17. and so are in the Transgression that would usurp authority over the Man Christ Jesus, and his Wife too, and would not have him to Reign; but the Judgment of the great Whore is come. But Christ, who is the Head of the Church, the True Woman which is his Wife, in it do Daughters Prophesie, who are above the Pope and his Wife and a top of them; And here Christ is the Head of the Male and Female, who may speak; and the Church is called *a Royal Priesthood;* so the Woman must offer as well as the Man, *Rev.* 22. 17. *The Spirit saith, Come, and the Bride saith, Come:* and so is not the Bride the Church? and doth the Church only consist of Men? you that deny Womens speaking, answer: Doth it not consist of Women as well as men? Is not the Bride compared to the whole Church? And doth not the Bride say, *Come?* Doth not the Woman speak then? the Husband Christ Jesus, the *Amen,* and doth not the false Church go about to stop the Brides Mouth? But it is not possible for the Bridegroom is with his Bride, and he opens her Mouth. Christ Jesus, who goes on Conquering, and to Conquer, who kill and slayes with the Sword, which is the words of his Mouth; the Lamb and the Saints shall have the Victory, the true Speakers of Men and Women over the false Speaker.

POSTSCRIPT

And you dark Priests, that are so mad against Womens Speaking and it's so grevious to you, did not God say to Abraham, Let it not be grevious in thy sight, because of the Lad, and because of thy bond-woman? In all that Sarah *hath said to thee, hearken to her voice (Mark here) the Husband must learn of the Woman and* Abraham *did so, and this was concerning the things of God for he saith in* Isaac *shall thy seed be called, and so* Abraham *did obey the voice of* Sarah, *as you may read in* Genesis 21. *and so he did not squench the good that was in his wife, for that which he spoke to* Abraham *was concerning the Church.*

And you may read Deborah *and* Barack, *and so how a Woman Preacht and sung* Judges 5. *what glorious triumphing expressions there was from a Woman, beyond all the Priests Servants, whom* Barack *did not bid be silent, for she Sung and Praised God, and declared to the Church of* Israel, *which now the hungry Priests that denyes Womens Speaking makes a trade of her words for a livlihood.*

And in Judges 13. *There you may see, how the Angel appeared to a Woman, and how the Woman came to her Husband and told him, saying, a man of God came to me, whose countenance was like the Countenance of a Man of God, and said that she should Conceive and bare a Son, and again the Angel of the Lord appeared to the Woman, and she made haste and ran, and shewed her Husband and said unto him, behold, he hath appeared unto me that came unto me the other day, and when the Angel of the Lord was gon, the Womans Husband said, we should surely dye because we had seen God, and then you may read how the woman comforted her Husband again, and said, if the Lord were pleased to kill us he would not have shewed us all these things, nor would this time have told us such things as these, and this was a Woman that taught.*

INTRODUCTION TO PETER RAMUS

Pierre de la Ramee, or Peter Ramus in Latin, was born in 1515 in France. He showed early promise as a scholar. In about 1523, Ramus went to study at the University of Paris, where he ended up teaching for the rest of his life. In 1572 Ramus, a convert to Protestantism, was killed in the St. Bartholomew's Day massacre.

In Augustine, Erasmus, and others, the trend to think of rhetoric as almost nothing but style is evident. Ramus is often taken as an extreme example of such a movement. Not only did he think of rhetoric in terms of style, but he rather explicitly denied it a role in generating substantive argument, a positive action against the status of rhetoric that goes beyond many other theorists.

To understand Ramus's stance, we must understand what had been happening to rhetoric and its twin verbal art of dialectic. You will recall that dialectic is an art of argument that depends upon classification and division, couched in the context of noncombative discussion. As early as Aristotle, theorists wrote about methods for classification and division as well as techniques for moving argument forward. During the Middle Ages, which was more concerned with developing theology than rhetoric, the arts of dialectic and logic were appropriated by theology. Dialectic became allied with, and virtually identical to, the verbal art of *logic*. Logic and dialectic were needed to help Church thinkers reason out the subtle intricacies of their dogmatic systems. The two arts thus became highly developed and, in the opinion of many, overdeveloped. Laborious disputations over minor theological and logical questions (sometimes parodied as, "How many angels can dance on the head of a pin?") occupied the attentions of arguers and theoreticians alike.

At the same time that dialectic and logic began developing huge and elaborate theoretical structures with seemingly little practical application, rhetoric abandoned development of its concerns for invention, or the art of thinking up what to say. It became preoccupied with *style* and with how to present information or beliefs discovered elsewhere, through other processes.

Between the hyperdevelopment of logic/dialectic and rhetoric's gradual atrophy of invention, the art of thinking up substantive arguments that could be directly addressed to practical issues deteriorated. Into this context Ramus came as a student at the University of Paris. He was brash and arrogant from the very start, publishing several works attacking the prevailing theories and methods of overly elaborate argument and dialectic. His vitriolic, slashing style is evident from the selection excerpted here from his book *Rhetoricae Distinctiones in Quintilianum,* or *Arguments in Rhetoric Against Quintilian.*

Ramus wrote this book attacking Quintilian specifically because of the regard that the educational establishment had for Quintilian and his educational methods. Quintilian was, in other words, a handy and popular target for Ramus to attack. Much of Ramus's attack early in the selection is against Quintilian's questionable definition of the orator as a good man skilled in speaking. Let us remember that although Quintilian's definition may be flawed, what lay behind it was an admiration for Cicero's model of the orator as a leader and public activist. Now, to be such a leader means that one must also generate ideas and think up answers to the important questions of the day; in other words, one must *invent* substantive arguments and one must help the public to *reason* together. When Ramus attacks Quintilian's vision of the good man skilled in speaking, then, he is attacking the idea that one skilled in *rhetoric* should be one in command of reason and argument. This is because the crucial, central point of Ramus's attack is to separate reason from rhetoric.

This attack on rhetoric's historic alliance with reason actually has two facets. One was Ramus's insistence that dialectical method, argument, and logic become simplified. Ramus saw logic as a possible universal method, which we noted earlier was an ideal of the Renaissance. He proposed a simpler system based on only "ten topics" that could ground all argument. The second facet of Ramus's attack was to make sure that these "topics" were not part of rhetoric, the verbal art which had historically had charge of topics, topoi, and commonplaces.

What it means to say that reason is not a part of rhetoric is that when one reasons, one is not doing that which is part of persuasion or influence. Ramus's attempt to split reason and rhetoric is not simply a matter of organizing discourses; it is an attempt to say what it is that we do when we influence one another. By seeing rhetoric only as style and verbal embellishment, Ramus essentially argued that style is how we are influenced in persuasion. Logic, reason, and argument he saw not as tools of persuasion, which can produce changeable and contradictory conclusions, but rather as tools of his universal method, which he thought would produce stable and absolute truths.

Ramus's attack on Quintilian is, then, a complicated maneuver: (1) It rejected the overly complicated argumentative systems of his time; (2) It argued for a replacement of those systems with his own, simpler, and he thought more powerful, universal system of ten topics; and (3) It effectively denied that his or any other system of argument produced persuasion; instead, it implied that such argumentative systems produced truth. Ramus achieved this last move by denying that rhetoric had anything to do with reason, which likewise must deny that reason is rhetorical. Ramus is best known for this separation of reason from rhetoric, a division of verbal arts that would have some influence for centuries as scholars pursued dreams of absolute and sure truth using the tools of what they saw as unshakeable reason and unbreakable argument.

PETER RAMUS

ARGUMENTS IN RHETORIC AGAINST QUINTILIAN

MOST EXCELLENT Maecenas, the Greeks have a wise proverb which teaches that each man should practice the art which he knows. Although I have been engaged in the study of rhetoric and dialectic for many years, I should not, like other people, care to boast about them; rather I feel ashamed to look back upon them due to the very meager results they produced. And so do I not seem to have some justification if in my studies of these arts I engage rather frequently in the very same argument? I have a single argument, a single subject matter, that the arts of dialectic and rhetoric have been confused by Aristotle, Cicero, and Quintilian. I have previously argued against Aristotle and Cicero. What objection then is there against calling Quintilian to the same account?

Aristotle's logic both lacked many virtues and abounded in faults. He left out many definitions and partitions of arguments; instead of one art of invention embracing the ten general topics—causes, effects, subjects, adjuncts, opposites, comparisons, names, divisions, definitions, witnesses—he created unfathomable darkness in his two books of *Posterior Analytics* and eight books of *Topics* with their confused account of predicables, predicaments, enunciations, abundance of propositions, and the invention of the middle term; in his treatment of simple syllogisms he did not collect the rarer ones; he gave no instruction on connections; he was completely silent about method; in a loud sophistic debate over quite useless rules he handed down to us nothing about the use of the art as a universal, but only as a particular. We have added to the art the virtues it lacked; we have uncovered these various faults and, I hope, have abolished them; we have revealed its true use and have shown it to be common to all things. Consequently, we have fought this dialectical contest over the art and its use with vigor and intelligence.

Translation by Carole Newlands

Our second contest was against Cicero. For he had transferred to rhetoric almost all Aristotle's obscurity concerning invention and arrangement, and indeed also style, confusedly making one art from the two, and then applying it confused in this way to the legal process of civil suits. Some time ago we had taught the virtues of invention and arrangement. By means of a defined, organized and illustrated classification of subjects, my close colleague Audomarus Talaeus cast light on style and delivery and pointed out their deficiencies. To this extent therefore we have here expelled the darkness.

Yet now Quintilian follows Aristotle's and Cicero's confusion of dialectic and rhetoric. Indeed he makes it worse by fabrications of his own, and by including in his teachings all the disputes concerning all the arts he had read or heard something about—grammar, mathematics, philosophy, drama, wrestling, rhetoric. We shall distinguish the art of rhetoric from the other arts, and make it a single one of the liberal arts, not a confused mixture of all arts; we shall separate its true properties, remove weak and useless subtleties, and point out the things that are missing. Thus, just as I previously attacked the Aristotelian obscurity in Cicero, so now in almost the same way I shall attack it in Quintilian. But since the same subject has already been handled in my attack on Aristotle and Cicero, I shall discuss the numerous points more briefly and less rigorously.

Finally, we shall rely on the supreme help of unwavering reason in our attempt to establish the true description and practice of the arts on which, up to this time, I have placed my energy and enthusiasm. For how many days, indeed how many years and ages do we suppose are wretchedly spent on false conjectures about these disciplines? I wish I had not known the wretchedness of wasting so much of my youth in this way. I wish that the scholars of rhetoric and dialectic would heed my advice and would sometimes think of the truth and usefulness of their subjects instead of tenaciously and obstinately quarreling over matters which they have naively accepted at a first hearing, without ever giving them proper consideration. As a result, if the arts were taught with greater conciseness they would certainly be more easily understood, and once the true method for their use was revealed, they would be more easy to practice.

But suppose someone should say, "By almighty God, do you attribute such greatness to yourself that you think you have seen faults or virtues in these arts which have escaped this array of such great men?" Indeed, Maecenas (for I address you and those like you, pure-minded judges unclouded by prejudice), if I were to say that Aristotle was a failure in philosophy, and Cicero and Quintilian each a failure in style, I would seem to be not quite sane. Therefore let us allow Aristotle as sharp an intelligence in various subjects and branches of knowledge as any Aristotelian could imagine, for I admit that that philosopher had an amazing fecundity of talent. Thanks to the generosity of Alexander, he compiled a natural science from the inventions and books of all nationalities; in his logic he questioned all philosophers, physical as well as moral and political; sometimes he showed as much syllogistic reasoning in judgment and as much method in arrangement as could be sought in the best of philosophers.

If you wish, attribute to Cicero these equal ornaments of dialectic, invention, and arrangement. I shall not demur. In fact I shall not only gladly but also perhaps truly admit that of all the men who are, have been, and will in the future be, he was the most eloquent. One could scarcely hope for such excellence of style (which we see in his books) and of delivery (which we learn from stories about him).

I would be acting impudently if I were to admit anything similar about Quintilian. For although he showed a certain shrewdness in the ability to conduct civil suits and although he usefully collected certain examples, nevertheless he differs vastly from Cicero in his style, which is possibly his chief virtue. For in individual words Quintilian does not possess the same purity, appropriateness or elegance. In consequence there is such a great difference that Cicero seems to have spoken in an age of gold, Quintilian in an age of iron. But nevertheless, compared to the eloquent men of that time, he was without doubt counted among the eloquent. I probably could not be like him, even if I should wish so; but in fact if I could, I would not even wish so. Such then were the qualities of Aristotle, Cicero, and Quintilian, and such was their stature. However, must those who excel in one or many virtues necessarily excel in them all? And is it necessary to think them not men, but gods in all things?

At present I am not inquiring after the supreme virtues of other kinds, such as those accorded the Apollos or the Jupiters. I am discussing now the precepts of dialectic and rhetoric, which I admit were almost all in fact either first discovered by those men, to the great glory of their names, or certainly were collected from others. Yet I add the observation that if they had applied as many months as I have years to judging these precepts accurately and to arranging them in order, I certainly do not doubt that they would have left us arts that are far truer and more distinct.

But the writings of these scholars reveal that while they indeed collected a lot of material, they did not evaluate it sufficiently, for in some places I look in vain for a syllogism. And they did not arrange it in a sufficiently fitting order, for elsewhere I find a lack of method. I confidently state that I have truly judged and correctly organized this same material in my teachings. Why so? Because the dialectical and rhetorical arts of Aristotle, Cicero, and Quintilian are fallacious and confused in their treatment of the dialectical and rhetorical usage of reason, and then of speech—the usage, I repeat, which one observes in their books. Mine are truthful and distinct, as both the art and its practice prove when they have been thoroughly investigated. This is the first, the middle, and the final support of my argument. I do not make evil use of the testimonies of men who can lie, but I establish my argument by the truthfulness of unwavering, natural usage, the usage, I repeat, which I have been following for so many years with the greatest effort through daily practice and by experience in the subject.

And so, Maecenas, since I am relying on the very pleasant knowledge of your most just wish, I would be embarrassed if I never wrote what I know about those arts. I shall explain them especially to you since you are not so much my patron as a mutual appreciator of good literature, sent by the grace of God to our France. But we delay too long on the threshold: let us take up the rhetorical controversies.

IT WILL PERHAPS seem to some people an enormous and very difficult task which I propose to undertake against Quintilian, for I shall undertake to teach that his instructions on oratory were not correctly ordered, organized, described—especially so since he seems to define an orator brilliantly at the start, then to divide elegantly the parts of the subjects covered by the definition and finally to delineate the property and nature of each part with extreme care and accuracy. Thus he seems to have looked at everything with especial thought, to have evaluated all things critically and to have organized them methodically. In this disputation, however, I shall, as far as I may, apply dialectic, the mentor of speaking with truth and constancy, in order that I may evaluate the subject with more incisiveness and wisdom. And so, all you dialecticians—that is, whoever can form a judgment about this question with truth and constancy—come here, pay attention, sharpen your wits, drive far away from you (in case passions of this kind have been ready to seize your minds), drive far away, I say, love, hate, prejudice, levity, fickleness, and rashness. Listen to me with willing and impartial minds to the extent that unwavering reason will convince, to the extent that certain conclusion will establish, finally to the extent that truth itself—which cannot be refuted or disproved—will hold firm.

And so first of all let us put forward the definition in which Quintilian outlined for us his ideal orator, and let us refer to this point of dispute everything relevant from all parts of his *Institutiones.* "I teach," he says, "that the orator cannot be perfect unless he is a good man. Consequently I demand from him not only outstanding skill in speaking but all the virtuous qualities of character." This is the type of orator that Quintilian constructs for us. Afterwards in the twelfth book, where he defines him in similar terms as a good man skilled in speaking well, he identifies those virtuous qualities of character as justice, courage, self-control, prudence, likewise knowledge of the whole of philosophy and of law, a thorough acquaintance with history, and many other attributes worthy of praise.

What then can be said against this definition of an orator? I assert indeed that such a definition of an orator seems to me to be useless and stupid: Why? Because a definition of any artist which covers more than is included in the rules of his art is superfluous and defective. For the artist must be defined according to the rules of his art, so that only as much of the art as the true, proper principles cover—this much is attributed to the artist, and nothing further. For a definition is not only a short, clear explanation of a subject but also it is so appropriate to the subject which is being defined that it perpetually agrees with it and is consistent within itself. The grammarian is defined as skilled in speaking and writing correctly; he is not defined as skilled in speaking, writing, and singing. Why not? Because grammar provides no precepts about the last. The geometrician is not defined as skilled in measurement and medicine. Why not? Because there is no precept in geometry which teaches how to cure illnesses.

Therefore let us hold to our axiom and let us lay down this first proposition of a syllogism:

> The definition of an artist which covers more than is included within the limits of the art is faulty.

Then let us add to the first proposition we have put down:

> But the definition of the artist of oratory handed down to us by Quintilian covers more than is included within the limits of the art.

For rhetoric is not an art which explains all the virtuous qualities of character. Moral philosophers speculate appropriately and judiciously on the numerous problems involving the moral virtues and the virtues of intelligence and the mind; mathematicians deal with arithmetic and geometry; men of learning and wisdom, not rhetoricians, discuss separately through their individual studies the remaining important branches of learning including the virtuous qualities of character. I conclude therefore:

> Quintilian's definition of the orator is as a result defective.

But suppose Quintilian should say that moral philosophy and the very theory of virtues are proper to rhetoricians, not to philosophers. Then the perfect orator is fashioned who cannot exist unless he has attained all the virtuous qualities of character. However, what if each of these statements is inappropriate and false? Shall we not then confirm the chief point in the conclusion of our syllogism? Accordingly, let us investigate whether instruction in virtues can be considered a part of rhetoric.

Is it because the orator ought to control the state and its citizens that moral training will therefore be a proper part of rhetoric? Undoubtedly it seems this way to Quintilian since he says:

> But I would not grant this, that (as certain men have thought) the principles of a good and upright life should be the responsibility of the philosophers since it is that citizen who is fitted for the administration of public and private matters, who can guide cities by his counsels, fortify them with his laws, and correct them with his judgments, who is assuredly none other than the orator. Accordingly, although I admit that I shall make use of certain things which are contained in the books of the philosophers, nevertheless let me argue that these truly and rightly fall within my field and properly belong to the art of oratory.

This is what Quintilian says, and consequently when he wishes to give a name to a human being who is an ideal leader in the republic and is perfect in every virtue and branch of knowledge, he calls him an "orator"—as if to make him a god rather than just a man skilled in a single art. Yet at this point Quintilian has proposed that he should give instructions about one certain art and virtue, not about perfection in every art and virtue. He thinks rhetoric is one of the liberal arts, not in fact a common art, and yet at the same time he deems rhetoric to be an art, a science, and a virtue. For in these books on oratory he has not described any science of civic skills, any theory of life and its duties, nor finally, in the sections dealing with rhetoric, any instruction in those virtues which he claims are parts of the art of oratory.

Quintilian decrees that there are five parts to the art of rhetoric—I shall talk about these afterwards—invention, arrangement, style, memory, delivery. He thinks there are no more and no less. Yet in no one of these parts does he fit in the moral philosophy which he now attributes to rhetoric. In fact this man was sadly lacking in a knowledge of dialectic. If he had learned from it that in every art and branch of knowledge one must seek out the true, proper, and primary causes of the subject, he would have decided that an orator should be defined quite differently, and he would have learned that he should speculate quite differently on the proper qualities of the arts.

There are two universal, general gifts bestowed by nature upon man, Reason and Speech; dialectic is the theory of the former, grammar and rhetoric of the latter. Dialectic therefore should draw on the general strengths of human reason in the consideration and the arrangement of the subject matter, while grammar should analyze purity of speech in etymology, syntax, and prosody for the purpose of speaking correctly, and also in orthography for the purpose of writing correctly. Rhetoric should demonstrate the embellishment of speech first in tropes and figures, second in dignified delivery. Next, from these general, universal so-called instruments other arts have been formed: arithmetic with its numbers, geometry with its diagrams, other arts with their other subjects. If these arts have been kept separate and enclosed within their own proper limits, then certainly what grammar will teach in its rightful province will not be confused with rhetoric, and dialectic will not encroach upon what each of the others has clearly described. In use these should be united, so that the same oration can expound purely, speak ornately, and express thought wisely. However, the precepts of pure diction, ornate delivery, and intelligent treatment must be kept separate and should not be confused.

Therefore, from this dialectical distinction of subjects, Quintilian should have defined rhetoric so that first of all he would grasp as a whole the material belonging strictly to the art and distinct and separate from all other art's material; then, when it was separated into parts, he could explain it. Thus to conclude this line of reasoning, I shall recall again two syllogisms:

> If moral philosophy were a part of rhetoric, it would have to be expounded in some part of rhetoric.
> But in fact Quintilian does this nowhere, nor should it be done at all.
> And therefore it is not a part of rhetoric.

Likewise,

> The parts of the material which belong to the art of rhetoric are only two, style and delivery.
> However, the parts of the art of rhetoric are the parts of its subject matter and they correspond completely to one another.
> Therefore there are only two parts of rhetoric, style and delivery.

But Quintilian will persist, as in fact he does, in the same proposition, and indeed he will urge even more keenly that rhetoric is a virtue—this is in the second chapter of the second book—and that no one can be an orator unless he is a good man (this is in the first chapter of the twelfth book) and for this reason, I believe, he will conclude that instruction in virtue is a part of rhetoric.

Nevertheless it must be seen that each of these statements of Quintilian's opinion is false. For although I admit that rhetoric is a virtue, it is virtue of the mind and the intelligence, as in all the true liberal arts, whose followers can still be men of the utmost moral depravity. Nor is rhetoric a moral virtue as Quintilian thinks, so that whoever possesses it is incapable of being a wicked man. Yet some Stoic philosophers seem to Quintilian—as he points out in the second book—to come cleverly to the following conclusions:

> To be self-consistent as regards what should or should not be done is a virtue, which we name prudence. Consequently, to be self-consistent as regards what should and should not be said will be a virtue. Likewise if a virtue is something whose rudiments have been provided by nature, rhetoric will be a virtue, because its rudiments are provided by nature.

But each one of these supposedly ingenious conclusions is twisted and false. For prudence is not a moral virtue but a virtue of the intelligence and mind. Therefore rhetoric will not be a moral virtue. Moreover it is absurd to think that these things are moral virtues whose their origins are from nature, as if vices instead of virtues did not rather have their origins in nature. Thus these philosophers deceive Quintilian in that they fabricate a fraudulent sophism instead of a sound syllogism.

For all that, Quintilian continues and maintains his own opinion that since dialectic is a virtue, so therefore is rhetoric. Quintilian should turn the whole thing around and should more correctly conclude that since dialectic is not a moral virtue which can shape a good man, so neither is rhetoric.

"An orator," he then adds, "cannot succeed in panegyric if he is not well versed in the distinctions between what is honorable and what is disgraceful; he cannot succeed in the law courts if he is ignorant of the nature of justice; and he cannot succeed amidst the turbulent threats of the people if he is timid." What then, O Quintilian? Is he who knows what is honest and just, himself honest and just? How few are the spendthrifts and cutthroats who do not know what is honest and just? If the orator should be fearful in the case of Milo, you say he will not speak well. What then is the result? Will rhetoric therefore mean bravery? Undoubtedly the grammarian will not be able to speak correctly if he is frightened, because when he is upset by fear he will pronounce syllables as long instead of short, or short instead of long. And because of his confused memory he will produce impurities of diction and solecisms. Is grammar therefore a moral virtue? Of what sort will the relationship between the two be? Indeed it is one thing to be something that is necessary to the other—quite another thing to be a part, a limb of it. I shall not object to your opinion that moral virtue is undoubtedly useful and suitable for the use of all arts, but in no way shall I admit that any art is a moral virtue.

Finally Quintilian scrapes together the most stupid trifles, saying that since virtue exists in beasts, and courage exists in robbers, it is therefore no wonder that eloquence is a moral virtue. But Quintilian no longer seems to be inexperienced and ignorant only of dialectic but rather of the whole of philosophy, especially of that main branch of philosophy which gives instruction in virtue. O Quintilian, although you say that moral virtue fashions good, respectable, and praiseworthy followers, nevertheless you do not give sufficient thought to what you say when you attribute moral virtue to beasts and robbers. For the future I expect better words than this, or you should think up better advice.

But Quintilian does not let the matter rest, for in the twelfth book he drifts back to that same problem and accumulates similar worthless ideas.

"An evil mind cannot have leisure to devote to rhetoric," he says. Or again, "The greatest part of rhetoric concerns goodness and justice," and "Virtue's authority prevails in persuasion." Of these the first two are absolutely ridiculous and absurd, while the third is like his statement that a timid orator will not plead well. However, let us pass these things by. Meanwhile let us maintain that moral philosophy is not a part of rhetoric, nor is rhetoric itself a moral virtue at all, as Quintilian thought.

Let us come rather to that part where he now says that he intends to fashion the perfect orator; such a man cannot exist unless he is equipped and embellished with all the virtuous qualities of character. Consequently moral philosophy is a part of rhetoric, and virtue must be included in a definition of the orator. It is in this last statement that this entire error can be checked. For truly, suppose that in the name of the perfect orator a politician is now imagined who can handle the public and private cases of his citizens by speaking, who by the authority of his virtue and by the smoothness of his oration can direct the minds of his audience wherever he wishes, who is indeed such a man as the poet describes:

> *Then if by chance they have noticed some man grave with his sense of duty and his merits, they fall silent and stand around him with ears pricked; he rules their minds with his words and charms their hearts. [Virgil, Aeneid 1.xv. 1–3]*

If, I say, that politician equipped with every art and virtue is the man defined by Quintilian, then Quintilian would have had to expound and describe not merely the one art of rhetoric from among so many arts and virtues, but all the arts and virtues (since that political ability is made up of these)—grammar, rhetoric, dialectic, mathematics, the whole of philosophy. But Quintilian did not do this.

Therefore Quintilian does not fashion the perfect orator about whom he talks, but, as I have said before, he examines only one of the liberal disciplines. In order to make it appear more admirable he confuses it in the following way and deceives himself by this line of reasoning: An orator cannot be perfect without philosophy; therefore philosophy is a part of rhetoric. But I point out—and I blame him for it—that Quintilian has erred here on two accounts, first because he so unwisely uses a false argument and then because he follows it with a fallacious proof. For it is not true that rhetoric cannot be practiced, nor, within reasonable limits, be perfected without moral philosophy. For even before a knowledge of moral philosophy has been acquired, the whole doctrine of style in both tropes and figures, and likewise the whole variety of delivery in both voice and gesture can be explained. At first those excellent qualities of oratory can be revealed and expounded by set examples from the orators and poets. Next, through the exercise of imitation they can be expressed first in writing and next in speaking; finally they can be generally handled and practiced as a whole in whatever kind of exercise you please.

However, those two parts, style and delivery, are the only true parts of the art of rhetoric, as I have demonstrated before. And the order in which the arts should be taught is as follows. The first is grammar, since it can be understood and practiced without the others; the second is rhetoric, which can be understood and practiced without all the others except for grammar.

Moreover, just as the perfect grammarian, one who is outstanding and exceptional (for there is nothing completely perfect either in nature or art or practice even though it is by these things that the art is perfected), just as I say again that the grammarian who has achieved every perfection in his art is to be called perfect, just so the orator who has acquired the consummate, fully developed virtues of oratorical theory clearly must be deemed perfect.

But if you were to add more arts, undoubtedly the man who masters them will have a greater perfection, though the perfection of each separate art will not be greater but the perfection derived from many arts will be joined. Perfect, consummate skill in arithmetic does not mean perfection in geometry, for perfection in the arts must be evaluated and measured from the arts themselves, not summoned outside from alien material. Therefore that pupil who in speaking has learned to vary and embellish his oration with tropes and figures, and likewise to declaim with voice and gesture in harmony, will be my perfect orator—if anything can be considered perfect in the arts—because he has grasped all the perfections of the art of oratory including its virtues and praiseworthy qualities.

In book two Quintilian confirms this very point—but how unwisely he does it! He says that the goal of the orator is not to persuade, because that depends on a chance result for which the art by its own power cannot be responsible, but rather to speak well. Consequently, although the orator may not win, still, if he has spoken well he has achieved his goal, because he has lived up to the ideals of his art. "For," he says, "the pilot wishes to reach port with his ship safe; if, however, he is swept out of his course by a storm, he will not on that account be a bad pilot, and he will utter the familiar saying, 'As long as I can keep a steady helm.' " Here Quintilian truly and generously realizes that the goal of rhetoric, complete perfection, is not found in alien and external matter but in the proper scope of the art itself. Therefore Quintilian should not be ashamed of being reprimanded for his great error—if not by us, then certainly by Quintilian himself. He says at the beginning that rhetoric is not perfect without philosophy; yet afterwards he says that the whole of rhetoric is directed towards itself, and that its goal of perfection does not depend on anything external but is completely and fully contained within the art itself. Therefore let us conclude that rhetoric can be perfected and completed without philosophy. Yet see how great is the advantage which the fairness and soundness of our judgment provides for us.

I have proved by so many arguments the falseness of the argument by which Quintilian was misled. At the same time I admit and allow that all this could be considered most true and certain if what Quintilian wishes could be accomplished in the following way.

Suppose therefore that the practice of rhetoric could not be perfect and complete without the remaining arts and virtues, especially philosophy—will it be right then to agree that whatever is useful and suitable to it is an integral part of rhetoric? Suppose we apply to the dialectician and the arithmetician what Quintilian says about the orator. Neither the dialectician nor the arithmetician can be perfect without a knowledge of all subjects, since the practice of all the arts which concern humanity is linked by a certain common bond and connected by a sort of kinship. Yet who believes that the dialectician and arithmetician are correctly defined if they are called "good men skilled in debate or in calculation" and perfect in every branch of knowledge and virtue? It is one thing to be something that is necessary, another to be an actual property. A house cannot be roofed without a foundation, without the soil of the land, and finally without God; therefore in defining "roof" shall I include all those things? This error would be too absurd. And so Quintilian errs both in argument and in proof.

And yes, as you may remark, I admit that the people labeled the orator according to Quintilian's conception, and I acknowledge that the stupidity inherent in this definition of the orator was due to the stupidity of the inexperienced common people. First of all he was called *rhetor* in Greece; then in Italy the orator was the man who conducted civil cases, like those we now call Advocates. And rhetoricians were named after rhetoric, grammarians after grammar, because at first rhetoric gave instruction in tropes and figures and in those subjects which are the property of rhetoric and common to no further discipline. Then, although the rhetoricians joined to their discipline the subjects of the dialectician—invention, arrangement and memory—and mixed in also many other things, they kept the name *rhetorician.* Finally, under the very same name, law, and philosophy, and the arts of mathematics, and history and the virtues were heaped together so that whoever had joined all these things with eloquence was called an orator.

But I believe that in treating the arts one should follow not the wavering error of the mob but the fixed law of truth. Therefore let us agree that Quintilian's definition for fashioning our orator is redundant and defective; let us agree that moral philosophy is not a part of rhetoric since it is not related to any part of it and is contained in no part of the relevant subject matter; let us agree that the Stoics' reasons are false and deceptive; finally let us agree that that magnificent definition of the orator is full of vain airs and devoid of truth. But enough about the definition of an orator. Although so far Quintilian does not seem to be sufficiently sharp-witted or to argue with sufficient accuracy, yet perhaps he will be sharper and wiser in the partition which follows.

Now the main partition of the work designed by Quintilian for creating an orator is its division into twelve books:

> My first book [he says] will contain those subjects which are preliminary to the task of the rhetorician. In my second I shall deal with the rudiments of the schools of rhetoric and with problems concerned with the essence of rhetoric itself. The next five books deal with Invention, and also with Arrangement. Four will be given over to Style, to which are joined Memory and Delivery. There will be one final book in which the orator himself is to be delineated so that, as far as I am able, I can discuss his character, the rules which guide him in undertaking,

> studying, and pleading cases, the type of style, the time at which he should cease to plead cases, and the pursuits he should follow afterwards.

In Quintilian's partition here, as indeed in his definition, I see his scrupulous care. For he has gathered together into one place everything which the Greeks and Romans handed down about the orator. However, I look in vain for sound judgment. I firmly assert that with the exception of a very few passages dealing with the theory of style and delivery, all the rest of his partition is partly false and partly stupid; certainly everything is confused, out of place, and lacking the illumination of dialectic.

The first book (he says) contains those subjects which are preliminary to the task of the rhetorician. These things therefore, I say, are alien to the art of rhetoric and, since the subject about which he is writing is rhetoric, they should not be placed among its precepts. Yet in these subjects alien to rhetoric Quintilian describes four forms of training for shaping the pupil who is to become an orator.

The first type of schooling, discussed in the first three chapters, concerns the first education of the infant boy: his nurses, parents, companions, proctors, the time, place, and method of learning Greek and Latin letters, and finally, the rudiments of the arts he will soon learn from the order of letters, from writing, from reading, from memory, and from delivery. Although among these there are some true and noteworthy things that are necessary to the first form of training in boys' education, and although so many Latin and Greek writers have produced numerous works dealing with this first education and schooling for boys, who has ever said that this belongs to instruction in rhetoric? Who has included this in rhetorical instructions as something proper to them? Is this method equally appropriate for the senator, the general, and the lawyer as well as for the orator? Arts must be fashioned not only by true but also by proper rules. It is one thing to be something useful, true, and praiseworthy, and another to be the property of some art.

Therefore this form of training has nothing to do with the art of rhetoric, and neither has his thought and understanding of the matter here. But Quintilian failed to analyze and to reason syllogistically, for this one conclusion could have annulled all those things:

> What should be included in the precepts of the arts are their properties;
> These things are not the properties of rhetoric;
> Therefore let them not be included here.

Nor should we keep coming back to this point, that an orator cannot exist without this boyhood education, for this cause is too remote from its effect. Perhaps a doctor cannot be perfect without the same training, yet I do not hear the doctor giving instructions in medicine that derive from that boyhood elementary schooling.

In the next nine chapters the subject of the second form of schooling, the grammatical school, is treated. First of all the same thing should be known about this as about the schooling discussed before. These instructions may be true, they may be useful, they may be necessary to the future orator, but what then? Should they therefore be mixed in with the teachings of oratory? Surely the same studies in grammar are necessary for the philosopher? But who would put up with a philosopher stammering in philosophy about the arts of the grammarians? Of course, the orator should not ignore the grammatical arts—I do not deny it. Indeed they are investigated by the grammarians, and once known are carried over into rhetoric. Let the same syllogism be the judge of this error as of the previous one. This training is not proper to the orator; therefore, let it be removed from the art of oratory.

But nonetheless, in this training Quintilian offends more deeply than in the first. For I say that here things are not only out of place and inappropriate, but that they are false both in the art and in the practice of the art. For in grammar Quintilian makes an almost equal and identical error as in the whole of rhetoric. He makes grammar have two parts, method (*methodicen*) and literary interpretation (*historicen*). To the former he attributes skill in speaking and writing correctly, to the latter interpretation of the poets. In that first part he gives some instructions—confusedly however—on the accent of letters and syllables, on the etymology of the parts of speech, on syntax, and on spelling. These are the complete and only parts of grammar. In addition to the regular subject of its second part (the task of interpreting the poets), he assigns to the grammarian history, music, astrology, philosophy, and finally rhetoric itself, whose handmaiden he wishes grammar to be.

This error arose from the mistaken notion of the unskilled common people—just as we said about the orator. For grammarians were once commonly said to be those men who instructed boys in letters and interpreted the poets for them; in this capacity they would use their knowledge of the various arts beyond grammar. However, the common people did not realize that the scholar who taught various arts in the course of explaining the poets was also a historian, a musician, an astrologer, a philosopher, a man skilled in rhetoric, and thus not merely a grammarian. Indeed in explaining the precepts of theory, Quintilian ought to have made a sharper distinction among these things than the common people could; and so he should have realized that literary interpretation—as he calls it—is no part of grammar. For if that teacher in explaining a poet not only practices the arts of etymology, syntax, prosody and orthography for the purposes of speaking and writing purely and correctly, but adds ethical knowledge in order to explain morality, adds astrology in order to demonstrate the rising and setting of stars, and adds other arts in order to explain matters related to them, certainly he will do this not by virtue of his skill in grammar but by virtue of his skill in those other disciplines. Quintilian almost says the same thing in chapter one of book two, but because of his lack of wisdom he confuses many things. In sum—so that I may be silent about several other things in these six chapters—that division of grammar into method and literary interpretation is false, just as that school on which he has spent so many chapters has nothing to do with rhetorical teaching.

From such an elegant, even dialectical description of the art of grammar Quintilian passes to its practice: that is, the interpretation of authors by the grammarian, the duty of the teacher, and the writing of the pupil. However, he orders the grammarian to lecture to his pupils on only the poets, especially Homer and Virgil. Here I strongly disagree with him. For although I believe that the reading of the poets serves both to arouse the still tender intelligence with various emotions and to make clear the rules of prosody (since the quantity of syllables is understood from the laws of verse), these however are only small and unimportant matters. For the purpose of acquiring an abundant vocabulary for speeches, a deliberative and forensic use of style, and an appropriateness and elegance of diction, I would prefer the pupil to read the letters of Cicero rather than the elegies of Ovid, and the stories of Terence (which are almost like daily speech) rather than the eclogues of Virgil.

Indeed, there is one style for poetry and another for oratory. And perhaps this display of irrelevant instruction explains why Quintilian's oratory was so vastly different from Cicero's, since he believed he should imitate the poets' style, not Cicero's and his followers'. Here therefore Quintilian makes his first mistake, in prescribing only the poets for his pupils.

Next he orders that in teaching and explicating a poet, the grammarian should grant importance to even those lesser functions of methodology such as the proper quality of metrical feet and the meaning of words. However, he says, "He should teach tropes and figures of speech and thought with greater care. Especially he will fix in their minds the value of proper arrangement and of graceful treatment of the subject matter, and he will show what is appropriate to each character, what is praiseworthy in thoughts and in words, where richness of style is to be commended, where restraint."

From what Quintilian says here about the duty of the grammarian, we see that of the two parts of grammar which he has made, methodology, the only real property of this art, is almost despised—while literary interpretation, which has nothing to do with grammar, is especially commended. But indeed, O Quintilian, this teacher should postpone and reserve those subjects—which, though more outstanding, are out of place—for the time when the pupil studies them in the proper sphere of the rhetoricians and philosophers. However, he should handle and practice with every diligence and care those subjects which do belong strictly to his discipline. Here he should spend time; here he should dwell. He should embellish this task in every way: he should explain the primary, original meaning in each expression; then he should illustrate the rules of diction and style with examples; he should constantly examine the sounds of letters, observe accent, and pay attention to spelling; finally he should realize that his sole, total responsibility is to teach the pupil committed to his training how to speak and write correctly. However, he should use those greater and more exalted subjects which you here so strongly recommend, only as far as is helpful for carrying out the methodology which you spurn.

Indeed, once the pupil has diligently practiced all the parts of grammar by speaking and writing, he will then use the wisdom of rhetoricians in tropes and figures, and the wisdom of philosophers in the remaining virtues. Quintilian himself says the same thing later, but, as so often elsewhere, he imprudently contradicts himself, saying as follows in the seventh chapter of this book:

> These parts of speaking and writing correctly are the most important; I do not indeed take away from the grammarians the two remaining parts of speaking with elegance and significance, but since I still have to deal with the tasks of the rhetorician, I am reserving these for a more important part of the work.

Then afterwards, in chapter one of book two, he complains that the duties of the rhetoricians have been taken over by the grammarians.

Quintilian says that grammar is the theory of speaking and writing correctly. Yet the same Quintilian also directs the grammarian to teach how to speak and write, not correctly, but rather decoratively by means of tropes and figures, and wisely and appropriately by means of planning, judgment, and prudence. But the first alone belongs to grammar, while the rest belongs to rhetoric and philosophy. Therefore Quintilian does not describe the proper duties of the teacher of grammar, but very unwisely mixes in those that are not proper and are out of place; he has fallen again into the snare of his previous error.

"The final part in the practice of the art of grammar," says Quintilian, "is that the pupil should analyze the verses of the poets he has been prescribed; next he should explain their meaning in different words; then with more boldness he should turn to a paraphrase; he should abbreviate certain lines and embellish others; and he should explain set aphorisms when the general scheme has been given."

But how will the Roman pupil who has been entrusted to the teacher of grammar explicate Homer in different words when he was not able to understand Homer's own words in the first place without his teacher's explanation? For the Roman pupil is not handed over to the instruction of a Greek grammarian in order to use his native gift of speech for other subjects—for where did the young child's native gift come from?—but in order to pursue the gift of speech by hearing, reading, imitating. And this third error as regards practice is equal to the second. For Quintilian imposes on the learner of grammar as well as on the teacher of the same art the functions not of grammar but of rhetoric, both its clearly established theory and its practice. And so Quintilian errs far more seriously in this second prescription than in the first. For there he recorded things that were out of place, whereas here he also muddles together things that are false, both in the art of grammar, of which he makes literary interpretation a part, and in its practice, first because he prescribes that only poets should be read, and then because he instructs the teacher and the pupil in that method. I am not saying here that Quintilian lacked care in seeking out and finding material, but I do very much long to see in him wisdom in judgment and syllogistic reasoning.

In the remaining three chapters of the first book two new fields are described for Quintilian's orator. In one of these he should learn mathematical arts, and in the other he should study teachers of comedy, tragedy, and wrestling in order to acquire dignity of voice and gesture. Such instructions concerning mathematics in the rhetorical arts are even more amazing than those concerning grammar, even though Quintilian says very little more on the subject. Nevertheless, if you imagine that Quintilian teaches mathematical arts separately, what sort of a sequence will this be for educating youth? Rhetoric in its rules of style and delivery, and dialectic in its instructions on invention and arrangement, are more general and common than all the mathematical arts, and from those universal sources of the sciences the mathematical arts, like fountains, have flowed separately. Therefore rhetoric and dialectic go first in the order of learning, and every branch of mathematics follows. On the other hand one cannot say on Quintilian's behalf that at one time the arts were handed down to pupils in this way. For mathematics were for a long time the first and only arts, and no others could be treated before them because there were none. For, as long as language was basic, there was virtually no grammar, and before Isocrates absolutely nothing was taught about rhetoric. But since subjects can not only be taught and understood, but can be easily taught and understood when the arts for this purpose have been discovered, I believe we must now inquire into what at this time ought to be done, not into what once was usually done. As if with one voice, all the schools of every master teach that progress and instruction in the arts develop from universals to particulars. Consequently grammar, rhetoric, and dialectic must go first; mathematics must follow. I pursue the fundament of truth, not the error of custom.

Quintilian sends us from the mathematicians to the comedians and tragedians and wrestlers. They could be useful if we lived in Quintilian's time, because then those men took great pains to develop properly the voice and body, though not in a manner suitable for the writer of an art. For arts ought to consist of subjects that are constant, perpetual, and unchanging, and they should consider only those concepts which Plato says are archetypal and eternal. There was, and will be, however, no time and no place in which refinement of voice and gesture could not be elegantly produced or studied. There were and will be many times and places, when there were, and will be, no comedians or tragedians or wrestlers. Therefore Quintilian does not act correctly when he hands over a constant and unchanging art to such impermanent teachers.

Now in all these remarks so far, we see that there is no lack of variety and abundance of subject matter, but rather that it is the rationale of the syllogism and of judgment that is missing. Quintilian has thrown together here whatever he believed would be useful to the orator, without considering whether those things were true properties of this branch of education.

We should refer all these teachings to dialectic and we should abide by its judgment: the first kind of training in infancy has nothing to do with rhetoric; the second concerning grammar is not only alien to rhetoric but is false in many parts; the third and fourth likewise are completely alien and muddled in a variety of ways. What therefore should we expect the opinion of dialectic to be except an order to drive out and abolish from rhetorical teachings all those studies which are not only inappropriate but are false and awkwardly confused? So much then for the first book.

In the second book, Quintilian says, he treats the first principles taught by the teacher of rhetoric and inquires into the very essence of rhetoric. But first of all, before anything is said about the first exercises in rhetoric, come three fulsome, expansive chapters about the age at which a boy should be sent to the rhetorician, about the character and duties of the instructor, and about whether the best instructor should be employed straight away. I grant that such things are dependable, true, praiseworthy, useful; but how can I grant that they are true properties of this art and doctrine, described to direct the pupil towards a short, clear way of speaking? Suppose Donatus investigated similar things in the treatment of his art, such as when the pupil should be taken from teaching at home to the grammarian, what kind of character the grammarian ought to have, and whether the best grammarian should be employed straight away; investigation of these problems would be as useful in grammar and every branch of learning as here in rhetoric. But not everything which can be investigated with truth and usefulness can also be investigated with strict appropriateness and relevance to the matter taught. The best teacher ought to follow a short, easy path in his teachings. Why then is such a thorny, such a twisty path with diversions and side tracks undertaken? I acknowledge here Quintilian's very great care and diligence in gathering together subject matter, but I acknowledge no dialectical skill at all in his discrimination and judgment of that subject matter.

In the next four chapters there is a completely muddled discussion about rhetorical training. First of all, the pupils should be given practice in the recounting of fictional and realistic narrative and of historical fact, by means of corroboration, refutation, praise, and blame. I denounce Quintilian's precept not wholly but in part, because it is not put in the right place or order. An art should first of all be described, and then the method of practicing the art, first in writing, secondly also in speaking, should be made clear. But nevertheless let us look at the entire instruction concerning practice which Quintilian recorded in this place.

Previously Quintilian had assigned only the poets for grammatical exercises. Now for rhetorical studies he prescribes first the historian and then the orator, so that pupils receive lectures on the poets first, then on the historians and finally on the orators. I previously spoke about the poets, and I am really surprised that it occurred to Quintilian to think that poets and historians were more suitable than orators for fashioning an orator, especially since Quintilian warns in his very own teachings that the orator should avoid several of the virtues of the poets and historians, not to mention their frequent rather licentious and loose treatment of their subjects. Will Livy or Sallust fashion the orator better than Cicero? Indeed in the shaping of a poet I would prefer Virgil and Homer and the other outstanding, famous poets, to any orator. Likewise in educating an orator I would prefer Cicero by far to all the historians and poets. Indeed, does an orator seem more at home among historians than among orators? Consequently I judge that this whole chapter is not only out of place but that its advice is false.

The next two chapters about the division of subject matter and about speaking are useful—let us hope they are also true! But as in the chapter above, these two are not put in the right place or order. Previously, Quintilian talked first about the art of grammar and then about its practice, and in this he was correct. For an art must be described and learned before its practice is discussed. However, the art of rhetoric has not yet been described by Quintilian; therefore his instructions on its practice are unsuitable at this point. Here as before I look in vain for judgment and syllogistic reasoning from Quintilian.

The next seven chapters contain investigations of learning, of the pupil's task, of the method of teaching the pupil, of the usefulness of declamation, of whether knowledge of the art is necessary, of the reason the uneducated often seem to the mob to have more talent, and of what boundary the art possesses. All these subjects are even more alien to the prescriptive description of the art of rhetoric than those we have discussed so far. The last part about the limit of the art seems especially true, namely that the teachings of rhetoric are not universal but changeable according to the variety of time, place, character, and case. But if the art of rhetoric were properly understood by its parts, style and delivery, this would be flagrantly wrong. For rhetoric will be an art almost as fixed as arithmetic or geometry, and its precepts concerning style and delivery will be as unchanging as Euclid's theorems of the plane and line. But Quintilian calls his teachings—which are a tightly packed, confused mixture of various arts aimed at Roman rules for forensic and civilian cases—the art of rhetoric; nor is it surprising that we say about such an art that its rules must not be trusted, since they are so deceptive and false, as well as inharmonious with every place, time, and character. Thus in the first book and in the thirteen chapters of the second book Quintilian treats things that are outside the main body of rhetoric.

Then, in a section rather like another preface, he says that the remaining eight chapters of the second book concern the essence of rhetoric; and without doubt in the fourteenth chapter the essence of rhetoric is treated to a certain extent. However, Quintilian does not go far enough when he appears to wish to explain the origin of the word *rhetoric,* for a person does not at all reveal its etymology by saying that in Latin *rhetoric* is translated as "oratoria" or "oratrix," but by explaining what the origin of the word is and from where it derived its meaning.

He divides the entire following theory into three parts so that he discusses the art, the artist, and the work—a totally ridiculous and senseless division. The second and the third part are understood from the definition of the first. In grammar the grammarian is not defined, nor the work of the grammarian. In arithmetic and geometry neither the instructors nor their work are defined because the art reveals what the artist and the special work of the art should be like. And so I look in vain here for Quintilian to give us dialectical rules of division.

Moreover, all the other points about the various disputed definitions of rhetoric—for instance, that rhetoric is a useful skill, what art it is and of what kind, that art bestows more than nature, whether rhetoric is a virtue, and what its subject matter is—these points are so confused and wordy that they are clearly the work of a teacher who wishes to scare away, break down, or deceive the ignorant novices of this art. Nevertheless, at the start of the eighth book Quintilian in fact strongly condemned this kind of teacher; in the same place he applauded the teacher who by a different way, simple and short, wishes to lead to the practical application of the art.

But what is the use of piling up, so to speak, the mistaken notions of so many people concerning the definition of rhetoric, its usefulness, and its art, and even of mixing in false notions such as the idea that the gift of art more than nature is responsible for the orator of consummate skill? For if, as is fitting, nature, art and practice are kept separate in this investigation of the perfect orator, then undoubtedly we would attribute the first importance to nature (as Cicero correctly realizes in the second book of *De oratore*), the second to practice, and the third and least to art. And we shall show that Quintilian's following sophism is false: when he says that instruction has more bearing on perfection than nature, he covers nature, art, and practice (under the art's single name), although nevertheless he compares nature with art in this investigation. Here there is not even a single grain of dialectical salt. This teacher can make no distinctions, no evaluations with any genuineness and constancy: in dialectic he is without doubt totally leaden.

Quintilian's arguments on the question of whether rhetoric is a virtue are quite ridiculous; but since these were discussed at the beginning it is not necessary to discuss them again.

In the final chapter Quintilian is completely preoccupied with investigating the subject matter of rhetoric and makes various remarks about the different opinions concerning this subject. In the end he concludes that the subject matter of rhetoric is everything which is brought before it as a subject of speech. This statement is hardly sound, complete or clear, first of all because the material of the art is one thing, the material of the artist truly another. The art of rhetoric assigns to itself natural usage observed in the examples of good stylists and explained by precepts; the artist, that is the orator trained in the art of rhetoric, assigns to himself everything that can be embellished by speech. In the same way the subject matter of the grammarian is everything which is laid down before him for speaking or writing correctly; the subject matter of the dialectician is everything which is laid before him for correct debate; the subject matter of the arithmetician is everything which is laid before him for calculation; the subject matter of the geometrician is everything which is laid before him for measurement. But then I do not deny that sometimes we talk figuratively—*tropikôs*—of the material of the art instead of the material of the artist. Hence this definition of subject matter does not receive sufficient explication; nevertheless, I approve and accept it as teaching appropriate to true rhetoric. In the two first books of the instructions in oratory, out of the many forms of training—domestic, grammatical, mathematical, with comic and tragic actors, with wrestling instructors, and finally with a rhetorician—there are only two statements which can be praised and approved of in true rhetoric. Rhetoric is the science of speaking well; the subject matter of the orator is whatever is laid before him as a subject for speech. Although indeed the many other things are true and useful in some places, nevertheless in an accurate description of the art of rhetoric they are all either completely out of place, or patently absurd.

My dispute with Quintilian's first two books has up until now dealt with the part where grammar in particular is confused. In the next five books the discussion concerns dialectic, specifically invention and arrangement. Therefore we must discuss these parts next, as well as the separate chapters. And so in the first chapter of the third book Quintilian gathers together the discoveries of all the Greek and Latin teachers about this art, and with intense but useless diligence he reviews the teachers themselves by name. For this list of so many names sheds no light on the theory of rhetoric, no more than if in grammar, through his love of vanity, he were to seek out by name all the writers about grammar; this catalogue, I say, sheds no light on the theory. A lack of judgment and of syllogistic reasoning has caused his vanity to overflow.

The next chapter is the same. Here Quintilian does not separate with sufficient sharpness rhetoric's cause and origins, its nature, its usefulness, its art, and its practice. What is the problem? Were Plato and Cicero wrong? Or was Quintilian himself wrong when in the fifth chapter of this book he teaches that rhetoric is perfected and completed by three things: nature, art, and practice? How is usefulness different from those three causes and origins? For nothing either conceived by nature, described by art, or handled by practice is futile and without some usefulness. This is a dialectical nicety of division indeed, that what you ought to explain in three parts you expand into four by a new creation.

In the third chapter rhetoric is separated into five parts: invention, arrangement, style, memory, delivery. I am now not at all surprised that Quintilian is so bereft of dialectic in this division, for he was unable to recognize that here he has confused dialectic itself with rhetoric, since invention, arrangement, and memory belong to dialectic and only style and delivery to rhetoric. Indeed, Quintilian's reason for dividing rhetoric into these five parts derived from the same single source of error as did the causes of the previous confusion. The orator, says Quintilian, cannot be perfected without virtue, without grammar, without mathematics, and without philosophy. Therefore, one must define the nature of the orator from all these subjects. The grammarian, the same man says, cannot be complete without music, astrology, philosophy, rhetoric and history. Consequently there are two parts of grammar, methodology and literary interpretation. As a result Quintilian now finally reasons that rhetoric cannot exist unless the subject matter is first of all discovered, next arranged, then embellished, and finally committed to memory and delivered. Thus these are the five parts of rhetoric.

This reasoning of Quintilian's often deceived and misled him without any need (as some men report). I propose rather—as I have already said—that we should argue and deliberate quite differently the questions concerning the proper nature and the true divisions of the arts. I consider the subject matters of the arts to be distinct and separate. The whole of dialectic concerns the mind and reason, whereas rhetoric and grammar concern language and speech. Therefore dialectic comprises, as proper to it, the arts of invention, arrangement, and memory; this is evident because, as we find among numerous dumb persons and many people who live without any outward speech, they belong completely to the mind and can be practiced inwardly without any help from language or oration. To grammar for the purposes of speaking and writing well belong etymology in interpretation, syntax in connection, prosody in the pronunciation of short and long syllables, and orthography in the correct rules for writing. From the development of language and speech only two proper parts will be left for rhetoric, style, and delivery; rhetoric will possess nothing proper and of its own beyond these.

And here I am not arguing like Quintilian on the basis of the *sine qua non* for the subject, but by a proper, legitimate line of reasoning:

> In every art one should teach as many parts as exist in its proper, natural subject matter, and no more.
> To the subject matter of the art of dialectic, that is to the natural use of reason, belongs the skill of inventing, arranging, and memorizing.
> Therefore it should deal with the same number of parts.

Likewise,

> To the subject matter of rhetoric pertains only the ascribed skill of style and delivery.
> Therefore it should deal with the same number of parts.

Likewise,

> The parts of another art should not be intermingled with the art of rhetoric.
> Invention, arrangement, and memory are parts of another discipline, namely dialectic.
> Therefore they should not be intermingled with rhetoric.

However, in other places Quintilian shows us with his very own testimony that those parts belong to dialectic. For in the last chapter of the fifth book he speaks as follows about dialecticians: "Those learned men, seeking for truth among men of learning, subject everything to a detailed, scrupulous inquiry, and they thus arrive at the clear, acknowledged truth so that they can claim for themselves the parts of invention and judgment, calling the former *topiké,* the latter *kritiké.*" Here Quintilian says that the dialecticians lay claim to invention and judgment (which contains a large part of arrangement in the conclusions of each argument and in syllogisms). And finally in the second chapter of the eleventh book he says that if memory belongs to any art, then it belongs completely to arrangement and order. Therefore he should say that the dialecticians could rightly claim this part also, because in dialectic that has been rightly described, one should teach the truest theory of order and arrangement according to the precepts of the syllogism and method.

In this chapter Quintilian disproves the various opinions concerning the number of these five parts, but he does this in such a way that he himself makes far worse mistakes than do those whose mistakes he censures. Some men added that judgment is rather different from invention and arrangement. Quintilian correctly censures these men, not however with a correct argument but with one that is very clumsy and ignorant of what true judgment is. Quintilian thinks that judgment is so inextricably mixed in with invention, arrangement, style, and delivery that it cannot be separated from them by theory or precepts; he does not recognize any theory of judgment at all but, as he explains later in the last chapter of the sixth book, he considers that judgment can no more be transmitted by art than can taste or smell.

In this way Quintilian reveals himself to be quite ignorant of dialectic, for he has either not heard or not read anything about the role of judging, and about the many types of syllogisms, both simple and complex. He has not remembered that Cicero said the following about the Stoics, that as long as they labored in only the one part of dialectic, they did not reach the arts of invention, and yet they did diligently follow the paths of judgment.

Nor indeed should we consider it possible that rhetorical judgment is one thing and dialectical judgment another, since for evaluating whether something is truly useful, suitable, fitting, or has the qualities it seems to have, there is one faculty of judgment which the syllogism alone executes and accomplishes. For something to be understood as true or false by the rule of the syllogism is no different than it would be for a subject of control and debate to be spoken truly or falsely. Why should I say here that Quintilian knew nothing of the theory of judgment or of the teaching of the syllogism when he himself denies that any at all can exist? Why should I now make a case with many arguments that Quintilian has no training in dialectic? For he not only confesses what I argue, but openly declares it. He says that two arts are claimed by the dialecticians—one invention, the other judgment—but he does not believe what he says, because he maintains that there is no art of judgment.

Therefore let us continue, and let us still use the art of judgment against this rhetorician who lacks the art and theory of judgment. Let us refer his opinion about the remaining subjects to the standard of dialectical judgment. His next instructions are indeed wonderfully confused.

In the fourth, fifth, sixth, tenth, and eleventh chapters he discusses the orator's subject matter and its separation into parts. Let us therefore first of all take up the debate over this question. First Quintilian decrees that there are three classes of causes, demonstrative, deliberative, and forensic. He uses Aristotle as the author of this division, the very man who—to repeat what I have already taught in my "Observation against Aristotle"—was virtually the sole author and inventor of all the obscurity in this art, who was the first to mix dialectical invention in with the art of rhetoric, and who organized his inquiries so awkwardly and so ridiculously.

I say first of all that this partition is false, since there are countless questions which are not contained in any part of these classes. Quintilian saw this when he said,

> But then a feeble attempt was made, first by certain Greeks, then by Cicero in his books of the *De oratore,* and now almost forcibly by the greatest authority of our times, to prove that there are not only more than these three kinds but also that they are practically countless. For if we place the task of praise and denunciation in the third division, in what kind of oratory shall we seem to be engaged when we complain, console, pacify, excite, terrify, encourage, instruct, explain obscurities, narrate, plead for mercy, give thanks, congratulate, reproach, vilify, describe, command, retract, express our desires and opinions, and so on? As a result I must ask pardon, so to speak, for remaining an adherent of the older view, and I must ask what were the motives which caused earlier writers to confine so closely a subject of such variety.

He recites these things with a certain grandeur, so that he appears to have solved a difficult matter; he does not seem to have understood the force of the argument which he uses against himself but, content with a fallacious, faulty solution, he has ensnared and deceived himself.

Quintilian, however, thinks he meets this objection in the following way: "In the course of a thorough examination of all these things," he says, "the following line of reasoning helped, that the entire task of the orator is either in the law courts, or outside the law courts." Agreed: and so? "The type of the objects of investigation in the law courts is obvious," he says. I admit this; what then? "Those matters which do not come before a judge either deal with past or future time," he says. Why, I ask? Can there not exist any question, any dispute, any occasion for speaking that deals with a contemporary subject? When there is an investigation of this syntax, this square, this star, this wound, this rhetoric, or countless matters of this kind, does the investigation concern a past or future rather than a contemporary matter? Consequently this is false.

But go on, nevertheless. "We praise or denounce past action," he says, "we deliberate about the future." But cannot the opportunity also be offered for investigating, consoling, pacifying, exciting, terrifying and doing countless other things that concern past and future? Thus Quintilian here concludes nothing, solves nothing, but confuses himself.

But another clear proof is added to the one above. "All subjects of speech," he says, "must either be certain or doubtful." What then, O Quintilian? What will you achieve by this division? "We praise or blame what is certain, according to each person's inclination," he says. Yet, like Cicero and Caesar in the Cato debate, we do praise and blame many uncertain things, and of course without either praising or blaming we treat many certain things, such as the almost limitless functions of the subjects covered by the liberal and practical arts. Therefore, part of this division is false.

"In some cases," he says, "dubious matters require deliberation, in other cases, litigation." Truly I look in vain here for the same statement as in the previous section, that the things which are doubtful to the ignorant are the countless subjects covered by the arts. Should a man who is ignorant of those arts guide the deliberation of the people or the judgment of the law courts according to Quintilian's precepts, instead of employing and seeking information from a learned, experienced man? O capricious and artless proposal! By this devious argument has Quintilian refuted the objections thrown against him? Has he in this way opposed the greatest author of his times? Yet his method is not to refute false arguments by true arguments, but rather to confirm true arguments by false sophisms.

Quintilian adds to this last quasi-solution one other. He abridges all those other species into the three kinds, but in a quite insolent manner that is inappropriate for a writer of the art. Indeed he wished to overrule us by the force of his authority, since he can prove nothing true by reason. I look in vain here for dialectical wisdom in his partition. Now I am saying not only that Quintilian errs without the art of judgment but also that he rambles on without any understanding of invention.

Partitions of questions of a similar but far greater uselessness follow in the whole of chapters five, six, and eleven. I have decided not to use up the greater part of my discourse against these by teaching that they are stupid and false, but rather I have decided that I should use one comprehensive refutation for so many foolish statements. I say therefore that the whole partition and division of these questions is clearly futile not only in the art of rhetoric, which is composed truly and appropriately from the parts of style and delivery, but also in this confused art of Quintilian's which is thrown together from the parts of invention, arrangement, style, memory and delivery. Since we indeed feel this way, let us repeat this line of argument from our "Observations against Aristotle."

> A theory common to the subjects laid before it for treatment seeks no partition of these subjects.

For instance, in grammar there is no division of the subjects laid before grammar for treatment, because grammar is a common art that deals with all aspects of writing and speaking.

> Rhetoric, though confused by Quintilian into five parts, is a theory completely common to the subjects laid before it for treatment.

For there is one art common to memory, delivery, and style, and their parts are not variously adapted to various questions—unless I do not know what is taught concerning the quality of style, and about the classification of arguments as either demonstration, deliberation, or adjudications; even then, there is not another art of tropes and figures, but another use. I shall demonstrate my proof concerning invention and judgment in their place.

But indeed I shall instead agree with Quintilian's opinion that rhetoric is defined as the science of speaking well, not about this or that, but about all subjects.

> Rhetoric therefore requires no partition of its areas of investigation.

Here I am not using fallacious or obscure proofs, but I am explaining the first and most important reason for dividing a question. If a question were to be divided in rhetoric, this would happen because some fixed arts are suited to fixed questions; not all parts of those arts as a whole would agree with all questions. But I contend that this is false, and I hold this to be plain and obvious first of all in respect to the three parts, style, memory, and delivery; in respect to the other two parts, invention and arrangement, I hold the same position about those things necessary for speaking.

Indeed the chief point of the whole confusion is in invention alone. The theory of memory and delivery is not repeated very often and is not confused in so many ways; it is dealt with once, and in one place only. The teaching of style through tropes and figures is not muddled by the same repeated and confused classifications; although Quintilian burdened this part with many unrelated subjects, still he did handle it altogether in a single place over the eighth and ninth books. In various places Quintilian says many things about the teaching of arrangement, proofs, questions, and the parts of a speech; he infers no universal and general (if I may use his word) precept. I say again that the chief point of this rhetorical confusion occurs entirely in invention; the reason for this we can see from reason and from the developments of history.

For I see that the scholars and teachers of this art have spent greater zeal in collecting the instructions of the ancients and in thinking up new instructions than they have used judgment in discriminating among their own and others' discoveries. The purpose of the early rhetoricians before Aristotle was not to record some general theory for speaking eloquently about all subjects, but only to draw up for forensic and civil cases some advice concerning the rules for amplification through tropes and figures. Other writers suggested other things about how to move the audience to anger, pity, envy, indignation, and similar passions, and about the classification of causes (demonstrative, deliberative, and judicial). Later Aristotle collected all their material together with great eagerness and care, and he mixed up these first arts with the universal, common topics of dialectical invention; he also gave some thought to delivery; later memory was added to rhetoric. Thus he entangled the arts of invention in as many ways as we have them now, despite the fact that only one general theory—separated into the ten topics of causes, results, subjects, adjuncts, opposites, comparisons, names, divisions, definitions, and witnesses—could be adapted to make clear most easily and plainly all questions, all parts of a speech, and finally all subjects.

But someone will say that in the classification of causes and the parts of a speech these lesser arts of invention are described for uneducated novices, whereas the more important and more common arts belonging to the universal topics are described for the pupils who have already made some progress in those studies. I hear them, I say, and I know that this is said in the second book of Cicero's *De oratore,* for there Antony speaks as follows about these topics of invention:

> If, however, I should wish that someone quite unskilled should be taught to speak, I would instead hammer with undivided zeal on the same anvil night and day, and I would thrust all the tiniest morsels, everything chewed very small,

> as the nurses say, down the young pupil's throat. But if he is generously instructed in the theory and already familiar with some usage, and if moreover he seems to be of sharp enough intelligence, I would snatch him away, not to some remote, landlocked rivulet, but to the source of the mighty, universal river. This site, as the home of all proofs, would reveal them to him through brief illustration and verbal definition.

Thus Cicero spoke there in Antony's voice.

Here I wish to lay down a comprehensive rebuttal to Cicero—namely, that in his rhetorical precepts there is almost nothing of Ciceronian judgment or intelligence; rather, he dealt merely with the rules of teachers and rhetoricians whom he had heard or read, Aristotle in particular. Cicero did not become eloquent from these rules, and his eloquence can easily be seen as splendid, not because of his own mixed-up rules but because of our own rules, which we make conform to his achievements. There is yet another point in respect to the authority of Cicero: Do we wish the authority of any man in a debate concerning an art to be superior to the truth of the case? Consider some similar proof in another body of instruction for an art. Suppose the grammarian should define a noun and should expound as a whole all the circumstantial adjuncts of the noun and its accidents. Because this is comprehensive, because it is general, we consider it sufficient for all nouns. We look for no lesser arts, nor could any particular art be more easily explained than that general one. The same proof obviously holds for the theory of invention.

INTRODUCTION TO DESIDERIUS ERASMUS

Erasmus lived in the middle of the Renaissance period, from 1469 to 1536. Born in Holland, he later moved to Italy and France to further his education. In 1499 he moved to England, where he lived and worked for sixteen years. During this period he write *On Copia,* which is excerpted here.

Erasmus was a priest in the Roman Catholic Church, a scholar, and a teacher. He both wrote and translated several important works that gained him a wide reputation. During a period in which he held an academic appointment at Cambridge University, he wrote *On Copia* as a textbook for a boys' school that was being founded by a friend.

The focus of *On Copia* is rhetorical style, which was typical of a preoccupation with language in rhetorical theory that had been gaining momentum ever since St. Augustine. By the Renaissance, rhetorical theorists were devising categories and schemes of hundreds of rhetorical tropes, figures of speech, and other stylistic devices. Fine distinctions were made among the many different ways to turn a phrase. There is evidence that the general population also responded to this fascination with verbal splendor, for this was the age of Shakespeare (who, after all, was writing for a popular audience).

Training in rhetorical style was central to the education of young people during the Renaissance. *On Copia* is best understood as a manual of training devices for application in school rather than as a "real life" rhetorical theory designed to guide actual practice. The theory and exercises here were meant to prepare students to be articulate and handy with a phrase; they were not meant for rhetorical application in and of themselves.

The word *copie* means "abundance" in Latin. Erasmus's book is instruction in how to achieve the ability to speak with an abundant style and also how to achieve the opposite effect of a lean and efficient style. The reading is divided into two books. The first book attempts to teach copia in style, the second to teach copia of subject matter. By abundance of style, Erasmus means the ability to express a word, phrase, or sentence in as many ways as possible. This kind of copia is a search for synonyms; it is a sort of thesaurus exercise. By abundance of subject matter, Erasmus means the ability to expand or contract a word, phrase, or sentence so as either to fully develop or efficiently summarize the content expressed in the language.

Erasmus offers different exercises to achieve both ends. Although he claims that the practice of copia allows *either* the expansion or compression of style and subject matter, by far his most common examples and techniques are directed towards expansion. You will find some marvelous examples of fairly simple sentences that are rephrased and paraphrased in different ways for page after page (copia of style). And you will find wonderful instances of simple sentences that are expanded exhaustively through copia of subject matter.

There are two reasons, Erasmus says, for learning the technique of copia. One is to acquire better verbal style in general, the second is to develop one's ability to speak extemporaneously. The educated person of the Renaissance would need both to achieve the desired fullness and well-roundedness that would prepare a person for participation in public life. Although this view of rhetoric is restricted to style, it shows rhetorical influence at work in the Renaissance.

DESIDERIUS ERASMUS OF ROTTERDAM

ON COPIA OF WORDS AND IDEAS

BOOK I

CHAPTER I

That the Aspiration to Copia Is Dangerous

Just as there is nothing more admirable or more splendid than a speech with a rich copia of thoughts and words overflowing in a golden stream, so it is, assuredly, such a thing as may be striven for at no slight risk, because, according to the proverb,

> Not every man has the luck to go to Corinth.[1]

Whence we see it befalls not a few mortals that they strive for this divine excellence diligently, indeed, but unsuccessfully, and fall into a kind of futile and amorphous loquacity, as with a multitude of inane thoughts and words thrown together without discrimination, they alike obscure the subject and burden the ears of their wretched hearers. To such a degree is this true that a number of writers, having gone so far as to deliver precepts concerning this very thing, if it please the gods, seem to have accomplished nothing else than, having professed copia (abundance) to have betrayed their poverty. And in truth this thing has so disturbed us, that partly selecting those from among the precepts of the art of Rhetoric suitable to this purpose, and partly adapting those which we have learned by a now long-continued experience in speaking and writing and have observed in our varied reading of a great many authors, we here set forth concerning each kind of copia, a number of principles, examples, and rules. We have not, to be sure, attempted to cover everything fully in a book, but have been content, in the publication of what one might call a brief treatise, to have opened the way to the learned and studious, and as it were to have furnished certain raw materials for other workers in the field. We have thus limited our efforts partly because we were moved to undertake this labor solely by the desire to be of service and

Translated from the Latin by Donald B. King, Ph.D., Professor of English, College of Mt. St. Joseph On-the-Ohio, and H. David Rix, Ph.D., Formerly Professor of English, Pennsylvania State University.

Many passages from the writings of ancient authors which Erasmus quoted as illustrations or examples, he repeated from the works of Quintilian or another, instead of directly from the works of the original author. In these notes, references to such secondary sources are enclosed in parentheses immediately following references to the primary sources.

[1] Horace *Epistles* i. 17, 36. Cf. Aulus Gellius *Attic Nights* i. 8, 4.

do not begrudge all the glory going to another if only we have produced something useful to youth eager for knowledge, and partly because we have been devoted to more serious studies to an extent that there is lacking very much leisure to spend on these lesser ones, most useful to be sure to the former kind, indeed of the greatest use, but nevertheless minute in themselves.

CHAPTER II

By Whom Copia Was Developed and by Whom Practiced

Further, lest anyone think this a modern device and to be disdained as lately born at our home, let him know that this method of diversifying speech is touched on lightly in a number of places by a very learned and likewise very diligent man, Quintilian,[1] and that many noted Sophists showed the way to the advantages of condensing speech. And they would not by any means have been able to do this without pointing out also a method of amplification; and if their books were extant, or if, as Quintilian suggests,[2] they had been willing to expound their doctrines fully, there would have been no need at all for these modest precepts of mine. It is a further recommendation of this thing that eminent men in every branch of learning have eagerly and diligently practiced this one. Thus there still survive several admirable efforts of Vergil about a mirror, about a stream frozen by the cold, about Iris, about the rising of the sun, about the four seasons of the year, about the heavenly constellations. That Aesopic fable about the fox and the crow which Apuleius narrates briefly with a wonderful economy of words, and also amplifies as fully as possible with a great many words, doubtless to exercise and display his genius, shows the same thing fully.[1] But come, who could find fault with this study when he sees that Cicero, that father of all eloquence, was so given to this exercise that he used to compete with his friend, the mimic actor, Roscius, to see whether the latter might express the same idea more times by means of various gestures, or he himself render it more often in speech varied through copia of eloquence.

CHAPTER III

How Authors Have Indulged in a Display of Copia

Moreover, the same authors, not only in school, but also in their serious work, sometimes indulged in a display of copia; while they at one time so compress a subject that you can take nothing away, at another, they so enrich and expand the same subject that you can add nothing to it. Homer, according to Quintilian,[2] is equally admirable at both—now copia, now brevity. Although it is not our intention here to cite examples, yet we will cite one of each from the peerless Vergil. What can have been said by anyone more concisely than this: "And the fields, where Troy was"?[3] With the fewest words, as Macrobius says, he consumed the state and engulfed it; not even a ruin was left.[4] On the other hand, listen to how fully he has treated the same topic:

> *The final day has come and the inescapable doom*
> *Of Troy; we were Trojans, there was Ilium and a great*
> *Glory of the Trojans, cruel Jupiter Argos, all has*

---

[1] See Quintilian *Education of an Orator* (hereinafter referred to as Quintilian) viii. 2; xii. 1; and in general, Books viii, ix and x.

[2] Quintilian iii. 1, 21.

[1] Apuleius *Prologue* to *On the God of Socrates* 4.

[2] Quintilian x. 1, 46.

[3] Vergil *Aeneid* iii. 11.

[4] Macrobius *Saturnalia* v. 1.

Taken away: the Greeks are supreme in a
burning city.
O fatherland, O home of the gods, Ilium, and
Trojans'
Walls, famed in war. . . .
Who the disaster of that night, who the
sorrows in words
Could express? or who could make its tears
equal to its sufferings?[1]

What fountain, what torrent, what sea has overflowed with as many waves as he has with words? But it might appear that this example should rather be referred to copia of thought. He indulged in profusion of words also when he said:

. . . Does he survive and breathe the upper
air,
Nor yet lie dead in the cruel shadows?[2]

But this thing is more common in Ovid, to such a degree that he is criticized on the score that he does not preserve due moderation in copia. However, he is criticized by Seneca, whose whole style Quintilian, Suetonius and Aulus Gellius condemn.[3]

CHAPTER IV

To Whom Unrestrained Copia Has Been Attributed As a Fault

Nor does it matter to me that some writers have been criticized for unduly and mistakenly striving for copia. For Quintilian notes too effusive and redundant copia in Stesichorus; but he mentions it in such a way as to confess that the fault should not be entirely avoided.[4] In Old Comedy Aeschylus is reproached because he said the same thing twice. "ηκω κὰι κατέρχομαι," that is, I am come back

[1] Vergil *Aeneid* ii. 324–27; 241–42; 361–62.

[2] Vergil *Aeneid* i, 546–47.

[3] Quintilian x. 1, 125. Aulus Gellius *Attic Nights* xiii 2. 2.

[4] Quintilian x. 1, 62.

and I am returned.[1] Seneca scarcely tolerates Vergil's repeating the same idea two or three times.[2] And, not to needlessly recount a long list, there have not been lacking those who condemned even Cicero as Asian and redundant and too extravagant in copia.[3] But these things, as I said, don't at all concern me, who indeed am not prescribing how one should write and speak, but am pointing out what to do for training, where, as everyone knows, all things ought to be exaggerated. Then I am instructing youth, in whom extravagance of speech does not seem wrong to Quintilian, because with judgment, superfluities are easily restrained, certain of them even, age itself wears away, while on the other hand, you cannot by any method cure meagerness and poverty.[4]

CHAPTER V

That It Is Characteristic of the Same Artist to Speak Both Concisely and Copiously

Now if there are any who fully approve the Homeric Menelaus, a man of few words, and who, on the other hand, disapprove of Ulysses, rushing on like a river swollen by the winter snows, that is, those whom laconism and conciseness greatly delight, not even they ought to object to our work, for in fact they themselves would find it not unprofitable, because it seems best to proceed by the same principle either to speak most concisely or most fully. If indeed it is true, as in Plato, Socrates acutely reasons, that the ability to lie and to tell the truth cleverly are talents of the same man, no artist will better compress speech to conciseness than he who has skill to enrich the same with as varied an ornamentation as possible. For as far as

[1] Aristophanes *Frogs* 1154 *seq.*

[2] Aulus Gellius *Attic Nights* xii. 2, 2.

[3] Quintilian xii. 10, 12 *ad fin.*

[4] Quintilian ii. 4. 5 *seq.*

conciseness of speech is concerned, who could speak more tersely than he who has ready at hand an extensive array of words and figures from which he can immediately select what is most suitable for conciseness? Or as far as concerns conciseness of thought, who would be more able at expressing any subject in the fewest possible words than one who has learned and studied what the matters of special importance in a case are, the supporting pillars, as it were, what are most closely related, what are appropriate for purposes of ornament. No one certainly will see more quickly and more surely what can be suitably omitted than he who has seen what can be added and in what ways.

CHAPTER VI

Concerning Those Who Strive for Either Conciseness or Copia Foolishly

But if we use either brevity or copia without method, there is the danger that there may befall us what we see happen to certain perverse affectors of laconism, although they speak but few words, yet even in those few, many, not to say all, are superfluous.[1] Just as in a different way it may happen to those who unskillfully strive for copia that although they are excessively loquacious, yet they say too little, leaving out many things that certainly need to be said.

Accordingly, our precepts will be directed to this, that you may be able in the fewest possible words so to comprehend the essence of a matter that nothing is lacking; that you may be able to amplify by copia in such a way that there is nonetheless no redundancy; and, the principle learned, that you may be free either to emulate laconism, if you wish, or to copy Asian exuberance, or to exhibit Rhodian moderation.

[1] See Quintilian viii. 3, 56, on κακοξήλια, excellence carried to excess.

CHAPTER VII

That Copia Is Twofold

Furthermore, I think it is clear that copia is twofold, as Quintilian himself declares, especially admiring among the other excellences of Pindar that most happy copia of thought and words.[1] And of these one consists in *Synonymia,* in *Heterosis* or *Enallage* of words, in metaphor, in change of word form, in *Isodynamia* and the remaining ways of this sort for gaining variety; the other depends upon the piling up, expanding and amplifying of arguments, *exempla, collationes,* similes, *dissimilia, contraria,* and other methods of this sort, which we will discuss in more detail in their proper place. Although these can be observed anywhere, so closely combined that you cannot tell them apart at all easily, so much does one serve the other, so that they might seem to be distinct only in theory, rather than in fact and in use, nevertheless, for the purpose of teaching, we shall make the distinction in such a way that we cannot deservedly be condemned for hair splitting in distinguishing, nor, on the other hand, for negligence.

CHAPTER VIII

For What Things This Training Is Useful

Now in order that studious youth may apply itself to this study with an eager disposition we shall make clear in a few words for what things it is of use. First of all then, this training in varying speech will be useful in every way for attaining good style, which is a matter of no little moment. In particular, however, it will be useful in avoiding tautology, that is, repetition of the same word or expression, a vice not only unseemly but also offensive. It not infrequently happens that we have to say the same thing several times, in which case,

[1] Quintilian x. 1. 61.

if destitute of copia we will either be at a loss, or, like the cuckoo, croak out the same words repeatedly, and be unable to give different shape or form to the thought. And thus betraying our want of eloquence we will appear ridiculous ourselves and utterly exhaust our wretched audience with weariness. Worse than tautology is *homologia,* as Quintilian says,[1] which does not lighten tedium with any charm of variety, and is wholly monotonous. Moreover, who is so patient a listener that he would even for a short time put up with a speech unvarying throughout? Variety everywhere has such force that nothing at all is so polished as not to seem rough when lacking its excellence. Nature herself especially rejoices in variety; in such a great throng of things she has left nothing anywhere not painted with some wonderful artifice of variety. And just as the eye is held more by a varying scene, in the same way the mind always eagerly examines whatever it sees as new. And if all things continually present themselves to the mind without variation, it will at once turn away in disgust. Thus the whole profit of a speech is lost. This great fault he will shun easily who is prepared to turn the same thought into many forms, as the famous Proteus is said to have changed his form. And in truth this training will contribute greatly to skill in extemporaneous speaking or writing; it will assure that we will not frequently hesitate in bewilderment or keep shamefully silent. Nor will it be difficult, with so many formulas prepared in readiness for action, to aptly divert even a rashly begun speech in any desired direction. Besides, in interpreting authors, in translating books from a foreign language, in writing verse, it will give us no little help, since in such matters, unless we are trained in the principles of copia, we shall often find ourselves either confused, or crude, or even silent.

[1] Quintilian viii. 3. 52.

CHAPTER IX

By What Methods of Training This Faculty May Be Developed

Next it remains to mention briefly by what methods of training this faculty may be developed. Having diligently committed the precepts to memory, we should often of set purpose select certain expressions and make as many variations of them as possible in the way Quintilian advises, "just as several different figures are commonly formed from the same piece of wax."[1] This work, moreover, will bear richer fruit, if several students compete with one another either orally or in writing, on a subject set for them. For then each individual will be aided by their common discoveries, and, the opportunity having been furnished, each one will discover many things. Again, we may treat some theme as a whole in many ways. And in this matter it will be well to emulate the ingenuity of Milo of Croton, so that making at first two variations, then three, then more and more, we may attain to such ability that at length we can without difficulty make a hundred or two hundred variations. In addition we will greatly increase the copia of our speech by translation from Greek authors, because the Greek language is especially rich in both word and thought. Moreover, it will occasionally be very useful to emulate them by paraphrasing. It will be of especial help to rewrite the verses of poets in prose; and on the other hand, to bind prose in meter, and put the same theme into first one and then another type of verse. And it will be very helpful for us to emulate and attempt by our own efforts to equal or even to improve upon that passage in any author which appears unusually rich in copia. Moreover, it will be especially useful if we peruse good authors night and day, particularly those who have excelled in copia of

[1] Quintilian x. 5. 9.

speech, such as Cicero, Aulus Gellius, Apuleius; and with vigilant eyes we should note all figures in them, store up in our memory what we have noted, imitate what we have stored up, and by frequent use make it a habit to have them ready at hand.

CHAPTER X

First Precept Concerning Copia

Having said these things as a sort of preface, it remains to address ourselves to the propounding of precepts, although the things we have already said can be regarded as precepts. However, it does not seem that we will be acting illogically if we commence the precepts here by forewarning the student of copia that, above all, care must be taken that speech be appropriate, be Latin, be elegant, be correct; and that he should not consider anything to belong to copia that is not consistent with the purity of the Roman language.

Elegance consists partly in words used by suitable authors; partly in using the right word; and partly in using it in the right expression. What clothing is to our body, diction is to the expression of our thoughts. For just as the fine appearance and dignity of the body are either set off to advantage or disfigured by dress and habit, just so thought is by words. Accordingly, they err greatly who think that it matters nothing in what words something is expressed, provided only it is in some way understandable. And the reason for changing clothes and for varying speech is one and the same. Consequently, let this be the primary concern, that the clothes be not dirty, or ill fitting, or improperly arranged. For it would be a shame if a figure good in itself should be displeasing because degraded by dirty clothes. And it would be ridiculous for a man to appear in public in a woman's dress, and unseemly for anyone to be seen with his clothes turned backside to and inside out. Therefore, if anyone should wish to strive for copia before he has acquired competence in the Latin language, that one, in my opinion at least, would be acting no less ridiculously than a pauper who did not own a single garment that he could wear without great shame, and who, suddenly changing his clothes, should appear in the forum covered by assorted rags, ostentatiously exhibiting his poverty instead of his riches. And will he not appear more senseless the more often he does this? I think he will. And yet no less absurdly do some of those who strive for copia act, who, although they are not able to express their thoughts even in one way in elegant phrases, nevertheless, just as if they were ashamed to appear insufficiently stammering, variously rephrase their stuttering in such a way as to make it more stuttering; as if they have undertaken a contest with themselves to speak as barbarously as possible. I want the furnishings of a rich house to exhibit the greatest variety; but I want it to be altogether in good taste, not with every corner crammed with willow and fig and Samian ware. At a splendid banquet I want various kinds of food to be served, but who could endure anyone serving a hundred different dishes not one of which but would move to nausea? I have deliberately given this warning at length, because I know the rash presumption of very many people who prefer to omit the fundamentals and (as the saying goes) with dirty feet to hasten to the heights straightway. Nor do they sin much less seriously who, mixing the sordid with the elegant, disfigure the purple with rags, and intersperse glass among precious stones, and combine garlic with Attic sweetmeats. Now we shall set forth formulas for varying, those of course that pertain to copia of words.

• • •

CHAPTER XXXIII

Practice

Now, to make the matter clearer, let us set forth an expression as an experiment and try how far it is possible to have it turn like Proteus into several forms; not that every method of varying is suitable in any one instance, but as many as are, we shall use. Let us take the following sentence for an example: *Your letter has delighted me very much. Your* does not admit of a synonym. Your fulness, your sublimity, your grandeur, are *periphrasis.* If you use a proper name, for instance, Faustus, it is *heterosis,* both of part of speech and of person, Faustus' letter. If Faustine letter, there is *heterosis* of the substantive in the epithet.

LETTER

Epistle, letter, writing are synonyms. Little letter, little epistle, little writing constitute *heterosis.* Written sheet is synecdoche; what you have written to me, *periphrasis.*

ME

My mind, my heart, my eyes is either *periphrasis* or synecdoche; us for me is enallage of number; Erasmus is *heterosis* of person.

VERY MUCH

Greatly, mightily, exceedingly, wonderfully, in a wonderful manner, etc. are synonyms. In the most profound manner, above measure, beyond measure, in an extraordinary degree, is *auxesis.* Not indifferently, not a little, not commonly is *contrarium* and negation. It is impossible to say how greatly, incredible to say, I cannot express in words, and others of that type savor of hyperbole.

HAS DELIGHTED

Has pleased, has refreshed, has exhilarated, are synonymous, except that there seems to be metaphor in has exhilarated. Has brought pleasure, has been a pleasure, has been a joy, etc. constitute *periphrasis.* Has imbued with joy, has been honeyed are metaphorical; has been not unpleasant, not disagreeable, substitutions of contraries.

Others cannot readily be illustrated without a context. Now then let us make trial. Your letter has delighted me very much. In a wonderful way your letter has delighted me; in an unusually wonderful way your letter has delighted me. Up to this point almost nothing has been varied except the word order. By your letter I have been greatly delighted. I have been delighted in an unusually wonderful way by your letter. Here only the voice of the verb has been changed. Your epistle has cheered me exceedingly. In truth by your epistle I have been exceedingly cheered. Your note has refreshed my spirit in no indifferent manner. By the writing of your humanity I have been refreshed in spirit in no indifferent manner. From your most pleasing letter I have had incredible joy. Your paper has been the occasion of an unusual pleasure for me. From your paper I have received a wondrous pleasure. What you wrote has brought me the deepest delight. From what you wrote the deepest joy has been brought me. From the letter of your excellency we have drunk a great joy; this is *relatio.* Anyone may easily compose others for himself. From the letter of my Faustus I have drunk the greatest joy. A by no means common joy has come to me from what you wrote. I have been uniquely delighted by your letter. I have received a wonderful delight from the letter of Faustus. How exceedingly your letter has delighted my spirit. Your paper has imbued me with ineffable delight. This is metaphor. Through your letter I have been imbued with an unusual delight. What you wrote has given me incredible pleasure. This is metaphor also. Your letter provided me with no little delight. I have been exceedingly delighted by reading your letter. The reading of your letter imbued my mind with singular joy. Your epistle was very delightful. Your letter was a source of extraordinary pleasure for me. From your letter I had a singular pleasure. You epistle was the greatest joy to me. What you wrote was the keenest delight to me. Your epistle was an incredible pleasure to me. Your epistle was immeasurably pleasing to me. You would scarcely believe how greatly I enjoy (*acquiescam*) what you wrote. Cicero frequently used *acquiescere* in this way for *oblectare.* Your epistle was the keenest enjoyment for me. Your letter has been most delightful. A singular pleasure has been provided for me by your letter. Your letter has been the occasion of glad joy for me. On receiving your letter I was carried away with joy. When your letter came I was filled with joy. On reading your most loving letter I was seized with an unusual pleasure. When I received your letter an incredible joy seized my spirit. Your epistle caressed me with extraordinary pleasure. What you wrote to me was most delightful. That you sent a letter to me was exceedingly pleasant. Nothing could have given me more pleasure than that you deemed me worthy of your letter. Your dear letter has made me rejoice exceedingly. By your letter I am made exceedingly joyful.

That you have informed me by your letter is not only acceptable to me, but in truth delightful. You should have seen me transported by the extent of my joy when your letter reached me. That you would greet me at least by letter was certainly delightful. Nothing more longed for than your letter could have come to me. Your very anxiously awaited letter has come. Nothing more desired than your letter could have come. In these last three there is *metalepsis* or at least synecdoche; for those things which we greatly desire are customarily considered pleasing. The letter of Faustus to Erasmus is unable not to be most pleasing. Not unpleasing to me was your letter. Your by no means disagreeable letter has come to me. Your writing in no way displeasing to me has come. Your letter was as charming to me as the most charming things. I have read your letter through with great pleasure. I have received your letter not without the keenest pleasure. He who handed me your letter, brought me a heap of joys. It is wonderful to say how your letter has taken hold of me. I have received the letter you sent; it lightens my heart with a new light of joys. Whatever there was of sadness in my heart, your letter cast out straightway. I felt a wondrous joy in my heart when your letter came to me. An uncommon pleasure entered my spirit from your letter. Your letter was the cause of my abundant rejoicing. Your letter made me rejoice exceedingly. It is scarcely possible to say how much joy came to me from your letter. I can hardly express in words how much pleasure was provided me by your letter. It is wonderful to say how much joy shone upon me from your letter. Immortal God! what great joy came to us from your letter? O wonderful, what great cause of joy your letter supplied! Good gods, what a great number of joys did your writing afford me? Your letter brought me greater joy than I can express. Your letter brought me very great pleasure. You would scarcely believe what a multitude of joys your letter brought to my spirit. I am not able to say in words with what great joys your letter loaded me. Why should I fear to speak thus when Terence spoke of "the day loaded with many advantages." Your letter has made me laden with joys. I rejoiced exceedingly in your letter. I took a unique pleasure in your letter. Your writing poured forth a most rich abundance of pleasure. Your letter was most pleasurable to me. By your letter the wrinkles were straightway wiped from my brow. Directly I saw your letter, I smoothed the brow of my spirit. While I read what you wrote to me, a wonderful pleasure stole into my heart. While I looked at your letter an extraordinary multitude of joys seized my mind. When I looked at your letter an incredible wave of joy entered my heart. When I received your most kind letter, a great joy possessed me entirely. I would die if anything more pleasing than your letter ever happened. I would perish if anything in life occurred more pleasurable than your letter. I call the muses to witness that nothing has ever before brought me more joy than your letter. Do not believe that Fortune can offer anything more pleasing than your letter. The delight your letter gives me is equalled only by the love I bear you. Oh wonderful! How much joy your letter aroused in me. What laughter, what applause, what exultant dancing your letter caused in me. Reading your most elegant letter I was touched with a strange joy. Your pen has sated me with joys. Your letter has afforded me much pleasure. Your so fine letter has wholly imbued me with joy. Your letter has imbued me with a rare pleasure. Your letter has covered my soul with an unusual pleasure. Nothing dearer than your letter has ever happened to me. I have never seen anything more joyful than your letter. There is nothing I shall receive with a gladder spirit than the next letter of my Faustus. With what joy do you suppose I am filled when I recognize your soul in your letter. When the letter carrier handed me your letter, my spirit at once began to thrill with an ineffable joy. How shall I tell you what joy titillated the spirit of your Erasmus when he received your letter. My spirit overflowed, as it were, with joy when your letter was given to me. How gladly I received your letter. After your note was brought to me, my spirit truly glowed with joy. I was almost insane with joy when I received your letter. The charm of your letter stays my spirit with extraordinary joy. I am unable to refrain from rejoicing exceedingly whenever your letters come to me. Your letter was pure honey to me. Whatever letters come from you seem to overflow with saccharin and honey. I am sumptuously refreshed by the rich banquets of your letters. Your writings are sweeter than any ambrosia. The letter of my Faustus was more sumptuous even than Sicilian feasts. There is no pleasure, no charm which I would compare with your letter. All things are sickening compared to your letter. The heart of Erasmus leaped with joy on reading your most affectionate letter. The papers covered with your writing completely filled me with joy. Whatever letter comes from you is pure joy to my heart. Your letter is alive with joy. He brought me a festal day who brought me your letter. I would have preferred what you wrote to any nectar. I would not have compared any Attic honey with your most affectionate letter. Saccharin is not sweet if it is compared with your letter. No draught of men has such a flavor as your letter has for me. What wine is to a man thirsting for it, your letter is to me. What clover is to bees, what willow boughs are to goats, what honey is to the bear, your letter is to me. The letter of your sublimity was sweeter to me than any honey. When I received your so eagerly awaited letter, you would have said that Erasmus was certainly drunk with joy. As soon as your letter came, you would have seen me as though drunk with excessive joy. As utterly as I love you, so utterly am I delighted by your letter. What you wrote seems nothing but pure charm to me. No dainty so caresses the palate as your letter charms my spirit. No luxuries titillate the palate more agreeably than what you wrote titillates my mind. ’Aμάξα ἡδονῶν, i.e., a wagon full of pleasures, he brought who brought your letter. Your letter brought me a *δάθον* (well) of pleasures when your letter was given to me. He carried a *θάλασσα* (sea) of joys who brought your letter. To me your letter was assuredly what *Διὸς ἐλκέφαλος*, i.e., brain of Zeus, was to the Persians.

If any of these appear to be of such a sort as would scarcely be considered suitable in prose, remember that this exercise is adapted to the composition of verse also.[1]

BOOK II

And Next Concerning the First Method of Embellishing

Now that we have stated our ideas on copia of words as briefly as we were able, it remains for us to touch upon copia of thought briefly. And so, to begin this part of the work with those matters that are most nearly related to the former, the first way to embellish thought is to relate at length and treat in detail something that could be expressed summarily and in general. And this, in fact, is the same as if one should display merchandise first through a latticework, or rolled up in carpets, then should unroll the carpets and disclose the merchandise, exposing it completely to sight. An example of this method follows:

> He lost everything through excess.

This expression, complete in itself, and, as it were, all rolled up, may be developed by enumerating a great many kinds of possessions, and by setting

---

[1] As explained in the Introduction (pp. 1–8) only the first thirty-three chapters of Book 1 are included in this translation.

forth various ways of losing property. Whatever had come by inheritance from father or mother, whatever had come by death of other relatives, whatever had been added from his wife's dowry, which was not at all mean, whatever had accrued from bequests (and considerable had accrued), whatever he had received from the liberality of his prince, whatever private property he had procured, all money, military equipment, clothes, estates, fields, together with farms and herds, in short, everything, whether movable or real estate, and finally even his immediate household property, in a short time he so consumed, wasted, and devoured in foulest passion for harlots, in daily banquets, in sumptuous entertainments, nightly drinking bouts, low taverns, delicacies, perfumes, dice, and gaming that what remained to him would not equal a farthing. In this case the words *everything* and *he lost by excess* are developed in detail. We will add yet another:

> He has finished his education.

This is a general statement. You will be able to develop this by recounting one by one the individual disciplines—every field of learning. There is no branch of learning at all in which he has not been elaborately trained, no discipline which he has not learned thoroughly to the smallest detail, and has so learned that he seems to have worked in that one alone. Further, he knows wonderfully well all the stories of the poets; and more, he has a rich fund of the ornaments of the rhetoricians, and has also studied the difficult canons of the grammarians. He is versed in the subtleties of the dialecticians; he has traced out the mysteries of natural philosophy, he has conquered the difficulties of metaphysics, he has penetrated the abstruseness of the theologians, he has learned the demonstrations of mathematics, likewise he is versed in the movements of the stars, the systems of numbers, the surveying of land, the location of cities, mountains, rivers and springs, their names and the distances between them, the harmonies and intervals of tones. Further, whatever of history there is, both ancient and modern, he knows. Whatever there is of good authors, of antiquity or of modern times, all that he has. Add to these an equal competence in Greek and Latin literature and languages; finally, whatever learning of any time has been acquired and handed down by eminent authors, all that, this man has completely comprehended and learned and holds in his mind. Another:

> Endowed with all the gifts of nature and fortune.

If anyone should wish to develop this, he will relate the individual physical advantages, then one by one the gifts of intellect and of character, lastly, family, wealth, country, success and whatever good fortune commonly brings. Again, a third example will be *omniscient Hippias*. If anyone wished to expand this, he could repeat with a varied copia of words all those things that Apuleius recounts in his description of Hippias in the *Florida*.

There survives a most appropriate example of this method in Lucian, in the *Harmonides*. For although he could have summarily said, "I have learned the whole art of flute playing," he preferred to display copia by developing details in this manner. "You have taught me how to play the flute correctly, and to blow on the mouthpiece lightly, as it were, and with harmony, then, with skilled and facile touch to use my fingers in frequent raising and lowering of the tone; morever you have taught me to keep time and, furthermore, to note what is proper to any type of harmony, the divine impetus of the Phrygian, the Bacchic fury of the Lydian, the sobriety and restraint of the Doric, the cheerfulness of the Ionic, so that the modes harmonize with the dance."[1] If in the last example above the author had seen fit to do in each branch of learning what Lucian did here in the one field of music, you can see how great copia of speech there would have been.

In this connection I should not think it out of place to make this suggestion, that a general state-

---

[1] Lucian *Harmonides* 1.

ment of the subject be placed at the beginning and that the same be then repeated in another form of speech, and that finally you should return to the general statement as though at last wearied of enumerating details, even though nothing has been omitted. Moreover, we must be careful not to confuse the regular succession of details with a chaotic mass of words, and we must take care not to make everything topsy-turvy, so that we do not accumulate an unmanageable multitude of words, wholly lacking in charm, but *do* prevent the boredom of our hearer or reader by skillful arrangement, or fitting distribution, or elegant description. To this class belongs also the case where the subject may not be divided into classes but must be partitioned. For example, he is wholly a monster, will be expanded by first dividing man into body and spirit, then mentioning the individual parts of the body, likewise the individual parts of the spirit: He is a monster in body and spirit; whatever you observe in his body or spirit you will find monstrous, a shaking head, a dog's eyes, the mouth of a serpent, the features of a fury, a distended paunch of a belly, hands hooked for rapine, twisted feet—finally even the whole shape of his body. What but a monster is displayed in all these? Note that beast's tongue and voice, you will say—a monstrosity; examine his nature, you will discover a monster. Consider his character, examine his life, you will find all things monstrous, and, not to pursue details, every inch of him is nothing but monster. Here if one wanted to linger over the painting, as it were, of the details, it is amply evident how much richness might be added to the speech. Another example also:

He was drenched.

From his topmost hair to the very bottom of his shoe he was wet with rain: Head, shoulders, chest, stomach, legs, in a word, his whole body was dripping with water. It may be worthwhile to mention that this first method can also be used for the sort of expression in which we add a generalization to some more specific statement. This is done chiefly for the purpose of amplifying: While every field of knowledge contributes much to the ornament and advantage of mortals, philosophy does so especially. Likewise, license is disgusting at every age to be sure, but it is by far most disgusting in old age. Likewise, while prudence is of great importance in everything, it is especially so in wars. For the simple statement was that prudence is of great importance in wars. Of this type is that example in Cicero's oration *For His House* before the Pontifices: "While many things, Pontifices, were discovered and established by our ancestors with the help of the gods, nothing was more striking than their decision that you be at the head of the religious rites of the immortal gods and also at the head of the state."[1] Although of what consequence is it to cite this one example of this class, since they are to be met with everywhere?

Second Method of Varying

The second method of varying is closely related to the first. Whenever we are not content to set forth briefly the conclusion of a matter, allowing the various things that lead up to it to be understood of themselves, we relate them one by one. The following will serve as an example of this precept: Cicero suppressed the undertakings of Catiline. You will enrich this thus: The nefarious undertakings of Catiline, who with the aid of the most abandoned young men plotted the destruction and extermination of the whole Roman state, Marcus Tullius Cicero, Consul, straightway suspected by his sagacity, investigated with singular vigilance, apprehended with greatest good judgment, revealed with wondrous zeal for the republic, proved clearly with incredible eloquence, put down with most weighty authority, destroyed with arms, abolished with great good fortune.

Likewise another: He was the father of a son by this girl. You may expand in this way: He was madly in love with this girl because she was of

---

[1] Cicero *For His House* 1. 1.

singular beauty. Then impatient of love, he tempted the mind of the simple girl with promises, enticed her with gifts, cajoled her with flattery, seduced her into mutual love by his favors, overcame her by wickedness, and finally had intercourse with her and deflowered her. Some time later the womb of the girl began to swell, a child doubtless having been conceived. At length in exactly nine months she was in labor and brought forth a boy.

Likewise another example: He took the city. This can be amplified thus: First, Fetiales are sent to demand restitution, and also to offer terms of peace; when the townspeople reject them, he levies troops everywhere, accumulates a very great force of military machines, moves the army together with the machines to the walls of the city. Those on the other side sharply repel the enemy from the walls, but at length he, superior in the fight, scales the walls, invades the city, and takes possession.

Third Method

From the second method again, the third method of amplification of speech does not differ a very great deal. In this one we do not just set forth a bare fact, but recount also the underlying causes, the beginnings from which it developed; as if it should not be sufficient for anyone to have said that he had waged war with the Neapolitan Gauls, but likewise he should add what the causes of hostility were, who the instigator, what the occasion for the outbreak of the war, what the hope of conquering, what the confidence on each side. This precept is so clear as not to need illustration and it would be difficult to give an example except in a great many words. Therefore we shall omit it and refer the reader to Sallust and Livy.

Fourth Method

And now greatly varying from the above methods is the fourth method of amplification: whenever we do not relate a matter simply, but enumerate likewise the concomitant or resultant circumstances. Suppose the general statement to be: We will charge the war to your account. You will be able to expand it in this way: A treasury exhausted against barbarian soldiers, a youth broken by hardships, crops trampled underfoot, herds driven off, burned villages and farms everywhere, fields lying waste, overturned walls, looted homes, pillaged shrines, so many childless old people, so many orphaned children, so many widowed matrons, so many virgins shamefully outraged, the character of so many young people ruined by license, such great sorrow, such great grief, so many tears, and moreover, the extinction of the arts, oppressive laws, the obliteration of religion, the chaos of all things human and divine, the government of the state corrupted, this whole array of evils that arises from war, I say, we shall lay to your charge alone, since indeed you were the author of the war.

Fifth Method

The fifth method of amplification concerns ἐνέργεια which is translated *Evidentia.* We use this whenever, for the sake of amplifying, adorning, or pleasing, we do not state a thing simply, but set it forth to be viewed as though portrayed in color on a tablet, so that it may seem that we have painted, not narrated, and that the reader has seen, not read. We will be able to do this well if we first conceive a mental picture of the subject with all its attendant circumstances. Then we should so portray it in words and fitting figures that it is as clear and graphic as possible to the reader. In this sort of excellence all the poets are eminent but especially Homer, as we shall point out in the proper places. The method consists chiefly of the description of things, times, places, and persons.

DESCRIPTION OF A THING

We shall enrich speech by description of a thing when we do not relate what is done, or has been done, summarily or sketchily, but place it before the reader painted with all the colors of rhetoric, so that at length it draws the hearer or reader outside himself as in the theatre. The Greeks call this ὑποτύπωσις from painting the picture of things. This word is commonly used, likewise, for whatever is brought before the eyes. For example, to quote from Quintilian, "if someone should say that a city was captured, he doubtless comprehends in that general statement everything that attends such fortune, but if you develop what is implicit in the one word, flames will appear pouring through homes and temples; the crash of falling buildings will be heard, and one indefinable sound of diverse outcries; some will be seen in bewildered flight, others clinging in the last embrace of their relatives; there will be the wailing of infants and women, old people cruelly preserved by fate till that day, the pillaging of profane and sacred objects, the running about of those carrying off booty and those seeking it, prisoners in chains before their captors, and the mother struggling to keep her infant, and fighting among the victors wherever there is greater plunder. For although the overthrow of a city involves all these things, it is nevertheless less effective to tell the whole at once than it is to relate all the particulars."[1] Thus far Quintilian. Likewise as illustration of this he cites this example from Caelius' *Against Antony:* "For they found him sunk in a drunken stupor, snoring with all his might, repeatedly belching, while the most beautiful of his dinner companions leaned toward him from all their various couches and the others lay about here and there. Half-dead with fright, having learned of the approach of the enemy, they were trying to arouse Antony. In vain they were shouting his name and raising his head; one whispered gently in his ear while another slapped him forcibly. But whenever he became aware of their voice and touch, he sought to embrace the neck of the nearest; having been aroused, he was unable to sleep, and being too drunk, he was unable to awaken, but was thrown about in a semiconscious sleep in the arms of his centurions

[1] Quintilian viii. 3. 67.

and concubines."[1] Nothing, says Quintilian, could be painted more credibly than this, nor could any reproach be more forceful, nor anything be pictured more clearly. He also presents a description of a luxurious banquet. "I seemed," he said, "to see some people entering, while others were going out, some reeling from wine, some sluggish from yesterday's drinking. The ground was filthy, muddy with wine, covered with withered garlands and the bones of fishes."[2] But there is a great abundance of this sort of example everywhere, especially in the poets, as has been said, and next to poets, in historians. But especially are the narratives of messengers in tragedies remarkably rich in this excellence, because they are presented instead of the spectacle and they report the things which it is either impossible or inappropriate to present on the stage. As when in Euripides' *Hecuba,* Talthybius relates to Hecuba how Polyxena was slain; and in the *Iphigenia in Aulis* the messenger tells how Iphigenia was killed. In the *Troades* of Seneca, the messenger reports to Andromache how her son Astyanax had perished. Enough examples have been pointed out, since all tragedies abound in narrations of this kind. Nor does it matter for this purpose whether they are true or false, as in the *Electra* of Sophocles, the old man tells Clytemnestra falsely how Orestes had perished in battle. Also Cicero is an admirable craftsman in this technique. I think it should be pointed out that this type of description consists chiefly in an exposition of details, of those in particular that most forcefully bring a thing before one's eyes, and produce an arresting narrative, and yet *collationes,* similes, *dissimilia, imagines,* metaphors, allegories and whatever other figures illustrate the matter may be advantageously employed. Even epithets are very effective for this purpose. As when we say lofty crags, turreted cities, cerulean or glassy sea, bending ploughman, proud philosopher, spreading

[1] Quintilian iv. 2. 123.

[2] Quintilian viii. 3. 66.

beech, dark chasm, and, in Homer, hateful war, and Hector with glancing helm, Ares, bane of men, and stormer of walls. The poet nowhere has any lack of this type. And in a description we do not include only what has preceded, what was contemporary with, and what followed an event, but likewise point out what did not happen or what could have happened if this or that had happened, or what can happen, as if someone should say, "See to what a crisis you have led the state, you who have rashly joined battle with the enemy." For indeed if by any chance of fortune the enemy had conquered, these things, and these would have happened. Or if someone should speak against monarchy, he would by description set before the eyes of his hearers all the tragedy of tyranny; from time to time he would admonish his audience to imagine that they actually saw all these things that would happen as soon as they changed democracy to monarchy. Furthermore, if it is a question of a serious matter, then *ὑποτυπώσεις*, i.e., delineations, should be employed in so far as they are profitable. But when the whole thing looks to pleasure, as is generally the case in poetry, one may indulge more freely in artifices of this sort, in *ἀποδέιξεις*, i.e., in demonstrations, and those things that are treated for the exercise or display of genius. To this class belong the descriptions of Homer, when he arms his gods or heroes, or describes the banquet, the battle, the rout, the council. For what he does not set before the eyes by suitable details, which although they sometimes seem minute, nevertheless, I know not how, bring the thing before your eyes in a marvelous manner, he does by epithets, as well as by use of similes. Then there are descriptions of whirlwinds, of storms, or of shipwrecks, such as occur in many places in Homer, in the first book of Vergil's *Aeneid,* in the eleventh book of Ovid's *Metamorphoses;* of barbarian combat in Juvenal, of pestilence, as in the third book of Vergil's *Georgics,* in Ovid, in Seneca's *Oedipus,* and in Thucydides; and of famine, of which type there is a brilliant example in a certain declamation of Quintilian; and of portents, eclipses of the sun, and of snow, rain, rivers, thunders, earthquakes, fires, floods, which sort is Ovid's description of the flood of Deucalion; of seditions, armies, battles, massacres, destruction, pillagings, single combat, naval warfare, such as in Lucan's third book; of a feast, banquets, weddings, funerals, triumphs, games, processions, of which kind is the description in Plutarch in his *Life of Antony* of the ship of Cleopatra; of sacred things, of ceremonies, incantations, of evil deeds as in the sixth book of Lucan. Likewise in Horace, in the *Satires,* in the role of Priapus telling what he has seen; of hunts, such as that of Cardinal Adrian, although scholars deny that the poem is his. Likewise of living things, such as the description of the electric ray and the porcupine in Claudian, and in the same author and likewise in Lactantius, of a Phoenix; of a parrot in Ovid's *Amores* and in Statius; of serpents in the ninth book of Lucan; of many fishes in Oppius; in Pliny, the description not only of numberless living things, their natures, conduct, battles, unions, but especially of a gnat; in Martial, the description of a horse and an ox, and an admirable one of bees; likewise of statues, e.g., the statute of an old man, as the one in the *Letters* of Pliny; of paintings and pictures such as that of Hercules Gallicus in Lucian; in Philostratus' various accounts of pictures; and similar accounts of woven things, and sculptures or like works of which there are innumerable examples in the poets and historians, as Arachne's web in Ovid's sixth book of the *Metamorphoses,* or the shield of Achilles, described by Homer, and of Aeneas by Vergil. Add to these, descriptions of a ship, garments, a panoply, a machine, a chariot, a colossus, a pyramid, or of any other similar things, the description of which would give pleasure. In my opinion this class should include descriptions of kinds of people and ways of life: as though one should place before your eyes a picture of the Scyths, the Androphagi, the Indians, the Troglodytes, or similar peoples. Or if you should paint a picture of the military life, the philosophic, the courtly, the rustic, the private, or the kingly. However, to express these things well, not only is art and genius necessary, but also it is of paramount importance to have actually seen what you wish to describe.

Also there are fabulous descriptions which nevertheless deal with actual things: such as descriptions of the golden age, of the silver, of the iron. Of this sort also is the picture of human life in Cebetes; of the court, of calumny, of education and several others in Lucian; of Rumor, Mischief, and the Prayers in Homer; of hunger and malice in Ovid; in the same author and likewise in Vergil, of Rumor. But if one prefers to classify these as descriptions of a person, concerning which I shall speak directly, I certainly do not greatly object.

DESCRIPTION OF A PERSON

After this comes description of persons, which is called prosopopoeia, although prosopographia or what is widely known by this name, is somewhat different from it. You might as well call those examples just mentioned concerning hunger and also envy and sleep prosopographia. For each is presented as a sort of personification. And to this class belong the figures of virtue and of pleasure that, according to Xenophon, Prodicus the Sophist represents in his *Hercules* as disputing with one another; and of death and life, that Ennius (according to Quintilian) introduces in his *Satires* as contestants. Likewise the figure of calumny, in Lucian, and in the same author, of learning, and of statuary; of opportunity, in Ausonius; of fortune, in Horace in the *Odes,* and in Q. Curtius; of greed, in Moschus; of poverty and wealth, in Aristophanes; of justice, in Chrysippus, according to Gellius; of philosophy, in Boethius; of a vampire, in Politian. Likewise of the muses, graces, furies, Bellona, the Sphinx, Scylla, Charybdis, and similar ones in the poets.

There are some closer to actuality, but yet quite suitable for display. Of this sort is the description of Hippias in Lucian and of the same person in Apuleius' *Florida;* but *notatio* is more suitable for the orator. For *notatio* is the name of these character sketches of a voluptuous lover, a miser, a glutton, a drunkard, a sluggard, a garrulous person, a braggart, a show off, an envious person, a sycophant, a parasite or a pimp. There is an example of this type in Book IV of the *Rhetoric for Herennius,* where a pseudomillionaire is depicted through his distinctive characteristics as a boaster of riches, although he was a pauper. In addition, one may take as many examples as he wishes from comedies. For comedy is concerned with nothing else. There exist, moreover, sketches useful for this purpose under the name of Theophrastus, although they seem to me to be the work of some *grammaticus* rather than of a philosopher. Hence, material for the portrait is drawn from all circumstances, but especially from these: From nationality or country, as if you should describe the appearance, culture, speech, language, bearing, gait, religious practices, temperament, and customs of a Carthaginian, Greek, Gaul, Scythian, Irishman, Spaniard, Scot, Englishman. Moreover, a Carthaginian is to be depicted as perfidious, sly, insolent, of ostentatious manner, and likewise with the others. And citizens of various countries have distinctive characteristics, as: effeminate Athenians, more versed in speech than action; austere Romans; thrifty Florentines. Such material is also drawn from sex, a man is painted as very austere, a woman very talkative, very changeable, very superstitious; from age, we depict such things as Horace points out in the *Art of Poetry;* from fortune, the wealthy man is drawn as very haughty, the poor man as very humble and timid; from disposition, the soldier is made vainglorious and immoderately boastful of his own deeds; the pimp, perjured; the rustic, too morose; the courtier, too cringing; the city man, too soft; the doctor, too anxious for gain; the poet, too eager for renown, delighting in fountains, groves, and retreats, a despiser of wealth and worldly goods; the sophist, more talkative than wise. Nor are the common affections to be overlooked: the feeling of a father for his children, a husband for his wife, a citizen for his country, a prince for his people, the people for the nobility, and others which Aristotle recounts in great detail in his *Rhetoric.* Moreover, there are also peculiar differences in each of these. It is not enough to understand what is appropriate to an old man, a youth, a slave, the father of a family, a pimp; otherwise the individuals in these classes would always be treated without individuality. The comic poets especially appear to have aimed at variety in persons of the same class. For how could two people be more dissimilar than Demea and Mitio in Terence; when the latter rebukes his son most severely, the former is pleasant; when the latter is especially pleasant, the former is severe. And yet each is an old man, and to that extent brothers. Who could be more different than Chremes, always calm and civil, and Simo, vehement and suspicious or, likewise, than prudent Pamphilius, and Charinus, destitute of spirit and wisdom? Who so unlike as Phaedria fighting vice, and Chaerea completely without scruples? Likewise, is there anything in common between Davus, most pertinacious author of hope, and Byrria, messenger of nothing but desperation? Or very much between Gnathas and Phormio? And the parasites of Plautus are far different from either one, just as the prostitutes of the latter also differ greatly from those of Terence. Terence depicts courtesans almost as good women—for example, Philotis and Bacchides in the *Hecyra;* Plautus, old men as loving and jovial, and cunning deceivers of their wives, although he makes Euclio extremely obstinate and suspicious of other women.

But if we treat a character used by another, the proper treatment is to be sought from those who depicted or described them before; for example, if you should treat Achilles you ought to depict him as impetuous, inexorable, frank, a foe of kings, a foe of the mendacious, swift of foot, for Homer painted him first thus; Ulysses, on the contrary, you ought to depict as crafty, deceptive, dissimulating, tolerant of everything; Agamemnon, less hard in spirit, but greedy for power, fearful of the people, more desirous of pleasure than war; Hector, sublime of spirit, careless of death and auguries, esteeming his fatherland above all things; Ajax, more prompt in deed than speech, impatient of abuse and denial. In short, as Homer has depicted the character of anyone, so ought the tragic poets to represent that person. Likewise, if anyone should desire to depict Aristotle, Themistocles, Phocion, Alcibiades, Pisistratus, Julius Caesar, Fabius or Camillus, or Timo, Socrates, Plato, or Epicurus, the proper treatment should be sought from the historians. This kind of exercise seems to have been approved by those who wrote the orations and epistles of Menelaus, Phaenix, Achilles, Phalaris, Brutus, Seneca and Paul. In the same way the writer of dialogue should be careful to what characters he attributes what speech. But what is proper in fictitious characters (for example, you should represent Philosophy as of sober countenance and full of authority; the Muses, simple and charming; the Graces, holding hands, and with flowing garments; Justice, upright and with steadfast glance; and others similarly) ought to be taken from the nature of the things in question. There is also a treatment proper to fables, which no one will rightly preserve unless he knows and has considered the natures of animals, so that he knows the elephant is docile and conscientious; the dolphin, an enemy of the crocodile, a friend of man; that the eagle builds his nest in high places; the beetle customarily pushes about the muck in which he gives birth and is born, and is not seen in seasons when eagles brood; the crested lark lays its eggs in grain fields; the hedgehog enjoys conversation, and is an enemy of snakes. And these things and others more recondite are easily found in Aristotle, Pliny, and Aelian. And this type is treated even by orators. But fables which attribute speech to inanimate things such as trees or rocks, seem rather forced. Prosopographies more characteristic of orators are those in which a certain character is depicted in his own colors, as it were, and to the extent which is necessary for the purpose, as in Sallust, Catilina; in Livy, Hannibal; in Plutarch, Trajan. *Effictiones,* i.e., descriptions of personal appearance, are employed sometimes, but less frequently. To this class belongs any detailed description of a beautiful woman, or on the other hand, of an ugly old woman. As Homer described Thersites, and Helen, at the request of Priam, points out from the walls many of the Greek chieftains; and Vergil, imitating him, in Book VI describes several Romans. To this class especially belongs the figure διαλογισμός, that is, *sermocinatio,* the attribution to an individual of language in harmony with his age, birth, country, life, purpose, spirit, and behavior. It is all right to compose speeches of this sort in history, for example; wherefore so many of the speeches of Thucydides, Sallust, Livy are composed, as well as letters and apophthegms, and, indeed, thoughts, as of the man talking with himself, although this is more common in the poets. It is properly called prosopopoeia whenever, with due regard to propriety, we present the character of a man far away, or long since dead, speaking. For example: what if we should now bring back to life the ancient noblemen of this city and they saw the morals of this generation, would they not burst out in these words? Then the speech would follow. What if that ancestor of yours were here now, would he not rebuke you deservedly with these words? What if Camillus should return to life, would he not rightly exhort us with these words? And now I seem to hear him talking to me thus. And imagine Plato himself expostulating with you in this way. Less extravagant are prosopopeia of the kind that represent people as saying those things which it is probable they would say if they were present. The figure is more strained (but nevertheless acceptable in serious orations as well as in exercises, if ever the seriousness of affairs should require it) when we represent nature or the state or the province or the fatherland as speaking. As does Cicero in his speech against Catiline: "What things and in what manner does it (the Fatherland) silently say to you Catiline?" again: "For if our country, which is far dearer to me than life, if all Italy, if the whole state, should speak thus, 'Marcus Tullius what are you doing?' "[1] Socrates in Plato's *Critias* portrays the laws as arguing with him. It is a figure of this type whenever we attribute speech to the gods themselves, or to places, or to other things without speech. But those which are properly called prosopographia are made more effective by metaphors, similes and *collationes.* Among the poets there are a great number of these.

DESCRIPTION OF PLACE

Speech is enriched also by descriptions of places; the Greeks call these *τοπογραφία.* Frequently they are used as an introduction to narrations not only by poets, but also by historians, and sometimes by orators. It is an example of this type whenever the whole appearance of a place is portrayed just as if it were in sight, as for example, the appearance of a city, a mountain, a region, a river, a port, a villa, gardens, an amphitheatre, a fountain, a cavern, a temple, a grove. And if these descriptions are of actual places they are to be called *topographia,* but if fictional, *topothesia.* Examples of the former are the description of the Laurentine villa in Pliny's *Letters,* in Statius of the Surrentine villa of Pollius and the Tiburtine villa of Manlius. Of the latter, the abode of sleep in Ovid, the home of Rumor and the palace of the sun; of the Lower Regions and the home of Cacus in Vergil; the home of Tenarus in Statius: the house in Lucian, palace of Psyche in Apuleius. To the former type should be referred, I think, the burning of Mt. Vesuvius described by Pliny the younger; of burning Aetna in Claudian; then any description of the Nile, or the cave of Sibyl, the rainbow and other things of that sort. The more unusual these things are the more pleasure they give, and one may linger longer over them, provided only that they are not wholly strange.

DESCRIPTION OF TIME

Further, we call a description of time *χρονογραφία.* And not infrequently this is used as a beginning. Sometimes it is employed simply for the sake of giving pleasure, for example, as the poets describe the day, the night, the dawn or the dusk, although even then another purpose ought not to be completely lacking. An example is the one in Vergil:

> *It was night, when the stars turn*
> *In mid-flight, when every field lies still;*
> *And tired bodies over the earth*

---

[1] Cicero *Against Catiline* 1. 7. 18 and 1. 11. 27 (Quintilian ix. 2. 32).

Were enjoying peaceful sleep; the woods
And wild seas were still,
The beasts and varicolored birds, those that far
And wide haunt the limpid lakes, and fields rough
With brambles, lay in sleep under the silent night,
Healed their cares, and hearts forgot their toil.[1]

For this description of nocturnal quiet tends to emphasize the grief of Dido who was not resting even then when all things else were resting. For immediately follows:

But not the distressed Phoenician queen, not
Ever was she lulled in sleep.

Descriptions of spring, winter, autumn, summer, the harvest, a holiday, the Saturnalia are of this type and they are often effective for demonstration. They are used in combination whenever we discuss the state of the times, for example, of peace, of war, of sedition, of faction, of monarchy, of democracy, when we show what virtues or vices especially would flourish then. These kinds of amplification, indeed, it is sometimes suitable for the student to compose separately as an exercise; but a complete description involves all of them. Horace, in that satire which I have just cited, for example, describes first the place, the Esquiline Hill, then the time, then the characters of Priapus and the wicked women; finally he vividly pictures the sacrifice and noisy flight of the frightened victims.

Egressio, Sixth Method of Amplifying

The sixth method of amplification connected with those above, which the Greeks call παρέκβασις, some of the Romans call *egressio;* others, *digressio;* and some, *excursus.* It is, by the definition of Quintilian, a discussion departing from the main subject but still pertinent and useful to the case; and it is used either to praise, for example, that famous recital of the virtues of Gnaius Pompey in Cicero's *For L. Cornelius* in which that divine orator (for I shall use the words of Quintilian) digresses abruptly from the speech he had begun, as if the thread of the speech were broken off by the mere mention of the name of the general, or to censure, or for adornment, or to charm, or to prepare for something that follows.[1] Digressions may be taken, moreover, for the most part from the same places that we have just considered. From the recounting of deeds, from the description of localities, countries, persons; likewise from the treatment of tales, fables; also from commonplaces whenever for the purpose of amplification we speak against pride, luxury, licentiousness, avarice, infamous passion, tyranny, anger and the rest of the vices, and spend time on these as though the main subject had been dropped for a time, or on the other hand, when we praise frugality, generosity, continence, the study of letters, piety and keeping silent. Those are of so much importance in speaking fluently that several famous authors have written about them; they call them χρεῖαι. And there are those commonplaces not unlike the above, when we contrast the advantages of freedom with the disadvantages of slavery, the mutability of fortune with the universal inevitableness of death, the great power of money in the affairs of mortals with the brevity of human life, and innumerable similar ones. Furthermore, it is permitted to delay longer in digression either at the beginning of a speech, as for instance, the description of Hercules Gallicus in Lucian, and of the Lamiae in Politian; or at the end, at which point the now tired hearer may be refreshed; Vergil does this commonly in the *Georgics.* In the middle, if it is ever proper to digress, a quick return should be made to that point whence the digression occurred, unless the part of the speech already completed offers occasion for a digression, as after the

[1] Vergil *Aeneid* iv. 522 seq.

[1] Quintilian iv. 3. 13-4.

narration, where the hearer may be rendered more eager for the argument that follows, or after the proof, or in general after uninteresting places where the weariness brought on by subtlety may be dispelled; or unless the matter itself freely offers an opportunity of this sort that invites to longer delay.

Seventh Method

The seventh method of amplification is taken from epithets. Diomedes made an epithet a species of *antonomasia* and defined it as a distinguishing word placed in front of a proper name for purposes of praise, attack, or information: For purposes of praise, as, divine Camilla; of attack, as, Ulysses, author of wicked deeds; of information, as, Larissaean Achilles. Epithets are taken from the mental powers, as, Plato, wisest of philosophers; from the body, Thersites, most deformed of all Greeks; from external goods, and that not in a general way but from all the different kinds of advantage that spring from fortune; from descent, as, noblest Maecenas; from wealth, as, Croesus, wealthiest of kings; from appearance, Nireus, most beautiful; from bodily strength, Milo, strongest of athletes; from one's country, Ulysses, the Ithacan; from achievement, Hercules, conqueror of monsters; from past events, twice captured Phrygians; in short from all the goods or troubles of fortune. Nor does it matter whether epithets are adjectival terms or not, provided only a certain characteristic be attributed in some way, not only to persons, but in truth even to things, as: headlong youth; headlong and mad counsellor, love; passion, food of evil men; sullen and difficult old age; philosophy, expeller of vices; comedy, mirror of human life; history, teacher of life. In poems it is permitted to use natural epithets, as: shining white snow, flowing fountains, freezing night, winding stream, golden sun. In prose they ought not to be employed unless they have a certain emphasis and affect the main point, as: you will not gain such an unjust request from Aristides, the most just; do you dare celebrate the Floralia before Cato, the most severe censor of morals? This is done chiefly in citations of examples or *sententiae:* Aristarchus, most learned and likewise most diligent; Cicero, prince of eloquence; Plato, most trustworthy author.

Eighth Method

The eighth method of enlarging is taken from circumstances, which the Greeks call *περιστάσεις*. These have to do partly with things: cause, place, occasion, instrument, time, mode and so on; partly with persons, as: race, country, sex, age, education, culture, physical appearance, fortune, position, quality of mind, desire, experiences, temperament, understanding and name. Timely and appropriate use of circumstances, moreover, has many advantages: First in amplifying and disparaging, about which we will speak briefly soon; then in vivid presentation, about which we spoke just above; and in addition, in confirmation and credibility. For it results in the whole speech being sown and fortified everywhere with close and frequent arguments, which although you do not develop, you lead forth, as it were, to the battle line; but they fight of themselves and help the cause not a little, so that, as it is possible for one, although he works in another field, to recognize, nevertheless, a man skilled in wrestling or music, so you can discern a rhetor anywhere from his skillful combining of this kind. Because they are spread throughout the whole speech, the method cannot be illustrated in a brief example.

Ninth Method of Enlarging

The ninth method of enlarging is by amplification. Several forms of this are considered by Quintilian. We shall touch briefly on those that are related to our present purpose. The first method of amplification is by *incrementum,* when by several steps not only is a climax reached, but sometimes, in some way, a point beyond the climax. There is an example of this in Cicero's fifth speech against Verres: "It is an offense to fetter a Roman citizen, a crime to flog him, treason to kill him, what shall I say it is to crucify him"[1]—there is no possible expression fully suitable to so wicked a deed. To this class belongs also that case in which, with circumstances accumulated in a regular order, something increasingly important continuously follows in the context and course (of the speech). An example of this is in Cicero's second *Philippic* about the vomiting of Antony: "O action not only disgusting to see, but also to hear. If this had happened to you at table during those monstrous drinking bouts of yours, who would not term it disgraceful? But actually in an assembly of the Roman people, the Master of the Horse, engaged in public business, for whom it would be disgraceful to belch, covered his chest and the whole tribunal with scraps of food smelling of wine."[2] Here single words carry the figure, for to vomit would have been loathsome in itself even if not in an assembly, even not an assembly of citizens, even not Romans, or even if he were not engaged in business, even if not public business, or even if he were not Master of Horse. If anyone should separate these and spend more time on the individual steps, he will certainly increase the copia of the speech, but yet he will amplify less effectively. The opposite of this is *comparatio*. For as *incrementum* looks to something higher, so *comparatio* seeks to rise from something lesser. Moreover, *comparatio* employs either a hypothetical or actual *exemplum*. An illustration of the hypothetical kind occurs in the first part of the example just quoted from Cicero. For he imagines this to have happened at table in private. There is also an example in the speech of the same orator against Catiline: "By Hercules, if my servants feared me the way all your fellow citizens fear you, I would think I ought to leave my house."[3] When using an actual *exemplum* we make the matter we are amplifying seem nearly as great or equal to or even greater than it. For example, Cicero in the *For Cluentius,* when he had related how a certain Milesian woman had taken a bribe from the alternate heirs to cause an abortion said: "Of how much greater punishment is Oppian deserving for the same injury. Since, indeed, she had attacked with violence her own body and harmed only herself; the latter, however, in committing the same offense harmed another."[1] In this type not only are parts compared with wholes, but also with parts, as in this passage from Cicero's first speech against Catiline: "Or in truth shall Scipio, that distinguished man, although a private citizen, have killed Tiberius Gracchus who was only slightly disturbing the State, and shall we who are consuls tolerate Catiline, who desires to lay waste the whole world with fire and slaughter?"[2] Here Catiline is compared to Gracchus, the situation of the State, to the whole world; a slight disturbance, to slaughter, fire, and laying waste; and a private citizen, to consuls. And if anyone should wish to, he can develop these fully through the use of details. And we amplify by *ratiocinatio,* when the one grows and the other is increased, in this way: "You, with that throat, that chest, that body with the strength of a gladiator, drank so much wine at the wedding of Hyppia that yesterday you had to vomit before the eyes of the Roman people."[3] Actually how great a quantity of wine Antony drank is inferred from the fact that his body with the strength of a gladiator was not able to endure or digest it. Under this heading should be classified those examples in which we raise the most hateful things to a peak of envy; we elevate them advisedly so that what is to follow may seem so much more grave. There is an example of this in Cicero: "The captain of a ship from a most noble city bought exemption from the terror of the scourge at a price. What humanity!"[4] Some extraordinarily hateful thing must be expected of

[1] Cicero *Against Verres* 5. 56 (Quintilian viii. 4. 4).

[2] Cicero *Philippics* 2. 25. 63 (Quintilian viii. 4. 8. and 10).

[3] Cicero *Against Catiline* 1. 7. 17 (Quintilian viii. 4. 10).

[1] Cicero *For Cluentius* 11. 32 (Quintilian viii. 4. 11).

[2] Cicero *Against Catiline* 1. 1. 3 (Quintilian viii. 4. 13).

[3] Cicero *Philippics* 2. 25. 63 (Quintilian viii. 4. 16).

[4] Cicero *Against Verres* 5. 44. 177 (Quintilian viii. 4. 19).

him to whom these things which are atrocities seem humane and usual by comparison. And we amplify by heaping up of words and likewise of significant *sententiae,* which method is close to the figure *συναθροισμός*, i.e., *accumulatio,* which was discussed above. Cicero uses this in his speech *For Ligarius:* "For what was that bared sword of yours doing on the battle front at Pharsalus, Tubero? Whose breast was that point seeking? What was the purpose of your arms? Upon what were your mind, your eyes, your hands, your bold spirit fixed? What did you desire? What were you hoping for?"[1] Here the speech was enlarged as though by a heaping up. The same result is accomplished, however, by a series of words rising higher and higher in meaning, as in this example: "There was the jailer, the executioner of the praetor, the death and terror of the allies and the Roman citizens, the lictor Sextius."[2] We amplify also by a device similar to the figure *correctio,* as in Cicero *Against Verres:* "For we have brought to your judgment not a thief, but a brigand; not an adulterer, but a violator of chastity; not an impious person, but an enemy of sacred and religious things; not an assassin, but a most cruel murderer of our fellow citizens and allies."[1]

[1] Cicero *For Ligarius* 3. 9 (Quintilian viii. 4. 27).

[2] Cicero *Against Verres* 2. 14. 118 (Quintilian viii. 4. 27).

Moreover, there are as many methods of attenuating as there are of amplifying. And common methods of amplification by adverbs, nouns, or other suitable parts of speech, used either in praise or attack, pertain to copia of speech: Cicero pleases me very greatly. How kindly your father-in-law behaves to you cannot be expressed in words. I should be unable to put into words how much Cicero pleases me. But we have discussed these methods of expansion in the first book.

And that method of amplifying is known and familiar in which we magnify a species contrasted with a class, as, while all the liberal disciplines gain a great deal of distinction or advantage for a man, above all does eloquence; but we touched upon this method also above.

• • •

[1] Cicero *Against Verres* 5. 66. 70 (Quintilian viii. 4. 27).

INTRODUCTION TO FRANCIS BACON

Francis Bacon was born in England in 1561 to a wealthy and privileged family. After an education at Cambridge, he became a lawyer and a politician. Bacon served in the House of Commons during the reign of Queen Elizabeth I, and later became Lord Chancellor under James I. He left public service in 1621 after a conviction for accepting bribes, and after a few years of the scholarly life died in 1626.

Bacon wrote widely in philosophy, politics, science, and in what amounted to rhetorical theory. His contributions to rhetoric are best understood by considering the fact that he was instrumental in the development of a way of thinking about the human mind that would be influential for hundreds of years: *faculty psychology.*

Faculty psychology offers a model of the human mind as divided into different abilities, tools, or instruments that are called *faculties.* Today, for instance, we might say that someone "has a faculty for music" or a "faculty for mathematics." What we are saying is that it is as if the person has an organ or "thing" in his or her mind that enables superior performance in music, mathematics, or some other activity or way of thinking. In the late Renaissance, several thinkers, Bacon prominently among them, developed comprehensive psychologies using this idea of faculties.

Different theorists proposed different configurations of various faculties. Among some of the faculties that were hypothesized were reason, imagination, will, appetite, memory, and so forth. Faculty psychology was a distinctly new innovation in theorizing about human thought, motivation, and response. This new psychology had wide reaching effects, not the least of which was application to rhetorical theory. Here we have excerpts from Bacon's book, *The Advancement of Learning,* which made use of faculty psychology to suggest some new rhetorical principles. Bacon defines rhetoric as the application of *reason* to the *imagination* for the moving of the *will.*

In this selection from *The Advancement of Learning,* we find Bacon discussing four "Intellectual Arts," by which he means four mental skills or purposes: invention, judgment, memory, and "elocution, or tradition." This last intellectual art is closest to rhetoric, and it is interesting that he refers to it as "tradition." He sees rhetoric as having the task of handing on to those who do not know it that which has been discovered. In Bacon's view, rhetoric does not invent knowledge so much as perpetuate it. Each of the four arts is discussed in terms of faculties used in their exercise, and in the discussion of rhetoric we find his definition of it as the application of reason to the imagination for the moving of the will.

We should note that towards the end of this selection Bacon distinguishes rhetoric from logic in saying that the former manages reason "in popular opinions and manners" while logic is for "reason exact and in truth." This distinction is similar to Aristotle's assignment of the contingent and everyday decisions to rhetoric, while decisions admitting of hard and fast conclusions are given to science. It is also important to note that in the late Renaissance, when science and logic are ascendant, Bacon puts rhetoric on a par with logic in that *both* manage reason.

The second selection from Bacon excerpted here is from his book *Novum Organum*. This reading is interesting for its use of faculty psychology and for its discussion of the ways in which public discourse is flawed. Today we are accustomed to complaining of the decay of public dialogue. Here is Bacon, in the seventeenth century, anticipating those views by analyzing the ways in which social conditions affect public discourse and decision making.

The *Novum Organum* is organized around four "idols." An idol in this sense is a preoccupation or fetish that turns out to be empty, false, or unreliable. These idols are limitations or barriers to human understanding; Bacon wants to explain why our knowledge will never be perfect. In that sense he was somewhat swimming against the tide of the late Renaissance, when many believed in the perfectability of knowledge.

The first idol Bacon discusses in the Idols of the Tribe: the ways in which human nature and the limitations inherent in all people prevent our ability to perceive and understand. Bacon reminds his contemporaries, then, of the limits of knowing that stem from human frailties. The second idol is the Idols of the Cave: individual biases and limitations. The third idol is the Idols of the Market-place: language. Bacon will say later in the reading that this is the worst idol in terms of preventing understanding: judgment is clouded because of the ways in which we use words. Finally, Bacon identifies the Idols of the Theatre: limitations in understanding stemming from systems of belief embodied in religion, philosophy, or any other organized way of thinking or living.

Later in the reading Bacon returns to the Idols of the Market-place, which are the most rhetorical of these barriers to understanding. He complains that words often do not fit reality as it really is. There are words for things that do not exist, and there are words that do not match very well things that do exist. This concern for matching language with reality will become a major preoccupation of Enlightenment rhetoric, as we will see in the next section.

Bacon is an early theorist of faculty psychology. He laid the groundwork for the use of that psychology in future rhetorical theories. As both a politician and an amateur scientist, he was ideally situated to propose theories that found a place for rhetoric in the increasingly scientific world of the late Renaissance.

FRANCIS BACON

THE ADVANCEMENT OF LEARNING

BOOK II

• • •

IX. 1. We come therefore now to that knowledge whereunto the ancient oracle directeth us, which is the knowledge of ourselves; which deserveth the more accurate handling, by how much it toucheth us more nearly. This knowledge, as it is the end and term of natural philosophy in the intention of man, so notwithstanding it is but a portion of natural philosophy in the continent of nature. And generally let this be a rule, that all partitions of knowledges be accepted rather for lines and veins than for sections and separations; and that the continuance and entireness of knowledge be preserved. For the contrary hereof hath made particular sciences to become barren, shallow, and erroneous, while they have not been nourished and maintained from the common fountain. So we see Cicero the orator complained of Socrates and his school, that he was the first that separated philosophy and rhetoric; whereupon rhetoric became an empty and verbal art. So we may see that the opinion of Copernicus touching the rotation of the earth, which astronomy itself cannot correct, because it is not repugnant to any of the *phainomena,* yet natural philosophy may correct. So we see also that the science of medicine if it be destituted and forsaken by natural philosophy, it is not much better than an empirical practice. With this reservation therefore we proceed to human philosophy or humanity, which hath two parts: the one considereth man segregate, or distributively; the other congregate, or in society. So as human philosophy is either simple and particular, or conjugate and civil. Humanity particular consisteth of the same parts whereof man consisteth; that is, of knowledges which respect the body, and of knowledges that respect the mind. But before we distribute so far, it is good to constitute. For I do take the consideration in general, and at large, of human nature to be fit to be emancipate and made a knowledge by itself: not so much in regard of those delightful and elegant discourses which have been made of the dignity of man, of his miseries, of his state and life, and the like adjuncts of his common and undivided nature; but chiefly in regard of the knowledge concerning the sympathies and concordances between the mind and body, which being mixed cannot be properly assigned to the sciences of either.

• • •

XII. 3. The arts intellectual are four in number; divided according to the ends whereunto they are referred: for man's labour is to invent that which is sought or propounded; or to judge that which is invented; or to retain that which is judged; or to deliver over that which is retained. So as the arts must be four: art of inquiry or invention: art of examination or judgement: art of custody or memory: and art of elocution or tradition.

• • •

XIII. 6. The invention of speech or argument is not properly an invention: for to invent is to discover that we know not, and not to recover or resummon that which we already know: and the use of this invention is no other but, out of the knowledge whereof our mind is already possessed, to draw forth or call before us that which may be pertinent to the purpose which we take into our consideration. So as to speak truly, it is no invention, but a remembrance or suggestion, with an application; which is the cause why the schools do place it after judgement, as subsequent and not precedent. Nevertheless, because we do account it a chase as well of deer in an inclosed park as in a forest at large, and that it hath already obtained the name, let it be called invention: so as it be perceived and discerned, that the scope and end of this invention is readiness and present use of our knowledge, and not addition or amplification thereof.

7. To procure this ready use of knowledge there are two courses, preparation and suggestion. The former of these seemeth scarcely a part of knowledge, consisting rather of diligence than of any artificial erudition. And herein Aristotle wittily, but hurtfully, doth deride the Sophists near his time, saying, *They did as if one that professed the art of shoe-making should not teach how to make up a shoe, but only exhibit in a readiness a number of shoes of all fashions and sizes.* But yet a man might reply, that if a shoemaker should have no shoes in his shop, but only work as he is bespoken, he should be weakly customed. But our Saviour, speaking of divine knowledge, saith, *That the kingdom of heaven is like a good householder, that bringeth forth both new and old store:* and we see the ancient writers of rhetoric do give it in precept, that pleaders should have the places, whereof they have most continual use, ready handled in all the variety that may be; as that, to speak for the literal interpretation of the law against equity, and contrary; and to speak for presumptions and inferences against testimony, and contrary. And Cicero himself, being broken unto it by great experience, delivereth it plainly, that whatsoever a man shall have occasion to speak of (if he will take the pains), he may have it in effect premeditate and handled *in thesi.* So that when he cometh to a particular he shall have nothing to do, but to put to names, and times, and places, and such other circumstances of individuals. We see likewise the exact diligence of Demosthenes; who, in regard of the great force that the entrance and access into causes hath to make a good impression, had ready framed a number of prefaces for orations and speeches. All which authorities and precedents may overweigh Aristotle's opinion, that would have us change a rich wardrobe for a pair of shears.

8. But the nature of the collection of this provision or preparatory store, though it be common both to logic and rhetoric, yet having made an entry of it here, where it came first to be spoken of, I think fit to refer over the further handling of it to rhetoric.

9. The other part of invention, which I term suggestion, doth assign and direct us to certain marks, or places, which may excite our mind to return and produce such knowledge as it hath formerly collected, to the end we may make use thereof. Neither is this use (truly taken) only to furnish argument to dispute probably with others, but likewise to minister unto our judgement to conclude aright within ourselves. Neither may these places serve only to apprompt our invention, but also to direct our inquiry. For a faculty of wise interrogating is half a knowledge. For as Plato saith, *Whosoever seeketh, knoweth that which he seeketh for in a general notion: else how shall he know it when he hath found it?* And therefore the larger your anticipation is, the more direct and compendious is your search. But the same places which will help us what to produce of that which we know already, will also help us, if a man of experience were before us, what questions to ask; or, if we have books and authors to instruct us, what points to search and revolve; so as I cannot report that this part of invention, which is that which the schools call topics, is deficient.

10. Nevertheless, topics are of two sorts, general and special. The general we have spoken to; but the particular hath been touched by some, but rejected generally as inartificial and variable. But leaving the humour which hath reigned too much in the schools (which is, to be vainly subtile in a few things which are within their command, and to reject the rest), I do receive particular topics, that is, places or directions of invention and inquiry in every particular knowledge, as things of great use, being mixtures of logic with the matter of sciences. For in these it holdeth, *ars inveniendi adolescit cum inventis;* for as in going of a way, we do not only gain that part of the way which is passed, but we gain the better sight of that part of the way which remaineth: so every degree of proceeding in a science giveth a light to that which followeth; which light if we strengthen by drawing it forth into questions or places of inquiry, we do greatly advance our pursuit.

XIV. 1. Now we pass unto the arts of judgement, which handle the natures of proofs and demonstrations; which as to induction hath a coincidence with invention. For in all inductions, whether in good or vicious form, the same action of the mind which inventeth, judgeth; all one as in the sense. But otherwise it is in proof by syllogism; for the proof being not immediate, but by mean, the invention of the mean is one thing, and the judgment of the consequence is another; the one exciting only, the other examining. Therefore, for the real and exact form of judgement, we refer ourselves to that which we have spoken of interpretation of nature.

2. For the other judgement by syllogism, as it is a thing most agreeable to the mind of man, so it hath been vehemently and excellently laboured. For the nature of man doth extremely covet to have somewhat in his understanding fixed and unmoveable, and as a rest and support of the mind. And therefore as Aristotle endeavoureth to prove, that in all motion there is some point quiescent, and as he elegantly expoundeth the ancient fable of Atlas (that stood fixed, and bare up the heaven from falling) to be meant of the poles or axle-tree of heaven, where upon the conversion is accomplished; so assuredly men have a desire to have an Atlas or axle-tree within to keep them from fluctuation, which is like to a perpetual peril of falling. Therefore men did hasten to set down some principles about which the variety of their disputations might turn.

• • •

XV. 1. The custody or retaining of knowledge is either in writing or memory; whereof writing hath two parts, the nature of the character, and the order of the entry. For the art of characters, or other visible notes of words or things, it hath nearest conjugation with grammar; and therefore I refer it to the due place. For the disposition and collocation of that knowledge which we preserve in writing, it consisteth in a good digest of common-places; wherein I am not ignorant of the prejudice imputed to the use of common-place books, as causing a retardation of reading, and some sloth or relaxation of memory. But because it is but a counterfeit thing in knowledges to be forward and pregnant, except a man be deep and full, I hold the entry of common-places to be a matter of great use and essence in studying, as that which assureth copie of invention, and contracteth judgement to a strength. But this is true, that of the methods of common-places that I have seen, there is none of any sufficient worth: all of them carrying merely the face of a school, and not of a world; and referring to vulgar matters and pedantical divisions, without all life or respect to action.

2. For the other principal part of the custody of knowledge, which is memory, I find that faculty in my judgement weakly inquired of. An art there is extant of it; but it seemeth to me that there are better precepts than that art, and better practices of that art than those received. It is certain the art (as it is) may be raised to points of ostentation prodigious: but in use (as it is now managed) it is barren, not burdensome, nor dangerous to natural memory, as is imagined, but barren, that is, not dexterous to be applied to the serious use of business and occasions. And therefore I make no more estimation of repeating a great number of names or words upon once hearing, or the pouring forth of a number of verses or rhymes *ex tempore,* or the making of a satirical simile of everything, or the turning of everything to a jest, or the falsifying or contradicting of everything by cavil, or the like (whereof in the faculties of the mind there is great copie, and such as by device and practice may be exalted to an extreme degree of wonder), than I do of the tricks of tumblers, funambuloes, baladines; the one being the same in the mind that the other is in the body, matters of strangeness without worthiness.

3. This art of memory is but built upon two intentions; the one prenotion, the other emblem. Prenotion dischargeth the indefinite seeking of that we would remember, and directeth us to seek in a narrow compass, that is, somewhat that hath congruity with our place of memory. Emblem reduceth conceits intellectual to images sensible, which strike the memory more; out of which axioms may be drawn much better practique than that in use; and besides which axioms, there are divers more touching help of memory, not inferior to them. But I did in the beginning distinguish, not to report those things deficient, which are but only ill managed.

XVI. 1. There remaineth the fourth kind of rational knowledge, which is transitive, concerning the expressing or transferring our knowledge to others; which I will term by the general name of tradition or delivery. Tradition hath three parts; the first concerning the organ of tradition; the second concerning the method of tradition; and the third concerning the illustration of tradition.

2. For the organ of tradition, it is either speech or writing: for Aristotle saith well, *Words are the images of cogitations, and letters are the images of words.* But yet it is not of necessity that cogitations be expressed by the medium of words. For whatsoever is capable of sufficient differences, and those perceptible by the senses is in nature competent to express cogitations. And therefore we see in the commerce of barbarous people, that understand not one another's language, and in the practice of divers that are dumb and deaf, that men's minds are expressed in gestures, though not exactly, yet it serve the turn. And we understand further, that it is the use of China, and the kingdoms of the High Levant to write in characters real, which express neither letters nor words in gross, but things or notions; insomuch as countries and provinces, which understand not one another's language, can nevertheless read one another's writings, because the characters are accepted more generally than the languages do extend; and therefore they have a vast multitude of characters, as many (I suppose) as radical words.

• • •

XVIII. 1. Now we descend to that part which concerneth the illustration of tradition, comprehended in the science which we call rhetoric, or art of eloquence, a science excellent, and excellently well laboured. But although in true value it is inferior to wisdom, as was said by God to Moses, when he disabled himself for want of this faculty, *Aaron shall be thy speaker, and thy shalt be to him as God;* yet with people it is the more mighty: for so Salomon saith, *Sapiens corde appellabitur prudens, sed dulcis eloquio majora reperiet;* signifying that profoundness of wisdom will help a man to a name or admiration, but that it is eloquence that prevaileth in an active life. And as to the labouring of it, the emulation of Aristotle with the rhetoricians of his time, and the experience of Cicero, hath made them in their works of rhetorics exceed themselves. Again, the excellency of examples of eloquence in the orations of Demosthenes and Cicero, added to the perfection of the precepts of eloquence, hath doubled the progression in this art; and therefore the deficiences which I shall note will rather be in some collections, which may as handmaids attend the art, than in the rules or use of the art itself.

2. Notwithstanding, to stir the earth a little about the roots of this science, as we have done of the rest; the duty and office of rhetoric is to apply reason to imagination for the better moving of the will. For we see reason is disturbed in the administration thereof by three means; by illaqueation or sophism, which pertains to logic; by imagination or impression, which pertains to rhetoric; and by passion or affection, which pertains to morality. And as in negotiation with others, men are wrought by cunning, by importunity, and by vehemency; so in this negotiation within ourselves, men are undermined by inconsequences, solicited and importuned by impressions or observations, and transported by passions. Neither is the nature of man so unfortunately built, as that those powers and arts should have force to disturb reason, and not to establish and advance it. For the end of logic is to teach a

form of argument to secure reason, and not to entrap it. The end of morality is to procure the affections to obey reason, and not to invade it. The end of rhetoric is to fill the imagination to second reason, and not to oppress it: for these abuses of arts come in but *ex obliquo,* for caution.

3. And therefore it was great injustice in Plato, though springing out of a just hatred to the rhetoricians of his time, to esteem of rhetoric but as a voluptuary art, resembling it to cookery, that did mar wholesome meats, and help unwholesome by variety of sauces to the pleasure of the taste. For we see that speech is much more conversant in adorning that which is good, than in colouring that which is evil; for there is no man but speaketh more honestly than he can do or think: and it was excellently noted by Thucydides in Cleon, that because he used to hold on the bad side in causes of estate, therefore he was ever inveighing against eloquence and good speech; knowing that no man can speak fair of courses sordid and base. And therefore as Plato said elegantly, *That virtue, if she could be seen, would move great love and affection;* so seeing that she cannot be showed to the sense by corporal shape, the next degree is to show her to the imagination in lively representation: for to show her to reason only in subtility of argument was a thing ever derided in Chrysippus and many of the Stoics, who thought to thrust virtue upon men by sharp disputations and conclusions which have no sympathy with the will of man.

4. Again, if the affections in themselves were pliant and obedient to reason, it were true there should be no great use of persuasions and insinuations to the will, more than of naked proposition and proofs; but in regard of the continual mutinies and seditions of the affections,

> Video meliora, proboque,
> Deteriora sequor,

reason would become captive and servile, if eloquence of persuasions did not practise and win the imagination from the affections' part, and contract a confederacy between the reason and imagination against the affections; for the affections themselves carry ever an appetite to good, as reason doth. The difference is, that the affection beholdeth merely the present; reason beholdeth the future and sum of time. And therefore the present filling the imagination more, reason is commonly vanquished; but after that force of eloquence and persuasion hath made things future and remote appear as present, then upon the revolt of the imagination reason prevaileth.

5. We conclude therefore that rhetoric can be no more charged with the colouring of the worse part, than logic with sophistry, or morality with vice. For we know the doctrines of contraries are the same, though the use be opposite. It appeareth also that logic differeth from rhetoric, not only as the fist from the palm, the one close, the other at large; but much more in this, that logic handleth reason exact and in truth, and rhetoric handleth it as it is planted in popular opinions and manners. And therefore Aristotle doth wisely place rhetoric as between logic on the one side, and moral or civil knowledge on the other, as participating of both: for the proofs and demonstrations of logic are toward all men indifferent and the same; but the proofs and persuasions of rhetoric ought to differ according to the auditors:

> Orpheus in sylvis, inter delphinas Arion.

Which application, in perfection of idea, ought to extend so far, that if a man should speak of the same thing to several persons, he should speak to them all respectively and several ways: though this politic part of eloquence in private speech it is easy for the greatest orators to want: whilst, by the observing their well-graced forms of speech, they leese the volubility of application: and therefore it shall not be amiss to recommend this to better inquiry, not being curious whether we place it here, or in that part which concerneth policy.

• • •

FRANCIS BACON

NOVUM ORGANUM

Aphorisms Concerning the Interpretation of Nature and the Kingdom of Man

• • •

XXXVIII

The idols and false notions which are now in possession of the human understanding, and have taken deep root therein, not only so beset men's minds that truth can hardly find entrance, but even after entrance obtained, they will again in the very instauration of the sciences meet and trouble us, unless men being forewarned of the danger fortify themselves as far as may be against their assaults.

XXXIX

There are four classes of idols which beset men's minds. To these for distinction's sake I have assigned names,—calling the first class *Idols of the Tribe;* the second, *Idols of the Cave;* the third, *Idols of the Market-place;* the fourth, *Idols of the Theater.*

XL

The formation of ideas and axioms by true induction is no doubt the proper remedy to be applied for the keeping off and clearing away of idols. To point them out, however, is of great use, for the doctrine of idols is to the interpretation of nature what the doctrine of the refutation of sophisms is to common logic.

XLI

The Idols of the Tribe have their foundation in human nature itself, and in the tribe or race of men. For it is a false assertion that the sense of man is the measure of things. On the contrary, all perceptions, as well of the sense as of the mind, are according to the measure of the individual and not according to the measure of the universe. And the human understanding is like a false mirror, which, receiving rays irregularly, distorts and discolors the nature of things by mingling its own nature with it.

XLII

The Idols of the Cave are the idols of the individual man. For everyone (besides the errors common to human nature in general) has a cave or den of his own, which refracts and discolors the light of nature; owing either to his own proper and peculiar nature or to his education and conversation with others; or to the reading of books, and the authority of those whom he esteems and admires; or to the differences of impressions, accordingly as they take place in a mind preoccupied and predisposed or in a mind indifferent and settled; or the like. So that the spirit of man (according as it is meted out to different individuals) is in fact a thing variable and full of perturbation, and governed as it were by chance. Whence it was well observed by Heraclitus that men look for sciences in their own lesser worlds, and not in the greater or common world.

XLIII

There are also idols formed by the intercourse and association of men with each other, which I call Idols of the Market-place, on account of the commerce and consort of men there. For it is by discourse that men associate; and words are imposed according to the apprehension of the vulgar. And therefore the ill and unfit choice of words wonderfully obstructs the understanding. Nor do the definitions or explanations wherewith in some things learned men are wont to guard and defend themselves, by any means set the matter right. But words plainly force and overrule the understanding, and throw all into confusion, and lead men away into numberless empty controversies and idle fancies.

XLIV

Lastly, there are idols which have immigrated into men's minds from the various dogmas of philosophies, and also from wrong laws of demonstration. These I call Idols of the Theater; because in my judgment all the received systems are but so many stage-plays, representing worlds of their own creation after an unreal and scenic fashion. Nor is it only of the systems now in vogue, or only of the ancient sects and philosophies, that I speak: for many more plays of the same kind may yet be composed and in like artificial manner set forth; seeing that errors the most widely different have nevertheless causes for the most part alike. Neither again do I mean this only of entire systems, but also of many principles and axioms in science, which by tradition, credulity, and negligence have come to be received.

But of these several kinds of idols I must speak more largely and exactly, that the understanding may be duly cautioned.

• • •

LIX

But the *Idols of the Market-place* are the most troublesome of all: idols which have crept into the understanding through the alliances of words and names. For men believe that their reason governs words; but it is also true that words react on the understanding; and this it is that has rendered philosophy and the sciences sophistical and inactive. Now words, being commonly framed and applied according to the capacity of the vulgar, follow those lines of division which are most obvious to the vulgar understanding. And whenever an understanding of greater acuteness or a more diligent observation would alter those lines to suit the true divisions of nature, words stand in the way and resist the change. Whence it comes to pass that the high and formal discussions of learned men end oftentimes in disputes about words and names; with which (according to the use and wisdom of the mathematicians) it would be more prudent to begin, and so by means of definitions reduce them to order. Yet even definitions cannot cure this evil in dealing with natural and material things; since the definitions themselves consist of words, and those words beget others: so that it is necessary to recur to individual instances, and those in due series and order; as I shall say presently when I come to the method and scheme for the formation of notions and axioms.

LX

The idols imposed by words on the understanding are of two kinds. They are either names of things which do not exist (for as there are things left unnamed through lack of observation, so likewise are there names which result from fantastic suppositions and to which nothing in reality corresponds), or they are names of things which exist, but yet confused and ill-defined, and hastily and irregularly derived from realities. Of the former kind are Fortune, the Prime Mover, Planetary Orbits, Elements of Fire, and like fictions which owe their origin to false and idle theories. And this class of idols is more easily expelled, because to get rid of them it is only necessary that all theories should be steadily rejected and dismissed as obsolete.

But the other class, which springs out of a faulty and unskillful abstraction, is intricate and deeply rooted. Let us take for example such a word as *humid,* and see how far the several things which the word is used to signify agree with each other; and we shall find the word *humid* to be nothing else than a mark loosely and confusedly applied to denote a variety of actions which will not bear to be reduced to any constant meaning.

• • •

❖

ENLIGHTENMENT THROUGH THE NINETEENTH CENTURY

INTRODUCTION TO THE ENLIGHTENMENT THROUGH THE NINETEENTH CENTURY

At the end of the Renaissance, the discoveries of natural science and mathematics began to increase rapidly. Whereas the Renaissance was a new age of wide learning across the arts, humanities, and sciences, the Enlightenment was a period in which, although the arts and humanities were by no means ignored, *reason* was widely taken to be the most valuable and most important human faculty. Enterprises that seemed especially to embody reasoning, such as science, became valued uppermost. The Enlightenment began in the late seventeenth century and continued into the nineteenth century. During the nineteenth century, some artists, scholars, and humanists rebelled against the focus on science and reason of the Enlightenment. Much of this rebellion was expressed in the Romantic movement in art, music, and literature. But paradoxically, the values of the Enlightenment continued to inform the practices of business, government, and much of everyday life even into the twentieth century. The Romantics of the nineteenth century may be seen as both a footnote to the Enlightenment and also as preparation for the changes in culture and thinking that came with the twentieth century.

Science and reason are ways of knowing. To understand the Enlightenment and the role that rhetorical theory found within it, we must begin by understanding attitudes towards knowledge during this period. The Enlightenment began as a period marked by significant changes in what people anticipated they could know about the natural world.

KNOWLEDGE

Imagine for a moment what it must be like to live in a world in which scientific instruments and knowledge were relatively crude. The way the world appeared to your *senses,* and your ways of understanding the world through *common sense,* would be the basis for knowledge for most ordinary people. If an apple *looked* clean and free of dirt or contamination you could assume that it *was* clean and you could eat it. If a table seemed hard and solid to you, you would have no reason to suppose that it was not what it seemed. Everyday experience had seemed a reliable source of knowledge to most people for centuries.

Imagine what a change it made when scientific instruments such as the microscope and telescope widely used in the late Renaissance revealed that the senses and common sense were not completely reliable sources of knowledge: That apple is *crawling* with bacteria, although it does not look like it. The earth orbits the sun, rather than vice versa, although common sense may not tell you so. Discoveries in chemistry and physics gave people to understand that the hard table you see before you is mainly "empty space" with molecules, atoms, and subatomic particles creating the physical structure you see (if one could squeeze all the space out from among the electrons, protons, neutrons, and so forth that make up the Sears Tower in Chicago, it would be the size of a toothpick—but it would weigh the same!).

During the late Renaissance, the Reformation had given further impetus to a process of questioning absolute, dogmatic religious doctrines. In sum, many people were coming to *doubt* truths upon which they had long relied. For the educated population that was aware of these changes, an intellectual crisis followed. The question arose as to what anyone could be *sure* of, and the search began for a foundation for certain knowledge. *Foundationalism* is a term that describes this search for that which we can be sure and certain of.

In the late Renaissance and early Enlightenment, the French philosopher René Descartes provoked a scholarly discussion that would last for centuries when he attempted to provide a sure foundation for knowledge. He could doubt anything, he argued, except the fact that he was doubting (that is to say, the fact that he was thinking about doubt). This knowledge of one's own thoughts, he felt, was the sure foundation for knowledge, and he summed his conclusion up in the famous phrase, "I think, therefore I am."

Others disagreed with Descartes's conclusions by arguing that people can be sloppy or misguided in their thoughts. Much better, these critics said, to depend on what is discovered by science about the external world. Note that this disagreement might be greatly simplified as a choice between "in here" and "out there." Some thinkers chose to depend on their ability to think and reflect "in here" (in your head) and reflect as a sure foundation for knowledge, while others placed their faith in knowledge of what is "out there" (in the external world). This *choice* between the in here and the out there is what is known as *dualism*. It is also expressed as seeing the world divided between the subjective and the objective, between mind and experience, between language and reality. Dualism is not which choice one makes between in here and out there, it is thinking that there is a choice to be made.

People have not always thought dualistically, and people in the twentieth century are only recently coming to question that choice. But dualism created a frame for thinking about how people can know about the world, a frame that western cultures stayed within for centuries. Whether the sure foundation for knowledge could be found in human thinking and feeling (in here) or in objective scientific examination of the physical world (out there) was the dualistic choice that shaped western thinking into this century.

Reason was central to dualism, whichever choice one made. If one argued that certainty could be found in human thinking, it was usually argued that only rational, cool, calm thinking could produce that certainty. If one believed, on the other hand, that certainty could be found in knowledge of the physical world, then reason was key to the scientific and mathematical models of research that were used to investigate that world. In either case, the Enlightenment was a period that enshrined reason as the highest human faculty.

Foundationalism and dualism also affected rhetorical theory. Foundationalism and rhetoric tend not to fit well together. As we have noted before, rhetoric questions the possibility of sure knowledge and tends to undermine certainties. What people think is foundational today they may be persuaded to question tomorrow. Rhetoric can only serve foundationalism as it served Augustine's Christian faith, as a second level discourse that passes on truths discovered elsewhere. To the extent that dualism privileges reason, rhetoric is suspect. This is because rhetoric has traditionally appealed to both reason and to emotion, to human aesthetic responses and to our reactions to the character of other people. Ramus's split in the Renaissance between reason and rhetoric would continue into the Enlightenment.

One of the most important ways in which rhetorical theory is affected by dualism is through *language purification*. Beginning with the theories of John Locke, some writers argued that language (which, as a product and medium of human thought is "in here") should precisely match the reality to which it refers (a reality "out there"). Others such as Giambattista Vico questioned whether language could ever precisely match reality, or whether language might in fact "create" reality in the ways that it influences us to see the world in different ways.

A final important development linking knowledge and rhetoric in the Enlightenment was the further growth of faculty psychology. Working on the base laid by Bacon and others, Enlightenment rhetorical theorists were able to use faculty psychology to develop elaborate, powerful ways of explaining how people respond to rhetorical appeals.

The legacy of the Enlightenment continued through the nineteenth century. Most of society, business, and government modeled itself on *rational* practices. The coldly "reasonable" logic of finance, profit, and the bottom line governed western culture as factories and homes alike were made to run like clockwork. The movie parody of the starched British banker arriving at work, leaving work, entering the home, and having dinner at precisely the exact hour and minute each day expresses the values, if not quite exactly the reality, of this rationalized western society. In reaction to this hyperdevelopment of the values of the Enlightenment, the Romantic movement began in the middle- to late-nineteenth century. This was largely an aesthetic movement in literature, art, and music designed to emphasize human emotions and artistic sensibilities so as to counterbalance the general social privileging of reason and rationality. The Romantic movement also had its effect on rhetorical theory and practice. The "sentimental style" of public speaking became popular in America, especially, but also in Europe. Although appeals to reason were still expected, heart wrenching emotional appeals could increasingly be found in rhetoric of all sorts. This tempering of reason with other ways of knowing and deciding was typical of a society preparing for its entry into the twentieth century.

Power

Changes in power distribution that were paradoxical occurred during the Enlightenment and through the nineteenth century. On the one hand, businesses and government grew, as did the power they wielded. Some corporations such as the British East Indies Corporation operated nearly independently of any sort of government controls, practically controlling colonies around the globe. The nineteenth century especially saw the rise of large, powerful, nearly autonomous businesses in Europe and the United States that served as the primary forces behind imperialist expansion. Such businesses needed rhetoric to appeal to consumers, especially in the nineteenth century when advertising became more prominent. But for the most part these businesses conducted their affairs dictatorially, with little debate or rhetorical argument as to the correct policies to pursue.

On the other hand, the Enlightenment and the nineteenth century were periods that saw a shrinking of the political and social "margin," periods in which people who were previously excluded from participation in public life began to do so more freely and openly. That meant that their participation in rhetorical exchange also widened. One such group was women. Women increasingly followed the earlier exhortations of Margaret Fell's to engage in public speaking. Not all women braved continuing public pressure discouraging them from speaking in public, though. Eliza Leslie's book, a portion of which you will read here, is an example of late-nineteenth century rhetorical theory for *domestic* application: It is a handbook for how privileged women should conduct themselves so as to exercise rhetorical influence at home, with families, and with spouses.

People in the economic margins came closer to the political mainstream and its rhetorical activities. The United States was created as an experiment in allowing a large number of people (although originally, only white males) to participate in self-government and therefore in public discourse. The French revolution also attempted, not as successfully, to include the poor and dispossessed in public decision making and the public discourse upon which that depends. The parliamentary tradition in Great Britain deepened as the right to elect representatives to Parliament was expanded beyond just property owners.

In the United States, most African-Americans spent all of the Enlightenment and half of the nineteenth century in slavery, yet their opportunities to participate in public decision making through rhetoric expanded slowly as well. Great speakers such as Frederick Douglass or Sojourner Truth arose to plead the cause of their people. American Indians were also eloquent in speaking in the interests of their people against the encroachments of Europeans. Although rhetorical *theory* did not develop or expand much during the late nineteenth century, rhetorical *practice* by previously marginalized groups enlarged gradually through the periods studied in this section.

DISCOURSE

In our section on the Roman rhetorical heritage, we read an early work of rhetorical critical theory by Longinus. During the Enlightenment, critical examination of art, literature, and music developed into a major discursive movement known as *belles lettres* or the *belletristic* school of thought. The belletristic school attempted to develop standards for judgment and improvement of *aesthetic* experience. Rhetoric was often taken to be one of the branches of literature, and so was the subject of critical analysis, as well.

In this book, Hugh Blair's work, *Lectures on Rhetoric and Belles Lettres,* is excerpted as an example of critical rhetorical theory. Blair argues for standards of *taste* so as to improve one's appreciation of art, music, and literature. We noted earlier that criticism is a kind of discourse that is facilitated by (1) a public that is increasingly more of an audience than it is a producer of texts, and (2) a grounding in the medium of print, so that a text may more easily be thought of and considered as an object for analysis. Both these conditions were true in the Enlightenment and especially through the nineteenth century, as populations and commitments to print both grew. The appearance of Romantic values and sensibilities late in the nineteenth century perpetuated the Enlightenment's concern for belles lettres. We will note when we introduce Blair's reading that critical theory itself is often rhetorical, because formulating a sense of taste can often have persuasive overtones relating to social and economic class.

Media

We have touched on media above, in noting that the critical impulses of belletrism are fueled in part by a culture committed to the print medium. That point may be emphasized by noting that the Enlightenment, and especially the nineteenth century, is the most print-oriented span of years in human history. Communication and storage of information were dedicated to the written word. Even some interpersonal communication was carried out through written notes rather than face-to-face communication, as one discovers by reading the literature of the period.

We have noted earlier how the print medium is consistent with an approach to knowledge that sees truths as objective and unchanging. We should therefore not be surprised to see the hyperrationalism of the Enlightenment and nineteenth century coexisting with such a strong commitment to the written word.

Several observers have also noted that especially the nineteenth century's immersion in print created in audiences a tolerance for lengthy, complicated argument. In Richard Whately's work excerpted here, written earlier in the nineteenth century, we see a growing interest in more elaborate theories of substantive argument. By mid-century, audiences could listen to complicated chains of argument in, for instance, the Lincoln and Douglas debates, that would last for hours. Rhetoric became lengthier, more expositional, and more verbal, many have argued, because of the social climate of print and writing in which it occurred.

For Further Reading

Gaillet, Lynee Lewis. 1997. *Scottish Rhetoric and Its Influences.* Mahwah, NJ: Lawrence Erlbaum.

Grassi, Ernest. 1988. *Rhetoric as Philosophy: The Humanist Tradition.* University Park, PA: Pennsylvania State University Press.

Howell, Wilbur Samuel. 1971. *Eighteenth-Century British Logic and Rhetoric.* Princeton, NJ: Princeton University Press.

Law, Jules David. 1993. *The Rhetoric of Empiricism: Language and Perception from Locke to I.A. Richards*. Ithaca, NY: Cornell University Press.

Mooney, Michael. 1994. *Vico in the Tradition of Rhetoric*. Mahwah, NJ: Lawrence Erlbaum.

Potkay, Adam. 1994. *The Fate of Eloquence in the Age of Hume*. Ithaca, NY: Cornell University Press.

Richard, Carl J. 1994. *The Founders and the Classics: Greece, Rome, and the American Enlightenment*. Cambridge, MA: Harvard University Press.

Sher, Richard B. 1985. *Church and University in the Scottish Enlightenment: The Moderate Literati of Edinburgh*. Princeton, NJ: Princeton University Press.

Warnick, Barbara. 1993. *The Sixth Canon: Belletristic Rhetorical Theory and Its French Antecedents*. Columbia, SC: University of South Carolina Press.

INTRODUCTION TO JOHN LOCKE

John Locke was an English philosopher of knowledge, logic, ethics, and language. He lived from 1632 to 1704. Locke was broadly educated and acquainted with the scholarly issues across many disciplines of his time in the arts, sciences, and humanities. Locke did not explicitly write works of rhetorical theory. Too many rhetoricians of his time taught rhetoric by having students learn lists of inflexible rules for speaking and writing. Because Locke thought that learning resulted from practice and habit—in other words, from experience—he disdained rhetoric because of this rule-centered approach taken by some rhetoricians of his time. Nevertheless, his philosophy contains much relevant material to our interests here. In this book we have excerpted part of his lengthy philosophical treatise, *An Essay Concerning Human Understanding,* with important links to rhetorical theory.

Locke's philosophy was important to the work of many other philosophers during the Enlightenment. One of his chief concerns, which informs the work excerpted here, was with the arbitrariness and conventionality of language. Some earlier theories of language, known as "Adamic" theories, held that language was in some sense naturally connected to the world to which it referred. Locke realized that this was not true, and that communities of speakers simply agreed conventionally that words would have the references that they had to reality. But since the links between language and reality were created rather than natural, the links could be created *faultily.* Therefore, Locke argued that language often posed obstacles to understanding and needed to be improved or purified to make words match reality more closely.

Clearly, Locke is working within the frame of dualism. He wants to make the words for thoughts *in* the human mind match an independent reality *out there* in the world. Without this precise linkage between words and reality, humans cannot know with certainty; Locke is therefore also operating within the foundationalist anxiety of the Enlightenment. The questions he considers and the answers he provides are thus typical of Enlightenment thinking about communication and rhetoric and their connections to knowledge.

The work excerpted here reveals some interesting assumptions that Locke makes from within his dualistic and foundationalist perspective. Early in the reading he presents two functions of language: to represent our thoughts to ourselves and to represent our thoughts to others. Consider this first function. Is it true that thoughts and language are separate in this sense, that we have the thought and then seek the word for it? Or do we have the thought *when* we have the word for it? In other words, does language refer to, or create, thoughts? Locke sees language as representational rather than fundamental; that is to say, it reflects both thought and reality but does not form either one.

Most of the reading explores the second function of representing our thoughts to other people. Notice that Locke argues that the purpose of communication is to be understood by using language that creates in the hearer the same idea that is in the mind of the speaker. We may want to question this assumption as well: Is it ever possible for *exactly* the same idea that began in one person's mind to be duplicated through communication in another person's mind? Furthermore, are our ideas exact to begin with? If I think about my dog, for instance, do I really have a precise and exact idea in my mind at any given time? If so, can I ever convey exactly that idea to you? If the answers to these questions are negative, it puts into question not only Locke's work but many of the premises of dualism and foundationalism.

Locke identifies four reasons why language might not serve to convey ideas precisely from mind to mind. These may also be understood as four reasons why rhetoric fails to work on an audience, if the audience does not understand what the speaker intends to say. First, the ideas for which words stand are often complex, and words may not capture that complexity in its entirety. Second, words may stand for ideas that have no connection in nature, ideas for such things as abstract concepts (we cannot find "justice" in nature, although we think about it and believe we know what it is). Third, words may refer to ideas that have a connection in nature, but discovering the connection is difficult (if God exists, comparing our word for God to the reality may be difficult!). Finally, "the signification of the word and the real essence of the thing are not exactly the same." This last difficulty occurs with colloquial expressions or ways of speaking that are imprecise, in which, for instance, people refer to a whale as a large "fish" even though it is not.

Explaining the significance of these four barriers to understanding occupies most of the remainder of Locke's excerpt here. Locke provides a clear explanation of why we might misunderstand one another. What is interesting is that, writing as he does from an Enlightenment perspective, he holds out the hope that perfect understanding might be achieved. Can we grant him that premise?

JOHN LOCKE

AN ESSAY CONCERNING HUMAN UNDERSTANDING

• • •

BOOK III

CHAPTER I

OF WORDS OR LANGUAGE IN GENERAL.

Man fitted to form articulate sounds.

§ 1. God having designed man for a sociable creature, made him not only with an inclination, and under a necessity to have fellowship with those of his own kind, but furnished him also with language, which was to be the great instrument and common tie of society. Man therefore had by nature his organs so fashioned as to be fit to frame articulate sounds, which we call words. But this was not enough to produce language; for parrots and several other birds will be taught to make articulate sounds distinct enough, which yet, by no means, are capable of language.

To make them signs of ideas.

§ 2. Besides articulate sounds, therefore, it was farther necessary that he should be able to use these sounds as signs of internal conceptions; and to make them stand as marks for the ideas within his own mind, whereby they might be made known to others, and the thoughts of men's minds be conveyed from one to another.

To make general signs.

§ 3. But neither was this sufficient to make words so useful as they ought to be. It is not enough for the perfection of language, that sounds can be made signs of ideas, unless those signs can be so made use of as to comprehend several particular things: for the multiplication of words would have perplexed their use, had every particular thing need of a distinct name to be signified by. To remedy this inconvenience, language had yet a farther improvement in the use of general terms, whereby one word was made to mark a multitude of particular existences: which advantageous use of sounds was obtained only by the difference of the ideas they were made signs of: those names becoming general, which are made to stand for general ideas, and those remaining particular, where the ideas they are used for are particular.

§ 4. Besides these names which stand for ideas, there be other words which men make use of, not to signify any idea, but the want or absence of some ideas simple or complex, or all ideas together; such as are *nihil* in Latin, and in English, ignorance and barrenness. All which negative or privative words cannot be said properly to belong to, or signify no ideas: for then they would be perfectly insignificant sounds; but they relate to positive ideas, and signify their absence.

Words ultimately derived from such as signify sensible ideas.

§ 5. It may also lead us a little towards the original of all our notions and knowledge, if we remark how great a dependence our words have on common sensible ideas; and how those, which are made use of to stand for actions and notions quite removed from sense, have their rise from thence, and from obvious sensible ideas are transferred to more abstruse significations, and made to stand for ideas that come not under the cognizance of our senses: *v.g.* to imagine, apprehend, comprehend, adhere, conceive, instil, disgust, disturbance, tranquillity, &c. are all words taken from the operations of sensible things, and applied to certain modes of thinking. Spirit, in its primary

signification, is breath: angel, a messenger: and I doubt not, but if we could trace them to their sources, we should find, in all languages, the names, which stand for things that fall not under our senses, to have had their first rise from sensible ideas. By which we may give some kind of guess what kind of notions they were, and whence derived, which filled their minds who were the first beginners of languages; and how nature, even in the naming of things, unawares suggested to men the originals and principles of all their knowledge: whilst, to give names that might make known to others any operations they felt in themselves, or any other ideas that came not under their senses, they were fain to borrow words from ordinary known ideas of sensation, by that means to make others the more easily to conceive those operations they experimented in themselves, which made no outward sensible appearances: and then when they had got known and agreed names, to signify those internal operations of their own minds, they were sufficiently furnished to make known by words all their other ideas; since they could consist of nothing, but either of outward sensible perceptions, or of the inward operations of their minds about them: we having, as has been proved, no ideas at all, but what originally come either from sensible objects without, or what we feel within ourselves, from the inward workings of our own spirits, of which we are conscious to ourselves within.

Distribution.

§ 6. But to understand better the use and force of language, as subservient to instruction and knowledge, it will be convenient to consider,

First, To what it is that names, in the use of language, are immediately applied.

Secondly, Since all (except proper) names are general, and so stand not particularly for this or that single thing, but for sorts and ranks of things; it will be necessary to consider, in the next place, what the sorts and kinds, or, if you rather like the Latin names, what the species and genera of things are; wherein they consist, and how they come to be made. These being (as they ought) well looked into, we shall the better come to find the right use of words, the natural advantages and defects of language, and the remedies that ought to be used, to avoid the inconveniences of obscurity or uncertainty in the signification of words, without which it is impossible to discourse with any clearness or order concerning knowledge: which being conversant about propositions, and those most commonly universal ones, has greater connexion with words than perhaps is suspected.

These considerations therefore shall be the matter of the following chapters.

CHAPTER II

OF THE SIGNIFICATION OF WORDS.

Words are sensible signs necessary for communication.

§ 1. Man, though he has great variety of thoughts, and such from which others, as well as himself, might receive profit and delight; yet they are all within his own breast, invisible and hidden from others, nor can of themselves be made appear. The comfort and advantage of society not being to be had without communication of thoughts, it was necessary that man should find out some external sensible signs, whereof those invisible ideas, which his thoughts are made up of, might be made known to others. For this purpose nothing was so fit, either for plenty or quickness, as those articulate sounds, which with so much ease and variety he found himself able to make. Thus we may conceive how words, which were by nature so well adapted to that purpose, come to be made use of by men, as the signs of their ideas; not by any natural connexion that there is between particular articulate sounds and certain ideas, for then there would be but one language amongst all men; but by a voluntary imposition, whereby such a word is made arbitrarily the mark of such an idea. The use then of words is to be sensible marks of ideas; and the ideas they stand for are their proper and immediate signification.

Words are the sensible signs of his ideas who uses them.

§ 2. The use men have of these marks being either to record their own thoughts for the assistance of their own memory, or as it were to bring out their ideas, and lay them before the view of others; words in their primary or immediate signification stand for nothing but the ideas in the mind of him that uses them, how imperfectly soever or carelessly those ideas are collected from the things which they are supposed to represent. When a man speaks to another, it is that he may be understood; and the end of speech is, that those sounds, as marks, may make known his ideas to the hearer. That then which words are the marks of are the ideas of the speaker: nor can any one apply them, as marks, immediately to any thing else but the ideas that he himself hath. For this would be to make them signs of his own conceptions, and yet apply them to other ideas; which would be to make them signs, and not signs of his ideas at the same time; and so in effect to have no signification at all. Words being voluntary signs, they cannot be voluntary signs imposed by him on things he knows not. That would be to make them signs of nothing, sounds without signification. A man cannot make his words the signs either of qualities in things, or of conceptions in the mind of another, whereof he has none in his own. Till he has some ideas of his own, he cannot suppose them to correspond with the conceptions of another man; nor can he use any signs for them: for thus they would be the signs of he knows not what, which is in truth to be the signs of nothing. But when he represents to himself other men's ideas by some of his own, if he consent to give them the same names that other men do, it is still to his own ideas; to ideas that he has, and not to ideas that he has not.

§ 3. This is so necessary in the use of language, that in this respect the knowing and the ignorant, the learned and unlearned, use the words they speak (with any meaning) all alike. They, in every man's mouth, stand for the ideas he has, and which he would express by them. A child having taken notice of nothing in the metal he hears called gold, but the bright shining yellow colour, he applies the word gold only to his own idea of that colour, and nothing else; and therefore calls the same colour in a peacock's tail gold. Another that hath better observed, adds to shining yellow great weight: and then the sound gold, when he uses it, stands for a complex idea of a shining yellow and very weighty substance. Another adds to those qualities fusibility: and then the word gold signifies to him a body, bright, yellow, fusible, and very heavy. Another adds malleability. Each of these uses equally the word gold, when they have occasion to express the idea which they have applied it to: but it is evident, that each can apply it only to his own idea; nor can he make it stand as a sign of such a complex idea as he has not.

Words often secretly referred, first to the ideas in other men's minds.

§ 4. But though words, as they are used by men, can properly and immediately signify nothing but the ideas that are in the mind of the speaker; yet they in their thoughts give them a secret reference to two other things.

First, They suppose their words to be marks of the ideas in the minds also of other men, with whom they communicate: for else they should talk in vain, and could not be understood, if the sounds they applied to one idea were such as by the hearer were applied to another; which is to speak two languages. But in this, men stand not usually to examine whether the idea they and those they discourse with have in their minds be the same: but think it enough that they use the word, as they imagine, in the common acceptation of that language; in which they suppose, that the idea they make it a sign of is precisely the same, to which the understanding men of that country apply that name.

Secondly, to the reality of things.

§ 5. Secondly, Because men would not be thought to talk barely of their own imaginations, but of things as really they are; therefore they often suppose the words to stand also for the reality of

things. But this relating more particularly to substances, and their names, as perhaps the former does to simple ideas and modes, we shall speak of these two different ways of applying words more at large, when we come to treat of the names of fixed modes, and substances in particular: though give me leave here to say, that it is a perverting the use of words, and brings unavoidable obscurity and confusion into their signification, whenever we make them stand for any thing but those ideas we have in our own minds.

Words by use readily excite ideas.

§ 6. Concerning words also it is farther to be considered: first, that they being immediately the signs of men's ideas, and by that means the instruments whereby men communicate their conceptions, and express to one another those thoughts and imaginations they have within their own breasts; there comes by constant use to be such a connexion between certain sounds and the ideas they stand for, that the names heard almost as readily excite certain ideas, as if the objects themselves, which are apt to produce them, did actually affect the senses. Which is manifestly so in all obvious sensible qualities; and in all substances that frequently and familiarly occur to us.

Words often used without signification.

§ 7. Secondly, That though the proper and immediate signification of words are ideas in the mind of the speaker, yet because by familiar use from our cradles we come to learn certain articulate sounds very perfectly, and have them readily on our tongues, and always at hand in our memories, but yet are not always careful to examine or settle their significations perfectly; it often happens that men, even when they would apply themselves to an attentive consideration, do set their thoughts more on words than things. Nay, because words are many of them learned before the ideas are known for which they stand; therefore some, not only children, but men, speak several words no otherwise than parrots do, only because they have learned them, and have been accustomed to those sounds. But so far as words are of use and signification, so far is there a constant connexion between the sound and the idea, and a designation that the one stands for the other; without which application of them, they are nothing but so much insignificant noise.

Their signification perfectly arbitrary.

§ 8. Words by long and familiar use, as has been said, come to excite in men certain ideas so constantly and readily, that they are apt to suppose a natural connexion between them. But that they signify only men's peculiar ideas, and that by a perfect arbitrary imposition, is evident, in that they often fail to excite in others (even that use the same language) the same ideas we take them to be the signs of: and every man has so inviolable a liberty to make words stand for what ideas he pleases, that no one hath the power to make others have the same ideas in their minds that he has, when they use the same words that he does. And therefore the great Augustus himself, in the possession of that power which ruled the world, acknowledged he could not make a new Latin word: which was as much as to say, that he could not arbitrarily appoint what idea any sound should be a sign of, in the mouths and common language of his subjects. It is true, common use by a tacit consent appropriates certain sounds to certain ideas in all languages, which so far limits the signification of that sound, that unless a man applies it to the same idea, he does not speak properly: and let me add, that unless a man's words excite the same ideas in the hearer, which he makes them stand for in speaking, he does not speak intelligibly. But whatever be the consequence of any man's using of words differently, either from their general meaning, or the particular sense of the person to whom he addresses them, this is certain, their signification, in his use of them, is limited to his ideas, and they can be signs of nothing else.

• • •

CHAPTER IX

OF THE IMPERFECTION OF WORDS.

Words are used for recording and communicating our thoughts.

§ 1. From what has been said in the foregoing chapters, it is easy to perceive what imperfection there is in language, and how the very nature of words makes it almost unavoidable for many of them to be doubtful and uncertain in their significations. To examine the perfection or imperfection of words, it is necessary first to consider their use and end: for as they are more or less fitted to attain that, so are they more or less perfect. We have, in the former part of this discourse, often upon occasion mentioned a double use of words.

First, one for the recording of our own thoughts.

Secondly, the other for the communicating of our thoughts to others.

Any words will serve for recording.

§ 2. As to the first of these, for the recording our own thoughts for the help of our own memories, whereby, as it were, we talk to ourselves, any words will serve the turn. For since sounds are voluntary and indifferent signs of any ideas, a man may use what words he pleases, to signify his own ideas to himself: and there will be no imperfection in them, if he constantly use the same sign for the same idea; for then he cannot fail of having his meaning understood, wherein consists the right use and perfection of language.

Communication by words civil or philosophical.

§ 3. Secondly, as to communication of words, that too has a double use.

I. Civil.

II. Philosophical.

First, by their civil use, I mean such a communication of thoughts and ideas by words, as may serve for the upholding common conversation and commerce, about the ordinary affairs and conveniences of civil life, in the societies of men one amongst another.

Secondly, by the philosophical use of words, I mean such an use of them as may serve to convey the precise notions of things, and to express, in general propositions, certain and undoubted truths, which the mind may rest upon, and be satisfied with, in its search after true knowledge. These two uses are very distinct; and a great deal less exactness will serve in the one than in the other, as we shall see in what follows.

The imperfection of words is the doubtfulness of their signification.

§ 4. The chief end of language in communication being to be understood, words serve not well for that end, neither in civil nor philosophical discourse, when any word does not excite in the hearer the same idea which it stands for in the mind of the speaker. Now since sounds have no natural connexion with our ideas, but have all their signification from the arbitrary imposition of men, the doubtfulness and uncertainty of their signification, which is the imperfection we here are speaking of, has its cause more in the ideas they stand for, than in any incapacity there is in one sound more than in another, to signify any idea: for in that regard they are all equally perfect.

That then which makes doubtfulness and uncertainty in the signification of some more than other words, is the difference of ideas they stand for.

Causes of their imperfection.

§ 5. Words having naturally no signification, the idea which each stands for must be learned and retained by those who would exchange thoughts, and hold intelligible discourse with others in any language. But this is hardest to be done where,

First, the ideas they stand for are very complex, and made up of a great number of ideas put together.

Secondly, where the ideas they stand for have no certain connexion in nature; and so no settled standard, any where in nature existing, to rectify and adjust them by.

Thirdly, when the signification of the word is referred to a standard, which standard is not easy to be known.

Fourthly, where the signification of the word, and the real essence of the thing, are not exactly the same.

These are difficulties that attend the signification of several words that are intelligible. Those which are not intelligible at all, such as names standing for any simple ideas, which another has not organs or faculties to attain,—as the names of colours to a blind man, or sounds to a deaf man,—need not here be mentioned.

In all these cases we shall find an imperfection in words, which I shall more at large explain, in their particular application to our several sorts of ideas: for if we examine them, we shall find that the names of mixed modes are most liable to doubtfulness and imperfection, for the two first of these reasons; and the names of substances chiefly for the two latter.

The names of mixed modes doubtful. First, because the ideas they stand for are so complex.

§ 6. First, the names of mixed modes are many of them liable to great uncertainty and obscurity in their signification.

I. Because of that great composition these complex ideas are often made up of. To make words serviceable to the end of communication, it is necessary (as has been said) that they excite in the hearer exactly the same idea they stand for in the mind of the speaker. Without this, men fill one another's heads with noise and sounds; but convey not thereby their thoughts, and lay not before one another their ideas, which is the end of discourse and language. But when a word stands for a very complex idea that is compounded and decompounded, it is not easy for men to form and retain that idea so exactly as to make the name in common use stand for the same precise idea, without any the least variation. Hence it comes to pass, that men's names of very compound ideas, such as for the most part are moral words, have seldom, in two different men, the same precise signification; since one man's complex idea seldom agrees with another's, and often differs from his own, from that which he had yesterday, or will have tomorrow.

Secondly, because they have no standards.

§ *7. II.* Because the names of mixed modes, for the most part, want standards in nature, whereby men may rectify and adjust their significations; therefore they are very various and doubtful. They are assemblages of ideas put together at the pleasure of the mind, pursuing its own ends of discourse, and suited to its own notions; whereby it designs not to copy any thing really existing, but to denominate and rank things, as they come to agree with those archetypes or forms it has made. He that first brought the word sham, or wheedle, or banter, in use, put together, as he thought fit, those ideas he made it stand for: and as it is with any new names of modes, that are now brought into any language, so it was with the old ones, when they were first made use of. Names therefore that stand for collections of ideas which the mind makes at pleasure, must needs be of doubtful signification, when such collections are no where to be found constantly united in nature, nor any patterns to be shown whereby men may adjust them. What the word murder, or sacrilege, &c. signifies, can never be known from things themselves: there be many of the parts of those complex ideas which are not visible in the action itself; the intention of the mind; or the relation of holy things, which make a part of murder or sacrilege, have no necessary connexion with the outward and visible action of him that commits either: and the pulling the trigger of the gun, with which the murder is committed, and is all the action that perhaps is visible, has no natural connexion with those other ideas that make up the complex one, named murder. They have their union and combination only from the understanding, which unites them under one name: but uniting them without any rule or pattern, it cannot be but that the signification of the name that stands for such voluntary collections should be often various in the minds of different men, who have scarce any standing rule to regulate themselves and their notions by, in such arbitrary ideas.

Propriety not a sufficient remedy.

§ 8. It is true, common use, that is the rule of propriety, may be supposed here to afford some aid, to settle the signification of language; and it cannot be denied but that in some measure it does. Common use regulates the meaning of words pretty well for common conversation; but nobody having an authority to establish the precise signification of words, nor determine to what ideas any one shall annex them, common use is not sufficient to adjust them to philosophical discourses; there being scarce any name of any very complex idea (to say nothing of others) which in common use has not a great latitude, and which, keeping within the bounds of propriety, may not be made the sign of far different ideas. Besides, the rule and measure of propriety itself being no where established, it is often matter of dispute whether this or that way of using a word be propriety of speech or no. From all which it is evident, that the names of such kind of very complex ideas are naturally liable to this imperfection, to be of doubtful and uncertain signification; and even in men that have a mind to understand one another, do not always stand for the same idea in speaker and hearer. Though the names glory and gratitude be the same in every man's mouth through a whole country, yet the complex collective idea, which every one thinks on, or intends by that name, is apparently very different in men using the same language.

The way of learning these names contributes also to their doubtfulness.

§ 9. The way also wherein the names of mixed modes are ordinarily learned, does not a little contribute to the doubtfulness of their signification. For if we will observe how children learn languages, we shall find that to make them understand what the names of simple ideas, or substances, stand for, people ordinarily show them the thing, whereof they would have them have the idea; and then repeat to them the name that stands for it, as white, sweet, milk, sugar, cat, dog. But as for mixed modes, especially the most material of them, moral words, the sounds are usually learned first; and then to know what complex ideas they stand for, they are either beholden to the explication of others or (which happens for the most part) are left to their own observation and industry; which being little laid out in the search of the true and precise meaning of names, these moral words are in most men's mouths little more than bare sounds; or when they have any, it is for the most part but a very loose and undetermined, and consequently obscure and confused signification. And even those themselves, who have with more attention settled their notions, do yet hardly avoid the inconvenience, to have them stand for complex ideas, different from those which other, even intelligent and studious men, make them the signs of. Where shall one find any, either controversial debate, or familiar discourse, concerning honour, faith, grace, religion, church, &c. wherein it is not easy to observe the different notions men have of them? which is nothing but this, that they are not agreed in the signification of those words, nor have in their minds the same complex ideas which they make them stand for: and so all the contests that follow thereupon are only about the meaning of a sound. And hence we see, that in the interpretation of laws, whether divine or human, there is no end; comments beget comments, and explications make new matter for explications; and of limiting, distinguishing, varying the signification of these moral words, there is no end. These ideas of men's making are, by men still having the same power, multiplied *in infinitum*. Many a man who was pretty well satisfied of the meaning of a text of scripture, or clause in the code, at first reading, has by consulting commentators quite lost the sense of it, and by these elucidations given rise or increase to his doubts, and drawn obscurity upon the place. I say not this, that I think commentaries needless; but to show how uncertain the names of mixed modes naturally are, even in the mouths of those who had both the intention and the faculty of speaking as clearly as language was capable to express their thoughts.

Hence unavoidable obscurity in ancient authors.

§ *10.* What obscurity this has unavoidably brought upon the writings of men, who have lived in remote ages and different countries, it will be needless to take notice; since the numerous volumes of learned men, employing their thoughts that way, are proofs more than enough to show what attention, study, sagacity, and reasoning are required, to find out the true meaning of ancient authors. But there being no writings we have any great concernment to be very solicitous about the meaning of, but those that contain either truths we are required to believe, or laws we are to obey, and draw inconveniences on us when we mistake or transgress; we may be less anxious about the sense of other authors, who writing but their own opinions, we are under no greater necessity to know them than they to know ours. Our good or evil depending not on their decrees, we may safely be ignorant of their notions: and therefore, in the reading of them, if they do not use their words with a due clearness and perspicuity, we may lay them aside, and, without any injury done them, resolve thus with ourselves:

"Si non vis intelligi, debes negligi."

Names of substances of doubtful signification.

§ *11.* If the signification of the names of mixed modes are uncertain, because there be no real standards existing in nature to which those ideas are referred, and by which they may be adjusted; the names of substances are of a doubtful signification, for a contrary reason, viz. because the ideas they stand for are supposed conformable to the reality of things, and are referred to standards made by nature. In our ideas of substances, we have not the liberty, as in mixed modes, to frame what combinations we think fit, to be the characteristical notes to rank and denominate things by. In these we must follow nature, suit our complex ideas to real existences, and regulate the signification of their names by the things themselves, if we will have our names to be signs of them, and stand for them. Here, it is true, we have patterns to follow, but patterns that will make the signification of their names very uncertain; for names must be of a very unsteady and various meaning, if the ideas they stand for be referred to standards without us, that either cannot be known at all, or can be known but imperfectly and uncertainly.

Names of substances referred, 1. To real essences that cannot be known.

§ *12.* The names of substances have, as has been shown, a double reference in their ordinary use.

First, sometimes they are made to stand for, and so their signification is supposed to agree to, the real constitution of things, from which all their properties flow, and in which they all centre. But this real constitution, or (as it is apt to be called) essence, being utterly unknown to us, any sound that is put to stand for it must be very uncertain in its application; and it will be impossible to know what things are, or ought to be called an horse, or anatomy, when those words are put for real essences that we have no ideas of at all. And therefore, in this supposition, the names of substances being referred to standards that cannot be known, their significations can never be adjusted and established by those standards.

2. To co-existing qualities, which are known but imperfectly.

§ *13.* Secondly, the simple ideas that are found to co-exist in substances being that which their names immediately signify, these, as united in the several sorts of things, are the proper standards to which their names are referred, and by which their significations may be best rectified. But neither will these archetypes so well serve to this purpose, as to leave these names without very various and uncertain significations: because these simple ideas that coexist, and are united in the same subject, being very numerous, and having all an equal right to go into the complex specific idea, which the specific name is to stand for; men, though they propose to themselves the very same subject to consider, yet frame very different ideas about it; and so the name they use for it unavoidably comes to have, in several men, very different significations. The simple qualities which make up the complex ideas, being most of them powers, in relation to changes, which they are apt to make in, or receive from, other bodies, are almost infinite. He that shall but observe what a great variety of alterations any one of the baser metals is apt to receive from the different application only of fire; and how much a greater number of changes any of them will receive in the hands of a chemist, by the application of other bodies; will not think it strange that I count the properties of any sort of bodies not easy to be collected, and completely known by the ways of inquiry, which our faculties are capable of. They being therefore at least so many that no man can know the precise and definite number, they are differently discovered by different men, according to their various skill, attention, and ways of handling; who therefore cannot choose but have different ideas of the same substance, and therefore make the signification of its common name very various and uncertain. For the complex ideas of substances being made up of such simple ones as are supposed to co-exist in nature, every one has a right to put into his complex idea those qualities he has found to be united together. For though in the substance of gold one satisfies himself with colour and weight, yet another thinks solubility in aq. regia as necessary to be joined with that colour in his idea of gold as any one does its fusibility; solubility in aq. regia being a quality as constantly joined with its colour and weight, as fusibility, or any other; others put in its ductility or fixedness, &c. as they have been taught by tradition or experience. Who of all these has established the right signification of the word gold? or who shall be the judge to determine? Each has its standard in nature, which he appeals to; and with reason thinks he has the same right to put into his complex idea, signified by the word gold, those qualities which upon trial he has found united, as another, who has not so well examined, has to leave them out; or a third, who has made other trials, has to put in others. For the union in nature of these qualities being the true ground of their union in one complex idea, who can say, one of them has more reason to be put in, or left out, than another? From hence it will always unavoidably follow, that the complex ideas of substances, in men using the same name for them, will be very various; and so the significations of those names very uncertain.

3. To co-existing qualities which are known but imperfectly.

§ 14. Besides, there is scarce any particular thing existing, which, in some of its simple ideas, does not communicate with a greater, and in others a less number of particular beings: who shall determine, in this case, which are those that are to make up the precise collection that is to be signified by the specific name; or can, with any just authority, prescribe which obvious or common qualities are to be left out; or which more secret, or more particular, are to be put into the signification of the name of any substance? All which together seldom or never fail to produce that various and doubtful signification in the names of substances, which causes such uncertainty, disputes, or mistakes, when we come to a philosophical use of them.

With this imperfection, they may serve for civil, but not well for philosophical use.

§ 15. It is true, as to civil and common conversation, the general names of substances, regulated in their ordinary signification by some obvious qualities, (as by the shape and figure in things of known seminal propagation, and in other substances, for the most part, by colour, joined with some other sensible qualities) do well enough to design the things men would be understood to speak

of; and so they usually conceive well enough the substances meant by the word gold, or apple, to distinguish the one from the other. But in philosophical inquiries and debates, where general truths are to be established, and consequences drawn from positions laid down—there the precise signification of the names of substances will be found, not only not to be well established, but also very hard to be so. For example, he that shall make malleableness, or a certain degree of fixedness, a part of his complex idea of gold, may make propositions concerning gold, and draw consequences from them, that will truly and clearly follow from gold, taken in such a signification; but yet such as another man can never be forced to admit, nor be convinced of their truth, who makes not malleableness, or the same degree of fixedness, part of that complex idea, that the name gold, in his use of it, stands for.

Instance liquor.

§ 16. This is a natural, and almost unavoidable imperfection in almost all the names of substances, in all languages whatsoever, which men will easily find, when once passing from confused or loose notions, they come to more strict and close inquiries: for then they will be convinced how doubtful and obscure those words are in their signification, which in ordinary use appeared very clear and determined. I was once in a meeting of very learned and ingenious physicians, where by chance there arose a question, whether any liquor passed through the filaments of the nerves. The debate having been managed a good while, by variety of arguments on both sides, I (who had been used to suspect that the greatest parts of disputes were more about the signification of words than a real difference in the conception of things) desired, that before they went any farther on in this dispute, they would first examine, and establish amongst them, what the word liquor signified. They at first were a little surprised at the proposal; and had they been persons less ingenious, they might perhaps have taken it for a very frivolous or extravagant one; since there was no one there that thought not himself to understand very perfectly what the word liquor stood for; which I think, too, none of the most perplexed names of substances. However, they were pleased to comply with my motion; and, upon examination, found that the signification of that word was not so settled and certain as they had all imagined, but that each of them made it a sign of a different complex idea. This made them perceive that the main of their dispute was about the signification of that term; and that they differed very little in their opinions concerning some fluid and subtile matter passing through the conduits of the nerves; though it was not so easy to agree whether it was to be called liquor or no—a thing which, when considered, they thought it not worth the contending about.

Instance gold.

§ 17. How much this is the case in the greatest part of disputes that men are engaged so hotly in, I shall perhaps have an occasion in another place to take notice. Let us only here consider a little more exactly the fore-mentioned instance of the word gold, and we shall see how hard it is precisely to determine its signification. I think all agree to make it stand for a body of a certain yellow shining colour; which being the idea to which children have annexed that name, the shining yellow part of a peacock's tail is properly to them gold. Others finding fusibility joined with that yellow colour in certain parcels of matter, make of that combination a complex idea, to which they give the name gold, to denote a sort of substances; and so exclude from being gold all such yellow shining bodies, as by fire will be reduced to ashes; and admit to be of that species, or to be comprehended under that name gold, only such substances, as having that shining yellow colour, will by fire be reduced to fusion, and not to ashes. Another, by the same reason, adds the weight; which being a quality as straitly joined with that colour as its fusibility, he thinks has the same reason to be joined in its idea, and to be signified by its name; and therefore the other made up of body, of such a colour and fusibility, to be

imperfect; and so on of all the rest: wherein no one can show a reason why some of the inseparable qualities, that are always united in nature, should be put into the nominal essence, and others left out; or why the word gold, signifying that sort of body the ring on his finger is made of, should determine that sort, rather by its colour, weight, and fusibility, than by its colour, weight, and solubility in aq. regia: since the dissolving it by that liquor is as inseparable from it as the fusion by fire; and they are both of them nothing but the relation which that substance has to two other bodies, which have a power to operate differently upon it. For by what right is it that fusibility comes to be a part of the essence signified by the word gold, and solubility but a property of it; or why is its colour part of the essence, and its malleableness but a property? That which I mean is this: That these being all but properties depending on its real constitution, and nothing but powers, either active or passive, in reference to other bodies; no one has authority to determine the signification of the word gold (as referred to such a body existing in nature) more to one collection of ideas to be found in that body than to another: whereby the signification of that name must unavoidably be very uncertain; since, as has been said, several people observe several properties in the same substance; and, I think, I may say nobody at all. And therefore we have but very imperfect descriptions of things, and words have very uncertain significations.

The names of simple ideas the least doubtful.

§ 18. From what has been said, it is easy to observe what has been before remarked, viz. That the names of simple ideas are, of all others, the least liable to mistakes, and that for these reasons. First, because the ideas they stand for, being each but one single perception, are much easier got, and more clearly retained, than the more complex ones; and therefore are not liable to the uncertainty which usually attends those compounded ones of substances and mixed modes, in which the precise number of simple ideas, that make them up, are not easily agreed, and so readily kept in the mind: and secondly, because they are never referred to any other essence, but barely that perception they immediately signify; which reference is that which renders the signification of the names of substances naturally so perplexed, and gives occasion to so many disputes. Men that do not perversely use their words, or on purpose set themselves to cavil, seldom mistake, in any language which they are acquainted with, the use and signification of the names of simple ideas: white and sweet, yellow and bitter, carry a very obvious meaning with them, which every one precisely comprehends, or easily perceives he is ignorant of, and seeks to be informed. But what precise collection of simple ideas modesty or frugality stand for in another's use, is not so certainly known. And however we are apt to think we well enough know what is meant by gold or iron; yet the precise complex idea others make them the signs of, is not so certain; and I believe it is very seldom that, in speaker and hearer, they stand for exactly the same collection: which must needs produce mistakes and disputes, when they are made use of in discourses, wherein men have to do with universal propositions, and would settle in their minds universal truths, and consider the consequences that follow from them.

And next to them, simple modes.

§ 19. By the same rule, the names of simple modes are, next to those of simple ideas, least liable to doubt and uncertainty, especially those of figure and number, of which men have so clear and distinct ideas. Who ever, that had a mind to understand them, mistook the ordinary meaning of seven, or a triangle? And in general the least compounded ideas in every kind have the least dubious names.

The most doubtful are the names of very compounded mixed modes and substances.

§ 20. Mixed modes, therefore, that are made up but of a few and obvious simple ideas,

have usually names of no very uncertain signification; but the names of mixed modes, which comprehend a great number of simple ideas, are commonly of a very doubtful and undetermined meaning, as has been shown. The names of substances, being annexed to ideas that are neither the real essences nor exact representations of the patterns they are referred to, are liable yet to greater imperfection and uncertainty, especially when we come to a philosophical use of them.

Why this imperfection charged upon words.

§ 21. The great disorder that happens in our names of substances, proceeding for the most part from our want of knowledge, and inability to penetrate into their real constitutions, it may probably be wondered, why I charge this as an imperfection rather upon our words than understandings. This exception has so much appearance of justice, that I think myself obliged to give a reason why I have followed this method. I must confess then, that when I first began this discourse of the understanding, and a good while after, I had not the least thought that any consideration of words was at all necessary to it. But when, having passed over the original and composition of our ideas, I began to examine the extent and certainty of our knowledge, I found it had so near a connexion with words, that, unless their force and manner of signification were first well observed, there could be very little said clearly and pertinently concerning knowledge; which being conversant about truth, had constantly to do with propositions; and though it terminated in things, yet it was for the most part so much by the intervention of words, that they seemed scarce separable from our general knowledge. At least, they interpose themselves so much between our understandings and the truth, which it would contemplate and apprehend, that, like the medium through which visible objects pass, their obscurity and disorder do not seldom cast a mist before our eyes, and impose upon our understandings. If we consider, in the fallacies men put upon themselves as well as others, and the mistakes in men's disputes and notions, how great a part is owing to words, and their uncertain or mistaken significations—we shall have reason to think this no small obstacle in the way to knowledge; which, I conclude, we are the more carefully to be warned of, because it has been so far from being taken notice of as an inconvenience, that the arts of improving it have been made the business of men's study, and obtained the reputation of learning and subtilty, as we shall see in the following chapter. But I am apt to imagine, that were the imperfections of language, as the instruments of knowledge, more thoroughly weighed, a great many of the controversies that make such a noise in the world, would of themselves cease; and the way to knowledge, and perhaps peace, too, lie a great deal opener than it does.

This should teach us moderation, in imposing our own sense of old authors.

§ 22. Sure I am, that the signification of words in all languages, depending very much on the thoughts, notions, and ideas of him that uses them, must unavoidably be of great uncertainty to men of the same language and country. This is so evident in the Greek authors, that he that shall peruse their writings will find in almost every one of them a distinct language, though the same words. But when to this natural difficulty in every country there shall be added different countries and remote ages, wherein the speakers and writers had very different notions, tempers, customs, ornaments, and figures of speech, &c. every one of which influenced the signification of their words then, though to us now they are lost and unknown; it would become us to be charitable one to another in our interpretations or misunderstanding of those ancient writings; which though of great concernment to be understood, are liable to the unavoidable difficulties of speech, which (if we except the names of simple ideas, and some very obvious things) is not capable, without a constant defining the terms, of conveying the sense and intention of the speaker, without any manner of doubt and uncertainty, to the hearer. And in dis-

courses of religion, law, and morality, as they are matters of the highest concernment, so there will be the greatest difficulty.

§ 23. The volumes of interpreters and commentators on the old and new Testament are but too manifest proofs of this. Though every thing said in the text be infallibly true, yet the reader may be, nay cannot choose but be, very fallible in the understanding of it. Nor is it to be wondered, that the will of God, when clothed in words, should be liable to that doubt and uncertainty which unavoidably attends that sort of conveyance; when even his Son, whilst clothed in flesh, was subject to all the frailties and inconveniences of human nature, sin excepted: and we ought to magnify his goodness, that he hath spread before all the world such legible characters of his works and providence, and given all mankind so sufficient a light of reason, that they to whom this written word never came, could not (whenever they set themselves to search) either doubt of the being of a God, or of the obedience due to him. Since then the precepts of natural religion are plain, and very intelligible to all mankind, and seldom come to be controverted; and other revealed truths, which are conveyed to us by books and languages, are liable to the common and natural obscurities and difficulties incident to words; methinks it would become us to be more careful and diligent in observing the former, and less magisterial, positive, and imperious, in imposing our own sense and interpretations of the latter.

INTRODUCTION TO GIAMBATTISTA VICO

Giambattista Vico was born in Naples, Italy, where he lived nearly his whole life (1668–1744). His family was of very modest means, and they could not afford expensive schooling for Vico. Nevertheless, he read voraciously and considered himself self-taught. This early independence of scholarship may have shaped his entire career. Although he was professor of Latin eloquence at the University of Naples, the position was a modest one that he had to supplement through writing and tutoring. While he was widely learned and wrote a book, *New Science,* he was not highly regarded by other European scholars during his lifetime. Vico was out of step with the concerns and interests of many other Enlightenment scholars, and was regarded by his contemporaries as having odd ideas.

Vico's duties as professor of eloquence were to train law students in public speaking and to deliver an oration in Latin once a year. The work excerpted here is a revision and expansion of one of those orations, *On the Study Methods of Our Time.* In this work, Vico examines the growing respect for scientific, mathematical, and logical methods of the Enlightenment and compares them with the more humanist, broader methods of the "ancients," the classical Greeks and Romans. His comparison of these two approaches to knowledge is informed by his work as a professor of rhetoric.

Vico's comparison is not intended to deny any worth to the methods employed by the scientists and mathematicians of his time. Instead, he intends to put those rationalist methods in perspective, a perspective that he felt was lost by many in his time who saw value *only* in science, reason, and detached observation. Vico wants to temper the pretensions of science and advance the claims of humanist, rhetorically-based learning as ways of knowing. It is important to recall that the new sciences of the Enlightenment claimed superiority chiefly in terms of the objective, rational *methods* that they used. Educational methods were likewise attuned to scientific assumptions and procedures. Vico wants his audience to think about the effects of these methods.

Vico gives science due praise early in this reading. But then he questions a key part of foundationalism and the scientific methods of his time: *doubt.* You will recall that Descartes's method was to seek out that which he could not doubt. Similarly, the scientific method attempts to establish hypotheses that, when tested, cannot be reasonably doubted. Science is a skeptical enterprise in its methods, Vico complains, and this may be true of our time as well as his. Vico is especially concerned that an early training in scientific methods would instill the habit of doubt and skepticism in young people, which he argues is undesirable.

In place of a method based on doubt and skepticism, Vico argues that an education that is keyed to *rhetoric* or "eloquence," as was the model of classical education among the Greeks and Romans, teaches young people more valuable habits that may then be supplemented by scientific skepticism at a later age. Rhetoric relies on having and using common sense, Vico argues, and common sense is more basic and valuable than is doubt. Young people should be taught to exercise the faculty of the imagination rather than doubting the products of imagining. Students should be trained in invention, or thinking up what *might* be said on any issue, before they are trained in doubting or criticizing what might be said.

Later in our excerpt, Vico directly compares training in rhetoric with training in skeptical science, and argues for the virtues of the former method. Science, he argues, discovers knowledge that is abstract, unambiguous, and for that reason relatively easy—but it is knowledge not connected to the real decisions and choices we must make every day. What he means is that a scientist wants to know in general, abstractly, what the chemical composition of water is. The scientist does not care about the state of water on a particular day, or what it might mean to an audience on a specific occasion. This latter concern for the here and now is rhetoric's domain, Vico claims. But the methods of rhetoric are more difficult than those of science because rhetoric works on shifting and uncertain human nature. The rhetorician must be a student of human affairs, which cannot be studied at the abstract level of science. The rhetorician's task is harder because the orator must advise particular audiences about specific, hard decisions. Yet rhetorical training is necessary because we all face such decisions that scientific methods cannot help us make.

Finally, Vico argues that because of the proliferation of arts and sciences (which is, of course, even more true for us than it was for him), there is a need for a way of thinking and knowing that integrates and unifies different branches of learning. Students of his time, he complained, lack coherence in their studies, learning disconnected and increasingly specialized subjects from different professors. As a solution, he explicitly offers rhetoric as a method of study, a way of thinking, and even a way of life that integrates different disciplines and ways of thinking. Rhetoric integrates and unifies because, since the orator might speak on any subject, rhetorical methods must be attuned to thinking about any subject—from the perspective of persuasion. This perspective holds the key to reunifying human knowledge and discourse, Vico argues. In taking such a stance, Vico returns to the Ciceronian model of the orator as widely-trained civic leader. Today, many scholars are rediscovering Vico's work and attempting to apply it to our own problems with specialized and disconnected learning. In that sense, Vico may be speaking more to our world than he was to his own.

GIAMBATTISTA VICO

ON THE STUDY METHODS OF OUR TIME

I

In his small but priceless treatise entitled *De dignitate et de augmentis scientiarum,*[1] Francis Bacon undertakes to point out what new arts and sciences should be added to those we already possess, and suggests how we may enlarge our stock of knowledge, [as far as necessary,] so that human wisdom may be brought to complete perfection.

Translated by Elio Gianturco, Associate Professor of Italian Literature, Hunter College

But, while he discovers a new cosmos of sciences, the great Chancellor proves to be rather the pioneer of a completely new universe than a prospector of this world of ours. His vast demands so exceed the utmost extent of man's effort that he seems to have indicated how we fall short of achieving an absolutely complete system of sciences rather than how we may remedy our cultural gaps.

This was so, I believe, because those who occupy the heights of power yearn for the immense and the infinite. Thus Bacon acted in the intellectual field like the potentates of mighty empires, who, having gained supremacy in human affairs, squander immense wealth in attempts against the

---

[1] (*Of the Dignity and Advancement of Learning.*) Bacon's project was of a striking, almost superhuman grandeur. He envisaged nothing less than the total reconstruction of the fabric of science: *Instauratio magna* (*The Great Instauration*). He was keenly conscious of the gigantic dimensions of his plan, for the realization of which he foresaw that a limited time would be utterly insufficient. "And certainly," he writes, "it may be objected to me with truth that my words require an age, a whole age, perhaps, to prove them, and many ages to perfect them."

The *De dignitate* was published in 1623, as an expansion of the *Two Books of Proficience and Advancement of Learning* which appeared in 1603–1605. It was meant to be Part I of the *Instauratio magna.* Part II is the *Novum organum* (*The New Organon*), i.e., the instrument to be substituted for the Ancients' superficial induction and the syllogistic method.

In order to achieve the reconstruction of science, as G. Fonsegrive points out, it was necessary, first, to dismantle traditional science (this was performed in the *De dignitate*); secondly, to establish the method by which true science can be attained (this was done in the *Novum organum*); finally, to construct modern science, and this would have been accomplished in the last part of the *Instauratio* which was left unfinished.

The general plan of the *Instauratio magna* was sketched (1620) in the Introduction of the *Novum organum.* An outline of Part I of *Instauratio* appears in the *Two Books of Proficience and Advancement of Learning* of 1603–1605.

In the *De dignitate,* after having defended science from the objections of theologians and writers on politics, Bacon extols its value (*dignitas*), and examines, one by one, the various branches of knowledge. What new sciences should be added to those already existing are listed in the prospectus of *desiderata* ("The New World of Sciences") affixed as an Appendix to this work. Among these new sciences are the history of culture, philosophical grammar, a treatise on the common principles (axioms) of the sciences, comparative anatomy, literary history, history of the arts, philosophy of law, etc.

The plan of the *Instauratio magna* called for six parts, as follows. Part I: a systematic division of all sciences, and a radical revision of their present status. Part II: explanation of principles which should guide our investigation and interpretation of nature, that is, an exposition of the new method. Part III: natural and experimental history destined for the establishment of philosophy, i.e., collection of the empirical materials to which the new method is to be applied. Part IV: "the ladder of the Intellect," showing the twofold use, inductive and deductive, of the human mind in the search for laws. Part V: anticipation of truth, i.e., the discoveries realized by the traditional method. Part VI: definite systematization of operational science.

As we stated, only Part I (*De dignitate*) and Part II (*Novum organum*) were composed; Part III is present in the form of a heterogeneous assemblage of scientific materials, *Sylva sylvarum* (*Forest of Materials*).

order of Nature herself, by paving the seas with stones, mastering mountains with sail, and other vain exploits forbidden by nature.

No doubt all that man is given to know is, like man himself, limited and imperfect. Therefore, if we compare our times with those of the Ancients—if we weigh, on both sides, the advantages and deficiencies of learning—our achievements and those of Antiquity would, by and large, balance.

We, the men of the modern age, have discovered many things of which the Ancients were entirely ignorant; the Ancients, on the other hand, knew much still unknown to us. We enjoy many techniques which enable us to make progress in some branch of intellectual or practical activity; they likewise had talents for progress in other fields. They devoted all their activity to certain arts which we almost totally neglect; we pursue some others which they apparently scorned. Many disciplines conveniently unified by the Ancients have been partitioned by us; a certain number which they inconveniently kept separate, we treat as unified. Finally, not a few sectors of culture have changed both appearance and name.

The foregoing provides the theme of the present discourse: Which study method is finer and better, ours or the Ancients'? In developing this topic I shall illustrate by examples the advantages and drawbacks of the respective methods. I shall specify which of the drawbacks of our procedures may be avoided, and how; and whether those which cannot be eliminated have their counterparts in particular shortcomings by which the Ancients were handicapped.

Unless I am mistaken, this theme is new; but the knowledge of it is so important, that I am amazed it has not been treated yet. In the hope of escaping censure, I ask you to give thought to the fact that my purpose is not to criticize the drawbacks of the study methods of our age or of those of antiquity, but rather to compare the advantages afforded by the study methods of the two epochs.

This matter is of direct concern to you: even if you know more than the Ancients in some fields, you should not accept knowing less in others. You should make use of a method by which you can acquire, on the whole, more knowledge than the Ancients, and, being aware of the shortcomings of ancient methods of study, you may endure the unavoidable inconveniences of our own.

The better to grasp the subject I am proposing to you, you should distinctly realize that in the present discourse I do not intend to draw parallels between individual branches of knowledge, single fields of sciences or arts of ancient and modern times.

My goal, instead, is to indicate in what respect our study methods are superior to those of the Ancients; to discover in what they are inferior, and how we may remedy this inferiority.

For our purpose we must, if not separate, at least set up a distinction between new arts, sciences, and inventions on one hand, and new *instruments* and aids to knowledge on the other. The former are the constituent material of learning; the latter are the way and the means, precisely the subject of our discourse.

Every study method may be said to be made up of three things: instruments, complementary aids, and the aim envisaged. The instruments presuppose and include a systematic, orderly manner of proceeding; the apprentice who, after suitable training, undertakes the task of mastering a certain art or science, should approach it in an appropriate and well-ordered fashion. Instruments are antecedent to the task of learning; complementary aids and procedures are concomitant with that task. As for the aim envisaged, although its attainment is subsequent to the process of learning, it should never be lost sight of by the learner, neither at the beginning nor during the entire learning process.

We shall arrange our discourse in corresponding order, and discuss first the instruments, then the aids to our method of study. As for the aim, it should circulate, like a blood-stream, through the entire body of the learning process. Consequently, just as the blood's pulsation may best be studied at the spot where the arterial beat is most perceptible, so the aim of our study methods shall be treated at the point where it assumes the greatest prominence.

Some of the new instruments of science are, themselves, sciences; others are arts; still others, products of either art or nature. Modern philosophical "critique" is the common instrument of all our sciences and arts.[1] The instrument of geometry is "analysis";[2] that of physics, geometry, plus the geometrical method (and, in a certain sense, modern mechanics). The instrument of medicine is chemistry and its off-shoot, pharmacological chemistry. The instrument of anatomy is the microscope; that of astronomy, the telescope; that of geography, the mariner's needle.

As for "complementary aids," I include among them the orderly reduction to systematic rules, of a number of subjects which the Ancients were wont

---

[1] Vico's reference is to the Cartesian method, the Cartesian "revolution of logic," in the famous four rules of the *Discourse on Method.* Method is defined by Descartes as "a set of certain and easy rules, such that anyone, who obeys them exactly, will, first, never take anything false for true, and secondly, will advance step by step, without waste of mental effort, until he has achieved the knowledge of everything which does not surpass his capacity of understanding" (*Rules for the Direction of the Mind,* Rule 4). In order to grasp the full, epochal significance of the Cartesian method, a study not only of the *Discourse* but also of the *Rules* is indispensable. It is furthermore necessary to keep in mind the specific features which distinguish the Cartesian from the Scholastic, syllogistic method. Descartes rejects "the Scholastic logic based on comprehension and connotation" (L. J. Beck, *The Method of Descartes: A Study of the Regulae* [Oxford: Clarendon Press, 1952], p. 106). As is well known, Descartes' method is based on the procedures of mathematics. "He attacks the idea of a science of method which assumes . . . that it can give rules and precepts for reasoning which are independent altogether of the nature of the content about which the reasoning occurs" (Beck, p. 105), that is, rules and precepts which are purely formal (*syllogismorum formae*). Aliquié points out that the Cartesian inference, being of the mathematical type, is utterly unlike the syllogism, "which operates by telescoping concepts different in extent and scope" (F. Aliquié, *Descartes, l'homme et l'oeuvre* [Paris: Hatier-Boivin, 1956], p. 32). In Descartes, the relationship which is at the basis of reasoning is not one of inherence. It is, most often, a relationship between quantities, which enables us to fix the place of such quantities within a certain "order" (Alquié). Most enlightening, for the purpose of understanding the character, nature, and scope of the Cartesian method, is an attentive examination of the *Geometry,* the *Dioptrics* and the *Meteorology,* where the Cartesian method may be seen in action, and where its function as a logic of scientific discovery can be observed at close range. The Cartesian method was amply elaborated (also in regard to the "moral" sciences) in the *Port-Royal Logic* (1662) by A. Arnauld and Pierre Nicole (Pascal is said to have contributed to the second edition of this book); and in Book VI of the *Recherche de la Vérité* (*The Search After Truth*) by Malebranche. A signally important variation of the Cartesian method is Spinoza's *Tractatus de intellectus emendatione* (*Treatise on the Improvement of the Understanding*). It has been remarked that, although Leibniz was mainly engaged in carrying out a reconciliation of the Aristotelian-Scholastic with the Cartesian method on the basis of the reciprocal relations of analysis and synthesis, he, notwithstanding his objections against Descartes, may be viewed as a continuator of the Cartesian method. It was this method which enabled him to develop universal mathematics *qua* logistics (mathematical logic) and logical calculus, under the name of *ars combinatoria.* (See S. Caramella, article "Metodo," in *Enciclopedia Filosofica* [Venice-Rome: Instituto per la Collaborazione Culturale, 1957], III, cols. 562–573.)

[2] Vico used the word "analysis" in two senses. The first is that of mathematical analysis (in geometry, the adjective "analytic" has come to mean "using algebraic methods"). It is important to distinguish the meaning that Vico attaches to "analysis" (a meaning identical to that assigned to it by Descartes) from the modern meaning, in which "analysis" is equivalent to "calculus." (Analytical geometry is the background for the calculus, invented by Newton and Leibniz.) Analysis is the first step of the Cartesian method. Rule 5 of the *Rules For the Direction of the Mind,* embodying the second and third Rule of the *Discourse,* asserts that "the exact observance of the method will be secured if (*a*) we reduce involved and obscure propositions, step by step, to more simple ones; and if then (*b*) we start from our intellectual intuition into the simplest propositions, and endeavor, by retracing our path through the same steps, to work out our way up to the knowledge of all the others." Descartes' method is the analytico-synthetic: in L. J. Beck's words, "every complex must be resolved by analysis into simple constituents or parts, and then, by the inverse process, synthesized, by combining those constituents in such an order that their interrelations or connexions, when they are combined together, are manifestly intelligible" (*The Method of Descartes,* pp. 278–279).

The second sense in which Vico uses the word "analysis" (in this passage of the *De nostri,* both senses are present) is that of "analytical geometry," a discipline, if not invented, triumphantly illustrated and applied by Descartes, and which, by a combination of algebra (*ars analytica*) and geometry, resulted in a method so powerful that, thanks to it, geometry made more progress in half a century than in the fifteen preceding centuries.

to entrust to practical common sense. Complementary aids are also works of literature and of the fine arts whose excellence designates them as patterns of perfection; the types used in the printing; and universities as institutions of learning.

In view of the easy accessibility, usefulness and value of the complementary aids, our study methods seem, beyond any doubt, to be better and more correct than those of the Ancients, whether in regard to facility, or to utility, or to merit.

As for the aim of all kinds of intellectual pursuits: one only is kept in view, one is pursued, one is honored by all: Truth.

II

Modern philosophical critique supplies us with a fundamental verity of which we can be certain even when assailed by doubt. That critique could rout the skepticism even of the New Academy.[1]

In addition, "analysis" (i.e., analytical geometry) empowers us to puzzle out with astonishing ease geometrical problems which the Ancients found impossible to solve.

Like us, the Ancients utilized geometry and mechanics as instruments of research in physics, but not as a constant practice. We apply them consistently, and in better form.

Let us leave aside the question whether geometry has undergone greater development by means of "*analysis,*" and whether modern mechanics constitutes something new. What cannot be denied is the fact that leading investigators have available to them a science enriched by a number of new and extremely ingenious discoveries. Modern scientists, seeking for guidance in their exploration of the dark pathways of nature, have introduced the geometrical method into physics. Holding to this method as to Ariadne's thread, they can reach the end of their appointed journey. Do not consider them as groping practitioners of physics: they are to be viewed, instead, as the grand architects of this limitless fabric of the world: able to give a detailed account of the ensemble of principles according to which God has built this admirable structure of the cosmos.

Chemistry, of which the Ancients were totally ignorant, has made outstanding contributions to medicine. Having observed the similarity which exists between the various phenomena of the human body and those of chemistry, the healing art has been able, not only to hazard guesses concerning many physiological functions and disorders, but to make these plainly discernible to the human eye.

Pharmacology, of course, a derivate of chemistry, was among the ancients merely a desideratum. Nowadays, we have converted that desideratum into a reality. Some of our researchers have applied chemistry to physics; others, mechanics to medicine. Our physical chemistry can faithfully, and, so to speak, *manually,* reproduce a number of meteors and other physical phenomena. Mechanical medicine can describe, by inferences drawn from the motions of machines, the diseases of the human body, and can treat them successfully. And anatomy clearly reveals not only the circulation of the blood, but the nerve-roots, countless humors, vessels and ducts of the human body (notice that such descriptions already constitute notable advances over ancient medicine), and moreover—thanks to the microscope—the nature of miliary glands, of the most minute internal organs, of plants, of silkworms, and of insects. To modern anatomy, furthermore, we are indebted for an insight into the process of generation, as

---

[1] The New Academy is the Second Platonic Academy (or School), whose major representatives were Arcesilaus (*ca.* 315–241 B.C.) and Carneades (*ca.* 214–129 B.C.), and which was marked by a radical epistemological skepticism (in contrast to the First and Third Platonic Academy, characterized by a predominantly dogmatic orientation of thought). Vico's allusion is to the Cartesian *cogito,* by which the certainty of existence is to be found in the depths of the doubting consciousness itself; be it noted that Vico did not believe that Descartes had put to flight, had "routed" skepticism; he demonstrates the contrary in his *De antiquissima Italiorum sapientia* (*On the Very Ancient Wisdom of the Italians,* which is a prosecution and expansion of the anti-Cartesian polemic broached in the *De nostri*).

demonstrated by the growth of the incubated egg. All these things were entirely outside of the narrow range of sight of the science of the Ancients; modern science throws a flood of light upon them.

As for astronomy, the modern telescope has brought within our ken a multitude of new stars, the variability of sun-spots, and phases of the planets. These discoveries have made us aware of several defects in the cosmological system of Ptolemy.[1]

In the domain of geographical exploration, the Ancients guessed vaguely, in a prophetic sort of way, at the existence of transoceanic lands. By the use of the mariner's compass, the modern age has actually discovered them. As a result, a wonderful luster has been bestowed upon geography.

It seems almost unbelievable that in our days men should not only be able to circumnavigate the globe along with the sun, but to outreach the sun's march and to negotiate its full course in less time than it takes that planet to complete it.[2]

From geometry and physics, taught by the present method, the science of mechanics has received major impulses and has rendered possible a great number of outstanding and marvelous inventions, which have vastly enriched human society. It may be said that it is from these three sciences that our technique of warfare derives. Our art of war is so immeasurably superior to that of the Ancients, that, compared with our technique of fortifying and attacking cities, Minerva would contemn her own Athenian citadel and Jupiter would scorn his three-pronged lightning as a blunt and cumbersome weapon.

Such are the "instruments" employed by our modern sciences; let us now turn to the complementary aids employed in the various sectors of our culture.

Systematic treatments (*artes*) have been set up of certain subjects which the Ancients left to unaided common sense. Among these subjects is the law, which the Ancients, balked by the difficulty of the task, gave up hope of organizing into a systematically arranged, methodical body of theory.

In the fields of poetry, oratory, painting, sculpture, and other fine arts, based on the imitation of nature, we possess a wealth of supremely accomplished productions, on which the admiration of posterity has conferred the prestige of archetypal exemplarity. Thanks to the guidance offered by these masterworks, we are able to imitate, correctly and easily, Nature at her best. The invention of printing places at our disposal an enormous number of books. Hence, our scholars are not compelled to restrict their competence to the knowledge of one or another author, but can master a multiple, diversified, almost boundless domain of culture.

Finally, we have great institutions of learning, i.e., universities, which are the repositories of all our sciences and arts, and where the intellectual, spiritual, and linguistic abilities of men may be brought to perfection. Almost all of these spheres of mental activity have as their single goal the inquiry after truth. Were I to set out to extol this inquiry, I would arouse wonder at my eulogizing something that no one ever thought of disparaging.

Let us now scrutinize these advantages of our study methods, and try to ascertain whether these methods lack some of the good qualities possessed by those of antiquity: or whether, instead, they are impaired by faults from which ancient methods were exempt. Let us examine whether we can avoid our deficiencies and appropriate the good points of the ancient methods, and

---

[1] Claudius Ptolemaeus (*ca.* A.D. 100–170), the most celebrated astronomer and geographer of antiquity, author of the *Almagest* (13 books) in which he develops the theory that the earth is stationary, with the sun, moon, and other planets revolving around it. This theory dominated scientific research in celestial phenomena for about 1400 years, until Copernicus.

[2] Vico means that in his epoch a voyage of circumnavigation could be performed in a lesser time than it takes the sun to revolve around the earth (four seasons). This does not mean that Vico did not believe in the heliocentric system: he speaks from the viewpoint of the Ancients, for whom geocentrism was the accepted dogma (in spite of Aristarchus of Samos, *ca.* 320–250 B.C., whose heliocentrism theory Copernicus had to rediscover).

by what means this may be done; and let us see whether those among our deficiencies which are unavoidable may be offset by the shortcomings of antiquity.

III

Let us begin with the *instruments* with which modern sciences operate.

Philosophical criticism is the subject which we compel our youths to take up first. Now, such speculative criticism, the main purpose of which is to cleanse its fundamental truths not only of all falsity, but also of the mere suspicion of error, places upon the same plane of falsity not only false thinking, but also those secondary verities and ideas which are based on probability alone, and commands us to clear our minds of them. Such an approach is distinctly harmful, since training in common sense is essential to the education of adolescents, so that that faculty should be developed as early as possible; else they break into odd or arrogant behavior when adulthood is reached. It is a positive fact that, just as knowledge originates in truth and error in falsity, so common sense arises from perceptions based on verisimilitude. Probabilities stand, so to speak, midway between truth and falsity, since things which most of the time are true, are only very seldom false.

Consequently, since young people are to be educated in common sense, we should be careful to avoid that the growth of common sense be stifled in them by a habit of advanced speculative criticism. I may add that common sense, besides being the criterion of practical judgment, is also the guiding standard of eloquence. It frequently occurs, in fact, that orators in a law court have greater difficulty with a case which is based on truth, but does not seem so, than with a case that is false but plausible. There is a danger that instruction in advanced philosophical criticism may lead to an abnormal growth of abstract intellectualism, and render young people unfit for the practice of eloquence.

Our modern advocates of advanced criticism rank the unadulterated essence of "pure," primary truth before, outside, above the gross semblances of physical bodies. But this study of primal philosophical truths takes place at the time when young minds are too immature, too unsure, to derive benefit from it.

Just as old age is powerful in reason, so is adolescence in imagination. Since imagination has always been esteemed a most favorable omen of future development, it should in no way be dulled. Furthermore, the teacher should give the greatest care to the cultivation of the pupil's memory, which, though not exactly the same as imagination, is almost identical with it. In adolescence, memory outstrips in vigor all other faculties, and should be intensely trained. Youth's natural inclination to the arts in which imagination or memory (or a combination of both) is prevalent (such as painting, poetry, oratory, jurisprudence) should by no means be blunted. Nor should advanced philosophical criticism, the common instrument today of all arts and sciences, be an impediment to any of them. The Ancients knew how to avoid this drawback. In almost all their schools for youths, the role of logic was fulfilled by geometry. Following the example of medical practitioners, who concentrate their efforts on seconding the bent of Nature, the Ancients required their youths to learn the science of geometry which cannot be grasped without a vivid capacity to form images. Thus, without doing violence to nature, but gradually and gently and in step with the mental capacities of their age, the Ancients nurtured the reasoning powers of their young men.

In our days, instead, philosophical criticism alone is honored. The art of "topics,"[1] far from being given first place in the curriculum, is utterly disregarded. Again I say, this is harmful, since the invention of arguments is by nature prior to the judgment of their validity, so that, in teaching, that

[1] See Introduction, note 1, p. xx.

invention should be given priority over philosophical criticism. In our days, we keep away from the art of inventing arguments, and think that this skill is of no use. We hear people affirming that, if individuals are critically endowed, it is sufficient to teach them a certain subject, and they will have the capacity to discover whether there is any truth in that subject. It is claimed that, without any previous training in the *ars topica,* any person will be able to discern the probabilities which surround any ordinary topic, and to evaluate them by *the same standard employed in the sifting of truth.* But who can be sure that he has taken into consideration every feature of the subject on hand? The most eulogizing epithet that can be given to a speech is that it is "comprehensive": praise is due to the speaker who has left nothing untouched, and has omitted nothing from the argument, nothing which may be missed by his listeners.

Nature and life are full of incertitude; the foremost, indeed, the only aim of our "arts" is to assure us that we have acted rightly. Criticism is the art of true speech; "*ars topica,*" of eloquence. Traditional "topics" is the art of finding "the *medium,*" i.e., the middle term: in the conventional language of scholasticism, "medium" indicates what the Latins call *argumentum.*[1] Those who know all the *loci,* i.e., the lines of argument to be used, are able (by an operation not unlike reading the printed characters on a page) to grasp extemporaneously the elements of persuasion inherent in any question or case. Individuals who have not achieved this ability hardly deserve the name of orators. In pressing, urgent affairs, which do not admit of delay or postponement, as most frequently occurs in our law courts—especially when it is a question of criminal cases, which offer to the eloquent orator the greatest opportunity for the display of his powers—it is the orator's business to give *immediate* assistance to the accused, who is usually granted only a few hours in which to plead his defense. Our experts in philosophical criticism, instead, whenever they are confronted with some dubious point, are wont to say: "Give me some time to think it over!"

[1] I.e., lines of reasoning along which the discussion of the subject is to be conducted.

I may add that in the art of oratory the relationship between speaker and listeners is of the essence. It is in tune with the opinions of the audience that we have to arrange our speech. It often happens that people unmoved by forceful and compelling reasons can be jolted from their apathy, and made to change their minds by means of some trifling line of argument. Consequently, in order to be sure of having touched all the soul-strings of his listeners, the orator, then, should run through the complete set of the *loci* which schematize the evidence. It is quite unfair to blame Cicero for having insisted on many a point of little weight. It was exactly by those points of little weight that he was able to dominate the law courts, the Senate, and (most important of all) the Assemblies of the people. It was by that method that he became the speaker most worthy of being considered a representative of Rome's imperial greatness. Is it not significant that it is precisely the orator whose only concern is the bare truth who gets stranded in cases in which a different speaker succeeds in extricating himself, by paying attention to credibility as well as the facts? The contrast of opinion between Marcus Brutus and Cicero, regarding the manner in which each of them thought that the defense of Milo should be conducted, provides an instructive case for reflection.

Marcus Brutus, who had been trained in a kind of philosophical, rationalistic criticism closely akin to ours (for he was a Stoic), thought that Milo[1] should be defended by throwing his

[1] Titus Annius Milo from Lanuvium. He was appointed tribune of the people in 57 B.C. and was a bitter opponent of the gang-leader Clodius, who, through his gladiators and henchmen, had established a reign of terror in Rome and its environs. Milo, in a battle near Bovillae (now Le Frattocchie) killed Clodius on January 20, 52 B.C. Previously, he had been instrumental in recalling Cicero from exile. Cicero composed a brilliant defense of

case upon the judges' mercy, and that he should seek acquittal on the ground of the distinguished services he had performed for the Republic, and on the ground of having rid Rome of Clodius, a noxious criminal.

Cicero, instead, an expert in the *ars topica,* deemed it unsafe to throw such a defendant upon the judges' indulgence, considering the conditions prevalent at that time. As a consequence, he based his defense speech entirely on conjectural reasons. Had he been given the chance of delivering that speech in court, he would certainly have brought about Milo's acquittal, as Milo himself declared.

Nevertheless, Antoine Arnauld,[1] a man of commanding scholarship, scorns the *ars topica,* and considers it of absolutely no use.

Whom shall we believe? Arnauld, who rejects the *ars topica,* or Cicero, who asserts that his own eloquence is chiefly due to the art of skillfully arraying a set of effective lines of argument? Let others decide; as for me, I am unwilling to award to the one what I would have to take away from the other: I shall limit myself to stating that a severely intellectualistic criticism enables us to achieve truth, while *ars topica* makes us eloquent. In antiquity, the Stoics devoted themselves entirely to philosophical criticism, while the Academics cultivated topics. Similarly, today the jejune and aridly deductive reasoning in which the Stoics specialized is followed by the moderns, whereas the Aristotelians of the recent past are characterized by the varied and multiform style of their utterance.

An argument presented by Pico della Mirandola, which a learned modern would contract into a single sorites, is rebutted by Cajetan in a string of one hundred syllogisms.[1]

It is significant that the representatives of the schools of ancient philosophy became the more eloquent in proportion as they were less inclined to a strictly philosophical criticism. The advocates of Stoicism (for whom, as for our *moderni,* pure reason is the regulative standard of truth), were the thinnest and leanest of all philosophers. The Epicureans, according to whom the regulative standard of truth resides in sense-perception, were simple in expression, and unfolded their doctrines in more detail. The ancient Academics instead, being disciples of Socrates who contended that he knew nothing but his own ignorance, were masters of an overflowing and lavishly embellished expression. As for the neo-Academics, who admitted that they did not even know that they did not know anything, they overwhelmed their listeners with torrential outbursts and snowdrifts of oratory.

Milo, but was prevented by fear from delivering it in the Forum. Milo was sent in banishment to Massilia (Marseilles). It is said that, being served an excellent fish meal, Milo ironically said: "Had it not been for Cicero, I would not now be enjoying these splendid mullets."

[1] Antoine Arnauld (1612–1694) was, after the death of Saint Cyran, the undisputed leader of Jansenism, and the most unbending adversary of the Jesuits. In the controversy concerning the *Augustinus* of Bishop Cornelius Jansenius, Arnauld defended Jansenius in his *Apologie de M. Jansenius* (1643–1644). Arnauld was the author of the famous distinction between *droit* (law) and *fait* (fact—the Church is not infallible in *questions de fait*). He wrote more than 320 works, the complete edition of which comprises 42 volumes: see *Œuvres de M. Antoine Arnauld,* ed. G. Dupac and J. Hautefage (Lausanne, 1775–1783). Arnauld, in collaboration with Nicole, was the author of the *Port-Royal Logic,* in which, contrary to what Vico states, the *ars topica* is not explicitly attacked. But, says Antonio Corsano, "it is undeniable that the *Art de penser,*" i.e., the *Logique de Port Royal,* "in which the logico-didactic trend of Jansenism is most clearly shown, is dominated by a fierce aversion to any sort of semi-skepticism or probabilism, to any compromise between truth and error: by a disinclination toward that confusion of reality and appearance on which the semi-rational (or altogether irrational) psychological spell of rhetoric is based" (Corsano edn. and trans. of *De nostri, Il metodo degli studi del tempo nostro* [Florence: Vallecchi, 1937]).

[1] Cardinal de Vio (1469–1534), called Gaetanus from his place of birth, Gaeta, was a General of the Dominican Order (1508), one of the most outstanding Catholic divines of his age, and a vehement enemy of Luther (De Vio was Apostolic legate to Germany in 1518). He was instrumental in bringing about the election to the imperial office of Charles V (June 28, 1519). De Vio was a prolific theological writer; the complete catalogue of his works is given by Mandonnet in *Dictionnaire de Théologie Catholique* (Paris: Letouizy et Ané, 1909–1950) Vol. II, cols. 1313–1329.

Both Stoics and Epicureans came out in support of only one side of the argument; Plato inclined towards one or the other side, depending on which appeared to him more probable; Carneades,[1] instead, was wont to embrace both of the sides of any given controversy. He would, for instance, affirm one day that justice exists, another day, that it does not, bringing forth equally compelling arguments for both positions and displaying an unbelievable power of argumentation. This was due to the fact that whereas truth is *one,* probabilities are many, and falsehoods numberless.

Each procedure, then, has its defects. The specialists in topics fall in with falsehood; the philosophical critics disdain any traffic with probability.

To avoid both defects, I think, young men should be taught the totality of sciences and arts, and their intellectual powers should be developed to the full; thus they will become familiar with the art of argument, drawn from the *ars topica.* At the very outset, their common sense should be strengthened so that they can grow in prudence and eloquence. Let their imagination and memory be fortified so that they may be effective in those arts in which fantasy and the mnemonic faculty are predominant. At a later stage let them learn criticism, so that they can apply the fullness of their personal judgment to what they have been taught. And let them develop skill in debating on either side of any proposed argument.

Were this done, young students, I think, would become exact in science, clever in practical matters, fluent in eloquence, imaginative in understanding poetry or painting, and strong in memorizing what they have learned in their legal studies.

They would not feel the impulse to step rashly into discussions while they are still in process of learning; nor would they, with pedestrian slavishness, refuse to accept any viewpoint unless it has been sanctioned by a teacher. In this sphere, the Ancients seem to me to be superior to us.

A five-year period of silence was enjoined upon all of Pythagoras' students.[1] After that time, they were allowed to maintain what they had learned, but had to ground their reasons only upon the authority of their master. "He said it," was their motto. The chief duty of a student of philosophy was to listen. Most appropriately were they called "auditors."

Arnauld himself, although his words seem to spurn this procedure, actually confirms and professes what I am stating. His treatise on *Logic*[2] is

---

[1] This view of Plato is somewhat akin to that expressed by Montaigne, with whose opinion Vico was probably not acquainted. Carneades of Cyrene (214–129 B.C.) integrated with the doctrine of probabilism the skeptical tradition initiated by Arcesilaus. Carneades went to Rome (together with Critolaus and Diogenes of Seleucia) in 156 B.C. in order to plead the defense of Athens, which the Romans had put under a heavy fine because of the plunder of Oropus. On that occasion, Carneades delivered two speeches, one in favor of justice, and one against it. Cicero (*Republic* III has left us a résumé of them. According to Guido Calogero, Carneades is one of the greatest and most complex figures in the history of ancient philosophy: his epistemological critique reveals an incomparably more rigorous subjectivism than that of Protagoras (article "Carneade," in *Enciclopedia Italiana,* Vol. IX [Rome: Treccani, 1931], p. 96). He was the harshest critic of Stoic epistemology. None of his numerous works is extant, but we know his doctrines through the notes of his disciples, Clitomachus of Carthage and Zeno of Alexandria.

---

[1] Pythagoras (*ca.* 580–500 B.C.), born at Samos, settled at Croton in South Italy, and there founded his famous school. The Pythagoreans were dogmatic worshippers of the authority of their master ("he said it"). Pythagoras was a strange combination of philosopher, mathematician, scientist, and mystic. Some of the precepts of his school were even more curious than that quoted by Vico (such is, for instance, the prohibition of eating horse beans). Pythagoras exerted a great influence on Plato.

[2] This is the famous *Art de penser,* also entitled *Logique de Port Royal,* co-authored by Antoine Arnauld and Pierre Nicole (1625–1695), and published in 1662. Cartesian influence on French education found in the *Port-Royal Logic* one of its most efficient vehicles. It has been noted that the analysis of language *qua* logical expression takes its starting point from this book. In Vico's Naples, the *Port-Royal Logic* had found enthusiastic endorsement on the part of the "innovators" (the pro-Cartesians), and had been scornfully rejected by the Jesuits (see Vincenzo de Ruvo edn. of *De nostri,* translated into Italian, with Introduction and notes [Padua: Cedam, 1941]).

replete with far-fetched and involved illustrations, with difficult examples drawn from the deep storehouses of each discipline. Naturally, these illustrations and examples prove to be unintelligible to the young student, unless he is already more than proficient in those arts and sciences from which those supporting materials are taken, and unless his teacher devotes great efforts and a great deal of eloquent skill to the explanation of them. If logic is studied at the terminal stage of the school curriculum, these deficiencies, besides those I have mentioned before, are avoided. What Arnauld presents, though he provides useful examples, is hardly to be understood; the materials offered by the Aristotelians, instead, though perfectly intelligible, are of no use whatever.[1]

• • •

VII

But the greatest drawback of our educational methods is that we pay an excessive amount of attention to the natural sciences and not enough to ethics. Our chief fault is that we disregard that part of ethics which treats of human character, of its dispositions, its passions, and of the manner of adjusting these factors to public life and eloquence. We neglect that discipline which deals with the differential features of the virtues and vices, with good and bad behavior-patterns, with the typical characteristics of the various ages of man, of the two sexes, of social and economic class, race and nation, and with the art of seemly conduct in life, the most difficult of all arts. As a consequence of this neglect, a noble and important branch of studies, i.e., the science of politics, lies almost abandoned and untended.

Since, in our time, the only target of our intellectual endeavors is truth, we devote all our efforts to the investigation of physical phenomena, because their nature seems unambiguous; but we fail to inquire into human nature which, because of the freedom of man's will, is difficult to determine. A serious drawback arises from the uncontrasted preponderance of our interest in the natural sciences.

Our young men, because of their training, which is focused on these studies, are unable to engage in the life of the community, to conduct themselves with sufficient wisdom and prudence; nor can they infuse into their speech a familiarity with human psychology or permeate their utterances with passion. When it comes to the matter of prudential behavior in life, it is well for us to keep in mind that human events are dominated by Chance and Choice, which are extremely subject to change and which are strongly influenced by simulation and dissimulation (both pre-eminently deceptive things). As a consequence, those whose only concern is abstract truth experience great difficulty in achieving their means, and greater difficulty in attaining their ends. Frustrated in their own plans, deceived by the plans of others, they often throw up the game. Since, then, the course of action in life must consider the importance of the single events and their circumstances, it may happen that many of these circumstances are extraneous and trivial, some of them bad, some even contrary to one's goal. It is therefore impossible to assess human affairs by the inflexible standard of abstract right; we must rather gauge them by the pliant Lesbic rule, which does not conform bodies to itself, but adjusts itself to their contours.

The difference, therefore, between abstract knowledge and prudence is this: in science, the outstanding intellect is that which succeeds in reducing a large multitude of physical effects to a single cause; in the domain of prudence, excellence is accorded to those who ferret out the greatest possible number of causes which may have produced a

[1] The Aristotelians referred to here were, according to Corsano, the Schoolmen, authors of the so-called *Summulae Logicales*. Nicolini mentions, among them, Petrus Hispanus (1226–1276), Paolo Nicoletti da Udine (1372–*ca.* 1429), whom Vico calls "the sharpest-minded of all composers of *Summulae*." Fausto Nicolini, edn. of *De nostri*, Vol. I (1914) of Vico's *Opere* (Laterza: Bari, 1914–1941).

single event, and who are able to conjecture which of all these causes is the true one. Abstract knowledge—science—is concerned with the highest verity; common sense, instead, with the lowliest. On the basis of this, the distinguished features of the various types of men should be marked out: the fool, the astute ignoramus, the learned man destitute of prudence, and the sage. In the conduct of life the fool, for instance, pays no attention to the highest or the meanest truths; the astute ignoramus notices the meanest but is unable to perceive the highest; the man who is learned but destitute of prudence, deduces the lowest truths from the highest; the sage, instead, derives the highest truths from the unimportant ones. Abstract, or general truths are eternal; concrete or specific ones change momentarily from truths to untruths. Eternal truths stand above nature; in nature, instead, everything is unstable, mutable. But congruity exists between goodness and truth; they partake of the same essence, of the same qualities. Accordingly, the fool, who is ignorant of both general and particular truths, constantly suffers prompt penalties for his arrogance. The astute ignoramus, who is able to grasp particular truths but incapable of conceiving a general truth, finds that cleverness, which is useful to him today, may be harmful to him tomorrow. The learned but imprudent individual, traveling in a straight line from general truths to particular ones, bulls his way through the tortuous paths of life. But the sage who, through all the obliquities and uncertainties of human actions and events, keeps his eye steadily focused on eternal truth, manages to follow a roundabout way whenever he cannot travel in a straight line, and makes decisions, in the field of action, which, in the course of time, prove to be as profitable as the nature of things permits.

Therefore, it is an error to apply to the prudent conduct of life the abstract criterion of reasoning that obtains in the domain of science. A correct judgment deems that men—who are, for the most part, but fools—are ruled, not by forethought, but by whim or chance. The doctrinaires judge human actions as they *ought* to be, not as they actually are (i.e., performed more or less at random). Satisfied with abstract truth alone, and not being gifted with common sense, unused to following probability, those doctrinaires do not bother to find out whether their opinion is held by the generality and whether the things that are truths to them are also such to other people.

This failure to concern themselves with the opinions of others has not only been a source of blame, but has proved to be extremely prejudicial, not only to private persons but to eminent leaders and great rulers as well. Let an example which is right to the point be quoted here: While the assembly of the French Estates was in session, Henry III, King of France, ordered Duke Henry de Guise, a very popular member of the French aristocracy, to be put to death, in spite of the fact that the Duke was under the protection of a safe conduct. Although just cause underlay that order of the king, such cause was not made manifest. The case having been brought up in Rome, Cardinal Ludovico Madruzzi, a man of great judgment in public affairs, commented: "Rulers should see to it not only that their actions are true and in conformity with justice, but that they also *seem* to be so."

Madruzzi's statement was proved true by the calamities which overtook France shortly after.[1]

The Romans, who were great experts in political matters, paid particular attention to appearances. Both their judges and their senators, on giving out an opinion, were always wont to say: "It seems."

---

[1] Henry de Lorraine, third Duke of Guise (1550–1588), a nephew of Charles de Guise, Cardinal of Lorraine, was murdered by Henri III of France. The background of this murder is lucidly epitomized in the article devoted to him in the *Columbia Encyclopedia* (3rd edn.; New York: Columbia University Press, 1963), p. 886: "Henri fought on the Catholic side in the wars of religion, and cooperated with Catherine de' Medici in planning the massacre of Saint Bartholomew's day. After the peace of 1576 he formed the Catholic League, of which Henri III, though secretly fearing it, became the nominal head. After the death of Francis, duke of Alençon (1584),

To summarize: It was because of their knowledge of the greatest affairs that philosophers were, by the Greeks, called "politici," i.e., experts in matters bearing on the total life of the body politic. Subsequently, philosophers were called Peripatetics and Academics, these names being derived from two small sections of the town of Athens, where their schools stood. Among the Ancients, the teaching of rational, physical, and ethical doctrines was entrusted to philosophers who took good care to adjust those doctrines to the practical common sense that should govern human behavior.

Today, on the contrary, we seem to have reverted to the type of physical research which was typical of pre-Socratic times.

There was an epoch when the "fourfold philosophy" (i.e., logic, physics, metaphysics, and ethics was handed down by its teachers in a manner fitted to foster eloquence: i.e., the attempt was made to fuse philosophy with eloquence. Demosthenes was a product of the Lyceum; Cicero, of the Academy: there is no doubt that they were the two foremost speakers of the two most splendid of languages. Today, those branches of philosophical theory are taught by such a method as to dry up every fount of convincing expression, of copious, penetrating, embellished, lucid, developed, psychologically effective, and impassionate utterance. The listeners' minds undergo a process of constriction, so as to assume the shape of those young virgins,

. . . whom their mothers compel to bend their shoulders, to stoop, to bind their bosom in order to achieve slimness;
if one of the girls is fleshier, they call her "the boxer"
and stint her on food;
if by nature she is healthy, they reduce her, by a special cure,
to the slenderness of a reed.
[Terence, The Eunuch *II.iii.23–26]*

Here some learned pundit might object that, in the conduct of life, I would have our young students become courtiers, and not philosophers; pay little attention to truth and follow not reality but appearances; and cast down morality and put on a deceitful "front" of virtue.

I have no such intention. Instead, I should like to have them act as philosophers, even at court; to care for truth that both is and has the appearance of truth, and to follow that which is morally good and which everybody approves.

As for eloquence, the same men assert that the modern study methods, far from being detrimental, are most useful to it. "How much preferable it is," they say, "to induce persuasion by solid arguments based on truth, to produce such an effect on the mind that, once that truth coalesces with reason, it can never again be separated from it, rather than to coerce the listener's soul by meretriciously eloquent allurements, by blazes of oratorical fire which, as soon as they are extinguished, cause him to revert to his original disposition!"

The answer is that eloquence does not address itself to the rational part of our nature, but almost entirely to our passions. The rational part in us may be taken captive by a net woven of purely intellectual reasonings, but the passional side of our nature can never be swayed and overcome unless this is done by more sensuous and materialistic means. The role of eloquence is to persuade; an orator is persuasive when he calls forth in his hearers the mood which he desires. Wise men induce this condition in themselves by an act of volition. This volition, in perfect obedience, follows the dictates of their intellect; consequently, it is enough

---

Henri de Lorraine revived (1585) the League in opposition to Henri of Navarre, the heir presumptive (later, King Henri IV). Guise, as the defender of the Catholic faith, became immensely popular and overshadowed the King, upon whom he attempted to force the complete program of the League. He instigated the revolt of the Parisians against the King on the Day of the Barricades (May 12, 1588), and took control of the city. He subsequently became reconciled to the King, who, however, brought about his assassination."

Ludovico Madruzzi (1532–1600), born in Trent, was a legate to the Diet of Augsburg; was ambassador to France; in 1561, was appointed cardinal. He took an active part in the Council of Trent, and was several times papal legate to Germany. His personal prestige and influence were deeply felt during the seventh Conclave.

for the speaker to point their duty to such wise men, and they do it. But the multitude, the *vulgus,* are overpowered and carried along by their appetite, which is tumultuous and turbulent; their soul is tainted, having contracted a contagion from the body, so that it follows the nature of the body, and is not moved except by bodily things. Therefore, the soul must be enticed by corporeal images and impelled to love; for once it loves, it is easily taught to believe; once it believes and loves, the fire of passion must be infused into it so as to break its inertia and force it to *will.* Unless the speaker can compass these three things, he has not achieved the effect of persuasion; he has been powerless to convince.

Two things only are capable of turning to good use the agitations of the soul, those evils of the inward man which spring from a single source: desire. One is philosophy, which acts to mitigate passions in the soul of the sage, so that those passions are transformed into virtues; the other is eloquence, which kindles these passions in the common sort, so that they perform the duties of virtue.

It may be objected that the form of government under which we live at present no longer allows eloquence to exercise its control over free peoples. To which I answer that we ought to be thankful to our monarchs for governing us not by fist but by laws. However, even under the republican form of government, orators have gained distinction by their fluent, broad, impassioned style of delivery in the law courts, the assemblies, and the religious convocations, to the greatest advantage of the state, and to the signal enrichment of our language.

But let us approach what may be a basic point. The French language is abundantly endowed with words designating abstract ideas. Now, abstraction is in itself but a dull and inert thing, and does not allow the comparative degree. This makes it impossible for the French to impart an ardently emotional tone to their ideas, inasmuch as such an effect can only be achieved by setting thought in motion, and a vehement motion at that; nor can they amplify or elevate their discourse. Nor can they invert the order of words: the conceptual abstraction being the most general category, it does not supply us with that "middle term" where the extreme points of a metaphor are able to meet and unite. It is therefore impossible in French for a single noun to be the vehicle of a metaphor; and metaphors composed of two nouns are, as a rule, somewhat stilted. Furthermore, when the French writers attempt the periodic style, they are unable to get very far, on account of the shortness of the sentence segments. Nor can French poets compose lines of greater breadth than those which are called "alexandrines"; and these alexandrines, besides consisting of two symmetrical portions, are more dragging and spindly than the Latin elegiac lines. (Each verse contains a simple thought, and they rhyme in pairs; the first feature reduces their scope, the second impairs their gravity.) French words have only two kinds of stress; they are accented on the ultima and on the penult, whereas Italian stresses the antepenult. In French the accent shifts to the penult, which results in a somewhat tenuous and thin sound. For these reasons, French is not fit for stately prose, nor for sublime verse. But though the French language cannot rise to any great sublimity or splendor, it is admirably suited to the subtle style. Rich in substantives, especially those denoting what the Scholastics call abstract essences, the French language can always condense into a small compass the essentials of things. Since arts and sciences are mostly concerned with general notions, French is therefore splendidly suited to the didactic genre. While we Italians praise our orators for fluency, lucidity, and eloquence, the French praise theirs for reasoning truly. Whenever the French wish to designate the mental faculty by which we rapidly, aptly, and felicitously couple things which stand apart, they call it *esprit,* and are inclined to view as a naive, simple trick what we consider as forceful power of combination; their minds, characterized by exceeding penetration, do not excel in synthetic power, but in piercing subtlety of reasoning. Consequently, if there is any truth in this statement, which is the theme of a famous debate, "genius is a product of language, not language of genius," we must recognize that the French are the only people who, thanks to the subtlety of their language, were able to invent the new philosophical criticism which seems so thoroughly intellectualistic, and analytical geometry, by which the subject matter of mathematics is, as far as possible, stripped of all concrete, figural elements, and reduced to pure rationality. The French are in the habit of praising the kind of eloquence which characterizes their language, i.e., an eloquence characterized by great fidelity to truth and subtlety, as well as by its notable deductive order. We Italians, instead, are endowed with a language which constantly evokes images. We stand far above other nations by our achievements in the fields of painting, sculpture, architecture, and music. Our language, thanks to its perpetual dynamism, forces the attention of the listeners by means of metaphorical expressions, and prompts it to move back and forth between ideas which are far apart. In the keenness of their perception, the Italians are second only to the Spaniards. Theirs is a language which, in the rich and elevated style (i.e., that of Herodotus, Livy, and Cicero), possesses a Guicciardini; in the grand and vehement style of Thucydides, Demosthenes, and Sallust, it has others; in Attic elegance, it has Boccaccio; in the new lyric style, Petrarch. Ariosto, in the grandeur of his plots and the ease of his diction, puts one in mind of Homer; while a poet like Tasso, by the enchantingly musical sublimity of his rhyme, comes fully up to Virgil. Shall we then not cultivate a language possessing such felicitous qualities?

In conclusion: whosoever intends to devote his efforts, not to physics or mechanics, but to a political career, whether as a civil servant or as a member of the legal profession or of the judiciary, a political speaker or a pulpit orator, should not waste too much time, in his adolescence, on those subjects which are taught by abstract geometry. Let him, instead, cultivate his mind with an ingenious method; let him study topics, and defend both sides of a controversy, be it on nature, man, or politics, in a freer and brighter style of expression. Let him not spurn reasons that wear a semblance of probability and verisimilitude. Let our efforts not be directed towards achieving superiority over the Ancients merely in the field of science, while they surpass us in wisdom; let us not be merely more exact and more true than the Ancients, while allowing them to be more eloquent than we are; let us equal the Ancients in the fields of wisdom and eloquence as we excel them in the domain of science.

• • •

XIV

As for universities, the amazing fact is that, whereas the Ancients possessed, so to speak, universities for the body, i.e., baths and athletic fields, where young men could develop their strength and agility by exercises such as racing, jumping, boxing, javelin- and discus-throwing, swimming and bathing, they never thought of establishing universities where young minds could be cultivated and strengthened.

In Greece, a single philosopher synthesized in himself a whole university. The Greek language, so fertile in potential developments that it was admirably fitted to express not only all the occurrences of common, everyday life, but the most recondite and abstruse ideas of all sciences and arts in apt terms, the beauty of which terms was commensurate with their appropriateness and felicity; the Greek genius for lawmaking, which was so exceptional that other nations came to borrow laws from Greece while Greece had no necessity to borrow from them—these fostered among the Hellenes the conviction of their immense superiority over other nations. They were wont to ask a question, acutely symptomatic of national conceit: "Art thou a Greek or a barbarian?" as if they esteemed themselves to be worth as much as half of the world, and to be the better part of it.

Things being so, since the Greeks devoted intense, undivided attention to the cultivation of philosophy, the mother, midwife, and nursling of all sciences and arts; since they did not, in the philosophical domain, rely on authority, but discussed all problems on no other merits but the intrinsic ones, each Greek philosopher was capable of achieving a mastery of all learning, both secular and religious, and it was from him alone that students learned thoroughly whatever it was necessary for them to know in the field of public affairs.

With the Romans, the case was different. Although their speech was not autochthonous but derived from other tongues, they proudly sprung all effort to prove that a Roman word derived from other languages. In the case of the words,

> . . . which fall from Grecian well-spring,
> but slightly changed,
> [Horace, *Ars poetica* 53]

they preferred the frivolous, erroneous, foolish interpretation, rather than admit that one of their terms had non-native origins. Although their laws had largely been borrowed from Greece, they expended great ingenuity in grafting those enactments onto their own political system, so that they seemed to spring spontaneously from their soil. In respect to both language and law, the Romans equaled the Greeks. The need for universities was felt by the Romans even less than by the Greeks, since, as I have pointed out, they thought that wisdom consisted in the art and practice of law, and learned to master it in the everyday experience of political affairs. Since the patricians kept law-lore concealed, as if it were an *arcanum* of state, far from feeling any need for universities, the Romans had no interest whatever in establishing them.

But with the transformation of republic into principate, it being in the interest of the emperors that the science of law should be propagated as legal doctrine, this discipline gradually attained greater range and compass through the multitude of writers and their division into doctrinal schools. Regular institutions of teaching were recognized, and the "Academies" of Rome, Constantinople, and Beirut were founded.

Our need for universities is considerably greater. We must have a thorough knowledge of the Scriptures and, in addition, of Eastern languages and of the canons of the ecclesiastic Councils, some of which were held in Asia, some in Europe, some in Africa, in different countries and cities, from apostolic to modern times. We must familiarize ourselves with the laws of Romans and Lombards, with feudal law, the theories of Greeks, Latins, and Arabs, which were introduced into our customary public law. We must guard against scribal garblings, plagiarisms, forgeries, interpolations of alien hands through which it is difficult for us to recognize the originals, and to grasp the author's true meaning. What we need to know is contained in so many books in languages that are extinct, composed by authors belonging to nations long since vanished. These books contain allusions to custom often unknown, in corrupted codices; therefore the attainment of any science or art has become so difficult for us, that at the present time no person can master even a single subject. This has made the establishment of universities necessary. In these universities, all branches of knowledge are taught by a number of scholars, each of whom is outstanding in his particular field. But this advantage is offset by a drawback. Arts and sciences, all of which in the past were embraced by philosophy and animated by it with a unitary spirit, are, in our day, unnaturally separated and disjointed. In antiquity, philosophers were remarkable for their coherence; their conduct was in full accord not only with the theories they professed but with their method of expounding them as well. Socrates, who maintained that "he knew nothing," never brought up any subject for discussion on his own initiative, but pretended to feel a desire to learn from the Sophists. His habit was to confine himself to advancing a series of minute questions, from the replies to which he drew his own inferences. The Stoics, instead, whose main principle was that the mind is the standard of all things, and that the sage should not entertain "mere opinions" about anything, established, in conformity with their requirements, a number of unquestionable truths, linking them, by continuous concatenation, through secondary propositions, to doubtful conclusions; and employed as their instrument of argumentation the figure of the *sorites*. Aristotle, who thought that in the attainment of truth the senses and the mind should co-operate, made use of the syllogism, by which he posited some universal propositions, so as to be able, in concrete cases, to eliminate dubiousness and to reach truth. Epicurus, for whom sense perception was the only avenue of approach to knowledge, neither granted any proposition to his opponents, nor allowed them to grant any to him, but explained phenomena in the simplest and most unadorned language.

Today, students who may be trained in the art of discourse by an Aristotelian, are taught physics by an Epicurean, metaphysics by a Cartesian. They may learn the theory of medicine from a Galenist, its practice from a chemist; they may receive instruction in the Institutes of Justinian from a disciple of Accursius, be trained in the Pandects by a follower of Antoine Favre,[1] in the *Codex* by a pupil of Alciati. Students' education is so warped and perverted as a consequence, that, although they may become extremely learned in some respects, their culture on the whole (and the whole is really the flower of wisdom) is incoherent. To avoid this serious drawback, I would suggest that our professors should so co-ordinate all disciplines into a single system so as to harmonize them with our religion and with the spirit of the political form under which we live. In this way, a coherent body of learning having been established, it will be possible to teach it according to the genius of our public polity.

[1] Antoine Favre (1557–1624) became famous for having pioneered in that domain of juridical learning that is referred to as "interpolationist research," i.e., for having pinpointed the alterations performed by the compilers of Justinian's codification on the texts of the Roman jurists of the "classical" epoch.

XV

I have now set forth the remarks suggested to me by the comparison of the study methods of our time with those of antiquity, and by a confrontation of their respective advantages and disadvantages, so that our methods may be more correct and finer in every respect.

If my ideas are true, I shall have reaped the supreme fruit of my existence. It has been my constant effort, within the very limited range of my powers, to be useful to human society. But if my remarks should be considered false or lacking in practicality, my unquestionably honorable ambition and my earnest efforts towards a grand goal shall earn me a pardon.

It may be objected that, whereas facing danger when necessary is a sign of courage, undertaking a risk when there is no need of doing so is a sign of foolhardiness. "Why should you have undertaken to treat this subject which involves a knowledge of all sciences?"—some one will ask.

In answer, I will say: As G. B. Vico, I have no concern; but as a professor of eloquence, great concern in this undertaking. Our ancestors, the founders of this University, clearly showed, by assigning the professor of eloquence the task of delivering every year a speech exhorting our students to the study of the principles of various sciences and arts, that they felt he should be well versed in all fields of knowledge. Nor was it without reason that the great man, Bacon, when called upon to give advice to James, King of England, concerning the organization of a university, insisted that young scholars should not be admitted to the study of eloquence unless they had previously studied their way through the whole curriculum of learning.

What is eloquence, in effect, but wisdom, ornately and copiously delivered in words appropriate to the common opinion of mankind? Shall the professor of eloquence, to whom no student may have access unless previously trained in all sciences and arts, be ignorant of those subjects which are required by his teaching duties? The man who is deputed to exhort young students to grapple with all kinds of disciplines, and to discourse about their advantages and disadvantages, so that they may attain those and escape these, should he not be competent to expound his opinions on such knowledge?

For these reasons, teachers willing to bear this burden (a burden, I fear, vastly surpassing the strength of my shoulders) deserve to be likened, I feel, to C. Cilnius Maecenas, Crispus Sallustius, and other *equites illustres,* who, though possessed of financial means superior to those which the law prescribed for admission to senatorial rank, insisted on their wish to remain within the equestrian order. It was, therefore, not my duty alone as professor of eloquence, but my right as well to take up the subject of this discourse. What determined me was by no means the desire to diminish the prestige of a colleague or to place myself in the spotlight.

As you saw, whenever drawbacks had to be pointed out, I passed individual authors in silence; and whenever it was necessary to mention these authors, I did it with the utmost respect, since it was not for an unimportant man like me to censure persons so eminently great. As for the drawbacks, I sedulously set them forth as unobtrusively as possible.

From childhood, I have imposed on myself this rule (which the weakness of my fellow men has made a sacred one), to be as indulgent to the shortcomings of others as I would like others to be indulgent to my own, especially since others may have done many important things well, and failed only in a few cases, whereas I may have been guilty of countless errors in matters requiring but little ability.

In the present discourse, I have carefully refrained from any boasting; though my speech could have been pompously entitled "On the reconciliation of the study methods of antiquity with those of our time," I have preferred a more modest and usual designation. My purpose has been

> not to draw smoke from the brightness of light, but to bring out light from smokey murk.
>
> [Horace, *Ars poetica* 143]

I chose not to clothe my thought in high-sounding words, lest I should offend the intelligence of this assembly of listeners, every member of which knows how to reason with his own head and is fully conscious of his right to judge any author as he thinks best.

But, someone will object, "You were certainly bragging when you said that your theme was new." Not in the least. The fact that a theme is new is not automatically a recommendation; monstrous and ridiculous things may also be novelties. But to bring forward new things and to treat them in the right manner is unquestionably worthy of praise. Whether I did so, or not, I shall leave to the judgment of my listeners and to the common judgment of scholars, from whom, I vow, I shall never depart. In my life I have always had the greatest apprehension of being alone in wisdom; this kind of solitude exposes one to the danger of becoming either a god or a fool.

But, it will be urged, you have shown yourself thoroughly presumptuous in choosing a subject where you had to show a mastery of all learned disciplines and where you had to pass peremptory and pretentious judgment on them, as if you had been fully and deeply familiar with every one of them. To fend off the objection, I beg whosoever wants to press it to reflect on the kinds of judgments I have passed. Let him observe that a certain doctrine may be either beneficial or prejudicial to some persons; let him ascertain how the harm that such doctrine is likely to cause may be avoided. He will find out that judgment cannot be passed except by a man who has studied all of these matters, but

> of all these things, no one more deeply than all others, yet all of them indeed, in moderation.
>
> [Terence, *The Lady of Andros* 58–59]

It is a common experience to see an individual who has concentrated all of his efforts on a single branch of study, and who has spent all his life on it, think that this field is, by far, more important than all others, and to see him inclined to make application of its specialty to matters wholly foreign to it. This may be due to the weakness of our nature, which prompts us to take an inordinate delight in ourselves and in our own pursuits.

Though I am afraid of delivering false judgments on all subjects, I am particularly afraid of advancing erroneous views on eloquence, since I profess it.

After stating this in defense of my assignment and of the way I have discharged it, permit me to say that I shall be greatly indebted to any one who wishes to criticize with pertinence and with concrete reference to their intrinsic purport, the points that I have brought up, so as to free me from eventual errors. He will be certain to enlist my gratitude by his mere intent to do so.

INTRODUCTION TO GEORGE CAMPBELL

George Campbell lived from 1719 to 1796 in Scotland. Campbell spent most of his life as a minister. That vocation helped to shape his views on rhetoric because, like Vico, he wanted to combat the prevailing skepticism and doubt of his era (not surprising in a man of the Church). It was his business to instill beliefs and values in people, often through the rhetorical enterprise of preaching. Campbell also participated in discussions and presented papers at the Aberdeen Philosophical Society in Scotland. This was a group of philosophers who wanted to develop a sophisticated philosophy of the mind, among other things. In some ways, they were among the first modern psychologists.

Campbell's treatise, *The Philosophy of Rhetoric,* is just such an attempt to create a complex psychological understanding of humans, in his case from a rhetorical perspective. Campbell is trying to explain how the human mind works by considering how the human mind is persuaded. This work, excerpted here, was well received by scholars and speakers, and has been regarded as extremely influential in shaping rhetorical theory ever since.

The rhetorical theorists since ancient times had made little progress, Campbell and his colleagues believed, in explaining persuasion. Campbell thought that more sophisticated explanations could be provided by *faculty psychology.* He therefore extends the project begun earlier by Francis Bacon.

Early in the reading from *The Philosophy of Rhetoric,* Campbell defines rhetoric or eloquence as "that art or talent by which the discourse is adapted to its end." Those "ends" of rhetoric are understood in terms of effects upon the faculties of audiences, and Campbell explains four such ends. The rhetor might want to appeal to, or activate an audience's *understanding, imagination, passion* (*emotions*), or *will.* Rhetoric appeals to the understanding so as to *inform* or convince, to the imagination so as to *please,* to the passion so as to *move,* and to the will so as to *persuade.* Campbell extensively discusses how rhetoric activates each faculty and how the different faculties interact so as to produce the desired ends.

The ways in which rhetoric as a discourse is situated against other discourses is an interesting part of Campbell's theory. Note that he describes the relationship of rhetoric to logic and to grammar. Both rhetoric and logic, he argues, are concerned with the sense or ideas behind communication. And both rhetoric and grammar are concerned with the expression or form of communication. With this formulation, Campbell restores invention to rhetoric, for as an ally of logic it must now help to formulate the "sense" of rhetorical messages. Rhetoric retains its traditional role of expression, working with grammar to put ideas into the most effective and pleasing form.

Campbell also cleverly puts rhetoric on a more equal footing with science. He argues that there are two kinds of evidence that people use to acquire knowledge. The first kind he calls "intuitive," which is the sort of evidence that instantly produces knowledge when we confront it. Types of intuitive evidence are mathematical axioms, simple consciousness of the physical world, and what he calls common sense, or fundamental rules for everyday action. The second kind of evidence is not as simple as is intuitive evidence, and that he calls "deductive." This is evidence that must be created through complicated chains of reasoning and by incorporating the simpler intuitive evidence. The two kinds of deductive evidence are scientific and moral reasoning. Science rarely simply observes and concludes; it experiments, compares, contrasts, and considers evidence in order to produce knowledge. Moral reasoning, by which Campbell means consideration of choices and difficult decisions, likewise weighs many different elements of intuitive evidence as it produces conclusions. Rhetoric is of this second kind of reasoning, Campbell argues. Campbell's reasoning therefore describes rhetoric as the same sort of reasoning as science! Both involve assembling evidence and premises, then reasoning them out towards a conclusion.

Pursuing this comparison of rhetoric and science in ways that are favorable for the former, Campbell argues that science is reasoning about abstract and independent truth, while moral reasoning (rhetoric) is reasoning about matters that are changeable in the here and now. Science tries to establish truths that are absolute, whereas rhetoric tries to establish conclusions that are "more or less" true, or matters of degree. Science, once it discovers a truth, can never entertain a conclusion to the contrary, while rhetoric always entertains contrary conclusions. Finally, science uses simpler evidence and reasoning, while rhetoric always uses more complicated evidence and strings of proof. Although we may wish to question some of Campbell's claims, he is clearly finding a theoretical role for rhetoric as a kind of discourse that is the equal of science.

Campbell's work pursues a logic of how rhetorical discourse might appeal to different faculties to produce desired ends. His rhetorical theory is the most sophisticated use of faculty psychology to date. Yet it retains rhetoric's ancient role of adaptation to the audience and the audience's situation of the moment. Campbell therefore helps to bridge the gap between ancient rhetoric and the new theories of the twentieth century.

GEORGE CAMPBELL

THE PHILOSOPHY OF RHETORIC

BOOK I

THE NATURE AND FOUNDATIONS OF ELOQUENCE.

CHAPTER I

Eloquence in the largest acceptation defined, its more general forms exhibited, with their different objects, ends, and characters.

In speaking there is always some end proposed, or some effect which the speaker intends to produce on the hearer. The word *eloquence* in its greatest latitude denotes, "That art or talent by which the discourse is adapted to its end[1]."

All the ends of speaking are reducible to four; every speech being intended to enlighten the understanding, to please the imagination, to move the passions, or to influence the will.

Any one discourse admits only one of these ends as the principal. Nevertheless, in discoursing on a subject, many things may be introduced, which are more immediately and apparently directed to some of the other ends of speaking, and not to that which is the chief intent of the whole. But then these other and immediate ends are in effect but means, and must be rendered conducive to that which is the primary intention. Accordingly, the propriety or the impropriety of the introduction of such secondary ends, will always be inferred from their subserviency or want of subserviency to that end, which is, in respect of them, the ultimate. For example, a discourse addressed to the understanding, and calculated to illustrate or evince some point purely speculative, may borrow aid from the imagination, and admit metaphor and comparison, but not the bolder and more striking figures, as that called vision or fiction[1], prosopopœia, and the like, which are not so much intended to elucidate a subject, as to excite admiration. Still less will it admit an address to the passions, which, as it never fails to disturb the operation of the intellectual faculty, must be regarded by every intelligent hearer as foreign at least, if not insidious. It is obvious, that either of these, far from being subservient to the main design, would distract the attention from it.

There is indeed one kind of address to the understanding, and only one, which, it may not be improper to observe, disdains all assistance whatever from the fancy. The address I mean is mathematical demonstration. As this does not, like moral reasoning, admit degrees of evidence, its perfection, in point of eloquence, if so uncommon an application of the term may be allowed, consists in perspicuity. Perspicuity here results entirely

Edited by Lloyd F. Bitzer

[1] "Dicere secundum virtutem orationis. Scientia bene dicendi." Quintilian The word *eloquence*, in common conversation, is seldom used in such a comprehensive sense. I have, however, made choice of this definition on a double account: 1st. It exactly corresponds to Tully's idea of a perfect orator; "Optimus est orator qui dicendo animos audientium et docet, et delectat, et permovet." 2dly. It is best adapted to the subject of these papers. See the note on page 4.

[1] By vision or fiction is understood, that rhetorical figure of which Quintilian says, "Quas φαντασιας Græci vocant, nos sane *visiones* appellamus, per quas imagines rerum absentium ita repræsentantur animo, ut eas cernere oculis ac præsentes habere videamur."

from propriety and simplicity of diction, and from accuracy of method, where the mind is regularly, step by step, conducted forwards in the same track, the attention no way diverted, nothing left to be supplied, no one unnecessary word or idea introduced.[1] On the contrary, an harangue framed for affecting the hearts or influencing the resolves of an assembly, needs greatly the assistance both of intellect and of imagination.

In general it may be asserted, that each preceding species, in the order above exhibited, is preparatory to the subsequent; that each subsequent species is founded on the preceding; and that thus they ascend in a regular progression. Knowledge, the object of the intellect, furnisheth materials for the fancy; the fancy culls, compounds, and, by her mimic art, disposes these materials so as to affect the passions; the passions are the natural spurs to volition or action, and so need only to be right directed. This connexion and dependency will better appear from the following observations.

When a speaker addresseth himself to the understanding, he proposes the *instruction* of his hearers, and that, either by explaining some doctrine unknown, or not distinctly comprehended by them, or by proving some position disbelieved or doubted by them.—In other words, he proposes either to dispel ignorance or to vanquish error. In the one, his aim is their *information;* in the other, their *conviction.* Accordingly the predominant quality of the former is *perspicuity;* of the latter, *argument.* By that we are made to know, by this to believe.

The imagination is addressed by exhibiting to it a lively and beautiful representation of a suitable object. As in this exhibition, the task of the orator may, in some sort, be said, like that of the painter, to consist in imitation, the merit of the work results entirely from these two sources; dignity, as well in the subject or thing imitated, as in the manner of imitation; and resemblance, in the portrait or performance. Now the principal scope for this class being in narration and description, poetry, which is one mode of oratory, especially epic poetry, must be ranked under it. The effect of the dramatic, at least of tragedy, being upon the passions, the drama falls under another species, to be explained afterwards. But that kind of address of which I am now treating, attains the summit of perfection in the *sublime,* or those great and noble images, which, when in suitable colouring presented to the mind, do, as it were, distend the imagination with some vast conception, and quite ravish the soul.

The sublime, it may be urged, as it raiseth admiration, should be considered as one species of address to the passions. But this objection, when examined, will appear superficial. There are few words in any language (particularly such as relate to the operations and feelings of the mind) which are strictly univocal. Thus admiration, when persons are the object, is commonly used for a high degree of esteem; but when otherwise applied, it denotes solely an internal taste. It is that pleasurable sensation which instantly ariseth on the perception of magnitude, or of whatever is great and stupendous in its kind. For there is a greatness in the degrees of quality in spiritual subjects, analagous to that which subsists in the degrees of quantity in material things. Accordingly, in all tongues, perhaps without exception, the ordinary terms, which are considered as literally expressive of the latter, are also used promiscuously to denote the former. Now admiration, when thus applied, doth not require to its production, as the passions generally do, any reflex view of motives or tendencies, or of any relation either to private interest, or to the good of others; and ought therefore to be numbered among those original feelings of the

---

[1] Of this kind Euclid hath given us the most perfect models, which have not, I think, been sufficiently imitated by later mathematicians. In him you find the exactest arrangement inviolably observed, the properest and simplest, and by consequence the plainest expressions constantly used, nothing deficient, nothing superfluous; in brief, nothing which in more, or fewer, or other words, or words otherwise disposed, could have been better expressed.

mind, which are denominated by some the reflex senses, being of the same class with a taste for beauty, an ear for music, or our moral sentiments. Now, the immediate view of whatever is directed to the imagination (whether the subject be things inanimate or animal forms, whether characters, actions, incidents, or manner) terminates in the gratification of some internal taste: as a taste for the wonderful, the fair, the good; for elegance, for novelty, or for grandeur.

But it is evident, that this creative faculty, the fancy, frequently lends her aid in promoting still nobler ends. From her exuberant stores most of those tropes and figures are extracted, which, when properly employed, have such a marvellous efficacy in rousing the passions, and by some secret, sudden, and inexplicable association, awakening all the tenderest emotions of the heart. In this case, the address of the orator is not ultimately intended to astonish by the loftiness of his images, or to delight by the beauteous resemblance which his painting bears to nature; nay, it will not permit the hearers even a moment's leisure for making the comparison, but as it were by some magical spell, hurries them, ere they are aware, into love, pity, grief, terror, desire, aversion, fury, or hatred. It therefore assumes the denomination of *pathetic,*[1] which is the characteristic of the third species of discourse, that addressed to the passions.

Finally, as that kind, the most complex of all, which is calculated to influence the will, and persuade to a certain conduct, is in reality an artful mixture of that which proposes to convince the judgment, and that which interests the passions, its distinguished excellency results from these two, the argumentative and the pathetic incorporated together. These acting with united force, and, if I may so express myself, in concert, constitute that passionate eviction, that *vehemence* of contention, which is admirably fitted for persuasion, and hath always been regarded as the supreme qualification in an orator.[1] It is this which bears down every obstacle, and procures the speaker an irresistible power over the thoughts and purposes of his audience. It is this which hath been so justly celebrated as giving one man an ascendant over others, superior even to what despotism itself can bestow; since by the latter the more ignoble part only, the body and its members are enslaved; whereas from

[1] I am sensible that this word is commonly used in a more limited sense, for that which only excites commiseration. *Perhaps* the word *impassioned* would answer better.

[1] This animated reasoning the Greek rhetoricians termed δεινοτης, which from signifying the principal excellency in an orator, came at length to denote oratory itself. And as vehemence and eloquence became synonymous, the latter, suitably to this way of thinking, was sometimes defined the *art of persuasion.* But that this definition is defective, appears even from their own writings, since in a consistency with it, their rhetorics could not have comprehended those orations called *demonstrative,* the design of which was not to persuade but to please. Yet it is easy to discover the origin of this defect, and that both from the nature of the thing, and from the customs which obtained among both Greeks and Romans. First, from the nature of the thing, for to persuade presupposes in some degree, and therefore may be understood to imply, all the other talents of an orator, to enlighten, to evince, to paint, to astonish, to inflame; but this doth not hold inversely; one may explain with clearness, and prove with energy, who is incapable of the sublime, the pathetic, and the vehement: besides, this power of persuasion, or, as Cicero calls it, "Posse voluntates hominum impellere quo velis, unde velis, deducere," as it makes a man master of his hearers, is the most considerable in respect of consequences. Secondly, from ancient customs. All their public orations were ranked under three classes, the demonstrative, the judiciary, and the deliberative. In the two last it was impossible to rise to eminence, without that important talent, the power of persuasion. These were in much more frequent use than the first, and withal the surest means of advancing both the fortune and the fame of the orator; for as on the judiciary the lives and estates of private persons depended, on the deliberative hung the resolves of senates, the fate of kingdoms, nay, of the most renowned republics the world ever knew. Consequently, to excel in these, must have been the direct road to riches, honours, and preferment. No wonder, then, that persuasion should almost wholly engross the rhetorician's notice.

the dominion of the former, nothing is exempted, neither judgment nor affection, not even the inmost recesses, the most latent movements of the soul. What opposition is he not prepared to conquer, on whose arms reason hath conferred solidity and weight, and passion such a sharpness as enables them, in defiance of every obstruction, to open a speedy passage to the heart?

It is not, however, every kind of pathos, which will give the orator so great an ascendancy over the minds of his hearers. All passions are not alike capable of producing this effect. Some are naturally inert and torpid; they deject the mind, and indispose it for enterprise. Of this kind are sorrow, fear, shame, humility. Others, on the contrary, elevate the soul, and stimulate to action. Such are hope, patriotism, ambition, emulation, anger. These, with the greatest facility, are made to concur in direction with arguments exciting to resolution and activity: and are, consequently, the fittest for producing, what for want of a better term in our language, I shall henceforth denominate the *vehement.* There is, besides, an intermediate kind of passions, which do not so congenially and directly either restrain us from acting, or incite us to act; but, by the art of the speaker, can, in an oblique manner, be made conducive to either. Such are joy, love, esteem, compassion. Nevertheless, all these kinds may find a place in suasory discourses, or such as are intended to operate on the will. The first is properest for dissuading; the second, as hath been already hinted, for persuading; the third is equally accommodated to both.

Guided by the above reflections, we may easily trace that connexion in the various forms of eloquence, which was remarked on, distinguishing them by their several objects. The imagination is charmed by a finished picture, wherein even drapery and ornament are not neglected; for here the end is pleasure. Would we penetrate further, and agitate the soul, we must exhibit only some vivid strokes, some expressive features, not decorated as for show (all ostentation being both despicable and hurtful here), but such as appear the natural exposition of those bright and deep impressions, made by the subject upon the speaker's mind; for here the end is not pleasure, but emotion. Would we not only touch the heart, but win it entirely to co-operate with our views, those affecting lineaments must be so interwoven with our argument, as that, from the passion excited our reasoning may derive importance, and so be fitted for commanding attention; and by the justness of the reasoning the passion may be more deeply rooted and enforced; and that thus both may be made to conspire in effectuating that persuasion which is the end proposed. For here, if I may adopt the schoolmen's language, we do not argue to gain barely the assent of the understanding, but, which is infinitely more important, the consent of the will.[1]

To prevent mistakes, it will not be beside my purpose further to remark, that several of the terms above explained are sometimes used by rhetoricians and critics in a much larger and more vague signification, than has been given them here. Sublimity and vehemence, in particular, are often confounded, the latter being considered as a species of the former. In this manner has this subject been treated by that great master Longinus, whose acceptation of the term *sublime* is extremely indefinite, importing an eminent degree of almost any excellence of speech, of whatever kind. Doubtless, if things themselves be understood, it does not seem material what names are assigned them. Yet it is both more accurate, and proves no inconsiderable aid to the right understanding of things, to discriminate by different signs such as are truly different. And that the two qualities above mentioned are of this number is undeniable, since we can produce passages full of vehemence, wherein no image is presented, which, with any

---

[1] This subordination is beautifully and concisely expressed by Hersan in Rollin, "Je conclus que la veritable eloquence est celle qui persuade; qu'elle ne persuade ordinairement qu'en touchant; qu'elle ne touche que par des choses et par des idées palpables."

propriety, can be termed great or sublime.[1] In matters of criticism, as in the abstract sciences, it is of the utmost consequence to ascertain, with precision, the meanings of words, and, as nearly as the genius of the language in which one writes will permit, to make them correspond to the boundaries assigned by Nature to the things signified. That the lofty and the vehement, though still distinguishable, are sometimes combined, and act with united force, is not to be denied. It is then only that the orator can be said to fight with weapons which are at once sharp, massive, and refulgent, which, like heaven's artillery, dazzle while they strike, which overpower the sight and the heart at the same instant. How admirably do the two forenamed qualities, when happily blended, correspond in the rational, to the thunder and lightning in the natural world, which are not more awfully majestical in sound and aspect, than irresistible in power.[1]

Thus much shall suffice for explaining the spirit, the intent, and the distinguishing qualities

---

[1] For an instance of this, let that of Cicero against Antony suffice. "Tu istis faucibus, istis lateribus, ista gladiatoria totius corporis firmitate, tantum vini in Hippiæ nuptiis exhauseras, ut tibi necesse esset in populi Romani conspectu vomere postridie. O rem non modo visu fœdam, sed etiam auditu! Si hoc tibi inter cœnam, in tuis immanibus illis poculis accidisset, quis non turpe duceret? In cætu vero populi Romani, negotium publicum gerens, magister equitum, cui ructare turpe esset, is vomens, frustis esculentis vinum redolentibus gremium suum et totum tribunal implevit." Here the vivacity of the address, in turning from the audience to the person declaimed against, the energy of the expressions, the repetition, exclamation, interrogation, and climax of aggravating circumstances, accumulated with rapidity upon one another, display in the strongest light the turpitude of the action, and thus at once convince the judgment and fire the indignation. It is therefore justly styled vehement. But what is the image it presents? The reverse in every respect of the sublime; what, instead of gazing on with admiration, we should avert our eyes from with abhorrence. For, however it might pass in a Roman senate, I question whether Ciceronian eloquence itself could excuse the uttering of such things in any modern assembly, not to say a polite one. With vernacular expressions, answering to these, "vomere, ructare, frustis esculentis vinum redolentibus," our more delicate ears would be immoderately shocked. In a case of this kind the more lively the picture is, so much the more abominable it is.

[1] A noted passage in Cicero's oration for Cornelius Balbus will serve as an example of the union of sublimity with vehemence. Speaking of Pompey, who had rewarded the valour and public services of our orator's client, by making him a Roman citizen, he says, "Utrum enim inscientem vultis contra fœdera fecisse, an scientem? Si scientem, O nomen nostri imperii, O populi Romani excellens dignitas, O Cneii Pompeii sie late longeque diffusa laus, ut ejus gloriæ domieilium communis imperii finibus terminetur: O nationes, urbes, populi, reges, tetrarelæ, tyranni, testes Cneii Pompeii non solum virtutis in bello, sed etiam religionis in pace: vos denique mutæ regiones imploro, et sola terrarum ultimarum, vos maria, portus, insulæ, littoraque; quæ est enim ora, quæ sedes, qui locus, in quo non extent hujus eum fortitudinis, tum vero humanitatis, tum animi, tum consilii, impressa vestigia! Hune quisquam incredibili quâdam at que inauditâ gravitate, virtute, constantiâ præditum fædera scientem neglexisse, violàsse, rupisæ, dicere audebit?" Here every thing conspires to aggrandize the hero, and exalt him to something more than mortal in the minds of the auditory; at the same time, every thing inspires the most perfect veneration for his character, and the most entire confidence in his integrity and judgment. The whole world is exhibited as no more than a sufficient theatre for such a superior genius to act upon. How noble is the idea! All the nations and potentates of the earth are, in a manner, produced as witnesses of his valour and his truth. Thus the orator at once fills the imagination with the immensity of the object, kindles in the breast an ardour of affection and gratitude, and, by so many accumulated evidences, convinces the understanding, and silences every doubt. Accordingly, the effect which the words above quoted, and some other things advanced in relation to the same personage, had upon the audience, as we learn from Quintilian, was quite extraordinary. They extorted from them such demonstrations of their applause and admiration, as he acknowledges to have been but ill-suited to the place and the occasion. He excuses it, however, because he considers it, not as a voluntary, but as a necessary consequence of the impression made upon the minds of the people. His words are remarkable, "Atque ego illos credo qui aderant, nee sensisse quid facerent, nee sponte judicioque plausisse; sed velut mente captos, et quo essent in loco ignaros, erupisse in hune voluntatis affectum," lib. viii. cap. 3. Without doubt, a considerable share of the effect ought to be ascribed to the immense advantage which the action and pronunciation of the orator would give to his expression.

of each of the forementioned sorts of address; all of which agree in this, an accommodation to affairs of a serious and important nature.

• • •

CHAPTER IV

Of the relation which eloquence bears to logic and to grammar.

In contemplating a human creature, the most natural division of the subject is the common division into soul and body, or into the living principle of perception and of action, and that system of material organs by which the other receives information from without, and is enabled to exert its powers, both for its own benefit and for that of the species. Analogous to this, there are two things in every discourse which principally claim our attention, the sense and the expression; or in other words, the thought and the symbol by which it is communicated. These may be said to constitute the soul and the body of an oration, or indeed of whatever is signified to another by language. For, as in man, each of these constituent parts hath its distinctive attributes, and as the perfection of the latter consisteth in its fitness for serving the purposes of the former, so it is precisely with those two essential parts of every speech, the sense and the expression. Now, it is by the sense that rhetoric holds of logic, and by the expression that she holds of grammar.

The sole and ultimate end of logic is the eviction of truth; one important end of eloquence, though, as appears from the first chapter, neither the sole, nor always the ultimate, is the conviction of the hearers. Pure logic regards only the subject, which is examined solely for the sake of information. Truth, as such, is the proper aim of the examiner. Eloquence not only considers the subject, but also the speaker and the hearers, and both the subject and the speaker for the sake of the hearers, or rather for the sake of the effect intended to be produced in them. Now, to convince the hearers is always either proposed by the orator, as his end in addressing them, or supposed to accompany the accomplishment of his end. Of the five sorts of discourses above mentioned, there are only two wherein conviction is the avowed purpose. One is that addressed to the understanding, in which the speaker proposeth to prove some position disbelieved or doubted by the hearers; the other is that which is calculated to influence the will, and persuade to a certain conduct; for it is by convincing the judgment that he proposeth to interest the passions and fix the resolution. As to the three other kinds of discourses enumerated, which address the understanding, the imagination, and the passions, conviction, though not the end, ought ever to accompany the accomplishment of the end. It is never formally proposed as an end where there are not supposed to be previous doubts or errors to conquer. But when due attention is not paid to it, by a proper management of the subject, doubts, disbelief, and mistake will be raised by the discourse itself, where there were none before, and these will not fail to obstruct the speaker's end, whatever it be. In explanatory discourses, which are of all kinds the simplest, there is a certain precision of manner which ought to pervade the whole, and which, though not in the form of argument, is not the less satisfactory, since it carries internal evidence along with it. In harangues pathetic or panegyrical, in order that the hearers may be moved or pleased, it is of great consequence to impress them with the belief of the reality of the subject. Nay, even in those performances where truth, in regard to the individual facts related, is neither sought nor expected, as in some sorts of poetry, and in romance, truth still is an object to the mind, the general truths regarding character, manners, and incidents. When these are preserved, the piece may justly be denominated true, considered as a picture of life; though false, considered as a narrative of particular events. And even these untrue events must be counterfeits of truth, and bear its image; for in cases wherein the proposed end can be rendered consistent with unbelief, it cannot be rendered compatible with incredibility. Thus, in order to satisfy the mind, in most cases, truth, and in every case, what bears the semblance of truth, must be presented to it. This holds equally, whatever be the declared aim of the speaker. I need scarcely add, that to prove a particular point is often occasionally necessary in every sort of discourse, as a subordinate end conducive to the advancement of the principal. If then it is the business of logic to evince the truth, to convince an auditory, which is the province of eloquence, is but a particular application of the logician's art. As logic therefore forges the arms which eloquence teacheth us to wield, we must first have recourse to the former, that being made acquainted with the materials of which her weapons and armour are severally made, we may know their respective strength and temper, and when and how each is to be used.

Now, if it be by the sense or soul of the discourse that rhetoric holds of logic, or the art of thinking and reasoning, it is by the expression or body of the discourse that she holds of grammar, or the art of conveying our thoughts in the words of a particular language. The observation of one analogy naturally suggests another. As the soul is of heavenly extraction and the body of earthly, so the sense of the discourse ought to have its source in the invariable nature of truth and right, whereas the expression can derive its energy only from the arbitrary conventions of men, sources as unlike, or rather as widely different, as the breath of the Almighty and the dust of the earth. In every region of the globe we may soon discover, that people feel and argue in much the same manner, but the speech of one nation is quite unintelligible to another. The art of the logician is accordingly, in some sense, universal; the art of the grammarian is always particular and local. The rules of argumentation laid down by Aristotle, in his Analytics, are of as much use for the discovery of truth in Britain or China as they were in Greece; but Priscian's rules of inflection and construction can assist us in learning no language but Latin. In propriety there cannot be such a thing as an universal grammar, unless there were such a thing as an universal language. The term hath sometimes, indeed, been applied to a collection of observations on the similar analogies that have been discovered in all tongues, ancient and modern, known to the authors of such collections. I do not mention this liberty in the use of the term with a view to censure it. In the application of technical or learned words, an author hath greater scope than in the application of those which are in more frequent use, and is only then thought censurable when he exposeth himself to be misunderstood. But it is to my purpose to observe that, as such collections convey the knowledge of no tongue whatever, the name *grammar,* when applied to them, is used in a sense quite different from that which it has in the common acceptation; perhaps as different, though the subject be language, as when it is applied to a system of geography.

Now, the grammatical art hath its completion in syntax; the oratorical, as far as the body or expression is concerned, in style. Syntax regards only the composition of many words into one sentence; style, at the same time that it attends to this, regards further the composition of many sentences into one discourse. Nor is this the only difference; the grammarian, with respect to what the two arts have in common, the structure of sentences, requires only purity; that is, that the words employed belong to the language, and that they be construed in the manner, and used in the signification, which custom hath rendered necessary for conveying the sense. The orator requires also beauty and strength. The highest aim of the former is the lowest aim of the latter; where grammar ends eloquence begins.

Thus the grammarian's department bears much the same relation to the orator's which the art of the mason bears to that of the architect. There is, however, one difference that well deserves our notice. As in architecture it is not necessary that he who designs should execute his own plans, he may be an excellent artist in this way who would handle very awkwardly the hammer and the trowel. But it is alike incumbent on the orator to design and to execute. He must, therefore, be master of the language he speaks or writes, and must be capable of adding to grammatic purity those higher qualities of elocution which will render his discourse graceful and energetic.

So much for the connexion that subsists between rhetoric and these parent arts, logic and grammar.

CHAPTER V

Of the different sources of Evidence, and the different Subjects to which they are respectively adapted.

LOGICAL truth consisteth in the conformity of our conceptions to their archetypes in the nature of things. This conformity is perceived by the mind, either immediately on a bare attention to the ideas under review, or mediately by a comparison of these with other related ideas. Evidence of the former kind is called intuitive; of the latter, deductive.

SECTION I.—OF INTUITIVE EVIDENCE.

PART I.—MATHEMATICAL AXIOMS.

Of intuitive evidence there are different sorts. One is that which results purely from *intellection.*[1] Of this kind is the evidence of these propositions: "One and four make five—Things equal to the same thing are equal to one another—The whole is greater than a part;" and, in brief, all axioms in arithmetic and geometry. These are, in effect, but so many different expositions of our own general notions, taken in different views. Some of them are no other than definitions, or equivalent to definitions. To say, "One and four make *five,*" is precisely the same as to say, "We give the name of *five* to one added to four." In fact, they are all, in some respect, reducible to this axiom, "Whatever is, is." I do not say they are deduced from it, for they have in like manner that original and intrinsic evidence, which makes them, as soon as the terms are understood, to be perceived intuitively. And if they are not thus perceived, no deduction of reason will ever confer on them any additional evidence. Nay, in point of time, the discovery of the less general truths has the priority, not from their superior evidence, but solely from this consideration, that the less general are sooner objects of perception to us, the natural progress of the mind, in the acquisition of its ideas, being from particular things to universal notions, and not inversely. But I affirm that, though not deduced from that axiom, they may be considered as particular exemplifications of it, and coincident with it, inasmuch as they are all implied in this, that the properties of our clear and adequate ideas can be no other than what the mind clearly perceives them to be.

But, in order to prevent mistakes, it will be necessary further to illustrate this subject. It might be thought that if axioms were propositions perfectly identical, it would be impossible to advance a step, by their means, beyond the simple ideas first perceived by the mind. And it must be owned, if the predicate of the proposition were nothing but a repetition of the subject, under the same aspect, and in the same or synonymous terms, no conceivable advantage could be made of it for the furtherance of knowledge. Of such propositions as these for instance, "Seven are seven," "eight are eight," and "ten added to eleven, are equal to ten added to eleven," it is manifest, that we could

---

[1] I have here adopted the term *intellection* rather than *perception,* because, though not so usual, it is both more apposite and less equivocal. *Perception* is employed alike to denote every immediate object of thought, or whatever is apprehended by the mind, our sensations themselves, and those qualities in body suggested by our sensations, the ideas of these upon reflection, whether remembered or imagined, together with those called general notions, or abstract ideas. It is only the last of these kinds which are considered as peculiarly the object of the understanding, and which, therefore, require to be distinguished by a peculiar name. Obscurity arising from an uncommon word is easily surmounted, whereas ambiguity, by misleading us, ere we are aware, confounds our notion of the subject altogether.

never avail ourselves of them for the improvement of science. Nor does the change of the name make any alteration in point of utility. The propositions, "Twelve are a dozen," "twenty are a score," unless considered as explications of the words *dozen* and *score,* are equally insignificant with the former. But when the thing, though in effect coinciding, is considered under a different aspect; when what is single in the subject is divided in the predicate, and conversely; or when what is a whole in the one is regarded as a part of something else in the other; such propositions lead to the discovery of innumerable and apparently remote relations. One added to four may be accounted no other than a definition of the word *five,* as was remarked above. But when I say, "Two added to three are equal to five," I advance a truth, which, though equally clear, is quite distinct from the preceding. Thus, if one should affirm, "Twice fifteen make thirty," and again, "Thirteen added to seventeen make thirty," nobody would pretend that he had repeated the same proposition in other words. The cases are entirely similar. In both, the same thing is predicated of ideas which, taken severally, are different. From these again result other equations, as, "One added to four are equal to two added to three," and "twice fifteen are equal to thirteen added to seventeen."

Now, it is by the aid of such simple and elementary principles, that the arithmetician and the algebraist proceed to the most astonishing discoveries. Nor are the operations of the geometrician essentially different. By a very few steps you are made to perceive the equality, or rather the coincidence, of the sum of the two angles formed by one straight line falling on another, with two right angles. By a process equally plain you are brought to discover, first, that if one side of a triangle be produced, the external angle will be equal to both the internal and opposite angles, and then, that all the angles of a triangle are equal to two right angles. So much for the nature and use of the first kind of intuitive evidence, resulting from pure intellection.

PART II.—CONSCIOUSNESS.

The next kind is that which ariseth from *consciousness.* Hence every man derives the perfect assurance that he hath of his own existence. Nor is he only in this way assured that he exists, but that he thinks, that he feels, that he sees, that he hears, and the like. Hence his absolute certainty in regard to the reality of his sensations and passions, and of every thing whose essence consists in being perceived. Nor does this kind of intuition regard only the truth of the original feelings or impressions, but also many of the judgments that are formed by the mind, on comparing these one with another. Thus the judgments we daily and hourly form, concerning resemblances or disparities in visible objects, or size in things tangible, where the odds is considerable, darker or lighter tints in colours, stronger or weaker tastes or smells, are all self-evident, and discoverable at once. It is from the same principle that, in regard to ourselves, we judge infallibly concerning the feelings, whether pleasant or painful, which we derive from what are called the internal senses, and pronounce concerning beauty or deformity, harmony or discord, the elegant or the ridiculous. The difference between this kind of intuition and the former will appear on the slightest reflection. The former concerns only abstract notions and ideas, particularly in regard to number and extension, the objects purely of the understanding; the latter concerns only the existence of the mind itself, and its actual feelings, impressions or affections, pleasures or pains, the immediate subjects of sense, taking that word in the largest acceptation. The former gives rise to those universal truths, first principles or axioms, which serve as the foundation of abstract science; whereas the latter, though absolutely essential to the individual, yet as it only regards particular perceptions, which represent no distinct genus or species of objects, the judgments resulting thence cannot form any general positions to which a chain of reasoning may be fastened, and consequently are not of the nature of axioms, though both similar and equal in respect of evidence.

Part III.—Common Sense.

The third sort is that which ariseth from what hath been termed properly enough, *common sense,*[1] as being an original source of knowledge common to all mankind. I own, indeed, that in different persons it prevails in different degrees of strength; but no human creature hath been found originally and totally destitute of it, who is not accounted a monster in his kind; for such, doubtless, are all idiots and changelings. By madness, a disease which makes terrible havoc on the faculties of the mind, it may be in a great measure, but is never entirely lost.

---

[1] The first among the moderns who took notice of this principle, as one of the genuine springs of our knowledge, was Buffier, a French philosopher of the present century, in a book entitled *Traité des premières Vérités;* one who to an uncommon degree of acuteness in matters of abstraction added that solidity of judgment which hath prevented in him, what had proved the wreck of many great names in philosophy, his understanding becoming the dupe of his ingenuity. This doctrine hath lately, in our own country, been set in the clearest light, and supported by invincible force of argument, by two very able writers in the science of man, Dr. Reid, in his *Inquiry into the Human Mind,* and Dr. Beattie, in his *Essay on the Immutability of Truth.* I beg leave to remark in this place, that, though for distinction's sake, I use the term *common sense* in a more limited signification than either of the authors last mentioned, there appears to be no real difference in our sentiments of the thing itself. I am not ignorant that this doctrine has been lately attacked by Dr. Priestley in a most extraordinary manner, a manner which no man, who has any regard to the name either of Englishman or of philosopher, will ever desire to see imitated, in this or any other country. I have read the performance, but have not been able to discover the author's sentiments in relation to the principal point in dispute. He says expressly, [Examination of Dr. Reid's Inquiry, &c. p. 119,] "Had these writers," Messieurs Reid, Beattie, and Oswald, "assumed as the elements of their common sense certain truths which are so plain that no man could doubt of them, (without entering into the ground of our assent to them,) their conduct would have been liable to very little objection." And is not this the very thing which these writers have done? What he means to signify by the parenthesis, "(without entering into the ground of our assent to them,)" it is not easy to guess. By a ground of assent to any proposition is commonly understood a reason or argument in support of it. Now, by his own hypothesis, there are truths so plain, that no man can doubt of them. If so, what ground of assent beyond their own plainness ought we to seek; what beside this can we ever hope to find, or what better reason needs be given for denominating such truths the dictates of common sense? If something plainer could be found to serve as evidence of any of them, then this plainer truth would be admitted as the first principle, and the other would be considered as deduced by reasoning. But notwithstanding the mistake in the instance, the general doctrine of primary truths would remain unhurt. It seems, however, that though their conduct would have been liable to very little, it would have been liable to some objection. "All that could have been said would have been, that, without any necessity, they had made an innovation in the received use of the term." I have a better opinion of these gentlemen than to imagine, that if the thing which they contend for be admitted, they will enter into a dispute with any person about the name: though, in my judgment, even as to this, it is not they, but he, who is the innovator. He proceeds, "For no person ever denied that there are self-evident truths, and that these must be assumed, as the foundation of all our reasoning. I never met with any person who did not acknowledge this, or heard of any argumentative treatise that did not go on the supposition of it." Now, if this be the case, I would gladly know what is the great point he controverts. Is it, whether such self-evident truths shall be denominated principles of Common Sense, or be distinguished by some other appellation? Was it worth any man's while to write an octavo of near 400 pages, for the discussion of such a question as this? And if, as he assures us, they have said more than is necessary, in proof of a truth which he himself thinks indisputable, was it no more than necessary in Dr. Priestley to compose so large a volume, in order to convince the world that too much had been said already on the subject? I do not enter into the examination of his objections to some of the particular principles produced as primary truths. An attempt of this kind would be foreign to my purpose; besides that the authors he has attacked are better qualified for defending their own doctrine, and no doubt will do it, if they think there is occasion. I shall only subjoin two remarks on this book. The first is, that the author, through the whole, confounds two things totally distinct, certain associations of ideas, and certain judgments implying belief, which, though in some, are not in all cases, and therefore not necessarily, connected with association. And if so, merely to account for the association is in no case to account for the belief with which it is attended. Nay, admitting his plea, [page 86,] that by the principle of association not only the ideas but the concomitant

It is purely hence that we derive our assurance of such truths as these: "Whatever has a beginning has a cause"—"When there is in the effect a manifest adjustment of the several parts to a certain end, there is intelligence in the cause." "The course of nature will be the same to-morrow that it is to-day; or, the future will resemble the past"—"There is such a thing as body; or, there are material substances independent of the mind's conceptions"—"There are other intelligent beings in the universe besides me"—"The clear representations of my memory, in regard to past events, are indubitably true." These, and a great many more of the same kind, it is impossible for any man by reasoning to evince, as might easily be shown, were this a proper place for the discussion. And it is equally impossible, without a full conviction of them, to advance a single step in the acquisition of knowledge, especially in all that regards mankind, life, and conduct.

I am sensible that some of these, to men not accustomed to inquiries of this kind, will appear at first not to be primary principles, but conclusions from other principles; and some of them will be thought to coincide with the other kinds of intuition above mentioned. Thus the first, "Whatever hath a beginning hath a cause," may be thought to stand on the same footing with mathematical axioms. I acknowledge that in point of evidence they are equal, and it is alike impossible, in either case, for a rational creature to withhold his assent. Nevertheless, there is a difference in kind. All the axioms in mathematics are but the enunciations of certain properties in our abstract notions, distinctly perceived by the mind, but have no relation to any thing without themselves, and can never be made the foundation of any conclusion concerning actual existence; whereas, in the axiom last specified, from the existence of one thing we intuitively conclude the existence of another. This proposition, however, so far differs, in my apprehension, from others of the same order, that I cannot avoid considering the opposite assertion as not only false but contradictory; but I do not pretend to explain the ground of this difference.

The faith we give to memory may be thought, on a superficial view, to be resolvable into consciousness, as well as that we give to the immediate impressions of sense. But on a little attention one may easily perceive the difference. To believe the report of our senses doth indeed commonly imply to believe the existence of certain external and corporeal objects, which give rise to our particular sensations. This, I acknowledge, is a principle which doth not spring from consciousness, (for consciousness cannot extend be-

---

belief may be accounted for, even this does not invalidate the doctrine he impugns. For, let it be observed that it is one thing to assign a cause which, from the mechanism of our nature, has given rise to a particular tenet or belief, and another thing to produce a reason by which the understanding has been convinced. Now, unless this be done as to the principles in question, they must be considered as primary truths, in respect of the understanding, which never deduced them from other truths, and which is under a necessity, in all moral reasonings, of founding upon them. In fact, to give any other account of our conviction of them is to confirm instead of confuting the doctrine, that in all argumentation they must be regarded as primary truths, or truths which reason never inferred, through any medium, from other truths previously perceived. My second remark is, that though this examiner has, from Dr. Reid, given us a catalogue of first principles, which he deems unworthy of the honourable place assigned them, he has no where thought proper to give us a list of those self-evident truths which, by his own account, and in his own express words, "must be assumed as the foundation of all our reasoning." How much light might have been thrown upon the subject by the contrast! Perhaps we should have been enabled, on the comparison, to discover some distinctive characters in his genuine axioms, which would have preserved us from the danger of confounding them with their spurious ones. Nothing is more evident than that, in whatever regards matter of fact, the mathematical axioms will not answer. These are purely fitted for evolving the abstract relations of quantity. This he in effect owns himself [page 39]. It would have been obliging, then, and would have greatly contributed to shorten the controversy, if he had given us at least a specimen of those self-evident principles, which, in his estimation, are the *ne plus ultra* of moral reasoning.

yond sensation,) but from common sense, as well as the assurance we have in the report of memory. But this was not intended to be included under the second branch of intuitive evidence. By that firm belief in sense, which I there resolved into consciousness, I meant no more than to say, I am certain that I see, and feel, and think, what I actually see, and feel, and think. As in this I pronounce only concerning my own present feelings, whose essence consists in being felt, and of which I am at present conscious, my conviction is reducible to this axiom, or coincident with it, "It is impossible for a thing to be and not to be at the same time." Now when I say, I trust entirely to the clear report of my memory, I mean a good deal more than, "I am certain that my memory gives such a report, or represents things in such a manner," for this conviction I have indeed from consciousness; but I mean, "I am certain that things happened heretofore at such a time, in the precise manner in which I now remember that they then happened." Thus there is a reference in the ideas of memory to former sensible impressions, to which there is nothing analogous in sensation. At the same time it is evident, that remembrance is not always accompanied with this full conviction. To describe, in words, the difference between those lively signatures of memory, which command an unlimited assent, and those fainter traces which raise opinion only, or even doubt, is perhaps impracticable; but no man stands in need of such assistance to enable him in fact to distinguish them, for the direction of his own judgment and conduct. Some may imagine that it is from experience we come to know what faith in every case is due to memory. But it will appear more fully afterwards, that unless we had implicitly relied on the distinct and vivid informations of that faculty, we could not have moved a step towards the acquisition of experience. It must, however, be admitted, that experience is of use in assisting us to judge concerning the more languid and confused suggestions of memory; or, to speak more properly, concerning the reality of those things, of which we ourselves are doubtful whether we remember them or not.

In regard to the primary truths of this order, it may be urged that it cannot be affirmed of them all at least, as it may of the axioms in mathematics, or the assurances we have from consciousness, that the denial of them implies a manifest contradiction. It is, perhaps, physically possible that the course of nature will be inverted the very next moment; that my memory is no other than a delirium, and my life a dream; that all is mere illusion; that I am the only being in the universe, and that there is no such thing as body. Nothing can be juster than the reply given by Buffier, "It must be owned," says he,[1] "that to maintain propositions, the reverse of the primary truths of common sense, doth not imply a contradiction; it only implies insanity." But if any person, on account of this difference in the nature of these two classes of axioms, should not think the term intuitive so properly applied to the evidence of the last mentioned, let him denominate it, if he please, instinctive: I have no objection to the term; nor do I think it derogates in the least from the dignity, the certainty, or the importance of the truths themselves. Such instincts are no other than the oracles of eternal wisdom.

For, let it be observed further, that axioms of this last kind are as essential to moral reasoning, to all deductions concerning life and existence, as those of the first kind are to the sciences of arithmetic and geometry. Perhaps it will appear afterwards that, without the aid of some of them, these sciences themselves would be utterly inaccessible to us. Besides, the mathematical axioms can never extend their influence beyond the precincts of abstract knowledge, in regard to number and extension, or assist us in the discovery of any matter of fact: whereas, with knowledge of the latter kind, the whole conduct and business of human life is principally and intimately connected. All reasoning

[1] Premières Vérités, Part i. Chap. xi.

necessarily supposes that there are certain principles in which we must acquiesce, and beyond which we cannot go—principles clearly discernible by their own light, which can derive no additional evidence from any thing besides. On the contrary supposition, the investigation of truth would be an endless and a fruitless task; we should be eternally proving, whilst nothing could ever be proved; because, by the hypothesis, we could never ascend to premises which require no proof. "If there be no first truths," says the author lately quoted,[1] "there can be no second truths, nor third, nor indeed any truth at all."

So much for intuitive evidence, in the extensive meaning which hath here been given to that term, as including every thing whose evidence results from the simple contemplation of the ideas or perceptions which form the proposition under consideration, and requires not the intervention of any third idea as a medium of proof. This, for order's sake, I have distributed into three classes, the truths of pure intellection, of consciousness, and of common sense. The first may be denominated metaphysical, the second physical, the third moral; all of them natural, original, and unaccountable.

[1] 1b. Dessein de l'Ouvrage.

SECTION II.—OF DEDUCTIVE EVIDENCE.

PART I.—DIVISION OF THE SUBJECT INTO SCIENTIFIC AND MORAL, WITH THE PRINCIPAL DISTINCTIONS BETWEEN THEM.

All rational or deductive evidence is derived from one or other of these two sources: from the invariable properties or relations of general ideas; or from the actual, though perhaps variable connexions subsisting among things. The former we call demonstrative, the latter moral. Demonstration is built on pure intellection, and consisteth in an uninterrupted series of axioms. That propositions formerly demonstrated are taken into the series, doth not in the least invalidate this account; inasmuch as these propositions are all resolvable into axioms, and are admitted as links in the chain; not because necessary, but merely to avoid the useless prolixity which frequent and tedious repetition of proofs formerly given would occasion. Moral evidence is founded on the principles we have from consciousness and common sense, improved by experience; and as it proceeds on this general presumption or moral axiom, that the course of nature in time to come will be similar to what it hath been hitherto, it decides, in regard to particulars, concerning the future from the past, and concerning things unknown from things familiar to us. The first is solely conversant about number and extension, and about those other qualities which are measurable by these. Such are duration, velocity, and weight. With regard to such qualities as pleasure and pain, virtue and vice, wisdom and folly, beauty and deformity, though they admit degrees, yet, as there is no standard or common measure, by which their differences and proportions can be ascertained and expressed in numbers, they can never become the subject of demonstrative reasoning. Here rhetoric, it must be acknowledged, hath little to do. Simplicity of diction, and precision in arrangement, whence results perspicuity, are, as was observed already,[1] all the requisites. The proper province of rhetoric is the second, or moral evidence; for to the second belong all decisions concerning fact, and things without us.

But that the nature of moral evidence may be better understood, it will not be amiss to remark a few of the most eminent differences between this and the demonstrative.

[1] Chap. i.

The first difference that occurs is in their subjects. The subject of the one is, as hath been observed, abstract independent truth, or the unchangeable and necessary relations of ideas; that of the other, the real but often changeable and contingent connexions that subsist among things actually existing. Abstract truths, as the properties of quantity, have no respect to time or to place, no dependence on the volition of any being, or on any cause whatever, but are eternally and immutably the same. The very reverse of all this generally obtains with regard to fact. In consequence of what has been now advanced, assertions opposite to truths of the former kind, are not only false, but absurd. They are not only not true, but it is impossible they should be true, whilst the meanings of the words (and consequently the ideas compared) remain the same. This doth not hold commonly in any other kind of evidence. Take, for instance, of the first kind, the following affirmations, "The cube of two is the half of sixteen,"—"The square of the hypothenuse is equal to the sum of the squares of the sides,"—"If equal things be taken from equal things, the remainders will be equal." Contrary propositions, as, "The cube of two is more than the half of sixteen,"—"The square of the hypothenuse is less than the sum of the squares of the sides,"—"If equal things be taken from equal things, the remainders will be unequal," are chargeable, not only with falsity, but with absurdity, being inconceivable and contradictory. Whereas, to these truths which we acquire by moral evidence, "Cæsar overcame Pompey,"—"The sun will rise to-morrow,"—"All men will die,"—the opposite assertions, though untrue, are easily conceivable without changing, in the least, the import of the words, and therefore do not imply a contradiction.

The second difference I shall remark is, that moral evidence admits degrees, demonstration doth not. This is a plain consequence of the preceding difference. Essential or necessary truth, the sole object of the latter, is incompatible with degree. And though actual truth, or matter of fact, be the ultimate aim of the former, likelihood alone, which is susceptible of degree, is usually the utmost attainment. Whatever is exhibited as demonstration is either mere illusion, and so no evidence at all, or absolutely perfect. There is no medium. In moral reasoning we ascend from possibility, by an insensible gradation, to probability, and thence, in the same manner, to the summit of moral certainty. On this summit, or on any of the steps leading to it, the conclusion of the argument may rest. Hence the result of that is, by way of eminence, denominated science, and the evidence itself is termed scientific; the result of this is frequently (not always) entitled to no higher denomination than opinion. Now, in the mathematical sciences, no mention is ever made of opinions.

The third difference is, that in the one there never can be any contrariety of proofs; in the other, there not only may be, but almost always is. If one demonstration were ever capable of being refuted, it could be solely by another demonstration, this being the only sort of evidence adapted to the subject, and the only sort by which the former could be matched. But to suppose that contraries are demonstrable, is to suppose that the same proposition is both true and false, which is a manifest contradiction. Consequently, if there should ever be the appearance of demonstration on opposite sides, that on one side must be fallacious and sophistical. It is not so with moral evidence, for, unless in a few singular instances, there is always real, not apparent evidence on both sides. There are contrary experiences, contrary presumptions, contrary testimonies, to balance against one another. In this case, the probability, upon the whole, is in the proportion which the evidence on the side that preponderates bears to its opposite. We usually say, indeed, that the evidence lies on such a side of the question, and not on the reverse; but by this expression is only meant the overplus of evidence, on comparing both sides. In like manner, when we affirm of an event, that it is probable, we say the contrary is only possible, although, when they are severally considered, we do not scruple to say, This is more probable than that; or, The probabilities on one side outweigh those on the other.

The fourth and last difference I shall observe is, that scientific evidence is simple, consisting of only one coherent series, every part of which depends on the preceding, and, as it were, suspends the following: moral evidence is generally complicated, being in reality a bundle of independent proofs. The longest demonstration is but one uniform chain, the links whereof, taken severally, are not to be regarded as so many arguments, and consequently when thus taken, they conclude nothing; but taken together, and in their proper order, they form one argument, which is perfectly conclusive. It is true, the same theorem may be demonstrable in different ways, and by different mediums; but as a single demonstration, clearly understood, commands the fullest conviction, every other is superfluous. After one demonstrative proof, a man may try a second, purely as an exercise of ingenuity, or the better to assure himself that he hath not committed an oversight in the first. Thus it may serve to warrant the regular procedure of his faculties, but not to make an addition to the former proof, or supply any deficiency perceived in it. So far is it from answering this end, that he is no sooner sensible of a defect in an attempt of this nature, than the whole is rejected as good for nothing, and carrying with it no degree of evidence whatever. In moral reasoning, on the contrary, there is often a combination of many distinct topics of argument, no way dependent on one another. Each hath a certain portion of evidence belonging to itself, each bestows on the conclusion a particular degree of likelihood, of all which accumulated the credibility of the fact is compounded. The former may be compared to an arch, no part of which can subsist independently of the rest. If you make any breach in it, you destroy the whole. The latter may be compared to a tower, the height whereof is but the aggregate of the heights of the several parts reared above one another, and so may be gradually diminished, as it was gradually raised.

So much for the respective natures of scientific and of moral evidence, and those characteristical qualities which discriminate them from each other. On a survey of the whole, it seems indubitable, that if the former is infinitely superior in point of authority, the latter no less excels in point of importance. Abstract truth, as far as it is the object of our faculties, is almost entirely confined to quantity, concrete or discrete. The sphere of Demonstration is narrow, but within her sphere she is a despotic sovereign, her sway is uncontrollable. Her rival, on the contrary, hath less power but wider empire. Her forces, indeed, are not always irresistible; but the whole world is comprised in her dominions. Reality or fact comprehends the laws and the works of nature, as well as the arts and the institutions of men; in brief, all the beings which fall under the cognizance of the human mind, with all their modifications, operations, and effects. By the first, we must acknowledge, when applied to things, and combined with the discoveries of the second, our researches into nature in a certain line are facilitated, the understanding is enlightened, and many of the arts, both elegant and useful, are improved and perfected. Without the aid of the second, society must not only suffer but perish. Human nature itself could not subsist. This organ of knowledge, which extends its influence to every precinct of philosophy, and governs in most, serves also to regulate all the ordinary but indispensable concernments of life. To these it is admirably adapted, notwithstanding its inferiority in respect of dignity, accuracy, and perspicuity. For it is principally to the acquisitions procured by experience that we owe the use of language, and the knowledge of almost every thing that makes the soul of a man differ from that of a new-born infant. On the other hand, there is no despot so absolute as not to be liable to a check on some side or other; and that the prerogatives of demonstration are not so very considerable, as on a cursory view one is apt to imagine; and this, as well as every other operation of the intellect, must partake in the weakness incident to all our mental faculties, and inseparable from our nature, I shall afterwards take an opportunity particularly to evince.

PART. II.—THE NATURE AND ORIGIN OF EXPERIENCE.

I should now consider the principal tribes comprehended under the general name of moral evidence; but, that every difficulty may be removed, which might retard our progress in the proposed discussion, it will be necessary, in the first place, to explore more accurately those sources in our nature which give being to experience, and consequently to all those attainments, moral and intellectual, that are derived from it. These sources are two, sense and memory. The senses, both external and internal, are the original inlets of perception. They inform the mind of the facts, which in the present instant are situated within the sphere of their activity, and no sooner discharge their office in any particular instance than the articles of information exhibited by them are devolved on the memory. Remembrance instantly succeeds sensation, insomuch that the memory becomes the sole repository of the knowledge received from sense; knowledge which, without this repository, would be as instantaneously lost as it is gotten, and could be of no service to the mind. Our sensations would be no better than the fleeting pictures of a moving object on a camera obscura, which leave not the least vestige behind them. Memory, therefore, is the only original voucher extant of those past realities for which we had once the evidence of sense. Her ideas are, as it were, the prints that have been left by sensible impressions. But from these two faculties, considered in themselves, there results to us the knowledge only of individual facts, and only of such facts as either heretofore have come, or at present do come, under the notice of our senses.

Now, in order to render this knowledge useful to us, in discovering the nature of things, and in regulating our conduct, a further process of the mind is necessary, which deserves to be carefully attended to, and may be thus illustrated. I have observed a stone fall to the ground when nothing intervened to impede its motion. This single fact produces little or no effect on the mind beyond a bare remembrance. At another time, I observe the fall of a tile, at another of an apple, and so of almost every kind of body in the like situation. Thus my senses first, and then my memory, furnish me with numerous examples, which, though different in every other particular, are similar in this, that they present a body moving downwards, till obstructed either by the ground or by some intervenient object. Hence my first notion of gravitation. For, with regard to the similar circumstances of different facts, as by the repetition such circumstances are more deeply imprinted, the mind acquires a habit of retaining them, omitting those circumstances peculiar to each wherein their differences consist. Hence, if objects of any kind, in a particular manner circumstanced, are remembered to have been usually, and still more if uniformly, succeeded by certain particular consequences, the idea of the former, in the supposed circumstance introduced into the mind, immediately associates the idea of the latter; and if the object itself, so circumstanced, be presented to the senses, the mind instantly anticipates the appearance of the customary consequence. This holds also inversely. The retention and association above explained are called Experience. The anticipation is in effect no other than a particular conclusion from that experience. Here we may remark by the way, that though memory gives birth to experience, which results from the comparison of facts remembered, the experience or habitual association remains, when the individual facts on which it is founded are all forgotten. I know from an experience which excludes all doubt, the power of fire in melting silver, and yet may not be able at present to recollect a particular instance in which I have seen this effect produced, or even in which I have had the fact attested by a credible witness.

Some will perhaps object that the account now given makes our experimental reasoning look like a sort of mechanism, necessarily resulting from the very constitution of the mind. I acknowledge the justness of the remark, but do not think that it ought to be regarded as an objection. It is plain that our reasoning in this way, if you please to call it so, is very early, and precedes all reflection on our faculties, and the manner of applying them. Those who attend to the progress of human nature through its different stages, and through childhood in particular, will observe that children make great acquisitions in knowledge from experience long before they attain the use of speech. The beasts also, in their sphere, improve by experience, which hath in them just the same foundations of sense and memory as in us, and hath, besides, a similar influence on their actions. It is precisely in the same manner, and with the same success, that you might train a dog, or accustom a child to expect food on your calling to him in one tone of voice, and to dread your resentment when you use another. The brutes have evidently the rudiments of this species of rationality, which extends as far in them as the immediate purposes of self-preservation require, and which, whether you call it reason or instinct, they both acquire and use in the same manner as we do. That it reaches no further in them, seems to arise from an original incapacity of classing, and (if I may use the expression) generalizing their perceptions; an exercise which to us very quickly becomes familiar, and is what chiefly fits us for the use of language. Indeed, in the extent of this capacity, as much, perhaps, as in any thing, lies also the principal natural superiority of one man over another.

But that we may be satisfied, that to this kind of reasoning, in its earliest or simplest form, little or no reflection is necessary, let it be observed, that it is now universally admitted by opticians, that it is not purely from sight, but from sight aided by experience, that we derive our notions of the distance of visible objects from the eye. The sensation, say they, is instantaneously followed by a conclusion or judgment founded on experience. The point is determined from the different phases of the object found, in former trials, to be connected with different distances, or from the effort that accompanies the different conformations we are obliged to give the organs of sight, in order to obtain a distinct vision of the object. Now, if this be the case, as I think hath been sufficiently evinced of late, it is manifest that this judgment is so truly instantaneous, and so perfectly the result of feeling and association, that the forming of it totally escapes our notice. Perhaps in no period of life will you find a person, that, on the first mention of it, can be easily persuaded that he derives this knowledge from experience. Every man will be ready to tell you that he needs no other witnesses than his eyes, to satisfy him that objects are not in contact with his body, but are at different distances from him as well as from one another. So passive is the mind in this matter, and so rapid are the transitions which, by this ideal attraction, she is impelled to make, that she is, in a manner, unconscious of her own operations. There is some ground to think, from the exact analogy which their organs bear to ours, that the discovery of distance from the eye is attained by brutes in the same manner as by us. As to this, however, I will not be positive. But though, in this way, the mind acquires an early perception of the most obvious and necessary truths, without which the bodily organs would be of little use; in matters less important her procedure is much slower, and more the result of voluntary application; and as the exertion is more deliberate, she is more conscious of her own activity, or, at least, remembers it longer. It is then only that in common style we honour her operation with the name of *reasoning;* though there is no essential difference between the two cases. It is true, indeed, that the conclusions in the first way, by which also in infancy we learn language, are commonly more to be regarded as infallible, than those effected in the second.

PART III.—THE SUBDIVISIONS OF MORAL REASONING.

But to return to the proposed distribution of moral evidence. Under it I include these three tribes, experience, analogy, and testimony. To these I shall subjoin the consideration of a fourth, totally distinct from them all, but which appears to be a mixture of the demonstrative and the moral; or rather a particular application of the former, for ascertaining the precise force of the latter. The evidence I mean is that resulting from calculations concerning chances.

I.—EXPERIENCE.

The first of these I have named peculiarly the evidence of experience, not with philosophical propriety, but in compliance with common language, and for distinction's sake. Analogical reasoning is surely reasoning from a more indirect experience. Now, as to this first kind, our experience is either uniform or various. In the one case, provided the facts on which it is founded be sufficiently numerous, the conclusion is said to be morally certain. In the other, the conclusion, built on the greater number of instances, is said to be probable, and more or less so, according to the proportion which the instances on that side bear to those on the opposite. Thus we are perfectly assured that iron thrown into the river will sink, that deal will float; because these conclusions are built on a full and uniform experience. That in the last week of December next, it will snow in any part of Britain specified, is perhaps probable; that is, if, on inquiry or recollection, we are satisfied that this hath more frequently happened than the contrary; that some time in that month it will snow, is more probable, but not certain, because, though this conclusion is founded on experience, that experience is not uniform; lastly, that it will snow some time during winter will, I believe, on the same principles, be pronounced certain.

It was affirmed that experience, or the tendency of the mind to associate ideas under the notion of causes, effects, or adjuncts, is never contracted by one example only. This assertion, it may be thought, is contradicted by the principle on which physiologists commonly proceed, who consider one accurate experiment in support of a particular doctrine as sufficient evidence. The better to explain this phenomenon, and the further to illustrate the nature of experience, I shall make the following observations. First, whereas sense and memory are conversant only about individuals, our earliest experiences imply, or perhaps generate, the notion of a species, including all those individuals which have the most obvious and universal resemblance. From Charles, Thomas, William, we ascend to the idea of man; from Britain, France, Spain, to the idea of kingdom. As our acquaintance with nature enlarges, we discover resemblances, of a striking and important nature, between one species and another, which naturally begets the notion of a genus. From comparing men with beasts, birds, fishes, and reptiles, we perceive that they are all alike possessed of life, or a principle of sensation and action, and of an organized body, and hence acquire the idea of animal: in like manner, from comparing kingdoms with republics and aristocracies, we obtain the idea of nation, and thence again rise in the same track to ideas still more comprehensive. Further, let it be remembered, that by experience we not only decide concerning the future from the past, but concerning things uncommon from things familiar which resemble them.

Now, to apply this observation: a botanist, in traversing the fields, lights on a particular plant, which appears to be of a species he is not acquainted with. The flower, he observes, is monopetalous, and the number of flowers it carries is seven. Here are two facts that occur to his observation; let us consider in what way he will be disposed to argue from them. From the first he does not hesitate to conclude, not only as probable, but as certain, that this individual, and all of the same species, invariably produce monopetalous flowers. From the second, he by no means concludes, as either certain, or even probable, that the flowers which either this plant, or others of the same species, carry at once, will always be seven. This difference, to a superficial inquirer, might seem capricious, since there appears to be one example, and but one in either case, on which the conclusion can be founded. The truth is, that it is not from this example only that he deduces these inferences. Had he never heretofore taken the smallest notice of any plant, he could not have reasoned at all from these remarks. The mind recurs instantly from the unknown to all the other known species of the same genus, and thence to all the known genera of the same order or tribe; and having experienced in the one instance, a regularity in every species, genus, and tribe, which admits no exception; in the other a variety as boundless as that of season, soil, and culture, it learns hence to mark the difference.

Again, we may observe that, on a closer acquaintance with those objects wherewith we are surrounded, we come to discover that they are mostly of a compound nature, and that not only as containing a complication of those qualities called accidents, as gravity, mobility, colour, extension, figure, solidity, which are common almost to all matter, not only as consisting of different members, but as comprehending a mixture of bodies, often very different in their nature and properties, as air, fire, water, earth, salt, oil, spirit, and the like. These, perhaps, on deeper researches, will be found to consist of materials still simpler. Moreover, as we advance in the study of nature, we daily find more reason to be convinced of her constancy in all her operations, that like causes, in like circumstances, always produce like effects, and inversely, like effects always flow from like causes. The inconstancy which appears at first in some of nature's works, a more improved experience teacheth us to account for in this manner. As most of the objects we know are of a complex nature, on a narrower scrutiny we find, that the effects ascribed to them ought often solely to be ascribed to one or more of the component parts; that the others noway contribute to the production: that, on the contrary, they sometimes tend to hinder it. If the parts in the composition of similar objects were always in equal quantity, their being compounded would make no odds; if the parts, though not equal, bore always the same proportion to the whole, this would make a difference: but such as in many cases might be computed. In both respects, however, there is an immense variety. Perhaps every individual differs from every other individual of the same species, both in the quantities and in the proportions of its constituent members and component parts. This diversity is also found in other things, which, though hardly reducible to species, are generally known by the same name. The atmosphere in the same place at different times, or at the same time in different places, differs in density, heat, humidity, and the number, quality, and proportion of the vapours or particles with which it is loaden. The more then we become acquainted with elementary natures, the more we are ascertained by a general experience of the uniformity of their operations. And though perhaps it be impossible for us to attain the knowledge of the simplest elements of any body, yet when any thing appears so simple, or rather so exactly uniform, as that we have observed it invariably to produce similar effects; on discovering any new effects, though but by one experiment, we conclude, from the general experience of the efficient, a like constancy in this energy as in the rest. Fire consumes wood, melts copper, and hardens clay. In these instances it acts uniformly, but not in these only. I have always experienced hitherto, that whatever of any species is consumed by it once, all of the same species it will consume upon trial at any time. The like may be said of what is melted, or hardened, or otherwise altered by it. If then, for the first time, I try the influence of fire on any fossil, or other substance, whatever be the effect, I readily conclude that fire will always produce a similar effect on similar bodies. This conclusion is not founded on this single instance, but on this instance compared with a general experience of the regularity of this element in all its operations.

So much for the first tribe, the evidence of experience, on which I have enlarged the more, as it is, if not the foundation, at least the criterion of all moral reasoning whatever. It is, besides, the principal organ of truth in all the branches of physiology (I use the word in its largest acceptation), including natural history, astronomy, geography, mechanics, optics, hydrostatics, meteorology, medicine, chemistry. Under the general term I also comprehend natural theology and psychology, which, in my opinion, have been most unnaturally disjoined by philosophers. Spirit, which here comprises only the Supreme Being and the human soul, is surely as much included under the notion of natural object as body is, and is knowable to the philosopher purely in the same way, by observation and experience.

II.—ANALOGY.

The evidence of analogy, as was hinted above, is but a more indirect experience, founded on some remote similitude. As things, however, are often more easily comprehended by the aid of example than by definition, I shall in that manner illustrate the difference between experimental evidence and analogical. The circulation of the blood in one human body is, I shall suppose, experimentally discovered. Nobody will doubt of this being a sufficient proof from experience, that the blood circulates in every human body. Nay, further, when we consider the great similarity which other animal bodies bear to the human body, and that both in the structure and in the destination of the several organs and limbs; particularly when we consider the resemblance in the blood itself, and blood-vessels, and in the fabric and pulsation of the heart and arteries, it will appear sufficient experimental evidence of the circulation of the blood in brutes, especially in quadrupeds. Yet, in this application, it is manifest, that the evidence is weaker than in the former. But should I from the same experiment infer the circulation of the sap in vegetables, this would be called an argument only from analogy. Now, all reasonings from experience are obviously weakened in proportion to the remoteness of the resemblance subsisting between that on which the argument is founded, and that concerning which we form the conclusion.

The same thing may be considered in a different way. I have learnt from experience, that like effects sometimes proceed from objects which faintly resemble, but not near so frequently as from objects which have a more perfect likeness. By this experience I have been enabled to determine the degrees of probability from the degrees of similarity in the different cases. It is presumable that the former of these ways has the earliest influence, when the mind, unaccustomed to reflection, forms but a weak association, and consequently but a weak expectation of a similar event from a weak resemblance. The latter seems more the result of thought, and is better adapted to the ordinary forms of reasoning.

It is allowed that an analogical evidence is at best but a feeble support, and is hardly ever honoured with the name of proof. Nevertheless, when the analogies are numerous, and the subject admits not evidence of another kind, it doth not want efficacy. It must be owned, however, that it is generally more successful in silencing objections than in evincing truth, and on this account may more properly be styled the defensive arms of the orator than the offensive. Though it rarely refutes, it frequently repels refutation, like those weapons which, though they cannot kill the enemy, will ward his blows.[1]

III.—TESTIMONY.

The third tribe is the evidence of testimony, which is either oral or written. This also hath been thought by some, but unjustly, to be solely and originally derived from the same source, experience.[2] The utmost in regard to this, that can be affirmed with truth, is that the evidence of testimony is to be considered as strictly logical, no further than

---

[1] Dr. Butler, in his excellent treatise called *The Analogy of Religion natural and revealed, to the Constitution and Course of Nature,* hath shown us how useful this mode of reasoning may be rendered, by the application he hath so successfully made of it for refuting the cavils of infidelity.

[2] I had occasion to make some reflections on this subject formerly. See Dissertation on Miracles, Part i. Sect. 1. There are several ingenious observations on the same subject in Reid's Inquiry, Ch. vi. Sect. 23.

human veracity in general, or the veracity of witnesses of such a character, and in such circumstances in particular, is supported, or perhaps more properly, hath not been refuted, by experience. But that testimony, antecedently to experience, hath a natural influence on belief, is undeniable. In this it resembles memory; for though the defects and misrepresentations of memory are corrected by experience, yet that this faculty hath an innate evidence of its own we know from this, that if we had not previously given an implicit faith to memory, we had never been able to acquire experience. This will appear from the revisal of its nature, as explained above. Nay, it must be owned, that in what regards single facts, testimony is more adequate evidence than any conclusions from experience. The immediate conclusions from experience are general, and run thus: "This is the ordinary course of nature;"—"Such an event may reasonably be expected, when all the attendant circumstances are similar." When we descend to particulars, the conclusion necessarily becomes weaker, being more indirect. For though all the *known* circumstances be similar, all the *actual* circumstances may not be similar; nor is it possible in any case to be assured, that all the actual circumstances are known to us. Accordingly, experience is the foundation of philosophy; which consists in a collection of general truths, systematically digested. On the contrary, the direct conclusion from testimony is particular, and runs thus: "This is the fact in the instance specified." Testimony, therefore, is the foundation of history, which is occupied about individuals. Hence we derive our acquaintance with past ages, as from experience we derive all that we can discover of the future. But the former is dignified with the name of knowledge, whereas the latter is regarded as matter of conjecture only. When experience is applied to the discovery of the truth in a particular incident, we call the evidence presumptive; ample testimony is accounted a positive proof of the fact. Nay, the strongest conviction built merely on the former is sometimes overturned by the slightest attack of the latter. Testimony is capable of giving us absolute certainty (Mr. Hume himself being judge[1]) even of the most miraculous fact, or of what is contrary to uniform experience. For, perhaps, in no other instance can experience be applied to individual events with so much certainty, as in what relates to the revolutions of the heavenly bodies. Yet, even this evidence, he admits, may not only be counterbalanced, but destroyed by testimony.

But to return. Testimony is a serious intimation from another, of any fact or observation, as being what he remembers to have seen or heard or experienced. To this, when we have no positive reasons of mistrust or doubt, we are, by an original principle of our nature (analogous to that which compels our faith in memory), led to give an unlimited assent. As on memory alone is founded the merely personal experience of the individual, so on testimony in concurrence with memory is founded the much more extensive experience which is not originally our own, but derived from others.[2] By the first, I question not, a man might acquire all the knowledge necessary for mere animal support, in that rudest state of human nature (if ever such a state existed) which was without speech and without society; to the last, in conjunction with the other, we are indebted for every thing which distinguishes the man from the brute, for language, arts, and civilization. It hath been observed, that from experience we learn to confine our belief in human testimony within the proper bounds. Hence we are taught to consider many attendant circumstances, which serve either to corroborate or to invalidate its evidence. The reputation of the attester, his manner of address, the nature of the fact attested, the occasion of giving the testimony, the possible or probable design in giving it, the disposition of the hearers to whom it was given, and several other circumstances, have all considerable influence in fixing the degree of credibility. But of these I shall have occasion to

[1] Essay on Miracles, p. 2.

[2] Dissertation on Miracles, Part i. Sect. 2.

take notice afterwards. It deserves likewise to be attended to on this subject, that in a number of concurrent testimonies (in cases wherein there could have been no previous concert), there is a probability distinct from that which may be termed the sum of the probabilities resulting from the testimonies of the witnesses, a probability which would remain even though the witnesses were of such a character as to merit no faith at all. This probability arises purely from the concurrence itself. That such a concurrence should spring from chance is as one to infinite; that is, in other words, morally impossible. If therefore concert be excluded, there remains no other cause but the reality of the fact.

Now to this species of evidence, testimony, we are first immediately indebted for all the branches of philology, such as, history, civil, ecclesiastic, and literary; grammar, languages, jurisprudence, and criticism; to which I may add revealed religion, as far as it is to be considered as a subject of historical and critical inquiry, and so discoverable by natural means: and secondly, to the same source we owe, as was hinted above, a great part of that light which is commonly known under the name of experience, but which is, in fact, not founded on our own personal observations, or the notices originally given by our own senses, but on the attested experiences and observations of others. So that as hence we derive entirely our knowledge of the actions and productions of men, especially in other regions and in former ages, hence also we derive, in a much greater measure than is commonly imagined, our acquaintance with Nature and her works.—Logic, rhetoric, ethics, economics, and politics are properly branches of pneumatology, though very closely connected with the philological studies above enumerated.

IV.—CALCULATIONS OF CHANCES.

The last kind of evidence I proposed to consider, was that resulting from calculations of chances. Chance is not commonly understood, either in philosophic or in vulgar language, to imply the exclusion of a cause, but our ignorance of the cause. It is often employed to denote a bare possibility of an event, when nothing is known either to produce or to hinder it. But in this meaning it can never be made the subject of calculation. It then only affords scope to the calculator, when a cause is known for the production of an effect, and when that effect must necessarily be attended with this or that or the other circumstance; but no cause is known to determine us to regard one particular circumstance in preference to the rest, as that which shall accompany the supposed effect. The effect is then considered as necessary, but the circumstance as only casual or contingent. When a die is thrown out of the hand, we know that its gravity will make it fall; we know also that this, together with its cubical figure, will make it lie so, when intercepted by the table, as to have one side facing upwards. Thus far we proceed on the certain principles of a uniform experience; but there is no principle which can lead me to conclude that one side rather than another will be turned up. I know that this circumstance is not without a cause; but is, on the contrary, as really effected by the previous tossing which it receives in the hand or in the box, as its fall and the manner of its lying are by its gravity and figure. But the various turns or motions given it, in this manner, do inevitably escape my notice; and so are held for nothing. I say, therefore, that the chance is equal for every one of the six sides. Now, if five of these were marked with the same figure, suppose a dagger [†], and only one with an asterisk [*], I should in that case say, there were five chances that the die would turn up the dagger, for one that it would turn up the asterisk. For the turning up each of the six sides being equally possible, there are five cases in which the dagger, and only one in which the asterisk would be uppermost.

This differs from experience, inasmuch as I reckon the probability here, not from numbering and comparing the events after repeated trials, but without any trial, from balancing the possibilities on both sides. But though different from experience, it is so similar, that we cannot wonder that it should produce a similar effect upon the mind. These different positions being considered as equal, if any of five shall produce a similar effect, and but the sixth another, the mind, weighing the different events, resteth in an expectation of that in which the greater number of chances concur; but still accompanied with a degree of hesitancy, which appears proportioned to the number of chances on the opposite side. It is much after the same manner that the mind, on comparing its own experiences, when five instances favour one side to one that favours the contrary, determines the greater credibility of the former. Hence, in all complicated cases, the very degree of probability may be arithmetically ascertained. That two dice marked in the common way will turn up seven, is thrice as probable as that they will turn up eleven, and six times as probable as that they will turn up twelve.[1] The degree of probability is here determined demonstratively. It is indeed true that such mathematical calculations may be founded on experience, as well as upon chances. Examples of this we have in the computations that have been made of the value of annuities, insurances, and several other commercial articles. In such cases a great number of instances is necessary, the greatest exactness in collecting them on each side, and due care that there be no discoverable peculiarity in any of them, which would render them unfit for supporting a general conclusion.

[1] Call one die A, the other B. The chances for 7 are

A 1. B 6.	A 4. B 3.
A 2. B 5.	A 5. B 2.
A 3. B.4.	A 6. B 1.

The chances for eleven are

A 6. B 5.

A 5. B 6.

The only chance for 12 is A 6. B 6. The 1st is to the 2nd as 6 to 2; to the 3rd, as 6 to 1.

PART IV.—THE SUPERIORITY OF SCIENTIFIC EVIDENCE RE-EXAMINED.

After the enumeration made in the first part of this section, of the principal differences between scientific evidence and moral, I signified my intention of resuming the subject afterwards, as far at least as might be necessary to show, that the prerogatives of demonstration are not so considerable, as on a cursory view one is apt to imagine. It will be proper now to execute this intention. I could not attempt it sooner, as the right apprehension of what is to be advanced will depend on a just conception of those things which have lately been explained. In the comparison referred to, I contrasted the two sorts of evidence, as they are in themselves, without considering the influence which the necessary application of our faculties in using both, has, and ought to have, on the effect. The observations then made in that abstracted view of the subject, appear to be well founded. But that view, I acknowledge, doth not comprehend the whole with which we are concerned.

It was observed of memory, that as it instantly succeeds sensation, it is the repository of all the stores from which our experience is collected, and that without an implicit faith in the clear representations of that faculty, we could not advance a step in the acquisition of experimental knowledge. Yet we know that memory is not infallible: nor can we pretend that in any case there is not a physical possibility of her making a false report. Here, it may be said, is an irremediable imbecility in the very foundation of moral reasoning. But is it less so in demonstrative reasoning? This point deserves a careful examination.

It was remarked concerning the latter, that it is a proof consisting of an uninterrupted series of axioms. The truth of each is intuitively perceived as we proceed. But this process is of necessity gradual, and these axioms are all brought in succession. It must then be solely by the aid of memory, that they are capable of producing conviction in the mind. Nor by this do I mean to affirm, that we can remember the preceding steps with their connexions, so as to have them all present to our view at one instant; for then we should, in that instant, perceive the whole intuitively. Our remembrance, on the contrary, amounts to no more than this, that the perception of the truth of the axiom to which we are advanced in the proof, is accompanied with a strong impression on the memory of the satisfaction that the mind received from the justness and regularity of what preceded. And in this we are under a necessity of acquiescing; for the understanding is no more capable of contemplating and perceiving at once the truth of all the propositions in the series, than the tongue is capable of uttering them at once. Before we make progress in geometry, we come to demonstrations, wherein there is a reference to preceding demonstrations; and in these perhaps to others that preceded them. The bare reflection, that as to these we once were satisfied, is accounted by every learner, and teacher too, as sufficient. And if it were not so, no advancement at all could be made in this science. Yet, here again, the whole evidence is reduced to the testimony of memory. It may be said that, along with the remembrance now mentioned, there is often in the mind a conscious power of recollecting the several steps, whenever it pleases; but the power of recollecting them severally, and successively, and the actual instantaneous recollection of the whole, are widely different. Now, what is the consequence of this induction? It is plainly this, that, in spite of the pride of mathesis, no demonstration whatever can produce, or reasonably ought to produce, a higher degree of certainty than that which results from the vivid representations of memory, on which the other is obliged to lean. Such is here the natural subordination, however rational and purely intellectual the former may be accounted, however mysterious and inexplicable the latter. For it is manifest, that without a perfect acquiescence in such representations, the mathematician could not advance a single step beyond his definitions and axioms. Nothing therefore is more certain, however inconceivable it appeared to Dr. Priestley, than what was affirmed by Dr. Oswald, that *the possibility of error attends the most complete demonstration.*

If from theory we recur to fact, we shall quickly find, that those most deeply versed in this sort of reasoning are conscious of the justness of the remark now made. A geometrician, I shall suppose, discovers a new theorem, which, having made a diagram for the purpose, he attempts to demonstrate, and succeeds in the attempt. The figure he hath constructed is very complex, and the demonstration long. Allow me now to ask, Will he be so perfectly satisfied on the first trial as not to think it of importance to make a second, perhaps a third, and a fourth? Whence arises this diffidence? Purely from the consciousness of the fallibility of his own faculties. But to what purpose, it may be said, the reiterations of the attempt, since it is impossible for him, by any efforts, to shake off his dependence on the accuracy of his attention and fidelity of his memory? Or, what can he have more than reiterated testimonies of his memory, in support of the truth of its former testimony? I acknowledge, that after a hundred attempts he can have no more. But even this is a great deal. We learn from experience, that the mistakes or oversights committed by the mind in one operation, are sometimes, on a review, corrected on the second, or perhaps on a third. Besides, the repetition, when no error is discovered, enlivens the remembrance, and so strengthens the conviction. But, for this conviction, it is plain that we are in a great measure indebted to memory, and in some measure even to experience.

Arithmetical operations, as well as geometrical, are in their nature scientific; yet the most accurate accountants are very sensible of the possibility of committing a blunder, and therefore rarely fail, for securing the matter, when it is of importance, to prove what they have done, by trying to effect the same thing another way. You have employed yourself, I suppose, in resolving some difficult problem by algebra, and are convinced that your solution is just. One whom you know to be an expert algebraist, carefully peruses the whole operation, and acquaints you that he hath discovered an error in your procedure. You are that instant sensible that your conviction was not of such an impregnable nature, but that his single testimony, in consequence of the confidence you repose in his experienced veracity and skill, makes a considerable abatement in it.

Many cases might be supposed, of belief founded only on moral evidence, which it would be impossible thus to shake. A man of known probity and good sense, and (if you think it makes an addition of any moment in this case) an astronomer and philosopher, bids you look at the sun as it goes down, and tells you, with a serious countenance, that the sun which sets to-day will never again rise upon the earth. What would be the effect of this declaration? Would it create in you any doubts? I believe it might, as to the soundness of the man's intellects, but not as to the truth of what he said. Thus, if we regard only the effect, demonstration itself doth not always produce such immovable certainty, as is sometimes consequent on merely moral evidence. And if there are, on the other hand, some well known demonstrations, of so great authority, that it would equally look like lunacy to impugn, it may deserve the attention of the curious to inquire how far, with respect to the bulk of mankind, these circumstances, their having stood the test of ages, their having obtained the universal suffrage of those who are qualified to examine them (things purely of the nature of moral evidence), have contributed to that unshaken faith with which they are received.

The principal difference then, in respect of the result of both kinds, is reduced to this narrow point. In mathematical reasoning, provided you are ascertained of the regular procedure of the mind, to affirm that the conclusion is false implies a contradiction; in moral reasoning, though the procedure of the mind were quite unexceptionable, there still remains a physical possibility of the falsity of the conclusion. But how small this difference is in reality, any judicious person who but attends a little may easily discover. The geometrician, for instance, can no more doubt whether the book called Euclid's Elements is a human composition, whether its contents were discovered and digested into the order in which they are there disposed, by human genius and art, than he can doubt the truth of the propositions therein demonstrated. Is he in the smallest degree surer of any of the properties of the circle, than that if he take away his hand from the compasses with which he is describing it on the wall, they will immediately fall to the ground. These things affect his mind, and influence his practice, precisely in the same manner.

So much for the various kinds of evidence, whether intuitive or deductive; intuitive evidence, as divided into that of pure intellection, of consciousness, and of common sense, under the last of which that of memory is included; deductive evidence, as divided into scientific and moral, with the subdivisions of the latter into experience, analogy, and testimony, to which hath been added the consideration of a mixed species concerning chances. So much for the various subjects of discourse, and the sorts of eviction of which they are respectively susceptible. This, though peculiarly the logician's province, is the foundation of all conviction, and consequently of persuasion too. To attain either of these ends, the speaker must always assume the character of the close candid reasoner: for though he may be an acute logician who is no orator, he will never be a consummate orator who is no logician.

• • •

CHAPTER VII

Of the Consideration which the Speaker ought to have of the Hearers, as men in general.

Rhetoric, as was observed already, not only considers the subject, but also the hearers and the speaker.[1] The hearers must be considered in a

[1] Chap. iv.

twofold view, as men in general, and as such men in particular.

As men in general, it must be allowed there are certain principles in our nature, which, when properly addressed and managed, give no inconsiderable aid to reason in promoting belief. Nor is it just to conclude from this concession, as some have hastily done, that oratory may be defined, "The art of deception." The use of such helps will be found, on a stricter examination, to be in most cases quite legitimate, and even necessary, if we would give reason herself that influence which is certainly her due. In order to evince the truth considered by itself, conclusive arguments alone are requisite; but in order to convince me by these arguments, it is moreover requisite that they be understood, that they be attended to, that they be remembered by me; and in order to persuade me by them to any particular action or conduct, it is further requisite, that by interesting me in the subject, they may, as it were, be felt. It is not therefore the understanding alone that is here concerned. If the orator would prove successful, it is necessary that he engage in his service all these different powers of the mind, the imagination, the memory, and the passions. These are not the supplanters of reason, or even rivals in her sway; they are her handmaids, by whose ministry she is enabled to usher truth into the heart, and procure it there a favourable reception. As handmaids they are liable to be seduced by sophistry in the garb of reason, and sometimes are made ignorantly to lend their aid in the introduction of falsehood. But their service is not on this account to be dispensed with; there is even a necessity of employing it, founded on our nature. Our eyes and hands and feet will give us the same assistance in doing mischief as in doing good; but it would not therefore be better for the world, that all mankind were blind and lame. Arms are not to be laid aside by honest men, because carried by assassins and ruffians; they are to be used the rather for this very reason. Nor are those mental powers, of which eloquence so much avails herself, like the art of war or other human arts, perfectly indifferent to good and evil, and only beneficial as they are rightly employed. On the contrary, they are by nature, as will perhaps appear afterwards, more friendly to truth than to falsehood, and more easily retained in the cause of virtue, than in that of vice.[1]

SECTION I.—MEN CONSIDERED AS ENDOWED WITH UNDERSTANDING.

But to descend to particulars; the first thing to be studied by the speaker is, that his arguments may be understood. If they be unintelligible, the cause must be either in the sense or in the expression. It lies in the sense if the mediums of proof be such as the hearers are unacquainted with; that is, if the ideas introduced be either without the sphere of their knowledge, or too abstract for their apprehension and habits of thinking. It lies in the sense likewise, if the train of reasoning (though no unusual ideas should be introduced) be longer, or more complex, or more intricate, than they are accustomed to. But as the fitness of the arguments, in these respects, depends on the capacity, education, and attainments of the hearers, which in different orders of men are different, this properly

---

[1] "Notandum est enim, affectus ipsos ad bonum apparens semper ferri, atque hac ex parte aliquid habere cum ratione commune; verum illud interest, quod *affectus intuentur prœcipue bonum in prœsentia; ratio prospiciens in longum, etiam futurum, et in summa.* Ideoque cum quae in præsentia obversentur, impleant phantasiam fortius, succumbit plerumque ratio et subjugatur. Sed postquam eloquentiâ et suasionum vi effectum sit, ut futura et remota constituantur et conspiciantur tanquam præsentia, tum demum abeunte in partes rationis, phantasia ratio fit superior. Concludamus igitur, non deberi magis vitio verti *Rhetoricœ,* quod deteriorem partem cohonestare sciat quam *Dialecticœ,* quod sophismata concinnare doceat. Quis enim nescit contrariorum eandem rationem esse, licet usu opponantur?" De Aug. Scient. L. vi. c. 3. Τα *ὑποκειμενα πραγματα ουχ ὁμοιως εχει, αλλ' αιει τ' αληθη και τα βελτιω τη φυσει ευτυλλογιστοτερα και πιθανωτερα, ὡς ἁπλως ειπειν. — ει δ' ότι μεγαλα βλαψειεν αι ὁ χτμενος αδικως τη τοιαυτη δυναμει των λογων, τουτο τε κοινον εστι κατα παντων των αγαθων, πληv αρετης , και μαλιστα κατα των χρησιμωτατων, οίον ισχυος, ὑγιειας, πλουτου. στρατηγιας τοιουτοις γαρ αι τις ωψιλησειε τα μεγιστα, χοωμενος δικαιως, και βλαψειεν αδικως.* Arist. Rhet. L. i. c. 1.

belongs to the consideration which the speaker ought to have of his audience, not as men in general, but as men in particular. The obscurity which ariseth from the expression will come in course to be considered in the sequel.

SECTION II.—MEN CONSIDERED AS ENDOWED WITH IMAGINATION.

The second thing requisite is that his reasoning be attended to; for this purpose the imagination must be engaged. Attention is prerequisite to every effect of speaking, and without some gratification in hearing, there will be no attention, at least of any continuance. Those qualities in ideas which principally gratify the fancy, are vivacity, beauty, sublimity, novelty. Nothing contributes more to vivacity than striking resemblances in the imagery, which convey, besides, an additional pleasure of their own.

But there is still a further end to be served by pleasing the imagination, than that of awakening and preserving the attention, however important this purpose alone ought to be accounted. I will not say with a late subtle metaphysician,[1] that "Belief consisteth in the liveliness of our ideas." That this doctrine is erroneous, it would be quite foreign to my purpose to attempt here to evince.[2] Thus much however is indubitable, that belief commonly enlivens our ideas; and that lively ideas have a stronger influence than faint ideas to induce belief. But so far are these two from being coincident, that even this connexion between them, though common, is not necessary. Vivacity of ideas is not always accompanied with faith, nor is faith always able to produce vivacity. The ideas raised in my mind by the Œdipus Tyrannus of Sophocles, or the Lear of Shakespeare, are incomparably more lively than those excited by a cold but faithful historiographer. Yet I may give full credit to the languid narrative of the latter, though I believe not a single sentence in those tragedies. If a proof were asked of the greater vivacity in the one case than in the other (which, by the way, must be finally determined by consciousness), let these effects serve for arguments. The ideas of the poet give greater pleasure, command closer attention, operate more strongly on the passions, and are longer remembered. If these be not sufficient evidences of greater vivacity, I own I have no apprehension of the meaning which that author affixes to the term. The connexion, however, that generally subsisteth between vivacity and belief will appear less marvellous, if we reflect that there is not so great a difference between argument and illustration as is usually imagined. The same ingenious writer says, concerning moral reasoning, that it is but a kind of comparison. The truth of this assertion any one will easily be convinced of, who considers the preceding observations on that subject.

Where then lies the difference between addressing the judgment and addressing the fancy? and what hath given rise to the distinction between ratiocination and imagery? The following observations will serve for an answer to this query. It is evident, that though the mind receives a considerable pleasure from the discovery of resemblance, no pleasure is received when the resemblance is of such a nature as is familiar to every body. Such are those resemblances which result from the specific and generic qualities of ordinary objects. What gives the principal delight to the imagination, is the exhibition of a strong likeness, which escapes the notice of the generality of people. The similitude of man to man, eagle to eagle, sea to sea, or in brief, of one individual to another individual of the same species, affects not the fancy in the least. What poet would ever think of comparing a combat between two of his heroes to a combat between other two? Yet no where else will he find so strong a resemblance. Indeed, to the faculty of imagination, this resemblance appears rather under the notion of identity; although it be the foundation of the strongest reasoning from experience. Again, the similarity of one species to an-

[1] The author of a Treatise of Human Nature, in 3 vols.

[2] If one is desirous to see a refutation of this principle, let him consult Reid's Inquiry, Chap. ii. Sect. 5.

other of the same genus, as of the lion to the tiger, of the alder to the oak, though this too be a considerable fund of argumentation, hardly strikes the fancy more than the preceding, inasmuch as the generical properties, whereof every species participates, are also obvious. But if from the experimental reasoning we descend to the analogical, we may be said to come upon a common to which reason and fancy have an equal claim. "A comparison," says Quintilian,[1] "hath almost the effect of an example." But what are rhetorical comparisons, when brought to illustrate any point inculcated on the hearers,—what are they, I say, but arguments from analogy? In proof of this let us borrow an instance from the forementioned rhetorician, "Would you be convinced of the necessity of education for the mind, consider of what importance culture is to the ground: the field which, cultivated, produceth a plentiful crop of useful fruits, if neglected, will be overrun with briars and brambles, and other useless or noxious weeds."[2] It would be no better than trifling to point out the argument couched in this passage. Now if comparison, which is the chief, hath so great an influence upon conviction, it is no wonder that all those other oratorical tropes and figures addressed to the imagination, which are more or less nearly related to comparison, should derive hence both life and efficacy.[3] Even antithesis implies comparison. Simile is a comparison in epitome.[4] Metaphor is an allegory in miniature. Allegory and prosopopeia are comparisons conveyed under a particular form.

[1] Instit. lib. v. cap. 11. Proximas exempli vires habet similitudo.

[2] Ibid. Ut si animum dicas excolendum, similitudine utaris terræ, quæ neglecta sentes atque dumos, exculta fructus creat.

[3] Præterea, nescio quomodo etiam credit facilius, quæ audienti jucunda sunt, et voluptate ad fidem ducitur. Quint. L. iv. c. 2.

[4] Simile and comparison are in common language frequently confounded. The difference is this: Simile is no more than a comparison suggested in a word or two; as, He fought like a lion: His face shone as the sun. Comparison is a simile circumstantiated and included in one or more separate sentences.

SECTION III.—MEN CONSIDERED AS ENDOWED WITH MEMORY.

Further, vivid ideas are not only more powerful than languid ideas in commanding and preserving attention, they are not only more efficacious in producing conviction, but they are also more easily retained. Those several powers, understanding, imagination, memory, and passion, are mutually subservient. That it is necessary for the orator to engage the help of memory, will appear from many reasons, particularly from what was remarked above, on the fourth difference between moral reasoning and demonstrative.[1] It was there observed, that in the former the credibility of the fact is the sum of the evidence of all the arguments, often independent of one another, brought to support it. And though it was shown that demonstration itself, without the assistance of this faculty, could never produce conviction; yet here it must be owned, that the natural connexion of the several links in the chain renders the remembrance easier. Now, as nothing can operate on the mind which is not in some respect present to it, care must be taken by the orator that, in introducing new topics, the vestiges left by the former on the minds of the hearers may not be effaced. It is the sense of this necessity which hath given rise to the rules of composition.

Some will perhaps consider it as irregular, that I speak here of addressing the memory, of which no mention at all was made in the first chapter, wherein I considered the different forms of eloquence, classing them by the different faculties of the mind addressed. But this apparent irregularity will vanish, when it is observed, that, with regard to the faculties there mentioned, each of them may not only be the direct, but even the

[1] Chap. v. Sect. ii. P. 1.

ultimate object of what is spoken. The whole scope may be at one time to inform or convince the understanding, at another to delight the imagination, at a third to agitate the passions, and at a fourth to determine the will. But it is never the ultimate end of speaking to be remembered, when what is spoken tends neither to instruct, to please, to move, nor to persuade. This therefore is of necessity no more on any occasion than a subordinate end; or, which is precisely the same thing, the means to some further end; and as such, it is more or less necessary on every occasion. The speaker's attention to this subserviency of memory is always so much the more requisite, the greater the difficulty of remembrance is, and the more important the being remembered is to the attainment of the ultimate end. On both accounts, it is of more consequence in those discourses whose aim is either instruction or persuasion, than in those whose design is solely to please the fancy, or to move the passions. And if there are any which answer none of those ends, it were better to learn to forget them than to teach the method of making them to be retained.

The author of the treatise above quoted hath divided the principles of association in ideas into resemblance, contiguity, and causation. I do not here inquire into all the defects of this enumeration, but only observe that, even on his own system, order both in space and time ought to have been included. It appears at least to have an equal title with causation, which, according to him, is but a particular modification and combination of the other two. Causation, considered as an associating principle, is, in his theory, no more than the contiguous succession of two ideas, which is more deeply imprinted on the mind by its experience of a similar contiguity and succession of the impressions from which they are copied. This therefore is the result of resemblance and vicinity united. Order in place is likewise a mode of vicinity, where this last tie is strengthened by the regularity and simplicity of figure; which qualities arise solely from the resemblance of the corresponding parts of the figure; or the parts similarly situated. Regular figures, besides the advantages they derive from simplicity and uniformity, have this also, that they are more familiar to the mind than irregular figures, and are therefore more easily conceived. Hence the influence which order in place hath upon the memory. If any person question this influence, let him but reflect, how much easier it is to remember a considerable number of persons, whom one hath seen ranged on benches or chairs, round a hall, than the same number seen standing promiscuously in a crowd: and how natural it is, for assisting the memory in recollecting the persons, to recur to the order wherein they were placed.

As to order in time, which in composition is properly styled Method, it consisteth principally in connecting the parts in such a manner as to give vicinity to things in the discourse which have an affinity; that is, resemblance, causality, or other relation in nature; and thus making their customary association and resemblance, as in the former case, co-operate with their contiguity in duration, or immediate succession in the delivery. The utility of method for aiding the memory, all the world knows. But besides this, there are some parts of the discourse, as well as figures of speech, peculiarly adapted to this end. Such are the division of the subject, the rhetorical repetitions of every kind, the different modes of transition and recapitulation.

SECTION IV.—MEN CONSIDERED AS ENDOWED WITH PASSIONS.

To conclude; when persuasion is the end, passion also must be engaged. If it is fancy which bestows brilliancy on our ideas, if it is memory which gives them stability, passion doth more, it animates them. Hence they derive spirit and energy. To say that it is possible to persuade without speaking to the passions, is but at best a kind of specious nonsense. The coolest reasoner always in persuading addresseth himself to the passions some way or other. This he cannot avoid doing, if he speak to the purpose. To make me believe it is enough to show me that things are so; to make me act, it is necessary to show that the action will answer some end. That can never be an end to me which gratifies no passion or affection in my nature. You assure me, "It is for my honour." Now you solicit my pride, without which I had never been able to understand the word. You say, "It is for my interest." Now you bespeak my self-love. "It is for the public good." Now you rouse my patriotism. "It will relieve the miserable." Now you touch my pity. So far therefore it is from being an unfair method of persuasion to move the passions, that there is no persuasion without moving them.

But if so much depend on passion, where is the scope for argument? Before I answer this question, let it be observed that, in order to persuade, there are two things which must be carefully studied by the orator. The first is, to excite some desire or passion in the hearers; the second is to satisfy their judgment that there is a connexion between the action to which he would persuade them, and the gratification of the desire or passion which he excites. This is the analysis of persuasion. The former is effected by communicating lively and glowing ideas of the object; the latter, unless so evident of itself as to supersede the necessity, by presenting the best and most forcible arguments which the nature of the subject admits. In the one lies the pathetic, in the other the argumentative. These incorporated together (as was observed in the first chapter) constitute that vehemence of contention, to which the greatest exploits of eloquence ought doubtless to be ascribed. Here then is the principal scope for argument, but not the only scope, as will appear in the sequel. When the first end alone is attained, the pathetic without the rational, the passions are indeed roused from a disagreeable languor by the help of the imagination, and the mind is thrown into a state which, though accompanied with some painful emotions, rarely fails, upon the whole, to affect it with pleasure. But, if the hearers are judicious, no practical effect is produced. They cannot by such declamation be influenced to a particular action, because not convinced that that action will conduce to the gratifying of the passion raised. Your eloquence hath fired my ambition, and makes me burn with public zeal. The consequence is, there is nothing which at present I would not attempt for the sake of fame, and the interest of my country. You advise me to such a conduct; but you have not shown me how that can contribute to gratify either passion. Satisfy me in this, and I am instantly at your command. Indeed, when the hearers are rude and ignorant, nothing more is necessary in the speaker than to inflame their passions. They will not require that the connexion between the conduct he urges and the end proposed be evinced to them. His word will satisfy. And therefore bold affirmations are made to supply the place of reasons. Hence it is that the rabble are ever the prey of quacks and impudent pretenders of every denomination.

On the contrary, when the other end alone is attained, the rational without the pathetic, the speaker is as far from his purpose as before. You have proved, beyond contradiction, that acting thus is the sure way to procure such an object. I perceive that your reasoning is conclusive: but I am not affected by it. Why? I have no passion for the object. I am indifferent whether I procure it or not. You have demonstrated that such a step will mortify my enemy. I believe it; but I have no resentment, and will not trouble myself to give pain to another. Your arguments evince that it would gratify my vanity. But I prefer my ease. Thus passion is the mover to action, reason is the guide. Good is the object of the will, truth is the object of the understanding.[1]

---

[1] Several causes have contributed to involve this subject in confusion. One is the ambiguity and imperfection of language. Motives are often called arguments, and both motives and arguments are promiscuously styled reasons. Another is, the idle disputes that have arisen among philosophers concerning the nature of good, both physical and moral. "Truth and good are one," says the author of the Pleasures of Imagination, an author whose poetical merit will not be questioned by persons of taste. The expression might have been passed in the poet, whose right to the use of *catachresis,* one of the many privileges comprehended under the name of *poetic license,* prescription hath fully established. But by philosophizing on this passage in his notes, he warrants us to canvass his reasoning, for no such privilege hath as yet

It may be thought that when the motive is the equity, the generosity, or the intrinsic merit of the action recommended, argument may be employed to evince the reasonableness of the end, as well as the fitness of the means. But this way of speaking suits better the popular dialect than the philosophical. The term *reasonableness,* when used in this manner, means nothing but the goodness, the amiableness, or moral excellency. If therefore the hearer hath no love of justice, no benevolence, no regard to right, although he were endowed with the perspicacity of a cherub, your harangue could never have any influence on his mind. The reason is, when you speak of the fitness of the means, you

---

been conceded to philosophers. Indeed, in attempting to illustrate, he has, I think, confuted it, or, to speak more properly, shown it to have no meaning. He mentions two opinions concerning the connexion of truth and beauty, which is one species of good. "Some philosophers," says he, "assert an independent and invariable law in nature, in consequence of which *all rational beings must alike perceive beauty in some certain proportions, and deformity in the contrary.*" Now, though I do not conceive what is meant either by an *independent law,* or by *contrary proportions,* this, if it proves any thing, proves as clearly that deformity and truth are one, as that beauty and truth are one; for those *contrary proportions* are surely as much proportions, or, if you will, as true proportions, as *some certain proportions* are. Accordingly, if, in the conclusion deduced, you put the word *deformity* instead of *beauty,* and the word *beauty* instead of *deformity,* the sense will be equally complete. "Others," he adds, "there are, who believe beauty to be merely a relative and arbitrary thing; and that it is not impossible, in a physical sense, that two beings of equal capacities for truth, should perceive, one of them beauty, and the other deformity, in the same relations. And upon this supposition, by that truth which is always connected with beauty, nothing more can be meant than the conformity of any object to those proportions, upon which, after a careful examination, the beauty of that species is found to depend." This opinion, if I am able to comprehend it, differs only in one point from the preceding. It supposes the standard or law of beauty not invariable or universal. It is liable to the same objection, and that rather more glaringly; for if the same relations must be always equally *true relations,* deformity is as really one with truth as beauty is, since the very same relations can exhibit both appearances. In short, no hypothesis hitherto invented hath shown that by means of the discursive faculty, without the aid of any other mental power, we could ever obtain a notion of either the beautiful or the good; and till this be shown, nothing is shown to the purpose. The author aforesaid, far from attempting this, proceeds on the supposition, that we first perceive beauty, he says not how, and then having, by a careful examination, discovered the proportions which give rise to the perception, denominate them *true;* so that all those elaborate disquisitions with which we are amused, amount only to a few insignificant identical propositions very improperly expressed. For out of a vast profusion of learned phrase, this is all the information we can pick, that "Beauty is—*truly* beauty," and that "Good is—*truly* good." "Moral good," says a celebrated writer, "consisteth in *fitness.*" From this account any person would at first readily conclude, that morals, according to him, are not concerned in the ends which we pursue, but solely in the choice of means for attaining our ends; that if this choice be judicious the conduct is moral; if injudicious, the contrary. But this truly pious author is far from admitting such an interpretation of his words. *Fitness* in this sense hath no relation to a further end. It is an absolute fitness, a fitness in itself. We are obliged to ask, What then is that fitness, which you call absolute? for the application of the word in every other case invariably implying the proper direction of means to an end, far from affording light to the meaning it has here, tends directly to mislead us. The only answer, as far as I can learn, that hath ever been given to this question, is neither more nor less than this, "That alone is absolutely fit which is morally good:" so that in saying moral good consisteth in fitness, no more is meant than that it consisteth in moral good. Another moralist appears, who hath made a most wonderful discovery. It is, that there is not a vice in the world but lying, and that acting virtuously in any situation is but one way or other of telling truth. When this curious theory comes to be explained, we find the practical lie results solely from acting contrary to what those moral sentiments dictate, which, instead of deducing, he everywhere presupposeth to be known and acknowledged by us. Thus he reasons perpetually in a circle, and without advancing a single step beyond it, makes the same things both causes and effects reciprocally. Conduct appears to be false for no other reason than because it is immoral, and immoral for no other reason but because it is false. Such philosophy would not have been unworthy those profound ontologists, who have blest the world with the discovery that "One being is but *one* being," that "A being is *truly* a being," and that "Every being has all the *properties* that it has," and who, to the unspeakable increase of useful knowledge, have denominated these the general attributes of being, and distinguished them by the titles, *unity, truth,* and *goodness.* This, if it be any thing, is the very sublimate of science.

address yourself only to the head; when you speak of the goodness of the end, you address yourself to the heart, of which we supposed him destitute. Are we then to class the virtues among the passions? By no means. But without entering into a discussion of the difference, which would be foreign to our purpose, let it suffice to observe, that they have this in common with passion. They necessarily imply an habitual propensity to a certain species of conduct, an habitual aversion to the contrary: a veneration for such a character, an abhorrence of such another. They are, therefore, though not passions, so closely related to them, that they are properly considered as motives to action, being equally capable of giving an impulse to the will. The difference is akin to that, if not the same, which rhetoricians observe between *pathos* and *ethos,* passion and disposition.[1] Accordingly, what is addressed solely to the moral powers of the mind, is not so properly denominated the pathetic, as the *sentimental.* The term, I own, is rather modern, but is nevertheless convenient, as it fills a vacant room, and doth not, like most of our new-fangled words, justle out older and worthier occupants, to the no small detriment of the language. It occupies, so to speak, the middle place between the pathetic and that which is addressed to the imagination, and partakes of both, adding to the warmth of the former the grace and attractions of the latter.

Now, the principal questions on this subject are these two:—How is a passion or disposition that is favourable to the design of the orator, to be excited in the hearers? How is an unfavourable passion or disposition to be calmed? As to the first it was said already in general, that passion must be awakened by communicating lively ideas of the object. The reason will be obvious from the following remarks: A passion is most strongly excited by sensation. The sight of danger, immediate or near, instantly rouseth fear; the feeling of an injury, and the presence of the injurer, in a moment kindle anger. Next to the influence of sense is that of memory, the effect of which upon passion, if the fact be recent, and remembered distinctly and circumstantially, is almost equal. Next to the influence of memory is that of imagination; by which is here solely meant the faculty of apprehending what is neither perceived by the senses, nor remembered. Now, as it is this power of which the orator must chiefly avail himself, it is proper to inquire what those circumstances are, which will make the ideas he summons up in the imaginations of his hearers, resemble, in lustre and steadiness, those of sensation and remembrance. For the same circumstances will infallibly make them resemble also in their effects; that is, in the influence they will have upon the passions and affections of the heart.

Section V.—The Circumstances that Are Chiefly Instrumental in Operating on the Passions.

These are perhaps all reducible to the seven following, probability, plausibility, importance, proximity of time, connexion of place, relation of the actors or sufferers to the hearers or speaker, interest of the hearers or speaker in the consequences.[1]

Part I.—Probability.

The first is *probability,* which is now considered only as an expedient for enlivening passion. Here

[1] This seems to have been the sense which Quintilian had of the difference between πaθος and ηθος, when he gave *amor* for an example of the first, and *charitas* of the second. The word μθος is also sometimes used for moral sentiment. Inst. L. vi. c. 2.

[1] I am not quite positive as to the accuracy of this enumeration, and shall therefore freely permit my learned and ingenious friend Dr. Reid, to annex the *et cætera* he proposes in such cases, in order to supply all defects. See Sketches of the History of Man, B. iii. Sk. 1. Appendix, c. ii. sect. 2.

again there is commonly scope for argument.[1] Probability results from evidence, and begets belief. Belief invigorates our ideas. Belief raised to the highest becomes certainty. Certainty flows either from the force of the evidence, real or apparent, that is produced: or without any evidence produced by the speaker, from the previous notoriety of the fact. If the fact be notorious, it will not only be superfluous in the speaker to attempt to prove it, but it will be pernicious to his design. The reason is plain. By proving he supposeth it questionable, and by supposing actually renders it so to his audience: he brings them from viewing it in the stronger light of certainty, to view it in the weaker light of probability: in lieu of sunshine he gives them twilight. Of the different means and kinds of probation I have spoken already.

PART II.—PLAUSIBILITY.

The second circumstance is *plausibility,* a thing totally distinct from the former, as having an effect upon the mind quite independent of faith or probability. It ariseth chiefly from the consistency of the narration, from its being what is commonly called natural and feasible. This the French critics have aptly enough denominated in their language *vraisemblance,* the English critics more improperly in theirs *probability.* In order to avoid the manifest ambiguity there is in this application of the word, it had been better to retain the word *verisimilitude,* now almost obsolete. That there is a relation between those two qualities must, notwithstanding, be admitted. This, however, is an additional reason for assigning them different names. An homonymous term, whose different significations have no affinity to one another, is very seldom liable to be misunderstood.

But as to the nature and extent of this relation, let it be observed, that the want of plausibility implies an internal improbability, which it will require the stronger external evidence to surmount. Nevertheless, the implausibility may be surmounted by such evidence, and we may be fully ascertained of what is in itself exceedingly implausible. Implausibility is, in a certain degree, positive evidence against a narrative; whereas plausibility implies no positive evidence for it. We know that fiction may be as plausible as truth. A narration may be possessed of this quality to the highest degree, which we not only regard as improbable, but know to be false. Probability is a light darted on the object, from the proofs, which for this reason are pertinently enough styled *evidence.* Plausibility is a native lustre issuing directly from the object. The former is the aim of the historian, the latter of the poet. That every one may be satisfied that the second is generally not inferior to the first, in its influence on the mind, we need but appeal to the effects of tragedy, of epic, and even of romance, which, in its principal characters, participates of the nature of poesy, though written in prose.

It deserves, however, to be remarked, that though plausibility alone hath often greater efficacy in rousing the passions than probability, or even certainty; yet, in any species of composition wherein truth, or at least probability, is expected, the mind quickly nauseates the most plausible tale, which is unsupported by proper arguments. For this reason it is the business of the orator, as much as his subject will permit, to avail himself of both qualities. There is one case, and but one, in which plausibility itself may be dispensed with; that is, when the fact is so incontestible that it is impossible to entertain a doubt of it; for when implausibility is incapable of impairing belief, it hath sometimes, especially in forensic causes, even a good effect. By presenting us with something monstrous in its kind, it raiseth astonishment, and thereby heightens every passion which the narrative is fitted to excite.

---

[1] In the judiciary orations of the ancients, this was the principal scope for argument. That to condemn the guilty, and to acquit the innocent, would gratify their indignation against the injurious, and their love of right, was too manifest to require a proof. The fact that there was guilt in the prisoner, or that there was innocence, did require it. It was otherwise in deliberative orations, as the conduct recommended was more remotely connected with the emotions raised.

But to return to the explication of this quality. When I explained the nature of experience, I showed that it consisteth of all the general truth collected from particular facts remembered; the mind forming to itself, often insensibly, and as it were mechanically, certain maxims, from comparing, or rather associating the similar circumstances of different incidents.[1] Hence it is, that when a number of ideas relating to any fact or event are successively introduced into my mind by a speaker; if the train he deduceth coincide with the general current of my experience; if in nothing it thwart those conclusions and anticipations which are become habitual to me, my mind accompanies him with facility, glides along from one idea to another, and admits the whole with pleasure. If, on the contrary, the train he introduceth run counter to the current of my experience; if in many things it shock those conclusions and anticipations which are become habitual to me, my mind attends him with difficulty, suffers a sort of violence in passing from one idea to another, and rejects the whole with disdain:

> *For while upon such monstrous scenes we gaze,*
> *They shock our faith, our indignation raise.*[2]
> FRANCIS.

In the former case I pronounce the narrative natural and credible, in the latter I say it is unnatural and incredible, if not impossible; and, which is particularly expressive of the different appearances in respect of connexion made by the ideas in my mind, the one tale I call coherent, the other incoherent. When therefore the orator can obtain no direct aid from the memory of his hearers, which is rarely to be obtained, he must, for the sake of brightening, and strengthening, and if I may be permitted to use so bold a metaphor, cementing his ideas, bespeak the assistance of experience. This, if properly employed, will prove a potent ally, by adding the grace of *verisimilitude* to the whole. It is therefore first of all requisite, that the circumstances of the narration, and the order in which they are exhibited, be what is commonly called natural, that is, congruous to general experience.

Where passion is the end, it is not a sufficient reason for introducing any circumstance that it is natural; it must also be pertinent. It is pertinent, when either necessary for giving a distinct and consistent apprehension of the object, at least for obviating some objection that may be started, or doubt that may be entertained concerning it; or when such as, in its particular tendency, promotes the general aim. All circumstances, however plausible, which serve merely for decoration, never fail to divert the attention, and so become prejudicial to the proposed influence on passion.

But I am aware that, from the explication I have given of this quality, it will be said, that I have run into the error, if it be an error, which I intended to avoid, and have confounded it with probability, by deriving it solely from the same origin, experience. In answer to this, let it be observed, that in every plausible tale which is unsupported by external evidence, there will be found throughout the whole, when duly canvassed, a mixture of possibilities and probabilities, and that not in such a manner as to make one part or incident probable, another barely possible, but so blended as equally to affect the whole, and every member. Take the Iliad for an example. That a haughty, choleric, and vindictive hero, such as Achilles is represented to have been, should, upon the public affront and injury he received from Agamemnon, treat that general with indignity, and form a resolution of withdrawing his troops, remaining thenceforth an unconcerned spectator of the calamities of his countrymen, our experience of the baleful influences of pride and anger renders in some degree probable; again, that one of such a character as Agamemnon, rapacious, jealous of his pre-eminence as commander-in-chief, who envied the superior merit of Achilles, and harboured resentment against him—that such a one,

[1] Chap. V. Sect. ii. Part 2.

[2] Quodcunque ostendis mihi sic, incredulus odi. Hor. De Arte Poet.

I say, on such an occurrence as is related by the poet, should have given the provocation, will be acknowledged also to have some probability. But that there were such personages, of such characters, in such circumstances, is merely possible. Here there is a total want of evidence. Experience is silent. Properly indeed the case comes not within the verge of its jurisdiction. Its general conclusions may serve in confutation, but can never serve in proof of particular or historical facts. Sufficient testimony, and that only, will answer here. The testimony of the poet in this case goes for nothing. His object we know is not truth but likelihood. Experience, however, advances nothing against those allegations of the poet, therefore we call them possible; it can say nothing for them, therefore we do not call them probable. The whole at most amounts to this—if such causes existed, such effects probably followed. But we have no evidence of the existence of the causes; therefore we have no evidence of the existence of the effects. Consequently, all the probability implied in this quality is a hypothetical probability, which is in effect none at all. It is an axiom among dialecticians, in relation to the syllogistic art, that the conclusion always follows the weaker of the premises. To apply this to the present purpose, an application not illicit, though unusual,—if one of the premises, suppose the major, contain an affirmation that is barely possible, the minor, one that is probable, possibility only can be deduced in the conclusion.

These two qualities, therefore, PROBABILITY and PLAUSIBILITY, (if I may be indulged a little in the allegoric style), I shall call sister-graces, daughter of the same father *Experience,* who is the progeny of *Memory,* the first-born and heir of *Sense.* These daughters *Experience* had by different mothers. The elder is the offspring of *Reason,* the younger is the child of *Fancy.* The elder, regular in her features, and majestic both in shape and mien, is admirably fitted for commanding esteem, and even a religious veneration: the younger, careless, blooming, sprightly, is entirely formed for captivating the heart, and engaging love. The conversation of each is entertaining and instructive, but in different ways. Sages seem to think that there is more instruction to be gotten from the just observations of the elder; almost all are agreed that there is more entertainment in the lively sallies of the younger. The principal companion and favourite of the first is *Truth,* but whether *Truth* or *Fiction* share most in the favour of the second it were often difficult to say. Both are naturally well-disposed, and even friendly to *Virtue,* but the elder is by much the more steady of the two; the younger, though perhaps not less capable of doing good, is more easily corrupted, and hath sometimes basely turned procuress to *Vice.* Though rivals, they have a sisterly affection to each other, and love to be together. The elder, sensible that there are but few who can for any time relish her society alone, is generally anxious that her sister be of the party; the younger, conscious of her own superior talents in this respect, can more easily dispense with the other's company. Nevertheless, when she is discoursing on great and serious subjects, in order to add weight to her words, she often quotes her sister's testimony, which she knows is better credited than her own, a compliment that is but sparingly returned by the elder. Each sister hath her admirers. Those of the younger are more numerous, those of the elder more constant. In the retinue of the former you will find the young, the gay, the dissipated; but these are not her only attendants. The middle-aged, however, and the thoughtful, more commonly attach themselves to the latter. To conclude; as something may be learned of characters from the invectives of enemies, as well as from the encomiums of friends, those who have not judgment to discern the good qualities of the first-born, accuse her of dulness, pedantry, and stiffness; those who have not taste to relish the charms of the second, charge her with folly, levity, and falseness. Meantime, it appears to be the universal opinion of the impartial, and such as have been best acquainted with both, that though the attractives of the younger be more irresistible at sight, the virtues of the elder will be longer remembered.

So much for the two qualities *probability* and *plausibility*, on which I have expatiated the more, as they are the principal, and in some respect, indispensable. The others are not compatible with every subject; but as they are of real moment, it is necessary to attend to them, that so they may not be overlooked in cases wherein the subject requires that they be urged.

PART III.—IMPORTANCE.

The third circumstance I took notice of was *importance,* the appearance of which always tends, by fixing attention more closely, to add brightness and strength to the ideas. The importance in moral subjects is analogous to the quantity of matter in physical subjects, as on quantity the moment of moving bodies in a great degree depends. An action may derive importance from its own nature, from those concerned in it as acting or suffering, or from its consequences. It derives importance from its own nature, if it be stupendous in its kind, if the result of what is uncommonly great, whether good or bad, passion or invention, virtue or vice, as what in respect of generosity is godlike, what in respect of atrocity is diabolical: it derives importance from those concerned in it, when the actors or the sufferers are considerable, on account either of their dignity or of their number, or of both: it derives importance from its consequences, when these are remarkable in regard to their greatness, their multitude, their extent, and that either as to the many and distant places affected by them, or as to the future and remote periods to which they may reach, or as to both.

All the four remaining circumstances derive their efficacy purely from one and the same cause, the connexion of the subject with those occupied, as speaker or hearers, in the discourse. *Self* is the centre here, which hath a similar power in the ideal world to that of the sun in the material world, in communicating both light and heat to whatever is within the sphere of its activity, and in a greater or less degree according to the nearness or remoteness.

PART IV.—PROXIMITY OF TIME.

First, as to *proximity of time,* every one knows that any melancholy incident is the more affecting that it is recent. Hence it is become common with story-tellers, that they may make a deeper impression on the hearers, to introduce remarks like these; that the tale which they relate is not old, that it happened but lately, or in their own time, or that they are yet living who had a part in it, or were witnesses of it. Proximity of time regards not only the past but the future. An event that will probably soon happen hath greater influence upon us than what will probably happen a long time hence. I have hitherto proceeded on the hypothesis, that the orator rouses the passions of his hearers by exhibiting some past transaction; but we must acknowledge that passion may be as strongly excited by his reasonings concerning an event yet to come. In the judiciary orations there is greater scope for the former, in the deliberative for the latter; though in each kind there may occasionally be scope for both. All the seven circumstances enumerated are applicable, and have equal weight, whether they relate to the future or to the past. The only exception that I know of is, that probability and plausibility are scarcely distinguishable, when used in reference to events in futurity. As in these there is no access for testimony, what constitutes the principal distinction is quite excluded. In comparing the influence of the past upon our minds, with that of the future, it appears in general, that if the evidence, the importance, and the distance of the objects be equal, the latter will be greater than the former. The reason, I imagine, is, we are conscious that as every moment, the future, which seems placed before us, is approaching; and the past, which lies, as it were, behind, is retiring, our nearness or relation to the one constantly increaseth as the other decreaseth. There is something like attraction in the first case, and repulsion in the second. This tends to interest us more in the future than in the past, and consequently to the present view aggrandizes the one and diminishes the other.

What, nevertheless, gives the past a very considerable advantage, is its being generally susceptible of much stronger evidence than the future. The lights of the mind are, if I may so express myself, in an opposite situation to the lights of the body. These discover clearly the prospect lying before us, but not the ground we have already passed. By the memory, on the contrary, that great luminary of the mind, things past are exhibited in retrospect: we have no correspondent faculty to irradiate the future: and even in matters which fall not within the reach of our memory, past events are often clearly discoverable by testimony, and by effects at present existing; whereas we have nothing equivalent to found our arguments upon in reasoning about things to come. It is for this reason, that the future is considered as the province of conjecture and uncertainty.

PART V.—CONNEXION OF PLACE.

Local *connexion,* the fifth in the above enumeration, hath a more powerful effect than proximity of time. Duration and space are two things, (call them entities or attributes, or what you please,) in some respects the most like, and in some respects the most unlike to one another. They resemble in continuity, divisibility, infinity, in their being deemed essential to the existence of other things, and in the doubts that have been raised as to their having a real or independent existence of their own. They differ, in that the latter is permanent, whereas the very essence of the former consisteth in transitoriness; the parts of the one are all successive, of the other all co-existent. The greater portions of time are all distinguished by the memorable things which have been transacted in them, the smaller portions by the revolutions of the heavenly bodies: the portions of place, great and small, (for we do not here consider the regions of the fixed stars and planets,) are distinguished by the various tracts of land and water, into which the earth is divided and subdivided; the one distinction intelligible, the other sensible; the one chiefly known to the inquisitive, the other in a great measure obvious to all.

Hence perhaps it arises, that the latter is considered as a firmer ground of relation than the former. Who is not more curious to know the notable transactions which have happened in his own country from the earliest antiquity, than to be acquainted with those which have happened in the remotest regions of the globe, during the century wherein he lives? It must be owned, however, that the former circumstance is more frequently aided by that of personal relation than the latter. Connexion of place not only includes vicinage, but every other local relation, such as being in a province under the same government with us, in a state that is in alliance with us, in a country well known to us, and the like. Of the influence of this connexion in operating on our passions we have daily proofs. With how much indifference, at least with how slight and transient emotion, do we read in newspapers the accounts of the most deplorable accidents in countries distant and unknown! How much, on the contrary, are we alarmed and agitated on being informed that any such accident hath happened in our neighbourhood, and that even though we be totally unacquainted with the persons concerned!

PART VI.—RELATION TO THE PERSONS CONCERNED.

Still greater is the power of *relation* to the persons concerned, which was the sixth circumstance mentioned, as this tie is more direct than that which attacheth us to the scene of action. It is the persons, not the place, that are the immediate objects of the passions love or hatred, pity or anger, envy or contempt. Relation to the actors commonly produces an effect contrary to that produced by relation to the sufferers, the first in extenuation, the second in aggravation of the crime alleged. The first makes for the apologist, the second for the accuser. This I say is commonly the case, not always. A remote relation to the actors, when the offence is heinous, especially if the sufferers be more nearly related, will sometimes rather aggravate than extenuate the guilt in our estimation. But it is impossible with any precision to reduce these effects to rules; so much depending on the different tempers and sentiments of different audiences. Personal relations are of various kinds. Some have generally greater influence than others; some again have greater influence with one person, others with another. They are consanguinity, affinity, friendship, acquaintance, being fellow-citizens, countrymen, of the same surname, language, religion, occupation, and innumerable others.

PART VII.—INTEREST IN THE CONSEQUENCES.

But of all the connective circumstances, the most powerful is *interest,* which is the last. Of all relations, personal relation, by bringing the object very near, most enlivens that sympathy which attacheth us to the concerns of others; interest in the effects brings the object, if I may say so, into contact with us, and makes the mind cling to it as a concern of its own. Sympathy is but a reflected feeling, and therefore, in ordinary cases, must be weaker than the original. Though the mirror be ever so true, a lover will not be obliged to it for presenting him with the figure of his mistress when he hath an opportunity of gazing on her person. Nor will the orator place his chief confidence in the assistance of the social and sympathetic affections, when he hath it in his power to arm the selfish.

Men universally, from a just conception of the difference, have, when self is concerned, given a different name to what seems originally the same passion in a higher degree. Injury, to whomsoever offered, is to every man that observes it, and whose sense of right is not debauched by vicious practice, the natural object of *indignation.* Indignation always implies *resentment,* or a desire of retaliating on the injurious person, so far at least as to make him repent the wrong he hath committed. This indignation in the person injured is, from our knowledge of mankind, supposed to be, not indeed universally, but generally so much stronger, that it ought to be distinguished by another appellation, and is, accordingly, denominated *revenge.* In like manner beneficence, on whomsoever exercised, is the natural object of our *love;* love always implies *benevolence,* or a desire of promoting the happiness of the beneficent person; but this passion in the person benefited is conceived to be so much greater, and to infer so strong an obligation to a return of good offices to his benefactor, that it merits to be distinguished by the title *gratitude.* Now by this circumstance of *interest* in the effects, the speaker, from engaging *pity* in his favour, can proceed to operate on a more powerful principle, *self-preservation.* The *benevolence* of his hearers he can work up into *gratitude,* their *indignation* into *revenge.*

The two last-mentioned circumstances, personal relation and interest, are not without influence, as was hinted in the enumeration, though they regard the speaker only, and not the hearers. The reason is, a person present with us, whom we see and hear, and who, by words, and looks, and gestures, gives the liveliest signs of his feelings, has the surest and most immediate claim upon our sympathy. We become infected with his passions. We are hurried along by them, and not allowed leisure to distinguish between his relation and our relation, his interest and our interest.

SECTION VI.—OTHER PASSIONS, AS WELL AS MORAL SENTIMENTS, USEFUL AUXILIARIES.

So much for those circumstances in the object presented by the speaker, which serve to awaken and inflame the passions of the hearers.[1] But when a passion is once raised, there are also other means

---

[1] To illustrate most of the preceding circumstances, and show the manner of applying them, I shall take an example from Cicero's last oration against Verres, where, after relating the crucifixion of Gavius, a Roman citizen, he exclaims, "1. O nomen dulce libertatis! O jus eximium nostræ civitatis! O lex Porcia, legesque Semproniæ! O graviter desiderata, et aliquando reddita plebi Romanæ tribunitia potestas! 2. Huccine tandem omnia reciderunt, ut civis Romanus in provincia populi Romani, in oppido fœderatorum, ab eo qui beneficio populi Romani fasces et secures haberet, deligatus in foro virgis cæderetur?——3. Sed quid ego plura de Gavio? quasi tu Gavio tum fueris infestus, ac non nomini, generi, juri

by which it may be kept alive, and even augmented. Other passions or dispositions may be called in as auxiliaries. Nothing is more efficacious in this respect than a sense of justice, a sense of public utility, a sense of glory; and nothing conduceth more to operate on these, than the sentiments of sages whose wisdom we venerate, the example of heroes whose exploits we admire. I shall conclude what relates to the exciting of passion when I have remarked, that pleading the importance and the other pathetic circumstances, or pleading the authority of opinions or precedents, is usually considered, and aptly enough, as being likewise a species of reasoning.

This concession, however, doth not imply, that by any reasoning we are ever taught that such an object ought to awaken such a passion. This we must learn originally from feeling, not from argument. No speaker attempts to prove it; though he sometimes introduceth moral considerations, in order to justify the passion when raised, and to prevent the hearers from attempting to suppress it. Even when he is enforcing their regard to the pathetic circumstances above mentioned, it is not so much his aim to show that these circumstances ought to augment the passion, as that these circumstances are in the object. The effect upon their minds he commonly leaves to nature; and is not

---

civium hostis, non illi inquam homini, sed causæ communi libertatis inimicus fuisti. 4. Quid enim attinuit, cum Mamertini more atque instituto suo, crucem fixissent post urbem, in via Pompeia; te jubere in ea parte figere, quæ ad fretum spectat; et hoc addere, quod negare nullo modo potes, quod omnibus audientibus dixisti palam, te idcirco illum locum deligere, ut ille qui se civem Romanum esse diceret, ex cruce Italiam cerneret, ac domum suam prospicere posset? 5. Itaque illa crux sola, judices, post conditam Messanam illo in loco fixa est. 6. Italiæ conspectus ad eam rem ab isto delectus est, ut ille in dolore cruciatuque moriens, perangusto freto divisa servitutis ac libertatis jura cognosceret; Italia autom alumnum suum, servitutis extremo summoque supplicio affectum videret. 7. Facinus est vincire civem Romanum, scelus verberare, prope parricidium necare, quid dicam, in crucem tollere? verbo satis digno tam nefaria res appellari nullo modo potest. 8. Non fuit his omnibus iste contentus. Spectet, inquit, patriam; in conspectu legum libertatisque moriatur. 9. Non tu hoc loco Gavium, non unum hominem, nescio quem, civem Romanum, sed communem libertatis et civitatis causam in illum cruciatum et crucem egisti. 10. Jam vero videte hominis audaciam! Nonne enim graviter tulisse arbitramini, quod illam civibus Romanis crucem non posset in foro, non in comitio, non in rostris defigere? 11. Quod enim his locis in provincia sua celebritate simillimum, regione proximum, potuit, elegit. 12. Monumentum sceleris—audaciæque suæ voluit esse in conspectu Italiæ, prætervectione omnium qui ultro citroque navigarent. 13. Paulo ante, judices, lacrymas in morte miserâ atque indignissimâ navarchorum non tenebamus: et recte de merito sociorum innocentium miseriâ commovebamur. 14. Quid nunc in nostor sanguine tandem facere debemus? nam civium Romanorum sanguis conjunctus existimandus est.——15. Omnes hoc loco cives Romani, et qui adsunt et qui ubicunque sunt, vestram severitatem desiderant, vestram fidem implorant, vestrum auxilium requirunt. 16. Omnia sua jura, commoda, auxilia, totam denique libertatem in vestris sententiis versari arbitrantur."——I shall point out the pathetic circumstances exemplified in this passage, observing the order wherein they were enumerated. I have numbered the sentences in the quotation to prevent repetition on referring to them. It must be remarked, first of all, that in judiciary orations, such as this, the proper place for plausibility is the narration; for probability, the confirmation or proof: the other five, though generally admissible into either of those places, shine principally in peroration. I shall show how the orator hath availed himself of these in the passage now cited. First, *importance;* and that first in respect of the enormity of the action, No. 7; of the disposition of the actor, No. 3, 9, 10; and to render probable what might otherwise appear merely conjectural, No. 4, 5, 8, 11, 12; in respect of consequences, their greatness, No. 1, 2: where the crime is most artfully though implicitly represented as subversive of all that was dear to them, liberty, the right of citizens, their most valuable laws, and that idol of the people, the tribunitian power; their extent, No. 15, 16. Secondly, *proximity of time;* there is but an insinuation of this circumstance in the word *tandem,* No. 2. There are two reasons which probably induced the orator in this particular to be so sparing. One is, the recency of the crime, as if the criminal's prætorship was notorious; the other and the weightier is, that of all relations this is the weakest; and even what influence it hath, reflection serves rather to correct than to confirm. In appearing to lay stress on so slight a circumstance, a speaker displays rather penury of matter than abundance. It is better, therefore, in most cases, to suggest it as it were by accident, than to insist on it as of design. It deserves also to be remarked, that the word here employed is very emphatical, as it conveys at the same time a tacit comparison of their so recent degeneracy with the freedom, security, and glory which they had long enjoyed. The same word is again introduced, No.

afraid of the conclusion, if he can make every aggravating circumstance be, as it were, both perceived and felt by them. In the enthymeme, (the syllogism of orators, as Quintilian[1] terms it,) employed in such cases, the sentiment that such a quality or circumstance ought to rouse such a passion, though the foundation of all, is generally assumed without proof, or even without mention. This forms the major proposition, which is suppressed as obvious. His whole art is exerted in evincing the minor, which is the antecedent in his argument, and which maintains the reality of those attendant circumstances in the case in hand. A careful attention to the examples of vehemence in the first chapter, and the quotation in the foregoing note, will sufficiently illustrate this remark.

SECTION VII.—HOW AN UNFAVOURABLE PASSION MUST BE CALMED.

I come now to the second question on the subject of passion. How is an unfavourable passion, or disposition, to be calmed? The answer is, either, first, by annihilating, or at least diminishing the object which raised it; or secondly, by exciting some other passion which may counterwork it.

By proving the falsity of the narration, or the utter incredibility of the future event, on the supposed truth of which the passion was founded, the object is annihilated. It is diminished by all such circumstances as are contrary to those by which it is increased. These are, improbability, implausibility, insignificance, distance of time, remoteness of place, the persons concerned such as we have no connexion with, the consequences such as we have no interest in. The method recommended by Gorgias, and approved by Aristotle, though peculiar in its manner, is, in those cases wherein it may properly be attempted, coincident in effect with that now mentioned. "It was a just opinion of Gorgias, that the serious argument of an adversary should be confounded by ridicule, and his ridicule by serious argument."[1] For this is only endeavouring, by the aid of laughter and contempt, to diminish, or even quite undo, the unfriendly emotions that have been raised in the minds of the hearers; or, on the contrary, by satisfying them of the seriousness of the subject, and of the importance of its consequences, to extinguish the contempt, and make the

---

14, to the same intent. Thirdly, *local connexion;* in respect of vicinage, how affectingly, though indirectly, is it touched, No. 4, 6, 8, 11, 12! indirectly, for reasons similar to those mentioned on the circumstance of time; as to other local connexions, No. 2, "in provincia populi Romani, in oppido fœderatorum." Fourthly, *personal relation;* first of the perpetrator, No. 2, "ab eo qui beneficio," &c. his crime therefore more atrocious and ungrateful, the most sacred rights violated by one who ought to have protected them; next of the sufferer, No. 2, "civis Romanus." This is most pathetically urged, and, by a comparison introduced, greatly heightened, No. 13, 14. Fifthly, the *interest,* which not the hearers only, but all who bear the Roman name, have in the consequences, No. 15, 16. We see, in the above example, with what uncommon address and delicacy those circumstances ought to be sometimes blended, sometimes but insinuated, sometimes, on the contrary, warmly urged, sometimes shaded a little, that the art may be concealed; and, in brief; the whole conducted so as that nothing material may be omitted, that every sentiment may easily follow that which precedes, and usher that which follows it, and that every thing said may appear to be the language of pure nature. The art of the rhetorician, like that of the philosopher, is analytical; the art of the orator is synthetical. The former acts the part of the skilful anatomist, who, by removing the teguments, and nicely separating the parts, presents us with views at once naked, distinct, and hideous, now of the structure of the bones, now of the muscles and tendons, now of the arteries and veins, now of the bowels, now of the brain and nervous system. The latter imitates Nature in the constructing of her work, who, with wonderful symmetry, unites the various organs, adapts them to their respective uses, and covers all with a decent veil, the skin. This, though she hide entirely the more minute and the interior parts, and show not to equal advantage even the articulations of the limbs, and the adjustment of the larger members, adds inexpressible beauty, and strength, and energy to the whole.

[1] Instit. 1. i. c. 9.

---

[1] *Δειν, εφη Γοργιας, την μεν σπουδην διαφθειρειν τωτ εναντιων γελωτι, τω δε γελωτα σπουδη ορθως λεγων.* Rhet. 1. iii. c. 18.

laughter, which the antagonist wanted to excite, appear when examined, no better than madness.

The second way of silencing an unfavourable passion or disposition, is by conjuring up some other passion or disposition, which may overcome it. With regard to conduct, whenever the mind deliberates, it is conscious of contrary motives impelling it in opposite directions; in other words, it finds that acting thus would gratify one passion; not acting, or acting otherwise, would gratify another. To take such a step, I perceive, would promote my interest, but derogate from my honour. Such another will gratify my resentment, but hurt my interest. When this is the case, as the speaker can be at no loss to discover the conflicting passions, he must be sensible that whatever force he adds to the disposition that favours his design, is in fact so much subtracted from the disposition that opposeth it, and conversely; as in the two scales of a balance, it is equal in regard to the effect, whether you add so much weight to one scale, or take it from the other.

Thus we have seen in what manner passion to an absent object may be excited by eloquence, which, by enlivening and invigorating the ideas of imagination, makes them resemble the impressions of sense and the traces of memory; and in this respect hath an effect on the mind similar to that produced by a telescope on the sight; things remote are brought near, things obscure rendered conspicuous. We have seen also in what manner a passion already excited may be calmed; how, by the oratorical magic, as by inverting the telescope, the object may be again removed and diminished.

It were endless to enumerate all the rhetorical figures that are adapted to the pathetic. Let it suffice to say, that most of those already named may be successfully employed here. Of others the principal are these, correction, climax, vision, exclamation, apostrophe, and interrogation. The three first, correction, climax, and vision, tend greatly to enliven the ideas, by the implicit, but animated comparison and opposition conveyed in them. Implicit and indirect comparison is more suitable to the disturbed state of mind required by the pathetic, than that which is explicit and direct. The latter implies leisure and tranquillity, the former rapidity and fire. Exclamation and apostrophe operate chiefly by sympathy, as they are the most ardent expressions of perturbation in the speaker. It at first sight appears more difficult to account for the effect of interrogation, which, being an appeal to the hearers, though it might awaken a closer attention, yet could not, one would imagine, excite in their minds any emotion that was not there before. This, nevertheless, it doth excite, through an oblique operation of the same principle. Such an appeal implies in the orator the strongest confidence in the rectitude of his sentiments, and in the concurrence of every reasonable being. The auditors, by sympathizing with this frame of spirit, find it impracticable to withhold an assent which is so confidently depended on. But there will be occasion afterwards for discussing more particularly the rhetorical tropes and figures, when we come to treat of elocution.

Thus I have finished the consideration which the speaker ought to have of his hearers as men in general; that is, as thinking beings endowed with understanding, imagination, memory, and passions, such as we are conscious of in ourselves, and learn from the experience of their effects to be in others. I have pointed out the arts to be employed by him in engaging all those faculties in his service, that what he advanceth may not only be understood, not only command attention, not only be remembered, but, which is the chief point of all, may interest the heart.

CHAPTER VIII

Of the Consideration which the Speaker ought to have of the Hearers, as such men in particular.

It was remarked in the beginning of the preceding chapter, that the hearers ought to be considered in a twofold view, as men in general, and as such men in particular. The first consideration I have despatched, I now enter on the second.

When it is affirmed that the hearers are to be considered as such men in particular, no more is meant, than that regard ought to be had by the speaker to the special character of the audience, as composed of such individuals; that he may suit himself to them, both in his style and in his arguments.[1] Now, the difference between one audience and another is very great, not only in intellectual but in moral attainments. That may be clearly intelligible to a House of Commons, which would appear as if spoken in an unknown tongue to a conventicle of enthusiasts. That may kindle fury in the latter, which would create no emotion in the former but laughter and contempt. The most obvious difference that appears in different auditories, results from the different cultivation of the understanding; and the influence which this, and their manner of life, have both upon the imagination and upon the memory.

But even in cases wherein the difference in education and moral culture hath not been considerable, different habits afterwards contracted, and different occupations in life, give different propensities, and make one incline more to one passion, another to another. They consequently afford the intelligent speaker an easier passage to the heart, through the channel of the favourite passion. Thus liberty and independence will ever be prevalent motives with republicans, pomp and splendour with those attached to monarchy. In mercantile states, such as Carthage among the ancients, or Holland among the moderns, interest will always prove the most cogent argument; in states solely or chiefly composed of soldiers, such as Sparta and ancient Rome, no inducement will be found a counterpoise to glory. Similar differences are also to be made in addressing different classes of men. With men of genius the most successful topic will be fame; with men of industry, riches; with men of fortune, pleasure.

[1] He must be "Orpheus in sylvis, inter delphinas Arion." VIRG.

But as the characters of audiences may be infinitely diversified, and as the influence they ought to have respectively upon the speaker must be obvious to a person of discernment, it is sufficient here to have observed thus much in the general concerning them.

CHAPTER IX

Of the Consideration which the Speaker ought to have of Himself.

THE last consideration I mentioned, is that which the speaker ought to have of himself. By this we are to understand, not that estimate of himself which is derived directly from consciousness or self-acquaintance, but that which is obtained reflexively from the opinion entertained of him by the hearers, or the character which he bears with them. Sympathy is one main engine by which the orator operates on the passions.

With them who laugh, our social joy
appears;
With them who mourn, we sympathize in
tears;
If you would have me weep, begin the strain,
Then I shall feel your sorrows, feel your
pain.[1]

FRANCIS.

Whatever, therefore, weakens that principle of sympathy, must do the speaker unutterable prejudice in respect of his power over the passions of his audience, but not in this respect only. One source, at least, of the primary influence of testimony on faith, is doubtless to be attributed to the

[1] Ut ridentibus arrident, ita flentibus adflent
Humani vultus. Si vis me flere, dolendum est
Primum ipsi tibi: tunc tua me infortunia lædent.
Hor. De Arte Poet.

same communicative principle. At the same time it is certain, as was remarked above, that every testimony doth not equally attach this principle; that in this particular the reputation of the attester hath a considerable power. Now, the speaker's apparent conviction of the truth of what he advanceth, adds to all his other arguments an evidence, though not precisely the same, yet near akin to that of his own testimony.[1] This hath some weight even with the wisest hearers, but is every thing with the vulgar. Whatever therefore lessens sympathy, must also impair belief.

Sympathy in the hearers to the speaker may be lessened several ways, chiefly by these two; by a low opinion of his intellectual abilities, and by a bad opinion of his morals. The latter is the more prejudicial of the two. Men generally will think themselves in less danger of being seduced by a man of weak understanding, but of distinguished probity, than by a man of the best understanding who is of a profligate life. So much more powerfully do the qualities of the heart attach us, than those of the head. This preference, though it may be justly called untaught and instinctive, arising purely from the original frame of the mind, reason, or the knowledge of mankind acquired by experience, instead of weakening, seems afterwards to corroborate. Hence it hath become a common topic with rhetoricians, that, in order to be a successful orator, one must be a good man; for to be good is the only sure way of being long esteemed good, and to be esteemed good is previously necessary to one's being heard with due attention and regard. Consequently, the topic hath a foundation in human nature. There are indeed other things in the character of the speaker, which, in a less degree, will hurt his influence; youth, inexperience of affairs, former want of success, and the like.

But of all the prepossessions in the minds of the hearers which tend to impede or counteract the design of the speaker, party-spirit, where it happens to prevail, is the most pernicious, being at once the most inflexible and the most unjust. This prejudice I mention by itself, as those above recited may have place at any time, and in any national circumstances. This hath place only when a people is so unfortunate as to be torn by faction. In that case, if the speaker and the hearers, or the bulk of the hearers, be of contrary parties, their minds will be more prepossessed against him, though his life were ever so blameless, than if he were a man of the most flagitious manners, but of the same party. This holds but too much alike of all parties, religious and political. Violent party-men not only lose all sympathy with those of the opposite side, but contract an antipathy to them. This, on some occasions, even the divinest eloquence will not surmount.

As to personal prejudices in general, I shall conclude with two remarks. The first is, the more gross the hearers are, so much the more susceptible they are of such prejudices. Nothing exposes the mind more to all their baneful influences than ignorance and rudeness; the rabble chiefly consider who speaks, men of sense and education what is spoken. Nor are the multitude, to do them justice, less excessive in their love than in their hatred, in their attachments than in their aversions. From a consciousness, it would seem, of their own incapacity to guide themselves, they are ever prone blindly to submit to the guidance of some popular orator, who hath had the address first, either to gain their approbation by his real or pretended virtues, or, which is the easier way, to recommend himself to their esteem by a flaming zeal for their favourite distinctions, and afterwards by his eloquence to work upon their passions. At the same time it must be acknowledged, on the other hand, that even men of the most improved intellects, and most refined sentiments, are not altogether beyond the reach of preconceived opinion, either in the speaker's favour or to his prejudice.

The second remark is, that when the opinion of the audience is unfavourable, the speaker hath need to be much more cautious in every step he takes, to show more modesty, and greater defer-

[1] Ne illud quidem præteribo, quantam afferat fidem expositioni narrantis auctoritas. QUINT. lib. iv. cap. 2.

ence to the judgment of his hearers; perhaps in order to win them, he may find it necessary to make some concessions in relation to his former principles or conduct, and to entreat their attention from pure regard to the subject; that, like men of judgment and candour, they would impartially consider what is said, and give a welcome reception to truth, from what quarter soever it proceed. Thus he must attempt, if possible, to mollify them, gradually to insinuate himself into their favour, and thereby imperceptibly to transfuse his sentiments and passions into their minds.

The man who enjoys the advantage of popularity needs not this caution. The minds of his auditors are perfectly attuned to his. They are prepared for adopting implicitly his opinions, and accompanying him in all his most passionate excursions. When the people are willing to run with you, you may run as fast as you can, especially when the case requires impetuosity and despatch. But if you find in them no such ardour, if it is not even without reluctance that they are induced to walk with you, you must slacken your pace and keep them company, lest they either stand still or turn back. Different rules are given by rhetoricians as adapted to different circumstances. Differences in this respect are numberless. It is enough here to have observed those principles in the mind on which the rules are founded.

CHAPTER X

The different kinds of public speaking in use among the moderns compared, with a view to their different advantages in respect of eloquence.

THE principal sorts of discourses which here demand our notice, and on which I intend to make some observations, are the three following: orations delivered at the bar, those pronounced in the senate, and those spoken from the pulpit. I do not make a separate article of the speeches delivered by judges to their colleagues on the bench; because, though there be something peculiar here, arising from the difference in character that subsists between the judge and the pleader, in all the other material circumstances, the persons addressed, the subject, the occasion, and the purpose in speaking, there is in these two sorts a perfect coincidence. In like manner, I forbear to mention the theatre, because so entirely dissimilar, both in form and in kind, as hardly to be capable of a place in the comparison. Besides, it is only a cursory view of the chief differences, and not a critical examination of them all, that is here proposed; my design being solely to assist the mind both in apprehending rightly, and in applying properly, the principles above laid down. In this respect, the present discussion will serve to exemplify and illustrate those principles. Under these five particulars, therefore, the speaker, the hearers or persons addressed, the subject, the occasion, and the end in view, or the effect intended to be produced by the discourse, I shall arrange, for order's sake, the remarks I intend to lay before the reader.

SECTION I.—IN REGARD TO THE SPEAKER.

The first consideration is that of the character to be sustained by the speaker. It was remarked in general, in the preceding chapter, that for promoting the success of the orator, (whatever be the kind of public speaking in which he is concerned,) it is a matter of some consequence that, in the opinion of those whom he addresseth, he is both a wise and a good man. But though this in some measure holds universally, nothing is more certain than that the degree of consequence which lies in their opinion, is exceedingly different in the different kinds. In each it depends chiefly on two circumstances, the nature of his profession as a public speaker, and the character of those to whom his discourses are addressed.

As to the first, arising from the nature of the profession, it will not admit a question, that the preacher hath in this respect the most difficult task; inasmuch as he hath a character to support, which is much more easily injured than that either of the senator, or the speaker at the bar. No doubt the reputation of capacity, experience in affairs, and as much integrity as is thought attainable by those called men of the world, will add weight to the words of the senator; that of skill in his profession, and fidelity in his representation, will serve to recommend what is spoken by the lawyer at the bar; but if these characters in general remain unimpeached, the public will be sufficiently indulgent to both in every other respect. On the contrary, there is little or no indulgence, in regard to his own failings, to be expected by the man who is professedly a sort of authorized censor, who hath it in charge to mark and reprehend the faults of others. And even in the execution of this so ticklish a part of his office, the least excess on either hand exposeth him to censure and dislike. Too much lenity is enough to stigmatize him as lukewarm in the cause of virtue, and too much severity as a stranger to the spirit of the gospel.

But let us consider more directly what is implied in the character, that we may better judge of the effect it will have on the expectations and demands of the people, and consequently on his public teaching. First, then, it is a character of some authority, as it is of one educated for a purpose so important as that of a teacher of religion. This authority, however, from the nature of the function, must be tempered with moderation, candour, and benevolence. The preacher of the gospel, as the very terms import, is the minister of grace, the herald of divine mercy to ignorant, sinful, and erring men. The magistrate, on the contrary, (under which term may be included secular judges and counsellors of every denomination,) is the minister of divine justice and of wrath. *He beareth not the sword in vain.*[1] He is on the part of heaven the avenger of the society with whose protection he is intrusted, against all who invade its rights. The first operates chiefly on our love, the second on our fear. *Minister of religion,* like angel of God, is a name that ought to convey the idea of something endearing and attractive; whereas the title *minister of justice* invariably suggests the notion of something awful and unrelenting. In the former, even his indignation against sin ought to be surmounted by his pity of the condition, and concern for the recovery, of the sinner. Though firm in declaring the will of God, though steady in maintaining the cause of truth, yet mild in his addresses to the people, condescending to the weak, using rather entreaty than command, beseeching them by the lowliness and gentleness of Christ, knowing that "the servant of the Lord must not strive, but be gentle to all men, apt to teach, patient, in meekness instructing those that oppose themselves."[1] He must be grave without moroseness, cheerful without levity. And even in setting before his people the terrors of the Lord, affection ought manifestly to predominate in the warning which he is compelled to give. From these few hints it plainly appears, that there is a certain delicacy in the character of a preacher, which he is never at liberty totally to overlook, and to which, if there appear any thing incongruous, either in his conduct or in his public performances, it will never fail to injure their effect. On the contrary, it is well known, that as, in the other professions, the speaker's private life is but very little minded, so there are many things which, though they would be accounted nowise unsuitable from the bar or in the senate, would be deemed altogether unbefitting the pulpit.

It ought not to be overlooked, on the other hand, that there is one peculiarity in the lawyer's professional character, which is unfavourable to conviction, and consequently gives him some disadvantage both of the senator and the preacher. We know that he must defend his client, and argue on the side on which he is retained. We know also

[1] Romans xiii. 4.

[1] 2 Tim. ii. 24, 25.

that a trifling and accidental circumstance, which nowise affects the merit of the cause, such as a prior application from the adverse party, would probably have made him employ the same acuteness, and display the same fervour, on the opposite side of the question. This circumstance, though not considered as a fault in the character of the man, but a natural, because an ordinary, consequent of the office, cannot fail, when reflected on, to make us shyer of yielding our assent. It removes entirely what was observed in the preceding chapter to be of great moment, our belief of the speaker's sincerity. This belief can hardly be rendered compatible with the knowledge that both truth and right are so commonly and avowedly sacrificed to interest. I acknowledge that an uncommon share of eloquence will carry off the minds of most people from attending to this circumstance, or at least from paying any regard to it. Yet Antony is represented by Cicero,[1] as thinking the advocate's reputation so delicate, that the practice of amusing himself in philosophical disputations with his friends is sufficient to hurt it, and consequently to affect the credibility of his pleadings. Surely the barefaced prostitution of his talents, (and in spite of his commonness, what else can we call it?) in supporting indifferently, as pecuniary considerations determine him, truth or falsehood, justice or injustice, must have a still worse effect on the opinion of his hearers.

It was affirmed that the consequence of the speaker's own character, in furthering or hindering his success, depends in some measure on the character of those whom he addresseth. Here indeed it will be found, on inquiry, that the preacher labours under a manifest disadvantage. Most congregations are of that kind, as will appear from the article immediately succeeding, which, agreeably to an observation made in the former chapter, very much considers who speaks; those addressed from the bar, or in the senate, consider more what is spoken.

Section II.—In Regard to the Persons Addressed.

The second particular mentioned as a ground of comparison, is the consideration of the character of the hearers, or more properly the persons addressed. The necessity which a speaker is under of suiting himself to his audience, both that he may be understood by them, and that his words may have influence upon them, is a maxim so evident as to need neither proof nor illustration.

Now, the first remark that claims our attention here is, that the more mixed the auditory is, the greater is the difficulty of speaking to them with effect. The reason is obvious—what will tend to favour your success with one, may tend to obstruct it with another. The more various therefore the individuals are, in respect of age, rank, fortune, education, prejudices, the more delicate must be the art of preserving propriety in an address to the whole. The pleader has, in this respect, the simplest and the easiest task of all; the judges, to whom his oration is addressed, being commonly men of the same rank, of similar education, and not differing greatly in respect of studies or attainments. The difference in these respects is much more considerable when he addresses the jury. A speaker in the house of peers hath not so mixed an auditory as one who harangues in the house of commons. And even here, as all the members may be supposed to have been educated as gentlemen, the audience is not nearly so promiscuous as were the popular assemblies of Athens and of Rome, to which their demagogues declaimed with so much vehemence, and so wonderful success. Yet, even of these, women, minors, and servants made no part.

We may therefore justly reckon a christian congregation in a populous and flourishing city, where there is a great variety in rank and education, to be of all audiences the most promiscuous. And though it is impossible that, in so mixed a multitude, every thing that is advanced by the

[1] De Orat. Lib. 2. Ego ista studia non improbo, moderata modo sint. Opinionem istorum studiorum, et suspicionem omnium artificii apud eos qui res judicent, oratori adversariam esse arbitror. Imminuit enim et oratoris auctoritatem, et orationis fidem.

speaker should, both in sentiment and in expression, be adapted to the apprehension of every individual hearer, and fall in with his particular prepossessions, yet it may be expected, that whatever is advanced shall be within the reach of every class of hearers, and shall not unnecessarily shock the innocent prejudices of any. This is still, however, to be understood with the exception of mere children, fools, and a few others who, through the total neglect of parents or guardians in their education, are grossly ignorant. Such, though in the audience, are not to be considered as constituting a part of it. But how great is the attention requisite in the speaker in such an assembly, that, whilst on the one hand he avoids, either in style or in sentiment, soaring above the capacity of the lower class, he may not, on the other, sink below the regard of the higher. To attain simplicity without flatness, delicacy without refinement, perspicuity without recurring to low idioms and similitudes, will require his utmost care.

Another remark on this article that deserves our notice is, that the less improved in knowledge and discernment the hearers are, the easier it is for the speaker to work upon their passions, and by working on their passions, to obtain his end. This, it must be owned, appears, on the other hand, to give a considerable advantage to the preacher, as in no congregation can the bulk of the people be regarded as on a footing, in point of improvement, with either house of parliament, or with the judges in a court of judicature. It is certain, that the more gross the hearers are, the more avowedly may you address yourself to their passions, and the less occasion there is for argument; whereas, the more intelligent they are, the more covertly must you operate on their passions, and the more attentive must you be in regard to the justness, or at least the speciousness of your reasoning. Hence some have strangely concluded, that the only scope for eloquence is in haranguing the multitude; that in gaining over to your purpose men of knowledge and breeding, the exertion of oratorical talents hath no influence. This is precisely as if one should argue, because a mob is much easier subdued than regular troops, there is no occasion for the art of war, nor is there a proper field for the exertion of military skill, unless when you are quelling an undisciplined rabble. Every body sees in this case, not only how absurd such a way of arguing would be, but that the very reverse ought to be the conclusion. The reason why people do not so quickly perceive the absurdity in the other case is, that they affix no distinct meaning to the word *eloquence,* often denoting no more by that term than simply the power of moving the passions. But even in this improper acceptation, their notion is far from being just; for wherever there are men, learned or ignorant, civilized or barbarous, there are passions; and the greater the difficulty is in affecting these, the more art is requisite. The truth is, eloquence, like every other art, proposeth the accomplishment of a certain end. Passion is for the most part but the means employed for effecting the end, and therefore, like all other means, will no further be regarded in any case, than it can be rendered conducible to the end.

Now the preacher's advantage even here, in point of facility, at least in several situations, will not appear, on reflection, to be so great as on a superficial view it may be thought. Let it be observed, that in such congregations as were supposed, there is a mixture of superior and inferior ranks. It is therefore the business of the speaker, so far only to accommodate himself to one class, as not wantonly to disgust another. Besides, it will scarcely be denied that those in the superior walks of life, however much by reading and conversation improved in all genteel accomplishments, often have as much need of religious instruction and moral improvement, as those who in every other particular are acknowledged to be their inferiors. And doubtless the reformation of such will be allowed to be, in one respect, of greater importance, (and therefore never to be overlooked,) that in consequence of such an event, more good may redound to others, from the more extensive influence of their authority and example.

SECTION III.—IN REGARD TO THE SUBJECT.

The third particular mentioned was the subject of discourse. This may be considered in a twofold view; first, as implying the topics of argument, motives, and principles, which are suited to each of the different kinds, and must be employed in order to produce the intended effect on the hearers; secondly, as implying the person or things in whose favour, or to whose prejudice, the speaker purposes to excite the passions of the audience, and thereby to influence their determinations.

On the first of these articles, I acknowledge the preacher hath incomparably the advantage of every other public orator. At the bar, critical explications of dark and ambiguous statutes, quotations of precedents sometimes contradictory, and comments on jarring decisions and reports, often necessarily consume the great part of the speaker's time. Hence the mixture of a sort of metaphysics and verbal criticism, employed by lawyers in their pleadings, hath come to be distinguished by the name *chicane,* a species of reasoning too abstruse to command attention of any continuance even from the studious, and consequently not very favourable to the powers of rhetoric. When the argument doth not turn on the common law, or on nice and hypercritical explications of the statute, but on the great principles of natural right and justice, as sometimes happens, particularly in criminal cases, the speaker is much more advantageously situated for exhibiting his rhetorical talents than in the former case. When, in consequence of the imperfection of the evidence, the question happens to be more question of fact than either of municipal law or of natural equity, the pleader hath more advantages than in the first case, and fewer than in the second.

Again, in the deliberations in the senate, the utility or the disadvantages that will probably follow on a measure proposed, if it should receive the sanction of the legislature, constitute the principal topics of debate. This, though it sometimes leads to a kind of reasoning rather too complex and involved for ordinary apprehension, is in the main more favourable to the display of pathos, vehemence, and sublimity than the much greater part of the forensic causes can be said to be. That these qualities have been sometimes found in a very high degree in the orations pronounced in a British senate, is a fact incontrovertible.

But beyond all question, the preacher's subject of argument, considered in itself, is infinitely more lofty and more affecting. The doctrines of religion are such as relate to God, the adorable Creator and Ruler of the world, his attributes, government, and law. What science to be compared with it in sublimity? It teaches also the origin of man, his primitive dignity, the source of his degeneracy, the means of his recovery, the eternal happiness that awaits the good, and the future misery of the impenitent. Is there any kind of knowledge in which human creatures are so deeply interested? In a word, whether we consider the doctrines of religion or its documents, the examples it holds forth to our imitation, or its motives, promises, and threatenings, we see on every hand a subject that gives scope for the exertion of all the highest powers of rhetoric. What are the sanctions of any human laws, compared with the sanctions of the divine law, with which we are brought acquainted by the gospel? Or where shall we find instructions, similitudes, and examples, that speak so directly to the heart, as the parables and other divine lessons of our blessed Lord?

In regard to the second thing which I took notice of as included under the general term *subject,* namely the persons or things in whose favour, or to whose prejudice the speaker intends to excite the passions of the audience, and thereby to influence their determinations, the other two have commonly the advantage of the preacher. The reason is, that his subject is generally things; theirs, on the contrary, is persons. In what regards the painful passions, indignation, hatred, contempt, abhorrence, this difference invariably obtains. The preacher's business is solely to excite your detestation of the crime; the pleader's business is principally to make you detest the criminal. The former paints vice to you in all its odious colours; the latter paints the vicious. There is a degree of abstraction, and consequently a much greater degree of attention, requisite to enable us to form just conceptions of the ideas and sentiments of the former; whereas, those of the latter, referring to an actual, perhaps a living, present, and well-known subject, are much more level to common capacity, and therefore not only are more easily apprehended by the understanding, but take a stronger hold of the imagination. It would have been impossible even for Cicero to inflame the minds of the people to so high a pitch against *oppression,* considered in the abstract, as he actually did inflame them against Verres the *oppressor;* nor could he have incensed them so much against *treason* and *conspiracy,* as he did incense them against Catiline the *traitor* and *conspirator.* The like may be observed of the effects of his orations against Antony, and in a thousand other instances.

Though the occasions in this way are more frequent at the bar, yet, as the deliberations in the senate often proceed on the reputation and past conduct of individuals, there is commonly here also a much better handle for rousing the passions than that enjoyed by the preacher. How much advantage Demosthenes drew from the known character and insidious arts of Philip king of Macedon, for influencing the resolves of the Athenians, and other Grecian states, those who are acquainted with the Philippics of the orator, and the history of that period, will be very sensible. In what concerns the pleasing affections, the preacher may sometimes, not often, avail himself of real human characters, as in funeral sermons, and in discourses on the patterns of virtue given us by our Saviour, and by those saints of whom we have the history in the sacred code. But such examples are comparatively few.

SECTION IV.—IN REGARD TO THE OCCASION.

The fourth circumstance mentioned as a ground of comparison, is the particular occasion of speaking. And in this I think it evident, that both the pleader and the senator have the advantage of the preacher. When any important cause comes to be tried before a civil judicatory, or when any important question comes to be agitated in either house of parliament, as the point to be discussed hath generally for some time before been a topic of conversation in most companies, perhaps throughout the kingdom, (which of itself is sufficient to give consequence to any thing,) people are apprized beforehand of the particular day fixed for the discussion. Accordingly, they come prepared with some knowledge of the case, a persuasion of its importance, and a curiosity which sharpens their attention, and assists both their understanding and their memory.

Men go to church without any of these advantages. The subject of the sermon is not known to the congregation, till the minister announce it just as he begins, by reading the text. Now, from our experience of human nature, we may be sensible that whatever be the comparative importance of the things themselves, the generality of men cannot here be wrought up, in an instant, to the like anxious curiosity about what is to be said, nor can be so well prepared for hearing it. It may indeed be urged, in regard to those subjects which come regularly to be discussed at stated times, as on public festivals, as well as in regard to assize-sermons, charity-sermons, and other occasional discourses, that these must be admitted as exceptions. Perhaps in some degree they are, but not altogether: for first, the precise point to be argued, or proposition to be evinced, is very rarely known. The most that we can say is, that the subject will have a relation (sometimes remote enough) to such an article of faith, or to the obligations we lie under to the practice of such a duty. But further, if the topic were ever so well known, the frequent recurrence of such occasions, once a year at least, hath long familiarized us to them, and, by destroying their novelty, hath abated exceedingly of that ardour which ariseth in the mind for hearing a discussion, conceived to be of importance, which one never had access to hear before, and probably never will have access to hear again.

I shall here take notice of another circumstance, which, without great stretch, may be classed under this article, and which likewise gives some advantage to the counsellor and the senator. It is the opposition and contradiction which they expect to meet with. Opponents sharpen one another, as iron sharpeneth iron. There is not the same spur either to exertion in the speaker, or to attention in the hearer, where there is no conflict, where you have no adversary to encounter with equal terms. Mr. Bickerstaff would have made but small progress in the science of defence, by pushing at the human figure which he had chalked upon the wall,[1] in comparison of what he might have made by the help of a fellow combatant of flesh and blood. I do not, however, pretend that these cases are entirely parallel. The whole of an adversary's plea may be perfectly known, and may, to the satisfaction of every reasonable person, be perfectly confuted, though he hath not been heard by the counsel at the bar.

SECTION V.—IN REGARD TO THE END IN VIEW.

The fifth and last particular mentioned, and indeed the most important of them all, is the effect in each species intended to be produced. The primary intention of preaching is the reformation of mankind. "The grace of God, that bringeth salvation, hath appeared to all men, teaching us that, denying ungodliness and worldly lusts, we should live soberly, righteously, and godly in this present world."[2] Reformation of life and manners—of all things that which is the most difficult by any means whatever to effectuate; I may add, of all tasks ever attempted by persuasion, that which has the most frequently baffled its power.

What is the task of any other orator compared with this? It is really as nothing at all, and hardly deserves to be named. An unjust judge, gradually worked on by the resistless force of human eloquence, may be persuaded, against his inclination, perhaps against a previous resolution, to pronounce an equitable sentence. All the effect on him, intended by the pleader, was merely momentary. The orator hath had the address to employ the time allowed him in such a manner as to secure the happy moment. Notwithstanding this, there may be no real change wrought upon the judge. He may continue the same obdurate wretch he was before. Nay, if the sentence had been delayed but a single day after hearing the cause, he would perhaps have given a very different award.

Is it to be wondered at, that when the passions of the people were agitated by the persuasive powers of a Demosthenes, whilst the thunder of his eloquence was yet sounding in their ears, the orator should be absolute master of their resolves? But an apostle or evangelist (for there is no anachronism in a bare supposition) might have thus addressed the celebrated Athenian, "You do, indeed, succeed to admiration, and the address and genius which you display in speaking justly entitle you to our praise. But however great the consequences may be of the measures to which, by your eloquence, they are determined, the change produced in the people is nothing, or next to nothing. If you would be ascertained of the truth of this, allow the assembly to disperse immediately after hearing you; give them time to cool, and then collect their votes, and it is a thousand to one you shall find that the charm is dissolved."

But very different is the purpose of the christian orator. It is not a momentary, but a permanent effect at which he aims. It is not an immediate and favourable suffrage, but a thorough change of heart and disposition, that will satisfy his view. That man would need to be possessed of oratory superior to human, who would effectually persuade him that stole to steal no more, the sensualist to forego his pleasures, and the miser his hoards, the insolent and haughty to become meek and humble, the vindictive forgiving, the cruel and unfeeling merciful and humane.

---

[1] Tatler.

[2] Tit. ii. 11, 12.

I may add to these considerations, that the difficulty lies not only in the permanency, but in the very nature of the change to be effected. It is wonderful, but it is too well vouched to admit of a doubt, that by the powers of rhetoric you may produce in mankind almost any change more easily than this. It is not unprecedented that one should persuade a multitude, from mistaken motives of religion, to act the part of ruffians, fools, or madmen; to perpetrate the most extravagant, nay, the most flagitious actions; to steel their hearts against humanity, and the loudest calls of affection: but where is the eloquence that will gain such an ascendant over a multitude, as to persuade them, for the love of God, to be wise, and just, and good? Happy the preacher whose sermons, by the blessing of Heaven, have been instrumental in producing even a few such instances! Do but look into the annals of church history, and you will soon be convinced of the surprising difference there is in the two cases mentioned—the amazing facility of the one, and the almost impossibility of the other.

As to the foolish or mad extravagances, hurtful only to themselves, to which numbers may be excited by the powers of persuasion, the history of the flagellants, and even the history of monachism, afford many unquestionable examples. But what is much worse, at one time you see Europe nearly depopulated at the persuasion of a fanatical monk, its inhabitants rushing armed into Asia, in order to fight for Jesus Christ, as they termed it, but as it proved in fact, to disgrace, as far as lay in them, the name of Christ and of Christian amongst infidels; to butcher those who never injured them, and to whose lands they had at least no better title than those whom they intended, by all possible means, to dispossess; and to give the world a melancholy proof, that there is no pitch of brutality and rapacity to which the passions of avarice and ambition, consecrated and inflamed by religious enthusiasm, will not drive mankind. At another time you see multitudes, by the like methods, worked up into a fury against innocent countrymen, neighbours, friends, and kinsmen, glorying in being most active in cutting the throats of those who were formerly held dear to them.

Such were the crusades preached up but too effectually, first against the Mahometans in the East, and next against Christians whom they called heretics, in the heart of Europe. And even in our own time, have we not seen new factions raised by popular declaimers, whose only merit was impudence, whose only engine of influence was calumny and self-praise, whose only moral lesson was malevolence? As to the dogmas whereby such have at any time affected to discriminate themselves, these are commonly no other than the *shibboleth,* the watchword of the party, worn, for distinction's sake, as a badge, a jargon unintelligible alike to the teacher and to the learner. Such apostles never fail to make proselytes. For who would not purchase heaven at so cheap rate? There is nothing that people can more easily afford. It is only to think very well of their leader and of themselves, to think very ill of their neighbour, to calumniate him freely, and to hate him heartily.

I am sensible that some will imagine that this account itself throws an insuperable obstacle in our way, as from it one will naturally infer, that oratory must be one of the most dangerous things in the world, and much more capable of doing ill than good. It needs but some reflection to make this mighty obstacle entirely vanish.—Very little eloquence is necessary for persuading people to a conduct to which their own depravity hath previously given them a bias. How soothing is it to them not only to have their minds made easy under the indulged malignity of their disposition, but to have that very malignity sanctified with a good name! So little of the oratorical talent is required here, that those who court popular applause, and look upon it as the pinnacle of human glory to be blindly followed by the multitude, commonly recur to defamation, especially of superiors and brethren, not so much for a subject on which they may display their eloquence, as for a succedaneum to supply their want of eloquence, a succedaneum which never yet was found to fail. I knew a preacher who, from this expedient alone, from being long the aversion of the populace, on account of his dulness, awkwardness, and coldness, all of a sudden became their idol. Little force is necessary to push down heavy bodies placed on the verge of a declivity, but much force is requisite to stop them in their progress, and push them up.

If a man should say, that because the first is more frequently effected than the last, it is the best trial of strength, and the only suitable use to which it can be applied, we should at least not think him remarkable for distinctness in his ideas. Popularity alone, therefore, is no test at all of the eloquence of the speaker, no more than velocity alone would be of the force of the external impulse originally given to the body moving. As in this the direction of the body, and other circumstances, must be taken into the account; so in that, you must consider the tendency of the teaching, whether it favours or opposes the vices of the hearers. To head a sect, to infuse party-spirit, to make men arrogant, uncharitable, and malevolent, is the easiest task imaginable, and to which almost any blockhead is fully equal. But to produce the contrary effect, to subdue the spirit of faction, and that monster spiritual pride, with which it is invariably accompanied, to inspire equity, moderation, and charity into men's sentiments and conduct with regard to others, is the genuine test of eloquence. Here its triumph is truly glorious, and in its application to this end lies its great utility:

> *The gates of hell are open night and day;*
> *Smooth the descent, and easy is the way:*
> *But to return and view the cheerful skies,*
> *In this the task and mighty labour lies.*[1]
>
> DRYDEN.

Now in regard to the comparison, from which I fear I shall be thought to have digressed, between the forensic and senatorian eloquence, and that of the pulpit, I must not omit to observe, that in what I say of the difference of the effect to be produced by the last mentioned species, I am to be understood as speaking of the effect intended by preaching in general, and even of that which, in whole or in part, is, or ought to be, either more immediately or more remotely, the scope of all discourses proceeding from the pulpit. I am, at the same time, sensible that in some of these, beside the ultimate view, there is an immediate and outward effect which the sermon is intended to produce. This is the case particularly in charity-sermons, and perhaps some other occasional discourses. Now of these few, in respect of such immediate purpose, we must admit, that they bear a pretty close analogy to the pleadings of the advocate, and the orations of the senator.

Upon the whole of the comparison I have stated, it appears manifest that, in most of the particulars above enumerated, the preacher labours under a very great disadvantage. He hath himself a more delicate part to perform than either the pleader or the senator, and a character to maintain which is much more easily injured. The auditors, though rarely so accomplished as to require the same accuracy of composition, or acuteness of reasoning, as may be expected in the other two, are more various in age, rank, taste, inclinations, sentiments, prejudices, to which he must accommodate himself. And if he derives some advantages from the richness, the variety, and the nobleness of the principles, motives, and arguments with which his subject furnishes him, he derives also some inconveniences from this circumstance, that almost the only engine by which he can operate on the passions of his hearers, is the exhibition of abstract qualities, virtues, and vices, whereas that chiefly employed by other orators is the exhibition of real persons, the virtuous and the vicious. Nor are the occasions of his addresses to the people equally fitted with those of the senator and of the pleader for exciting their curiosity and riveting their attention. And, finally, the task assigned him, the effect which he ought ever to have in view, is so great, so important, so durable, as seems to bid defiance to the strongest efforts of oratorical genius.

---

[1] _____ Facilis descensus Averni:
Noctes atque dies patet atri janua Ditis:
Sed revocare gradum, superasque evadere ad auras,
Hic labor, hoc opus est. VIRG. ÆN. lib vi.

Nothing is more common than for people, I suppose without reflecting, to express their wonder that there is so little eloquence amongst our preachers, and that so little success attends their preaching. As to the last, their success, it is a matter not to be ascertained with so much precision as some appear fondly to imagine. The evil prevented, as well as the good promoted, ought here, in all justice, to come into the reckoning. And what that may be, it is impossible in any supposed circumstances to determine. As to the first, their eloquence, I acknowledge that for my own part, considering how rare the talent is among men in general, considering all the disadvantages preachers labour under, not only those above enumerated, but others, arising from their different situations, particularly considering the frequency of this exercise, together with the other duties of their office, to which the fixed pastors are obliged, I have been for a long time more disposed to wonder, that we hear so many instructive and even eloquent sermons, than that we hear so few.

• • •

INTRODUCTION TO HUGH BLAIR

Hugh Blair was a Scottish theorist who lived from 1718 to 1800. He was the first Regius Professor of Rhetoric and Belles Lettres at Edinburgh University. Blair was also a minister, and in that capacity was an active preacher who published four books of sermons. Blair's interests included philosophy, and he was instrumental in defending fellow philosophers such as David Hume against charges of heresy made by the Church of Scotland.

Here you will find an excerpt from Blair's book, *Lectures on Rhetoric and Belles Lettres*. This was quite popular and influential in Blair's time, even though the theory presented in it is not strikingly original. Blair has been compared to Quintilian for his efforts at summarizing the rhetorical thinking of his time and making it accessible to the public for educational purposes.

The line of rhetorical theory concerned with critical judgment of texts, first exemplified in this book by Longinus, runs through Blair. His most interesting contributions to rhetorical theory are found in the material excerpted here. Blair attempts to develop a critical method for understanding *taste*.

Blair's reading begins with an interesting argument in praise of the human ability to communicate. Communication is valuable because *reason* is so much enhanced by communication; note that Blair describes reason as in need of assistance from communication. In this way he allies reason, rhetoric, and logic. Blair's argument for the importance of communicating reason, not just reasoning itself, stands in contrast to Descartes's model of a solitary thinker or doubter, and finds a place for rhetoric alongside reason, which was so valued in the Enlightenment.

Progress, Blair argues, is a major beneficial result of the new science of his age. But he claims that progress may be made in artistic, humanist affairs as well. His purpose here is to suggest a way to progress in thinking analytically about non-scientific matters, specifically the arts. In doing so, he is also claiming to be thinking rhetorically. Note that Blair argues that rhetoric is a speculative, rather than a practical, art. In other words, it is a tool of analysis rather than a guide to actually practicing something, namely public speaking. Blair's stance reflects the shift in the Enlightenment from a focus on speakers to a focus on audiences who might have more use for a speculative rather than a practical discourse.

Blair turns his attention to *taste,* which is a faculty. He uses faculty psychology to describe taste as a power in humans—the power to experience beauty. Although taste is a faculty, it is stronger in some people than in others. However, it is also a faculty that can be developed, and suggesting ways to do so is Blair's purpose. He offers several techniques for developing taste, such as its conscious exercise in artistic experience and taking special notice of models of aesthetic excellence.

Watch carefully Blair's theme of linking taste to *moral virtues.* Criticism has a moral dimension, he argues, because it achieves a proper balance between the senses and the intellect, unlike "low" pleasures that appeal only to our baser instincts. Taste is marked by "delicacy" and "correctness," he argues, and these dimensions also have moral as well as political weightings. Delicacy in artistic experience is likely to be something more often found among upper classes whose members, in Enlightenment England, had very little physical work to do. Compare the pleasures economically available to a coal worker of the period to those economically available to the idle rich, and the political and moral freight of a term like "delicacy" or "correctness" becomes apparent.

If one is to develop taste, then one requires a *standard of taste,* according to Blair. It is unthinkable, in his view, that one pleasure should be as good as another. There must be some way, Blair argues, to distinguish between these pleasures. Note that he supports his argument by comparing the pleasures of an "Addison" (a noted esthete of his time, much admired by the elite of British society) with the pleasures of "Laplanders" or "Hottentots." Surely the former pleasures are better, but how can we distinguish them from these "low" alternatives? Let us bear in mind that Britain during this period was colonizing and conquering people all over the globe. One way to justify this imperialism was to draw distinctions between "superior" British culture and the "degraded" cultures of those conquered people (in short, Laplanders and Hottentots). In this way we see Blair using criticism in rhetorical ways to prop up the cultural pretensions of British imperialism.

Blair wrestles with the issue of how a standard of taste might be found and justified. He considers the standard of what most people agree upon as good or beautiful, but he ends up rejecting that standard. Think about the classism inherent in his arguments against letting the general population set standards of taste. He finally argues that the preferences of the most civilized and cultured people should be used as the standards of taste. Those were, of course, Blair's social and economic cohorts.

The reading ends with Blair's reflections upon rhetoric as a particular kind of aesthetic or artistic activity, subject to standards of taste as was any other art. He follows Campbell in stressing the importance of appealing to different faculties to achieve different ends. Blair echoes Augustine in arguing that there are three levels of rhetorical purposes.

Throughout history, people have used artistic and aesthetic standards to achieve political ends. In our times, think about which pleasurable artistic experiences and which sorts of entertainment are deemed better or worse, more or less acceptable, high or low. Those judgments are likely to be weighted in terms of who has power, who is in a privileged economic class, which groups are closer to the mainstream, and so forth. In Blair we find an interesting rhetorical theory in the service of criticism, but we also find the rhetorical uses of rhetorical theory in the moral weightings he inserts into his standards of taste.

HUGH BLAIR

LECTURES ON RHETORIC AND BELLES LETTRES

LECTURE I

INTRODUCTION

One of the most distinguished privileges which Providence has conferred upon mankind, is the power of communicating their thoughts to one another. Destitute of this power, reason would be a solitary, and, in some measure, an unavailable principle. Speech is the great instrument by which man becomes beneficial to man: and it is to the intercourse and transmission of thought, by means of speech, that we are chiefly indebted for the improvement of thought itself. Small are the advances which a single unassisted individual can make towards perfecting any of his powers. What we call human reason, is not the effort or ability of one, so much as it is the result of the reason of many, arising from lights mutually communicated, in consequence of discourse and writing.

It is obvious, then, that writing and discourse are objects entitled to the highest attention. Whether the influence of the speaker, or the entertainment of the hearer, be consulted; whether utility or pleasure be the principal aim in view, we are prompted, by the strongest motives, to study how we may communicate our thoughts to one another with most advantage. Accordingly we find, that in almost every nation, as soon as language had extended itself beyond that scanty communication which was requisite for the supply of men's necessities, the improvement of discourse began to attract regard. In the language even of rude uncultivated tribes, we can trace some attention to the grace and force of those expressions which they used, when they sought to persuade or to affect. They were early sensible of a beauty in discourse, and endeavoured to give it certain decorations, which experience had taught them it was capable of receiving, long before the study of those decorations was formed into a regular art.

But, among nations in a civilized state, no art has been cultivated with more care, than that of language, style, and composition. The attention paid to it may, indeed, be assumed as one mark of the progress of society towards its most improved period. For, according as society improves and flourishes, men acquire more influence over one another by means of reasoning and discourse; and in proportion as that influence is felt to enlarge, it must follow, as a natural consequence, that they will bestow more care upon the methods of expressing their conceptions with propriety and eloquence. Hence we find, that in all the polished nations of Europe, this study has been treated as highly important, and has possessed a considerable place in every plan of liberal education.

Indeed, when the arts of speech and writing are mentioned, I am sensible that prejudices against them are apt to rise in the minds of many. A sort of art is immediately thought of, that is ostentatious and deceitful; the minute and trifling study of words alone; the pomp of expression; the studied fallacies of rhetoric; ornament substituted in the room of use. We need not wonder, that, under such imputations, all study of discourse as an art, should have suffered in the opinion of men of understanding; and I am far from denying, that rhetoric and criticism have sometimes been so managed as to tend to the corruption, rather than to the improvement, of good taste and true eloquence. But sure it is equally possible to apply the principles of reason and good sense to this art, as to any other that is cultivated among men. If the following Lectures have any merit, it will consist in an endeavour to substitute the application of these principles in the place of artificial and scholastic rhetoric; in an endeavour to explode false ornament, to direct attention more towards substance than show, to recommend good sense as the foundation of all good composition, and simplicity as essential to all true ornament.

When entering on this subject, I may be allowed, on this occasion, to suggest a few thoughts concerning the importance and advantages of such studies, and the rank they are entitled to possess in academical education.[1] I am under no temptation, for this purpose, of extolling their importance at the expense of any other department of science. On the contrary, the study of Rhetoric and Belles Lettres supposes and requires a proper acquaintance with the rest of the liberal arts. It embraces them all within its circle, and recommends them to the highest regard. The first care of all such as wish either to write with reputation, or to speak in public so as to command attention, must be, to extend their knowledge; to lay in a rich store of ideas relating to those subjects of which the occasions of life may call them to discourse or to write. Hence, among the ancients, it was a fundamental principle, and frequently inculcated, "Quod omnibus disciplinis et artibus debet esse instructus orator;" that the orator ought to be an accomplished scholar, and conversant in every part of learning. It is indeed impossible to contrive an art, and very pernicious it were if it could be contrived, which should give the stamp of merit to any composition rich or splendid in expression, but barren or erroneous in thought. They are the wretched attempts towards an art of this kind, which have so often disgraced oratory, and debased it below its true standard. The graces of composition have been employed to disguise or to supply the want of matter; and the temporary applause of the ignorant has been courted, instead of the lasting approbation of the discerning. But such imposture can never maintain its ground long. Knowledge and science must furnish the materials that form the body and substance of any valuable composition. Rhetoric serves to add the polish; and we know that none but firm and solid bodies can be polished well.

Of those who peruse the following Lectures, some by the profession to which they addict themselves, or in consequence of their prevailing inclination, may have the view of being employed in composition, or in public speaking. Others, without any prospect of this kind, may wish only to improve their taste with respect to writing and discourse, and to acquire principles which will enable them to judge for themselves in that part of literature called the Belles Lettres.

With respect to the former, such as may have occasion to communicate their sentiments to the public, it is abundantly clear that some preparation of study is requisite for the end which they have in view. To speak or to write perspicuously and agreeably with purity, with grace and strength, are attainments of the utmost consequence to all who purpose, either by speech or writing, to address the public. For without being master of those attainments, no man can do justice to his own conceptions; but how rich soever he may be in knowledge and in good sense, will be able to avail himself less of those treasures, than such as possess not half his store, but who can display what they possess with more propriety. Neither are these attainments of that kind for which we are indebted to nature merely. Nature has, indeed, conferred upon some a very favourable distinction in this respect, beyond others. But in these, as in most other talents she bestows, she has left much to be wrought out by every man's own industry. So conspicuous have been the effects of study and improvement in every part of eloquence; such remarkable examples have appeared

[1] The author was the first who read lectures on this subject in the university of Edinburgh. He began with reading them in a private character in the year 1759. In the following year he was chosen Professor of Rhetoric by the magistrates and town-council of Edinburgh; and, in 1762, his Majesty was pleased to erect and endow a Profession of Rhetoric and Belles Lettres in that university, and the author was appointed the first Regius Professor.

of persons surmounting, by their diligence, the disadvantages of the most untoward nature, that among the learned it has long been a contested, and remains still an undecided point, whether nature or art confer most towards excelling in writing or discourse.

With respect to the manner in which art can most effectually furnish assistance for such a purpose, there may be diversity of opinions. I by no means pretend to say that mere rhetorical rules, how just soever, are sufficient to form an orator. Supposing natural genius to be favourable, more by a great deal will depend upon private application and study, than upon any system of instruction that is capable of being publicly communicated. But at the same time, though rules and instructions cannot do all that is requisite, they may, however, do much that is of real use. They cannot, it is true, inspire genius; but they can direct and assist it. They cannot remedy barrenness; but they may correct redundancy. They point out proper models for imitation. They bring into view the chief beauties that ought to be studied, and the principal thoughts that ought to be avoided; and thereby tend to enlighten taste, and to lead genius from unnatural deviations, into its proper channel. What would not avail for the production of great excellencies, may at least serve to prevent the commission of considerable errors.

All that regards the study of eloquence and composition, merits the higher attention upon this account, that it is intimately connected with the improvement of our intellectual powers. For I must be allowed to say, that when we are employed, after a proper manner, in the study of composition, we are cultivating reason itself. True rhetoric and sound logic are very nearly allied. The study of arranging and expressing our thoughts with propriety, teaches to think as well as to speak accurately. By putting our sentiments into words, we always conceive them more distinctly. Every one who has the slightest acquaintance with composition knows, that when he expresses himself ill on any subject, when his arrangement is loose, and his sentences become feeble, the defects of his style can, almost on every occasion, be traced back to his indistinct conception of the subject: so close is the connexion between thoughts and the words in which they are clothed.

The study of composition, important in itself at all times, has acquired additional importance from the taste and manners of the present age. It is an age wherein improvements in every part of science, have been prosecuted with ardour. To all the liberal arts much attention has been paid; and to none more than to the beauty of language, and the grace and elegance of every kind of writing. The public ear is become refined. It will not easily bear what is slovenly and incorrect. Every author must aspire to some merit in expression, as well as in sentiment, if he would not incur the danger of being neglected and despised.

I will not deny that the love of minute elegance, and attention to inferior ornaments of composition, may at present have engrossed too great a degree of the public regard. It is indeed my opinion, that we lean to this extreme; often more careful of polishing style, than of storing it with thought. Yet hence arises a new reason for the study of just and proper composition. If it be requisite not to be deficient in elegance or ornament in times when they are in such high estimation, it is still more requisite to attain the power of distinguishing false ornament from true, in order to prevent our being carried away by that torrent of false and frivolous taste, which never fails, when it is prevalent, to sweep along with it the raw and ignorant. They who have never studied eloquence in its principles, nor have been trained to attend to the genuine and manly beauties of good writing, are always ready to be caught by the mere glare of language; and when they come to speak in public, or to compose, have no other standard on which to form themselves, except what chances to be fashionable and popular, how corrupted soever, or erroneous, that may be.

But as there are many who have no such objects as either composition or public speaking in view, let us next consider what advantages may be derived by them, from such studies as form the subject of these lectures. To them, rhetoric is not so much a practical art as a speculative science; and the same instructions which assist others in composing, will assist them in discerning and relishing the beauties of composition. Whatever enables genius to execute well, will enable taste to criticise justly.

When we name criticising, prejudices may perhaps arise, of the same kind with those which I mentioned before with respect to rhetoric. As rhetoric has been sometimes thought to signify nothing more than the scholastic study of words, and phrases, and tropes, so criticism has been considered as merely the art of finding faults; as the frigid application of certain technical terms, by means of which persons are taught to cavil and censure in a learned manner. But this is the criticism of pedants only. True criticism is a liberal and humane art. It is the offspring of good sense and refined taste. It aims at acquiring a just discernment of the real merit of authors. It promotes a lively relish of their beauties, while it preserves us from that blind and implicit veneration which would confound their beauties and faults in our esteem. It teaches us, in a word, to admire and to blame with judgment, and not to follow the crowd blindly.

In an age when works of genius and literature are so frequently the subjects of discourse, when every one erects himself into a judge, and when we can hardly mingle in polite society without bearing some share in such discussions; studies of this kind, it is not to be doubted, will appear to derive part of their importance from the use to which they may be applied in furnishing materials for those fashionable topics of discourse, and thereby enabling us to support a proper rank in social life.

But I should be sorry if we could not rest the merit of such studies on somewhat of solid and intrinsical use, independent of appearance and show. The exercise of taste and of sound criticism is, in truth, one of the most improving employments of the understanding. To apply the principles of good sense to composition and discourse; to examine what is beautiful and why it is so; to employ ourselves in distinguishing accurately between the specious and the solid, between affected and natural ornament, must certainly improve us not a little in the most valuable part of all philosophy, the philosophy of human nature. For such disquisitions are very intimately connected with the knowledge of ourselves. They necessarily lead us to reflect on the operations of the imagination, and the movements of the heart; and increase our acquaintance with some of the most refined feelings which belong to our frame.

Logical and ethical disquisitions move in a higher sphere; and are conversant with objects of a more severe kind; the progress of the understanding in its search after knowledge, and the direction of the will in the proper pursuit of good. They point out to man the improvement of his nature as an intelligent being; and his duties as the subject of moral obligation. Belles Lettres and criticism chiefly consider him as a being endowed with those powers of taste and imagination, which were intended to embellish his mind, and to supply him with rational and useful entertainment. They open a field of investigation peculiar to themselves. All that relates to beauty, harmony, grandeur, and elegance; all that can sooth the mind, gratify the fancy, or move the affections, belongs to their province. They present human nature under a different aspect from that which it assumes when viewed by other sciences. They bring to light various springs of action, which, without their aid, might have passed unobserved; and which, though of a delicate nature, frequently exert a powerful influence on several departments of human life.

Such studies have also this peculiar advantage, that they exercise our reason without fatiguing it. They lead to inquiries acute, but not painful; profound, but not dry nor abstruse. They strew flowers in the path of science; and while they keep the mind bent, in some degree, and active, they relieve it at the same time from that more toilsome labour to which it must submit in the acquisition of necessary erudition, or the investigation of abstract truth.

The cultivation of taste is farther recommended by the happy effects which it naturally tends to produce on human life. The most busy man, in the most active sphere, cannot be always occupied by business. Men of serious professions cannot always be on the stretch of serious thought. Neither can the most gay and flourishing situations of fortune afford any man the power of filling all his hours with pleasure. Life must always languish in the hands of the idle. It will frequently languish even in the hands of the busy, if they have not some employments subsidiary to that which forms their main pursuit. How then shall these vacant spaces, those unemployed intervals, which more or less, occur in the life of every one, be filled up? How can we contrive to dispose of them in any way that shall be more agreeable in itself, or more consonant to the dignity of the human mind, than in the entertainments of taste, and the study of polite literature? He who is so happy as to have acquired a relish for these, has always at hand an innocent and irreproachable amusement for his leisure hours, to save him from the danger of many a pernicious passion. He is not in hazard of being a burden to himself. He is not obliged to fly to low company, or to court the riot of loose pleasures, in order to cure the tediousness of existence.

Providence seems plainly to have pointed out this useful purpose to which the pleasures of taste may be applied, by interposing them in a middle station between the pleasures of sense, and those of pure intellect. We were not designed to grovel always among objects so low as the former; nor are we capable of dwelling constantly in so high a region as the latter. The pleasures of taste refresh the mind after the toils of the intellect, and the labours of abstract study; and they gradually raise it above the attachments of sense, and prepare it for the enjoyments of virtue.

So consonant is this to experience, that in the education of youth, no object has in every age appeared more important to wise men, than to tincture them early with a relish for the entertainments of taste. The transition is commonly made with ease from these to the discharge of the higher and more important duties of life. Good hopes may be entertained of those whose minds have this liberal and elegant turn. It is favourable to many virtues. Whereas to be entirely devoid of relish for eloquence, poetry, or any of the fine arts, is justly construed to be an unpromising symptom of youth; and raises suspicions of their being prone to low gratifications, or destined to drudge in the more vulgar and illiberal pursuits of life.

There are indeed few good dispositions of any kind with which the improvement of taste is not more or or less connected. A cultivated taste increases sensibility to all the tender and humane passions, by giving them frequent exercise while it tends to weaken the more violent and fierce emotions.

> These polish'd arts have humaniz'd mankind,
> Soften'd the rude, and calm'd the boist'rous mind

The elevated sentiments and high examples which poetry, eloquence, and history, are often bringing under our view, naturally tend to nourish in our minds public spirit, the love of glory, contempt of external fortune, and the admiration of what is truly illustrious and great.

I will not go so far as to say that the improvement of taste and of virtue is the same; or that they may always be expected to co-exist in an equal degree. More powerful correctives than taste can apply, are necessary for reforming the corrupt propensities which too frequently prevail among mankind. Elegant speculations are sometimes found to float on the surface of the mind, while bad passions possess the interior regions of the heart. At the same time this cannot but be admitted, that the exercise of taste is, in its native tendency, moral and purifying. From reading the most admired productions of genius, whether in poetry or prose, almost every one rises with some good impressions left on his mind; and though these may not always be durable, they are at least to be ranked among the means of disposing the heart to virtue. One thing is certain, and I shall hereafter have occasion to illustrate it more fully, that, without possessing the virtuous affections in a strong degree, no man can attain eminence in the sublime parts of eloquence. He must feel what a good man feels, if he expects greatly to move, or to interest mankind. They are the ardent sentiments of honour, virtue, magnanimity, and public spirit, that only can kindle that fire of genius, and call up into the mind those high ideas, which attract the admiration of ages; and if this spirit be necessary to produce the most distinguished efforts of eloquence, it must be necessary also to our relishing them with proper taste and feeling.

On these general topics I shall dwell no longer; but proceed directly to the consideration of the subjects which are to employ the following Lectures. They divide themselves into five parts. First, some introductory dissertations on the nature of taste, and upon the sources of its pleasures. Secondly, the consideration of language. Thirdly, of style. Fourthly of eloquence, properly so called, or public speaking in its different kinds. Lastly, a critical examination of the most distinguished species of composition, both in prose and verse.

LECTURE II

TASTE

The nature of the present undertaking leads me to begin with some inquiries concerning taste, as it is this faculty which is always appealed to, in disquisitions concerning the merit of discourse in writing.

There are few subjects on which men talk more loosely and indistinctly than on taste; few which it is more difficult to explain with precision; and none which in this course of Lectures will appear more dry or abstract. What I have to say on the subject, shall be in the following order. I shall first explain the Nature of Taste as a power or faculty in the human mind. I shall next consider, how far it is an improveable faculty. I shall show the sources of its improvement, and the characters of taste in its most perfect state. I shall then examine the various fluctuations to which it is liable, and inquire whether there be any standard to which we can bring the different tastes of men, in order to distinguish the corrupted from the true.

Taste may be defined "The power of receiving pleasure from the beauties of nature and of art." The first question that occurs concerning it is, whether it is to be considered as an internal sense, or as an exertion of reason? Reason is a very general term; but if we understand by it, that power of the mind which in speculative matters discovers truth, and in practical matters judges of the fitness of means to an end, I apprehend the question may be easily answered. For nothing can be more clear, than that taste is not resolvable into any such operation of reason. It is not merely through a discovery of the understanding or a deduction of argument, that the mind receives pleasure from a beautiful prospect or a fine poem. Such objects often strike us intuitively, and make a strong impression, when we are unable to assign the reasons of our being pleased. They sometimes strike in the same manner the philosopher and the peasant; the boy and the man. Hence the faculty by which we relish such beauties, seems more nearly allied to a feeling of sense, than to a process of the understanding; and accordingly from an external sense it has borrowed its name; that sense by which we receive and distinguish the pleasures of food, having, in several languages, given rise to the word taste, in the metaphorical meaning under which we now consider it. However, as in all subjects which regard the operations of the mind, the inaccurate use of words is to be carefully avoided, it must not be inferred from what I have said, that reason is entirely excluded from the exertions of taste. Though taste, beyond doubt, be ultimately founded on a certain natural and instinctive sensibility to beauty, yet reason, as I shall show hereafter, assists taste in many of its operations, and serves to enlarge its power.[1]

---

[1] See Dr. Gerard's *Essay on Tastes*—D'Alembert's Reflections on the use and abuse of Philosophy in matters which relate to Taste:—*Reflections Critiques sur la Poésie et sur la Peinture,* tome ii. ch. 22–31:—*Elements of Criticism,* chap. 25:—Mr. Hume's *Essay on the Standard of Taste*—Introduction to the *Essay on the Sublime and Beautiful.*

Taste, in the sense in which I have explained it, is a faculty common in some degree to all men. Nothing that belongs to human nature is more general than the relish of beauty of one kind or other; of what is orderly, proportioned, grand, harmonious, new, or sprightly. In children, the rudiments of taste discover themselves very early in a thousand instances; in their fondness for regular bodies, their admiration of pictures and statues, and imitations of all kinds; and their strong attachment to whatever is new or marvellous. The most ignorant peasants are delighted with ballads and tales, and are struck with the beautiful appearance of nature in the earth and heavens. Even in the deserts of America, where human nature shows itself in its most uncultivated state, the savages have their ornaments of dress, their war and their death songs, their harangues and their orators. We must therefore conclude the principles of taste to be deeply founded in the human mind. It is no less essential to man to have some discernment of beauty, than it is to possess the attributes of reason and of speech.[1]

But although none be wholly devoid of this faculty, yet the degrees in which it is possessed are widely different. In some men only the feeble glimmerings of taste appear; the beauties which they relish are of the coarsest kind; and of these they have but a weak and confused impression; while in others, taste rises to an acute discernment, and a lively enjoyment of the most refined beauties. In general, we may observe, that in the powers and pleasures of taste, there is a more remarkable inequality among men than is usually found in point of common sense, reason, and judgment. The constitution of our nature in this, as in all other respects, discovers admirable wisdom. In the distribution of those talents which are necessary for man's well-being, nature hath made less distinction among her children. But in the distribution of those which belong only to the ornamental part of life, she hath bestowed her favours with more frugality. She hath both sown the seeds more sparingly; and rendered a higher culture requisite for bringing them to perfection.

This inequality of taste among men is owing, without doubt, in part, to the different frame of their natures; to nicer organs, and finer internal powers, with which some are endowed beyond others. But, if it be owing in part to nature, it is owing to education and culture still more. The illustration of this leads to my next remark on this subject, that taste is a most improveable faculty, if there be any such in human nature; a remark which gives great encouragement to such a course of study as we are now proposing to pursue. Of the truth of this assertion we may easily be convinced, by only reflecting on that immense superiority which education and improvement give to civilized, above barbarous nations, in refinement of taste; and on the superiority which they give in the same nation to those who have studied the liberal arts, above the rude and untaught vulgar. The difference is so great, that there is perhaps no one particular in which these two classes of men are so far removed from each other, as in respect of the powers and the pleasures of taste: and assuredly for this difference no other general cause can be assigned, but culture and education. I shall now proceed to show what the means are by which taste becomes so remarkably susceptible of cultivation and progress.

Reflect first upon that great law of our nature, that exercise is the chief source of improvement in all our faculties. This holds both in our bodily, and in our mental powers. It holds even in our external senses, although these be less the subject of cultivation than any of our other faculties. We see how acute the senses become in persons whose trade or business leads to nice exertions of them. Touch, for instance, becomes infinitely more exquisite in men whose employment requires them to examine the polish of bodies, than it is in others. They who deal in microscopical observations, or are accustomed to engrave on precious stones, acquire surprising accuracy of sight in discerning

---

[1] On the subject of taste, considered as a power or faculty of the mind, much less is to be found among the ancient, than among the modern rhetorical and critical writers.

the minutest objects; and practice in attending to different flavours and tastes of liquors, wonderfully improves the power of distinguishing them, and of tracing their composition. Placing internal taste therefore on the footing of a simple sense, it cannot be doubted that frequent exercise, and curious attention to its proper objects, must greatly heighten its power. Of this we have one clear proof in that part of taste, which is called an ear for music. Experience every day shows, that nothing is more improvable. Only the simplest and plainest compositions are relished at first; use and practice extend our pleasure; teach us to relish finer melody, and by degrees enable us to enter into the intricate and compounded pleasures of harmony. So an eye for the beauties of painting is never all at once acquired. It is gradually formed by being conversant among pictures, and studying the works of the best masters.

Precisely in the same manner, with respect to the beauty of composition and discourse, attention to the most approved models, study of the best authors, comparisons of lower and higher degrees of the same beauties, operate towards the refinement of taste. When one is only beginning his acquaintance with works of genius, the sentiment which attends them is obscure and confused. He cannot point out the several excellencies or blemishes of a performance which he peruses; he is at a loss on what to rest his judgment: all that can be expected is, that he should tell in general whether he be pleased or not. But allow him more experience in works of this kind, and his taste becomes by degrees more exact and enlightened. He begins to perceive not only the character of the whole, but the beauties and defects of each part; and is able to describe the peculiar qualities which he praises or blames. The mist dissipates which seemed formerly to hang over the object; and he can at length pronounce firmly, and without hesitation, concerning it. Thus in taste, considered as mere sensibility, exercise opens a great source of improvement.

But although taste be ultimately founded on sensibility, it must not be considered as instinctive sensibility alone. Reason and good sense, as I before hinted, have so extensive an influence on all the operations and decisions of taste, that a thorough good taste may well be considered as a power compounded of natural sensibility to beauty, and of improved understanding. In order to be satisfied of this, let us observe, that the greater part of the productions of genius are no other than imitations of nature; representations of the characters, actions, or manners of men. The pleasure we receive from such imitations or representations is founded on mere taste: but to judge whether they be properly executed, belongs to the understanding, which compares the copy with the original.

In reading, for instance, such a poem as the *Aeneid,* a great part of our pleasure arises from the plan or story being well conducted, and all the parts joined together with probability and due connexion; from the characters being taken from nature, the sentiments being suited to the characters, and the style to the sentiments. The pleasure which arises from a poem so conducted, is felt or enjoyed by taste as an internal sense; but the discovery of this conduct in the poem is owing to reason; and the more that reason enables us to discover such propriety in the conduct, the greater will be our pleasure. We are pleased, through our natural sense of beauty. Reason shows us why, and upon what grounds, we are pleased. Wherever in works of taste, any resemblance to nature is aimed at, wherever there is any reference of parts to a whole, or of means to an end, as there is indeed in almost every writing and discourse, there the understanding must always have a great part to act.

Here then is a wide field for reason's exerting its powers in relation to the objects of taste, particularly with respect to composition, and works of genius; and hence arises a second and a very considerable source of the improvement of taste, from the application of reason and good sense to such productions of genius. Spurious beauties, such as unnatural characters, forced sentiments, affected style, may please for a little; but they please only because their opposition to nature and to good sense has not been examined, or attended to. Once show how nature might have been more justly imitated or represented; how the writer might have managed his subject to greater advantage; the illusion will presently be dissipated, and these false beauties will please no more.

From these two sources then, first, the frequent exercise of taste, and next the application of good sense and reason to the objects of taste, taste as a power of the mind receives its improvement. In its perfect state, it is undoubtedly the result both of nature and of art. It supposes our natural sense of beauty to be refined by frequent attention to the most beautiful objects, and at the same time to be guided and improved by the light of the understanding.

I must be allowed to add, that as a sound head, so likewise a good heart, is a very material requisite to just taste. The moral beauties are not only themselves superior to all others, but they exert an influence, either more near, or more remote, on a great variety of other objects of taste. Wherever the affections, characters, or actions of men are concerned, (and these certainly afford the noblest subjects to genius,) there can be neither any just or affecting description of them, nor any thorough feeling of the beauty of that description, without our possessing the virtuous affections. He whose heart is indelicate or hard, he who has no admiration of what is truly noble or praise-worthy, nor the proper sympathetic sense of what is soft and tender, must have a very imperfect relish of the highest beauties of eloquence and poetry.

The characters of taste, when brought to its most improved state, are all reducible to two, Delicacy and Correctness.

Delicacy of taste respects principally the perfection of that natural sensibility on which taste is founded. It implies those finer organs or powers which enable us to discover beauties that lie hid from a vulgar eye. One may have strong sensibility, and yet be deficient in delicate taste. He may be deeply impressed by such beauties as he perceives; but he perceives only what is in some degree coarse, what is bold and palpable; while chaster and simpler ornaments escape his notice. In this state, taste generally exists among rude and unrefined nations. But a person of delicate taste both feels strongly, and feels accurately. He sees distinctions and differences where others see none; the most latent beauty does not escape him, and he is sensible of the smallest blemish. Delicacy of taste is judged of by the same marks that we use in judging of the delicacy of an external sense. As the goodness of the palate is not tried by strong flavours, but by a mixture of ingredients, where, notwithstanding the confusion, we remain sensible of each; in like manner delicacy of internal taste appears, by a quick and lively sensibility to its finest, most compounded, or most latent objects.

Correctness of taste respects chiefly the improvement which that faculty receives through its connexion with the understanding. A man of correct taste is one who is never imposed on by counterfeit beauties; who carries always in his mind that standard of good sense which he employs in judging of every thing. He estimates with propriety the comparative merit of the several beauties which he meets with in any work of genius; refers them to their proper classes; assigns the principles, as far as they can be traced, whence their power of pleasing flows, and is pleased himself precisely in that degree in which he ought, and no more.

It is true, that these two qualities of taste, delicacy and correctness, mutally imply each other. No taste can be exquisitely delicate without being correct; nor can be thoroughly correct without being delicate. But still a predominancy of one or other quality in the mixture is often visible. The power of delicacy is chiefly seen in discerning the true merit of a work; the power of correctness, in rejecting false pretensions to merit. Delicacy leans more to feeling; correctness, more to reason and judgment. The former is more the gift of nature; the latter, more the product of culture and art. Among the ancient critics, Longinus possessed most delicacy; Aristotle, most correctness. Among the moderns, Mr. Addison is a high example of delicate taste; Dean Swift, had he written on the subject of criticism, would perhaps have afforded the example of a correct one.

Having viewed taste in its most improved and perfect state, I come next to consider its deviations from that state, the fluctuations and changes to which it is liable; and to inquire whether, in the midst of these, there be any means of distinguishing a true from a corrupted taste. This brings us to the most difficult part of our task. For it must be acknowledged, that no principle of the human mind is, in its operations, more fluctuating and capricious than taste. Its variations have been so great and frequent, as to create a suspicion with some, of its being merely arbitrary; grounded on no foundation, ascertainable by no standard, but wholly dependent on changing fancy; the consequence of which would be, that all studies or regular inquiries concerning the objects of taste were vain. In architecture, the Grecian models were long esteemed the most perfect. In succeeding ages, the Gothic architecture alone prevailed, and afterwards the Grecian taste revived in all its vigour, and engrossed the public admiration. In eloquence and poetry, the Asiatics at no time relished any thing but what was full of ornament, and splendid in a degree that we should denominate gawdy; whilst the Greeks admired only chaste and simple beauties, and despised the Asiatic ostentation. In our own country, how many writings that were greatly extolled two or three centuries ago, are now fallen into entire disrepute and oblivion. Without going back to remote instances, how very different is the taste of poetry which prevails in Great Britain now, from what prevailed there no longer ago than the reign of king Charles II, which the authors too of that time deemed an Augustan age: when nothing was in vogue but an affected brilliancy of wit; when the simple majesty of Milton was overlooked, and *Paradise Lost* almost entirely unknown; when Cowley's laboured and unnatural conceits were admired as the very quintessence of genius; Waller's gay sprightliness was mistaken for the tender spirit of love poetry; and such writers as Suckling and Etheridge were held in esteem for dramatic composition?

The question is, what conclusion we are to form from such instances as these? Is there any thing that can be called a standard of taste, by appealing to which we may distinguish between a good and a bad taste? Or, is there in truth no such distinction? and are we to hold that, according to the proverb, there is no disputing of tastes; but that whatever pleases is right, for that reason that it does please? This is the question, and a very nice and subtle one it is, which we are now to discuss.

I begin by observing, that if there be no such thing as any standard of taste, this consequence must immediately follow, that all tastes are equally good; a position, which, though it may pass unnoticed in slight matters, and when we speak of the lesser differences among the tastes of men, yet when we apply it to the extremes, presently shows its absurdity. For is there any one who will seriously maintain that the taste of a Hottentot or a Laplander is as delicate and as correct as that of a Longinus or an Addison? or, that he can be charged with no defect or incapacity who thinks a common newswriter as excellent an historian as Tacitus? As it would be held downright extravagance to talk in this manner, we are led unavoidably to this conclusion, that there is some foundation for the preference of one man's taste to that of another; or, that there is a good and a bad, a right and a wrong in taste, as in other things.

But to prevent mistakes on this subject, it is necessary to observe next, that the diversity of tastes which prevails among mankind, does not in every case infer corruption of taste, or oblige us to seek for some standard in order to determine who are in the right. The tastes of men may differ very considerably as to their object, and yet none of them be wrong. One man relishes poetry most; another takes pleasure in nothing but history. One prefers comedy; another, tragedy. One admires the simple; another, the ornamented style. The young are amused with gay and sprightly compositions. The elderly are more entertained with those of a graver cast. Some nations delight in bold pictures of manners, and strong representations of passion. Others incline to more correct and regular elegance both in description and sentiment. Though all differ, yet all pitch upon some one beauty which peculiarly suits their turn of mind; and therefore no one has a title to condemn the rest. It is not in matters of taste, as in questions of mere reason, where there is but one conclusion that can be true, and all the rest are erroneous. Truth, which is the object of reason, is one; beauty, which is the object of taste, is manifold. Taste, therefore, admits of latitude and diversity of objects, in sufficient consistency with goodness or justness of taste.

But then, to explain this matter thoroughly, I must observe farther that this admissible diversity of tastes can only have place where the objects of taste are different. Where it is with respect to the same object that men disagree, when one condemns that as ugly, which another admires as highly beautiful; then it is no longer diversity, but direct opposition of taste that takes place; and therefore one must be in the right, and another in the wrong, unless that absurd paradox were allowed to hold, that all tastes are equally good and true. One man prefers Virgil to Homer. Suppose that I, on the other hand, admire Homer more than Virgil. I have as yet no reason to say that our tastes are contradictory. The other person is more struck with the elegance and tenderness which are the characteristics of Virgil; I, with the simplicity and fire of Homer. As long as neither of us deny that both Homer and Virgil have great beauties, our difference falls within the compass of that diversity of tastes, which I have showed to be natural and allowable. But if the other man shall assert that Homer has no beauties whatever; that he holds him to be a dull and spiritless writer, and that he would as soon peruse any old legend of knight-errantry as the *Iliad;* then I exclaim, that my antagonist either is void of all taste, or that his taste is corrupted in a miserable degree; and I appeal to whatever I think the standard of taste, to show him that he is in the wrong.

What that standard is to which, in such opposition of tastes, we are obliged to have recourse, remains to be traced. A standard properly signifies, that which is of such undoubted authority as to be the test of other things of the same kind. Thus a standard weight or measure, is that which is appointed by law to regulate all other measures and weights. Thus the court is said to be the standard of good breeding; and the scripture of theological truth.

When we say that nature is the standard of taste, we lay down a principle very true and just, as far as it can be applied. There is no doubt, that in all cases where an imitation is intended of some object that exists in nature, as in representing human characters or actions, conformity to nature affords a full and distinct criterion of what is truly beautiful. Reason hath in such cases full scope for exerting its authority; for approving or condemning; by comparing the copy with the original. But there are innumerable cases in which this rule cannot be at all applied; and conformity to nature, is an expression frequently used, without any distinct or determinate meaning. We must therefore search for somewhat that can be rendered more clear and precise, to be the standard of taste.

Taste, as I before explained it, is ultimately founded on an internal sense of beauty, which is natural to men, and which, in its application to particular objects, is capable of being guided and enlightened by reason. Now were there any one person who possessed in full perfection all the powers of human nature, whose internal senses were in every instance exquisite and just, and whose reason was unerring and sure, the determinations of such a person concerning beauty, would, beyond doubt, be a perfect standard for the taste of all others. Wherever their taste differed from his, it could be imputed only to some imperfection in their natural powers. But as there is no such living standard, no one person to whom all mankind will allow such submission to be due, what is there of sufficient authority to be the standard of the various and opposite tastes of men? Most certainly there is nothing but the taste, as far as it can be gathered, of human nature. That which men concur the most in admiring, must be held to be beautiful. His taste must be esteemed just and true, which coincides with the general sentiments of men. In this standard we must rest. To the sense of mankind the ultimate appeal must ever lie, in all works of taste. If any one should maintain that sugar was bitter and tobacco was sweet, no reasonings could avail to prove it. The taste of such a person would infallibly be held to be diseased, merely because it differed so widely from the taste of the species to which he belongs. In like manner, with regard to the objects of sentiment or internal taste, the common feelings of men carry the same authority, and have a title to regulate the taste of every individual.

But have we then, it will be said, no other criterion of what is beautiful, than the approbation of the majority? Must we collect the voices of others, before we form any judgment for ourselves, of what deserves applause in eloquence or poetry? By no means; there are principles of reason and sound judgment which can be applied to matters of taste, as well as to the subjects of science and philosophy. He who admires or censures any work of genius, is always ready, if his taste be in any degree improved, to assign some reasons for his decision. He appeals to principles, and points out the grounds on which he proceeds. Taste is a sort of compound power, in which the light of the understanding always mingles, more or less, with the feelings of sentiment.

But though reason can carry us a certain length in judging concerning works of taste, it is not to be forgotten that the ultimate conclusions to which our reasonings lead, refer at last to sense and perception. We may speculate and argue concerning propriety of conduct in a tragedy, or an epic poem. Just reasonings on the subject will correct the caprice of unenlightened taste, and establish principles for judging of what deserves praise. But, at the same time, these reasonings appeal always in the last resort, to feeling. The foundation upon which they rest, is what has been found from experience to please mankind universally. Upon this ground we prefer a simple and natural, to an artificial and affected style; a regular and well-connected story, to loose and scattered narratives; a catastrophe which is tender and pathetic, to one which leaves us unmoved. It is from consulting our own imagination and heart, and from attending to the feelings of others, that any principles are formed which acquire authority in matters of taste.

When we refer to the concurring sentiments of men as the ultimate taste of what is to be accounted beautiful in the arts, this is to be always understood of men placed in such situations as are favourable to the proper exertions of taste. Every one must perceive, that among rude and uncivilized nations, and during the ages of ignorance and darkness, any loose notions that are entertained concerning such subjects, carry no authority. In those states of society, taste has no materials on which to operate. It is either totally suppressed, or appears in its lower and most imperfect form. We refer to the sentiments of mankind in polished and flourishing nations; when arts are cultivated and manners refined; when works of genius are subjected to free discussion, and taste is improved by science and philosophy.

Even among nations, at such a period of society, I admit that accidental causes may occasionally warp the proper operations of taste; sometimes the taste of religion, sometimes the form of government, may for a while pervert; a licentious court may introduce a taste for false ornaments, and dissolute writings. The usage of one admired genius may procure approbation for his faults, and even render them fashionable. Sometimes envy may have power to bear down, for a little, productions of great merit; while popular humour, or party spirit, may, at other times, exalt to a high, though short-lived reputation, what little deserved it. But though such casual circumstances give the appearance of caprice to the judgments of taste, that appearance is easily corrected. In the course of time, the genuine taste of human nature never fails to disclose itself and to gain the ascendant over any fantastic and corrupted modes of taste which may chance to have been introduced. These may have currency for a while, and mislead superficial judges; but being subjected to examination, by degrees they pass away; while that alone remains which is founded on sound reason, and the native feelings of men.

I by no means pretend, that there is any standard of taste, to which, in every particular instance, we can resort for clear and immediate determination. Where, indeed, is such a standard to be found for deciding any of those great controversies in reason and philosophy, which perpetually divide mankind? In the present case, there was plainly no occasion for any such strict and absolute provision to be made. In order to judge of what is morally good or evil, of what man ought, or ought not in duty to do, it was fit that the means of clear and precise determination should be afforded us. But to ascertain in every case with the utmost exactness what is beautiful or elegant, was not at all necessary to the happiness of man. And therefore some diversity in feeling was here allowed to take place; and room was left for discussion and debate, concerning the degree of approbation to which any work of genius is entitled.

The conclusion, which it is sufficient for us to rest upon, is, that taste is far from being an arbitrary principle, which is subject to the fancy of every individual, and which admits of no criterion for determining whether it be false or true. Its foundation is the same in all human minds. It is built upon sentiments and perceptions which belong to our nature; and which, in general, operate with the same uniformity as our other intellectual principles. When these sentiments are perverted by ignorance and prejudice, they are capable of being rectified by reason. Their sound and natural state is ultimately determined, by comparing them with the general taste of mankind. Let men declaim as much as they please concerning the caprice and the uncertainty of taste, it is found, by experience, that there are beauties, which, if they be displayed in a proper light, have power to command lasting and general admiration. In every composition, what interests the imagination, and touches the heart, pleases all ages and all nations. There is a certain string to which, when properly struck, the human heart is so made as to answer.

Hence the universal testimony which the most improved nations of the earth have conspired, throughout a long tract of ages, to give to some few works of genius; such as the Iliad of Homer, and the Aeneid of Virgil. Hence the authority which such works have acquired, as standards in some degree of poetical composition; since from them we are enabled to collect what the sense of mankind is, concerning those beauties which give them the highest pleasure, and which therefore poetry ought to exhibit. Authority or prejudice may, in one age or country, give a temporary reputation to an indifferent poet or a bad artist; but when foreigners, or when posterity examine his works, his faults are discerned, and the genuine taste of human nature appears. *Opinionum commenta delet dies; naturæ judicia confirmat.* (Time overthrows the illusions of opinion, but establishes the decisions of nature.)

• • •

LECTURE X

STYLE—PERSPICUITY AND PRECISION

Having finished the subject of language, I now enter on the consideration of style, and the rules that relate to it.

It is not easy to give a precise idea of what is meant by style. The best definition I can give of it, is, the peculiar manner in which a man expresses his conceptions, by means of language. It is different from mere language, or words. The words which an author employs, may be proper and faultless; and his style may, nevertheless, have great faults: it may be dry, or stiff, or feeble, or affected. Style has always some reference to an author's manner of thinking. It is a picture of the ideas which arise in his mind, and of the manner in which they rise there; and hence, when we are examining an author's composition, it is, in many cases, extremely difficult to separate the style from the sentiment. No wonder these two should be so intimately connected, as style is nothing else than that sort of expression which our thoughts most readily assume. Hence, different countries have been noted for peculiarities of style, suited to their different temper and genius. The eastern nations animated their style with the most strong and hyperbolical figures. The Athenians, a polished and acute people, formed a style accurate, clear, and neat. The Asiatics, gay and loose in their manners, affected a style florid and diffuse. The like sort of characteristical differences are commonly remarked in the style of the French, the English, and the Spaniards. In giving the general characters of style, it is usual to talk of a nervous, a feeble, or a spirited style; which are plainly the characters of a writer's manner of thinking, as well as of expressing himself: so difficult it is to separate these two things from one another. Of the general characters of style, I am afterwards to discourse; but it will be necessary to begin with examining the more simple qualities of it; from the assemblage of which, its more complex denominations, in a great measure, result.

All the qualities of good style may be ranged under two heads, perspicuity and ornament. For all that can possibly be required of language is, to convey our ideas clearly to the minds of others, and, at the same time, in such a dress, as by pleasing and interesting them, shall most effectually strengthen the impressions which we seek to make. When both these ends are answered, we certainly accomplish every purpose for which we use writing and discourse.

Perspicuity, it will be readily admitted, is the fundamental quality of style, a quality so essential in every kind of writing, that for the want of it, nothing can atone. Without this, the richest ornaments of style only glimmer through the dark; and puzzle, instead of pleasing the reader. This, therefore, must be our first object, to make our meaning clearly and fully understood, and understood without the least difficulty. "*Oratio*," says Quintilian, "*debet negligenter quoque audientibus esse aperta; ut in animum audientis, sicut sol in oculos, etiamsi in eum non intendatur, occurat. Quare non solum ut intelligere possit, sed ne omnino possit non intelligere curandum.*"[1] If we are obliged to follow a writer with much care, to pause, and read over his sentences a second time, in order to comprehend them fully, he will never please us long. Mankind are too indolent to relish so much labour. They may pretend to admire the author's depth, after they have discovered his meaning; but they will seldom be inclined to take up his work a second time.

Authors sometimes plead the difficulty of their subject as an excuse for the want of perspicuity. But the excuse can rarely, if ever, be admitted. For whatever a man conceives clearly, that, it is in his power, if he will be at the trouble, to put into distinct propositions, or to express clearly to others: and upon no subject ought any man to write, where he cannot think clearly. His ideas, indeed, may, very excusably, be on some subjects incomplete or inadequate; but still, as far as they go, they ought to be clear; and wherever this is the case, perspicuity in expressing them is always attainable. The obscurity which reigns so much among many metaphysical writers, is, for the most part, owing to the indistinctness of their own conceptions. They see the object but in a confused light; and, of course, can never exhibit it in a clear one to others.

Perspicuity in writing, is not to be considered as merely a sort of negative virtue, or freedom from defect. It has higher merit: it is a degree of positive beauty. We are pleased with an author, we consider him as deserving praise, who frees us from all fatigue of searching for his meaning; who carries us through his subject without any embarrassment or confusion; whose style flows always like a limpid stream, where we see to the very bottom.

The study of perspicuity requires attention, first, to single words and phrases, and then to the construction of sentences. I begin with treating of the first, and shall confine myself to it in this lecture.

---

1 "Discourse ought always to be obvious, even to the most careless and negligent hearer: so that the sense shall strike his mind, as the light of the sun does our eyes, though they are not directed upwards to it. We must study not only that every hearer may understand us, but that it shall be impossible for him not to understand us."

Perspicuity, considered with respect to words and phrases, requires these three qualities in them, *purity, propriety,* and *precision.*

Purity and propriety of language, are often used indiscriminately for each other; and, indeed, they are very nearly allied. A distinction, however, obtains between them. Purity is the use of such words, and such constructions, as belong to the idiom of the language which we speak; in opposition to words and phrases that are imported from other languages, or that are obsolete, or new coined, or used without proper authority. Propriety is the selection of such words in the language, as the best and most established usage has appropriated to those ideas which we intend to express by them. It implies the correct and happy application of them, according to that usage, in opposition to vulgarisms or low expressions; and to words and phrases, which would be less significant of the ideas that we mean to convey. Style may be pure, that is, it may all be strictly English, without Scoticisms or Gallicisms, or ungrammatical irregular expressions of any kind, and may, nevertheless, be deficient in propriety. The words may be ill chosen; not adapted to the subject, nor fully expressive of the author's sense. He has taken all his words and phrases from the general mass of English language; but he has made his selection among these words unhappily. Whereas, style cannot be proper without being also pure; and where both purity and propriety meet, besides making style perspicuous, they also render it graceful. There is no standard, either of purity or of propriety, but the practice of the best writers and speakers in the country.

When I mentioned obsolete or new coined words, as incongruous with purity of style, it will be easily understood, that some exceptions are to be made. On certain occasions, they may have grace. Poetry admits of greater latitude than prose, with respect to coining, or, at least, new compounding words; yet, even here, this liberty should be used with a sparing hand. In prose, such innovations are more hazardous, and have a worse effect. They are apt to give style an affected and conceited air; and should never be ventured upon, except by such, whose established reputation gives them some degree of dictatorial power over language.

The introduction of foreign and learned words, unless where necessity requires them, should always be avoided. Barren languages may need such assistances; but ours is not one of these. Dean Swift, one of our most correct writers, valued himself much on using no words but such as were of native growth: and his language may, indeed, be considered as a standard of the strictest purity and propriety, in the choice of words. At present, we seem to be departing from this standard. A multitude of Latin words have, of late, been poured in upon us. On some occasions, they give an appearance of elevation and dignity to style. But often, also, they render it stiff and forced: and, in general, a plain, native style, as it is more intelligible to all readers, so, by a proper management of words, it may be made equally strong and expressive with this Latinised English.

Let us now consider the import of precision in language, which, as it is the highest part of the quality denoted by perspicuity, merits a full explication; and the more, because distinct ideas are, perhaps, not commonly formed about it.

The exact import of precision, may be drawn from the etymology of the word. It comes from "*præcidere,*" to cut off: it imports retrenching all superfluities, and pruning the expression, so as to exhibit neither more nor less than an exact copy of his idea who uses it. I observed before, that it is often difficult to separate the qualities of style from the qualities of thought; and it is found so in this instance. For, in order to write with precision, though this be properly a quality of style, one must possess a very considerable degree of distinctness and accuracy in his manner of thinking.

The words which a man uses to express his ideas, may be faulty in three respects; they may either not express that idea which the author intends, but some other which only resembles, or is akin to it; or, they may express that idea, but not quite fully and completely; or, they may express it, together with something more than he intends. Precision stands opposed to all these three faults;

but chiefly to the last. In an author's writing with propriety, his being free from the two former faults seems implied. The words which he uses are proper; that is, they express that idea which he intends, and they express it fully; but to be precise, signifies, that they express that idea, and no more. There is nothing in his words which introduces any foreign idea, any superfluous unseasonable accessory, so as to mix it confusedly with the principal object, and thereby to render our conception of that object loose and indistinct. This requires a writer to have, himself, a very clear apprehension of the object he means to present to us; to have laid fast hold of it in his mind; and never to waver in any one view he takes of it; a perfection to which, indeed, few writers attain.

The use and importance of precision, may be deduced from the nature of the human mind. It never can view, clearly and distinctly, above one object at a time. If it must look at two or three together, especially objects among which there is resemblance or connexion, it finds itself confused and embarrassed. It cannot clearly perceive in what they agree, and in what they differ. Thus, were any object, suppose some animal, to be presented to me, of whose structure I wanted to form a distinct notion, I would desire all its trappings to be taken off, I would require it to be brought before me by itself, and to stand alone, that there might be nothing to distract my attention. The same is the case with words. If, when you would inform me of your meaning, you also tell me more than what conveys it; if you join foreign circumstances to the principal object; if, by unnecessarily varying the expression, you shift the point of view, and make me see sometimes the object itself, and sometimes another thing that is connected with it; you thereby oblige me to look on several objects at once, and I lose sight of the principal. You load the animal you are showing me, with so many trappings and collars, and bring so many of the same species before me, somewhat resembling, and yet somewhat differing, that I see none of them clearly.

This forms what is called a loose style; and is the proper opposite to precision. It generally arises from using a superfluity of words. Feeble writers employ a multitude of words to make themselves understood, as they think, more distinctly; and they only confound the reader. They are sensible of not having caught the precise expression, to convey what they would signify; they do not, indeed, conceive their own meaning very precisely themselves; and therefore help it out, as they can, by this and the other word, which may, as they suppose, supply the defect, and bring you somewhat nearer to their idea: they are always going about it, and about it, but never just hit the thing. The image, as they set it before you, is always seen double; and no double image is distinct. When an author tells me of his hero's *courage* in the day of battle, the expression is precise, and I understand it fully. But if, from the desire of multiplying words, he will needs praise his *courage* and *fortitude;* at the moment he joins these words together, my idea begins to waver. He means to express one quality more strongly; but he is, in truth, expressing two. *Courage* resists danger; *fortitude* supports pain. The occasion of exerting each of these qualities is different; and being led to think of both together, when only one of them should be in my view, my view is rendered unsteady, and my conception of the object indistinct.

From what I have said, it appears that an author may, in a qualified sense, be perspicuous, while yet he is far from being precise. He uses proper words, and proper arrangement; he gives you the idea as clear as he conceives it himself; and so far he is perspicuous: but the ideas are not very clear in his own mind; they are loose and general; and, therefore, cannot be expressed with precision. All subjects do not equally require precision. It is sufficient, on many occasions, that we have a general view of the meaning. The subject, perhaps, is of the known and familiar kind; and we are in no hazard of mistaking the sense of the author, though every word which he uses be not precise and exact.

Few authors, for instance, in the English language, are more clear and perspicuous, on the whole, than Archbishop Tillotson, and Sir William Temple; yet neither of them are remarkable for precision. They are loose and diffuse; and accustomed to express their meaning by several words, which show you fully whereabouts it lies, rather than to single out those expressions, which would convey clearly the idea which they have in view, and no more. Neither, indeed, is precision the prevailing character of Mr. Addison's style; although he is not so deficient in this respect as the other two authors.

Lord Shaftesbury's faults, in point of precision, are much greater than Mr. Addison's; and the more unpardonable, because he is a professed philosophical writer; who, as such, ought, above all things, to have studied precision. His style has both great beauties and great faults; and, on the whole, is by no means a safe model for imitation. Lord Shaftesbury was well acquainted with the power of words; those which he employs are generally proper and well sounding; he has great variety of them; and his arrangement, as shall be afterwards shown, is commonly beautiful. His defect, in precision, is not owing so much to indistinct or confused ideas, as to perpetual affectation. He is fond, to excess, of the pomp and parade of language; he is never satisfied with expressing any thing clearly and simply; he must always give it the dress of state and majesty. Hence perpetual circumlocutions, and many words and phrases employed to describe somewhat, that would have been described much better by one of them. If he has occasion to mention any person or author, he very rarely mentions him by his proper name. In the treatise, entitled, Advice to an Author, he descants for two or three pages together upon Aristotle, without once naming him in any other way, than the master critic, the mighty genius and judge of art, the prince of critics, the grand master of art, and consummate philologist. In the same way, the grand poetic sire, the philosophical patriarch, and his disciple of noble birth and lofty genius, are the only names by which he condescends to distinguish Homer, Socrates, and Plato, in another passage of the same treatise. This method of distinguishing persons is extremely affected; but it is not so contrary to precision, as the frequent circumlocutions he employs for all moral ideas; attentive, on every occasion, more to the pomp of language, than to the clearness which he ought to have studied as a philosopher. The moral sense, for instance, after he had once defined it, was a clear term; but, how vague becomes the idea, when, in the next page, he calls it, "That natural affection, and anticipating fancy, which makes the sense of right and wrong?" Self examination, or reflection on our own conduct, is an idea conceived with ease; but when it is wrought into all the forms of "A man's dividing himself into two parties, becoming a self-dialogist, entering into partnership with himself, forming the dual number practically within himself;" we hardly know what to make of it. On some occasions, he so adorns, or rather loads with words, the plainest and simplest propositions, as, if not to obscure, at least, to enfeeble them.

In the following paragraph, for example, of the inquiry concerning virtue, he means to show, that, by every ill action we hurt our mind, as much as one who should swallow poison, or give himself a wound, would hurt his body. Observe what a redundancy of words he pours forth: "Now if the fabric of the mind or temper appeared to us such as it really is; if we saw it impossible to remove hence any one good or orderly affection, or to introduce any ill or disorderly one, without drawing on, in some degree, that dissolute state which, at its height, is confessed to be so miserable; it would then, undoubtedly, be confessed, that since no ill, immoral, or unjust action, can be committed, without either a new inroad and breach on the temper and passions, or a further advancing of that execution already done: whoever did ill, or acted in prejudice to his integrity, good nature, or worth, would, of necessity, act with greater cruelty towards himself, than he who scrupled not to swallow what was poisonous, or who, with his own hands, should voluntarily mangle or wound his outward form or constitution, natural limbs, or body."[1] Here, to commit a bad

---

[1] Characteristics, Vol. II, p. 85.

action, is, first, "To remove a good and orderly affection, and to introduce an ill or disorderly one;" next, it is, "To commit an action that is ill, immoral, and unjust;" and in the next line, it is, "To do ill, or to act in prejudice of integrity, good nature, and worth;" nay, so very simple a thing as a man's wounding himself, is, "To mangle, or wound, his outward form or constitution, his natural limbs or body." Such superfluity of words is disgustful to every reader of correct taste; and serves no purpose but to embarrass and perplex the sense. This sort of style is elegantly described by Quintilian: "A crowd of unmeaning words is brought together by some authors, who, afraid of expressing themselves after a common and ordinary manner, and allured by an appearance of splendour, surround every thing which they mean to say with a certain copious loquacity."

The great source of a loose style, in opposition to precision, is the injudicious use of those words termed synonymous. They are called synonymous, because they agree in expressing one principal idea; but, for the most part, if not always, they express it with some diversity in the circumstances. They are varied by some accessary idea which every word introduces, and which forms the distinction between them. Hardly, in any language, are there two words that convey precisely the same idea; a person thoroughly conversant in the propriety of the language, will always be able to observe something that distinguishes them. As they are like different shades of the same colour, an accurate writer can employ them to great advantage, by using them, so as to heighten and to finish the picture which he gives us. He supplies by one, what was wanting in the other, to the force, or to the lustre of the image which he means to exhibit. But, in order to this end, he must be extremely attentive to the choice which he makes of them. For the bulk of writers are very apt to confound them with each other; and to employ them carelessly, merely for the sake of filling up a period, or of rounding and diversifying the language, as if their signification were exactly the same, while, in truth, it is not. Hence a certain mist and indistinctness is unwarily thrown over style.

From all that has been said on this head, it will now appear, that, in order to write or speak with precision, two things are especially requisite: one, that an author's own ideas be clear and distinct; and the other, that we have an exact and full comprehension of the force of those words which he employs. Natural genius is here required; labour and attention still more. Dean Swift is one of the authors, in our language, most distinguished for precision of style. In his writings, we seldom or never find vague expressions and synonymous words carelessly thrown together. His meaning is always clear, and strongly marked.

I had occasion to observe before, that though all subjects of writing or discourse demand perspicuity, yet all do not require the same degree of that exact precision which I have endeavoured to explain. It is, indeed, in every sort of writing, a great beauty to have, at least, some measure of precision, in distinction from that loose profusion of words which imprints no clear idea on the reader's mind. But we must, at the same time, be on our guard, lest too great a study of precision, especially in subjects where it is not strictly requisite, betray us into a dry and barren style; lest, from the desire of pruning too closely, we retrench all copiousness and ornament. Some degree of this failing may, perhaps, be remarked in Dean Swift's serious works. Attentive only to exhibit his ideas clear and exact, resting wholly on his sense and distinctness, he appears to reject, disdainfully, all embellishment, which, on some occasions, may be thought to render his manner somewhat hard and dry. To unite copiousness and precision, to be flowing and graceful, and at the same time correct and exact in the choice of every word, is, no doubt, one of the highest and most difficult attainments in writing. Some kinds of composition may require more of copiousness and ornament; others, more of precision and accuracy; nay, in the same composition, the different parts of it may demand a proper variation of manner. But we must study never to sacrifice, totally, any one of these qualities to the other; and by a proper management, both of them may be made fully consistent, if our own ideas be precise, and our knowledge and stock of words be, at the same time, extensive.

• • •

FROM LECTURE XIX

DIRECTIONS FOR FORMING A STYLE

It will be more to the purpose, that I conclude these dissertations upon style, with a few directions concerning the proper method of attaining a good style, in general; leaving the particular character of that style to be either formed by the subject on which we write, or prompted by the bent of genius.

The first direction which I give for this purpose, is, to study clear ideas on the subject concerning which we are to write or speak. This is a direction which may at first appear to have small relation to style. Its relation to it, however, is extremely close. The foundation of all good style, is good sense, accompanied with a lively imagination. The style and thoughts of a writer are so intimately connected, that, as I have several times hinted, it is frequently hard to distinguish them. Wherever the impressions of things upon our minds are faint and indistinct, or perplexed and confused, our style in treating of such things will infallibly be so too. Whereas, what we conceive clearly and feel strongly, we shall naturally express with clearness and with strength. This, then, we may be assured, as a capital rule as to style, to think closely of the subject, till we have attained a full and distinct view of the matter which we are to clothe in words, till we become warm and interested in it; then and not till then, shall we find expression begin to flow. Generally speaking, the best and most proper expressions, are those which a clear view of the subject suggests, without much labour or inquiry after them. This is Quintilian's observation, Bk. VIII, chap. 1: "The most proper words for the most part adhere to the thoughts which are to be expressed by them, and may be discovered as by their own light. But we hunt after them, as if they were hidden, and only to be found in a corner. Hence instead of conceiving the words to lie near the subject, we go in quest of them to some other quarter, and endeavour to give force to the expressions we have found out."

In the second place, in order to form a good style, the frequent practice of composing is indispensably necessary. Many rules concerning style I have delivered, but no rules will answer the end, without exercise and habit. At the same time, it is not every sort of composing that will improve style. This is so far from being the case, that by frequent, careless, and hasty composition, we shall acquire certainly a very bad style; we shall have more trouble afterwards in unlearning faults, and correcting negligences, than if we had not been accustomed to composition at all. In the beginning, therefore, we ought to write slowly and with much care. Let the facility and speed of writing, be the fruit of longer practice. Says Quintilian, with the greatest reason, "I enjoin, that such as are beginning the practice of composition, write slowly and with anxious deliberation. Their great object at first should be, to write as well as possible; practice will enable them to write speedily. By degrees, matter will offer itself still more readily; words will be at hand; composition will flow; every thing as in the arrangement of a well-ordered family, will present itself in its proper place. The sum of the whole is this; by hasty composition, we shall never acquire the art of composing well; by writing well, we shall come to write speedily."

We must observe, however, that there may be an extreme, in too great and anxious care about words. We must not retard the course of thought, nor cool the heat of imagination, by pausing too long on every word we employ. There is, on certain occasions, a glow of composition which should be kept up, if we hope to express ourselves happily, though at the expense of allowing some inadvertencies to pass. A more severe examination of these must be left to be the work of correction. For, if the practice of composition be useful, the laborious work of correcting is no less so: it is indeed absolutely necessary to our reaping any benefit from the habit of composition. What we have written, should be laid by for some little time, till the ardour of composition be past, till the fondness for the expressions we have used be worn off, and the expressions themselves be forgotten; and then, reviewing our work with a cool and critical eye, as if it were the performance of another, we shall discern many imperfections which at first escaped us. Then is the season for pruning redundances; for weighing the arrangement of sentences; for attending to the juncture and connecting particles; and bring style into a regular, correct, and supported form. This "*Limœ Labor,*" must be submitted to by all who would communicate their thoughts with proper advantage to others; and some practice in it will soon sharpen their eye to the most necessary objects of attention, and render it a much more easy and practicable work than might at first be imagined.

In the third place, with respect to the assistance that is to be gained from the writings of others, it is obvious, that we ought to render ourselves well acquainted with the style of the best authors. This is requisite both in order to form a just taste in style, and to supply us with a full stock of words on every subject. In reading authors with a view to style, attention should be given to the peculiarities of their different manners; and in this, and former lectures, I have endeavoured to suggest several things that may be useful in this view. I know no exercise that will be found more useful for acquiring a proper style, than to translate some passages from an eminent English author, into our own words. What I mean is, to take, for instance, some page of one of Mr. Addison's Spectators, and read it carefully over two or three times, till we have got a firm hold of the thoughts contained in it; then to lay aside the book; to attempt to write out the passage from memory, in the best way we can; and having done so, next to open the book, and compare what we have written with the style of the author. Such an exercise will, by comparison, show us where the defects of our style lie; will lead us to the proper attentions for rectifying them, and, among the different ways in which the same thought may be expressed, will make us perceive that which is the most beautiful.

In the fourth place, I must caution, at the same time, against a servile imitation of any author whatever. This is always dangerous. It hampers genius; it is likely to produce a stiff manner; and those who are given to close imitation, generally imitate an author's faults as well as his beauties. No man will ever become a good writer or speaker, who has not some degree of confidence to follow his own genius. We ought to beware, in particular, of adopting any author's noted phrases, or transcribing passages from him. Such a habit will prove fatal to all genuine composition. Infinitely better it is to have something that is our own, though of moderate beauty, than to affect to shine in borrowed ornaments, which will, at last, betray the utter poverty of our genius. On these heads of composing, correcting, reading, and imitating, I advise every student of oratory to consult what Quintilian has delivered in the tenth book of his Institutions, where he will find a variety of excellent observations and directions, that well deserve attention.

In the fifth place, it is an obvious, but material rule, with respect to style, that we always study to adapt it to the subject, and also to the capacity of our hearers, if we are to speak in public. Nothing merits the name of eloquent or beautiful, which is not suited to the occasion, and to the persons to whom it is addressed. It is to the last degree awkward and absurd, to attempt a poetical florid style, on occasions when it should be our business only to argue and reason; or to speak with elaborate pomp of expression, before persons who comprehend nothing of it, and who can only stare at our unseasonable magnificence. These are defects not so much in point of style, as, what is much worse, in point of common sense. When we begin to write or speak, we ought previously to fix in our minds a clear conception of the end to be aimed at; to keep this steadily in our view, and to suit our style to it. If we do not sacrifice to this great object every ill-timed ornament that may occur to our fancy, we are unpardonable; and though children and fools may admire, men of sense will laugh at us and our style.

In the last place, I cannot conclude the subject without this admonition, that in any case, and on any occasion, attention to style must not engross us so much, as to detract from a higher degree of attention to the thoughts. "*Curam verborum,*" says the great Roman critic, "rerum volo esse solicitudinem." (To your expressions be attentive: but about your matter be solicitous.) A direction the more necessary, as the present taste of the age in writing, seems to lean more to style than to thought. It is much easier to dress up trivial and common sentiments with some beauty of expression, than to afford a fund of vigorous, ingenious, and useful thoughts. The latter, requires true genius; the former may be attained by industry, with the help of very superficial parts. Hence, we find so many writers frivolously rich in style, but wretchedly poor in sentiment. The public ear is now so much accustomed to a correct and ornamented style, that no writer can, with safety, neglect the study of it. But he is a contemptible one who does not look to something beyond it; who does not lay the chief stress upon his matter, and employ such ornaments of style to recommend it, as are manly, not foppish. As Quintilian says, "A higher spirit ought to animate those who study eloquence. They ought to consult the health and soundness of the whole body, rather than bend their attention to such trifling objects as paring the nails, and dressing the hair. Let ornament be manly and chaste, without effeminate gayety, or artificial colouring; let it shine with the glow of health and strength."

• • •

INTRODUCTION TO RICHARD WHATELY

Richard Whately was English, born in London in 1787. He died in 1863. Whately was by profession a minister of the Church of England and an academic, holding appointments at Oxford. He was one of the most prolific writers of his time, publishing almost one hundred works. Whately wrote books of theology, philosophy, politics, finance, logic, and rhetoric. His book *Elements of Rhetoric,* written in 1828, is excerpted here. Whately was certainly the most important rhetorical theorist of the nineteenth century.

Whately's selection begins with his observation that throughout history there have been many widely varying definitions of rhetoric. He offers several reasons for this, such as the possibility that writers are actually referring to different things, or that a switch in dominant media from speaking to writing created a shift in what is rhetoric. Whatever the cause for such variety of definition, Whately objects to the position taken by many theorists whom we have read that rhetoric entails the study of a wide range of arts and sciences. Although rhetors may speak or write on many subjects, the study of rhetoric itself is a narrower discipline, Whately argues.

Whately's narrower definition of rhetoric is that it is "argumentative composition" and therefore an "offshoot from Logic." This definition accomplishes several interesting goals. It allies rhetoric with logic, making it a particular kind of reasoning. In this way, Whately is effectively reversing Ramus by reestablishing the historical affinity between rhetoric and reason. The definition conceptualizes rhetoric in a very focused way as argument, thereby also putting considerations such as language style or emotional appeals on a secondary level.

Whately distinguishes between inferring truth for oneself from evidence or propositions and inferring truth for the benefit of another person. The latter is the realm of rhetoric, he argues. Yet it is also the realm of all "philosophical works," and that would include the sciences. When any reasoning process, including science, must communicate its results to people, then rhetoric is at work. Whately thereby places rhetoric at the heart of the scientific reasoning process in an age still enamored of science.

Observing that rhetoric is not studied in his day as much as it was in ancient times, Whately considers some likely reasons for that difference: ancient Greece was more democratic; politics used to be carried out exclusively through rhetorical means; and the tricks or artifices of rhetoric are out of favor in his time. This last claim has to do with rhetorical theory. Whately argues that all such theory should be based on observation of successful rhetoric, and should simply supply advice that would assist and develop natural abilities. He provides several examples of fruitful rhetorical theory stemming from natural observations.

Whately's most original contributions to rhetorical theory may be found in the latter part of the selection included here. Basing his theory on observations of actual argument, especially in the courts, Whately presents two linked ideas: *burden of proof* and *presumption.* His formulation of these two principles is still a central part of the rhetorical theory of argument.

Presumption is the ability to assume that one's current course of action, stance, or belief is sufficient and not in need of change. Presumption is a very good thing to have. If you are walking down the street and a stranger begs one hundred dollars from you, *you* have presumption: You may assume that you need not give up your money unless you hear good reasons to do so. Another way to put this is to say that presumption means that, initially at least, one need not present arguments in favor of one's "side." The "other side" must do so. Since it is difficult to construct persuasive rhetorical arguments and harder still to effect change in people, one usually prefers to have presumption on one's side.

Presumption is vital to our understanding of how argument works, especially in the courts. Those who are accused in American and British legal systems have presumption. They need not prove their guilt—rather, their accusers must do so. Beyond the legal system, someone who runs for public office must say why she should be elected—it is not up to the voters to summon up arguments as to why she should not!

The usual bases for presumption are the *status quo* (the way things are), *rights and powers,* and *common knowledge.* If you have always visited your sister on Friday night but you do not intend to do so next Friday night, your sister has presumption and you will usually need to explain why you will not see her. If you ask your son to carry out the garbage, you as a parent typically have presumption because of the rights and powers belonging to parents; if your son has good reason not to take the trash away, he must come up with an argument to that effect. If you believe that the earth is round, you need not come up with arguments to defend that point to a flat-earther. Since it is common knowledge that the earth is round, you have presumption.

The corresponding principle of *burden of proof* in a disagreement belongs to the other side. If one does not have presumption, one must accept the burden of proof. The prosecution in criminal trials has the burden of proving that the defendant (who has presumption) is guilty beyond a reasonable doubt. If you believe your neighbor's dog dug up your tulips, you likely have the burden of proof to demonstrate that sad fact to your neighbor.

Whately explains these two principles in some detail. Let us note that although Whately is writing about reason and argument, the ideas of presumption and burden of proof are nevertheless completely rhetorical. That is because they depend on understanding and adapting discourse to social customs, practices, and expectations. There are no hard and fast rules to say what "counts" as presumption or burden of proof. It is a matter of how society thinks about or defines the status quo, rights and powers, and common knowledge that determines what is presumption or burden of proof in a given argument. Furthermore, as circumstances change during an argument, presumption and burden of proof may shift. Understanding how either concept actually works requires the quintessentially rhetorical tactic of examining particular circumstances. Whately therefore truly merges rhetoric and logic on an equal footing, with neither one subordinate to the other.

RICHARD WHATELY

ELEMENTS OF RHETORIC

INTRODUCTION

1

Various Definitions of Rhetoric

Of Rhetoric various definitions have been given by different writers; who, however, seem not so much to have disagreed in their conceptions of the nature of the same thing, as to have had different things in view while they employed the same term. Not only the word Rhetoric itself, but also those used in defining it, have been taken in various senses; as may be observed with respect to the word "Art" in Cicero's *De Oratore,* where a discussion is introduced as to the applicability of that term to Rhetoric; manifestly turning on the different senses in which "Art" may be understood.

To enter into an examination of all the definitions that have been given, would lead to much uninteresting and uninstructive verbal controversy. It is sufficient to put the reader on his guard against the common error of supposing that a general term has some real object, properly corresponding to it, independent of our conceptions;—that, consequently, some one definition in every case is to be found which will comprehend everything that is rightly designated by that term;—and that all others must be *erroneous:* whereas, in fact, it will often happen, as in the present instance, that both the wider, and the more restricted sense of a term, will be alike sanctioned by use (the only competent authority), and that the consequence will be a corresponding variation in the definitions employed; none of which perhaps may be fairly chargeable with error, though none can be framed that will apply to every acceptation of the term.

It is evident that in its primary signification, Rhetoric had reference to public *Speaking* alone, as its etymology implies. But as most of the rules for Speaking are of course applicable equally to Writing, an extension of the term naturally took place; and we find even Aristotle, the earliest systematic writer on the subject whose works have come down to us, including in his Treatise rules for such compositions as were not intended to be publicly recited.[1] And even as far as relates to Speeches, properly so called, he takes, in the same Treatise, at one time, a wider, and at another, a more restricted view of the subject; including under the term Rhetoric, in the opening of his work, nothing beyond the finding of topics of Persuasion, as far as regards the *matter* of what is spoken; and afterwards embracing the consideration of Style, Arrangement, and Delivery.

The invention of Printing, by extending the sphere of operation of the Writer, has of course contributed to the extension of those terms which, in their primary signification, had reference to Speaking alone. Many objects are now accomplished through the medium of the Press, which formerly came under the exclusive province of the Orator; and the qualifications requisite for success are so much the same in both cases, that we apply the term "Eloquent" as readily to a Writer as to a Speaker; though, etymologically considered, it could only belong to the latter. Indeed "Eloquence" is often attributed even to such composition,—*e.g.* Historical works,—as have in view an object entirely different from any that could be proposed by an Orator; because *some part* of the rules to be observed in Oratory, or rules analogous to these, are applicable to such compositions. Conformably to this view, therefore, some writers have

[1] Aristotle, *Rhetoric,* Bk. III.

spoken of Rhetoric as the Art of Composition, universally; or, with the exclusion of Poetry alone, as embracing all Prose-composition.

A still wider extension of the province of Rhetoric has been contended for by some of the ancient writers; who, thinking it necessary to include, as belonging to the Art, everything that could conduce to the attainment of the object proposed, introduced into their systems, Treatises on Law, Morals, Politics, &c., on the ground that a knowledge of these subjects was requisite to enable a man to speak well on them: and even insisted on Virtue[1] as an essential qualification of a perfect Orator; because a good character, which can in no way be so surely established as by deserving it, has great weight with the audience.

Aristotle's Censure of His Predecessors

These notions are combated by Aristotle; who attributes them either to the ill-cultivated understanding of those who maintained them, or to their arrogant and pretending disposition *i.e.* a desire to extol and magnify the Art they professed. In the present day, the extravagance of such doctrines is so apparent to most readers, that it would not be worth while to take much pains in refuting them. It is worthy of remark, however, that the very same erroneous view is, even now, often taken of Logic;[2] which has been considered by some as a kind of system of universal knowledge, on the ground that Argument may be employed on all subjects, and that no one can argue well on a subject which he does not understand; and which has been complained of by others for not supplying any such universal instruction as its unskilful advocates have placed within its province; such as in fact no one Art or System can possibly afford.

The error is precisely the same in respect of Rhetoric and of Logic; both being *instrumental* arts; and, as such, *applicable* to various kind of subject-matter, which do not properly *come under* them.

So judicious an author as Quintilian would not have failed to perceive, had he not been carried away by an inordinate veneration for his own Art, that as the possession of building materials is no part of the art of Architecture, though it is impossible to build without materials, so, the knowledge of the subjects on which the Orator is to speak, constitutes no part of the art of Rhetoric, though it be essential to its successful employment; and though virtue, and the good reputation it procures, add materially to the Speaker's influence, they are no more to be, for that reason, considered as belonging to the Orator, as such, than wealth, rank, or a good person, which manifestly have a tendency to produce the same effect.

Extremes in the Limitation and Extension of the Province of Rhetoric

In the present day, however, the province of Rhetoric, in the widest acceptation that would be reckoned admissible, comprehends all "Composition in Prose;" in the narrowest sense, it would be limited to "Persuasive Speaking."

Object of the Present Treatise

I propose in the present work to adopt a middle course between these two extreme points; and to treat of "Argumentative Composition," *generally,* and *exclusively;* considering Rhetoric (in conformity with the very just and philosophical view of Aristotle) as an off-shoot from Logic.

Philosophy and Rhetoric Compared

I remarked in treating of that Science, that Reasoning may be considered as applicable to two purposes, which I ventured to designate respectively by the terms "Inferring," and "Proving;" *i.e.* the *ascertainment* of the truth by investigation, and the *establishment* of it to the satisfaction of *another:* and I there remarked, that Bacon, in his

---

[1] See Quintilian.

[2] Whately, *Elements of Logic,* Introd.

Organon, has laid down rules for the conduct of the former of these processes, and that the latter belongs to the province of Rhetoric: and it was added, that to *infer* is to be regarded as the proper office of the Philosopher, or the Judge;—to *prove,* of the Advocate. It is not however to be understood that Philosophical works are to be excluded from the class to which Rhetorical rules are applicable; for the Philosopher who undertakes, by writing or speaking, to convey his notions to others, assumes, for the time being, the character of Advocate of the doctrines he maintains. The process of *investigation* must be supposed completed, and certain conclusions arrived at by that process, *before* he begins to impart his ideas to others in a treatise or lecture; the object of which must of course be to *prove* the justness of those conclusions. And in doing this, he will not always find it expedient to adhere to the same course of reasoning by which his own discoveries were originally made; other arguments may occur to him afterwards, more clear, or more concise, or better adapted to the understanding of those he addresses. In explaining therefore, and establishing the truth, he may often have occasion for rules of a different kind from those employed in its discovery. Accordingly, when I remarked, in the work above alluded to, that it is a common fault, for those engaged in Philosophical and Theological inquiries, to forget their own peculiar office, and assume that of the Advocate, improperly, this caution is to be understood as applicable to the process of *forming their own opinions;* not, as excluding them from advocating by all fair arguments, the conclusions at which they have arrived by candid investigation. But if this candid investigation do not take place in the first instance, no pains that they may bestow in searching for arguments, will have any tendency to ensure their attainment of truth. If a man begins (as is too plainly a frequent mode of proceeding) by hastily adopting, or strongly leaning to, some opinion which suits his inclination, or which is sanctioned by some authority that he blindly venerates, and then studies with the utmost dilgence, not as an Investigator of Truth, but as an Advocate labouring to prove his point, his talents and his researches, whatever effect they may produce in making converts to his notions, will avail nothing in enlightening his own judgment, and securing him from error.[1]

Composition, however, of the Argumentative kind, may be considered (as has been above stated) as coming under the province of Rhetoric. And this view of the subject is the less open to objection, inasmuch as it is not likely to lead to discussions that can be deemed superfluous, even by those who may choose to consider Rhetoric in the most restricted sense, as relating only to "Persuasive Speaking;" since it is evident that *Argument* must be, in most cases at least, the basis of Persuasion.

Plan of the Present Treatise

I propose then to treat, first and principally, of the Discovery of ARGUMENTS, and of their Arrangement; secondly, to lay down some Rules respecting the excitement and management of what are commonly called the *Passions,* (including every kind of Feeling, Sentiment, or Emotion,) with a view to the attainment of any object proposed,—principally, Persuasion, in the strict sense, *i.e.* the influencing of the WILL; thirdly, to offer some remarks on STYLE; and, fourthly, to treat of ELOCUTION.

• • •

3

From a general view of the history of Rhetoric, two questions naturally suggest themselves, which, on examination, will be found very closely connected together: first, what is the cause of the careful and extensive cultivation, among the ancients, of an Art which the moderns have comparatively neglected; and secondly, whether the former or the

---

[1] See "Essay on the Love of Truth," 2nd Series.

latter are to be regarded as the wiser in this respect;—in other words, whether Rhetoric be *worth* any diligent cultivation.

Assiduous Cultivation of Rhetoric by the Ancients

With regard to the first of these questions, the answer generally given is, that the nature of the Government in the ancient democratical States caused a demand for public speakers, and for such speakers as should be able to gain influence not only with educated persons in dispassionate deliberation, but with a promiscuous multitude; and accordingly it is remarked that the extinction of liberty brought with it, or at least brought after it, the decline of Eloquence; as is justly remarked (though in a courtly form) by the author of the dialogue on Oratory, which passes under the name of Tacitus: "What need is there of long discourses in the Senate, when the best of its members speedily come to an agreement? or of numerous harangues to the people, when deliberations on public affairs are conducted, not by a multitude of unskilled persons, but by a single individual, and that, the wisest?"

The Ancients Hearers Rather than Readers

This account of the matter is undoubtedly correct as far as it goes; but the importance of public speaking is so great, in our own, and all other countries that are not under a despotic Government, that the apparent neglect of the study of Rhetoric seems to require some further explanation. Part of this explanation may be supplied by the consideration that the difference in this respect between the ancients and ourselves is not so great in reality as in appearance. When the *only* way of addressing the Public was by orations, and when all political measures were debated in popular assemblies, the characters of Orator, Author, and Politician, almost entirely coincided; he who would communicate his ideas to the world, or would gain political power, and carry his legislative schemes into effect, was necessarily a Speaker; since, as Pericles is made to remark by Thucydides, "one who forms a judgment on any point, but cannot explain himself clearly to the people, might as well have never thought at all on the subject."[1] The consequence was, that almost all who sought, and all who professed to give, instruction, in the principles of Government, and the conduct of judicial proceedings, combined these, in their minds and in their practice, with the study of Rhetoric, which was necessary to give effect to all such attainments; and in time the Rhetorical writers (of whom Aristotle makes that complaint) came to consider the Science of Legislation and of Politics in general, as part of their own Art.

Much therefore of what was formerly studied under the name of Rhetoric, is still, under other names, as generally and as diligently studied as ever. Much of what we now call Literature or "Belles Lettres," was formerly included in what the ancients called Rhetorical studies.

Disavowal of Rhetorical Studies among the Moderns

It cannot be denied however that a great difference, though less, as I have said, than might at first sight appear, does exist between the ancients and the moderns in this point;—that what is strictly and properly called Rhetoric, is much less studied, at least less systematically studied, now, than formerly. Perhaps this also may be in some measure accounted for from the circumstances which have been just noticed. Such is the distrust excited by any suspicion of Rhetorical artifice, that every speaker or writer who is anxious to carry his point, endeavours to disown or to keep out of sight any superiority of skill; and wishes to be considered as relying rather on the strength of his

[1] Thucydides, book ii. See the Motto.

cause, and the soundness of his views, than on his ingenuity and expertness as an advocate. Hence it is, that even those who have paid the greatest and the most successful attention to the study of Composition and of Elocution, are so far from encouraging others by example or recommendation to engage in the same pursuit, that they labour rather to conceal and disavow their own proficiency; and thus theoretical rules are decried, even by those who owe the most to them. Whereas among the ancients, the same cause did not, for the reasons lately mentioned, operate to the same extent; since, however careful any speaker might be to disown the artifices of Rhetoric, properly so called, he would not be ashamed to acknowledge himself, generally, a student, or a proficient, in an Art which was understood to include the elements of Political wisdom.

4

Utility of Rhetoric

With regard to the other question proposed, viz. concerning the utility of Rhetoric, it is to be observed that it divides itself into two; first, whether Oratorical skill be, on the whole, a public benefit, or evil; and secondly, whether any artificial system of Rules is conducive to the attainment of that skill.

The former of these questions was eagerly debated among the ancients; on the latter, but little doubt seems to have existed. With us, on the contrary, the state of these questions seems nearly reversed. It seems generally admitted that skill in Composition and in speaking, liable as it evidently is to abuse, is to be considered, on the whole, as advantageous to the Public; because that liability to abuse is, neither in this, nor in any other case, to be considered as conclusive against the utility of any kind of art, faculty, or profession;—because the evil effects of misdirected power require that equal powers should be arrayed on the opposite side;—and because truth, having an intrinsic superiority over falsehood, may be expected to prevail when the skill of the contending parties is equal; which will be the more likely to take place, the more widely such skill is diffused.[1]

Eloquence Supposed to Be Something that Cannot Be Taught

But many, perhaps most persons, are inclined to the opinion that Eloquence, either in writing or speaking, is either a natural gift, or, at least, is to be acquired by mere practice, and is not to be attained or improved by any system of rules. And this opinion is favoured not least by those (as has been just observed) whose own experience would enable them to decide very differently; and it certainly seems to be in a great degree practically adopted. Most persons, if not left entirely to the disposal of chance in respect of this branch of education, are at least left to acquire what they can by *practice,* such as school or college-exercises afford, without much care being taken to initiate them systematically into the principles of the Art; and that, frequently, not so much from negligence in the conductors of education, as from their doubts of the utility of any such regular system.

Erroneous Systems of Rules

It certainly must be admitted, that rules not constructed on broad philosophical principles, are more likely to cramp than to assist the operations of our faculties;—that a pedantic display of technical skill is more detrimental in this than in any other pursuit, since by exciting distrust, it counteracts the very purpose of it;—that a system of

---

[1] Aristotle, *Rhetoric* ch. 1. He might have gone further; for it will very often happen that, before a popular audience, a *greater* degree of skill is requisite for maintaining the cause of truth than of falsehood. There are cases in which the arguments which lie most on the surface, and are, to superficial reasoners, the most easily set forth in a plausible form, are those on the wrong side. It is often difficult to a Writer, and still more, to a Speaker, to point out and exhibit, in their full strength, the delicate distinctions on which truth sometimes depends.

rules imperfectly comprehended, or not familiarized by practice, will (while that continues to be the case) prove rather an impediment than a help; as indeed will be found in all other arts likewise;—and that no system can be expected to equalize men whose natural powers are different. But none of these concessions at all invalidate the positions of Aristotle; that some succeed better than others in explaining their opinions, and bringing over others to them; and that, not merely by superiority of natural gifts, but by acquired habit; and that consequently if we can discover the causes of this superior success,—the means by which the desired end is attained by all who *do* attain it,—we shall be in possession of rules capable of general application; which is, says he, the proper office of an Art. Experience so plainly evinces, what indeed we might naturally be led antecedently to conjecture, that a right judgment on any subject is not necessarily accompanied by skill in effecting conviction,—nor the ability to discover truth, by a facility in explaining it,—that it might be matter of wonder how any doubt should ever have existed as to the possibility of devising, and the utility of employing, a System of Rules for "Argumentative Composition" generally; distinct from any system conversant about the subject-matter of each composition.

Knowledge of Facts No Remedy for Logical Inaccuracy

I have remarked in the Lectures on Political Economy (Lect. 9.) that "some persons complain, not altogether without reason, of the prevailing *ignorance* of facts, relative to this and to many other subjects; and yet it will often be found that the parties censured, though possessed of less knowledge than they ought to have, yet possess more than they know what to do with. Their deficiency in arranging and applying their knowledge,—in combining facts,—and correctly deducing and employing general principles, shall be greater than their ignorance of facts. Now to attempt remedying this fault by imparting to them additional knowledge,—to confer the advantage of wider experience on those who have not the power of profiting by experience,—is to attempt enlarging the prospect of a short-sighted man by bringing him to the top of a hill.

"In the tale of Sandford and Merton, where the two boys are described as amusing themselves with building a hovel with their own hands, they lay poles horizontally on the top, and cover them with straw, so as to make a flat roof: of course the rain comes through; and Master Merton then advises to *lay on more straw:* but Sandford, the more intelligent boy, remarks that as long as the roof is flat, the rain must, sooner or later, soak through; and that the remedy is to make a new *arrangement,* and form the roof sloping. Now the idea of enlightening incorrect reasoners by additional knowledge, is an error similar to that of the flat roof; it is merely laying on *more straw:* they ought first to be taught the right way of raising the roof. Of course knowledge is necessary; so is straw to thatch the roof: but no quantity of materials will supply the want of knowing how to build.

"I believe it to be a prevailing fault of the present day, not indeed to seek too much for knowledge, but to trust to accumulation of facts as a *substitute* for accuracy in the logical processes. Had Bacon lived in the present day, I am inclined to think he would have made his chief complaint against unmethodized inquiry and illogical reasoning. Certainly he would *not* have complained of *Dialectics* as corrupting Philosophy. To guard *now* against the evils prevalent in *his* time, would be to fortify a town against battering-rams, instead of against cannon. But it is remarkable that even that abuse of Dialectics which he complains of, was rather an error connected with the reasoning-process than one arising from a want of knowledge. Men were led to false conclusions, not through mere ignorance, but from hastily assuming the correctness of the data they reasoned from, without sufficient grounds. And it is remarkable that the revolution brought about in philosophy by Bacon, was not the *effect,* but the *cause,* of increased knowledge of physical facts: it was not that men were taught to think correctly by having new phenomena brought to light; but on the contrary, they discovered new phenomena in *consequence* of a new system of philosophizing."

It is probable that the existing prejudices on the present subject may be traced in great measure to the imperfect or incorrect notions of some writers, who have either confined their attention to trifling minutiæ of style, or at least have in some respect failed to take a sufficiently comprehensive view of the principles of the Art. One distinction especially is to be clearly laid down and carefully borne in mind by those who would form a correct idea of those principles; viz. the distinction already noticed in the *Elements of Logic,* between *an* Art, and *the* Art. "*An* Art of Reasoning" would imply, "a Method or System of Rules by the observance of which one may reason correctly;" "*the* Art of Reasoning" would imply a System of Rules to which every one *does* conform (whether knowingly, or not,) who reasons correctly: and such is Logic, considered as an Art.

A Rightly-Formed System Does Not Cramp the Natural Powers

In like manner "*an* Art of Composition" would imply "a System of Rules by which a good Composition may be produced;" "*the* Art of Composition,"—"such rules as *every* good Composition must conform to," whether the author of it had them in his mind or not. Of the former character appear to have been (among others) many of the Logical and Rhetorical Systems of Aristotle's predecessors in those departments. He himself evidently takes the other and more philosophical view of both branches: as appears (in the case of Rhetoric) both from the plan he sets out with, that of investigating the causes of the success of *all* who do succeed in effecting conviction, and from several passages occurring in various parts of his treatise; which indicate how sedulously he was on his guard to conform to that plan. Those who have not attended to the important distinction just alluded to, are often disposed to feel wonder, if not weariness, at his reiterated remarks, that "*all* men effect persuasion either in this way or in that;" "it is *impossible* to attain such and such an object in any other way," &c.; which doubtless were intended to remind his readers of the nature of his design; viz. not to teach *an* Art of Rhetoric, but *the* Art; not to instruct them merely how conviction *might* be produced, but how it *must.*[1]

If this distinction were carefully kept in view by the teacher and by the learner of Rhetoric, we should no longer hear complaints of the natural powers being fettered by the formalities of a System; since no such complaint can lie against a System whose rules are drawn from the invariable practice of all who succeed in attaining their proposed object.

No one would expect that the study of Sir Joshua Reynolds's lectures would cramp the genius of the painter. No one complains of the rules of Grammar as fettering Language; because it is understood that correct use is not founded on Grammar, but Grammar on correct use. A just system of Logic or of Rhetoric is analogous, in this respect, to Grammar.

Popular Objections

One may still however sometimes hear—though less, now, than a few years back—the hackneyed objections against Logic and Rhetoric, and even Grammar also. Cicero has been gravely cited (as Aristotle might have been also, in the passage just above alluded to, in his very treatise on Rhetoric) to testify that rhetorical rules are derived from the practice of Oratory, and not *vice versâ;* and that consequently there must have been—as there still is—such a thing as a speaker ignorant of those rules. A drayman, we are told, will taunt a comrade by saying, "you're a pretty fellow," without having learnt that he is employing the figure called Irony; and may employ "will" and "shall" correctly, without being able to explain the principle that guides him. And it might have been added, that perhaps he will go home whistling a

---

[1] See Appendix, note (AA.).

tune, though he does not know the name of a Note; that he will stir his fire, without knowing that he is employing the first kind of Lever; and that he will set his kettle on it to boil, though ignorant of the theory of Caloric, and of all the technical vocabulary of Chemistry. In short, of the two premises requisite for the conclusion contended for, the one about which there can be no possible doubt, is dwelt on, and elaborately proved; and the other, which is very disputable, is tacitly assumed. That the systems of Logic, Rhetoric, Grammar, Music, Mechanics, &c. must have been preceded by the practice of speaking, singing, &c., which no one ever did or can doubt, is earnestly insisted on; but that every system of which this can be said must consequently be mere useless trifling, which is at least a paradox, is quietly taken for granted; or, at least, is supposed to be sufficiently established, by repeating, in substance, the poet's remark, that

> "*. . . all a Rhetorician's rules*
> *But teach him how to name his tools:*"

and by observing that, for the most difficult points of all, natural genius and experience must do everything, and Systems of Art nothing.

To this latter remark it might have been added, that in *no* department can Systems of Art equalize men of different degrees of original ability and of experience; or teach us to accomplish all that is aimed at. No system of Agriculture can create Land; nor can the Art Military teach us to produce, like Cadmus, armed soldiers out of the Earth; though Land, and Soldiers, are as essential to the practice of these Arts, as the well-known preliminary admonition in the Cookery-book, "first take your carp," is to the culinary art. Nor can all the books that ever were written bring to a level with a man of military genius and experience, a person of ordinary ability who has never seen service.

As for the remark about "naming one's tools," which—with fair allowance for poetical exaggeration—may be admitted to be near the truth, it should be remembered, that if an inference be thence drawn of the uselessness of being thus provided with *names,* we must admit, by parity of reasoning, that it would be no inconvenience to a carpenter, or any other mechanic, to have no names for the several operations of *sawing, planing, boring,* &c. in which he is habitually engaged, or for the tools with which he performs them; and in like manner, that it would also be no loss to be without names—or without precise, appropriate, and brief names—for the various articles of dress and furniture that we use,—for the limbs and other bodily organs, and the plants, animals, and other objects around us;—in short, that it would be little or no evil to have a Language as imperfect as Chinese, or no Language at all.

Technical Terms

The simple truth is, TECHNICAL TERMS are a PART OF LANGUAGE. Now any portion of one's Language that relates to employments and situations foreign from our own, there is little need to be acquainted with. Nautical terms, *e.g.* it is little loss to a land-man to be ignorant of; though, to a sailor, they are as needful as any part of Language is to any one. And again, a deficiency in the proper Language of some *one* department, even though one we are not wholly unconcerned in, is not felt as a very heavy inconvenience. But if it were absolutely no disadvantage at all, then, it is plain the same might be said of a still *further* deficiency of a like character; and ultimately we should arrive at the absurdity above noticed,—the uselessness of Language altogether.

Real Use of Language

But though this is an absurdity which all would perceive,—though none would deny the importance of Language,—the full extent and real character of that importance is far from being universally understood. There are still (as is remarked in the Logic, Introd. § 5.) many,—though I believe not near so many as a few years back,—who, if questioned on the subject, would answer that the use of Language is to *communicate* our thoughts to each other; and that it is peculiar to Man: the truth being that *that* use of Language is *not* peculiar to

Man, though enjoyed by him in a much higher degree than by the Brutes; while that which does distinguish Man from Brute, is another, and quite distinct, use of Language, viz. as an *instrument* of *thought,*—a system of General-Signs, without which the Reasoning-process could not be conducted. The full importance, consequently, of Language, and of precise technical Language,—of having accurate and well-defined "names for one's tools,"—can never be duly appreciated by those who still cling to the theory of "Ideas;" those imaginary objects of thought in the mind, of which "Common-terms" are merely the names, and by means of which we are supposed to be able to do what I am convinced is impossible; to carry on a train of Reasoning without the use of Language, or of any General-Signs whatever.

But each, in proportion as he the more fully embraces the doctrine of *Nominalism,* and consequently understands the real character of Language, will become the better qualified to estimate the importance of an accurate system of nomenclature.

CHAP. II—OF ARGUMENTS

1

Proper Province of Rhetoric

The *finding* of suitable ARGUMENTS to prove a given point, and the skilful *arrangement* of them, may be considered as the immediate and proper province of Rhetoric, and of that alone.[1]

[1] Aristotle's division of Persuasives into "artificial" and "inartificial," including under the latter head, "Witnesses, Laws, Contracts," &c., is strangely unphilosophical. The one class, he says, the Orator is to make use of; the other, to devise. But it is evident that, in all cases alike, the *data* we argue *from* must be something already existing, and which we are not to make, but to use; and that the *arguments* derived from these data are the work of Art. Whether these data are general maxims or particular testimony—Laws of Nature, or Laws of the Land—makes, in this respect, no difference.

The business of Logic is, as Cicero complains, to *judge* of arguments, not to *invent* them: ("in inveniendis argumentis muta nimium est; in judicandis, nimium loquax)."[1] The knowledge, again, in each case, of the subject in hand, is essential; but it is evidently borrowed from the science or system conversant about that subject-matter, whether Politics, Theology, Law, Ethics, or any other. The art of addressing the feelings, again, does not belong exclusively to Rhetoric; since Poetry has at least as much to do with that branch. Nor are the considerations relative to Style and Elocution confined to argumentative and persuasive compositions. The art of *inventing* and *arranging Arguments* is, as has been said, the only province that Rhetoric can claim entirely and exclusively.

Various Divisions of Arguments

Arguments are divided according to several different principles; *i.e.* logically speaking, there are *several divisions* of them. And these *cross-divisions* have proved a source of endless perplexity to the Logical and Rhetorical student, because there is perhaps no writer on either subject that has been aware of their character. Hardly any thing perhaps has contributed so much to lessen the interest and the utility of systems of Rhetoric, as the indistinctness hence resulting. When in any subject the members of a division are not *opposed,* [contradistinguished,] but are in fact members of *different* divisions, *crossing* each other, it is manifestly impossible to obtain any clear notion of the Species treated of; nor will any labour or ingenuity bestowed on the subject be of the least avail, till the original source of perplexity is removed;—till, in short, the cross-division is detected and explained.

Arguments then may be divided.

First, into Irregular, and Regular, *i.e.* Syllogisms; these last into Categorical and Hypothetical; and the Categorical, into Syllogisms in the first Figure, and in the other Figures, &c. &c.

[1] Cicero, *De Oratore.*

Secondly, They are frequently divided into "Probable," [or "Moral,"] and "Demonstrative," [or "Necessary."]

Thirdly, into the "Direct," and the "Indirect;" [or *reductio ad absurdum,*]—the Deictic, and the Elenctic, of Aristotle.

Fourthly, into Arguments from "Example," from "Testimony," from "Cause to Effect," from "Analogy," &c. &c.

It will be perceived, on attentive examination, that several of the different species just mentioned will occasionally *contain* each other; *e.g.* a Probable Argument may be at the same time a Categorical Argument, a Direct Argument, and an Argument from Testimony, &c.; this being the consequence of Arguments having been divided on *several different principles;* a circumstance so obvious the moment it is distinctly stated, that I apprehend such of my readers as have not been conversant in these studies will hardly be disposed to believe that it could have been (as in the fact) generally overlooked, and that eminent writers should in consequence have been involved in inextricable confusion. I need only remind them however of the anecdote of Columbus breaking the egg. That which is perfectly obvious to any man of common sense, as soon as it is mentioned, may nevertheless fail to occur, even to men of considerable ingenuity.

Division of Forms of Arguments

It will also be readily perceived, on examining the principles of these several divisions, that the last of them alone is properly and strictly a division of *Arguments as such.* The First is evidently a division of the *Forms of stating them;* for every one would allow that the *same* Argument may be either stated as an enthymeme, or brought into the strict syllogistic form; and that, either categorically or hypothetically, &c.; *e.g.* "Whatever has a beginning has a cause; the earth had a beginning, therefore it had a cause; or, *If* the earth had a beginning, it had a cause: it had a beginning," &c. every one would call the *same* Argument, differently stated. This, therefore, evidently is not a division of Arguments *as such.*

Subject-Matter of Arguments

The Second is plainly a division of Arguments according to their *subject-matter,* whether Necessary or Probable, [certain or uncertain.] In Mathematics, *e.g.* every proposition that can be stated is either an immutable truth, or an absurdity and self-contradiction; while in human affairs the propositions which we assume are only true for the most part, and as general rules; and in Physics, though they must be true as long as the laws of nature remain undisturbed, the contradiction of them does not imply an absurdity; and the conclusions, of course, in each case, have the same degree and kind of certainty with the premises. This therefore is properly a division, not of *Arguments* as such, but of the *Propositions* of which they consist.

Purposes of Arguments

The Third is a division of Arguments according to the purpose for which they are employed; according to the *intention* of the reasoner; whether that be to establish "directly" [or "ostensively"] the conclusion drawn, or ["indirectly"] by means of an absurd conclusion to disprove one of the premises; (*i.e.* to prove its contradictory:) since the alternative proposed in *every* valid Argument is, *either* to admit the Conclusion, or to deny one of the Premises. Now it may so happen that in some cases, one person will choose the former, and another the latter, of these alternatives. It is probable, *e.g.* that many have been induced to admit the doctrine of Transubstantiation, from its clear connexion with the infallibility of the Romish Church; and many others, by the very same Argument, have surrendered their belief in that infallibility. Again, Berkeley and Reid seem to have alike admitted that the non-existence of matter was a necessary consequence of Locke's Theory of Ideas: but the former was hence led, *bonâ fide,* to admit and advocate that non-existence; while the latter was led by the very same Argument to reject the Ideal Theory. Thus, we see it is possible for the very same Argument to be Direct to one person, and Indirect to another; leading them to different results, according as they judge the original conclusion, or the contradictory of a premise, to be the more probable. This, therefore, is not properly a division of Arguments as such, but a division of *the purposes for which* they are on each occasion employed.

Division of Arguments as Such

The Fourth, which alone is properly a division of Arguments *as such*, and accordingly will be principally treated of, is a division according to the "relation of the subject-matter of the premises to that of the conclusion." I say, "of the subject-matter," because the *logical* connexion between the premises and conclusion is independent of the meaning of the terms employed, and may be exhibited with letters of the alphabet substituted for the terms; but the relation I am now speaking of between the premises and conclusion, (and the varieties of which form the several species of Arguments,) is in respect of their *subject-matter:* as *e.g.* an "Argument from Cause to Effect" is so called and considered, in reference to the relation existing between the premise, which is the Cause, and the conclusion, which is the Effect; and an "Argument from Example," in like manner, from the relation between a *known* and an *unknown* instance, both belonging to the same class. And it is plain that the present division, though it has a reference to the subject-matter of the premises, is yet not a division of *propositions* considered by themselves, (as in the case with the division into "probable" and "demonstrative,") but of *Arguments* considered as such; for when we say, *e.g.* that the premise is a Cause, and the conclusion the Effect, these expressions are evidently *relative,* and have no meaning, except in reference to each other; and so also when we say that the premise and the conclusion are two *parallel* cases, that very expression denotes their relation to each other.

In the Table [on the next page] I have sketched an outline of the several divisions of arguments here treated of.

2

Two Classes of Arguments

In distributing, then, the several kinds of Arguments, according to this division, it will be found convenient to lay down first two great classes, under one or other of which all can be brought; viz. first, such Arguments as might have been employed—not *as* arguments, but—to *account for* the fact or principle maintained, supposing its truth granted: secondly, such as could *not* be so employed. The former class (to which in this Treatise the name of "*A priori*" Argument will be confined) is manifestly Argument from *Cause* to Effect; since to *account* for any thing, signifies, to assign the Cause of it. The other class, of course, comprehends all other Arguments; of which there are several kinds, which will be mentioned hereafter.

The two sorts of proof which have been just spoken of, Aristotle seems to have intended to designate by the titles of ὅτι for the latter, and διότι for the former; but he has not been so clear as could be wished in observing the distinction between them. The only decisive test by which to distinguish the Arguments which belong to the one, and to the other, of these classes, is, to ask the question, "Supposing the proposition in question to be admitted, would this statement here used as an Argument, serve to *account* for and explain the truth, or not?" It will then be readily referred to the former or to the latter class, according as the answer is in the affirmative or the negative; as, *e.g.* if a murder were imputed to any one on the grounds of his "having a hatred to the deceased, and an interest in his death," the Argument would belong to the former class; because, *supposing* his guilt to be *admitted,* and an inquiry to be made how he can commit the murder, the circumstances just mentioned would serve to *account* for it; but not so, with respect to such an Argument as his

TABLE

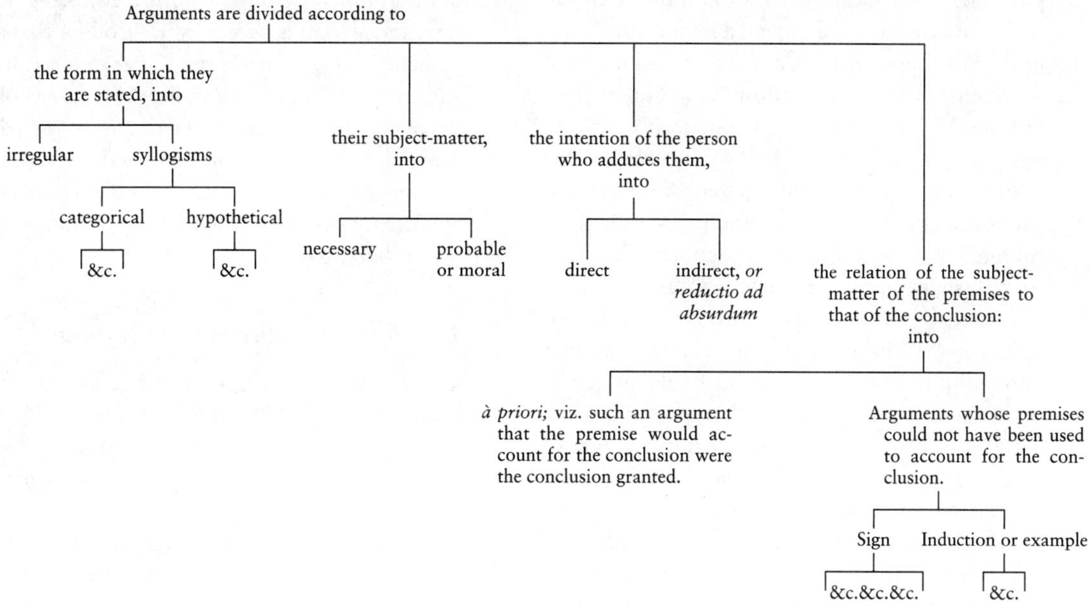

"having blood on his clothes;" which would therefore be referred to the other class.

And here let it be observed, once for all, that when I speak of arguing from Cause to Effect, it is not intended to maintain the real and proper efficacy of what are called Physical Causes to produce their respective Effects, nor to enter into any discussion of the controversies which have been raised on that point; which would be foreign from the present purpose. The word "Cause," therefore, is to be understood as employed in the popular sense; as well as the phrase of "accounting for" any fact.

Argument from Cause to Effect

As far, then, as any Cause, popularly speaking, has a tendency to produce a certain Effect, so far its existence is an Argument for that of the Effect. If the Cause be fully *sufficient,* and no *impediments* intervene, the Effect in question follows certainly; and the nearer we approach to this, the stronger the Argument.

Plausibility

This is the kind of Argument which produces (when short of absolute certainty) that species of the Probable which is usually called the "*Plausible.*" On this subject Dr. Campbell has some valuable remarks in his "*Philosophy of Rhetoric,*" (book i. § 5. ch. vii.) though he has been led into a good deal of perplexity, partly by not having logically analysed the two species of probabilities he is treating of, and partly by departing, unnecessarily, from the ordinary use of terms, in treating of the Plausible as something *distinct from* the Probable, instead of regarding it as a *species* of Probability.[1]

[1] I do not mean, however, that *every thing* to which the term "plausible" would apply would be in strict propriety called "probable"; as *e.g.* if we had fully ascertained some story that had been told us to be an imposition, we might still say, it was a "plausible" tale; though, subsequent to the detection, the word "probable" would not be so properly applied. But certainly common usage warrants the use of "probable" in many cases, on the ground

This is the chief kind of Probability which poets, or other writers of fiction, aim at; and in such works it is often designated by the term "natural."[1] Writers of this class, as they aim not at producing belief, are allowed to take their "Causes" for granted, (*i.e.* to assume any hypothesis they please,) provided they make the Effects follow naturally; representing, that is, the personages of the fiction as acting, and the events as resulting, in the same manner as might have been expected, supposing the assumed circumstances to have been real. And hence, the great Father of Criticism establishes his paradoxical maxim, that impossibilities which appear probable, are to be preferred to possibilities which appear improbable. For, as he justly observes, the impossibility of the hypothesis, as *e.g.* in Homer, the familiar intercourse of gods with mortals, is no bar to the kind of Probability (*i.e.* Verisimilitude) required, if those mortals are represented as acting in the manner men naturally would have done under those circumstances.

The Probability, then, which the writer of fiction aims at, has, for the reason just mentioned, no tendency to produce a *particular,* but only a *general,* belief; *i.e.* not that these particular events actually took place, but that *such* are likely, generally, to take place under such circumstances:[1] this kind of belief (unconsciously entertained) being necessary, and all that is necessary, to produce that sympathetic feeling which is the writer's object. In Argumentative Compositions, however, as the object of course is to produce conviction as to the particular point in question, the Causes from which our Arguments are drawn must be such as are either admitted, or may be proved, to be actually existing, or likely to exist.

The Unnatural Mistaken for Natural

It is worthy of remark, in reference to this kind of Probability—the "Plausible" or "Natural"—that men are apt to judge amiss of situations, persons, and circumstances, concerning which they have no exact knowledge, by applying to these the measure of their own feelings and experience:[2] the result of which is, that a correct account of these will often appear to them unnatural, and an erroneous one, natural. *E.G.* A person born with the usual endowments of the senses, is apt to attribute to the blind-born, and the deaf-mutes, such habits of thought, and such a state of mind, as his own would be, if he were to *become* deaf or blind, or to be left in the dark: which would be very wide of the truth. That a man born blind would not, on obtaining sight, know apart, on seeing them, a ball, and a cube, which he had been accustomed to handle, nor distinguish the dog from the cat, would appear to most persons unacquainted with the result of experiments, much less "natural" than the reverse. So it is also with those brought up free, in reference to the feelings and habits of thought of born-slaves;[3] with civilized men, in ref-

of this plausibility alone; viz. the adequacy of some cause, known, or likely to exist, to produce the effect in question. I could have wished that there had been some other word to designate what I have called, after Dr. Campbell's example, the "plausible," because it sometimes suggests the idea of "untrue." But "*likely,*" which, according to etymology, ought to be the suitable term, is often used to denote the "probable," generally.

When however we have clearly *defined* the technical sense in which we propose to employ a certain term, it may fairly be so taken, even though not invariably bearing that sense in common usage.

[1] It is also important for them, though not so essential, to keep clear of the improbable air produced by the introduction of events, which, though not unnatural, have a great *preponderance of chances* against them. The distinction between these two kinds of faults is pointed out in a passage in the *Quarterly Review,* for which see Appendix, [B.]

[1] On which ground Aristotle contends that the end of Fiction is more Philosophical than that of History, since it aims at general, instead of particular, Truth.

[2] See Part II. ch. ii. § 2.

[3] This has, in various ways, proved an obstacle to the abolition of Slavery. It has also caused great difficulty to some readers of the Book of Exodus.

erence to Savages; and of men living in Society, in reference to one who passes whole years in total solitude. I have no doubt that the admirable fiction of Robinson Crusoe would have been not only much less amusing, but, to most readers less apparently *natural,* if Friday and the other Savages had been represented with the indocility and other qualities which really belong to such Beings as the Brazilian Cannibals; and if the hero himself had been represented with that half-brutish apathetic despondency, and carelessness about all comforts demanding steady exertion, which are the really natural results of a life of utter solitude: and if he had been described as almost losing the use of his own language, instead of remembering the Spanish.

Again, I remember mentioning to a very intelligent man the description given by the earliest Missionaries to New Zealand, of their introduction of the culture of wheat; which he derided as an absurd fabrication, but which appeared to me what might have been reasonably conjectured. The Savages were familiar with bread, in the form of ship-biscuit; and accordingly, *roots* being alone cultivated by them, and furnishing their chief food, they expected to find at the roots of the wheat, tubers which could be made into biscuits. They accordingly dug up the wheat; and were mortified at the failure of their hopes. The idea of collecting small seeds, pulverizing these, and making the powder into a paste which was to be hardened by fire, was quite foreign from all their experience. Yet here, an unnatural representation would, to many, have appeared the more natural.

Much pains therefore must in many cases be taken in giving such explanations as may put men on their guard against this kind of mistake, and enable them to see the improbability, and sometimes utter impossibility, of what at the first glance they will be apt to regard as perfectly natural; and to satisfy them that something which they were disposed to regard as extravagantly unnatural, is just what might have been reasonably anticipated.

One way in which the unnatural is often made to appear, for a time, natural, is, by giving a lively and striking description which is correct in its several *parts,* and unnatural only when these are combined into a *whole;* like a painter who should give an exact picture of an English country-house, of a grove of Palm-trees, an Elephant and an Iceberg, all in the same Landscape. Thus, a vivid representation of a den of infamy and degradation, and of an ingenuous and well-disposed youth, may each be, in itself, so natural, as to draw off, for a time, the attention from the absurdity of making the one arise out of the other.

Employment of the Phrase a Priori

On the appropriate use of the kind of Argument now before us, (which is probably the εἰκὸς of Aristotle, though unfortunately he has not furnished any example of it,) some Rules will be laid down hereafter; my object at present having been merely to ascertain the nature of it. And here it may be worth while to remark, that though I have applied to this mode of Reasoning the title of "*a priori,*" it is not meant to be maintained that all such arguments as have been by other writers so designated correspond precisely with what has been just described. The phrase, "*a priori*" Argument, is not indeed employed by all in the same sense; it would, however, generally be understood to extend to any argument drawn from an *antecedent* or *forerunner,* whether a Cause or not; *e.g.* "the mercury sinks, therefore it will rain." Now this Argument being drawn from a circumstance which, though an antecedent, is in no sense a Cause, would fall not under the former, but the latter, of the classes laid down; since when rain comes, no one would *account* for the phenomenon by the falling of the mercury; which they would call a *Sign* of rain; and yet most, perhaps, would class this among "*a priori*" Arguments. In like manner the expression, "*a posteriori*" Arguments, would not in its ordinary use coincide precisely, though it would very nearly, with the second class of Arguments.

The division, however, which has here been adopted, appears to be both more philosophical, and also more precise, and consequently more practically useful, than any other; since there is so easy and decisive a test by which an Argument may be at once referred to the one or to the other of the classes described.

3

The second, then, of these classes, (viz. "Arguments drawn from such topics as could not be used to account for the fact, &c. in question, supposing it granted,") may be subdivided into two kinds; which will be designated by the terms "Sign" and "Example."

Sign

By "Sign" is meant, what may be described as an "argument from an *Effect* to a *Condition:*"—a species of Argument of which the analysis is as follows: As far as any circumstance is, what may be called a *Condition* of the existence of a certain effect or phenomenon, so far it may be inferred from the existence of that Effect: if it be a Condition *absolutely essential,* the Argument is, of course, demonstrative; and the probability is the stronger in proportion as we approach to that case.

Of this kind is the Argument in the instance lately given: a man is suspected as the perpetrator of the supposed murder, from the circumstance of his clothes being bloody; the murder being considered as in a certain degree a probable *condition* of that appearance; *i.e.* it is presumed that his clothes would *not otherwise* have been bloody. Again, from the appearance of ice, we infer, decidedly, the existence of a temperature not above freezing-point; that temperature being an essential Condition of the crystallization of water.

Proof of a Cause

Among the circumstances which are conditional to any Effect, must evidently come the Cause or Causes; and if there be only one possible Cause, this being absolutely essential, may be demonstratively proved from the Effect: if the same Effect might result from other Causes, then the Argument is, at best, but probable. But it is to be observed, that there are also many circumstances which have no tendency to *produce* a certain Effect, though it cannot exist *without* them, and from which Effect, consequently, they may be inferred, as Conditions, though not Causes; *e.g.* a man's "being alive one day," is a circumstance necessary, as a Condition, to his "dying the next;" but has no tendency to produce it; his having been alive, therefore, on the former day, may be proved from his subsequent death, but not *vice versa.*[1]

It is to be observed, therefore, that though it is very common for the Cause to be proved from its Effect, it is never so proved, *so far forth as* it is a *Cause,* but so far forth as it is a *condition,* or necessary circumstance.

A Cause, again, may be employed to prove an Effect, (this being the first class of Arguments already described,) so far as it *has a tendency* to produce the Effect, even though it be not at all *necessary* to it; (*i.e.* when other Causes may produce the same Effect;) and in this case, though the Effect may be inferred from the Cause, the Cause cannot be inferred from the Effect: *e.g.* from a mortal wound you may infer death; but not *vice versâ.*

---

[1] It is however very common, in the carelessness of ordinary language, to mention, as the Causes of phenomena, circumstances which every one would allow, on consideration, to be not Causes, but only conditions, of the Effects in question: *e.g.* it would be said of a tender plant, that it was destroyed in consequence of not being covered with a mat; though every one would mean to imply that the *frost* destroyed it; this being a Cause too well known to need being mentioned; and that which is spoken of as the Cause, viz. the absence of a covering, being only the Condition, without which the real Cause could not have operated.

How common it is to confound a Sign with a Cause is apparent in the resentment men are prone to feel against the prophets of evil; as Ahab "hated" the Prophet Micaiah, and gave as a reason "he doth not prophesy good concerning me, but evil."

Lastly, when a Cause is also a necessary or probable *condition, i.e.* when it is the *only* possible or only likely Cause, then we may argue both ways: *e.g.* we may infer a General's success from his known skill, or, his skill, from his known success: (in this, as in all cases, assuming what is the *better known* as a proof of what is less-known, denied, or doubted,) these two Arguments belonging, respectively, to the two classes originally laid down.

Logical and Physical Sequence

And it is to be observed, that, in such Arguments from Sign as this last, the conclusion which *follows, logically,* from the premise, being the Cause from which the premise *follows,* physically, (*i.e.* as a natural Effect,) there are in this case two different kinds of *Sequence* opposed to each other; *e.g.* "With many of them God was not well pleased; for they were overthrown in the wilderness." In Arguments of the first class, on the contrary, these two kinds of Sequence are combined, *i.e.* the Conclusion which follows logically from the premise, is also the Effect following physically from it as a Cause; a General's skill, *e.g.* being both the Cause and the Proof of his being likely to succeed.

Importance of Distinguishing the Two Kinds of Sequence

It is most important to keep in mind the distinction between these two kinds of Sequence, which are, in Argument, sometimes *combined,* and sometimes *opposed.* There is no more fruitful source of confusion of thought than that ambiguity of the language employed on these subjects, which tends to confound together these two things, so entirely distinct in their nature. There is hardly any argumentative writer on subjects involving a discussion of the Causes or Effects of anything, who has clearly perceived and steadily kept in view the distinction I have been speaking of, or who has escaped the errors and perplexities thence resulting. The wide extent accordingly, and the importance, of the mistakes and difficulties arising out of the ambiguity complained of, is incalculable. Of all the "Idola Fori"[1] none is perhaps more important in its results. To dilate upon this point as fully as might be done with advantage, would exceed my present limits; but it will not be irrelevant to offer some remarks on the origin of the ambiguity complained of, and on the cautions to be used in guarding against being misled by it.

Logical Sequence

The Premise by which anything is proved, is not necessarily the Cause of the fact's *being* such as it is; but it is the cause of our *knowing,* or being convinced, that it is so; *e.g.* the wetness of the earth is not the Cause of rain, but it is the Cause of our knowing that it has rained. These two things,—the Premise which produces *our conviction,* and the Cause which produces that *of which* we are convinced,—are the more likely to be confounded together, in the looseness of colloquial language, from the circumstance that (as has been above remarked) they frequently coincide; as, *e.g.* when we *infer* that the ground will be wet, from the fall of rain which *produces* that wetness. And hence it is that the same words have come to be applied, in common, to each kind of Sequence; *e.g.* an Effect is said to "follow" from a Cause, and a Conclusion to "follow" from the Premises; the words "Cause" and "Reason," are each applied indifferently, both to a Cause, properly so called, and to the Premise of an Argument; though "Reason," in strictness of speaking, should be confined to the latter. "Therefore," "hence," "consequently," &c., and also, "since," "because," and "why," have likewise a corresponding ambiguity.

Ambiguity of "Because," "Therefore," &c

The multitude of the words which bear this double meaning (and that, in all languages) greatly

[1] Bacon's "*Idols of the Marketplace.*"

increases our liability to be misled by it; since thus the very means men resort to for ascertaining the sense of any expression, are infected with the very same ambiguity; *e.g.* if we inquire what is meant by a "Cause," we shall be told that it is that from which something "follows;" or, which is indicated by the words "therefore," "consequently," &c., all which expressions are as equivocal and uncertain in their signification as the original one. It is in vain to attempt ascertaining by the balance the true amount of any commodity, if uncertain weights are placed in the opposite scale. Hence it is that so many writers, in investigating the Cause to which any fact or phenomenon is to be attributed, have assigned that which is not a *Cause,* but only a *Proof* that the fact is so; and have thus been led into an endless train of errors and perplexities.

Several, however, of the words in question, though employed indiscriminately in both significations, seem (as was observed in the case of the word ("Reason") in their primary and strict sense to be confined to one. "Δή," in Greek, and "ergo,"[1] or "itaque," in Latin, seem originally and properly to denote the Sequence of Effect from Cause; "ἄρα,"[2] and "igitur," that of conclusion from premises. The English word "*accordingly,*" will generally be found to correspond with the Latin "itaque."

Ambiguity of "Why"

The interrogative "why," is employed to inquire, either, first, the "Reasons," (or "Proof;") secondly, the "Cause;" or thirdly, the "object proposed," or Final-Cause: *e.g.* first, Why are the angles of a triangle equal to two right angles? secondly, Why are the days shorter in winter than in summer? thirdly, Why are the works of a watch constructed as they are?[1]

It is to be observed that the discovery of *Causes* belongs properly to the province of the Philosopher; that of "Reasons," strictly so called, (*i.e.* Arguments,) to that of the Rhetorician; and that, though each will have frequent occasion to assume the character of the other, it is most important that these two objects should not be confounded together.

4

Of Signs then there are some which from a certain Effect or phenomenon, infer the "Cause" of it; and others which, in like manner, infer some "Condition" which is not the Cause.

Testimony a Kind of Sign

Of these last, one species is the Argument from Testimony: the premise being the existence of the Testimony; the Conclusion, the truth of what is attested; which is considered as a "Condition" of the Testimony having been given: since it is evident that so far only as this allowed, (*i.e.* so far only as it is allowed, that the Testimony would not have been given, had it not been true,) can this Argument have any force. Testimony is of various kinds; and may possess various degrees of force,[2] not only in reference to its own intrinsic character, but in reference also to the kind of conclusion that it is brought to support.

---

[1] Most Logical writers seem not to be aware of this, as they generally, in Latin Treatises, employ "ergo" in the other sense. It is from the Greek ἐργῳ *i.e.* "in fact."

[2] "Ἀρα having a signification of *fitness* or *coincidence;* whence ἄρω.

---

[1] See the article WHY, in the Appendix to the Treatise on Logic.

[2] Locke has touched on this subject, though slightly and scantily. He says, "In the testimony of others, is to be considered,—1. The number. 2. The integrity. 3. The skill of the witnesses. 4. The design of the author, where it is a testimony out of a book cited. 5. The consistency of the parts and circumstances of the relation. 6. Contrary testimonies."

Matters of Fact, and of Opinion

In respect of this latter point, the first and great distinction is, between Testimony to *matters of Fact,* and, to *matters of Opinion,* or Doctrines.

The expressions "Matter [or Question] of Fact," and "Matter of Opinion," are not employed by all persons with precision and uniformity. But the notion most nearly conformable to ordinary usage seems to be this: by a "Matter of Fact" is meant, something which might, *conceivably,* be submitted to the *senses;* and about which it is supposed there could be no disagreement among persons who should be *present,* and to whose senses it should be submitted: and by a "Matter [or Question] of Opinion" is understood, anything respecting which an exercise of *judgment* would be called for on the part of those who should have certain objects before them, and who might conceivably disagree in their judgment thereupon.

No Greater Certainty about Facts, than Opinions

This, I think, is the description of what people in general intend to denote (though often without having themselves any very clear notion of it) by these phrases. Decidedly it is *not* meant, by those at least who use language with any precision, that there is greater *certainty,* or more general and ready *agreement,* in the one case than in the other. *E.G.* That one of Alexander's friends did, or did not, administer poison to him, every one would allow to be a question of *fact;* though it may be involved in inextricable doubt: while the question, *what sort of an act* that was, supposing it to have taken place, all would allow to be a question of *opinion;* though probably all would agree in their opinion thereupon.

A Question of Fact, One which Might Conceivably Be Submitted to the Senses

Again, it is not, apparently, necessary that a "Matter of Fact," in order to constitute it such, should have ever been actually submitted—or likely to be so—to the senses of any human Being; only, that it should be one which *conceivably might* be so submitted. *E.G.* Whether there is a lake in the centre of New Holland,—whether there is land at the South Pole—whether the Moon is inhabited,—would generally be admitted to be questions of *fact;* although no one has been able to bear testimony concerning them; and, in the last case, we are morally certain that no one ever will.

Questions of Opinion May Relate to Facts

The circumstance that chiefly tends to produce indistinctness and occasional inconsistency in the use of these phrases, is, that there is often much room for the exercise of judgment, and for difference of *opinion,* in *reference* to things which are, *themselves,* matters of *fact. E.G.* The degree of *credibility* of the *witnesses* who attest any fact, is, itself, a matter of Opinion; and so, in respect of the degree of weight due to any other kind of probabilities. That there *is,* or *is not,* land at the South Pole, is a matter of Fact; that the existence of land there is *likely,* or *unlikely,* is a matter of Opinion.

And in this, and many other cases, *different* questions very closely connected, are very apt to be confounded together,[1] and the proofs belonging to one of them brought forward as pertaining to the other. *E.G.* A case of alleged prophecy shall be in question: the event, said to have been foretold, shall be established as a fact; and also, the utterance of the supposed prediction *before* the event; and this will perhaps be assumed as proof of that which is in reality another question, and a "question of opinion;" whether the supposed prophecy *related* to the event in question; and again, whether it were merely a *conjecture* of human sagacity, or such as to imply superhuman prescience.

Again, whether a certain passage occurs in certain MSS. of the Greek Testament, is evidently a question of Fact; but whether the words imply

---

[1] See Treatise on Fallacies, "Irrelevant Conclusion."

such and such a doctrine,—however indubitable it may justly appear to us,—is evidently a "matter of opinion."[1]

Facts May Relate to Opinions

It is to be observed also, that, as there may be (as I have just said) questions of Opinion *relative* to Facts, so, there may also be questions of Fact, relative to Opinions: *i.e.* that such and such Opinions were, or were not, *maintained* at such a time and place, by such and such persons, is a question of Fact.

When the question is as to a Fact, it is plain we have to look chiefly to the *honesty* of a witness, his accuracy, and his means of gaining information. When the question is about a matter of Opinion, it is equally plain that his *ability to form a judgment* is no less to be taken into account.[2] But though this is admitted by all, it is very common with inconsiderate persons to overlook, in practice, the distinction, and to mistake as to, *what it is,* that, in each case, is attested. *Facts,* properly so called, are, we should remember, *individuals;* though the term is often extended to *general* statements; especially when these are well established. And again, the *causes* or other circumstances connected with some event or phenomenon, are often stated as a part of the very fact attested. If, for instance, a person relates his having found coal in a certain stratum; or if he states, that in the East Indies he saw a number of persons who had been sleeping exposed to the moon's rays, afflicted with certain symptoms, and that after taking a certain medicine they recovered,—he is bearing testimony as to simple matters of fact: but if he declares that the stratum in question *constantly* contains coal;—or, that the patients in question were so affected in *consequence* of the moon's rays,—that such is the *general* effect of them in that climate,[1] and that that medicine is a *cure* for such symptoms, it is evident that his testimony,—however worthy of credit—is borne to a *different kind of conclusion;* namely, not an individual, but a *general,* conclusion, and one which must rest, not solely on the veracity, but also on the judgment, of the witness.

Character of Witnesses

Even in the other case, however,—when the question relates to what is strictly a matter of fact,—the intellectual character of the witness is not to be wholly left out of the account. A man strongly influenced by prejudice, to which the weakest men are ever the most liable, may even fancy he sees what he does not. And some degree of suspicion may thence attach to the testimony of prejudiced, though honest men, when *their prejudices are on the same side with their testimony:* for otherwise their testimony may even be the stronger. *E.G.* The early disciples of Jesus were, mostly, ignorant, credulous, and prejudiced men; but all their expectations,—all their early prejudices,—ran counter to almost every thing that they attested. They were, in that particular case, harder to be convinced than more intelligent and enlightened men would have been. It is most important, therefore, to remember—what is often forgotten—that Credulity and Incredulity are the *same* habit considered in *reference to different things*. The more easy of belief any one is in respect of what falls in with his wishes or preconceived notions, the harder of belief he will be of anything that opposes these.[2]

---

[1] See Preface to vol. ii. of *Translation of Neander.*

[2] Testimony to matters of opinion usually receives the name of *Authority;* which term however is also often applied when facts are in question; as when we say, indifferently, "the account of this transaction rests on the Authority"—or "on the Testimony—of such and such an historian." See *Logic,* Appendix, Art. "Authority."

[1] Such is the prevailing, if not universal, belief of those who have resided in the East Indies.

[2] See *Logic,* b. ii. c. 2. §.

Number of Witnesses

Again, in respect of the *number* of witnesses, it is evident that,—other points being equal,—many must have more weight than one, or a few; but it is no uncommon mistake to imagine many witnesses to be bearing *concurrent* testimony to the *same* thing, when in truth they are attesting different things. One or two men may be bearing original testimony to some fact or transaction; and one or two hundred, who are repeating what they have heard from these, may be, in reality, only bearing witness to their *having heard it,* and to their own belief. Multitudes may agree in maintaining some system or doctrine, which perhaps one out of a million may have convinced himself of by research and reflection; while the rest have assented to it in implicit reliance on authority. These are not, in reality, attesting the same thing. The one is, in reality, declaring that so and so is, as he conceives, a conclusion fairly established by *reasons* pertaining to the subject-matter; the rest, that so and so is the established belief; or is held by persons on whose authority they rely. These last may indeed have very good ground for their belief: for no one would say that a man who is not versed in Astronomy is not justified in believing the Earth's motion; or that the many millions of persons who have never seen the sea, are credulous in believing, on testimony, its existence: but still it is to be remembered that they are not, in reality, bearing witness to the *same* thing as the others.

Undesigned Testimony

Undesigned testimony is manifestly, so far, the stronger; the suspicion of fabrication being thus precluded. Slight incidental hints therefore, and oblique allusions to any fact, have often much more weight than distinct formal assertions of it. And, moreover, such allusions will often go to indicate not only that the fact is *true,* but that it was, at the time when so alluded to, *notorious* and undisputed. The account given by Herodotus, of Xerxes's cutting a canal through the isthmus of Athos, which is ridiculed by Juvenal, is much more strongly attested by Thucydides in an incidental mention of a place "near which some remains of the canal might be seen," than if he had distinctly recorded his conviction of the truth of the narrative.

So also, the many slight allusions in the Apostolic Epistles to the sufferings undergone, and the miracles wrought, by Disciples, as things familiar to the readers, are much more decisive than distinct descriptions, narratives, or assertions, would have been.

Small Circumstances May Have Great Weight

Paley, in that most admirable specimen of the investigation of this kind of evidence, the "*Horæ Paulinæ,*" puts in a most needful caution against supposing that because it is on very *minute points* this kind of argument turns, therefore the *importance* of these points in establishing the conclusion, is *small.*[1] The reverse, as he justly observes, is the truth; for the more minute, and intrinsically trifling, and likely to escape notice, any point is, the more does it preclude the idea of design and fabrication. Imitations of natural objects,—flowers, for instance,—when so skilfully made as to deceive the naked eye, are detected by submitting the natural and the artificial to a *microscope.*

The same remarks will apply to other kinds of Sign also. The number and position of the nails in a man's shoe, corresponding with a foot-mark, or a notch in the blade of a knife, have led to the detection of a murderer.

---

[1] Thus Swift endeavoured (in Gulliver's Voyage to Laputa, and in some of his poems,) to cast ridicule on some of the evidence on which Bishop Atterbury's treasonable correspondence was brought home to him; the medium of proof being certain allusions, in some of the letters, to a lame lap-dog; as if the importance of the *evidence* were to be measured by the intrinsic importance of the *dog.* But Swift was far too acute a man probably to have fallen himself into such an error as he was endeavouring, for party-purposes, to lead his readers into.

Testimony of Adversaries

The Testimony of Adversaries,[1]—including under this term all who would be unwilling to admit the conclusion to which their testimony tends,—has, of course, great weight derived from that circumstance. And as it will, oftener than not, fall under the head of "undesigned," much minute research will often be needful, in order to draw it out.

Cross-Examination

In oral examination of witnesses, a skilful cross-examiner will often elicit from a reluctant witness most important truths, which the witness is desirous of concealing or disguising. There is another kind of skill, which consists in so alarming, misleading, or bewildering an honest witness as to throw discredit on his testimony, or pervert the effect of it.[2] Of this kind of art, which may be characterised as the most, or one of the most, base and depraved of all possible employments of intellectual power, I shall only make one further observation. I am convinced that the most effectual mode of eliciting *truth,* is quite different from that by which an honest, simple-minded witness is most easily baffled and confused. I have seen the experiment tried, of subjecting a witness to such a kind of cross-examination by a practised lawyer, as would have been, I am convinced, the most likely to alarm and perplex many an honest witness; without any effect in shaking the testimony: and afterwards, by a totally opposite mode of examination, such as would not have at all perplexed one who was honestly telling the truth, that same witness was drawn on, step by step, to acknowledge the utter falsity of the whole.

Generally speaking, I believe that a quiet, gentle, and straightforward, though full and careful examination, will be the most adapted to elicit *truth;* and that the manœuvres, and the browbeating, which are the most adapted to confuse an honest witness, are just what the dishonest one is the best prepared for. The more the storm blusters, the more carefully he wraps round him the cloak, which a warm sunshine will often induce him to throw off.

Testimony of Adversaries Usually Incidental

In any testimony (whether oral or written) that is unwillingly borne, it will more frequently consist in something *incidentally implied,* than in a distinct statement. For instance, the generality of men, who are accustomed to cry up Common-sense as preferable to Systems of Art, have been brought to bear witness, collectively, (see Preface to "Elements of Logic,") on the opposite side; inasmuch as each of them gives the preference to the latter, in the subject,—whatever it may be,—in which he is most conversant.

Sometimes, however, an adversary will be compelled distinctly to admit something that makes against him, in order to contest some other point. Thus, the testimony of the Evangelists, that the miracles of Jesus were acknowledged by the unbelievers, and attributed to magic, is confirmed by the Jews, in a Work called "Toldoth Jeschu;" (the "Generation of Jesus;") which must have been compiled (at whatever period) from *traditions existing from the very first;* since it is incredible that if those *contemporaries* of Jesus who opposed Him, had denied the *fact* of the miracles having been wrought, their *descendants* should have admitted the facts, and resorted to the hypothesis of magic.

Negative Testimony

The *negative* testimony, either of adversaries, or of indifferent persons, is often of great weight.

---

[1] *E.G.* I have seen in a professedly argumentative Work, a warning inserted against the alleged unsound doctrine contained in the Article "Person" in Appendix to the *Logic;* which being unaccompanied by any *proofs* of unsoundness, may be regarded as a strong testimony to the unanswerable character of the reasons I have there adduced.

[2] See an extract from a valuable pamphlet on the "License of Counsel," cited in the Lecture appended to Part II.

When statements or arguments, publicly put forth, and generally known, remain *uncontradicted,* an appeal may fairly be made to this circumstance, as a confirmatory testimony on the part of those acquainted with the matter, and interested in it; especially if they are likely to be unwilling to admit the conclusion.[1]

Concurrent Testimony

It is manifest that the concurrent testimony, positive or negative, of several witnesses, when there can have been no concert, and especially when there is any rivalry or hostility between them, carries with it a weight independent of that which may belong to each of them considered separately. For though, in such a case, each of the witnesses should be even considered as wholly undeserving of credit, still the chances might be incalculable against their all agreeing in the *same* falsehood. It is in this kind of testimony that the generality of mankind believe in the motions of the earth, and of the heavenly bodies, &c. Their belief is not the result of their own observations and calculations; nor yet again of their implicit reliance on the skill and the good-faith of any one or more astronomers; but it rests on the agreement of many independent and rival astronomers; who want neither the ability nor the will to detect and expose each other's errors. It is on similar grounds, as Dr. Hinds has justly observed, that all men, except about two or three in a million, believe in the existence and in the genuineness of manuscripts of ancient books, such as the Scriptures. It is not that they have themselves examined these; or again, (as some represent) that they rely implicitly on the good faith of those who profess to have done so; but they rely on the *concurrent* and *uncontradicted* testimony of all who have made, or who *might make,* the examination; both unbelievers, and believers of various hostile sects; any one of whom would be sure to seize any opportunity to expose the forgeries or errors of his opponents.

[1] See Hinds on the "Inspiration of Scripture."

This observation is the more important, because many persons are liable to be startled and dismayed on its being pointed out to them that they have been believing something—as they are led to suppose—on very insufficient reasons; when the truth is perhaps that they have been misstating their reasons.[1]

A remarkable instance of the testimony of adversaries,—both positive and negative,—has been afforded in the questions respecting penal-colonies. The pernicious character of the system was proved in various publications, and subsequently, before two committees of the House of Commons, from the testimony of persons who were *friendly* to that system: the report and evidence taken before those committees was published; and all this remained uncontradicted for years; till, on motions being made for the abolition of the system,[2] persons had the effrontery to come forward at the eleventh hour and deny the truth of the representations given: thus pronouncing on themselves a heavy condemnation, for having either left that representation—supposing they thought it false,—so long unrefuted, or else, denying what they knew to be true.

Misrepresentation, again, of argument,—attempts to suppress evidence, or to silence a speaker by clamour,—reviling and personality, and false charges—all these are presumptions of the same kind; that the cause against which they are brought, is,—in the opinion of adversaries at least,—unassailable on the side of truth.

Character of Things Attested

As for the character of the particular things that in any case may be attested, it is plain that we have to look to the probability or improbability, on the

[1] See Appendix, [D.].

[2] See "Substance of a Speech on Transportation, delivered in the House of Lords, on the 19th of May, 1840," &c.

one hand, of their being real, and, on the other hand, of their having been either imagined or invented by the persons attesting them.

Things Intrinsically Improbable, the Less Likely to Be Feigned

Anything unlikely to *occur,* is, so far, the less likely to have been feigned or fancied: so that its antecedent improbability may sometimes add to the credibility of those who bear witness to it.[1] And again, anything which, however likely to *take place,* would not have been likely, *otherwise,* to enter the mind of *those particular* persons who attest to it, or would be at variance with their interest or prejudices, is thereby rendered the more credible. Thus, as has been above remarked, when the disciples of Jesus record occurrences and discourses, such as were both foreign to all the notions, and at variance with all the prejudices, of any man living in those days, and of Jews more especially, this is a strong confirmation of their testimony.

Things Not Understood, or Not Believed, by Those Who Attest Them

It is also, in some cases, a strongly confirmatory circumstance that the witness should appear not to *believe,* himself, or not to *understand,* the thing he is reporting, when it is such as is, to *us, not* unintelligible nor incredible. *E.G.* When an ancient historian records a report of certain voyagers having sailed to a distant country in which they found the shadows falling on the opposite side to that which they had been accustomed to, and regards the account as incredible, from not being able to understand how such a phenomenon could occur, *we*—recognising at once what we know takes place in the Southern Hemisphere, and perceiving that *he* could not have *invented* the account—have the more reason for believing it. The report thus becomes analogous to the copy of an inscription in a language unknown to him who copied it.

The negative circumstance also, of a witness's *omitting* to mention such things as it is morally certain he *would* have mentioned had he been inventing, adds great weight to what he does say.

[1] See Sermon IV on "A Christian Place of Worship."

Superior Force of Negative Probabilities

And it is to be observed[1] that, in many cases, silence, omission, absence of certain statements, &c. will have even greater weight than much that we do find stated. *E.G.* Suppose we meet with something in a passage of one of Paul's Epistles, which indicates with a certain degree of probability the existence of such and such a custom, institution, &c., and suppose there is just the same degree of probability that such and such another custom, institution, or event, which he does *not* mention anywhere, *would* have been mentioned by him in the same place, supposing it to have really existed, or occurred; this omission, and the *negative* argument resulting, has incomparably the more weight than the other, *if we also find* that same omission in *all the other* epistles, and in every one of the Books of the New Testament.

E.G. The universal omission of all notice of the office of Hiereus (a sacerdotal priest) among the Christian ministers[2]—of all reference to one supreme Church bearing rule over all the rest[3]—of all mention of any transfer of the Sabbath from the seventh day to the first[4]—are instances of decisive negative arguments of this kind.

[1] See Essay on the "Omission of Creeds," &c.

[2] See Discourse on the Christian Priesthood appended to the Bampton Lectures. Also, Bernard's translation of Vitringa on the "Synagogue and the Church."

[3] See Essay II on the "Kingdom of Christ."

[4] See "Thoughts on the Sabbath."

So also, the omission of all allusion to a Future State, in those parts of the writings of Moses in which he is urging the Israelites to obedience by appeals to their hopes and fears; and again, in the whole of the early part of the Book of Job, in which that topic could not have failed to occur to persons believing in the doctrine,—this is a plain indication that no revelation of the doctrine was intended to be given in those Books; and that the passage, often cited, from the Book of Job, as having reference to the resurrection, must be understood as relating to that *temporal* deliverance which is narrated immediately after: since else it would (as Bishop Warburton has justly remarked) make all the rest of the Book unintelligible and absurd.[1]

Again, "although we do not admit the *positive* authority of antiquity in favour of any doctrine or practice which we do not find sanctioned by Scripture, we may yet, without inconsistency, appeal to it *negatively,* in refutation of many errors. . . . It is no argument in favour of the Millennium, that it was a notion entertained by Justin Martyr, since we do not believe him to have been inspired, and he may therefore have drawn erroneous inferences from certain texts of Scripture: but it is an argument against the doctrine of Transubstantiation, that we find no traces of it for above six centuries; and against the adoration of the Virgin Mary, that in like manner it does not appear to have been inculcated till the sixth century. It is very credible that the first Christian writers, who were but men, should have made mistakes to which all men are liable, in their interpretation of Scripture: but it is not credible that such important doctrines as Transubstantiation and the adoration of the Virgin Mary should have been transmitted from the Apostles, if we find no trace of them for five or six centuries after the birth of our Saviour."[2]

[1] See "Essay on a Future State" (First Series).

[2] Bishop Pepys's Charge, 1845.

Absence of All Records of Savages Having Civilized Themselves

To take another instance: I have remarked in the Lectures on Political Economy (Lect. 5), that the descriptions some writers give of the Civilization of Mankind, by the spontaneous origin, among tribes of Savages, of the various arts of life, one by one, are to be regarded as wholly imaginary, and not agreeing with anything that ever did, or can, actually take place; inasmuch as there is no record or tradition of any race of savages having ever civilized themselves without external aid. Numerous as are the accounts we have, of Savages who have *not* received such aid, we do not hear, in any one instance, of their having ceased to be Savages. And again, abundant as are the traditions (though mostly mixed up with much that is fabulous) of the origin of civilization in various nations, all concur in tracing it up to some foreign, or some superhuman, instructor. If ever a nation did emerge, unassisted, from the savage state, all memory of such an event is totally lost.

Now the *absence* of all such records or traditions, in a case where there is every reason to expect that an instance could be produced if any had ever occurred,—this *negative* circumstance (in conjunction with the other indications there adduced) led me, many years ago, to the conclusion, that it is impossible for mere Savages to civilize themselves—that consequently Man must at some period have received the rudiments of civilization from a *superhuman* instructor,—and that Savages are probably the descendants of civilized men, whom wars and other afflictive visitations have degraded.[1]

It might seem superfluous to remark that none but very general rules, such as the above, can be profitably laid down; and that to attempt to supersede the discretion to be exercised on each

[1] See an extract in the Appendix DD from the Lecture above alluded to.

individual case, by *fixing precisely* what degree of weight is to be allowed to the testimony of such and such persons, would be, at least, useless trifling, and, if introduced in practice, a most mischievous hindrance of a right decision. But attempts of this kind have actually been made, in the systems of Jurisprudence of some countries; and with such results as might have been anticipated. The reader will find an instructive account of some of this unwise legislation in an article on "German Jurisprudence" in the Edinburgh Review; from which an extract is subjoined in the Appendix.[1]

Testimony on *Oath* is commonly regarded as far more to be relied on—other points being equal—than any that is not sworn to. This however holds good, not universally, but only in respect of certain *intermediate* characters between the truly respectable and the worthless. For, these latter will either not scruple to take a false Oath, or, if they do, will satisfy their conscience by various *evasions* and *equivocations,* such as are vulgarly called "cheating the Devil"; so as to give, substantially, false testimony, while they cheat (in reality) *themselves,* by avoiding literal perjury. An upright man, again, considers himself as, virtually, on his Oath, whenever he makes a deliberate solemn assertion; and feels bound to guard against conveying any false impression.

But, even in respect of those intermediate characters, the influence of an Oath in securing veracity, is, I conceive, far less than some suppose. Let any one compare the evidence given on Oath, with that of those religionists who are allowed by law to substitute a "solemn Affirmation," and he will find no signs of the advantage of Sworn-testimony. Or, if he consider these religionists as, generally, more conscientious than the average, let him compare the evidence (of which we have such voluminous records) given before Committees of the House of *Lords,* which is on Oath, with that before Committees of the *Commons,* which is not; and he will find about the same proportion of honest and of dishonest testimony in each.

[1] Appendix DDD.

Still, there doubtless are persons who would scruple to swear to a falsehood which they would not scruple deliberately to affirm. But I doubt whether this proves much, in favour of the practice of requiring Oaths;—whether its chief effect is not to lower men's sense of the obligations to veracity on occasions when they are *not* on Oath. The expressions which the practice causes to be so much in use, of "*calling* God to witness," and of "*invoking* the Divine judgment," tend to induce men to act as if they imagined that God does *not* witness their conduct *unless* specially "called on"; and that He will not judge false testimony unless with our permission: and thus an habitual disregard for veracity is fostered. If Oaths were abolished—leaving the *penalties* for false-witness (no unimportant part of our security) unaltered—I am convinced that, on the whole, Testimony would be more trust-worthy than it is.

Still, since there are, as I have said, persons whose Oath—as matters now stand—is more worthy of credit than their Word, this circumstance must be duly considered in weighing the value of Testimony.[1]

Concurrent Signs of Other Kinds

The remark above made, as to the force of *concurrent* testimonies, even though each, separately, might have little or none,[2] but whose *accidental* agreement in a falsehood would be extremely improbable, is not solely applicable to the Argument

[1] See Appendix, Note DDD.

[2] It is observed by Dr. Campbell that "It deserves likewise to be attended to on this subject, that in a number of concurrent testimonies, (in cases wherein there could have been no previous concert,) there is a probability distinct from that which may be termed the sum of the probabilities resulting from the testimonies of the witnesses, a probability which would remain even though the witnesses were of such a character as to merit no faith at all. This probability arises purely from the concurrence itself. That such a concurrence should spring from chance, is as

from *Testimony,* but may be extended to many arguments of other kinds also; in which a similar calculation of chances will enable us to draw a conclusion, sometimes even amounting to moral certainty, from a combination of data which singly would have had little or no weight. *E.G.* If any one out of a hundred men throw a stone which strikes a certain object,[1] there is but a slight probability, from that fact alone, that he aimed at that object; but if all the hundred threw stones which struck the *same* object, no one would doubt that they aimed at it. It is from such a combination of arguments that we infer the existence of an intelligent Creator, from the marks of contrivance visible in the Universe, though many of these are such as, taken singly, might well be conceived undesigned and accidental; but that they should *all* be such, is morally impossible.

Testimonies Mutually Confirmatory

And here it may be observed that there may be such a concurrence of Testimonies or other Signs as shall have very considerable weight, even though they do not relate directly to *one* individual conclusion, but to *similar* ones. *E.G.* Before the reality of aërolites [meteoric stones] was established as it now is, we should have been justified in not giving at once full credit to some report, resting on ordinary evidence, of an occurrence so antecedently improbable as that of a stone's falling from the sky. But if twenty distinct accounts had reached us, from various parts of the globe, of a like phenomenon, though no two of the accounts related to the *same individual* stone, still, we should have judged this a decisive concurrence; (and this is in fact the way in which the reality of the phenomenon was actually established;) because each testimony, though given to an individual case, has a tendency towards the general conclusion in which all concur; viz. the *possibility* of such an event; and this being once admitted, the antecedent objection against each individual case is removed. The same reasoning applies to several of the New Testament Parables, as that of the Prodigal Son, the Labourers in the Vineyard, the Rich Man and Lazarus, &c., each of which contains an allusion to the future Call of the Gentiles, so little obvious however that it would have been hardly warrantable so to interpret any one of them, if it had stood alone.

Great care is requisite in setting forth clearly, especially in any popular discourse, arguments of this nature; the generality of men being better qualified for understanding (to use Lord Bacon's words) "particulars, one by one," than for taking a comprehensive view of a whole; and therefore in a *Galaxy* of evidence, as it may be called, in which the brilliancy of no single star can be pointed out, the lustre of the combination is often lost on them.

Fallacy of Composition

Hence it is, as was remarked in the Treatise on Fallacies, that the sophism of "Composition," as it is called, so frequently misleads men. It is not improbable, (in the above example,) that *each* of the stones, considered *separately,* may have been thrown at random; and therefore the same is concluded of *all,* considered in *conjunction.* Not that in such an instance as this, any one would reason so weakly; but that a still greater absurdity of the very same kind is involved in the rejection of the evidences of our religion, will be plain to any one who considers, not merely the individual force, but the *number* and *variety* of those evidences.[1]

---

one to infinite; that is, in other words, morally impossible. If therefore concert be excluded, there remains no other cause but the reality of the fact."—Campbell's *Philosophy of Rhetoric,* chap. V, bk. i, part 3.

[1] If I recollect rightly, these are the words of Mr. Dugald Stewart.

[1] Mr. Davison, in the introduction to his work on Prophecy, states strongly the cumulative force of a multitude of small particulars. See ch. iii. § 4. of this Treatise.

• • •

CHAP. III

2

Presumption and Burden of Proof

It is a point of great importance to decide in each case, at the outset, in your own mind, and clearly to point out to the hearer, as occasion may serve, on which side the *Presumption* lies, and to which belongs the [*onus probandi*] *Burden of Proof*. For though it may often be expedient to bring forward more proofs than can be fairly *demanded* of you, it is always desirable, when this is the case, that it should be *known*, and that the strength of the cause should be estimated accordingly.

According to the most correct use of the term, a "Presumption" in favour of any supposition, means, not (as has been sometimes erroneously imagined) a preponderance of probability in its favour, but, such a *preoccupation* of the ground, as implies that it must stand good till some sufficient reason is adduced against it; in short, that the *Burden of proof* lies on the side of him who would dispute it.

Thus, it is a well-known principle of the Law, that every man (including a prisoner brought up for trial) is to be *presumed* innocent till his guilt is established. This does not, of course, mean that we are to *take for granted* he is innocent; for if that were the case, he would be entitled to immediate liberation: nor does it mean that it is antecedently *more likely than not* that he is innocent; or, that the majority of these brought to trial are so. It evidently means only that the "burden of proof" lies with the accusers;—that he is not to be called on to prove his innocence, or to be dealt with as a criminal till he has done so; but that they are to bring their charges against him, which if he can repel, he stands acquitted.

Thus again, there is a "presumption" in favour of the right of any individuals or bodies-corporate to the property of which they are in *actual possession*. This does not mean that they are, or are not, *likely* to be the rightful owners: but merely, that no man is to be disturbed in his possessions till some claim against him shall be established. He is not to be called on to prove his right; but the claimant, to disprove it; on whom consequently the "burden of proof" lies.

Importance of Deciding on Which Side Lies the Onus Probandi

A moderate portion of common-sense will enable any one to perceive, and to show, on which side the Presumption lies, when once his attention is called to this question; though, for want of attention, it is often overlooked: and on the determination of this question the whole character of a discussion will often very much depend. A body of troops may be perfectly adequate to the defence of a fortress against any attack that may be made on it; and yet, if, ignorant of the advantage they possess, they sally forth into the open field to encounter the enemy, they may suffer a repulse. At any rate, even if strong enough to act on the offensive, they ought still to keep possession of their fortress. In like manner, if you have the "Presumption" on your side, and can but *refute* all the arguments brought against you, you have, for the present at least, gained a victory: but if you abandon this position, by suffering this Presumption to be forgotten, which is in fact *leaving out one of, perhaps, your strongest arguments,* you may appear to be making a feeble attack, instead of a triumphant defence.

Such an obvious case as one of those just stated, will serve to illustrate this principle. Let any one imagine a perfectly unsupported accusation of some offence to be brought against himself; and then let him imagine himself—instead of replying (as of course he would do) by a simple denial, and a defiance of his accuser to prove the charge,—setting himself to establish a negative,—taking on himself the burden of proving his own innocence, by collecting all the circumstances indicative of it that he can muster: and the result would be, in many cases, that this evidence would fall far short of establishing a certainty, and might even have the effect of raising a suspicion against him,[1] he having in fact kept out of sight the important circumstance, that these probabilities in one scale, though of no great weight perhaps in themselves, are to be weighed against absolutely nothing in the other scale.

The following are a few of the cases in which it is important, though very easy, to point out where the Presumption lies.

Presumption in Favour of Existing Institutions

There is a Presumption in favour of every *existing* institution. Many of these (we will suppose, the majority) may be susceptible of alteration for the better; but still the "Burden of proof" lies with him who proposes an alteration; simply, on the ground that since a change is not a good in itself, he who demands a change should show cause for it. No one is *called on* (though he may find it advisable) to defend an existing institution, till some argument is adduced against it; and that argument ought in fairness to prove, not merely an actual inconvenience, but the possibility of a change for the better.

Presumption of Innocence

Every book again, as well as person, ought to be presumed harmless (and consequently the copyright protected by our courts) till something is proved against it. It is a hardship to require a man to prove, either of his book, or of his private life, that there is no ground for any accusation; or else to be denied the protection of his Country. The Burden of proof, in each case, lies fairly on the accuser. I cannot but consider therefore as utterly unreasonable the decisions (which some years ago excited so much attention) to refuse the interference of the Court of Chancery in cases of piracy, whenever there was even any *doubt* whether the book pirated *might* not contain something of an immoral tendency.

[1] Hence the French proverb, "Qui s'excuse, s'accuse."

Presumption against a Paradox

There is a "Presumption" against any thing *paradoxical,* i.e. contrary to the prevailing opinion: it may be true; but the Burden of proof lies with him who maintains it; since men are not to be expected to abandon the prevailing belief till some reason is shown.

Hence it is, probably, that many are accustomed to apply "Paradox" as if it were a term of reproach, and implied absurdity or falsity. But correct use is in favour of the etymological sense. If a Paradox is unsupported, it can claim no attention; but if false, it should be censured on *that* ground; but not for being *new.* If true, it is the more important, for being a truth not generally admitted. "*Interdum vulgus rectum videt; est ubi peccat.*" Yet one often hears a charge of "paradox and nonsense" brought forward, as if there were some close connexion between the two. And indeed, in one sense this is the case; for to those who are too dull, or too prejudiced, to admit any notion at variance with those they have been used to entertain, *that* may appear nonsense, which to others is sound sense. Thus "Christ crucified" was "to the Jews, a stumbling-block," (paradox,) "and to the Greeks, foolishness;" because the one "required a sign" of a different kind from any that appeared; and the others "sought after wisdom" in their schools of philosophy.

Christianity, Presumptions against and For

Accordingly there was a Presumption against the Gospel in its first announcement. A Jewish peasant claimed to be the promised Deliverer, in whom all the nations of the Earth were to be blessed. The Burden of proof lay with Him. No one could be fairly called on to admit his pretensions till He showed cause for believing in Him. If He "had not done among them the *works* which none other man did, they had not had sin."

Now, the case is reversed. Christianity *exists;* and those who deny the divine origin attributed to it, are bound to show some reasons for assigning to it a human origin: not indeed to prove that it *did* originate in this or that way, without supernatural aid; but to point out some conceivable way in which it *might* have so arisen.

It is indeed highly expedient to bring forward evidences to establish the divine origin of Christianity: but it ought to be more carefully kept in mind than is done by most writers, that all this is an argument "ex abundanti," as the phrase is,—over and above what can fairly be called for, till some hypothesis should be framed, to account for the origin of Christianity by human means. The Burden of proof, *now,* lies plainly on him who rejects the Gospel: which, if it were not established by miracles, demands an explanation of the greater miracle,—its having been established, in defiance of all opposition, by human contrivance.

The Reformation

The Burden of proof, again, lay on the authors of the Reformation: they were bound to show cause for every *change* they advocated; and they admitted the fairness of this requisition, and accepted the challenge. But they were *not* bound to show cause for *retaining* what they left unaltered. The Presumption was, in those points, on their side; and they had only to reply to objections. This important distinction is often lost sight of, by those who look at the "doctrines, &c. of the Church of England as constituted at the Reformation," in the mass, without distinguishing the altered from the unaltered parts. The framers of the Articles kept this in mind in their expression respecting infant-baptism, that it "ought by all means to be *retained.*" They did not introduce the practice, but left it as they found it; considering the burden to lie on those who denied its existence in the primitive church, to show *when* it did arise.

The case of Episcopacy is exactly parallel: but Hooker seems to have overlooked this advantage: he sets himself to *prove* the apostolic origin of the institution, as if his task had been to *introduce* it.[1] Whatever force there may be in arguments so adduced, it is plain they must have far *more* force if the important Presumption be kept in view, that the institution had notoriously existed many ages, and that consequently, even if there had been no direct evidence for its being coeval with Christianity, it might fairly be at least supposed to be so, till some other period should be pointed out at which it had been introduced as an innovation.

Tradition

In the case of any *doctrines* again, professing to be essential parts of the Gospel-revelation, the fair *presumption* is, that we shall find all such distinctly declared in Scripture. And again, in respect of commands or prohibitions as to any point, which our Lord or his Apostles did deliver, there is a presumption that Christians are bound to comply. If any one maintains, on the ground of Tradition, the necessity of some additional article of faith (as for instance that of Purgatory) or the propriety of a departure from the New Testament precepts (as for instance in the denial of the cup to the Laity in the Eucharist) the burden of proof lies with him. We are not called on to prove that there is no tradition to the purpose;—much less, that no tradition can have any weight at all in *any* case. It is for *him* to prove, not merely generally, that there is such a thing as Tradition, and that it is entitled to respect, but that there is a tradition relative to each of the points which he thus maintains; and that such tradition is, in each point, sufficient to establish that point. For want of observing this rule, the most

---

[1] On the ambiguous employment of the phrase "divine origin"—a great source of confused reasoning among theologians—I have offered some remarks in Essay II. "On the Kingdom of Christ," § 17. 4th edit.

vague and interminable disputes have often been carried on respecting Tradition, generally.

It should be also remarked under this head, that in any one question the Presumption will often be found to lie on different sides, in respect of different parties. *E.G.* In the question between a member of the Church of England, and a Presbyterian, or member of any other Church, on which side does the Presumption lie? Evidently, to each, in favour of the religious community to which he at present belongs. He is not to separate from the Church of which he is a member, without having some sufficient reason to allege.

A Presumption evidently admits of various degrees of strength, from the very faintest, up to a complete and confident acquiescence.

Deference

The person, Body, or book, in favour of whose decisions there is a certain Presumption, is said to have, so far, "Authority"; in the strict sense of the word.[1] And a recognition of this kind of Authority,—an *habitual* Presumption in favour of such a one's decisions or opinions—is usually called "Deference."

It will often happen that this deference is not recognized by either party. A man will perhaps disavow with scorn all deference for some person,—a son or daughter perhaps, or an humble companion,—whom he treats, in manner, with familiar superiority; and the other party will as readily and sincerely renounce all pretension to Authority; and yet there may be that "habitual Presumption" in the mind of the one, in favour of the opinions, suggestions, &c. of the other, which we have called Deference. These parties however are not using the *words* in a different sense, but are unaware of the state of the *fact*. There is a Deference; but *unconscious*.

Arrogance

Those who are habitually wanting in Deference towards such as we think entitled to it, are usually called "*arrogant*"; the word being used as distinguished from self-*conceited, proud, vain,* and other kindred words. Such persons may be described as having an habitual and exclusive "self-deference."

Of course the persons and works which are looked up to as high authorities, or the contrary, will differ in each Age, Country, and Class of men. But most people are disposed,—measuring another by their own judgment,—to reckon *him* arrogant who disregards what *they* deem the best authorities. That man however may most fairly and strictly be so called who has no deference for those whom he *himself* thinks most highly of. And instances may be found of this character; *i.e.* of a man who shall hold in high estimation the ability and knowledge of certain persons—rating them perhaps above himself—whose most deliberate judgments, even on matters they are most conversant with, he will nevertheless utterly set at nought, in *each particular case* that arises, if they happen not to coincide with the idea that first strikes his mind.

Admiration and Deference, Distinct

For it is to be observed that *admiration, esteem,* and *concurrence in opinion,* are quite distinct from "Deference," and not necessarily accompanied by it. If any one makes what appears to us to be a very just remark, or if we acquiesce in what he proposes on account of the reasons he alleges,—this is not Deference. And if this has happened many times, and we thence form a high opinion of his ability, this again neither implies, nor even necessarily produces Deference; though in reason, such *ought* to be the result. But one may often find a person conversant with two others, A, and B, and estimating A without hesitation as the superior man of the two; and yet, in any case whatever that may arise, where A and B differ in their judgment, taking for granted at once that B is in the right.

---

[1] See article "Authority," in Appendix to *Elements of Logic.*

Grounds of Deference

Admiration, esteem, &c. are more the result of a judgment of the *understanding;* (though often of an erroneous one;) "Deference" is apt to depend on *feelings;*—often, on whimsical and unaccountable feelings. It is often yielded to a vigorous *claim,*—to an authoritative and overbearing demeanour. With others, of an opposite character, a soothing, insinuating, flattering, and seemingly submissive demeanour will often gain great influence. They will yield to those who seem to yield to them; the others, to those who seem resolved to yield to no one. Those who seek to gain adherents to their School or Party by putting forth the claim of *antiquity* in favour of their tenets, are likely to be peculiarly successful among those of an arrogant disposition. A book or a Tradition of a thousand years old, appears to be rather a *thing* than a *person;* and will thence often be regarded with blind deference by those who are prone to treat their contemporaries with insolent contempt, but who "will not go to compare with an old man." They will submit readily to the authority of men who flourished fifteen or sixteen centuries ago, and whom, if now living, they would not treat with decent respect.

With some persons, again, Authority seems to act according to the law of Gravitation; inversely as the squares of the *distances.* They are inclined to be of the opinion of the person who is *nearest.* Personal *Affection,* again, in many minds, generates Deference. They form a habit of first, *wishing,* secondly, *hoping,* and thirdly, *believing* a person to be in the right, whom they would be *sorry* to think mistaken. In a state of morbid depression of spirits, the same cause leads to the opposite effect. To a person in that state, whatever he would be "sorry to think" appears probable; and consequently there is a Presumption in his mind *against* the opinions, measures, &c. of those he is most attached to. That the degree of Deference felt for any one's Authority ought to depend not on our feelings, but on our judgment, it is almost superfluous to remark; but it is important to remember that there is a danger on *both* sides;—of an unreasonable Presumption either on the side of our wishes, or *against* them.

Deference as to Particular Points

It is obvious that Deference ought to be, and usually is, felt in reference to particular points. One has a deference for his physician, in questions of medicine; and for his bailiff, in questions of farming; but not *vice versâ.* And accordingly, Deference may be misplaced in respect of the *subject,* as well as of the person. It is conceivable that one may have a *due* degree of Deference, and an *excess* of it, and a *deficiency* of it, all towards the same person, but in respect of different points.

Men Often Self-Deceived As to Their Feelings of Deference

It is worth remarking, as a curious fact, that men are liable to deceive themselves as to the degree of Deference they feel towards various persons. But the case is the same (as I shall have occasion hereafter to point out[1]) with many other feelings also, such as pity, contempt, love, joy, &c.; in respect of which we are apt to mistake the *conviction* that such and such an object *deserves* pity, contempt, &c. for the *feeling* itself; which often does not accompany that conviction. And so also, a person will perhaps describe himself (with sincere good faith) as feeling great Deference towards some one, on the ground of his *believing* him to be *entitled* to it; and perhaps being really indignant against *any one else* who does not manifest it. Sometimes again, one will mistake for a feeling of Deference his *concurrence* with another's views, and admiration of what is said or done by him. But this, as has been observed above, does not imply Deference, if the same approbation would have been bestowed on the same views, supposing

[1] Part II. ch. 1. § 2.

them stated and maintained in an anonymous paper. The converse mistake is equally natural. A man may fancy that, in each case, he acquiesces in such a one's views or suggestions from the dictates of judgment, and for the reasons given; ("What she does seems wisest, virtuousest, discreetest, best"[1];) when yet perhaps the very same reasons, coming from another, would have been rejected.

Statements of Facts Liable to Be Disregarded, When Coming from Those Whose Judgment Is Undervalued

It is worth observing also, that though, as has been above remarked, (ch. ii. § 4) questions of *fact,* and of *opinion,* ought to be decided on very different grounds, yet, with many persons, a statement of facts is very little attended to when coming from one for whose judgment (though they do not deliberately doubt his veracity) they have little or no Deference. For, by common minds, the above distinction, between matters of fact and of opinion, is but imperfectly apprehended.[2] It is not therefore always superfluous to endeavour to raise a Presumption in favour of the judgment of one whom you wish to obtain credit, even in respect of matters in which judgment has, properly, little or no concern.

It is usual, and not unreasonable, to pay more Deference—other points being equal—to the decisions of a *Council,* or *Assembly* of any kind, (embodied in a Manifesto, Act of Parliament, Speech from the Throne, Report, Set of Articles, &c.,) than to those of an individual, equal, or even superior to any member of such Assembly. But in one point,—and it is a very important one, though usually overlooked,—this rule is subject to something of an exception; which may be thus stated: in any composition of an individual who is deemed worthy of respect, we presume that whatever he says must have *some* meaning,—must tend towards *some* object which could not be equally accomplished by *erasing* the whole passage. He is expected never to lay down a rule, and then add exceptions, nearly, or altogether coextensive with it; nor in any way to have so modified and explained away some assertion, that each portion of a passage shall be virtually neutralized by the other. Now if we interpret in this way any *joint*-production of several persons, we shall often be led into mistakes. For, those who have had experience as members of any deliberative Assembly, know by that experience (what indeed any one might conjecture) how much *compromise* will usually take place between conflicting opinions, and what will naturally thence result. One person, *e.g.* will urge the insertion of something, which another disapproves; and the result will usually be, after much debate, something of what is popularly called "splitting the difference:" the insertion will be made, but accompanied with such limitations and modifications as nearly to nullify it. A fence will be erected in compliance with one party, and a *gap* will be left in it, to gratify another. And again, there will often be, in some document of this class, a total *silence* on some point whereon, perhaps, most of the Assembly would have preferred giving a decision, but could not agree *what* decision it should be.

A like character will often be found also in the composition of a single individual, when his object is to *conciliate several parties* whose views are conflicting. He then *represents,* as it were, in his own mind, an Assembly composed of those parties.

Any one therefore who should think himself bound in due deference for the collective wisdom of some august Assembly, to interpret any joint-composition of it, exactly as he would that of a respectable individual, and never to attribute to it anything of that partially-inconsistent and almost nugatory character which the writings of a sensible and upright man would be exempt from,—any

[1] Milton.

[2] It is a curious characteristic of some of our older writers, that they are accustomed to cite authorities,—and that most profusely,—for matters of opinion, while for facts they often omit to cite any.

one, I say, who should proceed (as many do) on such a principle, would be often greatly misled.[1]

It may be added, that the Deference due to the decisions of an Assembly, is sometimes, erroneously, transferred to those of some individual member of it; that is, it is sometimes taken for granted, that what they have, jointly, put forth, is to be interpreted by what he, in his own writings, may have said on the same points. And yet it may sometimes be the fact, that the strong expressions of his sentiments in his own writings, may have been omitted in the *joint*-production of the Assembly, precisely because *not* approved by the majority in that Assembly.

Transferring the Burden of Proof

It is to be observed, that a Presumption may be *rebutted* by an opposite Presumption, so as to shift the Burden of proof to the other side. *E.G.* Suppose you had advised the removal of some *existing* restriction: you might be, in the first instance, called on to take the Burden of proof, and allege your reasons for the change, on the ground that there is a Presumption against every Change. But you might fairly reply, "True, but there is another Presumption which rebuts the former; every *Restriction* is in itself an evil;[2] and therefore there is a Presumption in favour of its removal, unless it can be shown necessary for prevention of some greater evil: I am not bound to allege any *specific* inconvenience; if the restriction is *unnecessary, that* is reason enough for its abolition: its defenders therefore are fairly called on to prove its necessity."[3]

Again, in reference to the prevailing opinion, that the "*Nathanael*" of John's Gospel was the same person as the Apostle "*Bartholomew*" mentioned in the others, an intelligent friend once remarked to me that *two names* afford a *prima facie* Presumption of two persons. But the name of *Bar*tholomew, being a "Patronymic," (like Simon Peter's designation *Bar*Jona, and Joseph's surname of *Bar*sabas, mentioned in Acts;—he being probably the same with the Apostle "Joseph Barnabas," &c.,) affords a Counter-presumption that he must have had *another* name, to distinguish him from his own kindred. And thus we are left open to the arguments drawn from the omission, by the other Evangelists, of the name of Nathanael,—evidently a very eminent disciple,—the omission by John of the name of the Apostle Bartholomew,—and the recorded intimacy with the Apostle Philip.

Presumption against Logic

In one of Lord Dudley's (lately published) letters to Bishop Copleston, of the date of 1814, he adduces a presumption against the Science of Logic, that it was sedulously cultivated during the dark periods when the intellectual powers of mankind seemed nearly paralysed,—when no discoveries were made, and when various errors were widespread and deep-rooted: and that when the mental activity of the world revived, and philosophical inquiry flourished, and bore its fruits, Logical studies fell into decay and contempt. To many minds this would appear a decisive argument. The author himself was too acute to see more in it than—what it certainly is—a fair Presumption. And he would probably have owned that it might be met by a counter-presumption.

Counter-Presumption

When any science or pursuit has been unduly and unwisely followed, to the neglect of others, and has even been intruded into their province, we may presume that a *re-action* will be likely to ensue

---

[1] In studying the Scriptures we must be on our guard against the converse mistake, of interpreting the Bible as if it were *one* Book, the joint-work of the Sacred Writers, instead of, what it is, several distinct books, written by individuals independently of each other.

[2] See *Charges and Other Tracts,* p. 447.

[3] See Essay II. "On the Kingdom of Christ," § 33.

and an equally excessive contempt, or dread, or abhorrence, to succeed.[1] And the same kind of reaction occurs in every department of life. It is thus that the thraldom of gross superstition, and tyrannical priestcraft, have so often led to irreligion. It is thus that "several valuable medicines, which when first introduced, were proclaimed, each as a panacea, infallible in the most opposite disorders, fell, consequently, in many instances, for a time, into total disuse; though afterwards they were established in their just estimation, and employed conformably to their real properties."[2]

So, it might have been said, in the present case, the mistaken and absurd cultivation of Logic during ages of great intellectual darkness, might be expected to produce, in a subsequent age of comparative light, an association in men's minds, of Logic, with the idea of apathetic ignorance, prejudice, and adherence to error; so that the legitimate uses and just value of Logic, supposing it to have any, would be likely to be scornfully overlooked. Our ancestors, it might have been said, having neglected to raise fresh crops of corn, and contented themselves with vainly thrashing over and over again the same straw, and winnowing the same chaff, it might be expected that their descendants would, for a time, regard the very operations of thrashing and winnowing with contempt, and would attempt to grind corn, chaff, and straw, altogether.

Such might have been, at that time, a statement of the counter-presumptions on this point.

Presumption Overthrown

Subsequently, the presumption in question has been completely done away. And it is a curious circumstance that the very person to whom that letter was addressed should have witnessed so great a change in public opinion, brought about (in great measure through *his own* instrumentality) within a small portion of the short interval between the writing of that letter and its publication, that the whole ground of Lord Dudley's argument is cut away. During that interval the Article on Logic in the *Encyclopaedia Metropolitana* (great part of the matter of it having been furnished by Bishop Copleston) was drawn up; and attracted so much attention as to occasion its publication in a separate volume: and this has been repeatedly reprinted both at home and in the United States of America, (where it is used as a textbook in, I believe, every College throughout the Union,) with a continually increasing circulation, which all the various attempts made to decry the study, seem only to augment: while sundry abridgements, and other elementary treatises on the subject, have been appearing with continually increased frequency.

Certainly, Lord Dudley, were he *now* living, would not speak of the "general neglect and contempt" of Logic at present: though so many branches of Science, Philosophy, and Literature, have greatly flourished during the interval.

The popularity indeed, or unpopularity, of any study, does not furnish, alone, a decisive proof as to its value: but it is plain that a presumption—whether strong or weak—which is based on the fact of general neglect and contempt, is destroyed, when these have ceased.

It has been alleged, however, that "the Science of Mind" has not flourished during the last twenty years; and that consequently the present is to be accounted such a dark period as Lord Dudley alludes to.

Supposing the statement to be well-founded, it is nothing to the purpose; since Lord Dudley was speaking, not, of any one science in particular, but of the absence or presence of intellectual cultivation, and of knowledge, generally;—the depressed or flourishing condition of Science, Arts, and Philosophy on the whole.

But as for the state of the "science of mind" at any given period, *that* is altogether a matter of opinion. It was probably considered by the

[1] I dwelt on this subject in a Charge to the Diocese of Dublin, 1843.

[2] *Elements of Logic,* Pref. p. x.

Schoolmen to be most flourishing in the ages which we call "dark." And it is not unlikely that the increased attention bestowed, of late years, on Logic, and the diminished popularity of those Metaphysicians who have written against it, may appear to the disciples of these last a proof of the low state (as it is, to Logical students, a sign of the improving state) of "the Science of Mind." That is, regarding the prevalence at present of logical studies as a sign that ours is "a dark age," this supposed darkness, again, furnishes in turn a sign that these studies flourish only in a dark age!

Presumptions for and against the Learned

Again, there is a presumption, (and a fair one) in respect of each question, in favour of the judgment of the most eminent men in the department it pertains to;—of eminent physicians, *e.g.* in respect to medical questions,—of theologians, in theological, &c. And by this presumption many of the Jews in our Lord's time seem to have been influenced, when they said, "have any of the Rulers, or of the Pharisees believed on Him?"

But there is a counter-presumption, arising from the circumstance that men eminent in any department are likely to regard with jealousy any one who professes to bring to light something unknown to themselves; especially if it promise to *supersede,* if established, much of what they have been accustomed to learn, and teach, and practise. And moreover, in respect of the medical profession, there is an obvious danger of a man's being regarded as a dangerous experimentalist who adopts any novelty, and of his thus losing practice even among such as may regard him with admiration as a philosopher. In confirmation of this, it may be sufficient to advert to the cases of Harvey and Jenner. Harvey's discovery of the circulation of the blood is said to have lost him most of his practice, and to have been rejected by every physician in Europe above the age of forty. And Jenner's discovery of vaccination had, in a minor degree, similar results.

There is also this additional counter-presumption against the judgment of the proficients in any department; that they are prone to a bias in favour of everything that gives the most palpable *superiority* to themselves over the uninitiated, (the Idiotae) and affords the greatest scope for the employment and display of their own peculiar acquirements. Thus, *e.g.* if there be two possible interpretations of some Clause in an Act of Parliament, one of which appears obvious to every reader of plain good sense, and the other can be supported only by some ingenious and far-fetched legal subtlety, a practised lawyer will be liable to a bias in favour of the latter, as setting forth the more prominently his own peculiar qualifications. And on this principle in great measure seems founded Bacon's valuable remark; "*harum artium saepe pravus fit usus,* ne sit nullus." Rather than let their knowledge and skill lie idle, they will be tempted to misapply them; like a schoolboy, who, when possessed of a knife, is for trying its edge on everything that comes in his way. On the whole, accordingly, I think that of these two opposite presumptions, the counter-presumption has often as much weight as the other, and sometimes more.

No Necessary Advantage to the Side on Which the Presumption Lies

It might be hastily imagined that there is necessarily an *advantage* in having the presumption on one's side, and the burden of proof on the adversary's. But it is often much the reverse. *E. G.* "In no other instance perhaps" (says Dr. Hawkins, in his valuable "Essay on Tradition,") "besides that of Religion, do men commit the very illogical mistake, of first canvassing all the objections against any particular system whose pretensions to truth they would examine, before they consider the direct arguments in its favour." (p. 82.) But why, it may be asked, *do* they make such a mistake in *this* case? An answer which I think would apply to a large proportion of such persons, is this: because a man having been brought up in a Christian-Country, has lived perhaps among such as have been accustomed from their infancy to *take for granted* the truth of their religion, and even to regard an *uninquiring* assent as a mark of commendable *faith;* and hence he has probably never even thought of proposing to himself the question,—Why should I receive Christianity as a divine revelation? Christianity being nothing new to him, and the *presumption* being in favour of it, while the burden of proof lies on its opponents, he is not stimulated to seek reasons for believing it, till he finds it controverted. And when it *is* controverted,—when an opponent urges—How do you reconcile this, and that, and the other, with the idea of a divine revelation? these objections strike by their *novelty,*—by their being opposed to what is generally received. He is thus excited to inquiry; which he sets about,—naturally enough, but very unwisely,—by seeking for answers to all these objections: and fancies that unless they can all be satisfactorily solved, he ought not to receive the religion.[1] "As if (says the Author already cited) there could not be truth, and truth supported by irrefragable arguments, and yet at the same time obnoxious to objections, numerous, plausible, and by no means easy of solution." "There are objections (said Dr. Johnson) against a *plenum* and objections against a *vacuum;* but one of them must be true." He adds that "sensible men really desirous of discovering the truth, will perceive that reason directs them to examine first the argument in favour of that side of the question, where the first presumption of truth appears. And the presumption is manifestly in favour of that religious creed already adopted by the country. . . . Their very earliest inquiry therefore must be into the direct arguments, for the authority of that book on which their country rests its religion."

But reasonable as such a procedure is, there is, as I have said, a strong temptation, and one which should be carefully guarded against, to adopt the opposite course;—to attend first to the objections which are brought against what is established, and which, for that very reason, rouse the mind from a state of apathy. Accordingly, I have not found that this "very illogical mistake" is by any means peculiar to the case of religion.

When Christianity was first preached, the state of things was reversed. The Presumption was against it, as being a novelty. "Seeing that these things *cannot be spoken against,* ye ought to be *quiet,*" was a sentiment which favoured an indolent acquiescence in the old Pagan worship. The stimulus of novelty was all on the side of those who came to overthrow this, by a new religion. The first inquiry of any one who at all attended to the subject, must have been, not,—What are the objections to Christianity?—but on what grounds do these men call on me to receive them as divine messengers? And the same appears to be the case with those Polynesians among whom our Missionaries are labouring: they begin by inquiring—"Why should we receive this religion?" And those of them accordingly who *have* embraced it, appear to be Christians on a much more rational and deliberate conviction than many among *us,* even of those who, in general maturity of intellect and civilisation, are advanced considerably beyond those Islanders.

I am not depreciating the inestimable advantages of a religious education; but, pointing out the *peculiar* temptations which accompany it. The Jews and Pagans had, in their early prejudices, greater difficulties to surmount than ours; but they were difficulties *of a different kind.*[1]

Thus much may suffice to show the importance of taking this preliminary view of the state of each question to be discussed.

---

[1] See the Lessons on Objections, in the *Easy Lessons on Christian Evidences* (published by Parker, West Strand, and also by the Christian Knowledge Society).

[1] *Logic,* Appendix.

INTRODUCTION TO ELIZA LESLIE

We have noted earlier that rhetoric is a fundamental human activity. Although some groups of people in different societies have been barred from mainstream rhetorical practices throughout history, they nevertheless have continued to behave rhetorically *somewhere, somehow.* We have noted that this is true for women, who have until fairly recently been denied the opportunity to participate equally in the most open public forums of rhetoric. In the Renaissance, women expressed their rhetorical natures at home, or in the courts by practicing courtly rhetoric. In the nineteenth century, the increasing leisure time of middle and upper class households gave women more freedom to interact socially. Visiting, entertaining, and maintaining appropriate relationships with others became major preoccupations with privileged women of the late-nineteenth century. These activities are inherently rhetorical, depending as they do on influence and persuasion, and they were thus an important outlet for women denied access to the more mainstream arenas of male rhetorical practice.

What might be described as a kind of domestic rhetorical theory arose to guide women in these rhetorical practices: handbooks or guidebooks addressed to "ladies" advising them on how best to manage their households and their interactions with others for best rhetorical effect. We include here an example excerpted from one of the more popular such books of its day, Eliza Leslie's *Miss Leslie's Behavior Book.*

Eliza Leslie was born in Philadelphia in 1787, where she lived most of her life. She was an eccentric and respected fixture of Philadelphia society until her death in 1858. Leslie was middle class, although her family suffered some financial hardships in her early adulthood. She was educated at home, and wrote and published some poetry, although it was not critically acclaimed. However, it was an early attempt at writing a cookbook that made her fortune. Leslie wrote one of the earliest published American cookbooks, which was so successful that it created financial independence for her. She continued to publish cookbooks throughout her life. Leslie also wrote successful children's books.

Later in life Leslie began writing for a new type of publication—women's magazines. She found success at this endeavor, and in 1853 collected some of her advice to women in *The Behavior Book,* which was revised shortly before her death as *Miss Leslie's Behavior Book*. In the excerpts from that volume printed here, you will find Leslie's advice specifically relating to communication and rhetorical practices for the middle- and upper-class woman. This is hardly a feminist text; much of her advice is couched in terms of making use of traditional female roles and expectations so as to achieve desired effects. Although she wrote during a period when strong feminist public speakers such as Susan B.

Anthony and Elizabeth Cady Stanton were becoming well known, Leslie's advice was heeded by many women who chose or were forced to follow a conventional path in life. We may read her advice to them as rhetorical theory from, and directed towards, the political margin of her time.

ELIZA LESLIE

MISS LESLIE'S BEHAVIOUR BOOK

A Guide and Manual for Ladies

• • •

CHAPTER XV

CONVERSATION.

Conversation is the verbal interchange of thoughts and feelings. To form a *perfect* conversationist, many qualifications are requisite. There must be knowledge of the world, knowledge of books, and a facility of imparting that knowledge; together with originality, memory, an intuitive perception of what is best to say, and best to omit, good taste, good temper, and good manners. An agreeable and instructive talker has the faculty of going "from gay to grave, from lively to serene," without any apparent effort; neither skimming so slightly over a variety of topics as to leave no impression of any, or dwelling so long upon one subject as to weary the attention of the hearers. Persons labouring under a monomania, such as absorbs their whole mind into one prevailing idea, are never pleasant or impressive talkers. They defeat their own purpose by recurring to it perpetually, and rendering it a perpetual fatigue. A good talker should cultivate a temperance in talking; so as not to talk too much, to the exclusion of other good talkers. Conversation is dialogue, not monologue. It was said of Madame de Stael that she did not converse, but delivered orations.

To be a perfect conversationist, a good voice is indispensable—a voice that is clear, distinct, and silver-toned. If you find that you have a habit of speaking too low, "reform it altogether." It is a bad one; and will render your talk unintelligible.

Few things are more delightful than for one intelligent and well-stored mind to find itself in company with a kindred spirit—each understanding the other, catching every idea, and comprehending every allusion. Such persons will become as intimate in half an hour, as if they had been personally acquainted for years.

On the other hand, the pleasure of society is much lessened by the habit in which many persons indulge, of placing themselves always in the opposition, controverting every opinion, and doubting every fact. They talk to you as a lawyer examines a witness at the bar; trying to catch you in some discrepancy that will invalidate your testimony; fixing their scrutinizing eyes upon your face "as if they would look you through," and scarcely permitting you to say, "It is a fine day," without making you prove your words. Such people are never popular. Nobody likes perpetual contradiction, especially when the subject of argument is of little or no consequence. In young people this dogmatic practice is generally based upon vanity and impertinence. In the old it is prompted by pride and selfishness. We doubt if in the present day the talk and manners of Johnson would have been tolerated in really good society.

Unless he first refers to it himself, never talk to a gentleman concerning his profession; at least do not question him about it. For instance, you must not expect a physician to tell you how his patients are affected, or to confide to you any particulars of their maladies. These are subjects that he will discuss only with their relatives, or their nurses. It is also very improper to ask a lawyer about his clients, or the cases in which he is employed. A clergyman does not like always to be talking about the church. A merchant, when away from his counting-house, has no wish to engage in business-talk with ladies; and a mechanic is ever willing "to leave the shop behind him." Every American is to be supposed capable of conversing on miscellaneous subjects; and he considers it no compliment to be treated as if he knew nothing but what the Scotch call his "bread-winner." Still, there are some few individuals who like to talk of their bread-winner. If you perceive this disposition, indulge them, and listen attentively. You will learn something useful, and worth remembering.

Women who have begun the world in humble life, and have been necessitated to give most of their attention to household affairs, are generally very shy in talking of housewifery, after their husbands have become rich, and are living in style, as it is called. Therefore, do not annoy them by questions on domestic economy. But converse as if they had been ladies always.

Lord Erskine, having lived a bachelor to an advanced age, finally married his cook, by way of securing her services, as she had frequently threatened to leave him. After she became Lady Erskine she lost all knowledge of cookery, and it was a mortal affront to hint the possibility of her knowing how any sort of eatable should be prepared for the table.

Never remind any one of the time when their situation was less genteel, or less affluent than at present, or tell them that you remember their living in a small house, or in a remote street. If they have not moral courage to talk of such things themselves, it is rude in you to make any allusion to them.

On the other hand, if invited to a fashionable house, and to meet fashionable company, it is not the time or place for you to set forth the comparative obscurity of your own origin, by way of showing that you are not proud. If *you* are not proud, it is most likely that your entertainers may be, and they will not be pleased at your ultra-magnanimity in thus lowering yourself before their aristocratic guests. These communications should be reserved for *tête-à-têtes* with old or familiar friends, who have no more pride than yourself.

When listening to a circumstance that is stated to have actually occurred to the relater, even if it strikes you as being very extraordinary, and not in conformity to your own experience, it is rude to reply, "Such a thing never happened to *me*." It is rude because it seems to imply a doubt of the narrator's veracity; and it is foolish, because its not having happened to *you* is no proof that it could not have happened to any body else. Slowness in belief is sometimes an evidence of ignorance, rather than of knowledge. People who have read but little, travelled but little, and seen but little of the world out of their own immediate circle, and whose intellect is too obtuse to desire any new accession to their own small stock of ideas, are apt to think that nothing can be true unless it has fallen under their own limited experience. Also, they may be so circumstanced that nothing in the least out of the common way is likely to disturb the still water of their pond-like existence.

A certain English nobleman always listens incredulously when he hears any person descanting on the inconveniences of travelling on the continent, and relating instances of bad accommodations and bad fare; uncomfortable vehicles, and uncomfortable inns; the short beds and narrow sheets of Germany; the slow and lumbering diligence-riding of France; the garlicky stews of Spain with a feline foundation; the little vine-twig fires in the chilly winters of Northern Italy; and various other ills which the flesh of travellers is heir to;—the duke always saying, "Now really *I* never experienced any of these discomforts, much as I have traversed the continent. None of these inconveniences ever come in my way." And how should they, when, being a man of enormous wealth, he always travels with a cavalcade of carriages; a retinue of servants; a wagon-load of bedding and other furniture; a cook, with cooking-utensils, and lots of luxurious eatables to be cooked at stopping-places—his body-coach (as it is called) being a horse-drawn palace. What inconveniences can possibly happen to *him?*

When you hear a gentleman speak in praise of a lady whom you do not think deserving of his commendations, you will gain nothing by attempting to undeceive him; particularly if she is handsome. Your dissenting from his opinion he will, in all probability, impute to envy, or ill-nature; and therefore the only impression you can make will be against yourself.

Even if you have reason to dislike the lady, recollect that few are without some good points both of person and character. And it will be much better for you to pass over her faults in silence, and agree with him in commending what is really commendable about her. What he would, perhaps, believe implicitly if told to him by a man, he would attribute entirely to jealousy, or to a love of detraction if related by a woman. Above all, if a gentleman descants on the beauty of a lady, and in your own mind you do not coincide with his opinion, refrain, on your part, from criticizing invidiously her face and figure, and do not say that "though her complexion may be fine, her features are not regular;" that "her nose is too small," or "her eyes too large," or "her mouth too wide." Still less disclose to him the secret of her wearing false hair, artificial teeth, or tinging her cheeks with rouge. If she is a bold, forward woman, he will find that out as soon as yourself, and sooner too,—and you may be sure that though he may amuse himself by talking and flirting with her, he in reality regards her as she deserves.

If a foreigner chances, in your presence, to make an unfavourable remark upon some custom or habit peculiar to your country, do not immediately take fire and resent it; for, perhaps, upon reflection, you may find that he is right, or nearly so. All countries have their national character, and no character is perfect, whether that of a nation or an individual. If you know that the stranger has imbibed an erroneous impression, you may calmly, and in a few words, endeavour to convince him of it. But if he shows an unwillingness to be convinced, and tells you that what he has said he heard from good authority; or that, before he came to America, "his mind was made up," it will be worse than useless for you to continue the argument. Therefore change the subject, or turn and address your conversation to some one else.

Lady Morgan's Duchess of Belmont very properly checks O'Donnell for his ultra-nationality, and advises him not to be always running a tilt with every Englishman he talks to, continually seeming as if ready with the war-cry of "St. Patrick for Ireland, against St. George for England."

Dr. Johnson was speaking of Scotland with his usual severity, when a Caledonian who was present, started up, and called out, "Sir, *I* was born in Scotland." "Very well, sir," said the cynic calmly, "I do not see why so small a circumstance should make any change in the national character."

English strangers complain (and with reason) of the American practice of imposing on their credulity, by giving them false and exaggerated accounts of certain things peculiar to this country, and telling them, as truths, stories that are absolute impossibilities; the amusement being to see how the John Bulls swallow these absurdities. Even General Washington diverted himself by mystifying Weld the English traveller, who complained to him at Mount Vernon of musquitoes so large and fierce that they bit through his cloth coat. "Those are nothing," said Washington, "to musquitoes I have met with, that bite through a thick leather boot." Weld expressed his astonishment, (as well he might;) and, when he "put out a book," inserted the story of the boot-piercing insects, which he said *must* be true, as he had it from no less a person than General Washington.

It is a work of supererogation to furnish falsehoods for British travellers. They can manufacture them fast enough. Also, it is ungenerous thus to sport with their ignorance, and betray them into ridiculous caricatures, which they present to the

English world in good faith. We hope these tricks are not played upon any of the best class of European travel-writers.

When in Europe, (in England particularly,) be not over sensitive as to remarks that may be made on your own country; and do not expect every one around you to keep perpetually in mind that you are an American; nor require that they should guard every word, and keep a constant check on their conversation, lest they should chance to offend your republican feelings. The English, as they become better acquainted with America, regard us with more favour, and are fast getting rid of their old prejudices, and opening their eyes as to the advantages to be derived from cultivating our friendship instead of provoking our enmity. They have, at last, all learned that our language is theirs, and they no longer compliment newly-arrived Americans on speaking English "quite well." It is not many years since two young ladies from one of our Western States, being at a party at a very fashionable mansion in London, were requested by the lady of the house to talk a little American; several of her guests being desirous of hearing a specimen of that language. One of the young ladies mischievously giving a hint to the other, they commenced a conversation in what school-girls call *gibberish;* and the listeners, when they had finished, gave various opinions on the American tongue, some pronouncing it very soft, and rather musical; others could not help saying candidly that they found it rather harsh. But all agreed that it resembled no language they had heard before.

There is no doubt that by the masses, better English is spoken in America than in England.

However an Englishman or an Englishwoman may boast of their intimacy with "the nobility and gentry," there is one infalliable rule by which the falsehood of these pretensions may be detected. And that is in the misuse of the letter H, putting it where it should not be, and omitting it where it should. This unaccountable practice prevails, more or less, in all parts of England, but is unknown in Scotland and Ireland. It is never found but among the middle and lower classes, and by polished and well-educated people is as much laughed at in England as it is with us. A relative of ours being in a stationer's shop in St. Paul's Church Yard, (the street surrounding the cathedral,) heard the stationer call his boy, and tell him to "go and take the babby out, and give him a *hairing*—the babby having had no *hair* for a week." We have heard an Englishman talk of "taking an *ouse* that should have an *ot* water pipe, and a *hoven.*" The same man asked a young lady "if she had *eels* on her boots." We heard an Englishwoman tell a servant to "bring the *arth* brush, and sweep up the *hashes.*" Another assured us that "the American ladies were quite *hignorant* of *hetiquette.*"

We have actually seen a ridiculous bill sent seriously by a Yorkshireman who kept a livery-stable in Philadelphia. The items were, *verbatim*—

	D. C.
anosafada	2 50
takinonimome	0 37

No reader can possibly guess this—so we will explain that the first line, in which all the words run into one, signifies "An orse af a day,"—or "A horse half a day." The second line means "takin on im ome,"—or "Taking of him home."

English travellers are justly severe on the tobacco-chewing and spitting, that though exploded in the best society, is still too prevalent among the million. All American ladies can speak feelingly on this subject, for they suffer from it in various ways. First, the sickening disgust without which they cannot witness the act of expectoration performed before their faces. Next, the danger of tobacco-saliva falling on their dresses in the street, or while travelling in steamers and rail-cars. Then the necessity of walking through the abomination when leaving those conveyances; treading in it with their shoes; and wiping it up with the hems of their gowns. We know an instance of the crown of a lady's white-silk bonnet being bespattered with tobacco-juice, by a man spitting out of a window in one of the New York hotels. A lady on the second seat of a box at the Chestnut-street theatre, found, when she went home, the back of her pelisse entirely spoilt, by some man behind not having succeeded in trying to spit past her—or perhaps he did not try. Why should ladies endure all this, that men may indulge in a vulgar and deleterious practice, pernicious to their own health, and which they cannot acquire without going through a seasoning of disgust and nausea?

It is very unmannerly when a person begins to relate a circumstance or an anecdote, to stop them short by saying, "I have heard it before." Still worse, to say you do not wish to hear it at all. There are people who set themselves against listening to any thing that can possibly excite melancholy or painful feelings; and profess to hear nothing that may give them a sad or unpleasant sensation. Those who have so much tenderness for themselves, have usually but little tenderness for others. It is impossible to go through the world with perpetual sunshine over head, and unfading flowers under foot. Clouds will gather in the brightest sky, and weeds choke up the fairest primroses and violets. And we should all endeavour to prepare ourselves for these changes, by listening with sympathy to the manner in which they have affected others.

No person of good feelings, good manners, or true refinement, will entertain their friends with minute descriptions of sickening horrors, such as barbarous executions, revolting punishments, or inhuman cruelties perpetrated on animals. We have never heard an officer dilate on the dreadful spectacle of a battlefield; a scene of which no description can ever present an adequate idea; and which no painter has ever exhibited in all its shocking and disgusting details. Physicians do not talk of the dissecting-room.

Unless you are speaking to a physician, and are interested in a patient he is attending, refrain in conversation from entering into the particulars of revolting diseases, such as scrofula, ulcers, cutaneous afflictions, &c. and discuss no terrible operations—especially at table. There are women who seem to delight in dwelling on such disagreeable topics.

If you are attending the sick-bed of a friend, and are called down to a visiter, speak of her illness with delicacy, and do not disclose all the unpleasant circumstances connected with it; things which it would grieve her to know, may, if once told, be circulated among married women, and by them repeated to their husbands. In truth, upon most occasions, a married woman is not a safe confidant. She will assuredly tell every thing to her husband; and in all probability to his mother and sisters also—that is, every thing concerning her friends—always, perhaps, under a strict injunction of secrecy. But a secret entrusted to more than two or three persons, is soon diffused throughout the whole community.

A man of some humour was to read aloud a deed. He commenced with the words, "Know one woman by these presents." He was interrupted, and asked why he changed the words, which were in the usual form, "Know all men by these presents." "Oh!" said he, "'tis very certain that all men will soon know it, if one woman does."

Generally speaking, it is injudicious for ladies to attempt arguing with gentlemen on political or financial topics. All the information that a woman can possibly acquire or remember on these subjects is so small, in comparison with the knowledge of men, that the discussion will not elevate them in the opinion of masculine minds. Still, it is well for a woman to desire enlightenment, that she may comprehend something of these discussions, when she hears them from the other sex; therefore let her listen as understandingly as she can, but refrain from controversy and argument on such topics as the grasp of a female mind is seldom capable of seizing or retaining. Men are very intolerant toward women who are prone to contradiction and contention, when the talk is of things considered out of their sphere; but very indulgent toward a modest and attentive listener, who only asks questions for the sake of information. Men like to dispense knowledge; but few of them believe that in departments exclusively their own, they can profit much by the suggestions of women. It is true there are and have been women who have distinguished themselves greatly in the higher branches of science and literature, and on whom the light of genius has clearly descended. But can the annals of woman produce a female Shakspeare, a female Milton, a Goldsmith, a Campbell, or a Scott? What woman has painted like Raphael or Titian, or like the best artists of our own times? Mrs. Damer and Mrs. Siddons had a talent for sculpture; so had Marie of Orleans, the accomplished daughter of Louis Philippe. Yet what are the productions of these talented ladies compared to those of Thorwaldsen, Canova, Chantrey, and the master chisels of the great American statuaries. Women have been excellent musicians, and have made fortunes by their voices. But is there among them a Mozart, a Bellini, a Michael Kelly, an Auber, a Boieldieu? Has a woman made an improvement on steam-engines, or on any thing connected with the mechanic arts? And yet these things have been done by men of no early education—by self-taught men. A good tailor fits, cuts out, and sews better than the most celebrated female dress-maker. A good man-cook far excels a good woman-cook. Whatever may be their merits as assistants, women are rarely found who are very successful at the head of any establishment that requires energy and originality of mind. Men make fortunes, women make livings. And none make poorer livings than those who waste their time, and bore their friends, by writing and lecturing upon the equality of the sexes, and what they call "Women's Rights." How is it that most of these ladies live separately from their husbands; either despising them, or being despised by them?

Truth is, the female sex is really as inferior to the male in vigour of mind as in strength of body; and all arguments to the contrary are founded on a few anomalies, or based on theories that can never be reduced to practice. Because there was a Joan of Arc, and an Augustina of Saragossa, should females expose themselves to all the dangers and terrors of "the battle-field's dreadful array." The women of the American Revolution effected much good to their country's cause, without encroaching upon the province of its brave defenders. They were faithful and patriotic; but they left the conduct of that tremendous struggle to abler heads, stronger arms, and sterner hearts.

We envy not the female who can look unmoved upon physical horrors—even the sickening horrors of the dissecting-room.

Yet women are endowed with power to meet misfortune with fortitude; to endure pain with patience; to resign themselves calmly, piously, and hopefully to the last awful change that awaits every created being; to hazard their own lives for those that they love; to toil cheerfully and industriously for the support of their orphan children, or their aged parents; to watch with untiring tenderness the sick-bed of a friend, or even of a stranger; to limit their own expenses and their own pleasures, that they may have something to bestow on deserving objects of charity; to smooth the ruggedness of man; to soften his asperities of temper; to refine his manners; to make his home a happy one; and to improve the minds and hearts of their children. All this women can—and do. And this is their true mission.

In talking with a stranger, if the conversation should turn toward sectarian religion, enquire to what church he belongs; and then mention your own church. This, among people of good sense and good manners, and we may add of true piety, will preclude all danger of remarks being made on either side which may be painful to either party. Happily we live in a land of universal toleration, where all religions are equal in the sight of the law and the government; and where no text is more powerful and more universally received than the wise and incontrovertible words—"By their fruits ye shall know them." He that acts well is a good man, and a religious man, at whatever altar he may worship. He that acts ill is a bad man, and has no true sense of religion; no matter how punctual his attendance at church, if of that church he is an unworthy member. Ostentatious sanctimony may deceive man, but it cannot deceive God.

On this earth there are many roads to heaven; and each traveller supposes his own to be the best. But they must all unite in one road at the last. It is only Omniscience that can decide. And it will then be found that no sect is excluded because of its faith; or if its members have acted honestly and conscientiously according to the lights they had, and molesting no one for believing in the tenets of a different church. The religion of Jesus, as our Saviour left it to us, was one of peace and good-will to men, and of unlimited faith in the wisdom and goodness, and power and majesty of God. It is not for a frail human being to place limits to his mercy, and say what church is the only true one—and the only one that leads to salvation. Let all men keep in mind this self-evident truth—"He can't be wrong whose life is in the right;" and try to act up to the Divine command of "doing unto all men as you would they should do unto you."

In America, no religious person of good sense or good manners ever attempts, in company, to controvert, uncalled for, the sectarian opinions of another. No clergyman that is a gentleman, (and they all are so, or ought to be,) ever will make the drawing-room an arena for religious disputation, or will offer a single deprecatory remark, on finding the person with whom he is conversing to be a member of a church essentially differing from his own. And if clergymen have that forbearance, it is doubly presumptuous for a woman, (perhaps a silly young girl,) to take such a liberty. "Fools rush in, where angels fear to tread."

Nothing is more apt to defeat even a good purpose than the mistaken and ill-judged zeal of those that are not competent to understand it in all its bearings.

Truly does the Scripture tell us—"There is a time for all things." We know an instance of a young lady at a ball attempting violently to make a proselyte of a gentleman of twice her age, a man of strong sense and high moral character, whose church (of which he was a sincere member) differed materially from her own. After listening awhile, he told her that a ballroom was no place for such discussions, and made his bow and left her. At another party we saw a young girl going round among the matrons, and trying to bring them all to a confession of faith.

Religion is too sacred a subject for discussion at balls and parties.

If you find that an intimate friend has a leaning toward the church in which you worship, first ascertain truly if her parents have no objection, and then, but not else, you may be justified in inducing her to adopt your opinions. Still, in most cases, it is best not to interfere.

In giving your opinion of a new book, a picture, or a piece of music, when conversing with a distinguished author, an artist or a musician, say modestly, that "so it appears to *you*,"—that "it has given *you* pleasure," or the contrary. But do not positively and dogmatically assert that it *is* good, or that it *is* bad. The person with whom you are talking is, in all probability, a far more competent judge than yourself; therefore, listen attentively, and he may correct your opinion, and set you right. If he fail to convince you, remain silent, or change the subject. Vulgar ladies have often a way of saying, when disputing on the merits of a thing they are incapable of understanding, "Any how, *I* like it," or, "It is quite good enough for *me*."—Which is no proof of its being good enough for any body else.

In being asked your candid opinion of a person, be very cautious to whom you confide that opinion; for if repeated as yours, it may lead to unpleasant consequences. It is only to an intimate and long-tried friend that you may safely entrust certain things, which if known, might produce mischief. Even very intimate friends are not always to be trusted, and when they have actually told something that they heard under the injunction of secrecy, they will consider it a sufficient atonement to say, "Indeed I did not mean to tell it, but somehow it slipped out;" or, "I really intended to guard the secret faithfully, but I was so questioned and cross-examined, and bewildered, that I knew not how to answer without disclosing enough to make them guess the whole. I am very sorry, and will try to be more cautious in future. But these slips of the tongue will happen."

The lady whose confidence has been thus betrayed, should be "more cautious in future," and put no farther trust in she of the slippery tongue—giving her up, entirely, as unworthy of farther friendship.

No circumstances will induce an honourable and right-minded woman to reveal a secret after promising secrecy. But she should refuse being made the depository of any extraordinary fact which it may be wrong to conceal, and wrong to disclose.

We can scarcely find words sufficiently strong to contemn the heinous practice, so prevalent with low-minded people, of repeating to their friends whatever they hear to their disadvantage. By low-minded people, we do not exclusively mean persons of low station. The low-minded are not always "born in a garret, in a kitchen bred." Unhappily, there are (so-called) ladies—ladies of fortune and fashion—who will descend to meannesses of which the higher ranks ought to be considered incapable, and who, without compunction, will wantonly lacerate the feelings and mortify the self-love of those whom they call their friends, telling them what has been said about them by other friends.

It is sometimes said of a notorious tatler and mischief-maker, that "she has, notwithstanding, a good heart." How is this possible, when it is her pastime to scatter dissension, ill-feeling, and unhappiness among all whom she calls her friends? She may, perhaps, give alms to beggars, or belong to sewing circles, or to Bible societies, or be officious in visiting the sick. All this is meritorious, and it is well if there is some good in her. But if she violates the charities of social life, and takes a malignant pleasure in giving pain, and causing trouble—depend on it, her show of benevolence is mere ostentation, and her acts of kindness spring not from the heart. She will convert the sewing circle into a scandal circle. If she is assiduous in visiting her sick friends, she will turn to the worst account, particulars she may thus acquire of the sanctities of private life and the humiliating mysteries of the sick-chamber.

If indeed it can be possible that tatling and mischief-making may be only (as is sometimes alleged) a bad habit, proceeding from an inability to govern the tongue—shame on those who have allowed themselves to acquire such a habit, and who make no effort to subdue it, or who have encouraged it in their children, and perhaps set them the example.

If you are so unfortunate as to know one of these pests of society, get rid of her acquaintance as soon as you can. If allowed to go on, she will infallibly bring you into some difficulty, if not into disgrace. If she begins by telling you—"I had a hard battle to fight in your behalf last evening at Mrs. Morley's. Miss Jewson, whom you believe to be one of your best friends, said some very severe things about you, which, to my surprise, were echoed by Miss Warden, who said she knew them to be true. But I contradicted them warmly. Still they would not be convinced, and said I must be blind and deaf not to know better. How very hard it is to distinguish those who love from those who hate us!"

Instead of encouraging the mischief-maker to relate the particulars, and explain exactly what these severe things really were, the true and dignified course should be to say as calmly as you can—"I consider no person my friend, who comes to tell such things as must give me pain and mortification, and lessen my regard for those I have hitherto esteemed, and in whose society I have found pleasure. I have always liked Miss Jewson and Miss Warden, and am sorry to hear that they do not like *me*. Still, as I am not certain of the exact truth, (being in no place where I could myself overhear the discussion,) it will make no difference in my behaviour to those young ladies. And now then we will change the subject, never to resume it. My true friends do not bring me such tales."

By-the-bye, tatlers are always listeners, and are frequently the atrocious writers of anonymous letters, for which they should be expelled from society.

Let it be remembered that all who are capable of detailing unpleasant truths, (such as can answer no purpose but to produce bad feeling, and undying enmity,) are likewise capable of exaggerating and misrepresenting facts, that do not seem quite strong enough to excite much indignation. Talebearing always leads to lying. She who begins with the first of these vices, soon arrives at the second.

Some prelude these atrocious communications with—"I think it my duty to tell how Miss Jackson and Mrs. Wilson talk about you, for it is right that you should know your friends from your enemies." You listen, believe, and from that time become the enemy of Miss Jackson and Mrs. Wilson—having too much pride to investigate the truth, and learn what they really said.

Others will commence with—"I'm a plain-spoken woman, and consider it right, for your own sake, to inform you that since your return from Europe, you talk quite too much of your travels."

You endeavour to defend yourself from this accusation, by replying that "having seen much when abroad, it is perfectly natural that you should allude to what you have seen."

"Oh! but there should be moderation in all things. To be candid—your friend Mrs. Willet says she is tired of hearing of France and Italy."

"Why then does she always try to get a seat next to me, and ask me to tell her something more of those countries?"

"Well, I don't know. People are so deceitful! There is Mr. Liddard, who says you bore him to death with talking about England."

"And yet whenever I do talk about England, I always find him at the back of my chair. And when I pause, he draws me on to say more."

"Men are such flatterers! Well, I always tell the plain truth. So it is best you should know Colonel Greenfield declares that since your return from Europe you are absolutely intolerable. Excuse my telling you these things. It is only to show that every body else thinks just as I do. Mrs. Gray says it is a pity you ever crossed the Atlantic."

Do not excuse her—but drop her acquaintance as soon as you can, without coming to a quarrel, in which case you will most probably get the worst. A plain-spoken woman is always to be dreaded. Her cold-blooded affectation of frankness is only a pretext to introduce something that will wound your feelings; and then she will tell you "that Mrs. A. B. C. and D., and Mr. E. and Mr. F. also, have said a hundred times that you are a woman of violent temper, and cannot listen to advice without flying into a passion."

And she will quietly take her leave, informing you that she is your best friend, and that all she has said was entirely for your own good, and that she shall continue to admonish you whenever she sees occasion.

A plain-spoken woman will tell you that you were thought to look very ill at Mrs. Thomson's party, your dress being rather in bad taste; that you ought to give up singing in company, your best friends saying that your style is now a little old-fashioned; that you should not attempt talking French to French ladies, as Mr. Leroux and Mr. Dufond say that your French is not quite Parisian, &c. &c. She will say these things upon no authority but her own.

When any one prefaces an enquiry by the vulgarism, "If it is a fair question?" you may be very certain that the question is a most *un*fair one—that is, a question which it is impertinent to ask, and of no consequence whatever to the asker.

If a person begins by telling you, "Do not be offended at what I am going to say," prepare yourself for something that she knows will certainly offend you. But as she has given you notice, try to listen, and answer with calmness.

It is a delicate and thankless business to tell a friend of her faults, unless you are certain that, in return, you can bear without anger to hear her point out your own. She will undoubtedly recriminate.

It is not true that an irritable temper cannot be controlled. It can, and is, whenever the worldly interest of the *enragée* depends on its suppression.

Frederick the Great severely reprimanded a Prussian officer for striking a soldier at a review. "I could not refrain," said the officer. "I have a high temper, your majesty, and I cannot avoid showing it, when I see a man looking sternly at me." "Yes, you can," replied the king. "I am looking sternly at you, and I am giving you ten times as much cause of offence as that poor soldier—yet you do not strike *me*."

A naturally irritable disposition can always be tamed down, by a strong and persevering effort to subdue it, and by determining always to check it on its first approaches to passion. The indulgence of temper renders a man (and still more a woman) the dread and shame of the whole house. It wears out the affection of husbands, wives, and children—of brothers and sisters; destroys friendship; disturbs the enjoyment of social intercourse; causes incessant changing of servants; and is a constant source of misery to that most unhappy of all classes, poor relations.

That a violent temper is generally accompanied by a good heart, is a popular fallacy. On the contrary, the indulgence of it hardens the heart. And even if its ebullitions are always succeeded by "compunctious visitings," and followed by apologies and expressions of regret, still it leaves wounds that time cannot always efface, and which we may forgive, but cannot forget.

Ill-tempered women are very apt to call themselves nervous, and to attribute their violent fits of passion to a weakness of the nerves. This is not true. A real nervous affection shows itself "more in sorrow than in anger," producing tears, tremor, and head-ache, fears without adequate cause, and general depression of spirits—the feelings becoming tender to a fault.

When a woman abandons herself to terrible fits of anger with little or no cause, and makes herself a frightful spectacle, by turning white with rage, rolling up her eyes, drawing in her lips, gritting her teeth, clenching her hands, and stamping her feet, depend on it, she is not of a nervous, but of a furious temperament. A looking-glass held before her, to let her see what a shocking object she has made herself, would, we think, have an excellent effect. We have seen but a few females in this revolting state, and only three of them were ladies—but we have heard of many.

When the paroxysm is over, all the atonement she can make is to apologize humbly, and to pray contritely. If she has really any goodness of heart, and any true sense of religion, she will do this promptly, and prove her sincerity by being very kind to those whom she has outraged and insulted—and whose best course during these fits of fury is to make no answer, or to leave the room.

As out of nothing, nothing can come, to be a good conversationist, you must have a well-stored mind, originality of ideas, and a retentive memory. Without making a lumber-room of your head, and stuffing it with all manner of useless and unnecessary things not worth retaining, you should select only such as are useful or ornamental, interesting or amusing. Your talk must flow as if spontaneously; one subject suggesting another, none being dwelt upon too long. Anecdotes may be introduced with much effect. They should be short, and related in such words as will give them the most point. We have heard the same anecdote told by two persons. With one it became prosy and tiresome, and the point was not perceptible from its being smothered in ill-chosen words. With the other narrator, the anecdote was "all light and spirit; soon told, and not soon forgotten." Brevity is the soul of wit, and wit is the soul of anecdote. And where wit is wanting, humour is an excellent substitute. Every body likes to laugh, or ought to. Yet there is a time for all things; and after listening to a serious or interesting incident well related, it is exceedingly annoying to hear some silly and heartless girl follow it with a ridiculous remark, intended to be funny—such as "Quite solemncolly!"—or, "We are all getting into the doldrums."

You may chance to find yourself in a company where no one is capable of appreciating the best sort of conversation, and where to be understood, or indeed to keep them awake, you must talk down to the capacities of your hearers. You must manage this adroitly, or they may find you out, and be offended. So, after all, it is, perhaps, safest to go on and scatter pearls where wax beads would be equally valued. Only in such society, do not introduce quotations from the poets, especially from Shakspeare, or your hearers may wonder what queer words you are saying. Another time, and with congenial companions, you can indulge in "the feast of reason, and the flow of soul."

If placed beside a lady so taciturn that no effort on your part can draw her out, or elicit more than a monosyllable, and that only at long intervals, you may safely conclude that there is nothing in her, and leave her to her own dullness, or to be enlivened by the approach of one of the other sex. That will make her talk.

Few persons are good talkers who are not extensive and miscellaneous readers. You cannot attentively read the best authors without obtaining a great command of words, so that you can always, with ease and fluency, clothe your ideas in appropriate language.

Knowledge is of course the basis of conversation—the root whose deepened strength and vigour gives life to the tree, multiplicity to its branches, and beauty to its foliage.

Much that is bad and foolish in women would have no existence if their minds were less barren. In a waste field, worthless and bitter weeds will spring up which it is hard to eradicate; while a soil that is judiciously cultivated produces abundant grain, luxuriant grass, and beautiful flowers.

There are ladies so exceedingly satisfied with themselves, and so desirous of being thought the special favourites of Providence, that they are always desiring to hold out an idea "that pain and sorrow can come not near them," and that they enjoy a happy exemption from "all the ills that flesh is heir to." They complain of nothing, for they profess to have nothing to complain of. They feel not the cold of winter, nor the heat of summer. The temperature is always exactly what *they* like. To them the street is never muddy with rain, nor slippery with ice. Unwholesome food agrees perfectly with *them*. They sleep soundly in bad beds, or rather no beds are bad. Travelling never fatigues them. Nobody imposes on them, nobody offends them. Other people may be ill—they are always in good health and spirits. To them all books are delightful—all pictures beautiful—all music charming. Other people may have trouble with their children—*they* have none. Other people may have bad servants—*theirs* are always excellent.

Now if all this were true, the lot of such persons would indeed be enviable, and we should endeavour to learn by what process such complete felicity has been attained—and why they see every thing through such a roseate medium. But it is not true. This is all overweening vanity, and a desire "to set themselves up above the rest of the world." We have always noticed that these over-fortunate, over-happy women have, in reality, a discontented, care-worn look, resulting from the incessant painful effort to seem what they are not. And if any body will take the trouble, it is very easy to catch them in discrepancies and contradictions. But it is not polite to do so. Therefore let them pass.

As mothers are always on the *qui vive,* (and very naturally,) be careful what you say of their children. Unless he is a decidedly handsome man, you may give offence by remarking, "The boy is the very image of his father." If the mother is a vain woman, she would much rather hear that all the children are the very image of herself. Refrain from praising too much the children of another family, particularly if the two sets of children are cousins. It is often dangerous to tell a mother that "little Willy is growing quite handsome." She will probably answer, "I had hoped my child was handsome always." With some mothers it is especially imprudent to remark that "little Mary looks like her aunt, or her grandmother." Again, if you prudently say nothing about the looks of the little dears, you may be suspected and perhaps accused of taking no interest in children. Young ladies, when in presence of gentlemen, are too apt to go on the other extreme, and over-act their parts, in the excessive fondling and kissing and hugging of children not in the least engaging, or even good-looking. We cannot believe that any female, not the mother, can really fall into raptures with a cross, ugly child. But how pleasant it is to play with and amuse, an intelligent, affectionate, and good-tempered little thing, to hear its innocent sayings, and to see the first buddings of its infant mind.

When you are visiting another city, and receiving civilities from some of its inhabitants, it is an ill requital for their attentions to disparage their place, and glorify your own. In every town there is something to praise; and in large cities there is a great deal to amuse, to interest, and to give pleasure. Yet there are travellers who (like Smelfungus) are never satisfied with the place they are in—who exclaim all the time against the east winds of Boston, the sea-air of New York, the summer heats of Philadelphia, the hilly streets of Baltimore, and the dusty avenues of Washington. We have heard people from New Orleans call Philadelphia the hottest city in the Union, and people from Quebec call it the coldest. If there are two successive days of rain, then poor Philadelphia is the rainiest of all places. If it snows twice in two weeks, then it is the snowiest. If a fire breaks out, it is the city of fires. If there is an Irish fight in Moyamensing, it is the city of perpetual riots. By-the-bye, after that summer when we really had several successive riots up-town, and down-town, we saw an English caricature of the City of Brotherly Love, where the spirit of William Penn, in hat and wig, was looking down sadly from the clouds at the rioters, who were all represented as Quakers, in strait, plain clothes, and broad brims, knocking each other about with sticks and stones, firing pistols, and slashing with bowie-knives. Alas, poor Quakers! how guiltless ye were of all this! It is a common belief in England, that of this sect are *all* the people of Pennsylvania.

In talking to an elderly lady, it is justly considered very rude to make any allusion to her age; even if she is unmistakeably an old woman, and acknowledges it herself. For instance, do not say—"This silk of yours is very suitable for an elderly person"—or—"Will you take this chair?—an old lady like you will find it very comfortable"—or—"Look, baby—is not that grandma?"—or—"I told the servant to attend first to you, on account of your age"—or—"Children, don't make such a noise—have you no respect for old people?"

All this we have heard.

Twentieth Century

INTRODUCTION TO THE TWENTIETH CENTURY

The twentieth century is arguably the most interesting and momentous period in human history. The wars have been more destructive, the pace of scientific and technological change has been faster, the social upheavals have been more fundamental than in any other era. Such far-reaching changes must also affect the ways in which rhetoric is practiced and theorized, since rhetoric is such a central human activity. In this century, there has been more innovative and important rhetorical theory written than at any other time since the ancient Greeks and Romans.

Widespread changes around the world have changed the ways that rhetoric is practiced. Theories to help the understanding of that rhetorical practice have likewise proliferated throughout the twentieth century. The rhetorical tradition that we have been following, grounded in western, European-influenced cultures, has been enriched and expanded through the expansion of audiences and messages to a global scale. People now talk to one another and influence one another around the world. We begin our discussion of rhetorical theory in the twentieth century by considering a key issue that enabled great changes in rhetorical practice, *media*.

Media

As the nineteenth century changed into the twentieth, print still reigned as the dominant medium. But important changes were coming in the form of *electronic media*. Early examples of electronic media, some appearing even before the turn of the century, were the telegraph, telephone, motion pictures, sound recording, and radio. As the century progressed, new electronic media such as television, computers, and video were introduced.

There are several important characteristics of electronic media that set them apart from other media such as print or the spoken word. These differences changed communication patterns fundamentally in the twentieth century. First, electronic media allow a sender of messages to reach millions of people efficiently. Speaking interpersonally, one can influence only a few people at a time. Public speakers can reach only a few thousands with their unamplified voices. An urban newspaper editorial writer might have a readership of half a million. But one talk show host or television news broadcaster can reach millions, and can do so instantaneously if necessary. These facts place great rhetorical power in the hands of those who could generate persuasive messages that could reach more people than has ever been possible before.

Second, electronic media are relatively easy for the audience to use although relatively difficult for the producers of messages to use. It may seem difficult to learn how to use a new video player, but not nearly as difficult as it is to learn how to read! Most electronic media are very easily used: It is as simple as turning on a television or sitting down in a movie theater. Yet consider the difficulty involved in learning how to *produce* music videos, television programs, or films. Electronic media shift the difficulty factor from receivers to senders of messages, in comparison to print's more even balance.

Third, electronic media are relatively expensive to use as senders of messages but relatively cheap to use as receivers of messages. Nearly everybody can afford to buy a radio or compact disc player. The programming on television and radio, once one owns a set, is free. But only a few people own radio stations or recording companies. Production facilities for messages conveyed electronically are typically owned by the wealthy or by large corporations.

Taken together, these three characteristics of electronic media mean that in the twentieth century more people have been audience members than have been speakers. One of the dramatic changes in rhetoric in the twentieth century has been the conversion of most people into receivers of the most important rhetoric, whereas most of us are not really able to produce and widely distribute meaningful persuasive messages. We have all *received* television commercials that cost millions to make, but how many of us have ever *produced* one? We are accustomed to hearing Bernard Shaw or Jay Leno speak to us on television, but how many of us could direct messages at millions of our fellow citizens? Rhetorical theory in the twentieth century has therefore changed dramatically to offer relatively less advice to people as to how to *produce* messages. Rhetorical theory is correspondingly more concerned to describe the ways in which people receive messages and to advise people as to how to receive messages more critically.

Another way to describe this change is to say that electronic media create more one-way rhetoric, with most people on the receiving end. Older rhetoric more often assumed that people would be involved in a two-way process of both speaking and listening. How people use media has created huge social and political changes in the twentieth century. Although many theorists are working to explain the effect of media on communication practices, we excerpt here the influential and engaging Canadian theorist Marshall McLuhan, whose theories written in the 1960s revolutionized thinking about media.

As we move into the twenty-first century, new forms of electronic media may actually be changing the rules yet again. Computers are giving more and more people access to the Internet and the World Wide Web. These venues allow people to generate messages very cheaply that may reach thousands or even millions of people. The growing popularity of technologies such as video and remote control for television sets is increasingly allowing people to make their own messages from the material provided for them by broadcasters. Channel cruising and taping programs for viewing under one's own preferred conditions is often the way that people use these electronic media. The new century, therefore, may again rewrite the rules to describe how new dominant media affect communication patterns.

Power

If the dominance of electronic media makes more of us into audience members and fewer of us into producers of messages, changes in power distributions must inevitably occur. To understand these changes, we must examine two trends that began at the end of the nineteenth century and have intensified, with no discernible signs of ceasing, in the twentieth century. These trends are the increase in size and power of big business and of big government. Both trends have serious rhetorical implications.

For most of human history, *production* of goods barely kept pace, if at all, with *needs and requirements* for goods. A medieval cobbler could more or less keep pace with the demand for shoes, but would be hard pressed to make twenty pairs per customer. Very few people needed more than one or two good pairs of shoes, nor was it economically feasible for them to purchase them. The same was true with most other consumer goods.

But as a result of the Industrial Revolution in the nineteenth century, the capacity of factories to produce goods began to grow at an enormous pace. By the end of the nineteenth century, it became clear that business could produce far more goods than people *needed.* To continue the expansion of business, it became necessary for corporations to induce people to buy goods on the basis of *desire* rather than *need.* People had to be persuaded to buy things on the basis of fantasy, style, and luxury rather than on the basis of what they minimally required. Although few people *need* ten pairs of shoes, if they can be persuaded to *want* a variety of shoes in different styles and colors, then large shoe making corporations can sell that much more of their products.

How to persuade people to buy more goods than they need, even more goods than they can use? Modern advertising was born, with tremendous rhetorical effect. Furthermore, as corporations needed more than ever to win the good graces of the public so as to retain their markets, public relations as a rhetorical discipline was also created by such pioneers as Edward Bernays early in the twentieth century.

As population increased, so did the size and complexity of government. Centralized, powerful governments arose to manage the affairs of increasingly large nation states around the world. There have always been dictators and monarchs in history with strong, centralized control over their nations. But in the twentieth century governments have developed an ability to influence citizens more powerfully than ever before precisely because of the development of new techniques of one-way persuasion, sometimes called *propaganda.* Powerful dictatorships such as those in Nazi Germany or the Soviet Union arose with the ability to keep their huge populations under control not only through force of arms but through skillful persuasion. It is a sad fact of life, never more true than in the twentieth century, that most repressive, genocidal, and violent regimes win the support of their people through persuasion at least as much as through the barrel of a gun. More open societies such as the United States often wage war with those dictatorships on a rhetorical basis, trying to persuade their own and their opponents' populations of the superiority of their cause. Rhetoric as an instrument of governmental control came into its own in the twentieth century.

One final rhetorical issue affecting the distribution of power has been the dramatic shrinking of the rhetorical margin in the twentieth century. This has happened in two ways. First, everyday rhetoric has moved out of the margins. Types of communication and rhetorical practices previously considered either not capable of influencing important public decisions or not worth studying have garnered the respect and attention of scholars and the public alike. The rhetorical impact of popular culture in television and popular film is now recognized as an important factor—in the late twentieth century perhaps *the* important factor—in managing public meanings and decisions. Scholars increasingly study, and bookstore shelves are full of books offering advice on practices of everyday communication in homes and offices. An example of domestic rhetorical theory from the mid-twentieth century is Amy Vanderbilt's book on "etiquette," an heir to Christine de Pisan's advice on courtly rhetoric. Rhetoric is now being identified in many different manifestations beyond the traditional forms of public speaking. One of the most influential theorists attempting to explain the power dimensions of everyday discourse is the French scholar Michel Foucault, whose work is excerpted here.

A second way in which the rhetorical margin has shrunk in the twentieth century is with the inclusion of many more groups in those rhetorical practices judged to be influential in managing public decisions. Racial minorities, women, gays and lesbians, and many other groups previously silenced or ignored by the rhetorical mainstream now have more of a voice. At the same time, rhetorical theorists recognize that the rhetoric of people in these groups may not be identical to that practiced in the empowered mainstream for many years. New theories designed to explain the special properties of the rhetoric of women, of African, Asian, or Latino Americans and of American Indians, and of other previously marginalized groups have proliferated recently. Excerpts from works by Molefi Kete Asante, Helene Cixous, Karlyn Kohrs Campbell, Carole Spitzack, and Kathryn Carter are included here as illustrations of these vigorous new lines of rhetorical theory.

DISCOURSE

Changes in media, society, and politics in the twentieth century have changed the forms or manifestations taken by rhetoric. Earlier we noted that some forms of communication such as popular music, television, and film are increasingly being regarded as rhetoric. This means that not only are the persuasive dimensions of those discourses now recognized, but the ways in which they are *important* in managing public decisions and meanings is also now understood. Theorists are now realizing that when the president gives a televised speech, the free-for-all journalists' commentaries that follow the speech and the commercial advertisement that follows the commentary may all affect public opinion quite as much as does the traditional rhetorical form of the speech itself. Therefore, rhetoric is being recognized in many more discursive forms than ever before.

The structure of the rhetorical transaction itself has changed for many kinds of persuasive experiences during the twentieth century. Rhetoric traditionally followed a model of a speaker or writer crafting a message that would go to a more or less determinate audience. That is to say, a speaker would know that she was to address the city council tomorrow, and would know who her audience was and what sort of beliefs and values she could appeal to for rhetorical effect. A writer would create a newspaper editorial that would speak to more or less predictable predispositions among subscribers to the paper.

This model is valid in circumstances where audiences are more or less predictable. By predictable I mean that the identity, makeup, values, beliefs, and predispositions of the audience are in general identifiable. Such an audience is usually cohesive in time and space: They are this specific nation hearing a speech now, they are a particular group of soldiers awaiting battle, they are exactly *this* Senate debating legislation. When an audience is more or less predictable, the *speaker* creates a *message* so as to appeal to the given *audience,* and the *purpose* of the appeal is for the audience to accept some belief or action.

Much rhetorical practice in the twentieth century is perforce based on a different model: The *purpose* of the speech is to *create the audience* by bringing hitherto disconnected aggregates of people together on a common ground of belief or action. To understand this new configuration of rhetorical discourse, we need to think about audiences in the twentieth century.

Audiences are increasingly *fluid, complex, dispersed,* and *active.* Imagine a person preparing a speech that is delivered on national television. Think about the audience that will receive the speech in terms of how most people use television. The audience is *fluid* because people rarely sit still even for twenty-second commercials, much less twenty-minute speeches. People consume pieces of messages and are then replaced by new people who consume different pieces of the message. Today's fluid audience is like a fast-moving, ever-changing line of cars zooming by billboards that are quickly seen and partially noticed. In other words, the physical makeup of the audience (the actual bodies composing the audience) come and go for many rhetorical messages today.

Today's rhetorical audiences are increasingly *complex.* One obvious reason is that the number of people receiving a message may well number in the millions. Another reason is that around the world, people increasingly live in heterogeneous societies; that is to say, highly mixed. Compared to even one hundred years ago, people today are more likely to live and work among and to interact with people of different races, ages, economic class, national origin, religion, and so forth. What this means for a rhetor is that prediction of an audience's needs, values, beliefs, and predispositions, which traditionally was taken as a vital condition for rhetorical appeal, may be difficult or impossible because there are so many needs, values, and so forth in the people attending to a rhetorical message.

Today's audiences are *dispersed* because they are not in one time and place. Television commercials reach people around the world at any given moment, and they reach people in different changing circumstances as they are rebroadcast. This means that analyzing an audience's context or situation, another traditional condition for rhetorical appeal, may become impossible. The rhetor may not find at all predictable, even foreseeable, what the situations are in which receivers of the message will find themselves.

Today's audiences are active because they increasingly have the means and use the opportunity to take speakers' messages and fashion them into their own messages. Consider the example of a television watcher with remote control. This person channel surfs through carefully-crafted messages, ignoring the wishes of those who spent millions putting together the shows and commercials through which she so blithely cruises, assembling an evening of entertainment (which is another way to say, assembling *her own message*) from the "stuff" provided on cable television. Consider the example of a president who gives what is considered a major foreign policy speech, only to find twenty seconds of that message excised, spliced into a news program, and followed by commentary. The intermediate audience of the television news program has already actively changed the message, even before it reaches our more active, channel surfing viewer.

Under these circumstances, what is created by rhetorical messages today is increasingly *the audience itself*. What a persuasive message for Nike shoes really tries to do is to create a group of Nike customers from out of a fluid, complex melange of potential consumers all around the world. Those previously random customers become a united audience, they cohere, around a base of allegiance to a product. The hopeful senatorial candidate Jones throws a message into the rhetorical environment hoping that the ideas and values in it provide a basis upon which people can unite or cohere as an audience of Jones voters.

New theories of rhetoric have developed to account for the ways in which rhetoric provides a place for audiences to gather. These theories are not attuned to the old rhetorical model of *competition* and *victory* so much as they attempt to show how *community* and *cooperation* are created out of the social chaos of the twentieth century. The greatest rhetorical theorist of the century is Kenneth Burke, who focuses on the ways in which identification and cooperation are created rhetorically, in addition to the more traditional goals of success for a single rhetor. I. A. Richards has written theories of meaning that show how rhetoric can remove misunderstandings among people and increase communities of consensus. Theorists of language such as Mikhail Bakhtin show how social and political structures form around the ways in which language is used rhetorically. These and other writers have made the twentieth century an exceptionally fertile period of innovation and progress in rhetorical theory.

Even though new patterns of rhetoric typify the twentieth century, the practices of persuasion are so varied and complex that older, more traditional forms of discourse have endured as well. Rhetorical theories have therefore developed to account for them, and also for the ways these older forms have changed to match changing social and political conditions. The twentieth century has seen the emergence of many popular rhetorical theorists such as William Hoffman, whose practical advice on public speaking and sales persuasion has continued to inspire the public throughout most of the century. Besides public speaking, argument continues to be studied. Two theorists here examine the ways in which argument emerges in everyday persuasion. Stephen Toulmin developed a model of argument out of legal persuasive practices that has been widely influential. Chaim Perelman and L. Olbrechts-Tyteca have updated many of the classical forms of argument and figures of speech, retheorizing how they are used in everyday persuasion in the twentieth century.

The twentieth century has seen lots of social, political, scientific, and technological changes. The twenty-first century will likely see even more! Our survey of the history of rhetorical theory has been a survey of the human condition and how thoughtful people have responded to it. As the human condition continues to change in the twenty-first century, so will rhetorical practice and the theories designed to understand it. We study rhetorical theory now and in the future not just to understand persuasion, but to understand ourselves through the lens of rhetoric.

KNOWLEDGE

In turning to our last major theme of knowledge, several developments in twentieth century rhetorical theory come together. We have seen that theorists have come to the realization that rhetoric occurs in significant ways in many different episodes and dimensions of life, not only in the peak moments of grand oratory. A corresponding realization is that the *effects* of rhetorical discourse are more widespread, long term, and fundamental than previous theory realized. Indeed, the most important effect of rhetoric, twentieth century theorists have realized, may be the changes it brings about in social knowledge.

For centuries, theorists looked to readily identifiable audience reactions to specific rhetorical messages as an index of the effect of those messages. If a speaker urged an audience to support a declaration of war, and they did so, their agreement was taken to be the effect of that message. Effects in the long term, or results that were out of the conscious awareness and choice of an audience, were taken to be too difficult to discover and assess.

Theorists of language such as Bakhtin, Richards, and Burke, however, have argued that there is a rhetoric inherent in the very words that people use in everyday discourse. The rhetoric of language use lies in the ways that it structures our perceptions, our categories of thinking, and our basic assumptions and predispositions. In other words, the rhetoric of language use affects *what we know and how we know.*

Traditional rhetoric would examine a political speech on behalf of a gubernatorial candidate to determine whether it had the effect of persuading the audience to vote for the candidate. But attention to the effects of rhetoric have expanded in the twentieth century. Analysis might now also include identifying the ways that such a speech, and hundreds more like it, instilled in the audience the idea that voting is a good thing, that democracy is viable, that one's vote counts, and so forth. In other words, a speech not only supports a candidate in an election but it affects social knowledge of what elections are all about. Likewise, television advertisements are not only selling a particular product, they are selling the knowledge that consumer goods are a high priority in life, that buying for pleasure is acceptable, and that satisfying desire is a primary goal in life.

The realization that the effects of rhetoric lie not only in particular decisions but in the knowledge that structures perception and social life has dramatically widened the scope of twentieth century rhetorical theory. Theorists and critics now have ways to identify effects at deeper, more long-term levels than ever before. In the process of doing so, they have placed rhetoric at the core of what it means to think and to experience the world as human beings.

FOR FURTHER READING

Bitzer, Lloyd F., and Edwin Black. 1971. *The Prospect of Rhetoric.* Englewood Cliffs, NJ: Prentice Hall.

Black, Edwin. 1965. *Rhetorical Criticism: A Study in Method.* NY: Macmillan.

Black, Edwin. 1992. *Rhetorical Questions: Studies of Public Discourse.* Chicago: University of Chicago Press.

Cherwitz, Richard A., ed. 1990. *Rhetoric and Philosophy.* Hillsdale, NJ: Lawrence Erlbaum.

Covino, William A., and David A. Jolliffe. 1995. *Rhetoric: Concepts, Definitions, Boundaries.* Boston: Allyn & Bacon.

Edelstein, Alex S. 1997. *Total Propaganda: From Mass Culture to Popular Culture.* Mahwah, NJ: Lawrence Erlbaum.

Enos, Theresa, and Stuart Brown, eds. 1993. *Defining the New Rhetoric.* Newbury Park, CA: Sage.

Enos, Theresa, Richard McNabb, Roxanne Mountford, and Carolyn Miller, eds. 1997. *Making and Unmaking the Prospects for Rhetoric.* Mahwah, NJ: Lawrence Erlbaum.

Farrell, Thomas B. 1993. *Norms of Rhetorical Culture.* New Haven: Yale University Press.

Foss, Karen A., and Sonja K. Foss. 1991. *Women Speak: The Eloquence of Women's Lives.* Prospect Heights, IL: Waveland.

Gill, Ann. 1994. *Rhetoric and Human Understanding.* Prospect Heights, IL: Waveland.

Hart, Roderick P. 1990. *Modern Rhetorical Criticism.* Glenview, IL: Scott, Foresman.

Kinneavy, James L. 1971. *A Theory of Discourse.* NY: Prentice Hall.

Lunsford, Andrea A., ed. 1995. *Reclaiming Rhetorica: Women in the Rhetorical Tradition.* Pittsburgh: University of Pittsburgh Press.

McPhail, Mark Lawrence. 1996. *Zen in the Art of Rhetoric: An Inquiry into Coherence.* Albany: State University of New York Press.

Medhurst, Martin J., and Thomas W. Benson, eds. 1991. *Rhetorical Dimensions in Media,* 2nd ed. Dubuque, IA: Kendall Hunt.

Scott, Robert L. 1967. "On Viewing Rhetoric as Epistemic." *Central States Speech Journal, 18:* 9–17.

INTRODUCTION TO MIKHAIL BAKHTIN

Rhetorical theorists throughout history have been interested in language. Much of the attention paid to language, however, has been to figures of speech, stylistic devices, or literary applications. Even more substantive treatments of language, such as St. Augustine's, linked persuasive purposes with variations in style.

One of the biggest changes in twentieth century rhetorical theory has been an attempt to theorize ordinary language use as fundamentally rhetorical. Theorists have argued that beyond the stylistic or decorative function of language there is rhetorical force in the basic vocabularies of everyday social and political discourse. Ordinary speech, at a basic level of grammar, syntax, and word choice, predisposes people to see the world in different ways. Since nobody lives outside of language, some theorists claim that language actually creates human reality by creating those predispositions. Therefore, language itself is rhetorical, and people will struggle over the words we use that not only describe but also create our realities. This theoretical development is a significant change from the language purifiers of the Enlightenment such as Locke, who saw the role of language as merely reflecting an objective reality.

One of the earliest and most influential theorists to see language as fundamentally shaping human realities was the Russian philosopher Mikhail Bakhtin (1895–1975). Bakhtin would likely *not* have called himself a rhetorical theorist because his views on language departed from those of the rhetorical tradition. Bakhtin saw language as *dialogue.* Its essential nature was to be found in the ongoing give-and-take of exchanges of messages. The meaning of an utterance can never be understood in isolation but always as a response to a previous utterance and as an invitation to a following statement, according to Bakhtin.

Bakhtin viewed rhetoric as hostile to his view of dialogue. He once argued, "In rhetoric there is the unconditionally innocent and the unconditionally guilty; there is complete victory and destruction of the opponent." Of course, Bakhtin was being unfair in regarding rhetoric as producing unconditional conclusions. And the rhetorical tradition has been well-attuned to the idea of rhetoric as responding to previous messages and anticipating new ones. But it is true that the rhetorical tradition has also tended to see persuasive force residing in monologic, extended arguments more than in the give-and-take of dialogic, everyday communication. Although he might not have called it rhetoric, Bakhtin is actually extending the rhetorical tradition by explaining how the dialogical nature of all communication has an impact on people that we would be justified in calling rhetorical.

Here you will find an excerpt from Bakhtin's book *Marxism and the Philosophy of Language,* originally published in 1929. You will notice early in the reading and in the title the term *Marxism.* For some, this word has connotations of failed East European economies. However, Bakhtin is using the word in the sense of a technique of social and political analysis, which is different from its economic applications.

The method of Marxism, Bakhtin says, attempts to show how everyday experience produces *ideologies,* or belief systems. It does so because objects and events in everyday life function as *signs.* The word *signs* is taken from the discipline of *semiotics* or *semiology,* which is the study of how language and experience come to have meaning. Semiotics, founded by the French linguist Ferdinand de Saussure late in the nineteenth century, has been very influential in twentieth century theory. Bakhtin wants to focus our attention on the ways in which actual experience of particular actions, objects, and events, including language, is the basis for whole systems of beliefs and values such as political, religious, or commercial ways of thinking.

Bakhtin argues in this reading that language is a set of special signs. That is because it is a sign not only of actions, objects, and events, but of our internal thoughts at the same time. By placing language across both thought and the world in this way, Bakhtin is part of the twentieth century effort to collapse Enlightenment dualism and avoid splitting experience into an "in here" and an "out there." The rest of this selection discusses the ways in which language works to create ideologies.

Bakhtin's central idea here is that language is always *addressed* from one person to another—it is always dialogical. It follows from the dialogical nature of language that it is *social.* We can never express an idea in our "own" language. Rather, the social groups and cultures to which we belong give us ways to speak that constrain how we think and act. Bakhtin gives a brilliant example of this in saying that the physical sensation of *hunger* can become, depending on how a society talks about it, either an "I-experience" or a "we-experience." If a homeless person is hungry, in other words, does a society (and the person himself) talk about that experience as something that only that particular individual is experiencing, or as something that a whole group of people (the poor, the homeless, etc.) experience *as* a group? Think about the political and social difference it might make whether one thought of one's hunger as something that had happened to only an individual, or something that regularly happened to a whole group of people. That choice in how we think about hunger is grounded, Bakhtin claims, in the *language* we have for talking about hunger.

Bakhtin explains how different levels of experiences can generate different levels of meaning, which add up to ideologies. Our grandest and most abstract political views, in other words, are grounded in how we experience everyday objects, actions, events, and in how we talk about those experiences.

Bakhtin's reading concludes with a chapter that distinguishes between two semiotic concepts, *meaning* and *theme.* Theme is what an utterance is about; meaning is how the words and signs in an utterance work together to create the theme. "What time is it?" is an utterance that has meaning, but only in potential; the theme says what the meaning is in a particular situation. "What time is it?" means different things depending on whether it is said (1) to one's spouse in the morning upon discovering that she has overslept and will be late for work, (2) to a friend who has shown up seriously late for a date, or (3) to a coworker who is passing in the hall.

As we have noted, Bakhtin would not call his work rhetorical theory. His ideas, however, have been taken as a fruitful advance on rhetorical theory by many thinkers in the twentieth century. Casual everyday comments and conversation may not seem especially rhetorical, particularly from the point of view of traditional rhetorical theory. But Bakhtin was instrumental in creating the idea that even ordinary, casual use of language has serious impact in shaping political, social ideology. His work has been seminal in shaping a rhetorical theory of the everyday use of language.

MIKHAIL BAKHTIN WRITING AS V. N. VOLOŠINOV

MARXISM AND THE PHILOSOPHY OF LANGUAGE

FROM PART I

CHAPTER I

THE STUDY OF IDEOLOGIES AND PHILOSOPHY OF LANGUAGE

The problem of the ideological sign. The ideological sign and consciousness. The word as an ideological sign par excellence. The ideological neutrality of the word. The capacity of the word to be an inner sign. Summary.

Problems of the philosophy of language have in recent times acquired exceptional pertinence and importance for Marxism. Over a wide range of the most vital sectors in its scientific advance, the Marxist method bears directly upon these problems and cannot continue to move ahead productively without special provision for their investigation and solution.

First and foremost, the very foundations of a Marxist theory of ideologies—the bases for the studies of scientific knowledge, literature, religion, ethics, and so forth—are closely bound up with problems of the philosophy of language.

Any ideological product is not only itself a part of a reality (natural or social), just as is any physical body, any instrument of production, or any product for consumption, it also, in contradistinction to these other phenomena, reflects and refracts another reality outside itself. Everything ideological possesses *meaning:* it represents, depicts, or stands for something lying outside itself. In other words, it is a *sign. Without signs, there is no ideology.* A physical body equals itself, so to speak; it does not signify anything but wholly coincides with its particular, given nature. In this case there is no question of ideology.

However, any physical body may be perceived as an image; for instance, the image of natural inertia and necessity embodied in that particular thing. Any such artistic-symbolic image to which a particular physical object gives rise is already an ideological product. The physical object is converted into a sign. Without ceasing to be a part of material reality, such an object, to some degree, reflects and refracts another reality.

The same is true of any instrument of production. A tool by itself is devoid of any special meaning; it commands only some designated function—to serve this or that purpose in production. The tool serves that purpose as the particular, given thing

Translated by
Ladislav Matejka and I.R. Titunik
Department of Slavic Languages and Literatures
University of Michigan
Ann Arbor, Michigan

that it is, without reflecting or standing for anything else. However, a tool also may be converted into an ideological sign. Such, for instance, is the hammer and sickle insignia of the Soviet Union. In this case, hammer and sickle possess a purely ideological meaning. Additionally, any instrument of production may be ideologically decorated. Tools used by prehistoric man are covered with pictures or designs—that is, with signs. So treated, a tool still does not, of course, itself become a sign.

It is further possible to enhance a tool artistically, and in such a way that its artistic shapeliness harmonizes with the purpose it is meant to serve in production. In this case, something like maximal approximation, almost a coalescence, of sign and tool comes about. But even here we still detect a distinct conceptual dividing line: the tool, as such, does not become a sign; the sign, as such, does not become an instrument of production.

Any consumer good can likewise be made an ideological sign. For instance, bread and wine become religious symbols in the Christian sacrament of communion. But the consumer good, as such, is not at all a sign. Consumer goods, just as tools, may be combined with ideological signs, but the distinct conceptual dividing line between them is not erased by the combination. Bread is made in some particular shape; this shape is not warranted solely by the bread's function as a consumer good; it also has a certain, if primitive, value as an ideological sign (e.g., bread in the shape of a figure eight [*krendel*] or a rosette).

Thus, side by side with the natural phenomena, with the equipment of technology, and with articles for consumption, there exists a special world—the *world of signs*.

Signs also are particular, material things; and, as we have seen, any item of nature, technology, or consumption can become a sign, acquiring in the process a meaning that goes beyond its given particularity. A sign does not simply exist as a part of a reality—it reflects and refracts another reality. Therefore, it may distort that reality or be true to it, or may perceive it from a special point of view, and so forth. Every sign is subject to the criteria of ideological evaluation (i.e., whether it is true, false, correct, fair, good, etc.). The domain of ideology coincides with the domain of signs. They equate with one another. Wherever a sign is present, ideology is present, too. *Everything ideological possesses semiotic value.*

Within the domain of signs—i.e., within the ideological sphere—profound differences exist: it is, after all, the domain of the artistic image, the religious symbol, the scientific formula, and the judicial ruling, etc. Each field of ideological creativity has its own kind of orientation toward reality and each refracts reality in its own way. Each field commands its own special function within the unity of social life. *But it is their semiotic character that places all ideological phenomena under the same general definition.*

Every ideological sign is not only a reflection, a shadow, of reality, but is also itself a material segment of that very reality. Every phenomenon functioning as an ideological sign has some kind of material embodiment, whether in sound, physical mass, color, movements of the body, or the like. In this sense, the reality of the sign is fully objective and lends itself to a unitary, monistic, objective method of study. A sign is a phenomenon of the external world. Both the sign itself and all the effects it produces (all those actions, reactions, and new signs it elicits in the surrounding social milieu) occur in outer experience.

This is a point of extreme importance. Yet, elementary and self-evident as it may seem, the study of ideologies has still not drawn all the conclusions that follow from it.

The idealistic philosophy of culture and psychologistic cultural studies locate ideology in the consciousness.[1] Ideology, they assert, is a fact of consciousness; the external body of the

---

[1] It should be noted that a change of outlook in this regard can be detected in modern neo-Kantianism. We have in mind the latest book by Ernst Cassirer, *Philosophie der symbolischen Formen,* Vol. 1, 1923. While remaining on the grounds of consciousness, Cassirer considers its dominant trait to be representation. Each

sign is merely a coating, merely a technical means for the realization of the inner effect, which is understanding.

Idealism and psychologism alike overlook the fact that understanding itself can come about only within some kind of semiotic material (e.g., inner speech), that sign bears upon sign, that *consciousness itself can arise and become a viable fact only in the material embodiment of signs.* The understanding of a sign is, after all, an act of reference between the sign apprehended and other, already known signs; in other words, understanding is a response to a sign with signs. And this chain of ideological creativity and understanding, moving from sign to sign and then to a new sign, is perfectly consistent and continuous: from one link of a semiotic nature (hence, also of a material nature) we proceed uninterruptedly to another link of exactly the same nature. And nowhere is there a break in the chain, nowhere does the chain plunge into inner being, nonmaterial in nature and unembodied in signs.

This ideological chain stretches from individual consciousness to individual consciousness, connecting them together. Signs emerge, after all, only in the process of interaction between one individual consciousness and another. And the individual consciousness itself is filled with signs. Consciousness becomes consciousness only once it has been filled with ideological (semiotic) content, consequently, only in the process of social interaction.

Despite the deep methodological differences between them, the idealistic philosophy of culture and psychologistic cultural studies both commit the same fundamental error. By localizing ideology in the consciousness, they transform the study of ideologies into a study of consciousness and its laws; it makes no difference whether this is done in transcendental or in empirical-psychological terms. This error is responsible not only for methodological confusion regarding the interrelation of disparate fields of knowledge, but for a radical distortion of the very reality under study as well. Ideological creativity—a material and social fact—is forced into the framework of the individual consciousness. The individual consciousness, for its part, is deprived of any support in reality. It becomes either all or nothing.

For idealism it has become all: its locus is somewhere above existence and it determines the latter. In actual fact, however, this sovereign of the universe is merely the hypostatization in idealism of an abstract bond among the most general forms and categories of ideological creativity.

For psychological positivism, on the contrary, consciousness amounts to nothing: It is just a conglomeration of fortuitous, psychophysiological reactions which, by some miracle, results in meaningful and unified ideological creativity.

The objective social regulatedness of ideological creativity, once misconstrued as a conformity with laws of the individual consciousness, must inevitably forfeit its real place in existence and depart either up into the superexistential empyrean of transcendentalism or down into the presocial recesses of the psychophysical, biological organism.

However, the ideological, as such, cannot possibly be explained in terms of either of these superhuman or subhuman, animalian, roots. Its real place in existence is in the special, social material of signs created by man. Its specificity consists precisely in its being located between organized individuals, in its being the medium of their communication.

Signs can arise only on *interindividual territory.* It is territory that cannot be called "natural" in the direct sense of the word:[1] signs do not arise between any two members of the species *Homo sapiens.* It is essential that the two individuals be

---

element of consciousness represents something, bears a symbolic function. The whole exists in its parts, but a part is comprehensible only in the whole. According to Cassirer, an idea is just as sensory as matter; the sensoriness involved, however, is that of the symbolic sign, it is representative sensoriness. [Au.]

[1] Society, of course, is also a *part of nature,* but a part that is qualitatively separate and distinct and possesses its own *specific* systems of laws. [Au.]

organized socially, that they compose a group (a social unit); only then can the medium of signs take shape between them. The individual consciousness not only cannot be used to explain anything, but, on the contrary, is itself in need of explanation from the vantage point of the social, ideological medium.

The individual consciousness is a social-ideological fact. Not until this point is recognized with due provision for all the consequences that follow from it will it be possible to construct either an objective psychology or an objective study of ideologies.

It is precisely the problem of consciousness that has created the major difficulties and generated the formidable confusion encountered in all issues associated with psychology and the study of ideologies alike. By and large, consciousness has become the *asylum ignorantiae* for all philosophical constructs. It has been made the place where all unresolved problems, all objectively irreducible residues are stored away. Instead of trying to find an objective definition of consciousness, thinkers have begun using it as a means for rendering all hard and fast objective definitions subjective and fluid.

The only possible objective definition of consciousness is a sociological one. Consciousness cannot be derived directly from nature, as has been and still is being attempted by naive mechanistic materialism and contemporary objective psychology (of the biological, behavioristic, and reflexological varieties). Ideology cannot be derived from consciousness, as is the practice of idealism and psychologistic positivism. Consciousness takes shape and being in the material of signs created by an organized group in the process of its social intercourse. The individual consciousness is nurtured on signs; it derives its growth from them; it reflects their logic and laws. The logic of consciousness is the logic of ideological communication, of the semiotic interaction of a social group. If we deprive consciousness of its semiotic, ideological content, it would have absolutely nothing left. Consciousness can harbor only in the image, the word, the meaningful gesture, and so forth. Outside such material, there remains the sheer physiological act unilluminated by consciousness, i.e., without having light shed on it, without having meaning given to it, by signs.

All that has been said above leads to the following methodological conclusion: *the study of ideologies does not depend on psychology to any extent and need not be grounded in it.* As we shall see in greater detail in a later chapter, it is rather the reverse: *objective psychology must be grounded in the study of ideologies.* The reality of ideological phenomena is the objective reality of social signs. The laws of this reality are the laws of semiotic communication and are directly determined by the total aggregate of social and economic laws. Ideological reality is the immediate superstructure over the economic basis. Individual consciousness is not the architect of the ideological superstructure, but only a tenant lodging in the social edifice of ideological signs.

With our preliminary argument, disengaging ideological phenomena and their regulatedness from individual consciousness, we tie them in all the more firmly with conditions and forms of social communication. The reality of the sign is wholly a matter determined by that communication. After all, the existence of the sign is nothing but the materialization of that communication. Such is the nature of all ideological signs.

But nowhere does this semiotic quality and the continuous, comprehensive role of social communication as conditioning factor appear so clearly and fully expressed as in language. *The word is the ideological phenomenon par excellence.*

The entire reality of the word is wholly absorbed in its function of being a sign. A word contains nothing that is indifferent to this function, nothing that would not have been engendered by it. A word is the purest and most sensitive medium of social intercourse.

This indicatory, representative power of the word as an ideological phenomenon and the exceptional distinctiveness of its semiotic structure would already furnish reason enough for advancing the word to a prime position in the study of ideologies. It is precisely in the material of the word that the basic, general-ideological forms of semiotic communication could best be revealed.

But that is by no means all. The word is not only the purest, most indicatory sign but is, in addition, *a neutral sign*. Every other kind of semiotic material is specialized for some particular field of ideological creativity. Each field possesses its own ideological material and formulates signs and symbols specific to itself and not applicable in other fields. In these instances, a sign is created by some specific ideological function and remains inseparable from it. A word, in contrast, is neutral with respect to any specific ideological function. It can carry out ideological functions of *any* kind—scientific, aesthetic, ethical, religious.

Moreover, there is that immense area of ideological communication that cannot be pinned down to any one ideological sphere: the area of *communication in human life, human behavior.* This kind of communication is extraordinarily rich and important. On one side, it links up directly with the processes of production; on the other, it is tangent to the spheres of the various specialized and fully fledged ideologies. In the following chapter, we shall speak in greater detail of this special area of behavioral, or life ideology. For the time being, we shall take note of the fact that the material of behavioral communication is preeminently the *word*. The locale of so-called conversational language and its forms is precisely here, in the area of behavioral ideology.

One other property belongs to the word that is of the highest order of importance and is what makes the word the primary medium of the individual consciousness. Although the reality of the word, as is true of any sign, resides between individuals, a word, at the same time, is produced by the individual organism's own means without recourse to any equipment or any other kind of extracorporeal material. This has determined the role of word as *the semiotic material of inner life—of consciousness* (inner speech). Indeed, the consciousness could have developed only by having at its disposal material that was pliable and expressible by bodily means. And the word was exactly that kind of material. The word is available as the sign for, so to speak, inner employment: it can function as a sign in a state short of outward expression. For this reason, the problem of individual consciousness as the *inner word* (as an *inner sign* in general) becomes one of the most vital problems in philosophy of language.

It is clear, from the very start, that this problem cannot be properly approached by resorting to the usual concept of word and language as worked out in nonsociological linguistics and philosophy of language. What is needed is profound and acute analysis of the word as social sign before its function as the medium of consciousness can be understood.

It is owing to this exclusive role of the word as the medium of consciousness that *the word functions as an essential ingredient accompanying all ideological creativity whatsoever.* The word accompanies and comments on each and every ideological act. The processes of understanding any ideological phenomenon at all (be it a picture, a piece of music, a ritual, or an act of human conduct) cannot operate without the participation of inner speech. All manifestations of ideological creativity—all other nonverbal signs—are bathed by, suspended in, and cannot be entirely segregated or divorced from the element of speech.

This does not mean, of course, that the word may supplant any other ideological sign. None of the fundamental, specific ideological signs is replacable wholly by words. It is ultimately impossible to convey a musical composition or pictorial image adequately in words. Words cannot wholly substitute for a religious ritual; nor is there any really adequate verbal substitute for even the simplest gesture in human behavior. To deny this would lead to the most banal rationalism and simplisticism. Nonetheless, at the very same time, every single one of these ideological signs, though not supplantable by words, has support in and is accompanied by words, just as is the case with singing and its musical accompaniment.

No cultural sign, once taken in and given meaning, remains in isolation: it becomes part of the *unity of the verbally constituted consciousness.* It is in the capacity of the consciousness to find verbal access to it. Thus, as it were, spreading ripples of verbal responses and resonances form around each and every ideological sign. Every *ideological refraction of existence in process of generation,* no matter what the nature of its significant material, *is accompanied by ideological refraction in word* as an obligatory concominant phenomenon. Word is present in each and every act of understanding and in each and every act of interpretation.

All of the properties of word we have examined—*its semiotic purity, its ideological neutrality, its involvement in behavioral communication, its ability to become an inner word and, finally, its obligatory presence, as an accompanying phenomenon, in any conscious act*—all these properties make the word the fundamental object of the study of ideologies. The laws of the ideological refraction of existence in signs and in consciousness, its forms and mechanics, must be studied in the material of the word, first of all. The only possible way of bringing the Marxist sociological method to bear on all the profundities and subtleties of "immanent" ideological structures is to operate from the basis of the philosophy of language as the *philosophy of the ideological sign.* And that basis must be devised and elaborated by Marxism itself.

• • •

CHAPTER 4

THEME AND MEANING IN LANGUAGE

Theme and meaning. The problem of active perception. Evaluation and meaning. The dialectics of meaning.

The problem of meaning is one of the most difficult problems of linguistics. Efforts toward solving this problem have revealed the one-sided monologism of linguistic science in particularly strong relief. The theory of passive understanding precludes any possibility of engaging the most fundamental and crucial features of meaning in language.

The scope of the present study compels us to limit ourselves to a very brief and perfunctory examination of this issue. We shall attempt only to map out the main lines of its productive treatment.

A definite and unitary meaning, a unitary significance, is a property belonging to any utterance *as a whole.* Let us call the significance of a whole utterance its *theme.*[1] The theme must be unitary, otherwise we would have no basis for talking about any one utterance. The theme of an utterance itself is individual and unreproducible, just as the utterance itself is individual and unreproducible. The theme is the expression of the concrete, historical situation that engendered the utterance. The utterance "What time is it?" has a different meaning each time it is used, and hence, in accordance with our terminology, has a different theme, depending on the concrete historical situation ("historical" here in microscopic dimensions) during which it is enunciated and of which, in essence, it is a part.

It follows, then, that the theme of an utterance is determined not only by the linguistic forms that comprise it—words, morphological and syntactic structures, sounds, and intonation—but also by extraverbal factors of the situation. Should we miss these situational factors, we would be as little able to understand an utterance as if we were to miss its most important words. The theme of an utterance is concrete—as concrete as the historical instant to which the utterance belongs. *Only an utterance taken in its full, concrete scope as an historical phenomenon possesses a theme.* That is what is meant by the theme of an utterance.

However, if we were to restrict ourselves to the historical unreproducibility and unitariness of

[1] The term is, of course, a provisional one. *Theme* in our sense embraces its implementation as well; therefore, our concept must not be confused with that of a theme in a literary work. The concept of "thematic unity" would be closer to what we mean.

each concrete utterance and its theme, we would be poor dialecticians. Together with theme or, rather, within the theme, there is also the *meaning* that belongs to an utterance. By meaning, as distinguished from theme, we understand all those aspects of the utterance that are *reproducible* and *self-identical* in all instances of repetition. Of course, these aspects are abstract: they have no concrete, autonomous existence in an artificially isolated form, but, at the same time, they do constitute an essential and inseparable part of the utterance. The theme of an utterance is, in essence, indivisible. The meaning of an utterance, on the contrary, does break down into a set of meanings belonging to each of the various linguistic elements of which the utterance consists. The unreproducible theme of the utterance "What time is it?" taken in its indissoluble connection with the concrete historical situation, cannot be divided into elements. The meaning of the utterance "What time is it?"—a meaning that, of course, remains the same in all historical instances of its enunciation—is made up of the meanings of the words, forms of morphological and syntactic union, interrogative intonations, etc., that form the construction of the utterance.

Theme is a complex, dynamic system of signs that attempts to be adequate to a given instant of generative process. Theme is reaction by the consciousness in its generative process to the generative process of existence. Meaning is *the technical apparatus for the implementation of theme.* Of course, no absolute, mechanistic boundary can be drawn between theme and meaning. There is no theme without meaning and no meaning without theme. Moreover, it is even impossible to convey the meaning of a particular word (say, in the course of teaching another person a foreign language) without having made it an element of theme, i.e., without having constructed an "example" utterance. On the other hand, a theme must base itself on some kind of fixity of meaning; otherwise it loses its connection with what came before and what comes after—i.e., it altogether loses its significance.

The study of the languages of prehistoric peoples and modern semantic paleontology have reached a conclusion about the so-called "complex-ness" of prehistoric thinking. Prehistoric man used one word to denote a wide variety of phenomena that, from our modern point of view, are in no way related to one another. What is more, the same word could be used to denote diametrically opposite notions—top and bottom, earth and sky, good and bad, and so on. Declares Marr:

> Suffice it to say that contemporary paleontological study of language has given us the possibility of reaching, through its investigations, back to an age when a tribe had only one word at its disposal for usage in all the meanings of which mankind was aware.[1]

"But was such an all-meaning word in fact a word?" we might be asked. Yes, precisely a word. If, on the contrary, a certain sound complex had only one single, inert, and invariable meaning, then such a complex would not be a word, not a sign, but only a signal.[2] *Multiplicity of meanings is the constitutive feature of word.* As regards the all-meaning word of which Marr speaks, we can say the following: *such a word, in essence, has virtually no meaning; it is all theme.* Its meaning is *inseparable from the concrete situation of its implementation.* This meaning is different each time, just as the situation is different each time. Thus the theme, in this case, subsumed meaning under itself and dissolved it before meaning had any chance to consolidate and congeal. But as language developed further, as its stock of sound complexes expanded, meaning began to congeal

---

[1] N. Ja. Marr, *Japhetic Theory,* (1926), p. 278.

[2] It is clear that even that earliest of all words, about which Marr speaks, is not in any way like a signal (to which a number of investigators endeavor to reduce language). After all, a signal that meant everything would be minimally capable of carrying out the function of a signal. The capacity of a signal to adapt to the changing conditions of a situation is very low. By and large, change in a signal means replacement of one signal by another.

along lines that were basic and most frequent in the life of the community for the thematic application of this or that word.

Theme, as we have said, is an attribute of a whole utterance only; it can belong to a separate word only inasmuch as that word operates in the capacity of a whole utterance. So, for instance, Marr's all-meaning word always operates in the capacity of a whole (and has no fixed meanings precisely for that reason). Meaning, on the other hand, belongs to an element or aggregate of elements in their relation to the whole. Of course, if we entirely disregard this relation to the whole (i.e., to the utterance), we shall entirely forfeit meaning. That is the reason why a sharp boundary between theme and meaning cannot be drawn.

The most accurate way of formulating the interrelationship between theme and meaning is in the following terms. Theme is the *upper, actual limit of linguistic significance;* in essence, only theme means something definite. Meaning is the *lower limit* of linguistic significance. Meaning, in essence, means nothing; it only possesses potentiality—the possibility of having a meaning within a concrete theme. Investigation of the meaning of one or another linguistic element can proceed, in terms of our definition, in one of two directions: either in the direction of the upper limit, toward theme, in which case it would be investigation of the contextual meaning of a given word within the conditions of a concrete utterance; or investigation can aim toward the lower limit, the limit of meaning, in which case it would be investigation of the meaning of a word in the system of language or, in other words, investigation of a dictionary word.

A distinction between theme and meaning and a proper understanding of their interrelationship are vital steps in constructing a genuine science of meanings. Total failure to comprehend their importance has persisted to the present day. Such discriminations as those between a word's *usual* and *occasional* meanings, between its central and lateral meanings, between its denotation and connotation, etc., are fundamentally unsatisfactory. The basic tendency underlying all such discriminations—the tendency to ascribe greater value to the central, usual aspect of meaning, presupposing that that aspect really does exist and is stable—is completely fallacious. Moreover, it would leave theme unaccounted for, since theme, of course, can by no means be reduced to the status of the occasional or lateral meaning of words.

The distinction between theme and meaning acquires particular clarity in connection with the *problem of understanding,* which we shall now briefly touch upon.

We have already had occasion to speak of the philological type of passive understanding, which excludes response in advance. Any genuine kind of understanding will be active and will constitute the germ of a response. Only active understanding can grasp theme—a generative process can be grasped only with the aid of another generative process.

To understand another person's utterance means to orient oneself with respect to it, to find the proper place for it in the corresponding context. For each word of the utterance that we are in process of understanding, we, as it were, lay down a set of our own answering words. The greater their number and weight, the deeper and more substantial our understanding will be.

Thus each of the distinguishable significative elements of an utterance and the entire utterance as a whole entity are translated in our minds into another, active and responsive, context. *Any true understanding is dialogic in nature.* Understanding is to utterance as one line of a dialogue is to the next. Understanding strives to match the speaker's word with a *counter word.* Only in understanding a word in a foreign tongue is the attempt made to match it with the "same" word in one's own language.

Therefore, there is no reason for saying that meaning belongs to a word as such. In essence, meaning belongs to a word in its position between speakers; that is, meaning is realized only in the process of active, responsive understanding. Meaning does not reside in the word or in the soul of the speaker or in the soul of the listener. Meaning is the *effect of interaction between speaker and listener produced via the material of a particular sound complex.* It is like an electric spark that occurs only when two different terminals are hooked together. Those who ignore theme (which is accessible only to active, responsive understanding) and who, in attempting to define the meaning of a word, approach its lower, stable, self-identical limit, want, in effect, to turn on a light bulb after having switched off the current. Only the current of verbal intercourse endows a word with the light of meaning.

Let us now move on to one of the most important problems in the science of meanings, the problem of the *interrelationship between meaning and evaluation.*

Any word used in actual speech possesses not only theme and meaning in the referential, or content, sense of these words, but also value judgment: i.e., all referential contents produced in living speech are said or written in conjunction with a specific *evaluative accent.* There is no such thing as word without evaluative accent.

What is the nature of this accent, and how does it relate to the referential side of meaning?

The most obvious, but, at the same time, the most superficial aspect of social value judgement incorporated in the word is that which is conveyed with the help of *expressive intonation.* In most cases, intonation is determined by the immediate situation and often by its most ephemeral circumstances. To be sure, intonation of a more substantial kind is also possible. Here is a classic instance of such a use of intonation in real-life speech. Dostoevskij, in *Diary of a Writer,* relates the following story.

> One Sunday night, already getting on to the small hours, I chanced to find myself walking alongside a band of six tipsy artisans for a dozen paces or so, and there and then I became convinced that all thoughts, all feelings, and even whole trains of reasoning could be expressed merely by using a certain noun, a noun, moreover, of utmost simplicity in itself [Dostoevskij has in mind here a certain widely used obscenity.—*V. V.*]. Here is what happened. First, one of these fellows voices this noun shrilly and emphatically by way of expressing his utterly disdainful denial of some point that had been in general contention just prior. A second fellow repeats this very same noun in response to the first fellow, but now in an altogether different tone and sense—to wit, in the sense that he fully doubted the veracity of the first fellow's denial. A third fellow waxes indignant at the first one, sharply and heatedly sallying into the conversation and shouting at him that very same noun, but now in a pejorative, abusive sense. The second fellow, indignant at the third for being offensive, himself sallies back in and cuts the latter short to the effect: "What the hell do you think you're doing, butting in like that?! Me and Fil'ka were having a nice quiet talk and just like that you come along and start cussing him out!" And in fact, this whole train of thought he conveyed by emitting just that very same time-honored word, that same extremely laconic designation of a certain item, and nothing more, save only that he also raised his hand and grabbed the second fellow by the shoulder. Thereupon, all of a sudden a fourth fellow, the youngest in the crowd, who had remained silent all this while, apparently having just struck upon the solution to the problem that had originally occasioned the dispute, in a tone of rapture, with one arm half-raised, shouts—What do you think: "Eureka!"? "I found it, I found it!"? No, nothing at all like "Eureka," nothing like "I found it." He merely repeats that very same unprintable noun, just that one single word, just that one word alone, but with rapture, with a squeal of ecstacy, and apparently somewhat excessively so, because the sixth fellow, a surly character and the oldest in the bunch, didn't think it seemly and in a trice stops the young fellow's rapture cold by turning

> on him and repeating in a gruff and expostulatory bass—yes, that very same noun whose usage is forbidden in the company of ladies, which, however, in this case clearly and precisely denoted: "What the hell are you shouting for, you'll burst a blood vessel!" And so, without having uttered one other word, they repeated just this one, but obviously beloved, little word of theirs six times in a row, one after the other, and they understood one another perfectly.[1]

All six "speech performances" by the artisans are different, despite the fact that they all consisted of one and the same word. That word, in this instance, was essentially only a vehicle for intonation. The conversation was conducted in intonations expressing the value judgments of the speakers. These value judgments and their corresponding intonations were wholly determined by the immediate social situation of the talk and therefore did not require any referential support. In living speech, intonation often does have a meaning quite independent of the semantic composition of speech. Intonational material pent up inside us often does find outlet in linguistic constructions completely inappropriate to the particular kind of intonation involved. In such a case, intonation does not impinge upon the intellectual, concrete, referential significance of the construction. We have a habit of expressing our feelings by imparting expressive and meaningful intonation to some word that crops up in our mind by chance, often a vacuous interjection or adverb. Almost everybody has his favorite interjection or adverb or sometimes even a semantically full-fledged word that he customarily uses for purely intonational resolution of certain trivial (and sometimes not so trivial) situations and moods that occur in the ordinary business of life. There are certain expressions like "so-so," "yes-yes," "now-now," "well-well" and so on that commonly serve as "safety valves" of that sort. The doubling usual in such expressions is symptomatic; i.e., it represents an artificial prolongation of the sound image for the purpose of allowing the pent up intonation to expire fully. Any one such favorite little expression may, of course, be pronounced in an enormous variety of intonations in keeping with the wide diversity of situations and moods that occur in life.

In all these instances, theme, which is a property of each utterance (each of the utterances of the six artisans had a theme proper to it), is implemented entirely and exclusively by the power of expressive intonation without the aid of word meaning or grammatical coordination. This sort of value judgment and its corresponding intonation cannot exceed the narrow confines of the immediate situation and the small, intimate social world in which it occurs. Linguistic evaluation of this sort may rightly be called an accompaniment, an accessory phenomenon, to meaning in language.

However, not all linguistic value judgments are like that. We may take any utterance whatsoever, say, an utterance that encompasses the broadest possible semantic spectrum and assumes the widest possible social audience, and we shall still see that, in it, an enormous importance belongs to evaluation. Naturally, value judgment in this case will not allow of even minimally adequate expression by intonation, but it will be the determinative factor in the choice and deployment of the basic elements that bear the meaning of the utterance. No utterance can be put together without value judgment. Every utterance is above all an *evaluative orientation.* Therefore, each element in a living utterance not only has a meaning but also has a value. Only the abstract element, perceived within the system of language and not within the structure of an utterance, appears devoid of value judgment. Focusing their attention on the abstract system of language is what led most linguists to divorce evaluation from meaning and to consider evaluation an accessory factor of meaning, the ex-

---

[1] *Polnoe sobranie sočinenij F. M. Dostoevskogo* [The Complete Works of F. M. Dostoevskij], Vol. IX, pp. 274–275, 1906.

pression of a speaker's individual attitude toward the subject matter of his discourse.[1]

In Russian scholarship, G. Špett has spoken of evaluation as the *connotation* of a word. Characteristically, he operates with a strict division between referential denotation and evaluative connotation, locating this division in various spheres of reality. This sort of disjuncture between referential meaning and evaluation is totally inadmissible. It stems from failure to note the more profound functions of evaluation in speech. Referential meaning is molded by evaluation; it is evaluation, after all, which determines that a particular referential meaning may enter the purview of speakers—both the immediate purview and the broader social purview of the particular social group. Furthermore, with respect to changes of meaning, it is precisely evaluation that plays the creative role. A change in meaning is, essentially, always a *reevaluation:* the transposition of some particular word from one evaluative context to another. A word is either advanced to a higher rank or demoted to a lower one. The separation of word meaning from evaluation inevitably deprives meaning of its place in the living social process (where meaning is always permeated with value judgment), to its being ontologized and transformed into ideal Being divorced from the historical process of Becoming.

Precisely in order to understand the historical process of generation of theme and of the meanings implementing theme, it is essential to take social evaluation into account. The generative process of signification in language is always associated with the generation of the evaluative purview of a particular social group, and the generation of an evaluative purview—in the sense of the totality of all those things that have meaning and importance for the particular group—is entirely determined by expansion of the economic basis. As the economic basis expands, it promotes an actual expansion in the scope of existence which is accessible, comprehensible, and vital to man. The prehistoric herdsman was virtually interested in nothing, and virtually nothing had any bearing on him. Man at the end of the epoch of capitalism is directly concerned about everything, his interests reaching the remotest corners of the earth and even the most distant stars. This expansion of evaluative purview comes about dialectically. New aspects of existence, once they are drawn into the sphere of social interest, once they make contact with the human word and human emotion, do not coexist peacefully with other elements of existence previously drawn in, but engage them in a struggle, reevaluate them, and bring about a change in their position within the unity of the evaluative purview. This dialectical generative process is reflected in the generation of semantic properties in language. A new significance emanates from an old one, and does so with its help, but this happens so that the new significance can enter into contradiction with the old one and restructure it.

The outcome is a constant struggle of accents in each semantic sector of existence. There is nothing in the structure of signification that could be said to transcend the generative process, to be independent of the dialectical expansion of social purview. Society in process of generation expands its perception of the generative process of existence. There is nothing in this that could be said to be absolutely fixed. And that is how it happens that meaning—an abstract, self-identical element—is subsumed under theme and torn apart by theme's living contradictions so as to return in the shape of a new meaning with a fixity and self-identity only for the while, just as it had before.

---

[1] That is how Anton Marty defines evaluation, and it is Marty who gives the most acute and detailed analysis of word meanings; see his *Untersuchungen zur Grundlegung der allgemeinen Grammatik und Sprachphilosophie* (Halle, 1908).

INTRODUCTION TO AMY VANDERBILT

An important theme in twentieth century rhetoric has been examining the ways in which everyday speech and action has rhetorical power. We learned from Mikhail Bakhtin that every utterance has ideological importance. One can also understand everyday speech and action as rhetorical from a more traditional point of view by theorizing the ways in which ordinary experience influences the ways that others think and behave towards us. How can we conduct ourselves so as to influence others favorably, not in the traditional rhetorical venues of the public speaking platform, but in our social interactions with others?

Another important theme in twentieth century rhetoric has been the development of popular rhetorical theories. One need only go to bookstores to find shelves of rhetorical advice for conduct in business and personal life. Many of these theories are not written by, nor for, academics but are instead directed at popular audiences. Likewise, seminars by motivational speakers draw millions of people each year who pay to hear advice on successful rhetorical presentations in sales, real estate, and personal affairs.

The selection included here is an early example of this sort of popular rhetorical theory, although its author did not call it by that name. Amy Vanderbilt was born in 1908 to a prominent New York family, related to the wealthy Cornelius Vanderbilt clan. Vanderbilt studied in Switzerland and at New York University. She had a long career as a publicist, advertising executive, and journalist. In the late 1940s she was asked by the Doubleday publishing company to publish a book on etiquette, which was published in 1952.

Vanderbilt stressed the idea that etiquette is fundamentally kindness, or consideration for other people. Consistent with that central idea, her advice showed a willingness to adapt traditional rules for polite behavior to changing social norms and circumstances. This stance is thoroughly rhetorical with its stress upon adaptation to circumstances and the needs and desires of others so as to achieve the desired ends of creating a favorable impression or preserving one's social standing. Vanderbilt wrote popular rhetorical theory to guide many aspects of everyday interaction with others.

Vanderbilt wrote for a general, popular audience, although many of her readers were women. In that sense she is in the line of rhetorical theorists of the margin from Christine de Pisan to Margaret Fell to Eliza Leslie. But in the twentieth century women were beginning more and more to enter the rhetorical mainstream and their margin began to shrink. Vanderbilt was aware of these changes. The book *Current Biographies* of 1954 quotes her as saying that "women are getting more and more into worthwhile community activities as their home lives are becoming simplified and informal." From her large book on general etiquette, therefore, we have selected part of a chapter advising women on their growing role as public speakers. Vanderbilt must also therefore be considered in the context of a popular rhetorical theorist, an early example of what has become today a large group of writers giving practical rhetorical advice to ordinary people.

AMY VANDERBILT

AMY VANDERBILT'S COMPLETE BOOK OF ETIQUETTE

• • •

SPEAKING BEFORE AN AUDIENCE

CHAPTER SIXTY

Like death and taxes, some form of public speaking comes at one time or another to all of us. We may only find ourselves on our feet at the Parent-Teacher meeting or at our club, but for the uninitiated, the shy, the unsure even this mild public appearance is agony in anticipation and often in actuality.

Extemporaneous speaking is an art fostered by plentiful practice. It is said that George Bernard Shaw, struck dumb when he first tried to speak in public, joined the contentious Fabian Society in England, and on any and all occasions rose to his feet until glibness became through constant practice part and parcel of his personality. Many a seemingly extemporaneous speech has been carefully memorized and lengthily extolled beforehand so that it comes forth smoothly—but not so smoothly as to seem well-prepared.

It is cheering to know from the testimony of experts that people do not wish us to be completely perfect in our delivery. Many excellent public speakers deliberately stumble or stutter occasionally to make their performance seem more humanly fallible. The man who speaks with too much assurance in his own performance sometimes finds his audience somewhat hostile. Perhaps this is because each person in the audience at some time mentally puts himself in the place of the speaker and suffers what he believes to be his diffidence or embarrassment, his strangeness in these surroundings or circumstances. For this reason the speaker starting his talk with too much self-assurance or brashness often finds his audience is not with him at all.

INTRODUCING YOUR SPEECH It takes an audience a few minutes to get used to you, so when you get on your feet you do not immediately proceed to the matter at hand. People are adjusting to your appearance, the tone of your voice, your bearing, and in my opinion they don't actually hear your opening words. I think it is this, rather than the routine dullness of most speech openings, that focuses the audience's attention so slowly on what you are saying. For the first few minutes the practiced speaker, therefore, fills in time with his "Thank you" to the chairman introducing him, calling him or her by name—"Thank you, Mrs. Wirk." Then come his formal salutations, "Mr. President, honored guests [if there are any], ladies and gentlemen." Some speakers, at this point, drag in some pointless joke or anecdote to tide them through what I think of as the inspection period, but as the preoccupied audience rarely gets the point of it and just laughs automatically, it seems better technique to begin with a little appropriate preamble that leads logically to the heart of what you have to say. One way of doing this is to prepare in advance an outline of what you plan to discuss. It is perfectly sound technique to state categorically what you have been asked to speak about and to indicate what you hope to prove or what points you wish to develop, but not at such length as to dull people's anticipation of your talk.

CLICHÉS The speech that is studded with clichés, especially those old saws of public speaking, "I come before you today," "Unaccustomed as I am to public speaking," "I point with pride," "We view with alarm," ". . . and in conclusion let me say," etc., is dreary. More is expected of us since the development of radio and television than the old-fashioned arm-waving oratorical approach. The more natural your speaking voice, the simpler your language and presentation, the more believable you will be.

USING THE VOICE CORRECTLY If a microphone is placed before you, it is well if you have noted how the person who introduced you used it. Properly, microphones are tested beforehand for volume and the speaker is told just how to speak into the one presented to him. Because of the wide use of the public address system and of radio microphones, the well-versed public speaker knows he must avoid the shouting that he used to do from the old lecture platform when he wanted to emphasize a point. He knows, too, that he must stand quietly and talk at all times directly into the microphone. Turning his head from side to side to take in the full sweep of the audience often partially blots out what he is trying to say. If he raises his voice perceptibly for emphasis, he must step back a little from the microphone to avoid blasting his hearer's eardrums. But often greater emphasis is made, when a mike is in use, by the lowering of the voice, even to a whisper. This technique, occasionally and artfully used, causes the audience to hang literally on each softly spoken word.

COUGHING DURING A SPEECH If a speaker must cough or sneeze or blow his nose during the course of a speech, he need not be embarrassed but may think of it as a useful, human diversion that brings a perhaps needed little break in the flow of his speech. He of course turns his head away, especially from a microphone, and excuses himself in the case of a cough or sneeze but not if he blows his nose or takes a sip of water. Some accomplished speakers use the drinking of water as a way of heightening suspense before making some dramatic charge or assertion. "And now I am going to tell you something that will shake every one of you, that will bring tears to the eyes of every man and woman in this hall—" (drink of water).

READING A SPEECH No speech should ever be read if you want your audience to listen to what you have to say. It is sometimes quite satisfactory to have before you a written speech the gist of which, at least, and phrases from it, have been committed to memory. But to read it verbatim, unless you are in a radio studio and the reading of a script is required, is to lose your audience at the start. Even if you read well, the audience will be bored and restless if it sees you in the act. Using an outline or notes on small cards held in the palm of the hand is much better and makes for a more believable, more personal presentation of your ideas. Many good speakers use the written speech before them as a reminder or a guide, especially when discussing scientific or political matters or in presenting professional papers, but they make it a point to look up frequently, to develop little techniques that make them at least seem to be extemporizing.

DIRECTING YOUR TALK Some speakers find it disconcerting to talk generally to an audience, so, before they rise, they select one face, sometimes one they know, and direct the entire discourse to it. This device may be effective for the speaker but works better, I think, if he chooses several faces in opposite parts of the hall and directs his words sometimes this way, sometimes that, to lend a little variation.

THE USE OF JOKES, ILLUSTRATIONS, AND ANECDOTES Jokes and anecdotes, if at all appropriate, do have a function in that they loosen up an audience—and the speaker too—especially at the difficult beginning of a speech. But they are better omitted if a speaker tells a story badly and self-consciously. And if they have nothing whatsoever to do with the case, they are certainly better omitted. Otherwise members of the audience may be so puzzled by the introduction of the stories that they will spend the rest of the time trying to determine the connection and so not hear, as consciously as they should, whatever else you have to say. It is good, in making a speech, to remember that many, many people are not ear-minded, that is, they don't easily digest what they get through the ears alone. For this reason points need to be made more than once, propositions put in several ways. Wherever possible, illustrate what you are saying visually in some way, with charts, graphs, slides, motion pictures, or some form of illustration in which you take part—sketches, exhibits, instruction in techniques. The action involved breaks up a too smooth presentation and makes the audience feel more at ease—and you will, too. A spotlight pointer where slides or movies are used is the most effective way of calling attention to certain details.

CLOSING A SPEECH Many a speech loses its effectiveness if the closing is too greatly drawn out or if, on the other hand, it is too abruptly terminated. Give some indication that you have said about all you are going to say on the subject a few minutes before sitting down. Many graceful speakers say something like this, "You have been kind enough to give me this amount of time, and, while I could develop this subject to a much greater extent, we are all anxious to hear what the next speaker has to say, etc." Then comes some brief summing-up point or points and a final statement of conclusion, but never say, without preamble, "I guess that's all," or "That's all I have to say." A speech should end on a point the hearer will take away with him, if possible, or on an anecdote that sums up in capsule form part, at least, of what the speaker was trying to say.

MAKING YOUR DEPARTURE Often a principal speaker will end his speech and almost without pause make his getaway from the speakers' table. He may have to make a train or fulfill another engagement, and, if so, the chairman should, if possible, prepare the audience for such a sudden departure when he thanks the speaker. The chairman in thanking him should repeat the speaker's name for late-comers or those who may not have caught it correctly before. "Thank you, Mr. Graham Saunders" is better than "Thank you, Mr. Saunders." Otherwise, it is courteous for the speaker to hear out his successors, if any, with at least a show of interest and to linger after the speeches to receive the felicitations or answer the questions of those assembled whenever this seems advisable.

DRESS OF THE SPEAKER

A MAN'S DRESS A man making an evening speech inquires beforehand what those at the speakers' table will wear—business suits, tuxedos, or full dress. It frequently happens that people at the speakers' table wear full dress and the others at the dinner come in dinner jackets. At public dinners it is never incorrect for the speaker, the chairman, and those at the speakers' table to wear full evening dress, even if the body of the assemblage comes informally attired. For the same reason, a lecturer, a conductor, or any personage making a public appearance in the evening wears formal clothes if there is any possibility of some of his hearers doing likewise. He should set the highest sartorial standard for the occasion so as not to embarrass any who come formally attired to do him proper honor.

A WOMAN SPEAKER'S DRESS A woman speaking in the evening wears a long or short dinner dress or a formal evening gown, depending on the occasion and on what the majority of women present will be wearing. If she is to open the opera season with an appeal for subscriptions she wears formal evening dress and her finest jewels. If she is to get up in the high school auditorium to explain the functioning of the Girl Scouts she dresses in street clothes and usually wears a hat.

Clothes so vivid or spectacular that they distract the hearers' attention from what you are saying are certainly a mistake. At the same time you should look your best, being sure that your clothes are not so new and high style that you are at all conscious of them. Overdressing is more likely to be criticized than underdressing for the occasion. For most speaking occasions, when in doubt, wear a good, tailored, but not sport, suit. Many younger women speak without a hat, or, if they wear a hat, they are careful to choose one that does not in any way shield the face. Shoes should be suitable to the costume, of course, but should not have spike heels if the talk is to take any length of time.

• • •

INTRODUCTION TO EDWARD L. BERNAYS

The introductory essay to this book drew a distinction between academic and popular rhetorical theory. Included in the "popular" side of that distinction would be theorists writing not just for the general public but for professional practitioners of rhetoric. The twentieth century has seen a remarkable explosion of such professionals in the fields of *advertising* and *public relations,* which are now billion dollar businesses. These thoroughly rhetorical professions have their own schools, training programs, and literature of advice for successful practice. We include here an example of some pioneering work in popular rhetorical theory directed at professional persuaders, written by Edward L. Bernays.

Edward L. Bernays lived a long and remarkable life, from 1891 to 1995. He was born in Vienna, Austria, the nephew of famed psychoanalyst Sigmund Freud. Bernays migrated to the United States at an early age, and earned a degree from Cornell University in Ithaca, New York in 1912. Bernays has been called the "father of public relations," which is the rhetorical practice of securing good relations between the public and a group, corporation, celebrity, or other entity. He earned that title because he was one of the first rhetorical practitioners to make systematic use of the newly burgeoning arts of advertising and persuasion early in this century.

Advertising and public relations have always been part of human history. But the needs of business to increase markets for their expanding productive capacities, beginning at the end of the nineteenth century, created an expanding need for applied commercial persuasion that even today shows no signs of tapering off. Also early in this century, the discipline of psychology began developing new understandings of how people are motivated through new models such as behavioral psychology. These new social sciences of human thought and behavior were immediately adapted by rhetoricians for use in advertising, sales, public relations, and other applied rhetorical practices.

Bernays was at the forefront of that new rhetorical movement. As a practitioner, he worked for major corporations such as General Electric, General Motors, Time, CBS, and NBC. Bernays was instrumental in the successful advertising and introduction of new products such as Ivory Soap for Procter and Gamble and Lucky Strike cigarettes for the American Tobacco Company. As a rhetorical theorist, Bernays wrote several useful books to guide the new applied rhetorics. One of his major concerns was the application of emerging social sciences to the persuasion of mass audiences. Excerpted here is a selection from his book on that subject, *Propaganda.*

Bernays's rhetorical theories are in the tradition of Cicero and Whately in that they are grounded in observations of rhetorical techniques that actually work. There are few inflexible rules for rhetorical practice here, except for some conclusions drawn from the new psychological sciences. The professionals who took guidance from

Bernays in these writings were instead offered practical applications of principles drawn from Bernays's own long experience and observations of other successful persuaders. This rhetorical theory was seminal in founding some of the most vigorous rhetorical practice in history.

EDWARD L. BERNAYS

PROPAGANDA

• • •

CHAPTER IV

THE PSYCHOLOGY OF PUBLIC RELATIONS

The systematic study of mass psychology revealed to students the potentialities of invisible government of society by manipulation of the motives which actuate man in the group. Trotter and Le Bon, who approached the subject in a scientific manner, and Graham Wallas, Walter Lippmann and others who continued with searching studies of the group mind, established that the group has mental characteristics distinct from those of the individual, and is motivated by impulses and emotions which cannot be explained on the basis of what we know of individual psychology. So the question naturally arose: If we understand the mechanism and motives of the group mind, is it not possible to control and regiment the masses according to our will without their knowing it?

The recent practice of propaganda has proved that it is possible, at least up to a certain point and within certain limits. Mass psychology is as yet far from being an exact science and the mysteries of human motivation are by no means all revealed. But at least theory and practice have combined with sufficient success to permit us to know that in certain cases we can effect some change in public opinion with a fair degree of accuracy by operating a certain mechanism, just as the motorist can regulate the speed of his car by manipulating the flow of gasoline. Propaganda is not a science in the laboratory sense, but it is no longer entirely the empirical affair that it was before the advent of the study of mass psychology. It is now scientific in the sense that it seeks to base its operations upon definite knowledge drawn from direct observation of the group mind, and upon the application of principles which have been demonstrated to be consistent and relatively constant.

The modern propagandist studies systematically and objectively the material with which he is working in the spirit of the laboratory. If the matter in hand is a nation-wide sales campaign, he studies the field by means of a clipping service, or of a corps of scouts, or by personal study at a crucial spot. He determines, for example, which features of a product are losing their public appeal, and in what new direction the public taste is veering. He will not fail to investigate to what extent it is the wife who has the final word in the choice of her husband's car, or of his suits and shirts.

Scientific accuracy of results is not to be expected, because many of the elements of the situation must always be beyond his control. He may know with a fair degree of certainty that under favorable circumstances an international flight will produce a spirit of good will, making possible even the consummation of political programs. But he cannot be sure that some unexpected event will not overshadow this flight in the public interest, or that some other aviator may not do something more spectacular the day before. Even in his restricted field of public psychology there must always be a wide margin of error. Propaganda, like economics and sociology, can never be an exact science for the reason that its subject-matter, like theirs, deals with human beings.

If you can influence the leaders, either with or without their conscious coöperation, you automatically influence the group which they sway. But men do not need to be actually gathered together in a public meeting or in a street riot, to be subject to the influences of mass psychology. Because man is by nature gregarious he feels himself to be a member of a herd, even when he is alone in his room with the curtains drawn. His mind retains the patterns which have been stamped on it by the group influences.

A man sits in his office deciding what stocks to buy. He imagines, no doubt, that he is planning his purchases according to his own judgment. In actual fact his judgment is a mélange of impressions stamped on his mind by outside influences which unconsciously control his thought. He buys a certain railroad stock because it was in the headlines yesterday and hence is the one which comes most prominently to his mind; because he has a pleasant recollection of a good dinner on one of its fast trains; because it has a liberal labor policy, a reputation for honesty; because he has been told that J. P. Morgan owns some of its shares.

Trotter and Le Bon concluded that the group mind does not *think* in the strict sense of the word. In place of thoughts it has impulses, habits and emotions. In making up its mind its first impulse is usually to follow the example of a trusted leader. This is one of the most firmly established principles of mass psychology. It operates in establishing the rising or diminishing prestige of a summer resort, in causing a run on a bank, or a panic on the stock exchange, in creating a best seller, or a box-office success.

But when the example of the leader is not at hand and the herd must think for itself, it does so by means of clichés, pat words or images which stand for a whole group of ideas or experiences. Not many years ago, it was only necessary to tag a political candidate with the word interests to stampede millions of people into voting against him, because anything associated with "the interests" seemed necessarily corrupt. Recently the word Bolshevik has performed a similar service for persons who wished to frighten the public away from a line of action.

By playing upon an old cliché, or manipulating a new one, the propagandist can sometimes swing a whole mass of group emotions. In Great Britain, during the war, the evacuation hospitals came in for a considerable amount of criticism because of the summary way in which they handled their wounded. It was assumed by the public that a hospital gives prolonged and conscientious attention to its patients. When the name was changed to evacuation posts the critical reaction vanished. No one expected more than an adequate emergency treatment from an institution so named. The cliché hospital was indelibly associated in the public mind with a certain picture. To persuade the public to discriminate between one type of hospital and another, to dissociate the cliché from the picture it evoked, would have been an impossible task. Instead, a new cliché automatically conditioned the public emotion toward these hospitals.

Men are rarely aware of the real reasons which motivate their actions. A man may believe that he buys a motor car because, after careful study of the technical features of all makes on the market, he has concluded that this is the best. He is almost certainly fooling himself. He bought it, perhaps, because a friend whose financial acumen he respects bought one last week; or because his neighbors believed he was not able to afford a car of that class; or because its colors are those of his college fraternity.

It is chiefly the psychologists of the school of Freud who have pointed out that many of man's thoughts and actions are compensatory substitutes for desires which he has been obliged to suppress. A thing may be desired not for its intrinsic worth or usefulness, but because he has unconsciously come to see in it a symbol of something else, the desire for which he is ashamed to admit to himself. A man buying a car may think he wants it for purposes of locomotion, whereas the fact may be that he would really prefer not to be burdened with it, and would rather walk for the sake of his health. He may really want it because it is a symbol of social position, an evidence of his success in business, or a means of pleasing his wife.

This general principle, that men are very largely actuated by motives which they conceal from themselves, is as true of mass as of individual psychology. It is evident that the successful propagandist must understand the true motives and not be content to accept the reasons which men give for what they do.

It is not sufficient to understand only the mechanical structure of society, the groupings and cleavages and loyalties. An engineer may know all about the cylinders and pistons of a locomotive, but unless he knows how steam behaves under pressure he cannot make his engine run. Human desires are the steam which makes the social machine work. Only by understanding them can the propagandist control that vast, loose-jointed mechanism which is modern society.

The old propagandist based his work on the mechanistic reaction psychology then in vogue in our colleges. This assumed that the human mind was merely an individual machine, a system of nerves and nerve centers, reacting with mechanical regularity to stimuli, like a helpless, will-less automaton. It was the special pleader's function to provide the stimulus which would cause the desired reaction in the individual purchaser.

It was one of the doctrines of the reaction psychology that a certain stimulus often repeated would create a habit, or that the mere reiteration of an idea would create a conviction. Suppose the old type of salesmanship, acting for a meat packer, was seeking to increase the sale of bacon. It would reiterate innumerable times in full-page advertisements: "Eat more bacon. Eat bacon because it is cheap, because it is good, because it gives you reserve energy."

The newer salesmanship, understanding the group structure of society and the principles of mass psychology, would first ask: "Who is it that influences the eating habits of the public?" The answer, obviously, is: "The physicians." The new salesman will then suggest to physicians to say publicly that it is wholesome to eat bacon. He knows as a mathematical certainty, that large numbers of persons will follow the advice of their doctors, because he understands the psychological relation of dependence of men upon their physicians.

The old-fashioned propagandist, using almost exclusively the appeal of the printed word, tried to persuade the individual reader to buy a definite article, immediately. This approach is exemplified in a type of advertisement which used to be considered ideal from the point of view of directness and effectiveness:

"YOU (perhaps with a finger pointing at the reader) *buy O'Leary's rubber heels*—NOW."

The advertiser sought by means of reiteration and emphasis directed upon the individual, to break down or penetrate sales resistance. Although the appeal was aimed at fifty million persons, it was aimed at each as an individual.

The new salesmanship has found it possible, by dealing with men in the mass through their group formations, to set up psychological and emotional currents which will work for him. Instead of assaulting sales resistance by direct attack, he is interested in removing sales resistance. He creates circumstances which will swing emotional currents so as to make for purchaser demand.

If, for instance, I want to sell pianos, it is not sufficient to blanket the country with a direct appeal, such as:

"YOU *buy a Mozart piano now. It is cheap. The best artists use it. It will last for years.*"

The claims may all be true, but they are in direct conflict with the claims of other piano manufacturers, and in indirect competition with the claims of a radio or a motor car, each competing for the consumer's dollar.

What are the true reasons why the purchaser is planning to spend his money on a new car instead of on a new piano? Because he has decided that he wants the commodity called locomotion more than he wants the commodity called music?

Not altogether. He buys a car, because it is at the moment the group custom to buy cars.

The modern propagandist therefore sets to work to create circumstances which will modify that custom. He appeals perhaps to the home instinct which is fundamental. He will endeavor to develop public acceptance of the idea of a music room in the home. This he may do, for example, by organizing an exhibition of period music rooms designed by well known decorators who themselves exert an influence on the buying groups. He enhances the effectiveness and prestige of these rooms by putting in them rare and valuable tapestries. Then, in order to create dramatic interest in the exhibit, he stages an event or ceremony. To this ceremony key people, persons known to influence the buying habits of the public, such as a famous violinist, a popular artist, and a society leader, are invited. These key persons affect other groups, lifting the idea of the music room to a place in the public consciousness which it did not have before. The juxtaposition of these leaders, and the idea which they are dramatizing, are then projected to the wider public through various publicity channels. Meanwhile, influential architects have been persuaded to make the music room an integral architectural part of their plans with perhaps a specially charming niche in one corner for the piano. Less influential architects will as a matter of course imitate what is done by the men whom they consider masters of their profession. They in turn will implant the idea of the music room in the mind of the general public.

The music room will be accepted because it has been made the thing. And the man or woman who has a music room, or has arranged a corner of the parlor as a musical corner, will naturally think of buying a piano. It will come to him as his own idea.

Under the old salesmanship the manufacturer said to the prospective purchaser, "Please buy a piano." The new salesmanship has reversed the process and caused the prospective purchaser to say to the manufacturer, "Please sell me a piano."

The value of the associative processes in propaganda is shown in connection with a large real estate development. To emphasize that Jackson Heights was socially desirable every attempt was made to produce this associative process. A benefit performance of the Jitney Players was staged for the benefit of earthquake victims of Japan, under the auspices of Mrs. Astor and others. The social advantages of the place were projected—a golf course was laid out and a clubhouse planned. When the post office was opened, the public relations counsel attempted to use it as a focus for national interest and discovered that its opening fell coincident with a date important in the annals of the American Postal Service. This was then made the basis of the opening.

When an attempt was made to show the public the beauty of the apartments, a competition was held among interior decorators for the best furnished apartment in Jackson Heights. An important committee of judges decided. This competition drew the approval of well known authorities, as well as the interest of millions, who were made cognizant of it through newspaper and magazine and other publicity, with the effect of building up definitely the prestige of the development.

One of the most effective methods is the utilization of the group formation of modern society in order to spread ideas. An example of this is the nationwide competitions for sculpture in Ivory soap, open to school children in certain age groups as well as professional sculptors. A sculptor of national reputation found Ivory soap an excellent medium for sculpture.

The Procter and Gamble Company offered a series of prizes for the best sculpture in white soap. The contest was held under the auspices of the Art Center in New York City, an organization of high standing in the art world.

School superintendents and teachers throughout the country were glad to encourage the movement as an educational aid for schools. Practice among school children as part of their art courses was stimulated. Contests were held between schools, between school districts and between cities.

Ivory soap was adaptable for sculpturing in the homes because mothers saved the shavings and the imperfect efforts for laundry purposes. The work itself was clean.

The best pieces are selected from the local competitions for entry in the national contest. This is held annually at an important art gallery in New York, whose prestige with that of the distinguished judges, establishes the contest as a serious art event.

In the first of these national competitions about 500 pieces of sculpture were entered. In the third, 2,500. And in the fourth, more than 4,000. If the carefully selected pieces were so numerous, it is evident that a vast number were sculptured during the year, and that a much greater number must have been made for practice purposes. The good will was greatly enhanced by the fact that this soap had become not merely the concern of the housewife but also a matter of personal and intimate interest to her children.

A number of familiar psychological motives were set in motion in the carrying out of this campaign. The esthetic, the competitive, the gregarious (much of the sculpturing was done in school groups), the snobbish (the impulse to follow the example of a recognized leader), the exhibitionist, and—last but by no means least—the maternal.

All these motives and group habits were put in concerted motion by the simple machinery of group leadership and authority. As if actuated by the pressure of a button, people began working for the client for the sake of the gratification obtained in the sculpture work itself.

This point is most important in successful propaganda work. The leaders who lend their authority to any propaganda campaign will do so only if it can be made to touch their own interests. There must be a disinterested aspect of the propagandist's activities. In other words, it is one of the functions of the public relations counsel to discover at what points his client's interests coincide with those of other individuals or groups.

In the case of the soap sculpture competition, the distinguished artists and educators who sponsored the idea were glad to lend their services and their names because the competitions really promoted an interest which they had at heart—the cultivation of the esthetic impulse among the younger generation.

Such coincidence and overlapping of interests is as infinite as the interlacing of group formations themselves. For example, a railway wishes to develop its business. The counsel on public relations makes a survey to discover at what points its interests coincide with those of its prospective customers. The company then establishes relations with chambers of commerce along its right of way and assists them in developing their communities. It helps them to secure new plants and industries for the town. It facilitates business through the dissemination of technical information. It is not merely a case of bestowing favors in the hope of receiving favors; these activities of the railroad, besides creating good will, actually promote growth on its right of way. The interests of the railroad and the communities through which it passes mutually interact and feed one another.

In the same way, a bank institutes an investment service for the benefit of its customers in order that the latter may have more money to deposit with the bank. Or a jewelry concern develops an insurance department to insure the jewels it sells, in order to make the purchaser feel greater security in buying jewels. Or a baking company establishes an information service suggesting recipes for bread to encourage new uses for bread in the home.

The ideas of the new propaganda are predicated on sound psychology based on enlightened self-interest.

I have tried, in these chapters, to explain the place of propaganda in modern American life and something of the methods by which it operates—to tell the why, the what, the who and the how of the invisible government which dictates our thoughts, directs our feelings and controls our actions. In the following chapters I shall try to show how propaganda functions in specific departments of group activity, to suggest some of the further ways in which it may operate.

• • •

INTRODUCTION TO I. A. RICHARDS

Ivor Armstrong Richards was English and lived from 1893 to 1979. Richards was educated at Cambridge University, where he also taught, and for a time was on the faculty of Harvard University. In the early years of the twentieth century there were new developments in the discipline of literary criticism as theorists developed new methods for the study of literature. Richards was part of this new discipline, and directed his attention to meaning in language. That interest led Richards to the study of rhetoric as well. He belongs with Bakhtin among those theorists in the twentieth century who studied the ways that language is inherently rhetorical.

The rhetorical tradition has always been keyed to the idea of persuasion, in which one party attempts to win over the other party through discourse. Rhetorical success becomes a zero sum game, in which one side wins and the other loses. This model is tenable as long as there is an underlying social order and civility that can afford such wins and losses. But many theorists in the violent and divisive twentieth century have felt that what is needed is discourse that unifies and reduces division rather than a discourse that defeats others. Richards is part of a school of thought that redefines rhetoric as influence that unites and brings together different parties.

You will find here excerpts from two of Richards's books. The first is from *The Meaning of Meaning,* written with C. K. Ogden and first published in 1923. This book was not directly about rhetoric, but because it sets out some important principles concerning how language carries meaning, it is certainly useful as rhetorical theory.

Ogden and Richards begin by saying that all symbols, and they mean primarily language, has meaning only in a context. The context includes how the word is used as well as who is using it and hearing it and the thoughts that those people have. The word "sling," for instance, cannot really be understood outside of the context in which it is used: It could be a support for a broken arm or it could be a throwing action. Meaning can be referential or emotive, Ogden and Richards argue. Emotive meaning expresses our inner states and feelings. Referential meaning is more complicated, because it involves both our thoughts and things in the world to which language refers. Ogden and Richards focus on explaining referential meaning.

To explain referential meaning, the authors propose a very useful model of symbolic meaning. The model is a triangle expressing the relationships among symbols, thoughts or references, and actions or objects in the world that are called referents. A symbol such as a word refers *directly* only to our thoughts, or references. A word refers *indirectly* to objects or events in the world. Only our thoughts or references refer *directly* to objects or events in the world.

This simple model of meaning nevertheless has great usefulness in explaining rhetoric and communication in general. Simply stated, it says that words refer directly to what people think about the world and only indirectly to the world itself. Notice that this is another theoretical merger of the dualism that preoccupied the Enlightenment, for it makes it impossible to separate mind from reality when it comes to language. Notice also that the model clarifies what it is that people talk about, argue about, and may disagree over. If you and a friend go to see a movie and you refer to the movie as "wonderful" while your friend calls it "trash," the model would remind us that those words for describing the *movie* are actually directly describing each of your *thoughts* about the movie. If your friend misses a lunch date and describes her action as "forgetfulness" while you call it "rudeness" you are both referring not to the missed lunch but to what each of you thinks about the missed lunch. This understanding of how meaning works is a tool for analyzing why people understand or misunderstand one another, and it is of help in assisting people to achieve greater clarity in their communication with one another.

Ogden and Richards argue that the need to clarify what words mean goes far beyond simple interpersonal misunderstandings. Great advances in science have been made, they claim, when scientists realized that some terms and concepts they were using referred to mistaken assumptions in their minds and *not* directly to any sort of reality. Because words are most directly about our perceptions and not about things in and of themselves, rhetorical analysts should be able to identify the reasons for misunderstandings and failed communication. We might think about terms that are widely used today, such as words for different *races,* that may relate more directly to popular perceptions than to any physical reality. Knowing how such terms work could inspire new rhetorics to overcome misunderstandings.

Misunderstanding is a key term in the next selection, which is from Richards's book *The Philosophy of Rhetoric.* Early in that volume he defines rhetoric not in terms of its traditional role as persuasion but more broadly as "a study of misunderstanding and its remedies." That definition is repeated early in this excerpt: Rhetoric is the "study of verbal understanding and misunderstanding." Richards makes an early distinction between the "macroscopic" and the "microscopic" study of rhetoric. Traditional rhetoric was macroscopic: It studied lengthy development of arguments, the organization of whole discourses, the inventional patterns of entire speeches. The new rhetoric that he proposes is microscopic because it studies particular words and vocabularies to identify the potential within word usage for creating understanding or misunderstanding. Such a view of rhetoric, Richards claims, goes beyond the traditional view of persuasion.

Richards begins a review of the "aims of discourses" to note that what is needed in his world (and ours) is a variety of rhetorical purposes or aims that go beyond just persuasion. Richards pins his hopes on rhetorical discourse because of his conception of meaning, and here he further develops the basic ideas he put forth with Ogden. Richards proposes a "theorem" of linguistic meaning.

What words mean is always *abstract,* he argues. Even seemingly concrete words like "pen" are always about several different sorts of things. Concrete words for particular objects, such as your friend "Joan," are also abstractions since they refer to several different Joans (in different moods, across time, and so forth). People can never speak a word that refers directly and concretely to the world; instead, we always speak at a certain level of abstraction. But since our *thoughts* are embodied in language, this means that our experience of the world is always at some level of abstraction. Richards clarifies this last claim with the startling claim that we never have sensations! What he means by that is that we are never aware of raw sensation until it has entered our consciousness as an *idea,* at some level of abstraction from immediate reality. Therefore, for Richards, language comes first in importance, before reality, in human thought. Notice that he explicitly applies this theorem to deny Enlightenment dualism.

Richards moves to a more applied level of theory in further developing his ideas of how words have meaning. Meaning is always taken from context, he argues, repeating a theme from *The Meaning of Meaning.* One way to phrase that idea is to say that the meaning of a word is its "delegated efficacy"; that is to say, what a word means is the effect (efficacy) delegated to it by its context. Another way to stress this idea is to say that the meaning of a word is "the missing part of its context"; in other words, to say that meaning is always taken from what is around a word and not from the word itself.

This selection concludes with another chapter from *The Philosophy of Rhetoric* on metaphor. Rather than treating metaphor as a special use of language for purposes of embellishment as the rhetorical tradition had done, Richards argues instead that metaphor is the essential principle behind all language. Metaphor, in claiming that "my love is a red rose," always operates at some level of abstraction by putting together two things that are *not* the same (my love, a red rose). Yet every word does this, he claims; indeed, "thought is metaphoric." When we refer to a "telephone," we are bringing together many different instruments under one word and saying that they are the "same" thing: All of them are telephones. Richards uses this more wide ranging understanding of metaphor to show how "microscopic" uses of language in texts might be better understood.

Richards was one of the most important theorists of language in the twentieth century. He expanded our understanding of rhetoric beyond persuasion and argument to make rhetoric almost coterminous with language and thought itself. In doing so he gave reasons to think about rhetoric as the most fundamental human activity, central to how we think and act.

CHARLES K. OGDEN AND I. A. RICHARDS

THE MEANING OF MEANING

A Study of the Influence of Language upon Thought and of the Science of Symbolism

CHAPTER I

THOUGHTS, WORDS AND THINGS

Let us get nearer to the fire, so that we can see what we are saying.
—THE BUBIS OF FERNANDO PO.

The influence of Language upon Thought has attracted the attention of the wise and foolish alike, since Lao Tse came long ago to the conclusion—

"He who knows does not speak, he who speaks does not know."

Sometimes, in fact, the wise have in this field proved themselves the most foolish. Was it not the great Bentley, Master of Trinity College, Cambridge, Archdeacon of Bristol, and holder of two other livings besides, who declared: "We are sure, from the names of persons and places mentioned in Scripture before the Deluge, not to insist upon other arguments, that Hebrew was the primitive language of mankind"? On the opposite page are collected other remarks on the subject of language and its Meaning, and whether wise or foolish, they at least raise questions to which, sooner or later, an answer is desirable. In recent years, indeed, the existence and importance of this problem of Meaning have been generally admitted, but by some sad chance those who have attempted a solution have too often been forced to relinquish their ambition—whether through old age, like Leibnitz, or penury, like C. S. Peirce, or both. Even the methods by which it is to be attacked have remained in doubt. Each science has tended to delegate the unpleasant task to another. With the errors and omissions of metaphysicians we shall be much concerned in the sequel, and philologists must bear their share of the guilt. Yet it is a philologist who, of recent years, has, perhaps, realized most clearly the necessity of a broader treatment.

"Throughout the whole history of the human race," wrote the late Dr Postgate, "there have been no questions which have caused more heart-searchings, tumults, and devastation than questions of the correspondence of words to facts. The mere mention of such words as 'religion,' 'patriotism,' and 'property' is sufficient to demonstrate this truth. Now, it is the investigation of the nature of the correspondence between word and fact, to use these terms in the widest sense, which is the proper and the highest problem of the science of meaning. That every living word is rooted in facts of our mental consciousness and history it would be impossible to gainsay; but it is a very different matter to determine what these facts may be. The primitive conception is undoubtedly that the name is indicative, or descriptive, of the thing. From which it would follow at once that from the presence of the name you could argue to the existence of the thing. This is the simple conception of the savage."

In thus stressing the need for a clear analysis of the relation between words and facts as the essential of a theory of Meaning, Dr Postgate himself was fully aware that at some point the philosophical and psychological aspects of that theory cannot be avoided. When he wrote (1896), the hope was not unreasonable that the science of Semantics would do something to bridge the gulf. But, although M. Bréal's researches drew attention to a number of fascinating phenomena in the history of language, and awakened a fresh interest in the educational possibilities of etymology, the net result was disappointing. That such disappointment was inevitable may be seen, if we consider the attitude to language implied by such a passage as the following. The use of words as though their meaning were fixed, the constant resort to loose metaphor, the hypostatization of leading terms, all indicate an unsuitable attitude in which to approach the question.

> *"Substantives are signs attached to things: they contain exactly that amount of truth which can be contained by a name, an amount which is of necessity small in proportion to the reality of the object. That which is most adequate to its object is the abstract noun, since it represents a simple operation of the mind. When I use the two words* compressibility, immortality, *all that is to be found in the idea is to be found also in the word. But if I take a real entity, an object existing in nature, it will be impossible for language to introduce into the word all the ideas which this entity or object awakens in the mind. Language is therefore compelled to choose. Out of all the ideas it can choose one only; it thus creates a name which is not long in becoming a mere sign.*
>
> *"For this name to be accepted it must, no doubt, originally possess some true and striking characteristic on one side or another; it must satisfy the minds of those to whom it is first submitted. But this condition is imperative only at the outset. Once accepted, it rids itself rapidly of its etymological signification; otherwise this signification might become an embarrassment. Many objects are inaccurately named, whether through the ignorance of the original authors, or by some intervening change which disturbs the harmony between the sign and the thing signified. Nevertheless, words answer the same purpose as though they were of faultless accuracy. No one dreams of revising them. They are accepted by a tacit consent of which we are not even conscious" (Bréal's* Semantics, *pp. 171–2).*

What exactly is to be made of substantives which "contain" truth, "that amount of truth which can be contained by a name"? How can "all that is found in the idea be also found in the word"? The conception of language as "compelled to choose an idea," and thereby creating "a name, which is not long in becoming a sign," is an odd one; while 'accuracy' and 'harmony' are sadly in need of elucidation when applied to naming and to the relation between sign and thing signified respectively. This is not mere captious criticism. The locutions objected to conceal the very facts which the science of language is concerned to elucidate. The real task before that science cannot be successfully attempted without a far more critical consciousness of the dangers of such loose verbiage. It is impossible to handle a scientific matter in such metaphorical terms, and the training of philologists has not, as a rule, been such as to increase their command of analytic and abstract language. The logician would be far better equipped in this respect were it not that his command of language tends to conceal from him what he is talking about and renders him prone to accept purely linguistic constructions, which serve well enough for his special purposes, as ultimates.

How great is the tyranny of language over those who propose to inquire into its workings is well shown in the speculations of the late F. de Saussure, a writer regarded by perhaps a majority of French and Swiss students as having for the first time placed linguistic upon a scientific basis. This author begins by inquiring, "What is the object at once integral and concrete of linguistic?" He does not ask whether it has one, he obeys blindly the primitive impulse to infer from a word some object for which it stands, and sets out determined to find it. But, he continues, speech (*le langage*), though concrete enough, as a set of events is not integral. Its sounds imply movements of speech, and both, as instruments of thought, imply ideas. Ideas, he adds, have a social as well as an individual side, and at each instant language implies both an established system and an evolution. "Thus, from whatever side we approach the question, we nowhere find the integral object of linguistic." De Saussure does not pause at this point to ask himself what he is looking for, or whether there is any reason why there should be such a thing. He proceeds instead in a fashion familiar in the beginnings of all sciences, and concocts a suitable object—'*la langue,*' the language, as opposed to speech. "What is *la langue?* For us, it is not to be confounded with speech (*le langage*); it is only a determinate part of this, an essential part, it is true. It is at once a social product of the faculty of speech, and a collection of necessary conventions adopted by the social body to allow the exercise of this faculty by individuals. . . . It is a whole in itself and a principle of classification. As soon as we give it the first place among the facts of speech we introduce a natural order in a whole which does not lend itself to any other classification." *La langue* is further "the sum of the verbal images stored up in all the individuals, a treasure deposited by the practice of speaking in the members of a given community; a grammatical system, virtually existing in each brain, or more exactly in the brains of a body of individuals; for *la langue* is not complete in any one of them, it exists in perfection only in the mass."[1]

Such an elaborate construction as *la langue* might, no doubt, be arrived at by some Method of Intensive Distraction analogous to that with which Dr Whitehead's name is associated, but as a guiding principle for a young science it is fantastic. Moreover, the same device of inventing verbal entities outside the range of possible investigation proved fatal to the theory of signs which followed.[1]

As a philologist with an inordinate respect for linguistic convention, de Saussure could not bear to tamper with what he imagined to be a fixed meaning, a part of *la langue.* This scrupulous regard for fictitious 'accepted' uses of words is a frequent trait in philologists. Its roots go down very deep into human nature, as we shall see in the two chapters which follow. It is especially regrettable that a technical equipment, otherwise excellent, should have been so weak at this point, for the initial recognition of a general science of signs, 'semiology,' of which linguistic would be a branch, and the most important branch, was a very notable attempt in the right direction. Unfortunately this theory of signs, by neglecting entirely the things for which signs stand, was from the beginning cut off from any contact with scientific methods of verification. De Saussure, however,

---

[1] *Cours de Linguistique Générale,* pp. 23–31.

[1] A sign for de Saussure is twofold, made up of a concept (signifié) and an acoustic image (signifiant), both psychical entities. Without the concept, he says, the acoustic image would not be a sign (p. 100). The disadvantage of this account is, as we shall see, that the process of interpretation is included by definition in the sign!

De Saussure actually prided himself upon having "defined things and not words." The definitions thus established "have nothing to fear," he writes, "from certain ambiguous terms which do not coincide in one language and another. Thus in German *Sprache* means '*langue*' and '*langage.*' . . . In Latin *sermo* rather signifies *langage et parole* while *lingua* designates '*la langue,*' and so on. No word corresponds exactly to any of the notions made precise above; this is why every definition made apropos of a word is idle; it is a bad method, to start from words to define things" (*ibid.*, p. 32). The view of definition here adopted implies, as will be shown later, remarkable ignorance of the normal procedure—the substitution, namely, of better understood for obscure symbols. Another specimen of this naivety is found in the rejection of the term 'symbol' to designate the linguistic sign (p. 103). "The symbol has the character of never being quite arbitrary. It is not empty; there is the rudiment of a natural tie between the signifying and the signified. The symbol for justice, the scales, could not be replaced by something else at random, a carriage for instance."

does not appear to have pursued the matter far enough for this defect to become obvious. The same neglect also renders the more recent treatise of Professor Delacroix, *Le Langage et la Pensée,* ineffective as a study of the influence of language upon thought.

Philosophers and philologists alike have failed in their attempts. There remains a third group of inquirers with an interest in linguistic theory, the ethnologists, many of whom have come to their subject after a preliminary training in psychology. An adequate account of primitive peoples is impossible without an insight into the essentials of their languages, which cannot be gained through a mere transfer of current Indo-European grammatical distinctions, a procedure only too often positively misleading. In the circumstances, each field investigator might be supposed to reconstruct the grammar of a primitive tongue from his own observations of the behaviour of a speaker in a given situation. Unfortunately this is rarely done, since the difficulties are very great; and perhaps owing to accidents of psychological terminology, the worker tends to neglect the concrete environment of the speaker and to consider only the 'ideas' which are regarded as 'expressed.' Thus Dr Boas, the most suggestive and influential of the group of ethnologists which is dealing with the vast subject-matter provided by the American-Indian languages, formulates as the three points to be considered in the objective discussion of languages—

> First, the constituent phonetic elements of the language;
>
> Second, the groups of ideas expressed by phonetic groups;
>
> Third, the method of combining and modifying phonetic groups.

"All speech," says Dr Boas explicitly, "is intended to serve for the communication of ideas." Ideas, however, are only remotely accessible to outside inquirers, and we need a theory which connects words with things through the ideas, if any, which they symbolize. We require, that is to say, separate analyses of the relations of words to ideas and of ideas to things. Further, much language, especially primitive language, is not primarily concerned with ideas at all, unless under 'ideas' are included emotions and attitudes—a procedure which would involve terminological inconveniences. The omission of all separate treatment of the ways in which speech, besides conveying ideas, also expresses attitudes, desires and intentions,[1] is another point at which the work of this active school is at present defective.

In yet another respect all these specialists fail to realize the deficiencies of current linguistic theory. Preoccupied as they are—ethnologists with recording the details of fast vanishing languages; philologists with an elaborate technique of phonetic laws and principles of derivation; philosophers with 'philosophy'—all have overlooked the pressing need for a better understanding of what actually occurs in discussion. The analysis of the

---

[1] Not that definitions are lacking which include more than ideas. Thus in one of the ablest and most interesting of recent linguistic studies, that of E. Sapir, Chief of the Anthropological Section, Geological Survey of Canada, an ethnologist closely connected with the American school, language is defined as "a purely human and non-instinctive method of communicating ideas, emotions and desires by means of a system of voluntarily produced symbols" (*Language,* 1922, p. 7). But so little is the emotive element considered that in a discussion of grammatical form, as shown by the great variation of word-order in Latin, we find it stated that the change from 'hominem femina videt' to 'videt femina hominem' makes "little or no difference beyond, *possibly,* a rhetorical or a *stylistic* one" (p. 65). The italics are ours; and the same writer sums up his discussion of the complex symbol 'The farmer kills the duckling,' with the remark: "In this short sentence of five words there are expressed thirteen distinct concepts" (p. 93). As will be noted at a later stage, the use of the term 'concept' is particularly unfortunate in such an analysis, and a vocabulary so infested with current metaphysical confusions leads unavoidably to incompleteness of treatment.

By being forced to include under 'concepts' both 'concrete concepts'—material objects, and 'Pure relational concepts' (abstract ways of referring), Sapir is unable in this work—which is, however, only a preliminary to his *Language as Symbol and as Expression*—to make even the distinctions which are essential inside symbolic language (cf. Chapter V., p. 101 *infra*); and when we come to deal with translation (Chapter X., p. 228) we shall find that this vocabulary has proved equally unserviceable to him.

process of communication is partly psychological, and psychology has now reached a stage at which this part may be successfully undertaken. Until this had happened the science of Symbolism necessarily remained in abeyance, but there is no longer any excuse for vague talk about Meaning, and ignorance of the ways in which words deceive us.

Throughout the Western world it is agreed that people must meet frequently, and that it is not only agreeable to talk, but that it is a matter of common courtesy to say something even when there is hardly anything to say. "Every civilized man," continues the late Professor Mahaffy, to whose *Principles of the Art of Conversation* we owe this observation, "feels, or ought to feel, this duty; it is the universal accomplishment which all must practise"; those who fail are punished by the dislike or neglect of society.

There is no doubt an Art in saying something when there is nothing to be said, but it is equally certain that there is an Art no less important of saying clearly what one wishes to say when there is an abundance of material; and conversation will seldom attain even the level of an intellectual pastime if adequate methods of Interpretation are not also available.

Symbolism is the study of the part played in human affairs by language and symbols of all kinds, and especially of their influence on Thought. It singles out for special inquiry the ways in which symbols help us and hinder us in reflecting on things.

Symbols direct and organize, record and communicate. In stating what they direct and organize, record and communicate we have to distinguish as always between Thoughts and Things.[1] It is Thought (or, as we shall usually say, *reference*) which is directed and organized, and it is also Thought which is recorded and communicated. But just as we say that the gardener mows the lawn when we know that it is the lawn-mower which actually does the cutting, so, though we know that the direct relation of symbols is with thought, we also say that symbols record events and communicate facts.

By leaving out essential elements in the language situation we easily raise problems and difficulties which vanish when the whole transaction is considered in greater detail. Words, as every one now knows, 'mean' nothing by themselves, although the belief that they did, as we shall see in the next chapter, was once equally universal. It is only when a thinker makes use of them that they stand for anything, or, in one sense, have 'meaning.' They are instruments. But besides this referential use which for all reflective, intellectual use of language should be paramount, words have other functions which may be grouped together as emotive. These can best be examined when the framework of the problem of strict statement and intellectual communication has been set up. The importance of the emotive aspects of language is not thereby minimized, and anyone chiefly concerned with popular or primitive speech might well be led to reverse this order of approach. Many difficulties, indeed, arising through the behaviour of words in discussion, even amongst scientists, force us at an early stage to take into account these 'non-symbolic' influences. But for the analysis of the senses of 'meaning' with which we are here chiefly concerned, it is desirable to begin with the relations of thoughts, words and things as they are found in cases of reflective speech uncomplicated by emotional, diplomatic, or other disturbances; and with regard to these, the indirectness

[1] The word 'thing' is unsuitable for the analysis here undertaken, because in popular usage it is restricted to material substances—a fact which has led philosophers to favour the terms 'entity,' 'ens' or 'object' as the general name for whatever is. It has seemed desirable, therefore, to introduce a technical term to stand for whatever we may be thinking of or referring to. 'Object,' though this is its original use, has had an unfortunate history. The word 'referent,' therefore, has been adopted, though its etymological form is open to question when considered in relation to other participial derivatives, such as agent or reagent. But even in Latin the present participle occasionally (e.g. *vehens* in equo) admitted of variation in use; and in English an analogy with substantives, such as 'reagent,' 'extent,' an 'incident' may be urged. Thus the fact that 'referent' in what follows stands for a thing and not an active person, should cause no confusion.

of the relations between words and things is the feature which first deserves attention.

This may be simply illustrated by a diagram, in which the three factors involved whenever any statement is made, or understood, are placed at the corners of the triangle, the relations which hold between them being represented by the sides. The point just made can be restated by saying that in this respect the base of the triangle is quite different in composition from either of the other sides.

Between a thought and a symbol causal relations hold. When we speak, the symbolism we employ is caused partly by the reference we are making and partly by social and psychological factors—the purpose for which we are making the reference, the proposed effect of our symbols on other persons, and our own attitude. When we hear what is said, the symbols both cause us to perform an act of reference, and to assume an attitude which will, according to circumstances, be more or less similar to the act and the attitude of the speaker.

Between the Thought and the Referent there is also a relation; more or less direct (as when we think about or attend to a coloured surface we see), or indirect (as when we 'think of' or 'refer to' Napoleon), in which case there may be a very long chain of sign-situations intervening between the act and its referent: word—historian—contemporary record—eye-witness—referent (Napoleon).

Between the symbol and the referent there is no relevant relation other than the indirect one, which consists in its being used by someone to stand for a referent. Symbol and Referent, that is to say, are not connected directly (and when, for grammatical reasons, we imply such a relation, it will merely be an imputed,[1] as opposed to a real, relation) but only indirectly round the two sides of the triangle.[2]

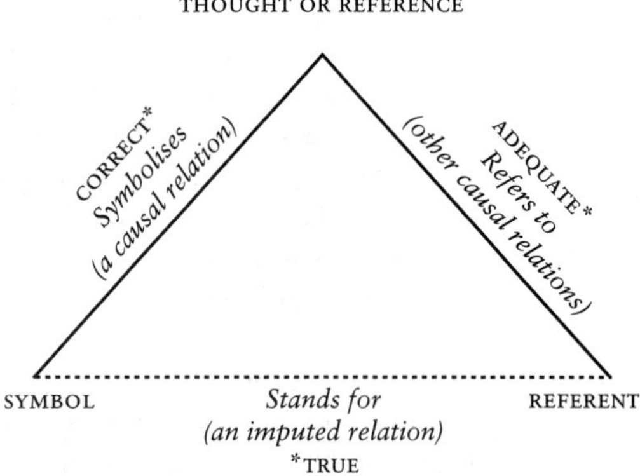

It may appear unnecessary to insist that there is no direct connection between say 'dog,' the word, and certain common objects in our streets, and that the only connection which holds is that which consists in our using the word when we refer to the animal. We shall find, however, that the kind of simplification typified by this once universal theory of direct meaning relations between words and things is the source of almost all the difficulties

[1] See Chapter VI., p. 116.

[2] An exceptional case occurs when the symbol used is more or less directly like the referent for which it is used, as for instance, it may be when it is an onomatopœic word, or an image, or a gesture, or a drawing. In this case the triangle is completed; its base is supplied, and a great simplification of the problem involved appears to result. For this reason many attempts have been made to reduce the normal language situation to this possibly more primitive form. Its greater completeness does no doubt account for the immense superiority in efficiency of gesture languages, within their appropriate field, to other languages not supportable by gesture within *their* fields. Hence we know far more perfectly what has occurred if a scene is well re-enacted than if it be merely described. But in the normal situation we have to recognize that our triangle is without its base, that between Symbol and Referent no direct relation holds; and, further, that it is through this lack that most of the problems of language arise. Simulative and non-simulative languages are entirely distinct in principle. Standing for and representing are different relations. It is, however, convenient to speak at times as though there were some direct relation holding between Symbol and Referent. We then say, on the analogy of the lawn-mower, that a Symbol refers to a Referent. Provided that the telescopic nature of the phrase is not forgotten, confusion need not arise. In Supplement I., Part V. *infra,* Dr Malinowski gives a valuable account of the development of the speech situation in relation to the above diagram.

* Cf. Chapter V., pp. 101–2.

which thought encounters. As will appear at a later stage, the power to confuse and obstruct, which such simplifications possess, is largely due to the conditions of communication. Language if it is to be used must be a *ready* instrument. The handiness and ease of a phrase is always more important in deciding whether it will be extensively used than its accuracy. Thus such shorthand as the word 'means' is constantly used so as to imply a direct simple relation between words and things, phrases and situations. If such relations could be admitted then there would of course be no problem as to the nature of Meaning, and the vast majority of those who have been concerned with it would have been right in their refusal to discuss it. But too many interesting developments have been occurring in the sciences, through the rejection of everyday symbolizations and the endeavour to replace them by more accurate accounts, for any naïve theory that 'meaning' is just 'meaning' to be popular at the moment. As a rule new facts in startling disagreement with accepted explanations of other facts are required before such critical analyses of what are generally regarded as simple satisfactory notions are undertaken. This has been the case with the recent revolutions in physics. But in addition great reluctance to postulate anything *sui generis* and of necessity undetectable[1] was needed before the simple natural notion of simultaneity, for instance, as a two-termed relation came to be questioned. Yet to such questionings the theory of Relativity was due. The same two motives, new discrepant facts, and distaste for the use of obscure kinds of entities in eking out explanations, have led to disturbances in psychology, though here the required restatements have not yet been provided. No Copernican revolution has yet occurred, although several are due if psychology is to be brought into line with its fellow sciences.

It is noteworthy, however, that recent stirrings in psychology have been mainly if not altogether concerned with feeling and volition. The popular success of Psycho-analysis has tended to divert attention from the older problem of thinking. Yet in so far as progress here has consequences for all the other sciences and for the whole technique of investigation in psychology itself, this central problem of knowing or of 'meaning' is perhaps better worth scrutiny and more likely to promote fresh orientations than any other that can be suggested. As the Behaviourists have also very properly pointed out, this question is closely connected with the use of words.

But the approach to Meaning, far more than the approach to such problems as those of physics, requires a thorough-going investigation of language. Every great advance in physics has been at the expense of some generally accepted piece of metaphysical explanation which had enshrined itself in a convenient, universally practised, symbolic shorthand. But the confusion and obstruction due to such shorthand expressions and to the naïve theories they protect and keep alive, is greater in psychology, and especially in the theory of knowledge, than elsewhere; because no problem is so infected with so-called metaphysical difficulties—due here, as always, to an approach to a question through symbols without an initial investigation of their functions.

We have now to consider more closely what the causes and effects of symbols are.[1] Whatever may be the services, other than conservative and retentive, of symbolization, all experience shows that there are also disservices. The grosser forms of verbal confusion have long been recognized; but

---

[1] Places and instants are very typical entities of verbal origin.

[1] Whether symbols in some form or other are necessary to thought itself is a difficult problem, and is discussed in *The Meaning of Psychology* (Chapter XIII.) as well as in Chapter X. of the present work. But certainly the recording and the communication of thought (telepathy apart) require symbols. It seems that thought, so far as it is transitive and not in the form of an internal dialogue, can dispense with symbols, and that they only appear when thought takes on this monologue form. In the normal case the actual development of thought is very closely bound up with the symbolization which accompanies it.

less attention has been paid to those that are more subtle and more frequent. In the following chapters many examples of these will be given, chosen in great part from philosophical fields, for it is here that such confusions become, with the passage of time, most apparent. The root of the trouble will be traced to the superstition that words are in some way parts of things or always imply things corresponding to them, historical instances of this still potent instinctive belief being given from many sources. The fundamental and most prolific fallacy is, in other words, that the base of the triangle given above is filled in.

The completeness of any reference varies; it is more or less close and clear, it 'grasps' its object in greater or less degree. Such symbolization as accompanies it—images of all sorts, words, sentences whole and in pieces—is in no very close observable connection with the variation in the perfection of the reference. Since, then, in any discussion we cannot immediately settle from the nature of a person's remarks what his opinion is, we need some technique to keep the parties to an argument in contact and to clear up misunderstandings—or, in other words, a Theory of Definition. Such a technique can only be provided by a theory of knowing, or of reference, which will avoid, as current theories do not, the attribution to the knower of powers which it may be pleasant for him to suppose himself to possess, but which are not open to the only kind of investigation hitherto profitably pursued, the kind generally known as scientific investigation.

Normally, whenever we hear anything said we spring spontaneously to an immediate conclusion, namely, that the speaker is referring to what we should be referring to were we speaking the words ourselves. In some cases this interpretation may be correct; this will prove to be what he has referred to. But in most discussions which attempt greater subtleties than could be handled in a gesture language this will not be so. To suppose otherwise is to neglect our subsidiary gesture languages, whose accuracy within their own limited provinces is far higher than that yet reached by any system of spoken or written symbols, with the exception of the quite special and peculiar case of mathematical, scientific and musical notations. Words, whenever they cannot directly ally themselves with and support themselves upon gestures, are at present a very imperfect means of communication. Even for private thinking thought is often ready to advance, and only held back by the treachery of its natural symbolism; and for conversational purposes the latitude acquired constantly shows itself to all those who make any serious attempts to compare opinions.

We have not here in view the more familiar ways in which words may be used to deceive. In a later chapter, when the function of language as an instrument for the *promotion of purposes* rather than as a means of *symbolizing references* is fully discussed, we shall see how the intention of the speaker may complicate the situation. But the *honnête homme* may be unprepared for the lengths to which verbal ingenuity can be carried. At all times these possibilities have been exploited to the full by interpreters of Holy Writ who desire to enjoy the best of both worlds. Here, for example, is a specimen of the exegetic of the late Dr Lyman Abbott, pastor, publicist and editor, which, through the efforts of Mr Upton Sinclair, has now become classic. Does Christianity condemn the methods of twentieth-century finance? Doubtless there are some awkward words in the Gospels, but a little 'interpretation' is all that is necessary.

> "Jesus did not say 'Lay not up for yourselves treasures upon earth.' He said 'Lay not up for yourselves treasures upon earth *where moth and rust doth corrupt and where thieves break through and steal.*' And no sensible American does. Moth and rust do not get at Mr Rockefeller's oil wells, and thieves do not often break through and steal a railway. What Jesus condemned was hoarding wealth."

Each investment, therefore, every worldly acquisition, according to one of the leading divines of the New World, may be judged on its merits. There is no hard and fast rule. When moth and rust have been eliminated by science the Christian investor will presumably have no problem, but in the meantime it would seem that Camphorated Oil fulfils most nearly the synoptic requirements. Burglars are not partial to it; it is anathema to moth; and the risk of rust is completely obviated.

Another variety of verbal ingenuity closely allied to this, is the deliberate use of symbols to misdirect the listener. Apologies for such a practice in the case of the madman from whom we desire to conceal the whereabouts of his razor are well known, but a wider justification has also been attempted. In the Christian era we hear of "falsifications of documents, inventions of legends, and forgeries of every description which made the Catholic Church a veritable seat of lying.'[1] A play upon words in which one sense is taken by the speaker and another sense intended by him for the hearer was permitted.[2] Indeed, three sorts of equivocations were distinguished by Alfonso de Liguori, who was beatified in the nineteenth century, which might be used with good reason;[3] a good reason being "any honest object, such as keeping our goods, spiritual or temporal."[4] In the twentieth century the intensification of militant nationalism has added further 'good reason'; for the military code includes all transactions with hostile nations or individuals as part of the process of keeping spiritual and temporal goods. In war-time words become a normal part of the mechanism of deceit, and the ethics of the situation have been aptly summed up by Lord Wolseley: "We will keep hammering along with the conviction that 'honesty is the best policy,' and that truth always wins in the long run. These pretty sentences do well for a child's copy-book, but the man who acts upon them in war had better sheathe his sword for ever."[1]

The Greeks, as we shall see, were in many ways not far from the attitude of primitive man towards words. And it is not surprising to read that after the Peloponnesian war the verbal machinery of peace had got completely out of gear, and, says Thucydides, could not be brought back into use—"The meaning of words had no longer the same relation to things, but was changed by men as they thought proper." The Greeks were powerless to cope with such a situation. We in our wisdom seem to have created institutions which render us more powerless still.[2]

On a less gigantic scale the technique of deliberate misdirection can profitably be studied with a view to corrective measures. In accounting for Newman's *Grammar of Assent* Dr E. A. Abbott had occasion to describe the process of 'lubrication,' the art of greasing the descent from the premises to the conclusion, which his namesake cited above so aptly employs. In order to lubricate well, various qualifications are necessary:

> "First a nice discrimination of words, enabling you to form, easily and naturally, a great number of finely graduated propositions, shading away, as it were, from the assertion 'x is white' to the

---

[1] Westermarck, *The Origin and Development of Moral Ideas,* Vol. II., p. 100.

[2] Alagona, *Compendium Manualis D. Navarri* XII., 88, p. 94.

[3] Alfonso di Liguori, *Theologia Moralis,* III., 151, Vol. I., p. 249.

[4] Meyrick, *Moral and Devotional Theology of the Church of Rome,* Vol. I., p. 3. Cf. further Westermarck, *loc. cit.*

---

[1] *Soldier's Pocket Book for Field Service,* p. 69.

[2] To-day, as Mr Montague (*Disenchantment,* p. 101) well puts it, "the only new thing about deception in war is modern man's more perfect means for its practice. The thing has become, in his hand, a trumpet more efficacious than Gideon's own. . . . To match the Lewis gun with which he now fires his solids, he has to his hand the newspaper Press, to let fly at the enemy's head the thing which is not." But this was a temporary use of the modern technique of misdirection, and with the return of peace the habit is lost? Not so, says Mr Montague. "Any weapon you use in a war leaves some bill to be settled in peace, and the Propaganda arm has its cost like another." The return of the exploiters of the verbal machine to their civil posts is a return in triumph, and its effects will be felt for many years in all countries where the power of the word amongst the masses remains paramount.

> assertion 'x is black.' Secondly an inward and absolute contempt for logic and for words. . . . And what are words but toys and sweetmeats for grown-up babies who call themselves men?"[1]

But even where the actual referents are not in doubt, it is perhaps hardly realized how widespread is the habit of using the power of words not only for *bona fide* communications, but also as a method of misdirection; and in the world as it is to-day the naïve interpreter is likely on many occasions to be seriously misled if the existence of this unpleasing trait—equally prevalent amongst the classes and the masses without distinction of race, creed, sex, or colour—is overlooked.

Throughout this work, however, we are treating of *bona fide* communication only, except in so far as we shall find it necessary in Chapter IX. to discuss that derivate use of Meaning to which misdirection gives rise. For the rest, the verbal treachery with which we are concerned is only that involved by the use of symbols as such. As we proceed to examine the conditions of communication we shall see why any symbolic apparatus which is in general use is liable to incompleteness and defect.

But if our linguistic outfit is treacherous, it nevertheless is indispensable, nor would another complete outfit necessarily improve matters, even if it were ten times as complete. It is not always new words that are needed, but a means of controlling them as symbols, a means of readily discovering to what in the world on any occasion they are used to refer, and this is what an adequate theory of definition should provide.

But a theory of Definition must follow, not precede, a theory of Signs, and it is little realized how large a place is taken both in abstract thought and in practical affairs by sign-situations. But if an account of sign-situations is to be scientific it must take its observations from the most suitable instances, and must not derive its general principles from an exceptional case. The person actually interpreting a sign is not well placed for observing what is happening. We should develop our theory of signs from observations of other people, and only admit evidence drawn from introspection when we know how to appraise it. The adoption of the other method, on the ground that all our knowledge of others is inferred from knowledge of our own states, can only lead to the *impasse* of solipsism from which modern speculation has yet to recoil. Those who allow beyond question that there are people like themselves also interpreting signs and open to study should not find it difficult to admit that their observation of the behaviour of others may provide at least a framework within which their own introspection, that special and deceptive case, may be fitted. That this is the practice of all the sciences need hardly be pointed out. Any sensible doctor when stricken by disease distrusts his own introspective diagnosis and calls in a colleague.

There are, indeed, good reasons why what is happening in ourselves should be partially hidden from us, and we are generally better judges of what other people are doing than of what we are doing ourselves. Before we looked carefully into other people's heads it was commonly believed that an entity called the soul resided therein, just as children commonly believe that there is a little man inside the skull who looks out at the eyes, the windows of the soul, and listens at the ears. The child has the strongest introspective evidence for this belief, which, but for scalpels and microscopes, it would be difficult to disturb. The tacitly solipsistic presumption that this naïve approach is in some way a necessity of method disqualifies the majority of philosophical and psychological discussions of Interpretation. If we restrict the subject-matter of the inquiry to 'ideas' and words, *i.e.,* to the left side of our triangle, and omit all frank recognition of the world outside us, we inevitably introduce confusion on

---

[1] *Philomythus,* p. 214.

such subjects as knowledge in perception, verification and Meaning itself.[1]

If we stand in the neighbourhood of a cross road and observe a pedestrian confronted by a notice *To Grantchester* displayed on a post, we commonly distinguish three important factors in the situation. There is, we are sure, (1) a Sign which (2) refers to a Place and (3) is being interpreted by a person. All situations in which Signs are considered are similar to this. A doctor noting that his patient has a temperature and so forth is said to diagnose his disease as influenza. If we talk like this we do not make it clear that signs are here also involved. Even when we speak of symptoms we often do not think of these as closely related to other groups of signs. But if we say that the doctor interprets the temperature, etc., as a Sign of influenza, we are at any rate on the way to an inquiry as to whether there is anything in common between the manner in which the pedestrian treated the object at the cross road and that in which the doctor treated his thermometer and the flushed countenance.

On close examination it will be found that very many situations which we do not ordinarily regard as Sign-situations are essentially of the same nature. The chemist dips litmus paper in his test-tube, and interprets the sign red or the sign blue as meaning acid or base. A Hebrew prophet notes a small black cloud, and remarks "We shall have rain." Lessing scrutinizes the Laocoön, and concludes that the features of Laocoön *père* are in repose. A New Zealand school-girl looks at certain letters on a page in her *Historical Manual for the use of Lower Grades* and knows that Queen Anne is dead.

[1] This tendency is particularly noticeable in such works as Baldwin's elaborate treatise on *Thoughts and Things*, where a psychological apparatus of 'controls' and 'contents' is hard to reconcile with the subsequent claim to discuss communication. The twist given to grammatical analysis by Aristotle's similar neglect of Reference is dealt with in Appendix A.

The method which recognizes the common feature of sign-interpretation[1] has its dangers, but opens the way to a fresh treatment of many widely different topics.

As an instance of an occasion in which the theory of signs is of special use, the subject dealt with in our fourth chapter may be cited. If we realize that in *all* perception, as distinguished from mere awareness, sign-situations are involved, we shall have a new method of approaching problems where a verbal deadlock seems to have arisen. Whenever we 'perceive' what we name 'a chair,' we are interpreting a certain group of data (modifications of the sense-organs), and treating them as signs of a referent. Similarly, even before the interpretation of a word, there is the almost automatic interpretation of a group of successive noises or letters as a word. And in addition to the external world we can also explore with a new technique the sign-situations involved by mental events, the 'goings on' or processes of interpretation themselves.

[1] In all these cases a sign has been interpreted rightly or wrongly, *i.e.*, something has been not only experienced or enjoyed, but understood as referring to something else. Anything which can be experienced can also be thus understood, *i.e.*, can also be a sign; and it is important to remember that interpretation, or what happens to (or in the mind of) an Interpreter is quite distinct both from the sign and from that for which the sign stands or to which it refers. If then we speak of the meaning of a sign we must not, as philosophers, psychologists and logicians are wont to do, confuse the (imputed) relation between a sign and that to which it refers, either with the referent (what is referred to) or with the process of interpretation (the 'goings on' in the mind of the interpreter). It is this sort of confusion which has made so much previous work on the subject of signs and their meaning unfruitful. In particular, by using the same term 'meaning' *both* for the 'Goings on' inside their heads (the images, associations, etc., which enabled them to interpret signs) and for the Referents (the things to which the signs refer) philosophers have been forced to locate Grantchester, Influenza, Queen Anne, and indeed the whole Universe equally inside their heads—or, if alarmed by the prospect of cerebral congestion, at least 'in their minds' in such wise that all these objects become conveniently 'mental.' Great care, therefore, is required in the use of the term 'meaning,' since its associations are dangerous.

We need neither confine ourselves to arbitrary generalizations from introspection after the manner of classical psychology, nor deny the existence of images and other 'mental' occurrences to their signs with the extreme Behaviourists.[1] The Double language hypothesis, which is suggested by the theory of signs and supported by linguistic analysis, would absolve Dr Watson and his followers from the logical necessity of affecting general anæsthesia. Images, etc., are often most useful signs of our present and future behaviour—notably in the modern interpretation of dreams.[2] An improved Behaviourism will have much to say concerning the chaotic attempts at symbolic interpretation and construction by which Psycho-analysts discredit their valuable labours.

The problems which arise in connection with any 'sign-situation' are of the same general form. The relations between the elements concerned are no doubt different, but they are of the same sort. A thorough classification of these problems in one field, such as the field of symbols, may be expected, therefore, to throw light upon analogous problems in fields at first sight of a very different order.

When we consider the various kinds of Sign-situations instanced above, we find that those signs which men use to communicate one with another and as instruments of thought, occupy a peculiar place. It is convenient to group these under a distinctive name; and for words, arrangements of words, images, gestures, and such representations as drawings or mimetic sounds we use the term *symbols*. The influence of Symbols upon human life and thought in numberless unexpected ways has never been fully recognized, and to this chapter of history we now proceed.

---

[1] That the mind-body problem is due to a duplication of symbolic machinery is maintained in Chapter IV., p. 81. Cf. also *The Meaning of Psychology,* by C. K. Ogden (1926), Chapter II., where this view is supported with reference to contemporary authorities who hold it.

[2] In the terminology of the present work, many of the analyst's 'symbols' are, of course, signs only; they are not used for purposes of communication. But in the literature of psycho-analysis there is much valuable insistence on the need of wider forms of interpretation, especially in relation to emotional overcharge. Cf., for example, Dr Jelliffe's "The Symbol as an Energy Condenser" (*Journal of Nervous and Mental Diseases,* December 1919), though the metaphor, like many other psychoanalytic locutions, must not be stretched too far in view of what has been said above and of what is to follow (of. pages 102–3 and 200 *infra*).

I. A. RICHARDS

The Philosophy of Rhetoric

LECTURE II

THE AIMS OF DISCOURSE AND TYPES OF CONTEXT

In my introductory lecture I urged that there is room for a persistent, systematic, detailed inquiry into how words work that will take the place of the discredited subject which goes by the name of Rhetoric. I went on to argue that this inquiry must be philosophic, or—if you hesitate with that word, I do myself—that it must take charge of the criticism of its own assumptions and not accept them, more than it can help, ready-made from other studies. How words mean, is not a question to which we can safely accept an answer either as an inheritance from common sense, that curious growth, or as something vouched for by another science, by psychology, say—since other sciences use words themselves and not least delusively when they address themselves to these questions. The result is that a revived Rhetoric, or study of verbal understanding and misunderstanding, must itself undertake its own inquiry into the modes of meaning—not only, as with the old Rhetoric, on a macroscopic scale, discussing the effects of different disposals of large parts of a discourse—but also on a microscopic scale by using theorems about the structure of the fundamental conjectural units of meaning and the conditions through which they, and their interconnections, arise.

In the old Rhetoric, of course, there is much that a new Rhetoric finds useful—and much besides which may be advantageous until man changes his nature, debates and disputes, incites, tricks, bullies and cajoles his fellows less. Aristotle's notes on the forensic treatment of evidence elicited under torture are unhappily not without their utility still in some very up-to-date parts of the world.

Among the general themes of the old Rhetoric there is one which is especially pertinent to our inquiry. The old Rhetoric was an offspring of dispute; it developed as the rationale of pleadings and persuadings; it was the theory of the battle of words and has always been itself dominated by the combative impulse. Perhaps what it has most to teach us is the narrowing and blinding influence of that preoccupation, that debaters' interest.

Persuasion is only one among the aims of discourse. It poaches on the others—especially on that of *exposition,* which is concerned to state a view, not to persuade people to agree or to do anything more than examine it. The review and correspondence columns of the learned and scientific journals are the places in which to watch this poaching at its liveliest. It is no bad preparation for any attempt at exposition—above all of such debatable and contentious matters as those to which I am soon to turn—to realize how easily the combative impulse can put us in mental blinkers and make us take another man's words in the ways in which we can down him with least trouble.

I can point this moral—call it defensive if you will—with a small specimen from one of the many little books which in the Nineteenth Century attempted a reform of Rhetoric. It is from Benjamin Humphrey Smart's *Practical Logic,* a little book written for and used for a few decades in the best young ladies' seminaries through the middle of the Nineteenth Century and now as dead as any book well can be. Smart is discussing the conduct of exposition. He has listed a number of faults commonly committed and comes to the

TENTH FAULT TO BE AVOIDED, namely: *Forgetting the Proposition.*

"Of this error," he writes, "the following instance may suffice:

> 'Anger has been called a short madness; and people of the weakest understanding are the most subject to it. It is remarkable that when a disputant is in the wrong, he tries to make up in violence what he wants in argument. This arises from his pride. He will not own his error, and because he is determined not to be convicted of it, he falls into a passion.'

Here, (Smart comments) instead of going on to show why Anger has been called a short madness, the writer wanders into reflections which have no necessary connection with the particular proposition. He should have reasoned thus:

> 'Anger has been called a short madness. To be convinced that the appellation is just, let us look to the effects of anger. It disturbs a man's judgment, so that he inflicts an injury on his dearest friend, who, the next moment, he loads with caresses. It makes him run headlong into dangers, which, if his mind were clear, he would be the first to see and avoid. It is true that anger does not always disturb the mind to this degree, but that it always disturbs the mind in a degree proportional to its violence, is certain; and therefore it may be justly characterised as a madness.' "

What necessary connection with the proposition, may we ask, has this sketch of some scenes from an early Victorian Novel? And whence comes this certainty that anger *always* disturbs the mind in a degree proportional to its violence? However, it is better perhaps to take its lesson to heart and remember that anger is not the only warping passion. Risibility and tedium, too, I think Smart would have said, can disturb the judgment.

Warned now of the dangers both of forgetting the proposition and of the 'short madness' that the combative and other passions induce, let me sketch, to use Hobbes' words, a theorem about meanings which may be useful in constructing the most general problems of a new Rhetoric.

I had better put in another warning, though, here. What follows is unavoidably abstract and general in the extreme. It may therefore rather illustrate the difficulties of communicating with such highly abstract language than achieve as much communication as we would wish. If so the fault will not lie, I hope and believe, either in my stupidity or in our joint stupidity. It will lie in the abstractness of the language. It has to be abstract here. What it is trying to say cannot, I think, be put safely in more concrete terms, for it is not talking about this or that mode of meaning but about all meanings. And I cannot here start with illustrations, because all things equally illustrate what I am saying; and how they are to be taken is just the problem. But, after this bout of abstractions, the applications I shall be making in the later Lectures will, I believe, clear up this dark patch. In brief, how we use this theorem best shows us what the theorem is.

If, then, you seem in the next half hour at times merely to be hearing words as sounds that come and go, I must beg your indulgence, or buy it with the promise that we *shall* come out again to practical problems in the everyday conduct of words. Meanwhile this very difficulty is an illustration of a chief practical problem.

What I am now going to try to say is something which, if it is right, we all in a sense know extremely well already. "It is not sufficiently considered," said Dr. Johnson, "that men more frequently require to be reminded than informed." I shall be trying to remind you of something so simple that it is hard to think of. Something as simple as possible, and, to quote Hobbes again, "clear and perspicuous to all men—save only to those who studying the hard writings of the metaphysicians, which they believe to be some egregious learning, think they understand not when they do." And it may be comforting to recall that Lotze began a course of lectures on an allied subject by saying that "The simplest of the conceptions here employed, that of a thing and that of its being, however lucid they appear at first, on closer consideration grow always more and more obscure."

For 'always' I would say 'for a time.' We return to lucidity. But now to work.

I have two sets of problems in view: one set I have just been talking about—the division of the various aims of discourse, the purposes for which we speak or write; in brief, the functions of language. The other set of problems goes deeper, and, if we can set it rightly, the problems about the language functions are best approached from it. I can indicate these deeper problems in many ways: What is the connection between the mind and the world by which events in the mind mean other events in the world? Or "How does a thought come to be 'of' whatever it is that it is a thought of?" or "What is the relation between a thing and its name?" The last indication may not seem to carry as far as the others; but they are all the same problem and I put the 'name'-formulation in because an over-simple view of naming, or rather a treatment of words in general as though they were names (usually of ideas) has been a main defect in the traditional study. These are, you will see, really deep problems. As such we shall not expect any answers which will be satisfactory. We must be content if the answers we get are to some degree useful—useful among other things in improving themselves.

I can start the theorem safely by remarking that we are things peculiarly responsive to other things. To develop this we have to consider the peculiarities of our responsiveness. We are responsive in all sorts of ways. Some of these ways are relatively simple, if cut short enough; as when we jump at a loud noise or respond to changes of temperature. But even here, if we compare ourselves to thermometers, we see that our responses are of a different order of complexity. A thermometer responds, the length of its thread of mercury varies with the temperature, but only with the present temperature—unless the thermometer is a bad one. What has happened to it in the past, what temperatures it formerly recorded, and the order in which it recorded them, all that has no bearing upon and does not interfere with its present response to changes of temperature. We can imagine, though, a thermometer that, whenever the temperature went up and down like this, M, did something that could only be explained by bringing in other things that happened to it in the past when the temperature went up and down so, M. And correspondingly did something else whenever the temperature went down and up, W. Such an imaginary thermometer would be on the way to showing characteristics of the behavior of living systems, of the systems which, we say, have a mind.

Now consider our own minds' simplest operations. Do we ever respond to a stimulus in a way which is not influenced by the other things that happened to us when more or less similar stimuli struck us in the past? Probably never. A new kind of stimulus might perhaps give rise to a new kind of sensation, a new kind of pain, say. But even so we should probably recognize it as a pain of some sort. Effects from more or less similar happenings in the past would come in to give our response its character and this as far as it went would be meaning. Meaning of a lowly kind, no doubt, the kind of meaning that the least developed animals live by. It is important—and that is why I have started so far back with these elementaries—to realize how far back into the past all our meanings go, how they grow out of one another much as an organism grows, and how inseparable they are from one another.

I can make the same point by denying that we have any sensations. That sounds drastic but is almost certainly true if rightly understood. A sensation would be something that just was *so,* on its own, a datum; as such we have none. Instead we have perceptions, responses whose character comes to them from the past as well as the present occasion. A perception is never just of an *it;* perception takes whatever it perceives as a thing of a certain sort. All thinking from the lowest to the highest—whatever else it may be—is sorting.

That is an important part of the theorem because it removes, if it is accepted, one of the worst troubles which have distorted traditional accounts of the meanings of words—the troubles that gave rise to the Nominalist, Realist, Conceptual controversies best known to us through the great British philosophical battle of the Eighteenth Century about whether we have and how we come by abstract ideas and what they are. This theorem alleges that meanings, from the very beginning, have a primordial generality and abstractness; and it follows William James in saying that the lowliest organism—a polyp or an amoeba—if it learns at all from its past, if it exclaims in its acts, "Hallo! Thingembob again!" thereby shows itself to be a conceptual thinker. It is behaving or thinking with a concept—not, of course, *of* one. Its act is abstractive and general; disregards in some respects the former situations and so is abstractive, and applies in some respects not to one single thing but to any of a sort and so is general.

The theorem settles the Eighteenth Century problem by standing it on its head. That problem was, How do we manage, from this particular concrete thing and that particular concrete thing and the other particular concrete thing, to arrive at the general abstract anything? The theorem holds that we *begin* with the general abstract anything, split it, as the world makes us, into sorts and then arrive at concrete particulars by the overlapping or common membership of these sorts. This bit of paper here now in my hand is a concrete particular to us so far as we think of it as paperish, hereish, nowish and in my hand; it is the more concrete as we take it as of more sorts, and the more specific as the sorts are narrower and more exclusive.

The next step in the theorem takes us on to words and their meanings. If we sum up thus far by saying that meaning is *delegated efficacy,* that description applies above all to the meaning of words, whose virtue is to be substitutes exerting the powers of what is not there. They do this as other signs do it, though in more complex fashions, through their contexts.

I must explain now the rather special and technical sense I am giving to this word 'context.' This is the pivotal point of the whole theorem. The word has a familiar sense in 'a literary context,' as the other words before and after a given word which determine how it is to be interpreted. This is easily extended to cover the rest of the book. I recall the painful shock I suffered when I first came across, in a book by Dr. Bosanquet, what he called the Golden Rule of Scholarship, "Never to quote or comment on anything in a book which you have not read from cover to cover." As with other Golden Rules a strange peace would fall upon the world if that were observed. I cannot honestly say I either practice the Rule or recommend it. There is a middle way wiser for the Children of this World. However, as I neither am nor hope to be a scholar, I have no occasion to practise it.

The familiar sense of 'context' can be extended further to include the circumstances under which anything was written or said; wider still to include, for a word in Shakespeare, say, the other known uses of the word about that time, wider still finally to include anything whatever about the period, or about anything else which is relevant to our interpretation of it. The technical use I am going to make of this term 'context' is none of these—though it has something in common with them as having to do with the governing conditions of an interpretation. We can get to it best, perhaps, by considering those recurrences in nature which statements of causal laws are about.

Put very simply, a causal law may be taken as saying that, under certain conditions, of two events if one happens the other does. We usually call the first the cause and the second the effect, but the two may happen together, as when I clap my hands and both palms tingle. If we are talking about final causes we reverse them, and the lecture you are going to hear was the cause of your coming hither. There is a good deal of arbitrariness at several points here which comes from the different purposes for which we need causal laws. We decide, to suit these purposes, how we shall divide up events; we make the existence of the earth one event and the tick of a clock another, and so on. And we distribute the titles of 'cause' and 'effect' as we please. Thus we do not please to say that night causes day or day night. We prefer to say that given the conditions the rotation of the earth is the cause of their succession. We are especially arbitrary in picking out the cause from among the whole group, or context, of conditions—of prior and subsequent events which hang together. Thus the coroner decides that the cause of a man's death was the act of a murderer and not the man's meeting with the murderer, or the stopping of his heart, or the fact that he was not wearing a bullet-proof waistcoat. That is because the coroner is interested in certain kinds of causal laws but not in others. So here, in sketching this causal theorem of meaning, I am interested only in certain kinds of law and am not necessarily saying anything about others.

Now for the sense of 'context.' Most generally it is a name for a whole cluster of events that recur together—including the required conditions as well as whatever we may pick out as cause or effect. But the modes of causal recurrence on which meaning depends are peculiar through that delegated efficacy I have been talking about. In these contexts one item—typically a word—takes over the duties of parts which can then be omitted from the recurrence. There is thus an abridgement of the context only shown in the behavior of living things, and most extensively and drastically shown by man. When this abridgement happens, what the sign or word—the item with these delegated powers—means is the missing parts of the context.

If we ask how this abridgement happens, how a sign comes to stand for an absent cause and conditions, we come up against the limits of knowledge at once. No one knows. Physiological speculation has made very little progress towards explaining *that,* though enormous strides have been made this century in analysing the complexities of the conditioned reflex. The shift, the handing over, is left still as inexplicable. Probably this 'learning problem' goes down as deep as the nature of life itself. We can suppose, if we like, that some sorts of residual effects are left behind from former occurrences which later co-operate with the sign in determining the response. To do so is to use a metaphor drawn from the gross behavior, taken macroscopically, of systems that are not living—printed things, gramaphone records and such. We can be fairly ingenious with these metaphors, invent neural archives storing up impressions, or neural telephone exchanges with fantastic properties. But how the archives get consulted or how in the telephone system A gets on to the B it needs, instead of to the whole alphabet at once in a jumble, remain utterly mysterious matters.

Fortunately linguistics and the theory of meaning need not wait until this is remedied. They can probably go much further than we have yet imagined without any answer to this question. It is enough for our purposes to say that what a word means is the missing parts of the contexts from which it draws its delegated efficacy.

At this point I must remind you of what I said a few minutes ago about the primordial generality and abstractness of meaning and about how, when we mean the simplest-seeming concrete object, its concreteness comes to it from the way in which we are bringing it simultaneously into a number of sorts. The sorts grow together in it to form that meaning. Theory here, as so often, can merely exploit the etymological hint given in the word 'concrete.'

If we forget this and suppose that we start with discrete impressions of particulars ('fixities and definites' as Coleridge called them) and then build these up into congeries, the theorem I am recommending collapses at once into contradictions and absurdities. That was the fault of the old Hartleian Associationism I complained of last time. It did not go back far enough, it took particular impressions as its initial terms. But the initial terms for this theorem are not impressions; they are sortings, recognitions, laws of response, recurrences of like behaviors.

A particular impression is already a product of concrescence. Behind, or in it, there has been a coming together of *sortings.* When we take a number of particular impressions—of a number of different white things, say—and abstract from them an idea of whiteness, we are explicitly reversing a process which has already been implicitly at work in our perception of them as all white. Our risk is to confuse the abstractness we thus arrive at intellectually with the primordial abstractness out of which these impressions have already grown—before ever any conscious explicit reflection took place.

Things, in brief, are instances of laws. As Bradley said, association marries only universals, and out of these laws, these recurrent likenessess of behavior, in our minds and in the world—not out of revived duplicates of individual past impressions—the fabric of our meanings, which is the world, is composed.

So much for the theorem. What are the problems we must use it to construct?

Since the whole business of Rhetoric comes down to comparisons between the meanings of words, the first problem, I think, should be this. How, if the meaning of a word is, in this sense, the missing parts of its contexts, how then should we compare the meanings of two words? There is opportunity for a grand misunderstanding here. It is not proposed that we should try to make these comparisons by a process of discovering, detailing, and then comparing these missing parts. We could not do it and, if we could, it would be waste of time. The theorem does not pretend to give us quite new ways of distinguishing between meanings. It only bars out certain practices and assumptions which are common and misleading.

The office of the theorem is much more negative than positive; but is not the less useful for that. It will not perhaps tell us how to do much that we cannot do without it already; but it will prevent us from doing stupid things which we are fond of doing. So a theory of evolution at least makes it more difficult to believe that The Dog Fritz in the German account really did the children's sums for them, or reminded them to salute their 'dear German flag.' So even an elementary physics puts in its place among superstitions Mr. Gladstone's firm belief that snow has "a peculiar power of penetrating leather," a power not possessed by water! For lack of that knowledge of physics in Mr. Gladstone, Lord Rayleigh found it quite impossible to persuade him it was not so.

The context theorem of meaning would prevent our making hundreds of baseless and disabling assumptions that we commonly make about meanings, over-simplifications that create false problems interfering with closer comparisons—and that is its main service. In this, it belongs with a number of other theorems which may be called policeman doctrines—because they are designed on the model of an ideal police-force, not to make any of us do anything but to prevent other people from interfering unduly with our lawful activities. The organization of impulses doctrine of values for literary criticism is in the same position. These policeman doctrines keep assumptions that are out of place from frustrating and misleading sagacity. I shall be illustrating the restraint of these bullying assumptions in most parts of Rhetoric later. We had one simple instance with Lord Kames' peacock's feather, last time, where what was discouraged was a naïve view of imagery as the stuff of meaning.

We shall have others in discussing the claims of usage next week. Preëminently what the theorem would discourage, is our habit of behaving as though, if a passage means one thing it cannot at the same time mean another and an incompatible thing. Freud taught us that a dream may mean a dozen different things; he has persuaded us that some symbols are, as he says, 'over-determined' and mean many different selections from among their causes. This theorem goes further, and regards all discourse—outside the technicalities of science—as over-determined, as having multiplicity of meaning. It can illustrate this view from almost any of the great controversies. And it offers us—by restraining the One and Only One True Meaning Superstition—a better hope, I believe, of profiting from the controversies. A controversy is normally an exploitation of a systematic set of misunderstandings for war-like purposes. This theorem suggests that the swords of dispute might be turned into plough shares; and a way found by which we may (to revert to Hobbes) "make use to our benefit of effects formerly seen—for the commodity of human life."

The next problem concerns what happens when we put words together in sentences. At least that is a common way of stating it. The theorem recommends us rather to turn the problem round and ask what happens when, out of the integral utterance which is the sentence, we try to isolate the discrete meanings of the words of which it is composed. That problem, the analysis of sentences and the interaction between words in the sentence, is my subject for next week. It is there that the most deep-rooted, systematic and persistent misunderstandings arise.

A third set of problems concerns rivalries between different types of context which supply the meaning for a single utterance. These start with the plain equivoque—as when the word 'reason' may mean either a cause or an argument. I am simplifying this here to make it a type of a really simple ambiguity. Actually in most occurrences it would be much more complex and not so easily cleared up, as the shifting meanings of 'cause' and 'argument' themselves show. The context theorem of meaning will make us expect ambiguity to the widest extent and of the subtlest kinds nearly everywhere, and of course we find it. But where the old Rhetoric treated ambiguity as a fault in language, and hoped to confine or eliminate it, the new Rhetoric sees it as an inevitable consequence of the powers of language and as the indispensable means of most of our most important utterances—especially in Poetry and Religion. And that too I shall be illustrating later.

Of course ambiguities are a nuisance in exposition as, in spite of my efforts, you have certainly been feeling. But neutral exposition is a very special limited use of language, comparatively a late development to which we have not (outside some parts of the sciences) yet adapted it. This brings me to those large-scale rivalries between contexts which shift the very aims of discourse. When the passions—the combative passion and others—intervene, either in the formation of an utterance or in its interpretation, we have examples of context action just as much as when the word 'paper,' say, takes its meaning from its contexts. The extra meaning that comes in when a sentence, in addition to making a statement, is meant to be insulting, or flattering, or is interpreted so—we may call it emotive meaning—is not so different from plain statement as we are apt to suppose. As the word means the missing part of its contexts and is a substitute for them, so the insulting intention may be the substitute for a kick,—the missing part of its context. The same general theorem covers all the modes of meaning.

I began tonight by speaking of the poaching of the other language functions on the preserve of pure exposition. Pure exposition has its guardian passions no doubt—though I do not know their names. But they are not often as strong as the poachers and are easily beguiled by them. It has been so necessary to us, especially since the physical basis of civilization became technical, to care at least sometimes for the truth only and keep the poachers sometimes out, that we have exaggerated enormously the extent of pure exposition. It is a relatively rare occurrence outside the routine of train services and the tamer, more settled parts of the sciences. We have exaggerated our success for strategic reasons—some of them good, because encouraging, if we do not too much hoodwink ourselves. I have aimed at points tonight to be merely expository in my remarks, but I know better than to suppose I have succeeded. We shall find, preëminently in the subject of rhetoric, that interpretations and opinions about interpretations that are not primarily steps of partisan policy are excessively hard to arrive at. And thereby we rediscover that the world—so far from being a solid matter of fact—is rather a fabric of conventions, which for obscure reasons it has suited us in the past to manufacture and support. And that sometimes is a dismaying re-discovery which seems to unsettle our foundations.

Anyone who publishes a book with the word 'Meaning' in its title becomes the recipient of a fan-mail of peculiar character. In comes a dribble of letters ever after from people who are quite unmistakably lunatics. Indeed, it seems that the subject is a dangerous one. Intense preoccupation with the sources of our meanings is disturbing, increasing our sense that our beliefs are a veil and an artificial veil between ourselves and something that otherwise than through a veil we cannot know. Something of the same sort can happen in travel. Anyone who has visited a sufficiently strange country and come into close contact with its life knows how unsettling and disorientating is the recognition of the place of conventions in our mental world. And the effect is deeper as the contact is closer. Few men have come into closer and more active contact with an alien world than Colonel Lawrence and when, at the end of the Introduction to *The Seven Pillars of Wisdom,* he writes of the selves which converse in the void, he says, "Then madness was very near, as I believe it would be near the man who could see things through the veils at once of two customs, two educations, two environments." He is writing of fatigue, and the page reeks of the extremities of war and of the desert—the desert which pushes man down to the limits of his endurance. The meditation of a single code of meanings is not so devastating, and I have seen already enough of Bryn Mawr to realize that it bears no least resemblance to a desert. We may then continue undeterred by the implications of my fan-mail.

The subject of the next lecture will be the Doctrine of Usage and the Interinanimation of Words and, as the rest of the course will be literary rather than philosophical and will attempt rather to practise than to theorize, I may close here with some lines from George Chapman about the theoretic principles of Rhetoric, the conduct of interpretation and "impartial contention" and their proper relation to action. It comes in a poem entitled

TO YOUNG IMAGINARIES IN KNOWLEDGE.

This rather were the way, if thou wouldst be
A true proficient in philosophy
Dissemble what thou studiest until
By thy impartial contention
Thou provest thee fit to do as to profess
And if thou still profess it not, what less
Is thy philosophy if in thy deeds
Rather than signs and shadows, it proceeds.

I must apologize if in this Lecture I have departed from the spirit of his recommendation.

• • •

LECTURE V

METAPHOR

It was Aristotle, no lesser man, who said, in *The Poetics,* "The greatest thing by far is to have a command of metaphor." But he went on to say, "This alone cannot be imparted to another: it is the mark of genius, for to make good metaphors implies an eye for resemblances." I do not know how much influence this remark has had: or whether it is at all responsible for our feeling that what it says is common-sense. But question it for a moment and we can discover in it, if we will to be malicious, here at the very beginning of the subject, the evil presence of three of the assumptions which have ever since prevented the study of this 'greatest thing by far' from taking the place it deserves among our studies and from advancing, as theory and practice, in the ways open to it.

One assumption is that 'an eye for resemblances' is a gift that some men have but others have not. But we all live, and speak, only through our eye for resemblances. Without it we should perish early. Though some may have better eyes than others, the differences between them are in degree only and may be remedied, certainly in some measure, as other differences are, by the right kinds of teaching and study. The second assumption denies this and holds that, though everything else may be taught, "This alone cannot be imparted to another." I cannot guess how seriously Aristotle meant this or what other subjects of teaching he had in mind as he spoke. But, if we consider how we all of us attain what limited measure of a command of metaphor we possess, we shall see that no such contrast is valid. As individuals we gain our command of metaphor just as we learn whatever else makes us distinctively human. It is all imparted to us from others, with and through the language we learn, language which is utterly unable to aid us except through the command of metaphor which it gives. And that brings up the third and worst assumption—that metaphor is something special and exceptional in the use of language, a deviation from its normal mode of working, instead of the omnipresent principle of all its free action.

Throughout the history of Rhetoric, metaphor has been treated as a sort of happy extra trick with words, an opportunity to exploit the accidents of their versatility, something in place occasionally but requiring unusual skill and caution. In brief, a grace or ornament or *added* power of language, not its constitutive form. Sometimes, it is true, a writer will venture on speculations that go deeper. I have just been echoing Shelley's observation that "Language is vitally metaphorical; that is, it marks the before unapprehended relations of things and perpetuates their apprehension, until words, which represent them, become, through time, signs for portions or classes of thought instead of pictures of integral thoughts: and then, if no new poets should arise to create afresh the associations which have been thus disorganised, language will be dead to all the nobler purposes of human intercourse." But that is an exceptional utterance and its implications have not yet been taken account of by rhetoricians. Nor have philosophers, as a body, done much better, though historians of language have long taught that we can find no word or description for any of the intellectual operations which, if its history is known, is not seen to have been taken, by metaphor, from a description of some physical happening. Only Jeremy Bentham, as successor to Bacon and Hobbes, insisted—with his technique of archetypation and phraseoplerosis—upon one inference that might be drawn; namely, that the mind and all its doings are fictions. He left it to Coleridge, F. H. Bradley and Vaihinger to point to the further inference; namely, that matter and its adventures, and all the derivative objects of contemplation, are fictions too, of varied rank because of varied service.

I have glanced for a moment at these deep waters into which a serious study of metaphor may plunge us, because possibly fear of them may be one cause why the study has so often not been enterprising and why Rhetoric traditionally has limited its inquiry to relatively superficial problems. But we shall not advance in even these surface problems unless we are ready to explore, as best we can, the depths of verbal interaction which give rise to them.

That metaphor is the omnipresent principle of language can be shown by mere observation. We cannot get through three sentences of ordinary fluid discourse without it, as you will be noticing throughout this lecture. Even in the rigid language of the settled sciences we do not eliminate or prevent it without great difficulty. In the semi-technicalised subjects, in aesthetics, politics, sociology, ethics, psychology, theory of language and so on, our constant chief difficulty is to discover how we are using it and how our supposedly fixed words are shifting their senses. In philosophy, above all, we can take no step safely without an unrelaxing awareness of the metaphors we, and our audience, may be employing; and though we may pretend to eschew them, we can attempt to do so only by detecting them. And this is the more true, the more severe and abstract the philosophy is. As it grows more abstract we think increasingly by means of metaphors that we profess *not* to be relying on. The metaphors we are avoiding steer our thought as much as those we accept. So it must be with any utterance for which it is less easy to know what we are saying than what we are not saying. And in philosophy, of which this is almost a definition, I would hold with Bradley that our pretence to do without metaphor is never more than a bluff waiting to be called. But if that is a truth, it is easier to utter than to accept with its consequences or to remember.

The view that metaphor is omnipresent in speech can be recommended theoretically. If you recall what I tried to say in my Second Lecture about the context theorem of meaning; about meaning as the delegated efficacy of signs by which they bring together into new unities the abstracts, or aspects, which are the missing parts of their various contexts, you will recollect some insistence that a word is normally a substitute for (or means) not one discrete past impression but a combination of general aspects. Now that is itself a summary account of the principle of metaphor. In the simplest formulation, when we use a metaphor we have two thoughts of different things active together and supported by a single word, or phrase, whose meaning is a resultant of their interaction.

"As to metaphorical expression," said Dr. Johnson, "that is a great excellence in style, when it is used with propriety, for it gives you two ideas for one." He is keeping, you see, to the limited traditional view of metaphor. As to the excellence of a style that gives you two ideas for one, that depends on what the two ideas do to one another, or conjointly do for us. We find, of course, when we look closer that there is an immense variety in these modes of interaction between co-present thoughts, as I will call them, or, in terms of the context theorem, between different missing parts or aspects of the different contexts of a word's meaning. In practice, we distinguish with marvellous skill between these modes of interaction, though our skill varies. The Elizabethans, for example, were far more widely skilled in the use of metaphor—both in utterance and in interpretation—than we are. A fact which made Shakespeare possible. The 18th Century narrowed its skill down, defensively, to certain modes only. The early 19th Century revolted against this and specialized in other modes. The later 19th Century and my generation have been recovering from these two specializations. That, I suggest, is a way of reformulating the Classic-Romantic antithesis which it would be interesting to try out.

But it could not be tried out without a better developed theory of metaphor than is yet available. The traditional theory noticed only a few of the modes of metaphor; and limited its application of the term *metaphor* to a few of them only. And thereby it made metaphor seem to be a verbal matter, a shifting and displacement of words, whereas fundamentally it is a borrowing between and intercourse of *thoughts,* a transaction between contexts. *Thought* is metaphoric, and proceeds by comparison, and the metaphors of language derive therefrom. To improve the theory of metaphor we must remember this. And the method is to take more note of the skill in thought which we possess and are intermittently aware of already. We must translate more of our skill into discussable science. Reflect better upon what we do already so cleverly. Raise our implicit recognitions into explicit distinctions.

As we do so we find that all the questions that matter in literary history and criticism take on a new interest and a wider relevance to human needs. In asking how language works we ask about how thought and feeling and all the other modes of the mind's activity proceed, about how we are to learn to live and how that "greatest thing of all," a command of metaphor—which is great only because it is a command of life—may best, in spite of Aristotle, "be imparted to another." But to profit we must remember, with Hobbes, that "the scope of all speculation is the performance of some action or thing to be done" and, with Kant, that—"We can by no means require of the pure practical reason to be subordinated to the speculative, and thus to reverse the order, since every interest is at last practical, and even that of the speculative reason is but conditional, and is complete only in its practical use." Our theory, as it has its roots in practice, must also have its fruit in improved skill. "I am the child," says the Sufi mystic, "whose father is his son, and the wine whose vine is its jar," summing up so the whole process of that meditation which does not forget what it is really about.

This much has been an introduction or preparation to put the theory of metaphor in a more important place than it has enjoyed in traditional Rhetoric. It is time to come down from these high speculations to consider some simple steps in analysis which may make the translation of our skill with metaphor into explicit science easier. A first step is to introduce two technical terms to assist us in distinguishing from one another what

Dr. Johnson called the two ideas that any metaphor, at its simplest, gives us. Let me call them the tenor and the vehicle. One of the oddest of the many odd things about the whole topic is that we have no agreed distinguishing terms for these two halves of a metaphor—in spite of the immense convenience, almost the necessity, of such terms if we are to make any analyses without confusion. For the whole task is to compare the different relations which, in different cases, these two members of a metaphor hold to one another, and we are confused at the start if we do not know which of the two we are talking about. At present we have only some clumsy descriptive phrases with which to separate them. 'The original idea' and 'the borrowed one'; 'what is really being said or thought of' and 'what it is compared to'; 'the underlying idea' and 'the imagined nature'; 'the principal subject' and 'what it resembles' or, still more confusing, simply 'the meaning' and 'the metaphor' or 'the idea' and 'its image.'

How confusing these must be is easily seen, and experience with the analysis of metaphors fully confirms the worst expectations. We need the word 'metaphor' for the whole double unit, and to use it sometimes for one of the two components in separation from the other is as injudicious as that other trick by which we use 'the meaning' here sometimes for the work that the whole double unit does and sometimes for the other component—the tenor, as I am calling it—the underlying idea or principal subject which the vehicle or figure means. It is not surprising that the detailed analysis of metaphors, if we attempt it with such slippery terms as these, sometimes feels like extracting cube-roots in the head. Or, to make a more exact comparison, what would the most elementary arithmetic feel like, if we used the word *twelve* (12) sometimes for the number one (1), sometimes for the number two (2) and sometimes for the number twenty-one (21) as well, and had somehow to remember, or see, unassisted by our notation, which uses we were making of it at different places in our calculations? All these words, *meaning, expression, metaphor, comparison, subject, figure, image,* behave so, and when we recognize this we need look no further for a part, at least, of the explanation of the backward state of the study. Why rhetoricians have not long ago remedied this defect of language for their purpose, would perhaps be a profitable matter for reflection. I do not know a satisfactory answer. As the best teacher I ever knew, G. E. Moore, once remarked, "Why we should use the same form of verbal expression to convey such different meanings is more than I can say. It seems to me very curious that language should have grown up as if it were expressly designed to mislead philosophers; and I do not know why it should have."

The words 'figure' and 'image' are especially and additionally misleading here. They both sometimes stand for the whole double unit and sometimes for one member of it, the vehicle, as opposed to the other. But in addition they bring in a confusion with the sense in which an image is a copy or revival of a sense-perception of some sort, and so have made rhetoricians think that a figure of speech, an image, or imaginative comparison, must have something to do with the presence of images, in this other sense, in the mind's eye or the mind's ear. But, of course, it need not. No images of this sort need come in at any point. We had one instance of the vicious influence of this red-herring in my first lecture—Lord Kames' antic with the mental picture he supposed we must form of Shakespeare's peacock-feather. Whole schools of rhetoric and criticism have gone astray after it. Lessing's discussion of the relations of the arts, for example, is grievously spoilt by it. We cannot too firmly recognize that how a figure of speech works has nothing necessarily to do with how any images, as copies or duplicates of sense perceptions, may, for reader or writer, be backing up his words. In special cases for certain readers they may come in—then is a long chapter of individual psychology which is relevant here. But the words can do almost anything without them, and we must put no assumption about their necessary presence into our general theory.

I can illustrate both the convenience of such technical terms as *tenor* and *vehicle* and the evil influence of the imagery assumption, with another citation from Lord Kames, from Chapter 20, paragraph 6, of his *Elements of Criticism.* You will see from the very difficulty of making out just what he is saying, how much we need rigid technicalities here. His point is, I think, evidently mistaken; but before we can be satisfied that it is mistaken, we have to be certain what it is; and what I want first to direct your attention upon is the clumsy and distracting language in which he has to state it. He is preparing to set up a rule to be observed by writers in 'constructing a metaphor.' He says, "In the fourth place, the comparison . . . being in a metaphor sunk by imagining the principal subject to be that very thing which it only resembles; an opportunity is furnished to describe it (i.e., the principal subject) in terms taken strictly or literally with respect to its imagined nature."

To use my proposed terms—we can describe or qualify the tenor by describing the vehicle. He goes on, "This suggests another rule: That in constructing a metaphor, the writer ought to make use of such words only as are applicable literally to the imagined nature of his subject." That is, he must not use any further metaphor in describing the vehicle. "Figurative words," he says, "ought carefully to be avoided; for such complicated figures, instead of setting the principal subject in a strong light, involve it in a cloud; and it is well if the reader, without rejecting by the lump, endeavour patiently to gather the plain meaning, regardless of the figures."

Let me invite you to consider what is being done here very carefully, for it illustrates, I believe, most of the things which have made the traditional studies of metaphor not very profitable. And notice first how it shows the 18th Century assumptions that figures are a mere embellishment or added beauty and that the plain meaning, the tenor, is what alone really matters and is something that, 'regardless of the figures,' might be gathered by the patient reader.

A modern theory would object, first, that in many of the most important uses of metaphor, the copresence of the vehicle and tenor results in a meaning (to be clearly distinguished from the tenor) which is not attainable without their interaction. That the vehicle is not normally a mere embellishment of a tenor which is otherwise unchanged by it but that vehicle and tenor in co-operation give a meaning of more varied powers than can be ascribed to either. And a modern theory would go on to point out that with different metaphors the relative importance of the contributions of vehicle and tenor to this resultant meaning varies immensely. At one extreme the vehicle may become almost a mere decoration or coloring of the tenor, at the other extreme, the tenor may become almost a mere excuse for the introduction of the vehicle, and so no longer be 'the principal subject.' And the degree to which the tenor is imagined "to be that very thing which it only resembles" also varies immensely.

These are differences I return to next week. Let us study Lord Kames a little longer first: How about this suggested rule that we should carefully avoid mounting metaphor upon metaphor? What would be the effect of taking it seriously? It would, if we accepted and observed it, make havoc of most writing and speech. It is disregarding—under cover of the convenient excuse that they are dead—the most regular sustaining metaphors of all speech. It would make, I think, Shakespeare the faultiest writer who ever held a pen; and it turns an obstinately blind eye upon one of the most obvious features of current practice in every minute of our speech. Look, for example, at Lord Kames' own sentence. "Such complicated figures, instead of setting the principal subject in a strong light, involve it in a cloud." What about that 'strong' light? The light is a vehicle and is described—without anyone experiencing the least difficulty—by a secondary metaphor, a figurative word. But you may say, "No! *Strong* is no longer a figurative word as applied to light. It is as literally descriptive of light as it is of a man or a horse. It carries not two ideas but one only. It has become 'adequated,' or is dead, and is no longer a metaphor." But however stone dead such metaphors seem, we can easily wake them up, and, if Kames were right, to wake them up would be to risk involving the tenor in a cloud, and nothing of the sort happens. This favourite old distinction between dead and living metaphors (itself a two-fold metaphor) is, indeed, a device which is very often a hindrance to the play of sagacity and discernment throughout the subject. For serious purposes it needs a drastic re-examination.

We are in fact immeasurably more adroit in handling complicated metaphors than Kames will allow us to be. He gives an example of a breach of his rule which is worth examining if only to show how easily a theory can paralyse normal aptitude in such things. He takes these two lines

> A stubborn and unconquerable flame
> Creeps in his veins and drinks the streams of life.

"Let us analyse this expression," he says. "That a fever may be imagined a flame, I admit; though more than one step is necessary to come at the resemblance." I, for my part, would have supposed, on the contrary, that we could hardly find a simpler transference, since both a fever and a flame are instances of a rise in temperature! But he goes on to detail these steps. "A fever by heating the body, resembles fire; and it is no stretch to imagine a fever to be a fire. Again, by a figure of speech, flame may be put for fire, because they are commonly conjoined; and therefore a fever may be termed a flame. But now, admitting a fever to be a flame, its effects ought to be explained in words that agree literally to a flame. This rule is not observed here; for a flame drinks figuratively only, not properly."

Well and good! But who, for all that, has any difficulty in understanding the lines? The interactions of tenor and vehicle are not in the least hampered by the secondary vehicle.

I have taken this instance of vain pedantry chiefly to accustom you to my use of these technical terms, but partly too to support the contention that the best part of the traditional discussion of metaphor is hardly more than a set of cautionary hints to overenthusiastic schoolboys, hints masquerading as fundamental theory of language. Lord Kames is not exceptionally limited in his treatment or abnormally obtuse. You will find similar things in Johnson when he discusses Cowley and Donne for example, in Monboddoe, and Harris and Withers, and Campbell, in all the chief 18th Century Rhetoricians.

Not until Coleridge do we get any adequate setting of these chief problems of language. But Coleridge's thought has not even yet come into its own. And, after Coleridge, in spite of the possibilities which he opened, there was a regrettable slackening of interest in the questions. The 18th Century was mistaken in the way it put them and in the technique it attempted to use, but it at least knew that they were important questions and that there is unlimited work to be done upon them. And so Lord Kames' *Elements of Criticism,* though I may seem to have been making fun of it in places, and though it is so full of similar things as to be most absorbing reading, is still a very valuable and instructive book offering a model not only of misconceptions to be avoided but of problems to be taken up, reframed and carried forward. Turning his pages you will again and again find points raised, which, if his treatment of them is unsatisfactory, are none the less points that no serious study of language should neglect. One such will serve me as a peg for a pair of warnings or morals of which any ambitious attempt to analyse metaphors is constantly in need.

Kames quotes from *Othello* the single line

> Steep'd me in poverty to the very lips

and comments, "The resemblance is too faint to be agreeable— Poverty must here be conceived to be a fluid which it resembles not in any manner." Let us look at Othello's whole speech. We shall find that it is not an easy matter to explain or justify that 'steep'd.' It comes, you will recall, when

Othello first openly charges Desdemona with unfaithfulness,

Had it pleas'd heaven
To try me with affliction, had he rain'd
All kinds of sores, and shames, on my bare head,
Steep'd me in poverty to the very lips,
Given to captivity me and my utmost hopes,
I should have found in some part of my soul
A drop of patience; but alas! to make me
The fixed figure for the time of scorn
To point his slow and moving finger at;
Yet could I bear that too; well, very well.
But there, where I have garner'd up my heart,
Where either I must live or bear no life,
The fountain from the which my current runs,
Or else dries up; to be discarded thence!
Or keep it as a cistern for foul toads
To knot and gender in!

What are we to say of that word *steep,* how answer Kames? He is indeed too mild, in saying "the resemblance is too faint to be agreeable." It's not a case of a lack of resemblance but of too much diversity, too much sheer oppositeness. For Poverty, the tenor, is a state of deprivation, of desiccation; but the vehicle—the sea or vat in which Othello is to be steeped—gives an instance of superfluity. In poverty all is outgoing, without income; were we "steeped to the very lips" it would be the incomings that we would have to fight against.* You will have noticed that the whole speech returns again and again to these liquid images: "had they rained," "a drop of patience," "The fountain from the which my current runs, Or else dries up." None of these helps *steep* out, and one of them "a drop of patience" makes the confused, disordered effect of *steep* seem much worse. I do not myself find any defence of the word except this, which seems indeed quite sufficient—as dramatic necessities commonly are—that Othello is himself horribly disordered, that the utterance is part of "the storm of horrour and outrage" with which he is assailing Desdemona and that a momentarily deranged mind speaks so and *is* obsessed with images regardless of their fittingness. Othello, we might say, is drowning in this storm, (Cf. Act II, i, 212–21) and knows it.

The morals I would point with this instance are: First, that not to see how a word *can* work is never by itself sufficient proof that it will not work. Second, conversely, that to see how it ought to work will not prove that it does. Any detailed examination of metaphor brings us into such risk of pedantry and self-persuasion, that these morals seem worth stress. Yet a critical examination of metaphor, with these morals in mind, is just now what literary criticism chiefly needs.

To come back to Kames, his objection that "the resemblance is too faint to be agreeable" (notice the amusing assumption that a writer must of course always aim to be agreeable!)—assumed that tenor and vehicle must be linked by their resemblance and that their interaction comes about through their resemblance one to another. And yet Kames himself elsewhere takes some pride, and justifiably, in pointing out a type of figure which does not depend upon resemblance but upon other relations between tenor and vehicle. He says that it has been overlooked by former writers, and that it must be distinguished from other figures as depending on a different principle.

"*Giddy brink, jovial wine, daring wound* are examples of this figure. Here are adjectives that cannot be made to signify any quality of the substantives to which they are joined: a *brink,* for example, cannot be termed *giddy* in a sense, either proper or figurative, that can signify any of its qualities or attributes. When we examine attentively the expression, we discover that a *brink* is termed *giddy* from producing that effect in those who stand on it . . . How," he asks, "are we to ac-

* In the partly parallel 'And steep my senses in forgetfulness' (*Henry IV,* P. II, III, i) Lethe, by complicating the metaphor, removes the difficulty.

count for this figure, which we see lies in the thought (I am not sure what *lies* means here. I think he means 'has its ground or explanation in the thought' not 'utters falsehood.') and to what principle shall we refer it? Have the poets a privilege to alter the nature of things, and at pleasure to bestow attributes upon a subject to which they do not belong?" Most moderns would say "Of course, they have!" But Kames does not take that way out. He appeals instead to a principle of contiguous association. "We have had often occasion to inculcate, that the mind passeth easily and sweetly along a train of connected objects, and, when the objects are intimately connected, that it is disposed to carry along the good or bad properties of one to another, especially when it is in any degree inflamed with these properties." He then lists eight varieties of these contiguous inflammations—without, I think, at all clearly realizing what an immense extension of the theory of possibilities of metaphoric interaction he has made with this new principle. Once we begin 'to examine attentively' interactions which do not work through *resemblances* between tenor and vehicle, but depend upon other relations between them including *disparities,* some of our most prevalent, over-simple, ruling assumptions about metaphors as comparisons are soon exposed.

But let us take one more glance at this *giddy brink* first. Is Kames right in saying that a *brink* cannot be termed *giddy* in a sense that can signify any of its qualities or attributes? Is he right in turning *giddy* into *giddy-making*—"a brink is termed giddy from producing that effect in those who stand on it"? Is it not the case that at the moment of giddiness the brink itself is perceived as swimming? As the man totters in vertigo, the world spins too and the brink becomes not merely giddy-making but actually vertiginous, seems itself to stagger with a dizziness and to whirl with a bewildering rapidity. The eyes nystagmically rolling give away their motion to the world—including the brink. Thus the brink as perceived, which is the brink that the poet is speaking of, actually itself acquires a giddiness. If so, we may doubt for a moment whether there is a metaphor here at all—until we notice how this whirling that infects the world as we grow giddy comes to it by a process which is itself radically metaphoric. Our eyes twitch, but it is the world which seems to spin. So it is with a large part, perhaps, in the final account, with *all* our perceptions. Our world is a projected world, shot through with characters lent to it from our own life. "We receive but what we give." The processes of metaphor in language, the exchanges between the meanings of words which we study in explicit verbal metaphors, are superimposed upon a perceived world which is itself a product of earlier or unwitting metaphor, and we shall not deal with them justly if we forget that this is so. That is why, if we are to take the theory of metaphor further than the 18th Century took it, we must have some general theorem of meaning. And since it was Coleridge who saw most deeply and clearly into this necessity, and, with his theory of the imagination, has done most to supply it, I may fittingly close this Lecture with a passage from Appendix C of *The Statesman's Manual,* in which Coleridge is stating that theory symbolically.

A symbol, for him, is a translucent instance, which "while it enunciates the whole, abides itself as a living part of that unity of which it is the representative." So here he takes the vegetable kingdom, or any plant, as an object of meditation through and in which to see the universal mode of imagination—of those metaphoric exchanges by which the individual life and its world grow together. If we can follow the meditation we are led, I believe, to Coleridge's conception of imaginative growth more easily and safely than by any other road. For, as the plant here is a symbol, in his sense, of all growth, so the passage too is itself a symbol, a translucent instance, of imagination.

He has been speaking of the book of Nature that "has been the music of gentle and pious minds in all ages, it is the poetry of all human nature, to read it likewise in a figurative sense, and to find therein correspondences and symbols of the spiritual world.

"I have at this moment before me, in the flowery meadow, on which my eye is now reposing, one of its most soothing chapters, in which there is no lamenting word, no one character of guilt or anguish. For never can I look and meditate on the vegetable creation, without a feeling similar to that with which we gaze at a beautiful infant that has fed itself asleep at its mother's bosom, and smiles in its strange dream of obscure yet happy sensations. The same tender and genial pleasure takes possession of me, and this pleasure is checked and drawn inward by the like aching melancholy, by the same whispered remonstrance, and made restless by a similar impulse of aspiration. It seems as if the soul said to herself: From this state hast *thou* fallen! Such shouldst thou still become, thy Self all permeable to a holier power! thy self at once hidden and glorified by its own transparency, as the accidental and dividuous in this quiet and harmonious object is subjected to the life and light of nature which shines in it, even as the transmitted power, love and wisdom, of God over all, fills and shines through nature! But what the plant is, by an act not its own and unconsciously—that must thou make thyself to become! must by prayer and by a watchful and unresisting spirit, join at least with the preventive and assisting grace to make thyself, in that light of conscience which inflameth not, and with that knowledge which puffeth not up!

"But further . . . I seem to myself to behold in the quiet objects on which I am gazing, more than an arbitrary illustration, more than a mere simile, the work of my own fancy. I feel an awe, as if there were before my eyes the same power as that of the reason—the same power in a lower dignity, and therefore a symbol established in the truth of things. I feel it alike, whether I contemplate a single tree or flower, or meditate on vegetation throughout the world, as one of the great organs of the life of nature. Lo!—with the rising sun it commences its outward life and enters into open communion with all the elements at once assimilating them to itself and to each other. At the same moment it strikes its roots and unfolds its leaves, absorbs and respires, steams forth its cooling vapour and finer fragrance, and breathes a repairing spirit, at once the food and tone of the atmosphere, into the atmosphere that feeds *it*. Lo!—at the touch of light how it returns an air akin to light, and yet with the same pulse effectuates its own secret growth, still contracting to fix what expanding it had refined. Lo!—how upholding the ceaseless plastic motion of the parts in the profoundest rest of the whole, it becomes the visible *organismus* of the whole silent or elementary life of nature and therefore, in incorporating the one extreme becomes the symbol of the other; the natural symbol of that higher life of reason."

What Coleridge has here said of this "open communion" is true also of the word—in the free metaphoric discursive sentence. "Are not words," he had asked nineteen years before, "Are not words parts and germinations of the plant?"

INTRODUCTION TO WILLIAM G. HOFFMAN

The first half of the twentieth century saw a remarkable number of books and articles published offering advice to ordinary people on the subject of public speaking. The most famous of these was Dale Carnegie's *How to Win Friends and Influence People* (1936), which had sold five million copies by his death and is still available.

Carnegie was not alone in dispensing applied rhetorical theory. Among the dozens of other practical theorists empowering ordinary people to speak in public was William G. Hoffman. Hoffman was a professor of English and Public Speaking at Boston University, and the first chapter to his book, *Public Speaking for Business Men* (1931) is excerpted here. Hoffman and his book are offered here as typical examples of the many applied theories that were widely published at this time.

Like Vanderbilt, Bernays, Leslie, and others, Hoffman is an example of a popular, applied rhetorical theorist. He breaks no new theoretical ground. In fact, his ideas are a recovery of the ancient art of public speaking. But the strength of his ideas lies in his practical application of that tradition to the rhetorical requirements of his time.

Hoffman stresses the importance of the personal in rhetorical contacts, whether that be on the public speaking platform or in direct sales. Confidence in one's own abilities and establishing a strong personal presence with those one wishes to influence are stressed. In this sense, Hoffman recovers the classical idea of *ethos* and applies it to modern rhetorical practice. He also stresses the personal in terms of the classical idea of adaptation to an audience. One must adapt to what the audience wants to hear, talk about what interests the audience, and make the audience feel good about themselves, Hoffman argues. Notice his emphasis on a more conversational style to meet the changing demands of the business environment. In these emphases on the personal dimensions of rhetorical practice, Hoffman was the kind of rhetorical theorist who advised millions of people throughout the twentieth century.

WILLIAM G. HOFFMAN

PUBLIC SPEAKING FOR BUSINESS MEN

CHAPTER I

THE RIGHT POINT OF VIEW

Lord Chesterfield was disturbed because his nineteen-year-old son was shy and awkward. He sent him to France with a tutor and wrote him a good many letters of advice, which, like most advice, did not function very noticeably. One of his favorite themes was public speaking. In a letter dated August, 1741, he says:

> It is certain that, by study and application, every man can make himself a pretty good Orator; eloquence depending upon observation and care. Every man, if he pleases, may chuse good words instead of bad ones, may speak properly instead of improperly, may be clear and perspicuous in his recitals, instead of dark and muddy; he may have grace instead of awkwardness in his motions and gestures; and, in short, he may be a very agreeable, instead of a very disagreeable speaker, if he will take care and pains. And surely it is very well worth while to take a great deal of pains to excel other men in that particular article in which they excel beasts.

The words *orator* and *eloquence* are in some disrepute today. They connote the windbaggery of politics or the solemn fustian of anniversaries, but Chesterfield had in mind a sensible and modest kind of speaking. He was a man of humor and good taste.

Eloquence is still the test of a good speech. Webster, to be sure, defines it, in part, as "lofty, noble, or impassioned utterance." That sounds a bit too lofty for most of us, but he goes on to say that it is "complete fusion of thought or feeling with verbal expression." He closes the definition by describing eloquence as "discourse characterized by force, art, and persuasiveness." And that is the very thing that manuals of advertising, business-letter writing, salesmanship and public speaking try to teach.

However we look at it, public speaking is more and more of personal concern to the ambitious or successful business man. It is no longer merely the professional art of lawyers, preachers, teachers and entertainers. It is an art of amateurs who need a little professional understanding. The executive who cannot speak with authority and skill in a conference, before a group of associates or a board of directors, at a dinner or convention, is failing in a major responsibility. He is unable to get a satisfactory hearing for needed changes and policies or is missing opportunities for expanding the goodwill of his company and of advertising it in a dignified and effective way.

Leaders as Speakers.—There is another practical demand for trained speakers. Business is beginning a deliberate effort to get back from the "soulless corporation" attitude to something like the more social, intimate, man-to-man conditions of other days. The industrial engineer has succeeded the efficiency expert. "Humanizing" industry is no longer a vague sentimentality, but a real and important problem. Employment management and the promotion of cooperative associations and enterprises require men who can talk well to groups large or small. The rank and file of employees who possess initiative and exceptional ability are being encouraged to come forward with their helpful ideas.

The "cog in the machine" is urged to be somebody, to show and use his individual capability.

Leadership must first express itself in speech. One must know how to ask for things, how to explain things and how to speak persuasively enough to win the active support of others. Doing business is chiefly talking business. Resourcefulness and adaptability in speech may be regarded as essential to success in every occupation. The remarkable growth of interest in oral English and public speaking is evidence enough that men and women everywhere appreciate this fact. Many expect too much, however, from a few hours of study. Glibness, mere fluency, is of little value. Good speech is founded on good thinking, and the tree of knowledge is not a mushroom growth.

Business is a much more comprehensive matter than it used to be. Politicians wait upon it; peace conferences anxiously seek its advice; domestic and international affairs revolve about it. The business world, directly or indirectly, includes everybody in civilized countries. Business talks are more numerous than any other kind, and the ever increasing complexity of society will bring its members together more and more for counsel and inspiration. Not long ago it was thought that the printed page would make public speaking almost obsolete, but man is too social and emotional to be satisfied with the silent page alone. He will always need the personal presence and the living voices of leaders to guide and arouse him. Print, pictures, telephone and radio are added uses and pleasures but they cannot alter the fundamental importance of public speaking. The business man studies it as a necessity, not as a luxury. He would avoid it if he could but he recognizes the fact that more and more such evasion will handicap the intelligent conduct of his affairs.

Characteristics of the Business Talk.—The discussion of local and more immediate problems has given rise to a comparatively new type of public speaking. It is more informal, colloquial and conversational than most of the classic, or traditional, models. In fact, the content and form of the ordinary business address are so different from those of the older types that at first glance there seems to be little value in studying them. There are no new principles involved, however; there is only a readjustment such as we have in "business English." The art of composition and presentation is applied to another and a more homogeneous and restricted subject matter.

Public speaking today is less exhibitional and more truly communicative. It lacks the "grand manner" associated with well-known orators, but its greater simplicity may be just as eloquent. This same change in style is noticeable in fiction, drama, acting and other speech arts. Practicality and realism are the fashion in this day of wider education and industrial expansion. Speaking is apparently easier, a fact which has misled many into wrong conceptions of the basic nature of the art. Indeed, they make no art of it at all. Their speeches retain the diffuseness and lack of studied organization characteristic of conversation. Their language is not accurate and vivid, their voices lack force and distinction, their bearing on the platform is without authority and poise. Art that is long and sometimes laborious is needed to correct these defects.

Plato defined public speaking as the "art of persuading men." We speak for the same purpose today and need the same tools to accomplish the desired result. Thought, language, voice and action must coordinate for concentration, clearness, conciseness and completeness. Problems of selection, arrangement and emphasis, of enunciation, energy and resonance, are present in the most unpretentious talks. A great deal of thoughtful, intelligent practice is necessary to acquire a confident and ready skill in effectively solving them. The schools of Greece and Rome required the most rigorous course of study for the public speaker. Before the orator was allowed to go before the public he had to gain a sound fundamental knowledge of all the arts and sciences available and had to spend years in the study and practice of his own art. Cicero and Quintilian were philosophers and scholars, the most broadly educated men of their day, and the greatest orators. Their books on public speaking are still the basis of our modern writings on the subject, and much of the filler, too. The same kind of comprehensive training is perhaps not necessary in our time, but the best speakers must still be philosophers and students, cosmopolitan in their interests and accurate and detailed in the knowledge of their subjects and their presentations.

The Conversational Style.—Public speaking is commonly described today as heightened conversation. This is a good definition if the implications in both words are fully understood. A speech should be forthright and sensible, good-humored and enthusiastic—conversation at its best. The conversational idea reminds you that you are talking to a specific audience and with a definite purpose, in much the same way that you would engage in a spirited discussion with an individual. It emphasizes communicativeness, sincerity and directness. It condemns empty rhetoric, conventional and artificial language.

On Being Natural.—But remember that the exhortation to be conversational also has its limitations. It sounds like the futile advice, "Be natural." For most of us to be natural is to be in some measure awkward, slouchy, indistinct, dull, slow or monotonous. The natural thing is often so inferior that man has to cultivate it and make it artistic—useful and beautiful. In speech we see the whole struggle for civilization reflected. Compare the grunts of the savage with the highly complex language we speak, the vocabulary of the illiterate with that of the educated man, the meager words and ideas of the child with the equipment of the adult. To be natural is not enough for most men. They need cultivation before they are ready for public appearance. That easy, natural manner that characterizes the work of the best actors and public speakers, and which makes one think that anybody can do it, is simply the highest art—the art that conceals art—and is the fine product, as a rule, of years of study and experience.

Misconceptions.—The business man too often thinks it is only the showy, declamatory, elocutionary speaking that has art. This is usually bad art because it distracts, deflects attention from the purpose and the subject of the speech to the manner, and fails to attain the desired end. But it is almost as serious a mistake to be satisfied with the trite formula: Have something to say and say it. That sounds honest and easy and is responsible for much dull speaking. It is only the trained speaker who combines the critic sense with the creative faculty, and who knows whether he has something to say (of interest to his audience) and whether he is saying it (convincingly and persuasively).

The Definition Defined.—In addressing an audience the conversational element and attitude must be *heightened*. Heightened means intensified, elevated, exalted. On the platform the speaker is raised to a leadership that demands, for one thing, much greater knowledge of the subject. He should have also skill in deciding what to omit and what to stress, and understanding of the principles of attention, of unity and variety. In other words, the business man must realize first of all that public speaking has a technique just as definite and substantial as have salesmanship, advertising and letter writing. He must seek proficiency through conscious and properly directed effort. He will avoid the casual, slipshod, unprepared manner of ordinary conversation and give his speech the focus and energy of heightened conversation.

Acquiring Confidence.—Perhaps this topic should be considered first in every textbook of public speaking because fear so occupies the mind of the average beginner that he cannot pay attention to anything else. Well, you have just considered the first comforting idea about it. Public speaking is conversational. You think nothing of talking three or four minutes at a time in a little argument in the office or the shop. You may have just returned from a convention and some one asks you what Smith said in his speech about the big sales campaign his firm put over so conspicuously. The details are fresh in your mind and before you know it you are in the midst of a pretty long speech. A few others come into the office and listen. Several clerks from the next office stand at the door. Presently you have an audience of twenty-five, but you don't mind. You are not making a speech. They have asked you for some practical information and you are giving it. If they interrupt with questions, you will answer them and go right on. Indeed, the speeches in Congress are like that. Members rise from their chairs to ask questions or to call attention to some weakness in the argument of the member on the platform.

Now suppose the advertising club of your city wanted to hear about this campaign. They invite you to speak at a luncheon. Perhaps you are a member and may know several of those present. This crowd has the same attitude that your friends in the office had. These people expect nothing from you but a plain straightforward talk of plans, methods, results, and some idea of how the thing struck you personally. If, when you have finished your dessert, somebody at the other end of the table might call out, "Say, Jim, tell us about that sales campaign of the A.B.C. Company," you could just take that cue, begin, and talk for an hour without any signs of palsy. Instead, you are introduced and rise, as a matter of convenience and courtesy, so that everybody can see and hear you. You may be a trifle ill at ease. You are more conspicuous than you have ever been before. But you go ahead with a story that you are perfectly at home with. You are a bit awkward in speech and manner, but that will get you more good will than a glib and smart performance. Presently you notice that the faces before you are friendly, relaxed, uncritical. They do not think of you as a public speaker or as an exhibition. They have asked you to give them a few facts, quite informally, and you are giving them in a modest, colloquial and perhaps offhand way.

Self-consciousness is only a kind of vanity. This excessive preoccupation about oneself implies a lack of humor. Look out, not in. Talk to and with your audience, not at it. You may in a very real sense converse with it. It replies, even though it does not speak aloud. Its looks and attitudes bespeak approval, indifference or question. You anticipate queries, objections, difficulties. Your problems in pointing out to your listeners the possibilities of your subject absorb your attention and lead you to active, purposeful concentration and study. This is what the business-letter writer calls "the you attitude." "Keep your mind on the other man" is a slogan of salesmanship.

We may not altogether talk away the fear of the platform, but worse fears have been removed by the power of suggestion. That very human psychologist, William James, in "Talks to Teachers," has a passage that should be deeply engraved in the mind of any one who can not "think on his feet." Here it is:

> Stated technically, the law is this: *That strong feeling about one's self tends to arrest the free association of one's objective ideas and motor processes.* We get the extreme example of this in the mental disease called melancholia.
>
> A melancholic patient is filled through and through with intensely painful emotion about himself. He is threatened, he is guilty, he is doomed, he is annihilated, he is lost. His mind is fixed as if in a clamp on these feelings of his own situation, and in all the books on insanity you may read that the usual varied flow of his thoughts has ceased. His associative processes, to use the technical phrase, are inhibited; and his ideas stand stock-still, shut up to their one monotonous function of reiterating inwardly the fact of the man's desperate estate . . .
>
> Now from all this we can draw an extremely practical conclusion. If, namely, we wish our trains of ideation and volition to be copious and varied and effective, we must form the habit of freeing them from the inhibitive influence of reflection upon them, of egotistic preoccupation about their results. Such a habit, like other habits; can be formed. Prudence and duty and self-regard, emotions of ambition and emotions of anxiety, have, of course, a needful part to play in our lives. But confine them as far as possible to the

occasions when you are making your general resolutions and deciding on your plans of campaign, and keep them out of the details. When once a decision is reached and execution is the order of the day, dismiss absolutely all responsibility and care about the outcome. *Unclamp*, in a word, your intellectual and practical machinery, and let it run free; and the service it will do you will be twice as good. Who are the scholars who get "rattled" in the recitation-room? Those who think of the possibilities of failure and feel the great importance of the act. Who are those who do recite well? Often those who are most indifferent. *Their* ideas reel themselves out of their memory of their own accord. Why do we hear the complaint so often that social life in New England is either less rich and expressive or more fatiguing than it is in some other parts of the world? To what is the fact, if fact it be, due unless to the overactive conscience of the people, afraid of either saying something too trivial and obvious, or something insincere, or something unworthy of one's interlocutor, or something in some way or other not adequate to the occasion? How can conversation possibly steer itself through such a sea of responsibilities and inhibitions as this?

Relax.—One way to confidence, then, is through cultivating objective thought. Get ready calmly and relax. Do not attack your assignment grimly or desperately. The young speaker is often urged to summon his will to the task, to remember what others have done, etc. Reinforce your self-respect by all means, but do not dwell upon it overmuch. You may fail to attend properly to the business you have with the audience. How far would a singer or a ball player get if he spent most of his time worrying about the moment of stepping out before his public? Of course he thinks about it, but with a sense of proportion. He knows that his salvation is in preparation and study and practice, and when he is ready he is eager to go. He discounts his nervousness. He knows that what he has done he can do again, even though he does not do it quite so easily or quickly or skilfully as he hopes to do. Preparation is the mother of confidence. The prepared speaker knows what he is going to say and do.

The Advantage of Fear.—The man who lacks any fear of an audience often lacks imagination and sensitiveness. He may not appreciate his responsibility and may be easily satisfied with an indifferent performance. Many great speakers have confessed to nervousness, depression and fear of failure. They always had a wholesome respect for their audience, and this state of mind drove them to careful preparation for every occasion, great or small.

Diffidence.—There are comparatively few persons who are not diffident—afflicted with embarrassment before some person or group, even though they are at ease and freely communicative with others. The professor and the iceman may be dumb in each other's presence in spite of the fact that they are voluble enough elsewhere. The wisest or wittiest man may seem dull among men of different training or experience. He has little to say and is keenly aware of his self-consciousness and futility. There is simply no common ground of interest large enough to promote "shop talk" of comparison, disagreement, question and narration, whether the talk is of a common occupation or stimulated by common interest in religion, politics, baseball or fishing.

Diffidence is converted into confidence by an atmosphere of congeniality. Dr. Richard C. Cabot in "What Men Live By" speaks interestingly of this:

> You can "get the jump on" another's diffidence if you shoot into his soul a message of welcome, of encouragement, of faith in his power to do something better than he has yet done. You do not wait for him to show his best. Your impulse of welcome breaks down his reserve, melts his shyness and brings him nearer to the thing that you expect of him. This is mirrored in his face. You see it, and your original faith is reinforced. You follow up the trail of sparks which you have

> spied within him; the spirit and exuberance of your quest redoubling in him the fire which you seek.

Diffident Persons Often Good Speakers.—This bit of psychology explains the fact that many shy persons are nevertheless excellent public speakers. On the platform they are free of the aggressive or challenging or competing or impatient personalities who press them too closely in conversation. The larger audience is comparatively remote and impersonal, and yet it is near enough to encourage with its attention, sympathy, patience and approval. The speaker is not hurried or interrupted. The faces about him are kindly, helpful, expectant.

Sympathy between Speaker and Audience.—For the same reason public speaking may be more intimate and personal than conversation. Most people are reticent when it comes to talking about the facts and emotions that really govern them. They are afraid of sounding silly or bookish. They fear the jibe or cynical smile.

The author and the public speaker have the time and the means to create moods and attitudes in their readers or audiences. Suspicion and the conventional suppression of feeling are not present to discourage warmth of expression. Conversations in the best plays or novels seem natural enough and absorb us and thrill us with their wisdom or smartness, humor or pathos. If these were actual conversations of real life, they would probably be called stilted or sentimental, affected or impossible.

In the next chapter will be noted the importance of planning and preparing for a definitely visualized audience. There is no distortion of the essential elements of the picture if the speaker imagines his audience to be thoroughly congenial and sympathetic.

Have a Plan.—We have not finished with this matter of courage and composure. Going back to your imaginary talk on the convention address you will probably agree that what kept you going was your thorough preparation. You knew the subject inside out. It had become a part of your own experience. You had a simple arrangement of topics. You jotted them down in the order in which the campaign progressed. You discussed the "prospects" who were to be reached, the way to get live mailing lists, the newspaper and magazine "copy," the letters and the "follow-ups," the folders that were enclosed, the special offer, the check-up on inquiries, the costs, the sales, the things that might have been done better, the application of the methods to other lines of business. You did not have to think on your feet. You thought in your chair in the office, at home, on the street—anywhere before you got to the platform. You unraveled the tangled skein of ideas at your leisure.

When Buffon, the scientist, delivered his address on style to the French Academy, he presented the scientist's characteristic point of view—order and system in thinking. He said:

> It is from lack of plan, from lack of reflection on his purpose, that a man of sheer intelligence finds himself embarrassed and does not know at what point to begin to write. ["Or to speak," he might have added.] He perceives, all at the same time, a great number of ideas; and, since he has neither compared them nor subordinated them, nothing leads him to prefer any of them to the others; so he remains in perplexity.

The experienced public speaker is like the experienced salesman. He has a pattern of description, explanation and argument that is so detailed and definite through reflection and familiarity that his talk is pretty nearly automatic. He seldom has to really think on his feet.

George Herbert Palmer, in "Self-cultivation in English," puts this idea strikingly in advising you to "lean upon your subject." When you have considered your subject enough to give it body and form, it will support you. You can lean on it, stand on it, get behind it, hide in it. "The play's the thing." The audience is absorbed in the story. The actor is absorbed in his part—his message—and the audience forgets him or takes him for granted.

Practice.—The best way to overcome the sinking spells that afflict all novices is to speak as often as you can. Remember that most public speakers are made, not born. Speaking is just one more job and we learn how to do it as we learn everything else—by doing it. In every walk of business the man who improves is the man who fights his own cowardice before some new problem or responsibility. His fear shames him, and with knocking heart and shaking legs he tackles the job to save his self-respect. His excitement and fear of quitting keep him going. Suddenly he becomes calm and finds he has greatly overrated the difficulty and the terror. Presently a new rut of use and habit is grooved, and the man turns to something else to worry about.

Summary.—The A B C, then, of promoting confidence on the platform is: (*a*) the conversational, not the exhibitional, attitude toward the audience; (*b*) preparation; (*c*) practice. The opportunities for practice are almost unlimited. Beginning with the small jobs will give you poise and assurance for the larger, more responsible ones. Give short informal talks to the members of your club, fraternity or other organization. Take part in debating a motion, act as secretary or chairman, speak at a dinner or introduce a guest. Students gain enormously in ease after their first talks. They begin to feel that "there's nothing to it" and often enough fall victims to overconfidence and laziness.

INTRODUCTION TO KENNETH BURKE

Kenneth Burke (1897–1993) is the most influential rhetorical theorist and critic of the twentieth century. Most of the major themes of twentieth century rhetoric come together in Burke's writings, which spanned nearly the entire century. Burke was born in Pittsburgh. He attended the Ohio State University and Columbia University briefly, but never earned a university degree. He did, however, receive many honorary degrees and taught at a number of colleges and universities. In addition to teaching, Burke was a literary critic, translator, music reviewer, book reviewer, novelist, poet, and essayist. His description of himself as a "word man" fairly summed up the center of his many interests and competencies.

It is difficult to synthesize the work of such a prolific theorist, but a good place to begin is with the idea, found throughout Burke's writings, that the most fundamental human reality is grounded in symbol usage, primarily language. Burke believed that how people speak generates their perceptions, social organization, beliefs, attitudes, and values. The observations of scientists are already inherent in the vocabularies they use, he argued. Our motives for reacting to any situation arise not from the situation itself but from what we *call* the situation. Writing during the Great Depression, he argued that a faulty economic language led to that social catastrophe, and that different ways of speaking about finance and money could lead the nation out of it. Burke sometimes called his system of thought *logology* because it was the study of language systems, and he sometimes called it *dramatism* because it treated human action as if it were dramatic action, or a play. But whatever he called his thought, it was based on the centrality of language.

The power of language to generate reality and thought is the theme underlying the Burkean works selected for inclusion in this book. When Adolph Hitler's book *Mein Kampf* was published in the 1930s, it was widely criticized for its fascist, intolerant views. Rather than simply joining the chorus of condemnations, Burke wrote a classic critical essay, "The Rhetoric of Hitler's 'Battle,'" in which he argued that the world could predict what Hitler and his followers would do by analyzing the language they were using. Burke argued that Hitler's language followed an ancient pattern called scapegoating, and that he would use the Jews to take the blame for the failings of the German people themselves.

Before the twentieth century, the discourse of criticism was largely directed at better understanding of literature, art, and other aesthetic experiences. Burke was in the forefront of critics who broke with that tradition to think critically about the *rhetoric* of art and literature. We turn to books, films, television, and other aesthetic experiences not only for enjoyment but also for the ways in which they help us to confront real-life problems. Burke's essay on Hitler is an influential example of how such criticism can advise the public on how to react to the serious effects of discourse.

The idea of literature as rhetorical is also central to the next essay included here, "Literature as Equipment for Living." Burke's view of what was "literature" was very broad; he really means any text. That definition not only opens up the field of literature to include political speeches, television shows and commercials, and technical manuals, but it makes criticism relevant to texts not traditionally considered aesthetic. So Burke introduces this essay by claiming that he is outlining a "sociological" criticism, by which he means a method for appraisal of a text with social (that is to say, rhetorical) implications.

Burke starts with the example of *proverbs*. He shows how proverbs sum up situations that people face and offer them motives for reacting to those situations. In other words, proverbs are rhetorical, for they give people the resources for responding to real-life problems and decisions. Then Burke extends the principle beyond proverbs: All texts, he argues, size up situations and suggest ways of responding to them. Some texts size those situations up accurately, and some do not. Some suggest desirable responses, some do not. The role of the critic, then, is to evaluate whether a text is valuable as "equipment for living" through the challenges of everyday life.

Criticism was not Burke's only rhetorical concern; he was also a rhetorical theorist of great influence in the twentieth century. The next essay included here is the introduction to Burke's book, *A Grammar of Motives*. The *grammar* of a language is its basic components. You have learned that English is based on a grammar of nouns, verbs, adverbs, and so forth. We know that all nouns behave in a certain way, and they facilitate thinking in a certain way; likewise, so do verbs and the other parts of speech.

Perhaps Burke's most original and influential theory holds that any language may be organized not only according to its nouns, verbs, adjectives, and so forth, but *also* according to groups of words that generate motives for perceiving and reacting to the world. If we think about the language spoken by any society we can think in terms of different ways for seeing and responding to the world that are embodied in that language. This is because every time anybody speaks, the language they use is making attributions about why the world is the way it is and how one should respond to the world. Burke begins this essay with that point by considering what is happening when we *say* what people are doing and why they are doing it.

What happens when we refer to the world in this way, Burke argues, is that our language explains the world to ourselves and others from one or a combination of five different perspectives. This scheme of five perspectives is called Burke's *pentad*. It consists of *act* (something that is done), *agent* (someone who does the act), *agency* (the means by which the act is carried out), *purpose* (the purpose served by the act), and *scene* (the context within which the act takes place). Every time we talk about crime, welfare, global warming, our neighbor's behavior, our cousin's new job—every time we talk about *anything*, our language unavoidably speaks of the world as if it is the way it is because of acts, agents, agencies, purposes, scenes, or some combination of those terms (in his later years Burke expanded the pentad to a "hexad," adding *attitude* as a sixth term). Critics have found Burke's pentad enormously useful in explaining a rhetorical dimension of texts that may be out of people's conscious awareness but nevertheless powerfully effective.

It is not possible to survey Burke's entire system of rhetorical theories, but one final set of theoretical concepts must be examined. These concepts are contained in the final selection reprinted here: three chapters from Burke's book, *A Rhetoric of Motives.* We have noted that in the divisive and divided twentieth century, rhetoric has often sought to establish common ground, in contrast to traditional rhetoric that could assume common ground already existing in an audience as a basis for further appeal. Theorists such as Richards in the twentieth century have therefore sought to explain ways in which rhetoric might foster cooperation and coming together as much as the more traditional view of the triumph of a single persuader over others. In *A Rhetoric of Motives,* we find much of Burke's theoretical work in support of that new way of understanding rhetoric.

Acknowledging that "persuasion" was the key term for older, more traditional rhetoric, Burke argues here that a wider, more inclusive term, especially for the rhetoric of his and our time, is *identification.* Identification occurs when people perceive that their interests are joined, and that they share ways of thinking and valuing. This sharing is embodied in shared ways of *speaking.* Burke expresses this idea through use of the term *substance.* Substance is what something is made of: The substance of this book is largely paper and ink, for instance. But the substance of people cannot really be defined physically or chemically: A list of the carbon and other materials of which our bodies are made would scarcely do justice to what a human *is.* People are made out of motives, values, beliefs, ideas, emotions, reasoning, and above all, *language.* Another way of thinking of the word "substance" is to divide it: "sub" and "stance." If one takes a physical stance, there must be something underneath (sub) that stance to hold one up. Likewise, if one takes a stance on some social or political matter, there must be a set of motives, values, and so forth "holding up" that stance.

Burke puts these terms together ingeniously: To achieve *identification* with each other, we must share *substance* with others, which means we must become *consubstantial* with other people. Identification through consubstantiality is therefore Burke's master vision of how rhetoric might work, beyond the narrower purposes of persuasion and gaining advantage. Rhetoric seeks to create a common substance, or a set of motives and values, upon which people may jointly take a stance to address the problems they face. Successful rhetoric allows people a way to achieve identification with one another on the basis of consubstantiality. The vehicle for achieving that consubstantiality is a shared language, or a common vocabulary.

More than any other rhetorical theorist of the twentieth century, Burke has helped us imagine what rhetoric might become as it changes to meet new social challenges and conditions. His theories integrate new interests in criticism, language, and a more inclusive view of rhetoric. No critic has written more, or more influentially, about rhetoric in the twentieth century than has Kenneth Burke.

KENNETH BURKE

THE PHILOSOPHY OF LITERARY FORM

THE RHETORIC OF HITLER'S "BATTLE"

THE appearance of *Mein Kampf* in unexpurgated translation has called forth far too many vandalistic comments. There are other ways of burning books than on the pyre—and the favorite method of the hasty reviewer is to deprive himself and his readers by inattention. I maintain that it is thoroughly vandalistic for the reviewer to content himself with the mere inflicting of a few symbolic wounds upon this book and its author, of an intensity varying with the resources of the reviewer and the time at his disposal. Hitler's "Battle" is exasperating, even nauseating; yet the fact remains: If the reviewer but knocks off a few adverse attitudinizings and calls it a day, with a guaranty in advance that his article will have a favorable reception among the decent members of our population, he is contributing more to our gratification than to our enlightenment.

Here is the testament of a man who swung a great people into his wake. Let us watch it carefully; and let us watch it, not merely to discover some grounds for prophesying what political move is to follow Munich, and what move to follow that move, etc.; let us try also to discover what kind of "medicine" this medicine-man has concocted, that we may know, with greater accuracy, exactly what to guard against, if we are to forestall the concocting of similar medicine in America.

Already, in many quarters of our country, we are "beyond" the stage where we are being saved from Nazism by our *virtues*. And fascist integration is being staved off, rather, by the *conflicts among our vices*. Our vices cannot get together in a grand united front of prejudices; and the result of this frustration, if or until they succeed in surmounting it, speaks, as the Bible might say, "in the name of" democracy. Hitler found a panacea, a "cure for what ails you," a "snakeoil," that made such sinister unifying possible within his own nation. And he was helpful enough to put his cards face up on the table, that we might examine his hands. Let us, then, for God's sake, examine them. This book is the well of Nazi magic; crude magic, but effective. A people trained in pragmatism should want to inspect this magic.

1

Every movement that would recruit its followers from among many discordant and divergent bands, must have some spot towards which all roads lead. Each man may get there in his own way, but it must be the one unifying center of reference for all. Hitler considered this matter carefully, and decided that this center must be not merely a centralizing hub of *ideas*, but a mecca geographically located, towards which all eyes could turn at the appointed hours of prayer (or, in this case, the appointed hours of prayer-in-reverse, the hours of vituperation). So he selected Munich, as the *materialization* of his unifying panacea. As he puts it:

> The geo-political importance of a center of a movement cannot be overrated. Only the presence of such a center and of a place, bathed in the magic of a Mecca or a Rome, can at length give a movement that force which is rooted in the inner unity and in the recognition of a hand that represents this unity.

If a movement must have its Rome, it must also have its devil. For as Russell pointed out years ago, an important ingredient of unity in the Middle Ages (an ingredient that long did its unifying work despite the many factors driving towards disunity) was the symbol of a *common enemy,* the Prince of Evil himself. Men who can unite on nothing else can unite on the basis of a foe shared by all. Hitler himself states the case very succinctly:

> As a whole, and at all times, the efficiency of the truly national leader consists primarily in preventing the division of the attention of a people, and always in concentrating it on a single enemy. The more uniformly the fighting will of a people is put into action, the greater will be the magnetic force of the movement and the more powerful the impetus of the blow. It is part of the genius of a great leader to make adversaries of different fields appear as always belonging to one category only, because to weak and unstable characters the knowledge that there are various enemies will lead only too easily to incipient doubts as to their own cause.
>
> As soon as the wavering masses find themselves confronted with too many enemies, objectivity at once steps in, and the question is raised whether actually all the others are wrong and their own nation or their own movement alone is right.
>
> Also with this comes the first paralysis of their own strength. Therefore, a number of essentially different enemies must always be regarded as one in such a way that in the opinion of the mass of one's own adherents the war is being waged against one enemy alone. This strengthens the belief in one's own cause and increases one's bitterness against the attacker.

As everyone knows, this policy was exemplified in his selection of an "international" devil, the "international Jew" (the Prince was international, universal, "catholic"). This *materialization* of a religious pattern is, I think, one terrifically effective weapon of propaganda in a period where religion has been progressively weakened by many centuries of capitalist materialism. You need but go back to the sermonizing of centuries to be reminded that religion had a powerful enemy long before organized atheism came upon the scene. Religion is based upon the "prosperity of poverty," upon the use of ways for converting our sufferings and handicaps into a good—but capitalism is based upon the prosperity of acquisitions, the only scheme of value, in fact, by which its proliferating store of gadgets could be sold, assuming for the moment that capitalism had not got so drastically in its own way that it can't sell its gadgets even after it has trained people to feel that human dignity, the "higher standard of living," could be attained only by their vast private accumulation.

So, we have, as unifying step No. 1, the international devil materialized, in the visible, point-to-able form of people with a certain kind of "blood," a burlesque of contemporary neo-positivism's ideal of meaning, which insists upon a *material* reference.

Once Hitler has thus essentialized his enemy, all "proof" henceforth is automatic. If you point out the enormous amount of evidence to show that the Jewish worker is at odds with the "international Jew stock exchange capitalist," Hitler replies with one hundred per cent regularity: That is one more indication of the cunning with which the "Jewish plot" is being engineered. Or would you point to "Aryans" who do the same as his conspiratorial Jews? Very well; that is proof that the "Aryan" has been "seduced" by the Jew.

The sexual symbolism that runs through Hitler's book, lying in wait to draw upon the responses of contemporary sexual values, is easily characterized: Germany in dispersion is the "dehorned Siegfried." The masses are "feminine." As such, they desire to be led by a dominating male. This male, as orator, woos them—and, when he has won them, he commands them. The rival male, the villainous Jew, would on the contrary "seduce" them. If he succeeds, he poisons their blood by intermingling with them. Whereupon, by purely associative connections of ideas, we are moved into attacks upon syphilis, prostitution, incest, and other similar misfortunes, which are introduced as a kind of "musical" argument when he is on the subject of "blood-poisoning" by intermarriage or, in its "spiritual" equivalent, by the infection of "Jewish" ideas, such as democracy.[1]

The "medicinal" appeal of the Jew as scapegoat operates from another angle. The middle class contains, within the mind of each member, a duality: its members simultaneously have a cult of money and a detestation of this cult. When capitalism is going well, this conflict is left more or less in abeyance. But when capitalism is balked, it comes to the fore. Hence, there is "medicine" for the "Aryan" members of the middle class in the projective device of the scapegoat, whereby the "bad" features can be allocated to the "devil," and one can "respect himself" by a distinction between "good" capitalism and "bad" capitalism, with those of a different lodge being the vessels of the "bad" capitalism. It is doubtless the "relief" of this solution that spared Hitler the necessity of explaining just how the "Jewish plot" was to work out. Nowhere does this book, which is so full of war plans, make the slightest attempt to explain the steps whereby the triumph of "Jewish Bolshevism," which destroys *all* finance, will be the triumph of "*Jewish*" finance. Hitler well knows the point at which his "elucidations" should rely upon the lurid alone.

The question arises, in those trying to gauge Hitler: Was his selection of the Jew, as his unifying devil-function, a purely calculating act? Despite the quotation I have already given, I believe that it was *not*. The vigor with which he utilized it, I think, derives from a much more complex state of affairs. It seems that, when Hitler went to Vienna, in a state close to total poverty, he genuinely suffered. He lived among the impoverished; and he describes his misery at the spectacle. He was *sensitive* to it; and his way of manifesting this sensitiveness impresses me that he is, at this point, wholly genuine, as with his wincing at the broken family relationships caused by alcoholism, which he in turn relates to impoverishment. During this time he began his attempts at political theorizing; and his disturbance was considerably increased by the skill with which Marxists tied him into knots. One passage in particular gives you reason, reading between the lines, to believe that the dialecticians of the class struggle, in their skill at blasting his muddled speculations, put him into a state of uncertainty that was finally "solved" by rage:

> The more I argued with them, the more I got to know their dialectics. First they counted on the ignorance of their adversary; then, when there was no way out, they themselves pretended stupidity. If all this was of no avail, they refused to understand or they changed the subject when driven into a corner; they brought up truisms, but they immediately transferred their acceptance to quite different subjects, and, if attacked again, they gave way and pretended to know nothing exactly. Wherever one attacked one of these prophets, one's hands seized slimy jelly; it slipped through one's fingers only to collect again in the next moment. If one smote one of them so thoroughly that, with the bystanders watching, he could but agree, and if one thus thought he had advanced at least one step, one was greatly astonished the following day. The Jew did not in the least remember the day before, he continued to talk in the same old strain as if nothing had happened, and if indignantly confronted, he pretended to be astonished and could not remember anything except that his assertions had already been proved true the day before.
>
> Often I was stunned.
>
> One did not know what to admire more: their glibness of tongue or their skill in lying.
>
> I gradually began to hate them.

At this point, I think, he is tracing the *spontaneous* rise of his anti-Semitism. He tells how, once he had discovered the "cause" of the misery about

---

[1] Hitler also strongly insists upon the total identification between leader and people. Thus, in wooing the people, he would in a roundabout way be wooing himself. The thought might suggest how the Führer, dominating the feminine masses by his diction, would have an incentive to remain unmarried.

him, he could *confront it.* Where he had had to avert his eyes, he could now *positively welcome* the scene. Here his drastic structure of *acceptance* was being formed. He tells of the "internal happiness" that descended upon him.

> This was the time in which the greatest change I was ever to experience took place in me.
>
> From a feeble cosmopolite I turned into a fanatical anti-Semite,

and thence we move, by one of those associational tricks which he brings forth at all strategic moments, into a vision of the end of the world—out of which in turn he emerges with his slogan: "I am acting in the sense of the Almighty Creator: *By warding off Jews I am fighting for the Lord's work*" (italics his).

He talks of this transition as a period of "double life," a struggle of "reason" and "reality" against his "heart."[1] It was as "bitter" as it was "blissful." And finally, it was "reason" that won! Which prompts us to note that those who attack Hitlerism as a cult of the irrational should emend their statements to this extent: irrational it is, but it is carried on under the *slogan* of "Reason." Similarly, his cult of war is developed "in the name of" humility, love, and peace. Judged on a quantitative basis, Hitler's book certainly falls under the classification of hate. Its venom is everywhere, its charity is sparse. But the rationalized family tree for this hate situates it in "Aryan love." Some deep-probing German poets, whose work adumbrated the Nazi movement, did gravitate towards thinking *in the name of* war, irrationality, and hate. But Hitler was not among them. After all, when it is so easy to draw a doctrine of war out of a doctrine of peace, why should the astute politician do otherwise, particularly when Hitler has slung together his doctrines, without the slightest effort at logical symmetry? Furthermore, Church thinking always got to its wars in Hitler's "sounder" manner; and the patterns of Hitler's thought are a bastardized or caricatured version of religious thought.

I spoke of Hitler's fury at the dialectics of those who opposed him when his structure was in the stage of scaffolding. From this we may move to another tremendously important aspect of his theory: his attack upon the *parliamentary.* For it is again, I submit, an important aspect of his medicine, in its function as medicine for him personally and as medicine for those who were later to identify themselves with him.

---

[1] Other aspects of the career symbolism: Hitler's book begins: "Today I consider it my good fortune that Fate designated Braunau on the Inn as the place of my birth. For this small town is situated on the border between those two German States, the reunion of which seems, at least to us of the younger generation, a task to be furthered with every means our lives long," an indication of his "transitional" mind, what Wordsworth might have called the "borderer." He neglects to give the date of his birth, 1889, which is supplied by the editors. Again there is a certain "correctness" here, as Hitler was not "born" until many years later—but he does give the exact date of his war wounds, which were indeed formative. During his early years in Vienna and Munich, he foregoes protest, on the grounds that he is "nameless." And when his party is finally organized and effective, he stresses the fact that his "nameless" period is over (i.e., he has shaped himself an identity). When reading in an earlier passage of his book some generalizations to the effect that one should not crystallize his political views until he is thirty, I made a note: "See what Hitler does at thirty." I felt sure that, though such generalizations may be dubious as applied to people as a whole, they must, given the Hitler type of mind (with his complete identification between himself and his followers), be valid statements about himself. One *should* do what he *did.* The hunch was verified: about the age of thirty Hitler, in a group of seven, began working with the party that was to conquer Germany. I trace these steps particularly because I believe that the orator who has a strong sense of his own "rebirth" has this to draw upon when persuading his audiences that his is offering them the way to a "new life." However, I see no categorical objection to this attitude; its menace derives solely from the values in which it is exemplified. They may be wholesome or unwholesome. If they are unwholesome, but backed by conviction, the basic sincerity of the conviction acts as a sound virtue to reinforce a vice—and this combination is the most disastrous one that a people can encounter in a demagogue.

There is a "problem" in the parliament—and nowhere was this problem more acutely in evidence than in the pre-war Vienna that was to serve as Hitler's political schooling. For the parliament, at its best, is a "babel" of voices. There is the wrangle of men representing interests lying awkwardly on the bias across one another, sometimes opposing, sometimes vaguely divergent. Morton Prince's psychiatric study of "Miss Beauchamp," the case of a woman split into several sub-personalities at odds with one another, variously combining under hypnosis, and frequently in turmoil, is the allegory of a democracy fallen upon evil days. The parliament of the Habsburg Empire just prior to its collapse was an especially drastic instance of such disruption, such vocal diaspora, with movements that would reduce one to a disintegrated mass of fragments if he attempted to encompass the totality of its discordancies. So Hitler, suffering under the alienation of poverty and confusion, yearning for some integrative core, came to take this parliament as the basic symbol of all that he would move away from. He damned the tottering Habsburg Empire as a "State of Nationalities." The many conflicting voices of the spokesmen of the many political blocs arose from the fact that various separationist movements of a nationalistic sort had arisen within a Catholic imperial structure formed prior to the nationalistic emphasis and slowly breaking apart under its development. So, you had this Babel of voices; and, by the method of associative mergers, *using ideas as imagery,* it became tied up, in the Hitler rhetoric, with "Babylon," Vienna as the city of poverty, prostitution, immorality, coalitions, half-measures, incest, democracy (i.e., majority rule leading to "lack of personal responsibility"), death, internationalism, seduction, and anything else of thumbs-down sort the associative enterprise cared to add on this side of the balance.

Hitler's way of treating the parliamentary babel, I am sorry to say, was at one important point not much different from that of the customary editorial in our own newspapers. Every conflict among the parliamentary spokesmen represents a corresponding conflict among the material interests of the groups for whom they are speaking. But Hitler did not discuss the babel from this angle. He discussed it on a purely *symptomatic* basis. The strategy of our orthodox press, in thus ridiculing the cacophonous verbal output of Congress, is obvious: by thus centering attack upon the *symptoms* of business conflict, as they reveal themselves on the dial of political wrangling, and leaving the underlying cause, the business conflicts themselves, out of the case, they can gratify the very public they would otherwise alienate: namely, the businessmen who are the activating members of their reading public. Hitler, however, went them one better. For not only did he stress the purely *symptomatic* attack here. He proceeded to search for the "cause." And this "cause," of course, he derived from his medicine, his racial theory by which he could give a noneconomic interpretation of a phenomenon economically engendered.

Here again is where Hitler's corrupt use of religious patterns comes to the fore. Church thought, being primarily concerned with matters of the "personality," with problems of moral betterment, naturally, and I think rightly, stresses as a necessary feature, the act of will upon the part of the individual. Hence its resistance to a purely "environmental" account of human ills. Hence its emphasis upon the "person." Hence its proneness to seek a noneconomic explanation of economic phenomena. Hitler's proposal of a non-economic "cause" for the disturbances thus had much to recommend it from this angle. And, as a matter of fact, it was Lueger's Christian-Social Party in Vienna that taught Hitler the tactics of tying up a program of social betterment with an anti-Semitic "unifier." The two parties that he carefully studied at that time were this Catholic faction and Schoenerer's Pan-German group. And his analysis of their attainments and shortcomings, from the standpoint of demagogic efficacy, is an extremely astute piece of work, revealing how carefully this man used the current situation in Vienna as an experimental laboratory for the maturing of his plans.

His unification device, we may summarize, had the following important features:

(1) Inborn dignity. In both religious and humanistic patterns of thought, a "natural born" dignity of man is stressed. And this categorical dignity is considered to be an attribute of *all* men, if they will but avail themselves of it, by right thinking and right living. But Hitler gives this ennobling attitude an ominous twist by his theories of race and nation, whereby the "Aryan" is elevated above all others by the innate endowment of his blood, while other "races," in particular Jews and Negroes, are innately inferior. This sinister secularized revision of Christian theology thus puts the sense of dignity upon a fighting basis, requiring the conquest of "inferior races." After the defeat of Germany in the World War, there were especially strong emotional needs that this compensatory doctrine of an *inborn* superiority could gratify.

(2) *Projection* device. The "curative" process that comes with the ability to hand over one's ills to a scapegoat, thereby getting purification by dissociation. This was especially medicinal, since the sense of frustration leads to a self-questioning. Hence if one can hand over his infirmities to a vessel, or "cause," outside the self, one can battle an external enemy instead of battling an enemy within. And the greater one's internal inadequacies, the greater the amount of evils one can load upon the back of "the enemy." This device is furthermore given a semblance of reason because the individual properly realizes that he is not alone responsible for his condition. There *are* inimical factors in the scene itself. And he wants to have them "placed," preferably in a way that would require a minimum change in the ways of thinking to which he had been accustomed. This was especially appealing to the middle class, who were encouraged to feel that they could conduct their businesses without any basic change whatever, once the businessmen of a different "race" were eliminated.

(3) Symbolic rebirth. Another aspect of the two features already noted. The projective device of the scapegoat, coupled with the Hitlerite doctrine of inborn racial superiority, provides its followers with a "positive" view of life. They can again get the feel of *moving forward,* towards a *goal* (a promissory feature of which Hitler makes much). In Hitler, as the group's prophet, such rebirth involved a symbolic change of lineage. Here, above all, we see Hitler giving a malign twist to a benign aspect of Christian thought. For whereas the Pope, in the familistic pattern of thought basic to the Church, stated that the Hebrew prophets were the *spiritual ancestors* of Christianity, Hitler uses this same mode of thinking in reverse. He renounces this "ancestry" in a "materialistic" way by voting himself and the members of his lodge a different "blood stream" from that of the Jews.

(4) Commercial use. Hitler obviously here had something to sell—and it was but a question of time until he sold it (i.e., got financial backers for his movement). For it provided a *noneconomic interpretation of economic ills.* As such, it served with maximum efficiency in deflecting the attention from the economic factors involved in modern conflict; hence by attacking "Jew finance" instead of *finance,* it could stimulate an enthusiastic movement that left "Aryan" finance in control.

Never once, throughout his book, does Hitler deviate from the above formula. Invariably, he ends his diatribes against contemporary economic ills by a shift into an insistence that we must get to the "true" cause, which is centered in "race." The "Aryan" is "constructive"; the Jew is "destructive"; and the "Aryan," to continue his *construction,* must *destroy* the Jewish *destruction.* The Aryan, as the vessel of *love,* must *hate* the Jewish *hate.*

Perhaps the most enterprising use of his method is in his chapter, "The Causes of the Collapse," where he refuses to consider Germany's plight as in any basic way connected with the consequences of war. Economic factors, he insists, are "only of second or even third importance," but "political, ethical-moral, as well as factors of blood and race, are of the first importance." His rhetorical steps are especially interesting here, in that he begins by seeming to flout the national susceptibilities: "The military defeat of the German people is not an undeserved catastrophe, but rather a deserved punishment by eternal retribution." He then proceeds to present the military collapse as but a "consequence of moral poisoning, visible to all, the consequence of a decrease in the instinct of self-preservation . . . which had already begun to undermine the foundations of the people and the Reich many years before." This moral decay derived from "a sin against the blood and the degradation of the race," so its innerness was an outerness after all: the Jew, who thereupon gets saddled with a vast amalgamation of evils, among them being capitalism, democracy, pacifism, journalism, poor housing, modernism, big cities, loss of religion, half measures, ill health, and weakness of the monarch.

2

Hitler had here another important psychological ingredient to play upon. If a State is in economic collapse (and his theories, tentatively taking shape in the pre-war Vienna, were but developed with greater efficiency in post-war Munich), you cannot possibly derive dignity from economic stability. Dignity must come first—and if you possess it, and implement it, from it may follow its economic counterpart. There is much justice to this line of reasoning, so far as it goes. A people in collapse, suffering under economic frustration and the defeat of nationalistic aspirations, with the very midrib of their integrative efforts (the army) in a state of dispersion, have little other than some "spiritual" basis to which they could refer their nationalistic dignity. Hence, the categorical dignity of superior race was a perfect recipe for the situation. It was "spiritual" in so far as it was "above" crude economic "interests," but it was "materialized" at the psychologically "right" spot in that "the enemy" was something you could *see.*

Furthermore, you had the desire for unity, such as a discussion of class conflict, on the basis of conflicting interests, could not satisfy. The yearning for unity is so great that people are always willing to meet you halfway if you will give it to them by fiat, by flat statement, regardless of the facts. Hence, Hitler consistently refused to consider internal political conflict on the basis of conflicting interests. Here again, he could draw upon a religious pattern, by insisting upon a *personal* statement of the relation between classes, the relation between leaders and followers, each group in its way fulfilling the same commonalty of interests, as the soldiers and captains of an army share a common interest in victory. People so dislike the idea of internal division that, where there is a real internal division, their dislike can easily be turned against the man or group who would so much as *name* it, let alone proposing to act upon it. Their natural and justified resentment against internal division itself, is turned against the diagnostician who states it as a *fact.* This diagnostician, it is felt, is the *cause* of the disunity he named.

Cutting in from another angle, therefore, we note how two sets of equations were built up, with Hitler combining or coalescing *ideas* the way a poet combines or coalesces *images.* On the one side, were the ideas, or images, of disunity, centering in the parliamentary wrangle of the Habsburg "State of Nationalities." This was offered as the antithesis of German nationality, which was presented in the curative imagery of unity, focused upon the glories of the Prussian Reich, with its mecca now moved to "folkish" Vienna. For though Hitler at first attacked the many "folkish" movements, with their hankerings after a kind of Wagnerian mythology of Germanic origins, he subsequently took "folkish" as a basic word by which to conjure. It was, after all, another noneconomic basis of reference. At first we find him objecting to "those who drift about with the word 'folkish' on their caps," and asserting that "such a Babel of opinions cannot serve as the basis of a political fighting movement." But later he seems to have realized, as he well should, that its vagueness was a major point in its favor. So it was incorporated in the grand coalition of his ideational imagery, or imagistic ideation; and Chapter XI ends with the vision of "a State which represents not a mechanism of economic considerations and interests, alien to the people, but a folkish organism."

So, as against the disunity equations, already listed briefly in our discussion of his attacks upon the parliamentary, we get a contrary purifying set; the wrangle of the parliamentary is to be stilled by the giving of *one* voice to the whole people, this to be the "inner voice" of Hitler, made uniform throughout the German boundaries, as leader and people were completely identified with each other. In sum: Hitler's inner voice, equals leader-people identification, equals unity, equals Reich, equals the mecca of Munich, equals plow, equals sword, equals work, equals war, equals army as midrib, equals responsibility (the personal responsibility of the absolute ruler), equals sacrifice, equals the theory of "German democracy" (the free popular choice of the leader, who then accepts the responsibility, and demands absolute obedience in exchange for his sacrifice), equals love (with the masses as feminine), equals idealism, equals obedience to nature, equals race, nation.[1]

And, of course, the two keystones of these opposite equations were Aryan "heroism" and "sacrifice" vs. Jewish "cunning" and "arrogance." Here again we get an astounding caricature of religious thought. For Hitler presents the concept of "Aryan" superiority, of all ways, in terms of "Aryan humility." This "humility" is extracted by a very delicate process that requires, I am afraid, considerable "good will" on the part of the reader who would follow it:

The Church, we may recall, had proclaimed an integral relationship between Divine Law and Natural Law. Natural Law was the expression of the Will of God. Thus, in the middle age, it was a result of natural law, working through tradition, that some people were serfs and other people nobles. And every good member of the Church was "obedient" to this law. Everybody resigned himself to it. Hence, the serf resigned himself to his poverty, and the noble resigned himself to his riches. The monarch resigned himself to his position as representative of the people. And at times the Churchmen resigned themselves to the need of trying to represent the people instead. And the pattern was made symmetrical by the consideration that each traditional "right" had its corresponding "obligations." Similarly, the Aryan doctrine is a doctrine of resignation, hence of humility. It is in accordance with the laws of nature that the "Aryan blood" is superior to all other bloods. Also, the "law of the survival of the fittest" is God's law, working through natural law. Hence, if the Aryan blood has been vested with the awful responsibility of its inborn superiority, the bearers of this "culture-creating" blood must resign themselves to struggle in behalf of its triumph. Otherwise, the laws of God have been disobeyed, with human decadence as a result. We must fight, he says, in order to "deserve to be alive." The Aryan "obeys" nature. It is only "Jewish arrogance" that thinks of "conquering" nature by democratic ideals of equality.

This picture has some nice distinctions worth following. The major virtue of the Aryan race was its instinct for self-preservation (in obedience to natural law). But the major vice of the Jew was his

[1] One could carry out the equations further, on both the disunity and unity side. In the aesthetic field, for instance, we have expressionism on the thumbs-down side, as against aesthetic hygiene on the thumbs-up side. This again is a particularly ironic moment in Hitler's strategy. For the expressionist movement was unquestionably a symptom of unhealthiness. It reflected the increasing alienation that went with the movement towards world war and the disorganization after the world war. It was "lost," vague in identity, a drastically accurate reflection of the response to material confusion, a pathetic attempt by sincere artists to make their wretchedness bearable at least to the extent that comes of giving it expression. And it attained its height during the period of wild inflation, when the capitalist world, which bases its morality of work and savings upon the soundness of its money structure, had this last prop of stability removed. The anguish, in short, reflected precisely the kind of disruption that made people *ripe* for a Hitler. It was the antecedent in a phrase of which Hitlerism was the consequent. But by thundering against this *symptom* he could gain persuasiveness, though attacking the very *foreshadowings of himself*.

instinct for self-preservation; for, if he did not have this instinct to a maximum degree, he would not be the "perfect" enemy—that is, he wouldn't be strong enough to account for the ubiquitousness and omnipotence of his conspiracy in destroying the world to become its master.

How, then, are we to distinguish between the benign instinct of self-preservation at the roots of Aryanism, and the malign instinct of self-preservation at the roots of Semitism? We shall distinguish thus: The Aryan self-preservation is based upon *sacrifice,* the sacrifice of the individual to the group, hence, militarism, army discipline, and one big company union. But Jewish self-preservation is based upon individualism, which attains its cunning ends by the exploitation of peace. How, then, can such arrant individualists concoct the world-wide plot? By the help of their "herd instinct." By their sheer "herd instinct" individualists can band together for a common end. They have no real solidarity, but unite opportunistically to seduce the Aryan. Still, that brings up another technical problem. For we have been hearing much about the importance of the *person.* We have been told how, by the "law of the survival of the fittest," there is a sifting of people on the basis of their individual capacities. We even have a special chapter of pure Aryanism: "The Strong Man is Mightiest Alone." Hence, another distinction is necessary: The Jew represents individualism; the Aryan represents "super-individualism."

I had thought, when coming upon the "Strong Man is Mightiest Alone" chapter, that I was going to find Hitler at his weakest. Instead, I found him at his strongest. (I am not referring to *quality,* but to *demagogic effectiveness.*) For the chapter is not at all, as you might infer from the title, done in a "rise of Adolph Hitler" manner. Instead, it deals with the Nazis' gradual absorption of the many disrelated "folkish" groups. And it is managed throughout by means of a spontaneous identification between leader and people. Hence, the Strong Man's "aloneness" is presented as a *public* attribute, in terms of tactics for the struggle against the *Party's* dismemberment under the pressure of rival saviors. There is no explicit talk of Hitler at all. And it is simply *taken for granted* that *his* leadership is the norm, and all other leaderships the abnorm. There is no "philosophy of the superman," in Nietzschean cast. Instead, Hitler's blandishments so integrate leader and people, commingling them so inextricably, that the politician does not even present himself as candidate. Somehow, the battle is over already, the decision has been made. "German democracy" has chosen. And the deployments of politics are, you might say, the chartings of Hitler's private mind translated into the vocabulary of nationalistic events. He says *what he thought* in terms of *what parties did.*

Here, I think, we see the distinguishing quality of Hitler's method as an instrument of persuasion, with reference to the question whether Hitler is sincere or deliberate, whether his vision of the omnipotent conspirator has the drastic honesty of paranoia or the sheer shrewdness of a demagogue trained in *Realpolitik* of the Machiavellian sort.[1] Must we choose? Or may we not, rather, replace

---

[1] I should not want to use the word "Machiavellian," however, without offering a kind of apology to Machiavelli. It seems to me that Machiavelli's *Prince* has more to be said in extenuation than is usually said of it. Machiavelli's strategy, as I see it, was something like this: He accepted the values of the Renaissance rule as a *fact.* That is: whether you like these values or not, they were there and operating, and it was useless to try persuading the ambitious ruler to adopt other values, such as those of the Church. These men believed in the cult of material power, and they had the power to implement their beliefs. With so much as "the given," could anything in the way of benefits for the people be salvaged? Machiavelli evolved a typical "Machiavellian" argument in favor of popular benefits, on the basis of the prince's own scheme of values. That is: the ruler, to attain the maximum strength, requires the backing of the populace. That this backing be as effective as possible, the populace should be made as strong as possible. And that the populace be as strong as possible, they should be well treated. Their gratitude would further repay itself in the form of increased loyalty.

It was Machiavelli's hope that, for this roundabout project, he would be rewarded with a well-paying office in the prince's administrative bureaucracy.

the "either—or" with a "both—and"? Have we not by now offered grounds enough for our contention that Hitler's sinister powers of persuasion derive from the fact that he spontaneously evolved his "cure-all" in response to inner necessities?

3

So much, then, was "spontaneous." It was further channelized into the anti-Semitic pattern by the incentives he derived from the Catholic Christian-Social Party in Vienna itself. Add, now, the step into *criticism.* Not criticism in the "parliamentary" sense of doubt, of hearkening to the opposition and attempting to mature a policy in the light of counter-policies; but the "unified" kind of criticism that simply seeks for conscious ways of making one's position more "efficient," more thoroughly itself. This is the kind of criticism at which Hitler was an adept. As a result, he could *spontaneously* turn to a scapegoat mechanism, and he could, by conscious planning, perfect the symmetry of the solution towards which he had spontaneously turned.

This is the meaning of Hitler's diatribes against "objectivity." "Objectivity" is interference-criticism. What Hitler wanted was the kind of criticism that would be a pure and simple coefficient of power, enabling him to go most effectively in the direction he had chosen. And the "inner voice" of which he speaks would henceforth dictate to him the greatest amount of realism, as regards the tactics of efficiency. For instance, having decided that the masses required certainty, and simple certainty, quite as he did himself, he later worked out a 25-point program as the platform of his National Socialist German Workers Party. And he resolutely refused to change one single item in this program, even for purposes of "improvement." He felt that the *fixity* of the platform was more important for propagandistic purposes than any revision of his slogans could be, even though the revisions in themselves had much to be said in their favor. The astounding thing is that, although such an attitude gave good cause to doubt the Hitlerite promises, he could explicitly explain his tactics in his book and still employ them without loss of effectiveness.[1]

Hitler also tells of his technique in speaking, once the Nazi party had become effectively organized, and had its army of guards, or bouncers, to maltreat hecklers and throw them from the hall. He would, he recounts, fill his speech with *provocative* remarks, whereat his bouncers would promptly swoop down in flying formation, with swinging fists, upon anyone whom these provocative remarks provoked to answer. The efficiency of Hitlerism is the efficiency of the one voice, implemented throughout a total organization. The trinity of government which he finally offers is: *popularity* of the leader, *force* to back the popularity, and popularity and force maintained together long enough to become backed by a *tradition.* Is such thinking spontaneous or deliberate—or is it not rather both?[2]

---

[1] On this point Hitler reasons as follows: "Here, too, one can learn from the Catholic Church. Although its structure of doctrines in many instances collides, quite unnecessarily, with exact science and research, yet it is unwilling to sacrifice even one little syllable of its dogmas. It has rightly recognized that its resistibility does not lie in a more or less great adjustment to the scientific results of the moment, which in reality are always changing, but rather in a strict adherence to dogmas, once laid down, which alone give the entire structure the character of creed. Today, therefore, the Catholic Church stands firmer than ever. One can prophesy that in the same measure in which the appearances flee, the Church itself, as the resting pole in the flight of appearances, will gain more and more blind adherence."

[2] Hitler also paid great attention to the conditions under which political oratory is most effective. He sums up thus:

"All these cases involve encroachments upon man's freedom of will. This applies, of course, most of all to meetings to which people with a contrary orientation of will are coming, and who now have to be won for new intentions. It seems that in the morning and even during the day men's will power revolts with highest energy against an attempt at being forced under another's will and another's opinion. In the evening, however, they succumb more easily to the dominating force of a stronger will. For truly every such meeting presents a wrestling match between two opposed forces. The superior

Freud has given us a succinct paragraph that bears upon the spontaneous aspect of Hitler's persecution mania. (A persecution mania, I should add, different from the pure product in that it was constructed of *public* materials; all the ingredients Hitler stirred into his brew were already rife, with spokesmen and bands of followers, before Hitler "took them over." Both the pre-war and post-war periods were dotted with saviors, of nationalistic and "folkish" cast. This proliferation was analogous to the swarm of barter schemes and currency-tinkering that burst loose upon the United States after the crash of 1929. Also, the commercial availability of Hitler's politics was, in a low sense of the term, a *public* qualification, removing it from the realm of "pure" paranoia, where the sufferer develops a wholly *private* structure of interpretations.)

I cite from *Totem and Taboo:*

> Another trait in the attitude of primitive races towards their rulers recalls a mechanism which is universally present in mental disturbances, and is openly revealed in the so-called delusions of persecution. Here the importance of a particular person is extraordinarily heightened and his omnipotence is raised to the improbable in order to make it easier to attribute to him responsibility for everything painful which happens to the patient. Savages really do not act differently towards their rulers when they ascribe to them power over rain and shine, wind and weather, and then dethrone them or kill them because nature has disappointed their expectation of a good hunt or a ripe harvest. The prototype which the paranoiac reconstructs in his persecution mania is found in the relation of the child to its father. Such omnipotence is regularly attributed to the father in the imagination of the son, and distrust of the father has been shown to be intimately connected with the heightened esteem for him. When a paranoiac names a person of his acquaintance as his "persecutor," he thereby elevates him to the paternal succession and brings him under conditions which enable him to make him responsible for all the misfortune which he experiences.

I have already proposed my modifications of this account when discussing the symbolic change of lineage connected with Hitler's project of a "new way of life." Hitler is symbolically changing from the "spiritual ancestry" of the Hebrew prophets to the "superior" ancestry of "Aryanism," and has given his story a kind of bastardized modernization, along the lines of naturalistic, materialistic "science," by his fiction of the special "blood-stream." He is voting himself a new identity (something contrary to the wrangles of the Habsburg Babylon, a soothing national unity); whereupon the vessels of the old identity become a "bad" father, i.e., the persecutor. It is not hard to see how, as his enmity becomes implemented by the backing of an organization, the rôle of "persecutor" is transformed into the rôle of persecuted, as he sets out with his like-minded band to "destroy the destroyer."

Were Hitler simply a poet, he might have written a work with an anti-Semitic turn, and let it go at that. But Hitler, who began as a student of painting, and later shifted to architecture, himself treats his political activities as an extension of his artistic ambitions. He remained, in his own eyes, an "architect," building a "folkish" State that was to match, in political materials, the "folkish" architecture of Munich.

We might consider the matter this way (still trying, that is, to make precise the relationship between the drastically sincere and the deliberately scheming): Do we not know of many authors who seem, as they turn from the rôle of citizen to the

---

oratorical talent of a domineering apostolic nature will now succeed more easily in winning for the new will people who themselves have in turn experienced a weakening of their force of resistance in the most natural way, than people who still have full command of the energies of their minds and their will power.

"The same purpose serves also the artificially created and yet mysterious dusk of the Catholic churches, the burning candles, incense, censers, etc."

rôle of spokesman, to leave one room and enter another? Or who has not, on occasion, talked with a man in private conversation, and then been almost startled at the transformation this man undergoes when addressing a public audience? And I know persons today, who shift between the writing of items in the class of academic, philosophic speculation to items of political pamphleteering, and whose entire style and method changes with this change of rôle. In their academic manner, they are cautious, painstaking, eager to present all significant aspects of the case they are considering; but when they turn to political pamphleteering, they hammer forth with vituperation, they systematically misrepresent the position of their opponent, they go into a kind of political trance, in which, during its throes, they throb like a locomotive; and behold, a moment later, the mediumistic state is abandoned, and they are the most moderate of men.

Now, one will find few pages in Hitler that one could call "moderate." But there are many pages in which he gauges resistances and opportunities with the "rationality" of a skilled advertising man planning a new sales campaign. Politics, he says, must be sold like soap—and soap is not sold in a trance. But he did have the experience of his trance, in the "exaltation" of his anti-Semitism. And later, as he became a successful orator (he insists that revolutions are made solely by the power of the spoken word), he had this "poetic" rôle to draw upon, plus the great relief it provided as a way of slipping from the burden of logical analysis into the pure "spirituality" of vituperative prophecy. What more natural, therefore, than that a man so insistent upon unification would integrate this mood with less ecstatic moments, particularly when he had found the followers and the backers that put a price, both spiritual and material, upon such unification?

Once this happy "unity" is under way, one has a "logic" for the development of a method. One knows when to "spiritualize" a material issue, and when to "materialize" a spiritual one. Thus, when it is a matter of materialistic interests that cause a conflict between employer and employee, Hitler here disdainfully shifts to a high moral plane. He is "above" such low concerns. Everything becomes a matter of "sacrifices" and "personality." It becomes crass to treat employers and employees as different *classes* with a corresponding difference in the classification of their interests. Instead, relations between employer and employee must be on the "personal" basis of leader and follower, and "whatever may have a divisive effect in national life should be given a unifying effect through the army." When talking of national rivalries, however, he makes a very shrewd materialistic gauging of Britain and France with relation to Germany. France, he says, desires the "Balkanization of Germany" (i.e., its breakup into separationist movements—the "disunity" theme again) in order to maintain commercial hegemony on the continent. But Britain desires the "Balkanization of *Europe*," hence would favor a fairly strong and unified Germany, to use as a counter-weight against French hegemony. *German* nationality, however, is unified by the *spiritual* quality of Aryanism (that would produce the national organization via the Party) while this in turn is *materialized* in the myth of the blood-stream.

What are we to learn from Hitler's book? For one thing, I believe that he has shown, to a very disturbing degree, the power of endless repetition. Every circular advertising a Nazi meeting had, at the bottom, two slogans: "Jews not admitted" and "War victims free." And the substance of Nazi propaganda was built about these two "complementary" themes. He describes the power of spectacle; insists that mass meetings are the fundamental way of giving the individual the sense of being protectively surrounded by a movement, the sense of "community." He also drops one wise hint that I wish the American authorities would take in treating Nazi gatherings. He says that the presence of a special Nazi guard, in Nazi uniforms, was of great importance in building up, among the followers, a tendency to place the center of authority in the Nazi party. I believe that we should take him at his word here, but use the advice in reverse, by insisting that, where Nazi meetings are to be permitted, they be policed by the authorities alone, and that uniformed Nazi guards to enforce the law be prohibited.

And is it possible that an equally important feature of appeal was not so much in the repetitiousness per se, but in the fact that, by means of it, Hitler provided a "world view" for people who had previously seen the world but piecemeal? Did not much of his lure derive, once more, from the *bad* filling of a *good* need? Are not those who insist upon a purely *planless* working of the market asking people to accept far too slovenly a scheme of human purpose, a slovenly scheme that can be accepted so long as it operates with a fair degree of satisfaction, but becomes abhorrent to the victims of its disarray? Are they not then psychologically ready for a rationale, *any* rationale, if it but offer them some specious "universal" explanation? Hence, I doubt whether the appeal was in the sloganizing element alone (particularly as even slogans can only be hammered home, in speech after speech, and two or three hours at a stretch, by endless variations on the themes). And Hitler himself somewhat justifies my interpretation by laying so much stress upon the *half-measures* of the middle-class politicians, and the contrasting *certainty* of his own methods. He was not offering people a *rival* world view; rather, he was offering a world view to people who had no other to pit against it.

As for the basic Nazi trick: the "curative" unification by a fictitious devil-function, gradually made convincing by the sloganizing repetitiousness of standard advertising technique—the opposition must be as unwearying in the attack upon it. It may well be that people, in their human frailty, require an enemy as well as a goal. Very well: Hitlerism itself has provided us with such an enemy—and the clear example of its operation is guaranty that we have, in him and all he stands for, no purely fictitious "devil-function" made to look like a world menace by rhetorical blandishments, but a reality whose ominousness is clarified by the record of its conduct to date. In selecting his brand of doctrine as our "scapegoat," and in tracking down its equivalents in America, we shall be at the very center of accuracy. The Nazis themselves have made the task of clarification easier. Add to them Japan and Italy, and you have *case histories* of fascism for those who might find it more difficult to approach an understanding of its imperialistic drives by a vigorously economic explanation.

But above all, I believe, we must make it apparent that Hitler appeals by relying upon a bastardization of fundamentally religious patterns of thought. In this, if properly presented, there is no slight to religion. There is nothing in religion proper that requires a fascist state. There is much in religion, when misused, that does lead to a fascist state. There is a Latin proverb, *Corruptio optimi pessima,* "the corruption of the best is the worst." And it is the corruptors of religion who are a major menace to the world today, in giving the profound patterns of religious thought a crude and sinister distortion.

Our job, then, our anti-Hitler Battle, is to find all available ways of making the Hitlerite distortions of religion apparent, in order that politicians of his kind in America be unable to perform a similar swindle. The desire for unity is genuine and admirable. The desire for national unity, in the present state of the world, is genuine and admirable. But this unity, if attained on a deceptive basis, by emotional trickeries that shift our criticism from the accurate locus of our trouble, is no unity at all. For, even if we are among those who happen to be "Aryans," we solve no problems even for ourselves by such solutions, since the factors pressing towards calamity remain. Thus, in Germany, after all the upheaval, we see nothing beyond a drive for ever more and more upheaval, precisely because the "new way of life" was no new way, but the dismally oldest way of sheer deception—hence, after all the "change," the factors driving towards unrest are left intact, and even strengthened. True, the Germans had the resentment of a lost war to increase their susceptibility to Hitler's rhetoric. But in a wider sense, it has repeatedly been observed, the whole world lost the War—and the accumulating ills of the capitalist order were but accelerated in their movements towards confusion. Hence, here too there are the resentments that go with frustration of men's ability to work and earn. At that point a certain kind of industrial or financial monopolist may, annoyed by the contrary voices of our parliament, wish for the momentary peace of one voice, amplified by social organizations, with all the others not merely quieted, but given the quietus. So he might, under Nazi promptings, be tempted to back a group of gangsters who, on becoming the political rulers of the state, would protect him against the necessary demands of the workers. His gangsters, then, would be his insurance against his workers. But who would be his insurance against his gangsters?

• • •

LITERATURE AS EQUIPMENT FOR LIVING

HERE I shall put down, as briefly as possible, a statement in behalf of what might be catalogued, with a fair degree of accuracy, as a *sociological* criticism of literature. Sociological criticism in itself is certainly not new. I shall here try to suggest what partially new elements or emphasis I think should be added to this old approach. And to make the "way in" as easy as possible, I shall begin with a discussion of proverbs.

1

Examine random specimens in *The Oxford Dictionary of English Proverbs.* You will note, I think, that there is no "pure" literature here. Everything is "medicine." Proverbs are designed for consolation or vengeance, for admonition or exhortation, for foretelling.

Or they name typical, recurrent situations. That is, people find a certain social relationship recurring so frequently that they must "have a word for it." The Eskimos have special names for many different kinds of snow (fifteen, if I remember rightly) because variations in the quality of snow greatly affect their living. Hence, they must "size up" snow much more accurately than we do. And the same is true of social phenomena. Social structures give rise to "type" situations, subtle subdivisions of the relationships involved in competitive and coöperative acts. Many proverbs seek to chart, in more or less homey and picturesque ways, these "type" situations. I submit that such naming is done, not for the sheer glory of the thing, but because of its bearing upon human welfare. A different name for snow implies a different kind of hunt. Some names for snow imply that one should not hunt at all. And similarly, the names for typical, recurrent social situations are not developed out of "disinterested curiosity," but because the names imply a command (what to expect, what to look out for).

To illustrate with a few representative examples:

Proverbs designed for consolation: "The sun does not shine on both sides of the hedge at once." "Think of ease, but work on." "Little troubles the eye, but far less the soul." "The worst luck now, the better another time." "The wind in one's face makes one wise." "He that hath lands hath quarrels." "He knows how to carry the dead cock home." "He is not poor that hath little, but he that desireth much."

For vengeance: "At length the fox is brought to the furrier." "Shod in the cradle, barefoot in the stubble." "Sue a beggar and get a louse." "The higher the ape goes, the more he shows his tail." "The moon does not heed the barking of dogs." "He measures another's corn by his own bushel." "He shuns the man who knows him well." "Fools tie knots and wise men loose them."

Proverbs that have to do with foretelling: (The most obvious are those to do with the weather.) "Sow peas and beans in the wane of the moon, Who soweth them sooner, he soweth too soon." "When the wind's in the north, the skilful fisher goes not forth." "When the sloe tree is as white as a sheet, sow your barley whether it be dry or wet." "When the sun sets bright and clear, An easterly wind you need not fear. When the sun sets in a bank, A westerly wind we shall not want."

In short: "Keep your weather eye open": be realistic about sizing up today's weather, because your accuracy has bearing upon tomorrow's weather. And forecast not only the meteorological weather, but also the social weather: "When the moon's in the full, then wit's in the wane." "Straws show which way the wind blows." "When the fish is caught, the net is laid aside." "Remove an old tree, and it will wither to death." "The wolf may lose his teeth, but never his nature." "He that bites on every weed must needs light on poison." "Whether the pitcher strikes the stone, or the stone the pitcher, it is bad for the pitcher." "Eagles catch no flies." "The more laws, the more offenders."

In this foretelling category we might also include the recipes for wise living, sometimes moral, sometimes technical: "First thrive, and then wive." "Think with the wise but talk with the vulgar." "When the fox preacheth, then beware your geese." "Venture a small fish to catch a great one." "Respect a man, he will do the more."

In the class of "typical, recurrent situations" we might put such proverbs and proverbial expressions as: "Sweet appears sour when we pay." "The treason is loved but the traitor is hated." "The wine in the bottle does not quench thirst." "The sun is never the worse for shining on a dunghill." "The lion kicked by an ass." "The lion's share." "To catch one napping." "To smell a rat." "To cool one's heels."

By all means, I do not wish to suggest that this is the only way in which the proverbs could be classified. For instance, I have listed in the "foretelling" group the proverb, "When the fox preacheth, then beware your geese." But it could obviously be "taken over" for vindictive purposes. Or consider a proverb like, "Virtue flies from the heart of a mercenary man." A poor man might obviously use it either to console himself for being poor (the implication being, "Because I am poor in money I am rich in virtue") or to strike at another (the implication being, "When he got money, what else could you expect of him but deterioration?"). In fact, we could even say that such symbolic vengeance would itself be an aspect of solace. And a proverb like "The sun is never the worse for shining on a dunghill" (which I have listed under "typical recurrent situations") might as well be put in the vindictive category.

The point of issue is not to find categories that "place" the proverbs once and for all. What I want is categories that suggest their active nature. Here there is no "realism for its own sake." There is realism for promise, admonition, solace, vengeance, foretelling, instruction, charting, all for the direct bearing that such acts have upon matters of welfare.

2

Step two: Why not extend such analysis of proverbs to encompass the whole field of literature? Could the most complex and sophisticated works of art legitimately be considered somewhat as "proverbs writ large"? Such leads, if held admissible, should help us to discover important facts about literary organization (thus satisfying the requirements of technical criticism). And the kind of observation from this perspective should apply beyond literature to life in general (thus helping to take literature out of its separate bin and give it a place in a general "sociological" picture).

The point of view might be phrased in this way: Proverbs are *strategies* for dealing with *situations*. In so far as situations are typical and recurrent in a given social structure, people develop names for them and strategies for handling them. Another name for strategies might be *attitudes*.

People have often commented on the fact that there are contrary *proverbs*. But I believe that the above approach to proverbs suggests a necessary modification of that comment. The apparent contradictions depend upon differences in *attitude* involving a correspondingly different choice of *strat-*

egy. Consider, for instance, the *apparently* opposite pair: "Repentance comes too late" and "Never too late to mend." The first is admonitory. It says in effect: "You'd better look out, or you'll get yourself too far into this business." The second is consolatory, saying in effect: "Buck up, old man, you can still pull out of this."

Some critics have quarreled with me about my selection of the word "strategy" as the name for this process. I have asked them to suggest an alternative term, so far without profit. The only one I can think of is "method." But if "strategy" errs in suggesting to some people an overly *conscious* procedure, "method" errs in suggesting an overly "*methodical*" one. Anyhow, let's look at the documents:

Concise Oxford Dictionary: "Strategy: Movement of an army or armies in a compaign, art of so moving or disposing troops or ships as to impose upon the enemy the place and time and conditions for fighting preferred by oneself" (from a Greek word that refers to the leading of an army).

New English Dictionary: "Strategy: The art of projecting and directing the larger military movements and operations of a campaign."

André Cheron, *Traité Complet d'Echecs: "On entend par stratégie les manoeuvres qui ont pour but la sortie et le bon arrangement des pièces."*

Looking at these definitions, I gain courage. For surely, the most highly alembicated and sophisticated work of art, arising in complex civilizations, could be considered as designed to organize and command the army of one's thoughts and images, and to so organize them that one "imposes upon the enemy the time and place and conditions for fighting preferred by oneself." One seeks to "direct the larger movements and operations" in one's campaign of living. One "maneuvers," and the maneuvering is an "art."

Are not the final results one's "strategy"? One tries, as far as possible, to develop a strategy whereby one "can't lose." One tries to change the rules of the game until they fit his own necessities. Does the artist encounter disaster? He will "make capital" of it. If one is a victim of competition, for instance, if one is elbowed out, if one is willy-nilly more jockeyed against than jockeying, one can by the solace and vengeance of art convert this very "liability" into an "asset." One tries to fight on his own terms, developing a strategy for imposing the proper "time, place, and conditions."

But one must also, to develop a full strategy, be *realistic.* One must *size things up* properly. One cannot accurately know how things *will be,* what is promising and what is menacing, unless he accurately knows how things *are.* So the wise strategist will not be content with strategies of merely a self-gratifying sort. He will "keep his weather eye open." He will not too eagerly "read into" a scene an attitude that is irrelevant to it. He won't sit on the side of an active volcano and "see" it as a dormant plain.

Often, alas, he will. The great allurement in our present popular "inspirational literature," for instance, may be largely of this sort. It is a strategy for easy consolation. It "fills a need," since there is always a need for easy consolation—and in an era of confusion like our own the need is especially keen. So people are only too willing to "meet a man halfway" who will *play down* the realistic naming of our situation and *play up* such strategies as make solace cheap. However, I should propose a reservation here. We usually take it for granted that people who consume our current output of books on "How to Buy Friends and Bamboozle Oneself and Other People" are reading as *students* who will attempt applying the recipes given. Nothing of the sort. *The reading of a book on the attaining of success is in itself the symbolic attaining of that success.* It is *while they read* that these readers are "succeeding." I'll wager that, in by far the great majority of cases, such readers make no serious attempt to apply the book's recipes. The lure of the book resides in the fact that the reader, while reading it, is then living in the aura of success. What he wants is *easy* success; and he gets it in symbolic form by the mere reading itself. To attempt applying such stuff in real life would be very difficult, full of many disillusioning difficulties.

Sometimes a different strategy may arise. The author may remain realistic, avoiding too easy a form of solace—yet he may get as far off the track in his own way. Forgetting that realism is an aspect for foretelling, he may take it as an end in itself. He is tempted to do this by two factors: (1) an *ill-digested* philosophy of science, leading him mistakenly to assume that "'relentless" naturalistic "truthfulness" is a proper end in itself, and (2) a merely *competitive* desire to outstrip other writers by being "more realistic" than they. Works thus made "efficient" by tests of competition internal to the book trade are a kind of academicism not so named (the writer usually thinks of it as the *opposite* of academicism). Realism thus stepped up competitively might be distinguished from the proper sort by the name of "naturalism." As a way of "sizing things up," the naturalistic tradition tends to become as inaccurate as the "inspirational" strategy, though at the opposite extreme.

Anyhow, the main point is this: A work like *Madame Bovary* (or its homely American translation, *Babbitt*) is the strategic naming of a situation. It singles out a pattern of experience that is sufficiently representative of our social structure, that recurs sufficiently often *mutandis mutatis*, for people to "need a word for it" and to adopt an attitude towards it. Each work of art is the addition of a word to an informal dictionary (or, in the case of purely derivative artists, the addition of a subsidiary meaning to a word already given by some originating artist). As for *Madame Bovary*, the French critic Jules de Gaultier proposed to add it to our *formal* dictionary by coining the word "Bovarysme" and writing a whole book to say what he meant by it.

Mencken's book on *The American Language*, I hate to say, is splendid. I console myself with the reminder that Mencken didn't write it. Many millions of people wrote it, and Mencken was merely the amanuensis who took it down from their dictation. He found a true "vehicle" (that is, a book that could be greater than the author who wrote it). He gets the royalties, but the job was done by a collectivity. As you read that book, you see a people who were up against a new set of typical recurrent situations, situations typical of their business, their politics, their criminal organizations, their sports. Either there were no words for these in standard English, or people didn't know them, or they didn't "sound right." So a new vocabulary arose, to "give us a word for it." I see no reason for believing that Americans are unusually fertile in word-coinage. American slang was not developed out of some exceptional gift. It was developed out of the fact that new typical situations had arisen and people needed names for them. They had to "size things up." They had to console and strike, to promise and admonish. They had to describe for purposes of forecasting. And "slang" was the result. It is, by this analysis, simply *proverbs not so named*, a kind of "folk criticism."

3

With what, then, would "sociological criticism" along these lines be concerned? It would seek to codify the various strategies which artists have developed with relation to the naming of situations. In a sense, much of it would even be "timeless," for many of the "typical, recurrent situations" are not peculiar to our own civilization at all. The situations and strategies framed in Aesop's Fables, for instance, apply to human relations now just as fully as they applied in ancient Greece. They are, like philosophy, sufficiently "generalized" to extend far beyond the particular combination of events named by them in any one instance. They name an "essence." Or, as Korzybski might say, they are on a "high level of abstraction." One doesn't usually think of them as "abstract," since they are usually so concrete in their stylistic expression. But they invariably aim to discern the "general behind the particular" (which would suggest that they are good Goethe).

The attempt to treat literature from the standpoint of situations and strategies suggests a variant of Spengler's notion of the "contemporaneous." By "contemporaneity" he meant corresponding stages of different cultures. For instance, if modern New York is much like decadent Rome, then we are "contemporaneous" with decadent Rome, or with some corresponding decadent city among the Mayas, etc. It is in this sense that situations are "timeless," "non-historical," "contemporaneous." A given human relationship may be at one time named in terms of foxes and lions, if there are foxes and lions about; or it may now be named in terms of salesmanship, advertising, the tactics of politicians, etc. But beneath the change in particulars, we may often discern the naming of the one situation.

So sociological criticism, as here understood, would seek to assemble and codify this lore. It might occasionally lead us to outrage good taste, as we sometimes found exemplified in some great sermon or tragedy or abstruse work of philosophy the same strategy as we found exemplified in a dirty joke. At this point, we'd put the sermon and the dirty joke together, thus "grouping by situation" and showing the range of possible particularizations. In his exceptionally discerning essay, "A Critic's Job of Work," R. P. Blackmur says, "I think on the whole his (Burke's) method could be applied with equal fruitfulness to Shakespeare, Dashiell Hammett, or Marie Corelli." When I got through wincing, I had to admit that Blackmur was right. This article is an attempt to say for the method what can be said. As a matter of fact, I'll go a step further and maintain: You can't properly put Marie Corelli and Shakespeare apart until you have first put them together. First genus, then differentia. The strategy in common is the genus. The *range* or *scale* or *spectrum* of particularizations is the differentia.

Anyhow, that's what I'm driving at. And that's why reviewers sometime find in my work "intuitive" leaps that are dubious as "science." They are not "leaps" at all. They are classifications, groupings, made on the basis of some strategic element common to the items grouped. They are neither more nor less "intuitive" than *any* grouping or classification of social events. Apples can be grouped with bananas as fruits, and they can be grouped with tennis balls as round. I am simply proposing, in the social sphere, a method of classification with reference to *strategies*.

The method has these things to be said in its favor: It gives definite insight into the organization of literary works; and it automatically breaks down the barriers erected about literature as a specialized pursuit. People can classify novels by reference to three kinds, eight kinds, seventeen kinds. It doesn't matter. Students patiently copy down the professor's classification and pass examinations on it, because the range of possible academic classifications is endless. Sociological classification, as herein suggested, would derive its relevance from the fact that it should apply both to works of art and to social situations outside of art.

It would, I admit, violate current pieties, break down current categories, and thereby "outrage good taste." But "good taste" has become *inert*. The classifications I am proposing would be *active*. I think that what we need is active categories.

These categories will lie on the bias across the categories of modern specialization. The new alignment will outrage in particular those persons who take the division of faculties in our universities to be an exact replica of the way in which God himself divided up the universe. We have had the Philosophy of the Being; and we have had the Philosophy of the Becoming. In contemporary specialization, we have been getting the Philosophy of the Bin. Each of these mental localities has had its own peculiar way of life, its own values, even its own special idiom for seeing, thinking, and "proving." Among other things, a sociological approach should attempt to provide a reintegrative point of view, a broader empire of investigation encompassing the lot.

What would such sociological categories be like? They would consider works of art, I think, as strategies for selecting enemies and allies, for socializing losses, for warding off evil eye, for purification, propitiation, and desanctification, consolation and vengeance, admonition and exhortation, implicit commands or instructions of one sort or another. Art forms like "tragedy" or "comedy" or "satire" would be treated as *equipments for living,* that size up situations in various ways and in keeping with correspondingly various attitudes. The typical ingredients of such forms would be sought. Their relation to typical situations would be stressed. Their comparative values would be considered, with the intention of formulating a "strategy of strategies," the "over-all" strategy obtained by inspection of the lot.

KENNETH BURKE

A Grammar of Motives

INTRODUCTION: THE FIVE KEY TERMS OF DRAMATISM

WHAT is involved, when we say what people are doing and why they are doing it? An answer to that question is the subject of this book. The book is concerned with the basic forms of thought which, in accordance with the nature of the world as all men necessarily experience it, are exemplified in the attributing of motives. These forms of thought can be embodied profoundly or trivially, truthfully or falsely. They are equally present in systematically elaborated metaphysical structures, in legal judgments, in poetry and fiction, in political and scientific works, in news and in bits of gossip offered at random.

We shall use five terms as generating principle of our investigation. They are: Act, Scene, Agent, Agency, Purpose. In a rounded statement about motives, you must have some word that names the *act* (names what took place, in thought or deed), and another that names the *scene* (the background of the act, the situation in which it occurred); also, you must indicate what person or kind of person (*agent*) performed the act, what means or instruments he used (*agency*), and the *purpose*. Men may violently disagree about the purposes behind a given act, or about the character of the person who did it, or how he did it, or in what kind of situation he acted; or they may even insist upon totally different words to name the act itself. But be that as it may, any complete statement about motives will offer *some kind of* answers to these five questions: what was done (act), when or where it was done (scene), who did it (agent), how he did it (agency), and why (purpose).

If you ask why, with a whole world of terms to choose from, we select these rather than some others as basic, our book itself is offered as the answer. For, to explain our position, we shall show how it can be applied.

Act, Scene, Agent, Agency, Purpose. Although, over the centuries, men have shown great enterprise and inventiveness in pondering matters of human motivation, one can simplify the subject by this pentad of key terms, which are understandable almost at a glance. They need never to be abandoned, since all statements that assign motives can be shown to arise out of them and to terminate in them. By examining them quizzically, we can range far; yet the terms are always there for us to reclaim, in their everyday simplicity, their almost miraculous easiness, thus enabling us constantly to begin afresh. When they might become difficult, when we can hardly see them, through having stared at them too intensely, we can of a sudden relax, to look at them as we always have, lightly, glancingly. And having reassured ourselves, we can start out again, once more daring to let them look strange and difficult for a time.

In an exhibit of photographic murals (*Road to Victory*) at the Museum of Modern Art, there was an aerial photograph of two launches, proceeding side by side on a tranquil sea. Their wakes crossed and recrossed each other in almost an infinity of lines. Yet despite the intricateness of this tracery, the picture gave an impression of great simplicity, because one could quickly perceive the generating principle of its design. Such, ideally, is the case with our pentad of terms, used as generating principle. It should provide us with a kind of simplicity that can be developed into considerable complexity, and yet can be discovered beneath its elaborations.

We want to inquire into the purely internal relationships which the five terms bear to one another, considering their possibilities of transformation, their range of permutations and combinations—and then to see how these various resources figure in actual statements about human motives. Strictly speaking, we mean by a Grammar of motives a concern with the terms alone, without reference to the ways in which their potentialities have been or can be utilized in actual statements about motives. Speaking broadly we could designate as "philosophies" any statements in which these grammatical resources are specifically utilized. Random or unsystematic statements about motives could be considered as fragments of a philosophy.

One could think of the Grammatical resources as *principles,* and of the various philosophies as *casuistries* which apply these principles to temporal situations. For instance, we may examine the term Scene simply as a blanket term for the concept of background or setting *in general,* a name for *any* situation in which acts or agents are placed. In our usage, this concern would be "grammatical." And we move into matters of "philosophy" when we note that one thinker uses "God" as his term for the ultimate ground or scene of human action, another uses "nature," a third uses "environment," or "history," or "means of production," etc. And whereas a statement about the grammatical principles of motivation might lay claim to a universal validity, or complete certainty, the choice of any one philosophic idiom embodying these principles is much more open to question. Even before we know what act is to be discussed, we can say with confidence that a rounded discussion of its motives must contain a reference to *some kind of* background. But since each philosophic idiom will characterize this background differently, there will remain the question as to which characterization is "right" or "more nearly right."

It is even likely that, whereas one philosophic idiom offers the best calculus for one case, another case answers best to a totally different calculus. However, we should not think of "cases" in too restricted a sense. Although, from the standpoint of the grammatical principles inherent in the internal relationships prevailing among our five terms, any given philosophy is to be considered as a casuistry, even a cultural situation extending over centuries is a "case," and would probably require a much different philosophic idiom as its temporizing calculus of motives than would be required in the case of other cultural situations.

In our original plans for this project, we had no notion of writing a "Grammar" at all. We began with a theory of comedy, applied to a treatise on human relations. Feeling that competitive ambition is a drastically over-developed motive in the modern world, we thought this motive might be transcended if men devoted themselves not so much to "excoriating" it as to "appreciating" it. Accordingly, we began taking notes on the foibles and antics of what we tended to think of as "the Human Barnyard."

We sought to formulate the basic stratagems which people employ, in endless variations, and consciously or unconsciously, for the outwitting or cajoling of one another. Since all these devices had a "you and me" quality about them, being "addressed" to some person or to some advantage, we classed them broadly under the heading of a Rhetoric. There were other notes, concerned with modes of expression and appeal in the fine arts, and with purely psychological or psychoanalytic matters. These we classed under the heading of Symbolic.

We had made still further observations, which we at first strove uneasily to class under one or the other of these two heads, but which we were eventually able to distinguish as the makings of a Grammar. For we found in the course of writing that our project needed a grounding in formal considerations logically prior to both the rhetorical and the psychological. And as we proceeded with this introductory groundwork, it kept extending its claims until it had spun itself from an intended few hundred words into nearly 200,000, of which the present book is revision and abridgement.

Theological, metaphysical, and juridical doctrines offer the best illustration of the concerns we place under the heading of Grammar; the forms and methods of art best illustrate the concerns of Symbolic; and the ideal material to reveal the nature of Rhetoric comprises observations on parliamentary and diplomatic devices, editorial bias, sales methods and incidents of social sparring. However, the three fields overlap considerably. And we shall note, in passing, how the Rhetoric and the Symbolic hover about the edges of our central theme, the Grammar.

A perfectionist might seek to evolve terms free of ambiguity and inconsistency (as with the terministic ideals of symbolic logic and logical positivism). But we have a different purpose in view, one that probably retains traces of its "comic" origin. We take it for granted that, insofar as men cannot themselves create the universe, there must remain something essentially enigmatic about the problem of motives, and that this underlying enigma will manifest itself in inevitable ambiguities and inconsistencies among the terms for motives. Accordingly, what we want is *not terms that avoid ambiguity,* but *terms that clearly reveal the strategic spots at which ambiguities necessarily arise.*

Occasionally, you will encounter a writer who seems to get great exaltation out of proving, with an air of much relentlessness, that some philosophic term or other has been used to cover a variety of meanings, and who would smash and abolish this idol. As a general rule, when a term is singled out for such harsh treatment, if you look closer you will find that it happens to be associated with some cultural or political trend from which the writer would dissociate himself; hence there is a certain notable ambiguity in this very charge of ambiguity, since he presumably feels purged and strengthened by bringing to bear upon this particular term a kind of attack that could, with as much justice, be brought to bear upon any other term (or "title") in philosophy, including of course the alternative term, or "title," that the writer would swear by. Since no two things or acts or situations are exactly alike, you cannot apply the same term to both of them without thereby introducing a certain margin of ambiguity, an ambiguity as great as the difference between the two subjects that are given the identical title. And all the more may you expect to find ambiguity in terms so "titular" as to become the marks of a philosophic school, or even several philosophic schools. Hence, instead of considering it our task to "dispose of" any ambiguity by merely disclosing the fact that it is an ambiguity, we rather consider it our task to study and clarify the *resources* of ambiguity. For in the course of this work, we shall deal with many kinds of *transformation*—and it is in the areas of ambiguity that transformations take place; in fact, without such areas, transformation would be impossible. Distinctions, we might say, arise out of a great central moltenness, where all is merged. They have been thrown from a liquid center to the surface, where they have congealed. Let one of these crusted distinctions return to its source, and in this alchemic center it may be remade, again becoming molten liquid, and may enter into new combinations, whereat it may be again thrown forth as a new crust, a different distinction. So that A may become non-A. But not merely by a leap from one state to the other. Rather, we must take A back into the ground of its existence, the logical substance that is its causal ancestor, and on to a point where it is consubstantial with non-A; then we may return, this time emerging with non-A instead.

And so with our five terms: certain formal interrelationships prevail among these terms, by reason of their role as attributes of a common ground or substance. Their participation in a common ground makes for transformability. At every point where the field covered by any one of these terms overlaps upon the field covered by any other, there is an alchemic opportunity, whereby we can put one philosophy or doctrine of motivation into the alembic, make the appropriate passes, and take out another. From the central moltenness, where all the elements are fused into one togetherness, there are thrown forth, in separate crusts, such distinctions as those between freedom and necessity, activity and passiveness, coöperation and competition, cause and effect, mechanism and teleology.

Our term, "Agent," for instance, is a general heading that might, in a given case, require further subdivision, as an agent might have his act modified (hence partly motivated) by friends (co-agents) or enemies (counter-agents). Again, under "Agent" one could place any personal properties that are assigned a motivational value, such as "ideas," "the will," "fear," "malice," "intuition," "the creative imagination." A portrait painter may treat the body as a property of the agent (an expression of personality), whereas materialistic medicine would treat it as "scenic," a purely "objective material"; and from another point of view it could be classed as an agency, a means by which one gets reports of the world at large. Machines are obviously instruments (that is, Agencies); yet in their vast accumulation they constitute the industrial scene, with its own peculiar set of motivational properties. War may be treated as an Agency, insofar as it is a means to an end; as a collective Act, subdivisible into many individual acts; as a Purpose, in schemes proclaiming a cult of war. For the man inducted into the army, war is a Scene, a situation that motivates the nature of his training; and in mythologies war is an Agent, or perhaps better a super-agent, in the figure of the war god. We may think of voting as an act, and of the voter as an agent; yet votes and voters both are hardly other than a politician's medium or agency; or from another point of view, they are a part of his scene. And insofar as a vote is cast without adequate knowledge of its consequences, one might even question whether it should be classed as an activity at all; one might rather call it passive, or perhaps sheer motion (what the behaviorists would call a Response to a Stimulus).

Or imagine that one were to manipulate the terms, for the imputing of motives, in such a case as this: The hero (agent) with the help of a friend (co-agent) outwits the villain (counter-agent) by using a file (agency) that enables him to break his bonds (act) in order to escape (purpose) from the room where he has been confined (scene). In selecting a casuistry here, we might locate the motive in the agent, as were we to credit his escape to some trait integral to his personality, such as "love of freedom." Or we might stress the motivational force of the scene, since nothing is surer to awaken thoughts of escape in a man than a condition of imprisonment. Or we might note the essential part played by the *co-agent,* in assisting our hero to escape—and, with such thoughts as our point of departure, we might conclude that the motivations of this act should be reduced to social origins.

Or if one were given to the brand of speculative enterprise exemplified by certain Christian heretics (for instance, those who worshipped Judas as a saint, on the grounds that his betrayal of Christ, in leading to the Crucifixion, so brought about the opportunity for mankind's redemption) one might locate the necessary motivational origin of the act in the *counter-agent.* For the hero would not have been prodded to escape if there had been no villain to imprison him. Inasmuch as the escape could be called a "good" act, we might find in such motivational reduction to the counter-agent a compensatory transformation whereby a bitter fountain may give forth sweet waters. In his *Anti-Dühring* Engels gives us a secular variant which no one could reasonably call outlandish or excessive:

> It was slavery that first made possible the division of labour between agriculture and industry on a considerable scale, and along with this, the flower of the ancient world, Hellenism. Without slavery, no Greek state, no Greek art and science; without slavery, no Roman Empire. But without Hellenism and the Roman Empire as a basis, also no modern Europe.

> We should never forget that our whole economic, political and intellectual development has as its presupposition a state of things in which slavery was as necessary as it was universally recognized. In this sense we are entitled to say: Without the slavery of antiquity, no modern socialism.

Pragmatists would probably have referred the motivation back to a source in *agency.* They would have noted that our hero escaped by using an *instrument,* the file by which he severed his bonds; then in this same line of thought, they would have observed that the hand holding the file was also an instrument; and by the same token the brain that guided the hand would be an instrument, and so likewise the educational system that taught the methods and shaped the values involved in the incident.

True, if you reduce the terms to any one of them, you will find them branching out again; for no one of them is enough. Thus, Mead called his pragmatism a philosophy of the *act.* And though Dewey stresses the value of "intelligence" as an instrument (agency, embodied in "scientific method"), the other key terms in his casuistry, "experience" and "nature," would be the equivalents of act and scene respectively. We must add, however, that Dewey is given to stressing the *overlap* of these two terms, rather than the respects in which they are distinct, as he proposes to "replace the traditional separation of nature and experience with the idea of continuity." (The quotation is from *Intelligence and the Modern World.*)

As we shall see later, it is by reason of the pliancy among our terms that philosophic systems can pull one way and another. The margins of overlap provide opportunities whereby a thinker can go without a leap from any one of the terms to any of its fellows. (We have also likened the terms to the fingers, which in their extremities are distinct from one another, but merge in the palm of the hand. If you would go from one finger to another without a leap, you need but trace the tendon down into the palm of the hand, and then trace a new course along another tendon.) Hence, no great dialectical enterprise is necessary if you would merge the terms, reducing them even to as few as one; and then, treating this as the "essential" term, the "causal ancestor" of the lot, you can proceed in the reverse direction across the margins of overlap, "deducing" the other terms from it as its logical descendants.

This is the method, explicitly and in the grand style, of metaphysics which brings its doctrines to a head in some over-all title, a word for being in general, or action in general, or motion in general, or development in general, or experience in general, etc., with all its other terms distributed about this titular term in positions leading up to it and away from it. There is also an implicit kind of metaphysics, that often goes by the name of No Metaphysics, and aims at reduction not to an over-all title but to some presumably underlying atomic constituent. Its vulgar variant is to be found in techniques of "unmasking," which would make for progress and emancipation by applying materialistic terms to immaterial subjects (the pattern here being, "X is nothing but Y," where X designates a higher value and Y a lower one, the higher value being thereby reduced to the lower one).

The titular word for our own method is "dramatism," since it invites one to consider the matter of motives in a perspective that, being developed from the analysis of drama, treats language and thought primarily as modes of action. The method is synoptic, though not in the historical sense. A purely historical survey would require no less than a universal history of human culture; for every judgment, exhortation, or admonition, every view of natural or supernatural reality, every intention or expectation involves assumptions about motive, or cause. Our work must be synoptic in a different sense: in the sense that it offers a system of placement, and should enable us, by the systematic manipulation of the terms, to "generate," or "anticipate" the various classes of motivational theory. And a treatment in these terms, we hope to show, reduces the subject synoptically while still permitting us to appreciate its scope and complexity.

It is not our purpose to import dialectical and metaphysical concerns into a subject that might otherwise be free of them. On the contrary, we hope to make clear the ways in which dialectical and metaphysical issues *necessarily* figure in the subject of motivation. Our speculations, as we interpret them, should show that the subject of motivation is a philosophic one, not ultimately to be solved in terms of empirical science.

• • •

KENNETH BURKE

A RHETORIC OF MOTIVES

IDENTIFICATION

We considered, among those "uses" to which Samson Agonistes was put, the poet's identification with a blind giant who slew himself in slaying enemies of the Lord; and we saw identification between Puritans and Israelites, Royalists and Philistines, identification allowing for a ritualistic kind of historiography in which the poet could, by allusion to a Biblical story, "substantially" foretell the triumph of his vanquished faction. Then we came upon a more complicated kind of identification: here the poet presents a motive in an essentially magnified or perfected form, in some way tragically purified or transcended; the imagery of death reduces the motive to ultimate terms, dramatic equivalent for an "entelechial" pattern of thought whereby a thing's nature would be classed according to the fruition, maturing, or ideal fulfillment, proper to its kind.

As seen from this point of view, then, an imagery of slaying (slaying of either the self or another) is to be considered merely as a special case of identification in general. Or otherwise put: the imagery of slaying is a special case of transformation, and transformation involves the ideas and imagery of *identification*. That is: the *killing* of something is the *changing* of it, and the statement of the thing's nature before and after the change is an *identifying* of it.

Perhaps the quickest way to make clear what we are doing here is to show what difference it makes. Noting that tragic poets identify motives in terms of killing, one might deduce that "they are essentially killers." Or one might deduce that "they are essentially identifiers." Terms for identification in general are wider in scope than terms for killing. We are proposing that our rhetoric be reduced to this term of wider scope, with the term of narrower scope being treated as a species of it. We begin with an anecdote of killing, because invective, eristic, polemic, and logomachy are so pronounced an aspect of rhetoric. But we use a dialectical device (the shift to a higher level of generalization) that enables us to transcend the narrower implications of this imagery, even while keeping them clearly in view. We need never deny the presence of strife, enmity, faction as a characteristic motive of rhetorical expression. We need not close our eyes to their almost tyrannous ubiquity in human relations; we can be on the alert always to see how such temptations to strife are implicit in the institutions that condition human relationships; yet we can at the same time always look beyond this order, to the principle of identification in general, a terministic choice justified by the fact that the identifications in the order of love are also characteristic of rhetorical expression. We may as well be frank about it, since our frankness, if it doesn't convince, will at least serve another important purpose of this work: it will reveal a strategic resource of terminology. Being frank, then: Because of our choice, we can treat "war" as a "*special case of peace*"—not as a primary motive in itself, not as *essentially* real, but purely as a *derivative* condition, a *perversion.*

IDENTIFICATION AND "CONSUBSTANTIALITY"

A is not identical with his colleague, B. But insofar as their interests are joined, A is *identified* with B. Or he may *identify himself* with B even when their interests are not joined, if he assumes that they are, or is persuaded to believe so.

Here are ambiguities of substance. In being identified with B, A is "substantially one" with a person other than himself. Yet at the same time he remains unique, an individual locus of motives. Thus he is both joined and separate, at once a distinct substance and consubstantial with another.

While consubstantial with its parents, with the "firsts" from which it is derived, the offspring is nonetheless apart from them. In this sense, there is nothing abstruse in the statement that the offspring both is and is not one with its parentage. Similarly, two persons may be identified in terms of some principle they share in common, an "identification" that does not deny their distinctness.

To identify A with B is to make A "consubstantial" with B. Accordingly, since our *Grammar of Motives* was constructed about "substance" as key term, the related rhetoric selects its nearest equivalent in the areas of persuasion and dissuasion, communication and polemic. And our third volume, *Symbolic of Motives,* should be built about *identity* as titular or ancestral term, the "first" to which all other terms could be reduced and from which they could then be derived or generated, as from a common spirit. The thing's *identity* would here be its uniqueness as an entity in itself and by itself, a demarcated unit having its own particular structure.

However, "substance" is an abstruse philosophic term, beset by a long history of quandaries and puzzlements. It names so paradoxical a function in men's systematic terminologies, that thinkers finally tried to abolish it altogether—and in recent years they have often persuaded themselves that they really did abolish it from their terminologies of motives. They abolished the *term,* but it is doubtful whether they can ever abolish the *function* of that term, or even whether they should *want* to. A doctrine of *consubstantiality,* either explicit or implicit, may be necessary to any way of life. For substance, in the old philosophies, was an *act;* and a way of life is an *acting-together;* and in acting together, men have common sensations, concepts, images, ideas, attitudes that make them *consubstantial.*

The *Grammar* dealt with the universal paradoxes of substance. It considered resources of placement and definition common to all thought. The *Symbolic* should deal with unique individuals, each its own peculiarly constructed act, or form. These unique "constitutions" being capable of treatment in isolation, the *Symbolic* should consider them primarily in their capacity as singulars, each a separate universe of discourse (though there are also respects in which they are consubstantial with others of their kind, since they can be classed with other unique individuals as joint participants in common principles, possessors of the same or similar properties).

The *Rhetoric* deals with the possibilities of classification in its *partisan* aspects; it considers the ways in which individuals are at odds with one another, or become identified with groups more or less at odds with one another.

Why "at odds," you may ask, when the titular term is "identification"? Because, to begin with "identification" is, by the same token, though roundabout, to confront the implications of *division.* And so, in the end, men are brought to that most tragically ironic of all divisions, or conflicts, wherein millions of cooperative acts go into the preparation for one single destructive act. We refer to that ultimate *disease* of cooperation: *war.* (You will understand war much better if you think of it, not simply as strife come to a head, but rather as a disease, or perversion of communion. Modern war characteristically requires a myriad of constructive acts for each destructive one; before each culminating blast there must be a vast network of interlocking operations, directed communally.)

Identification is affirmed with earnestness precisely because there is division. Identification is compensatory to division. If men were not apart from one another, there would be no need for the rhetorician to proclaim their unity. If men were wholly and truly of one substance, absolute communication would be of man's very essence. It would not be an ideal, as it now is, partly embodied in material conditions and partly frustrated by these same conditions; rather, it would be as natural, spontaneous, and total as with those ideal prototypes of communication, the theologian's angels, or "messengers."

The *Grammar* was at peace insofar as it contemplated the paradoxes common to all men, the universal resources of verbal placement. The *Symbolic* should be at peace, in that the individual substances, or entities, or constituted acts are there considered in their uniqueness, hence outside the realm of conflict. For individual universes, as such, do not compete. Each merely *is,* being its own self-sufficient realm of discourse. And the *Symbolic* thus considers each thing as a set of inter-related terms all conspiring to round out their identity as participants in a common substance of meaning. An individual does in actuality compete with other individuals. But within the rules of Symbolic, the individual is treated merely as a self-subsistent unit proclaiming its peculiar nature. It is "at peace," in that its terms *cooperate* in modifying one another. But insofar as the individual is involved in conflict with other individuals or groups, the study of this same individual would fall under the head of *Rhetoric.* Or considered rhetorically, the victim of a neurotic conflict is torn by parliamentary wrangling; he is heckled like Hitler within. (Hitler is said to have confronted a constant wrangle in his private deliberations, after having imposed upon his people a flat choice between conformity and silence.) Rhetorically, the neurotic's every attempt to legislate for his own conduct is disorganized by rival factions within his own dissociated self. Yet, considered Symbolically, the same victim is technically "at peace," in the sense that his identity is like a unified, mutually adjusted set of terms. For even antagonistic terms, confronting each other as parry and thrust, can be said to "cooperate" in the building of an over-all form.

The *Rhetoric* must lead us through the Scramble, the Wrangle of the Market Place, the flurries and flare-ups of the Human Barnyard, the Give and Take, the wavering line of pressure and counterpressure, the Logomachy, the onus of ownership, the Wars of Nerves, the War. It too has its peaceful moments: at times its endless competition can add up to the transcending of itself. In ways of its own, it can move from the factional to the universal. But its ideal culminations are more often beset by strife as the condition of their organized expression, or material embodiment. Their very universality becomes transformed into a partisan weapon. For one need not scrutinize the concept of "identification" very sharply to see, implied in it at every turn, its ironic counterpart: division. Rhetoric is concerned with the state of Babel after the Fall. Its contribution to a "sociology of knowledge" must often carry us far into the lugubrious regions of malice and the lie.

THE IDENTIFYING NATURE OF PROPERTY

Metaphysically, a thing is identified by its *properties*. In the realm of Rhetoric, such identification is frequently by property in the most materialistic sense of the term, economic property, such property as Coleridge, in his "Religious Musings," calls a

> twy-streaming fount,
> Whence Vice and Virtue flow, honey and gall.

And later:

> From Avarice thus, from Luxury and War
> Sprang heavenly Science; and from Science, Freedom.

Coleridge, typically the literary idealist, goes one step further back, deriving "property" from the workings of "Imagination." But meditations upon the dual aspects of property as such are enough for our present purposes. In the surrounding of himself with properties that name his number or establish his identity, man is ethical. ("Avarice" is but the scenic word "property" translated into terms of an agent's attitude, or incipient act.) Man's moral growth is organized through properties, properties in goods, in services, in position or status, in citizenship, in reputation, in acquaintanceship and love. But however ethical such an array of identifications may be when considered in itself, its relation to other entities that are likewise forming their identity in terms of property can lead to turmoil and discord. Here is *par excellence* a topic to be considered in a rhetoric having "identification" as its key term. And we see why one should expect to get much insight from Marxism, as a study of capitalistic rhetoric. Veblen is also, from this point of view, to be considered a theorist of rhetoric. (And we know of no better way to quickly glimpse the range of rhetoric than to read, in succession, the articles on "Property" and "Propaganda" in *The Encyclopaedia of the Social Sciences.*)

Bentham's utilitarian analysis of language, treating of the ways in which men find "eulogistic coverings" for their "material interests," is thus seen to be essentially rhetorical, and to bear directly upon the motives of property as a rhetorical factor. Indeed, since it is so clearly a matter of rhetoric to persuade a man by identifying your cause with his interests, we note the ingredient of rhetoric in the animal experimenter's ways of conditioning, as animals that respond avidly at a food signal suggest, underlying even human motives, the inclination, like a house dog, to seek salvation in the Sign of the Scraped Plate. But the lessons of this "animal rhetoric" can mislead, as we learn from the United States' attempts to use food as an instrument of policy in Europe after the war. These efforts met with enough ill will to suggest that the careful "screening" of our representatives, to eliminate reformist tendencies as far as possible and to identify American aid only with conservative or even reactionary interests, practically *guaranteed* us a dismal rhetoric in our dealings with other nations. And when Henry Wallace, during a trip abroad, began earning for our country the genuine good will of Europe's common people and intellectual classes, the Genius of the Screening came into its own: our free press, as at one signal, began stoutly assuring the citizens of both the United States and Europe that Wallace did not truly represent us. What did represent us, presumably, was the policy of the Scraped Plate, which our officialdom now and then bestirred themselves to present publicly in terms of a dispirited "idealism," as heavy as a dead elephant. You see, we were not to be identified with very resonant things; our press assured our people that the outcome of the last election had been a "popular mandate" to this effect. (We leave this statement unrevised. For the conditions of Truman's reelection, after a campaign in which he out-Wallaced Wallace, corroborated it "in principle.")

In pure identification there would be no strife. Likewise, there would be no strife in absolute separateness, since opponents can join battle only through a mediatory ground that makes their communication possible, thus providing the first condition necessary for their interchange of blows. But put identification and division ambiguously together, so that you cannot know for certain just where one ends and the other begins, and you have the characteristic invitation to rhetoric. Here is a major reason why rhetoric, according to Aristotle, "proves opposites." When two men collaborate in an enterprise to which they contribute different kinds of services and from which they derive different amounts and kinds of profit, who is to say, once and for all, just where "cooperation" ends and one partner's "exploitation" of the other begins? The wavering line between the two cannot be "scientifically" identified; rival rhetoricians can draw it at different places, and their persuasiveness varies with the resources each has at his command. (Where public issues are concerned, such resources are not confined to the intrinsic powers of the speaker and the speech, but depend also for their effectiveness upon the purely technical means of communication, which can either aid the utterance or hamper it. For a "good" rhetoric neglected by the press obviously cannot be so "communicative" as a poor rhetoric backed nation-wide by headlines. And often we must think of rhetoric not in terms of some one particular address, but as a general *body of identifications* that owe their convincingness much more to trivial repetition and dull daily reënforcement than to exceptional rhetorical skill.)

If you would praise God, and in terms that happen also to sanction one system of material property rather than another, you have forced Rhetorical considerations upon us. If you would praise science, however exaltedly, when that same science is at the service of imperialist-militarist expansion, here again you bring things within the orbit of Rhetoric. For just as God has been identified with a certain worldly structure of ownership, so science may be identified with the interests of certain groups or classes quite *unscientific* in their purposes. Hence, however "pure" one's motives may be actually, the impurities of identification lurking about the edges of such situations introduce a typical Rhetorical wrangle of the sort that can never be settled once and for all, but belongs in the field of moral controversy where men properly seek to "prove opposites."

Thus, when his friend, Preen, wrote of a meeting where like-minded colleagues would be pres-ent and would all be proclaiming their praise of science, Prone answered: "You fail to mention another colleague who is sure to be there too, unless you take care to rule him out. I mean John Q. Militarist-Imperialist." Whereat, Preen: "This John Q. Militarist-Imperialist must be quite venerable by now. I seem to have heard of him back in Biblical times, before Roger B. Science was born. Doesn't he get in everywhere, unless he is explicitly ruled out?" He does, thanks to the ways of identification, which are in accordance with the nature of property. And the rhetorician and the moralist become one at that point where the attempt is made to reveal the undetected presence of such an identification. Thus in the United States after the second World War, the temptations of such an identification became particularly strong because so much scientific research had fallen under the direction of the military. To speak merely in praise of science, without explicitly dissociating oneself from its reactionary implications, is to identify oneself with these reactionary implications by default. Many reputable educators could thus, in this roundabout way, *function* as "conspirators." In their zeal to get federal subsidies for the science department of their college or university, they could help to shape educational policies with the ideals of war as guiding principle.

• • •

INTRODUCTION TO RICHARD M. WEAVER

Richard Weaver (1910–1953) was a champion of conservative, Platonic, and Southern ideas. Born and educated in the southern United States, most of his career was spent at the University of Chicago. Weaver was by profession a professor of English, and he wrote and taught explicitly about rhetoric and the role that it might have in revitalizing an American culture that he saw as mistaken in its values. Weaver wrote several books and articles, and here, excerpted, is one of his best known essays, "Language Is Sermonic."

One of the mainstays of conservative thought is a concern for values. Weaver felt that American culture was losing many values that were worth preserving. One of those values was a concern for humanity, which was being replaced by adulation of science. Although Weaver did not oppose science, he thought that excessive dependence on it could lead to "scientism," or the application of scientific principles to matters that were not really scientific. Such matters included public decisions, ethics, and moral choices. Weaver argued that rhetoric was a better discourse than science to guide human experience in those cases.

Some of the specific values that Weaver sought to restore we might find questionable. As part of the "Agrarian Movement," Weaver idolized the culture of the Old South, apparently ignoring its basis in slavery at the same time that he praised its values of learning, gentility, and decorum. Regardless of the specific values he preferred, Weaver's rhetorical theory is keyed to the idea that rhetoric must examine the values and principles upon which it bases its appeals.

Weaver was a Platonic idealist. You will recall that Plato believed that a world of forms was the most basic reality. Following Plato, Weaver thought that principles and ideas were more important than particular experiences or the accidents of circumstance. It is better to try to make decisions on the basis of timeless truths and transcendent principles, Weaver argued, than on the basis of changeable circumstances. This idealism shapes his rhetorical theory, for Weaver strongly felt that rhetoric should base its appeals primarily on principles and values rather than on the present circumstances of the moment.

In the selection excerpted here, Weaver begins by complaining of a decline in the value of rhetoric in his time; he looks upon the eighteenth century (the Enlightenment) as a vanished golden age of rhetoric. This decline is due to "an alteration of man's image of man," says Weaver. That image is one that devalues human emotion and values and instead attempts to apply scientific values and standards to human actions and decisions. This application of science to inappropriate domains such as how people think and act Weaver calls "scientism."

Scientism, Weaver claims, proceeds from the assumption that one can acquire knowledge and make decisions without values; that, after all, is what the objective scientist tries to do in the laboratory. But one can neither be human nor understand the human without taking into consideration humanity's values and ideals. Science can tell us about rocks and stars, argues Weaver, but it cannot inform the decisions people must make.

A better discourse to guide human actions, and a better method for understanding humanity, is *rhetoric.* Weaver asserts this claim because rhetoric has traditionally appealed to the full range of humanity: to our reason and logic as well as to our emotions and values. But as Plato also argued, not all rhetoric is equally acceptable. As a Platonic idealist, Weaver claims that only that rhetoric which appeals on the basis of timeless, enduring principles is acceptable.

To explain that stance, Weaver defines rhetoric as "an art of emphasis embodying an order of desire." This useful definition calls to our attention the fact that rhetoric emphasizes certain things: the softness of this paper towel, the honesty of that politician, the weight of this legal evidence, and so forth. Rhetoric persuades by way of emphasizing some things and not others. But to emphasize something also asserts an "order of desire," a logic or ranking of those things that the audience *should* desire. For this reason, the rhetorician has two duties. The first is to educate the audience as to the principles and values that should be used in making a decision. The second duty is to advise the audience as to how to apply those principles and values to the particular case or decision that lies before them.

These two duties of the rhetor are really commonsensical. A car salesperson, for instance, should first advise the customer as to what one ideally looks for in a car, and then advise the customer that *this* creampuff being test-driven meets those principles. Weaver requires these two duties of rhetoricians not only because they make for successful rhetoric but because they are the most ethical way to persuade, from the point of view of a Platonic idealist. Arguments based on principles will always be preferable to arguments that ignore transcendent values and instead appeal only to the passing feelings of the moment.

Because of his preference for argument that appeals to enduring principles, Weaver claims that there is a hierarchy of preferable arguments in rhetoric. The most desirable is argument from definition, because definitions are timeless and enduring. The second most desirable argument is from relationship or similitude, because a similarity or relationship is always abstract, cutting across particulars of the moment. The third most desirable argument is from cause and effect; such an argument asserts an abstract principle, but is wrapped up in particular circumstances of what caused which effect, and is therefore less desirable. The least desirable argument is from circumstance: a simple appeal to what is happening or what one feels at the moment, with no appeal to principles.

Weaver's ideas have been influential among rhetorical theorists throughout this century. A Platonic idealist who was nevertheless much friendlier to rhetoric than was Plato, Weaver reminds theorists of the ethical dimension of both theory and practice. If his ethically-informed theories were relevant earlier in the twentieth century, they are surely relevant in our own times.

RICHARD M. WEAVER

LANGUAGE IS SERMONIC

LANGUAGE IS SERMONIC

Our age has witnessed the decline of a number of subjects that once enjoyed prestige and general esteem, but no subject, I believe, has suffered more amazingly in this respect than rhetoric. When one recalls that a century ago rhetoric was regarded as the most important humanistic discipline taught in our colleges—when one recalls this fact and contrasts it with the very different situation prevailing today—he is forced to see that a great shift of valuation has taken place. In those days, in the not-so-distant Nineteenth Century, to be a professor of rhetoric, one had to be *somebody.* This was a teaching task that was thought to call for ample and varied resources, and it was recognized as addressing itself to the most important of all ends, the persuading of human beings to adopt right attitudes and act in response to them. That was no assignment for the plodding sort of professor. That sort of teacher might do a middling job with subject matter courses, where the main object is to impart information, but the teacher of rhetoric had to be a person of gifts and imagination who could illustrate, as the need arose, how to make words even in prose take on wings. I remind you of the chairs of rhetoric that still survive in title in some of our older universities. And I should add, to develop the full picture, that literature was then viewed as a subject which practically anyone could teach. No special gift, other than perhaps industry, was needed to relate facts about authors and periods. That was held to be rather pedestrian work. But the instructor in rhetoric was expected to be a man of stature. Today, I scarcely need point out, the situation has been exactly reversed. Today it is the teacher of literature who passes through a long period of training, who is supposed to possess the mysteries of a learned craft, and who is placed by his very speciality on a height of eminence. His knowledge of the intricacies of Shakespeare or Keats or Joyce and his sophistication in the critical doctrines that have been developed bring him the esteem of the academy. We must recognize in all fairness that the elaboration of critical techniques and special approaches has made the teaching of literature a somewhat more demanding profession, although some think that it has gone in that direction beyond the point of

Edited by
Richard L. Johannesen
Rennard Strickland
Ralph T. Eubanks

diminishing returns. Still, this is not enough to account for the relegation of rhetoric. The change has gone so far that now it is discouraging to survey the handling of this study in our colleges and universities. With a few honorable exceptions it is given to just about anybody who will take it. The "inferior, unlearned, mechanical, merely instrumental members of the profession"—to recall a phrase of a great master of rhetoric, Edmund Burke—have in their keeping what was once assigned to the leaders. Beginners, part-time teachers, graduate students, faculty wives, and various fringe people, are now the instructional staff of an art which was once supposed to require outstanding gifts and mature experience. (We must note that at the same time the course itself has been allowed to decline from one dealing philosophically with the problems of expression to one which tries to bring below-par students up to the level of accepted usage.) Indeed, the wheel of fortune would seem to have turned for rhetoric; what was once at the top is now at the bottom, and because of its low estate, people begin to wonder on what terms it can survive at all.

We are not faced here, however, with the wheel of fortune; we are faced with something that has come over the minds of men. Changes that come over the minds of men are not inscrutable, but have at some point their identifiable causes. In this case we have to deal with the most potent of cultural causes, an alteration of man's image of man. Something has happened in the recent past to our concept of what man is; a decision was made to look upon him in a new light, and from this decision new bases of evaluation have proceeded, which affect the public reputation of rhetoric. This changed concept of man is best described by the word "scientistic," a term which denotes the application of scientific assumptions to subjects which are not wholly comprised of naturalistic phenomena. Much of this is a familiar tale, but to understand the effect of the change, we need to recall that the great success of scientific or positivistic thinking in the Nineteenth Century induced a belief that nothing was beyond the scope of its method. Science, and its off-spring applied science, were doing so much to alter and, it was thought, to improve the material conditions of the world, that a next step with the same process seemed in order. Why should not science turn its apparatus upon man, whom all the revelations of religion and the speculations of philosophy seemed still to have left an enigma, with the promise of much better result? It came to be believed increasingly that to think validly was to think scientifically, and that subject matters made no difference.

Now the method of scientific investigation is, as T. H. Huxley reminded us in a lecture which does great credit to him as a rhetorician, merely the method of logic. Induction and deduction and causal inference applied to the phenomena of nature yielded the results with which science was changing the landscape and revolutionizing the modes of industry. From this datum it was an easy inference that men ought increasingly to become scientists, and again, it was a simple derivative from this notion that man at his best is a logic machine, or at any rate an austerely unemotional thinker. Furthermore, carried in the train of this conception was the thought, not often expressed of course, that things would be better if men did not give in so far to being human in the humanistic sense. In the shadow of the victories of science, his humanism fell into progressive disparagement. Just what comprises humanism is not a simple matter for analysis. Rationality is an indispensable part to be sure, yet humanity includes emotionality, or the capacity to feel and suffer, to know pleasure, and it includes the capacity for aesthetic satisfaction, and, what can be only suggested, a yearning to be in relation with something infinite. This last is his religious passion, or his aspiration to feel significant and to have a sense of belonging in a world that is productive of much frustration. These at least are the properties of humanity. Well, man had been human for some thousands of years, and where had it gotten him? Those who looked forward to a scientific Utopia were inclined to think that his humanness had been a drag on his progress; human qualities were weaknesses, except for that special quality of rationality, which might be expected to redeem him.

However curious it may appear, this notion gained that man should live down his humanity and make himself a more efficient source of those logical inferences upon which a scientifically accurate understanding of the world depends. As the impulse spread, it was the emotional and subjective components of his being that chiefly came under criticism, for reasons that have just been indicated. Emotion and logic or science do not consort; the latter must be objective, faithful to what is out there in the public domain and conformable to the processes of reason. Whenever emotion is allowed to put in an oar, it gets the boat off true course. Therefore emotion is a liability.

Under the force of this narrow reasoning, it was natural that rhetoric should pass from a status in which it was regarded as of questionable worth to a still lower one in which it was positively condemned. For the most obvious truth about rhetoric is that its object is the whole man. It presents its arguments first to the rational part of man, because rhetorical discourses, if they are honestly conceived, always have a basis in reasoning. Logical argument is the plot, as it were, of any speech or composition that is designed to persuade. Yet it is the very characterizing feature of rhetoric that it goes beyond this and appeals to other parts of man's constitution, especially to his nature as a pathetic being, that is, a being feeling and suffering. A speech intended to persuade achieves little unless it takes into account how men are reacting subjectively to their hopes and fears and their special circumstances. The fact that Aristotle devotes a large proportion of his *Rhetoric* to how men feel about different situations and actions is an evidence of how prominently these considerations bulked even in the eyes of a master theorist.

Yet there is one further fact, more decisive than any of these, to prove that rhetoric is addressed to man in his humanity. Every speech which is designed to move is directed to a special audience in its unique situation. (We could not except even those radio appeals to "the world." Their audience has a unique place in time.) Here is but a way of pointing out that rhetoric is intended for historical man, or for man as conditioned by history. It is part of the *conditio humana* that we live at particular times and in particular places. These are productive of special or unique urgencies, which the speaker has got to recognize and to estimate. Hence, just as man from the point of view of rhetoric is not purely a thinking machine, or a mere seat of rationality, so he is not a creature abstracted from time and place. If science deals with the abstract and the universal, rhetoric is near the other end, dealing in significant part with the particular and the concrete. It would be the height of wishful thinking to say that this ought not be so. As long as man is born into history, he will be feeling and responding to historical pressures. All of these reasons combine to show why rhetoric should be considered the most humanistic of the humanities. It is directed to that part of our being which is not merely rational, for it supplements the rational approach. And it is directed to individual men in their individual situations, so that by the very definitions of the terms here involved, it takes into account what science deliberately, to satisfy its own purposes, leaves out. There is consequently no need for wonder that, in an age that has been influenced to distrust and disregard what is characteristically human, rhetoric should be a prime target of attack. If it is a weakness to harbor feelings, and if furthermore it is a weakness to be caught up in historical situations, then rhetoric is construable as a dealer in weaknesses. That man is in this condition religion, philosophy, and literature have been teaching for thousands of years. Criticism of it from the standpoint of a scientistic Utopia is the new departure.

The incompleteness of the image of man as a creature who should make use of reason only can be demonstrated in another way. It is a truism that logic is a subject without a subject matter. That is to say, logic is a set of rules and devices which are equally applicable whatever the data. As the science of the forms of reasoning, it is a means of interpreting and utilizing the subject matters of the various fields which do have their proper contents.

Facts from science or history or literature, for example, may serve in the establishment of an inductive generalization. Similar facts may be fed into a syllogism. Logic is merely the mechanism for organizing the data of other provinces of knowledge. Now it follows from this truth that if a man could convert himself into a pure logic machine or thinking machine, he would have no special relation to any body of knowledge. All would be grist for his mill, as the phrase goes. He would have no inclination, no partiality, no particular affection. His mind would work upon one thing as indifferently as upon another. He would be an eviscerated creature or a depassionated one, standing in the same relationship to the realities of the world as the thinking technique stands to the data on which it is employed. He would be a thinking robot, a concept which horrifies us precisely because the robot has nothing to think about.

A confirmation of this truth lies in the fact that rhetoric can never be reduced to symbology. Logic is increasingly becoming "symbolic logic"; that is its tendency. But rhetoric always comes to us in well-fleshed words, and that is because it must deal with the world, the thickness, stubbornness, and power of it.[1]

Everybody recognizes that there is thus a formal logic. A number of eminent authorities have written of rhetoric as if it were formal in the same sense and degree. Formal rhetoric would be a set of rules and devices for persuading anybody about anything. If one desires a certain response, one uses a certain device, or "trick" as the enemies of the art would put it. The set of appeals that rhetoric provides is analogized with the forms of thought that logic prescribes. Rhetoric conceived in this fashion has an adaptability and virtuosity equal to those of logic.

But the comparison overlooks something, for at one point we encounter a significant difference. Rhetoric has a relationship to the world which logic does not have and which forces the rhetorician to keep an eye upon reality as well as upon the character and situation of his audience. The truth of this is seen when we begin to examine the nature of the traditional "topics." The topics were first formulated by Aristotle and were later treated also by Cicero and Quintilian and by many subsequent writers on the subject of persuasion. They are a set of "places" or "regions" where one can go to find the substance for persuasive argument. Cicero defines a topic as "the seat of an argument." In function they are sources of content for speeches that are designed to influence. Aristotle listed a considerable number of them, but for our purposes they can be categorized very broadly. In reading or interpreting the world of reality, we make use of four very general ideas. The first three are usually expressed, in the language of philosophy, as being, cause, and relationship. The fourth, which stands apart from these because it is an external source, is testimony and authority.

One way to interpret a subject is to define its nature—to describe the fixed features of its being. Definition is an attempt to capture essence. When we speak of the nature of a thing, we speak of something we expect to persist. Definitions accordingly deal with fundamental and unchanging properties.

Another way to interpret a subject is to place it in a cause-and-effect relationship. The process of interpretation is then to affirm it as the cause of some effect or as the effect of some cause. And the attitudes of those who are listening will be affected according to whether or not they agree with our cause-and-effect analysis.

A third way to interpret a subject is in terms of relationships of similarity and dissimilarity. We say that it is like something which we know in fuller detail, or that it is unlike that thing in important respects. From such a comparison conclusions regarding the subject itself can be drawn. This is a very common form of argument, by which probabilities can be established. And since

---

[1] I might add that a number of years ago the Mathematics Staff of the College at the University of Chicago made a wager with the English Staff that they could write the Declaration of Independence in mathematical language. They must have had later and better thoughts about this, for we never saw the mathematical rendition.

probabilities are all we have to go on in many questions of this life, it must be accounted a usable means of persuasion.

The fourth category, the one removed from the others by the fact of its being an external source, deals not with the evidence directly but accepts it on the credit of testimony or authority. If we are not in position to see or examine, but can procure the deposition of some one who is, the deposition may become the substance of our argument. We can slip it into a syllogism just as we would a defined term. The same is true of general statements which come from quarters of great authority or prestige. If a proposition is backed by some weighty authority, like the Bible, or can be associated with a great name, people may be expected to respond to it in accordance with the veneration they have for these sources. In this way evidence coming from the outside is used to influence attitudes or conduct.

Now we see that in all these cases the listener is being asked not simply to follow a valid reasoning form but to respond to some presentation of reality. He is being asked to agree with the speaker's interpretation of the world that is. If the definition being offered is a true one, he is expected to recognize this and to say, at least inwardly, "Yes, that is the way the thing is." If the exposition of cause-and-effect relationship is true, he may be expected to concur that X is the cause of such a consequence or that such a consequence has its cause in X. And according to whether this is a good or a bad cause or a good or a bad consequence, he is disposed to preserve or remove the cause, and so on. If he is impressed with the similarity drawn between two things, he is as a result more likely to accept a policy which involves treating something in the same way in which its analogue is treated. He has been influenced by a relationship of comparability. And finally, if he has been confronted with testimony or authority from sources he respects, he will receive this as a reliable, if secondary, kind of information about reality. In these four ways he has been persuaded to read the world as the speaker reads it.

At this point, however, I must anticipate an objection. The retort might be made: "These are extremely formal categories you are enumerating. I fail to see how they are any less general or less indifferently applicable than the formal categories of logic. After all, definitions and so on can be offered of anything. You still have not succeeded in making rhetoric a substantive study."

In replying, I must turn here to what should be called the office of rhetoric. Rhetoric seen in the whole conspectus of its function is an art of emphasis embodying an order of desire. Rhetoric is advisory; it has the office of advising men with reference to an independent order of goods and with reference to their particular situation as it relates to these. The honest rhetorician therefore has two things in mind: a vision of how matters should go ideally and ethically and a consideration of the special circumstances of his auditors. Toward both of these he has a responsibility.

I shall take up first how his responsibility to the order of the goods or to the hierarchy of realities may determine his use of the topics.

When we think of rhetoric as one of the arts of civil society (and it must be a free society, since the scope for rhetoric is limited and the employment of it constrained under a despotism) we see that the rhetorician is faced with a choice of means in appealing to those whom he can prevail upon to listen to him. If he is at all philosophical, it must occur to him to ask whether there is a standard by which the sources of persuasion can be ranked. In a phrase, is there a preferred order of them, so that, in a scale of ethics, it is nobler to make use of one sort of appeal than another? This is of course a question independent of circumstantial matters, yet a fundamental one. We all react to some rhetoric as "untruthful" or "unfair" or "cheap," and this very feeling is evidence of the truth that it is possible to use a better or a worse style of appeal. What is the measure of the better style? Obviously this question cannot be answered at all in the absence of some conviction about the nature and destiny of man. Rhetoric inevitably impinges upon morality and politics; and if it is one of the means by which we endeavor to improve the character and the lot of men, we have to think of its methods and sources in relation to a scheme of values.

To focus the problem a little more sharply, when one is asking men to cooperate with him in thinking this or doing that, when is he asking in the name of the highest reality, which is the same as saying, when is he asking in the name of their highest good?

Naturally, when the speaker replies to this question, he is going to express his philosophy, or more precisely, his metaphysics. My personal reply would be that he is making the highest order of appeal when he is basing his case on definition or the nature of the thing. I confess that this goes back to a very primitive metaphysics, which holds that the highest reality is being, not becoming. It is a quasi-religious metaphysics, if you will, because it ascribes to the highest reality qualities of stasis, immutability, eternal perdurance—qualities that in Western civilization are usually expressed in the language of theism. That which is perfect does not change; that which has to change is less perfect. Therefore, if it is possible to determine unchanging essences or qualities and to speak in terms of these, one is appealing to what is most real in so doing. From another point of view, this is but getting people to see what is most permanent in existence, or what transcends the world of change and accident. The realm of essence is the realm above the flux of phenomena, and definitions are of essences and genera.

I may have expressed this view in somewhat abstruse language in order to place it philosophically, yet the practice I am referring to is everyday enough, as a simple illustration will make plain. If a speaker should define man as a creature with an indefeasible right to freedom and should upon this base an argument that a certain man or group of men are entitled to freedom, he would be arguing from definition. Freedom is an unchanging attribute of his subject; it can accordingly be predicated of whatever falls within the genus man. Stipulative definitions are of the ideal, and in this fact lies the reason for placing them at the top of the hierarchy. If the real progress of man is toward knowledge of ideal truth, it follows that this is an appeal to his highest capacity—his capacity to apprehend what exists absolutely.

The next ranking I offer tentatively, but it seems to me to be relationship or similitude and its subvarieties. I have a consistent impression that the broad resource of analogy, metaphor, and figuration is favored by those of a poetic and imaginative cast of mind. We make use of analogy or comparison when the available knowledge of the subject permits only probable proof. Analogy is reasoning from something we know to something we do not know in one step; hence there is no universal ground for predication. Yet behind every analogy lurks the possibility of a general term. The general term is never established as such, for that would change the argument to one of deductive reasoning with a universal or distributed middle. The user of analogy is hinting at an essence which cannot at the moment be produced. Or, he may be using an indirect approach for reason of tact; analogies not infrequently do lead to generalizations; and he may be employing this approach because he is respectful of his audience and desires them to use their insight.

I mentioned a moment earlier that this type of argument seems to be preferred by those of a poetic or non-literal sort of mind. That fact suggests yet another possibility, which I offer still more diffidently, asking your indulgence if it seems to border on the whimsical. The explanation would be that the cosmos *is* one vast system of analogy, so that our profoundest intuitions of it are made in the form of comparisons. To affirm that something is like something else is to begin to talk about the unitariness of creation. Everything is like everything else somehow, so that we have a ladder of similitude mounting up to the final oneness—to something like a unity in godhead. Furthermore, there is about this source of argument a kind of decent reticence, a recognition of the unknown along with the known. There is a recognition that the unknown may be continuous with the known, so that man is moving about in a world only partly realized, yet real in all its parts. This is the mood of poetry and mystery, but further adumbration of it I leave to those more gifted than I.

Cause and effect appears in this scale to be a less exalted source of argument, though we all have to use it because we are historical men. Here I must recall the metaphysical ground of this organization and point out that it operates in the realm of becoming. Causes are causes having effect and effects are resulting from causes. To associate this source of argument with its habitual users, I must note that it is heard most commonly from those who are characteristically pragmatic in their way of thinking. It is not unusual today to find a lengthy piece of journalism or an entire political speech which is nothing but a series of arguments from consequence—completely devoid of reference to principle or defined ideas. We rightly recognize these as sensational types of appeal. Those who are partial to arguments based on effect are under a temptation to play too much upon the fears of their audience by stressing the awful nature of some consequence or by exaggerating the power of some cause. Modern advertising is prolific in this kind of abuse. There is likewise a temptation to appeal to prudential considerations only in a passage where things are featured as happening or threatening to happen.

An even less admirable subvariety of this source is the appeal to circumstance, which is the least philosophical of all the topics of argument. Circumstance is an allowable source when we don't know anything else to plead, in which cases we say, "There is nothing else to be done about it." Of all the arguments, it admits of the least perspicaciousness. An example of this which we hear nowadays with great regularity is: "We must adapt ourselves to a fast-changing world." This is pure argument from circumstance. It does not pretend, even, to offer a cause-and-effect explanation. If it did, the first part would tell us why we must adapt ourselves to a fast-changing world; and the second would tell us the result of our doing so. The usually heard formulation does neither. Such argument is preeminently lacking in understanding or what the Greeks called *dianoia*. It simply cites a brute circumstance and says, "Step lively." Actually, this argument amounts to a surrender of reason. Maybe it expresses an instinctive feeling that in this situation reason is powerless. Either you change fast or you get crushed. But surely it would be a counsel of desperation to try only this argument in a world suffering from aimlessness and threatened with destruction.

Generally speaking, cause and effect is a lower-order source of argument because it deals in the realm of the phenomenal, and the phenomenal is easily converted into the sensational. Sensational excitements always run the risk of arousing those excesses which we deplore as sentimentality or brutality.

Arguments based on testimony and authority, utilizing external sources, have to be judged in a different way. Actually, they are the other sources seen through other eyes. The question of their ranking involves the more general question of the status of authority. Today there is a widespread notion that all authority is presumptuous. ("Authority is authoritarian" seems to be the root idea); consequently it is held improper to try to influence anyone by the prestige of great names or of sanctioned pronouncements. This is a presumption itself, by which every man is presumed to be his own competent judge in all matters. But since that is a manifest impossibility, and is becoming a greater impossibility all the time, as the world piles up bodies of specialized knowledge which no one person can hope to command, arguments based on authority are certainly not going to disappear. The sound maxim is that an argument based on authority is as good as the authority. What we should hope for is a new and discriminating attitude toward what is authoritative, and I would like to see some source recognized as having moral authority. This hope will have to wait upon the recovery of a more stable order of values and the re-recognition of qualities in persons. Speaking most generally, arguments from authority are ethically good when they are deferential toward real hierarchy.

With that we may sum up the rhetorical speaker's obligation toward the ideal, apart from particular determinations. If one accepts the possibility of this or any other ranking, one has to concede that rhetoric is not merely formal; it is realistic. It is not a playing with counters; its impulses come from insights into actuality. Its topic matter is existential, not hypothetical. It involves more than mere demonstration because it involves choice. Its assertions have ontological claims.

Now I return to the second responsibility, which is imposed by the fact that the rhetorician is concerned with definite questions. These are questions having histories, and history is always concrete. This means that the speaker or writer has got to have a rhetorical perception of what his audience needs or will receive or respond to. He takes into account the reality of man's composite being and his tendency to be swayed by sentiment. He estimates the pressures of the particular situation in which his auditors are found. In the eyes of those who look sourly upon the art, he is a man probing for weaknesses which he means to exploit.

But here we must recur to the principle that rhetoric comprehensively considered is an art of emphasis. The definite situation confronts him with a second standard of choice. In view of the receptivity of his audience, which of the topics shall he choose to stress, and how? If he concludes that definition should be the appeal, he tries to express the nature of the thing in a compelling way. If he feels that a cause-and-effect demonstration would stand the greatest chance to impress, he tries to make this linkage so manifest that his hearers will see an inevitability in it. And so on with the other topics, which will be so emphasized or magnified as to produce the response of assent.

Along with this process of amplification, the ancients recognized two qualities of rhetorical discourse which have the effect of impressing an audience with the reality or urgency of a topic. In Greek these appear as *energia* and *enargia*, both of which may be translated "actuality," though the first has to do with liveliness or animation of action and the second with vividness of scene. The speaker now indulges in actualization to make what he is narrating or describing present to the minds' eyes of his hearers.

The practice itself has given rise to a good deal of misunderstanding, which it would be well to remove. We know that one of the conventional criticisms of rhetoric is that the practitioner of it takes advantage of his hearers by playing upon their feelings and imaginations. He overstresses the importance of his topics by puffing them up, dwelling on them in great detail, using an excess of imagery or of modifiers evoking the senses, and so on. He goes beyond what is fair, the critics often allege, by this actualization of a scene about which the audience ought to be thinking rationally. Since this criticism has a serious basis, I am going to offer an illustration before making the reply. Here is a passage from Daniel Webster's famous speech for the prosecution in the trial of John Francis Knapp. Webster is actualizing for the jury the scene of the murder as he has constructed it from circumstantial evidence.

> The deed was executed with a degree of steadiness and self-possession equal to the wickedness with which it was planned. The circumstances now clearly in evidence spread out the scene before us. Deep sleep had fallen upon the destined victim and all beneath his roof. A healthful old man, to whom sleep was sweet, the first sound slumbers of the night held him in their soft but strong embrace. The assassin enters, through a window already prepared, into an unoccupied apartment. With noiseless foot he paces the lonely hall, half-lighted by the moon; he winds up the ascent of the stairs, and reaches the door of the chamber. Of this, he moves the lock by soft and continued pressure, till it turns on its hinges without noise; and he enters, and beholds the victim before him. The room is uncommonly open to the admission of light. The face of the innocent sleeper is turned from the murderer, and the beams of the moon, resting on the gray locks of the aged temple, show him where to strike. The fatal blow is given! and the victim passes, without a struggle or a motion, from the repose of sleep to the repose of death! It is the assassin's purpose to make sure work; and he plies the dagger, though it is obvious that life has

> been destroyed by the blow of the bludgeon. He even raises the aged arm, that he may not fail in his aim at the heart, and replaces it again over the wound of the poniard! To finish the picture, he explores the wrist for the pulse! He feels for it, and ascertains that it beats no longer! It is accomplished. The deed is done. He retreats, retraces his steps to the window, passes out through it as he came in, and escapes. He has done the murder. No eye has seen him, no ear has heard him. The secret is his own, and it is safe!

By depicting the scene in this fulness of detail, Webster is making it vivid, and "vivid" means "living." There are those who object on general grounds to this sort of dramatization; it is too affecting to the emotions. Beyond a doubt, whenever the rhetorician actualizes an event in this manner, he is making it mean something to the emotional part of us, but that part is involved whenever we are deliberating about goodness and badness. On this subject there is a very wise reminder in Bishop Whately's *Elements of Rhetoric:* "When feelings are strongly excited, they are not necessarily overexcited; it may be that they are only brought to the state which the occasion fully justifies, or even that they fall short of this." Let us think of the situation in which Webster was acting. After all, there is the possibility, or even the likelihood that the murder was committed in this fashion, and that the indicted Knapp deserved the conviction he got. Suppose the audience had remained cold and unmoved. There is the victim's side to consider and the interest of society in protecting life. We should not forget that Webster's "actualization" is in the service of these. Our attitude toward what is just or right or noble and their opposites is not a bloodless calculation, but a feeling for and against. As Whately indicates, the speaker who arouses feeling may only be arousing it to the right pitch and channeling it in the right direction.

To re-affirm the general contention: the rhetorician who practices "amplification" is not thereby misleading his audience, because we are all men of limited capacity and sensitivity and imagination. We all need to have things pointed out to us, things stressed in our interest. The very task of the rhetorician is to determine what feature of a question is most exigent and to use the power of language to make it appear so. A speaker who dwells insistently upon some aspect of a case may no more be hoodwinking me than a policeman or a doctor when he advises against a certain course of action by pointing out its nature or its consequences. He *should* be in a position to know somewhat better than I do.

It is strongly to be suspected that this charge against rhetoric comes not only from the distorted image that makes man a merely rationalistic being, but also from the dogma of an uncritical equalitarianism. The notion of equality has insinuated itself so far that it appears sometimes as a feeling, to which I would apply the name "sentimental plebeianism," that no man is better or wiser than another, and hence that it is usurpation for one person to undertake to instruct or admonish another. This preposterous (and we could add, wholly unscientific judgment, since our differences are manifold and provable) is propagated in subtle ways by our institutions of publicity and the perverse art of demagogic politics. Common sense replies that any individual who advises a friend or speaks up in meeting is exercising a kind of leadership, which may be justified by superior virtue, knowledge, or personal insight.

The fact that leadership is a human necessity is proof that rhetoric as the attempt through language to make one's point of view prevail grows out of the nature of man. It is not a reflection of any past phase of social development, or any social institution, or any fashion, or any passing vice. When all factors have been considered, it will be seen that men are born rhetoricians, though some are born small ones and others greater, and some cultivate the native gift by study and training, whereas some neglect it. Men are such because they are born into history, with an endowment of passion and a sense of the *ought.* There is ever some discrepancy, however slight, between the situation man is in and the situation he would like to realize. His life is therefore characterized by movement toward goals. It is largely the power of rhetoric which influences and governs that movement.

For the same set of reasons, rhetoric is cognate with language. Ever since I first heard the idea mentioned seriously it impressed me as impossible and even ridiculous that the utterances of men could be neutral. Such study as I have been able to give the subject over the years has confirmed that feeling and has led me to believe that what is sometimes held up as a desideratum—expression purged of all tendency—rests upon an initial misconception of the nature of language.

The condition essential to see is that every use of speech, oral and written, exhibits an attitude, and an attitude implies an act. "Thy speech bewrayeth thee" is aphoristically true if we take it as saying, "Your speech reveals your disposition," first by what you choose to say, then by the amount you decide to say, and so on down through the resources of linguistic elaboration and intonation. All rhetoric is a rhetoric of motives, as Kenneth Burke saw fit to indicate in the title of his book. At the low end of the scale, one may be doing nothing more than making sounds to express exuberance. But if at the other end one sits down to compose a *Critique of the Pure Reason,* one has the motive of refuting other philosophers' account of the constitution of being and of substituting one's own, for an interest which may be universal, but which nonetheless proceeds from the will to alter something.

Does this mean that it is impossible to be objective about anything? Does it mean that one is "rhetorical" in declaring that a straight line is the shortest distance between two points? Not in the sense in which the objection is usually raised. There are degrees of objectivity, and there are various disciplines which have their own rules for expressing their laws or their content in the most effective manner for their purpose. But even this expression can be seen as enclosed in a rhetorical intention. Put in another way, an utterance is capable of rhetorical function and aspect. If one looks widely enough, one can discover its rhetorical dimension, to put it in still another way. The scientist has some interest in setting forth the formulation of some recurrent feature of the physical world, although his own sense of motive may be lost in a general feeling that science is a good thing because it helps progress along.[1]

In short, as long as man is a creature responding to purpose, his linguistic expression will be a carrier of tendency. Where the modern semanticists got off on the wrong foot in their effort to refurbish language lay in the curious supposition that language could and should be outwardly determined. They were positivists operating in the linguistic field. Yet if there is anything that is going to keep on defying positivistic correlation, it is this subjectively born, intimate, and value-laden vehicle which we call language. Language is a system of imputation, by which values and percepts are first framed in the mind and are then imputed to things. This is not an irresponsible imputation; it does not imply, say, that no two people can look at the same clock face and report the same time. The qualities or properties have to be in the things, but they are not in the things in the form in which they are framed by the mind. This much I think we can learn from the great realist-nominalist controversy of the Middle Ages and from the little that contemporary semantics has been able to add to our knowledge. Language was created by the imagination for the purposes of man, but it may have objective reference—just how we cannot say

---

[1] If I have risked confusion by referring to "rhetoricians" and "rhetorical speakers," and to other men as if they were all non-rhetoricians, while insisting that all language has its rhetorical aspect, let me clarify the terms. By "rhetorician" I mean the deliberate rhetor: the man who understands the nature and aim and requirements of persuasive expression and who uses them more or less consciously according to the approved rules of the art. The other, who by his membership in the family of language users, must be a rhetorician of sorts, is an empirical and adventitious one; he does not know enough to keep invention, arrangement, and style working for him. The rhetorician of my reference is thus the educated speaker; the other is an untaught amateur.

until we are in possession of a more complete metaphysics and epistemology.

Now a system of imputation involves the use of predicates, as when we say, "Sugar is sweet" or "Business is good." Modern positivism and relativism, however, have gone virtually to the point of denying the validity of all conceptual predication. Occasionally at Chicago I purposely needle a class by expressing a general concept in a casual way, whereupon usually I am sternly reminded by some member brought up in the best relativist tradition that "You can't generalize that way." The same view can be encountered in eminent quarters. Justice Oliver Wendell Holmes was fond of saying that the chief end of man is to frame general propositions and that no general proposition is worth a damn. In the first of these general propositions the Justice was right, in the sense that men cannot get along without categorizing their apprehensions of reality. In the second he was wrong because, although a great jurist, he was not philosopher enough to think the matter through. Positivism and relativism may have rendered a certain service as devil's advocates if they have caused us to be more careful about our concepts and our predicates, yet their position in net form is untenable. The battle against general propositions was lost from the beginning, for just as surely as man is a symbol-using animal (and a symbol transcends the thing symbolized), he is a classifying animal. The morality lies in the application of the predicate.

Language, which is thus predicative, is for the same cause sermonic. We are all of us preachers in private or public capacities. We have no sooner uttered words than we have given impulse to other people to look at the world, or some small part of it, in our way. Thus caught up in a great web of inter-communication and inter-influence, we speak as rhetoricians affecting one another for good or ill. That is why I must agree with Quintilian that the true orator is the good man, skilled in speaking—good in his formed character and right in his ethical philosophy. When to this he adds fertility in invention and skill in the arts of language, he is entitled to that leadership which tradition accords him.

If rhetoric is to be saved from the neglect and even the disrepute which I was deploring at the beginning of this lecture, these primary truths will have to be recovered until they are a part of our active consciousness. They are, in summation, that man is not nor ever can be nor ever should be a depersonalized thinking machine. His feeling is the activity in him most closely related to what used to be called his soul. To appeal to his feeling therefore is not necessarily an insult; it can be a way to honor him, by recognizing him in the fulness of his being. Even in those situations where the appeal is a kind of strategy, it but recognizes that men—all men—are historically conditioned.

Rhetoric must be viewed formally as operating at that point where literature and politics meet, or where literary values and political urgencies can be brought together. The rhetorician makes use of the moving power of literary presentation to induce in his hearers an attitude or decision which is political in the very broadest sense. Perhaps this explains why the successful user of rhetoric is sometimes in bad grace with both camps. For the literary people he is too "practical"; and for the more practical political people he is too "flowery." But there is nothing illegitimate about what he undertakes to do, any more than it would be illegitimate to make use of the timeless principles of aesthetics in the constructing of a public building. Finally, we must never lose sight of the order of values as the ultimate sanction of rhetoric. No one can live a life of direction and purpose without some scheme of values. As rhetoric confronts us with choices involving values, the rhetorician is a preacher to us, noble if he tries to direct our passion toward noble ends and base if he uses our passion to confuse and degrade us. Since all utterance influences us in one or the other of these directions, it is important that the direction be the right one, and it is better if this lay preacher is a master of his art.

INTRODUCTION TO STEPHEN TOULMIN

Stephen Toulmin was born in England in 1922 and was educated at Cambridge University, majoring in mathematics and physics as an undergraduate and philosophy at the graduate level. Toulmin has taught at several American universities and is at this writing the Avalon Foundation Professor of the Humanities at Northwestern University. Many of Toulmin's writings are applicable to rhetorical theory, but the most influential is his book excerpted here, *The Uses of Argument,* published in 1958.

You will recall that the Enlightenment valued reason above other human capabilities and regarded most highly those activities that used reason most exclusively. Although many in the twentieth century came to moderate that faith in reason and its exercise in science and technology, nevertheless the values of the Enlightenment persisted among several philosophers. In different schools of thought, among them *logical positivism* and *analytic philosophy,* some theorists sought to order human life and thought around pure reason and logic. Some major theorists in different fields pursuing that goal were Rudolph Carnap, Bertrand Russell, and the behavioral psychologist B. F. Skinner. A "perfectly" logical standard for human thinking and acting is not consistent with rhetoric, since rhetoric has usually appealed to a wide range of human responses including aesthetic and emotional faculties.

Toulmin is, among other things, a student of argument. He became convinced that the model of pure reason and logic employed by the descendants of the Enlightenment in analytic philosophy had little to do with how people actually reason. Rationality in real life does not really use the highly-structured, rule-governed, deductive models urged as the standard for human reasoning by analytic and positivistic philosophers, Toulmin claimed.

Attempting to propose a theory for understanding argument as it is actually conducted (and by extension, a theory of human rationality), Toulmin's *The Uses of Argument* proposed a model of argument based upon observations of reason in legal and political rhetoric. Initially rejected by philosophers, Toulmin's work was adopted by rhetorical theorists and composition teachers and became influential in the informal logic movement. It would be fair to say that Toulmin's model is found in textbooks today second only to Aristotle's views on argument.

Toulmin's presentation of his model of argument is found in the passages from his book excerpted here. Every argument must include, he says, *data* (anything accepted as facts or evidence by an audience), a *claim* (a proposition the arguer wishes the audience to accept), and a *warrant* (a general rule or principle that justifies drawing the claim from the data). More complicated arguments may also include a *qualifier* (a statement of how strongly or under what conditions one should accept the claim), *backing* (reasons why the warrant is a valid rule or principle), and *rebuttal* (circumstances under which one would want to set the warrant aside temporarily).

This model of argument is completely rhetorical because it describes what is needed to persuade people rather than what is needed to match some abstract standard of logic. Nevertheless, an important contribution of Toulmin's work was his demonstration that the model explains how argument is conducted in enterprises such as science and the law that have been offered as paradigms of rationality. Reason is usually rhetorical rather than rigidly analytic, Toulmin shows us.

We should note that an important rhetorical dimension of the model is the extent to which it assumes that the audience participates in the reasoning process by combining their common sense and social knowledge with logic. Every part of the model need not be articulated explicitly, Toulmin claims, as long as the audience supplies the missing piece from their common sense. Suppose someone approaches you in a smoke-filled office building shouting, "The building is on fire (data), run for your life (claim)!" Any sensible person would be able to supply the "missing" warrant, which is something like "it is undesirable to burn." Indeed, we would think it strange were the arguer to explain this to us with an appeal to run from a burning building. Since Aristotle's explanation of enthymemes, audience participation in argument has been a hallmark of rhetorical appeals.

In applying his model of argument to audiences in the sciences and other academic disciplines, Toulmin claims that argument is "field dependent." That is because what counts as a warrant, or what is acceptable common sense and social knowledge, in one field may not count as a warrant in another field. The physicist follows different warrants in determining the existence of subatomic particles than does the engineer in deciding how to support a bridge or the artist in concluding how best to mix paints.

Toulmin's contribution is valuable for many reasons. He has perpetuated the ancient and honorable study of argument by providing a useful new theoretical model. Toulmin not only shows that rhetorical argument is rational, he demonstrates that rhetoric is fundamental to the conduct of reason in some activities, such as science, that have been assumed to be exempt from rhetorical influence. His idea of field dependence has demonstrated that what unifies reason is, because of field dependence, not one set of inflexible procedures so much as its rhetorical dimension. Toulmin is one of many philosophers in the twentieth century who have come to see that traditional philosophical issues such as logic can be informed more richly by understanding their rhetorical dimensions.

STEPHEN EDELSTON TOULMIN

THE USES OF ARGUMENT

• • •

THE LAYOUT OF ARGUMENTS

III

AN ARGUMENT is like an organism. It has both a gross, anatomical structure and a finer, as-it-were physiological one. When set out explicitly in all its detail, it may occupy a number of printed pages or take perhaps a quarter of an hour to deliver; and within this time or space one can distinguish the main phases marking the progress of the argument from the initial statement of an unsettled problem to the final presentation of a conclusion. These main phases will each of them occupy some minutes or paragraphs, and represent the chief anatomical units of the argument—its 'organs', so to speak. But within each paragraph, when one gets down to the level of individual sentences, a finer structure can be recognised, and this is the structure with which logicians have mainly concerned themselves. It is at this physiological level that the idea of logical form has been introduced, and here that the validity of our arguments has ultimately to be established or refuted.

The time has come to change the focus of our inquiry, and to concentrate on this finer level. Yet we cannot afford to forget what we have learned by our study of the grosser anatomy of arguments, for here as with organisms the detailed physiology proves most intelligible when expounded against a background of coarser anatomical distinctions. Physiological processes are interesting not least for the part they play in maintaining the functions of the major organs in which they take place; and micro-arguments (as one may christen them) need to be looked at from time to time with one eye on the macro-arguments in which they figure; since the precise manner in which we phrase them and set them out, to mention only the least important thing, may be affected by the role they have to play in the larger context.

In the inquiry which follows, we shall be studying the operation of arguments sentence by sentence, in order to see how their validity or invalidity is connected with the manner of laying them out, and what relevance this connection has to the traditional notion of 'logical form'. Certainly the same argument may be set out in quite a number of different forms, and some of these patterns of analysis will be more candid than others—some of them, that is, will show the validity or invalidity of an argument more clearly than others, and make more explicit the grounds it relies on and the bearing of these on the conclusion. How, then, should we lay an argument out, if we want to show the sources of its validity? And in what sense does the acceptability or unacceptability of arguments depend upon their 'formal' merits and defects?

We have before us two rival models, one mathematical, the other jurisprudential. Is the logical form of a valid argument something quasi-geometrical, comparable to the shape of a triangle or the parallelism of two straight lines? Or alternatively, is it something procedural: is a formally valid argument one *in proper form,* as lawyers would say, rather than one laid out in a tidy and simple *geometrical* form? Or does the notion of logical form somehow combine both these aspects, so that to lay an argument out in proper form necessarily requires the adoption of a particular geometrical layout? If this last answer is the right one, it at once creates a further problem for us: to see how and why proper procedure demands the adoption of simple geometrical shape, and how that shape guarantees in its turn the validity of our procedures. Supposing valid arguments can be cast in a geometrically tidy form, how does this help to make them any the more cogent?

These are the problems to be studied in the present inquiry. If we can see our way to unravelling them, their solution will be of some importance—particularly for a proper understanding of logic. But to begin with we must go cautiously, and steer clear of the philosophical issues on which we shall hope later to throw some light, concentrating for the moment on questions of a most prosaic and straightforward kind. Keeping our eyes on the categories of applied logic—on the practical business of argumentation, that is, and the notions it requires us to employ—we must ask what features a logically candid layout of arguments will need to have. The establishment of conclusions raises a number of issues of different sorts, and a practical layout will make allowance for these differences: our first question is—what are these issues, and how can we do justice to them all in subjecting our arguments to rational assessment?

Two last remarks may be made by way of introduction, the first of them simply adding one more question to our agenda. Ever since Aristotle it has been customary, when analysing the micro-structure of arguments, to set them out in a very simple manner: they have been presented three propositions at a time, 'minor premiss; major premiss; *so* conclusion'. The question now arises, whether this standard form is sufficiently elaborate or candid. Simplicity is of course a merit, but may it not in this case have been bought too dearly? Can we properly classify all the elements in our arguments under the three headings, 'major premiss', 'minor premiss' and 'conclusion', or are these categories misleadingly few in number? Is there even enough similarity between major and minor premisses for them usefully to be yoked together by the single name of 'premiss'?

Light is thrown on these questions by the analogy with jurisprudence. This would naturally lead us to adopt a layout of greater complexity than has been customary, for the questions we are asking here are, once again, more general versions of questions already familiar in jurisprudence, and in that more specialised field a whole battery of distinctions has grown up. 'What different sorts of propositions', a legal philosopher will ask, 'are uttered in the course of a law-case, and in what different ways can such propositions bear on the soundness of a legal claim?' This has always been and still is a central question for the student of jurisprudence, and we soon find that the nature of a legal process can be properly understood only if we draw a large number of distinctions. Legal utterances have many distinct functions. Statements of claim, evidence of identification, testimony about events in dispute, interpretations of a statute or discussions of its validity, claims to exemption from the application of a law, pleas in extenuation, verdicts, sentences: all these different classes of proposition have their parts to play in the legal process, and the differences between them are in practice far from trifling. When we turn from the special case of the law to consider rational arguments in general, we are faced at once by the question whether these must not be analysed in terms of an equally complex set of categories. If we are to set our arguments out with complete logical candour, and understand properly the nature of 'the logical process', surely we shall need to employ a pattern of argument no less sophisticated than is required in the law.

THE PATTERN OF AN ARGUMENT: DATA AND WARRANTS

'What, then, is involved in establishing conclusions by the production of arguments?' Can we, by considering this question in a general form, build up from scratch a pattern of analysis which will do justice to all the distinctions which proper procedure forces upon us? That is the problem facing us.

Let it be supposed that we make an assertion, and commit ourselves thereby to the claim which any assertion necessarily involves. If this claim is challenged, we must be able to establish it—that is, make it good, and show that it was justifiable. How is this to be done? Unless the assertion was made quite wildly and irresponsibly, we shall normally have some facts to which we can point in its support: if the claim is challenged, it is up to us to appeal to these facts, and present them as the foundation upon which our claim is based. Of course we may not get the challenger even to agree about the correctness of these facts, and in that case we have to clear his objection out of the way by a preliminary argument: only when this prior issue or 'lemma', as geometers would call it, has been dealt with, are we in a position to return to the original argument. But this complication we need only mention: supposing the lemma to have been disposed of, our question is how to set the original argument out most fully and explicitly. 'Harry's hair is not black', we assert. What have we got to go on? we are asked. Our personal knowledge that it is in fact red: that is our datum, the ground which we produce as support for the original assertion. Petersen, we may say, will not be a Roman Catholic: why?: we base our claim on the knowledge that he is a Swede, which makes it very unlikely that he will be a Roman Catholic. Wilkinson, asserts the prosecutor in Court, has committed an offence against the Road Traffic Acts: in support of this claim, two policemen are prepared to testify that they timed him driving at 45 m.p.h. in a built-up area. In each case, an original assertion is supported by producing other facts bearing on it.

We already have, therefore, one distinction to start with: between the *claim* or conclusion whose merits we are seeking to establish (C) and the facts we appeal to as a foundation for the claim—what I shall refer to as our *data* (D). If our challenger's question is, 'What have you got to go on?', producing the data or information on which the claim is based may serve to answer him; but this is only one of the ways in which our conclusion may be challenged. Even after we have produced our data, we may find ourselves being asked further questions of another kind. We may now be required not to add more factual information to that which we have already provided, but rather to indicate the bearing on our conclusion of the data already produced. Colloquially, the question may now be, not 'What have you got to go on?', but 'How do you get there?' To present a particular set of data as the basis for some specified conclusion commits us to a certain *step;* and the question is now one about the nature and justification of this step.

Supposing we encounter this fresh challenge, we must bring forward not further data, for about these the same query may immediately be raised again, but propositions of a rather different kind: rules, principles, inference-licences or what you will, instead of additional items of information. Our task is no longer to strengthen the ground on which our argument is constructed, but is rather to show that, taking these data as a starting point, the step to the original claim or conclusion is an appropriate and legitimate one. At this point, therefore, what are needed are general, hypothetical statements, which can act as bridges, and authorise the sort of step to which our particular argument commits us. These may normally be written very briefly (in the form 'If D, then C'); but, for candour's sake, they can profitably be expanded, and made more explicit: 'Data such as D entitle one to draw conclusions, or make claims, such as C', or alternatively 'Given data D, one may take it that C.'

Propositions of this kind I shall call *warrants* (W), to distinguish them from both conclusions and data. (These 'warrants', it will be observed, correspond to the practical standards or canons of argument referred to in our earlier essays.) To pursue our previous examples: the knowledge that Harry's hair is red entitles us to set aside any suggestion that it is black, on account of the warrant, 'If anything is red, it will not also be black.' (The very triviality of this warrant is connected with the fact that we are concerned here as much with a counter-assertion as with an argument.) The fact that Petersen is a Swede is directly relevant to the question of his religious denomination for, as we should probably put it, 'A Swede can be taken almost certainly not to be a Roman Catholic.' (The step involved here is not trivial, so the warrant is not self-authenticating.) Likewise in the third case: our warrant will now be some such statement as that 'A man who is proved to have driven at more than 30 m.p.h. in a built-up area can be found to have committed an offence against the Road Traffic Acts.'

The question will at once be asked, how absolute is this distinction between data, on the one hand, and warrants, on the other. Will it always be clear whether a man who challenges an assertion is calling for the production of his adversary's data, or for the warrants authorising his steps? Can one, in other words, draw any sharp distinction between the force of the two questions, 'What have you got to go on?' and 'How do you get there?'? By grammatical tests alone, the distinction may appear far from absolute, and the same English sentence may serve a double function: it may be uttered, that is, in one situation to convey a piece of information, in another to authorise a step in an argument, and even perhaps in some contexts to do both these things at once. (All these possibilities will be illustrated before too long.) For the moment, the important thing is not to be too cut-and-dried in our treatment of the subject, nor to commit ourselves in advance to a rigid terminology. At any rate we shall find it possible in *some* situations to distinguish clearly two different logical functions; and the nature of this distinction is hinted at if one contrasts the two sentences, 'Whenever A, one *has found* that B' and 'Whenever A, one *may take it* that B.'

We now have the terms we need to compose the first skeleton of a pattern for analysing arguments. We may symbolise the relation between the data and the claim in support of which they are produced by an arrow, and indicate the authority for taking the step from one to the other by writing the warrant immediately below the arrow:

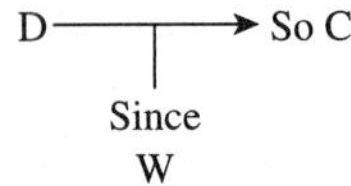

Or, to give an example:

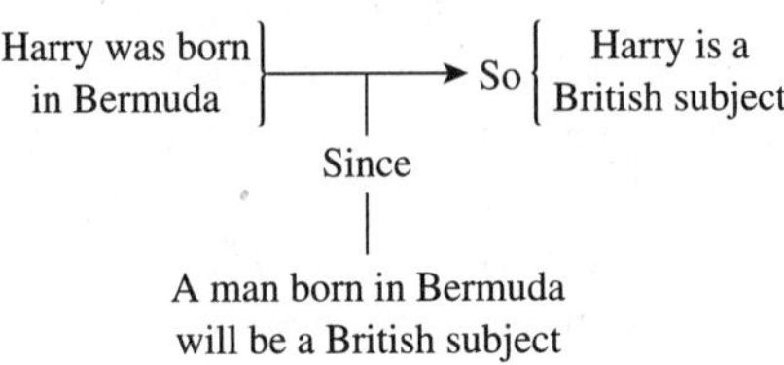

As this pattern makes clear, the explicit appeal in this argument goes directly back from the claim to the data relied on as foundation: the warrant is, in a sense, incidental and explanatory, its task being simply to register explicitly the legitimacy of the step involved and to refer it back to the larger class of steps whose legitimacy is being presupposed.

This is one of the reasons for distinguishing between data and warrants: data are appealed to explicitly, warrants implicitly. In addition, one may remark that warrants are general, certifying the soundness of *all* arguments of the appropriate type, and have accordingly to be established in quite a different way from the facts we produce as data. This distinction, between data and warrants, is similar to the distinction drawn in the law-courts between questions of fact and questions of law, and the legal distinction is indeed a special case of the more general one—we may argue, for instance, that a man whom we know to have been born in Bermuda is presumably a British subject, simply because the relevant laws give us a warrant to draw this conclusion.

One more general point in passing: unless, in any particular field of argument, we are prepared to work with warrants of *some* kind, it will become impossible in that field to subject arguments to rational assessment. The data we cite if a claim is challenged depend on the warrants we are prepared to operate with in that field, and the warrants to which we commit ourselves are implicit in the particular steps from data to claims we are prepared to take and to admit. But supposing a man rejects all warrants whatever authorising (say) steps from data about the present and past to conclusions about the future, then for him rational prediction will become impossible; and many philosophers have in fact denied the possibility of rational prediction just because they thought they could discredit equally the claims of all past-to-future warrants.

The skeleton of a pattern which we have obtained so far is only a beginning. Further questions may now arise, to which we must pay attention. Warrants are of different kinds, and may confer different degrees of force on the conclusions they justify. Some warrants authorise us to accept a claim unequivocally, given the appropriate data—these warrants entitle us in suitable cases to qualify our conclusion with the adverb 'necessarily'; others authorise us to make the step from data to conclusion either tentatively, or else subject to conditions, exceptions, or qualifications—in these cases other modal qualifiers, such as 'probably' and 'presumably', are in place. It may not be sufficient, therefore, simply to specify our data, warrant and claim: we may need to add some explicit reference to the degree of force which our data confer on our claim in virtue of our warrant. In a word, we may have to put in a *qualifier.* Again, it is often necessary in the law-courts, not just to appeal to a given statute or common-law doctrine, but to discuss explicitly the extent to which this particular law fits the case under consideration, whether it must inevitably be applied in this particular case, or whether special facts may make the case an exception to the rule or one in which the law can be applied only subject to certain qualifications.

If we are to take account of these features of our argument also, our pattern will become more complex. Modal qualifiers (Q) and conditions of exception or rebuttal (R) are distinct both from data and from warrants, and need to be given separate places in our layout. Just as a warrant (W) is itself neither a datum (D) nor a claim (C), since it implies in itself something about both D and C—namely, that the step from the one to the other is legitimate; so, in turn, Q and R are themselves distinct from W, since they comment implicitly on the bearing of W on this step—qualifiers (Q) indicating the strength conferred by the warrant on this step, conditions of rebuttal (R) indicating circumstances in which the general authority of the warrant would have to be set aside. To mark these further distinctions, we may write the qualifier (Q) immediately beside the conclusion which it qualifies (C), and the exceptional conditions which might be capable of defeating or rebutting the warranted conclusion (R) immediately below the qualifier.

To illustrate: our claim that Harry is a British subject may normally be defended by appeal to the information that he was born in Bermuda, for this datum lends support to our conclusion on account of the warrants implicit in the British Nationality Acts; but the argument is not by itself conclusive in the absence of assurances about his parentage and about his not having changed his nationality since birth. What our information does do is to establish that the conclusion holds good 'presumably', and subject to the appropriate provisos. The argument now assumes the form:

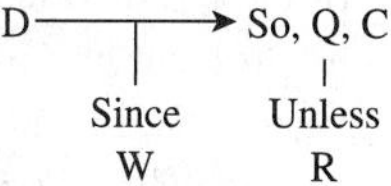
D
So, Q, C
Since
W
Unless
R

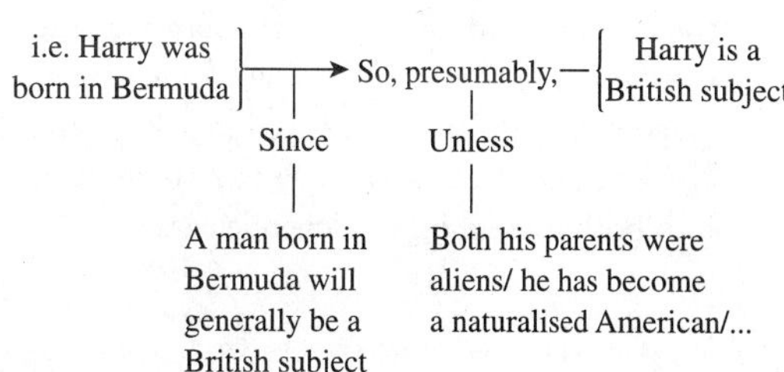
i.e. Harry was born in Bermuda
So, presumably,—
Harry is a British subject
Since
Unless
A man born in Bermuda will generally be a British subject
Both his parents were aliens/ he has become a naturalised American/...

We must remark, in addition, on two further distinctions. The first is that between a statement of a warrant, and statements about its applicability—

between 'A man born in Bermuda will be British', and 'This presumption holds good provided his parents were not both aliens, etc.' The distinction is relevant not only to the law of the land, but also for an understanding of scientific laws or 'laws of nature': it is important, indeed, in all cases where the application of a law may be subject to exceptions, or where a warrant can be supported by pointing to a general correlation only, and not to an absolutely invariable one. We can distinguish also two purposes which may be served by the production of additional facts: these can serve as further data, or they can be cited to confirm or rebut the applicability of a warrant. Thus, the fact that Harry was born in Bermuda and the fact that his parents were not aliens are both of them directly relevant to the question of his present nationality; but they are relevant in different ways. The one fact is a datum, which by itself establishes a presumption of British nationality; the other fact, by setting aside one possible rebuttal, tends to confirm the presumption thereby created.

One particular problem about applicability we shall have to discuss more fully later: when we set out a piece of applied mathematics, in which some system of mathematical relations is used to throw light on a question of (say) physics, the correctness of the calculations will be one thing, their appropriateness to the problem in hand may be quite another. So the question 'Is this calculation mathematically impeccable?' may be a very different one from the question 'Is this the relevant calculation?' Here too, the applicability of a particular warrant is one question: the result we shall get from applying the warrant is another matter, and in asking about the *correctness* of the result we may have to inquire into both these things independently.

THE PATTERN OF AN ARGUMENT: BACKING OUR WARRANTS

One last distinction, which we have already touched on in passing, must be discussed at some length. In addition to the question whether or on what conditions a warrant is applicable in a *particular* case, we may be asked why *in general* this warrant should be accepted as having authority. In defending a claim, that is, we may produce our data, our warrant, and the relevant qualifications and conditions, and yet find that we have still not satisfied our challenger; for he may be dubious not only about this particular argument but about the more general question whether the warrant (W) is acceptable at all. Presuming the general acceptability of this warrant (he may allow) our argument would no doubt be impeccable—if D-ish facts really do suffice as backing for C-ish claims, all well and good. But does not that warrant in its turn rest on something else? Challenging a particular claim may in this way lead on to challenging, more generally, the legitimacy of a whole range of arguments. 'You presume that a man born in Bermuda can be taken to be a British subject,' he may say, 'but why do you think that?' Standing behind our warrants, as this example reminds us, there will normally be other assurances, without which the warrants themselves would possess neither authority nor currency—these other things we may refer to as the *backing* (B) of the warrants. This 'backing' of our warrants is something which we shall have to scrutinise very carefully: its precise relations to our data, claims, warrants and conditions of rebuttal deserve some clarification, for confusion at this point can lead to trouble later.

We shall have to notice particularly how the sort of backing called for by our warrants varies from one field of argument to another. The *form* of argument we employ in different fields

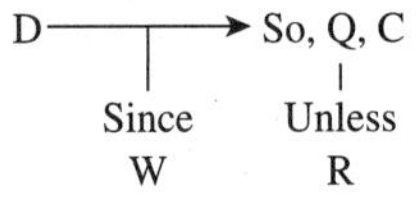

```
D ───┬───→ So, Q, C
     │          |
   Since      Unless
     W          R
```

need not vary very much as between fields. 'A whale will be a mammal', 'A Bermudan will be a Briton', 'A Saudi Arabian will be a Muslim': here are three different warrants to which we might appeal in the course of a practical argument, each of which can justify the same sort of straightforward step from a datum to a conclusion. We might add for variety examples of even more diverse sorts, taken from moral, mathematical or psychological fields. But the moment we start asking about the *backing* which a warrant relies on in each field, great differences begin to appear: the kind of backing we must point to if we are to establish its authority will change greatly as we move from one field of argument to another. 'A whale will be (i.e. *is classifiable as*) a mammal', 'A Bermudan will be (*in the eyes of the law*) a Briton', 'A Saudi Arabian will be (*found to be*) a Muslim'—the words in parentheses indicate what these differences are. One warrant is defended by relating it to a system of taxonomical classification, another by appealing to the statutes governing the nationality of people born in the British colonies, the third by referring to the statistics which record how religious beliefs are distributed among people of different nationalities. We can for the moment leave open the more contentious question, how we establish our warrants in the fields of morals, mathematics and psychology: for the moment all we are trying to show is the *variability* or *field-dependence* of the backing needed to establish our warrants.

We can make room for this additional element in our argument-pattern by writing it below the bare statement of the warrant for which it serves as backing (B):

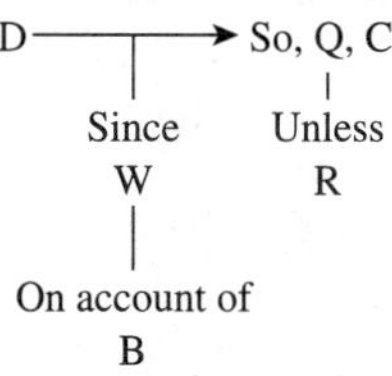
D
So, Q, C
Since
W
Unless
R
On account of
B

This form may not be final, but it will be complex enough for the purpose of our present discussions. To take a particular example: in support of the claim (C) that Harry is a British subject, we appeal to the datum (D) that he was born in Bermuda, and the warrant can then be stated in the form, 'A man born in Bermuda may be taken to be a British subject': since, however, questions of nationality are always subject to qualifications and conditions, we shall have to insert a qualifying 'presumably' (Q) in front of the conclusion, and note the possibility that our conclusion may be rebutted in case (R) it turns out that both his parents were aliens or he has since become a naturalised American. Finally, in case the warrant itself is challenged, its backing can be put in: this will record the terms and the dates of enactment of the Acts of Parliament and other legal provisions governing the nationality of persons born in the British colonies. The result will be an argument set out as follows:

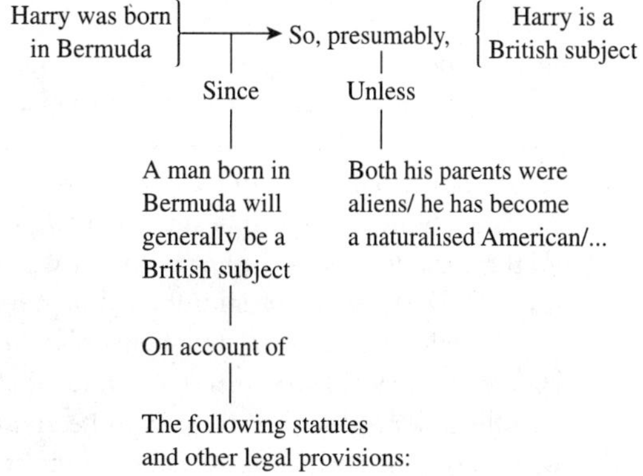
Harry was born in Bermuda
So, presumably,
Harry is a British subject
Since
Unless
A man born in Bermuda will generally be a British subject
Both his parents were aliens/ he has become a naturalised American/...
On account of
The following statutes and other legal provisions:

In what ways does the backing of warrants differ from the other elements in our arguments? To begin with the differences between B and W: statements of warrants, we saw, are hypothetical, bridge-like statements, but the backing for warrants can be expressed in the form of categorical statements of fact quite as well as can the data appealed to in direct support of our conclusions. So long as our statements reflect these functional differences explicitly, there is no danger of confusing the backing (B) for a warrant with the warrant itself (W): such confusions arise only when these differences are disguised by our forms of expression. In our present example, at any rate, there need be no difficulty. The fact that the relevant statutes have been validly passed into law, and contain the provisions they do, can be ascertained simply by going to the records of the parliamentary proceedings concerned and to the relevant volumes in the books of statute law: the resulting discovery, that such-and-such a statute enacted on such-and-such a date contains a provision specifying that people born in the British colonies of suitable parentage shall be entitled to British citizenship, is a straightforward statement of fact. On the other hand, the warrant which we apply *in virtue of* the statute containing this provision is logically of a very different character—'*If* a man was born in a British colony, he *may be presumed to be* British.' Though the facts about the statute may provide all the backing required by this warrant, the explicit statement of the warrant itself is more than a repetition of these facts: it is a general *moral* of a practical character, about the ways in which we can safely argue in view of these facts.

We can also distinguish backing (B) from data (D). Though the data we appeal to in an argument and the backing lending authority to our warrants may alike be stated as straightforward matters-of-fact, the roles which these statements play in our argument are decidedly different. Data of some kind must be produced, if there is to be an argument there at all: a bare conclusion, without any data produced in its support, is no argument. But the backing of the warrants we invoke need not be made explicit—at any rate to begin with: the warrants may be conceded without challenge, and their backing left understood. Indeed, if we demanded the credentials of all warrants at sight and never let one pass unchallenged, argument could scarcely begin. Jones puts forward an argument invoking warrant W_1, and Smith challenges that warrant; Jones is obliged, as a lemma, to produce another argument in the hope of establishing the acceptability of the first warrant, but in the course of this lemma employs a second warrant W_2; Smith challenges the credentials of this second warrant in turn; and so the game goes on. Some warrants must be accepted provisionally without further challenge, if argument is to be open to us in the field in question: we should not even know what sort of data were of the slightest relevance to a conclusion, if we had not at least a provisional idea of the warrants acceptable in the situation confronting us. The existence of considerations such as would establish the acceptability of the most reliable warrants is something we are entitled to take for granted.

Finally, a word about the ways in which B differs from Q and R: these are too obvious to need expanding upon, since the grounds for regarding a warrant as generally acceptable are clearly one thing, the force which the warrant lends to a conclusion another, and the sorts of exceptional circumstance which may in particular cases rebut the presumptions the warrant creates a third. They correspond, in our example, to the three statements, (i) that the statutes about British nationality *have in fact* been validly passed into law, and say this: . . . , (ii) that Harry *may be presumed* to be a British subject, and (iii) that Harry, having recently become a naturalised American, *is no longer covered* by these statutes.

INTRODUCTION TO CHAIM PERELMAN AND LUCIE OLBRECHTS-TYTECA

Chaim Perelman was a Belgian philosopher who lived from 1912 to 1984. He lived and taught at universities in that country. Perelman's work in many ways parallels that of Toulmin's. He was dissatisfied with the theories of argument prevalent among analytic philosophers and wanted to propose a theory to account for the ways in which argument actually worked in everyday life. His coauthor for two books and several articles was the Belgian social scientist Lucie Olbrechts-Tyteca (1899–1988). Included here are excerpts from their book, *The New Rhetoric: A Treatise on Argumentation,* published in 1958 and first translated into English in 1969.

Perelman and Olbrechts-Tyteca believed that dialectic and rhetoric were, as Aristotle put it, counterparts. Dialectic provided an underlying theory of how argument works, while rhetoric provided a theory of how argument might be applied in particular circumstances so as to influence human decisions. They drew material for their theory of argument from a wide array of everyday, scientific, and philosophical examples.

The theoretical structure used by Perelman and Olbrechts-Tyteca is much more traditional than that proposed by Toulmin. The categories and types of argument are systematically reviewed in their book, a representative sample of which is excerpted here. Many of those arguments are described in terms that seem very traditional and would not look out of place in Aristotle or Quintilian.

However, Perelman and Olbrechts-Tyteca are not simply repeating the classical formulas but are updating them for twentieth century rhetorical theory. One important dimension of their theory is a new application of the venerable idea of *dialectic:* They stress the nature of argument as responsive to previous statements and anticipatory of future replies. In that regard their theory is similar to Bakhtin's stress on dialogue, and its emphasis on the exchange of argument among people makes argument essentially rhetorical rather than merely formal. A second important dimension of Perelman and Olbrechts-Tyteca's theory is the *universal audience.* They claim that in addition to an appeal to a specific, flesh-and-blood audience, all argument also appeals to an ideal of all reasonable people, and how such people might weigh the appeal being made.

The rhetorical theories of Perelman and Olbrechts-Tyteca demonstrate the ongoing vitality of the classical tradition of argument and its flexibility in application to new social realities. They are part of a twentieth century approach to argument that studies it in actual use rather than as a formal structure of logic. In that sense they are part of the move of many philosophers to see human thought and reason as fundamentally rhetorical.

CHAIM PERELMAN AND LUCIE OLBRECHTS-TYTECA

THE NEW RHETORIC: A TREATISE ON ARGUMENTATION

PART ONE

• • •

§ 3. *The Speaker and His Audience*

The authors of scientific reports and similar papers often think that if they merely report certain experiments, mention certain facts, or enunciate a certain number of truths, this is enough of itself to automatically arouse the interest of their hearers or readers. This attitude rests on the illusion, widespread in certain rationalistic and scientific circles, that facts speak for themselves and make such an indelible imprint on any human mind that the latter is forced to give its adherence regardless of its inclination. An editor of a psychological journal, Katherine F. Bruner, likens such authors, who do not worry very much about their audience, to discourteous visitors:

> They slouch into a chair, staring glumly at their shoes, and abruptly announce, to themselves or not, we never know, "It has been shown by such and such . . . that the female of the white rat responds negatively to electric shock."
>
> "All right, sir," I say. "So what? Tell me first why I should care; then I will listen."[1]

It is true that these authors when addressing a learned society, or publishing an article in a specialized journal, can afford to neglect the means of entering into contact with their public, for the indispensable link between speaker and audience is provided by a scientific institution, the society, or the journal. In such a case, then, the author has merely to maintain, between himself and the public, the contact already established by the scientific institution.

But not everyone is in such a privileged position. For argumentation to develop, there must be some attention paid to it by those to whom it is directed. The prime concern of publicity and propaganda is to draw the attention of an indifferent public, this being the indispensable condition for carrying on any sort of argumentation. It is true that in a large number of fields—such as those of education, politics, science, the administration of justice—any society possesses institutions which facilitate and organize this contact of minds. But the importance of this preliminary problem must not be underrated on that account.

Under normal circumstances, some quality is necessary in order to speak and be listened to. In our civilization, where the printed word has become a commodity and utilizes economic organization to draw attention to itself, this preliminary condition is seen clearly only in cases where contact between the speaker and his audience cannot be brought about by the techniques of distribution. It is accordingly best seen where argumentation is developed by a speaker who is orally addressing a specific audience, rather than where it is contained in a book on sale in a bookstore. This quality in a speaker, without which he will not be listened to, or even, in many cases, allowed to

Translated by
John Wilkinson and Purcell Weaver
Center for the Study of Democratic Institutions

---

[1] Bruner, "Of Psychological Writing," *Journal of Abnormal and Social Psychology,* 37 (1942), 62.

speak, will vary with the circumstances. Sometimes it will be enough for the speaker to appear as a human being with a decent suit of clothes, sometimes he is required to be an adult, sometimes he must be a rank and file member of a particular group, sometimes the spokesman of this group. Under certain circumstances or before certain audiences the only admissible authority for speaking is the exercise of particular functions. There are fields where these matters of qualification to speak are regulated in very great detail.

This contact between the speaker and his audience is not confined to the conditions preliminary to argumentation: it is equally necessary if argumentation is to develop. For since argumentation aims at securing the adherence of those to whom it is addressed, it is, in its entirety, relative to the audience to be influenced.

How may such an audience be defined? Is it just the person whom the speaker addresses by name? Not always: thus, a member of Parliament in England must address himself to the Speaker, but he may try to persuade those listening to him in the chamber, and beyond that, public opinion throughout the country. Again, can such an audience be defined as the group of persons the speaker sees before him when he speaks? Not necessarily. He may perfectly well disregard a portion of them: a government spokesman in Parliament may give up any hope of convincing the opposition, even before he begins to speak, and may be satisfied with getting the adherence of his majority. And, on the other hand, a person granting an interview to a journalist considers his audience to be not the journalist himself but the readers of the paper he represents. The secrecy of deliberations, by modifying the speaker's opinion of his audience, may change the content of his speech. It is at once apparent from these few examples how difficult it is to determine by purely material criteria what constitutes a speaker's audience. The difficulty is even greater in the case of a writer's audience, as in most cases it is impossible to identify his readers with certainty.

For this reason we consider it preferable to define an audience, for the purposes of rhetoric, as *the ensemble of those whom the speaker wishes to influence by his argumentation.* Every speaker thinks, more or less consciously, of those he is seeking to persuade; these people form the audience to whom his speech is addressed.

§ 4. The Audience as a Construction of the Speaker

The audience, as visualized by one undertaking to argue, is always a more or less systematized construction. Efforts have been made to establish its psychological[1] or sociological[2] origins. The essential consideration for the speaker who has set himself the task of persuading concrete individuals is that his construction of the audience should be adequate to the occasion.

This does not hold for someone engaged in mere essay-making, without concern for real life. Rhetoric, which has then become an academic exercise, is addressed to conventional audiences, of which such rhetoric can afford to have stereotyped conceptions. However, it is this limited view of the audience, as much as artificiality of subject-matter, which is responsible for the degeneration of rhetoric.[3]

In real argumentation, care must be taken to form a concept of the anticipated audience as close as possible to reality. An inadequate picture of the audience, resulting from either ignorance or an unforeseen set of circumstances, can have very unfortunate results. Argumentation which an orator considers persuasive may well cause opposition in an audience for which "reasons for" are actually "reasons against." Thus, if one argues for a certain measure that it is likely to reduce social tension,

---

[1] Sullivan, *The Interpersonal Theory of Psychiatry.*

[2] Millioud, "La propagation des idées," *Revue philosophique,* 69 (1910), 580–600; 70 (1910), 168–191.

[3] Marrou, *Histoire de l'éducation dans l'Antiquité,* p. 278.

such argument will set against the measure all those who would like to see disturbances.

Accordingly, knowledge of those one wishes to win over is a condition preliminary to all effectual argumentation.

Concern with the audience transforms certain chapters in the classical treatises on rhetoric into veritable studies in psychology. For instance, in the passage in the *Rhetoric* dealing with the factors of age and fortune in audiences, Aristotle includes many shrewd descriptions of a differential-psychological nature that are still valid today.[1] Cicero shows the necessity of speaking differently to the class of men which is "coarse and ignorant, always preferring immediate advantage to what is honorable," and to "that other, enlightened and cultivated, which puts moral dignity above all else."[2] Later, Quintilian dwells on character differences, which are important to the orator.[3]

The study of audiences could also be a study for sociology, since a man's opinions depend not so much on his own character, as on his social environment, on the people he associates with and lives among. As M. Millioud has said: "If you want an uncultivated man to change his views, transplant him."[4] Every social circle or milieu is distinguishable in terms of its dominant opinions and unquestioned beliefs, of the premises that it takes for granted without hesitation: these views form an integral part of its culture, and an orator wishing to persuade a particular audience must of necessity adapt himself to it. Thus the particular culture of a given audience shows so strongly through the speeches addressed to it that we feel we can rely on them to a considerable extent for our knowledge of the character of past civilizations.

[1] Aristotle, *Rhetoric,* II, 12–17, 1388b–1391b. See also De Coster, "L'idéalisme des jeunes," *Morale et enseignement,* 1951–52, nos. 2, 3.

[2] Cicero, *Partitiones Oratoriae,* § 90.

[3] Quintilian, III, viii, 38 et seq.

[4] Millioud, "La propagation des idées," *Revue philosophique,* 70 (1910), 173.

Among the sociological considerations of possible use to an orator are those bearing on a very definite matter: the social functions exercised by his listeners. It is quite common for members of an audience to adopt attitudes connected with the role they play in certain social institutions. This fact has been stressed by the originator of the psychology of form:

> One can sometimes observe marvelous changes in individuals, as when some passionately biased person becomes a member of a jury, or arbitrator, or judge, and when his actions then show the fine transition from bias to an honest effort to deal with the problems at issue in a just and objective fashion.[1]

The same observation can be made of the mentality of a politician whose point of view changes when, after years spent in the opposition, he becomes a responsible member of the government.

The listener, then, in his new functions, assumes a new personality which the orator cannot afford to disregard. And what is true of the individual listener holds equally true of whole audiences, so much so that the theoreticians of rhetoric have found it possible to classify oratory on the basis of the role performed by the audience addressed. The writers of antiquity recognized three types of oratory, the deliberative, the forensic, and the epidictic, which in their view corresponded respectively to an audience engaged in deliberating, an audience engaged in judging, and an audience that is merely enjoying the unfolding of the orator's argument without having to reach a conclusion on the matter in question.[2]

We are presented here with a distinction of a purely practical order, whose defects and inadequacies are apparent. Particularly unsatisfactory is

[1] Wertheimer, *Productive Thinking,* pp. 135–136.

[2] Aristotle, *Rhetoric,* I, 3, 1358b, 2–7; Cicero, *Orator,* § 37; *Partitiones Oratoriae,* § 10; Quintilian, III, iv.

its characterization of the epidictic type of oratory, of which we shall have more to say later.[1] Though this classification cannot be accepted as such for the study of argumentation, it has nevertheless the merit of underlining the importance which a speaker must give to the functions of his audience.

It often happens that an orator must persuade a composite audience, embracing people differing in character, loyalties, and functions. To win over the different elements in his audience, the orator will have to use a multiplicity of arguments. A great orator is one who possesses the art of taking into consideration, in his argumentation, the composite nature of his audience. Examples of this art may be found on close reading of speeches made before parliamentary assemblies, a type of composite audience whose constituent elements are readily discernible.

However, an orator does not have to be confronted with several organized factions to think of the composite nature of his audience. He is justified in visualizing each one of his listeners as simultaneously belonging to a number of disparate groups. Even when an orator stands before only a few auditors, or indeed, before a single auditor, it is possible that he will not be quite sure what arguments will appear most convincing to his audience. In such a case, he will, by a kind of fiction, insert his audience into a series of different audiences. In *Tristram Shandy*—since argumentation is one of the main themes of this book, we shall often refer to it—Tristram describes an argument between his parents, in which his father wants to persuade his mother to have a midwife:

> He . . . placed his arguments in all lights; argued the matter with her like a Christian, like a heathen, like a husband, like a father, like a patriot, like a man. My mother answered everything only like a woman, which was a little hard upon her, for, as she could not assume and fight it out behind such a variety of characters, 'twas no fair match: 'twas seven to one.[1]

[1] Cf. § 11, infra: The Epidictic Genre.

Notice that it is not only the orator who so changes his mask: it is even more so his audience—his poor wife in this case—which his fancy transforms, as he seeks its most vulnerable points. However, as it is the speaker who takes the initiative in this "breaking down" of the audience, it is to him that the terms "like a Christian," "like a heathen," and so on, are applied.

When a speaker stands before his audience, he can try to locate it in its social setting. He may ask himself if all the members fall within a single social group, or if he must spread his listeners over a number of different—perhaps even opposed—groups. If division is necessary, several ways of proceeding are always possible: he may divide his audience ideally in terms of the social groups—political, occupational, religious, for example—to which the individual members belong, or in terms of the values to which certain members of the audience adhere. These ideal divisions are not mutually independent; they can, however, lead to the formation of very different partial audiences.

The breaking down of a gathering into subgroups will also depend on the speaker's own position. If he holds extremist views on a question, there is nothing to restrain him from considering all his interlocutors as forming a single audience. On the other hand, if he holds a moderate view, he will see them as forming at least two distinct audiences.[2]

Knowledge of an audience cannot be conceived independently of the knowledge of how to influence it. The problem of the nature of an audi-

[1] Sterne, *The Life and Opinions of Tristram Shandy*, bk. I, chap. 18, p. 42.

[2] Cf. the observations of L. Festinger on the lesser tendency toward communication found in those who hold moderate viewpoints: "Informal Social Communication," *Psychological Review*, vol. 57, no. 5, Sept. 1950, p. 275.

ence is indeed intimately connected with that of its conditioning. This term implies, at first sight, factors extrinsic to the audience. And all study of this conditioning assumes that this conditioning is considered as applying to an entity which would be the audience itself. But, on a closer view, knowledge of an audience is also knowledge of how to bring about its conditioning, as well as of the amount of conditioning achieved at any given moment of the discourse.

Various conditioning agents are available to increase one's influence on an audience: music, lighting, crowd effects, scenery, and various devices of stage management. These means have always been known and have been used in the past by primitive peoples, as well as by the Greeks, Romans, and men of the Middle Ages. In our own day, technical improvements have fostered the development of these conditioners to the point that they are regarded by some as the essential element in acting on minds.

Besides conditioning of this kind, which is beyond the scope of this work, there is the conditioning by the speech itself, which results in the audience no longer being exactly the same at the end of the speech as it was at the beginning. This form of conditioning can be brought about only if there is a continuous adaptation of the speaker to his audience.

§ 5. Adaptation of the Speaker to the Audience

Vico wrote, "the end sought by eloquence always depends on the speaker's audience, and he must govern his speech in accordance with their opinions."[1] In argumentation, the important thing is not knowing what the speaker regards as true or important, but knowing the views of those he is addressing. To borrow Gracian's simile, speech is

[1] Vico, *Opere*, ed. Ferrari, vol. II, *De Nostri Temporis Studiorum Ratione*, p. 10.

"like a feast, at which the dishes are made to please the guests, and not the cooks."[1]

The great orator, the one with a hold on his listeners, seems animated by the very mind of his audience. This is not the case for the ardent enthusiast whose sole concern is with what he himself considers important. A speaker of this kind may have some effect on suggestible persons, but generally speaking his speech will strike his audience as unreasonable. According to M. Pradines, the enthusiast's speech, even if capable of some effect, does not yield a "true" sound, the emotional reality "bursts through the mask of logic," for, he says, "passion and reasons are not commensurable."[2] The apparent explanation for this viewpoint is that the man swayed by passion argues without taking sufficiently into account the audience he is addressing: carried away by his enthusiasm, he imagines his audience to be susceptible to the same arguments that persuaded him. Thus, passion, in causing the audience to be forgotten, creates less an absence than a poor choice of reasons.

Because they adopted the techniques of the clever orator, Plato reproached the leaders of the Athenian democracy with "flattering" the populace when they should have led them. But no orator, not even the religious orator, can afford to neglect this effort of adaptation to his audience. "The making of a preacher," wrote Bossuet, "rests with his audience."[3] In his struggle against the demagogues at Athens, Demosthenes calls on the people to improve themselves so as to improve the performance of the orators:

> Your orators never make you either bad men or good, but you make them whichever you choose; for it is not you that aim at what they wish for, but they who aim at whatever they think you desire. You therefore must start with a

[1] Gracian, *L'homme de Cour*, p. 85.

[2] Pradines, *Traité de psychologie générale*, vol. II, pp. 324–325.

[3] Bossuet, *Sermons*, vol. II, *Sur la parole de Dieu*, p. 153.

> noble ambition and all will be well, for then no orator will give you base counsel, or else he will gain nothing by it, having no one to take him at his word.[1]

It is indeed the audience which has the major role in determining the quality of argument and the behavior of orators.[2]

Although orators, in their relationship to the listeners, have been compared to cooks, and even to parasites who "almost always speak a language contrary to their sentiments in order to be invited to fine meals,"[3] it must not be overlooked that the orator is nearly always at liberty to give up persuading an audience when he cannot persuade it effectively except by the use of methods that are repugnant to him. It should not be thought, where argument is concerned, that it is always honorable to succeed in persuasion, or even to have such an intention. The problem of harmonizing the scruples of the man of honor with submission to the audience received special attention from Quintilian.[4] To him rhetoric as *scientia bene dicendi*[5] implies that the accomplished orator not only is good at persuading, but also says what is good. If, then, one allows the existence of audiences of corrupt persons, whom one nonetheless does not want to give up convincing, and, at the same time, if one looks at the matter from the standpoint of the moral quality of the speaker, one finds oneself led, in order to solve the difficulty, to make distinctions and dissociations that do not come as a matter of course.

The coupling of obligation on the orator to adapt himself to his audience, with limitation of the audience to an incompetent mob, incapable of understanding sustained reasoning, or of maintaining attention if in the least distracted, has had two unfortunate results. It has discredited rhetoric, and has introduced into the theory of speech general rules which actually seem only to be valid in particular cases. We do not see, for instance, why, as a matter of principle, use of technical argumentation should lead away from rhetoric and dialectic.[1]

There is only one rule in this matter: adaptation of the speech to the audience, whatever its nature. Arguments that in substance and form are appropriate to certain circumstances may appear ridiculous in others.[2]

If the same event is described in a work that claims to be scientific and in a historical novel, the same method of proving its reality need not be adopted in the two cases. A reader who would have found Jules Romains' proofs of the voluntary suspension of the action of the heart ridiculous, had they appeared in a medical journal, might consider them an interesting hypothesis when developed in a novel.[3]

The procedures to be adopted in arguing are to some extent conditioned by the size of the audience, independently of considerations relating to the area of agreement taken as a basis for the argument, which vary from audience to audience. In discussing style as affected by the occasion of the speech, J. Marouzeau has drawn attention to

> a kind of deference and self-consciousness imposed by numbers, . . . as intimacy decreases, qualms increase, qualms about gaining the esteem of the listeners, about winning their applause or, at least, their approbation as expressed in looks and attitudes.[4]

Many other observations might pertinently be made on characteristics of audiences that influence a speaker's behavior and mode of argument. In

---

[1] Demosthenes, *On Organization,* § 36

[2] Cf. § 2, supra: The Contact of Minds.

[3] Saint-Évremond, vol. IX, p. 19, referring to Petronius, *The Satyricon,* chap. III, p. 3.

[4] Quintilian, III, viii; XII, i.

[5] Quintilian, II, xv, 34.

[1] Aristotle, *Rhetoric,* I, 2, 1357a, 1358a.

[2] Whately, *Elements of Rhetoric* (Harper), pt. III, chap. I, § 2, pp. 179 et seq.

[3] Reyes, *El Deslinde,* p. 40. Romains, *Les hommes de bonne volonté,* vol. XII: *Les créateurs,* chap I–VII. Cf. Belaval, *Les philosophes et leur langage,* p. 138.

[4] Marouzeau, *Précis de stylistique française,* p. 208.

our view, the value of our study depends on consideration being given to the many distinct aspects of particular audiences in as concrete a manner as possible. However, we wish to stress in the following four sections the characteristics of certain audiences selected for their unquestionable importance to all concerned with argumentation, and particularly to philosophers.

§ 6. *Persuading and Convincing*

We have said enough to show that audiences are almost infinite in their variety, and that, in the effort to adapt to their particular characteristics, a speaker faces innumerable problems. This is one reason, perhaps, why there is such tremendous interest in a technique of argumentation that would apply to all kinds of audiences, or at least to those composed of competent or rational people. Corresponding to this ideal, to this desire to transcend historical or local particularities so that theses defended may win universal acceptance, is the quest for objectivity, whatever the nature of this may be. In this endeavor, as Husserl says in a moving speech in which he defends the efforts of western rational thought, "we are, in our philosophical work, the *public servants of mankind.*"[1] In the same spirit, J. Benda accuses clerks of treason when they turn from concern with what is eternal and universal to defense of temporal and local values.[2] Here is resumed that age-old debate between those who stand for truth and those who stand for opinion, between philosophers seeking the absolute and rhetors involved in action. It is out of this debate that the distinction between *persuading* and *convincing* seems to arise. We wish to reconsider this distinction in the context of a theory of argumentation and of the role played by certain audiences.[3]

[1] Husserl, *Die Krisis der europäischen Wissenschaften* in *Gesammelle Werke,* vol. VI, p. 15.

[2] Benda, *La trahison des clercs.*

[3] Cf. Perelman and Olbrechts-Tyteca, "Logique et rhétorique," *Rhétorique et philosophie,* pp. 3 et seq.

To the person concerned with results, persuading surpasses convincing, since conviction is merely the first stage in progression toward action.[1] Rousseau considered it useless to convince a child "if you cannot also persuade him."[2]

On the other hand, to someone concerned with the rational character of adherence to an argument, convincing is more crucial than persuading. Furthermore, this rational character of conviction depends sometimes on the means used and sometimes on the faculties one addresses. In Pascal's view, persuasion is something applied to the automation—by which he means the body, imagination, and feeling, all, in fact, that is not reason.[3] Often persuasion is considered to be an unwarranted transposition of demonstration. Thus, according to Dumas, "in being persuaded, a person is satisfied with affective and personal reasons," and persuasion is often "sophistic."[4] But he does not specify in what respect this affective proof differs technically from objective proof.

The criteria relied on to distinguish between conviction and persuasion are always based on a decision requiring isolation from a totality, totality of procedures, totality of faculties, of certain elements conceived as rational. This process of isolation, it must be emphasized, is sometimes applied to the actual lines of reasoning. It may be shown, for instance, that a certain syllogism, while inducing conviction, will not induce persuasion: however, this way of speaking of a syllogism involves isolating it from an entire context, it supposes that the premises of the syllogism exist in the mind independently of the remainder, it transforms these premises into intangible and unshakable truths. We may be told, for example, that a certain person, although convinced of the dangers

[1] Whately, *Elements of Rhetoric* (Harper), pt. II, chap. I, § 1. Cf. Stevenson, *Ethics and Language* (Yale), pp. 139–140.

[2] Rousseau, *Emile* (Dent, Dutton), bk. III, p. 146.

[3] Pascal, *Pensées,* GBWW, vol. 33, p. 219, no. 252.

[4] Dumas, *Traité de psychologie,* vol. II, p. 740.

of too rapid mastication, will not on that account cease the practice.[1] Such a statement involves isolation, from the complete picture, of the reasoning which forms the basis of the conviction. It is overlooked, for instance, that this conviction may run up against another conviction affirming that time is gained by eating more quickly. It is apparent, then, that the concept of what constitutes conviction, though seemingly based on a singling out of the means of proof used or faculties called into play, often also involves the isolation of particular data from a far more complex totality.

However, even if one refuses, as we do, to adopt these distinctions in actual thought, one must recognize that our language makes use of two notions, convincing and persuading, and that there is a slight and perceptible difference in the meaning of the two terms.

We are going to apply the term *persuasive* to argumentation that only claims validity for a particular audience, and the term *convincing* to argumentation that presumes to gain the adherence of every rational being. The nuance involved is a delicate one and depends, essentially, on the idea the speaker has formed on the incarnation of reason. Every person believes in a set of facts, of truths, which he thinks must be accepted by every "normal" person, because they are valid for every rational being. But is this really the case? Does not this claim to an absolute validity for any audience composed of rational beings go too far? On this point, even the most conscientious writer can do no more than submit to the test of facts, to his readers' judgment.[2] In any case he will have done all he can to *convince,* if he thinks he is validly addressing such an audience.

Despite the similarity in their consequences, we prefer our criterion to that, quite different in principle, put forward by Kant in his *Critique of Pure Reason.* According to him, conviction and persuasion are two different kinds of belief:

> If a judgment is valid for every rational being, then its ground is objectively sufficient, and it is termed a *conviction.* If, on the other hand, it has its ground in the particular character of the subject, it is termed a *persuasion.* Persuasion is a mere illusion, the ground of the judgment, which lies solely in the subject, being regarded as objective. Hence a judgment of this kind has only private validity—is only valid for the individual who judges, and the holding of a thing to be true in this way cannot be communicated. . . . Persuasion, accordingly, cannot be *subjectively* distinguished from conviction, that is, so long as the subject views its judgment simply as a phenomenon of its own mind. But if we inquire whether the grounds of our judgment, which are valid for us, produce the same effect on the reason of others as on our own, we have then the means, though only subjective means, not, indeed, of producing conviction, but of detecting the merely private validity of the judgment; in other words, of discovering that there is in it the element of mere persuasion. . . . Persuasion I may keep for myself, if it is agreeable to me; but I cannot, and ought not, to attempt to impose it as binding upon others.[1]

The Kantian view, though rather close to ours in its consequences, differs from it in making the opposition of *subjective* and *objective* its criterion for distinguishing between persuasion and conviction. If conviction is based on the truth of its object, and is thereby valid for every rational being, then conviction alone can be proved, and persuasion has no more than individual significance. From this it is clear that Kant accepts only purely logical proof, and excludes from philosophy all argument that does not absolutely compel acceptance. Kant's

[1] Scott, *Influencing Men in Business. The Psychology of Argument and Suggestion* (1920), p. 31.

[2] Cf. Kant, *Critique of Pure Reason,* preface to the first edition, GBWW, vol. 42, p. 3.

[1] Kant, *Critique of Pure Reason,* GBWW, vol. 42, p. 240.

conception is defensible only if it is conceded that what is not necessary is not communicable, and this would exclude all argumentation directed to particular audiences: but argumentation of the latter kind is the chosen sphere of rhetoric. And from the moment one admits the existence of other means of proof than necessary proof, argumentation addressed to particular audiences assumes a significance beyond mere subjective belief.

The distinction that we propose between persuasion and conviction expresses indirectly the connection that is frequently established, though in a confused way, between persuasion and action, on the one hand, and, on the other, between conviction and intelligence. Indeed, the timeless character of certain audiences explains why arguments addressed to them make no call for immediate action.

At first sight, this distinction, based on the characteristics of the audience addressed, does not seem to explain the difference between conviction and persuasion as it is experienced by the hearer himself. But it will readily be seen that the same criterion can nevertheless apply, if one bears in mind that the hearer imagines the transfer to other audiences of the arguments presented to him and that he concerns himself with the reception they would obtain.

Our viewpoint has the advantage of showing that the difference between the terms *convincing* and *persuading* is always unprecise and in practice must remain so. For whereas the frontier between intelligence and will, between reason and the irrational, can be clearly drawn, the making of distinctions between different audiences is a far less certain matter, particularly as the representation the speaker makes of an audience is the result of an effort that can always be abandoned and replaced.

The distinction we make between persuading and convincing has many features in common with the distinctions made by writers in the past,[1] even though we have not adopted their criteria. It also explains the use some writers make, out of modesty, of the word persuasion as opposed to conviction. For instance, Claparède, in the preface to one of his books, tells us that his decision to let the manuscript see the light of day was in accession "to the request of Madame Antipoff, who persuaded (but did not convince) me that the publication of these investigations was desirable."[1] In so writing, the author has no thought of making a theoretical distinction between the two terms, but he makes use of the difference between them to express both the slight guaranteed objective value and the power of the reasons given by his collaborator. The difference in shades of meaning conveyed by Claparède may correspond to the Kantian concept, but seems to fit in even better with the fact that he was confronted with reasons that were convincing to him, but which he thought might not be convincing to everybody.

Thus the nature of the audience to which arguments can be successfully presented will determine to a great extent both the direction the arguments will take and the character, the significance that will be attributed to them. What formulation can we make of audiences, which have come to play a normative role, enabling us to judge on the convincing character of an argument? Three kinds of audiences are apparently regarded as enjoying special prerogatives as regards this function, both in current practice and in the view of philosophers. The first such audience consists of the whole of mankind, or at least, of all normal, adult persons; we shall refer to it as the *universal audience*. The second consists of the single *interlocutor* whom a speaker addresses in a dialogue. The third is the *subject himself* when he deliberates or gives himself reasons for his actions. We hasten to add that it is only when the interlocutor in a dialogue and the man debating with himself are regarded as an incarnation of the universal audience, that they can

---

[1] Cf., in particular, Fénelon, "Dialogues sur l'éloquence," *Oeuvres*, vol. XXI, p. 43.

[1] Claparède, "La genèse de l'hypothèse," *Archives de Psychologie*, vol. XXIV, introduction.

enjoy the philosophic privilege conferred to reason, by virtue of which argumentation addressed to them has often been assimilated to logical discourse. Each speaker's universal audience can, indeed, from an external viewpoint, be regarded as a particular audience, but it none the less remains true that, for each speaker at each moment, there exists an audience transcending all others, which cannot easily be forced within the bounds of a particular audience. On the other hand, the interlocutor in a dialogue or the person engaged in deliberation can be considered as a particular audience, with reactions that are known to us, or at least with characteristics we can study. Hence the primordial importance of the universal audience, as providing a norm for objective argumentation, since the other party to a dialogue and the person deliberating with himself can never amount to more than floating incarnations of this universal audience.

§ 7. *The Universal Audience*

Argumentation aimed exclusively at a particular audience has the drawback that the speaker, by the very fact of adapting to the views of his listeners, might rely on arguments that are foreign or even directly opposed to what is acceptable to persons other than those he is presently addressing. This danger is apparent in the case of a composite audience, which the speaker has to resolve into its constituent parts for the purposes of his argumentation. For a composite audience, such as a parliamentary assembly, will have to be regrouped as a single entity to make a decision, and it is extremely easy for the opponent of an incautious speaker to turn against him all the arguments he directed to the different parts of the audience, either by setting the arguments against each other so as to show their incompatibility or by presenting them to those they were not meant for. This explains the relative weakness of arguments that are accepted only by particular audiences and the value attached to opinions that enjoy unanimous approval, particularly approval by persons or groups who agree on very few matters.

Naturally, the value of this unanimity depends on the number and quality of those expressing it. Its highest point is reached when there is *agreement of the universal audience.* This refers of course, in this case, not to an experimentally proven fact, but to a universality and unanimity imagined by the speaker, to the agreement of an audience which should be universal, since, for legitimate reasons, we need not take into consideration those which are not part of it.

Philosophers always claim to be addressing such an audience, not because they hope to obtain the effective assent of all men—they know very well that only a small minority will ever read their works—but because they think that all who understand the reasons they give will have to accept their conclusions. *The agreement of a universal audience is thus a matter, not of fact, but of right.* The basis for relying on the adherence of those who submit to the data of experience or to the light shed by reason is the speaker's affirmation of that which corresponds to an objective fact, of that which constitutes a true and even necessary assertion.

Argumentation addressed to a universal audience must convince the reader that the reasons adduced are of a compelling character, that they are self-evident, and possess an absolute and timeless validity, independent of local or historical contingencies. "Truth," according to Kant, "depends upon agreement with the object, and consequently, with respect to this object, the judgments of all understandings must be in agreement." Every objective belief can be communicated, because it is "valid for the reason of every man." It is only such an assertion that can be *affirmed,* that is, be expressed "as necessarily valid for everyone."[1]

In fact, a judgment of this sort is deemed to be binding on everybody, because the speaker himself is convinced that it does not admit of any question. This Cartesian certitude has been described very expressively by Dumas:

[1] Kant, *Critique of Pure Reason,* GBWW, vol. 42, p. 240.

> Certitude is that complete belief, which entirely excludes doubt; it is necessary, universal affirmation; in other words, the man who is certain does not conceive the possibility of preferring the contrary affirmation, but imagines his affirmation as necessarily commanding the acceptance of everybody in the same circumstances. In short, it is the state in which we are conscious of thinking the truth, which is precisely this universal constraint, this mental obligation; subjectivity disappears, and man thinks as intelligence, as a man and no longer as an individual. The state of certitude has often been described with the help of such metaphors as light and luminosity; but the illumination brought by rational certitude carries its own explanation. It means rest and relaxation, even if the certitude is a painful one, as it puts an end to the tension and the worry of search and indecision. With it comes a feeling of power, but also of annihilation; one feels that prejudice, passion, and individual caprice have disappeared. . . . In rational belief the truth becomes ours and we become the truth.[1]

It is to be observed that where rational self-evidence comes into play, the adherence of the mind seems to be suspended to a compelling truth, and no role is played by the processes of argumentation. The individual, with his freedom of deliberation and of choice, defers to the constraining force of reason, which takes from him all possibility of doubt. Thus, maximally efficacious rhetoric, in the case of a universal audience, is rhetoric employing nothing but logical proof.

Rationalism, with its claim to completely eliminate rhetoric from philosophy, announced a very ambitious program which would bring about the agreement of minds through universal yielding to rational self-evidence. But the exigencies of the Cartesian method had hardly been stated when Descartes, in the name of these exigencies, made some very questionable assertions. How, indeed, does one distinguish between true and false self-evidence? Does a person suppose that there is really objective validity in what convinces a universal audience, of which he considers himself the ideal representative? Pareto has made the penetrating observation that the universal consensus invoked is often merely the unwarranted generalization of an individual intuition.[1] For this reason it is always hazardous for a writer or speaker to identify with logic the argumentation intended for the universal audience, as he himself has conceived it. The concepts that men have formed, in the course of history, of "objective facts" and "obvious truths" have sufficiently varied for us to be wary in this matter. Instead of believing in a universal audience, analogous to the divine mind which can assent only to the "truth," we might, with greater justification, characterize each speaker by the image he himself holds of the universal audience that he is trying to win over to his view.

Everyone constitutes the universal audience from what he knows of his fellow men, in such a way as to transcend the few oppositions he is aware of. Each individual, each culture, has thus its own conception of the universal audience. The study of these variations would be very instructive, as we would learn from it what men, at different times in history, have regarded as *real, true,* and *objectively valid.*

If argumentation addressed to the universal audience and calculated to convince does not convince everybody, one can always resort to *disqualifying the recalcitrant* by classifying him as stupid or abnormal. This approach, common among thinkers in the Middle Ages, is also used by some

---

[1] Dumas, *Traité de psychologie,* vol. II, pp. 197–198, 200.

[1] Pareto, *The Mind and Society,* vol. 1, §§589, 599, pp. 354, 361.

modern writers.[1] There can only be adherence to this idea of excluding individuals from the human community if the number and intellectual value of those banned are not so high as to make such a procedure ridiculous. If this danger exists, recourse must be had to another line of argumentation, and the universal audience must be set against an elite audience, endowed with exceptional and infallible means of knowledge. Those who pride themselves on possession of a supernatural revelation or mystical knowledge, as well as those who appeal to the virtuous, to believers, or to men endowed with grace, show their preference for an elite audience; this elite audience may even be confused with the perfect Being.

The elite audience is by no means always regarded as similar to the universal audience. Indeed, the elite audience often wishes to remain distinct from the common run of men: if this is so, the elite is characterized by its hierarchic position. But often also the elite audience is regarded as a model to which men should conform in order to be worthy of the name: in other words, the elite audience sets the norm for everybody. In this case, the elite is the vanguard all will follow and conform to. Its opinion is the only one that matters, for, in final analysis, it is the determining one.

The elite audience embodies the universal audience only for those who acknowledge this role of vanguard and model. For the rest it will be no more than a particular audience. The status of an audience varies with the concepts one has of it.

Certain specialized audiences are readily assimilated to the universal audience, such as the audience of the scientist addressing his fellow scientists. The scientist addresses himself to certain particularly qualified men, who accept the data of a well-defined system consisting of the science in which they are specialists. Yet, this very limited audience is generally considered by the scientist to be really the universal audience, and not just a particular audience. He supposes that everyone with the same training, qualifications, and information would reach the same conclusions.

The same holds good when we are dealing with morals. We expect our judgments to be confirmed by the reactions of others. However, the "others" to whom we appeal are not just any "others." We make our appeal solely to those who have duly "reflected" on the conduct we approve or disapprove. As Findlay says:

> We make our appeal above the unreflecting heads of present company, to the great company of reflecting persons, wherever they may be situated in space or time.[1]

This sort of appeal is criticized by J.-P. Sartre in his remarkable lectures on the audience of a writer:

> We have said that the writer addresses himself, in principle, to all men. But, immediately afterward, we observed that he is only read by some of them. From this gap between ideal public and real public originates the idea of abstract universality. In other words, the author postulates a perpetual repetition over an indefinite future of the handful of readers he has in the present . . . recourse to infinity in time tries to compensate for the failure in space (return to the infinite of the reasonable man of the seventeenth century writer, extension to infinity of the writers' club and of the public of specialists for the nineteenth century writer). . . . By concrete universality, on the other hand, is meant the totality of men living in a given society.[2]

[1] E. g. Lefebvre, *A la Lumiere du materialisme dialectique,* I, *Logique fromelle, logique dialectique,* p. 29.

[1] Findlay, "Morality by Convention," *Mind,* LIII, new series, 1944, p. 160. Cf. Prior, *Logic and the Basis of Ethics,* p. 84.

[2] Sarte, *Situations,* vol. II, pp. 192-193.

Sartre upbraids writers for neglecting the concrete universality to which they could, and should, address themselves, in favor of an illusory abstract universality. But is it not Sartre's universal audience which will have to judge the merits of this criticism and decide whether or not the writer has been harboring up to now a voluntary or involuntary illusion, whether up to now he has failed in his self-appointed "mission"? And it is Sartre's universal audience he himself addresses when he wants to explain his views on this question of abstract and concrete universality.

We believe, then, that audiences are not independent of one another, that particular concrete audiences are capable of validating a concept of the universal audience which characterizes them. On the other hand, it is the undefined universal audience that is invoked to pass judgment on what is the concept of the universal audience appropriate to such a concrete audience, to examine, simultaneously, the manner in which it was composed, which are the individuals who comprise it, according to the adopted criterion, and whether this criterion is legitimate. It can be said that audiences pass judgment on one another.

• • •

INTRODUCTION TO MARSHALL McLUHAN

Marshall McLuhan (1911–1980) was born in Canada, educated at Cambridge University in England, and taught at universities in the United States and Canada. McLuhan was trained in English literature and literary studies, including criticism. He was a student of the Renaissance. McLuhan was certainly familiar with rhetorical issues, since he taught rhetoric and interpretation. But it is as a theorist of media that McLuhan has been most influential internationally. McLuhan may be the academic theorist included in this book who has the most popular recognition.

McLuhan's central thesis was that every age and society has dominant media that shape the way the culture thinks. Rhetorical theorists have found this insight tremendously useful, for it essentially holds that there is a rhetorical effect inherent within usage of a medium, in addition to whatever effect may come from the content of the message alone. This idea is summed up in McLuhan's statement, widely publicized and familiar to millions, that "the medium is the message." McLuhan's theories mean that the same message will have different effects when watched on television as opposed to being read in a book. This effect is long term, fundamental, and bedrock deep in the thoughts, dispositions, values, and habits of every society.

McLuhan's most influential book, among many that he published, is excerpted here. *Understanding Media: The Extensions of Man* was published in 1964. McLuhan worked relatively soon after the mass introduction of television into western culture (television really began to achieve widespread circulation only in the late 1940s). By the time McLuhan began to think seriously about media, it was clear that television had become the dominant media in most western nations, including the United States, and was poised to dominate the entire world. Therefore, although he discusses the effects of different media such as print and the telephone, McLuhan's thought is mainly directed at explaining the effects of television on social, political, cultural, and psychological dimensions of the culture of his time.

Here you will find excerpted the second chapter of *Understanding Media.* McLuhan begins that book with several important ideas. He asserts the close connection between human thought and action, and media, by arguing that media are *extensions* of humans, specifically of the sensorium or human sensory organs. One wishes, for instance, to speak to someone across town, and can neither shout nor hear so far, so one extends one's voice and hearing through the telephone. But the media we use then affect us, for they contain messages; the medium *is* the message, as the chapter title claims. McLuhan even speaks of electric lights as having messages, as well! He goes on to compare the effects of *electric* media with other popular media such as print, to argue that a radical change has taken place in the twentieth century due to humanity's increased reliance on qualitatively distinct electric media.

An intriguing idea is introduced in the selection printed here: Media are either hot or cool. A hot medium extends a single human sense in "high definition," whereas a cool medium extends a sense in "low definition." A photograph is hot because it gives the eye a lot of information, while the telephone is cool because it gives the ear only a little information. The nature of media as hot or cool is an important dimension of the message that is embodied in merely using them, and McLuhan develops the effects of hot and cold media in the rest of the chapter. While one might disagree with his claims about specific media and the amount of information they give (for example, does the recent introduction of big screen television now mean that television is hot?), McLuhan's ideas are useful in prodding his reader to think about the rhetorical effect of exposure to media itself, regardless of the messages a given medium carries.

McLuhan has often been criticized for writing imprecisely, with more concern for crafting witty and provocative phrases than for scholarly precision. But it may well be McLuhan's willingness to take theoretical chances by proposing outrageous ideas that made him such a seminal thinker about media in the twentieth century. Among the poetry, extremism, and occasional silliness of his writing are some brilliant insights about the deep effects of media on how people think and live with one another. McLuhan has been instrumental in expanding the concerns of many rhetorical theorists to include issues relating to media.

MARSHALL McLUHAN

UNDERSTANDING MEDIA: THE EXTENSIONS OF MAN

• • •

2/MEDIA HOT AND COLD

"The rise of the waltz," explained Curt Sachs in the *World History of the Dance,* "was a result of that longing for truth, simplicity, closeness to nature, and primitivism, which the last two-thirds of the eighteenth century fulfilled." In the century of jazz we are likely to overlook the emergence of the waltz as a hot and explosive human expression that broke through the formal feudal barriers of courtly and choral dance styles.

There is a basic principle that distinguishes a hot medium like radio from a cool one like the telephone, or a hot medium like the movie from a cool one like TV. A hot medium is one that extends one single sense in "high definition." High definition is the state of being well filled with data. A photograph is, visually, "high definition." A cartoon is "low definition," simply because very little visual information is provided. Telephone is a cool medium, or one of low definition, because the ear is given a meager amount of information. And speech is a cool medium of low definition, because so little is given and so much has to be filled in by the listener. On the other hand, hot media do not leave so much to be filled in or completed by the audience. Hot media are, therefore, low in participation, and cool media are high in participation or completion by the audience. Naturally, therefore, a hot medium like radio has very different effects on the user from a cool medium like the telephone.

A cool medium like hieroglyphic or ideo-grammic written characters has very different effects from the hot and explosive medium of the phonetic alphabet. The alphabet, when pushed to a high degree of abstract visual intensity, became typography. The printed word with its specialist intensity burst the bonds of medieval corporate guilds and monasteries, creating extreme individualist patterns of enterprise and monopoly. But the typical reversal occurred when extremes of monopoly brought back the corporation, with its impersonal empire over many lives. The hotting-up of the medium of writing to repeatable print intensity led to nationalism and the religious wars of the sixteenth century. The heavy and unwieldy media, such as stone, are time binders. Used for writing, they are very cool indeed, and serve to unify the ages; whereas paper is a hot medium that serves to unify spaces horizontally, both in political and entertainment empires.

Any hot medium allows of less participation than a cool one, as a lecture makes for less participation than a seminar, and a book for less than dialogue. With print many earlier forms were excluded from life and art, and many were given strange new intensity. But our own time is crowded with examples of the principle that the hot form excludes, and the cool one includes. When ballerinas began to dance on their toes a century ago, it was felt that the art of the ballet had acquired a new "spirituality." With this new intensity, male figures were excluded from ballet. The role of women had also become fragmented with the advent of industrial specialism and the explosion of home functions into laundries, bakeries, and hospitals on the periphery of the community. Intensity or high definition engenders specialism and fragmentation in living as in entertainment, which explains why any intense experience must be "forgotten," "censored," and reduced to a very cool state before it can be "learned" or assimilated. The Freudian "censor" is less of a moral function than an indispensable condition of learning. Were we to accept fully and directly every shock to our various structures of awareness, we would soon be nervous wrecks, doing double-takes and pressing panic buttons every minute. The "censor" protects our central system of values, as it does our physical nervous system by simply cooling off the onset of experience a great deal. For many people, this cooling system brings on a life-long state of psychic *rigor mortis,* or of somnambulism, particularly observable in periods of new technology.

An example of the disruptive impact of a hot technology succeeding a cool one is given by Robert Theobald in *The Rich and the Poor.* When Australian natives were given steel axes by the missionaries, their culture, based on the stone axe, collapsed. The stone axe had not only been scarce but had always been a basic status symbol of male importance. The missionaries provided quantities of sharp steel axes and gave them to women and children. The men had even to borrow these from the women, causing a collapse of male dignity. A tribal and feudal hierarchy of traditional kind collapses quickly when it meets any hot medium of the mechanical, uniform, and repetitive kind. The medium of money or wheel or writing, or any other form of specialist speedup of exchange and information, will serve to fragment a tribal structure. Similarly, a very much greater speed-up, such as occurs with electricity, may serve to restore a tribal pattern of intense involvement such as took place with the introduction of radio in Europe, and is now tending to happen as a result of TV in America. Specialist technologies detribalize. The nonspecialist electric technology retribalizes. The process of upset resulting from a new distribution of skills is accompanied by much culture lag in which people feel compelled to look at new situations as if they were old ones, and come up with ideas of "population explosion" in an age of implosion. Newton, in an age of clocks, managed to present the physical universe in the image of a clock. But poets like Blake were far ahead of Newton in their response to the challenge of the clock. Blake spoke of the need to be delivered "from single vision and Newton's sleep," knowing very well that Newton's response to the challenge of the new mechanism was itself merely a mechanical repetition of the challenge. Blake saw Newton and Locke and others as hypnotized Narcissus types quite unable to meet the challenge of mechanism. W. B. Yeats gave the full Blakean version of Newton and Locke in a famous epigram:

> *Locke sank into a swoon;*
> *The garden died;*
> *God took the spinning jenny*
> *Out of his side.*

Yeats presents Locke, the philosopher of mechanical and lineal associationism, as hypnotized by his own image. The "garden," or unified consciousness, ended. Eighteenth-century man got an extension of himself in the form of the spinning machine that Yeats endows with its full sexual significance. Woman, herself, is thus seen as a technological extension of man's being.

Blake's counterstrategy for his age was to meet mechanism with organic myth. Today, deep in the electric age, organic myth is itself a simple and automatic response capable of mathematical formulation and expression, without any of the imaginative perception of Blake about it. Had he encountered the electric age, Blake would not have met its challenge with a mere repetition of electric form. For myth *is* the instant vision of a complex process that ordinarily extends over a long period. Myth is contraction or implosion of any process, and the instant speed of electricity confers the mythic dimension on ordinary industrial and social action today. We *live* mythically but continue to think fragmentarily and on single planes.

Scholars today are acutely aware of a discrepancy between their ways of treating subjects and the subject itself. Scriptural scholars of both the Old and New Testaments frequently say that while their treatment must be linear, the subject is not. The subject treats of the relations between God and man, and between God and the world, and of the relations between man and his neighbor—all these subsist together, and act and react upon one another at the same time. The Hebrew and Eastern mode of thought tackles problem and resolution, at the outset of a discussion, in a way typical of oral societies in general. The entire message is then traced and retraced, again and again, on the rounds of a concentric spiral with seeming redundancy. One can stop anywhere after the first few sentences and have the full message, if one is prepared to "dig" it. This kind of plan seems to have inspired Frank Lloyd Wright in designing the Guggenheim Art Gallery on a spiral, concentric basis. It is a redundant form inevitable to the electric age, in which the concentric pattern is imposed by the instant quality, and overlay in depth, of electric speed. But the concentric with its endless intersection of planes is necessary for insight. In fact, it is the technique of insight, and as such is necessary for media study, since no medium has its meaning or existence alone, but only in constant interplay with other media.

The new electric structuring and configuring of life more and more encounters the old lineal and fragmentary procedures and tools of analysis from the mechanical age. More and more we turn from the content of messages to study total effect. Kenneth Boulding put this matter in *The Image* by saying, "The meaning of a message is the change which it produces in the image." Concern with *effect* rather than *meaning* is a basic change of our electric time, for effect involves the total situation, and not a single level of information movement. Strangely, there is recognition of this matter of effect rather than information in the British idea of libel: "The greater the truth, the greater the libel."

The effect of electric technology had at first been anxiety. Now it appears to create boredom. We have been through the three stages of alarm, resistance, and exhaustion that occur in every disease or stress of life, whether individual or collective. At least, our exhausted slump after the first encounter with the electric has inclined us to expect new problems. However, backward countries that have experienced little permeation with our own mechanical and specialist culture are much better able to confront and to understand electric technology. Not only have backward and nonindustrial cultures no specialist habits to overcome in their encounter with electromagnetism, but they have still much of their traditional oral culture that has the total, unified "field" character of our new electromagnetism. Our old industrialized areas, having eroded their oral traditions automatically, are in the position of having to rediscover them in order to cope with the electric age.

In terms of the theme of media hot and cold, backward countries are cool, and we are hot. The "city slicker" is hot, and the rustic is cool. But in terms of the reversal of procedures and values in the electric age, the past mechanical time was hot, and we of the TV age are cool. The waltz was a hot, fast mechanical dance suited to the industrial time in its moods of pomp and circumstance. In contrast, the Twist is a cool, involved and chatty form of improvised gesture. The jazz of the period of the hot new media of movie and radio was hot jazz. Yet jazz of itself tends to be a casual dialogue form of dance quite lacking in the repetitive and mechanical forms of the waltz. Cool jazz came in quite naturally after the first impact of radio and movie had been absorbed.

In the special Russian issue of *Life* magazine for September 13, 1963, it is mentioned that in Russian restaurants and night clubs, "though the Charleston is tolerated, the Twist is taboo." All this is to say that a country in the process of industrialization is inclined to regard hot jazz as consistent with its developing programs. The cool and involved form of the Twist, on the other hand, would strike such a culture at once as retrograde and incompatible with its new mechanical stress. The Charleston, with its aspect of a mechanical doll agitated by strings, appears in Russia as an avant-garde form. We, on the other hand, find the *avant-garde* in the cool and the primitive, with its promise of depth involvement and integral expression.

The "hard" sell and the "hot" line become mere comedy in the TV age, and the death of all the salesmen at one stroke of the TV axe has turned the hot American culture into a cool one that is quite unacquainted with itself. America, in fact, would seem to be living through the reverse process that Margaret Mead described in *Time* magazine (September 4, 1954): "There are too many complaints about society having to move too fast to keep up with the machine. There is great advantage in moving fast if you move completely, if social, educational, and recreational changes keep pace. You must change the whole pattern at once and the whole group together—and the people themselves must decide to move."

Margaret Mead is thinking here of change as uniform speed-up of motion or a uniform hotting-up of temperatures in backward societies. We are certainly coming within conceivable range of a world automatically controlled to the point where we could say, "Six hours less radio in Indonesia next week or there will be a great falling off in literary attention." Or, "We can program twenty more hours of TV in South Africa next week to cool down the tribal temperature raised by radio last week. Whole cultures could now be programmed to keep their emotional climate stable in the same way that we have begun to know something about maintaining equilibrium in the commercial economies of the world.

In the merely personal and private sphere we are often reminded of how changes of tone and attitude are demanded of different times and seasons in order to keep situations in hand. British clubmen, for the sake of companionship and amiability, have long excluded the hot topics of religion and politics from mention inside the highly participational club. In the same vein, W. H. Auden wrote, ". . . this season the man of goodwill will wear his heart up his sleeve, not on it. . . . the honest manly style is today suited only to Iago" (Introduction to John Betjeman's *Slick But Not Streamlined*). In the Renaissance, as print technology hotted up the social *milieu* to a very high point, the gentleman and the courtier (Hamlet–Mercutio style) adopted, in contrast, the casual and cool nonchalance of the playful and superior being. The Iago allusion of Auden reminds us that Iago was the *alter ego* and assistant of the intensely earnest and very non-nonchalant General Othello. In imitation of the earnest and forthright general, Iago hotted up his own image and wore his heart on his sleeve, until General Othello read him loud and clear as "honest Iago," a man after his own grimly earnest heart.

Throughout *The City in History,* Lewis Mumford favors the cool or casually structured towns over the hot and intensely filled-in cities. The great period of Athens, he feels, was one during which most of the democratic habits of village life and participation still obtained. Then burst forth the full variety of human expression and exploration such as was later impossible in highly developed urban centers. For the highly developed situation is, by definition, low in opportunities of participation, and rigorous in its demands of specialist fragmentation from those who would control it. For example, what is known as "job enlargement" today in business and in management consists in allowing the employee more freedom to discover and define his function. Likewise, in reading a detective story the reader participates as co-author simply because so much has been left out of the narrative. The open-mesh silk stocking is far more sensuous than the smooth nylon, just because the eye must act as hand in filling in and completing the image, exactly as in the mosaic of the TV image.

Douglas Cater in *The Fourth Branch of Government* tells how the men of the Washington press bureaus delighted to complete or fill in the blank of Calvin Coolidge's personality. Because he was so like a mere cartoon, they felt the urge to complete his image for him and his public. It is instructive that the press applied the word "cool" to Cal. In the very sense of a cool medium, Calvin Coolidge was so lacking in any articulation of data in his public image that there was only one word for him. He was real cool. In the hot 1920s, the hot press medium found Cal very cool and rejoiced in his lack of image, since it compelled the participation of the press in filling in an image of him for the public. By contrast, F.D.R. was a hot press agent, himself a rival of the newspaper medium and one who delighted in scoring off the press on the rival hot medium of radio. Quite in contrast, Jack Paar ran a cool show for the cool TV medium, and became a rival for the patrons of the night spots and their allies in the gossip columns. Jack Paar's war with the gossip columnists was a weird example of clash between a hot and cold medium such as had occurred with the "scandal of the rigged TV quiz shows." The rivalry between the hot press and radio media, on one hand, and TV on the other, for the hot ad buck, served to confuse and to overheat the issues in the affair that pointlessly involved Charles Van Doren.

An Associated Press story from Santa Monica, California, August 9, 1962, reported how

> Nearly 100 traffic violators watched a police traffic accident film today to atone for their violations. Two had to be treated for nausea and shock. . . .
>
> Viewers were offered a $5.00 reduction in fines if they agreed to see the movie, *Signal* 30, made by Ohio State police.
>
> It showed twisted wreckage and mangled bodies and recorded the screams of accident victims.

Whether the hot film medium using hot content would cool off the hot drivers is a moot point. But it does concern any understanding of media. The effect of hot media treatment cannot include much empathy or participation at any time. In this connection an insurance ad that featured Dad in an iron lung surrounded by a joyful family group did more to strike terror into the reader than all the warning wisdom in the world. It is a question that arises in connection with capital punishment. Is a severe penalty the best deterrent to serious crime? With regard to the bomb and the cold war, is the threat of massive retaliation the most effective means to peace? Is it not evident in every human situation that is pushed to a point of saturation that some precipitation occurs? When all the available resources and energies have been played up in an organism or in any structure there is some kind of reversal of pattern. The spectacle of brutality used as deterrent can brutalize. Brutality used in sports may humanize under some conditions, at least. But with regard to the bomb and retaliation as deterrent, it is obvious that numbness is the result of any prolonged terror, a fact that was discovered when the fallout shelter program was broached. The price of eternal vigilance is indifference.

Nevertheless, it makes all the difference whether a hot medium is used in a hot or a cool culture. The hot radio medium used in cool or non-literate cultures has a violent effect, quite unlike its effect, say in England or America, where radio is felt as entertainment. A cool or low literacy culture cannot accept hot media like movies or radio as entertainment. They are, at least, as radically upsetting for them as the cool TV medium has proved to be for our high literacy world.

And as for the cool war and the hot bomb scare, the cultural strategy that is desperately needed is humor and play. It is play that cools off the hot situations of actual life by miming them. Competitive sports between Russia and the West will hardly serve that purpose of relaxation. Such sports are inflammatory, it is plain. And what we consider entertainment or fun in our media inevitably appears as violent political agitation to a cool culture.

One way to spot the basic difference between hot and cold media uses is to compare and contrast a broadcast of a symphony performance with a broadcast of a symphony rehearsal. Two of the finest shows ever released by the CBC were of Glenn Gould's procedure in recording piano recitals, and Igor Stravinsky's rehearsing the Toronto symphony in some of his new work. A cool medium like TV, when really used, demands this involvement in process. The neat tight package is suited to hot media, like radio and gramophone. Francis Bacon never tired of contrasting hot and cool prose. Writing in "methods" or complete packages, he contrasted with writing in aphorisms, or single observations such as "Revenge is a kind of wild justice." The passive consumer wants packages, but those, he suggested, who are concerned in pursuing knowledge and in seeking causes will resort to aphorisms, just because they are incomplete and require participation in depth.

The principle that distinguishes hot and cold media is perfectly embodied in the folk wisdom: "Men seldom make passes at girls who wear glasses." Glasses intensify the outward-going vision, and fill in the feminine image exceedingly, Marion the Librarian notwithstanding. Dark glasses, on the other hand, create the inscrutable and inaccessible image that invites a great deal of participation and completion.

Again, in a visual and highly literate culture, when we meet a person for the first time his visual appearance dims out the sound of the name, so that in self-defense we add: "How do you spell your name?" Whereas, in an ear culture, the *sound* of a man's name is the overwhelming fact, as Joyce knew when he said in *Finnegans Wake,* "Who gave you that numb?" For the name of a man is a numbing blow from which he never recovers.

Another vantage point from which to test the difference between hot and cold media is the practical joke. The hot literary medium excludes the practical and participant aspect of the joke so completely that Constance Rourke, in her *American Humor,* considers it as no joke at all. To literary people, the practical joke with its total physical involvement is as distasteful as the pun that derails us from the smooth and uniform progress that is typographic order. Indeed, to the literary person who is quite unaware of the intensely abstract nature of the typographic medium, it is the grosser and participant forms of art that seem "hot," and the abstract and intensely literary form that seems "cool." "You may perceive, Madam," said Dr. Johnson, with a pugilistic smile, "that I am well-bred to a degree of needless scrupulosity." And Dr. Johnson was right in supposing that "well-bred" had come to mean a white-shirted stress on attire that rivaled the rigor of the printed page. "Comfort" consists in abandoning a visual arrangement in favor of one that permits casual participation of the senses, a state that is excluded when any one sense, but especially the visual sense, is hotted up to the point of dominant command of a situation.

On the other hand, in experiments in which all outer sensation is withdrawn, the subject begins a furious fill-in or completion of senses that is sheer hallucination. So the hotting-up of one sense tends to result in hallucination.

• • •

INTRODUCTION TO MICHEL FOUCAULT

Michel Foucault (1926–1984) was a French scholar with degrees in psychology, psychiatry, and philosophy. Foucault studied the ways that societies use discourse to create structures of relationships that empower and disempower people. Different ways of speaking and writing make people and cultures what they are, he argued. Although Foucault did not call his work rhetorical, it has been taken as a fruitful rhetorical theory for understanding the effects of everyday language on society. Foucault shares with Bakhtin, Burke, and others a concern for the rhetorical effects of language, but Foucault looks for those effects at very broad social, institutional, and cultural levels.

Two of Foucault's many works are excerpted here, from his book *The Archaeology of Knowledge* and his essay "The Discourse on Language." An emphasis on *power* is especially clear in these two selections. Foucault attempts to show the power that resides in ways of speaking and writing.

The title of the first chapter from *The Archaeology of Knowledge* is revealing: "The Formation of Objects." Foucault argues that language and the ways language is used creates in our minds an awareness of objects, and actions that can actually be considered the creation of those entities. He uses the interesting example of "psychopathology," or mental illness. Foucault argues that mental illness is created by discursive practices, or how certain behaviors are talked about, so that different societies may actually have different ways to be mentally ill!

Much of Foucault's writing is organized around lists. He wants to reveal social structures created by language, and this way of thinking shows in his own discourse: He writes in a very structured way, creating taxonomies around his key theoretical concepts. The first list the reader finds here tells of three discursive characteristics that contribute to the creation of objects: First, "surfaces of their emergence," or the relevant contexts of illness. In the nineteenth century, Foucault argues, mental illness had to do with contexts of the family or with religion. In his time, he claims, it emerged on a surface of sexuality. Second, "authorities of delimitation," or who gets to say what is mental illness and what isn't. In his time, it is medical authorities. Third, "grids of specification," or types and categories of illness. Some illnesses today such as schizophrenia did not "exist" in the nineteenth century, just as some of that era's illnesses such as hysteria are not thought of as "real diseases" today.

The idea of *discursive formations* is key to Foucault's thought. These are ways of speaking and writing, similar to our idea of "discourse" as a language game or set of rules for speaking as explained in the introduction to this book. Foucault's next list is of four characteristics of discursive formations: They limit what one can talk about; they are established by institutions or social patterns; they are rules or expectations at an abstract rather than a primary level; and they generate but are not the same thing as actual discourses.

What does one do so as to use or activate the power of discursive formations? Foucault identifies three conditions for using discursive formations: One must adopt a certain role as speaker; institutional sites from which discourse proceeds must be identified; and the role of the speaker must be endowed with authority.

Because Foucault believes that power in any society flows from discursive formations, in the second reading ("The Discourse on Language") he makes the significant point that discourse is not the means or tools by which people seek power in some other context. Instead, discourse is power itself, and the power to control discourse is thus the master power in any society. Following his example, it is important how a society speaks of mental illness, for the discursive formations that create mental illness also grant speakers power over others. Because any society must control its mechanisms of power, granting access to some but not to all, Foucault's final set of lists is a summary of "principles of exclusion," or ways in which the power of discourse is granted to some but not to others. He identifies three sets of such principles of exclusion: external, internal, and speaker centered.

External principles of exclusion are "external" to the discourse itself, and Foucault names three external principles: prohibition of certain kinds of talk by certain people in certain places; a distinction between madness and reason; and a distinction between truth and falsity. Internal principles of exclusion arise internally from discourse, and they are: the fact that discourses all provide a commentary on other discourses; identifiable characteristics of particular authors; and organization of disciplines (perhaps better understood as genres of discourse). Finally, there are principles of exclusion pertaining to the person who is speaking or writing: rituals (what the speaker must say or do so as to use the formation); societies of discourse (which groups of speakers may speak); doctrines (what the speaker must believe to speak); and social appropriations of discourse (who is educated, how, where, and so forth).

Foucault's own vocabulary is often arcane and difficult to understand. Yet it has been influential in the late-twentieth century for rhetorical theorists who want to explain the ways in which whole societies, or large groups or institutions within societies, can be sites where power is created and molded. According to Foucault, we all participate in perpetuating the ways that power is organized in our schools, families, businesses, cities, and nations by the ways that we create and use discursive formations. There is, therefore, a rhetoric embedded in discursive formations, and theorists have found Foucault invaluable in identifying how that rhetoric works to distribute power.

MICHEL FOUCAULT

THE ARCHAEOLOGY OF KNOWLEDGE

PART II

CHAPTER I

THE UNITIES OF DISCOURSE

The use of concepts of discontinuity, rupture, threshold, limit, series, and transformation present all historical analysis not only with questions of procedure, but with theoretical problems. It is these problems that will be studied here (the questions of procedure will be examined in later empirical studies—if the opportunity, the desire, and the courage to undertake them do not desert me). These theoretical problems too will be examined only in a particular field: in those disciplines—so unsure of their frontiers, and so vague in content—that we call the history of ideas, or of thought, or of science, or of knowledge.

But there is a negative work to be carried out first: we must rid ourselves of a whole mass of notions, each of which, in its own way, diversifies the theme of continuity. They may not have a very rigorous conceptual structure, but they have a very precise function. Take the notion of tradition: it is intended to give a special temporal status to a group of phenomena that are both successive and identical (or at least similar); it makes it possible to rethink the dispersion of history in the form of the same; it allows a reduction of the difference proper to every beginning, in order to pursue without discontinuity the endless search for the origin; tradition enables us to isolate the new against a background of permanence, and to transfer its merit to originality, to genius, to the decisions proper to individuals. Then there is the notion of influence, which provides a support—of too magical a kind to be very amenable to analysis—for the facts of transmission and communication; which refers to an apparently causal process (but with neither rigorous delimitation nor theoretical definition) the phenomena of resemblance or repetition; which links, at a distance and through time—as if through the mediation of a medium of propagation—such defined unities as individuals, *œuvres*, notions, or theories. There are the notions of development and evolution: they make it possible to group a succession of dispersed events, to link them to one and the same organizing principle, to subject them to the exemplary power of life (with its adaptations, its capacity for innovation, the incessant correlation of its different elements, its systems of assimilation and exchange), to discover, already at work in each beginning, a principle of coherence and the outline of a future unity, to master time through a perpetually reversible relation between an origin and a term that are never given, but are always at work. There is the notion of 'spirit', which enables us to establish between the simultaneous or successive phenomena of a given period a community of meanings, symbolic links, an interplay of resemblance and reflexion, or which allows the sovereignty of collective consciousness to emerge as the principle of unity and explanation. We must question those ready-made syntheses, those groupings that we normally accept before any examination, those links whose validity is recognized from the outset; we must oust those forms and obscure forces by which we usually link the discourse of one man with that of another; they must be driven out from the darkness in which they reign. And instead of according them unqualified, spontaneous value, we must ac-

Translated from the French by A. M. Sheridan Smith

cept, in the name of methodological rigour, that, in the first instance, they concern only a population of dispersed events.

We must also question those divisions or groupings with which we have become so familiar. Can one accept, as such, the distinction between the major types of discourse, or that between such forms or genres as science, literature, philosophy, religion, history, fiction, etc., and which tend to create certain great historical individualities? We are not even sure of ourselves when we use these distinctions in our own world of discourse, let alone when we are analysing groups of statements which, when first formulated, were distributed, divided, and characterized in a quite different way: after all, 'literature' and 'politics' are recent categories, which can be applied to medieval culture, or even classical culture, only by a retrospective hypothesis, and by an interplay of formal analogies or semantic resemblances; but neither literature, nor politics, nor philosophy and the sciences articulated the field of discourse, in the seventeenth or eighteenth century, as they did in the nineteenth century. In any case, these divisions—whether our own, or those contemporary with the discourse under examination—are always themselves reflexive categories, principles of classification, normative rules, institutionalized types: they, in turn, are facts of discourse that deserve to be analysed beside others; of course, they also have complex relations with each other, but they are not intrinsic, autochthonous, and universally recognizable characteristics.

But the unities that must be suspended above all are those that emerge in the most immediate way: those of the book and the *œuvre.* At first sight, it would seem that one could not abandon these unities without extreme artificiality. Are they not given in the most definite way? There is the material individualization of the book, which occupies a determined space, which has an economic value, and which itself indicates, by a number of signs, the limits of its beginning and its end; and there is the establishment of an *œuvre,* which we recognize and delimit by attributing a certain number of texts to an author. And yet as soon as one looks at the matter a little more closely the difficulties begin. The material unity of the book? Is this the same in the case of an anthology of poems, a collection of posthumous fragments, Desargues' *Traité des Coniques,* or a volume of Michelet's *Histoire de France?* Is it the same in the case of Mallarmé's *Un Coup de dés,* the trial of Gilles de Rais, Butor's *San Marco,* or a Catholic missal? In other words, is not the material unity of the volume a weak, accessory unity in relation to the discursive unity of which it is the support? But is this discursive unity itself homogeneous and uniformly applicable? A novel by Stendhal and a novel by Dostoevsky do not have the same relation of individuality as that between two novels belonging to Balzac's cycle *La Comédie humaine;* and the relation between Balzac's novels is not the same as that existing between Joyce's *Ulysses* and the *Odyssey.* The frontiers of a book are never clear-cut: beyond the title, the first lines, and the last full stop, beyond its internal configuration and its autonomous form, it is caught up in a system of references to other books, other texts, other sentences: it is a node within a network. And this network of references is not the same in the case of a mathematical treatise, a textual commentary, a historical account, and an episode in a novel cycle; the unity of the book, even in the sense of a group of relations, cannot be regarded as identical in each case. The book is not simply the object that one holds in one's hands; and it cannot remain within the little parallelepiped that contains it: its unity is variable and relative. As soon as one questions that unity, it loses its self-evidence; it indicates itself, constructs itself, only on the basis of a complex field of discourse.

The problems raised by the *œuvre* are even more difficult. Yet, at first sight, what could be more simple? A collection of texts that can be designated by the sign of a proper name. But this designation (even leaving to one side problems of attribution) is not a homogeneous function: does the name of an author designate in the same way a text that he has published under his name, a text that he has presented under a pseudonym, another found after his death in the form of an unfinished draft, and another that is merely a collection of jottings, a notebook? The establishment of a complete *œuvre* presupposes a number of choices that are difficult to justify or even to formulate: is it enough to add to the texts published by the author those that he intended for publication but which remained unfinished by the fact of his death? Should one also include all his sketches and first drafts, with all their corrections and crossings out? Should one add sketches that he himself abandoned? And what status should be given to letters, notes, reported conversations, transcriptions of what he said made by those present at the time, in short, to that vast mass of verbal traces left by an individual at his death, and which speak in an endless confusion so many different languages (*langages*)?[1] In any case, the name 'Mallarmé' does not refer in the same way to his *thèmes* (translation exercises from French into English), his translations of Edgar Allan Poe, his poems, and his replies to questionnaires; similarly, the same relation does not exist between the name Nietzsche on the one hand and the youthful autobiographies, the scholastic dissertations, the philological articles, *Zarathustra, Ecce Homo,* the letters, the last postcards signed 'Dionysos' or 'Kaiser Nietzsche', and the innumerable notebooks with their jumble of laundry bills and sketches for aphorisms. In fact, if one speaks, so undiscriminately and unreflectingly of an author's *œuvre,* it is because one imagines it to be defined by a certain expressive function. One is admitting that there must be a level (as deep as it is necessary to imagine it) at which the *œuvre* emerges, in all its fragments, even the smallest, most inessential ones, as the expression of the thought, the experience, the imagination, or the unconscious of the author, or, indeed, of the historical determinations that operated upon him. But it is at once apparent that such a unity, far from being given immediately, is the result of an operation; that this operation is interpretative (since it deciphers, in the text, the transcription of something that it both conceals and manifests); and that the operation that determines the *opus,* in its unity, and consequently the *œuvre* itself, will not be the same in the case of the author of *Le Théâtre et son Double* (Artaud) and the author of the *Tractatus* (Wittgenstein), and therefore when one speaks of an *œuvre* in each case one is using the word in a different sense. The *œuvre* can be regarded neither as an immediate unity, nor as a certain unity, nor as a homogeneous unity.

One last precaution must be taken to disconnect the unquestioned continuities by which we organize, in advance, the discourse that we are to analyse: we must renounce two linked, but opposite themes. The first involves a wish that it should never be possible to assign, in the order of discourse, the irruption of a real event; that beyond any apparent beginning, there is always a secret origin—so secret and so fundamental that it can never be quite grasped in itself. Thus one is led inevitably, through the naïvety of chronologies, towards an ever-receding point that is never itself present in any history; this point is merely its own void; and from that point all beginnings can never be more than recommencements or occultation (in one and the same gesture, this *and* that). To this theme is connected another according to which all manifest discourse is secretly based on an 'already-said'; and that this 'already-said' is not merely a phrase that has already been spoken, or a text that has already been written, but a 'never-said', an incorporeal discourse, a voice as silent as a breath, a writing that is merely the hollow of its own mark. It is supposed therefore that everything that is formulated in discourse was already articulated in that semi-silence that precedes it, which continues to run obstinately beneath it, but which it covers

---

[1] The English word 'language' translates the French '*langue*' (meaning the 'natural languages: French, English, etc.) and '*langage*' (meaning either 'language in general' or 'kinds of language': philosophical, medical language, etc.). Where the meaning would otherwise be unclear, I have added the original French word in brackets. (Tr.)

and silences. The manifest discourse, therefore, is really no more than the repressive presence of what it does not say; and this 'not-said' is a hollow that undermines from within all that is said. The first theme sees the historical analysis of discourse as the quest for and the repetition of an origin that eludes all historical determination; the second sees it as the interpretation of 'hearing' of an 'already-said' that is at the same time a 'not-said'. We must renounce all those themes whose function is to ensure the infinite continuity of discourse and its secret presence to itself in the interplay of a constantly recurring absence. We must be ready to receive every moment of discourse in its sudden irruption; in that punctuality in which it appears, and in that temporal dispersion that enables it to be repeated, known, forgotten, transformed, utterly erased, and hidden, far from all view, in the dust of books. Discourse must not be referred to the distant presence of the origin, but treated as and when it occurs.

These pre-existing forms of continuity, all these syntheses that are accepted without question, must remain in suspense. They must not be rejected definitively of course, but the tranquillity with which they are accepted must be disturbed; we must show that they do not come about of themselves, but are always the result of a construction the rules of which must be known, and the justifications of which must be scrutinized: we must define in what conditions and in view of which analyses certain of them are legitimate; and we must indicate which of them can never be accepted in any circumstances. It may be, for example, that the notions of 'influence' or 'evolution' belong to a criticism that puts them—for the foreseeable future—out of use. But need we dispense for ever with the '*œuvre*', the 'book', or even such unities as 'science' or 'literature'? Should we regard them as illusions, illegitimate constructions, or ill-acquired results? Should we never make use of them, even as a temporary support, and never provide them with a definition? What we must do, in fact, is to tear away from them their virtual self-evidence, and to free the problems that they pose; to recognize that they are not the tranquil locus on the basis of which other questions (concerning their structure, coherence, systematicity, transformations) may be posed, but that they themselves pose a whole cluster of questions (What are they? How can they be defined or limited? What distinct types of laws can they obey? What articulation are they capable of? What sub-groups can they give rise to? What specific phenomena do they reveal in the field of discourse?). We must recognize that they may not, in the last resort, be what they seem at first sight. In short, that they require a theory, and that this theory cannot be constructed unless the *field* of the facts of discourse on the basis of which those facts are built up appears in its non-synthetic purity.

And I, in turn, will do no more than this: of course, I shall take as my starting-point whatever unities are already given (such as psychopathology, medicine, or political economy); but I shall not place myself inside these dubious unities in order to study their internal configuration or their secret contradictions. I shall make use of them just long enough to ask myself what unities they form; by what right they can claim a field that specifies them in space and a continuity that individualizes them in time; according to what laws they are formed; against the background of which discursive events they stand out; and whether they are not, in their accepted and quasi-institutional individuality, ultimately the surface effect of more firmly grounded unities. I shall accept the groupings that history suggests only to subject them at once to interrogation; to break them up and then to see whether they can be legitimately reformed; or whether other groupings should be made; to replace them in a more general space which, while dissipating their apparent familiarity, makes it possible to construct a theory of them.

Once these immediate forms of continuity are suspended, an entire field is set free. A vast field, but one that can be defined nonetheless: this field is made up of the totality of all effective statements (whether spoken or written), in their dispersion as events and in the occurrence that is proper to them. Before approaching, with any degree of certainty, a science, or novels, or political speeches, or the *œuvre* of an author, or even a single book, the material with which one is dealing is, in its raw, neutral state, a population of events in the space of discourse in general. One is led therefore to the project of a *pure description of discursive events* as the horizon for the search for the unities that form within it. This description is easily distinguishable from an analysis of the language. Of course, a linguistic system can be established (unless it is constructed artificially) only by using a corpus of statements, or a collection of discursive facts; but we must then define, on the basis of this grouping, which has value as a sample, rules that may make it possible to construct other statements than these: even if it has long since disappeared, even if it is no longer spoken, and can be reconstructed only on the basis of rare fragments, a language (*langue*) is still a system for possible statements, a finite body of rules that authorizes an infinite number of performances. The field of discursive events, on the other hand, is a grouping that is always finite and limited at any moment to the linguistic sequences that have been formulated; they may be innumerable, they may, in sheer size, exceed the capacities of recording, memory, or reading: nevertheless they form a finite grouping. The question posed by language analysis of some discursive fact or other is always: according to what rules has a particular statement been made, and consequently according to what rules could other similar statements be made? The description of the events of discourse poses a quite different question: how is it that one particular statement appeared rather than another?

It is also clear that this description of discourses is in opposition to the history of thought. There too a system of thought can be reconstituted only on the basis of a definite discursive totality. But this totality is treated in such a way that one tries to rediscover beyond the statements themselves the intention of the speaking subject, his conscious activity, what he meant, or, again, the unconscious activity that took place, despite himself, in what he said or in the almost imperceptible fracture of his actual words; in any case, we must reconstitute another discourse, rediscover the silent murmuring, the inexhaustible speech that animates from within the voice that one hears, reestablish the tiny, invisible text that runs between and sometimes collides with them. The analysis of thought is always *allegorical* in relation to the discourse that it employs. Its question is unfailingly: what was being said in what was said? The analysis of the discursive field is orientated in a quite different way; we must grasp the statement in the exact specificity of its occurrence; determine its conditions of existence, fix at least its limits, establish its correlations with other statements that may be connected with it, and show what other forms of statement it excludes. We do not seek below what is manifest the half silent murmur of another discourse; we must show why it could not be other than it was, in what respect it is exclusive of any other, how it assumes, in the midst of others and in relation to them, a place that no other could occupy. The question proper to such an analysis might be formulated in this way: what is this specific existence that emerges from what is said and nowhere else?

We must ask ourselves what purpose is ultimately served by this suspension of all the accepted unities, if, in the end, we return to the unities that we pretended to question at the outset. In fact, the systematic erasure of all given unities enables us first of all to restore to the statement the specificity of its occurrence, and to show that discontinuity is one of those great accidents that create cracks not only in the geology of history, but also in the simple fact of the statement; it emerges in its historical irruption; what we try to examine is the incision that it makes, that irreducible—and very often tiny—emergence. However banal it may be, however unimportant its consequences may appear to be, however quickly it may be forgotten after its appearance, however little heard or however badly deciphered we may suppose it to be, a statement is always an event that neither the language (*langue*) nor the meaning can quite exhaust. It is certainly a strange event: first, because on the one hand it is linked to the gesture of writing or to the articulation of speech, and also on the other hand it opens up to itself a residual existence in the field of a memory, or in the materiality of manuscripts, books, or any other form of recording; secondly, because, like every event, it is unique, yet subject to repetition, transformation, and reactivation; thirdly, because it is linked not only to the situations that provoke it, and to the consequences that it gives rise to, but at the same time, and in accordance with a quite different modality, to the statements that precede and follow it.

But if we isolate, in relation to the language and to thought, the occurrence of the statement/event, it is not in order to spread over everything a dust of facts. It is in order to be sure that this occurrence is not linked with synthesizing operations of a purely psychological kind (the intention of the author, the form of his mind, the rigour of his thought, the themes that obsess him, the project that traverses his existence and gives it meaning) and to be able to grasp other forms of regularity, other types of relations. Relations between statements (even if the author is unaware of them; even if the statements do not have the same author; even if the authors were unaware of each other's existence); relations between groups of statements thus established (even if these groups do not concern the same, or even adjacent, fields; even if they do not possess the same formal level; even if they are not the locus of assignable exchanges); relations between statements and groups of statements and events of a quite different kind (technical, economic, social, political). To reveal in all its purity the space in which discursive events are deployed is not to undertake to re-establish it in an isolation that nothing could overcome; it is not to close it upon itself; it is to leave oneself free to describe the interplay of relations within it and outside it.

The third purpose of such a description of the facts of discourse is that by freeing them of all the groupings that purport to be natural, immediate, universal unities, one is able to describe other unities, but this time by means of a group of controlled decisions. Providing one defines the conditions clearly, it might be legitimate to constitute, on the basis of correctly described relations, discursive groups that are not arbitrary, and yet remain invisible. Of course, these relations would never be formulated for themselves in the statements in question (unlike, for example, those explicit relations that are posed and spoken in discourse itself, as in the form of the novel, or a series of mathematical theorems). But in no way would they constitute a sort of secret discourse, animating the manifest discourse from within; it is not therefore an interpretation of the facts of the statement that might reveal them, but the analysis of their coexistence, their succession, their mutual functioning, their reciprocal determination, and their independent or correlative transformation.

However, it is not possible to describe all the relations that may emerge in this way without some guide-lines. A provisional division must be adopted as an initial approximation: an initial region that analysis will subsequently demolish and, if necessary, reorganize. But how is such a region to be circumscribed? On the one hand, we must choose, empirically, a field in which the relations are likely to be numerous, dense, and relatively easy to describe: and in what other region do discursive events appear to be more closely linked to one another, to occur in accordance with more easily decipherable relations, than in the region usually known as science? But, on the other hand, what better way of grasping in a statement, not the moment of its formal structure and laws of construction, but that of its existence and the rules that govern its appearance, if not by dealing with relatively unformalized groups of discourses, in which the statements do not seem necessarily to be built on the rules of pure syntax? How can we be sure of avoiding such divisions as the *œuvre,* or such categories as 'influence', unless, from the very outset, we adopt sufficiently broad fields and scales that are chronologically vast enough? Lastly, how can we be sure that we will not find ourselves in the grip of all those over-hasty unities or syntheses concerning the speaking subject, or the author of the text, in short, all anthropological categories?

Unless, perhaps, we consider all the statements out of which these categories are constituted—all the statements that have chosen the subject of discourse (their own subject) as their 'object' and have undertaken to deploy it as their field of knowledge?

This explains the *de facto* privilege that I have accorded to those discourses that, to put it very schematically, define the 'sciences of man'. But it is only a provisional privilege. Two facts must be constantly borne in mind: that the analysis of discursive events is in no way limited to such a field; and that the division of this field itself cannot be regarded either as definitive or as absolutely valid; it is no more than an initial approximation that must allow relations to appear that may erase the limits of this initial outline.

CHAPTER 2

DISCURSIVE FORMATIONS

I have undertaken, then, to describe the relations between statements. I have been careful to accept as valid none of the unities that would normally present themselves to anyone embarking on such a task. I have decided to ignore no form of discontinuity, break, threshold, or limit. I have decided to describe statements in the field of discourse and the relations of which they are capable. As I see it, two series of problems arise at the outset: the first, which I shall leave to one side for the time being and shall return to later, concerns the indiscriminate use that I have made of the terms statement, event, and discourse; the second concerns the relations that may legitimately be described between the statements that have been left in their provisional, visible grouping.

There are statements, for example, that are quite obviously concerned—and have been from a date that is easy enough to determine—with political economy, or biology, or psychopathology; there are others that equally obviously belong to those age-old continuities known as grammar or medicine. But what are these unities? How can we say that the analysis of headaches carried out by Willis or Charcot belong to the same order of discourse? That Petty's inventions are in continuity with Neumann's econometry? That the analysis of judgement by the Port-Royal grammarians belongs to the same domain as the discovery of vowel gradations in the Indo-European languages? What, in fact, are *medicine, grammar,* or *political economy?* Are they merely a retrospective regrouping by which the contemporary sciences deceive themselves as to their own past? Are they forms that have become established once and for all and have gone on developing through time? Do they conceal other unities? And what sort of links can validly be recognized between all these statements that form, in such a familiar and insistent way, such an enigmatic mass?

First hypothesis—and the one that, at first sight, struck me as being the most likely and the most easily proved: statements different in form, and dispersed in time, form a group if they refer to one and the same object. Thus, statements belonging to psychopathology all seem to refer to an object that emerges in various ways in individual or social experience and which may be called madness. But I soon realized that the unity of the object 'madness' does not enable one to individualize a group of statements, and to establish between them a relation that is both constant and describable. There are two reasons for this. It would certainly be a mistake to try to discover what could have been said of madness at a particular time by interrogating the being of madness itself, its secret content, its silent, self-enclosed truth; mental illness was constituted by all that was said in all the statements that named it, divided it up, described it, explained it, traced its developments, indicated its various correlations, judged it, and possibly gave it speech by articulating, in its name, discourses that were to be taken as its own. Moreover, this group of statements is far from referring to a single object, formed once and for all, and to preserving it indefinitely as its horizon of inexhaustible ideality; the object presented as their correlative by medical statements of the seventeenth or eighteenth century is not identical with the object that emerges in legal sentences or police action; similarly, all the objects of psychopathological discourses were modified from Pinel or Esquirol to Bleuler: it is not the same illnesses that are at issue in each of these cases; we are not dealing with the same madmen.

One might, perhaps one should, conclude from this multiplicity of objects that it is not possible to accept, as a valid unity forming a group of statements, a 'discourse, concerning madness'. Perhaps one should confine one's attention to those groups of statements that have one and the same object: the discourses on melancholia, or neurosis, for example. But one would soon realize that each of these discourses in turn constituted its object and worked it to the point of transforming it altogether. So that the problem arises of knowing whether the unity of a discourse is based not so much on the permanence and uniqueness of an object as on the space in which various objects emerge and are continuously transformed. Would not the typical relation that would enable us to individualize a group of statements concerning madness then be: the rule of simultaneous or successive emergence of the various objects that are named, described, analysed, appreciated, or judged in that relation? The unity of discourses on madness would not be based upon the existence of the object 'madness', or the constitution of a single horizon of objectivity; it would be the interplay of the rules that make possible the appearance of objects during a given period of time: objects that are shaped by measures of discrimination and repression, objects that are differentiated in daily practice, in law, in religious casuistry, in medical diagnosis, objects that are manifested in pathological descriptions, objects that are circumscribed by medical codes, practices, treatment, and care. Moreover, the unity of the discourses on madness would be the interplay of the rules that define the transformations of these different objects, their non-identity through time, the break produced in them, the internal discontinuity that suspends their permanence. Paradoxically, to define a group of statements in terms of its individuality would be to define the dispersion of these objects, to grasp all the interstices that separate them, to measure the distances that reign between them—in other words, to formulate their law of division.

Second hypothesis to define a group of relations between statements: their form and type of connexion. It seemed to me, for example, that from the nineteenth century medical science was characterized not so much by its objects or concepts as by a certain *style,* a certain constant manner of statement. For the first time, medicine no longer consisted of a group of traditions, observations, and heterogeneous practices, but of a corpus of knowledge that presupposed the same way of looking at things, the same division of the perceptual field, the same analysis of the pathological fact in accordance with the visible space of the body, the same system of transcribing what one perceived in what one said (same vocabulary, same play of metaphor); in short, it seemed to me that medicine was organized as a series of descriptive statements. But, there again, I had to abandon this hypothesis at the outset and recognize that clinical discourse was just as much a group of hypotheses about life and death, of ethical choices, of therapeutic decisions, of institutional regulations, of teaching models, as a group of descriptions; that the descriptions could not, in any case, be abstracted from the hypotheses, and that the descriptive statement was only one of the formulations present in medical discourse. I also had to recognize that this description has constantly been displaced: either because, from Bichat to cell pathology, the scales and guidelines have been displaced; or because from visual inspection, auscultation and palpation to the use of the microscope and biological tests, the information system has been modified; or, again, because, from simple anatomo-clinical correlation to the delicate analysis of physiopathological processes, the lexicon of signs and their decipherment has been entirely reconstituted; or, finally, because the doctor has gradually ceased to be himself the locus of the registering and interpretation of information, and because, beside him, outside him, there have appeared masses of documentation, instruments of correlation, and techniques of analysis, which, of course, he makes use of, but which modify his position as an observing subject in relation to the patient.

All these alterations, which may now lead to the threshold of a new medicine, gradually appeared in medical discourse throughout the nineteenth century. If one wished to define this discourse by a codified and normative system of statement, one would have to recognize that this medicine disintegrated as soon as it appeared and that it really found its formulation only in Bichat and Laennec. If there is a unity, its principle is not therefore a determined form of statements; is it not rather the group of rules, which, simultaneously or in turn, have made possible purely perceptual descriptions, together with observations mediated through instruments, the procedures used in laboratory experiments, statistical calculations, epidemiological or demographic observations, institutional regulations, and therapeutic practice? What one must characterize and individualize is the coexistence of these dispersed and heterogeneous statements; the system that governs their division, the degree to which they depend upon one another, the way in which they interlock or exclude one another, the transformation that they undergo, and the play of their location, arrangement, and replacement.

Another direction of research, another hypothesis: might it not be possible to establish groups of statements, by determining the system of permanent and coherent concepts involved? For example, does not the Classical analysis of language and grammatical facts (from Lancelot to the end of the eighteenth century) rest on a definite number of concepts whose content and usage had been established once and for all: the concept of *judgement* defined as the general, normative form of any sentence, the concepts of *subject* and *predicate* regrouped under the more general category of *noun,* the concept of *verb* used as the equivalent of that of *logical copula,* the concept of *word* defined as the sign of a representation, etc.? In this way, one might reconstitute the conceptual architecture of Classical grammar. But there too one would soon come up against limitations: no sooner would one have succeeded in describing with such elements the analyses carried out by the Port-Royal authors than one would no doubt be forced to acknowledge the appearance of new concepts; some of these may be derived from the first, but the others are heterogeneous and a few even incompatible with them. The notion of natural or inverted syntactical order, that of complement (introduced in the eighteenth century by Beauzée), may still no doubt be integrated into the conceptual system of the Port-Royal grammar. But neither the idea of an originally expressive value of sounds, nor that of a primitive body of knowledge enveloped in words and conveyed in some obscure way by them, nor that of regularity in the mutation of consonants, nor the notion of the verb as a mere name capable of designating an action or operation, is compatible with the group of concepts used by Lancelot or Duclos. Must we admit therefore that grammar only appears to form a coherent figure; and that this group of statements, analyses, descriptions, principles and consequences, deductions that has been perpetrated under this name for over a century is no more than a false unity? But perhaps one might discover a discursive unity if one sought it not in the coherence of concepts, but in their simultaneous or successive emergence, in the distance that separates them and even in their incompatibility. One would no longer seek an architecture of concepts sufficiently general and abstract to embrace all others and to introduce them into the same deductive structure; one would try to analyse the interplay of their appearances and dispersion.

Lastly, a fourth hypothesis to regroup the statements, describe their interconnexion and account for the unitary forms under which they are presented: the identity and persistence of themes. In 'sciences' like economics or biology, which are so controversial in character, so open to philosophical or ethical options, so exposed in certain cases to political manipulation, it is legitimate in the first instance to suppose that a certain thematic is capable of linking, and animating a group of discourses, like an organism with its own needs, its own internal force, and its own capacity for survival. Could one not, for example, constitute as a unity everything that has constituted the evolutionist theme from Buffon to Darwin? A theme that in the first instance was more philosophical, closer to cosmology than to biology; a theme that directed research from afar rather than named, regrouped, and explained results; a theme that always presupposed more than one was aware of, but which, on the basis of this fundamental choice, forcibly transformed into discursive knowledge what had been outlined as a hypothesis or as a necessity. Could one not speak of the Physiocratic theme in the same way? An idea that postulated, beyond all demonstration and prior to all analysis, the natural character of the three ground rents; which consequently presupposed the economic and political primacy of agrarian property; which excluded all analysis of the mechanisms of industrial production; which implied, on the other hand, the description of the circulation of money within a state, of its distribution between different social categories, and of the channels by which it flowed back into production; which finally led Ricardo to consider those cases in which this triple rent did not appear, the conditions in which it could form, and consequently to denounce the arbitrariness of the Physiocratic theme?

But on the basis of such an attempt, one is led to make two inverse and complementary observations. In one case, the same thematic is articulated on the basis of two sets of concepts, two types of analysis, two perfectly different fields of objects: in its most general formulation, the evolutionist idea is perhaps the same in the work of Benoît de Maillet, Bordeu or Diderot, and in that of Darwin; but, in fact, what makes it possible and coherent is not at all the same thing in either case. In the eighteenth century, the evolutionist idea is defined on the basis of a kinship of species forming a continuum laid down at the outset (interrupted only by natural catastrophes) or gradually built up by the passing of time. In the nineteenth century the evolutionist theme concerns not so much the constitution of a continuous table of species, as the description of discontinuous groups and the analysis of the modes of interaction between an organism whose elements are interdependent and an environment that provides its real conditions of life. A single theme, but based on two types of discourse. In the case of Physiocracy, on the other hand, Quesnay's choice rests exactly on the same system of concepts as the opposite opinion held by those that might be called utilitarists. At this period the analysis of wealth involved a relatively limited set of concepts that was accepted by all (coinage was given the same definition; prices were given the same explanation; and labour costs were calculated in the same way). But, on the basis of this single set of concepts, there were two ways of explaining the formation of value, according to whether it was analysed on the basis of exchange, or on that of remuneration for the day's work. These two possibilities contained within economic theory, and in the rules of its set of concepts, resulted, on the basis of the same elements, in two different options.

It would probably be wrong therefore to seek in the existence of these themes the principles of the individualization of a discourse. Should they not be sought rather in the dispersion of the points of choice that the discourse leaves free? In the different possibilities that it opens of reanimating already existing themes, of arousing opposed strategies, of giving way to irreconcilable interests, of making it possible, with a particular set of concepts, to play different games? Rather than seeking the permanence of themes, images, and opinions through time, rather than retracing the dialectic of their conflicts in order to individualize groups of statements, could one not rather mark out the dispersion of the points of choice, and define prior to any option, to any thematic preference, a field of strategic possibilities?

I am presented therefore with four attempts, four failures—and four successive hypotheses. They must now be put to the test. Concerning those large groups of statements with which we are so familiar—and which we call *medicine, economics,* or *grammar*—I have asked myself on what their unity could be based. On a full, tightly packed, continuous, geographically well-defined field of objects? What appeared to me were rather series full of gaps, intertwined with one another, interplays of differences, distances, substitutions, transformations. On a definite, normative type of statement? I found formulations of levels that were much too different and functions that were much too heterogeneous to be linked together and arranged in a single figure, and to simulate, from one period to another, beyond individual *œuvres,* a sort of great uninterrupted text. On a well-defined alphabet of notions? One is confronted with concepts that differ in structure and in the rules governing their use, which ignore or exclude one another, and which cannot enter the unity of a logical architecture. On the permanence of a thematic? What one finds are rather various strategic possibilities that permit the activation of incompatible themes, or, again, the establishment of the same theme in different groups of statement. Hence the idea of describing these dispersions themselves; of discovering whether, between these elements, which are certainly not organized as a progressively deductive structure, nor as an enormous book that is being gradually and continuously written, nor as the *œuvre* of a collective subject, one cannot discern a regularity: an order in their successive appearance, correlations in their simultaneity, assignable positions in a common space, a reciprocal functioning, linked and hierarchized transformations. Such an analysis would not try to isolate small islands of coherence in order to describe their internal structure; it would not try to suspect and to reveal latent conflicts; it would study forms of division. Or again: instead of reconstituting *chains of inference* (as one often does in the history of the sciences or of philosophy), instead of drawing up *tables of differences* (as the linguists do), it would describe *systems of dispersion.*

Whenever one can describe, between a number of statements, such a system of dispersion, whenever, between objects, types of statement, concepts, or thematic choices, one can define a regularity (an order, correlations, positions and functionings, transformations), we will say, for the sake of convenience, that we are dealing with a *discursive formation*—thus avoiding words that are already overladen with conditions and consequences, and in any case inadequate to the task of designating such a dispersion, such as 'science', 'ideology', 'theory', or 'domain of objectivity'. The conditions to which the elements of this division (objects, mode of statement, concepts, thematic choices) are subjected we shall call the *rules of formation.* The rules of formation are conditions of existence (but also of coexistence, maintenance, modification, and disappearance) in a given discursive division.

This, then, is the field to be covered; these the notions that we must put to the test and the analyses that we must carry out. I am well aware that the risks are considerable. For an initial probe, I made use of certain fairly loose, but familiar, groups of statement: I have no proof that I shall find them again at the end of the analysis, nor that I shall discover the principle of their delimitation and individualization; I am not sure that the discursive formations that I shall isolate will define medicine in its overall unity, or economics and grammar in the overall curve of their historical destination; they may even introduce unexpected boundaries and divisions. Similarly, I have no proof that such a description will be able to take account of the scientificity (or non-scientificity) of the discursive groups that I have taken as an attack point and which presented themselves at the outset with a certain pretension to scientific rationality; I have no proof that my analysis will not be situated at a quite different level, constituting a description that is irreducible to epistemology or to the history of the sciences. Moreover, at the end of such an enterprise, one may not recover those unities that, out of methodological rigour, one initially held in suspense: one may be compelled to dissociate certain *œuvres,* ignore influences and traditions, abandon definitively the question of origin, allow the commanding presence of authors to fade into the background; and thus everything that was thought to be proper to the history of ideas may disappear from view. The danger, in short, is that instead of providing a basis for what already exists, instead of going over with bold strokes lines that have already been sketched, instead of finding reassurance in this return and final confirmation, instead of completing the blessed circle that announces, after innumerable stratagems and as many nights, that all is saved, one is forced to advance beyond familiar territory, far from the certainties to which one is accustomed, towards an as yet uncharted land and unforeseeable conclusion. Is there not a danger that everything that has so far protected the historian in his daily journey and accompanied him until nightfall (the destiny of rationality and the teleology of the sciences, the long, continuous labour of thought from period to period, the awakening and the progress of consciousness, its perpetual resumption of itself, the uncompleted, but uninterrupted movement of totalizations, the return to an ever-open source, and finally the historico-transcendental thematic) may disappear, leaving for analysis a blank, indifferent space, lacking in both interiority and promise?

CHAPTER 3

THE FORMATION OF OBJECTS

We must now list the various directions that lie open to us, and see whether this notion of 'rules of formation'—of which little more than a rough sketch has so far been provided—can be given real content. Let us look first at the formation of objects. And in order to facilitate our analysis, let us take as an example the discourse of psychopathology from the nineteenth century onwards—a chronological break that is easy enough to accept in a first approach to the subject. There are enough signs to indicate it, but let us take just two of these: the establishment at the beginning of the century of a new mode of exclusion and confinement of the madman in a psychiatric hospital; and the possibility of tracing certain present-day notions back to Esquirol, Heinroth, or Pinel (paranoia can be traced back to monomania, the intelligence quotient to the initial notion of imbecility, general paralysis to chronic encephalitis, character neurosis to non-delirious madness); whereas if we try to trace the development of psychopathology beyond the nineteenth century, we soon lose our way, the path becomes confused, and the projection of Du Laurens or even Van Swieten on the pathology of Kraepelin or Bleuler provides no more than chance coincidences. The objects with which psychopathology has dealt since this break in time are very numerous, mostly very new, but also very precarious, subject to change and, in some cases, to rapid disappearance: in addition to motor disturbances, hallucinations, and speech disorders (which were already regarded as manifestations of madness, although they were recognized, delimited, described, and analysed in a different way), objects appeared that belonged to hitherto unused registers: minor behavioural disorders, sexual aberrations and disturbances, the phenomena of suggestion and hypnosis, lesions of the central nervous system, deficiencies of intellectual or motor adaptation, criminality. And on the basis of each of these registers a variety of objects were named, circumscribed, analysed, then rectified, re-defined, challenged, erased. Is it possible to lay down the rule to which their appearance was subject? Is it possible to discover according to which non-deductive system these objects could be juxtaposed and placed in succession to form the fragmented field—showing at certain points great gaps, at others a plethora of information—of psychopathology? What has ruled their existence as objects of discourse?

(a) First we must map the first *surfaces* of their *emergence:* show where these individual differences, which, according to the degrees of rationalization, conceptual codes, and types of theory, will be accorded the status of disease, alienation, anomaly, dementia, neurosis or psychosis, degeneration, etc., may emerge, and then be designated and analysed. These surfaces of emergence are not the same for different societies, at different periods, and in different forms of discourse. In the case of nineteenth-century psychopathology, they were probably constituted by the family, the immediate social group, the work situation, the religious community (which are all normative, which are all susceptible to deviation, which all have a margin of tolerance and a threshold beyond which exclusion is demanded, which all have a mode of designation and a mode of rejecting madness, which all transfer to medicine if not the responsibility for treatment and cure, at least the burden of explanation); although organized according to a specific mode, these surfaces of emergence were not new in the nineteenth century. On the other hand, it was no doubt at this period that new surfaces of appearance began to function: art with its own normativity, sexuality (its deviations in relation to customary prohibitions become for the first time an object of observation, description, and analysis for psychiatric discourse), penality (whereas in previous periods madness was carefully distinguished from criminal conduct and was regarded as an excuse, criminality itself becomes—and subsequent to the celebrated 'homicidal monomanias'—a form of deviance more or less related to madness). In these fields of initial differentiation, in the distances, the discontinuities, and the thresholds that appear within it, psychiatric discourse finds a way of limiting its domain, of defining what it is talking about, of giving it the status of an object—and therefore of making it manifest, nameable, and describable.

(b) We must also describe the authorities of delimitation: in the nineteenth century, medicine (as an institution possessing its own rules, as a group of individuals constituting the medical profession, as a body of knowledge and practice, as an authority recognized by public opinion, the law, and government) became the major authority in society that delimited, designated, named, and established madness as an object; but it was not alone in this: the law and penal law in particular (with the definitions of excuse, non-responsibility, extenuating circumstances, and with the application of such notions as the *crime passionel,* heredity, danger to society), the religious authority (in so far as it set itself up as the authority that divided the mystical from the pathological, the spiritual from the corporeal, the supernatural from the abnormal, and in so far as it practised the direction of conscience with a view to understanding individuals rather than carrying out a casuistical classification of actions and circumstances), literary and art criticism (which in the nineteenth century treated the work less and less as an object of taste that had to be judged, and more and more as a language that had to be interpreted and in which the author's tricks of expression had to be recognized).

(c) Lastly, we must analyse the *grids of specification:* these are the systems according to which the different 'kinds of madness' are divided, contrasted, related, regrouped, classified, derived from one another as objects of psychiatric discourse (in the nineteenth century, these grids of differentiation were: the soul, as a group of hierarchized, related, and more or less interpenetrable faculties; the body, as a three-dimensional volume of organs linked together by networks of dependence and communication; the life and history of individuals, as a linear succession of phases, a tangle of traces, a group of potential reactivations, cyclical repetitions; the interplays of neuropsychological correlations as systems of reciprocal projections, and as a field of circular causality).

Such a description is still in itself inadequate. And for two reasons. These planes of emergence, authorities of delimitation, or forms of specification do not provide objects, fully formed and armed, that the discourse of psychopathology has then merely to list, classify, name, select, and cover with a network of words and sentences: it is not the families—with their norms, their prohibitions, their sensitivity thresholds—that decide who is mad, and present the 'patients' to the psychiatrists for analysis and judgement; it is not the legal system itself that hands over certain criminals to psychiatry, that sees paranoia beyond a particular murder, or a neurosis behind a sexual offence. It would be quite wrong to see discourse as a place where previously established objects are laid one after another like words on a page. But the above enumeration is inadequate for a second reason. It has located, one after another, several planes of differentiation in which the objects of discourse may appear. But what relations exist between them? Why this enumeration rather than another? What defined and closed group does one imagine one is circumscribing in this way? And how can one speak of a 'system of formation' if one knows only a series of different, heterogeneous determinations, lacking attributable links and relations?

In fact, these two series of questions refer back to the same point. In order to locate that point, let us re-examine the previous example. In the sphere with which psychopathology dealt in the nineteenth century, one sees the very early appearance (as early as Esquirol) of a whole series of objects belonging to the category of delinquency: homicide (and suicide), *crimes passionels,* sexual offences, certain forms of theft, vagrancy—and then, through them, heredity, the neurogenic environment, aggressive or self-punishing behaviour, perversions, criminal impulses, suggestibility, etc. It would be inadequate to say that one was dealing here with the consequences of a discovery: of the sudden discovery by a psychiatrist of a resemblance between criminal and pathological behaviour, a discovery of the presence in certain delinquents of the classical signs of alienation, or mental derangement. Such facts lie beyond the grasp of contemporary research: indeed, the problem is how to decide what made them possible, and how these 'discoveries' could lead to others that took them up, rectified them, modified them, or even disproved them. Similarly, it would be irrelevant to attribute the appearance of these new objects to the norms of nineteenth-century bourgeois society, to a reinforced police and penal framework, to the establishment of a new code of criminal justice, to the introduction and use of extenuating circumstances, to the increase in crime. No doubt, all these processes were at work; but they could not of themselves form objects for psychiatric discourse; to pursue the description at this level one would fall short of what one was seeking.

If, in a particular period in the history of our society, the delinquent was psychologized and pathologized, if criminal behaviour could give rise to a whole series of objects of knowledge, this was because a group of particular relations was adopted for use in psychiatric discourse. The relation between planes of specification like penal categories and degrees of diminished responsibility, and planes of psychological characterization (faculties, aptitudes, degrees of development or involution, different ways of reacting to the environment, character types, whether acquired, innate, or hereditary). The relation between the authority of medical decision and the authority of judicial decision (a really complex relation since medical decision recognizes absolutely the authority of the judiciary to define crime, to determine the circumstances in which it is committed, and the punishment that it deserves; but reserves the right to analyse its origin and to determine the degree of responsibility involved). The relation between the filter formed by judicial interrogation, police information, investigation, and the whole machinery of judicial information, and the filter formed by the medical questionnaire, clinical examinations, the search for antecedents, and biographical accounts. The relation between the family, sexual and penal norms of the behaviour of individuals, and the table of pathological symptoms and diseases of which they are the signs. The relation between therapeutic confinement in hospital (with its own thresholds, its criteria of cure, its way of distinguishing the normal from the pathological) and punitive confinement in prison (with its system of punishment and pedagogy, its criteria of good conduct, improvement, and freedom). These are the relations that, operating in psychiatric discourse, have made possible the formation of a whole group of various objects.

Let us generalize: in the nineteenth century, psychiatric discourse is characterized not by privileged objects, but by the way in which it forms objects that are in fact highly dispersed. This formation is made possible by a group of relations established between authorities of emergence, delimitation, and specification. One might say, then, that a discursive formation is defined (as far as its objects are concerned, at least) if one can establish such a group; if one can show how any particular object of discourse finds in it its place and law of emergence; if one can show that it may give birth simultaneously or successively to mutually exclusive objects, without having to modify itself.

Hence a certain number of remarks and consequences.

1. The conditions necessary for the appearance of an object of discourse, the historical conditions required if one is to 'say anything' about it, and if several people are to say different things about it, the conditions necessary if it is to exist in relation to other objects, if it is to establish with them relations of resemblance, proximity, distance, difference, transformation—as we can see, these conditions are many and imposing. Which means that one cannot speak of anything at any time; it is not easy to say something new; it is not enough for us to open our eyes, to pay attention, or to be aware, for new objects suddenly to light up and emerge out of the ground. But this difficulty is not only a negative one; it must not be attached to some obstacle whose power appears to be, exclusively, to blind, to hinder, to prevent discovery, to conceal the purity of the evidence or the dumb obstinacy of the things themselves; the object does not await in limbo the order that will free it and enable it to become embodied in a visible and prolix objectivity; it does not preexist itself, held back by some obstacle at the first edges of light. It exists under the positive conditions of a complex group of relations.

2. These relations are established between institutions, economic and social processes, behavioural patterns, systems of norms, techniques, types of classification, modes of characterization; and these relations are not present in the object; it is not they that are deployed when the object is being analysed; they do not indicate the web, the immanent rationality, that ideal nervure that reappears totally or in part when one conceives of the object in the truth of its concept. They do not define its internal constitution, but what enables it to appear, to juxtapose itself with other objects, to situate itself in relation to them, to define its difference, its irreducibility, and even perhaps its heterogeneity, in short, to be placed in a field of exteriority.

3. These relations must be distinguished first from what we might call 'primary' relations, and which, independently of all discourse or all object of discourse, may be described between institutions, techniques, social forms, etc. After all, we know very well that relations existed between the bourgeois family and the functioning of judicial authorities and categories in the nineteenth century that can be analysed in their own right. They cannot always be superposed upon the relations that go to form objects: the relations of dependence that may be assigned to this primary level are not necessarily expressed in the formation of relations that makes discursive objects possible. But we must also distinguish the secondary relations that are formulated in discourse itself: what, for example, the psychiatrists of the nineteenth century could say about the relations between the family and criminality does not reproduce, as we know, the interplay of real dependencies; but neither does it reproduce the interplay of relations that make possible and sustain the objects of psychiatric discourse. Thus a space unfolds articulated with possible discourses: a system of *real* or *primary relations,* a system of *reflexive* or *secondary relations,* and a system of relations that might properly be called *discursive.* The problem is to reveal the specificity of these discursive relations, and their interplay with the other two kinds.

4. Discursive relations are not, as we can see, internal to discourse: they do not connect concepts or words with one another; they do not establish a deductive or rhetorical structure between propositions or sentences. Yet they are not relations exterior to discourse, relations that might limit it, or impose certain forms upon it, or force it, in certain circumstances, to state certain things. They are, in a sense, at the limit of discourse: they offer it objects of which it can speak, or rather (for this image of offering presupposes that objects are formed independently of discourse), they determine the group of relations that discourse must establish in order to speak of this or that object, in order to deal with them, name them, analyse them, classify them, explain them, etc. These relations characterize not the language (*langue*) used by discourse, nor the circumstances in which it is deployed, but discourse itself as a practice.

We can now complete the analysis and see to what extent it fulfils, and to what extent it modifies, the initial project.

Taking those group figures which, in an insistent but confused way, presented themselves as *psychology, economics, grammar, medicine,* we asked on what kind of unity they could be based: were they simply a reconstruction after the event, based on particular works, successive theories, notions and themes some of which had been abandoned, others maintained by tradition, and again others fated to fall into oblivion only to be revived at a later date? Were they simply a series of linked enterprises?

We sought the unity of discourse in the objects themselves, in their distribution, in the interplay of their differences, in their proximity or distance—in short, in what is given to the speaking subject; and, in the end, we are sent back to a setting-up of relations that characterizes discursive practice itself; and what we discover is neither a configuration, nor a form, but a group of *rules* that are immanent in a practice, and define it in its specificity. We also used, as a point of reference, a unity like *psychopathology:* if we had wanted to provide it with a date of birth and precise limits, it would no doubt have been necessary to discover when the word was first used, to what kind of analysis it could be applied, and how it achieved its separation from neurology on the one hand and psychology on the other. What has emerged is a unity of another type, which does not appear to have the same dates, or the same surface, or the same articulations, but which may take account of a group of objects for which the term psychopathology was merely a reflexive, secondary, classificatory rubric. Psychopathology finally emerged as a discipline in a constant state of renewal, subject to constant discoveries, criticisms, and corrected errors; the system of formation that we have defined remains stable. But let there be no misunderstanding: it is not the objects that remain constant, nor the domain that they form; it is not even their point of emergence or their mode of characterization; but the relation between the surfaces on which they appear, on which they can be delimited, on which they can be analysed and specified.

In the descriptions for which I have attempted to provide a theory, there can be no question of interpreting discourse with a view to writing a history of the referent. In the example chosen, we are not trying to find out who was mad at a particular period, or in what his madness consisted, or whether his disturbances were identical with those known to us today. We are not asking ourselves whether witches were unrecognized and persecuted madmen and madwomen, or whether, at a different period, a mystical or aesthetic experience was not unduly medicalized. We are not trying to reconstitute what madness itself might be, in the form in which it first presented itself to some primitive, fundamental, deaf, scarcely articulated[1] experience, and in the form in which it was later organized (translated, deformed, travestied, perhaps

---

[1] This is written against an explicit theme of my book *Madness and Civilization,* and one that recurs particularly in the Preface.

even repressed) by discourses, and the oblique, often twisted play of their operations. Such a history of the referent is no doubt possible; and I have no wish at the outset to exclude any effort to uncover and free these 'prediscursive' experiences from the tyranny of the text. But what we are concerned with here is not to neutralize discourse, to make it the sign of something else, and to pierce through its density in order to reach what remains silently anterior to it, but on the contrary to maintain it in its consistency, to make it emerge in its own complexity. What, in short, we wish to do is to dispense with 'things'. To 'depresentify' them. To conjure up their rich, heavy, immediate plenitude, which we usually regard as the primitive law of a discourse that has become divorced from it through error, oblivion, illusion, ignorance, or the inertia of beliefs and traditions, or even the perhaps unconscious desire not to see and not to speak. To substitute for the enigmatic treasure of 'things' anterior to discourse, the regular formation of objects that emerge only in discourse. To define these *objects* without reference to the *ground*, the *foundation of things*, but by relating them to the body of rules that enable them to form as objects of a discourse and thus constitute the conditions of their historical appearance. To write a history of discursive objects that does not plunge them into the common depth of a primal soil, but deploys the nexus of regularities that govern their dispersion.

However, to suppress the stage of 'things themselves' is not necessarily to return to the linguistic analysis of meaning. When one describes the formation of the objects of a discourse, one tries to locate the relations that characterize a discursive practice, one determines neither a lexical organization, nor the scansions of a semantic field: one does not question the meaning given at a particular period to such words as 'melancholia' or 'madness without delirium', nor the opposition of content between 'psychosis' and 'neurosis'. Not, I repeat, that such analyses are regarded as illegitimate or impossible; but they are not relevant when we are trying to discover, for example, how criminality could become an object of medical expertise, or sexual deviation a possible object of psychiatric discourse. The analysis of lexical contents defines either the elements of meaning at the disposal of speaking subjects in a given period, or the semantic structure that appears on the surface of a discourse that has already been spoken; it does not concern discursive practice as a place in which a tangled plurality—at once superposed and incomplete—of objects is formed and deformed, appears and disappears.

The sagacity of the commentators is not mistaken: from the kind of analysis that I have undertaken, *words* are as deliberately absent as *things* themselves; any description of a vocabulary is as lacking as any reference to the living plenitude of experience. We shall not return to the state anterior to discourse—in which nothing has yet been said, and in which things are only just beginning to emerge out of the grey light; and we shall not pass beyond discourse in order to rediscover the forms that it has created and left behind it; we shall remain, or try to remain, at the level of discourse itself. Since it is sometimes necessary to dot the 'i's of even the most obvious absences, I will say that in all these searches, in which I have still progressed so little, I would like to show that 'discourses', in the form in which they can be heard or read, are not, as one might expect, a mere intersection of things and words: an obscure web of things, and a manifest, visible, coloured chain of words; I would like to show that discourse is not a slender surface of contact, or confrontation, between a reality and a language (*langue*), the intrication of a lexicon and an experience; I would like to show with precise examples that in analysing discourses themselves, one sees the loosening of the embrace, apparently so tight, of words and things, and the emergence of a group of rules proper to discursive practice. These rules define not the dumb existence of a reality, nor the canonical use of a vocabulary, but the ordering of objects. 'Words and things' is the entirely serious title of a problem; it is the ironic title of a work that modifies its own form, displaces its own data, and reveals, at the end of the day, a quite different task. A task that consists of not—of no longer—treating discourses as groups of signs (signifying elements referring to contents or representations) but as practices that systematically form the objects of which they speak. Of course, discourses are composed of signs; but what they do is more than use these signs to designate things. It is this *more* that renders them irreducible to the language (*langue*) and to speech. It is this 'more' that we must reveal and describe.

CHAPTER 4

THE FORMATION OF ENUNCIATIVE MODALITIES

Qualitative descriptions, biographical accounts, the location, interpretation, and cross-checking of signs, reasonings by analogy, deduction, statistical calculations, experimental verifications, and many other forms of statement are to be found in the discourse of nineteenth-century doctors. What is it that links them together? What necessity binds them together? Why these and not others? Before attempting an answer to such questions, we must first discover the law operating behind all these diverse statements, and the place from which they come.

(a) First question: who is speaking? Who, among the totality of speaking individuals, is accorded the right to use this sort of language (*langage*)? Who is qualified to do so? Who derives from it his own special quality, his prestige, and from whom, in return, does he receive if not the assurance, at least the presumption that what he says is true? What is the status of the individuals who—alone—have the right, sanctioned by law or tradition, juridically defined or spontaneously accepted, to proffer such a discourse? The status of doctor involves criteria of competence and knowledge; institutions, systems, pedagogic norms; legal conditions that give the right—though not without laying down certain limitations—to practise and to extend one's knowledge. It also involves a system of differentiation and relations (the division of attributions, hierarchical subordination, functional complementarity, the request for and the provision and exchange of information) with other individuals or other groups that also possess their own status (with the state and its representatives, with the judiciary, with different professional bodies, with religious groups and, at times, with priests). It also involves a number of characteristics that define its functioning in relation to society as a whole (the role that is attributed to the doctor according to whether he is consulted by a private person or summoned, more or less under compulsion, by society, according to whether he practises a profession or carries out a function; the right to intervene or make decisions that is accorded him in these different cases; what is required of him as the supervisor, guardian, and guarantor of the health of a population, a group, a family, an individual; the payment that he receives from the community or from individuals; the form of contract, explicit or implicit, that he negotiates either with the group in which he practises, or with the authority that entrusts him with a task, or with the patient who requests advice, treatment, or cure). This status of the doctor is generally a rather special one in all forms of society and civilization: he is hardly ever an undifferentiated or interchangeable person. Medical statements cannot come from anybody; their value, efficacy, even their therapeutic powers, and, generally speaking, their existence as medical statements cannot be dissociated from the statutorily defined person who has the right to make them, and to claim for them the power to overcome suffering and death. But we also know that this status in western civilization was profoundly modified at the end of the eighteenth century when the health of the population became one of the economic norms required by industrial societies.

(b) We must also describe the institutional *sites* from which the doctor makes his discourse, and from which this discourse derives its legitimate source and point of application (its specific objects and instruments of verification). In our

societies, these sites are: the hospital, a place of constant, coded, systematic observation, run by a differentiated and hierarchized medical staff, thus constituting a quantifiable field of frequencies; private practice, which offers a field of less systematic, less complete, and far less numerous observations, but which sometimes facilitates observations that are more far-reaching in their effects, with a better knowledge of the background and environment; the laboratory, an autonomous place, long distinct from the hospital, where certain truths of a general kind, concerning the human body, life, disease, lesions, etc., which provide certain elements of the diagnosis, certain signs of the developing condition, certain criteria of cure, and which makes therapeutic experiment possible; lastly, what might be called the 'library' or documentary field, which includes not only the books and treatises traditionally recognized as valid, but also all the observations and case-histories published and transmitted, and the mass of statistical information (concerning the social environment, climate, epidemics, mortality rates, the incidence of diseases, the centres of contagion, occupational diseases) that can be supplied to the doctor by public bodies, by other doctors, by sociologists, and by geographers. In this respect, too, these various 'sites' of medical discourse were profoundly modified in the nineteenth century: the importance of the document continues to increase (proportionately diminishing the authority of the book or tradition); the hospital, which had been merely a subsidiary site for discourse on diseases, and which took second place in importance and value to private practice (in which diseases left in their natural environment were, in the eighteenth century, to reveal themselves in their vegetal truth), then becomes the site of systematic, homogeneous observations, large-scale confrontations, the establishment of frequencies and probabilities, the annulation of individual variants, in short, the site of the appearance of disease, not as a particular species, deploying its essential features beneath the doctor's gaze, but as an average process, with its significant guide-lines, boundaries, and potential development. Similarly, it was in the nineteenth century that daily medical practice integrated the laboratory as the site of a discourse that has the same experimental norms as physics, chemistry, or biology.

(c) The positions of the subject are also defined by the situation that it is possible for him to occupy in relation to the various domains or groups of objects: according to a certain grid of explicit or implicit interrogations, he is the questioning subject and, according to a certain programme of information, he is the listening subject; according to a table of characteristic features, he is the seeing subject, and, according to a descriptive type, the observing subject; he is situated at an optimal perceptual distance whose boundaries delimit the wheat of relevant information; he uses instrumental intermediaries that modify the scale of the information, shift the subject in relation to the average or immediate perceptual level, ensure his movement from a superficial to a deep level, make him circulate in the interior space of the body—from manifest symptoms to the organs, from the organs to the tissues, and finally from the tissues to the cells. To these perceptual situations should be added the positions that the subject can occupy in the information networks (in theoretical teaching or in hospital training; in the system of oral communication or of written document: as emitter and receiver of observations, case-histories, statistical data, general theoretical propositions, projects, and decisions). The various situations that the subject of medical discourse may occupy were redefined at the beginning of the nineteenth century with the organization of a quite different perceptual field (arranged in depth, manifested by successive recourse to instruments, deployed by surgical techniques or methods of autopsy, centred upon lesional sites), and with the establishment of new systems of registration, notation, description, classification, integration in numerical series and in statistics, with the introduction of new forms of teaching, the circulation of information, relations with other theoretical domains (sciences or philos-

ophy) and with other institutions (whether administrative, political, or economic).

If, in clinical discourse, the doctor is in turn the sovereign, direct questioner, the observing eye, the touching finger, the organ that deciphers signs, the point at which previously formulated descriptions are integrated, the laboratory technician, it is because a whole group of relations is involved. Relations between the hospital space as a place of assistance, of purified, systematic observation, and of partially proved, partially experimental therapeutics, and a whole group of perceptual codes of the human body—as it is defined by morbid anatomy; relations between the field of immediate observations and the domain of acquired information; relations between the doctor's therapeutic role, his pedagogic role, his role as an intermediary in the diffusion of medical knowledge, and his role as a responsible representative of public health in the social space. Understood as a renewal of points of view, contents, the forms and even the style of description, the use of inductive or probabilistic reasoning, types of attribution of causality, in short, as a renewal of the modalities of enunciation, clinical medicine must not be regarded as the result of a new technique of observation—that of autopsy, which was practised long before the advent of the nineteenth century; nor as the result of the search for pathogenic causes in the depths of the organism—Morgagni was engaged in such a search in the middle of the eighteenth century; nor as the effect of that new institution, the teaching hospital—such institutions had already been in existence for some decades in Austria and Italy; nor as the result of the introduction of the concept of tissue in Bichat's *Traité des membranes.* But as the establishment of a relation, in medical discourse, between a number of distinct elements, some of which concerned the status of doctors, others the institutional and technical site from which they spoke, others their position as subjects perceiving, observing, describing, teaching, etc. It can be said that this relation between different elements (some of which are new, while others were already in existence) is effected by clinical discourse: it is this, as a practice, that establishes between them all a system of relations that is not 'really' given or constituted *a priori;* and if there is a unity, if the modalities of enunciation that it uses, or to which it gives place, are not simply juxtaposed by a series of historical contingencies, it is because it makes constant use of this group of relations.

One further remark. Having noted the disparity of the types of enunciation in clinical discourse, I have not tried to reduce it by uncovering the formal structures, categories, modes of logical succession, types of reasoning and induction, forms of analysis and synthesis that may have operated in a discourse; I did not wish to reveal the rational organization that may provide statements like those of medicine with their element of intrinsic necessity. Nor did I wish to reduce to a single founding act, or to a founding consciousness the general horizon of rationality against which the progress of medicine gradually emerged, its efforts to model itself upon the exact sciences, the contraction of its methods of observation, the slow, difficult expulsion of the images or fantasies that inhabit it, the purification of its system of reasoning. Lastly, I have not tried to describe the empirical genesis, nor the various component elements of the medical mentality: how this shift of interest on the part of the doctors came about, by what theoretical or experimental model they were influenced, what philosophy or moral thematics defined the climate of their reflexion, to what questions, to what demands, they had to reply, what efforts were required of them to free themselves from traditional prejudices, by what ways they were led towards a unification and coherence that were never achieved, never reached, by their knowledge. In short, I do not refer the various enunciative modalities to the unity of the subject—whether it concerns the subject regarded as the pure founding authority of rationality, or the subject regarded as an empirical function of synthesis. Neither the 'knowing' (*le 'connaître'*), nor the 'knowledge' (*les 'connaissances'*).

In the proposed analysis, instead of referring back to *the* synthesis or *the* unifying function of *a* subject, the various enunciative modalities manifest his dispersion.[1] To the various statuses, the various sites, the various positions that he can occupy or be given when making a discourse. To the discontinuity of the planes from which he speaks. And if these planes are linked by a system of relations, this system is not established by the synthetic activity of a consciousness identical with itself, dumb and anterior to all speech, but by the specificity of a discursive practice. I shall abandon any attempt, therefore, to see discourse as a phenomenon of expression—the verbal translation of a previously established synthesis; instead, I shall look for a field of regularity for various positions of subjectivity. Thus conceived, discourse is not the majestically unfolding manifestation of a thinking, knowing, speaking subject, but, on the contrary, a totality, in which the dispersion of the subject and his discontinuity with himself may be determined. It is a space of exteriority in which a network of distinct sites is deployed. I showed earlier that it was neither by 'words' nor by 'things' that the regulation of the objects proper to a discursive formation should be defined; similarly, it must now be recognized that it is neither by recourse to a transcendental subject nor by recourse to a psychological subjectivity that the regulation of its enunciations should be defined.

• • •

THE DISCOURSE ON LANGUAGE*

I would really like to have slipped imperceptibly into this lecture, as into all the others I shall be delivering, perhaps over the years ahead. I would have preferred to be enveloped in words, borne way beyond all possible beginnings. At the moment of speaking, I would like to have perceived a nameless voice, long preceding me, leaving me merely to enmesh myself in it, taking up its cadence, and to lodge myself, when no one was looking, in its interstices as if it had paused an instant, in suspense, to beckon to me. There would have been no beginnings: instead, speech would proceed from me, while I stood in its path—a slender gap—the point of its possible disappearance.

Behind me, I should like to have heard (having been at it long enough already, repeating in advance what I am about to tell you) the voice of Molloy, beginning to speak thus: 'I must go on; I can't go on; I must go on; I must say words as long as there are words, I must say them until they find me, until they say me—heavy burden, heavy sin; I must go on; maybe it's been done already; maybe they've already said me; maybe they've already borne me to the threshold of my story, right to the door opening onto my story; I'd be surprised if it opened'.

A good many people, I imagine, harbour a similar desire to be freed from the obligation to begin, a similar desire to find themselves, right from the outside, on the other side of discourse, without having to stand outside it, pondering its particular, fearsome, and even devilish features. To this all too common feeling, institutions have an ironic reply, for they solemnise beginnings, surrounding them with a circle of silent attention; in order that they can be distinguished from far off, they impose ritual forms upon them.

Inclination speaks out: 'I don't want to have to enter this risky world of discourse; I want nothing to do with it insofar as it is decisive and final; I would like to feel it all around me, calm and transparent, profound, infinitely open, with others responding to my expectations, and truth emerging,

---

[1] In this respect, the term '*regard* médical' used in my *Naissance de la clinique* was not a very happy one.

* This lecture was delivered in French at the Collège de France on December 2, 1970. The original French text has been published with the title *L'ordre du discours* (Paris, Gallimard, 1971). The English translation by Rupert Swyer was first published in *Social Science Information*, April 1971, pp. 7–30.

one by one. All I want is to allow myself to be borne along, within it, and by it, a happy wreck'. Institutions reply: 'But you have nothing to fear from launching out; we're here to show you discourse is within the established order of things, that we've waited a long time for its arrival, that a place has been set aside for it—a place which both honours and disarms it; and if it should happen to have a certain power, then it is we, and we alone, who give it that power'.

Yet, maybe this institution and this inclination are but two converse responses to the same anxiety: anxiety as to just what discourse is, when it is manifested materially, as a written or spoken object; but also, uncertainty faced with a transitory existence, destined for oblivion—at any rate, not belonging to us; uncertainty at the suggestion of barely imaginable powers and dangers behind this activity, however humdrum and grey it may seem; uncertainty when we suspect the conflicts, triumphs, injuries, dominations and enslavements that lie behind these words, even when long use has chipped away their rough edges.

What is so perilous, then, in the fact that people speak, and that their speech proliferates? Where is the danger in that?

Here then is the hypothesis I want to advance, tonight, in order to fix the terrain—or perhaps the very provisional theatre—within which I shall be working. I am supposing that in every society the production of discourse is at once controlled, selected, organised and redistributed according to a certain number of procedures, whose role is to avert its powers and its dangers, to cope with chance events, to evade its ponderous, awesome materiality.

In a society such as our own we all know the rules of *exclusion*. The most obvious and familiar of these concerns what is *prohibited*. We know perfectly well that we are not free to say just anything, that we cannot simply speak of anything, when we like or where we like; not just anyone, finally, may speak of just anything. We have three types of prohibition, covering objects, ritual with its surrounding circumstances, the privileged or exclusive right to speak of a particular subject; these prohibitions interrelate, reinforce and complement each other, forming a complex web, continually subject to modification. I will note simply that the areas where this web is most tightly woven today, where the danger spots are most numerous, are those dealing with politics and sexuality. It is as though discussion, far from being a transparent, neutral element, allowing us to disarm sexuality and to pacify politics, were one of those privileged areas in which they exercised some of their more awesome powers. In appearance, speech may well be of little account, but the prohibitions surrounding it soon reveal its links with desire and power. This should not be very surprising, for psychoanalysis has already shown us that speech is not merely the medium which manifests—or dissembles—desire; it is also the object of desire. Similarly, historians have constantly impressed upon us that speech is no mere verbalisation of conflicts and systems of domination, but that it is the very object of man's conflicts.

But our society possesses yet another principle of exclusion; not another prohibition, but a division and a rejection. I have in mind the opposition: reason and folly. From the depths of the Middle Ages, a man was mad if his speech could not be said to form part of the common discourse of men. His words were considered nul and void, without truth or significance, worthless as evidence, inadmissible in the authentification of acts or contracts, incapable even of bringing about transubstantiation—the transformation of bread into flesh—at Mass. And yet, in contrast to all others, his words were credited with strange powers, of revealing some hidden truth, of predicting the future, of revealing, in all their naivete, what the wise were unable to perceive. It is curious to note that for centuries, in Europe, the words of a madman were either totally ignored or else were taken as words of truth. They either fell into a void—rejected the moment they were proffered—or else men deciphered in them a naive or cunning reason, rationality more rational than that of a rational man. At all events, whether excluded or secretly invested with reason, the madman's speech did not strictly exist. It was through his words that one recognised the madness of the madman; but they were certainly the medium within which this division became active; they were neither heard nor remembered. No doctor before the end of the eighteenth century had ever thought of listening to the content—how it was said and why—of these words; and yet it was these which signalled the difference between reason and madness. Whatever a madman said, it was taken for mere noise; he was credited with words only in a symbolic sense, in the theatre, in which he stepped forward, unarmed and reconciled, playing his role: that of masked truth.

Of course people are going to say all that is over and done with, or that it is in the process of being finished with, today; that the madman's words are no longer on the other side of this division; that they are no longer nul and void, that, on the contrary, they alert us to the need to look for a sense behind them, for the attempt at, or the ruins of some '*œuvre*'; we have even come to notice these words of madmen in our own speech, in those tiny pauses when we forget what we are talking about. But all this is no proof that the old division is not just as active as before; we have only to think of the systems by which we decipher this speech; we have only to think of the network of institutions established to permit doctors and psychoanalysts to listen to the mad and, at the same time, enabling the mad to come and speak, or, in desperation, to withhold their meagre words; we have only to bear all this in mind to suspect that the old division is just as active as ever, even if it is proceeding along different lines and, via new institutions, producing rather different effects. Even when the role of the doctor consists of lending an ear to this finally liberated speech, this procedure still takes place in the context of a hiatus between listener and speaker. For he is listening to speech invested with desire, crediting itself—for its greater exultation or for its greater anguish—with terrible powers. If we truly require silence to cure monsters, then it must be an attentive silence, and it is in this that the division lingers.

It is perhaps a little risky to speak of the opposition between true and false as a third system of exclusion, along with those I have mentioned already. How could one reasonably compare the constraints of truth with those other divisions, arbitrary in origin if not developing out of historical contingency—not merely modifiable but in a state of continual flux, supported by a system of institutions imposing and manipulating them, acting not without constraint, nor without an element, at least, of violence?

Certainly, as a proposition, the division between true and false is neither arbitrary, nor modifiable, nor institutional, nor violent. Putting the question in different terms, however—asking what has been, what still is, throughout our discourse, this will to truth which has survived throughout so many centuries of our history; or if we ask what is, in its very general form, the kind of division governing our will to knowledge—then we may well discern something like a system of exclusion (historical, modifiable, institutionally constraining) in the process of development.

It is, undoubtedly, a historically constituted division. For, even with the sixth century Greek poets, true discourse—in the meaningful sense—inspiring respect and terror, to which all were obliged to submit, because it held sway over all and was pronounced by men who spoke as of right, according to ritual, meted out justice and attributed to each his rightful share; it prophesied the future, not merely announcing what was going to occur, but contributing to its actual event, carrying men along with it and thus weaving itself into the fabric of fate. And yet, a century later, the highest truth no longer resided in what discourse *was*, nor in what it *did:* it lay in what was *said*. The day dawned when truth moved over from the ritualised act—potent and just—of enunciation to settle on what was enunciated itself: its meaning, its form, its object and its relation to what it referred to. A division emerged between Hesiod and Plato, separating true discourse from false; it was a new division for, henceforth, true discourse was no longer considered precious and desirable, since it had ceased to be discourse linked to the exercise of power. And so the Sophists were routed.

This historical division has doubtless lent its general form to our will to knowledge. Yet it has never ceased shifting: the great mutations of science may well sometimes be seen to flow from some discovery, but they may equally be viewed as the appearance of new forms of the will to truth. In the nineteenth century there was undoubtedly a will to truth having nothing to do, in terms of the forms examined, of the fields to which it addressed itself, nor the techniques upon which it was based, with the will to knowledge which characterised classical culture. Going back a little in time, to the turn of the sixteenth and seventeenth centuries—and particularly in England—a will to knowledge emerged which, anticipating its present content, sketched out a schema of possible, observable, measurable and classifiable objects; a will to knowledge which imposed upon the knowing subject—in some ways taking precedence over all experience—a certain position, a certain viewpoint, and a certain function (look rather than read, verify rather than comment), a will to knowledge which prescribed (and, more generally speaking, all instruments determined) the technological level at which knowledge could be employed in order to be verifiable and useful (navigation, mining, pharmacopoeia). Everything seems to have occurred as though, from the time of the great Platonic division onwards, the will to truth had its own history, which is not at all that of the constraining truths: the history of a range of subjects to be learned, the history of the functions of the knowing subject, the history of material, technical and instrumental investment in knowledge.

But this will to truth, like the other systems of exclusion, relies on institutional support: it is both reinforced and accompanied by whole strata of practices such as pedagogy—naturally—the book-system, publishing, libraries, such as the learned societies in the past, and laboratories today. But it is probably even more profoundly accompanied by the manner in which knowledge is employed in a society, the way in which it is exploited, divided and, in some ways, attributed. It is worth recalling at this point, if only symbolically, the old Greek adage, that arithmetic should be taught in democracies, for it teaches relations of equality, but that geometry alone should be reserved for oligarchies, as it demonstrates the proportions within inequality.

Finally, I believe that this will to knowledge, thus reliant upon institutional support and distribution, tends to exercise a sort of pressure, a power of constraint upon other forms of discourse—I am speaking of our own society. I am thinking of the way Western literature has, for centuries, sought to base itself in nature, in the plausible, upon sincerity and science—in short, upon true discourse. I am thinking, too, of the way economic practices, codified into precepts and recipes—as morality, too—have sought, since the eighteenth century, to found themselves, to rationalise and justify their currency, in a theory of wealth and production; I am thinking, again, of the manner in which such prescriptive ensembles as the Penal Code have sought their bases or justifications. For example, the Penal Code started out as a theory of Right; then, from the time of the nineteenth century, people looked for its validation in sociological, psychological, medical and psychiatric knowledge. It is as though the very words of the law had no authority in our society, except insofar as they are derived from true discourse. Of the three great systems of exclusion governing discourse—prohibited words, the division of madness and the will to truth—I have spoken at greatest length concerning the third. With good reason: for centuries, the former have continually tended toward the latter; because this last has, gradually, been attempting to assimilate the others in order both to modify them and to provide them with a firm foundation. Because, if the two former are continually growing more fragile and less certain to the extent that they are now invaded by the will to truth, the latter, in contrast, daily grows in strength, in depth and implacability.

And yet we speak of it least. As though the will to truth and its vicissitudes were masked by truth itself and its necessary unfolding. The reason is perhaps this: if, since the time of the Greeks, true discourse no longer responds to desire or to that which exercises power in the will to truth, in the will to speak out in true discourse, what, then, is at work, if not desire and power? True discourse, liberated by the nature of its form from desire and power, is incapable of recognising the will to truth which pervades it; and the will to truth, having imposed itself upon us for so long, is such that the truth it seeks to reveal cannot fail to mask it.

Thus, only one truth appears before our eyes: wealth, fertility and sweet strength in all its insidious universality. In contrast, we are unaware of the prodigious machinery of the will to truth, with its vocation of exclusion. All those who, at one moment or another in our history, have attempted to remould this will to truth and to turn it against truth at that very point where truth undertakes to justify the taboo, and to define madness; all those, from Nietzsche to Artaud and Bataille, must now stand as (probably haughty) signposts for all our future work.

There are, of course, many other systems for the control and delimitation of discourse. Those I have spoken of up to now are, to some extent, active on the exterior; they function as systems of exclusion; they concern that part of discourse which deals with power and desire.

I believe we can isolate another group: internal rules, where discourse exercises its own control; rules concerned with the principles of classification, ordering and distribution. It is as though we were now involved in the mastery of another dimension of discourse: that of events and chance.

In the first place, commentary. I suppose, though I am not altogether sure, there is barely a society without its major narratives, told, retold and varied; formulae, texts, ritualised texts to be spoken in well-defined circumstances; things said once, and conserved because people suspect some hidden secret or wealth lies buried within. In short, I suspect one could find a kind of gradation between different types of discourse within most societies: discourse 'uttered' in the course of the day and in casual meetings, and which disappears with the very act which gave rise to it; and those forms of discourse that lie at the origins of a certain number of new verbal acts, which are reiterated, transformed or discussed; in short, discourse which *is spoken* and remains spoken, indefinitely, beyond its formulation, and which remains to be spoken. We know them in our own cultural system: religious or juridical texts, as well as some curious texts, from the point of view of their status, which we term 'literary'; to a certain extent, scientific texts also.

What is clear is that this gap is neither stable, nor constant, nor absolute. There is no question of there being one category, fixed for all time, reserved for fundamental or creative discourse, and another for those which reiterate, expound and comment. Not a few major texts become blurred and disappear, and commentaries sometimes come to occupy the former position. But while the details of application may well change, the function remains the same, and the principle of hierarchy remains at work. The radical denial of this gradation can never be anything but play, utopia or anguish. Play, as Borges uses the term, in the form of commentary that is nothing more than the reappearance, word for word (though this time it is solemn and anticipated) of the text commented on; or again, the play of a work of criticism talking endlessly about a work that does not exist. It is a lyrical dream of talk reborn, utterly afresh and innocent, at each point; continually reborn in all its vigour, stimulated by things, feelings or thoughts. Anguish, such as that of Janet when sick, for whom the least utterance sounded as the 'word of the Evangelist', concealing an inexhaustible wealth of meaning, worthy to be broadcast, rebegun, commented upon indefinitely: 'When I think', he said on reading or listening; 'When I think of this phrase, continuing its journey through eternity, while I, perhaps, have only incompletely understood it . . .'

But who can fail to see that this would be to annul one of the terms of the relationship each time, and not to suppress the relationship itself? A relationship in continual process of modification; a relationship taking multiple and diverse forms in a given epoch: juridical exegesis is very different—and has been for a long time—from religious commentary; a single work of literature can give rise, simultaneously, to several distinct types of discourse. The *Odyssey,* as a primary text, is repeated in the same epoch, in Berand's translation, in infinite textual explanations and in Joyce's *Ulysses.*

For the time being, I would like to limit myself to pointing out that, in what we generally refer to as commentary, the difference between primary text and secondary text plays two interdependent roles. On the one hand, it permits us to create new discourses ad infinitum: the top-heaviness of the original text, its permanence, its status as discourse ever capable of being brought up to date, the multiple or hidden meanings with which it is credited, the reticence and wealth it is believed to contain, all this creates an open possibility for discussion. On the other hand, whatever the techniques employed, commentary's only role is to say *finally,* what has silently been articulated *deep down.* It must—and the paradox is ever-changing yet inescapable—say, for the first time, what has already been said, and repeat tirelessly what was, nevertheless, never said. The infinite rippling of commentary is agitated from within by the dream of masked repetition: in the distance there is, perhaps, nothing other than what was there at the point of departure: simple recitation. Commentary averts the chance element of discourse by giving it its due: it gives us the opportunity to say something other than the text itself, but on condition that it is the text itself which is uttered and, in some ways, finalised. The open multiplicity, the fortuitousness, is transferred, by the principle of commentary, from what is liable to be said to the number, the form, the masks and the circumstances of repetition. The novelty lies no longer in what is said, but in its reappearance.

I believe there is another principle of rarefaction, complementary to the first: the author. Not, of course, the author in the sense of the individual who delivered the speech or wrote the text in question, but the author as the unifying principle in a particular group of writings or statements, lying at the origins of their significance, as the seat of their coherence. This principle is not constant at all times. All around us, there are sayings and texts whose meaning or effectiveness has nothing to do with any author to whom they might be attributed: mundane remarks, quickly forgotten; orders and contacts that are signed, but have no recognisable author; technical prescriptions anonymously transmitted. But even in those fields where it is normal to attribute a work to an author—literature, philosophy, science—the principle does not always play the same role; in the order of scientific discourse, it was, during the Middle Ages, indispensable that a scientific text be attributed to an author, for the author was the index of the work's truthfulness. A proposition was held to derive its scientific value from its author. But since the seventeenth century this function has been steadily declining; it barely survives now, save to give a name to a theorem, an effect, an example or a syndrome. In literature, however, and from about the same period, the author's function has become steadily more important. Now, we demand of all those narratives, poems, dramas and comedies which circulated relatively anonymously throughout the Middle Ages, whence they come, and we virtually insist they tell us who wrote them. We ask authors to answer for the unity of the works published in their names; we ask that they reveal, or at least display the hidden sense pervading their work; we ask them to reveal their personal lives, to account for their experiences and the real story that gave birth to their writings. The author is he who implants, into the troublesome language of fiction, its unities, its coherence, its links with reality.

I know what people are going to say: 'But there you are speaking of the author in the same way as the critic reinvents him after he is dead and buried, when we are left with no more than a tangled mass of scrawlings. Of course, then you have to put a little order into what is left, you have to imagine a structure, a cohesion, the sort of theme you might expect to arise out of an author's consciousness or his life, even if it is a little fictitious. But all that cannot get away from the fact the author existed, irrupting into the midst of all the words employed, infusing them with his genius, or his chaos'.

Of course, it would be ridiculous to deny the existence of individuals who write, and invent. But I think that, for some time, at least, the individual who sits down to write a text, at the edge of which lurks a possible *œuvre,* resumes the functions of the author. What he writes and does not write, what he sketches out, even preliminary sketches for the work, and what he drops as simple mundane remarks, all this interplay of differences is prescribed by the author-function. It is from his new position, as an author, that he will fashion—from all he might have said, from all he says daily, at any time—the still shaky profile of his *œuvre.*

Commentary limited the hazards of discourse through the action of an *identity* taking the form of *repetition* and *sameness.* The author principle limits this same chance element through the action of an *identity* whose form is that of *individuality* and the *I.*

But we have to recognise another principle of limitation in what we call, not sciences, but 'disciplines'. Here is yet another relative, mobile principle, one which enables us to construct, but within a narrow framework.

The organisation of disciplines is just as much opposed to the commentary-principle as it is to that of the author. Opposed to that of the author, because disciplines are defined by groups of objects, methods, their corpus of propositions considered to be true, the interplay of rules and definitions, of techniques and tools: all these constitute a sort of anonymous system, freely available to whoever wishes, or whoever is able to make use of them, without there being any question of their meaning or their validity being derived from whoever happened to invent them. But the principles involved in the formation of disciplines are equally opposed to that of commentary. In a discipline, unlike in commentary, what is supposed at the point of departure is not some meaning which must be rediscovered, nor an identity to be reiterated; it is that which is required for the construction of new statements. For a discipline to exist, there must be the possibility of formulating—and of doing so ad infinitum—fresh propositions.

But there is more, and there is more, probably, in order that there may be less. A discipline is not the sum total of all the truths that may be uttered concerning something; it is not even the total of all that may be accepted, by virtue of some principle of coherence and systematisation, concerning some given fact or proposition. Medicine does not consist of all that may be truly said about disease; botany cannot be defined by the sum total of the truths one could say about plants. There are two reasons for this, the first being that botany and medicine, like other disciplines, consist of errors as well as truths, errors that are in no way residuals, or foreign bodies, but having their own positive functions and their own valid history, such that their roles are often indissociable from that of the truths. The other reason is that, for a proposition to belong to botany or pathology, it must fulfil certain conditions, in a stricter and more complex sense than that of pure and simple truth: at any rate, other conditions. The proposition must refer to a specific range of objects; from the end of the seventeenth century, for example, a proposition, to be 'botanical', had to be concerned with the visible structure of plants, with its system of close and not so close resemblances, or with the behavior of its fluids; (but it could no longer retain, as had still been the case in the sixteenth century, references to its symbolic value or to the virtues and properties accorded it in antiquity). But without belonging to any discipline, a proposition is obliged to utilize conceptual instruments and techniques of a well-defined type; from the nineteenth century onwards, a proposition was no longer medical—it became 'non-medical', becoming more of an individual fantasy or item of popular imagery—if it employed metaphorical or qualitative terms or notions of essence (congestion, fermented liquids, dessicated solids); in return, it could—it had to—appeal to equally metaphorical notions, though constructed according to a different functional and physiological model (concerning irritation, inflammation or the decay of tissue). But there is more still, for in order to belong to a discipline, a proposition must fit into a certain type of theoretical field. Suffice it to recall that the quest for primitive language, a perfectly acceptable theme up to the eighteenth century, was enough, in the second half of the nineteenth century, to throw any discourse into, I hesitate to say error, but into a world of chimera and reverie—into pure and simple linguistic monstrosity.

Within its own limits, every discipline recognises true and false propositions, but it repulses a whole teratology of learning. The exterior of a science is both more, and less, populated than one might think: certainly, there is immediate experience, imaginary themes bearing on and continually accompanying immemorial beliefs; but perhaps there are no errors in the strict sense of the term, for error can only emerge and be identified within a well-defined process; there are monsters on the prowl, however, whose forms alter with the history of knowledge. In short, a proposition must fulfil some onerous and complex conditions before it can be admitted within a discipline; before it can be pronounced true or false it must be, as Monsieur Canguilhem might say, 'within the true'.

People have often wondered how on earth nineteenth-century botanists and biologists managed not to see the truth of Mendel's statements. But it was precisely because Mendel spoke of objects, employed methods and placed himself within a theoretical perspective totally alien to the biology of his time. But then, Naudin had suggested that hereditary traits constituted a separate element before him; and yet, however novel or unfamiliar the principle may have been, it was nevertheless reconcilable, if only as an enigma, with biological discourse. Mendel, on the other hand, announced that hereditary traits constituted an absolutely new biological object, thanks to a hitherto untried system of filtrage: he detached them from species, from the sex transmitting them, the field in which he observed being that infinitely open series of generations in which hereditary traits appear and disappear with statistical regularity. Here was a new object, calling for new conceptual tools, and for fresh theoretical foundations. Mendel spoke the truth, but he was not *dans le vrai* (within the true) of contemporary biological discourse: it simply was not along such lines that objects and biological concepts were formed. A whole change in scale, the deployment of a totally new range of objects in biology was required before Mendel could enter into the true and his propositions appear, for the most part, exact. Mendel was a true monster, so much so that science could not even properly speak of him. And yet Schleiden, for example, thirty years earlier, denying, at the height of the nineteenth century, vegetable sexuality, was committing no more than a disciplined error.

It is always possible one could speak the truth in a void; one would only be in the true, however, if one obeyed the rules of some discursive 'policy' which would have to be reactivated every time one spoke.

Disciplines constitute a system of control in the production of discourse, fixing its limits through the action of an identity taking the form of a permanent reactivation of the rules.

We tend to see, in an author's fertility, in the multiplicity of commentaries and in the development of a discipline so many infinite resources available for the creation of discourse. Perhaps so, but they are nonetheless principles of constraint, and it is probably impossible to appreciate their positive, multiplicatory role without first taking into consideration their restrictive, constraining role.

There is, I believe, a third group of rules serving to control discourse. Here, we are no longer dealing with the mastery of the powers contained within discourse, nor with averting the hazards of its appearance; it is more a question of determining the conditions under which it may be employed, of imposing a certain number of rules upon those individuals who employ it, thus denying access to everyone else. This amounts to a rarefaction among speaking subjects: none may enter into discourse on a specific subject unless he has satisfied certain conditions or if he is not, from the outset, qualified to do so. More exactly, not all areas of discourse are equally open and penetrable; some are forbidden territory (differentiated and differentiating) while others are virtually open to the winds and stand, without any prior restrictions, open to all.

Here, I would like to recount a little story so beautiful I fear it may well be true. It encompasses all the constraints of discourse: those limiting its powers, those controlling its chance appearances and those which select from among speaking subjects. At the beginning of the seventeenth century, the Shogun heard tell of European superiority in navigation, commerce, politics and the military arts, and that this was due to their knowledge of mathematics. He wanted to obtain this precious knowledge. When someone told him of an English sailor possessed of this marvelous discourse, he summoned him to his palace and kept him there. The Shogun took lessons from the mariner in private and familiarised himself with mathematics, after which he retained power and lived to a very old age. It was not until the nineteenth century that there were *Japanese* mathematicians. But that is not the end of the anecdote, for it has its European aspect as well. The story has it that the English sailor, Will Adams, was a carpenter and an autodidact. Having worked in a shipyard he had learnt geometry. Can we see in this narrative the expression of one of the great myths of European culture? To the monopolistic, secret knowledge of oriental tyranny, Europe opposed the universal communication of knowledge and the infinitely free exchange of discourse.

This notion does not, in fact, stand up to close examination. Exchange and communication are positive forces at play within complex but restrictive systems; it is probable that they cannot operate independently of these. The most superficial and obvious of these restrictive systems is constituted by what we collectively refer to as ritual; ritual defines the qualifications required of the speaker (of who in dialogue, interrogation or recitation, should occupy which position and formulate which type of utterance); it lays down gestures to be made, behaviour, circumstances and the whole range of signs that must accompany discourse; finally, it lays down the supposed, or imposed significance of the words used, their effect upon those to whom they are addressed, the limitations of their constraining validity. Religious discourse, juridical and therapeutic as well as, in some ways, political discourse are all barely dissociable from the functioning of a ritual that determines the individual properties and agreed roles of the speakers.

A rather different function is filled by 'fellowships of discourse', whose function is to preserve or to reproduce discourse, but in order that it should circulate within a closed community, according to strict regulations, without those in possession being dispossessed by this very distribution. An archaic model of this would be those groups of Rhapsodists, possessing knowledge of poems to recite or, even, upon which to work variations and transformations. But though the ultimate object of this knowledge was ritual recitation, it was protected and preserved within a determinate group, by the, often extremely complex, exercises of memory implied by such a process. Apprenticeship gained access both to a group and to a secret which recitation made manifest, but did not divulge. The roles of speaking and listening were not interchangeable.

Few such 'fellowships of discourse' remain, with their ambiguous interplay of secrecy and disclosure. But do not be deceived; even in true discourse, even in the order of published discourse, free from all ritual, we still find secret-appropriation and non-interchangeability at work. It could even be that the act of writing, as it is institutionalised today, with its books, its publishing system and the personality of the writer, occurs within a diffuse, yet constraining, 'fellowship of discourse'. The separateness of the writer, continually opposed to the activity of all other writing and speaking subjects, the intransitive character he lends to his discourse, the fundamental singularity he has long accorded to 'writing', the affirmed dissymmetry between 'creation' and any use of linguistic systems—all this manifests in its formulation (and tends moreover to accompany the interplay of these factors in practice) the existence of a certain 'fellowship of discourse'. But there are many others, functioning according to entirely different schemas of exclusivity and disclosure: one has only to think of technical and scientific secrets, of the forms of diffusion and circulation in medical discourse, of those who have appropriated economic or political discourse.

At first sight, 'doctrine' (religious, political, philosophical) would seem to constitute the very reverse of a 'fellowship of discourse'; for among the latter, the number of speakers were, if not fixed, at least limited, and it was among this number that discourse was allowed to circulate and be transmitted. Doctrine, on the other hand, tends to diffusion: in the holding in common of a single ensemble of discourse that individuals, as many as you wish, could define their reciprocal allegiance. In appearance, the sole requisite is the recognition of the same truths and the acceptance of a certain rule—more or less flexible—of conformity with validated discourse. If it were a question of just that, doctrines would barely be any different from scientific disciplines, and discursive control would bear merely on the form or content of what was uttered, and not on the speaker. Doctrinal adherence, however, involves both speaker and the spoken, the one through the other. The speaking subject is involved through, and as a result of, the spoken, as is demonstrated by the rules of exclusion and the rejection mechanism brought into play when a speaker formulates one, or many, inassimilable utterances; questions of heresy and unorthodoxy in no way arise out of fanatical exaggeration of doctrinal mechanisms; they are a fundamental part of them. But conversely, doctrine involves the utterances of speakers in the sense that doctrine is, permanently, the sign, the manifestation and the instrument of a prior adherence—adherence to a class, to a social or racial status, to a nationality or an interest, to a struggle, a revolt, resistance or acceptance. Doctrine links individuals to certain types of utterance while consequently barring them from all others. Doctrine effects a dual subjection, that of speaking subjects to discourse, and that of discourse to the group, at least virtually, of speakers.

Finally, on a much broader scale, we have to recognise the great cleavages in what one might call the social appropriation of discourse. Education may well be, as of right, the instrument whereby every individual, in a society like our own, can gain access to any kind of discourse. But we well know that in its distribution, in what it permits and in what it prevents, it follows the well-trodden battle-lines of social conflict. Every educational system is a political means of maintaining or of modifying the appropriation of discourse, with the knowledge and the powers it carries with it.

I am well aware of the abstraction I am performing when I separate, as I have just done, verbal rituals, 'fellowships of discourse', doctrinal groups and social appropriation. Most of the time they are linked together, constituting great edifices that distribute speakers among the different types of discourse, and which appropriate those types of discourse to certain categories of subject. In a word, let us say that these are the main rules for the subjection of discourse. What is an educational system, after all, if not a ritualisation of the word; if not a qualification of some fixing of roles for speakers; if not the constitution of a (diffuse) doctrinal group; if not a distribution and an appropriation of discourse, with all its learning and its powers? What is 'writing' (that of 'writers') if not a similar form of subjection, perhaps taking rather different forms, but whose main stresses are nonetheless analogous? May we not also say that the judicial system, as well as institutionalised medicine, constitute similar systems for the subjection of discourse?

I wonder whether a certain number of philosophical themes have not come to conform to this activity of limitation and exclusion and perhaps even to reinforce it.

They conform, first of all, by proposing an ideal truth as a law of discourse, and an immanent rationality as the principle of their behaviour. They accompany, too, an ethic of knowledge, promising truth only to the desire for truth itself and the power to think it.

They then go on to reinforce this activity by denying the specific reality of discourse in general.

Ever since the exclusion of the activity and commerce of the sophists, ever since their paradoxes were muzzled, more or less securely, it would seem that Western thought has seen to it that discourse be permitted as little room as possible between thought and words. It would appear to have ensured that *to discourse* should appear merely as a certain interjection between speaking and thinking; that it should constitute thought, clad in its signs and rendered visible by words or, conversely, that the structures of language themselves should be brought into play, producing a certain effect of meaning.

This very ancient elision of the reality of discourse in philosophical thought has taken many forms in the course of history. We have seen it quite recently in the guise of many themes now familiar to us.

It seems to me that the theme of the founding subject permits us to elide the reality of discourse. The task of the founding subject is to animate the empty forms of language with his objectives; through the thickness and inertia of empty things, he grasps intuitively the meanings lying within them. Beyond time, he indicates the field of meanings—leaving history to make them explicit—in which propositions, sciences, and deductive ensembles ultimately find their foundation. In this relationship with meaning, the founding subject has signs, marks, tracks, letters at his disposal. But he does not need to demonstrate these passing through the singular instance of discourse.

The opposing theme, that of originating experience, plays an analogous role. This asserts, in the case of experience, that even before it could be grasped in the form of a *cogito*, prior significations, in some ways already spoken, were circulating in the world, scattering it all about us, and from the outset made possible a sort of primitive recognition. Thus, a primary complicity with the world founds, for us, a possibility of speaking of experience, in it, to designate and name it, to judge it and, finally, to know it in the form of truth. If there is discourse, what could it legitimately be if not a discrete reading? Things murmur meanings our language has merely to extract; from its most primitive beginnings, this language was already whispering to us of a being of which it forms the skeleton.

The theme of universal mediation is, I believe, yet another manner of eliding the reality of discourse. And this despite appearances. At first sight it would seem that, to discover the movement of a logos everywhere elevating singularities into concepts, finally enabling immediate consciousness to deploy all the rationality in the world, is certainly to place discourse at the centre of speculation. But, in truth, this logos is really only another discourse already in operation, or rather, it is things and events themselves which *insensibly* become discourse in the unfolding of the essential secrets. Discourse is no longer much more than the shimmering of a truth about to be born in its own eyes; and when all things come eventually to take the form of discourse, when everything may be said and when anything becomes an excuse for pronouncing a discourse, it will be because all things having manifested and exchanged meanings, they will then all be able to return to the silent interiority of self-consciousness.

Whether it is the philosophy of a founding subject, a philosophy of originating experience or a philosophy of universal mediation, discourse is really only an activity, of writing in the first case, of reading in the second and exchange in the third. This exchange, this writing, this reading never involve anything but signs. Discourse thus nullifies itself, in reality, in placing itself at the disposal of the signifier.

What civilization, in appearance, has shown more respect towards discourse than our own? Where has it been more and better honoured? Where have men depended more radically, apparently, upon its constraints and its universal character? But, it seems to me, a certain fear hides behind this apparent supremacy accorded, this apparent logophilia. It is as though these taboos, these barriers, thresholds and limits were deliberately disposed in order, at least partly, to master and control the great proliferation of discourse, in such a way as to relieve its richness of its most dangerous elements; to organise its disorder so as to skate round its most uncontrollable aspects. It is as though people had wanted to efface all trace of its irruption into the activity of our thought and language. There is undoubtedly in our society, and I would not be surprised to see it in others, though taking different forms and modes, a profound logophobia, a sort of dumb fear of these events, of this mass of spoken things, of everything that could possibly be violent, discontinuous, querulous, disordered even and perilous in it, of the incessant, disorderly buzzing of discourse.

If we wish—I will not say to efface this fear—but to analyse it in its conditions, its activity and its effects, I believe we must resolve ourselves to accept three decisions which our current thinking rather tends to resist, and which belong to the three groups of function I have just mentioned: to question our will to truth; to restore to discourse its character as an event; to abolish the sovereignty of the signifier.

These are the tasks, or rather, some of the themes which will govern my work in the years ahead. One can straight away distinguish some of the methodological demands they imply.

A principle of *reversal,* first of all. Where, according to tradition, we think we recognise the source of discourse, the principles behind its flourishing and continuity, in those factors which seem to play a positive role, such as the author discipline, will to truth, we must rather recognise the negative activity of the cutting-out and rarefaction of discourse.

But, once we have distinguished these principles of rarefaction, once we have ceased considering them as a fundamental and creative action, what do we discover behind them? Should we affirm that a world of uninterrupted discourse would be virtually complete? This is where we have to bring other methodological principles into play.

Next, then, the principle of *discontinuity.* The existence of systems of rarefaction does not imply that, over and beyond them lie great vistas of limitless discourse, continuous and silent, repressed and driven back by them, making it our task to abolish them and at last to restore it to speech. Whether talking in terms of speaking or thinking, we must not imagine some unsaid thing, or an unthought, floating about the world, interlacing with all its forms and events. Discourse must be treated as a discontinuous activity, its different manifestations sometimes coming together, but just as easily unaware of, or excluding each other.

The principle of *specificity* declares that a particular discourse cannot be resolved by a prior system of significations; that we should not imagine that the world presents us with a legible face, leaving us merely to decipher it; it does not work hand in glove with what we already know; there is no prediscursive fate disposing the word in our favour. We must conceive discourse as a violence that we do to things, or, at all events, as a practice we impose upon them; it is in this practice that the events of discourse find the principle of their regularity.

The fourth principle, that of *exteriority,* holds that we are not to burrow to the hidden core of discourse, to the heart of the thought or meaning manifested in it; instead, taking the discourse itself, its appearance and its regularity, that we should look for its external conditions of existence, for that which gives rise to the chance series of these events and fixes its limits.

As the regulatory principles of analysis, then, we have four notions: event series, regularity and the possible conditions of existence. Term for term we find the notion of event opposed to that of creation, the possible conditions of existence opposing signification. These four notions (signification, originality, unity, creation) have, in a fairly general way, dominated the traditional history of ideas; by general agreement one sought the point of creation, the unity of a work, of a period or a theme, one looked also for the mark of individual originality and the infinite wealth of hidden meanings.

I would like to add just two remarks, the first of which concerns history. We frequently credit contemporary history with having removed the individual event from its privileged position and with having revealed the more enduring structures of history. That is so. I am not sure, however, that historians have been working in this direction alone. Or, rather, I do not think one can oppose the identification of the individual event to the analysis of long term trends quite so neatly. On the contrary, it seems to me that it is in squeezing the individual event, in directing the resolving power of historical analysis onto official price-lists (*mercuriales*), title deeds, parish registers, to harbour archives analysed year by year and week by week, that we gradually perceive—beyond battles, decisions, dynasties and assemblies—the emergence of those massive phenomena of secular or multi-secular importance. History, as it is practised today, does not turn its back on events; on the contrary, it is continually enlarging the field of events, constantly discovering new layers—more superficial as well as more profound—incessantly isolating new ensembles—events, numerous, dense and interchangeable or rare and decisive: from daily price fluctuations to secular inflations. What is significant is that history does not consider an event without defining the series to which it belongs, without specifying the method of analysis used, without seeking out the regularity of phenomena and the probable limits of their occurrence, without enquiring about variations, inflexions and the slope of the curve, without desiring to know the conditions on which these depend. History has long since abandoned its attempts to understand events in terms of cause and effect in the formless unity of some great evolutionary process, whether vaguely homogeneous or rigidly hierarchised. It did not do this in order to seek out structures anterior to, alien or hostile to the event. It was rather in order to establish those diverse converging, and sometimes divergent, but never autonomous series that enable us to circumscribe the 'locus' of an event, the limits to its fluidity and the conditions of its emergence.

The fundamental notions now imposed upon us are no longer those of consciousness and continuity (with their correlative problems of liberty and causality), nor are they those of sign and structure. They are notions, rather, of events and of series, with the group of notions linked to these; it is around such an ensemble that this analysis of discourse I am thinking of is articulated, certainly not upon those traditional themes which the philosophers of the past took for 'living' history, but on the effective work of historians.

But it is also here that this analysis poses some, probably awesome philosophical or theoretical problems. If discourses are to be treated first as ensembles of discursive events, what status are we to accord this notion of event, so rarely taken into consideration by philosophers? Of course, an event is neither substance, nor accident, nor quality nor process; events are not corporeal. And yet, an event is certainly not immaterial; it takes effect, becomes effect, always on the level of materiality. Events have their place; they consist in relation to, coexistence with, dispersion of, the cross-checking accumulation and the selection of material elements; it occurs as an effect of, and in, material dispersion. Let us say that the philosophy of event should advance in the direction, at first sight paradoxical, of an incorporeal materialism. If, on the other hand, discursive events are to be dealt with as homogeneous, but discontinuous series, what status are we to accord this discontinuity? Here we are not dealing with a succession of instants in time, nor with the plurality of thinking subjects; what is concerned are those caesurae breaking the instant and dispersing the subject in a multiplicity of possible positions and functions. Such a discontinuity strikes and invalidates the smallest units, traditionally recognised and the least readily contested: the instant and the subject. Beyond them, independent of them, we must conceive—between these discontinuous series of relations which are not in any order of succession (or simultaneity) within any (or several) consciousnesses—and we must elaborate—outside of philosophies of time and subject—a theory of discontinuous systematisation. Finally, if it is true that these discursive, discontinuous series have their regularity, within certain limits, it is clearly no longer possible to establish mechanically causal links or an ideal necessity among their constitutive elements. We must accept the introduction of chance as a category in the production of events. There again, we feel the absence of a theory enabling us to conceive the links between chance and thought.

In the sense that this slender wedge I intend to slip into the history of ideas consists not in dealing with meanings possibly lying behind this or that discourse, but with discourse as regular series and distinct events, I fear I recognise in this wedge a tiny (odious, too, perhaps) device permitting the introduction, into the very roots of thought, of notions of *chance, discontinuity* and *materiality*. This represents a triple peril which one particular form of history attempts to avert by recounting the continuous unfolding of some ideal necessity. But they are three notions which ought to permit us to link the history of systems of thought to the practical work of historians; three directions to be followed in the work of theoretical elaboration.

Following these principles, and referring to this overall view, the analyses I intend to undertake fall into two groups. On the one hand, the 'critical' group which sets the reversal-principle to work. I shall attempt to distinguish the forms of exclusion, limitation and appropriation of which I was speaking earlier; I shall try to show how they are formed, in answer to which needs, how they are modified and displaced, which constraints they have effectively exercised, to what extent they have been worked on. On the other hand, the 'genealogical' group, which brings the three other principles into play: how series of discourse are formed, through, in spite of, or with the aid of these systems of constraint: what were the specific norms for each, and what were their conditions of appearance, growth and variation.

Taking the critical group first, a preliminary group of investigations could bear on what I have designated functions of exclusion. I have already examined one of these for a determinate period: the disjunction of reason and madness in the classical age. Later, we could attempt an investigation of a taboo system in language, that concerning sexuality from the sixteenth to the nineteenth century. In this, we would not be concerned with the manner in which this has progressively—and happily—disappeared, but with the way it has been altered and rearticulated, from the practice of confession, with its forbidden conduct, named, classified, hierarchised down to the smallest detail, to the belated, timid appearance of the treatment of sexuality in nineteenth-century psychiatry and medicine. Of course, these only amount to somewhat symbolic guidelines, but one can already be pretty sure that the stresses will not fall where we expect, and that taboos are not always to be found where we imagine them to be.

For the time being, I would like to address myself to the third system of exclusion. I will envisage it in two ways. Firstly, I would like to try to visualise the manner in which this truth within which we are caught, but which we constantly renew, was selected, but at the same time, was repeated, extended and displaced. I will take first of all the age of the Sophists and its beginning with Socrates, or at least with Platonic philosophy, and I shall try to see how effective, ritual discourse, charged with power and peril, gradually arranged itself into a disjunction between true and false discourse. I shall next take the turn of the sixteenth and seventeenth centuries and the age which, above all in England, saw the emergence of an observational, affirmative science, a certain natural philosophy inseparable, too, from religious ideology—for this certainly constituted a new form of the will to knowledge. In the third place, I shall turn to the beginning of the nineteenth century and the great founding acts of modern science, as well as the formation of industrial society and the accompanying positivist ideology. Three slices out of the morphology of our will to knowledge; three staging posts in our philistinism.

I would also like to consider the same question from quite another angle. I would like to measure the effect of a discourse claiming to be scientific—medical, psychiatric or sociological—on the ensemble of practices and prescriptive discourse of which the penal code consists. The study of psychiatric skills and their role in the penal system will serve as a point of departure and as basic material for this analysis.

It is within this critical perspective, but on a different level, that the analysis of the rules for the limitation of discourse should take place, of those among which I earlier designated the author principle, that of commentary and that of discipline. One can envisage a certain number of studies in this field. I am thinking, for example, of the history of medicine in the sixteenth to nineteenth centuries; not so much an account of discoveries made and concepts developed, but of grasping—from the construction of medical discourse, from all its supporting institutions, from its transmission and its reinforcement,—how the principles of author, commentary and discipline worked in practice; of seeking to know how the great author principle, whether Hippocrates, Galen, Paracelsus and Sydenham, or Boerhaave, became a principle of limitation in medical discourse; how, even late into the nineteenth century, the practice of aphorism and commentary retained its currency and how it was gradually replaced by the emphasis on case-histories and clinical training on actual cases; according to which model medicine sought to constitute itself as a discipline, basing itself at first on natural history and, later, on anatomy and biology.

One could also envisage the way in which eighteenth and nineteenth-century literary criticism and history have constituted the character of the author and the form of the work, utilising, modifying and altering the procedures of religious exegesis, biblical criticism, hagiography, the 'lives' of historical or legendary figures, of autobiography and memoirs. One day, too, we must take a look at Freud's role in psycho-analytical knowledge, so different from that of Newton in physics, or from that an author might play in the field of philosophy (Kant, for example, who originated a totally new way of philosophizing).

These, then, are some of the projects falling within the critical aspect of the task, for the analysis of instances of discursive control. The genealogical aspect concerns the effective formation of discourse, whether within the limits of control, or outside of them, or as is most frequent, on both sides of the delimitation. Criticism analyses the processes of rarefaction, consolidation and unification in discourse; genealogy studies their formation, at once scattered, discontinuous and regular. To tell the truth, these two tasks are not always exactly complementary. We do not find, on the one hand, forms of rejection, exclusion, consolidation or attribution, and, on a more profound level, the spontaneous pouring forth of discourse, which immediately before or after its manifestation, finds itself submitted to selection and control. The regular formation of discourse may, in certain conditions and up to a certain point, integrate control procedures (this is what happens, for example, when a discipline takes on the form and status of scientific discourse). Conversely, modes of control may take on life within a discursive formation (such as literary criticism as the author's constitutive discourse) even though any critical task calling instances of control into play must, at the same time, analyse the discursive regularities through which these instances are formed. Any genealogical description must take into account the limits at play within real formations. The difference between the critical and the genealogical enterprise is not one of object or field, but of point of attack, perspective and delimitation.

Earlier on I mentioned one possible study, that of the taboos in discourse on sexuality. It would be difficult, and in any case abstract, to try to carry out this study, without at the same time analysing literary, religious and ethical, biological and medical, as well as juridical discursive ensembles: wherever sexuality is discussed, wherever it is named or described, metaphorised, explained or judged. We are a very long way from having constituted a unitary, regular discourse concerning sexuality; it may be that we never will, and that we are not even travelling in that direction. No matter. Taboos are homogeneous neither in their forms nor their behaviour whether in literary or medical discourse, in that of psychiatry or of the direction of consciousness. Conversely, these different discursive regularities do not divert or alter taboos in the same manner. It will only be possible to undertake this study, therefore, if we take into account the plurality of series within which the taboos, each one to some extent different from all the others, are at work.

We could also consider those series of discourse which, in the sixteenth and seventeenth centuries, dealt with wealth and poverty, money, production and trade. Here, we would be dealing with some pretty heterogeneous ensembles of enunciations, formulated by rich and poor, the wise and the ignorant, protestants and catholics, royal officials, merchants or moralists. Each one has its forms of regularity and, equally, its systems of constraint. None of them precisely prefigures that other form of regularity that was to acquire the momentum of a discipline and which was later to be known, first as 'the study of wealth' and, subsequently, 'political economy'. And yet, it was from the foregoing that a new regularity was formed, retrieving or excluding, justifying or rejecting, this or that utterance from these old forms.

One could also conceive a study of discourse concerning heredity, such as it can be gleaned, dispersed as it was until the beginning of the twentieth century, among a variety of disciplines, observations, techniques and formulae; we would be concerned to show the process whereby these series eventually became subsumed under the single system, now recognised as epistemologically coherent, known as genetics. This is the work François Jacob has just completed, with unequalled brilliance and scholarship.

It is thus that critical and genealogical descriptions are to alternate, support and complete each other. The critical side of the analysis deals with the systems enveloping discourse; attempting to mark out and distinguish the principles of ordering, exclusion and rarity in discourse. We might, to play with our words, say it practises a kind of studied casualness. The genealogical side of discourse, by way of contrast, deals with series of effective formation of discourse: it attempts to grasp it in its power of affirmation, by which I do not mean a power opposed to that of negation, but the power of constituting domains of objects, in relation to which one can affirm or deny true or false propositions. Let us call these domains of objects positivist and, to play on words yet again, let us say that, if the critical style is one of studied casualness, then the genealogical mood is one of felicitous positivism.

At all events, one thing at least must be emphasised here: that the analysis of discourse thus understood, does not reveal the universality of a meaning, but brings to light the action of imposed rarity, with a fundamental power of affirmation. Rarity and affirmation; rarity, in the last resort of affirmation—certainly not any continuous outpouring of meaning, and certainly not any monarchy of the signifier.

And now, let those who are weak on vocabulary, let those with little comprehension of theory call all this—if its appeal is stronger than its meaning for them—structuralism.

I am well aware that I could never have begun to undertake these researches I have just outlined to you, were I not able to benefit from the aid of certain models and props. I believe I owe much to Monsieur Dumézil, for it was he who encouraged me to work at an age when I still thought writing a pleasure. But I owe a lot, too, to his work; may he forgive me if I have wandered from the meaning and rigour of his texts, which dominate us today. It is he who taught me to analyse the internal economy of discourse quite differently from the traditional methods of exegesis or those of linguistic formalism. It is he who taught me to refer the system of functional correlations from one discourse to another by means of comparison. It was he, again, who taught me to describe the transformations of a discourse, and its relations to the institution. If I have wished to apply a similar method to discourse quite other than legendary or mythical narratives, it is because before me lay the works of the historians of science, above all, that of Monsieur Canguilhem. I owe it to him that I understood that the history of science did not necessarily involve, either an account of discoveries, or descriptions of the ideas and opinions bordering science either from the side of its doubtful beginnings, or from the side of its fall-out; but that one could—that one should—treat the history of science as an ensemble, at once coherent, and transformable into theoretical models and conceptual instruments.

A large part of my indebtedness, however, is to Jean Hyppolite. I know that, for many, his work is associated with that of Hegel, and that our age, whether through logic or epistemology, whether through Marx or through Nietzsche, is attempting to flee Hegel: and what I was attempting to say earlier concerning discourse was pretty disloyal to Hegel.

But truly to escape Hegel involves an exact appreciation of the price we have to pay to detach ourselves from him. It assumes that we are aware of the extent to which Hegel, insidiously perhaps, is close to us; it implies a knowledge, in that which permits us to think against Hegel, of that which remains Hegelian. We have to determine the extent to which our anti-Hegelianism is possibly one of his tricks directed against us, at the end of which he stands, motionless, waiting for us.

If, then, more than one of us is indebted to Jean Hyppolite, it is because he has tirelessly explored, for us, and ahead of us, the path along which we may escape Hegel, keep our distance, and along which we shall find ourselves brought back to him, only from a different angle, and then, finally, be forced to leave him behind, once more.

First, Hyppolite took the trouble to give some presence to this great, slightly phantomlike shadow that was Hegel, prowling through the nineteenth century, with whom men struggled in the dark. He gave Hegel this presence with his translation of the *Phenomonology of the mind;* proof of the extent to which Hegel came to life in this text was the number of Germans who came to consult this text in order to understand what, for a moment at least, had become the German version.

From this text, Hyppolite sought out and explored all the issues, as though his chief concern had become: can one still philosophize where Hegel is no longer possible? Can any philosophy continue to exist that is no longer Hegelian? Are the non-Hegelian elements in our thought necessarily non-philosophical? Is that which is anti-philosophical necessarily non-Hegelian? As well as giving us this Hegelian presence, he sought not merely a meticulous historical description: he wanted to turn Hegel into a schema for the experience of modernity (is it possible to think of the sciences, politics and daily suffering as a Hegelian?) and he wanted, conversely, to make modernity the test of Hegelianism and, beyond that, of philosophy. For Hyppolite, the relationship with Hegel was the scene of an experiment, of a confrontation in which it was never certain that philosophy would come out on top. He never saw the Hegelian system as a reassuring universe; he saw in it the field in which philosophy took the ultimate risk.

From this stem, I believe, the alterations he worked, not within Hegelian philosophy, but upon it, and upon philosophy as Hegel conceived it; from this also, a complete inversion of themes. Instead of conceiving philosophy as a totality ultimately capable of dispersing and regrouping itself in the movement of the concept, Jean Hyppolite transformed it into an endless task, against the background of an infinite horizon. Because it was a task without end, it was also a task in process of continuous recommencement, given over to the forms and paradoxes of repetition. For Hyppolite, philosophy, as the thought of the inaccessible totality, was that which could be rejected in the extreme irregularity of experience; it was that which presents and reveals itself as the continually recurring question in life, death and in memory. Thus he transformed the Hegelian theme of the end of self-consciousness into one of repeated interrogation. But because it consisted in repetition, this philosophy did not lie beyond concepts; its task was not that of abstraction, it was, rather, to maintain a certain reticence, to break with acquired generalisations and continually to reestablish contact with the non-philosophical; it was to draw as close as possible, not to its final fulfilment, but to that which precedes it, that which has not yet stirred its uncertainty. In order not to reduce them, but to think them, this philosophy was to examine the singularity of history, the regional rationalities of science, the depths of memory in consciousness; thus arose the notion of a philosophy that was present, uncertain, mobile all along its line of contact with non-philosophy, existing on its own, however, and revealing the meaning this non-philosophy has for us. But, if it is in repeated contact with non-philosophy, where then lies the beginning of philosophy? Is it already there, secretly present in that which is not philosophy, beginning to formulate itself half under its breath, amid the murmuring of things? But, perhaps, from that point on, philosophy has no *raison d'être,* or, maybe, philosophy should start out on a priori foundations? We see, thus, the theme of the foundations of discourse and its formal structure substituting itself for the Hegelian one of present movement.

The final alteration Jean Hyppolite worked upon Hegelian philosophy was this: if philosophy really must begin as absolute discourse, then what of history, and what is this beginning which starts out with a singular individual, within a society and a social class, and in the midst of struggle?

These five alterations, leading to the very extremities of Hegelian philosophy, doubtless forcing it to spill over its own limits, evoke by turns the great figures of modern philosophy Jean Hyppolite ceaselessly opposed to Hegel: Marx, with his questions of history; Fichte, and the problem of the absolute beginnings of philosophy; Bergson's theme of contact with non-philosophy; Kierkegaard, with the problem of repetition and truth; Husserl, and the theme of philosophy as an infinite task, linked to the history of our rationality. Beyond these philosophical figures we can perceive all those fields of knowledge Hyppolite invoked around his own questions: psychoanalysis, with its strange logic of desire; mathematics and the formalisation of discourse; information theory and its application to the analysis of life—in short, all those fields giving rise to questions of logic and existence, continually intertwining and unravelling their links.

I think this work, articulated in a small number of major books, but, even more, invested in research, teaching, in a perpetual attentiveness, in an everyday alertness and generosity, in its apparently administrative and pedagogic responsibilities (*i.e.,* doubly political), has traversed and formulated the most fundamental problems of our age. Many of us are infinitely indebted to him.

It is because I have borrowed both the meaning and the possibility of what I am doing from him; because, often, he enlightened me when I struck out blindly; because I would like to dedicate my work to him, that I end this presentation of my projected work by invoking the name of Jean Hyppolite. It is towards him, towards that hiatus—where I feel at once his absence and my failings—that the questions I now ask myself are pointing.

Because I owe him so much, I well understand that your choice, in inviting me to teach here is, in good part, a homage to Jean Hyppolite. I am profoundly grateful to you for the honour you have done me, but I am no less equal to the challenge of succeeding him, I know nonetheless that, if that happiness should have been granted us, I should have been encouraged by his indulgence this evening.

I now understand better why I experienced so much difficulty when I began speaking, earlier on. I now know which voice it was I would have wished for, preceding me, supporting me, inviting me to speak and lodging within my own speech. I know now just what was so awesome about beginning; for it was here, where I speak now, that I listened to that voice, and where its possessor is no longer, to hear me speak.

INTRODUCTION TO MOLEFI KETE ASANTE

Molefi Kete Asante (born in 1942) is one of the leading proponents of *Afrocentric* cultural theory and criticism. Asante earned his Ph.D. at UCLA and has taught at several major American universities. At this writing Asante teaches at Temple University, where he founded an internationally known doctoral program in Afrocentric studies. Asante is the author of many books and articles (some in his former name of Arthur L. Smith) on African-American rhetoric, protest and political rhetoric, and Africology. Among leading Africologists, Asante is the most consistently rhetorical in his theoretical writings.

We have noted that one major development in twentieth century rhetorical theory and practice has been the recovery of speakers and writers from the margins of history. Other selections in this anthology attest to greater attention to the rhetoric of women in this century. Another important development has been greater attention to the rhetoric of racial and ethnic groups that have been marginalized, particularly in the United States. Often described as culture-centered rhetorical theories, scholarly work is proceeding on several fronts to understand the rhetorical practices of Americans of African, Asian, Native American, and Latino heritage. At this writing, the best developed literature in culture-centered rhetorical theory is Afrocentric, identifying the rhetorical practices and experiences of Americans of African cultural background. In that literature, Asante's contributions stand above the rest in both quantity and quality.

Two chapters from Asante's book *The Afrocentric Idea* are excerpted here. The idea of rhetorical condition is key to understanding Asante's Afrocentric rhetorical theory. Asante defines rhetorical condition as "the structure and power pattern, assumed or imposed, during a rhetorical situation by society." These rules and conditions for how rhetoric is practiced are culturally determined. The most visible rhetorical practices follow rhetorical conditions established by the Eurocentric (grounded in a European cultural heritage) condition. Asante argues that we need to know Afrocentric rhetorical conditions and how they differ from the Eurocentric if we are to understand African-American rhetorical practices.

Asante compares Eurocentric and Afrocentric rhetorical conditions on just a few key points in this selection, chiefly stressing the idea that Eurocentric rhetoric is hierarchical and Afrocentric rhetoric is not. The characteristics of Eurocentric rhetoric are traced to its theoretical birth in ancient Greece. Asante argues that Eurocentric culture in general is influenced by the conditions it would impose on rhetorical practice.

In the second chapter reprinted here, Asante develops at greater length the characteristics of an Afrocentric rhetorical condition. He is theorizing the chief categories for practicing, understanding, and critiquing Afrocentric rhetoric. The key to Afrocentric rhetoric, Asante argues, is its attempt "to create harmony and balance in the midst of disharmony and indecision." To understand how Afrocentric rhetoric does that, one must examine the categories of *rhythm, styling, language, improvisation, indirection,* and *sound.* Other Afrocentric theorists cited by Asante identify rhetorical appeals to humanism, communalism, empathy, and other values as typical characteristics of Afrocentric rhetoric. Asante's overall claim is that the "rules" for rhetoric, what will appeal to an audience, are different for those of Afrocentric cultural heritage than they are for those of Eurocentric cultural heritage. If one wishes to understand how rhetoric works for many different kinds of people, one must therefore be attuned to the conditions imposed on rhetorical practice by their culture.

We have noted that a major theoretical development in twentieth century rhetoric has been to think of rhetoric as something other than one speaker trying to get an advantage over others through persuasion. Richards has seen rhetoric as remedying misunderstanding, and Burke sees it as finding common ground. Asante's theories show us not only how to understand Afrocentric rhetoric, they also position Afrocentric rhetoric as "ahead of its time" insofar as it is an alternative to the traditional, hierarchic view of rhetoric. Mainstream rhetorical theory and practice in the twentieth century can be seen as *moving toward* an understanding of what rhetoric is and should be which has been held for centuries by people of African heritage.

MOLEFI KETE ASANTE

The Afrocentric Idea

RHETORICAL CONDITION AS A CONCEPTUAL FIELD

Einstein is quoted as having said modern quantum physics "is theory which decides what we can observe."[1] What Einstein meant was that the scientist's freedom is restricted by the language he accepts. It is impossible to break out of a narrow frame of reference if you are not given the capability to dream of what can be. Only certain kinds of information can be acquired if we employ certain kinds of theoretical rules. Noam Chomsky found this in language and Howard Gardner (of Project Zero) has indicated as much in the patterns of music. However, the linguistic and cognitive patterns are not the only generators of restriction; one can be restricted by the general political situation, where the rules of the game are different for different players.

The last five hundred years of world history have been devastating for the acquisition of knowledge about other than European cultures. Dominated by whites in Asia, Africa, and Latin America, victimized people have expressed their desire to redress their grievances. Paulo Freire has said (in *The Politics of Education*)[2] that true education is a liberating experience for the peasant. Beyond this, however, is the fact that certain political constructs impose definite limitations in concepts and content on all discourse about reality. Out of these limitations the oppressed, non-free people, who are exploited by ruling classes, those whose wills are enforced, are challenged to struggle against structural discourse that denies their right to freedom and, indeed, their right to existence. Ultimately, the acting out or the speaking out of the word is also confined to the categories established by the early power brokers for the dominant society. That is why I speak of the empowering of the oppressed by listening to their voices.

Rhetorical Conditions and Power Structures

Rhetoric has been tied to the linguistic postulate that the form of a public discourse must express a statement that is reasonably controlled by the emitter, and one that can potentially be understood by the receiver. This is a euro-linear construction, situated in a stimulus-response ideology, that places responsibility on both the sender and the receiver of a message's content and expression. This view explicates form in the common sense of order of sentence structure—in effect, the syntactical dimension. Yet as far as the African American communicator is concerned, perhaps the most authentic, overarching symbol in discourse is the structure of the rhetorical condition itself. Structure becomes a form of discourse, apart from its character, in the words of a discourse.

Rhetorical condition is the structure and power pattern, assumed or imposed, during a rhetorical situation by society. Although the condition may be negotiated by the communicators, different rhetorical situations produce different conditions because the inherent power relationships change from situation to situation. I do not mean traditional structural concerns of discourse, that is, arrangement and style; these follow almost naturally from the structure of the *discourse as discourse.* There is a rhetoric of structure, not in the sense of a rhetoric about structure, but rather a rhetoric of form about the rhetoric of words. While the structure affects all users of language, it functions to maintain white supremacist views in a rhetorical—that is, symbolic—as well as a political sense.

Structure constitutes a parallel message to the internal structure of discourse. Although Rosenthal was astute in his observations about corollary symbols, he never considered structure itself.[3] Bitzer, on the other hand, wanted to know the context out of which a speaker or writer created discourse.[4] Thus, Lloyd Bitzer is clear, the rhetorical situation is a natural context of persons, events, objects, relations, and an exigence that evokes an utterance. Both Paul Rosenthal and Lloyd Bitzer are ultimately interested in the context of discourse, yet neither recognizes the inherent structural constraints on the context.

Ordinary language philosophers such as Austin and Searle, unlike Rosenthal and Bitzer, have started from the concept of structure in detail, particularly as it relates to the postulates of philosophical reasoning.[5] They have provided some challenging concepts in grammatical usage, but their view is limited for our understanding of the large structural characteristics of a rhetorical condition. Interest in types of propositions may tell us something about the philosopher's linguistic inclinations but it does not get us closer to the question of the overarching condition of discourse in the African American or African context. One might discover, say, that in authoritarian discourse the imperative form is an obvious power set-up in a communicative situation. And we might admit that the use of an imperative in a rhetorical discourse establishes a social environment that signals power. But ultimately the structure of the rhetorical condition is chosen first. Those who listen to a discourse may choose to accept or to resist the structural form of the discourse, yet the choosing of the form—for example, *forensic, deliberate, ceremonial, sermonic,* or *agitational*—is itself the initial commitment to a certain outcome because the rhetorical condition is established as soon as the form is chosen. Madhubuti has said that the black American leaders tend to choose the sermonic form, which limits them in the arena of power. White leaders tend to emerge from business, the academy, and the professions, but blacks, because of the word, tend to find their leaders in the pulpit.[6]

The shortcomings of the sermonic form as a means to power are the least of our worries in the world of ideas. More importantly, the sermon itself is a captive of a larger, more politically significant context. Sermons exist within the framework of the political or ideological context in which the speaker exists. As such, the sermon as a discourse form pays homage to a meta-form of discourse that directs the details of what is possible at any given moment in the sermon. An imperialism of framework operates as viciously as any political or intellectual imperialism ever operated. There is, in the final analysis, a profound dilemma in discourse that articulates itself in the way we, as humans, choose to handle the structural condition. Rhetorical condition, therefore, is not an illusionary concept; it is the source of the subtle machinations of power and manipulation of words and lesser forms.

But how are we to understand discourse in this society, given the rhetorical condition? Daudi provides a significant insight into its nature when he contends that discourse "is the object of a struggle for power."[7] So the real question is "not what is said but who says? And why does he say so? Who takes possession of the discourse, and for what purpose does he do it?"[8] Daudi's point seems to be the importance of power in discourse. Who takes possession of the word? What use is made of the discourse? So now we must ask further, What constitutes a rhetoric of structure? How does one distinguish it from a rhetoric of words? Both are symbolic, yet a rhetoric of structure achieves its ends despite the modification of the stylistic elements of discourse so long as structure remains the same. For example, it does not matter if the language of the imperative is polite and gentle, so long as the imperative structure endures; a social environment has been created where one, for instance, gives orders and the other is expected to obey. Sometimes this occurs in social situations where political and economic power resides in one class or one race and powerlessness in another class or race, for example, South African whites and blacks. Such a rhetorical condition seldom allows reciprocity, despite the illusion, within the framework of a unidirectional perspective. Black communicators tend to seek a redress by moving to neutralize unidirectional rhetoric.

Take, for example, the power of a speaker in an imperative situation. Since the imperative mood in English normally finds its source in the indicative, which expresses a fact that is not in doubt, it becomes the task of the speaker to express that fact. However, whatever reality may exist in the future is held in abeyance by the speaker's attitude as he or she makes pertinent and prudent commands within the context of the rhetorical condition. The speaker, who therefore can control the future, controls a portion of time, and holds a key to the audience's knowledge. Thus, the imperative mood commands the listeners, directs their knowledge, and assesses their performance. An Afrocentric theory explains how one can disidentify from controlling structures, because it is so easy for structure to take over from content and manipulate the message, orchestrate it, at will. Although structure as discourse prevails in all rhetorical situations (Bitzerian), it is politics and religion that provide the more obvious examples. Goldschlager believes that the goal of both religion and politics is to win, not to convince reasonably.[9] He misunderstands the true purpose of rhetorical discourse and has little or no conception of black discourse, because he fails to see its operation in the practical world, that is, in the arena of human interactions in the give and take of decision making, one of the principal civilizing marks of our species.

The confirmation of our freedom and responsibility occurs in the decisions that we make. Therefore, both religion and politics, in the normal course of their activities, seek to win but seek to win reasonably, that is, in such a way as to be perceived as being reasonable. The fact that the reasons employed may not be good enough for the logician or the rhetorician who demands not merely a *perception of rationality* but rationality does not negate the fact that both the speaker and the audience in politics and religion assume credibility in their enterprise. However, the same discourse may be rejected by the audience as unconvincing in its reasons or reasoning. Of course, when significant persons possess "special" knowledge that is unavailable to us, we are more willing to defer to the priests, rabbis, shamans, and preachers. And in our communities we are not devoid of charismatic preachers who use language to demonstrate their special calling. Marcus Garvey, Martin Luther King Jr., Malcolm X, Maulana Karenga, Louis Farrakhan, and Jesse Jackson are consummate orators in the historical tradition.

Since power finds its efficacy in acquiescence, messages structured in a hierarchical manner reduce the leverage of the audience to respond to an incomplete or fragmentary discourse. There are several discourse forms that are hierarchical in the sense they assume that certain communicators hold higher positions of rank, for example, *criticism, sermons, lectures.* Each of these forms, as examples, operating in the rhetorical situation, is structural in character, apart from structure in the message organization. Discourse forms, such as criticism or sermons, are pragmatic and efficient and as such they support the established order, whatever that order happens to be. Marcuse contends that the political system dictates the mode of discourse.[10] In his analysis of the present era, human beings are pretty much manipulated by the architectonic industrial-political-technical environment. What comes out of the speaker's mouth is determined by the society. At another level, however, rhetorical structure dictates relationships, whether in a Marxist or a capitalist society. Marcuse asserts that the immense productivity of the modern economic system provides and satisfies human wants while checking any speculation or emergence that might challenge the established order.

It is clear that any criticism, whether Marxist or capitalist, implies the ability of the critic to judge, assess, evaluate the other. The act of criticizing, therefore, is an act of imposition: One imposes one's own standards onto the other. In order for critical discourse to be effective and valuable, the recipient must acquiesce. In fact, the entire history of Africans in the United States has been marked by a singular resistance to criticism from those who have sought to deny civil and human rights to blacks. Furthermore, this resistance is one supreme negation of the imposition of a racist and oppressive discourse. Nevertheless, the wielding of critical power confers authority in the practical arena of discourse, whether in legislative bodies, political meetings, or intellectual gatherings. It cannot do otherwise, because its natural form is autoreferential. The black politician who criticizes the political policies of the opposition sets herself or himself up as an authority capable of assessing the other. And while the challenge to the opposition is always cast in a hierarchical form, it is not necessarily sustained in the face of a counterchallenge.

Characteristics of Hierarchical Discourse

There are three characteristics for a condition of hierarchical discourse: control over the rhetorical territory through definition, establishment of a self-perpetuating initiation or *rite de passage,* and the stifling of opposing discourse. These characteristics may be seen in the rhetoric of domination. One way to create ambiguity is to redefine established terms in such a manner that the original meaning is lost. Wherever ambiguity exists, the established order is able to occupy the ground of clarity by contending that ambiguity did not exist prior to the rise of the opposition, although the established order may have participated in creating the ambiguous situation. In this manner, the established order can undercut the opposition and manipulate the pattern of communication for its own effect. By defining not only the terms of discussion but also the grounds upon which the discussion will be waged, the established order concentrates power in its own hands.

Octavio Paz has contended that the established order has the ability to impose one vision of the world while exterminating another vision.[11] This is a power unknown to the victims—as victims. It is reserved for the established order by will or power. Thus when one says—as Jerry Falwell, the American leader of the Moral Majority, said after a visit to South Africa in 1985—that the Western world should not impose democracy on the South Africans, one misunderstands the nature of the established order, the Nationalist government of Pieter Botha. No one can impose democracy from the outside; however, the government can prevent democracy from occurring from within by essentially preventing people from choosing it. This is the way the discourse of condition, of structure, operates to confound the best reasons of the victims; it prevents choice. And the prevention of choice is fundamentally an intellectual terrorism, carried on by the established order opposed to the liberation of Freire's peasant. Therefore, the imposition of one vision and the extermination of others must be confronted on intellectual grounds.

The second characteristic of hierarchical discourse is that it creates a self-perpetuating ritual whereby the truth, in effect, is reserved for those who are initiated. To be initiated, in this context, would mean to adhere to a given position. The votarists of a particular position will have received the "word" from some certifying authority. I am not suggesting that audiences are by definition not a part of the initiated; there are too many contrary examples where those defined as audients stand on the floor and speak to their fellows in a manner that sets up the structural pattern. Apart from whether or not the speaker from the floor supports the established order, the speaker, by virtue of *taking* the floor, participates in a hierarchical situation that provides its own message. Furthermore, it is a situation within a larger "fixed" situation where the rules are set, often against the interests of the new speaker.

There are several ways in which one may take the floor: One may raise a hand to "acquire" the floor; one may proceed to the front of an audience to speak; or one may shout a message from a position in the audience, without being recognized. Initially, such a person is assumed to have something to say, although, after listening, the audience might accept or reject the speaker's message. Nevertheless, the seizing of the ground is itself an act of assertion, and by that act the speaker establishes a hierarchical structure that mirrors the established order, although the message content may be different from what it would be if it emanated from established leaders.

On the other hand, all institutions, whether public or private, are fluid in their leadership structure and policies, and what may parade as the established order today may not be so tomorrow. Audiences have been known to shout speakers down as an attempt to strip them of power. The assumption of the floor is no guarantee of the permanence of structural advantage. Those who speak from the floor today, to criticize the established order, may indeed be the ones who are criticized tomorrow. This is true, even though a skillful rhetor may maneuver an audience by manipulating the rhetorical structure. A speaker whose rhetorical forte is counterargument may want to engage the audience in debate, thereby turning the structure to advantage.

The third characteristic of hierarchical discourse is the stifling of opposing discourse. Since no power position is permanent and all institutions seek to perpetuate themselves, institutions often choose to denounce all opposing views, through direct confrontation (as on a battlefield), through subterfuge (as in indirect attacks on the opposition's character or in the trenches of dialectical combat), or in giving the opposing view the illusion of a channel of expression (which is, in reality, controlled by the established order). Since only the votarists are uniquely qualified to expatiate on a given subject, the opposition's words are not to be taken seriously. This is the position that is assumed by those who occupy the summit of the established pyramid. At this rarefied height, knowledge increases, and the numbers decrease. Those who would oppose come from the broad base of the pyramid and consequently are devoid of the symbol of power, which is reserved only for those who have knowledge. Yet, the act of speaking to a group as opposition momentarily re-orders the structure of power.

To have the floor is valuable as a structural symbol of power, regardless of how briefly one holds the floor. To stifle the opposition, therefore, those in positions of power seek to keep the opposition away from every idiom of power. Thus, an individual who seeks to challenge authority will find that not only are the facts often inaccessible, but it is likely that the access to a message channel and access to a formal discourse situation are also unavailable. The established order prevails by demonstrating, in its absolute occupation of the symbolic and structural ground, that the opposition does not exist. Invisibility is the ultimate defense—out of sight, out of mind. It appears to the opposition that a tyranny of occupation sits astride its attempt to achieve equity. Thus the Afrocentric psychologist, Akbar, contends that intellectual oppression involves the use of abusive language, ideas, and concepts to degrade a people.[12] In reality, the entire social fabric of oppression is dictated by symbols of hierarchy and intellectual theories rooted in Eurocentric viewpoints.

More importantly, many blacks and most whites do not see that the symbols are dominated by European values, which creates "new speaker" or "different speaker" categories.

Hierarchical discourse operates in ideological contexts. But that is perhaps not to say much, since all discourse is contextual, and context is defined ideologically in most cases. However, what we mean is that hierarchical discourse that seeks to maintain its hierarchical position is supported by ideology. Without the ideological context, the discourse is vacuous, a hollow form without power. Given a context, the discourse assumes an awesome power as supporter of an entire worldview whose material base may be rooted in history. The more authoritarian these contexts, the more rigid the discourse structure.

This point can be clarified by examining hierarchical discourse in relationship to the common stimulus-response, sender-receiver, speaker-audience model. The paradigm itself hinges on hierarchy and a formidable structure is proposed that dictates the relationship between the message sender and receiver. This structure, I contend, is inherently unequal and constitutes an inequity that in one way mirrors cultural expansion. Daudi is clear on this issue when he says, "What we today call reason and rationalism have no intrinsic value. Our concept of reason was founded in relation to its exterior, in what reason defined as its opposite. Our culture, as its fundamental element, suddenly reveals itself to be founded on its margins."[13]

Daudi is, of course, stating an empirical view. While he condemns reason as the principal source of knowledge, thereby challenging the rationalist position, he enthrones empiricism. Neither rationalism nor empiricism encompasses all the ways of knowing; certainly the existential and so-called mystical ways of knowing constitute varieties of human knowing. Suffice it to say, at the moment, that when the sender-receiver model is adhered to, it is by nature one in which a tutor and a tutoree participate. What is potentially detrimental in that situation is the power-dependency formula that exists in so much discourse. To question the tutor, to challenge the sender, must remain a part of any liberating discourse.

At least two methods of discourse are open to the receiver in opposition to the speaking power. Both methods are based in the nature of the authority exercised over the structure by the speaking power. Since the ruling power tries to impose silence by presenting an "undebatable word," the receiver must present the most debatable symbol. This is why a culture that would refuse to exploit occupies a different ground than the exploiting culture. The second method of attack is the use of guerrilla rhetoric, the multifrontal verbal attacks on the structural symbol of the speaking power itself. To concentrate only on the words would be to allow the authoritarian discourse structure to continue as unassailable because of its superior ground position in determining how the battle should be waged. That is precisely why black students of the 1960s who successfully agitated for the establishment of Afro-American Studies departments had to resort to "nonnegotiable demands." Negotiation is the ground of the speaking power, the sender of the S–R model; consequently, students, and particularly black students, would be in an unequal position to negotiate with university administrators. In a larger sense, the receiver must attack the architectonics of authoritarian discourse, showing it to be an artificial structure. Most audiences are bound to linguistic and formal structures, not to content; and the ruling powers will seek to use parades, the flag, the star, torchlights, the swastika, the monkeytail swatter of the late Jomo Kenyatta, the cross, or the Ku Klux Klan hood as signs of omniscience.[14] The receiver who employs a substitute discourse or guerrilla rhetoric successfully against the voice of force, so that the voice itself falls silent, must guard against the inevitable temptation to employ the same discourse tactics as the fallen force.

A history of black protest in America and recently in South Africa has shown that the power that inheres in the rhetorical condition by virtue of its established position can be effectively challenged if the intended receivers of the message reject the message. Of course, this is asking that consciousness be elevated to the point where the receivers-victims know what is happening to them. There cannot be any effective power unless the victims of rhetorical dictatorship, by force or acquiescence, allow it to continue. Revolt—intellectual, moral, or rhetorical—is a sign of rejection. Daudi says, "All knowledge is political, not because it may have political consequences or be politically useful, but because knowledge has its conditions of possibility in power relations."[15] The rhetorical condition is symbolic of the political structure; it thrives on the same principles and it liberates or imprisons its interactants on the same philosophical grounds. Power relations create politics and politics creates, *inter alia,* power relations.

In establishing this perspective, you can see that I am proposing not only a new perspective but a different framework for understanding human behavior. A people who have been relegated to the fringes of the society must now be looked upon as players in the field, albeit players who have operated from a position of less power for the past four hundred years. Only an ample metatheory can adequately consider the multidimensions of the black communicative experience; and this metatheory is founded on Afrocentric bases.

The necessity of this world of thought can be seen by a simple analysis of the European philosophical outlook since Plato and Aristotle. Lovejoy's position is stated clearly when he writes (in *The Great Chain of Being*) that "the most fundamental of the group of ideas of which we are to review the history appears first in Plato; and nearly all that follows might therefore serve as an illustration of a celebrated remark of Professor Whitehead's, that 'the safest general characterization of the European philosophical tradition is that it consists of a series of footnotes to Plato.' "[16]

Unfortunately, these footnotes to Plato become central arguments in the European reach for intellectual exclusivity. All roads backwards supposedly lead to the Greeks, regardless of the discipline or field of study. I recall reading an essay on technology in which Daniel Bell argued that "the contemplative tradition of mind" goes back to Greece.[17] If one shows an interest in drama, the Eurocentric author points this person to Sophocles' comedies and tragedies; in art, to the perfection of Greek sculpture; in history, to Herodotus and Thucydides; in epic poetry, to Homer; in rhetoric, to Aristotle's *Rhetoric* and Plato's *Phaedrus* and *Gorgias—ad infinitum,* it seems. With this line of thinking and no intellectual correctives, the scholar will assume that no other universe of thought exists; and, in fact, it is impossible to conceive of another universe of thought so long as one is ensconced in this intellectual cocoon. Thus Ibn Battuta, who probably travelled as far and wide as Marco Polo (with as much significance) within the same general time frame, is hardly known by educated Westerners. Clever Aphrodite, as she had done with Narcissus because of his obstinacy, allows Eurocentric writers to see their own reflections and to fall violently in love with what they see.

So overwhelming is the impact of Greco-Roman traditions that almost every American student knows the Colosseum or Parthenon before he or she knows the Empire State Building, the Tiber before the Mississippi, and Aristotle before Du Bois. The "glory that was Greece" and "grandeur that was Rome" completely blinded the subsequent interpreters of the achievements of those cultures; but even worse, so handicapped the northern and western European thinkers that they could not see that Greece and Rome had more in common with Africa than, say, Scandinavia.

The academy is not yet fully alive to the important transformation being brought about by the developing African world consciousness. It is always difficult to recognize decisive steps in theoretical development when one is in immediate proximity and the steps are so gradual. Sustained by new information and innovative methodologies, Afrology will transform community and social sciences, as well as arts and humanities, and assist in constructing a new, perhaps more engaging, way to analyze and synthesize reality. Perhaps what is needed is a post-Western or meta-Western metatheory to disentangle us from the consuming monopoly of a limited intellectual framework, but first let us establish the idea of an Afrocentric metatheory.

THE IDEA OF A METATHEORY

A metatheory suggests the character and content of theories in the sense that it prescribes what a theory should explain (how African American language developed, or how it is used in urban communities, or what is its essence) and what analytical methodologies are required for revealing and establishing concepts such as symbolic engineering and expressive artifact. A metatheory, then, is the product of decision rather than discovery, and it is justified by the theories that are consonant to it.

The process of discovering "natural laws" is instructive, and discovery is based on observable phenomena. When observations seem to lead to the same generalization, the scientist says a law exists. Once the law is contradicted by new observations that lead to another generalization, it ceases being a natural law. As Steinmann understood, "without metaresearch, there can be no investigation of any phenomenon."[18] *Ebonics,* for example, could only find a theoretical base because of metagrammatical research. The prototypical language of African Americans has been named *Ebonics* in order to distinguish it from English. The word is a composite of *ebony* and *phonetics.*

Rhetoric, in an Afrocentric sense, is the productive thrust of language into the unknown in an attempt to create harmony and balance in the midst of disharmony and indecision. The uses of rhetoric are varied, and it is necessary to include the production of disharmony in its utility. The presence of counteracting rhetorics sets up tensions that often thrust one rhetoric in the role of creating disharmony. Language itself compounds the problems of the unknown, for it is being made as the speaker speaks. That is why it is possible to say that the black speaker, or any speaker who senses the nature of words as artifacts, glimpses the limits of rhetoric. In this sense, rhetoric is not a science; it is an art. That is to say, a certain inventive skill is needed in managing words and sentences to be effective as a communicator.

An inventional scheme for African communication behavior will have possible implications for a more general theory. Such a frame, in its metatheoretical dimensions, must be adequately broad to accommodate diverse and conflicting approaches to the generation of innovations. Every use of language is unlike any other; and some uses might even be contextually paradoxical. Adequacy of metatheory, therefore, is defined not by a single theoretical statement, but by its allowance for the self-aggrandizement of any theory. In this sense the metatheory becomes architectonic as an organizing scheme by which all else is explained. Such a metatheory must be inclusive in order to account for the prototypical language styles and myths of the culture. Beyond that, it must explain the peculiar social focus of black language in America and, by that explanation, become interpretative of symbolic engineering in a multiethnic situation. Accordingly, social or political change is nothing more than the transmitting of information as an act of power in this scheme.

As an inclusive plan, this metatheory, for example, places William Labov and Walt Wolfram's structural works in the same communication family as William Stewart's historical analysis of black language behavior.[19] This much is clear and surely reflective of traditional associative patterns along disciplinary lines. Even clearer, however, is the fact that Thomas Kochman's ethnography of black street language and the descriptive work on black spoken discourse, called *ethno-rhetoric,* belongs to the same inclusive plan.

This perspective employs ideas from numerous social scientists and humanists, particularly those who call themselves Afrologists, and regards them as pilots to comprehension of African American language and cultural behavior. Such a perspective begins with a linguistic foundation, in the sense of an explication of structure, and moves towards an understanding of the symbolisms employed in practical discourse. The path from one point to the other is tedious, but it is this process that must be explained if we are ever to know anything substantial about how African Americans use language and behave in public and private.

Practicable theories are developed on the basis of plausible, coherent principles that explain certain phenomena; so, clearly, one function of a metatheory would be to accommodate principles for the explanation of theoretical phenomena related to African American communication. The various social class constructs, language deficit models, and case histories, as well as surrealistic rhetoric and the lyrical quality of black discourse style, can be successfully conceptualized within the framework of the metatheory.[20]

The constituents of the metatheory are *frame of mind, scope of context, structure of code,* and *delivery of message.* This fundamental analytical system allows us to be open to the infinite potentialities of communication, and the constituents of this metatheory aid us in determining the innovations in African American communicative behavior without an undue concentration on either grammatical, syntactical, semantic, or lexical components.

The significance of any metatheory is that it not only explains a given cluster of theories but also provides opportunity for enlarging human understanding generally. It is now possible to explore the relationship among the constituents as they help to interpret the sweep of black language and discourse patterns within the context of the American society.

A metatheory is no more valid than the theories that are consonant to it; or more exactly, those theories justify the metatheory. Insofar as I have chosen the metatheory on the basis of the theories, the metatheory has been decided upon in terms of the character of the theories. For example, the claim by linguisticians that even when specific vocabularies are no longer employed, the phonological and morphological patterns of certain groups of African Americans reflect an African past, is consistent with the metatheoretical constituents. Yet also true is Henry Mitchell's contention that the prevailing rhetorical quality of the black preacher is lyrical. Mitchell argues that the black preacher is even required to use the black intonation and accent, because "no black man can truly identify with a God who speaks only the language of the white oppressor."[21]

Rhythm, Styling, and Sound

It would be nonsense to argue that theories which emerge about black language and discourse can claim uniformity in black behavior; but the variance among blacks is less than between blacks and non-blacks.[22] Dixon and Foster state that six essential elements comprise the black referent: (1) the value of humanism, (2) the value of communalism, (3) the attribute of oppression/paranoia, (4) the value of empathetic understanding, (5) the value of rhythm, and (6) the principle of limited reward.[23] There is, in addition, a seventh element:

the principle of styling. So in writing about the frame of mind I am emphasizing how certain social, creative, and psychological factors contribute to a total view of language. In isolating any part of this language for linguistic or rhetorical studies (I mean at the simplest level, structural or persuasive), the frame of mind of the language user is important for analytical consideration. I know, for instance, that to the African American preacher, speaking in the proper frame of mind, "Jesus is my subject" is not the same as saying "Jee-sas is my subject." Baraka has made a similar observation regarding the singing of the song "Just a Closer Walk with Thee" and the way one changes the word *yeh* by moving the tongue.[24]

It is not my intention to discuss each of these elements; rather, I will concentrate on two elements that are more obviously related to the matter of language and rhetoric. The concepts of *rhythm* and *styling* seem indicative, in terms of our discussion, of the frame of mind. Rhythm in spoken discourse is a basic measure of the successful speech. How well a speaker can regulate his flow of words with the proper pauses of audience "indentations" becomes the standard for the black speaker before a basically black audience. Henry Mitchell refers to this as establishing "a kind of intimate fellowship." Sound periodicity dictates the communicative terms of black language. The effective users of the language recognize, almost naturally, the need to employ some form of rhythm in vocal expression. Usually the speaker employs the characteristic style of his audience so that his cadences are familiar to his hearers. Martin Luther King utilized the spoken language of his followers and the "sounding good" quality, frequently noted by observers, contributed to his success. A basic element in *sounding good* is to know when *not* to sound. The rhetorical pause used so brilliantly by Malcolm X in his speeches is an essential factor in the black frame of mind as it relates to rhythm in language. And as we shall see, rhythm is also the basis of African American transcendence.[25]

The regular clustering of tones according to accent and time value explains only a portion of the rhythmic frame of mind. Mitchell has observed that the African American style is dependent upon the audience's permissiveness. Most audiences (if allowed to be) are definers of communicative boundaries. They establish the limits of the speaker's effectiveness by their behaviors. To "keep" the audience, a speaker must *style,* and a key element of style is rhythm created by tone, accent, and meaning. Thus *to style* is an action, and when one styles one is engaged in creating a relationship.[26]

Styling refers to the conscious or unconscious manipulation of language or mannerisms to influence favorably the hearers of a message. A variety of behaviors is permitted to achieve the desired end. They may be classified according to the receiver's principal way of responding: visual and audio. Visual styling is effected by gestural or symbolic mannerisms. While the most common type of gesture in communication is purposive movement for meaning and emphasis, conscious styling movement is highly regarded by black speakers and hearers. Conventional gesticulation is concerned with description and emphasis, as in "The fish was *this* size" or "The point is well made that . . ."

Symbolic mannerisms, such as Martin Luther King Jr. touching the small upper pocket on his coat, are also a matter of visual styling. This gesture lends presence to the speaker who, in taking this liberty, shows the audience that he is not an average speaker but someone capable of handling his platform tasks with ease. Every speaker is not gifted with ability to employ unconventional gestures during a speech. A certain amount of verbal skill accompanies the speaker who uses visual styling. Other forms of visual styling are environmental, in the sense that they are connected to the principal constituents of a rhetorical situation (speaker, message, and receivers), but are primarily effected by the arrangement of physical surroundings or the sartorial habits of the speaker or his friends (e.g., in the '60s we saw the black leather jackets of Bobby Seale's guards, dashiki-clad youths on the platform behind Maulana Karenga, etc.). The genius of the speaker determines the quality of the visual styling. Of course, writers have no such cadre of visual symbols; speech is much more a collective experience than writing. Metaphors must gather the soldiers for writers.

What people hear in a speech is what rhetorical critics chiefly evaluate. Because of this, the response to African American vocal cues is significant. These cues may take several forms, including variations of pronunciation, intercalations, and malapropisms. Words are frequently intoned to give them a "soulful" quality. In an education meeting at a university, where a young speaker gave his view of education, he began by saying "Education is for the C-O-M-M-U-N-I-T-Y. I mean com-mu-ni-ty." He was styling, and every person familiar with the "tradition" knew that the speaker had seized upon this stylistic device to have an impact. Between the speaker and the audience was an authentic bond, created by the spoken word.

Intercalations are the "filler" expressions that often appear as deliberate attempts at styling but become habitual with repeated use. In this category are "you know," "lookit," and "hey," which often find their way into the language mainstream. To be "cool" is to be capable of handling the verbal styling necessary to establish presence. Whereas rhythm and styling are major contributive factors in the African American speaker's frame of mind as it relates to language, the intercalations manifest in styling are interrelated to rhythm as a recurring sound or polyrhythms.[27] Historically, the expression "she sounded on him" underscored the importance of verbal expression. Although *sounding* carries the idea of verbal games, it is a precise description of both the rhythm and wit employed in language. Without rhythm or wit, one cannot "sound," since "sounding" is itself style.

The Context for Symbol Development

A second constituent in a metatheory would be the contextual scope of black language and rhetoric; it provides a basis for understanding how symbols are engineered. What are the social realities governing the development of black language? And what are the constraints upon black speakers against creating new rhetorics? The context must be comprised of the historical as well as the present moment in terms of resources for bringing about new language styles. One can describe the coming to be of a new object or event, whether new words or innovative phrases (or the "dozens"), by considering the creation in the light of these questions. What resources are available to the African American for inventing effective symbols? How does the inventing person recognize the effective use of symbols in a multiethnic society? What are the structuring considerations?

A speaker governs the use of language under tutelage from the audience, for it is the audience that determines effectiveness. Therefore, when King said "I've been to the Mountaintop" to a black audience in Memphis, it was something he would not perhaps—rhetorically speaking—have said if he had been speaking before a white audience at, say, Harvard Law School. The constraints upon him were ethnically or culturally determined. Black audiences demand to hear certain expressions, to see certain things, and to enjoy certain kinds of humor. Proverbs are also a part of the African American speaker's context, and good speakers find in their audiences the commonplaces that are appealing. To say that is to say something about the "folk talk" in the black community whether it is "Your momma sure was good to me" or "Brothers and Sisters, we got a Rock on our side. Pray with me."

In yet another turn upon the scope of the context, arguments and stylistic devices must be chosen within a certain framework by the black speaker. Despite the seemingly infinite variations upon language, the number of arguments are contextually constrained. Little wonder that the arguments of Martin Luther King and James Farmer in the late 1950s sounded like arguments of William Whipple in the 1830s; or that the positions taken by Malcolm X and Stokely Carmichael (Kwame Toure) were similar to those of Henry Highland Garnet and David Walker over a century before. Listen to Garnet in 1843:

> Two hundred and twenty seven years ago the first of our injured race were brought to the shores of America. They came not with their own consent, to find an unmolested enjoyment of the blessings of this fruitful soil. The first dealings they had with men calling themselves Christians exhibited to them the worst features of corrupt and sordid hearts: and convinced them that no cruelty is too great, no villainy and no robbery too abhorrent for even enlightened men to perform, when influenced by avarice and lust. Neither did they come flying upon the wings of liberty to a land of freedom. But they came with broken hearts, from their beloved native land, and were doomed to unrequited toil and deep degradation.[28]

This is the speech of a man who knew the horrors of American slavery and whose intense convictions brought forth a flood of protest.

What Garnet knew about America, Malcolm X also knew, and in the following statement Malcolm X put it more succinctly, perhaps more directly:

> I'm not going to sit at your table and watch you eat, with nothing on my plate, and call myself a diner. Sitting at the table doesn't make you a diner, unless you eat some of what's on the plate. Being here in America doesn't make you an American. Being born here in America doesn't make you an American.[29]

David Walker had expressed his hatred of the deeds of the "white Christian Americans" in *An Appeal to the Colored Citizens of the World.* In a speech in Boston in 1828, he said:

> The dejected, degraded and now enslaved children of Africa will have, in spite of all of their enemies, to take their stand among the nations of the earth.[30]

Walker—like Garnet, Carmichael, and Malcolm X—believed that the rise of Africans in America would be inevitable. Of course, changes in minute detail of style were present, but the external reality with which these black rhetors dealt was basically unchanged. There could be no enlargement of argumentative possibilities for the black speaker without the corresponding enlargement—or better, alteration—of the external reality. Black language and communication are framed by characteristic practices that are products of a special experience, environment, and heritage.

The contemporary cry, "Revolution now, education later!" in the South African townships shows the same response to external realities exhibited in the United States in the 1960s. A host of black speakers in South Africa have used powerfully dramatic language, hoping to shake the firmly established structure of white supremacy. The difficulty is that the appeal from within the metaphoric mind of white culture is tied to many of the assumptions of that culture. In effect, to make an appeal for liberation, political rights, and equality of blacks on the basis of Afrikaner Christian values is to be enslaved to the framework. I contend that change comes from altering circumstances or replacing the frameworks that created the conditions. In South Africa as in the United States, conceptual questions must assume a greater prominence.

The Lyrical Code

The making of a linguistic code is a cultural creation of a people's heritage. How ideas have been structured in the past dictates, to a large extent, how they will be structured in the future. Nuances are transmitted with the general fabric of the mores of a society. The three components to code structuring in the rhetorical behavior of black Americans are lyrical quality, vocal artifact, and indirection.

The African American's approach to language is principally lyrical, and this is the basic poetic and narrative response to reality. Numerous examples have been descriptively documented indicating the expressive quality of the preacher as the prototype of the black speaker. But it is not only the preacher who combines brilliant imagination with music to make it a lyrical style; this combination also predominates among public platform orators whose roots are firmly in the secular rhetoric of the urban streets. The closer a person moves to the white community psychologically, the further he moves from the lyrical approach to language. Among organizing patterns for platform speaking, narration is the most consistent form for a lyrical attitude. Thus the narrative, as similar as it appears to be to the African storyteller's constructions, is nevertheless most consonant with a lyrical approach to language. For example, consider James Weldon Johnson's famous rendition of an African American sermon:

THE CREATION

And God stepped out on space,
And he looked around and said:
I'm lonely—
I'll make me a world.

And far as the eye of God could see
Darkness covered everything,
Blacker than a hundred midnights
Down in a cypress swamp.

Then God smiled,
And the light broke,
And the darkness rolled up on one side,
And the light stood shining on the other,
And God said: That's good!

Then God reached out and took the light in his hands,
And God rolled the light around in his hands
Until he made the sun;
And he set that sun a-blazing in the heavens.
And the light that was left from making the sun
God gathered it up in a shining ball
And flung it against the darkness,
Spangling the night with the moon and stars.
Then down between
The darkness and the light
He hurled the world;
And God said: That's good!

Then God himself stepped down—
And the sun was on his right hand,
And the moon was on his left;
The stars were clustered about his head,
And the earth was under his feet.
And God walked, and where he trod
His footsteps hollowed the valleys out
And bulged the mountains up.

Then he stopped and looked and saw
That the earth was hot and barren.
So God stepped over to the edge of the world
And he spat out the seven seas—
He batted his eyes, and the lightnings flashed—
He clapped his hands, and the thunders rolled—
And the waters above the earth came down,
The cooling waters came down.

Then the green grass sprouted,
And the little red flowers blossomed,
The pine tree pointed his finger to the sky,
And the oak spread out his arms,
The lakes cuddled down in the hollows of the ground,
And the rivers ran down to the sea;
And God smiled again,
And the rainbow appeared,
And curled itself around his shoulder.

Then God raised his arm and he waved his hand
Over the sea and over the land,
And he said: Bring forth! Bring forth!
And quicker than God could drop his hand,
Fishes and fowls
And beasts and birds
Swam the rivers and the seas,
Roamed the forests and the woods,
And split the air with their wings.
And God said: That's good!

Then God walked around,
And God looked around
On all that he had made.
He looked at his sun,
And he looked at his moon,
And he looked at his little stars;
He looked on his world
With all its living things,
And God said: I'm lonely still.

Then God sat down—
On the side of a hill where he could think;
By a deep, wide river he sat down;
With his head in his hands,
God thought and thought,
Till he thought: I'll make me a man!

Up from the bed of the river
God scooped the clay;
And by the bank of the river
He kneeled him down;
And there the great God Almighty
Who lit the sun and fixed it in the sky,
Who flung the stars to the most far corner of
the night,
Who rounded the earth in the middle of his
hand;
This Great God,
Like a mammy bending over her baby,
Kneeled down in the dust
Toiling over a lump of clay
Till he shaped it in his own image;

Then into it he blew the breath of life,
And man became a living soul.
Amen. Amen.[31]

There is little wonder that our preachers are famous for sermons with titles such as "Dry Bones in the Valley," "The Three Hebrew Boys," "Daniel in the Lion's Den," "The Prodigal Son." These lyrically pregnant stories are demonstratively presented with emphatic diversions to instruct audiences. They are not unlike the narratives of Ananse or Brer Rabbit in their transmission of values and ideas. In fact, it may be argued, in a Herskovitian fashion, that these folk preachers retained for the African audiences the basic elements of the storytellers and, by applying their skills to new materials, made the proverbs and folktales operative in an alien context. The Afro-American speaker exhibits strong tendencies towards a lyrical approach to language, which is structured accordingly.

The power of the lyricism that dances in the sermons of the black preacher derives its vitality from two sources, and Hamilton correctly identifies one source as the oral tradition:

> The black culture is characterized by an oral tradition. Knowledge, attitudes, ideas, notions are traditionally transmitted orally, not through the written word. It is not unusual, then, that the natural leader among black people would be one with exceptional oratorical skills. He must be able to talk, to speak—to preach. In the black religious tradition, the successful black preacher is an expert orator. His role involves more, however. His relationship with his parishioners is reciprocal; he talks to them, and they talk back to him. That is expected. In many church circles this talk-back during a sermon is a firm measure of the preacher's effectiveness.[32]

An aspect of the oral tradition is the polyrhythms of the speech situation. The talk-back, hand clapping, and affirmations represent the complex movement of a whole audience towards unity with the speaker's message. Sometimes the audience shouts "That's right!" "Preach the truth!" "Yes, Lord!" "Help him, my Lord!" "Lordy, Lordy, Lord!" and "Make it plain!" Interspersing the speech with such interjections, the audience gives the speaker immediate feedback to complete the call-and-response patterns of the culture.

The lyricism, according to Henry Mitchell, "is traceable to Black African culture."[33] Moreover, Africa is at the heart of *all* African American behavior. Communication styles are reflective of the internal mythic clock, the epic memory, the psychic stain of Africa in our spirits. This is no great mystery inasmuch as similar memories exist in other people who maintain, however tangentially, a connection with their ancestral traditions. While African Americans may not consciously identify the lyricism with Africa, it is nevertheless a significant part of the communicative pattern, adding the elements of indirection and polyrhythms. In effect, the oral tradition and the call-and-response are both related to the African origin of the cultural behaviors. In this sense, they may be parts of the same phenomenon.

Another aspect of code structuring has to do with how the speaker uses voice—the idea that words and their sounds are products of human work and are, by this virtue, artifactitious. One understands that voice, much like the calimba, fonton-from, or flute, is merely an instrument for the conveying of ideas. There is no music, only tools for expressing concepts. When one speaks of the orator, as I do, it is necessary to see that, in the African culture, voice is an instrument just as significant as the lexical items spoken. Some lexical items cannot be powerful until they are powerfully spoken by the orator.

I believe that the difference between the European and the African understanding on this subject is profound. To "play jazz," you must have something to say or else you merely play music. The technical procession through the notes is not music as understood in African culture; the use of a technical style, dry and unimaginative, is not oratory. One must know how to use the voice. Intonation and tonal styling are substantive parts of most African American oratory. And the intelligent speaker knows that speaking is an emotional as well as an intellectual process, and that how one alters a phoneme or a word in vocal expression is significant. To know how to say "cat" or "man" is to know the secrets of word magic.

In such a sense, the black speaker knows what the ancestors knew with their use of *nommo:* that all magic is word magic, and the generation and transformation of sounds contribute to a speaker's power. Thus, we are ready to say that whatever a speaker does with a word is a fact unto itself, apart from any reality the word has separate from the particular speaker. A speaker can alter the meaning of a word—"basically the [same] way one can change the word *yeh* from simple response to stern challenge simply by moving the tongue slightly."[34] There are a number of one-syllable sounds that enhance or complement the African American speaker's timbre and pitch: "cat," "say," "man," "yeh," "hey," "what," "right," etc. What is unusual about these sounds is the specificity that accompanies them. Like the black preacher, the disc jockey who lives in the spirit of the people knows precisely what and how to say something.

The contemporary black disc jockey, like the rap musicians and the deejay rockers of Jamaica, operate out of the same collective Afrocentric response to words. In the United States, the rap was preceded by *signifying*. The "signifying monkey," which is legendary in the African American communication memory, gives birth to several forms of signifying, to rapping, and to variations of the "dozens." A common version of the signifying monkey goes like this:

> *Down in the jungle near a dried-up creek*
> *The signifying monkey hadn't slept for a week*
> *Remembering the ass-kicking he had got in the past*
> *He had to find somebody to kick the lion's ass.*
> *The monkey said to the lion one bright summer day,*
> *There's a bad motherfucker over the way.*
> *The way he talks about you can't be right.*
> *And when y'all meet there's bound to be a fight.*
> *He talks about your mother in a helluva way.*
> *He called her a no-good bitch and he meant it for a fight.*
> *Now if you ask me, I'll say, "man, it ain't right."*
> *Off went the lion in a terrible rage*
> *creating a breeze which shook the trees*
> *and knocked the giraffe to his knees.*
> *He confronted the elephant up under the tree,*
> *and said, "motherfucker, it's you or me."*
> *He drove at the elephant and made his pass.*
> *That's when the elephant knocked him flat on his ass.*
> *He kicked and stomped him all in his face*
> *Busted two ribs and pulled his tail out of place.*
> *They cursed and fought damn near all day.*
> *I still don't see how that lion got away.*[35]

Spoken with the melodious cadence of the poet, the signifying monkey, which is related to the tale of the lion and the rabbit from West Africa, becomes a ritualized form of aggression. The monkey, whose power is insignificant in relationship to the herds of the forest, knows how to neutralize those who possess greater physical power. In this way the African American, using the spiritual ancestor memory of African rhythms and tales, creates a reality through spoken language.

Paul Carter Harrison says in *The Drama of Nommo* that the signifying monkey "reflects the transformation of oral expression as the word passed from the south and caught up with the rhythms of the urban north."[36] The transformation referred to by Harrison is demonstrated in the cadences, rhythms, and lyricisms of black verbal art. In many instances, there is a profound immediacy in the artistic magic of saying something with meaning that is the same as saying something with feeling.

Jahn has understood the interrelationship between the art and activity in most African cultures, continental and diasporan. His appreciation of the aesthetic differences between Europe and Africa, for example, is revealing and helpful in our discussion of sound in the African American speech. Jahn says "an African aesthetic rests, therefore, on the aesthetics of Kuntu, and that means, on the harmony of meaning and rhythm, of sense and form."[37] He contends that the Europeans see the "work" as an object that *has* meaning and rhythm. But the African sees *kuntu* (art) in action: the poem as recited, the carving in its function as stimulus in the worship of an *orisha,* the mask in movement of the dance—that is, when it is *kuntu.* That is why oratory in African cultures is never a thing but always activity. Sound conveys the artistic attitude of the orator.[38]

Furthermore, sound is a rhetorical artifact inasmuch as it has a certain effect upon the hearers. Thus, when a speaker concludes a speech, the statement "He sure sounds good" is a proper approbation. A listener states approval of the energy (form and context being inseparable) expended in the speech. But the approbation is made with particular understanding of what glides and flights of sound were made. Effectiveness, therefore, is dependent upon vocal expression as a lasting impact, not upon gesture or supporting evidence, for obviously a speaker may claim evidence and perfect gesticulation and not be effective. Conversely, by appropriately modulating tones, a speaker can make the evidence and gesticulation accomplish the ends.

The third component to code structuring, observable in stylistic development, is *indirection.* In speaking before an audience, the African American speaker often approaches the central issues of talk in a circuitous fashion, in the manner of the cultural temperament, with lyricism and indirection. By "stalking" the issues, the speaker demonstrates skill and arouses hearers' interest. The person who goes directly to the issues is said to have little imagination and even less flair for rhetorical style.

Indirection is usually a matter of deduction, as the speaker toys with related ideas and concepts before focusing on his prime target:

> *I am not a Politician, nor the son of a*
> *Politician*
> *I am not a Republican, nor a Democrat*
> *Nor an American.*[39]

In this typical passage from Malcolm X we see the formula for indirection. What could have been simply put as "I know that I am not an American" is more elaborately clothed. Such embellishment in public speaking can also be derived from the speaker's metaphorical capabilities, or illustrations, or aphorisms, or a combination of these techniques. But whatever the speaker's choice, he is certainly playing in the right ball park if he "surrounds" his issue before focusing upon it. This behavior is true not only of the platform speaker, but also plays a role in dyadic conversation. Its true bases are the enthymematic products of our cultural experiences. One would be mistaken to speak of this linguistic behavior as "beating around the bush," because it is always *on* the bush, though at times tapping it exceedingly lightly.

Herskovits was one of the first to observe the use of indirection in black language. He comments in *The Myth of the Negro Past* that indirection may have been a characteristic the African Americans brought with them from Africa. In one example of the African fondness for indirection, the attitude of the French colonial authorities in Africa was shown to be unwise because of their straightforward manner. When the French directly asked, for tax purposes, how many people lived in the houses of each compound, the old people would respond that they were wiser than to ask a person directly to tell something that is a disadvantage to himself. Herskovits says:

> Whatever the African basis for this attitude, it must be made clear that slavery did nothing to diminish the force of its sanctions. Nor have the disabilities under which the negro has lived since slavery tended to decrease its appeal as an effective measure of protection. Nonetheless, certain characteristic reactions to life in Africa itself—on the part of the upper class as well as ordinary folk, which even take certain institutionalized forms in the political system of at least one well integrated African culture—make it essential that this tradition of indirection be regarded as a carry-over of aboriginal culture.[40]

Herskovits is convinced that African Americans came to America "equipped with the technique" of indirection.[41] Any Afrocentric analysis of black communication must consider the importance of limited revelation, holding back on what one knows, restraint in speaking directly to strangers in the African American culture. Of course, in contemporary society one has to consider also the influence of acculturation on black style.

The Art of Improvisation

Discourse spoken by African Americans is characterized by artistic instrumentation. As an art form, the speech, frequently interrupted by vocal responses from the hearers, is *made* with careful attention to effect. Like African art of the highest order, it is functional and is not made for art's sake alone but for its practical value to people.[42] Therefore, when audiences respond with outbursts of "Amen," "That's right," "Tell the Truth," etc., they are testifying to the impact of the delivery of the message. It is difficult to refer to these vocal outbursts as interruptions of the speech; more accurately, they are affirmations.

Speakers who succeed in arousing in their audiences the desire to give vocal assent are prototypes for the black community. And the audiences' vocal affirmations, which are regulatory, comprise a monitoring system (as feedback systems generally do) for effectiveness. This is similar to the common function of applause during certain American cultural events. When a speaker views delivery of a message as a performance, certain constraints and possibilities, which otherwise would *not* be, are placed upon him. Here, then, it is not just the linguistic code that a speaker must be concerned with, but presence as a speaker (appearance, countenance, grace, and manner). And presence is integrally related to how a person chooses to argue, contend, affirm, or entertain; and how the listener chooses to respond to his language. By using language common to the audiences, a speaker is not merely understandable, he is credible. This explains the success of folk preachers and some radical orators. But delivery, however animated, cannot substitute for a speaker's genuine sensitivity to audiences. This holds for every dyadic communication situation, whether speaker to audiences (many) or speaker to listener (one).

The kind of delivery indicates how a speaker regards the situation and audiences; that is, the choice of physical styles—*pompous* or *conversational*—reflects the rhetorical setting. Furthermore, the choice of modes—*impromptu, manuscript, extemporaneous,* or *memorized*—underscores the effect of situation and audiences upon the speaker. The typical rhetorical setting is persuasive and the proper decisions of the speaker influence the persuasive impact on audiences. As a consideration for a metatheory of African American black language and communication, it should be noted that our speakers generally prefer the extemporaneous mode of delivery, characterized by lively speaking and the coining of exact language at the moment of utterance. In oratory, as in music, the individualistic, the improvisational, is the soul of performance. This is not to say that memorized speeches are unheard of, or that manuscript speeches are not given. When exactness of language and careful timing are essential, the speaker must react in the most appropriate manner. In most cases, the manuscript speech serves a speaker's needs of exactness and definite timing. While presentation of a message is constrained by environmental conditions, it completes the speech act for the encoding person and is therefore essential to communication.

Just as with jazz, which is the classical music of America, the improvised voice, with spontaneity and variety, is the voice of African American oratory. An endless variety of presentation styles, all falling within the acceptable Afrocentric motif, speaks to the diversity of the orators, from Booker T. Washington to Louis Farrakhan. Their province is the spoken word, and in this province they excel at presentation of the message. This should not be confused with white styles, whose sources are different; the Afrocentric presentation forms are related to music, particularly the epic styles of blues and jazz. The forms may be seen further back, in the work songs, which predate the blues, spirituals, and jazz. In these folk-forms one finds the call-and-response, improvisation, and rhythm.

The political and cultural symbols of American society reflect the monoethnicity that has persisted in American cultural phenomena. Spoken discourse as conceptualized and as practiced apart from the new directions outlined above (frame of mind, context, structure of code, and delivery) is demonstratively unrepresentative symbolically. What is needed is an expansion of cultural perspectives and a reconceptualization of symbolic engineering in order to understand the role of African culture in African American behavior. Inasmuch as our perception of people, events, and objects can influence language, we surely must be cognizant that beyond the level of specific words in language that are monoethnic there are substantive influences upon language (a sort of Whorfian twist) that make our communicative habits sterile. The writers who have argued that the English language is our enemy have argued convincingly on the basis of "*black*ball," "*black*mail," "*black* Friday," etc.; but they have not argued thoroughly in terms of the total symbolic architecton of society. Only when we challenge the symbolic generation of monoethnic concepts in a multicultural society will we truly make progress.

As Eleanor W. Traylor shows in her essay on Toni Morrison's *Tar Baby*, Europeans have often imposed their symbols on blacks.

> The people of this fable-world imbibe toxic ideas . . . they are miseducated by cant; by historical, cultural, and political bias or ignorance of schoolish books; by insidious daily-diet propaganda sponsored by moneymongers; . . . by foolish slogans rampant in this world convincing many that "if you White, you right; if you Black, stand back or catchup."[43]

The imposition of a single symbol system onto a multiethnic society typifies the Eurocentrism in the conventional approach to language. By accepting the constituents of the African American communication patterns, we extend the understanding of human communication. On the other hand, it is difficult to have meaningful discourse when the points of reference are inherently biased. In fact, symbol imperialism, rather than institutional racism, is the major social problem facing multicultural societies. It is both linguistic and rhetorical in our use of communication. Santa Claus as an American symbol is one example. In terms of discourse, our perceptions of Santa Claus color our responses. As an ethnic symbol imposed as a universal symbol of benevolence, Santa is not adequate. But neither is Hanu-Claus, nor is Saint Soul—two versions of the symbol developed by ethnic and racial minority groups. Only a reevaluation of the constituents of communication for a multiethnic society can establish meaningful dialogue. "Flesh"-color Band-Aids, traditional American combs, sunglasses or regular eyeglasses, or the nude look—all of which disregard racial variations in skin color and bone structure—are indicative of such symbol imperialism. Language is the instrument of conveyance of attitudes and perceptions, and these symbols must play havoc with symbolic structure.

One can illustrate this point almost endlessly, but that is not my objective here. However, it should be sufficient to say that most of the so-called universal concepts fail transculturally, and without transcultural validity there is not universality. This is precisely the point Armstrong makes against Jung's archetypes.[44] Jung's archetypes could not be called universal because they could not be seen as classes of events across cultures, regardless of their substantive validity within cultures. Armstrong shows us that both Jung's archetypes and Lévi-Strauss's bipolar archetypes are to be rejected as universal.[45] He concludes that while Jung's archetypes as descriptive categories of the psyches of the Western European may be valid, they cannot be viewed as other than Western and "therefore not per se basic structures of man's mind."[46] This is not to say that archetypes are not possible in African or Asian culture, but only to declare that, unless one can establish transcultural validity for the archetype, it remains substantively culturally defined. Perhaps we should look at how Eurocentric perspectives assisted in the misunderstanding of black language behavior. The imposition of a view that is antithetical to the nature of the language emerged in the 1960s, as a result of a universalist conception.

In the discussion of African American language, some writers have obfuscated the tone and style of Ebonics. Good-natured endeavors to explain the persistence of Ebonics in African American culture have become crippled. In attempting to refute the negative views of black language, some neo-radical linguists of the 1960s adopted the idea of black language as nonstandard and inflicted a confusion about our culture that has proved difficult to eliminate. They not only accepted the dialectical structure of American racist ideology, which sees white as standard and others as nonstandard, even substandard, but borrowed from the twisted formulations of a supremacist logic. Such is the complexity of the material artifact of Ebonics. Hence, B. L. Bailey argued in the 1960s that black people used a nonstandard English.[47] This was not an unusual perspective because in the same journal, R. G. Kaplan, in "On a Note of Protest (in a Minor Key): Bidialectism vs. Bidialectism," expounded a similar position on black language. Kaplan adds a turn to the position, however, by insisting that "non-standard" language was not a racial but an economic issue.[48] Despite Kaplan's intentions, his argument seeks to demonstrate that the preservation of the white power structure is dependent upon the teaching of English grammar as a vehicle for assimilation and standardization; he errs when he does not see the cultural antecedents to Ebonics. The genius of the Africans who created this unique linguistic response to their environment cannot be gainsaid. Yoruba, Asante, Ibo, Hausa, Mandingo, Serere, and Wolof had to combine elements of their language in order to communicate with each other and the English. Ebonics was a creative enterprise, out of the materials of interrelationships and the energies of the African ancestral past.

Those interested in the social and political uses of speech must be flexible enough to accommodate this view. Of course, much has been done in this regard, particularly as it relates to the classroom teacher's understanding of Ebonics and its various dialects. Clearly, the statement of a metatheoretical position for African communication suggests how we can structure our symbols to be more useful. Ethno-rhetorics concerned with exploring the persuasive potentials of languages within certain ethnic/cultural groups may be stimulants for a broader philosophical consideration of symbolic utility for a more humanistic society. Therefore, the fundamental position we must assume is that of making an aggressive beginning, despite the political and economic constraints that tend to ensnare us. Eurocentric systems have functioned as directors of the social systems, holding an enormous grip on the advancement of social and intellectual thought.

I believe that the early black protest speakers understood that there had to be a fundamental refocusing of the social and intellectual environment in order to achieve true liberation. Although the literature of American origin was rich in the language of liberty and freedom, it was always a freedom totally within the framework of the Eurocentric view. This worked for whites from Europe; they could analyze the various possibilities inasmuch as a common cultural thread was shared. However, for the African American this thread represented a whole fabric based upon a strong apocalyptic-Viking mythology. Its exclusivity created (*inter alia*) the need for justifying rhetorics to support it.

Historically, our social and political protests have been emblems of resistance. The struggle has been to show that difference does not have to be oppositional. Quite frankly, this is difficult when the bombarding Eurocentricisms in the social sciences and humanities suggest the inability of the majority of whites to think beyond Eurocentric ideals. A music school that does not teach a course on Duke Ellington, a history department without any mention of Du Bois, or a philosophy department that refuses to consider Fanon or King reflect, in a direct manner, the imbedded abstraction of exclusivity.

NOTES

1. Quoted in Jeremy Campbell, *Grammatical Man* (New York: Simon and Schuster, 1982), p. 179.
2. Paulo Freire, *The Politics of Education* (Hadley, Mass.: Bergin and Garvey, 1985).
3. Paul Rosenthal, "The Concept of Paramessage in Persuasive Communication," *Quarterly Journal of Speech* 58 (1970): 15–30.
4. Lloyd Bitzer, "The Rhetorical Situation," *Philosophy and Rhetoric* 1, (1968), pp. 1–4.
5. See J. L. Austin, *How to Do Things with Words* (Oxford: Oxford University Press, 1955), and J. Searle, *Speech Acts* (Cambridge: Cambridge University Press, 1970).
6. Haki Madhubuti, *Earthquakes and Sunrise Missions* (Chicago: Third World Press, 1984). Madhubuti conceives the objective reality of African Americans in terms of the colonial metaphor. He sees an encapsulation of the political, economic, and cultural aspirations of the African American population. In a sense, the African American is at war against capture in quite dissimilar ways than other American national cultures. Madhubuti claims an assertive cultural nationalism as the only approach to intellectual and cultural liberation.
7. P. Daudi, "The Discourse of Power or the Power of Discourse," *Alternatives* (1983), p. 276.
8. Ibid., p. 277.
9. A. Goldschlager, "Towards a Semiotics of Authoritarian Discourse," *Poetics Today* 3, no. 1 (1982): 11–13.
10. Herbert Marcuse, *One Dimensional Man: Studies in the Ideology of Advanced Industrial Society* (Boston: Beacon Press, 1964). Marcuse's technological vise is credited for the lack of creative will in both the West and the socialist nations. There is only one dimension dictated by

the industrial and high-technological managed societies. A ready-made, built-in dictionary of thought and action governs the one-dimensional man.

11. Octavio Paz, *The Bow and the Lyre* (New York: McGraw-Hill, 1973).
12. Na'im Akbar, "Mental Disorder among African Americans," *Black Books Bulletin* 7, no. 2 (1981): 18–25.
13. Daudi, "Discourse," p. 274.
14. E. Buyssens, *La Communication et l'articulation linguistique* (Brussels, Presses Universitaires de Bruxelles, 1978).
15. Daudi, "Discourse," p. 277.
16. Arthur Lovejoy, *The Great Chain of Being* (Cambridge, Mass.: Harvard University Press, 1964), p. 24.
17. Daniel Bell, "Technology, Nature and Society," *American Scholar* 42, no. 3 (Summer 1973): 391.
18. Martin Steinmann, *New Rhetorics* (New York: Scribner's, 1967).
19. In Walt Wolfram and Marcia Whitemann, "The Role of Dialect Interference in Composition," *Florida FL Reporter* (Spring–Fall 1971), pp. 34–38.
20. Steinmann, *New Rhetorics,* p. 26.
21. Henry Mitchell, *Black Preaching* (New York: Lippincott, 1970), p. 24. Mitchell's presentation of the phenomenon of black preaching underscores variety in theme, tonal quality, and rhetorical qualities. Charles V. Hamilton's *The Black Preacher in America* (New York: Morrow and Co., 1972) places the black preacher into a political context, showing the relationship of the preacher to power. Mitchell's intention, on the contrary, is the elevation of the black preacher's style of eloquence in the mind of his readers. Both views are clearly within the scope of the African American preaching tradition.
22. Vernon Dixon and Badi Foster, *Beyond Black or White* (Boston: Little, Brown, 1971).
23. Ibid., *passim.*
24. LeRoi Jones (Imamu Amiri Baraka), *Blues People* (New York: Morrow and Co., 1963), p. 26.
25. Kariamu Asante, "Commonalities in African Dance: An Aesthetic Foundation," in M. Asante and K. W. Asante, eds., *African Culture: The Rhythms of Unity* (Westport, Conn.: Greenwood Press, 1985). The commonalities identified by Kariamu Asante in the traditional dance of Africa are found in music, religion, and relationships as well. Indeed, the thesis of *African Culture* is the idea that Africa presents one vast cultural river with numerous tributaries. Polyrhythm, according to Kariamu Asante, represents one of the seven principal senses of African aesthetics.
26. Henry Mitchell, *Black Preaching* (New York: Lippincott, 1970), p. 162.
27. See Jones, *Blues People,* p. 31.
28. Henry Highland Garnet, "An Address to the Slave," in Arthur Smith and Stephen Robb, *The Voice of Black Rhetoric* (Boston: Allyn & Bacon, 1970), pp. 22–32.
29. Malcolm X and George Breitman, *Malcolm X Speaks* (New York: Grove Press, 1966)
30. David Walker, "An Appeal to the Colored Citizens of the World," in Herbert Aptheker, *One Continual Cry* (New York: Humanities Press, 1965).
31. James Weldon Johnson, *God's Trombones* (New York: Viking, 1965), pp. 1–3.
32. Charles V. Hamilton, *The Black Preacher in America* (New York: William Morrow, 1972), p. 42.
33. Mitchell, *Black Preaching,* p. 14.
34. Jones, *Blues People,* p. 26.
35. A version of the signifying monkey I learned as a child in Nashville, Tennessee.
36. Paul Carter Harrison, *The Drama of Nommo* (New York: Grove Press, 1972), p. 48.
37. Janheinz Jahn, *Muntu: The New African Culture* (New York: Grove Press, 1961), pp. 170–173.

38. Ibid., p. 174.
39. Malcolm X, "Message from the Grass Roots." Record Album. (New York: Douglas Communications, n.d.).
40. Melville Herskovits, *The Myth of the Negro Past* (Boston: Beacon Press, 1958), p. 156.
41. Ibid., p. 158.
42. See Robert Farris Thompson, *Black Gods and Kings* (Bloomington: Indiana University Press, 1971), pp. 3–4, for a discussion of African art, symbolism, and society. Thompson's work seeks to provide an objective African interpretation of culture. In *The Flash of the Spirit* (New York: Random House, 1983), for example, he is content to allow the indigenous cultures of Africa to provide their own explanations of African art. In many ways Thompson follows the tradition begun by Melville Herskovits and the Northwestern School.
43. Eleanor W. Traylor, "The Fabulous World of Toni Morrison," in Amiri Baraka and Amina Baraka (eds.), *Confirmations* (New York: Quill, 1983), pp. 342–343.
44. Armstrong, *Wellspring,* pp. 102–103.
45. Ibid.
46. Ibid., p. 107.
47. B. L. Bailey, "Language and Communication Styles in Afro-American Children in the United States," *Florida FL Reporter* 7 (Spring/Summer 1969): 46.
48. R. G. Kaplan, "On a Note of Protest (in a Minor Key): Bidialectism vs. Bidialectism," *Florida FL Reporter* (Spring/Summer 1969).

INTRODUCTION TO HÉLÈNE CIXOUS

Hélène Cixous was born in 1937 in French colonial Algeria. She now lives in France, where she is a professor of English literature. Cixous is primarily known as a feminist theorist. Her essay, "The Laugh of the Medusa," is reprinted here, and is widely regarded as a feminist classic. This essay influenced the development of feminist rhetorical theories, as scholars attempt to complete the transition of women's rhetoric from the margin to the mainstream.

Cixous' work generally attempts to identify structures that perpetuate power inequities in society. Her feminist focus is on the ways that inequities between men and women are created and sustained, specifically through discursive structures. By attempting to identify ways of speaking and writing that perpetuate patriarchy (male dominance), and likewise to identify ways of speaking and writing that would affirm women, Cixous' work parallels that of Foucault.

The style of the selection reprinted here is poetic and hyperbolic. Through this style Cixous attempts to model a kind of language that she thinks would be liberating for women. Using this style as an example of how women should speak and write, she makes several points: Women's language is ideally expressive and liberating, allowing a voice that has been marginalized. However, few or no discourses at present display the full potential of that language, because the style of most language has been male, even if spoken by women.

Cixous argues that the work of male domination has been to marginalize women's language and to enlist women themselves to devalue it. Therefore, changing language is a site of resistance to patriarchy. Cixous claims that writing has traditionally been linked to reason. But women's writing follows a different kind of reason that is more poetic and keyed to narrative. Women's writing must be linked more closely to immediate lived experience; Cixous expresses this idea by saying that women must "return to the body." A recovery of groundedness in real experience of their bodies will empower women as well as challenge a patriarchy that has been based on physical sexual differences.

Cixous argues that women's language is more physically expressive than is men's. It is always addressed and dialogical rather than the more typical male monological style. Cixous also bases much of her argument on the work of Sigmund Freud and his French disciple Jacques Lacan. Her discussion of Freudian theory is technical and somewhat difficult for the lay person. In general, she is attempting to bend Freudian theory towards her own use as a feminist theorist.

Some feminist rhetorical theorists have argued that a truly feminine rhetorical theory must identify distinct ways in which women speak that are different from men's patterns of discourse. It is not enough simply to identify women public speakers, these theorists claim, since public speaking itself may be a male-centered activity. Of course, their claims are controversial and are challenged by other feminist scholars such as Karlyn Kohrs Campbell, whose work is also excerpted here. But for this line of feminist rhetorical theory, the work of Cixous is seminal in identifying distinctly female discursive practices.

HÉLÈNE CIXOUS

THE LAUGH OF THE MEDUSA

I shall speak about women's writing: about *what it will do*. Woman must write her self: must write about women and bring women to writing, from which they have been driven away as violently as from their bodies—for the same reasons, by the same law, with the same fatal goal. Woman must put herself into the text—as into the world and into history—by her own movement.

The future must no longer be determined by the past. I do not deny that the effects of the past are still with us. But I refuse to strengthen them by repeating them, to confer upon them an irremovability the equivalent of destiny, to confuse the biological and the cultural. Anticipation is imperative.

Since these reflections are taking shape in an area just on the point of being discovered, they necessarily bear the mark of our time—a time during which the new breaks away from the old, and, more precisely, the (feminine) new from the old (*la nouvelle de l'ancien*). Thus, as there are no grounds for establishing a discourse, but rather an arid millennial ground to break, what I say has at least two sides and two aims: to break up, to destroy; and to foresee the unforeseeable, to project.

This is a revised version of "Le Rire de la Méduse." which appeared in *L'Arc* (1975), pp. 39–54.

Translated by Keith Cohen and Paula Cohen

I write this as a woman, toward women. When I say "woman," I'm speaking of woman in her inevitable struggle against conventional man; and of a universal woman subject who must bring women to their senses and to their meaning in history. But first it must be said that in spite of the enormity of the repression that has kept them in the "dark"—that dark which people have been trying to make them accept as their attribute—there is, at this time, no general woman, no one typical woman. What they have *in common* I will say. But what strikes me is the infinite richness of their individual constitutions: you can't talk about *a* female sexuality, uniform, homogeneous, classifiable into codes—any more than you can talk about one unconscious resembling another. Women's imaginary is inexhaustible, like music, painting, writing: their stream of phantasms is incredible.

I have been amazed more than once by a description a woman gave me of a world all her own which she had been secretly haunting since early childhood. A world of searching, the elaboration of a knowledge, on the basis of a systematic experimentation with the bodily functions, a passionate and precise interrogation of her erotogeneity. This practice, extraordinarily rich and inventive, in particular as concerns masturbation, is prolonged or accompanied by a production of forms, a veritable aesthetic activity, each stage of rapture inscribing a resonant vision, a composition, something beautiful. Beauty will no longer be forbidden.

I wished that that woman would write and proclaim this unique empire so that other women, other unacknowledged sovereigns, might exclaim: I, too, overflow; my desires have invented new desires, my body knows unheard-of songs. Time and again I, too, have felt so full of luminous torrents that I could burst—burst with forms much more beautiful than those which are put up in frames and sold for a stinking fortune. And I, too, said nothing, showed nothing; I didn't open my mouth, I didn't repaint my half of the world. I was ashamed. I was afraid, and I swallowed my shame and my fear. I said to myself: You are mad! What's the meaning of these waves, these floods, these outbursts? Where is the ebullient, infinite woman who, immersed as she was in her naiveté, kept in the dark about herself, led into self-disdain by the great arm of parental-conjugal phallocentrism, hasn't been ashamed of her strength? Who, surprised and horrified by the fantastic tumult of her drives (for she was made to believe that a well-adjusted normal woman has a . . . divine composure), hasn't accused herself of being a monster? Who, feeling a funny desire stirring inside her (to sing, to write, to dare to speak, in short, to bring out something new), hasn't thought she was sick? Well, her shameful sickness is that she resists death, that she makes trouble.

And why don't you write? Write! Writing is for you, you are for you; your body is yours, take it. I know why you haven't written. (And why I didn't write before the age of twenty-seven.) Because writing is at once too high, too great for you, it's reserved for the great—that is, for "great men"; and it's "silly." Besides, you've written a little, but in secret. And it wasn't good, because it was in secret, and because you punished yourself for writing, because you didn't go all the way; or because you wrote, irresistibly, as when we would masturbate in secret, not to go further, but to attenuate the tension a bit, just enough to take the edge off. And then as soon as we come, we go and make ourselves feel guilty—so as to be forgiven; or to forget, to bury it until the next time.

Write, let no one hold you back, let nothing stop you: not man; not the imbecilic capitalist machinery, in which publishing houses are the crafty, obsequious relayers of imperatives handed down by an economy that works against us and off our backs; and not *yourself*. Smug-faced readers, managing editors, and big bosses don't like the true texts of women—female-sexed texts. That kind scares them.

I write woman: woman must write woman. And man, man. So only an oblique consideration will be found here of man; it's up to him to say where his masculinity and femininity are at: this will concern us once men have opened their eyes and seen themselves clearly.[1]

Now women return from afar, from always: from "without," from the heath where witches are kept alive; from below, from beyond "culture"; from their childhood which men have been trying desperately to make them forget, condemning it to "eternal rest." The little girls and their "ill-mannered" bodies immured, well-preserved, intact unto themselves, in the mirror. Frigidified. But are they ever seething underneath! What an effort it takes—there's no end to it—for the sex cops to bar their threatening return. Such a display of forces on both sides that the struggle has for centuries been immobilized in the trembling equilibrium of a deadlock.

---

[1] Men still have everything to say about their sexuality, and everything to write. For what they have said so far, for the most part, stems from the opposition activity/passivity, from the power relation between a fantasized obligatory virility meant to invade, to colonize, and the consequential phantasm of woman as a "dark continent" to penetrate and to "pacify." (We know what "pacify" means in terms of scotomizing the other and misrecognizing the self.) Conquering her, they've made haste to depart from her borders, to get out of sight, out of body. The way man has of getting out of himself and into her whom he takes not for the other but for his own, deprives him, he knows, of his own bodily territory. One can understand how man, confusing himself with his penis and rushing in for the attack, might feel resentment and fear of being "taken" by the woman, of being lost in her, absorbed, or alone.

Here they are, returning, arriving over and again, because the unconscious is impregnable. They have wandered around in circles, confined to the narrow room in which they've been given a deadly brainwashing. You can incarcerate them, slow them down, get away with the old Apartheid routine, but for a time only. As soon as they begin to speak, at the same time as they're taught their name, they can be taught that their territory is black: because you are Africa, you are black. Your continent is dark. Dark is dangerous. You can't see anything in the dark, you're afraid. Don't move, you might fall. Most of all, don't go into the forest. And so we have internalized this horror of the dark.

Men have committed the greatest crime against women. Insidiously, violently, they have led them to hate women, to be their own enemies, to mobilize their immense strength against themselves, to be the executants of their virile needs. They have made for women an antinarcissism! A narcissism which loves itself only to be loved for what women haven't got! They have constructed the infamous logic of antilove.

We the precocious, we the repressed of culture, our lovely mouths gagged with pollen, our wind knocked out of us, we the labyrinths, the ladders, the trampled spaces, the bevies—we are black and we are beautiful.

We're stormy, and that which is ours breaks loose from us without our fearing any debilitation. Our glances, our smiles, are spent; laughs exude from all our mouths; our blood flows and we extend ourselves without ever reaching an end; we never hold back our thoughts, our signs, our writing; and we're not afraid of lacking.

What happiness for us who are omitted, brushed aside at the scene of inheritances; we inspire ourselves and we expire without running out of breath, we are everywhere!

From now on, who, if we say so, can say no to us? We've come back from always.

It is time to liberate the New Woman from the Old by coming to know her—by loving her for getting by, for getting beyond the Old without delay, by going out ahead of what the New Woman will be, as an arrow quits the bow with a movement that gathers and separates the vibrations musically, in order to be more than her self.

I say that we must, for, with a few rare exceptions, there has not yet been any writing that inscribes femininity; exceptions so rare, in fact, that, after plowing through literature across languages, cultures, and ages,[1] one can only be startled at this vain scouting mission. It is well known that the number of women writers (while having increased very slightly from the nineteenth century on) has always been ridiculously small. This is a useless and deceptive fact unless from their species of female writers we do not first deduct the immense majority whose workmanship is in no way different from male writing, and which either obscures women or reproduces the classic representations of women (as sensitive—intuitive—dreamy, etc.)[2]

Let me insert here a parenthetical remark. I mean it when I speak of male writing. I maintain unequivocally that there is such a thing as *marked* writing; that, until now, far more extensively and repressively than is ever suspected or admitted, writing has been run by a libidinal and cultural—hence political, typically masculine—economy; that this is a locus where the repression of women has been perpetuated, over and over, more or less consciously, and in a manner that's frightening since it's often hidden or adorned with the mystifying charms of fiction; that this locus has grossly exaggerated all the signs of sexual opposition (and not sexual difference), where woman has never *her*

---

[1] I am speaking here only of the place "reserved" for women by the Western world.

2 Which works, then, might be called feminine? I'll just point out some examples: one would have to give them full readings to bring out what is pervasively feminine in their significance. Which I shall do elsewhere. In France (have you noted our infinite poverty in this field?—the Anglo-Saxon countries have shown resources of distinctly greater consequence), leafing through what's come out of the twentieth century—and it's not much—the only inscriptions of feminity that I have seen were by Colette, Marguerite Duras, . . . and Jean Genét,

turn to speak—this being all the more serious and unpardonable in that writing is precisely *the very possibility of change,* the space that can serve as a springboard for subversive thought, the precursory movement of a transformation of social and cultural structures.

Nearly the entire history of writing is confounded with the history of reason, of which it is at once the effect, the support, and one of the privileged alibis. It has been one with the phallocentric tradition. It is indeed that same self-admiring, self-stimulating, self-congratulatory phallocentrism.

With some exceptions, for there have been failures—and if it weren't for them, I wouldn't be writing (I-woman, escapee)—in that enormous machine that has been operating and turning out its "truth" for centuries. There have been poets who would go to any lengths to slip something by at odds with tradition—men capable of loving love and hence capable of loving others and of wanting them, of imagining the woman who would hold out against oppression and constitute herself as a superb, equal, hence "impossible" subject, untenable in a real social framework. Such a woman the poet could desire only by breaking the codes that negate her. Her appearance would necessarily bring on, if not revolution—for the bastion was supposed to be immutable—at least harrowing explosions. At times it is in the fissure caused by an earthquake, through that radical mutation of things brought on by a material upheaval when every structure is for a moment thrown off balance and an ephemeral wildness sweeps order away, that the poet slips something by, for a brief span, of woman. Thus did Kleist expend himself in his yearning for the existence of sister-lovers, maternal daughters, mother-sisters, who never hung their heads in shame. Once the palace of magistrates is restored, it's time to pay: immediate bloody death to the uncontrollable elements.

But only the poets—not the novelists, allies of representationalism. Because poetry involves gaining strength through the unconscious and because the unconscious, that other limitless country, is the place where the repressed manage to survive: women, or as Hoffmann would say, fairies.

She must write her self, because this is the invention of a *new insurgent* writing which, when the moment of her liberation has come, will allow her to carry out the indispensable ruptures and transformations in her history, first at two levels that cannot be separated.

a) Individually. By writing her self, woman will return to the body which has been more than confiscated from her, which has been turned into the uncanny stranger on display—the ailing or dead figure, which so often turns out to be the nasty companion, the cause and location of inhibitions. Censor the body and you censor breath and speech at the same time.

Write your self. Your body must be heard. Only then will the immense resources of the unconscious spring forth. Our naphtha will spread, throughout the world, without dollars—black or gold—nonassessed values that will change the rules of the old game.

To write. An act which will not only "realize" the decensored relation of woman to her sexuality, to her womanly being, giving her access to her native strength; it will give her back her goods, her pleasures, her organs, her immense bodily territories which have been kept under seal; it will tear her away from the superegoized structure in which she has always occupied the place reserved for the guilty (guilty of everything, guilty at every turn: for having desires, for not having any; for being frigid, for being "too hot"; for not being both at once; for being too motherly and not enough; for having children and for not having any; for nursing and for not nursing . . .)—tear her away by means of this research, this job of analysis and illumination, this emancipation of the marvelous text of her self that she must urgently learn to speak. A woman without a body, dumb, blind, can't possibly be a good fighter. She is reduced to being the servant of the militant male, his shadow. We must kill the false woman who is preventing the live one from breathing. Inscribe the breath of the whole woman.

b) An act that will also be marked by woman's *seizing* the occasion to *speak,* hence her shattering entry into history, which has always been based *on her suppression.* To write and thus to forge for herself the antilogos weapon. To become *at will* the taker and initiator, for her own right, in every symbolic system, in every political process.

It is time for women to start scoring their feats in written and oral language.

Every woman has known the torment of getting up to speak. Her heart racing, at times entirely lost for words, ground and language slipping away—that's how daring a feat, how great a transgression it is for a woman to speak—even just open her mouth—in public. A double distress, for even if she transgresses, her words fall almost always upon the deaf male ear, which hears in language only that which speaks in the masculine.

It is by writing, from and toward women, and by taking up the challenge of speech which has been governed by the phallus, that women will confirm women in a place other than that which is reserved in and by the symbolic, that is, in a place other than silence. Women should break out of the snare of silence. They shouldn't be conned into accepting a domain which is the margin or the harem.

Listen to a woman speak at a public gathering (if she hasn't painfully lost her wind). She doesn't "speak," she throws her trembling body forward; she lets go of herself, she flies; all of her passes into her voice, and it's with her body that she vitally supports the "logic" of her speech. Her flesh speaks true. She lays herself bare. In fact, she physically materializes what she's thinking; she signifies it with her body. In a certain way she *inscribes* what she's saying, because she doesn't deny her drives the intractable and impassioned part they have in speaking. Her speech, even when "theoretical" or political, is never simple or linear or "objectified," generalized: she draws her story into history.

There is not that scission, that division made by the common man between the logic of oral speech and the logic of the text, bound as he is by his antiquated relation—servile, calculating—to mastery. From which proceeds the niggardly lip service which engages only the tiniest part of the body, plus the mask.

In women's speech, as in their writing, that element which never stops resonating, which, once we've been permeated by it, profoundly and imperceptibly touched by it, retains the power of moving us—that element is the song: first music from the first voice of love which is alive in every woman. Why this privileged relationship with the voice? Because no woman stockpiles as many defenses for countering the drives as does a man. You don't build walls around yourself, you don't forego pleasure as "wisely" as he. Even if phallic mystification has generally contaminated good relationships, a woman is never far from "mother" (I mean outside her role functions: the "mother" as nonname and as source of goods). There is always within her at least a little of that good mother's milk. She writes in white ink.

Woman for women.—There always remains in woman that force which produces/is produced by the other—in particular, the other woman. *In* her, matrix, cradler; herself giver as her mother and child; she is her own sister-daughter. You might object, "What about she who is the hysterical offspring of a bad mother?" Everything will be changed once woman gives woman to the other woman. There is hidden and always ready in woman the source; the locus for the other. The mother, too, is a metaphor. It is necessary and sufficient that the best of herself be given to woman by another woman for her to be able to love herself and return in love the body that was "born" to her. Touch me, caress me, you the living noname, give me my self as myself. The relation to the "mother," in terms of intense pleasure and violence, is curtailed no more than the relation to childhood (the child that she was, that she is, that she makes, remakes, undoes, there at the point where, the same, she others herself). Text: my body—shot through with streams of song; I don't mean the overbearing, clutchy "mother" but, rather, what touches you, the equivoice that affects you, fills your breast with an urge to come to language and launches your force; the rhythm that laughs you; the intimate recipient who makes all metaphors possible and desirable; body (body? bodies?), no more describable than god, the soul, or the Other; that part of you that leaves a space between yourself and urges you to inscribe in language your woman's style. In women there is always more or less of the mother who makes everything all right, who nourishes, and who stands up against separation; a force that will not be cut off but will knock the wind out of the codes. We will rethink womankind beginning with every form and every period of her body. The Americans remind us, "We are all Lesbians"; that is, don't denigrate woman, don't make of her what men have made of you.

Because the "economy" of her drives is prodigious, she cannot fail, in seizing the occasion to speak, to transform directly and indirectly *all* systems of exchange based on masculine thrift. Her libido will produce far more radical effects of political and social change than some might like to think.

Because she arrives, vibrant, over and again, we are at the beginning of a new history, or rather of a process of becoming in which several histories intersect with one another. As subject for history, woman always occurs simultaneously in several places. Woman un-thinks[1] the unifying, regulating history that homogenizes and channels forces, herding contradictions into a single battlefield. In woman, personal history blends together with the history of all women, as well as national and world history. As a militant, she is an integral part of all liberations. She must be farsighted, not limited to a blow-by-blow interaction. She foresees that her liberation will do more than modify power relations or toss the ball over to the other camp; she will bring about a mutation in human relations, in thought, in all praxis: hers is not simply a class struggle, which she carries forward into a much vaster movement. Not that in order to be a woman-in-struggle(s) you have to leave the class struggle or repudiate it; but you have to split it open, spread it out, push it forward, fill it with the fundamental struggle so as to prevent the class struggle, or any other struggle for the liberation of a class or people, from operating as a form of repression, pretext for postponing the inevitable, the staggering alteration in power relations and in the production of individualities. This alteration is already upon us—in the United States, for example, where millions of night crawlers are in the process of undermining the family and disintegrating the whole of American sociality.

The new history is coming; it's not a dream, though it does extend beyond men's imagination, and for good reason. It's going to deprive them of their conceptual orthopedics, beginning with the destruction of their enticement machine.

It is impossible to *define* a feminine practice of writing, and this is an impossibility that will remain, for this practice can never be theorized, enclosed, coded—which doesn't mean that it doesn't exist. But it will always surpass the discourse that regulates the phallocentric system; it does and will take place in areas other than those subordinated to philosophico-theoretical domination. It will be conceived of only by subjects who are breakers of automatisms, by peripheral figures that no authority can ever subjugate.

Hence the necessity to affirm the flourishes of this writing, to give form to its movement, it's near and distant byways. Bear in mind to begin with (1) that sexual opposition, which has always worked for man's profit to the point of reducing writing, too, to his laws, is only a historico-cultural limit. There is, there will be more and more rapidly pervasive now, a fiction that produces irreducible effects of femininity. (2) That it is through ignorance that most readers, critics, and writers of both sexes hesitate to admit or deny outright the possibility or the pertinence of a distinction between feminine and masculine writing. It will usually be said, thus disposing of

---

[1] "*Dé-pense,*" a neologism formed on the verb *penser,* hence "unthinks," but also "spends" (from *dépenser*) (translator's note).

sexual difference: either that all writing, to the extent that it materializes, is feminine; or, inversely—but it comes to the same thing—that the act of writing is equivalent to masculine masturbation (and so the woman who writes cuts herself out a paper penis); or that writing is bisexual, hence neuter, which again does away with differentiation. To admit that writing is precisely working (in) the inbetween, inspecting the process of the same and of the other without which nothing can live, undoing the work of death—to admit this is first to want the two, as well as both, the ensemble of the one and the other, not fixed in sequences of struggle and expulsion or some other form of death but infinitely dynamized by an incessant process of exchange from one subject to another. A process of different subjects knowing one another and beginning one another anew only from the living boundaries of the other: a multiple and inexhaustible course with millions of encounters and transformations of the same into the other and into the in-between, from which woman takes her forms (and man, in his turn; but that's his other history).

In saying "bisexual, hence neuter," I am referring to the classic conception of bisexuality, which, squashed under the emblem of castration fear and along with the fantasy of a "total" being (though composed of two halves), would do away with the difference experienced as an operation incurring loss, as the mark of dreaded sectility.

To this self-effacing, merger-type bisexuality, which would conjure away castration (the writer who puts up his sign: "bisexual written here, come and see," when the odds are good that it's neither one nor the other), I oppose the *other bisexuality* on which every subject not enclosed in the false theater of phallocentric representationalism has founded his/her erotic universe. Bisexuality: that is, each one's location in self (*réperage en soi*) of the presence—variously manifest and insistent according to each person, male or female—of both sexes, nonexclusion either of the difference or of one sex, and, from this "self-permission," multiplication of the effects of the inscription of desire, over all parts of my body and the other body.

Now it happens that at present, for historico-cultural reasons, it is women who are opening up to and benefiting from this vatic bisexuality which doesn't annul differences but stirs them up, pursues them, increases their number. In a certain way, "woman is bisexual"; man—it's a secret to no one—being poised to keep glorious phallic monosexuality in view. By virtue of affirming the primacy of the phallus and of bringing it into play, phallocratic ideology has claimed more than one victim. As a woman, I've been clouded over by the great shadow of the scepter and been told: idolize it, that which you cannot brandish. But at the same time, man has been handed that grotesque and scarcely enviable destiny (just imagine) of being reduced to a single idol with clay balls. And consumed, as Freud and his followers note, by a fear of being a woman! For, if psychoanalysis was constituted from woman, to repress femininity (and not so successful a repression at that—men have made it clear), its account of masculine sexuality is now hardly refutable; as with all the "human" sciences, it reproduces the masculine view, of which it is one of the effects.

Here we encounter the inevitable man-with-rock, standing erect in his old Freudian realm, in the way that, to take the figure back to the point where linguistics is conceptualizing it "anew," Lacan preserves it in the sanctuary of the phallos (ϕ) "sheltered" from *castration's lack!* Their "symbolic" exists, it holds power—we, the sowers of disorder, know it only too well. But we are in no way obliged to deposit our lives in their banks of lack, to consider the constitution of the subject in terms of a drama manglingly restaged, to reinstate again and again the religion of the father. Because we don't want that. We don't fawn around the supreme hole. We have no womanly reason to pledge allegiance to the negative. The feminine (as the poets suspected) affirms: ". . . And yes," says Molly, carrying *Ulysses* off beyond any book and toward the new writing; "I said yes, I will Yes."

The Dark Continent is neither dark nor unexplorable.—It is still unexplored only because we've been made to believe that it was too dark to be explorable. And because they want to make us believe that what interests us is the white continent, with its monuments to Lack. And we believed. They riveted us between two horrifying myths: between the Medusa and the abyss. That would be enough to set half the world laughing, except that it's still going on. For the phallologocentric sublation[1] is with us, and it's militant, regenerating the old patterns, anchored in the dogma of castration. They haven't changed a thing: they've theorized their desire for reality! Let the priests tremble, we're going to show them our sexts!

Too bad for them if they fall apart upon discovering that women aren't men, or that the mother doesn't have one. But isn't this fear convenient for them? Wouldn't the worst be, isn't the worst, in truth, that women aren't castrated, that they have only to stop listening to the Sirens (for the Sirens were men) for history to change its meaning? You only have to look at the Medusa straight on to see her. And she's not deadly. She's beautiful and she's laughing.

Men say that there are two unrepresentable things: death and the feminine sex. That's because they need femininity to be associated with death; it's the jitters that gives them a hard-on! for themselves! They need to be afraid of us. Look at the trembling Perseuses moving backward toward us, clad in apotropes. What lovely backs! Not another minute to lose. Let's get out of here.

Let's hurry: the continent is not impenetrably dark. I've been there often. I was overjoyed one day to run into Jean Genêt. It was in *Pompes funèbres*.[2] He had come there led by his Jean. There are some men (all too few) who aren't afraid of femininity.

Almost everything is yet to be written by women about femininity: about their sexuality, that is, its infinite and mobile complexity, about their eroticization, sudden turn-ons of a certain miniscule-immense area of their bodies; not about destiny, but about the adventure of such and such a drive, about trips, crossings, trudges, abrupt and gradual awakenings, discoveries of a zone at one time timorous and soon to be forthright. A woman's body, with its thousand and one thresholds of ardor—once, by smashing yokes and censors, she lets it articulate the profusion of meanings that run through it in every direction—will make the old single-grooved mother tongue reverberate with more than one language.

We've been turned away from our bodies, shamefully taught to ignore them, to strike them with that stupid sexual modesty; we've been made victims of the old fool's game: each one will love the other sex. I'll give you your body and you'll give me mine. But who are the men who give women the body that women blindly yield to them? Why so few texts? Because so few women have as yet won back their body. Women must write through their bodies, they must invent the impregnable language that will wreck partitions, classes, and rhetorics, regulations and codes, they must submerge, cut through, get beyond the ultimate reserve-discourse, including the one that laughs at the very idea of pronouncing the word "silence," the one that, aiming for the impossible, stops short before the word "impossible" and writes it as "the end."

Such is the strength of women that, sweeping away syntax, breaking that famous thread (just a tiny little thread, they say) which acts for men as a surrogate umbilical cord, assuring them—otherwise they couldn't come—that the old lady is always right behind them, watching them make phallus, women will go right up to the impossible.

When the "repressed" of their culture and their society returns, it's an explosive, *utterly* destructive, staggering return, with a force never yet

---

[1] Standard English term for the Hegelian *Aufhebung*, the French *la relève*.

[2] Jean Genêt, *Pompes funèbres* (Paris, 1948), p. 185.

unleashed and equal to the most forbidding of suppressions. For when the Phallic period comes to an end, women will have been either annihilated or borne up to the highest and most violent incandescence. Muffled throughout their history, they have lived in dreams, in bodies (though muted), in silences, in aphonic revolts.

And with such force in their fragility; a fragility, a vulnerability, equal to their incomparable intensity. Fortunately, they haven't sublimated; they've saved their skin, their energy. They haven't worked at liquidating the impasse of lives without futures. They have furiously inhabited these sumptuous bodies: admirable hysterics who made Freud succumb to many voluptuous moments impossible to confess, bombarding his Mosaic statue with their carnal and passionate body words, haunting him with their inaudible and thundering denunciations, dazzling, more than naked underneath the seven veils of modesty. Those who, with a single word of the body, have inscribed the vertiginous immensity of a history which is sprung like an arrow from the whole history of men and from biblico-capitalist society, are the women, the supplicants of yesterday, who come as forebears of the new women, after whom no intersubjective relation will ever be the same. You, Dora, you the indomitable, the poetic body, you are the true "mistress" of the Signifier. Before long your efficacity will be seen at work when your speech is no longer suppressed, its point turned in against your breast, but written out over against the other.

In body.—More so than men who are coaxed toward social success, toward sublimation, women are body. More body, hence more writing. For a long time it has been in body that women have responded to persecution, to the familial-conjugal enterprise of domestication, to the repeated attempts at castrating them. Those who have turned their tongues 10,000 times seven times before not speaking are either dead from it or more familiar with their tongues and their mouths than anyone else. Now, I-woman am going to blow up the Law: an explosion henceforth possible and ineluctable; let it be done, right now, *in* language.

Let us not be trapped by an analysis still encumbered with the old automatisms. It's not to be feared that language conceals an invincible adversary, because it's the language of men and their grammar. We mustn't leave them a single place that's any more theirs alone than we are.

If woman has always functioned "within" the discourse of man, a signifier that has always referred back to the opposite signifier which annihilates its specific energy and diminishes or stifles its very different sounds, it is time for her to dislocate this "within," to explode it, turn it around, and seize it; to make it hers, containing it, taking it in her own mouth, biting that tongue with her very own teeth to invent for herself a language to get inside of. And you'll see with what ease she will spring forth from that "within"—the "within" where once she so drowsily crouched—to overflow at the lips she will cover the foam.

Nor is the point to appropriate their instruments, their concepts, their places, or to begrudge them their position of mastery. Just because there's a risk of identification doesn't mean that we'll succumb. Let's leave it to the worriers, to masculine anxiety and its obsession with how to dominate the way things work—knowing "how it works" in order to "make it work." For us the point is not to take possession in order to internalize or manipulate, but rather to dash through and to "fly."[1]

Flying is woman's gesture—flying in language and making it fly. We have all learned the art of flying and its numerous techniques; for centuries we've been able to possess anything only by flying; we've lived in flight, stealing away, finding, when desired, narrow passageways, hidden crossovers. It's no accident that *voler* has a double meaning, that it plays on each of them and thus throws off the agents of sense. It's no accident: women take after birds and robbers just as rob-

[1] Also, "to steal." Both meanings of the verb *voler* are played on, as the text itself explains in the following paragraph (translator's note).

bers take after women and birds. They (*illes*)[1] go by, fly the coop, take pleasure in jumbling the order of space, in disorienting it, in changing around the furniture, dislocating things and values, breaking them all up, emptying structures, and turning propriety upside down.

What woman hasn't flown/stolen? Who hasn't felt, dreamt, performed the gesture that jams sociality? Who hasn't crumbled, held up to ridicule, the bar of separation? Who hasn't inscribed with her body the differential, punctured the system of couples and opposition? Who, by some act of transgression, hasn't overthrown successiveness, connection, the wall of circumfusion?

A feminine text cannot fail to be more than subversive. It is volcanic; as it is written it brings about an upheaval of the old property crust, carrier of masculine investments; there's no other way. There's no room for her if she's not a he. If she's a her-she, it's in order to smash everything, to shatter the framework of institutions, to blow up the law, to break up the "truth" with laughter.

For once she blazes *her* trail in the symbolic, she cannot fail to make of it the chaosmos of the "personal"—in her pronouns, her nouns, and her clique of referents. And for good reason. There will have been the long history of gynocide. This is known by the colonized peoples of yesterday, the workers, the nations, the species off whose backs the history of men has made its gold; those who have known the ignominy of persecution derive from it an obstinate future desire for grandeur; those who are locked up know better than their jailers the taste of free air. Thanks to their history, women today know (how to do and want) what men will be able to conceive of only much later. I say woman overturns the "personal," for if, by means of laws, lies, blackmail, and marriage, her right to herself has been extorted at the same time as her name, she has been able, through the very movement of mortal alienation, to see more closely the inanity of "propriety," the reductive stinginess of the masculine-conjugal subjective economy, which she doubly resists. On the one hand she has constituted herself necessarily as that "person" capable of losing a part of herself without losing her integrity. But secretly, silently, deep down inside, she grows and multiplies, for, on the other hand, she knows far more about living and about the relation between the economy of the drives and the management of the ego than any man. Unlike man, who holds so dearly to his title and his titles, his pouches of value, his cap, crown, and everything connected with his head, woman couldn't care less about the fear of decapitation (or castration), adventuring, without the masculine temerity, into anonymity, which she can merge with without annihilating herself: because she's a giver.

I shall have a great deal to say about the whole deceptive problematic of the gift. Woman is obviously not that woman Nietzsche dreamed of who gives only in order to.[1] Who could ever think of the gift as a gift-that-takes? Who else but man, precisely the one who would like to take everything?

If there is a "propriety of woman," it is paradoxically her capacity to depropriate unselfishly: body without end, without appendage, without principal "parts." If she is a whole, it's a whole composed of parts that are wholes, not simple partial objects but a moving, limitlessly changing ensemble, a cosmos tirelessly traversed by Eros, an immense astral space not organized around any one sun that's any more of a star than the others.

This doesn't mean that she's an undifferentiated magma, but that she doesn't lord it over her body or her desire. Though masculine sexuality gravitates around the penis, engendering that

[1] *Illes* is a fusion of the masculine pronoun *ils,* which refers back to birds and robbers, with the feminine pronoun *elles,* which refers to women (translator's note).

[1] Reread Derrida's text, "Le Style de la femme," in *Nietzsche aujourd'hui* (Paris: Union Générale d'Editions, Coll. 10/18), where the philosopher can be seen operating an *Aufhebung* of all philosophy in its systematic reducing of woman to the place of seduction: she appears as the one who is taken for; the bait in person, all veils unfurled, the one who doesn't give but who gives only in order to (take).

centralized body (in political anatomy) under the dictatorship of its parts, woman does not bring about the same regionalization which serves the couple head/genitals and which is inscribed only within boundaries. Her libido is cosmic, just as her unconscious is worldwide. Her writing can only keep going, without ever inscribing or discerning contours, daring to make these vertiginous crossings of the other(s) ephemeral and passionate sojourns in him, her, them, whom she inhabits long enough to look at from the point closest to their unconscious from the moment they awaken, to love them at the point closest to their drives; and then further, impregnated through and through with these brief, identificatory embraces, she goes and passes into infinity. She alone dares and wishes to know from within, where she, the outcast, has never ceased to hear the resonance of fore-language. She lets the other language speak—the language of 1,000 tongues which knows neither enclosure nor death. To life she refuses nothing. Her language does not contain, it carries; it does not hold back, it makes possible. When id is ambiguously uttered—the wonder of being several—she doesn't defend herself against these unknown women whom she's surprised at becoming, but derives pleasure from this gift of alterability. I am spacious, singing flesh, on which is grafted no one knows which I, more or less human, but alive because of transformation.

Write! and your self-seeking text will know itself better than flesh and blood, rising, insurrectionary dough kneading itself, with sonorous, perfumed ingredients, a lively combination of flying colors, leaves, and rivers plunging into the sea we feed. "Ah, there's her sea," he will say as he holds out to me a basin full of water from the little phallic mother from whom he's inseparable. But look, our seas are what we make of them, full of fish or not, opaque or transparent, red or black, high or smooth, narrow or bankless; and we are ourselves sea, sand, coral, seaweed, beaches, tides, swimmers, children, waves. . . . More or less wavily sea, earth, sky—what matter would rebuff us? We know how to speak them all.

Heterogeneous, yes. For her joyous benefit she is erogenous; she is the erotogeneity of the heterogeneous: airborne swimmer, in flight, she does not cling to herself; she is dispersible, prodigious, stunning, desirous and capable of others, of the other woman that she will be, of the other woman she isn't, of him, of you.

Woman be unafraid of any other place, of any same, or any other. My eyes, my tongue, my ears, my nose, my skin, my mouth, my body-for-(the)-other—not that I long for it in order to fill up a hole, to provide against some defect of mine, or because, as fate would have it, I'm spurred on by feminine "jealousy"; not because I've been dragged into the whole chain of substitutions that brings that which is substituted back to its ultimate object. That sort of thing you would expect to come straight out of "Tom Thumb," out of the *Penisneid* whispered to us by old grandmother ogresses, servants to their father-sons. If they believe, in order to muster up some self-importance, if they really need to believe that we're dying of desire, that we are this hole fringed with desire for their penis—that's their immemorial business. Undeniably (we verify it at our own expense—but also to our amusement), it's their business to let us know they're getting a hard-on, so that we'll assure them (we the maternal mistresses of their little pocket signifier) that they still can, that it's still there—that men structure themselves only by being fitted with a feather. In the child it's not the penis that the woman desires, it's not that famous bit of skin around which every man gravitates. Pregnancy cannot be traced back, except within the historical limits of the ancients, to some form of fate, to those mechanical substitutions brought about by the unconscious of some eternal "jealous woman"; not to penis envies; and not to narcissism or to some sort of homosexuality linked to the ever-present mother! Begetting a child doesn't mean that the woman or the man must fall ineluctably into patterns or must recharge the circuit of reproduction. If there's a risk there's not an inevitable trap: may women be spared the pressure, under the guise of consciousness-raising, of a supplement of interdictions. Either you want a kid or you don't—*that's your business.* Let nobody threaten you; in satisfying your desire, let not the fear of becoming the accomplice to a sociality succeed the old-time fear of being "taken." And man, are you still going to bank on everyone's blindness and passivity, afraid lest the child make a father and, consequently, that in having a kid the woman land herself more than one bad deal by engendering all at once child—mother—father—family? No; it's up to you to break the old circuits. It will be up to man and woman to render obsolete the former relationship and all its consequences, to consider the launching of a brand-new subject, alive, with defamilialization. Let us dematerpaternalize rather than deny woman, in an effort to avoid the co-optation of procreation, a thrilling era of the body. Let us defetishize. Let's get away from the dialectic which has it that the only good father is a dead one, or that the child is the death of his parents. The child is the other, but the other without violence, bypassing loss, struggle. We're fed up with the reuniting of bonds forever to be severed, with the litany of castration that's handed down and genealogized. We won't advance backward anymore; we're not going to repress something so simple as the desire for life. Oral drive, anal drive, vocal drive—all these drives are our strengths, and among them is the gestation drive—just like the desire to write: a desire to live self from within, a desire for the swollen belly, for language, for blood. We are not going to refuse, if it should happen to strike our fancy, the unsurpassed pleasures of pregnancy which have actually been always exaggerated or conjured away—or cursed—in the classic texts. For if there's one thing that's been repressed here's just the place to find it: in the taboo of the pregnant woman. This says a lot about the power she seems invested with at the time, because it has always been suspected, that, when pregnant, the woman not only doubles her market value, but—what's more important—takes on intrinsic value as a woman in her own eyes and, undeniably, acquires body and sex.

There are thousands of ways of living one's pregnancy; to have or not to have with that still invisible other a relationship of another intensity. And if you don't have that particular yearning, it doesn't mean that you're in any way lacking. Each body distributes in its own special way, without model or norm, the nonfinite and changing totality of its desires. Decide for yourself on your position in the arena of contradictions, where pleasure and reality embrace. Bring the other to life. Women know how to live detachment; giving birth is neither losing nor increasing. It's adding to life an other. Am I dreaming? Am I mis-recognizing? You, the defenders of "theory," the sacrosanct yes-men of Concept, enthroners of the phallus (but not of the penis):

Once more you'll say that all this smacks of "idealism," or what's worse, you'll splutter that I'm a "mystic."

And what about the libido? Haven't I read the "Signification of the Phallus"? And what about separation, what about that bit of self for which, to be born, you undergo an ablation—an ablation, so they say, to be forever commemorated by your desire?

Besides, isn't it evident that the penis gets around in my texts, that I give it a place and appeal? Of course I do. I want all. I want all of me with all of him. Why should I deprive myself of a part of us? I want all of us. Woman of course has a desire for a "loving desire" and not a jealous one. But not because she is gelded; not because she's deprived and needs to be filled out, like some wounded person who wants to console herself or seek vengeance: I don't want a penis to decorate my body with. But I do desire the other for the other, whole and entire, male or female; because living means wanting everything that is, everything that lives, and wanting it alive. Castration? Let others toy with it. What's a desire originating from a lack? A pretty meager desire.

The woman who still allows herself to be threatened by the big dick, who's still impressed by the commotion of the phallic stance, who still leads a loyal master to the beat of the drum: that's the woman of yesterday. They still exist, easy and numerous victims of the oldest of farces: either they're cast in the original silent version in which, as titanesses lying under the mountains they make with their quivering, they never see erected that theoretic monument to the golden phallus looming, in the old manner, over their bodies. Or, coming today out of their *infans* period and into the second, "enlightened" version of their virtuous debasement, they see themselves suddenly assaulted by the builders of the analytic empire and, as soon as they've begun to formulate the new desire, naked, nameless, so happy at making an appearance, they're taken in their bath by the new old men, and then, whoops! Luring them with flashy signifiers, the demon of interpretation—oblique, decked out in modernity—sells them the same old handcuffs, baubles, and chains. Which castration do you prefer? Whose degrading do you like better, the father's or the mother's? Oh, what pwetty eyes, you pwetty little girl. Here, buy my glasses and you'll see the Truth-Me-Myself tell you everything you should know. Put them on your nose and take a fetishist's look (you are me, the other analyst—that's what I'm telling you) at your body and the body of the other. You see? No? Wait, you'll have everything explained to you, and you'll know at last which sort of neurosis you're related to. Hold still, we're going to do your portrait, so that you can begin looking like it right away.

Yes, the naives to the first and second degree are still legion. If the New Women, arriving now, dare to create outside the theoretical, they're called in by the cops of the signifier, fingerprinted, remonstrated, and brought into the line of order that they are supposed to know; assigned by force of trickery to a precise place in the chain that's always formed for the benefit of a privileged signifier. We are pieced back to the string which leads back, if not to the Name-of-the-Father, then, for a new twist, to the place of the phallic-mother.

Beware, my friend, of the signifier that would take you back to the authority of a signified! Beware of diagnoses that would reduce your generative powers. "Common" nouns are also proper nouns that disparage your singularity by classifying it into species. Break out of the circles; don't remain within the psychoanalytic closure. Take a look around, then cut through!

And if we are legion, it's because the war of liberation has only made as yet a tiny breakthrough. But women are thronging to it. I've seen them, those who will be neither dupe nor domestic, those who will not fear the risk of being a woman; will not fear any risk, any desire, any space still unexplored in themselves, among themselves and others or anywhere else. They do not fetishize, they do not deny, they do not hate. They observe, they approach, they try to see the other woman, the child, the lover—not to strengthen their own narcissism or verify the solidity or weakness of the master, but to make love better, to invent

Other love.—In the beginning are our differences. The new love dares for the other, wants the other, makes dizzying, precipitous flights between knowledge and invention. The woman arriving over and over again does not stand still; she's everywhere, she exchanges, she is the desire-that-gives. (Not enclosed in the paradox of the gift that takes nor under the illusion of unitary fusion. We're past that.) She comes in, comes-in-between herself me and you, between the other me where one is always infinitely more than one and more than me, without the fear of ever reaching a limit; she thrills in our becoming. And we'll keep on becoming! She cuts through defensive loves, motherages, and devourations: beyond selfish narcissism, in the moving, open, transitional space, she runs her risks. Beyond the struggle-to-the-death that's been removed to the bed, beyond the love-battle that claims to represent exchange, she scorns at an Eros dynamic that would be fed by hatred. Hatred: a heritage, again, a remainder, a duping subservience to the phallus. To love, to watch-think-seek the other in the other, to despecularize, to unhoard. Does this seem difficult? It's not impossible, and this is what nourishes life—a love that has no commerce with the apprehensive desire that provides against the lack and stultifies the strange; a love that rejoices in the exchange that multiplies. Wherever history still unfolds as the history of death, she does not tread. Opposition, hierarchizing exchange, the struggle for mastery which can end only in at least one death (one master—one slave, or two nonmasters ≠ two dead)—all that comes from a period in time governed by phallocentric values. The fact that this period extends into the present doesn't prevent woman from starting the history of life somewhere else. Elsewhere, she gives. She doesn't "know" what she's giving, she doesn't measure it; she gives, though, neither a counterfeit impression nor something she hasn't got. She gives more, with no assurance that she'll get back even some unexpected profit from what she puts out. She gives that there may be life, thought, transformation. This is an "economy" that can no longer be put in economic terms. Wherever she loves, all the old concepts of management are left behind. At the end of a more or less conscious computation, she finds not her sum but her differences. I am for you what you want me to be at the moment you look at me in a way you've never seen me before: at every instant. When I write, it's everything that we don't know we can be that is written out of me, without exclusions, without stipulation, and everything we will be calls us to the unflagging, intoxicating, unappeasable search for love. In one another we will never be lacking.

INTRODUCTION TO KARLYN KOHRS CAMPBELL

Karlyn Kohrs Campbell (born in 1937) is at this writing Professor of Speech-Communication at the University of Minnesota, where she also received her Ph.D. Campbell has taught at several American universities, including the California State University at Los Angeles, the State University of New York at Binghamton, and the University of Kansas. Widely published in rhetorical theory and criticism and in studies of American public address, Campbell has also emerged as a major theorist of women's rhetoric.

We have noted the attempts on several theoretical fronts to reclaim women's rhetoric from the margins. Campbell's work is at the forefront of one distinctive theme within that movement. Campbell is trying to identify skilled female speakers who have entered the traditional male domain of public speaking. Much of Campbell's work has been the recovery of female speakers who have been ignored by historians despite the effectiveness of their speaking. Her extensive critical studies of these speakers identifies rhetorical characteristics peculiar to their styles of speaking. However, in comparison to Cixous and others, Campbell is not attempting to theorize distinctly female patterns of rhetorical discourse. The rhetoric of women is diverse and multi-faceted, she argues, and can no more be characterized by single comprehensive theories than can the rhetoric of men.

Included in this anthology is part of the introduction to Campbell's monumental work, *Man Cannot Speak for Her,* a study of female orators with particular attention to feminist speakers. The selection begins with Campbell's observation that the history of rhetoric is written by and about men. This does not mean that there have been no female orators and rhetoricians, only that they have been lost in the margins of the history of rhetorical theory. Campbell's purpose is to reclaim some of those speakers from the margin.

The focus of Campbell's study is on female speakers in the women's rights movement, especially beginning in the nineteenth century in the United States. Campbell notes that this movement was linked to other political efforts on the part of women to create changes in society, such as the temperance and the abolitionist movements. The history of women in these rhetorical efforts in the nineteenth and twentieth centuries is reviewed by Campbell.

Campbell then explains the difficulties that women had in gaining access to the predominantly male forum of the public speaking platform. The constraints that those social conditions placed on women created distinctive rhetorical practices. Campbell focuses particularly on the style of these speakers as distinct rhetorical adaptations to the repression they faced in gaining both the right to speak and an audience that would allow them to do so.

Rhetorical theories of women's rhetoric are being developed on many fronts today. Campbell's ongoing work is an example of one vigorous strain that seeks to identify the rhetorical work of women in gaining access to the traditional male world of public speaking. Her work adds to our theoretical understanding of different dimensions of women's rhetoric.

KARLYN KOHRS CAMPBELL

MAN CANNOT SPEAK FOR HER

1

INTRODUCTION

Men have an ancient and honorable rhetorical history. Their speeches and writings, from antiquity to the present, are studied and analyzed by historians and rhetoricians. Public persuasion has been a conscious part of the Western male's heritage from ancient Greece to the present. This is not an insignificant matter. For centuries, the ability to persuade others has been part of Western man's standard of excellence in many areas, even of citizenship itself. Moreover, speaking and writing eloquently has long been the goal of the humanistic tradition in education.

Women have no parallel rhetorical history. Indeed, for much of their history women have been prohibited from speaking, a prohibition reinforced by such powerful cultural authorities as Homer, Aristotle, and Scripture. In the *Odyssey,* for example, Telemachus scolds his mother Penelope and tells her, "Public speech [*mythos*] shall be men's concern" (Homer 1980, 9).[1] In the *Politics,* Aristotle approvingly quotes the words, "Silence is a woman's glory" (1923, 1.13.12602a.30), and the epistles of Paul enjoin women to keep silent. As a result, when women began to speak outside the home on moral issues and on matters of public policy, they faced obstacles unknown to men. Further, once they began to speak, their words often were not preserved, with the result that many rhetorical acts by women are gone forever; many others can be found only in manuscript collections or rare, out-of-print publications. Even when reprinted, they frequently are treated as historical artifacts from which excerpts can be drawn rather than as artistic works that must be seen whole in order to be understood and appreciated. As a rhetorical critic I want to restore one segment of the history of women, namely the rhetoric of the early woman's rights movement that emerged in the United States in the 1830s, that became a movement focused primarily on woman suffrage after the Civil War, and whose force dissipated in the mid-1920s. I refer to this as the early movement in contrast to contemporary feminism.

This project is a rhetorical study, which means that all of the documents analyzed in the chapters that follow and anthologized in volume II are works through which woman's rights advocates sought to persuade others of the rightness of their cause. In the broadest sense, rhetoric is the study of the means by which symbols can be used to appeal to others, to persuade. The potential for persuasion exists in the shared symbolic and socioeconomic experience of persuaders (rhetors) and audiences; specific rhetorical acts attempt to exploit that shared experience and channel it in certain directions.

Rhetoric is one of the oldest disciplines in the Western tradition. From its beginnings in ancient

Greece, it has been a practical art, one that assesses a persuader's efforts in light of the resources available on a specific occasion in relation to a particular audience and in order to achieve a certain kind of end. As a result, rhetorical analysis has focused on invention, the rhetor's skill in selecting and adapting those resources available in language, in cultural values, and in shared experience in order to influence others.

The aim of the rhetorical critic is enlightenment—an understanding of the ways symbols can be used by analyzing the ways they were used in a particular time and place and the ways such usage appealed or might have appealed to other human beings—then or now. Rhetorical critics attempt to function as surrogates for audiences, both of the past and of the present. Based on their general knowledge of rhetorical literature and criticism, and based on familiarity with the rhetoric of a movement and its historical milieu, critics attempt to show how a rhetorical act has the potential to teach, to delight, to move, to flatter, to alienate, or to hearten.

The potential to engage another is the aesthetic or symbolic power of a piece of persuasive discourse. Such assessments are related to a work's actual effects. However, many rhetorical works fail to achieve their ends for reasons that have little to do with their style or content. In a social movement advocating controversial changes, failure to achieve specific goals will be common, no matter how able and creative the advocates, whether male or female. For example, a woman might urge legal changes to give a wife a right to her own earnings, but in a single speech to men opposed to the very idea of a woman speaking, she cannot succeed in practical terms, even though her speech is powerful and noteworthy. If she were extremely skillful, she might increase awareness of the plight of married women and arouse sympathy for them among some members of the audience. As a result, critics must judge whether the choices made by rhetors were skillful responses to the problems they confronted, not whether the changes they urged were enacted. Nevertheless, where evidence of impact exists, it will be noted, although such evidence is not a reliable measure of rhetorical skill, because it, too, can be the product of extrinsic factors.

Selecting appropriate terminology to refer to women in the early movement has proved something of a problem, because the meanings of some key terms have changed. I call the activists of the earlier movement feminists only in the sense that they worked to advance the cause of women. To themselves, they were woman's rights advocates (working for the rights of woman) or suffragists (working for woman suffrage), and for the most part, I shall retain these labels. In the United States, only their opponents called them "suffragettes," whereas in Great Britain, the radical wing of the movement, the Women's Social and Political Union, led by Emmeline and Christabel Pankhurst, adopted this epithet as their own. The term "feminism" existed in the mid-nineteenth century, but it meant only "having the qualities of a female." In the 1890s the term came into use, primarily by anti-suffragists, to refer negatively to woman's rights activists, that is, those committed to the legal, economic, and social equality of women. After the turn of the century, the term became more acceptable, and mainstream suffragists used the term but redefined it (Shaw 1918, in Linkugel 1960, 2:667–83; Cott 1987, 3–50); early in this century more radical feminists in the National Woman's Party claimed it as their own. As this study will demonstrate, women in the early movement differed over goals; my use of "feminism" here is inclusive and catholic, referring to all those who worked for the legal, economic, and political advancement of women, beginning in the 1830s.

References to individual women also required decisions. Except for chapter 2, in which I refer to Sarah and Angelina Grimké by their first names in order to distinguish between them, I have consistently referred to women by the names they used themselves, for example Ida B. Wells, Lucy Stone, and Carrie Chapman Catt, or I have used their birth and married names to refer to them after initial identification, for example Cady Stanton and

Coffin Mott. I do so to retain their identities as well as to indicate kinship, as in Martha Coffin Wright and Lucretia Coffin Mott. This may seem a bit cumbersome, but I can find no alternative that seems consistent with my principles and theirs. When names changed subsequent to or during movement activism, such changes are indicated in brackets, as in Antoinette Brown [Blackwell].

MOVEMENT HISTORY

Woman's rights agitation was in large measure a byproduct of women's efforts in other reform movements. Women seeking to end slavery, to attack the evils of alcohol abuse, and to improve the plight of prostitutes found themselves excluded from male reform organizations and attacked for involving themselves in concerns outside the home. A distinctive woman's rights movement began when women reformers recognized that they had to work for their own rights before they could be effective in other reform efforts.

Many early woman's rights advocates began as abolitionists, but because they were excluded from participation in male anti-slavery societies, they formed female anti-slavery societies and ultimately, as chapter 2 describes, they began to press for their own rights in order to be more effective in the abolitionist struggle (Hersh 1978). Both Lucretia Coffin Mott and Elizabeth Cady Stanton dated the beginnings of the woman's rights movement from 1840, the year when five female delegates from U.S. anti-slavery societies, one of whom was Coffin Mott, were refused seating at the World Anti-Slavery Convention in London. The outrage they felt at the debate that culminated in the denial of women's participation in the convention fueled their decision to call a woman's rights convention, a decision that eventuated in the Seneca Falls, New York, convention of 1848. Because the struggle to abolish slavery was so closely related to the earliest efforts for woman's rights, and because female abolitionists' speeches show them struggling to find ways to cope with proscriptions against speaking, the next chapter analyzes this connection, and texts by abolitionist women are included in volume II.

Woman's rights activism took an organized form at the 1848 Seneca Falls convention at which Elizabeth Cady Stanton made her first speech, and the movement's manifesto, the "Declaration of Sentiments," was introduced and ratified. Local, regional, and national woman's rights conventions were held until the outbreak of the Civil War in 1861. During the war, women activists bent all their efforts toward supporting the Union cause, primarily through work on the Sanitary Commission, and toward abolishing slavery, primarily through the Woman's National Loyal League. Because of their important contributions, women expected to be rewarded with suffrage. Instead, they were told that their dreams were to be deferred. Woman suffrage was so controversial that it was feared it would take suffrage for Afro-American males down to defeat. As a result, in 1868, the Fourteenth Amendment for the first time introduced the word "male" into the U.S. Constitution. Bitterness and frustration caused the movement to split into rival organizations in 1869. However, a final effort was made to obtain suffrage through the courts. Based on the argument that the Fourteenth Amendment had defined citizenship, and that citizenship implied suffrage, in 1872 Susan B. Anthony and other women registered and voted, or attempted to do so. In 1875, however, the Supreme Court rejected that argument, making a separate federal amendment necessary.

During this period a major impetus toward woman suffrage came from an unexpected source —the temperance movement. This reform effort, like abolitionism, was a major source of woman's rights advocates. The struggle against the evils of alcohol abuse caught fire in 1874, and the Woman's Christian Temperance Union (WCTU) was founded. Per capita consumption of alcohol by Americans in the 1820s is estimated to have been three times that of 1980, and by 1909, Americans spent almost as much on alcohol as they did on all food products and nonalcoholic beverages combined. In the 1820s, hard liquor was inexpensive, cheaper than beer, wine, milk, coffee, or tea; only water was cheaper, and it was often polluted. Consumption of alcoholic beverages had been an integral part of U.S. life since colonial times, and alcoholic beverages were thought to be nutritious and healthful. Such traditions and beliefs, combined with low cost, increased consumption (Rorabaugh 1980; Lender and Martin 1983). In 1870, there were some 100,000 saloons in the country, approximately one for every fifty inhabitants (Giele 1961, 41).

Women were vulnerable to the effects of alcohol abuse. Although some women became drunkards, primarily due to the high alcohol content of patent medicines, alcoholism among males was the major problem. Women married to drunkards were at the mercy of their husbands. As late as 1900, in thirty-seven states a woman had no rights to her children, and all her possessions and earnings belonged to her husband (Bordin 1981, 7).

Temperance was an acceptable outlet for the reformist energies of women during the last decades of the nineteenth century. Unlike earlier woman's rights and woman suffrage advocacy, which implied at least a redefinition of woman's sphere, temperance work could be done by a "true woman." Because brothels were often attached to saloons, alcohol was perceived as an inducement to immorality as well as a social and economic threat to the home. Women who struggled against its use were affirming their piety, purity, and domesticity. Because the sale and consumption of alcohol was associated with immorality, and because temperance work implied no change in woman's traditional role, churches that opposed other reforms supported temperance activities. WCTU branches often grew out of existing churchwomen's organizations. As a result, temperance efforts exacted fewer social costs from women than did work for other woman's rights. Although the WCTU accepted traditional concepts of womanhood, it came to argue that woman's distinctive influence should be extended outside the home via the vote. Consequently, woman suffrage became acceptable to more conservative women (and men), who had rejected it before, when presented as a means for woman to protect her domestic sphere from abuses related to alcohol.

In 1890, the rival suffrage organizations merged into the National American Woman Suffrage Association (NAWSA). Although 1890 was the year Wyoming became the first state to give women the right to vote, in the period around the turn of the century women activists made little progress. Anti-suffrage activity was at its height, and movement leadership was in transition as the initiators died and a younger generation took over. With the rise of the Progressive movement, particularly in the West, the climate for woman's rights improved. Women such as the Rev. Dr. Anna Howard Shaw traveled throughout the nation speaking in support of woman suffrage. In 1915, the skilled administrator Carrie Chapman Catt assumed leadership of NAWSA, developing a "Winning Plan" to maximize pressure on Congress to pass a suffrage amendment. Finally, Alice Paul and her cohorts in the National Woman's Party (NWP) paraded, picketed, and demonstrated in order to draw attention to the issue and to keep it at the top of the congressional agenda. These efforts, energized by the pressures of World War I, led to passage of an amendment and its ratification on August 26, 1920. For the first time, all U.S. women were eligible to vote in the 1920 elections.

Sadly, that achievement meant less than women activists had hoped. Few women voted, and in a short time it became clear that women did not form a distinct voting bloc or constituency. The limited meaning of woman suffrage was manifest in 1925 when an amendment prohibiting child labor failed to gain ratification, and that event symbolizes the end of the early movement.

Many causes contributed to the demise of the movement. In the "Red scare" of the 1920s, women activists were attacked for their support of progressive causes, including the Parent-Teacher Association (PTA) and the Young Women's Christian Association (YWCA). Activists also hastened their own end by bitterly dividing over the equal rights amendment, introduced in 1923 at the behest of the National Woman's Party. On the one hand, the NWP took an inflexible and absolute natural rights position, rejecting any special legal consideration for women. In opposition, the League of Women Voters, descendant of NAWSA, and women trade unionists, among others, fought to retain protective legislation, which would have been imperiled by such an amendment. Conflict over similar issues and over the ERA persists among U.S. women, underlining the links between the earlier movement and contemporary feminist concerns.

• • •

STRUGGLING FOR THE RIGHT TO SPEAK

Early woman's rights activists were constrained to be particularly creative because they faced barriers unknown to men. They were a group virtually unique in rhetorical history because a central element in woman's oppression was the denial of her right to speak (Lipking 1983). Quite simply, in nineteenth-century America, femininity and rhetorical action were seen as mutually exclusive. No "true woman" could be a public persuader.

The concept of "true womanhood" (Welter 1976), or the "woman-belle ideal" (Scott 1970), defined females as "other," as suited only for a limited repertoire of gender-based roles, and as the repository of cherished but commercially useless spiritual and human values. These attitudes arose in response to the urbanization and industrialization of the nineteenth century, which separated home and work. As the cult of domesticity was codified in the United States in the early part of the century, two distinct subcultures emerged. Man's place was the world outside the home, the public realm of politics and finance; man's nature was thought to be lustful, amoral, competitive, and ambitious. Woman's place was home, a haven from amoral capitalism and dirty politics, where "the heart was," where the spiritual and emotional needs of husband and children were met by a "ministering angel." Woman's nature was pure, pious, domestic, and submissive (Welter 1976, 21). She was to remain entirely in the private sphere of the home, eschewing any appearance of individuality, leadership, or aggressiveness. Her purity depended on her domesticity; the woman who was compelled by economic need or slavery to work away from her own hearth was tainted. However, woman's alleged moral superiority (Cott 1977, 120, 146–48, 170) generated a conflict out of which the woman's rights movement emerged.

As defined, woman's role contained a contradiction that became apparent as women responded to what they saw as great moral wrongs. Despite their allegedly greater moral sensitivity, women were censured for their efforts against the evils of prostitution and slavery (Berg 1978; Hersh 1978). Women who formed moral reform and abolitionist societies, and who made speeches, held conventions, and published newspapers, entered the public sphere and thereby lost their claims to purity and piety. What became the woman's rights/woman suffrage movement arose out of this contradiction.

Women encountered profound resistance to their efforts for moral reform because rhetorical action of any sort was, as defined by gender roles, a masculine activity. Speakers had to be expert and authoritative; women were submissive. Speakers ventured into the public sphere (the courtroom, the legislature, the pulpit, or the lecture platform); woman's domain was domestic. Speakers called attention to themselves, took stands aggressively, initiated action, and affirmed their expertise; "true women" were retiring and modest, their influence was indirect, and they had no expertise or authority. Because they were thought naturally incapable of reasoning, women were considered unsuited to engage in or to guide public deliberation. The public realm was competitive, driven by ambition; it was a sphere in which the desire to succeed could only be inhibited by humane concerns and spiritual values. Similarly, speaking was competitive, energized by the desire to win a case or persuade others to one's point of view. These were viewed as exclusively masculine traits related to man's allegedly lustful, ruthless, competitive, amoral, and ambitious nature. Activities requiring such qualities were thought to "unsex" women.

The extent of the problem is illustrated by the story of educational pioneer Emma Hart Willard (Scott 1978; Willard 1819). Encouraged by Governor De Witt Clinton in 1819 to present "A Plan for Improving Female Education" to the New York Legislature, Hart Willard presented her proposal to legislators, but carefully remained seated to avoid any hint that she was delivering a speech. In her biography of this influential educator, Alma Lutz writes: "Although this [oral presentation] was very unconventional for a woman, she did not hesitate, so great was her enthusiasm for her *Plan*. . . . She impressed them not as the much-scorned female politician, but as a noble woman inspired by a great ideal" (Lutz 1931, 28).

In other words, a woman who spoke displayed her "masculinity"; that is, she demonstrated that she possessed qualities traditionally ascribed only to males. When a woman spoke, she enacted her equality, that is, she herself was proof that she was as able as her male counterparts to function in the public sphere. That a woman speaking is such proof explains the outraged reactions to women addressing "promiscuous" audiences of men and women, sharing a platform with male speakers, debating, and preaching, even on such clearly moral issues as slavery, prostitution, and alcohol abuse. The hostility women experienced in reform efforts led them to found female reform organizations and to initiate a movement for woman's rights, at base a movement claiming woman's right to engage in public moral action.

Biology, or rather ignorance of biology, was used to buttress arguments limiting woman's role and excluding her from higher education and political activity. On average, women were smaller than men. As a result, it was assumed that they had smaller brains, and that therefore their brains presumably were too small to sustain the rational deliberation required in politics and business. Moreover, their smaller, and hence more delicate and excitable, nerves could not withstand the pressures of public debate or the marketplace. Menarche, the onset of menstruation, was viewed as a physical cataclysm that rendered women unfit for normal activity. For example, Harvard medical professor Dr. Edward Clarke (1873) argued against higher education for women on the grounds that the blood needed to sustain development of the ovaries and womb would be diverted to the brain, which he believed was a major cause of serious illness.

Because of the conceptions of their nature and the taboos that were part of the cult of domesticity, women who spoke publicly confronted extraordinary obstacles. For example, abolitionist Abby Kelley [Foster]

> faced such continuous and merciless persecution that she earned the title "our Joan of Arc" among her co-workers. Lucy Stone later described Kelley's career as "long, unrelieved, moral torture." . . . Because she often traveled alone, or (worse) with male agents, she was vilified as a "bad" woman. . . . She was further reviled when she continued to appear in public while pregnant. (Hersh 1978, 42–43)

On the one hand, a woman had to meet all the usual requirements of speakers, demonstrating expertise, authority, and rationality in order to show her competence and make herself credible to audiences. However, if that was all she did, she was likely to be judged masculine, unwomanly, aggressive, and cold. As a result, women speakers sometimes searched for ways to legitimate such "unwomanly" behavior and for ways to incorporate evidence of femininity into ordinary rhetorical action. In other instances, their own defiance and outrage overwhelmed their efforts at adaptation. In still other cases, rhetors found womanly ways of persuasion that were self-contradictory, and hence ultimately damaging to their cause. Yet on occasion, extraordinarily skilled women persuaders found symbolic means of responding to these contradictory expectations, and produced masterpieces. The problems women faced as speakers are a recurring theme of this book, a theme that remains relevant for contemporary women who still must struggle to cope with these contradictory expectations, albeit in somewhat modified forms.

FEMININE STYLE

Analysis of persuasion by women indicates that many strategically adopted what might be called a feminine style to cope with the conflicting demands of the podium. That style emerged out of their experiences as women and was adapted to the attitudes and experiences of female audiences. However, it was not, and is not today, a style exclusive to women, either as speakers or as audiences.

Deprived of formal education and confined to the home, a woman learned the crafts of housewifery and motherhood—cooking, cleaning, canning, sewing, childbearing, child-rearing, and the like—from other women through a supervised internship combining expert advice with trial and error. These processes are common to all craft-learning, including carpentry, horse training and plumbing, but craft-related skills cannot be expressed in universal laws; one must learn to apply them contingently, depending upon conditions and materials (McMillan 1982). Learning to adapt to variation is essential to mastery of a craft, and the highly skilled craftsperson is alert to variation, aware of a host of alternatives, and able to read cues related to specific conditions.

If the process of craft-learning is applied to the rhetorical situation (and rhetoric itself is a craft), it produces discourse with certain characteristics. Such discourse will be personal in tone (crafts are learned face-to-face from a mentor), relying heavily on personal experience, anecdotes, and other examples. It will tend to be structured inductively (crafts are learned bit by bit, instance by instance, from which generalizations emerge). It will invite audience participation, including the process of testing generalizations or principles against the experiences of the audience. Audience members will be addressed as peers, with recognition of authority based on experience (more skilled craftspeople are more experienced), and efforts will be made to create identification with the experiences of the audience and those described by the speaker. The goal of such rhetoric is empowerment, a term contemporary feminists have used to refer to the process of persuading listeners that they can act effectively in the world, that they can be "agents of change" (Bitzer 1968). Given the traditional concept of womanhood, which emphasized passivity, submissiveness, and patience, persuading women that they could act was a precondition for other kinds of persuasive efforts.[3]

Many of the qualities of the style just described are also part of the small-group phenomenon known as consciousness-raising, associated with contemporary feminism as well as other social movements, which is a communicative style that can be incorporated into speaking or prose writing (Farrell 1979). Because oppressed groups tend to develop passive personality traits, consciousness-raising is an attractive communication style to people working for social change. Whether in a small group, from the podium, or on the page, consciousness-raising invites audience members to participate in the persuasive process—it empowers them. It is a highly appealing form of discourse, particularly if identification between advocate and audience is facilitated by common values and shared experience.

Based on this description, it should be obvious that while there is nothing inevitably or necessarily female about this rhetorical style, it has been congenial to women because of the acculturation of female speakers and audiences.[4] It can be called "feminine" in this context because it reflects the learning experiences of women who were speakers and audiences in this period, and because, as a less authoritative and aggressive style, it was a less confrontational violation of taboos against public speaking by women.

Because the very act of speaking publicly violated concepts of womanhood, the rhetoric of early woman's rights advocates always had at least two dimensions—presentation of their grievances and justification of woman's right to function in the public sphere, to speak with authority in any area of human life. From the beginnings of the movement, women justified their demands based on what Aileen Kraditor (1965, 43–74) calls the argument from justice and the argument from expediency. The argument from justice was drawn from natural rights philosophy and affirmed the personhood of women and their right to all the civil and political privileges of citizenship.[5] It was a demand for rights affirming that, at least in law and politics, there were no differences between the sexes. By contrast, the argument from expediency presumed that women and men were fundamentally different, so that it would be beneficial, that is, desirable and prudent, to give women rights because of the effect on society. For example, it was argued that if women were educated, they would be better able to fulfill their obligations as wives and mothers; if married women had the right to sue, to enter into contracts, to control their earnings, and to own property, they would be able to protect themselves and their children against profligate husbands, or to fulfill their duties to their children in widowhood. If women were allowed to vote, they would bring to bear on politics their purity, piety, and domestic concerns, and thus purify government and make it more responsive to the needs of the home.

Most woman's rights advocates mixed these arguments, often in a somewhat self-contradictory way. In the earliest period, natural rights arguments predominated, but most advocates still assumed that women were naturally better suited to motherhood and that the aim of a woman's life was wifehood and motherhood. However, even in that period, some argued chiefly from the benefits that increased opportunities or rights would produce for woman's traditional qualities and duties—education would make women more virtuous, increased economic rights for married women would produce better mothers. In the 1870s, arguments from expediency predominated, with emphasis on the societal benefits of the woman's ballot, particularly in fighting the evils of alcohol. Yet as time passed, those who argued from benefits frequently incorporated arguments from natural rights into their rhetoric, and in this later period there were speakers, such as Dr. Anna Howard Shaw, who argued almost exclusively from the natural rights position (Linkugel 1963).

Natural rights arguments were perceived as less feminine. "True women" were unselfish—their efforts were for others, particularly their husbands and children. Women who claimed their rights were seen as selfish, as wanting to abandon their traditional womanly roles to enter the sphere of men, and this made such arguments and advocates particularly unappealing to many women (Camhi 1973, 113). Arguments from benefits were "feminine" in part because they presupposed the qualities of "true womanhood" and in part because they appeared unselfish. Women who argued from expediency did not seek rights for their own sake but only for the good that could be done with them for others. This argument achieved its fullest development in the WCTU's support for woman suffrage as a means to protect the home against the abuses of alcohol.

The obstacles early women persuaders faced persist, although in altered forms, in the present. As a result, my goals in this project are simultaneously scholarly and feminist. As a scholar, I wish to rescue the works of great women speakers from the oblivion to which most have been consigned; above all, I wish to show that the artistry of this rhetoric generated enduring monuments to human thought and creativity.[6] Because early feminists faced obstacles whose residues still haunt contemporary women, their rhetorical efforts are a rich source of illumination. As a feminist, I believe that the works analyzed in this volume and anthologized in volume II represent a particularly abundant mother lode of rhetorical creativity from which contemporary women speakers and activists may draw examples and inspiration.

NOTES

1. Translations of this line vary, but all render *mythos* similarly: "Talking must be men's concern." (1946, 34); "Speech shall be for men." (1935, 11); "Speech shall be the men's care" (1932, 11); and "Speech is man's matter." (1897 rpt. 1967, 20).
3. Passivity, modesty, patience, and submissiveness were integral parts of "true womanhood," concepts reinforced by nineteenth-century women's total lack of economic, social, legal, or political power. The impact of such attitudes is apparent in more contemporary studies of women's self-concepts (McClelland 1964). Freeman (1971) cites a study done in the 1950s in which women were asked to pick adjectives to describe themselves: they selected "uncertain, anxious, nervous, hasty, careless, fearful, childish, helpless, sorry, timid, clumsy, stupid, silly, domestic, understanding, tender, sympathetic, pure, generous, affectionate, loving, moral, kind, grateful, and patient" (165). Many of these qualities are at odds with a sense of being capable of effective action.
4. Unlike Farrell (1979, 917n), I do not presume that "feminine" style is rooted in biological differences.
5. Natural rights philosophy grew out of ancient and medieval doctrines of natural law that were modified by an emphasis on the individual in the seventeenth century. Fundamentally, natural rights philosophy took the view that individuals had rights no government could abridge or deny. As a result, the function of government was to protect such rights, requiring plebiscites to determine the consent of the governed and revolution if the government failed in its proper functions. Articulated in the writings of John Locke, natural rights philosophy was elaborated in the United States in the works of Thomas Jefferson, Samuel Adams, and Thomas Paine. Classic expressions of natural rights philosophy are the Declaration of Independence and the Bill of Rights. Concepts of natural rights infused the writings of Mary Wollstonecraft and were central to the Declaration of Sentiments adopted at Seneca Falls in 1848.
6. Rhetoric is not, of course, the only important element in a social movement (Freeman 1975, 1–43).

INTRODUCTION TO CAROLE SPITZACK AND KATHRYN CARTER

Comparison of the work of Karlyn Kohrs Campbell with Hélène Cixous reveals a healthy variety among the efforts of those who are recovering the rhetoric of women from the margins of theory and practice. The article reprinted here is a survey of that variety. The authors are Carole J. Spitzack, Professor of Communication at Tulane University, and Kathryn E. Carter, Professor of Communication Studies at the University of Nebraska.

Spitzack and Carter argue that theories of women's rhetoric are informed by assumptions about the nature of women. In a survey of the literature on female rhetoric, they identify five schools of thought based on five definitions of women. The first is "womanless communication," which ignores female rhetoric because it assumes it is unimportant in history. The second is "great women speakers," typified by the work of Campbell. The third is "woman as other," which sees women as essentially different from men and which then identifies ways in which those differences are manifest in rhetoric. The fourth is "the politics of woman as other," typified by Cixous, which not only identifies differences but celebrates them as politically desirable forms of communication. The final school of thought, "women as communicators," examines feminist scholarship itself and compares its findings to the recent practices and experiences of women as communicators.

Other writers might well identify a different taxonomy of approaches to the study of women's rhetoric. Scholarship changes over time, and eventually a new scheme of schools of thought may be proposed. But Spitzack and Carter provide a useful model for understanding the variety of perspectives on female rhetoric that has guided and will guide the development of women's rhetorical theory.

CAROLE SPITZACK AND KATHRYN CARTER

WOMEN IN COMMUNICATION STUDIES: A TYPOLOGY FOR REVISION

Studies by and about women are gaining increased visibility in the communication discipline. Courses in gender and communication are being added to departmental curricula, the number of women in professional organizations is growing, articles by women appear regularly in communication publications, and in recent years scholars have formed caucuses and journals that are devoted explicitly to the study of women's communication.[1] Although female visibility and diversity *may* contribute to a knowledge of women's communication, the suggestion that mere presence or strength in numbers signals understanding may be overly optimistic. Unless investigations of women serve to challenge and complicate depictions of human communication, the insights gained by gender and feminist scholars are easily placed back into the pre-established frameworks that have been found to distort women's communication. Improved understanding becomes possible when taken for granted assumptions concerning the questions asked and the strategies employed by researchers are critically examined. Such analysis not only demands attention to *women's* communication, but in the process of critique, dominant assumptive bases in communication research come under scrutiny. Within dominant paradigms and sex-role imagery female experience is restricted and excluded. Critical reflection on these paradigms challenges male *and* female researchers to design truly inclusive strategies.

Our aim is to describe five conceptualizations of women that are present in communication research: Womanless Communication; Great Women Communicators; Women as Other; The Politics of Woman as Other; Women as Communicators. Each conceptualization assumes a particular picture of women's "place" in communication studies, and more generally, in socio-cultural practices. By making assumptions and gender imagery explicit, we encourage self-consciousness regarding research choices, ultimately leading to the pluralism advocated by communication scholars.

Our typology is based in an adaptation of the model proposed by Peggy McIntosh in "Interactive Phases of Curriculum Re-Vision: A Feminist Perspective."[2] McIntosh uses the discipline of History to describe each phase in her model: Womanless History; Women in History; Women as Problem, Anomaly, or Absence in History; Woman as History; History Redefined or Reconstructed to Include Us All.[3] The model is subsequently applied by McIntosh to English, Biology, and Art History. Although McIntosh focuses specifically on curriculum development in areas other than communication, her phase model challenges all academicians to examine the relation between perceptions of women and research practices within their own disciplines. In the analysis to follow, the term *types* replaces McIntosh's *phases,* however, because earlier phases of communication research do not dissolve into later research. Each type is an important component in contemporary disciplinary definition. The final section, Women as Communicators, highlights the interrelation of the five conceptualizations of women by examining the concept of leadership as it might be approached within each type of communication research. We use research on leadership as the exemplar because it is an area of study within rhetoric, interpersonal communication, and small group communication, whether the methods are those of rhetorical criticism or empirical studies.

WOMANLESS COMMUNICATION

Womanless Communication research simply leaves women out of its account of human communication. The lives and experiences of women are omitted implicitly from such accounts because, McIntosh observes, scholarly attention is focused on "those who had most public power and whose lives were involved with laws, wars, acquisition of territory, and management of power."[4] Historically, by comparison to the influence of men, women have enjoyed only marginal participation in public realms. That womanless communication has for a long time been the academic norm is evident, for example, in a survey of 45 speech anthologies, where, among thousands of speeches, Karlyn Campbell found only 52 speeches or speech excerpts by women.[5] Similarly, Karen Foss and Sonja Foss reveal that in major publication outlets for communication scholars, there is a disproportionately low number of female authored articles and studies about women.[6] These observations, along with insights gained from numerous feminist communication scholars, help to frame two important questions: despite the appearance of increased female participation in recent years, why and in what sense has the study of communication remained *womanless?*

George Kennedy's comprehensive analysis of rhetoric warns that history documents a perspective since most of the world's population does not appear in records that describe cultural progress.[7] Kennedy's observation, combined with our field's focus on public communicative contexts, leads to the tendency to omit large numbers of people, both male and female, from historical records. Until recently, neither minority groups nor women held visibly powerful positions, for example, in political office, media, corporations, or academia.[8] Hence, to continue to use the public and the political as criteria for scholarly interest is to continue to exclude most people from cultural records.

In addition to exclusion as one of the general cultural omissions of minority groups, female stereotypes establish a double barrier for women. Presumptions regarding the role and/or nature of women are inconsistent with public power. Traditionally, femininity is associated with private domains such as home and family, while masculinity is at home in the public areas of politics and commerce.[9] Moreover, as Lea Stewart, Pamela Cooper, and Sheryl Friedley point out, "traditional sex roles have labeled males as aggressive, assertive, active, and independent and have labeled females as subjective, noncompetitive, and dependent."[10] Insofar as public career aspirations involving individual advancement and competitive instincts are thought to be secondary and perhaps even incompatible with femininity, the publicly visible woman becomes a contradiction in terms.

Even a woman who attains social visibility in a respected domain, such as Geraldine Ferraro in her bid for the 1984 vice presidency, finds much public attention centered on personal relationships, family, and appearance; in short, her ability to occupy a male role is questioned implicitly by highlighting her *female* obligations. The mere presence of a woman in a traditionally male domain complicates even routine communicative acts, evidenced, for example, in the controversy surrounding the greeting gestures of Ferraro and Mondale: should they kiss or shake hands? The public female figure who does not display feminine characteristics and concerns is suspect because within the confines of role prescriptions, she is deemed "unnatural"; at the same time her "natural" female qualities render her unsuitable for the public realm.[11]

Women are omitted from present communication studies when the field sets criteria that exclude critical comment because cultural stereotypes define women as poor communicators. The devaluation of women's communication rarely evolves by way of explicit sanctions against female participation. Rather, the logic that informs dominant world views assumes a basis in neutrality, providing claims of *human* truths which, in fact, reflect the interests and predispositions of privileged groups—namely men. Communication scholars contribute to female invisibility by the particular definitions of humanism and free speech. Here, tension exists between the demand for pluralism and the potentially exclusionary way in which pluralism has been defined. For example, Roderick Hart identifies communication practitioners as "liberals of the first order," persons who "accept all comers into the world of human discourse," humanists who "think about the resources of language as well as how to utter words."[12] He suggests that all individuals should have opportunities to achieve recognition through communicative competence because, "We are a pull-yourself-up-by-the-bootstraps profession."[13] To the extent that he emphasizes the need for diversity, Hart's portrayal is consistent with the works of numerous communication scholars who argue that knowledge is most accurate and valuable when multiple perspectives are considered.[14]

Although admirable in many respects, the call for diversity can be used to justify the *exclusion* of women. Because women may not *want* to pull themselves up to the place defined as "communicative competence" by the "liberals," they are excluded for a failure to meet the "objective" criteria. Mary Ann Fitzpatrick addresses a similar problem by observing that most empirical studies, in the quest for "objective" results, treat all persons identically, failing to account for variation based in gender socialization.[15] The unwillingness to recognize gender variables and the particular perspective that underlies investigation presents a distorted picture of homogeneity and impartiality that Fitzpatrick calls "communication science fiction." In essence, if all persons are accepted according to global definitions of competence which are in fact *particular* definitions, excluded social members are valued only when and if they display the characteristics of dominant culture.

Embedded in the bootstraps characterization of communication is a world view entrenched in values of individual strength, competition, and distinction. McIntosh argues that within social hierarchies, those who have not achieved individual recognition are "construed as not worth studying in a serious and sustained way."[16] Here, cultural organization can be viewed as a pyramidal structure in which a few persons occupy the uppermost areas or peaks, while the majority exists in the relatively immense and stratified base. The correlation between gender and social position is clearly defined by Ann Oakley: "Power is unequally distributed in most societies, and depends not only on personal qualities of the individual but on social position. Different people occupy different social positions and men occupy a different position in society from women: class inequality and gender inequality coexist."[17] The experience of persons who are dependent and powerless by societal standards is beneath the serious intellectual pursuits of those who occupy the peaks. By virtue of their base status, women have not demonstrated climbing capabilities and have thus failed as competitors. Even authors who tacitly promote female characteristics in depictions of humane and ethical communication, potentially revaluing women's experience, often take male figures as exemplars.[18] The very qualities that discount women are admirable in men who have managed to gain recognition in competitive cultures for their commitments to pacifism, community, and equality.

When the position of dominant culture is clothed in neutrality, the experience of those at the pyramidal base is named, evaluated, and dehistoricized within dominant codes. When pointing out, for example, that women have contributed to historical progress and thus their experience should be included in research and pedagogy, one is often asked to provide evidence for female contribution. If women have truly accomplished important tasks, the argument goes, they will gain the attention of researchers. But because the activism of muted group members is thought to be secondary and opposed to the feminine role centered on child care and family maintenance, their speech has often not been preserved in cultural records.[19] A case of the failure to preserve women's speech is found in Phyllis Japp's analysis of Angelina Grimke's feminist rhetoric, where the author notes that "only incomplete texts of two of Angelina's speeches remain extant."[20] The dynamics of this process are central to what Dale Spender calls "constructing women's silence."[21] Here, the historical chain of female influence is broken repeatedly "so that each new generation [has] to begin afresh to create its meanings, unaware of what had gone before."[22] A sustained history of female contribution is interrupted so that, according to Adrienne Rich, each wave of interest in women's lives is "received as if it emerged from nowhere: as if each of us had lived, thought and worked without any historical past or contextual present. This is one of the ways in which women's work and thinking has been made to seem sporadic, erratic, orphaned of any tradition of its own."[23] According to Spender, the likelihood of preservation is directly proportional to parity with the dominant culture: "Where the meanings of women have been discontinuous with the male version of reality they have not been retained."[24]

In womanless communication, strategies and styles of human interaction are made and reported by those who occupy cultural peaks. The base population in social ordering is labeled so that it is not only inferior, but has no means of escaping inferior status because the logic of inquiry has the privilege of discounting or marginalizing all that is essentially *different*. In so doing, McIntosh argues, the privilege enjoyed by dominant groups entails the ability to discount "types of power and versions of knowledge which this privileged class of men does not share."[25] If as a discipline we encourage diverse perspectives without simultaneously questioning the value or presumed validity of concepts such as neutrality and competition in the context of gender arrangements, the result is censorship of the very perspectives that could lead to enriched accounts of *human* communication.

GREAT WOMEN SPEAKERS

The second type of communication research shifts to a specific mode of female visibility. Because significant communication is often presumed to occur in public contexts, the women analyzed are characterized as *great women speakers*.[26] Here, women comprise part of our sociopolitical history and are thought to be influential. In communication studies, analyses of great women are most readily found in the area of rhetoric. Knowledge about women and their speaking activities lends richness and balance to research practices. Rather than excluding women as objects of study, these studies depict women as conscious actors who influence society. In addition to an identification of the barriers confronted by women speakers, rhetorical analyses reveal and clarify the history, style, and themes in public address by women.[27] The hostility encountered by female speakers, since they were entering a domain typically reserved for men, necessitated alternative rhetorical strategies.[28] Sustained investigations recognize the many women orators active in social and political causes. Thus, analyses of influential women serve two important purposes: a recognition of female influence in public domains and a reevaluation of taken for granted speaking domains and styles.

The study of women speakers is unquestionably valuable, but because of its capacity to focus attention on women's experience in a male-dominated area, caution is also necessary. Investigations of women who overcame obstacles in order to have a public voice, thus making their way into historical records and academic publications, do much to dismantle the assumption that only men are capable of greatness. Yet, the appearance of a few great women can easily support the presumption that the *majority* of women cannot rival male accomplishments. Great women are presumed to be atypical, and simultaneously they are thought to represent the concerns and styles of women. The addition of a few speeches by women to anthologies, journals, classrooms, "pretends to show us 'women' but really shows us only a famous few, or makes a place for a newly-declared or newly-resurrected famous few."[29] The very concept of greatness is exclusionary and to this extent, warns Mary Daly, it implies that women's speaking is motivated by a "desire to parallel the record of men's achievements."[30] The women who are not famous, exceptional, or great by male standards remain invisible. This is not to suggest that women as public orators should be ignored simply because a vast majority of women are unrepresented, nor do we suggest that great women speakers are ineffective. Rather, the very concept of greatness needs to be reevaluated, for such an assessment is often defined according to insidious criteria that often remain invisible.

Traditional rhetorical paradigms, observes Campbell, contain narrowly defined criteria for determining who and what is heard and studied.[31] The power wielded by particular institutions such as religion and politics, typically populated by men, is central in definitions of influence, significance, and timeliness. Great speeches, recorded and preserved with care, often focus on historical turning points, significant political or activist change, and economic issues.[32] Such topic areas or speeches are not problematical in principle, but because of concomitant assumptions concerning female domains of expertise, women are presumed to have no experiential credibility in political or social matters. In contemporary politics, women who advocate rights for women are viewed as a special interest group, since issues such as reproductive freedom are not deemed significant for the general populace. Conversely, spokespersons who rise above special interests and focus on the "real" issues of our times—war, the arms race, advances in high-powered weaponry—are seen to address the concerns of humanity at large. Female speaking is complicated by assigning to women the task of sustaining cultural moral values and preserving social order through duties involving support, nurturance, relationship maintenance, and procreative responsibility. Sanctions imposed against female speakers by clergy, for example, are grounded precisely in morality-related concerns.[33] Although women hold a vested interest in social issues, for instance in controversy surrounding temperance, abolition, and voting rights, their views are often placed in the category of special interest and thus easily dismissed as non-issues.

Many great-speaker paradigms support the devaluation of women because when assessing greatness, critical vision is trained to see what has already been deemed effective. For example, in a study of Francis Wright's oratory, Kathleen Kendall and Jeanne Fisher use Aristotelean categories in judging Wright's extrinsic ethos and conclude by noting, "Eloquence without extrinsic ethos produces museum pieces of oratory, not catalytic compositions that influence the course of history. Her one real accomplishment was to be remembered as an early pioneer in the history of the American women's movement."[34] Wright's "failure" as an important social influence is explained as a "failure to meet societal expectations," which in turn "lowered her ethos and thereby mitigated her effectiveness."[35] Kendall and Fisher's treatment of Wright's speaking, which could have led to a radical questioning of applicability between Aristotelean criteria and women's speech, instead finds Wright to be ineffective. Analyses of greatness are clothed in presumptions that complicate female participation by linking rhetorical effectiveness to overarching criteria and distinctive individuals. As Campbell asserts, "The questions have not been 'what is rhetoric'? or 'what speeches really illustrate great rhetorical inventions,'? but rather who our political leaders were and what they said on certain kinds of political occasions."[36] So long as women's speaking is judged according to criteria that exclude women, it will be deemed inconsequential, specialized, or lacking in persuasive appeal.

The investigation of female speakers requires a shift in the process of critical inquiry. We offer two possible alternatives to the great speaker paradigm. First, the rhetorical activities, strategies, and styles of women can be examined according to generative criteria that do not establish hierarchies of greatness. That is, the concept of greatness can be redefined with criteria that do not privilege male speakers. Second, we suggest that rhetorical competency need not define influence solely in the context of individual speakers and social institutions. Analyses of historical movements that concern the lives and choices of ordinary women, such as Celeste Condit Railsback's work on abortion, are valuable because they call attention to the means by which female identity is constructed in socio-rhetorical discourse.[37] From here, questions asked concerning effectiveness can move beyond singularity, focusing on female collectivities such as the contemporary women's movement. An analysis of women's groups does not abandon the individual altogether, but recognizes that individuals are enmeshed in, and defined by, everyday social and relationship networks. As Campbell argues, for example, the rhetoric of women's liberation merits study as a distinct genre because it evinces a fusion of substantive and stylistic features. Here, women's speaking

> is distinctive stylistically in rejecting certain traditional concepts of the rhetorical process. . . . Traditional or familiar definitions of persuasion do not satisfactorily account for the rhetoric of women's liberation. In relation to such definitions, feminist advocacy wavers between the rhetorical and the non-rhetorical, the persuasive and the non-persuasive. Rhetoric is usually defined as dealing with public issues, structural analyses, and social action, yet women's liberation emphasizes acts concerned with personal exigencies and private, concrete experience, and its goal is frequently limited to particular, autonomous action by individuals.[38]

Rules for speaking and determinations of significance become truly inclusive through a reassessment of the rhetorical tradition. Additionally, the inventiveness of female speakers offers an enriched understanding of rhetorical strategies and relevant historical issues. The challenge is not one of creating a place for women in an already existing framework of great speakers. As Gerda Lerner observes, an uncritical assimilation of women into intact social structures is limited because it "deals with women in male-defined society and tries to fit them into categories and value systems which consider man the measure of significance."[39] As McIntosh suggests, rhetoric can be studied not by asking *if* women say anything important, or *if* there are any great women speakers, but by asking, what women say, how women use the public platform, how women speak.[40] If, however, women's concerns and styles are granted no place in cultural discourse, they will retain the *mistaken* status of academic "museum pieces"—interesting to observe but where essential function is missed.

WOMAN AS OTHER

The third type of research, comprised predominantly of empirical studies, expands the parameters of the great women speaker domain by focusing on gender as a variable in public contexts, small group settings, organizational cultures, and interpersonal relationships. Female existence is here thought to be "other" than its male counterpart, and so researchers are obliged to examine both the dynamics of this otherness and the comparative relation between two differing realities. The precedent for male/female opposition in communication studies is set by a more general cultural view of the relation between masculine and feminine, culture and nature. Michael Zimmerman notes that "man's conception of himself as essentially cultural, non-female, non-natural, immortal, and transcendent, as opposed to the essentially natural, non-cultural, mortal woman, has continued in various guises for several thousands years."[41] The oppositions between masculine and feminine, culture and nature, frame difference in a mutually exclusive and hierarchical manner, constituting a major barrier for women attempting cultural inclusion.

Early studies in the area of male/female differences moved from biological to psychological arguments. In many respects, biological findings were translated into the domains of psychology and anthropology. Lionel Tiger's research on friendship is exemplary in this respect.[42] Because men are physically larger and stronger than women, he argued, they are better prepared to suffer "an array of humiliations, discomforts, fears and other oppressions," sealing the bonds of loyalty and camaraderie.[43] Because of the questionable nature of such conclusions, primarily the confusion of cause and effect which led to reliability problems, researchers turned almost completely to theories of psychological sex and sex-role orientation for explanations of male/female differences. Sandra Bem's investigation of androgyny and the Bem Sex-Role Inventory led to studies centered on psychological sex differences as manifested in communication situations.[44] A host of male/female psychological differences emerged, derived largely from experimental and observational techniques, suggesting that women are characterized by passivity, verbal ability, compliance, fear, dependence, and attentiveness, while men exhibit behaviors associated with aggressiveness, analytic or mathematical ability, high levels of activity, rebelliousness, and independence.[45]

The study of sex differences in communication behavior, often owing to the findings of psychologists, constitutes a rich body of research.[46] The most pervasive area of inquiry is comprised of language behavior analyses that address the syntactic and semantic disparities in male and female speech. Three distinct yet related issues in research of this type can be identified.

The first issue, framing the largest body of findings, locates sex differences by noting variance in phonology, pitch, intonation, lexicon, and meaning.[47] A second issue concerns the relation between perception and role expectation; in particular, researchers analyze the extent to which language behavior is perceived as "masculine" or "feminine."[48] When a woman uses profanity and shouts in anger, for example, her actions contradict the stereotypically feminine characteristics of passivity, politeness, and compliance. A final issue concerns an assessment of communicative competence based on gender differences in language use.[49] Identical communication behaviors, such as the use of tag questions, often lead to different competence evaluations depending on speaker sex. For example, when a woman says, "It's a nice day, isn't it?" she is thought to lack authority, thereby reducing her competence; when a man makes the same utterance, he is perceived as an open and congenial conversation partner, thus elevating his level of competence.

Studies focused on sex differences have recently come under attack by a number of scholars.[50] Criticism centers on the labeling process whereby women's language and communication behaviors are found to be deviant or deficient. As Barrie Thorne, Cheris Kramarae, and Nancy Henley suggest, gender scholars are now beginning to realize that early reliance on the findings of influential male linguists such as Jesperson is problematic because, in the very questions asked about sex differences, female deficiency is already presumed:

> Do women have a more limited vocabulary than men do, or do they use more—or different—adjectives and adverbs? Are women more apt to leave their sentences unfinished? Do they enunciate more properly? Do they use lots of "superficial" words? Are their sentences longer or shorter, than men's? Do they use more questioning, or uncertain notation?[51]

Arguably, not all of these questions suggest female inferiority, but in each case, male speech is the standard against which female or "other" speech is judged. The project of finding difference is highly contingent on more general assumptions that in many ways pre-establish relations between cultural members. Indeed, Joseph Pillota states, "to recognize differences it is necessary either to assume one of the cultures as a base and interpret others in terms of it or to assume common features across various cultures on the basis of which the variations are comprehensible."[52] Female difference, then, is comprehensible and judged to be deficient within the context of male communication behavior.

The female difference is viewed as a handicap when compared to a standard that finds deviation in all that is non-standard male usage. In Robin Lakoff's work, women are found to lack authority and seriousness in speaking, hence reducing their effectiveness.[53] Here, women's speech is ineffective because it is laden with weak expletives, trivializing particles, intensifiers and polite forms, tag questions, and hedges; in short, Lakoff finds women's language behavior to be tentative, uncertain, and indecisive. Dale Spender criticizes Lakoff's work by noting that the observations made, like those in Jesperson's work, are grounded in an implicit acceptance of masculine speech as the norm:

> Lakoff accepts that men's language is superior and she assumes that this is a feature of their linguistic performance and not of their sex. . . . She takes male language as the norm and measures women against it, and the outcome of this procedure is to classify any difference on the part of women as "deviation." Given these practices, it is unlikely that Lakoff could have arrived at positive findings for women, for any differences revealed, whether a product of language or of sex, would be predisposed to interpretation as yet more evidence of female deficiency.[54]

As Lakoff's work exemplifies, if women's speech is thought to be deficient, it will appear deficient since she presumes that *women* speak differently, not that women and men speak differently.

Frequently, sex difference researchers suggest male usage as the solution to female deficiency.[55] If women can be taught to communicate like men, they will become equally competent. However, women who adopt male usage are often evaluated as less successful and less likable than men. Even when actual behavior is identical, it is viewed differently depending on the source. In an analysis of male/female conversational dynamics in small groups, Patricia Bradley finds that qualifying devices "diminish discussants' positive reactions to *women* in small group settings. It cannot be argued on the basis of these findings, however, that tag questions and disclaimers are inherently 'weaker' or credibility deflating since men were able to use them with virtual impunity."[56] Moreover, as Martha Solomon points out, much research involves participants in tasks and situations that, given sex-role stereotypes, render female communication behavior less salient and less effective.[57] For instance, subjects may be asked to argue for a single position, select the best solution to a problem, or influence another person—all of which are part of the male sex-typed script in American culture.[58] Studies designed with implicit male norms, combined with negative evaluations of women's speech, make it impossible for a woman to attempt to speak like a man because her female identity is taken into account in evaluations of her speaking behavior.

An additional problem occurs when researchers begin by assuming female difference. Specifically, if men and women are thought to exist in an oppositional relation, findings are likely to highlight differences rather than similarities. "Researchers may tend to presume and overreport differences rather than similarities," suggest Kramer, Throne, and Henley, "because our culture is infused with stereotypes which polarize females and males."[59] Statistical procedures may be especially problematic when used in gender studies, Fitzpatrick indicates, because such research strategies "focus on testing and finding *differences* between people and ignore similarities."[60] An example illustrates. Fitzpatrick describes an investigation in which male and female subjects were tested to determine self-perceptions of communication behavior, along with perceptions of the behavior of same and opposite sex friends. Approximately ten dimensions of behavior, ranging from control to nurturance, were examined. Although researchers found difference in only two dimensions, "the entire discussion section of the paper focused on the two differences discovered between males and females."[61] A failure to find male-female disparity or "significance," especially when one begins by positing its existence, often results in an unpublishable article. Unfortunately, the dilemma is typically resolved by selecting new subjects, changing variables, or altering data collection techniques such that difference can be found.

While research in the area of sex differences provides an important source of knowledge about women's communication, its implicit characterization of woman as "other" risks further sedimentation of male-female stereotypes. When studies take women's speaking to be the problem and fail to question men's speaking with equal rigor, we can expect a storehouse of information that sings the praises of differences, but does little to challenge definitions of competence, influence, and success. Simply pointing to woman as a disadvantaged other falsely implies that women are passive victims, trapped in sex-typed communication constraints with no hope of escape, when in fact they can be viewed as active agents. Valid investigations of female communication behavior require a non-comparative approach which, by implication, not only questions the normative power of male experience, but views women as self-conscious actors, as co-producers of their communicative climates.

THE POLITICS OF WOMAN AS OTHER

The project of learning to value women's experience is an inherently political enterprise because it entails seeing women not as a problem but as valuable human beings.[62] Because the male/female opposition is inequitable, women are not only seen as deficient communicators, but their everyday lives are named by dominant culture. When women discuss their experiences, for example, their talk is often labeled "chit-chat," "gossip," or "girl talk"; when men do the same, they are "making a point," "stating a position," or imparting social knowledge.[63] A crucial task in learning to value women's communication first involves a critical questioning of female experience as defined within an androcentric framework, and second, a revaluing of women's experience *in its own terms.* Traumatic female experiences such as childbirth, when named within a culture that still in large measure both mandates and devalues motherhood, are either deemed unimportant in the overall scheme of scholarly interests, or if addressed, are stripped of their complexity. As Spender points out, childbirth is portrayed as an event of "rapturous joy," a life-completing achievement for women.[64] On television programs we might well see a young woman enduring mildly uncomfortable labor pains, immediately and miraculously followed by mother and child in a hospital bed. Neither the physical pain involved in giving birth nor the intense ambivalence is seen by viewers. In describing her own experience of giving birth, Rich critiques the long-standing silence concerning motherhood:

> No one mentions the psychic crises of bearing a first child, the excitation of long-buried feelings about one's own mother, the sense of confused power and powerlessness, of being taken over on the one hand and of touching new physical and psychic potentialities on the other, a heightened sensibility which can be exhilarating, bewildering, and exhausting.[65]

Within the *politics of woman as other* paradigm, researchers promote a critical female voice that speaks on behalf of its own complexity.

Sustained investigations of female experience reveal complex forms of communication, definitions of relationships, and styles of reasoning. Novel conceptions of human communication emerge from such studies. Female communication behaviors are transactional and cooperative rather than linear and competitive.[66] For example, Fern Johnson and Elizabeth Aries find that women's friendships are sustained by talk involving non-critical listening, mutual support, and enhancement of self-worth.[67] Storytelling as a conversational paradigm in women's communication serves to maintain horizontal power relationships such that closeness and inclusiveness are insured.[68] Through question-asking and affirming utterances, women's speaking promotes understanding.[69] Rather than defining a conversation partner as one who alternatively listens and speaks, which often results in a two-person monologue, the topics and experiences shared *between* female partners are woven together.[70] A dissatisfying conversation is one in which a partner attempts to gain distinction from the other, which is often taken implicitly as a request for distance or separation.

The preceding research on female interaction demonstrates unique strategies. These strategies are revealed when women's communication is studied in its own terms. When female relationship behavior enters the domain of traditional research in the area of interpersonal communication, the problem of deficiency is likely to occur because the weaving together of shared issues is not amenable to strict quantification and control. The predominance of exchange models and statistical assessments of communication behavior places the study of relationships into a realm filled with economic imagery.[71] Viewing interpersonal communication as something that is exchanged and that becomes comprehensively known only by isolating and testing variables is consistent with the experience of persons for whom individual control is central. In Gerald Miller's anthology, *Explorations in Interpersonal Communication,* there is much hope expressed for ongoing relational communication research.[72] On the one hand, Miller notes a "change in emphasis from the *individual,* as the primary unit of analysis, to the *relationship,*" which may indicate a willingness to decentralize issues of individual control and distinction; on the other hand, "powerful mathematical models" for use in studying relationships, "allow the researcher to milk maximum information from the data and permit closer approximation of the processual complexities of interpersonal communication."[73] Essentially, Miller advocates statistical analyses of relationship dynamics because the *researcher* is given greater control, "a precision and parsimony not found in verbal constructions," stating almost as a tangential point, "a major outstanding question, of course, concerns the extent to which certain assumptions of these models can be met in the domain of the 'real' world."[74]

Indeed, a "counting" approach to the study of female relationship behavior, emphasizing control, power, and static precision, may be inappropriate when everyday interactional emphasis is not centered on reducing relationship strategies to their essential components but on bringing together a great many experiences, emotions, expressions, and individuals within the space of a single conversation. Rather than viewing a relationship as an entity comprised of two individuals, women leave open possibilities for a rethinking of individual identities and relationship boundaries, depending on the directions taken in conversation. We are not suggesting that women do not engage in exchange-like relationships or that women are incapable of quantifying relationship behaviors. We are suggesting, however, that such approaches reflect a masculine view of relationships. In Kathryn Carter's research on perception in relationships, for example, men describe their involvements through the use of economic metaphors, while women use gardening metaphors.[75] Women discuss the process of tending, nurturing, weathering storms and seasons, and growing; men describe costs, benefits, trade-offs and losses, and often "rank" or "rate" the value of a relationship.

Women's perceptions of relationships continue to remain invisible not only when research relies on exchange approaches, but also when researchers assume that relationships are based in mutuality and equality. Michael Roloff defines a relationship as a "mutual agreement, imiplicit or explicit, between two people in order to maximize rewards."[76] In interpersonal communication textbooks, healthy relationships are typically defined as those in which definition is mutual, respect for the other is presumed, and mutual negotiation of rules and roles takes place. Even in the case of "complementary" relational structures, where one partner has more power than the other, both partners *mutually* designate superior and subordinate roles.[77] When gender as a social organizing force is incorporated into research of this kind, the concepts of equality and mutuality must be reexamined. Although part of the feminine stereotype defines women as controlling in relationships, the realities of economic dependence, the value placed on intimacy for women and independence for men, and the general devaluation of female communication behavior, do not promote mutuality or equality.

An understanding of women's relationship dynamics requires a move away from traditional conceptions of human communication research. Not only are concepts of equality and mutuality misleading when women are involved, but female relationships are often not experienced in terms of rules and exchanges. In Carol Gilligan's study of moral development, most women are found to negotiate relationships through an ethic of care.[78] Many women attempt to generate novel and inclusive interactional strategies which preserve networks of personal and social relationships. As studies of children's game playing reveal, boys are likely to place emphasis on abiding by rules; girls are apt to stop or alter a game when rules interfere with the preservation of relationship bonds.[79] The ethic of care, problematized by rules, has consequences for the larger question of ethics in communicative choices. One of Gilligan's respondents describes an immoral decision as one in which a person attempts to "decide carelessly or quickly or on the basis of one or two factors when you know that there are other things that are important and that will be affected."[80] Respected individuals are those who "are really connected to the concrete situations in their lives."[81]

A revaluing of the female ethics of care and connection depends on an assessment of who is in a position to define societal relationships between men and women. Lana Rakow observes that "men have been in a position to 'structure the structures,' to make their use of metaphors and metonyms count, and to construct a symbolic system which fits and explains their experiences, creating a gendered world within which we take our gendered places."[82] The relationship strategies of women are at once mandated and marginalized by male structures. That is, women are deemed healthy if they are nurturing and other-directed; simultaneously, male hierarchies of value equate feminine qualities with low levels of reasoning capacity and intellectual prowess. It is unlikely that *women* would have devised a gender system in which female relationship behaviors are seen as both essential and inferior. Moreover, a socially defined position of powerlessness does not give women the luxury of clothing female experience in neutrality in order to make claims about *human* experience.

The study of women's communication, because of its very lack of fit with traditional research paradigms, can serve to enrich and expand the repertory of research options found in the communication discipline. Female interaction styles, in fact, challenge scholars to reconsider the crucial issue of using methods that are appropriate to the questions asked in research studies. In Oakley's analysis of pregnancy, for example, where the goal is to understand women's experience of being pregnant and giving birth, many traditional guidelines for researcher-respondent interview interaction are found to be inadequate.[83] The intensely personal experience of pregnancy is difficult to share with a "neutral" data collector, especially if the researcher refuses to communicate with some degree of reciprocity. Studies by Carole Spitzack and Deanna Hall and Kristen Langellier, among others, reconsider the separation of researcher and respondent communication, and researchers opt instead to interact with their respondents.[84] These authors, like Oakley, conduct interviews with a particular subject area in mind, but allow respondents the freedom to reframe or refocus the direction of the interview, to ask questions and receive answers from the researcher, to introduce issues that are not part of the researcher's agenda. In short, the communication of these female researchers and female respondents matches the experience of woman-to-woman interaction that is characterized by a weaving together of experiences. In view of Gilligan's observations, we can expect a high degree of richness, complexity, and respondent involvement when such tactics are used because here the "rules of the game" can be influenced and redefined to preserve the relationship between interviewer and respondent.

An examination of the confrontation between women's communication and research practices does not suggest that women's communication is simply different or better than men's, but rather presents women's experience as valid and complex, posing the question: how can women's communication be examined so that it is seen as significant and richly competent? As Spender points out, "it is political choice on the part of feminist scholars to find in favour of women, but this is no different from non-feminist researchers who have exercised their political choice by almost always finding in favour of men."[85] The difference, Spender adds, "is that feminism acknowledges its politics."[86] Scholars who conduct studies on women's communication, like their colleagues, argue for a fit between research questions and methods. Given the social polarization of males and females, identical communication behaviors are unlikely; thus, presumably universal principles that guide inquiry are not universally applicable. The priority placed on objectivity in research practices serves dominant culture because registers of discourse "have been encoded by males for their own ends . . . women shall either be excluded, or made 'uncomfortable,' or serve those ends if, and when, they do participate."[87] The views and judgments contained within male registers are imposed on others who do not have male experiences. The practical side of research on women entails a focus on the everyday lives, experiences, and communication behaviors of women; the critical side calls attention to the imposition.

A number of communication scholars conduct feminist research, and current activities in our discipline suggest a gradual acceptance of women's communication as a valid area of investigation. At the 1985 Speech Communication Association Conference, participants in a seminar on women and communicative power spent considerable time discussing publication outlets for research on women. Taylor and Bate's forthcoming anthology, *Women Communicating,* provides analyses of female communication behavior, including mother-daughter interaction, women and appearance, and group dynamics among female adolescents.[88] Organizations such as the Society for the Study of Language, Gender, and Communication; the Organization for Research on Women's Communication; the Women's Caucus of the Speech Communication Association; and annual gatherings such as the Annual Conference for Gender and Communication Research, all promise to establish links and support networks among feminist researchers. The potential empowerment afforded by these forms of woman-to-woman communication, which gives visibility and legitimacy to the lives of women, is dependent on a more general willingness of non-feminist or anti-feminist scholars to rethink the rules of the research game.

The awareness generated by studying women's experience in its own terms challenges all disciplines, claim Marilyn Schuster and Susan Van Dyne, for the operation of "invisible paradigms" is made explicit in the very process of research.[89] Questions remain, however, as to how a new-found understanding of women becomes practical and truly empowering. At this point, answers must be speculative because women are not yet afforded the luxury of full inclusion. The study of women's communication, even though it addresses at least half the population, is still considered a specialty area. Communication departments may offer courses in gender studies, but by implication the separation of gender from presumably mainstream areas sends a strong message: the study of women is marginal and lacks import for the discipline as a whole. A reluctance on the part of communication scholars to identify and discuss sexism as a component of disciplinary practices outside the context of gender courses or gender issues also contributes to the problem of female marginality. In her examination of 55 communication textbooks with copyright dates of 1980 or later, Phyllis Randall finds that only "six confront the issue of sexism directly," and only nine mention sexist language.[90] These realities necessitate caution for researchers attempting to reposition female experience into the general framework of communication studies; before invisible paradigms can become visible, it is first necessary to have an audience that is willing to look.

A second complication in the mainstreaming of women in communication research concerns the possible co-opting of the findings derived from research on women. The concerns and speaking structures unearthed in women's communication can easily be renamed and transformed into evidence that supports female stereotypes. To suggest that women are "connected" to their everyday circumstances, for example, can support views that portray women as incapable of objective thinking. Alternatively, if experiences such as motherhood and pregnancy are examined and discussed to include contradictions and complexities, research findings can be read not only as further evidence for the "natural" female role, but also as support for labels often applied to women, such as "irrational" and "indecisive." Co-option and distortion can be diminished if women's experience is valued *within* communication studies, as an *already present* and valuable component of the discipline.

WOMEN AS COMMUNICATORS

In a recent conversation we were told that the problem with feminists is a tendency to push their "in group" politics on other people even when most people on the "outside" do not share their politics. This comment indicates the extent of work yet to be done in bringing about an inclusion of women in communication studies, but in its characterization of inside vs. outside perspectives, the remark also poses a challenge to feminist communication scholars. The general belief still seems to be that feminists mix politics and research, but most people who investigate human communication do not. In describing the first four conceptualizations of women in communication research we have climbed down the pyramid envisaged by McIntosh, dismantling it piece by piece, to show, as many feminists claim, that personal choices often have political significance. This is not to suggest that researchers, by virtue of affiliation with particular political systems, intentionally exclude female experience, but rather to suggest that a complex cultural process of silencing renders it impossible for women who support women to have a voice from the "inside" of contemporary communication studies. The very term "feminist," with its negative social implication, can be taken as yet another means of discounting research about and for women. The point at which all communication scholars acknowledge the culturally sedimented presumptions contained in their views is the point at which, as a discipline, women can be seen *as* communicators.

When women are viewed as communicators, researchers examine the relationship between sedimented assumptions and the degree of female visibility afforded by particular cultural definitions of men and women. The critical collaboration of researchers in diverse areas of communication studies—for example, rhetoric, interpersonal and group, mass communication—encourages analyses of the extent to which our scholarship promotes an inclusive understanding of women's communication. For purposes of illustrating how this analysis takes place, we outline the study of leadership as it may be approached within each kind of research presented in our typology. McIntosh stresses that disciplinary inclusiveness is contingent on seeing points of divergence and convergence, consciousness regarding differing and similar assumptions in the context of issues we share.[91] Leadership is an area of study within many divisions in our field, and an area that is approached from diverse perspectives. Our aim in describing approaches to leadership is at once disciplinary and cultural; that is, leadership is understood, and is opened to critical scrutiny, when it is connected to our shared and diverse *cultural* images of men and women.

We show that assumptions contained in each type of research are "connected" to culture at large by utilizing Edwin Ardener's model of the relation between dominant and muted groups.[92] Ardener suggests that "women constitute a *muted group,* the boundaries of whose culture and reality overlap, but are not wholly contained by, the *dominant* (*male*) *group.*"[93] The markers that separate the two groups are clear yet penetrable, indicating the possible vacillation by women between dominant and muted groups. Originally designed to depict the range of possible relationships between dominant and muted groups with particular cultures, Ardener's model is often adopted by feminist scholars to explain the places occupied by women in patriarchal cultures. "Women," Elaine Showalter explains, can then be seen not as persons who are "inside and outside the male tradition; they are inside two traditions simultaneously."[94] The "bilingual" nature of women's communication is called upon in differing contexts and in various degrees, depending, in the case of leadership, on the extent to which women's experiences are given a voice.

In *womanless communication,* the qualities of leadership are gender neutral. Researchers are careful to point out that an "ideal" leader does not exist, and to this extent, leadership is said to be situationally dependent. The shift from "leader" to "leadership," Robert Cathcart and Larry Samovar suggest, signals a growing awareness that "leadership is a function of group process rather than a series of traits residing in an individual."[95] While the focus appears to move away from individual leaders, leadership is often defined in the context of influence and personal power. Moreover, leadership is always something done by an individual, as is evident in the many arguments against shared or absent leadership positions. Leadership is often contrasted to followership, which assumes an inequitable division between the leader and the led. As Robert Tannenbaum, Irving Wechsler, and Fred Massarik observe, "Leadership always involves attempts on the part of a *leader* (influencer) to affect (influence) the behavior of a *follower* (influenced) or followers in a *situation.*"[96] The role of leader *or* follower will in all likelihood depend on status and power, given the presumption of inequity. Stuart Tubbs points out, for example, that "Higher status tends to result in greater personal power or ability to influence others. Increased power, in turn, tends to elevate an individual's status level. Power and status go hand in hand, reciprocally influencing each other."[97] In assessing the qualities of good leadership, then, researchers turn to individuals who demonstrate a capacity for influence or compliance gaining.

Given the positioning of persons within cultural hierarchies, the qualities of model leadership are epitomized by men. Leader effectiveness is often contingent on characteristics that are thought to be at variance with female socialization. Most women are not likely to wield individual influence or power as defined within culture; thus, female traits may well appear in definitions of poor leadership. James Kinder, for example, compares four types of leaders by combining four behavioral traits: dominance, submission, warmth, and hostility.[98] The traits are combined in order to present four styles of leadership, followed by evaluations of effectiveness. Leaders who are both dominant and warm are maximally effective because they show commitment to tasks and people. The submissive-warm leader, by contrast, fails because he is "a kindly soul who puts happy relationships above all other considerations. . . . He strives to create a warm, pleasant, social atmosphere where an easy-going work tempo may be maintained."[99] Given the socialization of women, which gives much attention to nurturing, preserving relationships at the cost of rules, and creating horizontal bonds between people, women may be viewed as ineffective leaders.

Leadership from a *great women speakers* paradigm begins by asking, "Who are the great leaders in history?" Here, the spheres of men and women cross to a negligible degree with the realization that some successful leaders are women, thus the following question, "Who are the great female leaders?" A small percentage of women gain access to dominant leadership studies. Membership is composed of privileged women who are acceptable by male standards, women whose leadership skills match those of their male counterparts. Geraldine Ferraro may exist in the privileged realm because, in running for the second-highest office in American politics, she proved to be an "exceptional" woman.

Yet, the model also explains the failure of greatness as it pertains to women. The extraordinary female, because of physiology and socialization, is grouped simultaneously with her muted counterparts. Her behavior is interpreted with gender in mind so that even the title that affirms dominant membership, "Great Women," provides assurance that most women are unqualified for greatness. Moreover, regardless of leadership capabilities, gender remains a salient feature of leadership evaluations. A woman's role and temperament, as seen in depictions of greatness in *womanless communication,* is thought to be incompatible with leadership. For example, when Ferraro called attention to Bush's patronage in the 1984 vice-presidential debate by saying, "Don't patronize me," critics remarked on the emotional and uncontrolled character of her response. The practical problem, as argued by Schuster and Van Dyne, is that within the dominant realm, "most women's histories . . . will not measure up to the preeminent male model: as writers, their production will seem minor in form or scope; as political activists, their participation in the sweep of history will appear sporadic."[100] The greatness paradigm, then, provides a relatively stable vision of male history; the few women deemed extraordinary must set themselves apart from, and identify with, the vast majority of invisible women.

If woman is defined as an *other,* male definitions of competent leadership are adopted and female leadership styles are compared to them. Research questions ask: How does female leadership differ from male leadership? Are women as competent as men in commanding roles? Do people respond more favorably to male or female leaders? The muted group is compared to the dominant group, but the reverse, which asks, "Are men as competent as women in leadership roles?" seldom occurs. Here, the muted status of women remains constant. Research activity centers on the elaboration of differences between the two spheres, with the dominant group serving a normative function. Assumptions concerning effectiveness are grounded in male sex-role stereotypes; thus good leaders are found to be aggressive, competitive, task-oriented, analytic, and logical.[101] Because leadership has been defined in public and corporate spheres, Fitzpatrick argues, the behavioral "script" required for leader competence is often perceived to be consistent with male socialization.[102] In fact, studies report that female leaders are generally found to be less effective, less competent, and less successful than their male counterparts.[103] Moreover, women who *do* follow the dictates of professional competence in leadership roles are often viewed as pushy, bitchy, hostile, overly-ambitious.[104] The great leader paradigm and the notion of women leaders as "others" are similar insofar as neither equalizes the status of dominant and muted groups. Rather, both implicitly presume universality based on male experience. Female leadership, then, appears deficient.

When scholars work to uncover the dynamics of female leadership without adopting the dominant paradigm, research questions and presumptions are radically altered. The study of leadership is simultaneously a critical analysis because competency assessments account for the *politics of woman as other.* Women's experience is validated and named such that it is seen to comprise half the world's history. Scholars focus on the female sphere, working to unearth richness and diversity among individual women. Inquiries are framed inclusively: How do women experience leadership? How do women define successful leadership? How are corporate and personal relationships affected when women lead? How do women work together? Addressing these questions may involve analyses of homemakers, teachers, managers, secretaries, and students. In general, women who have a capacity to direct and influence the course of daily events, either collectively or individually, are potential sources of data. Conceptions of leadership expand to include the everyday lives of women, incorporating such qualities as compassion, sensitivity, and trust. Fidelity to women's communication behavior allows researchers to describe ambiguities in female leadership, such as an ability to occupy both leader and led roles simultaneously. The circle of mutation becomes larger as women's styles of communication are found to be strong, effective, and valid.

When women are viewed *as* communicators, rather than as a deviant or mysterious subculture, disciplinary conceptions of men *and* women are found to have a basis in cultural practices. Showalter explains,

> Both muted and dominant groups generate beliefs or ordering of social reality at the unconscious level, but dominant groups control the forms or structures in which consciousness can be articulated. Thus muted groups must mediate their beliefs through the allowable forms of dominant structures. Another way of putting this would be to say that all language is the language of the dominant, and women, if they speak at all, must speak through it.[105]

The experience of muted groups is rich in critical potential because women are typically placed in a relation of exteriority with respect to dominant culture. By living as "outsiders" *within* culture, women are able to see the exclusive character of many claims about *human* behavior. They may find their communication behavior described in portrayals of ineffective leadership, for example, and conclude that they are ill-suited for leadership roles. However, the same observation can be used to point out the exclusionary nature of such seemingly "neutral" definitions. From here, women can begin to question the qualities proposed for leadership and conduct investigations which do not begin by assuming that female behaviors impede group progress. Female leadership may, in fact, *promote* cohesiveness, openness, trust, and commitment.

The study of women as communicators can expand the knowledge base of the communication discipline, providing men and women with both behavioral and research alternatives. An excellent example of the critical insight made possible when women are studied within culture is provided in Gillian Michell's investigation of Grice's conversational maxims.[106] Grice's maxims are supposedly general, widely cited rules for conversation, which make the implicit assumption that conversational participants are rational and equal. Michell analyzes each maxim and notes that women do not follow Grice's rules when conversing with men because there are social constraints present, limiting women's choices and positioning women hierarchically with respect to a male partner. It is only by *violating* Grice's maxims that women can achieve the maximally effective exchanges of information. Michell observes that women must "tell it slant" in order to converse in a sexist society. That is, they must "follow the rules" of dominant culture, *and* understand that the rules are not applicable to their own conversational vantagepoint.

The inclusion of women in communication studies is counter-productive if one form of exclusion is simply replaced with another. The proposal for a normative shift from male to female communication behaviors is based in a view which is both hierarchical and linear. Nor is it enough to simply acknowledge women's experience through the use of gendered examples and mixed-gender pronouns. These "add women and stir" solutions are often cosmetic, having no effect on the research process. Rather, we argue that female inclusion is dependent on a global disciplinary awareness of assumptions that exclude and devalue female communication. Female inclusion requires not only an understanding of women within the parameters of communication studies, but includes analyses of gender as an organizing force in social interaction.[107] Such inclusion may well involve an investigation of *researcher* communication, as evidenced in publications, classrooms, and everyday interaction, along with studies centered on the communication of others, because researchers, too, exist within socially defined gender arrangements.

The inclusion of women in communication studies is dependent on collaboration within our discipline. We endorse the view of Susan Bellrichard, who argues that socially excluded persons are "heard" through a formulation of "counter-discourse from the inside."[108] We do not suggest that a "counter-discourse" requires researchers to surrender traditional investigative approaches. Strategies designed to comprehend male versions of reality play an important role in disciplinary definition, as does our pluralistic tradition. We do, however, call for a specification of the presumptions contained in strategies that purport to be objective, along with concomitant assumptions that give the label of "subjective" or "soft" to alternative procedures. The challenge then involves more than conducting studies on women. The task is to analyze embedded assumptions concerning the objects of study, the methods of data collection, and the questions guiding research.[109] In so doing, portrayals of human communication are not found to be definitively right or wrong, but to reflect gendered and therefore *political* presumptions. The net gains resulting from self-reflexive criticism are substantial. First, as women become empowered as active agents in communication studies, possibilities for growth and disciplinary change are uncovered. Second, researchers will be better able to match research methods to the particularities of their research questions. Third, novel theories, investigative strategies and topic areas emerge when the perspectival nature of taken for granted assumptions comes under scrutiny. And perhaps most importantly, the critical activity we endorse promotes a *truly* pluralistic view of human communication.

NOTES

Carole Spitzack is Assistant Professor of Communication at Tulane University. Kathryn Carter is Associate Professor of Communication at Wayne State College.

1. For an overview of the past and present status of communication research on women, see Karen A. Foss and Sonja K. Foss, "The Status of Research on Women and Communication," *Communication Quarterly* 31 (1983): 195–204. See also, Barrie Thorne, Cheris Kramarae, and Nancy Henley, eds., "Language, Gender and Society: Opening a Second Decade of Research," in *Language, Gender and Society* (Rowley, MA: Newbury House, 1983), 7–24. Organizations such as the Women's Caucus of the Speech Communication Association; the Society for the Study of Language, Gender, and Communication; and the Organization for Research on Women's Communication add to female visibility in communication studies. In addition, *Women's Studies in Communication* is a journal devoted explicitly to analyses of female communication behavior and gender issues.
2. Peggy McIntosh, "Interactive Phases of Curriculum Re-Vision: A Feminist Perspective," Working Paper No. 124, Wellesly College Center for Research on Women (1983); reprinted as "Interactive Phases of Curricular Re-Vision," in *Toward a Balanced Curriculum,* eds. Bonnie Spanier, Alexander Bloom, and Darlene Boroviak (Cambridge: Schenkman, 1984), 25–34.
3. McIntosh, 3–23.
4. McIntosh, 7.
5. During a 1985 lecture titled, "Women Speaking: A Feminist Analysis of Rhetoric," given at Tulane University in New Orleans, Louisiana, Campbell presented the results from her survey of 45 speech anthologies with copyright dates of 1896–1981. No speeches by women appeared, for example, in books with the following titles: *Speeches in English; American Public Address, 1740–1952; Famous American Speeches; Speeches for Illustration and Example; Famous Speeches of American History; British and American Eloquence; The Library of Universal Literature, Vols. I and II; American Speeches; Contemporary Forms of American Speeches;* and *Twentieth Century Issues.* There were no speeches by Lucy Stone, Angelina Grimke, Anna Howard Shaw, or Lucretia Mott. Only incomplete versions of speeches by Elizabeth Cady Stanton appeared, along with one speech by Susan B. Anthony that was actually a congressional hearing.

6. Karen A. Foss and Sonja K. Foss, "Incorporating the Feminist Perspective in Communication Research," in *Doing Research on Women's Communication: Alternative Perspectives in Theory and Method,* eds. Kathryn Carter and Carole Spitzack (forthcoming).
7. George A. Kennedy, *Classical Rhetoric and its Christian and Secular Tradition from Ancient to Modern Times* (Chapel Hill: University of North Carolina Press, 1980), 3–17.
8. See, for example, Jo Freeman, ed., *Women: A Feminist Perspective,* 3rd ed. (Palo Alto, CA: Mayfield Publishing Co., 1984); Gerda Lerner, ed., *Black Women in White America* (New York: Vintage Books, 1972); Clyde W. Franklin, II, *The Changing Definitions of Masculinity* (New York: Plenum Press, 1984).
9. For comprehensive analyses of the feminine role in cultural practices and rituals, see Susan Brownmiller, *Feminity* (New York: Fawcett Columbine Press, 1984); Rosalind Coward, *Female Desires: How They are Sought, Bought and Packaged* (New York: Grove Press, 1985).
10. Lea P. Stewart, Pamela J. Cooper, and Sheryl A. Friedly, *Communication Between the Sexes: Sex Differences and Sex-Role Stereotypes* (Scottsdale, AZ: Gorsuch Scarisbrick, 1986), 27.
11. Brownmiller observes, "Femininity always demands more. It must constantly reassure its audience by a willing demonstration of difference, even if one does not exist in nature. . . . To fail at the feminine difference is to appear not to care about men, and to risk the loss of their attention and approval." *Femininity,* 15.
12. Roderick P. Hart, "The Politics of Communication Studies: An Address to Undergraduates," *Communication Education* 34 (1985): 164.
13. Hart, 164.
14. Cf. Wayne C. Booth, *Critical Understanding: The Powers and Limits of Pluralism* (Chicago: University of Chicago Press, 1979); Richard Cherwitz and James W. Hikins, "Rhetorical Perspectivism," *Quarterly Journal of Speech* 69 (1983): 249–266.
15. Mary Ann Fitzpatrick, "Effective Interpersonal Communication for Women in the Corporation: Think Like a Man, Talk Like a Lady," in *Women in Organizations: Barriers and Breakthroughs,* ed. Joseph J. Pilotta (Prospect Heights, IL: Waveland Press, 1983), 73.
16. McIntosh, 7.
17. Ann Oakley, *Subject Women* (New York: Pantheon, 1981), 281.
18. See Ronald C. Arnett, *Dwell in Peace: Applying Nonviolence to Everyday Relationships* (Elgin, IL: The Brethren Press, 1980). In a chapter titled, "The Dialogue of Peace," Arnett outlines the views of Martin Buber and Mahatma Gandhi to exemplify nonviolent resolutions to conflict, 125–126. See also, John Stewart, ed. *Bridges Not Walls: A Book About Interpersonal Communication,* 4th ed. (New York: Random House, 1986). In describing four central views of humanistic communication, Stewart presents exemplary essays by Leo Buscaglia, Carl R. Rogers, Erich Fromm, and Martin Buber, 337–392.
19. See Ann Crittenden Scott, "The Value of Housework," in *Feminist Frameworks: Alternative Theoretical Accounts of the Relations Between Women and Men,* 3rd ed., eds. Alison M. Jaggar and Paula Rothenberg Struhl (New York: McGraw-Hill, 1978), 227–231. In the *Dictionary of Occupational Titles,* observes Scott, "Each occupation is rated on a skill scale from a high of 1 to a low of 887. Listed at the 878 level are home-makers, foster mothers, child-care attendants, home health aids, nursery school teachers, and practical nurses," 229. This publication is compiled by the United States Department of Labor.
20. Phyllis M. Japp, "Esther or Isaiah?: The Abolitionist-Feminist Rhetoric of Angeline Grimke," *Quarterly Journal of Speech* 71 (1985): 336.
21. Dale Spender, *Man Made Language,* 2nd ed. (London: Routledge and Kegan-Paul, 1985), 52–75.
22. Spender, 53.
23. Cited in Spender, 53.
24. Spender, 53.

25. McIntosh, 7.
26. See, for example, Kathleen Edgerton Kendall and Jeanne Y. Fisher, "Francis Wright on Women's Rights: Eloquence Versus Ethos," *Quarterly Journal of Speech* 60 (1974); 58–68; Anthony Hillbruner, "Francis Wright: Egalitarian Reformer," *Southern Speech Communication Journal* 23 (1958): 193–205; Karlyn Kohrs Campbell, "Stanton's 'The Solitude of Self': A Rationale for Feminism," *Quarterly Journal of Speech* 66 (1980): 304–312.
27. See, for example, Karlyn Kohrs Campbell, "The Rhetoric of Women's Liberation: An Oxymoron," *Quarterly Journal of Speech* 59 (1973): 74–86; Brenda Robinson Hancock, "Affirmation by Negation in the Women's Liberation Movement," *Quarterly Journal of Speech* 58 (1972): 264–271.
28. Until recently there were numerous prohibitions against women speaking in public. Speakers such as Wright and Stanton encountered hostility because conventional norms held that women's place was in the home and not in the public sphere, particularly the speaking platform. See Campbell, "Women Speaking." Kendall and Fisher point out that Wright's "failure to meet societal expectations" greatly diminished her ethos, 58.
29. McIntosh, 7.
30. Mary Daly, *Gyn-Ecology: The Meta-Ethics of Radical Feminism* (Boston: Beacon Press, 1978), 24.
31. Campbell, "Women Speaking."
32. Examples include Nixon's "Checkers" speech; Martin Luther King, Jr.'s "I Have a Dream" speech; Reagan's 1982 speech in which a balanced budget was proposed.
33. Campbell, "Women Speaking."
34. Kendall and Fisher, 68.
35. Kendall and Fisher, 58.
36. Campbell, "Women Speaking."
37. Celeste Condit Railsback, "The Contemporary American Abortion Controversy: Stages in the Argument," *Quarterly Journal of Speech* 70 (1984): 410–424.
38. Campbell, "The Rhetoric of Women's Liberation," 78, 84–85.
39. Cited in Ellen Carole Dubois, et al., *Feminist Scholarship: Kindling in the Groves of Academe* (Urbana: University of Illinois Press, 1985), 55.
40. McIntosh, 17.
41. Michael Zimmerman, "Feminism, Deep Ecology, and Environmental Ethics," *Environmental Ethics* 9 (Spring 1987): 25.
42. A detailed analysis of Tiger's research is provided in, Robert R. Bell, *Worlds of Friendship* (Beverly Hills: Sage Publications, 1981), 75–94.
43. Cited in Bell, 76.
44. See, for example, Sandra L. Bem, "The Measurement of Psychological Androgyny," *Journal of Consulting and Clinical Psychology* 42 (1974): 155–162; Sandra L. Bem, "Sex-Role Adaptability: One Consequence of Psychological Androgyny," *Journal of Personality and Social Psychology* 31 (1975): 634–643; Donald G. Ellis and Linda McCallister, "Relational Control in Sex-Typed and Androgynous Groups," *Western Journal of Speech Communication* 44 (1980): 35–49; Lynda Greenblatt, James E. Haswnauer, and Vicki S. Freimuth, "Psychological Sex Type and Androgyny in the Study of Communication Variables: Self-Disclosure and Communication Apprehension," *Human Communication Research* 6 (1980): 117–129; Charles L. Montgomery and Michael Burgoon, "An Experimental Study of the Interactive Effectives of Sex and Androgyny on Attitude Change," *Communication Monographs* 44 (1977): 130–135; Mary A. Talley, Richmond Talley, and Virginia Peck, "The Relationship Between Psychological Gender Orientation and Communication Style," *Human Communication Research* 6 (1980): 326–339.
45. Stewart, Cooper, and Friedley, 24–26.

46. For a comprehensive bibliography on sex differences research in communication, see Susan B. Shimanoff, "Sex as a Variable in Communication Research 1970–1976: An Annotated Bibliography," *Women's Studies in Communication* 1 (1977): 8–20. For a survey and summary of research on women, gender, and sex differences published in communication journals, see Foss and Foss, "The Status of Research on Women." See also, Judith C. Pearson, *Gender and Communication* (Dubuque, IA: Wm. C. Brown Publishers, 1985) for an extensive bibliography on sex differences and gender research.
47. For bibliographies on linguistic studies in sex differences, see Nancy Henley and Barrie Thorne, "Sex Differences in Language, Speech, and Nonverbal Communication: An Annotated Bibliography," in *Language and Sex: Difference and Dominance,* eds. Barrie Thorne and Nancy Henley (Rowley, MA: Newbury House, 1975), 204–305. See also studies cited in a section titled "Phonetic Variants," in Nancy Henley and Barrie Thorne, *She Said/He Said* (Pittsburgh: Know, Inc., 1975). *She Said/He Said* is a reprint of Henley and Thorne's original work.
48. These studies fall under the general heading of "attribution." For a bibliography of attribution studies, see "Attribution," in Foss and Foss, 1983, 198.
49. See studies cited under "Evaluation" in Foss and Foss, 1983, 198.
50. See, for example, Spender; Linda L. Putnam, "In Search of Gender: A Critique of Communication and Sex Roles Research," *Women's Studies in Communication* 5 (1982): 1–9; Cheris Kramer, Barrie Thorne, and Nancy Henley, "Perspectives on Language and Communication," *Signs* 3 (1978): 638–651; *Women's Studies in Communication* 7 (1984), a special issue on papers selected from those prepared for the 1984 Conference on Gender and Communication Research, The Pennsylvania State University, University Park, Pennsylvania.
51. Thorne, Kramarae, and Henley, "Opening a Second Decade," 12.
52. Joseph J. Pilotta, ed., *Interpersonal Communication: Essays in Phenomenology and Hermeneutics* (Washington, DC: Center for Advanced Research in Phenomenology and the University Press of America, 1982), 49.
53. See Robin Lakoff, *Language and Women's Place* (New York: Harper and Row, 1975). See also Spender's critique of Lakoff's work, 8–9, 17, 18–19, 34–40, 86, 125.
54. Spender, 8.
55. For example, Pearson ends nearly every chapter in *Gender and Communication* by suggesting that women and men blend aspects of male and female communication styles, but inadvertently she accepts stereotyped sex-role characteristics. For example, women must learn to be logical and men must learn to be emotional. Given the presumed deficiency of women's communication, females must alter their communication considerably if they hope to achieve competence in social situations.
56. Patricia Hayes Bradley, "The Folk-Linguistics of Women's Speech: An Empirical Examination," *Communication Monographs* 48 (1981): 90.
57. Martha Solomon, "A Prolegomenon to Research on Gender Role Communication," *Women's Studies in Communication* 7 (1984): 98.
58. Solomon, 98.
59. Kramer, Thorne, and Henley, "Perspectives," 640.
60. Fitzpatrick, 74.
61. Fitzpatrick, 75.
62. McIntosh, 14.
63. See Kristin M. Langellier and Eric E. Peterson, "Spinstorying: A Communication Analysis of Women's Storytelling," Speech Communication Association Conference, Chicago, Illinois 1984. See also Dubois, et al., 23.
64. Spender, 52–74.

65. Adrienne Rich, *Of Woman Born: Motherhood as Experience and Institution* (New York: Bantam Books, 1977), 17.
66. See, for example, Susan Kalcik, " '. . . like Ann's gynecologist or the time I was almost raped': Personal Narrative in Women's Rap Groups," in *Women and Folklore,* ed. Claire R. Farrer (Austin: University of Texas Press, 1975), 3–11; Deborah Jones, "Gossip: Notes on Women's Oral Culture," in *The Voices and Words of Women and Men,* ed. Cheris Kramarae (Oxford: Pergamon Press, 1980), 193–198; Lee Jenkins and Cheris Kramer, "Small Group Processes: Learning from Women," *Women's Studies International Quarterly* 1 (1978): 67–84.
67. Fern L. Johnson and Elizabeth J. Aries, "The Talk of Women Friends," *Women's Studies International Forum* 6 (1983): 353–361.
68. See, for example, Carole Edelsky, "Who's Got the Floor," *Language in Society* 10 (1983): 383–421; Langellier and Peterson; Kalcik, 3–11.
69. See Paula A. Treichler and Cheris Kramarae, "Women's Talk in the Ivory Tower," *Communication Quarterly* 31 (1983): 118–132.
70. See Treichler and Kramarae, 118–132.
71. For a discussion of the problems created when an economic metaphor is used to explain social interaction, see Mercilee M. Jenkins and Cheris Kramarae, "A Thief in the House," in *Men's Studies Modified: The Impact of Feminism on the Academic Disciplines,* ed. Dale Spender (Oxford: Pergamon Press, 1981), 11–18.
72. Gerald R. Miller, ed., *Explorations in Interpersonal Communication* (Beverely Hills, CA: Sage Publications, 1976), 9–16.
73. Miller, 14.
74. Miller, 14.
75. Kathryn Carter, "The Experience of Relationships for Women and Men," Women's Studies Colloquia, Newcomb College Center for Research on Women, Tulane University, New Orleans, Louisiana, February, 1986.
76. Michael E. Roloff, "Communication Strategies, Relationships, and Relational Changes," in *Explorations in Interpersonal Communication,* ed. Gerald R. Miller (Beverely Hills, CA: Sage Publications, 1976), 182.
77. One example: Dennis R. Smith and Keith L. Williamson, *Interpersonal Communication: Roles, Rules, Strategies and Games,* 3rd ed. (Dubuque, IA: Wm. C. Brown Publishers, 1985), 88–90.
78. Carol Gilligan, *In a Different Voice: Psychological Theory and Women's Development* (Cambridge, MA: Harvard University Press, 1982), 5–23.
79. See Gilligan's discussion, 9–23.
80. Gilligan, 147.
81. Gilligan, 148.
82. Lana F. Rakow, "Rethinking Gender Research in Communication," *Journal of Communication* 36 (1986): 22–23.
83. Ann Oakley, "Interviewing Women: A Contradiction in Terms," in *Doing Feminist Research,* ed. Helen Roberts (London: Routledge and Kegan Paul, 1981), 30–61.
84. Carole Spitzack, "Body Talk: The Politics of Weight Loss and Female Identity," in *Women Communicating,* eds. Anita Taylor and Barbara Bate (Norwood, NJ: Ablex, Forthcoming); Deanna Hall and Kristin Langellier, "Storytelling Strategies in Mother-Daughter Communication," in *Women Communicating,* eds. Anita Taylor and Barbara Bate (Norwood, NJ: Ablex. Forthcoming).
85. Spender, 8.
86. Spender, 8.
87. Spender, 80.

88. Anita Taylor and Barbara Bate, eds., *Women Communicating* (Norwood, NJ: Ablex, Forthcoming).
89. Marilyn R. Schuster and Susan R. Van Dyne, eds., *Women's Place in the Academy: Transforming the Liberal Arts Curriculum* (Totowa, NJ: Rowman and Allanheld, 1985), 7, 24.
90. Phyllis R. Randall, "Sexist Language and Speech Communication Texts: Another Case of Benign Neglect," *Communication Education* 34 (1985): 128.
91. See McIntosh's discussion of plurality in curriculum development, 20–33.
92. Ardener's model is presented in, Elaine Showalter, "Feminist Criticism in the Wilderness," *Critical Inquiry* 8 (1983): 197–205.
93. Showalter, 199.
94. Showalter, 202.
95. Robert S. Cathcart and Larry A. Samovar, eds., *Small Group Communication: A Reader,* 4th ed. (Dubuque, IA: Wm. C. Brown Publishers, 1984), 368.
96. Robert Tannenbaum, Irving B. Wechsler, and Fred Massarik, "Leadership: A Frame of Reference," in *Small Group Communication: A Reader,* 4th ed., eds. Robert S. Cathcart and Larry A. Samovar, 371.
97. Stewart L. Tubbs, *A Systems Approach to Small Group Communication,* 2nd ed. (Reading, MA: Addison-Wesley Publishing, 1984), 154.
98. See James F. Kinder, "Styles of Leadership," in *Small Group Communication,* 4th ed., eds. Robert S. Cathcart and Larry A. Samovar, 400–406.
99. Kinder, 404.
100. Schuster and Van Dyne, 19.
101. See, for example, Gerald M. Phillips, Douglas J. Pedersen, and Julia T. Wood, *Group Discussion: A Practical Guide to Participation and Leadership* (Boston: Houghton Mifflin, 1979); Steven A. Beebe and John T. Masterson, *Communicating in Small Groups: Principles and Practices,* 2nd ed. (Glenview, IL: Scott, Foresman, 1986).
102. Fitzpatrick, 74–78.
103. See, for example, B. Bass, J. Krusell, and R. Alexander, "Male Managers' Attitudes Towards Working Women," *American Behavioral Scientists* 15 (1971): 221–236; V.E. Schein, "The Relationship Between Sex Role Stereotypes and Requisite Management Characteristics," *Journal of Applied Psychology* 57 (1973): 95–100; V.E. Schein, "Relationships Between Sex Role Stereotypes and Requisite Management Characteristics Among Female Managers," *Journal of Applied Psychology* 60 (1975): 340–344. For a review of male-female differences in small group communication, see also John E. Baird, "Sex Differences in Group Communication: A Review of Relevant Research," *Quarterly Journal of Speech* 62 (1976): 179–192.
104. See, for example, K. Deaux, "Self-Evaluations of Male and Female Managers," *Sex Roles* 5 (1979): 571–580; B. Rosen and T.H. Jerdee, "Influence of Sex-Role Stereotypes on Personnel Decisions," *Journal of Applied Psychology* 39 (1974): 9–14; K. Deaux and J. Taynor, "Evaluation of Male and Female Ability: Bias Works Two Ways," *Psychological Reports* 32 (1973): 261–262; D.M. Siegler and R.S. Siegler, "Stereotypes of Males' and Females' Speech," *Psychological Reports* 39 (1976): 167–170.
105. Showalter, 200.
106. Gillian Michell, "Women and Lying: A Pragmatic and Semantic Analysis of 'Telling it Slant,' " *Women's Studies International Forum* 7/5 (1984): 373–383.
107. Dubois et al., 47. See also Jenkins and Kramarae, "A Thief in the House."
108. Susan Bellrichard, "Voices From the Margin," *Canadian Journal of Political and Social Theory* 10 (1986): 1.
109. Dubois et al., 16.

Credits

Gorgias, *Encomium of Helen.* D.M. MacDowell trans. Copyright © 1982. Used by permission of Gerald Duckworth & Co. Ltd.

Isocrates, *Isocrates,* Vol. II, George Norlin trans., 1929. Reprinted by permission of the publishers and the Loeb Classical Library from Isocrates: *Isocrates,* Vol. II, translated by George Norlin, Cambridge, Mass.: Harvard University Press, 1929.

Plato, *Gorgias.* Reprinted by permission of the publishers and the Loeb Classical Library from Plato: *Gorgias,* Vol. III, translated by W.R. Lamb, Cambridge, Mass.: Harvard University Press, 1925.

Plato, *Phaedrus,* in *The Works of Plato,* Irwin Edman, ed. Copyright © 1928 Random House.

Aristotle, *The Rhetoric of Aristotle,* Richard Claverhouse Jebb trans. and John Edwin Sandys ed. Copyright © 1909. Reprinted with the permission of Cambridge University Press.

Cicero, *Cicero on Oratory and Orators,* J.S. Watson, trans. and ed., (1878). Copyright © 1878 HarperCollins Publishers.

Quintilian, *Institutio Oratoria.* Reprinted by permission of the publishers and the Loeb Classical Library from Quintilian: *Institutio Oratoria,* translated by H.E. Butler, Cambridge, Mass.: Harvard University Press, 1920.

Longinus, *On the Sublime,* in *Classical Literary Criticism:* Aristotle, Horace, Longinus translated by T.S. Dorsch (Penguin Classics, 1965) copyright T.S. Dorsch, 1965 reproduced by permission of Penguin Books Ltd.

St. Augustine, *On Christian Doctrine,* J.F. Shaw, trans., (1873). Reprinted by permission of T & T Clark Ltd.

De Pizan, Christine. *A Medieval Woman's Mirror of Honor: The Treasury of the City of Ladies,* Charity Cannon Willard trans., Madeleine Pelner Cosman ed., (1989). Reprinted by permission of Persea Books, Inc.

Ramus, Peter. *Arguments in Rhetoric Against Quintilian,* Carole Newlands trans. Copyright © 1986 by Northern Illinois University Press. Used by permission of the publisher.

Desiderius Erasmus of Rotterdam, *On Copia of Words and Ideas,* Donald B. King & H. David Rix trans. Copyright © 1963 Marquette University Press.

Bacon, Frances. *The Advancement of Learning,* William Aldis Wright ed., (1926). Reprinted by permission of Oxford University Press.

Bacon, Frances. *Novum Organum in Philosophic Classics,* Vol. II: Bacon to Kant, ed. by Walter Kaufmann, (1968). Reprinted by permission of Prentice-Hall, Inc., Upper Saddle River, NJ.

Locke, John. *An Essay Concerning Human Understanding,* Alexander Campbell Fraser, ed., (1959), Vol. II, Book III. Reprinted by permission of Dover Publications.

Locke, John. *The Works of John Locke,* Vol. II, Book 3, (1963). Reprinted by permission of Scientia Verlag und Antiquariat.

Vico, Giambattista. *On the Study Methods of Our Time,* Elio Gianturco trans., (1965). Used by permission of Cornell University Press.

Fell, Margaret. *Women's Speaking Justified,* (1667). Public domain.

Campbell, George. *The Philosophy of Rhetoric,* Lloyd F. Bitzer ed., (1963). Copyright © 1963 Southern Illinois University Press.

Blair, Hugh. *Lectures on Rhetoric and Belles Lettres* in *The Rhetoric of Blair, Campbell, and Whately*. James L. Golden and Edward P.J. Corbett eds., (1968). Reprinted by permission of James Golden.

Whately, Richard. *Elements of Rhetoric,* Douglas Ehinger ed., (1963). Copyright © 1963 Southern Illinois University Press.

Leslie, Eliza. *Miss Leslie's Behavior Book: A Guide and Manual for Ladies.* (1972; originally published in 1859). Reprinted by permission from Ayer Co. Publishers, No. Stratford, NH 03590.

Bakhtin, Mikhail (writing as V. N. Vološinov). *Marxism and the Philosophy of Language,* Ladislav Matejka & J.R. Titunik, trans., (1973). Reprinted by permission from Academic Press, Inc.

Vanderbilt, Amy. *Amy Vanderbilt's Complete Book of Etiquette,* (1954). Copyright © 1978 by Curtis B. Kellar & Lincoln G. Clark as executors of the estate of Amy Vanderbilt and Doubleday. Used by permission of Doubleday, a division of Random House, Inc.

Bernays, Edward L. *Propaganda,* (1928). Copyright © 1928 by Horace Liveright, Inc., renewed © 1956 by Edward L. Bernays. Reprinted by permission of Liveright Publishing Corporation.

Ogden, C.K. and I.A. Richards, *The Meaning of Meaning,* (1923). Reprinted with permission of Routledge Ltd.

Richards, I.A. *The Philosophy of Rhetoric,* (1936). Copyright © 1936 Oxford University Press. Reprinted by permission of Oxford University Press.

Burke, Kenneth. *The Philosophy of Literary Form,* 3rd. ed. rev., (1973; originally published 1941). Reprinted by permission of the University of California Press.

Burke, Kenneth. *A Grammar of Motives,* (1969; originally published 1945). Used by permission of the University of California Press.

Burke, Kenneth. *A Rhetoric of Motives,* (1969; originally published 1950). Reprinted by permission of the University of California Press.

Weaver, Richard M. *Language Is Sermonic: Richard M. Weaver on the Nature of Rhetoric,* Richard L. Johannesen, Rennard Strickland, Ralph T. Eubanks eds., (1970). Reprinted by permission of Louisiana State University Press. Copyright © 1970 by Louisiana State University Press.

Toulmin, Stephen. *The Uses of Argument,* (1958), III: "The Layout of Argument." Copyright © 1958 Cambridge University Press. Reprinted with the permission of Cambridge University Press.

Perelman, Chaim and L. Olbrechts-Tyteca, *The New Rhetoric: A Treatise on Argumentation.* Copyright © 1969 by University of Notre Dame Press, Notre Dame, IN. Reprinted by permission.

McLuhan, Marshall. *Understanding Media: The Extensions of Man,* (1964). Copyright © 1980 Corinne McLuhan.

Foucault, Michael. *The Archaeology of Knowledge and the Discourse on Language* (1972). Used by permission of the Georges Borchardt, Inc. Literary Agency.

Asante, Molefi Kete. *The Afrocentric Idea.* Copyright © 1987 by Temple University. Reprinted by permission of Temple University Press.

Campbell, Karlyn Kohrs. *Man Cannot Speak for Her.* Copyright © 1989 by Greenwood Press. Reproduced with permission of Greenwood Publishing Group, Inc., Westport, CT.

Cixous, Helene. "The Laugh of the Medusa," *Signs,* 1:4 (1976). Reprinted with permission of the University of Chicago Press.

Spitzack, Carol and Kathryn Carter. "Women in Communication Studies: A Typology for Revision," *Quarterly Journal of Speech,* Vol. 73, Number 4 (Nov., 1987). Used by permission of the National Communication Association.

INDEX